THE LIBRARY
ST. MARY'S COLLEGE OF MARYLAND
ST. MARY'S CITY, MARYLAND 20686

*The Rise and Fall of
the Political Press in Britain*

Volume Two:
The Twentieth Century

BY THE SAME AUTHOR

Lord Haldane, Scapegoat for Liberalism
John Morley at the India Office, 1905–1910
Sir John Brunner, Radical Plutocrat
Fleet Street Radical: A. G. Gardiner and the 'Daily News'
Nonconformity in Modern British Politics
Asquith
The Rise and Fall of the Political Press in Britain,
Volume I: The Nineteenth Century

Edited by Stephen Koss
The Pro-Boers: The Anatomy of an Anti-war Movement

STEPHEN KOSS

The Rise and Fall of The Political Press in Britain

Volume Two:
THE TWENTIETH CENTURY

THE UNIVERSITY OF NORTH CAROLINA PRESS
Chapel Hill and London

For Richard and Juliet

Copyright © 1984 by Stephen Koss

First published in the United States 1984
by The University of North Carolina Press
All rights reserved

Library of Congress Cataloging in Publication Data
(Revised for volume 2)

Koss, Stephen E.
  The rise and fall of the political press in Britain.

  Includes bibliographical references and index.
  Contents: [1] The nineteenth century – v. 2. the twentieth century.
  1. Press and politics – Great Britain – History – 19th century.   2. Press and politics – Great Britain – History – 20th century.   I. Title.
PN5124.P6K6   1981   072   81-1707
ISBN 0-8078-1483-0 (v. 1)
ISBN 0-8078-1598-5 (v. 2)

First published in Great Britain 1984
by Hamish Hamilton Ltd
Garden House, 57–59 Long Acre, London WC2E 9JZ

Typeset by Computape (Pickering) Ltd.
Printed in Great Britain by
St Edmundsbury Press, Bury St Edmunds, Suffolk

CONTENTS

	Acknowledgments	vii
	Introduction	1
1	'The Crowd of Joseph Chamberlains'	15
2	Effigies of Liberalism	54
3	Changing the Guard	84
4	The Peers, the People, and the Press	118
5	A Climacteric Year	152
6	Candid Friends	191
7	Declarations of War	238
8	From Coalition to Coalition	274
9	Squaring and Squashing	307
10	The Emergency Period	348
11	Interesting Coincidences	384
12	Troublemakers	422
13	The Wages of Harlotry	463
14	'In Queer Street'	505
15	Gentleman's Agreements	542
16	The Shiver Sisters Bow Out	577
17	The Road to 1947 and Beyond	614
18	Postscript and Post-mortem	657
	Manuscript Sources	687
	Index	690

ILLUSTRATIONS

Between pages 342 *and* 343

1a Alfred Harmsworth (1st Viscount Northcliffe)
1b Sir Edward Levy Lawson (1st Baron Burnham), proprietor of the *Daily Telegraph*
2   J L Garvin, editor of the *Observer* from 1908 to 1942 and the *Pall Mall Gazette* from 1912 to 1915
3a H A ('Taffy') Gwynne, editor of the *Standard* from 1904 to 1911 and the *Morning Post* from 1911 to 1937. 1929
3b C P ('Great') Scott, editor of the *Manchester Guardian* from 1872 to 1929. 1907
4a With Lord Birkenhead holding the lantern, Lords Rothermere and Beaverbrook dig to disinter the Lloyd George coalition. 1923
4b Lords Rothermere and Beaverbrook as uninvited guests at an 'End-of-the-Session Party at the Borgias'. 1923
5a Lord Beaverbrook depicted during the week that Stanley Baldwin accused him of seeking 'the prerogative of the harlot'. 1931
5b Lord Beaverbrook celebrating a Conservative victory
6   David Low's cartoon of the 'Shiver Sisters' performing their dance of appeasement under the direction of Herr Goebbels. 1938
7a Philip Zec's controversial cartoon in the *Daily Mirror*. 1942
7b A commentary on Fleet Street prospects. 1976
8   Rupert Murdoch, the new owner of Times Newspapers, with William Rees-Mogg, then editor of *The Times*

ACKNOWLEDGMENTS

'Why, oh why do Americans have to write such long books?' So a friendly critic, himself a distinguished English academic, asked himself two years ago as he unwrapped a review copy of the first of these two volumes. The answer, of course, owes nothing to the national origins of the author. There are some subjects that can be painted in miniature, others that require a broad canvas. In each case, the technique is dictated by the nature of the enterprise and, unavoidably, by the range of available sources.

In the nineteenth century, there was a multiplicity of newspapers, serving a diversity of political functions. Some of the least known were, in fact, among the most historically significant and therefore demanded extensive documentation. Some of the best known needed to be brought into perspective. In the twentieth century, there has been a precipitous decline in the number of newspapers, especially ones that have aspired to influence. Yet political activity has retained its complexity, and the personalities involved have been still more controversial. Not least, the archival materials exist in much greater profusion and frequently serve to contradict legends and memories.

Consequently, this second and concluding instalment is even more massive than its predecessor, and must be, if it is to provide a comprehensive survey of actions and motives. As a book, it is intended to stand on its own, but may help to tie together certain threads that were left dangling at the end of the first volume, which terminated somewhat artificially at the turn of the century. Basically, however, it tells a self-contained story. The political press continued to rise after 1901, though increasingly in uncharted directions. Its fall, by the criteria adopted here, is now complete.

The reader is offered these words not so much as an apology as an explanation. The real apologies must be reserved for those who assisted in the task and who, like the author, found it more demanding than they had perhaps anticipated. For this study has consumed many years as well as many pages, and it would have taken longer – with less satisfactory results – without the industry and encouragement of many friends and colleagues.

Peter Clarke, John Grigg, and Robert Webb uncomplainingly read the entire manuscript and offered an assortment of stimulating criticisms, which I have done my best to meet. My debts to them are incalculable. Various portions of the work were also subjected to vigorous scrutiny by Anthony Howard, Michael Leapman, F. M. Leventhal, John Stubbs, and A. J. P. Taylor, each of whom brought to bear his expertise. Their advice and admonitions were alike gratefully received, although I hasten to exempt any and all of them for whatever errors of fact or interpretation may persist.

Alan J. Lee, who was planning a sequel to his own book on the nineteenth-century press at the time of his premature death, was a valued counsellor. This book is humbly offered as a memorial to him and to Ivan Yates, a devoted friend with whom I first discussed the project long ago.

Philip Duncum and David Hubback, besides answering many queries, allowed me access to materials on which they were respectively working. With gracious hospitality, Mark Barrington-Ward and Vivian Brooks permitted me to consult their fathers' diaries, E. Peter Wright put the Arthur Mann Papers at my disposal, and Lord Bathurst and the late Lord Harcourt made available their family papers. Sir Adrian Cadbury volunteered to circularize his kinsmen on my behalf; among them, John Crosfield loaned me proof sheets from the family history he had written for private publication, and E. C. Hambly turned up an autobiographical note by Henry T. Cadbury. Joan Woods, whose contribution defies classification, rewarded me with her trust and the joy of her companionship.

Those who made accessible primary sources in their private or public keeping are far too numerous to list individually. All too few can be properly identified in the bibliography. But special mention must be made of certain professional archivists who performed services above and beyond the call of duty: Patrick Baird (City of Birmingham Reference Library), B. S. Benedikz (Birmingham University Library), Graham R. Hill (McMaster University Library), David J. Johnson (House of Lords Record Office), Gordon Phillips and Anne C. D. Piggott (*The Times* Archives), Angela Raspin (British Library of Economic and Political Science), Clare Stephens (Churchill College, Cambridge), and David Taylor (Manchester Central Library). The librarians at the Bodleian and Codrington libraries in Oxford and the Butler and Journalism School libraries at Columbia University were indispensable. Alan S. Bell assisted in different places and, always distinctively, in countless ways.

Others lent support in tracing archives and, in the process, dispensed useful suggestions. They include Paul Addison, the 3rd Earl of Birkenhead (who was as close as I came to the elusive Berry family), Geoffrey D. M. Block, Lord Briggs, John Hutcheson, Robert Maclennan, Herbert Nicholas, W. J. Reader, and Joan Stevenson. I benefited enormously, though sometimes indirectly, from interviews and informal conversations with Lord Ardwick, David Astor, Tom Baistow, Stanley Baron, James Cameron, Alexander Chancellor, Sir Christopher Chancellor, Michael Cudlipp, Michael Cummings, Michael Foot, William Forrest, Lord Gibson, John Grant, Sir Geoffrey Harmsworth,

Acknowledgments

Alastair Hetherington, Christopher Johnson, Lajos Lederer, Lord Marsh, Rupert Murdoch, Lord Robbins, Graham Watson, and David Wood. Among those whose kind responses to my letters helped to clarify points of detail were Vernon Bartlett, Lord Cowdray, Sir Roger Fulford, Maurice Gordon, Jo Grimond, Cecil King, Harold Macmillan, Sir Kenneth Preston, Donald Tyerman, Lord Willis, and Lord Wilson.

I shall resist a gnawing temptation to identify those very few individuals who denied their cooperation either by sealing off manuscript collections or by stipulating such conditions that I found unacceptable. In two instances, one involving a senior politician and the other (more shamefully and less explicably) a fellow academic, I was forbidden to quote directly from correspondence I had seen. Being charitable, which again has nothing to do with my nationality, I am disposed to think that the recalcitrance of these people owed more to indifference than to a desire to conceal information; but the frustrations were exactly the same. Needless to say, in no instance has my interpretation been altered by courtesies I received, much less by those I was refused.

Those who gave me permission to quote extracts from unpublished documents to which they hold copyright have received my private thanks. It was not always possible to trace copyright holders, and I beg the indulgence of any whom I may have missed.

Robin Quinville and John Copp, both graduate students at Columbia, checked and double-checked bibliographical references. Frank Beck cheerfully retyped pages that had been revised beyond intelligibility.

Jim Schoff at the Centre for the Study of Cartoon and Caricature, the University of Kent, helped me to obtain and identify the illustrations, which are published by arrangement with Mrs Eva Reichmann, McMaster University Library, *Punch*, the Thomson Organisation, Michael Cummings, Express Newspapers Ltd and the *Sunday Times*.

Acknowledgment is due, and most gladly made, to the Warden and Fellows of All Souls College, Oxford, who extended my visiting fellowship for an additional term to cover the final preparation of this volume. I was thus conveniently (and comfortably) situated to draw upon the advice of Sir Patrick Neill, then chairman of the Press Council, to partake of the inimitable kindnesses of John Simmons, and to resume my common-room tutorials. A research grant from the American Council of Learned Societies enabled me to take advantage of these privileges.

The forbearance of Christopher Sinclair-Stevenson, friend and publisher (in that order), cannot go unrecorded. It was exceeded only by that of my long-suffering family, who generously forgave my periodic absences and tolerated my continuous absences of mind. Other authors have paid sufficient tribute to my wife's editorial skills that they require no certification from me. No one, however, could have esteemed them more highly. Our children, Juliet and Richard, deserve full credit for their precocious professionalism, exercised by checking transcriptions, grappling with proofs, and helping to compile yet another index. For their dedication, thoughtful understanding, and mercilessly cynical banter, I am supremely grateful.

INTRODUCTION

Late in 1904, as if to prove that neither insight nor ingenuity had deserted him, W. T. Stead dignified the London daily newspapers as 'His Majesty's Public Councillors'.[1] He then divided them into four categories.

In the first rank, Stead placed *The Times* and the *Westminster Gazette*, both political papers 'read by men of both parties'; their circulations were relatively modest (hovering around 35,000 and 20,000 respectively), but their reputations were resounding. Immediately below, in descending order of importance, came the *Standard*, the *Daily News*, the *Morning Post*, the *Daily Chronicle*, the *Morning Leader*, the *St James's Gazette*, the *Daily Graphic*, the *Star*, the *Globe*, the *Echo*, and the *Pall Mall Gazette*, which Stead himself had edited in palmier days for both of them. Falling equally between morning and evening publication, and almost equally in terms of partisan allegiance, newspapers in this intermediate classification were distinguished by editorial excellence, parliamentary front-bench connections, or a healthy mixture of the two. To a third echelon, Stead consigned those journals that 'combine the maximum of advertising and of circulation with the minimum of influence': the *Daily Telegraph*, once the front-runner in Fleet Street; the *Daily Mail*, which had pre-empted it; and, 'hobbling painfully after', the *Daily Express*. Significantly, all three were better known for their proprietors (Lord Burnham, Sir Alfred Harmsworth, and C. Arthur Pearson) than for their editors. Finally, at the bottom, Stead put those dailies that were as much without pretence to influence as without serious capacity for it: the *Morning Advertiser*, the *Daily Mirror*, the *Sun*, the *Evening News*, and the *Evening Standard*. Although one may dispute Stead's value judgments in specific cases, his inventory – which pointedly excluded provincial and weekly newspapers – serves conveniently to provide a framework.

Of the twenty-one major metropolitan papers that celebrated Edward VII's accession in 1901, three did not survive long enough to report his death nine years later. In 1905, the *Echo* closed down, and the *St James's Gazette* was merged with the *Evening Standard*. The following year saw the setting of the *Sun*. Then, in 1912, the *Morning Leader* was absorbed by the *Daily News*.

[1] *Review of Reviews*, xxx (December 1904), 604–605.

After a heady burst of late-Victorian expansionism, Fleet Street began to retrench. On the whole, the evening papers were hardest hit. Most of them survived the thinning of the ranks, but wore an ominously leaner look. Through acquisitions, amalgamations, and closures, the base of proprietorial control continually narrowed. Yet, for the time being, the portents were more dramatic than the effects.

Competition steadily intensified, production costs soared, and the market – once considered illimitable – now seemed to have been saturated. Stead tried to reverse the trend in 1904 by founding his *Daily Paper*; dauntingly addressed to 'the abnormally scrupulous', it ran for a mere thirty-two issues. The *Tribune*, launched in 1906, was a costlier and more telling failure. All the same, there existed a staggering array of London-based dailies, especially if one takes into account the profusion of specialized journals that catered to the business community and other sectional interests. Upon closer inspection, one may see that the balance on the newsstands had shifted over the preceding generation. While those properties in Stead's third and fourth classifications had grown more numerous and usually more prosperous, those at or near the apex had become more vulnerable and perhaps expendable. Thus, proportionately fewer newspapers qualified as political organs with identifiable affiliations, and perpetually fewer seemingly aspired to do so.

With plethora giving the semblance of plenitude, the British press flourished by comparison with foreign models. Notwithstanding the exploits of Joseph Pulitzer and William Randolph Hearst in America, Fleet Street enjoyed an enviable popularity, a notable vitality, and, not least, an unmatched political authority. The last was conferred partly by a unique degree of centralization and partly by the persistence of nineteenth-century parliamentary ideals. The pre-eminence of Westminster, accented by the forms and practices of British journalism, reflected a contiguity that was no less ideological than geographical. Whether it created or merely reflected the climate of opinion, the British press was an integral part of political society.

Writing in 1914, R. A. Scott-James ascribed the political superiority of London newspapers over their dispersed counterparts in the United States to 'the simple reason that Englishmen are more interested in politics than Americans'. He might have drawn the same faulty conclusion from the regionalism of the French press under the Third Republic or from the arrangements that obtained in Imperial Germany. Cultural values, reinforced by considerations of economy and topography, made London far more of a journalistic nerve-centre than New York, Paris, or Berlin. To all intents and purposes, the London press was Britain's national press. 'Even to-day,' Edward Dicey, formerly editor of the *Observer*, declared in 1905, 'I am confident that north and south, east and west of the metropolis you will not find a single town in which a first-class daily local newspaper is found, provided that the London papers are obtainable there by breakfast time.'[1] Provincial journals, welded into chains, were being eclipsed within their own enclaves. A few oustanding ones preserved their independence and, with it, an integrity they could assert from time to time. As a rule, however, they were ignored with impunity by party officials.

'It is amazing how parochial are the London newspaper readers, even those with interests & connections in the north,' Gervase Beckett, the proprietor of the *Yorkshire Post*, remarked in the 1920s to Arthur Mann, his editor back in Leeds. Strewn across the table at the Carlton Club, where Beckett belonged as a veteran Conservative MP, were 'six copies of the *Daily Mail*, of the *Daily Express*, many of the *Mirror*, etc., etc.' Even the socialist *Daily Herald* was boldly on display in that Conservative holy of holies. To Beckett's dismay, only 'by ringing the bell & obtaining the assistance of a waitress' was it possible for a member of the Carlton to 'discover in a pigeon-hole below a side-table a single copy of the *Yorkshire Post, Glasgow Herald* or *Scotsman*. Yet no MP or other man from the north makes any protest.'[2]

Understandably, provincial editors did not like to think of themselves as practitioners of pigeon-hole journalism. Assisted by Collin Brooks, who went on to work for Lord Rothermere and ultimately to edit *Truth*, Mann fashioned the *Yorkshire Post* into 'an organ of modern Tory democracy' between the wars. Proud of his contribution, Brooks fancied 'how seriously the sheet is read by the majority of those who take it, and how closely it is scanned by people like the Central Unionist Office, and Baldwin and the Labour men.' Only after he had left Leeds did he realize his miscalculation. Mann, who eventually followed him to the metropolis, described an exchange with Neville Chamberlain in 1940. 'I'm afraid, Mr Prime Minister, you don't regard me as a friendly critic,' Mann opened the conversation. 'Neville said with palpable annoyance and contempt, "Oh, I'm much too busy to read the provincial newspapers".'[3] Few major politicians were so blunt, but most of them harboured the same perspective, which has accordingly shaped this book. If the provincial press receives short shrift in these chapters, it is because it received short shrift in reality.

With diminishing subservience and attenuated impact, British newspapers continued to promote political causes and to attend to the needs of electoral organization. In return, politicians remained deeply involved – sometimes embroiled – in newspaper management. 'Naturally the chief weapon of the various Parties is the Press,' wrote Carl Peters, a German visitor, in 1904. 'The Press plays a part in Great Britain that can be likened to its mission in no other European country,' he insisted. 'Everybody reads his newspaper in England,

---

[1] Scott-James, *The Influence of the Press* (London, 1914?), p. 213; Dicey, 'Journalism New and Old,' *Fortnightly Review*, lxxxiii (1905), 914.
[2] Beckett to Mann, 23 October [?], Mann Papers.
[3] Collin Brooks's diary, 13 August 1925 and 2 February 1940.

nay generally two, a morning and an evening paper.' With a mixture of incredulity and disdain, Peters found it 'very amusing to watch in passing trains, how almost every passenger has his face buried in his paper'.[1]

The operative assumption here was that railway passengers, including the legions of commuters from the spreading suburbs, were engrossed in political articles, not the crossword, sporting news, or any of the other multitudinous features that vied for attention. Nor did this view take into account the prevailing gradations in literacy as well as popular taste. That the British led the world as per capita consumers of newsprint was indisputable. That their addiction was a determinant of their partisan preferences, as Peters inferred, was altogether more questionable. Failing to discriminate among types of newspapers, he was by no means unusual in his propensity to characterize them primarily as political vehicles. That had been their assigned function in mid-Victorian times, and remained their dominant characteristic in Germany and elsewhere. But the network of interrelationships between politicians and journalists in Britain had gradually changed, along with patterns of readership. To buy a copy of a paper no longer implied a political gesture as it had done in the 1860s and '70s. To own or even to edit a paper no longer entailed a contractual obligation to toe a party line. Theory lagged behind practice, however, and contemporaries habitually strove to revive a system that had never existed quite as they imagined. This book, building on the foundations of its predecessor, will investigate those efforts and their effects.

Foreign observers like Peters may be forgiven for failing to discern such subtle adjustments, which were often obscured by an atavistic rhetoric. Similarly, Fleet Street professionals like Scott-James stood too close to comprehend fully the interplay of personal, social, and electoral dynamics. A discrete phase in the history of the political press had ended by the turn of the century, before the succeeding phase had obviously begun. The transition from official control of the press to 'ownership by a political tendency', as Sir Denis Hamilton has called it, occurred decisively in the 1850s, though not, as he has suggested, 'out of the belief in the political parties that private ownership did not serve them well'.[2] Rather, private ownership, subject to defined consensual limits, was the norm through the second half of the nineteenth century, once the 'taxes on knowledge' had been abolished. The commercial tendency accompanied and eventually superseded the political tendency as the driving force. This time, the transition was halting, and its ramifications were not completely manifest until after the First World War, if then.

All the while, familiar principles were more easily invoked than applied. Politicians continued to expect – occasionally to demand – obeisance. Newspapers gave it more and more stintingly, until it became too erratic to qualify as partisan support in the traditional sense. The rise of the political press, it will be

[1] Peters, *England and the English* (London, 1904), pp. 181, 193.
[2] Hamilton, *Who Is To Own the British Press?* (London, 1976), p. 10.

recalled, had been triggered off by legislation: the consecutive repeal of the advertisement duty in 1853, the stamp duty in 1855, and, as a pendant, the paper duty in 1861. By contrast, the fall of the political press was devoid of statutory landmarks. A fitful process that extended over generations, its catalysts were conflicts of interest and ambition, rooted in divergences of perception among politicians and journalists alike. Instead of a sudden break, there was an attrition, which awaits scrutiny.

Admittedly more difficult to delineate, these changes of attitude are best illustrated by comparison. In the 1890s, F. Carruthers Gould, the brilliant cartoonist of the *Westminster Gazette*, loyally declined to caricature his 'own people', by whom he meant Liberals, leaving that task to his 'Conservative friends'. In 1929, Lord Beaverbrook reserved space in the *Daily Express* for 'our supporters', by whom he meant advocates of Empire Free Trade, bidding his critics to 'Go to the opposition newspapers', by which he meant organs of orthodox Conservatism. Yet Beaverbrook's *Evening Standard* featured the cartoons of David Low, whose graphic assaults on party and proprietorial policy were cunningly tolerated. By then, allegiances had become – as they remain – less straightforward.[1]

From the politicians' standpoint, these changes were especially perplexing. In Victorian times, personalities as disparate as John Bright and Benjamin Disraeli had established newspapers; to the same purpose, other party leaders had variously nurtured pre-existing journals. Moral as well as financial imperatives led to a refinement of procedures, but not immediately to a redefinition of aims. On the understanding that spontaneous support – or, failing that, its facsimile – was more efficacious, politicians began to exercise control less blatantly and, as a rule, indirectly. What they could not accomplish by persuasion, they did not hesitate to attempt by more high-handed methods, usually behind a corporate smoke-screen. David Lloyd George, who had helped to effect the transfer of the *Daily News* in 1901, engineered the takeover of the *Daily Chronicle* in 1918, and thereafter pulled the strings of the United Newspapers syndicate. His Asquithian rivals, more modestly endowed, subscribed to the Westminster Group, with the *Westminster Gazette* as its flagship. Through the first quarter of the twentieth century, until commercial magnates bailed them out, the Unionist whips kept afloat a number of floundering properties, while the postwar *Daily Herald* subsisted on subsidies from the Labour Party and its trade-union affiliates.

These arrangements, which carried the seeds of their own destruction, could not last indefinitely: for one thing, newspaper investments proved too much of a drain on party coffers; for another, they returned diminishing satisfaction. Owing as much to a sense of frustration as to a sense of propriety, politicians withdrew from such commitments. Their self-denying ordinances came too

[1] F. C. Gould, draft autobiography; Beaverbrook to Sir William Bull, 19 December 1929, quoted in A. J. P. Taylor, *Beaverbrook* (London, 1972), p. 273.

late to make much difference, and merely confirmed the political autonomy of a weakened press. In 1967, confronted by the Thomson Organisation's acquisition of *The Times*, Harold Wilson 'took a strictly non-interventionist view' that contrasted with politicians' frenzied responses when that paper had changed hands in 1908 and 1922. Wilson asked his counsellors 'if there weren't any practical proposals for preventing, say, the *Guardian* or the *Mail* from folding up', and they 'looked very hard for some weeks and found nothing practical'.[1] Direct political interference was out of bounds.

The wonder is that the transformation did not come sooner. Towards the close of the nineteenth century, it already seemed as though the days of the political press were numbered, if not yet over. The twentieth century saw an unexpected revival. With the reassertion of the primacy of parties, politically attuned journals recovered a substantial measure of their former impetus. To be sure, their ground had been perceptibly eroded, but they stood it boldly. Their finances were often shaky, but their capacity for potential service could not be taken lightly. The Boer War, like the Crimean War earlier and each of the world wars that lay ahead, invigorated the press and disrupted its partisan attachments. Dissension within the Liberal and Conservative camps invited journalistic meddling. The emergence of the Labour Party, wedded to traditional concepts of publicity, was another restorative. The drift towards disengagement was therefore temporarily arrested. Collaboration between politicians and newspapers resumed, and was to be heightened by events.

The writing may have been on the wall, but it tended to be disregarded. Parliamentary strength was not linked to editorial favour, much less the fortunes of a particular paper to the depth of its political commitment. Circulation did not, in itself, either translate into votes or ensure solvency. 'The more copies we sold, the more money we lost,' George Lansbury wrote of the *Daily Herald*, which chronically suffered from insufficient advertising. Neither the *Westminster Gazette* nor *The Times* relied on sales for its prestige. The *Daily Mail*, making a virtue of necessity, started out by deliberately forsaking prestige for profitability. Like the *Herald* among the Labour faithful, the *Daily News* among Liberals and the *Standard* among Conservatives carried far greater weight inside their respective party folds than outside. As demonstrated by the *Manchester Guardian*, a paper might appeal to certain strata of intellectual or social opinion to the virtual exclusion of others. 'Among cultured and earnest people, on the one hand, and mere commercial men, on the other, the *M.G.* is undoubtedly a great force,' C. P. Scott, its editor-owner, was told by one of his employees. 'But the majority of the electors belong to the working class, and working men do not read the *M.G.*'[2]

---

[1] Richard Crossman, *The Diaries of a Cabinet Minister*, II (London, 1976), pp. 229–30.
[2] Lansbury, *The Miracle of Fleet Street* (London, 1925), p. 161; A. Yates to Scott, 10 August 1912, quoted in P. F. Clarke, *Lancashire and the New Liberalism* (Cambridge, 1971), p. 155, where Yates is identified as 'very likely a printer on the paper'.

How, in any instance, was this 'great force' to be measured? Or, from another perspective, how was it to be harnessed, and to what end? Exactly as contemporaries disagreed as to the relative merits of competing newspapers, historians have since disagreed as to their relative importance. Some have gone so far as to discount the cumulative influence of the press, or further to deny it categorically. The fact remains, however, that readers and writers alike believed not only that such an influence existed, but also that it was pervasive. Accordingly, political strategies were predicated on the assumption that newspaper comment, whether by quantity or quality, materially affected developments within, between, and beyond parliamentary groupings. Mistaken or not, this conviction created its own reality.

To a considerable extent, the power of the press was a conceit on the part of journalists, naturalized citizens of the Fourth Estate, who strove vaingloriously to live up to legend. Nevertheless, a conceit cannot be maintained in the face of overwhelming indifference, let alone scorn. Egotism – sometimes disguised as professional pride – does not suffice as an explanation. An outgrowth of the nineteenth-century parliamentary culture, the political press must be seen as a contrivance on the part of diverse public figures, all eager to bring pressure to bear on affairs of state. Seizing upon the press out of hope, out of desperation, or simply out of habit, they sedulously fostered newspapermen's self-images.

The exercise of that influence, however imperfectly or indeed impressionistically intuited, furthermore varied from case to case and from time to time. It depended upon newspapermen's contacts and the use they made of them. J. L. Garvin amused Mrs Austen Chamberlain with half an hour of 'all the inside gossip of politics – whereof I know more than she or her husband hear of or guess though she is a Cabinet Minister's wife & he Chancellor of the Exchequer'. It depended no less upon the willingness of politicians to take instruction. 'There is no need for the newspapers to tell me my faults,' protested A. J. Balfour; 'I know them all, but I can't alter them.' His cousin, Lord Hugh Cecil, could only 'hope there is a purgatory for otherwise journalists will all go to hell', which prompted Geoffrey Dawson to rejoin that 'the path of the poor journalist is hard enough in this world without being inevitably predestined to damnation or even to purgatory'. Neville Chamberlain, whose stoicism came late in the day, retired from office with a painful appreciation of the fickleness of press opinion: 'Of course I can't & don't expect journalists who are accustomed to deal only with the affairs of the moment to recollect the past.' That is the responsibility of the historian, here undertaken.[1]

Although there were no longer commercial fortunes to be won from partisan journalism, involvement in newspaper enterprises continued to pay political dividends, difficult to compute on any absolute scale. Alfred Harmsworth,

---

[1] Garvin to Viola Woods, 11 February 1920, Woods Papers; Beatrice Webb's diary, 17 April 1905, Passfield Papers; Cecil to Dawson, 16 December 1930, and Dawson to Cecil, 17 December 1930 (copy), Dawson Papers; Chamberlain to Simon, 6 October 1940, Simon Papers.

hardly as aloof from the scramble as he pretended, kept open the option of a second candidacy until it became clear that his Fleet Street operations afforded him the means of satisfying his ambition without the risk of incurring another electoral humiliation. Scott, whose lacklustre parliamentary career terminated in 1905, recognized journalism as a more conducive sphere for his progressivism. More typically, Sir George Newnes continued to give unexceptional service in the House of Commons, where his son joined him in 1906 and lived up to family tradition. 'It is 20 years since I first went there,' reflected the proprietor of the *Westminster Gazette*, who humbly described himself as 'a quiet Member,' though 'perhaps a useful one in many ways.'[1] His utility was primarily extra-mural. Like countless back-benchers, Newnes assumed newspaper obligations to amplify his public voice, to defend constituency interests, and generally to impress the party chiefs by his dedication. For aspiring politicians as well as apologetic ones, involvement with the press complemented parliamentary service. Some entertained a vague hope of helping to shape official policy. Others, with time on their hands and money in their pockets, sought amusement or companionship. All craved recognition of one sort or another. The motives were as varied as the personalities themselves.

The avowedly political journals of the early twentieth century were responsive – and responsible – to the educated and articulate classes within society, which were perceived essentially as cultural rather than economic entities. The majority of these publications were hothouse plants, doomed to perish in an increasingly democratic atmosphere. Meanwhile, they enjoyed an Indian summer. Within a restricted area, which encompassed the political community as it was then formally constituted, they were deemed capable of rousing the public conscience, facilitating (or retarding) the passage of legislation, and fuelling intra-party rivalries.

Three examples, all from the years 1902 and 1903, testify to these ideas. 'I think the journalists at home ought really to organize something like a regular campaign in favour of the decent organization of the British Empire,' Alfred (soon to become Viscount) Milner wrote from South Africa to E. B. Iwan-Müller, a leader-writer for the *Daily Telegraph* and a confidant of Balfour, then Prime Minister. A veteran of Stead's *Pall Mall Gazette*, Milner communicated his keen enthusiasm for newspaper agitations to his young disciples, many of whom gravitated to Fleet Street. Beatrice Webb, preparing the ground for London education proposals, deputized R. B. Haldane to inspire *The Times*, while her husband undertook the more mundane task of permeating the *Daily Mail*. The Fabians, like the Milnerites, thus helped to perpetuate the conventions of the political press. Lord Rosebery, a lingering – or malingering – presence in Edwardian political life, cultivated cordial relations with *The Times* and, despite a pose of lofty detachment, kept close watch on other

---

[1] Newnes to Gladstone, 19 December 1905, Viscount Gladstone Papers, Add. MSS. 46, 063, fol. 227b.

editorial offices. 'What *is* going on at the *Daily Chronicle*? Do tell me,' he asked E. T. Cook, who was reduced to writing leaders for that comparatively undistinguished paper. Whatever its influence, the press had certainly lost none of its mystique.[1]

As the makers of news, politicians fired the imaginations and captured the loyalties of journalists. As the purveyors of news to the general public, journalists were equally indispensable to politicians. At the point where their needs intersected, fascination gave way to obsession. This mutual attraction is not difficult to understand. Newspapers held a monopoly on the commodity of propaganda. Pamphleteering, as shown by the pitiable performance of the 'pro-Boers', had gone out of fashion; even Gladstone's famous tract against the Bulgarian Horrors in 1876 had required an orchestrated press campaign to realize its impact. Public speeches, no longer automatically accorded verbatim transcription, ceased to reverberate. With increasing secularization, the pulpit declined as a political force. Alternative mass media had not yet arisen. That left the press as the best available index to popular opinion as well as the single most convenient mechanism for guiding it.

At different levels, different newspapers afforded different channels of communication. Megaphones through which statesmen could broadcast their appeals, they were also ventriloquial devices through which hints could be dropped and dialogues could be conducted. A select and highly informed readership was reasonably assumed to be capable of interpreting the most casual intimation. Experts at home and abroad were adept at reading between the lines. The less sophisticated were allowed to glean what they could.

'Mass thinking is a strange and unaccountable affair,' concluded R. D. Blumenfeld in 1933, after more than a quarter of a century at the *Daily Express*. He was being realistic, not insouciant. Only at the end of that decade, with the improvization of market survey procedures, was it possible to say who was reading which newspapers and with how much comprehension. Before the Second World War, any assessment of day-to-day popular sentiment was inevitably impressionistic. Still more so was any estimate of the intrinsic value of newspaper support. Earlier on, these issues had been largely irrelevant, given the prevailing confines of political discourse. The stature of a journal was measured by the gratitude it received from those whom it praised, the resentment it incurred from those whom it censured, and 'above all' – according to J. A. Spender – by the number of lesser journals that duplicated its contents. Far from impeding the exercise of influence, these rarefied conditions had supposedly encouraged it. 'There could have been no better audience for the purpose of what is now called propaganda,' insisted Spender, recalling his halcyon days at the élitist *Westminster*, 'and the writers who

---

[1] Milner to Iwan-Müller, 4 January 1902, Milner Papers; Webb, *Our Partnership* (London, 1948), p. 257 (diary extract of 16 January 1903); Rosebery to Cook, 16 November 1903, Cook Papers.

addressed it had a direct influence which they could not possibly have had, if they had been speaking to the multitude.' His retrospective defensiveness was itself a commentary on the extent to which times had changed.[1]

The aura of the political press derived from its self-conscious exclusivity, which replicated the theatre of partisan debate. The doyen of political journalists, Spender embodied both the strengths and weaknesses of a proud tradition. As the intimate of H. H. Asquith and Sir Edward Grey, who shared his Balliol heritage, he further personified the constraints of the classical Liberal ethic. His front-page editorials, elegantly phrased and couched in modulated tones, commanded a respectful hearing from the enlightened few. They were not written with a view to persuade the unenlightened many, who were an unknown quantity.

The *Westminster Gazette*, as its name proclaimed, aimed at a circulation within Parliament and its environs. Although sympathetic to the plight of the masses, it would sooner write them off as customers than write down to them. The *Westminster* could pretend to influence so long as parliamentary Liberalism, of which it was more or less an accredited organ, could bank on the acquiescence of the electorate and the gentility of gentlemen. Neither, as we know, was immutable. The extension of the franchise in 1918, anticipated by prewar social turbulence and wartime dislocations, undermined the foundations of the Liberal order. The politics of class, anathema to Liberalism, supplanted the politics of conscience. By creed and temperament, Spender was ill equipped to raise his voice above the din. Without proper acoustics, his eloquence lacked resonance. The cohesion of the Liberal Party did not survive the pressures of war; his editorship ended in November 1921, not long after the break-up of the party; and the *Westminster*, converted from evening to morning publication, folded early in 1928.

Spender and Scott, with A.G. Gardiner of the *Daily News* and Robert Donald of the *Daily Chronicle* warily following suit, shone as editors by subordinating their professional and personal interests to the welfare of the Liberal cause. The allies of politicians, they defended policies and safeguarded secrets, which was a small price to pay for the confidences they enjoyed. On the Unionist side, editors evinced a comparable fidelity to party programmes, however contradictorily they expounded them. More overtly than their Liberal counterparts, who had to wait until the war for fissures to reappear, Tory journalists were often the perpetrators of intrigue. The golden age of great editors, as it has been commemorated, owed its lustre less to literary merit – though that was not a negligible commodity – than to the recognized status of its representatives as party or factional spokesmen. Spender was 'an unofficial member of the Liberal Cabinet', wrote Scott-James with pardonable exaggeration. 'Many of the most remarkable personalities in London journalism,' he

---

[1] Blumenfeld, *The Press in My Time* (London, 1933), p. 48; Spender, *Life, Journalism and Politics* (London, 1927), II, 135.

continued, 'derive their support not only from their journalistic talents, but from the fact that they are known to have personal influence in high political circles.'[1] In some cases, that influence transcended that of their papers. Garvin was the last of the breed, a political editor who held his chair through the ensuing age of great proprietors. But he eventually outlived his usefulness; and, in any case, the *Observer* was a weekly paper, not a daily.

The correlation between parliamentary mutations and newspaper orientations, emphasized in the previous volume of this study, remained constant through the first quarter of the century. Thereafter, without disappearing, it became less binding. The dependence of the press upon party agents for funds and favours gradually lessened, as did the dependence of party leaders on the press for endorsement. That is not to suggest that politicians came to spurn the goodwill of journalists, merely that they happily settled for more informal liaisons. Richard Crossman, who hosted 'journalist lunches at the Garrick', ridiculed his colleagues in Wilson's government who employed 'their own public relations officers'.[2] Such self-serving practices were a far cry from the coercive techniques of the past. The difference can be illustrated by the experiences of successive generations of the Harmsworth family. Lord Northcliffe, the chief of the tribe, assisted the overthrow of Asquith in 1916 and thereby confirmed his own power, which Lloyd George grudgingly recognized in the form of ministerial appointments. His brother, Lord Rothermere, joined Lord Beaverbrook in an attempt to topple Stanley Baldwin, who famously rebuked him for seeking 'the prerogative of the harlot'. Their nephew, Cecil Harmsworth King, turned ferociously against Wilson in 1968, only to be himself removed from the board of the *Daily Mirror* and the *Sun*. By then, not even a Harmsworth could get away with such audacity.

While personal factors cannot be ignored, they were less important than the contexts in which each of the Harmsworths operated. Northcliffe rode the crest of a wave, which had ebbed by the 1930s and evaporated by the 1960s. Politicians, including newspapermen who aspired to political authority, must be judged on the basis of the opportunities open to them. It is doubtful that Northcliffe would have succeeded where Rothermere and King failed. Nothing less than the First World War was required to fulfil his aspirations. Nothing less than the Second World War was required to accommodate Beaverbrook, who better appreciated the growing discrepancy between press power and public service.

We are talking here about newspaper owners, the notorious press lords, who had eclipsed editors as the formulators of newspaper policy. That was the most conspicuous change in the conduct of the press, but arguably not the most profound one. The relationship between editors and proprietors was one side of the coin, that between them and the politicians was another. Upheavals

---
[1] Scott-James, *Influence of the Press*, pp. 211, 213.
[2] Crossman, *Diaries*, II, 368, 373, and III (London, 1977), 255.

within the parties, precipitating realignments within an expanding electorate, necessarily affected the way newspapers were run. That part of the press that doted on Westminster could not help reflecting the convulsions that occurred there. Conflicts within the Unionist alliance, the dismemberment of the Liberal Party and its displacement by Labour, the cataclysms of two world wars, all left their mark and their casualties in Fleet Street. Paradoxically, so did the progressive enlargement of the democratic arena. 'Every extension of the franchise renders more powerful the newspaper and less powerful the politician,' trumpeted Alfred Harmsworth in 1903. On the contrary, the two declined, hand in hand. With a perception born of nostalgia, Winston Churchill recognized as much: 'before the liquefaction of the British political system set in,' he later recalled, 'we had a real political democracy led by a hierarchy of statesmen, and not a fluid mass distracted by newspapers. There was a structure in which statesmen, electors and the press all played their part.' His definitions were different from Harmsworth's, but not so different as both of theirs from ours.[1]

Needless to say, the contraction of the press was due basically to economic causes, beyond the control of politicians. That it took a disproportionately heavy toll on political newspapers – eliminating twelve of the top thirteen properties in Stead's roster as opposed to two of the bottom eight (with the *Evening News* following as a third in 1980) – lends credence to the view that a political stance was at least a disability. Newspapers, which had hitherto survived by virtue of their party identifications, ultimately collapsed under the weight of them. Or else they retreated from the political battlefield, taking up positions of guarded (in some cases feigned) neutrality. Declaring themselves independent, they expressed preferences, particularly at the time of general elections. Their support was volunteered and no longer commanded.

In their Victorian heyday, political journals had helped to inculcate a respect for Parliament by transmitting its proceedings to the nation and, still more, by celebrating them. In return for this estimable service, a quasi-constitutional dignity had been conferred on the press, as signalled by the capital letter that was commonly affixed to it. Eventually, when party disputes were waged out of doors, this dignity wore thin. Newspapers struggled to adapt themselves to new exigencies, invariably to their own disadvantage, and sometimes to their own discredit. Their debility mirrored the diminution of Parliament as an institution and a spreading disaffection with the party system. The majority of newspaper readers, indifferent to political transactions which appeared increasingly remote from their ordinary lives, demanded more succinct and frivolous reporting than the 'quality' papers were designed to provide. Radio and eventually television gave many people all the serious news they wanted to know. A minority, retaining an acute political awareness, demanded a more

[1] Arthur Lawrence, *Journalism as a Profession* (London, 1903), p. 172; Churchill, *A Roving Commission: My Early Life* (New York, 1930), p. 357.

objective presentation, equally incompatible with the historic functions of the political press, which had put a greater premium on views than news. Britain's decline as a world power further shifted the balance of newspaper coverage and, at another level, the patterns of proprietorial control. In the 1850s and '60s, it was considered detrimental for the *Morning Star* to be managed from Manchester. A century later, many British papers were owned by multinational conglomerates with headquarters abroad.

This book will attempt to trace and interpret these configurations. Its methodology was set forth by its predecessor, but presumably warrants recapitulation. The focus is upon the ever-shrinking cluster of newspapers with distinct political attributes, objectives, and connections. The intention is to evaluate journalism in its party political setting. It has not been considered feasible to undertake a full-scale history of the twentieth-century press, much less a survey of the events that newspapers have chronicled in their columns. Nor has it seemed useful for present purposes to engage in detailed content analysis, or to deal with such matters as distribution, staffing, labour relations, and technology, except in so far as they impinge on political performance. That is not to deny that each of these areas deserves investigation in its own right. To have attended to them here, however, would have been to alter the proportions of this book and, more seriously, to submerge its themes.

In the twentieth century, to an even greater extent that before, the political press was based in London and overwhelmingly metropolitan in its outlook. With certain exceptions, which may be taken to prove the rule, attention is firmly fixed on Fleet Street. Some of the people to be encountered there and elsewhere in public life, though perhaps fewer than one might have expected, are carry-overs from the previous century who were introduced in the previous volume. Without too much exaggeration, however, it may be said that they acquired distinctly new personalities along with new opportunities and responsibilities after 1901, none more dramatically than Alfred Harmsworth, who went on to achieve dominance as Lord Northcliffe. The reader who has been denied their prior acquaintance will not, therefore, labour under any serious disadvantage.

The starting point was determined by the terminal point of the companion volume. But the choice of a cut-off requires explanation and perhaps justification. Links between newspapers and party agencies, which held surprisingly well through the early decades of the century, weakened during the interwar period and thereafter snapped. 'The day of the old-fashioned party-tied daily rag is as dead as the pre-war world,' Garvin wrote in 1929 to Beaverbrook.[1] In fact, as the episode of appeasement was soon to reveal, this obituary was a shade premature. The Second World War put the invalid out of its misery. More emphatically than the general election of 1945 and more graphically than

---

[1] Garvin to Beaverbrook, 29 May 1929, Beaverbrook Papers.

the report of the Royal Commission of 1947–49, the elections of 1950 and 1951 proclaimed the demise of 'the old-fashioned party-tied daily rag'.

In 1961–62 and 1974–77, two subsequent Royal Commissions on the Press collected bountiful evidence, which social scientists have expropriated as grist for their mills. Once a neglected subject, shrouded in secrecy, the workings of the press have increasingly elicited official and scholarly inquiry. More often than not, the frames of reference are ideological and the conclusions are stridently tendentious. Newspapers have been considered as tools of capitalist oppression, just as they were once seen as manifestations of original sin. The ailments of the press, industrial as well as metaphysical, may be better diagnosed in the light of their historical antecedents. 'It's not easy to defend,' a character in Tom Stoppard's play, *Night and Day* (1978), remarks of modern British journalism, 'but it's mainly attacked for the wrong reasons'. This study does not purport to point out the right reasons, offering neither polemics nor a blueprint for reconstruction. If it manages to elucidate the wrongness of the wrong reasons, that will be success enough.

One

'THE CROWD OF JOSEPH CHAMBERLAINS'

'In the beginning of the twentieth century,' G. K. Chesterton observed, 'there were so many prophets and so many prophecies, that it was difficult to elude all their ingenuities.' Readers of the press, to which Chesterton himself was a lively contributor, could not have failed to be overwhelmed by this efflorescence, which was particularly striking in the realm of political ideas. Liberalism had emerged from W. E. Gladstone's giant shadow, as did Unionism from Lord Salisbury's, with new tensions and fecundity. Socialism, yet to register an electoral impact, already added to the intellectual ferment. Theories and counter-theories were propounded on every side. Newspapers were active participants in the debate. Free from parliamentary restraints, editors often anticipated the positions of party leaders. And, as Henry S. Lunn reminded W. M. Crook, whose brief tenure at the *Echo* ended in acrimony: 'Directors and proprietors of a paper have as much right to a conscience as an editor.'[1]

The fragility of newspaper enterprises gave greater scope for political intervention in the management of the press. At the same time, dissension within political parties presented irresistible temptations for newspapermen to advance themselves and their propositions. By airing controversies and, still more, by commenting provocatively on them, journalists undoubtedly exacerbated the divisions within parliamentary ranks. The wider the breaches, the bolder were their pronouncements and the more presumptuous their assorted 'ingenuities'.

In its ramshackle state, the Liberal Party left itself open to prophets and prophecies of every shape – including Chesterton's – and purpose. Until the close of 1905, when Sir Henry Campbell-Bannerman formed a government which was soon to enjoy a spectacular victory at the polls, the party had seemed bent on self-destruction. Apart from the well-publicized rift between the Liberal Imperialists and their 'pro-Boer' adversaries, there existed sharp disagreements between militant Nonconformists and scientific secularists, and between Gladstonian fundamentalists and younger collectivists. Lord Rosebery, who had resigned the party leadership in 1896, retained the loyalty

---

[1] Chesterton, *The Napoleon of Notting Hill* (London, 1904), p. 14; Lunn to Crook, 5 May 1900, Crook Papers.

of assorted Liberals, who expected him to resume command at some critical moment. The Liberal press was virtually unanimous in its adulation of Rosebery at the turn of the century, but thereafter turned portentously against him. On 15 February 1902, after two rapid changes of ownership and four of editorship, the *Daily News* was able to write off Rosebery as 'at best a useful and efficient critic of affairs, with undefined political principles, if, indeed, any principles at all'. The *Manchester Guardian* reached the same conclusion, much to the disquiet of J. E. Taylor, its venerable proprietor, who feared that Scott 'assumed rather too hastily that Lord Rosebery had gone over to the Unionists'.[1]

To despair of Rosebery was natural enough. To summon up enthusiasm for his rival required greater effort and perhaps a willing suspension of disbelief. 'Sir Henry Campbell-Bannerman would not himself claim to be a Bright or a Gladstone,' the *Daily News* conceded (6 March 1902). 'But there have been times when men of simple, straightforward honesty and transparent clearness of purpose have been more necessary to the salvation of the people than any great orator.' Like the leader whom it backhandedly praised, the *Daily News* showed greater integrity than dynamism during these troubled years. It was not until 1904, when – along with the *Daily Chronicle* – it reduced its price to a halfpenny, that the paper surged ahead. At that time, too, the *Chronicle* was invigorated by the appointment of Robert Donald to its editorship. In the case of each of these Liberal morning dailies, the reduction in price was obviously a stimulus, though arguably less powerful than the concurrent recovery of party morale.

Among the metropolitan evening papers, official Liberalism could count on varying degrees of support from the *Westminster Gazette*, which sold for a penny, and from the halfpenny *Star* and *Echo*. In the more crowded morning field, it relied on the halfpenny *Morning Leader* as well as the *Daily News* and the *Daily Chronicle*. None of these properties was then a commercial success, and the *Echo*, under the desultory editorship of F. W. Pethick-Lawrence (later a Labour MP and the 1st Baron Pethick-Lawrence), faded out in the summer of 1905. Ernest Parke edited the *Morning Leader* and the *Star* in tandem until 1908, when James Douglas began a twelve-year stint on the latter. At the *Daily News*, with which the *Morning Leader* merged in 1912, A. G. Gardiner held the chair through the First World War, when he – like Donald of the *Chronicle* – was displaced.

An unprepossessing figure, Gardiner did not have an easy time establishing himself, and typified the plight of political editors, especially those of the Liberal persuasion. He began in March 1902 with a ready-made staff that included Herbert Paul, a former MP, who had weathered successive storms in Bouverie Street. Within weeks, Paul was dismissed for having written a

---

[1] Taylor to Scott, 27 February 1902, *Guardian* Archives.

vitriolic obituary of Cecil Rhodes. J. A. Spender 'heard the rumour' and thought it 'a shame, for who, if not Paul, is to find shelter on an organ which prides itself on pro-Boerdom?' His brother Harold, who worked on the *Daily News*, confirmed that Paul had proved 'too much' for George Cadbury, 'the simple moral person who holds the reins'. H. W. Nevinson, then serving unhappily at the *Chronicle* and soon to join the *Daily News*, was 'sure that Gardiner himself had nothing to do with it, but there was a power on that paper behind the editor, as I was myself to discover in 1909'. A minor incident, Paul's dismissal illustrated the endemic disharmonies within and between Liberal newspaper offices.[1]

On no single issue were Liberals more vexed by conflicting 'ingenuities' and disingenuities than that of the perennial Irish question. After two futile attempts to legislate Home Rule, the party retreated from its commitment without corporately disavowing it. Front-bench Liberals privately confessed their disinclination to revive Gladstone's scheme, which had found little favour with the electorate. With the exception of J. A. Spender, who preached revisionism, Liberal publicists held firm, differing only with regard to a timetable. But their espousals, hedged with qualifications, carried neither conviction nor relevance. C. F. Moberly Bell, managing director of *The Times*, challenged the assertion of James Thursfield, a veteran leader-writer, that 'the mistake Unionists often seem to make is that Home Rulers don't believe in Home Rule'. As Bell saw it, the delusion was on the part of the Home Rulers themselves. He claimed to 'have searched in vain for a Home ruler who believed in Home rule and have failed to find one who combines what I call belief with intelligence and honesty'. Even John Morley, whose honesty was as proverbial as his fidelity to Gladstonian doctrine, did not fill the bill. He seemed to advocate Home Rule as 'a policy of despair', which Bell considered 'not a *policy* at all'. Bell supposed that 'one may call anything Home rule and by believing in that call yourself a Home ruler', but he argued that Thursfield's 'middle course "Home rule"' was not essentially different from the 'middle course "Union"' defended by *The Times*.[2]

Since 1886, the Irish controversy had given shape – if not substance – to parliamentary politics. At least superficially, politicians had divided between those who wished to maintain the Union unimpaired and those who wished either to terminate or modify it. Editorial opinion had divided along the same lines. But, by the new century, Home Rule had declined into an abstraction: the Liberals, assuming that they had the motivation, were too weak to implement it; and Irish nationalism had been deflected by measures of Unionist conciliation. Rosebery, for one, had called for a 'clean slate' as the first step towards the recasting of party programmes. However, his own ideas were

[1] Spender to Cook, 5 April 1902, Cook Papers; Nevinson, *Changes and Chances* (London, 1923), p. 315.
[2] Moberly Bell to Thursfield, 15 and 17 October 1901, *Times* Archives.

nebulous and his strategy was disconcertingly hesitant. While it was obvious that the Irish issue had grown stale, it was not clear what would replace it as the touchstone of party allegiance.

For a time, imperialism had seemed the answer. Enveloping the Irish question, it promised – or, depending on one's perspective, threatened – to overhaul parties and possibly to clear the ground between them. The vision of a global empire, efficiently run, proved as alluring to many Liberal and socialist intellectuals as to those who traced their spiritual descent from Disraeli. The Boer War clouded that vision. By discrediting imperialism as a benign and progressive force, that experience disqualified it as a basis for parliamentary realignment. As the war in South Africa dragged on, the slogans began to ring hollow. The politicians who coined them and the publicists who gave them currency soon reverted to their former labels, which had the virtue of familiarity. The few who resisted, like Rosebery and Cook, were banished to the wilderness.

One of the obstacles to change was Lord Salisbury, who carried nineteenth-century forms into a twentieth-century setting. A brake upon his colleagues, he continued until the end of his third premiership to manipulate press opinion. His private secretary, Schomberg McDonnell, made certain to see G. E. Buckle of *The Times* in March 1901, when two minor ministers were relieved of office. 'We parted good friends,' McDonnell reported to his chief. 'Harmsworth had access to Salisbury personally', according to the former's official biographers, who glorified their subject by claiming that McDonnell 'was constantly in his company'. Through McDonnell, Salisbury prevailed on various editors to mute their criticisms of the government and to explicate its policies. His age and reputation secured him a deference that his successors were denied.[1]

In the summer of 1902, Salisbury retired, and the Unionist leadership passed to his nephew, A. J. Balfour. Cracks immediately appeared which were to widen over the next decade. 'I have had great difficulty in discussing the Balfour succession in the *N[ational] R[eview]*,' confessed Leo Maxse, who had replaced Alfred Austin as owner-editor of that monthly journal in 1893, 'for on the one hand one is reluctant to attack a man who has just been chosen, and on the other hand it is of course impossible to approve of the arrangement.' A Liberal Unionist, Maxse would have preferred to see Joseph Chamberlain take command. Certainly Chamberlain, who temporarily continued at the Colonial Office, was a more arresting personality than Balfour, though potentially a more divisive one. Conservatives as well as Liberal Unionists thrilled to his appeal. 'I admire your spirit & the soundness of your views,' Reginald Lucas, Tory MP for Portsmouth, wrote to Lady Bathurst ('Lady Joe'), who was later to inherit control of the *Morning Post*. 'I regard Chamberlain as

---

[1] Memorandum by Macdonnell, 27 March 1901, Salisbury Papers; R. Pound and G. Harmsworth, *Northcliffe* (London, 1959), p. 252.

the ablest & strongest man, & the most unquestionable patriot, in the country.'[1]

During his three years as Prime Minister, Balfour achieved several notable reforms, none of the type to inspire popular enthusiasm. His 1902 Education Act was a case in point. A genuinely constructive measure, it displeased the government's friends and infuriated its enemies. Aggrieved Nonconformists organized to defeat ministerial candidates in a string of by-elections. 'The men who are engineering this agitation, the newspapers that are fostering it, are in the main pro-Boer leaders and pro-Boer press,' Dr Rutherfoord Harris stated in October 1902, when the National Union convened at Manchester; 'the *Daily News* has only changed the theme of its mischievous tirades.'[2] Chamberlain knew that matters were more serious. Liberals, who had bitterly fought each other over the South African war, came together to oppose the Education Act, which went far to restore solidarity in their ranks. Whether Chamberlain was seeking to defuse this controversy or merely to circumvent it, he shook the government by embarking on a crusade for imperial preference. He found few supporters among the elders of his party, but captured the imagination of the rank and file. Resigning from the Cabinet in September 1903 in order to stump the country on behalf of the fiscal proposals he had taken up the previous May, he orchestrated the press as never before or since.

Chamberlain's obsession with journalism was well known. To Sir Edward Hamilton, then Gladstone's private secretary, he had once 'disclaimed all desire to be at the head of affairs himself', saying that he 'preferred power behind the scenes, such as the editor of a powerful paper enjoys'.[3] In 1903, he combined the best of both worlds. 'There is nothing that I envy and admire more in Mr Chamberlain than his power and hold on the Press of this country,' declared Rosebery in a speech at Edinburgh on 12 December.

> At the beginning of last May I suppose there were hardly any newspapers in the country who realised that they were not as much attached to Free Trade as to the British Constitution and the Union Jack. All of a sudden there comes forward this magic musician, who plays a few notes on his pipe, and in a moment the whole mass of this highly respectable and, I thought, firm and convinced Free Trade Press begins to caper. Some are very old papers, who almost wore out their youth on behalf of Free Trade; some are middle-aged papers which I never suspected of these frolics; some are young and active and enterprising papers with enormous circulations. It matters very little what they are – large circulations or small – they all go hopping and bounding and skipping after the magic piper who has summoned them.

[1] Maxse to Cook, 29 July 1902, Cook Papers; Lucas to Lady Bathurst, 24 March 1902, Bathurst Papers. Lady Bathurst later commissioned Lucas to write the biography of her father, *Lord Glenesk and the 'Morning Post'* (London, 1910).
[2] National Union minutes, 14 October 1902.
[3] Sir Edward Hamilton's diary, 2 June 1886.

Rosebery, whose own magic pipes had rusted, made these remarks 'in a tone, not of disparagement, but of good humoured and conscientious envy'. Acknowledging that he was 'not one of those who affect to disparage the power or the influence of the Press', he contemplated that 'it must be delightful to be followed by this dance of adoring and convinced newspapers, but I confess I think it a very serious thing for the cause to which I am attached'. Where Rosebery's Liberal League had failed, Chamberlain's Tariff Reform League brilliantly succeeded. The obvious explanation was the talent of the piper and the rhythm of his tune. But there were some less obvious reasons, too.

Had he bestirred himself, Rosebery might have launched a counter-offensive. In early September 1903, J. A. Spender was staying with Rosebery at Mentmore, where 'a special courier' arrived with a message from Harmsworth, who proffered an alliance against protectionism. Spender recalled that his host had 'laughed, but he was also visibly angry'. Rebuffed by Rosebery, who seemed no better than the 'funny old men' who led the Liberal Party, Harmsworth developed an 'admiration for Chamberlain, as the one real business man among politicians, the man who did things on a big scale and knew how to put the waters in a roar'. As always, his commitment was more personal than ideological. 'He has ... no loyalties to anything but the wind that blows at the moment,' Gardiner afterwards wrote of him. 'When Mr Chamberlain opened his protection campaign, he [Harmsworth] came out against it with all his guns. ... He went to Chamberlain's Glasgow meeting, saw the vast audience ..., believed it spelled victory, and next morning came out in the *Daily Mail* as a sort of St Paul of the new gospel – only to desert it again directly the gospel began to wane.' On 7 October, the morning after Chamberlain's Glasgow speech, Harmsworth published a signed article in the *Daily Mail* in which he pledged general support, save for the proposed 'stomach taxes' which would have raised the price of foodstuffs. Chamberlain worked hard to allay Harmsworth's apprehensions. He sent 'leader suggestions' to H. W. Wilson, the chief leader-writer for the *Daily Mail*, and assured him that, 'just as Harmsworth knows what the public want to read, so I know what the elector wants; it is an instinct in both of us.'[1]

Chamberlain procured Harmsworth's allegiance – however 'fitful, transitory, and incomplete' – by flattery and 'by making it perfectly clear that by the aid of the tax on foreign manufactures much more taxation on food can be remitted than is going to be imposed'. That, as Wilson told Harmsworth, 'would meet your views'. This modest effort won Chamberlain the endorsement of the *Daily Mail*, the *Evening News*, and the *Daily Mirror*, which

[1] Gardiner, 'The Times,' *Atlantic Monthly*, cxix (1917), 116, which A. M. Gollin has described as 'an accurate reflection of the feeling about Harmsworth at this time', *The Observer and J. L. Garvin* (London, 1960), p. 4; Spender, *Life, Journalism and Politics*, II, 171–72, with dates corrected by Gollin, *Observer*, p. 6n.; Wilson to Harmsworth [October 1903], Northcliffe Papers. For Harmsworth's invasion of Fleet Street and its legendary significance, see Volume I (London, 1981), chapter 9.

Harmsworth was to launch on 2 November. Cecil and Hildebrand Harmsworth, who shared their eldest brother's disenchantment with Rosebery, took to championing Chamberlain in their *New Liberal Review*, its title notwithstanding. Yet Chamberlain did not rely on the Harmsworth brethren alone.[1]

Neglecting to inform his audience at Edinburgh of his own exchange with Harmsworth, Rosebery also distorted other matters. Of 'the very old papers' to which he imputed Chamberlainite loyalties, only the *Globe* and the *Morning Post* pledged full support to Tariff Reform, and it was fanciful to suggest that either had worn away its youth on behalf of Free Trade. The *Standard*, as we shall see, sided with the Tory Free Fooders until November 1904, when C. Arthur Pearson purchased control. *The Times*, which had grudgingly resigned itself to Free Trade, was a house divided. Such greybeards as W. F. Monypenny and Valentine Chirol, along with such younger men as Leo Amery, were dedicated to Chamberlain's proposals, which Professor W. A. S. Hewins extolled in a series of sixteen articles. Nevertheless, Buckle (who struck Hewins as 'wobbly') and Moberly Bell regretted Chamberlain's strategy as precipitate. For the sake of party unity, Bell tried at first to protect Chamberlain from his journalistic friends. 'The greater part of the press is rushing to the conclusion that Chamberlain's propositions involve a rapid & immediate revolution in our fiscal policy,' he complained in June to John St Loe Strachey, who flew the flag of Free Trade Unionism in the *Spectator*. 'My own belief – and after a good deal of talk with Mr Chamberlain I believe his – is that the change for many years to come would be hardly appreciable. Of course it is a revolution in ideas but in practice what would it amount to?' By August, Bell had come to see that 'Mr Chamberlain's Crusade ... threatens to transform entirely the position of parties', a not unwelcome prospect. Admitting that his own 'convictions are very strong that absolute Free Trade, if we could get it, would be the best thing for us', he was 'quite certain ... that there are difficulties in our existing system, and if we can help to cement the Empire, even by some financial sacrifice, we have got to do it'. A self-styled 'radical with Imperialistic leanings', Bell was more inclined to doubt the practicality than the merits of Chamberlain's formula. While '*The Times* was not definitely in favour of Tariff Reform', at least 'it was not antagonistic'.[2]

By contrast, the *Morning Post*, which had never quite forgiven Disraeli for acquiescing in Free Trade, hailed Chamberlain as a redeemer. Winston Churchill, the Conservative member for Oldham and 'an old friend', pleaded in vain with Oliver Borthwick, whose father was Lord Glenesk and owner of the paper,

---

[1] Gollin, *Observer*, p. 6; Wilson to Harmsworth, 1 October 1903 and telegrams of 3 October 1903, Northcliffe Papers; Pound and Harmsworth, p. 264.
[2] Moberly Bell to Strachey, 10 June 1903, Strachey Papers; Moberly Bell to [?], 5 August 1903, quoted in E. Moberly Bell, *Life and Letters of C. F. Moberly Bell* (London, 1927), pp. 225–26; *History of The Times*, IV, part 1 (London, 1952), 9–11.

not to commit the *Morning Post* to the support of Chamberlain's scheme. If it succeeded, it would break up the Empire, and in failing, as it is bound to do, it may do the most terrible injury to the Conservative party. .... Do not be dragged at the tail of *The Times*, which is simply a rampant Protectionist, and will, not for the first time, get badly left.

Churchill, soon to cross the floor to the Liberal benches, also tried to persuade Harmsworth. 'The *Daily Mail* is doing fine service; but there are many difficulties ahead,' he warned on 26 August. Calculating that 'this is the time for a central government', Churchill recommended that Harmsworth should 'have a talk' with Rosebery, his neighbour in Berkeley Square. Harmsworth again tried, only to be turned away. Still Churchill remained optimistic: 'With a little care we might very easily set up a great central government neither Protectionist nor Pro Boer, which will deal with the shocking administrative inefficiency which prevails.' To this end, he expressed the 'wish we had a Manchester paper!' Within weeks, Harmsworth had cast his lot with Chamberlain, in whose interest he eventually acquired the *Manchester Courier*. In congratulating him, Wilson wrote that 'it is excellent that you have held aloof from Winston, and are not in the camp of the stand-stills.'[1]

The *Daily Telegraph*, the *Pall Mall Gazette*, and the *St James's Gazette* were presumably the 'middle-aged papers' to which Rosebery alluded at Edinburgh. Never having known a system of protection, they were all the more attracted to it. The *Daily Express*, founded in 1900, was the baby of Fleet Street. At the start, it had explicitly eschewed politics. But Pearson, its proprietor and initially its titular editor, evinced early tendencies towards imperial preference. Alexander Paul, a migrant from the *Daily News*, lunched with him on 7 February 1901 to explore the possibility of employment. 'I am very sorry to see, however, that he is evidently going in for Protection,' Paul informed Cook, his former editor. 'I should not like to be associated with Protectionism. But I understand that Pearson is willing to keep his paper on independent lines and to give all sides a hearing.'[2] At the appropriate time, Pearson proved a natural recruit for Chamberlain's army.

In the summer of 1903, while Harmsworth stubbornly balked at food taxes, the Tariff Reformers astutely played off Pearson against him. Constant competitors, Harmsworth and Pearson were swashbucklers of comparable age and aggrandizement. Both had started out as contributors to Sir George Newnes's *Tit-Bits*, which was the model for Harmsworth's *Answers* and for *Pearson's Weekly*, designed 'to interest, to elevate, to amuse'. Pearson, a Wykehamist, was the better educated as well as the more philanthropic. No

---

[1] Churchill to Borthwick, 30 May 1903, quoted in Lucas, *Glenesk*, p. 406; Churchill to Harmsworth, 26 August and 1 September 1903, and Wilson to Harmsworth, 1 October 1903, Northcliffe Papers.
[2] Paul to Cook, 8 February 1901, Cook Papers.

less resourceful as a financier, he was more innovative in the areas of typography and merchandising: the *Express* had experimented by splashing news across its front page; and *Pearson's Weekly*, its circulation boosted by insurance schemes rather than the usual competitions, dabbed its copies with eucalyptus oil to afford its readers immunity against influenza.

R. D. Blumenfeld, an expatriate American, was the link between them. *De facto* editor of the *Express*, he was also a crony of Harmsworth, who had deputed him to make an offer for *The Times*. Taking credit for having invented the slogan 'Tariff Reform Means Work for All,' Blumenfeld conceived of journalism as public relations. 'Mr Chamberlain has not until now been able to secure the support of a single London daily,' he recorded in his diary on 23 June 1903, 'and we, who are ardent Tariff Reformers, felt that it was time to see to the support of his plans, particularly since Alfred Harmsworth thunders away about "stomach taxes".' Assisted by the Wilson brothers, H. W. who worked for the *Mail* and J. B. who worked for the *Express*, he fixed an interview between Chamberlain and Pearson, 'the hesitant newspaper proprietor'. Pearson gratified them by placing the *Express* at Chamberlain's disposal and, still more, by accepting the chairmanship of the fledgling Tariff Reform League. He subscribed to League funds and himself paid an annual salary of £1,200 to Hewins, secretary of Chamberlain's high-powered Tariff Commission. When Maxse subsequently proposed that Harmsworth should be conscripted as a member of the League's executive committee, Chamberlain demurred: 'Pearson joined us from the first and has done inestimable service. We cannot press for Harmsworth's inclusion unless Pearson himself is equally favourable to it.'[1]

There was no denying the importance of Pearson's adherence. Although the *Express* had yet to show a profit, its circulation – second only to the *Mail*'s – was particularly impressive among the artisan classes that Chamberlain needed to reconcile to the short-term prospect of 'dear food'. Moreover, an estimated million readers ostensibly accepted the premiss that 'if you see it in *Pearson's Weekly*, it is so'. Pearson compensated for his weak grasp of economic theory by ensuring that enthusiastic crowds were on hand to greet Chamberlain at every whistle-stop. Yet his crude methods of propaganda discomforted Amery and other intellectuals, disappointed by results in successive by-elections. For them, Pearson was little more than bait to catch a larger fish.

Harmsworth was slow to bite. In July, he commiserated with Strachey that 'we are being worsted at every turn in the fight so far, except in the matter of the Press which, with few exceptions, will turn round as they see [how] the contest goes'. To his annoyance, *The Times* and the *Standard* seemed to be tempering their objections 'to the food part of the tax', which he implored Chamberlain to

---

[1] Blumenfeld, *R.D.B.'s Diary* (London, 1930), pp. 194–95; Blumenfeld, *The Press in My Time*, pp. 48–49; Pearson to Hewins, 14 November 1903, Hewins Papers; Chamberlain to Maxse, 1 January 1904, Maxse Papers.

drop from the Tariff Reform package. 'Chamberlain can only gain by the divided state of the opposition to him,' Harmsworth grimly reckoned, '& he is the only man with a definite plan.' That Harmsworth should have made common cause with Strachey indicated how far he then stood from the protectionist camp. 'The *Spectator* is, no doubt, an influence, & its hostility to the new departure counts for something,' Milner conceded to Iwan-Müller, 'but for my own part I am glad to be quit of such an ally. ... An organ wh. can deliberately appeal to Hicks Beach (!!) to head a "Cave" for the salvation of the Empire, is no fit associate for the likes of me – or you.'[1]

Sir Michael Hicks Beach (now Viscount St Aldwyn) was an erstwhile Colonial Secretary who had accompanied Salisbury into retirement. Like other party notables who remained in office, Conservatives and Liberal Unionists alike, he ascribed paramount value to the maintenance of Free Trade. Balfour was able to stave off a confrontation until September, when Chamberlain quietly tendered his resignation. By a sleight-of-hand, the Prime Minister also obtained the resignations of Chamberlain's most prominent critics, thus ensuring the semblance of a balance within the Cabinet. Chamberlain did not wish to bring down the government, in which his son Austen was stationed at the Exchequer; rather he hoped to convert it to his views by demonstrating their electoral feasibility. 'I am glad you agree with me,' he wrote to Moberly Bell on 25 September, 'that if reconstruction goes on satisfactorily the Government will last some time yet.' Nevertheless, the effect was to weaken seriously Balfour's hand, while leaving Chamberlain free to 'carry the fiery cross into the constituencies'.[2]

For Harmsworth as for others, Chamberlain's departure from office was a signal that he meant business. More than that, it confirmed him as the pivotal figure in national politics. By throwing down the gauntlet, he had produced a new polarization. His speech at Glasgow on 6 October, as much by its fervency as by its simplifications, satisfied Harmsworth and the doubting Thomases of Printing House Square, who had been studiously briefed beforehand. Writing to Moberly Bell, Austen Chamberlain concurred that 'the movement in favour' of his father's policy was, 'as you say, marked indeed. The *Mail*'s change is I think of some significance.' Chamberlain took time off from his whirlwind campaign to collogue with Harmsworth and with his 'brother, Mr Hildebrand'. As a reward, the *Evening News*, which had previously railed against 'stomach taxes', filled seven columns on 4 November with a verbatim report of his speech that day at Birmingham, 'and was in the streets shortly after half-past ten at night'.[3]

[1] Harmsworth to Strachey, 16 and 17 July 1903, Strachey Papers; Milner to Iwan-Müller, 29 June 1903, Milner Papers.
[2] Chamberlain to Moberly Bell, 25 September 1903, *Times* Archives; Alan Sykes, *Tariff Reform in British Politics, 1903–1913* (Oxford, 1979), ch. 2.
[3] Austen Chamberlain to Moberly Bell, 15 October 1903, *Times* Archives; Chamberlain to Harmsworth, 3 December 1903 (copy), Chamberlain Papers; *Sell's* (1904).

But Chamberlain's lieutenants knew better than to trust either to chance or to Harmsworth's whims. What they wanted was unconditional support, which would not come unstuck. 'I quite understand your feelings about the possibility of the D[aily] T[elegraph] relapsing,' Amery told Garvin, who wrote leaders for that paper and pungent articles for the *National Review*. 'But isn't it even worse,' Amery asked, 'that the case should be lost by default in the columns of *The Times* which after all is politically more important?'[1] Determined not so much to educate as to overwhelm public opinion, the Tariff Reformers feared the damage that might be done by waverers. Many of them being newspapermen themselves, they set great store by the press. Short of a monopoly, they sought to obtain editorial predominance. Nothing less would allow them to impress their arguments on the country, on the parliamentary Unionist Party, and on one another.

As chairman of the Tariff Reform League, Pearson explained the situation to Harmsworth:

> The weakest point in our armour at present seems to be in the fact that definite statements made by Mr Chamberlain's principal opponents are reported in the Press generally, while owing to the fact that Mr Chamberlain is practically the only speaker on our side to whose speeches considerable space is given, replies to these statements do not reach the public.

The first step towards remedying this deficiency was the purchase of the *Sun* in November 1903 by a syndicate headed by Sir George Armstrong, who had run the *Globe* since 1871 and the Sunday *People* since 1881. But that, in itself, was hardly sufficient. Pearson's personal efforts were more substantial. That year, he bought the *St James's Gazette* from Edward Steinkopff, entrusting its editorship to Ronald McNeill (later Lord Cushendun), a staunch Chamberlainite. From the ashes of the *Newcastle Evening Leader*, he brought forth the *Newcastle Evening Mail*. He next entered into prolonged negotiations to buy the *Standard* and the *Evening Standard* from his relations, the Johnstones. Outbidding Harmsworth, who took it in good grace, Pearson clinched the deal in November 1904 and, the following May, amalgamated the *St James's* with the *Evening Standard*, which had an assured sale in the City. The penny *Standard* and the halfpenny *Daily Express*, addressed to markedly different readerships, remained separate, each expounding protectionism in its own way. Not for nothing, Churchill admitted, had Chamberlain saluted Pearson as 'the "champion hustler" of the Tariff Reform League'.[2]

The capture of the *Standard* created a greater stir than its dwindling circulation seemed to warrant. 'I cannot remember any one of the frequent

---

[1] Amery to Garvin, 2 February 1904, Garvin Papers.
[2] Pearson to Harmsworth, 25 November 1903, Northcliffe Papers; Churchill, speech at Glasgow, 10 November 1904, *The Times*, 11 November 1904.

transfers in the ownership of newspapers which caused nearly so much discussion as has been caused by the sale of the *Standard* to Mr Pearson,' reflected the writer of the 'London Letter' in the *Manchester Guardian* (7 November 1904). Besides its historic associations with Disraeli and Salisbury, frequently celebrated and rarely understood, the paper was considered the morning voice of middle-class Conservatism. Edited by Byron Curtis, with Sidney Low (formerly editor of the *St James's*) as its political leader-writer, the *Standard* had been the only penny morning journal on the ministerial side to dissent from Chamberlain's proposals. 'Its long and solitary defence of the blockhouse of Tory Free Trade has been watched as something heroic,' wrote the *Guardian*'s correspondent, who noted the 'amazing situation' – now that the *Daily News* and the *Daily Chronicle* were priced at a halfpenny – that 'there will not be a single penny morning Free Trade paper in London'.

Pearson had moved swiftly and decisively. 'The *Standard* is in the market and I have secured an option on it,' he notified Chamberlain on 12 October. 'The paper had, of course, gone down very much of late, but not too far to be saved from the total wreck which will befall it if it is left much longer under its present management.' His avowed motives were more political than commercial.

> The *Standard* among newspapers is like a free-fooder in the Cabinet. It is a powerful enemy in our ranks and very much more harmful than an open foe. In my judgment the *Standard* has from the point of view of newspaper influence done far more to impede the course of Tariff Reform than any other paper. It has still a great hold among the sober thinking classes and particularly among business men, for its commercial intelligence has always been looked upon as the very best.

Blumenfeld, who did not hesitate to put down the *Standard*'s 'precipitous decline to its continued espousal of Free Trade', heard on 3 November that Pearson had paid £700,000 for the property. Cook understood that the sum was 'not far short of £700,000', as opposed to Harmsworth's offer of £450,000. 'The present circulation is 80,000,' he remarked incredulously; 'last year's profits said to have been 10,000 – at one time 100,000.' There were rumours that Pearson, who 'has no capital of his own', was backed by South African investors; but Cook regarded that as 'mere surmise'. In fact, Pearson's outlay has been put at £300,000, less than half the amount that Chamberlain and Harmsworth were led to believe. And his principal backer was Sir Alexander Henderson (later Lord Faringdon), Liberal Unionist MP for West Staffordshire and treasurer of the Tariff Reform League.[1]

---

[1] Pearson to Chamberlain, 12 October 1904, quoted in Sidney Dark, *The Life of Sir Arthur Pearson* (London, 1922), p. 114; Blumenfeld, *R.D.B.'s Diary*, pp. 197–98; Cook's diary, 5 November 1904, Cook Papers; *History of The Times*, III (London, 1947), 122.

Mentioning a purchase price of £700,000, the *Daily Mail* broke the story on Saturday, 5 November. 'No alterations are contemplated in the price, appearance, or general tone of the paper,' the *Mail* stated, adding that Pearson ('a young man not only in years but in dominant force') had privately undertaken a 'business venture' and was not 'acting for the Tariff Reform League'. Aged thirty-eight (though he 'talks with the enthusiasm of twenty-five'), Pearson was identified as the publisher of 'numerous "weeklies" and monthly magazines', the founder of the *Daily Express*, the owner of five provincial dailies, and the holder of a 'controlling interest in the *St James's Gazette*'. Pearson, without correcting the *Mail*'s estimate of his expenditure, thanked Harmsworth 'for the nice things you say about me in this morning's *Daily Mail* and for the importance which you give to my purchase of the *Standard*'. He incidentally revealed that 'it had been intended to complete the business next Tuesday or Wednesday, but the announcement in your paper made it necessary to complete it at once'.[1]

Not everyone responded with such complaisance. Churchill protested that a staff of 'able writers' was to be 'scattered', and 'their places ... filled by the obedient scribes of a mammoth trust'. Pearson wrote to the *Spectator* on 9 November to deny these allegations, which his biographer contemptuously dismissed as 'windy rubbish'. Yet they were essentially true. Obviously, Curtis could not continue. He was replaced as editor of the *Standard* by H. A. Gwynne, whom Chamberlain recommended. A strong imperialist whose bond with Milner dated from his time as the Reuters war correspondent in South Africa, Gwynne went on to edit the *Morning Post* from 1911 to 1937. At the *Evening Standard*, S. J. Pryor was succeeded by William Woodward, Pearson's cousin. Although Sidney Low and Richardson Evans were retained as leader-writers for the *Standard*, the situation was more complicated than either Pearson or his biographer saw fit to relate. 'I have no idea what is going to happen, or indeed what *is* happening, at Shoe Lane,' Low wrote to Cook on 11 November. 'They have very courteously asked me to continue as before with the understanding that I am not to write Tariff Reform or anything else of which I disagree.' As recompense, Low was appointed literary editor. 'I can't tell you with what grief I heard about the *Standard* and with what sympathy for you,' Spender told him on the 17th. 'I am glad you still find literary work you can do, but what perverse waste of material that you should be shut off from writing on home politics!' This awkward arrangement lasted until Pearson terminated it at the end of 1908. Thereafter, on a free-lance basis, Low contributed a weekly quota of four leaders and one signed article to the *Standard*.[2]

[1] Pearson to Harmsworth, 5 November 1904, Northcliffe Papers.
[2] Dark, *Pearson*, pp. 117–19; Low to Cook, 11 November 1904, Cook Papers; Spender to Low, 17 November 1904, quoted in Desmond Chapman-Huston, *The Lost Historian: A Memoir of Sir Sidney Low* (London, 1936), p. 146.

Frederick Greenwood, whom Low had displaced in 1888 as editor of the *St James's Gazette*, lamented that the press was 'running down into disgrace as deep as it ever stood in, or deeper'. The new managers at Shoe Lane, he declared to David Hannay, once one of his band of 'Merry Men', were behaving 'after the manner of the mudlarks whom you may remember under the hotel-windows at Greenwich'. From an 'informant, who is behind the scenes', Greenwood learnt that plans were afoot to launch 'a new sixpenny weekly ... for the express purpose of advocating Chamberlain & all his works'. Conceived as a riposte to the *Spectator*, the projected journal was to be edited by 'the famous Mr Monypenny of *The Times* & South Africa'. Reportedly, 'the whole arrangement had been made in consultation with Mr Chamberlain personally'. In the event, the venture did not come off, and the Tariff Reformers had to make do with the *Outlook*. C. S. Goldman, its new proprietor (and later Unionist MP for Penryn), was 'very anxious to develop and improve it in order to make it the leading weekly representing our views', Amery told Garvin, who soon became its editor. Goldman had 'just been staying with Joe who seems to be very anxious that he should push on and be successful with it'. For his part, Garvin later recalled that 'Mr Chamberlain practically placed me in the editorial chair of the *Outlook* like a soldier at his post'.[1]

In *The Man Who Was Thursday*, his 'nightmare' novel of 1908, Chesterton fantasized over how 'a murmur of "Mr Joseph Chamberlain"' was amplified into a roar, as 'the crowd of Joseph Chamberlains (a solemn thought) could be heard trampling down the corridor'. That was a perfect metaphor for Fleet Street a few years earlier. In a tally on 10 November 1904, the *Manchester City News* counted fifteen 'Protectionist' metropolitan dailies, four of them controlled by Pearson and three by Harmsworth. On the Free Trade side, there were but six papers, all Liberal. Henry Labouchere's *Truth* (30 November) professed unconcern: 'The general public seldom read leading articles, and it is only by those that a newspaper proprietor can endeavour to promote the cause he supports. ... So long as there are grievances and scandals a newspaper will be a Radical agent, whatever may be the opinions expressed in the leading articles.' This interpretation, arguably more realistic than cynical, failed to convince contemporaries, just as it has since failed to mollify those who criticize the press for an inherent conservative bias. Least of all did it quiet the rage of the Unionist Free Traders, whose platform had been wrested from them.

On the evening of 2 December, Hicks Beach (as he was still known in political circles) called on J. S. ('Jack') Sandars, Balfour's private secretary. In 'full cry about the *Standard*', he unveiled a scheme to start a Free Trade rival. Sandars, who 'deprecated' the idea, 'told him of the thousands of Party money sunk in these inglorious enterprises'. As Sandars recounted the conversation to

---

[1] Greenwood to Hannay, 7 November 1904, Hannay Papers; Amery to Garvin, 4 October 1904, and Garvin to Arthur Steel-Maitland, 24 April 1912, Garvin Papers.

Balfour, 'Beach did not disagree, and then went on to discuss Pearson's policy'. Sandars, thinking it 'only right to be quite frank with him as an old colleague and friend', disclosed that Balfour 'had seen Pearson . . . *after the transaction of purchase was complete*'. Pearson had purportedly requested an interview with the Prime Minister, who was 'merely the listener to a man of business talking with the enthusiasm of an expert upon his own business'. The stress that Sandars laid on the sequence of events implied an element of obfuscation or possibly deception. In any case, Hicks Beach was smoothed down. After talking to Sandars, he dined at Lady Jeune's, where he was introduced to Gwynne, 'Pearson's new Editor'. The spell was broken. The next morning, Hicks Beach returned to tell Sandars, 'in his own powerful language, that this man was one of the biggest fools he had ever met'. Gwynne had 'talked, according to Beach, with the greatest recklessness. He announced that Pearson would very shortly make a very rapid change of front, and that the *Standard* would become a Protectionist organ in a very short space of time.'[1] So much for Sandars's assurances that Pearson was first and foremost a businessman. By depicting Balfour as an honest broker, Sandars had made him seem a dupe.

In fact, Balfour was an astute tactician who was playing a waiting game. That he ultimately lost does not detract from the skill of his performance, much less from its grace. Personally sympathetic to Chamberlain's protectionist designs, he was reluctant to declare himself prematurely for fear of frightening the electorate, colonial opinion, or his orthodox associates. For himself as well as his party, he demanded 'liberty of fiscal negotiation', leaving his objectives conveniently vague. Tariff Reform had to be brought within the realm of 'practical politics' before any attempt could be made to legislate it.[2] Newspapers were uniquely equipped to achieve this necessary consensus. Moreover, their own reactions could be taken as an index to the political mood.

Appearances to the contrary, Balfour was keenly attentive to the press. Less of a favourite than Chamberlain, who was 'Joe' to his Fleet Street admirers, Balfour kept contact with journalists who supplied him with information and guidance. His lines of communication criss-crossed Chamberlain's. It was not so much that the two men competed for newspaper support as that they drew on many of the same sources. In March 1903, when Balfour considered the possibility of nominating the Duke of Connaught as adjutant-general, he procured Buckle's promise 'that the appointment will not be seriously attacked by *The Times*'. (Buckle urged him to 'avoid making the appointment, at any rate at present', and Balfour complied.)[3] Resolved to tread a middle course and thereby to avert an open rupture, he made extensive use of journalists in his own languid way.

[1] Sandars to Balfour, 3 December 1904, Balfour Papers.
[2] Balfour used these phrases in his letter to the King, 15 September 1903, quoted in Sykes, *Tariff Reform*, p. 51.
[3] Buckle to Balfour, 3 March 1903, Sandars Papers.

Since his university days, Balfour had enjoyed a warm friendship with Iwan-Müller, whose career he advanced. From 1884 to 1896, Iwan-Müller was the political leader-writer for the *Manchester Courier* and, in that capacity, cast an eye on affairs in Balfour's local constituency. Restless in Manchester, he had persuaded Balfour to put forward his name for the editorship of the *Morning Post*, then served as second-in-command to Cust on the *Pall Mall Gazette*. Eventually, he found a berth on the *Daily Telegraph*. In the eventful summer of 1903, when Balfour drew up his 'Economic Notes on Insular Free Trade', he sent Iwan-Müller a draft copy. 'I have read and re-read the "Notes" with deep sympathy and absolute concurrence,' replied Iwan-Müller, who in turn submitted 'a sketch for some things I'm going to say to the world' on the vexing subject of tariffs. Iwan-Müller advised Balfour to delay the promulgation of his views until the critical moment, and it was only in September that the 'Economic Notes' saw publication in pamphlet form. Apart from his services as an adviser, Iwan-Müller also functioned as Balfour's intermediary with other journalists. On 10 August, for example, he broached Balfour's proposals with J. Nicol Dunn, the editor of the *Morning Post*, and 'the result of that conference' meant that he could 'sleep less disturbed this night'. Dunn was on the point of leaving his office 'for the usual month's holiday', and Iwan-Müller instructed Sandars 'to be very careful about the *Morning Post* in Dunn's absence. I think you should write to him 'to be forwarded' asking to where you should commit "in advance" a very confidential minute.' With Dunn's approval, presumably delivered behind Borthwick's back, Iwan-Müller undertook to 'write the article on the notes wherever I am'.[1]

These cloak-and-dagger activities were part of a network of intrigues, mostly played out in the press. The *Daily Telegraph*, representing the Unionist Party in microcosm, was torn between Iwan-Müller's Balfourite leanings and Garvin's espousal of Chamberlainism. Besides his unsigned leaders in the *Telegraph*, Garvin wrote in those pages – as in the *Fortnightly Review* – as "Calchas", and he was also 'Our Special Inquirer' for the *National Review*, where he collaborated with Maxse to produce a supplement on 'The Economics of Empire' that weighed down the September number. Suggesting 'A Tariff Reformer' as a suitable by-line, Garvin was instead fancifully dignified as 'The Assistant Editor'. Maxse was Garvin's 'chief personal link with Chirol and *The Times* generally', much as Garvin was Maxse's link with Harmsworth. *The Times* praised the September supplement to the *National Review* and stated that 'no thoughtful reader will deny that the facts which it adduces and the arguments it employs are of the gravest and most impressive kind' (1 September). Thus, a good deal of press comment was patently manufactured. Under a variety of signatures that scarcely preserved

---

[1] Iwan-Müller to Balfour, 9 August 1903, Dunn to Iwan-Müller, 10 August 1903, and Iwan-Müller to Sandars, 10 August 1903, Sandars Papers.

anonymity, a handful of publicists debated with one another and sometimes with themselves. It amused Garvin to recall his

> second and most daring interview with Mr Chamberlain. He was just upon the point of devouring me, when I told him for the first time that I was 'Calchas' and various other pseudonyms and anonyms, who had been like a whole train of followers. He said to me across the table 'I did not know you were my unknown supporter,' and all was right and a great hour followed.

To Andrew Bonar Law, Garvin pointed up the moral: 'You will sometimes know who is your supporter, sometimes you will not.' If the politicians were occasionally bemused, how much more was the general public?[1]

Balfour might comfortably ignore the vast outpouring of articles. 'I have read Spender (he is the Editor of the *Westminster*) hastily,' he wrote on 6 September 1903 to the Duke of Devonshire. 'At first sight I am not impressed: partly because I never read "Calchas" to whom he is replying.' Nevertheless, Balfour could not ignore what journalists were thinking, and especially on whose behalf they were thinking it. It was Sandars's job to keep him abreast. In addition, Chamberlain forwarded 'secret and dictated' copies of vital correspondence. J. Parker Smith, Liberal Unionist MP for the Partick division of Lanarkshire and Chamberlain's parliamentary private secretary, visited Edinburgh on 8 September, '& called on [Charles] Cooper of the *Scotsman*'. He reported the interview to Chamberlain, who promptly remitted word to Balfour. A weathercock in 1886, when he had forsaken Gladstonianism for Unionism, Cooper delivered 'his opinion' that Chamberlain's cause was 'winning all along the line. He said that he had been brought up himself on the very milk of Cobden, had heard Cobden & Bright on that subject & had always been a Free Trader of the straitest – till recent years when he had had doubts, but put them aside as impossible.' When Chamberlain repudiated Free Trade, the *Scotsman* staff instinctively proposed to denounce him, only to incur an editorial veto. 'No,' Cooper told his colleagues. 'I have known Mr Ch. for many years & am not going against him without being very sure of my reasons!' The leader-writers of the *Scotsman*, 'at a loss what to do', received firm instructions: 'Attack the people who are attacking Mr Ch. but don't commit yourselves.' In the same post, Chamberlain forwarded to Balfour a letter he had received from Moberly Bell, who had returned to Printing House Square after a month's holiday to discover a 'change of tone ... in all my reports from

---

[1] Maxse to Garvin, 3 August 1903, Garvin Papers; Garvin to Maxse, 29 August 1903, Maxse Papers; Garvin to Stanley Morison, 6 June 1943 (copy), *Times* Archives; Garvin to Bonar Law, 20 November 1906 (copy), Garvin Papers. Garvin proved less tolerant of pluralism on the part of others. R. M. Barrington-Ward, assisting him at the *Observer* between stints on *The Times*, hoped 'to employ my week (as opposed to my week-end) more fully by working as Secretary or quasi-editor of *The Round Table*. Garvin, however, took the view that it was impossible to be in the counsels of two political journals at once, even two journals as sympathetic and cooperative as these.' Entry of September-October 1919, Barrington-Ward's diary.

the country. We are I'm afraid going to lose on that ridiculous fiction – the big loaf,' Bell anticipated. 'On the mere question of a tariff on manufactured goods we could I believe win all along the line, but the taxation of food proposals give the enemy a tremendous weapon.' On 9 September, Chamberlain cited these letters to Balfour as evidence of the mutual advantages to be gained should he withdraw from the Cabinet and stump the country. That day, he offered his resignation, which Balfour made public a week later. Neither Cooper nor Moberly Bell had induced Chamberlain's decision, but both had given an added push.[1]

Balfour was in direct contact with Cooper, whom he sent another advance copy of his 'Economic Notes'. On 12 September, two days before the Cabinet assembled to pass judgment, Cooper had already assured Balfour that he could 'count on the support of the *Scotsman*'. Claiming to 'have read much on the subject, with strong Free Trade predilections not to say prejudices', Cooper professed himself 'satisfied that the policy foreshadowed in your paper (which I have read with great interest, and shall certainly read again) is the policy that Great Britain ought to adopt'. So that he could guard against misunderstandings, Cooper requested 'such information, either for us or for my guidance, as you may feel at liberty to give'.[2] The *Scotsman* was therefore entitled to infer on the 14th that Balfour 'looks approvingly on the object Mr Chamberlain has in view'. Anticipating 'that resignations may ... be tendered', the paper scoffed at 'wild speculation' that the ministry would fall, that Parliament would be dissolved, or that 'the resignations would throw the whole Constitution into the melting pot'. Soon afterwards, when resignations were actually announced, the *Scotsman* was convinced 'that both Mr Chamberlain and Mr Balfour have taken the course that was best in the circumstances'. Brushing aside other departures from the Cabinet as 'comparatively unimportant', it authoritatively declared that Chamberlain would continue to give 'his perfect sympathy and his cordial support' to the Prime Minister, who accepted 'in spirit and principle' the policy of protectionism (18 September).

In spite of its distance from London, the *Scotsman* had a particular bearing on this crisis. 'With regard to the general feeling among Liberal Unionists, I have consulted the *Scotsman*'s representative, who is very much in touch with that group of the Party,' Sandars told Balfour. In seceding from the government, the Duke of Devonshire had threatened to 'carry the Liberal Unionists in a body out of our ranks'. But the *Scotsman*'s parliamentary expert discerned 'that the Duke's active adherents will be relatively few', and that 'Chamberlain can get on very well' without recourse to 'the Liberal Unionist machine'. Such counsel was extremely useful to Balfour, who was balancing one faction against

---

[1] Balfour to Devonshire, 6 September 1903, Devonshire Papers; Parker Smith to Chamberlain, 8 September 1903, and Moberly Bell to Chamberlain, 8 September 1903 (copies), enclosed in Chamberlain to Balfour, 9 September 1903, Sandars Papers.

[2] Cooper to Balfour, 12 September 1903, Sandars Papers.

another. Others who rendered assistance included Henry Cust, who had returned to the backbenches after an earlier stint at the *Pall Mall Gazette*. But the Prime Minister's mainstay was Iwan-Müller, who enhanced the status of any paper for which he wrote. In April 1904, when the Anglo-French entente was negotiated, Iwan-Müller and Chirol both received, 'merely for their guidance', copies of all but the most secret communiqués. The following October, when Balfour undertook to clarify his economic position in a speech to the Scottish Conservative Club at Edinburgh, Sandars 'had a long turn with Iwan-Müller . . . so that he can write appropriately'. The effort was repaid with lavish coverage in the *Daily Telegraph*, which was 'convinced that the Premier's rallying cry will not only heal all the schisms, and reunite the Unionist party, but that it will attract to his standard many who have hitherto been indifferent, or even hostile' (4 October).[1]

Iwan-Müller's effectiveness depended on the disposition of his proprietor, Edward Levy Lawson, a baronet since 1892 and Baron Burnham since the previous year. 'Müller says he fears old Lawson has been suffering from an overdose of Asquith & Metternich,' Sandars remarked after the owner of the *Telegraph* had accepted hospitality first from the Liberal politician and then from the German ambassador. He had good reason for concern. Within weeks, Iwan-Müller described to Sandars how his 'connection with the *D.T.* was "as near as nothing" severed . . . because I would not write more violently than the circumstances seemed to me to warrant – and I fear I see the end coming though as I told the chief I would do nothing to provoke it'. It was well understood that the chief to whom Iwan-Müller referred was Balfour, not Burnham.[2]

The elevation of Lawson to the peerage elicited an amount of anti-Semitic chaff, but no serious criticism. More controversial was the conferment in 1903 of a baronetcy on Alfred Harmsworth. Strenuous denials failed to quash rumours that the honour, long coveted, was purchased by a contribution to Unionist Party funds. Harmsworth had more to offer than the mere bounty of his cheque-book. Deriving his fortune and reputation from a chain of popular periodicals, he acquired the *Evening News* in 1894 and, two years later, struck gold with the *Daily Mail*. The *Daily Mirror* was his next exploit. It began on 2 November 1903 as a morning penny daily for, by, and about women. Advance publicity generated a first-day sale of more than 265,000 copies, which quickly melted away. Circulation plummeted below 25,000, and Harmsworth confessed to have 'dropped £100,000' before 26 January 1904, when this 'flat, rank, and unmitigated failure' was successfully transformed into a halfpenny illustrated paper. Mary Howarth was replaced as editor by Hamilton Fyfe, who

---

[1] Sandars to Balfour, 6 October 1903, 11 April and 1 October 1904, Balfour Papers; and Cust to Balfour, 22 September 1903, Sandars Papers.
[2] Sandars to Balfour, 1 October 1904, and Iwan-Müller to Sandars, 26 October 1904, Balfour Papers.

came from the *Morning Advertiser* on a five-year contract and afterwards shifted to the *Daily Mail*. Refloated, the *Daily Mirror* gratified its proprietor by attaining 'a splendid reaction', with sales rising to over 143,000 within weeks.[1]

Apart from these three metropolitan properties and his lowbrow magazines, Harmsworth held the *Southern Daily Mail* at Portsmouth as a souvenir of his abortive candidacy there in 1895. He had twice bid for *The Times*, which was to fall to him in 1908. For a pittance of £4,000, he picked up the Sunday *Observer* in May 1905. Obviously, he was not a man whom the politicians could afford to ignore, much less offend. Churchill, after decrying Pearson's take-over of the *Standard*, assured Harmsworth that 'my remarks about "mammoth newspaper trusts" were intended to be general in their reference & certainly not personal to yourself'. Estranged from his party leaders, Churchill watched as they drew Harmsworth into their protectionist net. In November 1904, Harmsworth justified his baronetcy and paved the way for his barony by expanding his operations in Manchester, the cradle of Free Trade, where he already published a northern edition of the *Daily Mail*. According to his official biographers, he invested in the ailing *Manchester Courier* expressly to make it 'the leading Conservative organ of the North'. The Sowler family, who had borne the burden since the 1830s, were grateful to be relieved of their shareholding. But local Unionist MPs, divided on the fiscal issue, had mixed feelings. W. J. Galloway, who sat for Manchester South-West, was 'disgusted' by 'the Harmsworth agreement', and predicted to Sandars that 'Tariff Reform in Manchester will ruin us'. Sandars tried to calm him down by pointing out that 'Harmsworth's Tariff Reform was of the moderate kind'. Reporting the exchange to Balfour, Sandars observed that

> Galloway was very anxious to be acquitted of political indifference inasmuch as he had not contributed to the project. You know some time ago he (Galloway) offered to find £60,000 and take over the paper. He says to-day he congratulates himself on being well out of it.

After the next election, Galloway was out of Parliament as well. Better than either Harmsworth or Balfour, who was beaten at Manchester East, he had sensed the antipathy of Lancashire to protectionism.[2]

Dunn resigned the editorship of the *Morning Post* and accepted Harmsworth's invitation 'to become part-proprietor and editor of the *Manchester Courier*'. At a luncheon to celebrate the new régime, he proclaimed that he had travelled north on a single ticket, and did not contemplate a return to London. In fact, he left Manchester in 1910 to become editor of the Johannesburg *Star*.

---

[1] Fyfe to Harmsworth, 4 November 1903, Northcliffe Papers; Harmsworth, 'How I Dropped £100,000 on the "Mirror",' *Daily Mirror*, 27 February 1904; Viscount Camrose, *British Newspapers and Their Controllers* (London, 1947), pp. 57–60.

[2] Churchill to Harmsworth, 16 November 1904, Northcliffe Papers; Pound and Harmsworth, p. 291; Sandars to Balfour, 30 November 1904, Balfour Papers.

Six years later, Harmsworth liquidated the *Manchester Courier*, having tired of its losses. His involvement with the *Observer* was even briefer, though more fruitful. On the market since 1903, the property – London's oldest Sunday newspaper – came into his possession in the spring of 1905. With a weekly circulation that fluctuated between 2,000 and 4,000, the *Observer* had been losing £12,000 to £15,000 a year. In the first financial year under Harmsworth's management, its sales were insufficient to meet the cost of newsprint. Harmsworth, however, did not seek a profit, but rather a share of 'public power', which – as Garvin recognized – could never come from 'the *Daily Mail* as it is'. Before the contracts were signed, he telephoned Garvin, whom he esteemed as 'the greatest journalist in England', offering him the editorship and a one-third interest. Garvin's commitments precluded his acceptance at this time. Harmsworth's second choice was Amery, whom he offered 'more than twice as much salary' as he was being paid by *The Times*, 'as well as a tenth share in the ownership'. Amery gave 'serious consideration' to 'the *Observer* business', but decided to remain at Printing House Square, where he could hope to succeed Buckle. Austin Harrison was thereupon appointed editor without a stake in the company, making it easier to discharge him in January 1908, when Garvin was at last ready to assume command. By then, the price of the *Observer* had been reduced to a penny, and sales had climbed to approximately 20,000 a week. Surviving Harmsworth's divestiture in 1911, Garvin's marathon reign was to last for thirty-four years.[1]

For Garvin, the *Observer* provided a supreme opportunity for making propaganda. 'This is flinging the die,' he informed Northcliffe (as Harmsworth had become) with characteristic gusto. 'If you are really going to remodel that editorial page so as to enable me to be of adequate use to you, I will come into your organisation entirely and never look back.' The financial terms were relatively unimportant: 'For paper guarantees on policy I won't stickle', so long as there was the chance for 'putting grip and stiffening into editorial policy. *Consistency Compels Conviction*.' Northcliffe, for whom consistency was never a strong suit, had other considerations. Whereas a loss was unacceptable to him, except as a momentary challenge, he was no longer content to be identified with cheap and cheapening journalism. Through the *Daily Mail*, the *Daily Mirror*, and the *Evening News*, he could collect dividends, but not the respectability with which he sought to impress his widening circle of social and political contacts. Only by achieving such respectability might he realize his dream of owning *The Times*. After 1905, when he reached the sobering age of forty, Northcliffe craved nothing so much as to be taken seriously. His purchase of the *Manchester Courier* had been calculated to win the respect and

[1] Dunn to Glenesk, 23 December 1904, Bathurst Papers; Camrose, *British Newspapers*, p. 118; Garvin to Northcliffe, 1 December 1906, Northcliffe Papers; Amery to Garvin, 4 October 1904, Garvin Papers; Gollin, *Observer*, pp. 8–10; Amery, *My Political Life* (London, 1953), I, 267; Amery to Moberly Bell, 19 June 1905, *Times* Archives; H. Simonis, *The Street of Ink* (London, 1917), pp. 126–27.

gratitude of party officials. With the same objective, he had sunk £10,000 into the East of England Newspaper Company at Norwich. For £14,000, he also acquired the *World*, a gossipy weekly with snob appeal, which promised him 'social prestige and influence'. There were those who suspected that Northcliffe, once ennobled, had taken leave of his senses. When he had bought the *Observer*, he reminded Garvin, he was 'regarded as a D. F. for doing so'. For the time being, at any rate, there was distinctly a method to his madness.[1]

The ministerial Unionists, with the Chamberlainites hovering behind them, were reasonably satisfied. Harmsworth and Pearson, each a so-called 'partisan of non-partyism', had come to their rescue. Deeply divided in Parliament and in the constituencies, Unionism presented a united front in the columns of the daily press. To one degree or another, every newspaper that supported the government was an advocate of protectionism. All the same, certain advocates of protectionism resisted classification as supporters of the government. A twentieth-century definition of editorial sovereignty required no less.

Moberly Bell, after protesting to Spender over a similar aspersion in the *Westminster Gazette*, reproved Strachey for remarking in the *Spectator* that *The Times* had 'unfortunately become of late very much of a partisan organ' (28 May 1904). Insisting that he was not 'journalistically thinskinned', he conceded that the *Spectator* had

> a perfect right to say that we do not reflect accurately the saner side of public opinion – it is obvious that every paper must think that of every other paper with which it differs in opinion. ...
>
> What you have no right to say is that *The Times* has 'dropped its better tradition of impartiality' because that is a statement which is absolutely untrue and therefore unjust and offensive.

James Thursfield, taking his manager's part, concurred that *The Times* had never been a 'party paper' in the ordinary sense. 'Nevertheless', there was no mistaking that

> the paper ... has now for some years been in sharp conflict with the party represented by the present Opposition; & the necessity under which it has lain of withstanding & criticizing the policy & proceedings of the Opposition has I think often given it a tone which the mere party man is likely to mistake for partisanship.

Moberly Bell despaired of convincing Strachey: 'I am afraid that like a good many people you only recognize impartiality when it is on your side.' Yet he could not deny that, if the paper was not strictly Unionist, 'of late years it has

---

[1] Garvin to Northcliffe, 15 November 1907 (copy), Garvin Papers; Gollin, *Observer*, p. 8n.; Northcliffe to Garvin, 17 March 1908, Garvin Papers.

been more exclusively identified with the Unionist party because the question of Home Rule was regarded as a vital one'. This identification became an anachronism after 1903, when tariffs eclipsed Ireland as the divisive issue in British politics.[1]

Without going so far as to extend the same courtesy to Liberals, who had their own newspapers to represent them, Moberly Bell devised a scheme to accommodate the Unionist Free Traders, who 'have now no organ in the morning London press'. With the approval of the Duke of Devonshire, whom he chanced to meet at Marseilles, he and Buckle asked Arthur Elliot to supervise 'a certain amount of space in *The Times* each week . . . that we should place at the disposal of our Unionist adversaries'. Elliot, Liberal Unionist MP for Durham, 'refused on the ground of other occupations'. Moberly Bell next turned to Strachey: 'I want to ask whether you can suggest anyone else – or whether you would undertake it yourself.' The idea, as he elaborated it, was 'to have something like 6 cols. a week at the complete control & disposal' of a Unionist Free Trade spokesman. These columns, which might vary in length and day of appearance from week to week,

> would be headed by some formula showing that they were under the control of x, represented the views of x's party & not those of *The Times*. The matter in them might consist of letters to the Editor, or of articles approved by x as a fair statement of the case, or fuller reports of speeches. . . . Fair criticism would be allowed of our own articles. On the other hand we should be equally free to criticise those published by x.

It was presumptuous for Moberly Bell's daughter to conclude that this 'offer was refused on the grounds that *The Times* gave both sides so impartially that it was not worth while to accept it'. Strachey, who believed that an editor should be master in his own house, was too proud and certainly too practical to submit to such terms. One set of strong views, strongly held, was surely enough for any paper. It was also enough for any party, as the Unionists were to learn at the next general election.[2]

With respect to Harmsworth and Pearson, it was more the case of strong views, weakly held. The *Daily Mail*, a self-styled 'whispering gallery', constantly threatened to backslide on the vexing issue of food taxes. The *Standard*, possibly out of deference to recalcitrant readers, took its own tack. In a series of articles that ran from 6 to 9 February 1905, the journal diverged from Chamberlain's blueprint for a 10 per cent duty on foreign manufactures, calling instead for a 5 per cent tax on all imports, with enumerated exemptions for colonial suppliers. 'Pearson has been thinking of something of this sort since he

---

[1] Moberly Bell to Strachey, 28 May and 1 June 1904, 9 February 1905, Strachey Papers; Thursfield to Moberly Bell, 30 May 1904, *Times* Archives.
[2] Moberly Bell to [Elliot], 11 January 1905, quoted in Moberly Bell, *Moberly Bell*, pp. 227–28; Moberly Bell to Strachey, 9 February 1905, Strachey Papers.

took over the paper,' Chamberlain bitterly suspected. Of course, a proprietor was permitted to say what he liked in his newspaper, but heterodoxy was not to be brooked from the chairman of the Tariff Reform League. 'I am much disappointed at Pearson's action and do not understand it,' Chamberlain wrote to Hewins on the day that the final article appeared.

> It will not do ... that the political cause which we have at heart should be in any way prejudiced in order to suit the exigencies of a newspaper, and while we have no right to press Mr Pearson to do anything against his own interest we must I think ask him to separate his fortunes from ours.

Pearson's resignation, tactfully attributed to 'pressure of business', was speedily forthcoming. Besides revealing the differences of emphasis and opinion that existed among Tariff Reformers, the incident confirmed the priorities of the political press, as Chamberlain effectively perpetuated them. Where 'the exigencies of a newspaper' as he called them, clashed with those of a party, it was clearly stipulated which should take precedence.[1]

* * *

In 1885, when James Joicey and a group of local Liberals had established the *Newcastle Daily Leader*, 'Radical Joe' Chamberlain was among the party spokesmen who sent congratulations. Eighteen years later, an apostate from Liberalism, he publicly welcomed its supersession by Pearson's 'new evening paper at Newcastle-on-Tyne which will support the policy of tariff reform which I am endeavouring to place before my countrymen'. The *Westminster Gazette* (20 October 1903) called attention to the irony: yet another 'Leader' had been lost, leaving Liberalism without representation in the Newcastle press.

The pattern was the same elsewhere. Provincial journalism, traditionally a Liberal preserve, fell to the protectionist battalions. Harold Spender, who undertook a roving commission for the *Daily News*, paused in his travels to note 'the wholesale defection of papers that once called themselves Liberal'. Throughout 'the whole of the centre of England', the situation struck him as appalling: 'Capital, shrewdly seeking her child, interest, has taken sides with the winners in the great towns. The mob wanted Jingoism; so Jingoism has been given to it in daily and weekly doses, at the lowest possible price.' Writing from Sheffield on 2 February 1903, he mourned the defection of the *Independent*, 'once a great organ of light' in a city of Tory darkness. At Birmingham, where the *Daily Post* had converted to Unionism in 1886, the *Daily Argus* had 'held up the flag' from 1891 until 1903, when it was absorbed by the Tory *Daily*

---

[1] Chamberlain to Hewins, 3 and 9 February 1905, Hewins Papers; Pearson to the Duke of Sutherland, 3 March 1905, quoted in Dark, *Pearson*, p. 102.

Gazette. The following year, Pearson's Midland Express Company purchased control of the *Daily Gazette*, and acquired the *Birmingham Evening Dispatch*, which had been Johnstone family property.

Commenting on the 'deeply interesting and illuminating' investigations by its 'Special Commissioner', the *Daily News* painted a bleak picture:

> It is a lamentable fact that Liberalism to-day has not one voice in the daily Press of Birmingham, and that throughout the North the papers have one after another either been captured by the Unionists or have succumbed to the infection of the shoddy Imperialism the shrine of which is fittingly at Birmingham.

There were two notable exceptions, the *Manchester Guardian* and the *Bradford Observer*, neither a thriving concern,

> together with one or two evening papers which have never bowed the knee to Baal [and] still keep the flag of a real and strenuous Liberalism flying; but there are whole tracts of country, densely populated, where Liberalism is silent. Its guns have been spiked by the plutocrats. ... There is no greater need to-day throughout the land than a more plentiful supply of newspapers which are not in the control of plutocrats and adventurers. (2 February 1903)

Writing in the July 1904 number of the *Nineteenth Century*. W. J. Fisher (recently discharged from the editorship of the *Daily Chronicle*) maintained that, 'from Glasgow to Bradford, there is no representative Liberal daily newspaper'. Whether or not that was technically correct, Herbert Gladstone, the Liberal chief whip, was dismayed to learn the following spring that the *Bradford Observer* was 'practically in the market' for £65,000. 'Obviously, there is a great field for newspaper enterprise on the Liberal side in the Leeds and Bradford Districts,' he wrote to C. P. Scott, whom he asked to provide 'management' to keep the *Bradford Observer* on a Liberal keel. Scott was in no position to comply. At the time, he was locked in combat with J. E. Taylor, the proprietor of the *Manchester Guardian*, who wanted to take G. B. Dibblee into partnership. When Taylor died in October 1905, Scott continued his battle with Taylor's four trustees, who would neither sell the copyright nor consent to Scott's continuation 'as editor except with Mr Dibblee in Manchester to represent them as Manager'. After weeks of wrangling, during which both sides took legal advice, the trustees gave Scott an option to purchase at an inflated price, which left him heavily – and happily – in debt.[1]

If the state of the Liberal press was not quite so dire as certain Cassandras made out, it was dire enough for Campbell-Bannerman to complain at the time

---

[1] Fisher, 'The Liberal Press and the Party,' *Nineteenth Century*, lvi (1904), 203; Gladstone to Scott, 3 April 1905, *Guardian* Archives; Laurence Scott to Ensor, 27 November, 11 and 14 December 1905, Ensor Papers; David Ayerst, *Guardian* (London, 1971), pp. 308–15.

of the 1906 election that 'the newspaper press had largely (and he thought it was a great misfortune) got into the hands of combinations of capitalists and others'. In the aftermath of the Boer War, denunciations of capitalism became a *leitmotiv* of Liberal rhetoric, and the prevalence of newspaper monopolies was held to exemplify the danger to the interests of the community. Though not without foundation, these lamentations implied an incongruity and perhaps a tinge of envy. Did Campbell-Bannerman, among others, suppose that the modern press had ever been in other hands? Liberals had been content when free market forces had operated in their favour. They had owed their predominance in Victorian journalism to 'plutocrats and adventurers' of the sort – if not of the persuasion – that the *Daily News* now castigated; they had encouraged and rewarded the 'capitalists and others' whom Campbell-Bannerman now scorned. Only when the system had seemingly turned against them did Liberals discover its iniquities. Before then, as the minutes of the National Union annually attested, the Conservatives had been the anti-monopolists.[1]

Hardly a twentieth-century phenomenon, the process of 'trustification' could be traced at least as far back as 1828, when it was calculated that William Innell Clement owned 10 per cent of all newspapers published in England. Bright, whose Liberal credentials were unimpeachable, had welcomed plutocratic control as the guarantee of a free press and sought to build a chain on that basis. A generation later, Samuel Storey and Andrew Carnegie went far towards succeeding. Where would the nineteenth-century Liberal press have been without such adventurers as Labouchere or such plutocrats as Samuel Morley, Sir John Brunner, and J. J. Colman? Edward Lloyd (whose *Lloyd's Weekly News* had passed the million mark in 1896) and Newnes must be recognized as the forerunners of Harmsworth and Pearson, who may be seen in turn as the beneficiaries of Liberal experiments.

A few of these magnates maintained an interest in Liberal journalism, but most had withdrawn. Storey had eschewed Chamberlain's Unionism in Parliament and the press only to imbibe his protectionism. Carnegie, separated from British politics by the wide Atlantic, declined to get involved. In May 1903, Stead appealed to him for help in 'the founding of a newspaper & news agency which would undertake in serious earnest the work of counterworking the propaganda that makes for war'. Reviving a stillborn project of 1893, he envisaged a London journal that would 'not only have its own circulation', but also 'be in a position to supply the provincial press'. Undeterred by Carnegie's refusal, Stead proceeded with plans for his *Daily Paper*, anticipating 'an opportunity of daily utterance in London on political affairs' and, more grandiosely, distribution 'in Paris and Berlin and perhaps in Rome and Vienna,

---

[1] Campbell Bannerman, speech at Culross, 12 January 1906, *The Times*, 13 January 1906. See Alan J. Lee, *The Origins of the Popular Press 1855–1914* (London, 1976), pp. 76–77, for an attempt 'to put Liberal anxieties in perspective'.

etc.' After five weeks, the *Daily Paper* ceased publication on 9 February 1904, leaving its creator distraught and destitute.[1]

Wealthy Liberals, who had formerly served their party by subsidizing its press, found it easier to write a cheque and be done with it. Sir George Newnes agreed 'to subscribe largely to the Election Fund' at the close of 1905, though he had already given more than his share. 'When the *Pall Mall Gazette* was bought by the American millionaire, Mr Astor,' he reminded Gladstone,

> I took over the entire staff – and gave them a habitation & a home, and founded the *Westminster Gazette*. I wrote to many of the leading friends of Liberalism: but the responses were so small that it would have been absolutely impossible to carry out the enterprise. For ten years I lost £10,000 per annum, and never asked any one of the party for any help. .... I believe it is admitted that the *Westminster Gazette* has supplied an effective weapon to the Liberal party, and has been a powerful influence for the principles which we advocate. This could not have been achieved unless I had personally taken upon myself a great responsibility.

Having shouldered this burden since 1893, never permitting Spender to see how he 'was straining his fortunes', Newnes was growing weary. In February 1907, there was 'a persistent rumour that the Harmsworths are going to purchase the whole of Newnes' business, including the *Westminster Gazette*'. John Buchan dismissed it as 'probably only the usual *canard*, but it is believed that Newnes is rather short of money'. The following year, Newnes sold the *Westminster* to a Liberal syndicate headed by Sir Alfred Mond (later 1st Baron Melchett).[2]

Mond, then MP for Chester, was also to succeed Newnes as member for Swansea, where he found a safer seat. His father had been the business partner of Brunner, MP for Northwich and reportedly the largest single contributor to the 1906 campaign chest. Brunner, too, had been a benefactor of the Liberal press. In 1888, he had helped to found the *Star* and, from 1890 to 1899, he had sustained the weekly *Speaker*. According to hearsay evidence, he had had a stake in starting the *Morning Leader* in 1892. Though his name was continually mentioned in connection with newspaper ventures, Brunner had since found other outlets for his energy and capital. At most, he was willing to make a token commitment. When a constituent advised him in November 1906 that Cheshire Conservatives had tendered an offer for the *Warrington Guardian*, Brunner 'promised £3,000, provided £16,000 in all be

---

[1] Stead to Carnegie, 18 May 1903, Carnegie Papers; J. M. Robertson Scott, *The Life and Death of a Newspaper* (London, 1952), pp. 158–59, 246–51.

[2] Newnes to Gladstone, 19 December 1905, Viscount Gladstone Papers, Add. MSS. 46,063, fol. 227b; Spender, *Life, Journalism and Politics*, II, 139; Buchan to Strachey, 2 February 1907, Strachey Papers.

found' for a counter-bid. Ever the philanthropist, he was no longer prepared to be a proprietor.[1]

For nearly two generations, Liberal industrialists had vied with one another for the privilege of investing in newspaper enterprises. Usually men of humble origins and Nonconformist background, they had accepted these obligations as an obvious way to render service and to secure social and political advancement. The early twentieth century saw a change of attitude, sometimes dictated by a change of affiliation. The result was a spate of closures and amalgamations, with newspapers passing from family into public hands. Hopes on the part of Lloyd George and others that the *Manchester Guardian* might spearhead a revival were dashed by its own financial difficulties. Except for George Cadbury, who had stepped forward in 1901 to save the soul of the *Daily News* from gambling and militarism, the Liberals seemed to have run out of rescuers. However much Cadbury's paper might sneer at the 'plutocrats and adventurers' on the Unionist side, the Liberal Party managers would have been grateful to enlist a few of them.

Help, however, was on its way. Charles Starmer was managing editor of the *Northern Echo* at Darlington, where he was the ex-mayor and secretary of the local Liberal association; in the short-lived Parliament of 1923, he was to sit in the Liberal interest for Cleveland. The *Echo*, on which Stead had risen to national prominence, was selling fewer than 5,000 copies in 1903, when Starmer appealed for assistance from Joseph Rowntree. Like Cadbury, Rowntree was a devout Quaker and a cocoa manufacturer. For the purpose of taking over the *Echo* and its two associated weeklies, he formed the North of England Newspaper Company, with himself as a director and his nephew Arnold, president of the York Liberal association and later Liberal MP for that city, as chairman. In 1904, Rowntree established his Social Service Trust, to which he transferred his interest. 'Perhaps the greatest danger to our national life arises from the power of selfish and unscrupulous wealth which influences public opinion largely through the press,' he minuted to his fellow trustees.

> If the funds permitted, and the directors of the Social Service Trust were equal to the task, it would be quite in accordance with my wish that they should control, by purchase or otherwise, a newspaper or newspapers, conducting them not with a primary view to profit but with the object of influencing public thought in right channels.[2]

In exactly this spirit, the Trust acquired the *Speaker* in 1906, refurbishing it as the *Nation* in March 1907. In 1909, it relieved H. J. Wilson of his majority

---

[1] J. [?] Dodds to Brunner, 26 November 1906 (with comments), Brunner Papers.

[2] Joseph Rowntree, letter to Trustees, 1904, quoted in 'The *Star* and *Morning Leader* (1909) Limited,' memorandum dated 15 October 1929, Cowdray Papers; these paragraphs are otherwise based on a memorandum helpfully prepared for the author by A. P. Duncum, who quoted from the minutes and documents of the Joseph Rowntree Social Service Trust.

shareholding in the *Sheffield Independent*, and negotiated a bilateral agreement with the Cadburys to save the *Morning Leader* and the *Star* from Tory clutches.

With subsidies from the Trust, taking the form of loans that were regularly expunged from the ledgers, the *Northern Echo* continued with Starmer as manager. In 1909, he shifted to the *Sheffield Independent*. An employee of the Trust, he struck up a partnership with J. B. Morrell, the first director of Rowntree and Company to come from outside the family, a director of the North of England Newspaper Company, and, from 1906, a director of the Trust as well. Starmer and Morrell, acting independently of the Trust, interlocked with it. In 1912, they picked up the remnants of Pearson's empire in Birmingham; six years later, they replaced Sir Jesse Boot, the retail chemist, as the owners of Liberal morning and evening journals in Nottingham. Arnold Rowntree did not participate in either of these transactions, but privately helped to finance the purchase of weeklies in Durham, Lancaster, and Lincoln. In 1921, he, Starmer (now Sir Charles Starmer), and Morrell were named directors of the Westminster Press, formed and magnanimously funded by the 1st Viscount Cowdray. Save for the National Press Agency, which continued separately under Trust auspices for another decade, the newspaper holdings of the Trust were merged with those of the Starmer-Morrell group into the new company. The *Westminster Gazette*, converted from evening to morning publication, was its most distinguished appendage, though a drain on its resources.

When the Joseph Rowntree Social Service Trust was incorporated in 1904, its founder laid down specific guidelines: 'Ordinary subscriptions to political organizations will, I believe, be inexpedient, but occasional crises might arise when the funds of this Trust might rightly be called upon.' Although individual trustees made personal donations to the Liberal Party, the Trust limited its corporate contributions to the maintenance and development of Liberal journalism. Nor did the party provide subventions to Trust-owned newspapers. Closer collaboration came only after the war, when the Trust had exhausted its capital and Cowdray entered the picture. Before then, the Rowntree Trust jealously guarded its autonomy, restricting its activity to the provincial and high-toned periodical press. In these spheres, it promoted the Liberal ethic, if necessary against the electoral requirements of official Liberalism, as when the *Northern Echo* endorsed the Labour candidacy of Arthur Henderson in the 1903 by-election at Barnard Castle. Qualitatively, if not structurally, Rowntree's incursion had little in common with those of Harmsworth and Pearson. When Churchill inveighed against the 'mammoth newspaper trusts' that controlled and corrupted Edwardian journalism, the Social Service Trust was surely far from his mind.

Rowntree's altruism, a reminder that old-style Victorian paternalism had not died out, was not unique. In March 1905, a brigade of Yorkshire Liberals captured the *Leeds Daily News*, a proponent of Toryism since 1873. The ringleader was W. P. Byles, who had retired in 1899 as proprietor of the *Bradford Observer* (on which he began work in 1853 at the age of fourteen) and who was to return to the Commons in 1906 as member for Salford. To be sure, that was small compensation for the loss of the *Leeds Mercury*, which had no sooner celebrated its centenary than it was bought in 1902 by Leicester Harmsworth and transformed into an illustrated halfpenny paper. The result, in Gladstone's opinion, was that it 'entirely lost its old position'. Sir Christopher (later the 1st Baron) Furness, the shipping magnate who sat for the Hartlepools, kept the *Northern Daily Mail* from going over to protectionism, and secured the Newcastle *North Mail* from Pearson in January 1906. Not without local import, such isolated efforts had limited national effect. The penny morning papers in the provinces were overwhelmingly Unionist. The metropolitan press, which had cut deeply into their readerships, showed the same tendency. One historian, detecting 'signs from 1902 and 1903 onwards of a tilting of the balance back towards the Liberals', has reckoned that the London Unionist dailies in 1906 had an aggregate circulation of 1,605,000 as opposed to one of 550,000 for the Liberal rivals. The angle of the tilt was therefore relatively slight.[1]

A congeries of sectional interests, some inimical to others, the Liberal Party began to awake from its torpor. Its press, which had spurred earlier revivals, lagged behind. In part, this journalistic debility reflected economic realities, which made it exceedingly difficult to buy out established papers and virtually prohibitive to start new ones. In part, too, it reflected a shift of the centre of gravity within the party. The Liberal Imperialists, who had shown remarkable aptitude in cultivating editorial loyalties, were a waning force. Religious groups, which had traditionally infused the Liberal press with their fervour, had turned inwards. The February 1903 number of the *Crusader*, the monthly organ of Free Churchmen who passively resisted the 1902 Education Act, deemed only one London paper – the *Daily News* – worthy of Nonconformist patronage. Liberal Churchmen were no better supplied. Spender entreated the chief whip to find someone to keep alive the *Pilot*, 'a weekly review of ecclesiastical and general politics, literature and learning', founded in March 1900. 'It does on the whole make for Liberal views among a certain class of people who get no other impetus that way & the cost of maintaining it is quite small,' reasoned Spender. 'If there is any rich Liberal Churchman, he ought to help.' He pleaded in vain: on 21 May 1904, the *Pilot* discontinued publication.[2]

The oldest among Liberalism's diurnal standard-bearers, the *Daily News* was the first to feel a quickening pulse. Under Gardiner's quiet and purposeful

---

[1] Gladstone to Scott, 3 April 1905, *Guardian* Archives; Maurice Milne, *The Newspapers of Northumberland and Durham* (Newcastle-upon-Tyne, 1971?), pp. 185–86; A. K. Russell, *Liberal Landslide* (Newton Abbot, 1973), pp. 138–39.

[2] Spender to Gladstone, 3 March 1904, Viscount Gladstone Papers, Add. MSS. 46, 042, fol. 3.

guidance, the paper kept faith with its Nonconformist readers, improved its literary features, expanded its news coverage, and waged a militant campaign against social injustice. A member of the Rainbow Circle, a monthly dining society that was a breeding ground for the New Liberalism, Gardiner strove to reconcile the policies of Fabian reconstruction with the tenets of Radical individualism. He did not exaggerate when he later described his paper as 'the vehicle in the press of the new spirit which was soon to change the current of politics, ... a vehicle not merely of opinion but of action'. In this respect, he received resolute backing from his elderly proprietor, George Cadbury. Early in 1901, Cadbury had been induced by Lloyd George to assume a major shareholding in the *Daily News*, which had been following the primrose path of jingoism. A year later, after his advanced views on old-age pensions and other welfare issues had provoked discord within the directorship, Cadbury took full control and brought in Gardiner. Both men looked upon Chamberlain's proposals for Tariff Reform as a machiavellian attempt to divert national attention from pressing domestic problems. Liberal officials, too weak (and possibly too timorous) to venture pronouncements on social reform, were more grateful for the *Daily News*'s impassioned defence of Free Trade. 'You appear to me to be taking, if I may say so, quite the right line,' Campbell-Bannerman wrote to Gardiner.[1]

Cadbury, whose own success as a businessman testified to the moral and material benefits of Cobdenism, accepted his newspaper responsibilities as a sacred mission. 'It is a big undertaking,' he reflected when the decision was taken to reduce the price of the *Daily News* to a halfpenny,

> but I can enter into it with real pleasure and joy, as ... the opportunity for good is *vast*. The churches have not preached ethical Christianity & we must do it & bring them up to a higher standard, this must be the case before 'The kingdoms of this world shall become the kingdoms of our Lord, and of His Christ.'

Gardiner, whose inspiration was wholly secular, was more consciously the servant of party. Even so, he regularly found himself at loggerheads with the whips, who, for example, urged him to desist from the practice of publishing lists of Liberal MPs absent from the lobbies. 'It is very good for all of us to receive rebuke and criticism on the frequent occasions when we need it,' Gladstone scolded in 1902:

> But may I suggest that it is quite impossible either to secure a full or anything like a full attendance of our men every day, or to enact that there shall be no

---

[1] Gardiner, *Life of George Cadbury* (London, 1923), pp. 222, 225; Campbell-Bannerman to Gardiner, 18 December 1903, Gardiner Papers.

pairs. .... At least 25 per cent of our men by infirmity, occupation or temperament cannot attend from day to day.

Three years later, as a decade of Unionist rule neared its close, a group of backbenchers – including Labouchere, Lloyd George, and Churchill – implored Gardiner to resume this tactic: 'We are convinced that it is almost hopeless to attempt to turn out the Ministry, unless the Liberal attendance in the House be more regular than at present.' The *Daily News* pursued its objectives as much by confrontation as by accommodation.[1]

The *Daily Chronicle* took longer to turn round. Late in 1903, Frank Lloyd, its proprietor, offered the editorship to Donald, the prospective Liberal candidate at West Ham. Forced to choose between journalism and a parliamentary career, Donald accepted the more immediate prize, leaving the electors of West Ham to return C. F. G. Masterman, a leader-writer for the *Daily News*. In due course, Masterman's place at the *Daily News* was filled by H. W. Nevinson, who had left the *Chronicle* shortly before the shake-up. Fisher, who had been editor since 1899, was to stand unsuccessfully at Canterbury in the 1906 election. The traffic between newspaper offices and between them and party headquarters was unusually heavy.

E. T. Cook, who had taken refuge at the *Chronicle* after his eviction from the *Daily News*, took a dim view of these proceedings. 'The new editor is to be a man who was a reporter under me years ago at the *Pall Mall* and has recently been an advertisement agent,' he wrote sniffily to Rosebery on 16 November. Cook's own future on the paper was then unclear. 'Lloyd offers me a certain post under him. And, though I have not a particularly proud stomach, the offer is not appetizing.' His predisposition was to 'write and decline, and leave Lloyd to take the next step – viz. presumably three months' notice to terminate my contract as leader-writer'. But Lloyd easily persuaded him to reconsider. 'This is not a time when either for public or private reasons I should like to lose my "pulpit" and constant occupation,' Cook admitted to Rosebery a week later. By the end of the year, Cook had had a satisfactory interview with Donald, and had 'agreed to go on as at present for a while, until the new situation develops itself. ... I shall give the new régime unprejudiced trial.' In fact, his connection lasted until 1910. But the transition was as difficult for him as for others. 'The *D.C.* is paying like hot cakes, but it is going to the devil none the less,' J. H. Morgan, another member of the staff, complained the following spring. 'Cook's heart isn't in his work; Donald is rather a slack creature. The office swarms with irresponsible sub-editors and a legion of printers devils who all want sorting out. Of such is the kingdom of halfpenny papers.'[2]

[1] Cadbury to Gardiner, 11 February 1904, Gladstone to Gardiner, 24 June 1902, and Labouchere *et al.* to Gardiner, 2 March 1905, Gardiner Papers.
[2] Cook to Rosebery, 16 and 25 November, 29 December 1903, Rosebery Papers, Vol. 10, 117, fols. 170, 178, 195; Morgan to Ensor, 6 May 1904, Ensor Papers; H. A. Taylor, *Robert Donald* (London, 1934?), pp. 47–48.

The substitution of Donald for Fisher as editor of the *Daily Chronicle*, implying the further subordination of Cook, was a blow to Rosebery. In the press as in Parliament, his friends were deserting him. Spender remained an admirer of his statesmanlike bearing, but dedicated the *Westminster Gazette* to the task of Liberal reunification to which Rosebery was unmistakably an impediment. Asquith, who took an active part in the Free Trade rebuttal to Chamberlain, emerged as the Liberal Imperialist favourite. Rosebery's sporadic speeches still commanded attention, especially in the Unionist papers, which featured them as a means of exploiting persistent Liberal divergences. Yet his declining stature could be measured in column inches. 'Lord Rosebery, five years ago, was worth what is known professionally as a full report,' Alfred Kinnear of the Central News Agency observed in the March 1905 number of the *Contemporary Review*. 'He is now saleable usually at from half a column to three-quarters of a column to the Press as a whole.' Significantly enough, it was in the *Observer* that Henry Lucy found 'an excellent verbatim report' of Rosebery's speech at Trowbridge on 29 October 1904. 'It is one of the advantages of speaking on a Saturday,' remarked Lucy, 'that busy folk have opportunity on a Sabbath afternoon of reading four columns of small print, a privilege inaccessible by Moses when he advocated the day of rest.' Rosebery, however, knew all too well that the circulation of the *Observer* scarcely exceeded the size of his audience at Trowbridge. Monday's *Times*, ignoring his prepared text, facetiously found his 'position ... in the great united Liberal Party ... more difficult to define or understand'. The more isolated Rosebery became, the more he was obsessed by journalism. Charles Hobhouse, Liberal MP for Bristol East, dined with him the following March and noted in his diary 'one trait I learnt. He reads an enormous number of daily papers *himself*, & leaves or trusts nothing for his secretary to transact.'[1]

The same could not have been said of Campbell-Bannerman or Asquith, both of whom relied chiefly on Gladstone to maintain newspaper contacts. Their confidence was not misplaced. Famous for having flown the 'Hawarden Kite' in December 1885, when he prematurely signalled his father's conversion to Home Rule, Gladstone mobilized the press with the same assiduity he demonstrated in the sphere of constituency organization. The resources at his disposal were, to say the least, limited. The *Daily Chronicle* and the *Daily News* were restored to buoyancy, and the *Westminster Gazette* did not allow its commercial weakness to impair its partisan strength. With the demise of the *Echo* on 5 August 1905, the Liberals lost one of their four metropolitan dailies and their single halfpenny evening paper. Founded in 1868, it had passed through various owners and had boasted a circulation approaching 200,000 in the early 1880s. Its opposition to the Boer War had

---

[1] Kinnear, 'Parliamentary Reporting,' *Contemporary Review*, lxxxvii (1905), 369; Lucy to Rosebery, 30 October 1904, Rosebery Papers, Vol. 10, 118, fol. 146; Hobhouse's diary, 31 March 1905, *Inside Asquith's Cabinet* (ed. E. David; London, 1977), p. 52.

inflicted disabilities, managerial and financial, from which it never recovered, and the proprietors preferred to liquidate the company rather than to entertain a Unionist bid. By the time the *Echo* folded, plans were already being made to start the *Tribune*, a Liberal penny daily. But that experiment did not get under way until January 1906, when the Liberals were back in office.

In the interim, the depleted Liberal press did its utmost to minimize differences within its own party ranks, while it underscored the divisions over fiscal policy among the Unionists. Numerically superior, the ministerial press worked to project a countervailing image of Unionist solidarity and to expose Liberal discords. It was as steep a challenge for publicists on the one side to reconcile the conflicting views of Rosebery and Campbell-Bannerman (let alone to attune them to Lloyd George's notoriety as a 'pro-Boer' or John Burns's equally outrageous reputation as a trade-unionist firebrand) as it was for those on the other side to reconcile the conflicting views of Chamberlain and Balfour (let alone to assert their compatibility with the Free Trade remonstrances of the Duke of Devonshire and the Cecils). The *Westminster Gazette* was most adept among the Liberal organs at papering over cracks; *The Times* among the Unionist ones, though it was obliged to concede that 'Mr Chamberlain's confidence in a near victory ... may not be fully shared by those responsible for the unity of a party and its guidance in times of difficulty' (8 July 1905). As the official historians of *The Times* have acknowledged: 'The paper's task was to emphasize the folly of Liberal contentions, and to maintain harmony in the Unionist party', if necessary by obfuscation. To accomplish this purpose, there had to be close consultation with party officials. Writing to Moberly Bell on 21 August, Chirol expressed qualified approval for a leading article that morning – presumably the one on 'Unionism and Disunion in Ireland' – which 'was on the whole less unsatisfactory ... than I had ventured to hope for a few days ago, when Buckle first came back from his interview in Downing St.' So much, then, for Moberly Bell's adamant insistence on the paper's 'impartiality'.[1]

On both sides, patience wore thin as preparations were made for an electoral confrontation that could not be long postponed. In anticipation of the contest, Sir Alfred Hickman, Conservative MP for Wolverhampton West, refitted the *Midland Evening News* ('the only Conservative journal for seven divisions') with 'the costly machinery necessary for increasing the size of the paper from four to six pages' in order 'to increase its value for party purposes'; in the event, Hickman lost his own seat to a Labour challenger, again disproving any correlation between newspaper support and voting results. Conversely, the Liberals were poised to sweep Lancashire, where the *Manchester Guardian* was in desperate straits. Laurence Scott confided to R. C. K. Ensor 'about the end of the old *M.G.* and the break up more or less of my father's existence'. He

[1] Chirol to Moberly Bell, 21 August 1905, *Times* Archives; *History of The Times*, IV, part 1, 11.

gloomily forecast that the staff would disperse: 'My father, I think, will devote himself for a bit to my mother's health, but I hope that later he will take up Parliament again'; C. E. Montague, the chief leader-writer, 'will leave journalism & settle down cheaply in the country somewhere to write'; Herbert Sidebotham, another leader-writer, 'will, I hope, get on to the *Tribune*, which should probably live at any rate for a year or two'; and Laurence himself would 'probably try for a reviewing job on the *Tribune* too, but I am not sure'. Stricken by his wife's death on 27 November, C. P. Scott threw himself into the battle to save the *Guardian*. He had yet to clear his debts in May 1908, when Laurence, whom he was grooming as his successor, died of tuberculosis.[1]

During the second half of November, passions erupted to the surface. Meeting at Newcastle on the 14th, the National Union ignored Balfour's appeal for unity and instead passed a strongly worded resolution in favour of tariffs. The next day, the *Morning Post* was moved to ask how much longer a party could follow a general who 'led his troops up to but not across the Rubicon of fiscal reform'. Iwan-Müller, who had recently warned Balfour 'that the word had gone forth to the Chamberlainite press to attack *you* simultaneously', saw evidence of a carefully laid plot. While he did 'not for one moment believe that the word was suggested, hinted or even countenanced by Highbury', where Chamberlain resided, he alerted Balfour to the growing peril:

> The ardent spirits of the Tariff Reformers *are* disloyal to *you*. There is not a Tory amongst them: Leo Maxse, Garvin, Amery, Gwynne, Goldman are all Radicals inoculated with fiscalitis. Douglas Straight who edits the old rag, the *P.M.G.*, does not know what he is (he really *is* an *ass*), but his young men are of that persuasion, and the *Globe* is *Orange* and leans to Chamberlain because he is more anti-Irish than you are. So that all the Unionist papers are for the time engaged in denigrating you in the interest of Radical-Fiscal Reform-Unionism. And mark my words this rotten crusade will be developed with increasing malignancy *till* the Election.

Only *The Times* and his own *Daily Telegraph* escaped Iwan-Müller's censure, to which Maxse replied in the January number of the *National Review* by branding them a 'Balfour clique'. Iwan-Müller, professing his willingness 'to stretch compromise to its most elastic limits', drew the line at 'sacrific[ing] Toryism to an unknown Liberalism temporarily in alliance with my party. . . . If you and yours want to wrest predominance in the Unionist party from the Tories,' he defiantly proclaimed to Maxse, 'you will find in me a bitter and uncompromising opponent.' Enmities within parties ran as high as those

---

[1] H. Midgley to Balfour, 7 November 1905, Sandars Papers; L. Scott to Ensor [9 November 1905], Ensor Papers.

between them, and were stoked by what the *Standard* (25 November) deplored as 'a press created crisis'.[1]

Turning with relief from the problems of their own party, Unionist newspapers concentrated on the rekindled issue of Home Rule, which threatened a Liberal split and a rupture with the Irish Nationalists. It was this prospect, highlighted by Rosebery's declaration of independence at Bodmin on 25 November, that ultimately determined Balfour's strategy. By resigning on 4 December, he gave the Liberals the opportunity to form an administration and, in the process, to vent their disagreements so as to discredit themselves in the eyes of the electorate. As early as 31 March, the *Daily News* had scorned Balfour 'who by refusing to appeal to the country has continued to govern in defiance of popular will', the implicit assumption being that the Unionists, forced to stand on their dismal record, would pave the way for a Liberal resurgence. More to Balfour's liking was the procedure adumbrated by Garvin in the *Outlook* on 2 December: 'Ministers unmuzzled would be free to fight with more effect [and] a great Unionist rally would be certain.' Foisting upon his opponents the duty of dissolving Parliament, he stood to benefit from their discomfort and probable disarray.

The vast majority of Liberal editorial counsellors were eager to accept the challenge. Spender in the *Westminster Gazette* was a prominent exception, calling upon Campbell-Bannerman to decline the King's commission until proper conditions had been met. But Crook, a former editor of the *Echo*, joined with F. W. Hirst of the *Economist*, among others, in urging Campbell-Bannerman to reject this craven course. Hirst privately assured him that 'all honest Liberals will hope and trust that you will not be embarrassed or distracted by the Cornish fireworks' that Rosebery had ignited at Bodmin: 'I don't believe anyone outside the *Westminster Gazette* office takes them seriously.' Extensively reported, the Bodmin speech provoked Campbell-Bannerman to complain to Grey that 'as usual the press, not purely of malice, but as a mere matter of paper-selling has fanned the flames'. Accused by Rosebery of having 'hoisted once more in its most pronounced form the flag of Home Rule', Campbell-Bannerman was invited by Newnes to issue a categorical statement that 'you would not consent to separation between the two countries', Britain and Ireland. 'This letter of course would not be published,' Newnes explained, 'but if you consented it would be mentioned that your communication is in response to a request from the *Westminster Gazette*.'[2]

Campbell-Bannerman, whose genial exterior concealed a core of iron, was not disposed to take dictation. In any case, he had more pressing concerns. As

[1] Iwan-Müller to Balfour, 10 November 1905 (midnight), Balfour Papers; Iwan-Müller to Maxse, 1 January 1906, Maxse Papers.
[2] Crook to Campbell-Bannerman, 23 November 1905, Hirst to Campbell-Bannerman, 24 November 1905, Newnes to Campbell Bannerman, 27 November 1905, Campbell-Bannerman Papers, Add. MSS. 41, 238, fols. 84, 87, 89; Campbell-Bannerman to Grey, 1 December 1905, Asquith Papers.

soon as Balfour relinquished office on 4 December, he set about constructing a Liberal ministry – the first in a decade – in which he struck a balance between sections of the party. That Rosebery would stand aside was a foregone conclusion, though one that Spender and Strachey were loath to accept. Less predictable were the responses of the Liberal Imperialist triumvirs – Asquith, Haldane, and Grey – whose 'Relugas Compact' had stipulated terms for their participation. In particular, they held out for Campbell-Bannerman's elevation to the House of Lords, which would have made Asquith leader in the Commons. Finding Campbell-Bannerman immovable, Asquith contented himself with the Exchequer, which *The Times* mistakenly understood to be reserved for Morley, 'and no one in the party can prefer stronger claims, though the City may be surprised by his appointment' (7 December).

Haldane and especially Grey were more refractory: the former, though sorely tempted, would not go to the War Office unless his friend took the foreign secretaryship. Writing in the *Daily Chronicle* on 9 December as 'One Who Knew Him', Henry Norman dwelled upon Grey's unique attributes: 'as passionless as the pale moon ..., he has the superlative quality which has gained him in an extraordinary degree the confidence of his fellow-men ... – the quality of character'. The previous day, *The Times* had prematurely gloated that Grey, 'the man designated by popular opinion for that most important post', had definitely 'refused to join a Government constituted on the basis now deliberately chosen'. The effect was the reverse of that intended. '*The Times* did not help a difficult task this morning,' Haldane informed Campbell-Bannerman, 'but now that Grey has recognised his obligation, he has accepted it very wholeheartedly, and in a spirit which would give you great satisfaction could you have heard the conversation I have just had with him.' Sir Almeric Fitzroy, clerk to the Privy Council, confirmed that Haldane and Grey had been compelled to join by *The Times*'s 'deliberate attempt to smash the credit of the new Government from its inception'. In his view, '*The Times* has done more to give force and cohesion to Sir H. Campbell-Bannerman's Ministry than any other single agency.'[1]

Thanks to the clumsiness of *The Times*, Campbell-Bannerman was able to assemble a stronger, more broadly based team than his critics had expected. The inclusion of the leading Liberal Imperialists in prominent positions served as a counterpoise to the '*Daily News* men' – the likes of Morley, Lloyd George, and Burns – who held other major portfolios. But the contribution of the *Daily News* was more substantial. Unlike *The Times*, which had acted unwittingly to shore up the government, the *Daily News* gave the Prime Minister unstinted support. Perhaps its most outstanding service was rendered behind the scenes.

On the afternoon of 6 December, while Campbell-Bannerman was engaged in delicate negotiations with the Liberal Imperialists, Gardiner arrived at his

[1] Haldane to Campbell-Bannerman, 8 December 1905, Campbell-Bannerman Papers, Add. MSS. 41, 218, fol. 161; entry of 8 December 1905, in Fitzroy, *Memoirs* (London, 1925), I, 271.

office in Bouverie Street to find 'a message from Herbert Gladstone asking me to telephone him at a certain number that evening, not mentioning his name'. At ten o'clock, exactly as instructed, he 'rang the number and Herbert answered'. Gladstone correctly surmised that Gardiner had seen – and meant to answer – the leading article in that morning's *Times*, recommending that Campbell-Bannerman should take a peerage. 'May I suggest that you should not dismiss the idea too absolutely,' he told Gardiner, who later recalled his quandary:

> Gladstone was one of the most loyal of C.B.'s supporters & had already accepted the Home Secretaryship & I was puzzled by the singular request. I asked for more light, but he vouchsafed none & confined himself to repeating the hint. My intention had been to insist in the strongest terms on C.B. staying in the H. of C., but this communication put me into the deepest perplexity. If H.G. was in favour of C.B. going upstairs then C.B. himself must have given way.

Under the pressure of an impending deadline, Gardiner 'talked the matter over with Masterman, who was then on our leader writing staff, and we agreed that the best thing was to put the question bluntly to C.B. himself'. He hurriedly 'wrote a note referring to *The Times* leader, but not of course to the telephone conversation, and asking for a word of guidance'. His secretary delivered it to Grosvenor Place, 'and caught C.B. as he was going to bed'. Wrapped in his dressing gown, Campbell-Bannerman authorized Gardiner to publish a 'reply to *The Times* [that] was not wanting in vigour & firmness'. Gardiner never sought nor obtained from Gladstone an explanation for 'his intervention in favour of the other side', and was satisfied to have helped to thwart the manoeuvre.[1]

Deprived of Campbell-Bannerman's presence, the Upper House settled for that of Alfred Harmsworth, created Baron Northcliffe in Balfour's resignation honours list. 'Though we differ so profoundly in politics your elevation to the Peers was *a real pleasure to me*,' Strachey wrote to him. 'I always felt it was ridiculous to make old Levi Lawson a Peer & refuse the same honour to you. On public grounds the *D[aily] M[ail]* is worth ten of the *D[aily] T[elegraph]*.' Others were a good deal less complimentary. 'You probably saw without surprise yesterday that Harmsworth has become a peer,' Buckle wrote to his proprietor. 'How infinitely more distinguished you are as Mr Walter of *The Times*, the fourth of the dynasty, than the Glenesks, Burnhams, and Harmsworths.' For his own part, Buckle declined a baronetcy, though he was 'naturally pleased' that Balfour considered his services 'worthy of recognition

---

[1] Russell, *Liberal Landslide*, p. 35; memorandum by Gardiner [1940s], Gardiner Papers. J. A. Spender had received a similar summons from Gladstone the previous afternoon. Memorandum of 5 December 1905, Spender Papers, Add. MSS. 46, 388, fol. 63.

by the State. Absolute independence of Ministries and parties is one of the most cherished of our traditions in Printing House Square,' he instructed the outgoing premier. 'Such support as *The Times* has given to your Government has been given entirely on public, and not on party grounds, and is not a suitable subject for payment with party rewards.' Half platitude and half prophecy, Buckle's cherished tradition was put to the test by an election that returned an overwhelming Liberal majority, followed two years later by Northcliffe's acquisition of *The Times*.[1]

---

[1] Strachey to Northcliffe, 22 December 1905, Northcliffe Papers; Buckle to Walter, 10 December 1905, *Times* Archives; Buckle to Balfour, 5 December 1905, Balfour Papers.

Two

EFFIGIES OF LIBERALISM

Sobered by the adversity of later years, J. A. Spender was moved to reflect that, 'from the journalist's point of view', the revival of Liberalism in the general election of 1906 had been 'altogether too much'. Equipped with a massive majority in the new Parliament, 'Liberal politicians seemed to be in a position in which they were beyond the good or evil that newspapers could do, or the need of their assistance'. As a party loyalist, Spender had rejoiced at the result. As a Fleet Street professional, however, he had been struck by its disadvantages. 'The journalist, *qua* journalist, always prefers to have his party in Opposition,' he explained, keenly conscious of the paradox. 'Daily support of a Government – the "loyal" support which Governments expect from the newspapers on their side – is a weary business, which cannot be made effective or entertaining to any but devout party worshippers.'[1]

Through the January campaign, Spender worked indefatigably to put his party into power at the cost of putting himself into this editorial predicament. The *Westminster Gazette* dutifully concentrated on the Free Trade issue, which combined the greatest popular appeal with the least potential for causing disruption in Liberal ranks. With particular satisfaction, the paper reported the return of Sir George Newnes at Swansea and the election of his son Frank at Bassetlaw. The *Daily News*, too, plunged headlong into what it described as 'by far the greatest electoral struggle of our generation' (6 January). Three members of its staff (P. W. Wilson, C. F. G. Masterman, and L. G. Chiozza Money), 'to say nothing of half a dozen former members', won sets, and David Williamson's bid to capture the 'Tory citadel of Dulwich' was considered 'almost more honourable than victory' (29 January). Less reluctant than Spender to run the risk of opening wounds, Gardiner allowed his leader-writers free rein to denounce the Unionists for their imperial excesses, including the importation of 'Chinese slavery' to the Transvaal, and the *Daily News* fastened instinctively on Nonconformist grievances over licensing and education. On 9 January, readers were urged to 'realise that Chamberlainism and Balfourism are dying forces, and ... and to give them the fatal stroke' at the polls.

[1] Spender, *Life, Journalism and Politics*, I, 134.

Spender's ministerial allies, drawn mostly from the Liberal Imperialist wing, were disconcerted by attacks on Lord Milner's South African policies and relatively unmoved by Nonconformist demands. Gardiner's connections, like those of C. P. Scott, belonged to the overlapping Radical and 'pro-Boer' contingents. Temporarily muted, differences within the Liberal hierarchy continued to find expression in the columns of the Liberal press. The editors of the *Morning Leader* and the *Star*, lacking intimate contacts at this exalted level, were subject to still fewer restraints. The *Daily Chronicle*, by contrast, aimed to be more pragmatic than programmic. Robert Donald, feeling his way as editor, waited upon party leaders for directives on South African controversies: 'I have no voice, ... but we must be on the winning side. We must say nothing till the Cabinet decides,' he told E. T. Cook, his Roseberyite leader-writer, who deplored this 'degradation of journalism'.[1]

However degrading or constraining, subservience was accepted by political journalists as a fact of life, at least during the protracted trial of a general election. For the Liberals, who had taken office after a decade in the wilderness, a show of unity was deemed essential in order to dispel any lingering impression that the party was unfit to provide stable government. Moreover, the Liberal papers were painfully aware of their own inherent disadvantages. Fewer than their Unionist counterparts, and with a smaller aggregate circulation, they tried to maximize their impact by informal collaboration with front-bench spokesmen and with one another. To a distinguished group of politicians and journalists, who gathered at the National Liberal Club on 27 January to celebrate the *Daily News*'s diamond jubilee, Gardiner proclaimed that 'the Liberal Press of London will have no rivalry except that noble one of seeking how best to serve the people's cause'.

Among the guests on that occasion was L. T. Hobhouse, who had been considered for Gardiner's job, and who had more recently assumed the political editorship of the new penny *Tribune*. A welcome recruit to the depleted ranks of metropolitan Liberal papers, the *Tribune* had been set afoot the previous spring, when the party was still in opposition. E. C. Bentley had heard on 31 May 1905 that 'there *is* a new Lib. paper starting', and he promptly volunteered his services. 'This is a big thing, I think,' Bentley wrote in his diary. 'All depends on who is to edit.'[2]

Hobhouse was an admirable choice, though in some ways an awkward one. Upon his departure from the *Manchester Guardian* in 1902, he had moved south to London and into the orbit of Fabian intellectualism. 'It is strange,' he wrote to Scott, 'but I think I have realised the influence of the *M.G.* more since I came to London than when I was in M/c. The other Liberal papers are so futile.' Graham Wallas later recalled that Hobhouse, 'with his very human restlessness and fits of depression, was the kind of saint which modern

---

[1] Cook's diary, 31 January 1906, Cook Papers.
[2] Bentley's diary, 31 May 1905, Bentley Papers, Bodleian MS Eng. Misc. e. 870.

civilisation most requires'. It was not clear how either his saintliness or his progressivism would wash with the proprietors of the *Tribune*, who engaged him at an annual salary of £1,000. Hobhouse was sensitive to the anomalies of this arrangement. 'I am not sure that we shall always agree & there will be the eternal question of the ethics of compromise,' he informed his sister with due pessimism.[1]

J. E. Taylor, who had been Hobhouse's employer at the *Manchester Guardian*, took a dim view of the prospects for the *Tribune*, 'which is, I feel assured, foredoomed to failure'.[2] But Taylor's death soon put the *Guardian* in further jeopardy and, with the dissolution of the *Echo*, portended an availability of Liberal readers and writers. The *Tribune*, with its proud emphasis on quality, was therefore designed to fill a void which, happily enough, never arose. Scott's success in securing control of the *Guardian* from Taylor's trustees, a tribute to his perseverance and self-sacrifice, deprived the *Tribune* of a *raison d'être* as well as potential contributors, who stayed put in Manchester.

The first issue of the *Tribune* appeared on 15 January 1906, three days after polling had begun and after the Liberals had already registered sweeping gains in Lancashire. The chief proprietor was Franklin Thomasson, son and heir of the Bolton textile manufacturer who had helped George Cadbury to wrest the *Daily News* from jingo hands at the turn of the century. The younger Thomasson, as Sir Philip Gibbs recalled him, 'was a very tall, handsome, and melancholy young man', who 'started the *Tribune* as a kind of sacred duty which he had inherited with his money'. Campbell-Bannerman sent him a personal letter, which served to launch publication: 'We are all of us deeply indebted to you for the great public spirit you have shown in coming forward to undertake such an enterprise' (15 January). The whips afforded him more tangible gratification in the form of a safe seat at Leicester, conveniently vacated by Henry Broadhurst in March.[3]

Thomasson, a novice at the game, invited Augustine Birrell to dignify the venture as 'a kind of literary godfather'. But Birrell, returned to Parliament as member for Bristol North and newly installed as president of the Board of Education, had time only to advise Thomasson 'that if you pay £100,000 into my bank as a free gift, and do *not* start the *Tribune*, you will save a very great deal of money!' For more practical assistance, Thomasson turned to William Hill, formerly news editor of the *Westminster Gazette*. It was Hill, the editor-in-chief, to whom both Bentley and Gibbs applied for appointments, while Hobhouse was responsible for bringing in J. L. Hammond, J. A. Hobson, and H. N. Brailsford. This bifurcation may explain, but cannot

[1] *New Statesman*, 25 April 1931; Hobhouse to Scott, 18 June 1905, and Hobhouse to Emily Hobhouse, 28 August 1905, quoted in Peter Clarke, *Liberals and Social Democrats* (Cambridge, 1978), p. 101.
[2] Taylor to Scott, 18 August 1905, *Guardian* Archives.
[3] Gibbs, *Adventures in Journalism* (London, 1923), p. 96; *Sell's* (1907).

excuse, the chaos that resulted in the hiring of two literary editors and two news editors. Gibbs, one of the literary editors, claimed credit for commissioning a regular article from Chesterton, and for featuring work by Kipling and Conrad, all without effect on sales. 'We were long, and serious, and "highbrow", and – to tell the truth – dull,' he confessed in his memoirs. 'The public utterly refused to buy the *Tribune*,' and advertisers kept their distance.[1]

Despite its failure to realize either the hopes of its sponsors or a profit on its investment, the *Tribune* was greeted with respectful attention. Meeting on 2 February 1906, the general committee of the Oxford and Cambridge University Club considered a suggestion from John Mansfield (later 3rd Baron Sandhurst), a barrister, 'that one or two copies of the new penny Liberal Paper, the *Tribune*, be taken by the Club, and that a copy of each of the *Daily News* and the *Chronicle* be discontinued'. The decision was taken 'to order two copies of the *Tribune*' and, in the interests of economy, 'to discontinue one copy each of the *Standard*, the *Daily News*, and the *Chronicle*'.[2] Yet a Clubland clientele, though regarded as a prerequisite to the exertion of political influence, was obviously no assurance of solvency and implicitly perhaps a bar to it. Within the first two months, there was a catastrophic drop in circulation from 239,000 to 52,000 copies.

Thomasson, seeing his father's legacy dissipated, renewed his quest for secondary shareholders. He had failed initially to secure backing from five 'Liberal capitalists', who – according to Cook – had demanded nothing less than Cook as editor and baronetcies for themselves. (By the time Scott heard the story secondhand from Lord Loreburn, the price had been inflated to '4 or 5 peerages'.) After further setbacks, Thomasson negotiated an infusion of capital from American commercial sources, men who were 'not interested as Englishmen in English political questions', but who were connected with the Free Trade Union. Hammond resigned in protest, contrary to advice from his father-in-law, who was unable to see

> that there is any harm in American capital, as such, being risked in an English paper. If the object is solely to promote a mutual understanding between the two nations it would even seem to me to be a good thing. ... I was afraid that Harmsworth was going to get a finger in the pie & I was rather relieved when I heard the new share-holders were Yanks, though I naturally distrust the Yanks: still I suppose there are decent ones.

Vaughan Nash, who had left the *Daily News* to become Campbell-Bannerman's private secretary, gave the same counsel with greater authority, but still to no avail: 'If the Americans aren't going to have any voice in the

[1] Gibbs, *Adventures*, pp. 97–99; Harold Herd, *The March of Journalism* (London, 1952), p. 261; *also see* Alan J. Lee, 'Franklin Thomasson and the *Tribune*,' *Historical Journal*, xvi (1973), 341–60.
[2] Minutes, Oxford and Cambridge University Club, 2 February 1906.

shares, are not your scruples too scrupulous? ... So far as I know Thomasson has an absolutely free hand as regards policy.' Hammond, who no longer trusted Thomasson's free hand, saw a vital issue at stake. He regarded the paper 'as an organ for propa- ganda' and himself as 'part of its permanent political machinery'. While that did not entitle him to 'disregard the commercial interest of the paper', he was 'a politician first and a journalist afterwards' and therefore could not 'reconcile myself to a course which would put me in what I regard as a funda- mentally false position & I find myself obliged with great regret to leave the *Tribune*'.[1]

Hammond was behaving somewhat priggishly, but all too logically. The relationship between commercial management and editorial control was a vexing problem. 'Every paper ... must have money behind it to begin with,' his father-in-law supposed,

> & that money must always be connected with some interests which might at any given moment be found to be incompatible with the common good: e.g. it *might* be discovered that chocolate was largely responsible for cancer & in that case the *Daily News*'s brief for chocolate would not be convincing; but the possibility of the discovery being made wouldn't keep me off the *Daily News*.

Nor, for that matter, was the *Pall Mall Gazette*'s 'advocacy of Protection' made suspect by the fact that 'the paper is owned by Astor – at least I never thought of the *PMG* as being on a different footing from other Protectionist papers'. Hammond, however, could not divorce the piper from the tune. 'It is all drip, drip, drip,' he complained to Gilbert Murray, the Oxford classicist and a Liberal activist. In 'this world of mercenary journalism', he saw 'much less danger of men strutting too much than there is of their crawling too much'. With Brailsford in tow, he shifted to the *Daily News*, where he found it 'a great relief to be on a paper where people are Liberals'.[2]

In large part, the dispute over American funding was more pretext than cause. At the start of 1907, Hobhouse had finally quit the *Tribune*, as frequently threatened, and Hammond was feeling increasingly uncomfortable. Temperamentally unsuited to the rigours of daily journalism, Hobhouse – as Barbara Hammond put it – had 'an unfortunate way of treating fellow workers as "the dirt beneath his feet"' and gave the impression that 'he wld. be unhappy without some kind of a crisis on'. Presumably with Thomasson rather than Scott in mind, Hobhouse – now Martin White professor of sociology at the

---

[1] Cook's diary, n.d. (referring to events of 'Jan. or Feb.' 1906), Cook Papers; Scott's diary [29] June 1914, *Guardian* Archives; Hammond to Thomasson, 29 January 1907 (draft copy), E. H. Bradby to Hammond, 30 January 1907, and Nash to Hammond, 28 January 1907, Hammond Papers.

[2] Bradby to Hammond, 30 January 1907, Hammond Papers; Hammond to Murray, 30 January 1907, and Barbara Hammond to Mary Murray, 1 March 1907, Murray Papers.

London School of Economics – concluded bitterly that 'journalism is a profession which may be carried on (a) by people with independent means, (b) by people without convictions'. Hobson, similarly disillusioned, had withdrawn even sooner. Brailsford held on longest. 'Hobhouse's departure has distressed me very deeply and though I am going to give the new order of things a trial I am not at all sanguine,' he wrote to Scott on 1 February. 'Hammond is going too, and that does not make things easier.' To redress the balance, Brailsford nominated Nevinson to share leader-writing duties, but Nevinson was 'refused ... as too expensive', an 'excuse' that was taken as 'insincere'.[1]

Passing over Hammond's superior claims for the political editorship, Thomasson filled the vacancy by appointing S. J. Pryor, 'a charming little man' in Gibbs's estimation, but a person of no fixed allegiance. 'Felt humiliated at my rejection even by such a creature as Pryor,' Nevinson confided to his diary. After a transatlantic apprenticeship on the *New York Sun*, where he allegedly specialized in articles critical of British policy, Pryor had returned to his native country to work for Harmsworth on the *Daily Mail* and then, briefly, for Pearson on the *Daily Express* and the *Evening Standard*; he was eventually to take up a position on *The Times*. Thomasson must have hoped that Pryor would inject some Harmsworthian dynamism into the failing concern, and conceivably that he might help to attract more Yankee dollars. Instead, Pryor presided over the *Tribune*'s slow demise.[2]

Under the stewardship of Pryor, who was designated both editor and managing director, the *Tribune* cut free from its Radical moorings and drifted rightwards. Strachey, editor of the Unionist Free Trade *Spectator*, invited Pryor to lunch at Brooks's in July 1907, and was pleased to confirm 'that his views are very much those represented to me by the member of his staff, that is, he is altogether a left-centre man in his private opinions, and also he is strongly of opinion that the proper position for the *Tribune* is the left-centre position'. Pursuing the will-o'-the-wisp of a centre party, neither Radical nor protectionist, Strachey informed Rosebery 'that Pryor would very much like to work on our lines and that he thinks he may gradually be able to do so but that the process would necessarily be a slow one'. Thomasson, whose 'views are very much more moderate than they were', could probably be brought round. Already Pryor had braved 'a great many angry protests from the extremists who looked upon the paper as their appanage', but he had stood firm with Thomasson's support. While it was not to be expected that the *Tribune* would 'come out as a non-Party organ or at any rate to break away from official Liberalism', there was the prospect that it would occupy 'a national position

---

[1] Barbara Hammond to Mary Murray, 2 August and 30 November 1906, Murray Papers; Hobhouse to Barbara Hammond, 4 September 1907, Hammond Papers; Brailsford to Scott, 1 February 1907, *Guardian* Archives; Nevinson's diary, 12 February 1907.
[2] Gibbs, *Adventures*, p. 99; Nevinson's diary, 12 February 1907.

just as *The Times* used to' so as 'to represent public opinion in the widest and best sense and not Party opinions'. To accomplish this purpose, Strachey urged Rosebery to meet Pryor, who

> was very naturally anxious to see you and would feel greatly honoured if you would let him call upon you. . . . You will find him a typical journalist of the new school, primarily interested in the sale and production of the newspaper. At the same time he seemed to me a shrewd and capable little man. . . . I was struck by one remark of his which was that he was always trying to persuade the *Tribune* people that the world was not composed of politicians, and that the newspapers which succeeded were those which appealed to ordinary men and women and not to politicians pure and simple.

More controversially, Strachey also thought it would be 'a very good thing' if Pryor could meet Lord Hugh Cecil, to whom he sent a copy of his letter to Rosebery. 'Pryor seemed to be quite hopeful that Thomasson may gradually come to see that his paper will succeed far better as an independent organ than as a Party journal,' Strachey told Cecil, the *fons et origo* of Hughliganism', who recommended in turn that Rosebery should see 'not only Pryor but Thomasson ... to talk him over. I don't think it matters at all in present circumstances what exact line the *Tribune* takes,' Cecil reasoned, 'so long as it is a line clearly different from the Party line on either side.'[1]

All the while, the finances of the *Tribune* were going from bad to worse. Members of the staff made desperate efforts to keep the vessel afloat. Gibbs struck a bargain with the Countess of Carlisle, 'a gallant old lady', who subscribed a fortnight's expenses to endow the *Tribune*'s temperance crusade. One of his colleagues journeyed to Dublin, where Birrell had been transferred as Irish Secretary, in a vain attempt to enlist official Liberal patronage. 'Mr Birrell, is the *Tribune* going to die?' the emissary asked pleadingly. 'Twinkling through his eyeglasses', the statesman intoned: 'May the *Tribune* die the death it so richly deserves.' In January 1908, Thomasson 'decided to cut his losses', which Gibbs reckoned to amount to £300,000. Blumenfeld, shedding no crocodile tears, calculated that the *Tribune* ('one of the outstanding journalistic failures of our time') had run through £400,000 of Thomasson's fortune. Wickham Steed later put the sum at £600,000. Northcliffe repeated to Archibald Marshall a rumour that 'Thomasson is said to have dropped three-quarters of a million'. Kennedy Jones hazarded a relatively conservative estimate of £200,000 and asked rhetorically: 'Could there be

---

[1] Strachey to Rosebery, 22 July 1907 (copy), Strachey to Cecil, 22 July 1907 (copy), and Cecil to Strachey, 26 July 1907, Strachey Papers; no correspondence with Pryor or Thomasson survives among the Rosebery Papers.

more convincing proof that political opinion no longer possessed intrinsic commercial value in Fleet Street?'[1]

The moral drawn by Jones was, at best, premature, and no less debatable than Alan J. Lee's fatalistic assertion that the *Tribune* 'succumbed in the end to forces which threatened all the Radical press, and to which they all, in the end, succumbed'.[2] For the first half of its two-year existence, the paper was only half-Radical – Hobhouse's half – and, under Pryor, its partisan edge grew blunt. Arguably, had its devotion to party been more pronounced, Birrell and other Liberal leaders might have responded more sympathetically. In any case, a penny Radical organ was something of a contradiction in terms. Whereas the *Daily News* and the *Daily Chronicle* tapped new popular readerships (and advertising revenues) by lowering their prices, the *Tribune* strove to be the morning counterpart of the *Westminster Gazette*, which had neither the inclination nor the capacity for Radicalism. Its pretensions, reflected in its price, proved a greater disability than its political orientation.

In a larger sense, the fate of the *Tribune* may be seen to reflect the distress of Radicalism, which had lost its electoral thrust and ideological coherence. Older Radicals, who adhered to the Gladstonian tradition, had little in common with younger social democrats, whose Radicalism was of a more fiery hue. The emergence of an independent Labour Party, which had won twenty-nine seats in the 1906 elections, pre-empted the Radicals from their place on the extreme left of the parliamentary spectrum. Although 'Radical' retained its currency as an epithet, Radical doctrines were increasingly difficult to define, except by process of elimination. In many areas, most notably those of foreign policy and defence expenditure, Radicalism had evolved into a negative creed. To say, therefore, that the *Tribune* was a Radical voice – supposing this to have been the case – was to say more about its tone than about its content.

There existed no clear-cut division or any irreconcilable difference between Radicals, especially those who styled themselves as 'New Liberals', and Labour men, including those who espoused theories of socialism. Labour politicians were looked upon, and indeed nurtured, as representatives of a working-class Liberalism, and usually saw themselves in that light. Even when they stood on their own, they accepted shelter beneath the proverbial 'Liberal umbrella'. Although Liberal constituency associations were sometimes unresponsive to Labour aspirations, the parliamentary Liberal leadership was generally well disposed. And at least since 1888, when T. P. O'Connor had launched the *Star*, the views of organized labour received due attention in the pages of the Liberal press.

In 1903, the lopsided alliance between the Liberal and Labour parties was

---

[1] Gibbs, *Adventures*, pp. 99–101; Blumenfeld, *R.D.B.'s Diary*, entry of 8 February 1908 (London, 1930), p. 214; Steed, *The Press* (Harmondsworth, 1938), p. 84; Marshall, *Out and About* (London, 1933), p. 85; Jones, *Fleet Street and Downing Street*, pp. 322–23.

[2] Lee, 'The Radical Press,' in A. J. A. Morris, ed., *Edwardian Radicalism* (London, 1974), p. 56.

ratified by an electoral pact between Herbert Gladstone and Ramsay MacDonald, secretary of the Labour Representation Committee. George Cadbury, proprietor of the *Daily News* and a generous benefactor of the ILP, had acted as an intermediary. His paper, which gave extensive coverage to trade union activity, raised campaign funds for Labour candidates and, along with the Rowntrees' *Northern Echo* at Darlington, endorsed Arthur Henderson in that symbolic by-election at Barnard Castle. Gardiner, during earlier days at Blackburn, had cooperated with Philip Snowden, and he had since made MacDonald's acquaintance through the Rainbow Circle. It implied no betrayal of the Labour cause for MacDonald to propose himself to Gardiner in 1905 for the position relinquished by Nash at the *Daily News*. Rather, it attested to the intimacy at the time between the forces of progressivism.[1]

Like many Irish MPs and not a few impecunious Liberals, Labour politicians often dabbled in journalism as a means of eking out a livelihood. With the influx of Labour members in 1906, journalists became the third largest occupational component in the House of Commons.[2] From all indications, however, a high proportion of these professionals plied their trade on an occasional or free-lance basis. Those who held regular appointments tended, necessarily, to belong to the staffs of Liberal papers. The Labour Party, unlike the Irish Nationalists, had no daily organ of their own until the *Daily Herald* and the *Daily Citizen* began in 1912. There were, of course, various Labour (or socialist) weeklies and monthlies; but they were stamped by sectional or regional interests, antagonistic to one another, haphazardly distributed, and altogether no substitute for a metropolitan political newspaper. Through the Edwardian period, Labour spokesmen depended on such national platforms as the *Echo*, the *Morning Leader*, the *Daily News*, and the *Nation*.

Keir Hardie, who campaigned year after year to remedy this deficiency, had founded the weekly *Labour Leader* in 1894 from the wreckage of *The Miner*, and made it his 'unique source of personal authority over British socialists' until the end of 1903, when he lost editorial control. In the words of his accomplished biographer, Hardie 'had from the outset of his career been firmly convinced of the power of the printed word in making converts to socialism'. In his emphasis on the political function of the press, as in other respects, Hardie was clearly a traditionalist. He was also a realist, who recognized the problems involved in establishing an accredited ILP journal. 'The solid sermon and newspaper articles of even half-a-hundred years ago would not now be tolerated,' he wrote in 1907; 'not because of their dulness, but because of the mental effort needed to follow and understand them. A snippety press and a sensational public are outstanding marks of modern times.' Along with a

---

[1] Koss, *Fleet Street Radical: A. G. Gardiner and the 'Daily News'* (London, 1973), pp. 50, 57; F. Bealey and H. Pelling, *Labour and Politics 1900–1906* (London, 1958), pp. 140–47; E. C. Bentley, *Those Days* (London, 1940), pp. 227–28.

[2] J. A. Thomas, *The House of Commons 1906–1911* (Cardiff, 1958), pp. 22–23.

common religious impulse, Labour and Radicalism shared a despondency over the conduct of the popular press. 'There can be no regeneration of the world by a new journalism,' J. A. Hobson told the 225th meeting of the Rainbow Circle on 8 May 1918. 'Labour papers are as bad as others.'[1]

In some ways, Labour papers were even worse. Tied to faction, they articulated the ideals and resentments of mercurial personalities. Usually, they were crippled by this attribute: the *Labour Elector*, commenced as a monthly in June 1888 and converted to a weekly the following November, was dominated by H. H. Champion and could not survive his abrupt departure for Australia in April 1890: *Justice*, the weekly organ of the Social Democratic Federation, was too much the mouthpiece of H. M. Hyndman and his vendettas; and *Commonweal*, a monthly from February 1885 to May 1886, when it became a weekly, served the 'variegated membership' of the Socialist League until February 1891, when William Morris stepped aside and the paper reverted to monthly publication as 'A Revolutionary Journal of Anarchic Communism'. Only in one instance did the cult of personality pay off. Robert Blatchford, a jovial and brazenly undoctrinaire socialist, produced the first issue of the *Clarion* in Manchester on 2 December 1891, and sold nearly 40,000 copies. Proclaiming its dedication to 'a policy of humanity; a policy not of party, sect or creed', the *Clarion* did not conform to the conventions of political journalism, but none the less proved 'a great propagandist force'. Idiosyncratic to the point of giving boisterous support to the Boer War, Blatchford was ready in November 1904 to remake the *Clarion* as 'The Great Bi-Weekly'. There were, however, difficulties, which he spelled out to A. M. ('Alec') Thompson, his colleague:

> We are unpopular with the Labour and Socialist leaders. We are unknown, almost, to the Trade Unions. We are anathema to the Liberals & Tories, the Teetotalers, the Roman Catholics, the Methodists. *And we are no use to the fools.*

Despite persistent overtures, the *Clarion* kept its distance from any organized socialist movement, while it preached the benefits of working-class solidarity. 'What have we to do with the Labour Party, with the Socialist Party, with the ILP, with the SDF?' Blatchford asked Thompson as the general election approached. 'Nothing,' he himself answered. 'We never notice them.' Yet the *Clarion* gained from Labour's electoral breakthrough by a rise in circulation to 74,000 copies. Among the new subscribers was the Reform Club, where it was decided on 6 February 1906 that 'the *Clarion* Newspaper', still a '1d. weekly', should 'be taken on'.[2]

[1] K. O. Morgan, *Keir Hardie* (London, 1975), p. 234; Hardie, *From Serfdom to Socialism* (London, 1907), p. 50; Rainbow Circle minutes, 8 May 1918.
[2] Paul Thompson, *Socialists, Liberals and Labour* (London, 1967), pp. 149–50; E. P. Thompson, *William Morris* (rev. ed., London, 1977), pp. 391–92, 588; Ensor, *England*

As Labour expanded its operations in the constituencies, an array of local periodicals had sprung up with little effective coordination between them. They ranged from Hardie's *Merthyr Pioneer* to the *Chelsea Pick and Shovel*, from the *Bradford Labour Echo* and the *Nottingham Labour Echo* (both sponsored by Labour Church agencies) to the atheistic *Torch of Anarchy*, from the *Dunfermline Worker* (owned by a tobacconist) to the *Plymouth Socialist* (nominally attached to the local United Democratic Club, but in fact an ILP paper, edited by a prominent member of the SDF). As one historian has observed, 'even those who supported the idea of a socialist press were often unhappy at the proliferation of socialist newspapers and its diluting effect on the socialist cause'.[1] The challenge was to obtain financial resources and technical facilities without falling victim to capitalist pressures, to achieve a measure of uniformity without losing spontaneity, and to attract working-class readerships without pandering to a taste for sensationalism.

The election to Parliament of twenty-nine LRC candidates, accompanied by two dozen auxiliaries whom *The Times* (30 January 1906) classified as 'Labour' on grounds of trade-union sponsorship, loomed as a development of major significance. But contemporaries differed in their inferences. As late as 9 January, *The Times* had ascribed 'socialist' intentions to those whom it labelled as 'Radicals'. Ten days later, confronted by the genuine article, it warned that socialism was inimical to Radical individualism. Echoing Chamberlain's pronouncement that socialism posed a threat that only Tariff Reform could ward off, the paper professed less concern with the advent of a Labour Party, manifesting 'the determination of the wage-earning classes to have representatives of their own in the House of Commons', than with the 'tendency to call the new party Socialists, a title which carries with it in many minds summary and contemptuous condemnation' (30 January). Without specifying whether this tendency was internal or external to the Labour Party, *The Times* joined with other Unionist publications in promoting it. The object was to sow the suspicion that the Liberal majority, owing to the gullibility or inertia of its leaders, left itself open to permeation and eventual supersedence by its aggressive Labour allies.

Labour politicians, many of whom disclaimed a socialist ideology, were altogether more modest. Recognizing that Labour candidates were 'more dependent on Liberal votes than ever', Bernard Shaw confessed in the *Clarion* (2 February 1906) his anticipation – or apprehension – that the parliamentary Labour Party would not act as 'anything more than a nominally independent Trade Unionist and Radical group'. That Labour gradually was to succeed in

---

1870–1914 (Oxford, 1963), p. 334; Blatchford to Thompson, 14 November 1904 and [1905], Blatchford Papers; minutes, Reform Club, 6 February 1906.

[1] Deian Hopkin, 'The Socialist Press in Britain, 1890–1910,' in G. Boyce, J. Curran, and P. Wingate, eds., *Newspaper History* (London, 1978), pp. 294–306; *also see* Stanley Harrison, *Poor Men's Guardians* (London, 1974), ch. 8.

absorbing the Radicals, much less that it was ultimately to undermine the Liberal consensus, could not have been foretold. Of course, the election results raised Labour's expectations and widened its base of operations. But Labour, itself a conglomerate, was prepared at this stage to work within the context of a partnership for progress, and as a junior partner at that.

Liberal patronage remained indispensable to Labour not only in the constituencies, but also in the provision of press exposure. The *Majority*, a halfpenny morning paper which billed itself as 'The Organ for All Who Work for Wages or Salary', began on 10 July 1906 and fizzled within the week. There was no choice but to rely on Liberal journals, which – to give them their due – fostered a spirit of Lib-Lab mutuality. In time, this reliance came to rankle precisely because it worked so well as to deter any independent Labour initiative. William Stewart, with experience on the *Dunfermline Worker* and the *Labour Leader*, complained that 'the lack of newspaper press capable of competing with the lavishly financed journalism of the vested interests has always been the chief handicap of the socialist movement'.[1] A retrospective judgment, rendered after the First World War, this view belongs – with the stories of the *Daily Citizen* and the *Daily Herald* – to a subsequent phase of Labour's development.

* * *

Valentine Chirol, head of *The Times*'s foreign department, heard the election news on his way back from India aboard HMS *Hyacinth*. 'The result seems to me more like an earthquake than a mere landslide! Surely it's the biggest thing that has happened at home since 1832! & the most alarming,' he wrote to Moberly Bell in Printing House Square. Deprived of a copy of *The Times*, he was 'looking forward with some curiosity to see what the big 'un will make of it all'. Chamberlain, whose supporters had gained ground within the diminished Unionist Party, was probably looking upon the smash-up with grim satisfaction and could be forgiven for smiling at Balfour's ejection from Manchester; 'but what about A.J.B. now? "Down amongst the dead men, down, down, down."'[2]

Back at his desk, Chirol expressed stern disapproval of the line *The Times* was taking. The suggestion by the official historians of that paper that 'the Foreign Department . . ., naturally, was more familiar with Socialist theory and action than the Home News Department or the Home leader-writers', does not carry conviction. Rather, Chirol's absence during the campaign had immunized him against the 'fanatical belief in the innate wickedness of the present Government, which to my regret seems to dominate Printing House Square'.[3]

[1] Stewart, *Keir Hardie* (London, 1921), p. 160.
[2] Chirol to Moberly Bell, 20 January 1906, *Times* Archives.
[3] *History of The Times*, IV, part 1 (London, 1952), 42; Chirol to Steed, 12 April 1906, quoted in *ibid*.

Under his conciliatory influence, *The Times* pledged to support the new administration in the areas of diplomacy and defence, where it confidently expected no reversals of policy. The *Daily News*, fearing the effect of such 'blandishments' on certain Cabinet ministers, advised *The Times* to 'look at the party whom it has helped to ruin. ... Let the Government obey the spirit that called it into existence, not the defeated powers against whom a tremendous national verdict has been secured' (29 January). Between the major parties as within the Unionist fold, *The Times* had to tread cautiously.

Having gone into the fray divided, the Unionists emerged shattered. Balfour and Chamberlain managed better than their respective followers to avoid open altercation. The Unionist Free Traders suffered especially heavy losses at the polls. With Balfour himself temporarily *hors de combat*, the Balfourites were outnumbered three-to-one by the Tariff Reformers in the new Parliament. In the press, their proportional disadvantage was still more overwhelming, which was assumed to be hardly coincidental.

Iwan-Müller read the January number of the *National Review* on New Year's Day and was 'finally driven to retort' to Maxse, its pugnacious editor: 'Twice have I written you long letters to try if we could not pull things together and twice have I torn them up', knowing the effort to be 'useless'. Garvin or indeed Chamberlain could verify how 'I laboured for peace & harmony in the Unionist ranks' to the point of arranging accommodation in the *Daily Telegraph* 'for the propagation of extreme Tariff Reform views'. In exchange, Maxse had now 'damned the *D.T.* and ... denounced the leader-writer (myself) as a member of a "Balfour clique"'. Unwilling to 'believe that there is any irreconcilable difference between A.J.B. and J.C.', Iwan-Müller accused Maxse's *National Review* and Garvin's *Outlook* of 'trying to make one. If so; if you want war, you shall have it,' he threatened. But, as he knew, the journalistic artillery was on their side.[1]

On 5 February, after the dust had settled, Iwan-Müller offered 'Some Thoughts upon the Present Discontent' in the form of a lengthy memorandum, addressed to Sandars, but obviously intended for Balfour's perusal. 'The last special cause' of the Unionist débâcle, and the one he surveyed most systematically, 'was what the French call a "bad press"'. The problem was put into historical perspective: 'From 1886 till Joe's retirement from the Ministry' in 1903,

> the Tory (Unionist) party was for the first time ... infinitely stronger in the support of the (London) press than its opponents. In the provinces we have never been so strong as the Radicals. The *Yorkshire Post*, the *Birmingham*

[1] Iwan-Müller to Maxse, 1 January 1906, Maxse Papers. G. K. Chesterton, who exhibited similar characteristics, recalled Maxse as 'a really good partisan, and for that reason a bad party man. For a good party man is not he who is ready to attack the other party; but he who is ready to spare the other party when commanded to do so by his own party.' *G.K.'s Weekly*, 30 January 1932.

Post (L.U.), the *Scotsman* and the *Glasgow Herald*, were most notable exceptions to our provincial weakness. But when the Fiscal problem was raised, our strength was turned into weakness.

As Iwan-Müller saw it, 'only two daily papers in London' could '*afford* to take an independent line in politics', by which he meant Unionist politics:

> *The Times* because it has a sort of recognised privilege of upholding the Government of the day ...; the *Daily Telegraph* because its popularity and circulation depend much more upon the variety and completeness of its general contents than upon its political articles, though it is a great assistance to a party to have on its side a paper which is read principally for other than political reasons. The *Telegraph* was loyal to the Chief throughout; *The Times* wobbled a good deal, but *until the elections were in sight* was definitely Chamberlainite.

Elsewhere in his treatise, he explained that '*The Times* rallied splendidly at the last, but it could not efface the marks of the pricks with which for reasons (not mainly political) it delighted to torment Cecilian Administrators'.

As for other Fleet Street properties, they were either 'organs of the Tariff Reform League', like the *Standard* and the *Daily Express*, or else had their policies 'dictated largely by business conditions of rivalry' that played into protectionist hands: the *Pall Mall Gazette*, 'incomprehensibly' hostile, 'always "crabbed" the Chief'; the *Globe* was 'Orange, Jingo, Protectionist and insular to the last degree'; the *Evening Standard* was routinely 'Chamberlainite'; and the *Morning Post*, 'owned by an ungrateful and dissatisfied Tory, ... was in some respects more "Joeite" than Joe himself'. Consequently,

> while no Daily paper rallied to the official Opposition, the strength of the Chamberlainite faction in the London press exaggerated and magnified beyond all reason the importance and depth of our internal divisions. And except in a few cases – not more than two or three – the London press exercised a great, perhaps unconscious influence over journalism in the provinces.

Dismissive of weekly journals, which 'count for very little in the development of public opinion', Iwan-Müller concluded that the 'only remedy' was 'to watch opportunities and seize the moment when one or other' of the pre-existing dailies 'is in the market – e.g. the *Standard* or *PMG* – and induce some wealthy man or men to buy it'. Perceiving that there was 'no room for a new paper (vide the *Tribune*)', he was also aware that, 'if undertaken', this 'scheme ... can only be carried out by shareholders whose first object is political and not financial'. Ideally, 'the interests of Toryism and moderate Fiscal Reform' should be served by 'at least one penny morning paper (other than the *D.T.*), one penny evening, and one six-penny weekly'. In addition, there was 'one task ... which must be grappled with immediately', namely the provision of a halfpenny evening paper, capable of swaying working-class votes. Perhaps such a paper could be produced in London, leaving 'space at discretion for local news' to be inserted as appropriate. The idea was not a new one, but the success of the *Daily Mail*'s northern edition commended the possibility.[1]

The Unionist Free Traders were still more impoverished in terms of the journals at their command and were subject to intensified recrimination after the *Spectator* (6 January) instructed its readers to vote for a Liberal in lieu of a Unionist Free Trade candidate. 'By the way what a devilish unpopular lot we Unionist Free Traders are with Joe's lot,' Eric Parker remarked to David Hannay, with whom he had worked on the defunct *St James's Gazette*.[2] Bereft of a London daily, the dissident Unionists were able to count on the *Glasgow Herald* (with a circulation of 52,000) and the Hultons' *Daily Dispatch* in Manchester. This was fortunate in that five of their fifty-six candidates were clustered in Glasgow and eleven in Lancashire. The *Dispatch* claimed a 'daily circulation' of 125,000, '*More than* that of Any Provincial Morning Newspaper.' Listed in *Sell's* directory as politically 'neutral', it lavishly praised the Duke of Devonshire's Free Trade manifesto and denounced 'pure protectionism' as an 'unsound policy' and a 'danger' (1 January). The notion that Balfour and Chamberlain had 'worked out a basis for common action, and will go into the struggle side by side', was derided as 'a great waste of breath. ... Let us assure the Chamberlainite newspapers that they need waste no more ink on the subject. ... True Free Traders are in no danger of being taken in' (3 January). On the 13th, the *Dispatch* concurred with the *Spectator* that a Liberal was preferable to a Tariff Reformer at the polls: 'If our Free Trade views are to have the least effect we must sink all other political prepossessions today.' Balfour's defeat was regretted because of 'strong personal ties', and all the more because it reduced the parliamentary Unionist Party to a Chamberlainite rump (15 January).

Chamberlain, however, was strangely reluctant to capitalize on Balfour's misfortune. In a letter to *The Times* on 2 February, he removed himself from the running for the leadership and proceeded instead to issue a list of demands for Balfour to consider. To Buckle, whom he saw beforehand, he was 'as usual, ... quite frank ... as to his resolves and wishes': first of all, he professed his determination 'to put an end to the dual headship of the party, Balfour recommending one cause while he recommends another'; secondly, he hoped 'to come to a complete agreement with Balfour, by Balfour's making a further

---

[1] Memorandum by Iwan-Müller, 5 February 1906, Balfour Papers.
[2] Parker to Hannay, 24 January 1906, Hannay Papers; for the Unionist Free Traders and their press in the general election of 1906, see R. A. Remple, *Unionists Divided* (Newton Abbot, 1972), ch. 9, and A. K. Russell, *Liberal Landslide*, pp. 140–41.

advance in his direction'. In the event that 'Balfour does not oblige', Chamberlain was ready to 'stand apart as the head of a group of Tariff Reformers', independent of the official Opposition and its whips.[1]

To Fabian Ware, editor of the 'Joeite' *Morning Post*, Chamberlain spoke more forcefully and perhaps more candidly. 'I have seen a good deal of Mr Chamberlain lately,' Ware reported on 3 February to Lady Bathurst, his proprietor's daughter:

> The leadership is his if he will take it, but he most emphatically *won't*. He says that he is not the right man, that the Church & the landed people would not really support him. That is a brief but absolutely accurate summary of his position. *But* he will only follow Mr Balfour if he (B) will publicly & definitely accept his (C's) policy. If he won't C will be forced to form a separate but 'friendly' group & fight every bye-election.

That morning, Chamberlain saw another of his Fleet Street confederates, Lord Northcliffe, then left London for a holiday. Upon arrival at Torquay, he promptly wrote to Northcliffe about a point that there had not been time to discuss. Convinced by Balfour's chilliness 'that he has finally decided to stand with the Free Traders rather than with the Tariff Reformers', Chamberlain was willing to consider the suggestion made by Garvin in the *Outlook* and allusively mooted in the *Morning Post* that Walter Long might qualify as a compromise leader. 'I doubt if this solution would commend itself to A.J.B.,' Chamberlain revealed, 'but I wanted you to know that, as far as I am concerned, I should see in it an acceptable arrangement.'[2]

Northcliffe was eminently deserving of Chamberlain's confidence. Apart from the backing he provided through his London papers, he had spent £50,000 to scoop up the ordinary shares of the *Manchester Courier*. On the same day that Chamberlain saw and wrote to him, Northcliffe was reminded by A. F. Stephenson, managing director of the Manchester concern, that 'one thing neither you nor anyone else can lose sight of is if it had not been for *you* there would have today been no *Manchester Courier*'. Save for Northcliffe's intervention, that property might have fallen into the hands of the Unionist Free Traders, from whom Northcliffe had already kept the *Observer* and from whom he was soon to keep *The Times*. Or else, like the *Manchester Evening Mail*, the morning *Courier* might have folded. Iwan-Müller, with firsthand experience of Manchester journalism, knew that 'the disappearance of the *Evening Mail* was most severely felt' by Unionist candidates in Lancashire, Balfour included. Plans to replace it were wrecked by Lord Stanley (soon to become the 17th Earl of Derby) and other 'Manchester Unionists'. Dunn, the

---

[1] Buckle to Walter, 1 February 1906, *Times* Archives.
[2] Ware to Lady Bathurst, 3 February 1906, Bathurst Papers; Chamberlain to Northcliffe, 3 February 1906 (copy), Chamberlain Papers.

editor of the *Courier*, characterized them as 'a wretched lot' who, 'as a rule, care for nothing except the comfortable state of their bellies and their bank-books'.[1]

The Unionist Free Traders implored Balfour to resist Chamberlain's demands, while the respective followers of the two leaders sank further into despair. Balfour's position was the more vulnerable. To fit him out with a safe seat would be relatively easy, but to generate enthusiasm for him was another matter. Iwan-Müller, always inclined to see matters from the journalistic angle, told Sandars: 'If there is no London daily evening ... paper of standing that gives a wholehearted support to the Chief I don't see how he is to carry on.' The Chamberlainites refused to accept their hero's self-denying ordinance as his last word. 'You and I are not represented by Balfour and never can be, never have been,' Ivor Maxse, Leo's older brother, insisted to Lady Bathurst. 'Therefore we must split the party for a time, and now is the time.' Leo Maxse solicited assistance from Buckle, who conceded that there was 'much to be said' in Chamberlain's favour, but who remonstrated that *The Times* could not say it unless Chamberlain first came forward. 'You apparently have made up your mind that, failing Chamberlain, anyone is better than Balfour,' replied Buckle, who thought it would be 'a great pity to take any irrevocable step at a moment when Unionists are sore after their defeat & anxious to show their spirit by smashing the crockery'. In desperation, the younger Maxse poured out his grief to Lady Bathurst: 'The Unionist Party seems to be completely paralysed by its leaders. What are we to do?'[2]

As Chamberlain confided to Northcliffe, one of his proposals was for the establishment of 'joint organisation', and Balfour had responded negatively. Rumours were rife that Balfour intended to install Sandars as head of the Central Office in tandem with Sir Alexander Acland Hood or, worse, Iwan-Müller. The *Standard* and the *Globe*, all too ready to believe the worst about Balfour's motives, stiffly protested, the *Globe* by impugning Sandars's competence. Sandars, who was 'doing my best to co-operate', wrote 'very civilly' to Maxse to deny these allegations: 'I told him that I knew he had, & deservedly had, a great influence in T.R. circles & their Press – wouldn't he persuade them to conduct their campaign agst. A.J.B. without bringing my name into it?'[3] If nothing else, this incident went to show how deeply rooted were the suspicions entertained by the Chamberlainites against the 'old gang' as well as how acute was the sensitivity to newspaper criticism.

[1] Pound and Harmsworth, p. 296; memorandum by Iwan-Müller, 5 February 1906, Balfour Papers; Stephenson to Northcliffe, 3 February 1906, and Dunn to Northcliffe and Sutton, 25 June 1907, Northcliffe Papers.
[2] Iwan-Müller to Sandars, 6 January 1906, Sandars Papers; Buckle to Maxse, 6 February 1906, Maxse Papers; Ivor Maxse to Lady Bathurst, 4 February 1906, and Maxse to Lady Bathurst, 7 February 1906, Bathurst Papers.
[3] Sandars to Iwan-Müller, 5 February 1906, Iwan-Müller Papers, Add. MSS. 51, 316, fols. 79–81.

Maxse, for all the influence he seemed to wield, put little trust in his fellow journalists. 'The worst of the London press is that so many of its editors are capable of making a strong start, but they are incapable of keeping at it,' he grumbled to Lady Bathurst. 'The weak-kneed and the wobbling politicians get hold of them and mislead them as to "public opinion".' Maxse, whose own pertinacity was never in doubt, thus inverted the process by which public opinion was brought to bear through the press. The *Morning Post*, however, escaped his censure. Adamantly Chamberlainite, even in the face of Chamberlain's tactical withdrawal, it would have no truck with intra-party concessions. Lady Bathurst, who was to inherit the proprietorship upon her father's death in 1908, took an increasing interest in editorial affairs. Her literary contribution was limited to the correspondence columns, where she published a letter signed 'Tariff Reformer' in February. She and her husband, together with Ivor Maxse, were designated executors of the Glenesk estate and, as such, directors of the *Morning Post* company. Another, less active director was L. V. ('Loulou') Harcourt, Sir William's son and Lady Glenesk's nephew, who held a junior ministry in the Campbell-Bannerman government. That a high-ranking Liberal should bear a titular responsibility for the *Morning Post* posed a potential embarrassment to all concerned. On taking office, Harcourt was constitutionally required to relinquish any commercial directorships. He explained his curious family obligations to the Prime Minister, who advised him 'to take the opinion of the new Lord Chancellor', Lord Loreburn. Receiving a special dispensation from the Woolsack, Harcourt was able to inform Glenesk, his 'dear Uncle Algy', that the arrangements could stand. For the time being, he remained a Liberal Trojan horse within the protectionist encampment.[1]

'Dear old Joe, he isn't deserting us!' Ware rejoiced to Lady Bathurst on 8 February. 'It's the last chance for the Unionist Party & I believe they will take it.' He had been heartened by Chamberlain's open letter to Lord Ridley, prominently featured in the *Morning Post*, calling for a party conference to resolve differences. Such a meeting was scheduled at Lansdowne House on the 15th and, the day before, Chamberlain and Balfour exchanged their famous 'Valentine' letters. Balfour was seen to have capitulated to the Tariff Reformers: 'the Balfour climb-down is a great triumph for the *Nat.*', Maxse was assured by Strachey, who curiously reasoned that 'it is also a triumph for the *Spec.* for, as you know, we have always declared that Balfour was in reality a Chamberlainite and that he had not the courage of his opinions'. Strachey took further consolation from the fact that 'we shall have no more tedious Balfourian psychology in the newspapers'.[2]

---

[1] Maxse to Lady Bathurst, 30 January 1906, and Harcourt to Glenesk, 13 December 1905, Bathurst Papers; Lucas, *Glenesk*, pp. 374–75, 413.
[2] Ware to Lady Bathurst, 8 February 1906, Bathurst Papers; Strachey to Maxse, 16 February 1906, Maxse Papers.

Yet Maxse kept up his attacks on the 'Balfour clique' in the *National Review*. The hopeless estrangement of the Unionist Free Traders was symbolized by the decision that Chamberlain would substitute as leader of the Opposition until Balfour negotiated a safe return to the Commons. Parker could 'quite agree' with Hannay 'that it's no use sitting still with Joe working the machine for all he's worth on the other side', but he balked at having to 'change ... opinions because Joe ordains that opinions must be changed'. Defiantly, he proclaimed his intention to attend a dinner in honour of Ronald McNeill, who had been defeated as a Tariff Reform candidate at West Aberdeen, 'and I'm rather looking forward to a fight with my old colleagues'. Parker recalled happier days on the *St James's Gazette* when McNeill, as editor, 'used to damn' one of their colleagues 'up and down stairs for perpetually committing the paper to Protection in those hastily written "notes" that we used to string off between 9 and 10.30 a.m.'[1] McNeill, now a different creature, bided his time as assistant editor on the *Encyclopaedia Britannica* until 1911, when he was elected Unionist MP for East Kent.

Balfour did not have so long to wait. In a by-election on 27 February, he was returned for the City of London. Suffering from influenza, he did not take his seat until 12 March and was then out of commission during subsequent weeks. The Tariff Reform press, anxious to consolidate its gains, mounted a campaign to subordinate the Balfourite Central Office to the Chamberlainite National Union. A committee considered proposals for an overhaul of party organization, and delivered its recommendations to the National Union in July. Acland Hood, the embattled chief whip, took strong exception to the *Morning Post*'s 'suggestion that the policy of the party should be managed by a committee': the implications were obvious, and the result 'would be disastrous'.[2]

By then, the situation had altered radically. Chamberlain, who had just celebrated his seventieth birthday, suffered a stroke and retired to Highbury. The seriousness of his condition was kept a secret, but his powers of speech and sight were too much impaired for him ever to resume an active political life. Dissatisfaction with Balfour persisted, but was diffused. That winter, a move to regroup the protectionist forces around Lord Milner proved a non-starter. (Sandars had a detailed account from Iwan-Müller and would have sent Balfour 'Iwan's letter but you could not read it!!') All the same, Sandars gloomily contemplated that, except for the *Daily Telegraph*, 'we have not a single organ of the London Press which wd. support the orthodox party & its leader' against the militants. 'The result of all this,' he warned Balfour on 22 January 1907, 'is that there has been a general weakening of your authority throughout the country.'[3]

---

[1] Parker to Hannay, 27 February 1906, Hannay Papers.
[2] National Union minutes, 27 July 1906.
[3] Sandars to Balfour, 13 and 22 January 1907, Balfour Papers.

The journalistic mood was shifting, however. Apart from Strachey, who was 'bound to say Mr Balfour in his capacity of leader of the Unionist Party fills me more and more with misgiving', critics tempered their resistance. Garvin, hitherto a relentless antagonist, saw no alternative to 'a hearty and final acceptance' of Balfour's leadership, though he feared it 'would cost me the support perhaps even of Maxse and the *Morning Post*'. Lord Glenesk, a maverick to the end, infuriated his editor by vetoing the publication of 'an unauthorised programme', the product of some 'very confidential meetings' between Ware and 'several leaders'. Maxse, with a nudge from Chamberlain, slowly swung round and celebrated Balfour's speech at Birmingham in November 1907 as 'a landmark in British policy, . . . acceptable to all reasonable tariff reformers', among whom he had the temerity to place himself. Northcliffe had perhaps the fewest scruples about championing Balfour, whose signed photograph adorned his 'square polished desk' at Sutton Place. 'You know that I am a very keen Tariff Reformer,' he said to Lord Robert Cecil, pointing out 'the brutal fact . . . that we are all under the influence of the invalid at Highbury, who is never allowed to hear the truth.'[1]

When Chamberlain 'was struck down, very difficult months followed' for Garvin. His relationship with Goldman, proprietor of the *Outlook*, rapidly deteriorated, and he was searching for someone who would buy out the journal without disrupting his editorship. In June, he sought to enlist Northcliffe, better equipped than any of the 'various people' who were interested for the essential reason that 'a first-class sixpenny review can only be made into . . . the *property* it ought to be by having a great distributing organisation at its back'. In November, Walter Long stepped forward. Too prudent to involve himself directly, he acted through his private secretary and persuaded Lord Iveagh to purchase the *Outlook* and to vest control in his son, Walter Guinness (later 1st Baron Moyne), soon to become Unionist MP for Bury St Edmunds. But the business disputes that had soured Garvin's partnership with Goldman led to an impasse with Guinness. Garvin denied that he was being mercenary: 'As Mr Chamberlain would tell you in a moment, if he were well, I am one of the few journalists who have made – and more than once – a serious sacrifice of money for principle.' In the event, Guinness acquired the *Outlook* and dispensed with the services of Garvin and Edward Grigg (later 1st Baron Altrincham), the assistant editor. Long, whose purpose had been to maintain the journal as a platform for Garvin's Irish views, was disconsolate. 'For me the *Outlook* meant you and Grigg,' he commiserated with Garvin; 'without this splendid combination it would have little if any value for me.'

---

[1] Strachey to Devonshire, 28 December 1906, Devonshire Papers; Garvin to Joseph Chamberlain, 24 September 1906, Austen Chamberlain Papers; Ware to Lady Bathurst, 25 February 1907, Bathurst Papers; Chamberlain to Maxse, 22 November 1907, Maxse Papers; *National Review*, December 1907; Tom Clarke, *My Northcliffe Diary* (London, 1931), pp. 46–47; Northcliffe to Cecil, n.d. (probably 1910), quoted in Pound and Harmsworth, pp. 289–90.

Garvin, of course, had other opportunities for gainful employment, including an invitation from Buckle to contribute articles on Tariff Reform. But *'The Times* people (suicidal imbeciles as they are)' dragged their heels. Garvin saw them as having been put off by his fulminations in the *National Review*, and 'only waiting for a pretext' to lead 'a great ratting movement'. Nor, at first flush, was Garvin attracted by a 'most splendid offer' to serve in a nebulous capacity as 'political right hand' to Northcliffe, whose 'own machine is too strong for him' and who was dominated by Kennedy Jones, 'the real power behind the scenes' and 'the master of all the lower arts of journalism'. Within the year, however, Northcliffe again proffered the editorship of the *Observer*, which lay outside Jones's bailiwick. In October 1907, Garvin revealed to Edward Goulding (later 1st Baron Wargrave) his plans

> to take over the *Observer*. It had once a great influence: it has a great name. It is the only first-class Sunday paper. I would make it a sort of penny rival to the sixpenny weekly reviews (as well as a thoroughly good *news*paper) and would run it with uncompromising independence upon Imperial-progressive-tariff reform-social reform lines. I should have a considerable share of the enterprise and I cannot help thinking it might be a great political influence as well as a great business success.

To Northcliffe, he expressed his eagerness 'to drive that machine until it smokes', yet 'to take care not to sacrifice the interests of the *Observer* as a general newspaper to tariff reform or any other fixed idea whatever'. Austen Chamberlain warmly approved: 'Once again the *Observer* will become interesting!' Garvin's appointment took effect at the end of January 1908, and he was soon crowing to Northcliffe that the *Observer* 'has far more immediate influence upon opinion than the *Outlook* ever had in its best days'.[1]

With Garvin gone, the *Outlook* demanded – and received – far less attention. Hannay gave Frederick Greenwood an unfavourable account of its performance. 'With so many lame ducks & other kinds of quack-quacks in the press,' replied Greenwood, 'here's a ... journal well-equipped for a career of independence & power, going wrong from the outset. So it seems.' To all intents and purposes, it had ceased to count as a significant exponent of Tariff Reform. The *Sun* was an earlier and more absolute loss. Since the autumn of

---

[1] The above paragraphs are based on Garvin to Steel-Maitland, 24 April 1912, Buckle to Garvin, 29 November 1906, and Long to Garvin, 10 November 1906, Garvin Papers; Garvin to Northcliffe, 20 June and 1 December 1906, 1 November 1907, and [February?] 1908, Northcliffe Papers; Garvin to Guinness, 16 November 1906, and Austen Chamberlain to Garvin, 13 January 1908, quoted in Gollin, *Observer*, pp. 136, 28; Garvin to Goulding, 25 October 1907, Wargrave Papers. Years later, Garvin recalled 'his early experience ... of the *Outlook* before the Guinnesses bought it and it became, as E. V. Lucas said, the *Stoutlook*'. His very 'first meeting with Lord Iveagh in a room lined with Romneys and Gainsboroughs and a pile of cashboxes in the middle' convinced him 'that he and Iveagh would not get on'. Barrington-Ward's diary, 1 December 1931.

1903, it had been managed without intellectual distinction by Sir George Armstrong and W. T. Madge, whose problems with the *Globe* and the *People* were more than they could handle. On 11 October 1906, they closed down the *Sun*. And, the following June, they sold the *Globe*, the oldest surviving metropolitan evening paper, to Hildebrand Harmsworth. The least energetic of Northcliffe's brothers, he reportedly paid £75,000 and lost £80,000 over the next three years. Charles Palmer was lifted out of the news-room to the editorship of the *Globe*.[1]

Eric Parker, a nostalgic veteran of London evening journalism, 'was enraged to see that the polluting hand of the Harmsworths was laid on the *Globe*, which though absurdly violent was at least a part of the older order of things'. Recently, 'at a hospital dinner', Parker had laid eyes on Harold Harmsworth, the second eldest of the brethren, who 'looked as if he had had a good go at the pig-trough. He is a vulgarly gross creature.'[2] But neither Harold (the future Lord Rothermere) nor Hildebrand could rival the appetite of Alfred, who – as the pseudonymous 'X' – was about to open negotiations which were to bring him custody of *The Times* in March 1908. The pig-trough then seemed to stretch from one end of Fleet Street to the other. Or, to substitute Chesterton's imagery for Parker's, 'the crowd of Joseph Chamberlains' had become a crowd of Harmsworths, another 'solemn thought'.

*   *   *

Liberal newspapers exulted at their party's spectacular electoral victory and enjoyed equally the spectacle of Unionist disunity, which they lost no opportunity to bring before the public. Nevertheless, they could not disguise their own deficiencies and relative disadvantages. Fleet Street, like the House of Lords and the Church, was recognized as a preponderantly Tory domain, however wide or deep the fissures on the Tory side. Few Liberal papers operated as commercially viable concerns, and fewer still could pretend to the influence of certain Unionist rivals. Lady Horner, the celebrated society hostess whose daughter married Asquith's eldest son, was not alone in bemoaning the 'powerful' influence of *The Times* and in wishing that the Liberal press 'were stronger and that someone read it!'[3] She exaggerated, of course; but her assessment was more valid than her snobbish tone might suggest.

The Liberal paper that carried greatest weight among the 'somebodies' was the *Westminster Gazette*, an evening equivalent to the morning *Times*. Alexander Murray, Master of Elibank and now Liberal MP for Selkirk and Peebles, was requested in his official capacity as Comptroller of the Royal Household to draft a memorandum on the subject of British newspapers. This document,

[1] Greenwood to Hannay, 14 January 1907, Hannay Papers; Pound and Harmsworth, p. 293; Simonis, *Street of Ink*, pp. 94–95.
[2] Parker to Hannay, 8 July 1907, Hannay Papers.
[3] Lady Horner to Elizabeth Haldane [13] January 1910, Haldane Papers, Vol. 6022, fol. 15.

'forwarded to the Emperor of Russia by Her Majesty the Queen', singled out the *Westminster Gazette* as 'the most powerful organ in England, voicing, as it does, the views of the Liberal Party, which was returned to power ... by the greatest majority ever known in English political history'. The Tsar, whose attention was called to a leading article in favour of the Duma and an extension of civil liberties in Russia, was further informed that 'the circulation of the paper is not confined to the Liberal Party, it is largely read in Conservative circles' as well. J. A. Spender, editor of the *Westminster*, would have been flattered, but he knew that his paper's reputation abroad as 'the organ of Sir Edward Grey' was hardly warranted, and that its circulation was limited, if select.[1]

Other Liberal dailies, for all the loyalty they commanded, were no better able to challenge the primacy of *The Times*. In upper-class drawing-rooms, they were eclipsed by the *Morning Post*, the *Standard*, and the *Pall Mall Gazette*. Among the suburban classes, increasingly visible within Edwardian society, they were no match for the *Daily Mail* or even the *Daily Express*. The *Manchester Guardian*, which raised its circulation to 37,000 in 1906, spoke in a northern dialect, as signalled by its proscription of the word 'provincial'. The *Daily Chronicle* showed spirit, but little sign of authority. The *Tribune*, as we have seen, was practically stillborn. The *Morning Leader* and the *Star* were easily discounted. The most vigorous of the lot was the *Daily News*, with an average sale of 153,600 copies in 1906. Its editor was privately addressed by a faithful reader, who was glad to see the paper 'sound & healthy & going strong', but who voiced a familiar complaint:

> Like many other radicals I take in *The Times*. I take it for its news & its letters. Is it not possible to get up a Liberal paper which will attract the best letter-writers? (Yes, your letters are good, but there are other kinds of letters.) Have you any idea of the number of people there are, like me, who take in *The Times* because of the news & the letters? The country is overwhelmingly Liberal. We need the halfpenny *Daily News*, but we also need the other kind of paper.
>
> No! I am not a snob. I ask for a liberal paper which will command the attention of the well-to-do liberals who are now compelled to take in *The Times*.
>
> You will say that the tax I pay, 3d a day, for *The Times* is not great. But it is a *tribute* paid to the enemy and I had rather pay ten times as much for a liberal paper.[2]

That the circulation of the *Daily News* was more than three times that of *The Times* compounded both the irony and the grievance.

[1] Memorandum by the Master of Elibank, 25 June 1906 (draft), Elibank Papers, Vol. 8801; Spender, *Life, Journalism and Politics*, I, 170.
[2] William Perry to 'My dear Old *Daily News*', 9 January 1908, Gardiner Papers.

Liberalism's weakness was especially evident among the quality Sunday papers. Yet, after Garvin left the *Outlook*, the Liberal position improved in weekly political journalism. The *Economist* kept faith with its Cobdenite heritage, and the *Spectator*'s adamant opposition to Tariff Reform compelled it to give the Liberals the benefit of many a doubt. For what it was worth, there was also *Truth*, with Horace Voules as *de facto* editor until his death in 1909, and Henry Labouchere as proprietor until 1910. Of far greater consequence, the *Speaker* acquired a new lease of life as the *Nation*. Hammond, in whom Sir John Brunner had vested the editorship, was pleased to report on 30 August 1906 that the majority of 'the shareholders have been bought out by a group of Liberals ... of the right general colour', who proposed to install F. W. Hirst as editor: 'There was no kind of quarrel, & ... though I differ from Hirst's ideas I have nothing but admiration for his disinterested public spirit, & nothing but goodwill for the future of the paper.' Acquired by the Joseph Rowntree Social Service Trust, the *Speaker* introduced popular features ('competitions, ... more commerce & less literature') as Hammond had predicted, but delayed an editorial appointment. Finally, late in January 1907, Massingham took charge, after Cadbury released him from his contract with the *Daily News*. The transmogrification followed on 2 March, when the *Nation* made its debut containing an article on the armaments question by Campbell-Bannerman.[1]

Leaving the employment of one Cocoa Quaker for that of another, Massingham did not imagine that the *Daily News* would have difficulty replacing him as lobby correspondent. 'I have been too much of the House, & a fresher eye & style will be a good change,' he told Gardiner. His new assignment gave him relief from the ardours of daily journalism, untrammelled editorial control, and an opportunity to assemble a remarkable group of contributors, who shone twice weekly, first in print and then at the *Nation* lunches. Conceiving of Liberalism as 'a critical force', Massingham never hesitated 'to interrogate the Government', with the result that his journal became a yardstick for measuring the distance between party philosophy and ministerial practice. Bernard Shaw, who lived in a flat above the editorial offices in Adelphi Terrace, joked that 'Mr Massingham emphasizing his commitment to the Liberal Party always reminds us of Mr Belloc who emphasizes his attachment to the Catholic Church by keeping us wondering how soon he will be excommunicated'. The *Economist* had been shortsighted to predict (9 March 1907) that Massingham's *Nation* would function as 'the new weekly organ of the united Liberal Party'.[2]

Nevinson, suitably querulous, wrote 'middles' for the *Nation* 'at good pay', but spent the better part of his week writing leaders on foreign affairs for the

[1] R. A. Bennett, 'Mr Labouchere as a Journalist,' in A. Thorold, *The Life of Labouchere* (London, 1913), pp. 462–63; Hammond to Ensor, 30 August 1906, Ensor Papers; *also see* A. F. Havighurst, *Radical Journalist: H. W. Massingham* (Cambridge, 1974), pp. 143–44.

[2] Massingham to Gardiner, 26 January 1907, Gardiner Papers; Havighurst, *Radical Journalist*, pp. 96, 175–76; Shaw, quoted in E. Hyams, *The New Statesman* (London, 1963), p. 30.

Daily Chronicle, which he found continually frustrating. On 14 July 1907, for example, he 'wrote on Japan & did [a] strong leader against [the] Russian alliance', only to have his article 'cut ... down to a few lines' on the grounds that it contradicted the 'policy of [the] paper'. Roused to indignation (not that many people would have noticed any difference in his demeanour), he withdrew the leader and fulminated against his superiors: 'I don't know why you call yourselves a Liberal paper. It is ludicrous.' The next day, he attended a *Nation* lunch, where Massingham 'strongly dissuaded' him from resigning his position on the *Daily Chronicle*: 'on no paper can one hope to agree with more than 3/5 of policy'. One of the fortunate few, 'H.W.M. said he was convinced the Rowntrees wd. run straight'.[1]

Not many editors or political leader-writers would have taken so confident a view of their proprietors' steadfastness. The more purposeful a journalist, the greater the likelihood of friction over which policies to pursue and how single-mindedly to pursue them. As a rule, editors were less respectful of party orthodoxies and more attracted to controversies that enlivened a paper.

Obviously enough, the proprietor had his investment at stake, the journalist his professional reputation; but that was only one of several related factors and, given the fact that many editors were also shareholders in the concern, not nearly as decisive as it may appear. Proprietors were often MPs or men with political ambitions, directly subject to various pressures from the whips. Then, too, they belonged to different wings or generations within their respective parties, and identified themselves accordingly. Hobhouse and Thomasson might both be Radicals, just as Garvin and Goldman might both be Unionists, but there were fundamental conflicts of definition and emphasis in each case. Hobhouse preserved his moral integrity by retreating into academic life, Garvin by doing battle with Northcliffe and eventually with the Astors on the *Observer*. Ware was increasingly at odds with the owners of the *Morning Post*; they were to replace him in 1911 with Gwynne, who bore the scars of his squabbles with Pearson on the *Standard*. Scott's long collaboration with Taylor on the *Manchester Guardian* had ended in acrimony over the Dibblee partnership, implicitly a political issue. At the *Daily Chronicle*, Donald did not always see eye-to-eye with Frank Lloyd. At the *Daily News*, Gardiner found intolerable the 'niggling criticisms' levelled by Henry Cadbury, manager of his father's paper.[2]

The least enviable of them all was probably Thomas Marlowe, who edited the *Daily Mail* for Northcliffe. 'I have carried on your paper, sometimes under circumstances of great difficulty, for eight years and I have always endeavoured to carry out your wishes when I have been informed of them,' Marlowe responded on 20 May 1907 to a reproof from his volatile employer. That morning, the *Mail* had reported – without comment – a speech at Edinburgh on

---

[1] Nevinson's diary, 31 January, 14 and 15 July 1907.
[2] Gardiner's diary, 17 January 1910, Gardiner Papers.

the 18th by Winston Churchill, who alleged that the paper 'misrepresents every action and motive of his Majesty's Government'. Churchill's 'outburst' mattered far less than Northcliffe's concurrence that the recent performance of the *Mail* had been 'unduly political'. Marlowe, declaring it his 'policy' to give the Liberal ministers 'all possible scope but to take the utmost advantage of their mistakes', rejected Northcliffe's imputations. To the contrary, he insisted, 'the course of events drives us into party politics & I believe that when we are dealing with party politics it is better to be strongly political rather than mild'. As Northcliffe was incapacitated by 'burning' eyes and insomnia, Marlowe's full-blooded views prevailed on the next day's leader page: 'Happily, no one takes Mr Churchill's abuse seriously,' not even Campbell-Bannerman, formerly the victim of his verbal assaults.[1]

The Liberals could hardly depend on the benevolence of the *Daily Mail*, although there were isolated instances when it lent itself to their immediate purposes. Northcliffe, as this incident implied, showed a tender regard for Churchill, much to the disgust of Maxse and others. On 29 October 1907, the paper cooperated with Lloyd George by advocating compulsory arbitration in the railway dispute. Less favourably received, John Burns was jealous of these 'two Romeos', who successfully courted newspaper opinion. Forsaking any hope of the *Daily Mail*, Burns looked to the *Daily News* to provide him with the sort of sympathetic support that Asquith and Grey ordinarily obtained from the *Westminster Gazette*, or Lloyd George from the *Manchester Guardian*. Stung by criticisms of his work at the Local Government Board, he deplored the 'Americanizing of [the] Press' and its editorial fickleness, which he held responsible for Liberal setbacks. 'If Tariff Reform and Reaction win at [the] next Election by 100 to 200 [seats],' he warned Gardiner in the spring of 1908,

> the reasons . . . will be 7
>   Vaughan Nash
>   H. W. M[assingham]
>   C. F. G. M[asterman]
>   A.G.G.
>   P. W. W[ilson, the *Daily News*'s labour columnist]
>   W. T. Stead
>   K[eir] H[ardie]
> And the worst of all [is] A.G.G. because he runs a paper and himself is run. Our Press urges us to bring in Bills. When done, they at once take the bloom off all our peaches, or when the Bill is passed they reveal to our enemies not what it has done, but what it did not do. . . . Why the *D.N.* is an enemy of Progress!

---

[1] Marlowe to Northcliffe, 20 May 1907, Northcliffe Papers; Pound and Harmsworth, pp. 301–302.

Complaining incessantly of Gardiner's partiality to Fabians, ILP leaders, and demagogues like Lloyd George, Burns ascribed his own unpopularity to the fact that 'every Paper wants its own tame Cabinet Minister' to leak information. Nevertheless, he scorned an invitation to defend his departmental record in a guest column: 'Cabinet Ministers must not write for money, they must only work for abuse.' In furthering the cause of Liberalism, the *Daily News* was thus called upon to massage the egos of Liberal statesmen, a task it found uncongenial and – in Burns's case – counter-productive.[1]

By the second half of 1907, the glow of Liberal victory and the jolt of Unionist defeat had alike begun to wear off. Newspapers were divided not only in their loyalties between parties, but also, if less conspicuously, in their loyalties within them. Numerically superior, the Opposition press had broken down into Balfourite and Chamberlainite blocs, with a small Unionist Free Trade component, largely confined to the provinces. Chamberlain's physical debility caused fragmentation among the Tariff Reformers, who operated at cross purposes through a plurality of journalistic channels. The *Morning Post* and the *National Review*, linked by the Maxse brothers, were organs of intransigence. The *Standard*, the *Daily Express*, and the *Daily Mail* were decidedly more equivocal, yet less amenable to front-bench influence than either the *Daily Telegraph* or *The Times*. Bonar Law, who was eventually to succeed Balfour as Unionist leader, had already established close connections with J. P. Croal, who had replaced Cooper at the *Scotsman* on the eve of the 1906 elections. 'The only regret I had about your speech was that we could not print the whole of it,' Croal apologized to Bonar Law on 10 October 1907. 'It struck me as a remarkably persuasive exposition of the Tariff Reform position.' Other editorial adjustments served Unionism less well. Sandars considered J. S. R. Phillips, who took charge of the *Yorkshire Post*, 'a good man of business – but, though he prides himself on his political acumen, his ability in this line is very moderate'. Describing Phillips as 'a devout Cobdenite with Radical sympathies', he was 'disposed to think' that 'Phillips' loyalty is a doubtful commodity'. Gervase Beckett, who owned the *Yorkshire Post* along with the *Saturday Review*, was known to be dissatisfied, as apparently were northern readers. 'Yorkshire does not like its *Yorkshire Post* articles as once it did,' Sandars told Balfour.[2]

Apart from the *Tribune*, a chastening fiasco, the Liberals made assorted efforts – and gestures – to develop their resources. On 25 May 1906, W. M. Thompson, editor of *Reynolds's News*, was guest of honour at a National

---

[1] John Grigg, *Lloyd George: The People's Champion* (London, 1978), p. 155, and various letters from Lloyd George about Board of Trade affairs, 1907 and 1908, Northcliffe Papers; Runciman to McKenna, 27 March 1910, McKenna Papers; Burns's diary, 14 October 1909, Add. MSS. 46, 327, fol. 43; Burns to Gardiner, 5 November 1907, 22 June and 7 July 1908, Gardiner Papers.

[2] Croal to Bonar Law, 10 October 1907, Bonar Law Papers 18/3/36; Sandars to Balfour, 5 November 1907, Balfour Papers.

Liberal Club banquet 'in recognition of his services to the cause of Liberalism'. The event marked an official attempt to broaden the social base of Liberal journalism. A vastly popular Sunday print, which declined to divulge its prewar circulation statistics, this paper had begun life in 1850 as *Reynolds's Weekly Newspaper* and later became *Reynolds's Illustrated News* before merging with the *Sunday Citizen* in 1962. The power behind Thompson's editorial chair was J. H. Dalziel, Liberal MP for Kirkcaldy from 1892 to 1921, who underwent similar changes of nomenclature: he was knighted in 1908, made a privy councillor in 1912, created a baronet in 1918, and raised to the peerage in 1921 as Baron Dalziel of Kirkcaldy. A fervent supporter of Lloyd George, he is not to be confused with Davison Dalziel, the Unionist MP for Brixton, who was proprietor of the *Evening Standard* from 1910 to 1915 and who became Baron Dalziel of Wooler. J.H. – or Henry – Dalziel, nominally business manager of *Reynolds's*, which he bought outright in 1914, figured prominently in a number of Liberal newspaper transactions. These must await scrutiny. Meanwhile, he can be taken to personify a new spirit of unabashed commercialism on the part of many who controlled the Liberal press. 'Really,' he expostulated in Parliament when asked about his shadowy role in the transfer of the *Daily Chronicle* in 1918, 'it is a matter for the House of Commons that they should sit down seriously and discuss my business operations?'[1]

Without Dalziel's financial assistance, the Liberals counted other achievements in the overhaul of their publicity apparatus. Arnold Bennett agreed with H. G. Wells, a fellow contributor, that the *Nation* – as the *Speaker* had been successfully reincarnated – 'had no circulation', but was 'admirable', especially on labour questions. In the spring of 1907, the *New Age* began anew as 'An Independent Socialist Review of Politics, Literature and Art' under the co-editorship of A. R. Orage and Holbrook Jackson: more influential in the sphere of aesthetics than in that of parliamentary activity, the *New Age* – with Orage exclusively in control from 1908 to 1922 – embraced ideas wholly compatible with those of an advanced Liberalism. By summer, Laurence Scott was able to assure Ensor that 'the *M.G.*'s affairs are all but established now. The contract of sale to my father has been agreed to in all particulars and only awaits signature which should not take many months.' In each of these three cases, a probable closure had been averted. The Newneses, father and son, were audibly complaining about the steady losses of the *Westminster Gazette*, and Hammond was chilled to overhear George Cadbury's remark that he might sell the *Daily News* if Henry Cadbury did not make 'a success of it'. On balance, however, the Liberal press was showing notable powers of resilience, coupled with what

---

[1] *Sell's* (1907); David Butler and Anne Sloman, *British Political Facts 1900–1979* (London, 1980), pp. 444, 453; *Parliamentary Debates* (Commons), 5th ser., cx, cols. 87–88 (15 October 1918).

the *Daily Chronicle* (7 February 1908) saw as 'a stronger sense of party loyalty'.[1]

Official Liberalism was the beneficiary of yet another source of editorial support, however conditional or circumscribed. True to its word, *The Times* took a bipartisan approach to foreign and imperial questions so long as the Government appeared to do the same. Radicals were dismayed to win applause for policies of 'continuity', a concept that testified to their impotence. To be sure, *The Times* accepted the new order with greater resignation than enthusiasm, dispensing backhanded compliments and often damning ministerial decisions with faint praise. On the one hand, it maintained its protectionist principles; on the other, it moderated them. Asquith's budget of 1907, which provided for a scheme of non-contributory old-age pensions and introduced a differentiated rate of taxation on earned and unearned incomes, was pilloried as 'the crudest system of finance known among civilized men' (4 May 1907); even so, as the official historians of the paper have pointed out, 'at this date *The Times* refrained from demanding a new fiscal system' on the Tariff Reform model. Grey, as Foreign Secretary, was treated solicitously. Haldane was justly extolled as an improvement upon his Unionist predecessors at the War Office by Colonel Charles à Court Repington, military correspondent of *The Times* since 1904, who prided himself on writing out of 'sincere conviction, independent of all personal, political and other bias'. With comparable magnanimity, *The Times* also acknowledged Morley's special qualifications for the India Office: when Morley spoke of enacting constitutional reforms, it noted with relief on 20 July 1907, 'he evidently does not mean radical alteration. He means the most cautious and gradual development, upon lines which are reasonably consistent with the past'. For his part, Morley was 'not sorry to have friendly words in newspapers'. Yet for *The Times* to dignify him as a Whig statesman was a provocation to his Radical critics on the backbenches.[2]

It is possible to impute a motive of cynicism to *The Times*'s leader-writers, who befriended certain Liberal ministers at the expense of doctrinaire Liberalism. There was, however, a more logical explanation. The old-timers at Printing House Square were less fiercely partisan and, in the last days of the *ancien régime*, theirs were the views that prevailed. The Chamberlainite bandwagon, deprived of its driver, had run aground, while the socialist chariot was seen to be gathering momentum. Some degree of accommodation with responsible Liberalism was therefore accepted as imperative. Chirol solemnly

---

[1] Hammond to Gardiner, 26 August 1907, Gardiner Papers; Bennett's journal, 2 March 1908 and 26 November 1909, Berg Collection, New York Public Library; L. P. Scott to Ensor, 17 July 1907, Ensor Papers; *also see* W. Martin, *'The New Age' Under Orage* (Manchester, 1967), pp. 24–29.

[2] Repington to Raymond Marker, 17 April 1905, Kitchener-Marker Papers, Add. MSS. 52, 277B, fols. 17–21; *History of The Times*, IV, part 1, 16; Morley to Campbell-Bannerman, 5 September 1907, Campbell-Bannerman Papers, Add. MSS. 41, 223, fol. 263.

reflected that 'this England of ours seems to me sometimes to be terribly out of joint', and the 'worst of it', he confessed to Wickham Steed,

> is that in many ways it is our own sins – speaking now as a Conservative – that are coming home to roost, our sins of commission & especially of omission during 20 years tenure of office – & I feel this so strongly that I cannot join in the indiscriminate abuse heaped on the present Govt. If we exhaust our epithets on a Govt. which has preserved the continuity of Imperial policy in foreign & Indian affairs, & even – *pace* the Transvaal – in colonial affairs, what shall we have left in our vocabulary when we have a Labour Govt. in office five or ten years hence which will cast every tradition & principle of Empire to the winds?[1]

The relative reasonableness of *The Times*, as personified by Chirol, was based largely on fear, no less real for being wildly exaggerated.

The threat to *The Times* itself was a good deal more immediate, and terrifyingly real. On 31 July 1907, twelve days after Chirol delivered this prognosis, the Chancery court ruled against the Walter family in a suit brought by several minority shareholders. The proprietary partnership of *The Times* was ordered to be dissolved, its accounts rendered, and its assets disposed of. Northcliffe soon heard of the matter when he dined with Sir Alexander Henderson. A financier associated with Pearson, Henderson sat in Parliament as a Unionist from 1898 to 1906 and again from 1913 to 1916. Something of a recluse, Northcliffe had been tempted out that evening by the promise of an after-dinner piano recital by Paderewski. The conversation at Henderson's table, where Lord Stuart of Wortley provocatively foretold the amalgamation of *The Times* with Pearson's *Standard*, drowned out any music that followed.[2]

---

[1] Chirol to Stead, 19 July 1907, *Times* Archives.
[2] Pound and Harmsworth, pp. 308–309. During 'a long interview' on 21 January 1910, Northcliffe told J. S. Sandars a slightly different version 'of the accident by which he became interested in *The Times*'; as Sandars repeated it to Balfour (24 January 1910, Balfour Papers), 'Charlie Wortley' was the host and Henderson was a fellow guest on the occasion.

Three

CHANGING THE GUARD

Suffering from a bout of poor health, Northcliffe was also laid low by legal difficulties during the second half of 1907. His popular newspapers – the *Daily Mail*, the *Evening News*, and the *Daily Mirror* – had vehemently attacked proposals by Lever Brothers to amalgamate with smaller firms in order to create a mammoth 'soap trust', inimical to the interests of the British consumer for whom cleanliness was proverbially next to godliness. Arguably, as cynics pointed out, the proposed merger was potentially injurious to the advertising receipts of the Harmsworth press as well. Throughout the spring and early summer, there were daily denunciations of Lever's business practices, coupled with appeals (which did not go unheeded) for a boycott of Lever products.

The crusade was not without political overtones. W. H. Lever (later 1st Viscount Leverhulme) was one of the mainstays of the Liberal Party in the north-west and MP for the Wirral division of Cheshire. A paternalistic employer, he was offended to see his workmen's community at Port Sunlight mocked by the *Daily Mirror*'s cartoonist as 'Port Moonshine'. An ardent Free Trader, he was furious at being accused of engaging in a form of underhand self-protectionism at the expense of the poor. A businessman above all else, he was provoked by the precipitous drop in his company's sales and by the consequent effect on the market price of its preference shares.

Lever consulted his lawyers, who took advice from F. E. Smith (later Lord Chancellor and 1st Earl of Birkenhead). 'There is no answer to this action for libel and the damages must be enormous,' declared Smith, after digesting the documents along with a bottle of champagne and two dozen oysters. Yet Smith, who sat as Conservative MP for the Walton division of Liverpool, was unwilling to take on the case, however conclusive the evidence or generous the fee. Northcliffe, he knew full well, 'can help me greatly', whereas Lever was 'of no use to me. I don't want his money. Would much rather never have seen him.' Instead, Lever was represented in court by another prominent Unionist, Sir Edward (later Baron) Carson, MP for Dublin University. Northcliffe, too, crossed party lines to find a lawyer.

To defend the *Daily Mail*, he chose Rufus Isaacs (later 1st Marquess of Reading), Liberal MP for Reading.[1]

The trial was held at Liverpool in July. Northcliffe was not present, having decamped to Paris to avoid being called as a witness. But Lever was there, determined to play out the drama. He gave Roscoe Brunner, Sir John's son, an account of the courtroom proceedings:

> It will gratify Sir John ... to know that no settlement was made with the *Daily Mail* and a settlement was refused, that when Rufus Isaacs got up and made his opening statement neither myself nor the Counsel had any idea, but that he was going to fight the case out. The *Daily Mail* simply surrendered horse, foot and artillery, and it was only a matter to decide whether there should be two or three days' wrangle over the damages, or name a sum which could be settled and done with. In addition I would like to point out that all through the case both Counsel and Solicitor have thrown and did throw the gravest doubt of any Jury awarding even as much as £50,000.

That, in fact, was the amount awarded to Lever Brothers. And Northcliffe had not yet heard the last of the affair. Lever, emulated by others whom the *Daily Mail* had maligned, brought further suits, leaving Northcliffe to pay damages and costs to a total of £151,000. In the words of Northcliffe's official biographers, 'the shadow of the soap litigation lay heavily across the year'.[2]

Struck down, Northcliffe had not been struck out by any means. As usual, there was nothing like a reversal to set his mind on bigger and better things. The story of his purchase of *The Times* has been told often, and there is no need here to recount it again in labyrinthine detail. Nevertheless, the political ingredients, which have tended to be overlooked, help to account for certain cloak-and-dagger aspects of the commercial transaction.

Before his tactical withdrawal to Paris, Northcliffe instructed his solicitors to keep close watch on developments at Printing House Square. They confirmed that Arthur Walter, without taking either Moberly Bell or Buckle into his confidence, had indeed entered into secret negotiatons with Pearson, who had outbid Northcliffe for the *Standard* in 1904. The politicians were attentive to the situation, carefully weighing one set of rumours against another. They did not know much more than Buckle, to whom Walter's disclosures came as 'a shock' the following January. From a Liberal perspective, Pearson and Northcliffe were equally deplorable prospects. From the standpoint of official Unionism, however, Northcliffe was more acceptable by virtue of his latent Balfourite sympathies. In any case, the projected transfer was viewed with profound apprehension. On 20 November 1908, three days after he had

---

[1] Pound and Harmsworth, pp. 303–304; H. Montgomery Hyde, *Lord Reading* (New York, 1967), pp. 72–74.

[2] Lever to R. Brunner, 23 July 1907, Brunner Papers; Pound and Harmsworth, p. 305.

described Pearson's control of *The Times* as a foregone conclusion, Sandars told Balfour of a conversation with Pearson, who 'says that he ... has decided to drop the proposed "acquisition" but that the paper is going into quite "desirable" hands. Now we *must* find whose hands these are – if possible.' There was a pregnant irony in the fact that Fleet Street, which made it a business to penetrate political smokescreens, should have managed so well to guard its own secrets.[1]

Pearson certainly owed Balfour no explanation and doubtless enjoyed leading him a merry chase. The 'quite "desirable" hands' to which he alluded belonged to Sir Alexander Henderson, who was his surrogate. Had Henderson become proprietor of *The Times*, Pearson would have succeeded in all but name. For all its probability, however, the scheme was aborted.

By the opening days of 1908, Pearson seemed to have clinched his deal. At that point, Northcliffe swung into action to have it unclinched. Conducted with the utmost cordiality, his campaign was shrewdly calculated to prejudice Pearson's arrangements with the Walters by exposing them to the glare of publicity. On 5 January, the *Observer* enigmatically informed its readers, including senior members of *The Times*'s staff, 'that important negotiations are taking place which will place the direction of *The Times* newspaper in the hands of a very capable proprietor of several popular magazines and newspapers'. From the phraseology and the source, it was instantly assumed that this person was Northcliffe. In order to allay apprehensions, or at least to clarify matters, *The Times* was obliged to issue a statement on the 7th. Acknowledging that plans were being made to form 'a limited company under the proposed chairmanship of Mr [Arthur] Walter', it further specified:

> The business management will be reorganized by Mr C. Arthur Pearson, the proposed managing director.
> The editorial character of the paper will remain unchanged, and will be conducted, as in the past, on lines independent of party politics.
> The contemplated arrangements will in all probability require the sanction of the Court before they become definitive.

As intended, the paragraph in the *Observer* fell like a bombshell. Northcliffe later gloated that it had 'exploded the Pearson *conspiracy*'. Buckle, his confidence shaken, reacted sharply. Over his objections, Pearson had been mentioned by name in *The Times*'s official announcement. Although he knew Pearson 'but little, and have not found him specially sympathetic, I am on quite friendly terms with him', he wrote to Walter, who was 'detained at Bear Wood by a bad cold'. Still, Buckle could not help wondering

---

[1] Buckle to Walter, 6 January 1908 (copy), *Times* Archives; Sandars to Balfour, 17 and 20 November 1907, Balfour Papers.

whether the advantage his experience of newspaper business will bring to the management of the Paper may not be outweighed by his association in the public mind (his connexion with the *Standard* being very recent) with a Press of very different aims and ideals. In other words, though I trust his ability may help us, I fear his *name* will do us harm.

(Interestingly, it was the *Standard* and not the *Daily Express* that he associated with Pearson's name.) Walter, in a circular addressed to the lesser shareholders, stressed the need 'to place the paper upon a sound financial footing' and Pearson's obvious qualifications on that score; rather unconvincingly, he went on to explain that 'a rumour to which publicity was prematurely given necessitated our announcement in The Times before it was possible to place the scheme before you'. Like Buckle, they could not have been appeased and must have recognized a debt of gratitude to Northcliffe.[1]

If the Lever dispute had indicated that Northcliffe was losing his grip, his intervention in the Walter-Pearson agreement showed him at the height of his powers. Maintaining an outward appearance of benevolent neutrality, he wrote to congratulate Pearson and proposed to feature an interview with him in the *Daily Mail*. Pearson nervously declined – or deferred – such a compliment. 'All this publicity for me is rubbing things in very much so far as the Walters are concerned,' he admitted, 'and from the point of their feelings I do not want to be seeming to push myself at all.' Northcliffe's aim, on the contrary, was to push Pearson as hard as possible so as to emphasize the implicit threat he posed to the gentlemanly traditions of Printing House Square. In lieu of a formal interview, the *Daily Mail* (8 January) presented a profile of Pearson who, it was recalled, had been immortalized by Chamberlain as 'a hustler'. That, of course, was not at all the image that Pearson wished to project under present circumstances. The following Sunday, the *Observer* chimed in by portraying Pearson as a young ('he is a little over forty') adventurer, who 'has done strong as well as sensational things'. According to Alfred Butes, Northcliffe's trusted secretary, the Chief had personally written this article in a mood of playful provocation: 'It was a piece of camouflage, a smoke-screen for Northcliffe himself.' Others, close to Northcliffe, denied any ulterior motive. Yet, by playing up Pearson's dynamism, no less than his political attachments, Northcliffe artfully discredited his rival.[2]

Garvin was at a loss to understand Northcliffe's subtle strategy. 'Where did this come from?' he asked G. A. Sutton, who delivered the text. 'It blew in the window,' came the reply. For once, Garvin underestimated Northcliffe's manipulative skills. 'I grieve infinitely that Pearson instead of you has rushed

[1] Memorandum by Northcliffe, 4 January 1909, quoted in Pound and Harmsworth, p. 309n.; Buckle to Walter, 6 January 1908 (copy), *Times* Archives; Walter to the proprietors, 9 January 1908, quoted in *History of The Times*, III, 515.
[2] Pearson to Northcliffe, 7 January 1908, and Butes's testimony, quoted in Pound and Harmsworth, p. 310.

Olympus and seized the thunder of Jupiter,' he wrote as if to console Northcliffe on 7 January:

> Has he got the instinct for it[?] Reduced to a penny and run with the right force and independence, I'm certain *The Times* could be made in seven years a greater power and property than it ever was before. We are at a turning point in journalism; and politics are becoming so tremendously real that playing at them is played out.

Garvin's opinion could only have fortified Northcliffe in his resolve. Perhaps, in some vague way, that was its purpose.[1]

Northcliffe paid backhanded compliments to Pearson, secure in the knowledge that others would take up cudgels. The *Westminster Gazette* (7 January) scoffed at the assurance that the advent of Pearson, drawing on capital from the likes of Henderson, would leave 'unchanged' the political character of *The Times*: 'This seems to us rather misleading.' Pearson's strenuous denial that he acted 'for a party of wealthy Tariff Reformers' served merely to bring his affiliations more openly into question. The old guard at Printing House Square was dead set against him. Asked what he proposed to do about 'this Pearson business', Moberly Bell growled: 'Smash it!' Buckle, whose own position was not directly at risk, notified Walter that Balfour, Lansdowne, Grey, Morley, and – oddly enough – Joseph and Austen Chamberlain, had joined 'a crowd of lesser personages . . . in deploring and strongly deprecating the introduction of Pearson'. By early February, some of the shareholders who had pledged their support had had second thoughts.[2]

With Pearson stymied, oher customers ventured forth. Moberly Bell's daughter recalled two rival schemes, one advanced by a group which 'sought to secure *The Times* in support of Free Trade, the other . . . interested in the paper chiefly as a potentially money-making concern, and . . . backed by German money'. In fact, these two groups were closely related, and Strachey was the link between them. The editor of the *Spectator*, who had gratified Pearson with 'a particularly nice letter' of congratulations, wrote in a totally different spirit to Chirol:

> I am of course nothing but exceedingly sorry that *The Times* should pass into the hands of a Tariff Reformer like Pearson and I am sure you will know I speak from the heart when I say how pained I am to think of the position in which you and many others on *The Times* find yourselves. Here again, however, I think that in justice to Pearson one must not lay the blame upon him but upon the Walters. . . . Why on earth didn't the Walters come to the left-centre people instead of going to Pearson? Of course one never knows

---

[1] Pound and Harmsworth, p. 310; Garvin to Northcliffe, 7 January 1908, Northcliffe Papers.
[2] Pound and Harmsworth, p. 311; *History of The Times*, III, 526–27.

but I cannot help thinking that if I had been approached I might have got a certain number of people of moderate and left-centre views to find the money required. At any rate I could and would have tried.

Chirol apparently intimated that it was not yet too late, for Strachey now immersed himself in '*The Times* intrigues', as he called them. With his connivance, Bernard Mallet and William Tyrrell persuaded their friend Emil ('Willy') Koch to act 'as a financier' in the event that 'the Pearson combination is upset'. Mallett and Tyrrell were both well-connected civil servants, with the latter deploying his 'Levantine methods' as principal private secretary to Sir Edward Grey. According to Mallet, Koch was 'a first rate man & would act from public motives without any idea of personal gain commercial or otherwise. But,' he reminded Strachey, 'it is not easy at short notice to get hold of the men who will guarantee the £180,000 or so required'. For this purpose, 'fresh men' would have to be found.[1]

Strachey promptly made contact with Lord Cromer, the retired proconsul, whose qualifications included a family connection with the Baring banking dynasty and a reputation for non-partisanship sufficient for Campbell-Bannerman to have offered him the foreign secretaryship in 1905. Just as he had declined to cast his lot with a Liberal administration, Cromer refused to sit 'upon any Board with Tariff Reformers'. Strachey tried to reason with him, pointing out that Unionist Free Traders and 'moderate Liberals' shared an obligation to safeguard *The Times* on the understanding that it would 'remain absolutely Unionist in regard to Ireland'. After all, he remonstrated,

> it would be impossible to expect *The Times* to come right round and be Free Trade at once, and further, that from the newspaper point of view, almost as much injury would be done to the influence of *The Times* if it were proclaimed that it had been bought by Free Traders as if it had been bought by Tariff Reformers, because the public would be suspicious of *The Times* controlled by any one political group.

While Strachey pleaded with Cromer, Koch reported to Mallet 'that he has now been promised most of the money' and requested permission to list Cromer and Strachey as directors of the projected company.[2]

For all Strachey's persuasion, Cromer had concluded by 26 February that the scheme was 'altogether too vague for him to lend his name to it'. That vagueness was increased by Strachey's further efforts to make the take-over of

---

[1] *History of The Times*, III, 518; Moberly Bell, *Life and Letters of C. F. Moberly Bell*, p. 290; Strachey to Chirol, 22 January 1908 (copy), and Mallet to Strachey, 25 January 1908, Strachey Papers; *also see* Zara S. Steiner, *The Foreign Office and Foreign Policy 1898–1914* (Cambridge, 1969), pp. 118–19.
[2] Strachey to Mallet, 3 February 1908 (copy), and Mallet to Strachey, 4 February 1908, Strachey Papers.

The Times the first step towards the creation of a centre coalition, 'Anti-Home Rule, Anti-Socialism, Anti-Protection & Anti-Little Englandism'. Week after week, Strachey commended the idea of fusion to the readers of the *Spectator*, who (he assured Lord Rosebery) 'form already a kind of Centre Party and I think I may say without egotism that they would very largely follow my lead'. To this end, he entered into collusion with F. W. Maude, a publicist for the Liberal League. Their strategy was first to restore the League to life, then to merge it into a wider grouping which would command support from Cromer and disaffected Unionists. Together, Strachey and Maude tried to rouse Rosebery, who 'rejoiced at . . . the diplomatic negotiations into which you have patriotically plunged', but who reaffirmed his determination 'to keep clear of politics, in fact to get out of them'. The most Rosebery would promise was to 'meditate on this new situation' and to 'see Cromer and consider the whole position'. Differences among the Unionists, with the Cecils clinging to the delusion that Balfour (their kinsman) might be won to the Free Trade side, doomed the movement, to the 'great relief' of Rosebery.[1]

Deprived of significant Unionist support for either of his designs, Strachey fell back on his Liberal accomplices. On 27 February, two days after Lord Hugh Cecil had 'upset the applecart', Strachey proposed J. A. Spender as editor of *The Times* under a Free Trade régime. Or perhaps, he speculated, it might prove possible 'to enlist Spender's great journalistic qualities in the capacity of manager while the editorial chair might be given to Chirol, whom . . . I consider the fittest man for editor and a man who could be trusted with a free hand'. Admittedly, there were differences of opinion between Spender and Chirol, but Strachey did not regard them as insuperable. Spender's name was frequently mentioned during these weeks, not necessarily with his knowledge or sanction. Herbert Gladstone naturally thought of him when 'asked to express an opinion, in connection with *The Times* re-organization, favourable to a possible Editor', but hesitated to hazard a nomination 'without ascertaining whether there is any hope left to us that *The Times* magnates may be wise enough' to entertain one. Lord Esher spread the rumour, which Buckle and Garvin were able to refute, that Spender was also 'Pearson's choice for Editor'. Years later, Spender himself revealed the existence of a Liberal syndicate, 'one of the moving spirits' being Campbell-Bannerman, 'and the last communication I ever received from him was a message from his sick-room to say that he hoped . . . it would result in my being editor of a Free Trade and independent *Times*'. According to Spender's recollection, belied by chronology, if the venture 'ever had a chance, Campbell-Bannerman's death extinguished it'.[2]

[1] Strachey to W. Sharp, solicitor, 26 February 1908 (copy), Strachey Papers; Strachey to Rosebery, 21 February 1908, and Rosebery to Strachey, 27 February 1908 (copy), Rosebery to Strachey, 24 February 1908 (copy), and Rosebery to Maude, 24 February 1908 (copy), Rosebery Papers, Vols. 10, 170, fols. 16–19, and 10, 172, fols. 11, 43; *also see* Sykes, *Tariff Reform*, pp. 168–71.

[2] Maude to Rosebery, 25 February 1908, Rosebery papers, Vol. 10, 172, fols. 37–40; Strachey to Sharp, 27 February 1908 (copy), Strachey Papers; Gladstone to Spender, 3 February 1908,

Campbell-Bannerman chaired his farewell Cabinet on 12 February and died on 22 April. By then, *The Times* had been secure in Northcliffe's grasp for over a month. Pearson's hopes had melted like the reproduction of *The Times*'s famous clock, which had been sculpted in ice by the chef at the Savoy as a centre-piece for Pearson's victory dinner. 'Many men I see tell me that the Pearson business is sure to fall through,' Maxse told Northcliffe on 7 February, 'and I have just heard of a dinner which was to have celebrated the event being postponed.' Within the week, Chirol could 'feel pretty confident that anyhow the Pearson combine will fall through. What will come in its stead I cannot yet say – certainly nothing worse, for that would be inconceivable!'[1]

Only Moberly Bell knew what to anticipate, and he was bound by an oath of secrecy. Resolved to resist Pearson, he was no less antagonistic towards Strachey's confederates, 'supported by Britons of the name of Koch and Speyer', whose origins as German Jews raised the spectre of cosmopolitanism. All things considered, Northcliffe seemed to him relatively unobjectionable: though his 'journalistic methods were alien to those of *The Times*', his politics were sufficiently flexible to allow the *Observer* to maintain its 'rather historic Cross-bench tradition'. Horace Hooper, an American consultant who had helped to set up *The Times* Book Club, brought them together. 'Mr Bell,' Northcliffe began the interview, 'I am going to buy *The Times*. With your help, if you will give it to me. In spite of you, if you don't.' Enid Moberly Bell summed up her father's predicament: 'The choice ... was not whether he should get the money from Northcliffe or another, but whether he should support Northcliffe's scheme or wash his hands of the whole business', leaving the Walters to contract a second unfortunate alliance or perhaps to revive the first. At this point (and not before, as Northcliffe's biographers have implied), Moberly Bell resorted to an 'expedient'. He drew up 'a list in alphabetical order of prominent people known to possess sufficient wealth to be possible purchasers of *The Times*', and circulated it among select friends (including Cromer and members of the Rothschild family), instructing them 'to cross off the names of any to whose connexion with *The Times* they would take serious exception'. Reportedly, none eliminated Northcliffe from the list. Encouraged by this response, Moberly Bell went to Arthur Walter on behalf of Northcliffe, whose identity he did not divulge. Walter was satisfied to accept his manager's assurances that 'I am acting solely in what I believe to be the best interests of *The Times*,' much as Moberly Bell was content to accept

---

Spender Papers, Add. MSS. 46, 391, fol. 232; Buckle to Garvin, 12 January 1935, Garvin Papers; Spender, *Life, Journalism and Politics*, II, 164–65. At lunch on 6 February 1914, Spender 'repeated' to Cook 'what he told me last time, how C.B. shortly before his death had got up a Liberal syndicate to buy *The Times* with J.A.S. as editor'. Cook's diary, 6 February 1914, Cook Papers.

[1] Maxse to Northcliffe, 7 February 1908, Northcliffe Papers; Chirol to Steed, 12 February 1908, *Times* Archives.

Northcliffe's assurances that the editorial integrity of the paper would be respected.[1]

From a hotel in Boulogne, where he took shelter under an assumed name, Northcliffe communicated with Moberly Bell in code while awaiting court clearance. Rather grandly designated as 'Atlantic', Northcliffe was privately referred to as 'X' by Moberly Bell, who was 'Canton'. For equally fanciful reasons, Walter was tagged as 'Manitoba', Kennedy Jones as 'Alberta', and Pearson as 'Dawson'. Chirol, too unimportant for a code-name, was aware 'that in some quarters exception is taken to ... the anonymity' of the principals in the transaction. But he, for one, was prepared to make a virtue of necessity:

> The strength of *The Times* has always lain largely in its anonymity, which as far as the editorial side of the paper is concerned has been hitherto maintained as far as humanly possible, & has been largely maintained even in connexion with the proprietary. ... If it were announced tomorrow that the money had been obtained from this or that individual, whatever might be his personal standing & reputation, it would be immediately assumed that *The Times* would henceforth be controlled in the interest of the political party or profession or creed or business with which he happened to be connected. If it were Lord Cromer, it would be said that *The Times* was going to be run for free trade; if the Duke of Norfolk, for Roman Catholic interests; if Rothschild, for the Jews; if Lord Iveagh, for the brewers; if Lord Rosebery, for his particular 'tabernacle', &c. &c.

Anonymity, therefore, was to be reckoned 'in this respect a valuable safeguard' so long as the paper continued 'to be conducted on the same lines ... & by the same staff'. In retrospect, Chirol held to this view. 'Some thought then, and a few may still think, that Lord Northcliffe was, after all, a very dubious *deus ex machina*,' he reflected in 1927. 'There were no abrupt changes in the editorial conduct of the paper', however, and Northcliffe had 'broad enough vision to see that, if the paper was to maintain something of its old authority, it could not be run on the same lines as the many other papers which he had created and fashioned after his own heart'.[2]

During the next fifteen years of Northcliffe's governing proprietorship of *The Times*, his 'vision' was generally too cloudy to inspire confidence, much less to permit any unequivocal appraisal of his intentions. Chirol gave him credit for having realized, however grudgingly or imperfectly, 'that *The Times* was not, and could not be, merely a threepenny *édition de luxe* of the *Daily Mail*'. But professional pride may have led Chirol to dignify the reasons. 'The *Mail* is in my judgment a very much greater power than *The Times* will ever be

[1] Pound and Harmsworth, pp. 311–12; Moberly Bell, *Moberly Bell*, pp. 290–91; Garvin to Rosebery [25 February 1908], Rosebery Papers, Vol. 10, 121, fols. 89–90.

[2] Chirol to Bell, 27 February 1908, *Times* Archives; Chirol, introduction to Moberly Bell, *Moberly Bell*, pp. 14–15.

and we can make it an infinitely greater thing than it is,' Northcliffe wrote on 9 January 1908 at the onset of negotiations with Moberly Bell. Given that the average daily sale of *The Times* was a paltry 38,000 and that the *Mail* was approaching the two-million mark, there can be no doubt which one he favoured. It was wishful thinking to suppose that his fundamental priorities had changed. Over dinner at the Ritz on 11 January, Morley amused Esher (whom Pearson had prematurely offered 'a seat on the new Board of *The Times*') by relating a conversation between Northcliffe and Robert Donald ('I think'), who professed his aim to run the *Daily Chronicle* 'on sound lines, no modern journalism, but good solid stuff, etc. "Yes," said Northcliffe, "and, my dear fellow, why not print it in Gothic type?"' To Garvin, whom he knew more intimately, Northcliffe expressed himself more bluntly on 2 March. 'I cannot help thinking that so many columns of politics ... will prevent your getting circulation,' he concluded a critique of the previous day's *Observer*, which sold fewer than 30,000 copies.

> Page 6 is entirely politics this week, *heavy* politics too. Page seven also political. If we are to get a circulation of 70,000 or 100,000 it is essential that we should interest *more people*. Remember the *women*. Our canvass, which is costing £3,000 a year, is aimed at the home. If we can get this paper into 70,000 homes every week, it will become a great power.

Transplanted to Printing House Square, this equation of circulation (including circulation among people excluded from the franchise) with power marked a more dramatic departure than any other single change in managerial structure or typography.[1]

On 17 March, *The Times* carried a cryptic announcement that a court order had sanctioned the formation of a new company 'to take over the business of the publication of *The Times* newspaper'. Arthur Walter would chair the Board of Directors to be composed exclusively of members of the pre-existing staff. 'There will be no change whatever in the political or editorial direction of the paper, which will be conducted by the same Staff on the indepent lines pursued uninterruptedly for so many years.' No mention was made of Northcliffe and, to ensure that none appeared elsewhere, Moberly Bell saw to it that the Press Association conveyed the dire warning that any revelation of the legal proceedings would be actionable as contempt of court. Walter, whom Northcliffe considered entitled to know the identity of his rescuer, infuriated him by sharing the secret with his family and with Buckle. Moberly Bell, however, '*effectually prevented further leakage*', as he wired to 'Atlantic'. Buckle, assisting in the pleasant task of 'collecting opinions about our noble selves',

---

[1] Moberly Bell, *Moberly Bell*, pp. 14–15; Northcliffe to Sutton, 9 January 1908, quoted in *History of The Times*, III, 538; *Journals and Letters of Reginald Viscount Esher*, II (ed. M. V. Brett; London, 1934), 273, 275; Northcliffe to Garvin, 2 March 1908, Garvin Papers.

reported to Moberly Bell that Rosebery was satisfied and 'recognized that, whoever X may be, for some time at any rate there are ample guarantees that *The Times* will remain *The Times*'. Buckle also received 'a cheering letter from John Morley, the most eminent of living journalists', who

> rejoice[d] that the ruinous schemes of a few weeks ago had been frustrated, and that you are where you were. A real public misfortune has been avoided and you may have been further gratified at the testimony so universally furnished to the hold your Olympian organ has upon the world's imagination & esteem.

For the time being, Northcliffe kept his distance from Printing House Square and so successfully preserved his cover that the hall porter gruffly turned away his emissary. Moberly Bell's 'reassuring letter' of 23 March reminded Chirol of what Strachey had once said about Northcliffe: 'He seems to me to be cast in much the same metal as Cecil Rhodes whose methods were often equally repugnant, but whom every one admits to have been a big man.'[1]

Tipping the scales at fourteen stone, Northcliffe was a big man in every sense. His acquisition of *The Times*, which would have exhausted the emotional and financial resources of any ordinary mortal, was one of several concerns at the time. His close scrutiny of the contents and accounts of the *Observer* has been noted. Nor did he neglect the management of the *Daily Mail*, the *Evening News*, and the *Daily Mirror*. In addition, recurrent squabbles within the Unionist Party, particularly as they affected his operations in Manchester, demanded his attention.

Balfour's leadership was again being disputed. 'No doubt, if the clamour which is now being raised by the *Standard & Morning Post* is extended to the whole of the Unionist press, Balfour's position may become impossible,' Buckle contemplated in a letter to Walter on 31 January. Averse to believe that Chamberlain, an invalid at Highbury, was privy to these attacks, Buckle knew that 'people are already talking of a Chamberlainite intrigue'. *The Times* was resigned to say nothing 'at present ... to prejudice the question', unlike Pearson's *Standard* or other metropolitan and provincial rivals.[2]

The *Manchester Courier*, which Northcliffe had salvaged as a service to the Unionist cause in Lancashire, was drawn into the fracas. On 14 January, it cautiously welcomed the appearance of the *Manchester Conservative and Unionist*, a new monthly magazine published under the auspices of the Manchester Conservative Association. Lord Stanley, a leading official of the Association, complicated matters by joining the directorate of Edward Hulton's *Daily Dispatch* and *Evening Chronicle*. 'These journals, as many will

---

[1] *History of The Times*, III, 570; Pound and Harmsworth, pp. 316–17; Buckle to Moberly Bell, 19 March 1908, and Chirol to Moberly Bell, 28 March 1908, *Times* Archives.
[2] Buckle to Walter, 31 January 1908, *Times* Archives.

remember, did their utmost two years ago to contribute to the Unionist reverses in this part of the world', and Hulton had recently reiterated his devotion to Free Trade. In the opinion of the *Courier* – 'the sole and official exponent of the Unionist policy . . . as defined by Mr Balfour and as accepted by every loyal Unionist' – Stanley was imprudent to associate with journals that were 'pledged to throw all their weight on the side of the Liberal Cobdenite candidates as against the Unionist champions of fiscal revision'.

A. F. Stephenson, co-partner in the management of the *Courier*, agreed with Northcliffe 'that no attack should be made on Lord Stanley personally'. The *Courier* had spoken out, he insisted, only after 'the majority of the prominent conservatives in Manchester had expressed their annoyance, and there was a good deal of talk on all sides'. Dunn, who edited the *Courier*, was rather more bellicose, recalling as he did 'the enormous attacks on Unionist leaders by the *Dispatch* & *Chronicle* before the general election, & their almost hysterical jubilation at the subsequent overthrow of the Unionist forces'. Willing to go easy on Stanley, he saw no reason to spare Hulton. He desisted only upon receipt of information 'that Lord Stanley joined Hulton's Board with the knowledge & approval of Mr Balfour' and others. Hulton was reportedly

> full of fears over the step he had taken. Papers that changed politics and had suffered for it seemed to form a sort of nightmare for him. He expressed some doubts as to whether his people had not gone too far in the direction of Toryism in commenting on the Mid-Devon [by-election] result! He also volunteered the statement that if he had the opportunity he would advise Stanley to be moderate in his speech on Saturday.

Stanley's address to the National Union at Liverpool on 25 January struck Dunn as 'comparatively brief and moderate', a fact he ascribed to 'action' on the part of Northcliffe, who discountenanced the movement for Unionist Free Trade separatism. Stanley 'had to admit that Hulton had not relinquished his "Free Trade principles", but announced that he had proposed him for the Carlton Club and hoped he would soon be converted'. Meanwhile, Dunn was given to understand that Hulton's Manchester papers 'will attack the Government and support the Opposition on general grounds, while maintaining a "policy of silence" on Tariff Reform'. That, under the circumstances, was the most a Balfourite could reasonably expect.[1]

Because *The Times* already coupled a policy of protectionism with a fidelity to the official Unionist leadership, there was no need for Northcliffe to tamper with its editorial independence. That situation, rather than his 'unbroken reverence for the idea of *The Times*' (as discerned by the paper's official historians), accounted for his initial self-restraint. Of course, he wanted to

---

[1] Stephenson to Northcliffe, 16 January 1908, Dunn to Sutton, 17, 19, 22, and 27 January 1908 (copies), Northcliffe Papers.

make the property more commercially successful by attracting advertisers and by making its coverage more topical. 'I have always said that *The Times* of the last forty years had as its mottoes "Abandon Scope all ye who enter here" and "News, like Wine, improves by keeping",' he quipped to Geoffrey Robinson, Buckle's eventual successor. The appointment of Edward Grigg, formerly assistant to Garvin on the *Outlook*, 'gave a new impulse to Imperial thinking in the office'. Fears that Northcliffe might tarnish the reputation of *The Times*, either by lowering its literary standards or by using it as the vehicle of his undisclosed ambitions, were quickly laid to rest, only to revive with a vengeance later on. Far from reducing *The Times* to the level of the *Daily Mail*, as some had predicted, he threatened to invest the *Mail* with an unbecoming air of respectability. Tom Clarke, who joined its staff in 1911, had the 'impression ... that we were trying to live up to our new rôle as a sort of sister to *The Times*', with sub-editors taken to task for their colloquialisms and jocularity.[1]

'We are suffering from lack of abuse,' complained Moberly Bell. 'Other papers used to attack us', with the result that sales had prospered and writers had been kept on their toes. 'Don't worry about a lack of abuse, Mr Bell,' replied Northcliffe. 'When I reveal my identity as controller of *The Times* you will get all the abuse you want.' That was no idle boast. By early summer, Northcliffe's veil was wearing thin, and telling questions began to be asked. On 9 July, an enquiry from 'a very high quarter' was conveyed by Esher, who shuttled between Windsor and the West End. Northcliffe responded candidly about '*The Times*, and the method, half skill and half luck, of its purchase', in a way that allowed his caller to conclude: 'His mind is that of an organiser and speculator, not of the politician.' As if to verify this view, Northcliffe took the unusual step of defining his 'position' in writing: it was

> merely that of one who wishes to see this country represented to the world by an absolutely independent newspaper, always, I trust, in my lifetime, worthy of its high traditions; the organ of neither parties, sects, nor financiers; its columns open to every shade of politics; a newspaper run not as a profit-making machine at all.
>
> *The Times* is, in fact, in my life, what a yacht or a racing stable is to others – it is merely my hobby.

Such noble sentiments could not have failed to please Esher and his royal mentor. By the same token, they were calculated to give 'very special satisfaction' to Buckle, who received a copy of the document and was happy 'to find that the things which I care most about in the Paper are highly valued by you'.[2]

These platitudes, repeated in casual conversations and in the leading articles

---

[1] *History of The Times*, III, 583, 769, IV, part 1, 16–17; Clarke, *Northcliffe Diary*, p. 51.
[2] Pound and Harmsworth, p. 320; *History of The Times*, III, 640; *Esher*, II, 327; Buckle to Northcliffe, 12 July 1908 (copy), *Times* Archives.

of *The Times*, carried little weight with Northcliffe's Liberal critics. Buckle called Moberly Bell's attention to a series, 'The Harmsworth Brand', that ran in the *Nation* from 18 July ('*The Times* under Northcliffe ... cannot well possess any moral or intellectual force') to 28 August. 'The articles are not at all fair,' Buckle admitted, 'but of course contain a good deal of truth.' Although Massingham's transparent design was to establish *The Times*'s guilt by association, Buckle expected these attacks to 'do us more good than harm, because they will seem to emphasize the necessity which X feels himself of keeping the two styles of journalism well apart'. The *Daily News*, which had protested at Northcliffe's elevation to the peerage, portrayed him savagely and, in the process, hit at *The Times*. Gardiner, enjoying 'the privilege of not knowing Lord Northcliffe', felt all the more qualified to recognize him as 'a man who understands material success and nothing else', as someone who 'blots out the foolish word "consistency" from his bright lexicon and repudiates his yesterdays with fearless indifference to criticism', secure in the knowledge 'that the mob has no memory and only asks for its daily sensation and its daily bread'. An apocryphal ride on the London underground gave Gardiner all he needed by way of acquaintance with Northcliffe:

> The fat gentleman on one side of me was reading the *Globe*; the slim lady on the other side the *Daily Mirror*; the smart office-boy in front the *Daily Mail*; the meek person next the *Sunday Companion*; the lad in the corner *Comic Cuts*. There were *Evening Newses*, and *Red Magazines*, *Puck*, and the *World*. The papers were different, but the accents were one.

And now, Gardiner asserted, 'the voice of *Answers* speaks in the thunders of *The Times*'. Here, in bountiful measure, was the abuse that Moberly Bell had hankered after.[1]

In fact, some of the publications enumerated by Gardiner were owned or managed by other Harmsworths. Moreover, Northcliffe was in the process of divesting himself of several properties. The *Southern Daily Mail* at Portsmouth had been liquidated in 1907. In the summer of 1908, the same fate seemed in store for the *Manchester Courier*, which – as Northcliffe told Balfour – had 'arrived at one of its quinquennial crisis [*sic*]'. After local Conservatives withdrew their support, Northcliffe saw no reason to go on. He relinquished the chairmanship of the company to Alderman W. T. Rothwell, but continued as a director 'against my better judgment throughout' until 1915, the year before the assets were finally sold off; 'the rapid rise in the price of paper' during wartime was the nominal reason for closure (*The Times*, 22 January 1916). Early in 1909, carrying 'upon my shoulders *The Times*', Northcliffe delegated responsibility for the *World* to Hamilton Edwards, the managing

---

[1] Buckle to Moberly Bell, 29 August 1908, *Times* Archives; Gardiner, *Prophets, Priests and Kings* (London, 1908), pp. 89–97.

editor of *Answers* and a director of Amalgamated Press, Ltd. 'As an old friend of Edmond Yates', whose name he misspelt, Northcliffe confessed to have 'rather foolishly assumed' custody of the *World*, 'thinking I should be able to devote a couple of days a week to it'. Overburdened, he had 'only been in the *World* office once since I purchased it' and decided to find an attentive editor, preferably one with 'sufficient capital wherewith to run the concern'. Edwards, allowing his own investment to remain in the enterprise, arranged the transfer 'to a new company under Lord Winterton, whom I have known to be a very able young man', and who began an eighteen-month tenure in April. The youngest member of the Commons in 1904, when he was elected as a Unionist, Winterton now became the youngest editor in Fleet Street. He had imbibed Tariff Reform as Chamberlain's parliamentary private secretary, and was to hold office in four governments in the course of a career that spanned nearly half a century. At his invitation, F. E. Smith became a director. Garvin contributed articles on foreign affairs and, for a time, retained a minor shareholding. 'It is an immense relief to me that you have got rid of the *World*,' he wrote to Northcliffe. 'Now for me to get rid of it.' Two years later, Northcliffe got rid of the *Observer* (inexplicably omitted from Gardiner's inventory), leaving Garvin to carry on under a new proprietorship.[1]

The Times was a peculiar outpost in Northcliffe's press empire, always more a dominion than a dependency. Morbidly conscious of his mortality, he spoke to Esher of leaving it in his will to the care of some national committee, like 'that of the British Museum', to ensure its permanence. Strachey, with whom he broached the subject, recommended a board of 'independent trustees', who would include the Lord Chancellor, the Speaker of the House of Commons, the Archbishop of Canterbury, and the vice-chancellors of the universities of Oxford and Cambridge; representing 'all the elements of the national life with which *The Times* is specially concerned', these public persons would be endowed to preserve the paper in accordance with Northcliffe's wish that it should 'remain an impartial, judicial and national organ of public opinion'. Yet, by his earlier proposals for a centrist *Times*, Strachey had revealed a discrepancy between his notion of impartiality and Northcliffe's, neither being constant. The relativity of that concept, particularly as it applied to political journalism, was to engender violent controversy in the years that followed. Northcliffe, if not *The Times*, thrived on it. On the third attempt, he had fulfilled an ambition, and that was evidently what mattered most to him.[2]

*   *   *

[1] Dunn to Sutton, 1 June and 15 July 1908 (copies), Northcliffe to Balfour, 29 July 1908 (copy), Northcliffe to Stephenson, 7 January 1913 (copy), Northcliffe to Edwards, 5 February and 23 March 1909 (copies), and Garvin to Northcliffe, 30 April 1909, Northcliffe Papers; *also see* Winterton, *Pre-War* (London, 1932), pp. 148–57.

[2] Northcliffe to Esher, 9 July 1908, quoted in *History of The Times*, IV, part 1, 787n.; Strachey to Northcliffe, 10 August 1908, Northcliffe Papers; *Spectator*, 22 September 1922.

If 1908 was Northcliffe's *annus mirabilis*, it was also Asquith's. At least since the formation of the Liberal government in December 1905, Asquith had been waiting to collect his prize. On 8 April, weeks after Northcliffe's clandestine triumph, he kissed hands as Prime Minister.

Welcomed by the Unionist press, which saw him as a brake upon the destructive forces of radicalism, socialism, and Irish nationalism, Asquith was thought by many Liberal journalists to lack the requisite dynamism and broad sympathies. 'He is the constructive engineer of politics, not the man of visions,' Gardiner had written shortly before Asquith's ascent. 'If he is wanting in any essential of statesmanship, it is a strong impulse to action. He has patience rather than momentum.' At a time when Liberal self-confidence appeared to have ebbed in the face of an intractable House of Lords, by-election reverses, and a depression in trade, Asquith seemed both temperamentally and ideologically unsuited to recapture the euphoria, much less to redeem the promises, of 1906. Least of all could he generate the affection enjoyed by his avuncular predecessor. The *Manchester Guardian* could neither forget his imperialist stance during the Boer War nor forgive his machinations before the Liberals took office. On 17 February, it guardedly implied its preference for Lloyd George, who personally inspired an editorial appeal on 6 March on behalf of 'adequate guarantees for the fullest representation in the councils of the party of the sounder and more decided Liberal traditions'. Scott accepted that Asquith 'was a sort of natural successor', but complained to Goldwin Smith on 15 March that 'the present Cabinet with Asquith simply substituted for Campbell-Bannerman' at the helm would be a set-back. Although, in the event, Asquith's changes in ministerial personnel were not extensive, the elevation of Lloyd George to the Exchequer went far to appease Scott and others of a Radical disposition. Nevertheless, the *Manchester Guardian* grumbled on 13 April: 'The Cabinet as a whole is still not representative of the party either in the country or in the House of Commons', and a further reshuffle was needed 'at no very distant date'.[1]

With a suspiciously unerring instinct, the *Daily Chronicle* revealed Asquith's Cabinet choices as they were being made and before they were submitted for royal approval. Margot Asquith, neatly described by John Grigg as 'the most intriguing (in both senses) of British Prime Ministers' wives', implored Churchill to 'do your d---dest' to restrain Lloyd George, who was presumed to be the culprit. Accepting Asquith's 'flattering' offer of the Exchequer, Lloyd George rejected 'the amiable suggestion that I had been responsible for the publication of the Cabinet list', and afterwards denied 'utterly' to Churchill that he was the *Chronicle*'s informant. 'It is unlikely that Lloyd George was totally innocent,' deduced Grigg, after carefully sifting through the evidence. On the other hand, 'the reasonable assumption would be that Lloyd George

---

[1] *Daily News*, 29 February 1908; *Political Diaries of C. P. Scott* (ed. T. Wilson; London, 1970), pp. 30–31; *also see* Bruce K. Murray, *The People's Budget 1909/10* (Oxford, 1980), ch. III.

was not the only source of the leak', which Asquith 'was a good deal annoyed to find' in print. The incident served to indicate not only a distrust of Lloyd George on the part of certain colleagues, most significantly Reginald McKenna and Walter Runciman, but also Asquith's reluctant concern with newspaper publicity. 'What are the social forces wh. count with the Prime Minister?' his wife – a social force in her own right – rhetorically asked W. T. Stead. 'I have been married 15 years to him & have never seen him interested in, much less moved by, any external opinion whether of the Press or the public.' His daughter Violet, no less given to hyperbole in the name of devotion, was fond of remarking that Asquith never deigned to take notice of newspaper comment. The women in Asquith's life were unreliable witnesses.[1]

From the start of his premiership, if not before, Asquith was keenly aware of the conduct of the Liberal press and eager to remedy its more glaring deficiencies. Owing to an exaggerated sense of propriety, which ultimately worked to his disadvantage, he was more reticent in his dealings with journalists than Lloyd George, who found them boon companions, or Churchill, who paid late-night calls to Bouverie Street and merrily helped Masterman polish off leaders for the *Daily News*. Initially, along with Grey, Asquith was treated by *The Times* and other opposition journals with a solicitude which tended to lessen his dependence on Liberal papers. Soon enough, he was left to rely on Liberal organs, inadequate to the task. Querulous by nature, these publications were rarely inclined to accord him unqualified support, and some were openly antagonistic. In 1912, when Churchill proposed 'to consolidate and encourage all our forces' by conferring honours on journalists as the Tories had done, Asquith vetoed the idea. 'No party was ever worse served than ours by its Press,' he fumed, making it clear that he was not oblivious to its performance.[2]

With the exception of the *Westminster Gazette*, compliantly edited by Spender, the major Liberal dailies and weeklies adhered to a Radical position and resisted discipline from the whips. Their potential for mischief enhanced by collaboration with dissenting elements within the Cabinet and on the backbenches, they were sharply critical of the policy of 'continuity' practised by Grey at the Foreign Office, the halting pace of Morley's Indian reforms, Burns's hidebound administration at the Local Government Board, the failure of successive presidents of the Board of Education to allay Nonconformist discontents, and especially of the spiralling expenditures on armaments. The *Manchester Guardian* considered it more reprehensible than ironic that in 1908, 'a year of profound peace', a Liberal Government should propose 'to spend sixty millions, or six millions more than we spent on normal military and

---

[1] Grigg, *Lloyd George: The People's Champion*, pp. 134–39; Margot Asquith to Stead [1909], Stead Papers.
[2] Churchill to Asquith, 12 August 1912 (draft), and Asquith to Churchill, 16 August 1912, in R. S. Churchill, ed., *Winston S. Churchill*, companion vol. 2, part 3, I (London, 1969), 627–29.

naval services in 1901, the worst year of the South African War' (3 March 1908). Along with the *Daily News*, the *Nation*, and *The Economist*, it waged a campaign to reduce service estimates and to effect a rapprochement with Germany.

Spender was sympathetic to the cause of international conciliation to the extent that he accompanied other Liberal and a few Unionist editors on a goodwill mission to Germany in the spring of 1907. But his dependability as a ministerial apologist was never in doubt. The problem was that his platform, the *Westminster Gazette*, threatened to collapse under him. Sir George Newnes, who refuted rumours that he was a bidder for *The Times*, let it be known that he had 'become weary of the *Westminster Gazette*', which he hoped to sell for £50,000 in order to realize capital for a new morning venture. In that case, the *Westminster* would shut down. William Robertson Nicoll, who owned and edited the *British Weekly* ('a journal of social and Christian progress'), reported to Scott on 31 March 'a strong movement going on just now to establish a penny morning Free Trade daily' to which Spender would presumably transfer his editorial services. 'The money seems likely to come in,' but 'the experience of the *Tribune*' as well as 'the complete failure of the *Pall Mall Gazette* to establish itself as a morning daily' back in 1870, made it 'most desirable that no false step should be taken'. An ally of Lloyd George, Robertson Nicoll thought it would be more logical to start a London edition of the *Manchester Guardian*, which would have the asset of being more aggressively Radical than anything Spender might edit.[1] Scott, whose resources were already stretched to the utmost, proved unreceptive to the scheme, which was periodically urged upon him. Like Cobden and Bright, he feared the contaminating influences of Fleet Street and, having emancipated himself from Taylor's yoke, shied away from partnerships that might inhibit his authority.

J. A. ('Jack') Pease, who was appointed chief whip in June 1908, attended to the *Westminster Gazette* as one of the first items on his agenda. On the 18th, he informed Asquith 'about negotiations for [the] purchase of [the] *Westminster*' from Newnes, whose plan for a morning paper had been abandoned. In his diary, Pease also recorded contacts with Oswald Partington and Charles Henry, both wealthy Liberal MPs, whom he hoped to recruit as investors. A week later, he told Asquith that Sir Christopher Furness, another backbench plutocrat, had advanced a 'scheme to acquire the *W. Gazette*' independently of 'others' (presumably Partington and Henry), who would not 'join him but run together on an equal footing, making themselves liable for £5000 down & later [a] further £5000'. If such a syndicate were formed, Pease 'thought I could find ten willing to go in', but declared it 'a pity to lose this money if Furness would do it all'. For unspecified reasons, Furness bowed out. 'Alick' Murray, the Master of Elibank and a more adept fund-raiser, thereupon introduced Pease

---

[1] Nicoll to Scott, 31 March 1908, *Guardian* Archives.

to Lord Allendale, who (as W. C. B. Beaumont) had been Liberal MP for Hexham from 1895 to 1907. Allendale undertook to subscribe £5,000 towards shares in the *Westminster Gazette*, pledging half the amount 'about 1st Sept. next' and the remainder two years hence. In return, Pease agreed to advance him the sum of £2,500, interest free, from party funds. As he reviewed the terms, Allendale was to assume liability 'for the first £5,000 and I will make myself liable for the further £5,000 if called up on the ... shares which will be allotted to you'. Put more succinctly by Murray, who followed Pease as chief whip, the party had underwritten Allendale's investment: 'in order to induce him to place money in the *Westminster Gazette*, we had to undertake to supply half while the whole amount stands in his name'. The whips' office, where the shares certificates were held as collateral, thus operated as a brokerage agency and a bank. That it did so successfully was celebrated on 28 July, when Asquith entertained Pease and Mr and Mrs J. A. Spender at lunch.[1]

These transactions, which involved party officials in unaccustomed capacities, were necessarily kept as quiet as Northcliffe's acquisition of *The Times*. Decades later, Spender's biographer glossed over the replacement of Newnes by 'a syndicate of well known Liberals', among whom he selectively identified Henry (but neither Partington nor Allendale), Sir W. D. Pearson (later 1st Viscount Cowdray), and Sir John Brunner. Alfred Mond, then Liberal MP for Chester, was designated chairman; and Donald Maclean, then Liberal MP for Bath and later deputy chairman of the party, was secretary. In fact, Brunner was not involved, though his son and namesake eventually joined the board. 'By an accident', he saw a copy of the *National Review* in which he and Ludwig Mond, 'gentlemen of alien extraction', were said to have taken control of the paper. In a letter that Maxse declined to publish, Brunner asserted his British birthright and remonstrated that neither he 'nor my old friend and partner Dr Mond [Alfred's father] holds a single share in the *Westminster*'. According to Spender, it was precisely because Brunner was 'supposed to have inspired the *Westminster* on its pro-German line' that he was made 'the innocent victim of Maxse's attacks'. Henry and Allendale disposed of their shares before or during the First World War; but Partington, Maclean, and Cowdray held on through the Liberal convulsions of the 1920s. Mond, eventually superseded by Cowdray as chairman, was a difficult master to serve. On 9 August 1909, Spender rebuked him for having broken – 'on two consecutive days ... last week' – what was 'almost an absolute rule among the proprietors of newspapers not to write over their own names in their own journals'. Arnold Bennett, ever the man about town, saw Mond closeted with his editor at the Reform Club: 'Spender looked as dry as he is'; and 'the employed and the

---

[1] Pease's diary, 18 and 25 June, and 28 July 1908, Allendale to Pease, 16 July 1908, and Pease to Allendale, 17 July 1908 (copy?), Pease Papers; Murray of Elibank to R. H. Davies, 28 January 1915, Asquith Papers.

employer', taking leave of each other, 'shook hands like not too intimate friends'.[1]

Against his inclination and possibly his better judgment, Asquith played an increasingly active role in each successive reconstruction of the *Westminster Gazette* board. Apart from presiding at congratulatory luncheons, he allowed his name to be used to attract investors. With preferments and dignities, he rewarded those who heeded the party call. As a last resort, he sanctioned the use of party funds. Taking over as chief whip, Pease was cautioned to avoid the fund-raising expedients of his predecessor, who 'had been skating on too thin ice in selling honours'. Within months, however, Pease recorded in his diary how the Prime Minister 'sent for me and told me' that George Riddell, proprietor of the *News of the World* since 1903, 'wanted a Knighthood'. For this modest price, Asquith reckoned, Riddell 'might help a hospital, & use his paper in our favour'. Riddell promptly received his knighthood, which Lloyd George upgraded to a baronetcy in 1918 and a barony in 1920. Appearances to the contrary, the fundamental difference between Asquith and Lloyd George was one of degree, not principle.[2]

Asquith's succession, bringing changes in the Cabinet and the whips' office, signalled a heightening of tensions between and within parliamentary groupings. Other newspaper configurations reflected this development more acutely than those behind the scenes at the *Westminster Gazette*. The Liberal provincial press, depleted and decayed, gave particular cause for anxiety. G. G. Armstrong, who edited the Rowntrees' *Northern Echo* at Darlington, berated 'Leeds Liberals for tolerating a Harmsworthian "Liberal" paper in their midst to fight against them at election times'. His taunt galvanized his cousin, Arnold Lupton, the Liberal MP for Sleaford, who canvassed the possibility that the *Leeds Mercury* might be restored to its historic Liberalism through an arrangement with Ernest Parke and the owners of the *Morning Leader*. Lupton broached the matter with Rowland H. Barran, the member for Leeds North, whom he assured that the *Mercury* could be made to 'pay if it were bought', but local assistance failed to materialize. Instead

---

[1] Wilson Harris, *J. A. Spender* (London, 1946), p. 28; Spender to Mond, 9 August 1909 (draft copy?), Spender Papers, Add. MSS. 46, 392, fol. 20; Brunner to Maxse, 9 March 1909, in the *Westminster Gazette*, 11 May 1909; Maxse to Brunner, 12 March 1909, and Spender to Brunner, 13 April 1909, Brunner Papers; Arnold Bennett's journal, 16 October 1912.

[2] Pease's diary, 5 June 1908 and 27 April 1909, Pease Papers. In response to subsequent criticisms of newspaper honours, Asquith maintained – somewhat disingenuously – that he had been

> obliged to act mainly on the advice of the whips and other such experts. The man you mention (I think his name is Riddell) was strongly recommended to me on the ground (amongst others) that his paper the *News of the World* had become definitely Liberal, and was a valuable party asset.

Asquith to Spender, 10 November 1909, Spender Papers, Add. MSS. 46, 388, fol. 92.

Armstrong moved from Darlington to Manchester, where he became managing editor of the *Daily News*'s northern edition.[1]

Whereas the *Manchester Guardian* was unwilling and perhaps unable to extend its operations to London, where its copies frequently arrived at midday, the *Daily News* saw the benefits to be gained from delivering London to Manchester. That the Cadburys were 'seriously contemplating' such a move had been 'a good deal rumoured' since May 1908, when John Scott predicted to his father that 'it would be foredoomed to failure'. He was happily mistaken. Publication began on 11 January 1909 and continued until March 1921, with a brief resumption in 1928. The Scotts really had little reason to fear the competition, for there existed a large potential readership in Lancashire from which the *Manchester Guardian* had excluded itself as much by content as by price. Both publicly and privately, the managers of the *Daily News* took pains to 'emphasise ... the fact that our coming [to Manchester] is in no spirit of rivalry to that great national champion of good causes, the *Manchester Guardian*'. Armstrong submitted to C. P. Scott a circular which he and Henry Cadbury had drafted for distribution among 'Liberal Agents, Trades Union secretaries, Ministers, &c. ... in the immediate Manchester district': professing a 'desire to supplement' the progressivism of the *Guardian*, it stated the case

> that a penny Liberal paper cannot adequately counteract the influence of its halfpenny Tory rivals, ... which, by their price, or place of publication, or both, are able to reach the masses in the North with very much greater ease than any of their competitors. It is this advantage which our firm desires to neutralise by its present step.

Produced at up-to-date premises in Dale Street, the northern edition of the *Daily News* reserved a proportion of its space for 'North country news and comment', but otherwise replicated its metropolitan parent.[2]

In Bouverie Street, where Gardiner's editorial sovereignty remained unaffected, the immediate impact of Asquith's premiership was felt through Masterman's appointment to an under-secretaryship at the Local Government Board. Nevinson advertised his availability to the *Daily News* as a leader-writer or war correspondent, but prejudiced his chances first by renouncing his membership in the Liberal Party 'in rage at their gradual approach to an understanding with the bloodthirsty Tsardom', and then by accusing the Cadburys of deriving their profits from 'cocoa slavery' in Angola. Reading the papers on 12 April 1908, Nevinson 'saw that Masterman had been summoned to Asquith, which almost certainly means I shall be offered his place on the

---

[1] Armstrong, *Memories* (London, 1944), p. 90.
[2] John Scott to C. P. Scott [15 May 1908], Armstrong to Scott, 22 December 1908, and draft circular dated January 1908, *Guardian* Archives; *also see* Koss, *Fleet Street Radical*, pp. 109–10.

D.N.'. To secure it, he 'cycled early to Gardiner's house' on the 17th and, without alluding to his purpose, strove to dispel the impression that he was hostile to the Cadburys and their assorted products. Gardiner, 'very straight & sensible', promised to let him 'hear something definite on Tuesday when Henry Cadbury wd. return from a family consultation'. Beginning in June, Nevinson wrote four leading articles a week for the *Daily News* at an annual salary of £500. His connection lasted only fourteen months, ending in a violent clash over the paper's policy with respect to the forced feeding of imprisoned suffragettes. Gardiner, whom he exonerated as 'a temperate and conciliatory editor', was caught in the middle. Ernest Parke had warned against the combination of Brailsford and Nevinson as political leader-writers ('What a pair to drive in tandem!'), and his advice was sound. Gardiner came to regard Nevinson as a baleful influence on Brailsford, just as he blamed Belloc for bringing out hidden weaknesses in Chesterton. In 1941, when Nevinson died, Gardiner could not resist saying that he did not envy St Peter, who 'will find him something of a handful, for I can't imagine him comfortable in heaven with no heroics to indulge in & nothing to do but twang a harp'.[1]

Employment opportunities for distinguished political journalists, especially those with a left-wing bent, were in too short supply for feuds to last very long. Nevinson proceeded to assignments on the *Daily Chronicle* and the *Manchester Guardian*, but was back on the *Daily News*'s payroll as Berlin correspondent when war broke out in 1914. In the brief period when he and Brailsford shared leader-writing responsibilities, the *Daily News* took on a more militant tone. Most pronounced in relation to the women's suffrage issue, where it inveighed against Home Office brutality and prime ministerial insensitivity, this attitude of moral outrage extended across a broad front of governmental policy. In common with many Liberal journals, the *Westminster Gazette* always excepted, the *Daily News* suspected the Cabinet, now dominated by Liberal Imperialist elements, of a reckless propensity to sacrifice social reform on the altar of national prestige. The controversial decision to equip the Royal Navy with costly new Dreadnoughts, in response to a public clamour provoked by the announcement of an acceleration in German shipbuilding, was decried as a wasteful provocation, which moreover siphoned appropriations from domestic welfare programmes. Although not without substance, these allegations were often reduced to simplisms, ignoring the financial and international predicaments in which policy-makers found themselves. If the Liberal leadership were to prevail over entrenched interests, it would require the active support of the democracy from which it claimed its mandate. The recalcitrance of Liberal newspapers, by adding to a mood of demoralization, was regarded as especially crippling.

---

[1] Nevinson's diary, 12 and 17 April 1908; Nevinson, *More Changes, More Chances* (London, 1925), pp. 283 ff.; Gardiner to Swinnerton, 16 November 1941, Swinnerton Papers.

Before leaving the Exchequer for the premiership, Asquith had effectively laid down the guidelines for Free Trade finance by introducing differentiated rates of taxation between earned and unearned incomes and thereby presaging a shift of the tax burden to the wealthier classes. It was left to Lloyd George to follow through by obtaining from land values and other direct taxes the necessary revenues for armaments, non-contributory old-age pensions, insurance schemes, and the like. It was freely admitted that the Liberals' ability to withstand the mounting pressure for Tariff Reform and to win the next election would hinge on Lloyd George's success or failure. The Unionists quickly realized as much. As early as November 1908, they began to mutter threats, which the Liberals tended to discount, that the House of Lords might reject the 1909 budget and so force an early election.

Long before they were unveiled on 29 April 1909, Lloyd George's proposals for 'democratic taxation' had registered a profound impact. On the Liberal side, they restored ministerial solidarity and an overriding sense of purpose. While divergences over naval estimates and other priorities persisted within the Cabinet and the party, they were temporarily swept aside. Nowhere was there greater ardour than among Liberal publicists, many of whom had been at odds with the government and consequently with each other. After backing Lloyd George against a majority of his colleagues in his vain attempt to resist Admiralty demands, they championed him as the official spokesman for Liberal interests. Gardiner was typical: dining with the Mastermans on 7 October 1908, he 'agreed that the line for the autumn for the press must be *attack*, on the land monopoly especially, not defence'. Scott's adulation of Lloyd George went without saying, and the prospect of a pitched battle with the Lords merely confirmed his loyalty. Massingham, whose articles in the *Nation* and the *Morning Leader* betrayed an impatience with 'the complete flabbiness of the party', was similarly heartened. The recipients of Lloyd George's various attentions, including his calculated indiscretions, Liberal newspapermen were easily won over. Charles Hobhouse, Financial Secretary to the Treasury and no admirer of the Chancellor's methods, noted disapprovingly in his diary on 7 March 1909 that, 'instead of working at the details of his budget', Lloyd George preferred

> to 'collect ideas' by talking to journalists and by confiding to the Editor of the *Daily Chronicle* his views of what the Budget should be. Together with Churchill he formed a cabal which was to pledge the Cabinet in advance and if they didn't agree, to offer resignation and a newspaper war on those who remained.

Prepared for any and every eventuality, Lloyd George exploited the press to overcome qualms on the part of certain timorous associates, to help goad the

Lords either into submission or a suicidal act of defiance, and finally to awaken the country to the blessings of his 'People's Budget'.[1]

The Unionists, thrown on the defensive, were equally dependent on journalistic weaponry; indeed, it has been suggested that, being 'largely without platform speakers comparable to Churchill and Lloyd George', the opposition banked on its press as a chief source of strength. Yet, divided among themselves, they could not keep their guns in Fleet Street from backfiring. Each Unionist paper adopted its own strategy predicated on the suppositions of the sectional interests with which it identified. The tactic of *The Times*, for example, was to play upon conflicts within Liberal ranks. Early in 1909, Buckle heard 'that the Winston-Lloyd George party are making another rally in the Cabinet' over naval estimates. 'We must strengthen the hands of Asquith, Grey, & the sensible men in the Govt. by a leader or two,' he directed Thursfield, who wrote to order. Had the ministerial balance been destroyed rather than merely tipped, there would have been no regrets in Printing House Square. On questions of naval policy, *The Times* was inspired by Sir John ('Jacky') Fisher, the irrepressible First Sea Lord, whose editorial alliances transcended party lines. In addition to Spender and Stead, Fisher's friends included Garvin (whom he supplied with 'magnificent secret stuff, chapter and verse') and Gardiner (to whom he spoke unguardedly, 'but kindly ... don't remember anything I said!'). The *Morning Post* and the *Standard* took the part of Fisher's bitter antagonist, Lord Charles Beresford, who alternated naval service with intermittent stints as a Tory MP. 'The *M.P.*'s antics about Beresford show that they have completely lost their heads and are suffering acutely from spleen and jealousy,' Monypenny remarked to Moberly Bell.[2]

It suited the Liberals, for purposes of propaganda, to portray the national press as a Conservative and unrepresentative monolith, akin to the House of Lords. 'The Liberal Party ... must not allow itself to be overawed by the hostility of the Press which is ranged against it,' Churchill told an audience at Birmingham on 13 January 1909. In fact, Unionist newspapers were badly divided within and among themselves. Their solid front was a thin veneer that cracked under pressure, disclosing doubts and vacillations that gave comfort to the enemy. The *Morning Post* was a case in point. On 6 May 1908, it hailed as 'remarkable ... the sweeping advance of the Tariff Reform movement since the early weeks of last year, when the whole body of its opponents and some even of its wavering supporters thought that it was flickering out'. Particular satisfaction was gleaned from Amery's by-election campaign at East Wolverhampton, where the Liberal majority was reduced to a single digit that

[1] Lucy Masterman, *C. F. G. Masterman* (London, 1968), p. 109; Havighurst, *Radical Journalist*, p. 191; *Inside Asquith's Cabinet*, p. 76.

[2] Gollin, *Observer*, p. 93; Buckle to Thursfield, 19 January 1909, *Times* Archives; Garvin to Northcliffe, 2 February 1908, Northcliffe Papers; Fisher to Gardiner, 20 June 1909, Gardiner Papers; Monypenny to Moberly Bell, 10 July 1908, *Times* Archives; *also see* Gollin, *Observer*, pp. 44–51, *and* A. Marder, *From the Dreadnought to Scapa Flow*, I (London, 1961), 77.

betokened 'the conversion of the Unionist Party from an enfeebled political machine to an animated force of rational patriotism'. Instead of the praise he expected, Fabian Ware received 'definite and far-reaching instructions' from Lord Glenesk that he was 'entirely to abandon that line'. The editor retorted 'quite nicely that I could not do this – that it was all I lived for & that men like Austen Chamberlain, Lord Milner & Bonar Law agreed with me', but his venerable proprietor remained adamant. 'What am I to do? I am at my wit's end,' Ware wrote to Lady Bathurst after the Maxse brothers had counselled him to ignore her father's injunctions. 'And now just when the paper is going better than it ever has (circulation *up* 3,000 a day)', he found himself 'kept awake at night by the worry of defending vital principles of policy'.[1]

These exertions to force the pace of protectionism were an embarrassment to the Balfourites, who were struggling to maintain a precarious unity in anticipation of a general election that they were resigned to lose. The *Spectator* (21 January 1909) warned that if the Unionists implemented the policy of proscription 'announced in the *Morning Post* . . . disaster must overtake the Party'. Ware, who would have no truck with either defeatism or Free Trade (which he held to be synonymous), also had to contend with differences among his staff. Richard Jebb, one of the principal leader-writers, was a hard-line Tariff Reformer who furnished the 'original draft' for an 'unauthorised programme' which was published with the emendation and approval of Austen Chamberlain, Milner, Amery, J. W. Hills, and Bonar Law, the last confessing to a 'personal inclination' against such an implicit challenge to Balfour. Spenser Wilkinson, who wrote leaders for the *Morning Post* after briefly serving as editor in 1905, disputed Ware's authority and rejected 'his dictation in matters of opinion'. The death of Glenesk, whose daughter succeeded to the proprietorship, fortified Ware's stand, with the result that the paper soon became an accessary to Leo Maxse's 'Balfour Must Go' agitation. W. P. Ward, the editor of the *Dublin Review* and a Tory publicist, was 'sure that there is a *very large* body of Unionist opinion against *violent* Tariff reform', but he was prevented from expressing his heretical views in the *Morning Post*. An article aimed at 'propping up A.J.B.' was vetoed by Ware after it had been accepted by H. Buller, the literary editor, who regretted the incident as 'really most unfortunate! ultimately proceeding from the stupidity of Ware who thought the campaign against Balfour to be something in the manner of Napoleon'.[2]

Far from rendering valuable support to Unionism in any of its shades, opposition newspapers disappointed everyone in turn. The 1908 Education Bill, surrendered by the government without a fight, enhanced neither party's reputation. 'The press – our press – is absolutely rotten, and must have been

[1] *Daily News*, 14 January 1909; Ware to Lady Bathurst, 6 May 1908, Bathurst Papers.
[2] Bonar Law to Ware, 8 September 1908 (copy), Bonar Law Papers 18/8/10; Ware to Bonar Law, 29 September 1908, Bonar Law Papers 18/4/75; Wilkinson to Lady Bathurst, 4 April 1909, Bathurst Papers; Ward to Sandars, 5 February 1909, enclosing Buller to Ward, 4 February 1909, Sandars Papers.

squared,' Sandars wrote to Balfour, 'or they could not have been so foolish as to write as they have done before the Bill was out.' When the *Morning Post* sought to stave off concessions to Irish nationalism by advancing a scheme for 'Imperial Home Rule', Garvin 'deplored and condemned that departure, and upon the earnest entreaty of Bonar Law himself, the whole disastrous thing was stopped. Fabian Ware,' he explained 'in confidence' to Strachey, 'is as independent a journalist as either of us, but the *Morning Post* in that matter was speaking for itself, and not for Tariff Reform or for any Tariff Reformer of standing outside its offices.' That it was necessary for Unionist politicians to bring Unionist papers to heel was itself a commentary on the dubious advantages that the party was said to enjoy. That Unionist politicians like Bonar Law were generally successful was no less a commentary on the limits of editorial independence.[1]

Garvin's estimation of Ware is especially interesting in the light of his own position. Since January 1908, he had been editing the *Observer* on the understanding that he would advise on the political conduct of the *Daily Mail* and other Harmsworth properties. At the time he had taken up his duties, it was not imagined that *The Times* would soon be added to Northcliffe's holdings. Useful in leaking information prejudicial to Pearson, Garvin had no responsibility for *The Times* and a lessened influence over Northcliffe. After a testy exchange with Moberly Bell, whom he accused of slighting the *Observer*, Garvin proclaimed to Northcliffe that 'apart from my interest in your interests and in the sheer drama of your recent performances I don't care *one damn* for *The Times* or anything about it!' Insinuations that Garvin was angling for the editorship of *The Times* 'marred the old frankness' of their relationship. Further tensions arose when Garvin complained that the business requirements of the *Observer* were being neglected. Arguably, however, it was on political grounds that Garvin felt the greatest discomfort.[2]

'For my part,' Northcliffe wrote affectionately to Garvin ('my dear Garvino') at year's end, '1909 has been a back-breaker. *The Times* has been my chief difficulty.' Parliamentary imbroglios, and his own erratic responses to them, did nothing to ease his task. Like the *Observer*, a staunch defender of McKenna's 'Big Navy' policies, *The Times* vigorously upheld the 'sensible men' against the Radical 'economists' who operated through the National Liberal Federation, various *ad hoc* committees, and the mainstream Liberal press. Lloyd George, who led the insurgents within the Cabinet, turned the tables on Asquith and stiffly protested when ministerial dissensions were leaked to the *Observer*, *The Times*, the *Daily Telegraph*, and the *Westminster Gazette*. With muted tolerance, *The Times* also accepted the Indian consti-

---

[1] Sandars to Balfour, 20 November 1908, Balfour Papers; Garvin to Strachey, 13 February 1909, Strachey Papers.
[2] Garvin to Northcliffe, 8 September 1908, Northcliffe Papers; Garvin to Northcliffe, 5 February 1909 (copy), Garvin Papers; *also see* Gollin, *Observer*, pp. 162–67.

tutional reforms introduced by Morley, who was relieved to report, after he and Lord Minto had appointed the first native member to the Viceroy's executive council: '*The Times*, which in India matters is almost the only journal that really counts, shakes its head a little solemnly, but without scare.'[1]

Towards Churchill, whom he embraced as a fellow swashbuckler and whose aristocratic background was perhaps a further endearment, Northcliffe maintained a stubborn cordiality. At least during the first half of the new year, however, Lloyd George was his *bête noire*. 'The emptiness of Lloyd George's head is becoming painfully apparent to the country,' Northcliffe declared on 11 January in a memorandum to the staff at Printing House Square. This outburst, obviously inspired by Lloyd George's dogged opposition to naval expansionism, has been further interpreted by Northcliffe's biographers as an expression of the 'prevailing fear that the Budget of 1909 would show class feeling being used as an instrument of policy'.[2] Without waiting for the details, *The Times* and other Northcliffe properties railed against the omnibus nature of the budget and its partisan ramifications.

On 27 February 1909, a private dinner was held at the Savoy Hotel to commemorate Buckle's twenty-fifth anniversary as editor of *The Times*. 'The occasion,' he wrote afterwards to Balfour, 'was also interesting as showing, what you already know from talks with Lord Northcliffe and with me, that there is to be no change of any kind, save in the way of improvement on the old lines, in the conduct of the Paper.' To the extent that these 'old lines' were independent, they hardly ran above party. Buckle conceded as much when he later recalled to Balfour 'a quarter of a century during which we were in constant & almost intimate relations'. He was to retire in 1912, 'while I still have some remnants of youth hanging about me'. In the twilight of his editorship, with his successor standing at his elbow, he was increasingly a figurehead whose directives were countermanded. In his absence, the board of directors decided on 3 September 1909 'that it would greatly facilitate matters if Buckle was not expected to attend ... the daily conference of heads of departments'.[3]

Northcliffe had his own ideas about electoral strategy, though he habitually contradicted them. There were reproaches from the Conservative Central Office in April, when *The Times* joined the *Morning Post* and the *Standard* in promoting the adoption of a Tariff Reform candidate at Stratford-on-Avon in place of Philip Foster, who was defeated in the 1906 election; in the event, Foster regained the seat in a May by-election. By then, Northcliffe was facetiously apologizing to Buckle for having

---

[1] Northcliffe to Garvin, 31 December 1909, Garvin Papers; Lloyd George to Asquith, 8 February 1909, Asquith Papers; Morley to Minto, 25 March 1909, Minto Papers.
[2] Pound and Harmsworth, p. 376.
[3] Buckle to Balfour, 31 March 1909, 28 July 1912, and 25 July 1928, Balfour Papers; Chirol to Moberly Bell, 3 September 1909, *Times* Archives.

to worry you about Politics when you ought to be busy trying to earn a dividend, but I see by the enclosed paragraph from my brother's paper, the *Globe*, that the extreme Tariff Reformers, of which he is one, not satisfied with their mischief in East Hertfordshire and Marylebone, are now trying to thrust upon Oxford University one of their own candidates, with the object, I suppose, of excluding Hugh Cecil. ... Personally, I would rather have Hugh Cecil, Free Fooder though he be, than fifty of these wealthy people who are buying their way into the House of Commons by means of the approaching Tariff.

Buckle, with all the diplomacy he could muster, concurred 'that Hugh Cecil, despite his heresies, ought to be in the House, and that University representation should not be dictated by the machine. At the same time', he ventured that Sir Charles Alfred Cripps (later 1st Baron Parmoor), the Tariff Reform favourite, 'would be a very suitable member for Oxford University' by virtue of his academic and theological qualifications.[1]

The steady advance of Tariff Reform in the constituencies and the press was arrested by the introduction of the budget, a brilliant counterstroke. Journalistic reactions faithfully reflected partisan allegiances. Save for *The Economist*, stamped by a congenital Cobdenism, Liberal papers were enthusiastic. On 30 April, the *Manchester Guardian* extolled 'one of the most evenly distributed schemes we have ever had', while the *Daily Chronicle* praised its consonance 'with democratic principle and with the dictates of justice'. Despite reservations about the 'complexity' of the measure, the *Westminster Gazette* endorsed the egalitarian objectives of what the *Nation* (1 May) acclaimed as 'the first democratic budget' in British history. The *Morning Post* and the *National Review* competed for the distinction of being the most aggressively vindictive, with the *Observer* almost temperate by comparison. In July, Garvin met Ware, who announced 'that the *Morning Post* means to start in the autumn a great campaign for drastic treatment of the Budget in the Lords. Everything looks as though we are going to get business,' Garvin advised Northcliffe. William Waldorf Astor, whose purchase of the *Observer* was soon to make him Garvin's employer, already owned the *Pall Mall Gazette*. Within the next three months, according to an American acquaintance, he 'remitted to New York a million and a half sterling ($7,500,000) which but for Mr Lloyd George's Budget I should have invested here'.[2]

---

[1] James Hargreaves to Austen Chamberlain, 24 April 1909, and Acland Hood to Austen Chamberlain, 26 April 1909, Austen Chamberlain Papers, 4/1/431-32; Northcliffe to Buckle, 16 May 1909 (copy), and Buckle to Northcliffe, 17 May 1909, Northcliffe Papers. 'As you know, I am continuing my support of Robert and Hugh Cecil,' Northcliffe told Marlowe. 'Unfortunately, there is no one at the *Daily Mail* who understands the matter.' Nor was there anyone at the *Observer*. Northcliffe to Marlowe, 14 June 1909 (copy), Northcliffe Papers.

[2] Garvin to Northcliffe, 19 July 1909, Northcliffe Papers; George Smalley, *Anglo-American Memories* (2nd ser.; London, 1912), pp. 273-74.

Poised to pounce, Northcliffe greeted the actual provisions of the budget with bombastic truculence. The initial pragmatism of the Balfourite leadership disturbed him. 'I was rather sorry to hear that the powers that be in the Unionist Party were against the Peers throwing out the Budget,' he wrote to H. W. Wilson of the *Daily Mail*, 'for, if that process be technically correct, I think it would be wise in the interests of the country that the people should have the matter placed before them at a General Election.' Wilson, adopting exactly this tack in his leading articles, could only 'hope . . . that the Lords will reject the Budget, even if it plunges us into a great political battle'.[1] Following Garvin's example in the *Observer*, Thomas Marlowe recommended that the *Mail* 'should make the issue the naval one', namely 'that the Budget does not make sufficient provision for the Navy, and that therefore it should be rejected'. But Garvin's argument, condemned by the *Daily Chronicle* as a 'thumping lie', was altogether too narrow to suit the purposes of the *Daily Mail*, which preferred to conjure up visions of a socialist menace. By contrast, *The Times* emphasized the constitutional implications, with younger Tariff Reformers like Amery and Grigg kept in check by Chirol and Buckle. These nuances were detected and ridiculed by the *Daily News* (3 May), which reminded its readers 'that *The Times*, the *Daily Mail*, and the *Observer*, not to mention a host of minor organs in London and the provinces, are all controlled by one man'.

That man foresaw a crucial place for himself in the impending struggle, but it was located in Fleet Street, not at Westminster. Flattered by Wilson's suggestion that he might lead the forces of patriotic resistance in the Upper House, Northcliffe modestly admitted that 'I shall never make an orator'. Since 1905, when he was raised to the peerage, he had shunned parliamentary exposure. 'I am one of those people who believe that journalists should be read and not seen,' he told Lloyd George, whose 'kind invitation' he politely declined. He made one of his rare appearances at Westminster on the afternoon of 3 August, but – avoiding the chamber to which he belonged – took a seat in the peers' gallery of the Commons. His brother Cecil, who sat for Droitwich as a Liberal, saw him above and coaxed him to stay to tea. Strange to the ways of Parliament, Northcliffe first required assurances that peers were permitted to trespass in the refreshment-room of the other place. His unusual presence there was immediately noticed by J. H. Dalziel, one of Lloyd George's newspaper cronies, who thought that the time had come for Northcliffe and Lloyd George to make each other's acquaintance. The Chancellor was waiting in his room behind the Speaker's chair and, Dalziel told Northcliffe, was 'very keen to meet you'. With Cecil Harmsworth as chaperon, the two men conversed amicably for 'upwards of an hour', during which 'the Wizard devoted all his powers to capturing Northcliffe'. On the subject of the budget,

[1] Northcliffe to Wilson, 19 May 1909 (copy) and Wilson to Northcliffe, 22 May 1909, Northcliffe Papers.

the younger Harmsworth recalled his brother's obduracy: 'He would have nothing to do with it. He was opposed to it himself, and it was most unpopular with his readers.' On the forthcoming Development of Roads Bill, a cause dear to his heart, Northcliffe was more accommodating and went so far as to volunteer press support. 'Then Lloyd George did a very bold thing,' according to Cecil's recollection. 'Would Northcliffe like to see the draft proposals that he was to submit to the House the next day?' he asked. Lloyd George 'waived all objections aside' and, to Northcliffe's amazement and delight, 'told him he might make any use of it he pleased in the *Daily Mail*'. This 'splendid impudence' achieved its desired effect. Northcliffe left 'with the precious draft' in his 'inner pocket'. But the bigger bulge, so to speak, was in Lloyd George's pocket.[1]

P. W. Wilson, the lobby correspondent for the *Daily News*, was among those who craned their necks at the sight of Northcliffe in the gallery. Reporting the event on the 5th, he described the impromptu confabulation in the room behind the Speaker's chair and deduced that the result would be 'a collapse of the obstruction' that Unionists had deployed against the budget. 'The *Daily News* statement is an entire concoction,' Northcliffe informed his staff at *The Times*, and his biographers have taken him at his word. Yet, even allowing for a measure of exaggeration, the threat of Northcliffe's defection was real enough for Garvin to send him a cutting of the offending article, along with an entreaty 'not to encourage by indirect means in your newspapers thoughts of a surrender on the Budget which would ruin the Empire'. What had upset Garvin was not so much the prophecy of the *Daily News*, but, more tangibly, statements that had crept into *The Times* and the *Daily Mail*: the former, in its 'Political Notes' on the 4th, acknowledged a change in public opinion favourable to the budget, 'a change comparable only to the turn of the tide upon an estuary when the moored boats swing slowly round'; the latter, on the 5th, featured a report from 'A Parliamentary Correspondent', who perceived the same trend, with the Development of Roads Bill qualifying as the trump card for the government.[2]

Hamilton Fyfe, who had worked for Northcliffe on the *Daily Mirror*, put down the equivocations of the *Daily Mail* as a journalistic stunt: 'People that day were talking about the *Mail* more than ever.' Nevertheless, most of those who were talking were bemused Unionists. It has been further asserted that Northcliffe's newspapers merely recorded, as objectivity obliged them to do, a growing support that they themselves neither encouraged nor condoned. Yet, as recognized by A. P. Nicholson, chief parliamentary correspondent for *The*

---

[1] Northcliffe to Wilson, 19 May 1909 (copy), Northcliffe Papers; Northcliffe to Lloyd George, 23 June 1909, quoted in Grigg, *Lloyd George: The People's Champion*, p. 214n.; Gollin, *Observer*, p. 106n. Tom Clarke (*Northcliffe in History*, pp. 87–88) describes 'this fateful meeting' from a text provided by Cecil Harmsworth; Pound and Harmsworth (pp. 366–67) cite identical passages, mentioning Cecil Harmsworth's diary as their source.

[2] Pound and Harmsworth, p. 377; Gollin, *Observer*, pp. 106–107.

Times (and, incidentally, the brother of a Liberal MP), 'in the case of the House of Lords and the Budget, ... news and policy seem to be inextricably intertwined'.[1]

There is reason to believe that the episode was a good deal more serious. Lloyd George had been buoyed up to 'hear that reports are coming in to the Tory headquarters from all parts of the country that the Budget is popular'. It is unlikely that he could have resisted the temptation to share this intelligence with Northcliffe, who himself must have heard it from diverse and reliable sources. Writing to his brother on the 4th, Lloyd George gave a markedly different version of his interview with Northcliffe, who 'came to see me last night. ... He told me that the Budget has completely destroyed the Tariff Reform propaganda in the country. He said that they had all miscalculated the popularity of the Land Clauses. He wants to trim.' Garvin's 'Pauline epistle' that day to Northcliffe (who sent a copy to Sandars for Balfour's enlightenment) corroborates this view of Northcliffe's sentiments and intention. On the 5th, after he had read both the *Daily News* and the *Daily Mail*, Garvin wrote still more heatedly. 'Is it Winston who is betraying you?' he demanded of Northcliffe. 'The whole tone of *The Times* and *Daily Mail* seems to me utterly, utterly disastrous.' Ware provided Lady Bathurst with a similar rendering of events: 'Northcliffe visited the Lobby of the House of Commons the other day & as a result gave instructions to *The Times* & the *Daily Mail* to announce that opposition to the Budget must be abandoned!' Fortunately, however, 'Garvin is evidently standing up to him'.[2]

To stop Northcliffe from wobbling, Garvin escorted him to an interview with Balfour, who endeavoured to undo Lloyd George's mischief. 'I saw Northcliffe today,' Balfour wrote playfully to Sandars on Friday, the 6th. He hoped that the session would prove

> useful. It certainly was in the highest degree entertaining. He was not so 'piano' as I expected. Garvin was there; and Garvin, in his most fighting mood, had (I suspect) talked to him before I arrived.
>
> After luncheon we three walked up and down the lawn discussing the situation. It was as good as a play. Northcliffe saying at intervals – 'I have got to write (or rather get written) an article against the budget every day: how am I to do it?' To which Garvin (speaking across me who was between them) would reply by a violent general onslaught on the iniquities of the measure; prospects of its fatal effect on the Empire, the Constitution and the Party if it were allowed to pass; the duty of the H. of Lords & so forth. All this was no

---

[1] Fyfe, *Northcliffe* (London, 1930), p. 166; Nicholson to Northcliffe, 23 July 1909, Northcliffe Papers.

[2] Lloyd George to his brother, 3 and 4 August 1909, quoted in William George, *My Brother and I* (London, 1958), p. 230; Garvin to Northcliffe, 4 August 1909 (copies), Garvin Papers and Sandars Papers; Garvin to Northcliffe, 5 August 1909, Northcliffe Papers; Ware to Lady Bathurst, 24 August 1909, Bathurst Papers.

use to poor Northcliffe who wanted 'sense' (as we called it at Eton) for leading articles, not general expositions of policy. But finally some practical suggestions were made: – which Garvin was to embody in his Saturday [sic] article in the *Observer* & which were to provide a text for the Harmsworth papers.

Sandars was suitably amused. 'The scene you so vividly described – you between the optimist & the pessimist journalist – the journalist who cares for the great issue and the one who only regards the market – interested me greatly,' he replied to Balfour on Sunday, the 8th. The *Observer*, he was glad to see, had 'played up magnificently' that morning: denouncing Lloyd George as 'a very fustian demagogue' and a trickster 'too clever by half', it predicted that his fulminations to an East End audience at Limehouse would induce 'the revolt of all moderate men'. Balfour communicated his warm approval and waited for the other Harmsworth properties to take their cue. His 'decision and dexterity', Garvin later recalled, 'were the master influences upon the situation from first to last, and . . . the journalistic interpreter of the mind of his party was at the best an assistant crisis-maker'.[1]

As promised, the *Daily Mail* returned to the charge, waxing more indignant than ever against the budget. On 16 August, it saluted 'Mr J. L. Garvin's Brilliant Work' in the *Observer*. Six days later, it afforded its readers a sampling of Garvin's prose in the form of a signed portrait of 'Mr Balfour a Man of Action'. *The Times*, a more complicated and perhaps rustier machine, took longer to change gears. 'If *The Times* does not care to take the *Observer* plunge – at least it ought to do nothing the other way,' Sandars whispered into Garvin's 'confidential ear' on 3 September. What exasperated him most of all was 'the want of precision' that enabled such journals as *The Times* and the *Spectator* to oppose the budget in principle, yet to hang back from urging its outright rejection. On the very same day, Chirol described to Moberly Bell 'a satisfactory and useful Board meeting yesterday' at Printing House Square: 'From several independent sources we gather that the Unionist leaders have made up their minds to have the Budget rejected by the Lords.' Like Lord Lansdowne, who led the Unionist majority in the Upper House, Chirol harboured misgivings about this 'very dangerous decision, for the weight of evidence appears to be in favour of the popularity of the Budget, and if we are beaten at the next General Election on that issue, it will be the triumph not of the Liberal party as we now know it, but of the radical wing'. Balfour blamed the prolonged hesitancy of *The Times* on Buckle, whom he saw on the 21st – the day before he delivered a fighting speech at Birmingham – and who struck him as 'dreadful'. (Buckle returned from that meeting 'very much perplexed as to what line the paper should take about the Lords and the Budget', but vaguely

---

[1] Balfour to Sandars, 6 August 1909, Sandars Papers; Sandars to Balfour, 8 August 1909, Balfour Papers; undated autobiographical fragment, Garvin Papers.

resigned to 'support rejection'.) Northcliffe, off on a five-week tour of North America, saw the culprit as Moberly Bell, inhibited by a wish to conciliate the 'vast body of the banking class, who have hitherto been Free Traders'. Kennedy Jones, 'rather sarcastic' about the paper's equivocations, pointed out 'that not to take the strong line after Mr Balfour had spoken would hurt *The Times*'. Putting conscience above convenience, *The Times* temporized until 1 October, when it drily observed that 'there can no longer . . . be much doubt as to the fate of the Finance Bill when it leaves the House of Commons'.[1]

With Balfour's passive assistance, Garvin had nudged Northcliffe back into line. *The Times* followed lamely and at a distance. Nevertheless, the harm was done. 'Never had there been such a *volte face*,' crowed the September number of the *Review of Reviews*. 'The Anti-Budget party felt as if their own familiar friend had treacherously smitten them under the fifth rib.' On 6 August, the *Daily News* applauded the spectacle of the Unionist troops 'In Full Flight'. It was only to be expected that Liberal journalists would mercilessly salt the wounds of their opponents. But Unionist journalists emitted cries of anguish that scarcely required amplification. The *Standard* (quoted with relish by the *Nation* on 7 August) hit out at 'journals supposed to be loyal to the Unionist Cause'. That day's *Spectator* attacked the *Daily Mail* for having presented 'what almost amounted to a panegyric of the Budget. The greater part read like a speech of the Chancellor of the Exchequer in one of his more chastened moods.'

The furore had abated by 26 August, when Sandars visited the lobby and saw 'several Pressmen, . . . nearly all' of whom said 'the same thing'. The correspondent for the *Yorkshire Post* was typical in requesting permission to state 'that the Budget is in certain peril'. Sandars 'asked him why he wanted to begin on this line; and his reply was that it was being said so generally that his paper wanted to get abreast of public opinion'. Yet it took time to restore momentum and morale. Acland Hood, the Unionist chief whip, enumerated five reasons why party activists were despondent: '(1) Disappointment at High Peak', where they had been over-confident of capturing a marginal seat in one of four July by-elections; (2) The idea that in the House we have been fighting the battle of the big landlords (especially urban) only; (3) The temporary eclipse of Tariff Reform by the Budget; (4) The loss of nerve by Northcliffe, which has re-acted on our own people, and given them the notion that the Budget is enthusiastically supported in the Country; (5) The eight Dreadnoughts conceded by the government in response to a naval scare, which the Unionists were alleged to have manufactured without consideration of the cost to the taxpayer. Four of these five items were impersonal forces. The exception was

---

[1] Sandars to Garvin, 3, 12, and 21 September 1909, Garvin Papers; Chirol to Moberly Bell, 3 and 22 September 1909, *Times* Archives; Northcliffe to Garvin, 16 [September] 1909 (copy), Northcliffe Papers; Sandars to Wilfrid Short, 21 September 1909, Balfour Papers.

an outsize individual, unreasonable and unreasoning, who protruded into each of the other factors as well.[1]

For neither the first time nor the last, Northcliffe was rated as significant by political strategists for reasons less obvious than he himself imagined. It was not so much that they considered him capable of exerting direct influence as that they credited him with a supernatural sensitivity to the popular mood. While few seriously believed that his intercession might affect the outcome of a parliamentary division or an election contest, there was the mystical notion that he knew – whether by instinct or by reference to his sales accounts – the preference of the unknown man in the street. His waverings, no less than his categoric pronouncements, were therefore presumed to represent underlying currents of opinion. A. P. Nicholson might have been 'much impressed' to discover from these mid-summer paroxysms 'that *The Times* can still exercise great power', but critics recognized it as the power to generate vexation and confusion.[2]

The power generally attributed to Northcliffe was something else. Emanating from Carmelite House, not Printing House Square, it was largely reflective and constantly shifting. If only in that respect, it resembled the power of Lloyd George, another tribune of the people, but one with better credentials than those conferred by the *Daily Mail*. Both men had attained new prominence in 1908, one by acquiring *The Times* and the other by his appointment to the Exchequer in Asquith's Liberal government. As a result, relations between Fleet Street and Downing Street entered a new phase.

---

[1] Sandars to Balfour, 26 August 1909, Balfour Papers; Acland Hood to Sandars, 8 August 1909, Sandars Papers.
[2] Wilson to Northcliffe, 30 June 1909, and Nicholson to Northcliffe, 13 August 1909, Northcliffe Papers.

Four

THE PEERS, THE PEOPLE, AND THE PRESS

From 29 April 1909, when Lloyd George – in a rambling four-and-a-half-hour speech – introduced his 'War Budget . . . for raising money to wage implacable warfare against poverty and squalidness', until August 1911, when the Parliament Act relieved the House of Lords of its veto, British politics displayed an unwonted savagery. Necessitating two general elections within a single year, itself an indication of an acute crisis, the battle was fought in a variety of interlocking spheres by participants who differed as profoundly in their strategies as in their objectives. To some, the episode marked a prelude to social reconstruction. To others, it was fundamentally the resolution of a constitutional conflict. There were those who dwelled on the partisan implications, conflictingly interpreted. Not a few were impelled by the promise – or, conversely, the threat – of Irish reform. Alternately, the prolonged controversy seemed a duel between personalities and a clash between cardinal principles. By its kaleidoscopic nature, the struggle defied easy characterization and thereby became all the more critical.

'Upon the development of the political parties the effect was substantial, although not in the most obvious directions,' Roy Jenkins has concluded.[1] The same held true for the political press, which provided channels of communication to the parties and to the divergent forces within them. Used to generate heat more often than light, newspapers were considered indispensable as a means of arousing public opinion. To an extent that warrants examination, they were employed no less deliberately, and perhaps more effectively, as tools to construct parliamentary platforms.

For all their talk about 'independence' from official control, editors and proprietors proved remarkably eager to endorse policies, which the most prominent among them actively helped to frame. Some, beholden to party managers, were in no position to do otherwise. Most, however, were motivated either by their strong allegiances or by vicarious ambitions. Day after day, week after week, journalists willingly undertook to harangue the enemy and to rally the faithful. Determined to stiffen the resolve of those whom they supported, they tended instead to stiffen the resistance of those whom they

---

[1] Jenkins, *Mr Balfour's Poodle* (London, 1954), p. 186.

opposed. At most, they clarified issues and, by presenting them in the starkest terms, simplified choices. At the very least, they forced the pace of the proceedings that they then assiduously chronicled and commented upon.

In anticipation of the show-down, which took longer to occur than anyone could have predicted, parties began to put their electoral machines in order. Newspapers, being the engines of the propaganda apparatus, commanded special attention. The previous general election, a disaster for the Unionists, had left them in disarray, with their adherents in the press divided and recriminative. While the Liberal press had received a fillip from the 1906 returns, its dynamism soon dribbled away, as the fate of the short-lived *Tribune* poignantly revealed. On both sides of the party barricades, estrangements had developed – or intensified – between front-bench 'mandarins' (as Leo Maxse scornfully dubbed them) and journalistic lieutenants, who felt let down and, in no small measure, betrayed. Less concerned with the niceties of parliamentary procedure and less inclined to compromise with practicality, publicists demanded fidelity to doctrine and pleaded for bold initiatives. These tensions were most pronounced in the Unionist camp, where Tariff Reform was espoused more ardently by newspapermen (usually the confederates of party dissidents) than their chiefs would have wished. Much the same disjunction was to be found among the Liberals, although it lacked equivalent focus. L. T. Hobhouse complained that Cabinet ministers, including Lloyd George and Morley, were too reluctant to take an emphatic stand against naval expansionism. 'Could you persuade them of the necessity of saying something,' he asked C. P. Scott, 'and not leaving the whole fight to the *Guardian* with the help of the *Nation* and an occasional faint bleat from the *D. News*? They really owe something to their Press which incurs all the obloquy.'[1]

The problems afflicting political journals were basically the same, their party preferences notwithstanding. Nevertheless, on the basis of those preferences, some were able to survive while others went under. The *Westminster Gazette* and *The Times*, neither capable of converting its authority into dividends, each received a new lease on life under reconstituted ownerships. In the case of the *Westminster*, the Liberal whips were instrumental in effecting the rescue. Northcliffe, in acquiring control of *The Times*, had received welcome encouragement from high quarters, but no monetary assistance. Within eighteen months of his purchase, he alarmed Buckle and Moberly Bell by casually stating that he contemplated the disposal of that white elephant 'to some one who would run it from a purely commercial point of view' if he did not soon see an improvement in its financial prospects. To Buckle's relief, Northcliffe confessed that his 'threat . . . was merely a bogey to frighten Bell'. That it could have been taken seriously by the editor was proof of the mood of uncertainty that hung over Printing House Square. A similar uneasiness dogged Spender at the *Westminster*, Ware at the *Morning Post*, Gardiner at the *Daily News*, Parke

---

[1] Hobhouse to Scott, 7 April 1909, *Guardian* Archives.

at the *Morning Leader*, Blumenfeld at the *Daily Express*, and numerous others. Not even Garvin was immune from anxieties. Doubting (with good reason, as it turned out) the strength of Northcliffe's commitment to the *Observer*, he saw 'no sensible alternative for me but to renew my contract with the *Daily Telegraph*', for which he wrote 'every day upon every variety of subject in heaven'. Taking care to 'do nothing incompatible with my *Observer* contract', Garvin also contributed regularly to the *National Review*, the *Fortnightly Review*, and a string of dependent periodicals. '*The Times* never stops nibbling and won't bite,' he told Northcliffe. 'The *Morning Post* asks for all kinds of articles, but won't pay decently, and a precious leader page they get from their cheap and academic scribblers.' Lloyd George hit home with his sarcastic comment that Garvin ran the risk of being 'a sort of Pooh-Bah of polemics' at the expense of his 'moral influence'.[1]

Northcliffe, showing less concern for moral influence than business sense, had already begun a process of divestment, partly for medical reasons. He was not tempted, therefore, when Amery brought word from H. S. Staveley Hill, Conservative MP for Kingswinford, that the *Midland Evening News* at Wolverhampton was available 'for a reasonable sum'. Its purchase by Northcliffe would have suited Amery, who had been narrowly defeated the previous spring in a by-election at Wolverhampton East, and who hoped for another try. Though Amery kept his promise to Hill 'to do my best in the matter', Northcliffe replied by expressing regret 'that I cannot embark on any more journals, directly or indirectly. I have too many already, and am warned by my oculist that if I do not relinquish a great deal of work, I shall shortly have to be led about by a blind man's dog.'[2]

Eye trouble was an affliction that Northcliffe shared with Pearson, who was going blind. Before 1908, the two tycoons had fought over the remains of pre-existing press empires. Then, after his mortifying loss to Northcliffe in *The Times* sweepstakes, Pearson's luck and health were broken. On neither score did Northcliffe show him much pity: 'For goodness sake, don't write me so often,' he reprimanded Pomeroy Burton, the general manager of Associated Newspapers, who informed him of Pearson's disability in the mistaken belief that 'you would like to know exactly what his terrible plight is'. The properties that Pearson had founded and collected were sold off or closed down. The *Standard*, a cornerstone of Tory journalism, was kept going after April 1910 by Davison Dalziel. He also acquired the *Evening Standard*, which had absorbed the *St James's Gazette*. Put up for auction, Pearson's multiple holdings in

---

[1] Buckle to Northcliffe, 9 and 11 August 1909 (copies), *Times* Archives; Garvin to Northcliffe, 9 August 1909 (copy), Garvin Papers; Garvin to Northcliffe, 15 August [1909] and 6 December 1909, Northcliffe Papers; *also see* the November 1909 number of *The Review of Reviews*, where Stead described Garvin as 'the Gadfly of the Opposition' and 'a striking illustration of the power of the pen'.
[2] Amery's diary, 21 May 1909, Amery Papers; Northcliffe to Amery, 19 June 1909 (copy), Northcliffe Papers.

Birmingham reverted to Liberal ownership under Morrell and Starmer, who obtained assistance from local party activists and a subvention from central party funds.[1]

The *Daily Express*, Pearson's answer to Harmsworth's *Daily Mail*, revealed – at least so far as it was possible to reveal – the evolution of a complicated relationship between party investors and the political press. Pearson had founded his halfpenny morning paper in 1900, merging it with the *Morning Herald*, which he detached from the *Echo*. In 1902, retaining the nominal editorship for himself, he hired Blumenfeld 'as responsible foreign Editor' at a salary of £20 a week. Gradually, as Pearson's energies were consumed by the Tariff Reform League and the two *Standards*, Blumenfeld attained a wider jurisdiction. 'The *Express* marks my entry into the daily newspaper field, and will always be a very pet child of mine,' Pearson wrote to him at the end of 1904. 'It is very gratifying that things go so smoothly in Tudor St., while I am so much occupied with getting matters straight in Shoe Lane.'[2]

It has been presumed that, 'stricken with blindness', Pearson 'withdrew his interest from the paper' as early as 1908, leaving Blumenfeld to carry on 'with his own financial resources', consisting mainly of loans. Yet Blumenfeld's recollection, eventually transmitted by his son, was imprecise and self-serving. The transition was not nearly so abrupt, let alone complete. Pearson stayed on as managing director until 1912. 'In the past,' he reflected in a letter to Blumenfeld on 28 January 1909, 'the *Express* has ... been a private concern, owned almost entirely by myself'; it had recently become a 'Public Company', with 'a very large sum of money invested in the business by the general public, and [we] have consequently to assume responsibilities which did not exist before'. The public from which the paper drew its capital, not nearly so general as he made out, determined the responsibilities to which he grandly referred.[3]

'Historians have often speculated where the political parties got their money from at this time, itself a difficult enough topic,' A. J. P. Taylor has observed. 'They have not gone on to enquire what the parties did with the money when they got it.' In this grey area, Taylor's biography of Lord Beaverbrook breaks new ground and digs beneath it. Subsidies to newspapers, 'disguised in the form of investment in the paper's shares by some individual', became more and more common. The Liberals, as we have seen, resorted to this subterfuge in the case of the *Westminster Gazette*. The Conservatives, better able to evoke nineteenth-century precedents, institutionalized the technique. In this way, periodic amounts ('sometimes as much as £10,000 a year') were siphoned to the *Standard*, the *Observer*, the *Globe*, the *Pall Mall Gazette*, and an assortment of

---

[1] Northcliffe to Burton [1912], quoted in Pound and Harmsworth, p. 432; memorandum on the Rowntree Trust, prepared for the author by A. P. Duncum, 16 August 1978.

[2] Blumenfeld to Pearson, 8 February 1902 (draft), and Pearson to Blumenfeld, 27 December 1904, Blumenfeld Papers.

[3] Information from Sir John Elliot, quoted in Taylor, *Beaverbrook*, p. 53; Pearson to Blumenfeld, 28 January 1909, Blumenfeld Papers; Dark, *Pearson*, p. 113.

provincial supplicants. Arthur Steel-Maitland, superintending the Unionist Central Office, encouraged these newspaper rescue missions. Because it was as important to keep up appearances as to achieve results, the 'recognized channel' (as Steel-Maitland euphemistically called him) 'had to be himself a man of substance so as to make the transaction plausible; and the individual usually added some genuine investment of his own'. Successful men of business, who drew no distinction between commercial and political morality, these front-men tended to be prospective candidates or parliamentary novices, hoping to ingratiate themselves. As a rule, they were also fervent protectionists, whom Northcliffe had had in mind when he gibed at 'these wealthy people who are buying their way into the House of Commons by means of the approaching Tariff'.[1]

Sir Alexander Henderson, the Glasgow magnate who had underwritten Pearson's bid for *The Times*, was one of the public shareholders in the *Express*; he was a Liberal Unionist MP from 1898 to 1908 and again from 1913 to 1916, when he retired with a peerage. Joining him was Oliver Locker Lampson, who entered the House (where he was to sit for thirty-five years) in January 1910 as the Conservative member for Huntingdonshire North. Claude Lowther, cousin of the 5th Earl of Lonsdale, was another major subscriber; he had lost his seat for the Eskdale division of Cumberland in the Liberal floodtide of 1906, failed to reclaim it in the election of January 1910, and came back the following December. Blumenfeld was a shareholder in his own right, but also in other people's. When the company was refloated in 1915, Wilfrid Ashley (later 1st Baron Mount Temple), the Conservative MP for Blackpool, consented to have his 'name substituted for Blumenfeld's' on a block of ordinary (i.e. non-voting) shares. Steel-Maitland recruited further backing for the *Express* from Lord Howard de Walden, the sportsman and littérateur. 'Of course I do not wish to make any comparisons or distinctions between the Press on the Unionist side and the help which they all give to the Party,' he averred in his pose as honest broker. 'But it is of such importance that we should not lose the assistance of any of them, that the help, which I understand you have so kindly offered, will be of real service to the Party.' Boasting an unaudited circulation in excess of 400,000, a figure accepted more readily by advertisers than by politicians in the know, the *Express* simply could not have met its normal operating expenses without these regular transfusions.[2]

What the company records deliberately failed to disclose is that neither Locker Lampson nor Lowther paid – or paid fully – for the shares registered in

---

[1] Taylor, *Beaverbrook*, pp. 61–62; Northcliffe to Buckle, 16 May 1909 (copy), Northcliffe Papers.

[2] Steel-Maitland to Howard de Walden, 14 June [1910?] (copy), Steel-Maitland Papers; Steel-Maitland to Bonar Law, 3 August 1915, Bonar Law Papers, 51/2/2. Whereas *T. B. Browne's Advertiser's ABC* (1910) put the circulation of the *Express* at 425,000. Steel-Maitland estimated that it had risen from 200,000 to 'two hundred and thirty odd thousand daily' by 1912. Memorandum, 'Mr Locker Lampson's Scheme,' Steel-Maitland Papers.

their respective names. The 2nd Duke of Westminster, whose backstairs involvement was eventually brought to light by his solicitors, paid £5,000 towards each of their subscriptions, though without implicating himself. Other 'trustees', usually country gentlemen for whom Tory politics was an avocation, purchased debentures that bore no names. That Lord Howard de Walden was not mentioned in any legal document may be taken to imply that he defaulted on his kind offer; more probably, however, it betokens that he – like Ashley later on – contributed in Blumenfeld's name or possibly in no name at all.

There can be no doubt that this circuitous procedure, suitable to the purposes of all concerned, was undertaken at the instigation of party officials, anxious to establish firm and broad foundations for their press. The ultimate personification of this method was Beaverbrook, then Max Aitken and Unionist MP for Ashton-under-Lyne. On 2 January 1911, in response to an urgent appeal from Bonar Law, he handed Blumenfeld a cheque for £25,000 as a personal loan, and thereby inadvertently initiated a long association with the *Daily Express*. At the time, Aitken ostentatiously possessed the resources, but not yet the inclination, to cut a figure as a press lord. Before acquiring an outright interest in the *Express*, the Canadian millionaire served from 1911 to 1914 as 'a sort of trustee' for the *Globe*, which had gone to wreck under the management of Hildebrand Harmsworth. As a 'recognized channel' *par excellence*, Aitken was obliged to provide only £15,000 of the *Globe*'s £40,000 purchase price, the balance coming from anonymous Unionists or directly from party funds.[1]

The pitched battle over the Lloyd George budget enhanced the value and self-esteem of newspapers. As organs of partisan propaganda, they were closely bound to the whips' office by ties that entangled the back benches. Party managers, whether Liberals like Pease and Illingworth or Unionists like Acland Hood and Steel-Maitland, considered it imperative not only to perpetuate journals which might ordinarily have been left to languish, but also to orchestrate their performances. With Walter Long as titular president, a Budget Protest League was formed in June 1909; overlapping with the Tariff Reform League, arguably to its prejudice, it mined the same lode of Fleet Street talent.

The Liberals quickly countered with a Budget League 'so as to spread the light regarding the Budget' in the words of Haldane, its president. Amply funded by Mond and R. C. Lehmann, among others, the Budget League was directed by Sir Henry Norman, an experienced journalist who had been Liberal MP for Wolverhampton South since 1900. Masterman, another newspaperman turned politician, chaired its sub-committee for 'literature', responsible for supplying 'powder and shot' (as it was called by F. N. Curran of the *Yorkshire Evening News*) to clients in the evening and weekly press. On 9 July, Norman summoned a conference attended by members of the League execu-

[1] Beaverbrook Papers, H/16; Taylor, *Beaverbrook*, p. 53.

tive and twenty-four Liberal editors, who afterwards took tea with the Prime Minister. Within weeks, he could boast that the League's 'Weekly Column' was being taken by 140 weeklies throughout the country, and that numerous dailies had agreed to run a half-column of 'Budget Notes' compiled by Harold Spender. The *South Wales Daily News* (25 September) paid tribute to Norman's 'triumph of organisation', as did Asquith and Lloyd George. Prepared for either eventuality, Norman suggested to Liberal editors 'that your paper should appear the day after the Lords have rejected the Budget with its chief editorial and news pages in mourning – that is, with turned rules'.[1]

The Unionists, sharply divided in the merits of Tariff Reform as an antidote to the implicit 'socialism' of the budget, had the harder time mobilizing effective press support. Garvin, who had frequent occasion to discuss 'the whole Unionist position in thorough detail' with Acland Hood and Sandars, remained convinced that a protectionist programme offered Balfour the best means to turn back the Radical onslaught. Kennedy Jones, whom Garvin suspected of 'anti-Imperialist' tendencies, thought that Balfour would be better advised to exploit the misgivings of moderate Liberals (whom he imagined as likely to follow Rosebery's wayward lead) without further exacerbating tensions in Unionist ranks; striking Chirol as 'quite sanguine – in fact positive – about the result of the elections', he predicted a Unionist 'majority of anything between 20 & 100 over Radicals, Lab[our] & Nationalists combined!' Chirol, ruefully acknowledging an inability to compete with 'K.J.' for Northcliffe's ear, admitted 'that mere denunciation of the Budget especially in bearing on the propertied classes is futile', yet resisted the idea that *The Times* should pin its hopes to Tariff Reform, to which he imputed motives of 'selfishness' akin to those of the confiscatory socialists. Finding the budget 'much more objectionable in the way in which it does things than as to the things that it proposes to do', he blamed *The Times*'s dilemma and the party's predicament on Balfour, who, 'with all his brilliant abilities, ... has not hitherto shown himself a skilful leader, though he is, undoubtedly, a brilliant parliamentarian'.[2]

Other opposition journalists would not have conceded half so much in Balfour's favour. His equivocations, coupled with his willingness to confer behind closed doors with Asquith, provoked new rumblings against him. Sandars, anxious to allay the discontent, was kept busy 'to a late hour' on 14 October, seeing a succession of editors. The first on his agenda was Buckle, whose leading article on 'The Crown and the Constitution' contained 'a strong

---

[1] Asquith to Norman, 18 June 1909, Pease to Norman, 29 June 1909, memorandum of 9 July 1909, minutes of the executive committee of the Budget League, 21 July 1909, and circular letter by Norman, 24 November 1909, Norman Papers; *Daily Telegraph*, 24 June 1909.

[2] Garvin to Northcliffe, 13 August 1909, and Chirol to Northcliffe, 12 October 1909, Northcliffe Papers; Garvin to Goulding, 25 October 1907, Wargrave Papers; Chirol to Moberly Bell, 25 September 1909, and Chirol to Steed, 9 October 1909 (copy), *Times* Archives.

set of observations' which did not so much defend as clarify Balfour's position. 'After he had gone,' Sandars reported to Balfour, 'I saw representatives of the *Telegraph*, *Daily Mail*, *Daily Express* and *Standard*', all of whom had been 'hopelessly on the wrong tack' and were put 'on reasonable lines'. The prevailing impression, which Sandars endeavoured to dispel, was that Balfour was prepared 'to surrender to the Government' under threat of royal pressure.[1] It was to meet such pressure, real or imagined, that militant Tariff Reformers set to work.

The leading parliamentary protectionists held their fire, understandably reluctant to foment disruption – and thus endanger their seats – in the face of an impending election. The 'Whole Hoggers' in the press felt no comparable compunction, and strove to fill the vacuum, as they variously perceived it. However elementary, the point bears repetition that they acted, at least in part, out of a professional obligation. Unlike politicians, who might retire into a guarded silence, newspapermen were required to address their publics at appointed intervals. Forced to meet deadlines, they could not wait for the dust to settle before making their pronouncements. There was no time for their passions to cool. Yet there was a good deal more to their truculence than merely that.

The centre of gravity had shifted more markedly in the Unionist press than in the party as a whole. Free Trade Unionism, which remained an intellectually substantive force at Westminster (and, to a lesser extent, a factor in scattered constituencies), had ceased to count for much in the helter-skelter world of political journalism. Led by Frederick Huth Jackson, a director of the Bank of England, 'a group of . . . capitalists' explored the possibility of buying the *Daily Graphic* or, better still, the *Standard*, and running it as 'a daily organ of central opinion'. Neither proposal bore fruit: the *Standard* held to a protectionist course through changes of ownership; the *Daily Graphic* stood as a house divided, with an editor, W. A. Ackland – who advocated Free Trade and House of Lords reform – 'worried by Directors who are Tariff Reformers' and diehards. Hulton's retreat from Free Trade orthodoxy in Lancashire has been noted. In April 1909, the *Glasgow Herald*, an adherent of Free Trade in 1906, pledged itself 'in future [to] support Mr Balfour in regard to Tariff Reform and also advocate a strong naval policy'. Having kept close contact with his home town and former consitituency, Bonar Law was invited to contribute protectionist articles to the *Herald*: 'these can be published anonymously, if necessary,' he was advised. Whether or not he complied (that the request was renewed in 1911 suggests that he did not turn it down flat), he typified those disgruntled members of the opposition who dared not proclaim on

---

[1] Sandars to Balfour, 14 October 1909, Balfour Papers; Strachey to Jackson, 1 March 1909 (copy), Strachey Papers. On the Liberal side, the *Daily News* infuriated Burns by its implacable resistance to any 'surrender . . . to the pretensions of the Peers' and by its determination to force a confrontation at any cost. Burns to Gardiner, 2 November 1909, Gardiner Papers.

public platforms what their supporters unabashedly declared in print.[1]

While organs like the Manchester *Daily Dispatch*, the *Glasgow Herald*, and the *Spectator* edged into line behind Balfour, whom they saw to offer the best available prospect for Tory latitudinarianism, the organs of Chamberlainite fundamentalism moved beyond him. Courting official rebuke, the *Morning Post*, the *Standard*, and the *National Review* hoisted to varying heights the tattered flag of rebellion. For them, Balfour was no hope, but an impediment to the reconstruction of the party on a new right-wing axis. While few of them cared to admit – even among themselves – that their aim was anything more than to strengthen Balfour's limp hand, the implications were clear enough.

The *Morning Post* hesitated to go too far, once the slide in its readership became a matter of 'frank concern'. In September 1909, when Edward Goulding, the Conservative MP for Worcester City, claimed to have 'heard that the line we were taking against the Party leaders was sending the circulation down', Ware was 'able to laugh in his face without acting'; in mid-October, after the business manager had corroborated Goulding's prognosis, Ware could no longer laugh with conviction. The chief difficulty, or so he airily suggested to Lady Bathurst, was that the paper got dragged into controversies on the coat-tails of its two leader-writers, Wilkinson and Jebb. Wilkinson, 'a first-rate man', was away from his desk for long stretches while he fulfilled his academic duties as Chichele professor of military history at Oxford; his articles were often stale by the time they were delivered to the office, and his views could be characterized as 'being *de*structive rather than *con*structive'. Jebb's capacity for destruction was far greater. At 'a very considerable financial sacrifice', he undertook to 'stop the rot' by offering himself as an independent candidate at Marylebone East, where Lord Robert Cecil was the incumbent. Far from disapproving, Ware applauded Jebb's 'disinterested strength', which he confidently expected to administer a 'fearful shock' to the party leaders, Balfourites and Tariff Reformers alike. 'It is a great score for us to be able to show that we not only write things but are able actually to do them,' he told his proprietor.[2]

The contest at Marylebone East has been described as 'the most acrimonious of the five Unionist intra-party conflicts' in the general election of January 1910. The outbreak of local hostilities long anticipated the formal campaign, which oddly figured as an anticlimax. Jebb's insurgency was sufficiently successful to persuade Cecil to withdraw with dignity, but not to secure his own adoption by the Marylebone Constitutional Union. That association turned instead to Lord Charles Beresford, who had represented the constituency back in the 1880s. Condemning Jebb as 'a dangerous lunatic', Beresford decided to

---

[1] Harold Cox to Cromer, 31 January 1910, Cromber Papers, PRO/FO 633/19/9–10; James Kennedy to Bonar Law, 4 April 1909, and F. Harcourt Kitchin to Bonar Law, 11 and 15 September 1909, and 31 October 1911, Bonar Law Papers, 18/5/94, 18/5/102–103, and 18/7/205.

[2] Ware to Lady Bathurst, 4 and 15 October 1909, Bathurst Papers.

stand at Portsmouth, a seat more appropriate to his naval image, rather than to risk a clash with the *Morning Post*. As second choice, the Unionists at Marylebone selected James Boynton, a moderate protectionist who was able to draw on residual Cecilian support. Twice bypassed, Jebb none the less persevered. 'So Jebb & the *Morning Post* are to have their way in Marylebone. I wonder what will come of it,' Austen Chamberlain mused to his step-mother.[1]

In the event, nothing came of it: Jebb polled 702 votes to finish in third place behind Boynton and a Liberal contender. However, the circumstances were vastly more significant than the showing, especially as a commentary on the pretensions of the press. To all intents and purposes, the *Morning Post* was Jebb's party platform, and thus furnished a precedent for later electoral interventions by Lords Beaverbrook and Rothermere. On 6 November, the paper announced 'that there was a movement on foot to start a Unionist Democratic League on the basis of Marylebone and Oxford', where another unsuccessful challenge was mounted against the candidacy of Lord Hugh Cecil. Encouraged by 'letters from people who took it seriously and wished to be enrolled', Ware foresaw the growth of 'an organisation ready to back' Jebb and others 'should the Unionist party – as seems certain – definitely refuse them support or recognition'. Envisioning a movement 'clothed in Tariff Reform, National Service and Unionism (i.e. union of Classes, Nation and Empire)', he was confident that 'it would spread like wildfire, particularly among those Unionists whom Mr Balfour has alienated since Mr Chamberlain dropped out of the fight'. So eager was he 'to try my hand at controlling it' that he wrote to Lady Bathurst on the 8th, asking her to consider 'making me Manager ... and appointing a more sedate and less pugnacious Editor' in order to preserve 'arms' length' between the paper and the proposed organization. 'Please don't think this League is just a sudden whim,' he implored; 'the sort of thing has been in my mind for long.' Quite apparently, it was not in Lady Bathurst's mind, for, three days later, Ware mollified her with firm assurances that he would 'do nothing without consulting you & in any case I should oppose with every power at my disposal any action that might lessen the chances of success of our Party at the General Election'. Although the paper persisted in its support of Jebb's forlorn candidacy, the idea of a breakaway movement was shelved. All the same, Sandars found it difficult to forgive Ware's 'vain and disloyal action in East Marylebone, where in order to advertise his own contentions, he did his best to lose us one of the safest seats in London'.[2]

With the same objectives and rhetoric, the *Standard* set up a Working-Men Candidates Fund. One of its beneficiaries, John Dumphreys, captured Bermondsey from the Liberals (who soon regained the seat in the general election)

[1] Neal Blewett, *The Peers, the Parties and the People: The General Elections of 1910* (London, 1972), pp. 219–20; Beresford to Balfour, 6 November 1909, Balfour Papers; Austen Chamberlain to Mary Chamberlain, 22 October 1909, Chamberlain Papers, 4/1/459.

[2] Ware to Lady Bathurst, 8 and 11 November 1909, Bathurst Papers; Sandars to Balfour, 26 January 1910, Balfour Papers.

in an October by-election. 'His victory has given an immense impetus to the movement for democratising the Unionist Party,' exulted the December number of Maxse's *National Review*, which greatly preferred working-class Tories to blueblooded Cecils on the one hand, but adamantly opposed payment for MPs on the other, Gwynne, the editor of the *Standard*, collected over £6,000 through his paper. His purse, together with his protectionist principles, commended him to other malcontents, including Ware, whom he was to succeed as editor of the *Morning Post*. Amery, always eclectic in his memberships, was joint treasurer of the Trades Unionist Tariff Reform Association, dedicated to the advancement of Maxse's proposition that 'working class Conservatives are neither Cobdenites nor Socialists'. It would be useful, he reckoned to Maxse, 'to collar hold some of Gwynne's fund in order to run one of our people. If we can get even two or three good Unionist working men into the House it will make a lot of difference.' The party whips dared take no exception to the idea, which carried the blessing of Lord Milner; but they revealed their wariness by allocating constituencies which were, for the most part, impregnable Liberal strongholds.[1]

On 30 November, the House of Lords inflicted a crushing defeat on the Lloyd George budget. Parliament was prorogued on 3 December and, a week later, Asquith opened the election campaign with a rousing speech at the Albert Hall, from which women were carefully excluded as a precaution against suffragette demonstrations. The press on either side was not so easily controlled. At the outset, journalists attempted to close ranks, but solidarity wore thin as the gruelling campaign wore on. Garvin, at his most helpful, urged Sandars to arrange for prominent Unionists to take to the rostrum on Saturdays so that 'not only my own paper but all the cheaper Sunday papers with a vast total circulation' could be 'stuffed with speeches on the day of the week when democracy lazes and reads'. In the *Observer*, he coined the slogan, 'A New Government for the New Year!' Strachey, equally 'convinced that it is the essential duty, in the interests of the country, to turn out the present Government', volunteered 'to use every power at my command to secure that end'. Reversing its stand of 1906, the *Spectator* called upon Unionist Free Traders to support Tariff Reformers over any Liberal. For all that, it suffered abuse in 'the Tariff Reform Press', particularly the *Daily Express*. LeSage of the *Daily Telegraph*, awaiting Asquith's kick-off speech, stood ready to 'deal with him in the temperate Christian tone we always adopt towards a bitter political opponent'.[2]

[1] *Standard*, 14 December 1909; *Morning Post*, 19 November 1909; Amery to Maxse, 12 November 1909, Maxse Papers; Blewett, p. 272.

[2] Garvin to Sandars, 29 November 1909, and Strachey to Balfour, 30 November 1909, Balfour Papers; LeSage to Garvin, 8 December 1909, Garvin Papers. Garvin's advice to Sandars was later adopted by R. H. S. Crossman, who 'realized that Saturday midday is the ideal time to launch a statement if you want publicity, since you get it in the Saturday evening papers, the

Northcliffe had returned from his travels in time for the struggle. He was 'unfortunately very unwell since landing', Garvin informed Sandars, 'but from his pillow he is driving things splendidly, taking in hand himself the Lancashire campaign; and the *Daily Mail* as a political organ was never half so good as now'. As Northcliffe personally detailed his master-plan to Sandars, it included 'special editions of my *Daily Mail* for Lancashire, East Anglia and North East England during the Election. We shall also concentrate on Liverpool.' Another of his projects was to 'gather together, perhaps £2,000' to 'run a temporary evening newspaper – one edition only during the Election' – at Newcastle. Taken with the idea, Sandars offered him 'a grant of £500 from our Funds' if it would 'be of any service'. Northcliffe's physical ailments were as nothing to the animus he bore towards Hulton and the 17th Earl of Derby (formerly Lord Stanley) in Manchester. Despite their agreement to 'issue very strong Tariff Reform articles' in the *Daily Dispatch* and the *Evening Chronicle*, those papers were allegedly 'advertising themselves on immense placards in Manchester as *Independent*', and their weakness laid open the Lancashire market to the northern edition of the *Daily News*. Northcliffe's view that Derby had 'been very badly out manoeuvred by the enemy' was not disputed by Sandars, who recalled having warned Acland Hood that 'Eddy Stanley' (as Derby was still known in top circles) 'had not qualifications, either of character or technical knowledge, to guide so difficult an affair as he has undertaken'.[1]

More than ever, Northcliffe required – and received – special handling. S. J. Pryor, his 'watchdog', acquainted him with the discourtesy shown 'at the Conservative Central Office when a *Times* reporter called to get a copy of Mr Balfour's Election Address'. More than 'a case in point of where *The Times* is losing the privileges it previously had', the incident gave evidence of 'very poor Election organisation' with respect to newspaper publicity. Late in the day, the Unionist Party managers started to build the 'more practical relations' which Northcliffe enviously saw to 'have been cultivated on the Liberal side by Sir Henry Norman'. By arrangement with Northcliffe, Pryor spent an hour and a half advising Sandars, who consequently missed his 'train home: but it was well worth it'. In addition, J. Percival Hughes, the principal agent at the Central Office, 'had interviews with the leading London daily Unionist newspapers with a view to obtaining better reports of speeches from our leading speakers'. During the third week of December, he canvassed party spokesmen for lists of their forthcoming public engagements so that editors could be properly alerted. Sandars admitted to Northcliffe that 'the nature of our old traditions with regard to the Press' posed an obstacle to effective collaboration, though

---

Sunday papers and the Monday papers, if it's any good'. Entry of 3 November 1960, Crossman, *Backbench Diaries* (ed. J. Morgan; London, 1981), p. 898.

[1] Northcliffe to Sandars [December 1909] (copy), and Sandars to Northcliffe, 25 December 1909, Northcliffe Papers; Garvin to Sandars, 1 December 1909, and Sandars to Balfour, 22 December 1909, Balfour Papers.

his 'own desire' was 'to attach to our Central Office some machinery which could establish both an intimate and general communication with the higher authorities of the friendly Newspapers'. Instructed by Pryor that there was 'no time to establish any Press bureau or system with our office before the Election is over', he tried to remedy the deficiency by issuing a series of confidential bulletins. Garvin, the recipient of one of them, dismissed it as 'a mass of verbiage like a string of inferior leading articles useless to newspapers, and though marked "Confidential" contain[ing] no confidences at all'.[1]

To better effect, and in harness with Garvin, Sandars worked to stabilize Northcliffe. That was almost a full-time job. 'One word of conclusion,' he wound up a lengthy review of electoral strategy and party affairs on 13 December:

> Let me say how admirably our Party is served by the *Daily Mail*. It is the most potent auxiliary. Everyone reads it: it is a brief for all our speakers. Its arguments, its facts, its criticisms supply the best and most modern ammunition. I told Mr Balfour of its leading articles last week, and he said he would read them if I wd. have them put together for him: and he will.

Conscience would not have allowed Sandars to pay the same compliment to *The Times*. That was just as well, given that the *Daily Mail* was closer to Northcliffe's heart. Only three days later, Sandars 'made a strong representation to Northcliffe about the great prominence' that *The Times* had accorded to a slashing oration by Churchill, whom Garvin considered an egregious self-publicist. To atone, *The Times* responded 'handsomely' to Lord Curzon's next platform appearance. Garvin and Sandars, regarding Northcliffe as something of an innocent, were 'determined ... to save him from the embraces of Winston who flatters him & toadies him in a sickening way, and then laughs at him behind his back'. In moments of exasperation, Sandars could 'only wish Northcliffe knew as much about politics as he does about business'.[2]

The bond between Garvin and Sandars was a common devotion to Balfour. When Amery mildly suggested that the Unionist leader might be induced to 'come out more strongly', Garvin rejected the notion as 'not only useless but unpardonable to A.J.B.', who 'alone saved tariff reform and everything else in August and September, when everything was at stake and the *Morning Post* was in favour of surrender – as bad as *The Times* or worse'. Perpetually resentful of *The Times*, which he denounced to Sandars at year's end as 'a national curse', Garvin was powerless to deflect its defeatist course. Northcliffe

---

[1] Pryor to Northcliffe, 11 December 1909, Northcliffe to Sandars [December 1909] (copy), Sandars to Northcliffe, 18 December 1909, and Garvin to Northcliffe, 3 January 1910, Northcliffe Papers; Hughes to Bonar Law, 21 December 1909, Bonar Law Papers, 18/5/108; Sandars to Balfour, 18 December 1909, Balfour Papers.

[2] Sandars to Northcliffe, 13 December 1909, Northcliffe Papers; Sandars to Balfour [16 December 1909] and 18 December 1909, Balfour Papers.

was 'in Paris on his way to [a] rest cure', he lamented. 'I can't bother him now and "K.J." is in Glasgow', attending to business matters. 'But remember,' he told Sandars, 'they have no Editorial Control: and my absolute conviction is that those who have the Control desire a Unionist disaster in order to justify an attitude on the Budget to which they had not the courage to stick.' On 6 January, after *The Times* had given short shrift to Balfour's 'excellent' speech at Hanley on naval preparedness, Garvin summoned up the courage to intrude on Northcliffe's 'hibernation'. Professing that he 'could only talk freely' to his chief 'on paper just because you are not likely to take it amiss or to misunderstand' his motives, he offered an analysis of the situation at Printing House Square. 'There are two very distinct kinds of impartiality – one real and illuminating, the other spurious and irritating,' he argued. *The Times*, specializing in the latter, produced 'frigid, niggling, reluctant stuff, affecting judgment yet devoid of power'. Of course, he appreciated all Northcliffe had achieved: 'I would have to be a very blind journalist no[t] to see that you have done wonders with it – more than I for one . . . had thought possible.' But the fact remained that, in its political stance, *The Times* had withstood Northcliffe's impact. As A. P. Nicholson, its parliamentary correspondent, put it, the task was to 'change a brick wall into a yielding mattress'.[1]

Sandars had his own opportunity to confront Northcliffe, who was between rest cures, on Friday, 21 January. After a weekend's recuperation, he dictated a 'very confidential' account for the benefit of Balfour.[2] At Northcliffe's invitation, Sandars had arrived 'at a quarter to ten in the evening and stayed till half past twelve!!', again missing his train. His host

> was very interesting, as he usually is, especially when his conversation has reference to those matters which relate to his own special province.
>
> He began by commenting upon our successes, and contended that Garvin had been right throughout. He argued that now that the Counties had got hold of Tariff Reform, they would never rest until that policy was accomplished, and he seemed confident that it would only be a question of time before that cause was espoused by the Northern constituencies. He laid stress on the value of your speeches, which he considered were the outstanding features of the campaign and which had, he said, attracted a widespread admiration not confined to the people of these islands.
>
> Our conversation drifted to the attitude of *The Times*. He said that he had more than once when abroad telegraphed to remonstrate with the occasional ambiguity of view which marked the leading articles in that paper; and that while an improvement was at once recorded, the paper subsequently showed

[1] Amery to Garvin, 18 November 1909, and Garvin to Northcliffe, 6 January 1910 (copy), Garvin Papers; Garvin to Amery, 30 November 1909, Amery Papers; Garvin to Sandars, 31 December 1909, Balfour Papers; Nicholson to Butes, 4 March 1910, Northcliffe Papers.

[2] The two following paragraphs, except where otherwise noted, are based on Sandars to Balfour, 24 January 1910, Balfour Papers.

a tendency to drift away from a tone of clear pronouncement. He reflected with some disapproval upon the attitude of Buckle and his staff, observing that they wanted what he called 'vision', and he contended that the whole policy of the paper, when left alone, indicated the extraordinarily old fashioned system upon which it had been worked for generations.

From further remarks, Sandars gathered that much more could not be reasonably expected from Northcliffe, whose immediate concern with *The Times* was essentially mercantile.

As always, business and politics went hand in hand in the conduct of the Harmsworth press. *The Manchester Courier*, was 'doing well out of the Election', having netted 'about £1,300 extra in payments and advertisements', which included a subvention of '£500 from the Conservative Headquarters and the £200 ... collected ... from the Candidates' in the vicinity.[1] According to Northcliffe, *The Times* had already 'secured a great deal of the advertisements of the *Morning Post*', and he anticipated that, 'before long', the spoils would be divided between himself and Lord Burnham. This had happened because of 'the extraordinary folly of the *Morning Post*. Owing to its policy of quarrelling with the Unionist leaders and the organisation of the party ..., they had lost and were losing a great deal of money.' Northcliffe, who considered it a case of just retribution, 'could not conceive why a paper which in former days had been such a fine property, should deliberately throw away the fruits of an established success'. He entertained 'no opinion of Fabian Ware either as a practical man or as one of journalistic ability', but 'spoke slightingly of the *Standard*, and said that its part in the daily press was quite insignificant'. On this score, Sandars 'ventured with respect to demur', pointing out 'the value of the assistance it had rendered to the Party during this election'. This interjection gave pause to Northcliffe, who wrote the next day to temper his judgment: 'I think I did not do justice to my friend Pearson and his newspapers. I should like to say that I believe his newspapers have had a very excellent effect during these elections.' That was hardly a retraction in that it dealt collectively with Pearson's properties and omitted any specific reference to the *Standard*.

Northcliffe, whose indisposition was diagnosed by Sandars as 'indigestion, probably caused by over-work', had obviously endeared himself to Garvin, who thrilled anew to his appeal. Apologizing to Sanders for a 'silence this last fortnight', he wrote on 29 January: 'Every bit of me was occupied by our business and by newspapers and by Northcliffe in one way or another.... The said N. grows in my affections.' In the *Observer* and the *Daily Telegraph* (where he had just paid Balfour 'the best tribute I could'), as well as behind the scenes, Garvin had given indefatigable service to his party. No Unionist, and certainly no Unionist journalist, had done more. Now, he could relax. The election had been fought, and he had 'helped to manoeuvre' Northcliffe 'into a

[1] S. R. Crapnell to Sutton, 12 January 1910, Northcliffe Papers.

real rest where they even take away his pencils; and if he is well and cheerful and assured of more enjoyment of life, he will do priceless things for us'. For the treatment of his mysteriously persistent 'neurasthenia', Northcliffe entered a London nursing home, where his newspaper diet was restricted to the *Daily Mail* and the *Observer*. It was 'like a prison', he scribbled (perhaps with a purloined pencil) from his confinement. His withdrawal and the return of a diminished Liberal majority restored a semblance of calm in Fleet Street.[1]

* * *

Polling extended from 14 January until 9 February 1910, resulting in the highest proportional turn-out of voters of any twentieth-century general election. The campaign, hinging on the constitutional issue though hardly confined to it, was fiercely fought on all sides. From the moment that the House of Lords rejected the budget, journalists had their work cut out for them. C.E. Montague, the chief leader-writer for the *Manchester Guardian* (and, incidentally, Scott's son-in-law), led 'rather a dog's life' through the long ordeal; 'with all the speeches there are to be read every night', he found it impossible to 'write any imperishable masterpieces in my mornings'. Nevertheless, as he remarked to Francis Dodd, it was 'good to have something worth trying for in politics', and the excitement gripped him.[2]

The politicians, anxious to whip up support, saw to it that the pace of newspaper activity did not slacken. On the one hand, they prodded their own publicists to perform more vigorously; on the other, they indicted their opponents on the grounds of journalistic evidence. Lloyd George, reciting the saga of his budget in a speech at the National Liberal Club on 3 December, recalled: 'All the weightiest papers on the Conservative side were against it.' Among the offenders, he counted *The Times*, the *Birmingham Post*, the *Glasgow Herald*, the *Spectator*, and 'I think the *Yorkshire Post*'. Edited by the ubiquitous Garvin, the maddest of the 'Mad Mullahs', the *Observer* 'was the rabidest of the lot'. The *Daily Mail*, having 'hesitated, . . . only came in at the last moment', when it 'placed at the disposal of the wreckers that passion for accuracy of statement which has been so dear to it'. According to Lloyd George's interpretation, these organs of intransigence had prevailed over 'the wise men, . . . the reflecting men of the Unionist Party', whom he presumed still to exist.[3]

It suited Lloyd George's purpose to assign culpability, and selectively at that, to allegedly irresponsible – though persuasive – journalists rather than to the official Unionist leaders, whom he would have to confront in the parlia-

[1] Garvin to Sandars, 29 January 1910, Sandars Papers; Pound and Harmsworth, pp. 391–92.
[2] Montague to Dodd, 8 December 1909, Montague-Dodd Correspondence, Add. MSS. 45, 910, fol. 48.
[3] *Daily Chronicle*, 4 December 1909.

mentary arena. Garvin, who practised his craft anonymously, was singled out for special condemnation, and thought it best to lie low for a time so as to be 'free to give ... denial'. The *Daily Mail* (4 December) professed unconcern either on his part or its own: Lloyd George's 'attack ... does not disturb our peace of mind, and we have no doubt that Mr J. L. Garvin, the distinguished editor of the *Observer*, whom the Chancellor also assailed in a very unusual manner, is capable of taking care of himself'. To deny complicity would have been to disclaim influence, and that was something that no newspaper was prepared to do, even had circumstances permitted. Yet, to play safe, the *Daily Mail* shifted its emphasis from the constitutional dispute to the more emotive theme of naval defence. From 13 to 24 December, it featured a series of daily articles by Robert Blatchford, whose homespun socialism proved no deterrent to chauvinism. 'Nothing that has appeared in the *Daily Mail* in recent years has attracted more attention, has aroused more discussion, or has been followed by our readers with closer interest,' the paper asserted on the 23rd. Reprinted as a penny pamphlet, Blatchford's inflammatory warnings against the German peril had sold 1,600,000 copies by 22 January 1910, and nearly a quarter of a million complimentary copies were distributed by various party agencies. The *Observer* and other Unionist journals likewise appreciated the value of the naval question as a rallying cry.[1]

The *Morning Post* tended to plough its own furrow, even with regard to the naval issue, on which it faithfully followed Beresford and distanced itself from 'the Fisher press'. At 'a meeting of picked Tariff Reformers', including Bonar Law and F. E. Smith, Ware demanded pride of place for the cause of protectionism. He was convinced that his political associates 'all agreed with me but most of them have to obey Balfour in the hope of getting office or because of their seats'. That, however, seemed to him no reason for the *Morning Post* to reorder its priorities, especially as advertising revenues were 'looking up again'. The *Standard*, without any commercial stimulus, also revived the tactics of 1906. In the closing months of Pearson's ownership, it was sued for libel by the Cadburys over its charge that they had exploited slave labour in the cocoa plantations of Portuguese Africa. Represented in court by Isaacs, with Carson appearing for the defence, the plaintiffs were awarded a farthing damages plus costs. More willingly than certain Radical critics, *The Times* credited the Cadburys' good faith, but expressed 'regret' that the *Daily News*, a 'newspaper which was not unconnected with them, did not reserve a little of the fierce indignation which it poured upon Chinese slavery' in South Africa 'for the unmistakable form of it which existed in San Thomé and Principe'.[2]

[1] Garvin to Northcliffe, 6 December 1909, Northcliffe Papers; *Daily Mail*, 4 and 23 December 1909, and 22 January 1910.
[2] Ware to Lady Bathurst, undated fragment [probably February 1910], Bathurst Papers; *The Times*, 7 December 1909.

Reynolds's News, its own outpourings restricted to the sabbath day, complained on 2 January 1910: 'The daily newspapers have ceased to be retailers of news – they are merely mammoth political pamphlets of the most partisan type.' On the basis of a quantitative analysis, Neal Blewett has concurred with this assessment:[1] 'For eight weeks from 3 December 1909', when Lloyd George spoke at the National Liberal Club, 'the press was literally dominated by the elections. . . . Only the death of Leopold of the Belgians on 17 December 1909 and the great Paris floods of late January 1910 displaced the first election as the major news topic of the day.' By Blewett's calculation, the *Manchester Guardian* led the morning pack, devoting 36,900 column inches, or 40 per cent of its editorial space, to election coverage during this eight-week period; this reflected not only the strength of its commitment and connections, but also the fact that the quality provincial dailies, 'with their unrivalled local sources', grasped at the 'opportunity to compete with the expanding national press'. The *Standard* came second, with 26,000 column inches or 29 per cent of its editorial content. The *Daily Telegraph* and the *Daily Chronicle* followed with 25,700 column inches (23 per cent) and 24,200 column inches (39 per cent) respectively. Directly below, with wider columns, came the *Daily News*, *The Times*, and the *Morning Post*, ranging from 23,500 to 20,400 inches. The *Daily Mail* (11,500 column inches or 24 per cent) was in tenth place, behind the *Morning Leader* and the *Daily Express*, but ahead of the *Daily Graphic* and the *Daily Mirror*. Bearing in mind that the allocation of space 'in any newspaper was chiefly a function of its size', the most remarkable factor was that 'no London morning newspaper gave less than one-fifth of its total editorial space to election material'.

Yet, as Blewett himself has readily acknowledged, such a quantitative analysis can neither establish 'the quality of press partisanship' nor elucidate 'factional undertones'. While it provides conclusive testimony to 'an extraordinary preoccupation with things electoral', it does not take account of certain discrepancies. The threepenny *Times*, along with its penny rivals, had relatively more space to make available and, besides, a tradition of electoral involvement to uphold. The halfpenny morning dailies, like the greater number of evening and Sunday journals, were restricted on both counts. With the exception of the *Morning Leader*, the Liberal papers were 'more politicised than the Unionist', owing to the 'Radical tendency to political engagement, the Liberals' idealistic belief in the efficacy of reasoned argument, and perhaps a desire to offset their numerical inferiority, as well as particular personal factors'. Nevertheless, the degree of politicization varied from case to case, sometimes from day to day, with effects that frequently contradicted the official party line. Exactly the same held true on the Unionist side of journalism, where 'particular personal factors' were equally manifest against the contrasting background of an overwhelming numerical superiority. As for the

[1] Blewett, pp. 309–11, provides the framework for the ensuing paragraphs.

suggestion that one party had a more pronounced tendency towards political engagement or a stronger 'belief in the efficacy of reasoned argument', the nature of the political press would admit to no such distinctions.

In the final reckoning, quality of support surely mattered more than quantity, though it notoriously resists statistical measurement. Blewett, having expertly quantified 'this flow of words', does not pretend to be able

> to determine the impact ... on the voter. The bias of most of the press was such that it is difficult to imagine that it provided much help to the genuinely undecided. Rather than change votes, it is more likely that it confirmed existing prejudices and provided rationalisations for established loyalties.

Even that conclusion must logically depend on what was said, with what emphasis or urgency, and on whose authority. The number of grey column inches allotted to a political appeal might have counted as an irrelevance or, worse, a disadvantage. About the rôle of the press, as distinct from its hypothetical impact, Blewett 'can be a little more definite'. By the slogans to which they gave currency, newspapers 'provided the cues and tokens of party loyalty and partisan reactions'. Furthermore, they were instrumental 'in structuring the national debate', as when the Unionist press deflected attention 'from the constitutional issue to fiscal and naval questions'. Neither of these contributions should be discounted. All the same, neither necessarily correlates with any scale of newspaper support.

The intensity of press feeling was probably more of a determinant than its amplitude, much less its distribution. For antithetical reasons, newspapers declared in unison that crucial issues were at stake, and that the future of the nation depended on the outcome. 'Never have the two parties been separated by differences so vital and profound,' insisted the *Morning Post* (3 January 1910); 'never has there been so wide a gulf between their professed aims and between the policies for which they are appealing.' Chesterton, writing in the *Daily News* on 15 January, distinguished it as 'the one historical election that I have seen since I was born, and perhaps the only one I shall see before I die'. A *soi-disant* Cavalier, he was more modest than the latter-day Puritans on that paper who, the same day, hailed the contest as the most momentous since the Civil War. The *Daily Mail* (15 January), evincing an uncharacteristic regard for history, drew a more apposite analogy with the events of 1832.

Among Liberal metropolitan dailies, according to Blewett, the *Morning Leader* was unsurpassed in its 'crudities'. More surprisingly, he also found that 'no Unionist papers equalled the savagery of the penny *Daily Telegraph*, most virulent of all the Unionist press in its assault on the Ministry and the Ministers'. One would have expected the contrary from the *Telegraph*, dowdy in appearance and stolid in its Toryism; but a sense of Balfourite desperation, combined with promptings from Garvin, shook its equanimity. Execrating the

'Yellow Parliament' of 1906, 'born in the mendacity of the pigtail elections' and marked by 'a policy of social bribes and Imperial betrayal' (11 January), the paper reserved its compliments exclusively for Unionist statesmen. On 15 January, it published Balfour's 'message to the country', accompanied by a 'joint manifesto' signed by him and Joseph Chamberlain: 'No Englishman with an ear to hear the trumpet call of patriotism can fail to respond to the ringing summons of the Unionist leaders,' the *Telegraph* proclaimed in a leading article.

The *Daily News* reversed the formula, memorializing the late Parliament and castigating those who aimed to set back the clock. 'It might have been said that the judgment of 1906 was the judgment of men merely weary of the rule of a discredited party,' it wrote on 19 January, in the wake of inconclusive returns from the boroughs and before the earliest county returns were declared:

> We know now that the judgment was positive and not negative, and that it expressed the determination of industrial England to open a new era in which the conquests of the past should be preserved, but the work be taken in hand of producing a new England, in which every citizen should have the hope of a larger life.

To assist the rural voter in his choice, a series on 'Mr Balfour's Logic' underscored the contradictions in the Unionist leader's successive statements on the topic of agricultural protection. 'I think this appeal by the *Daily News* is one of the wickedest things I have seen,' fumed Balfour's secretary, who conveyed word from Iwan-Müller that a 'letter to Harry Lawson was *very* helpful' in getting the *Daily Telegraph* to fight back.[1] Its leading article on 18 January, entitled 'Mr Balfour on Election Issues', was everything (and more) that its subject could have wished:

> By the stupendous majority of 13,284, a record in the annals of the constituency, the City returns Mr Balfour to the House of Commons, and reminds his followers thoughout the country of the greatness of their debt to their leader. Whatever the final issue at the polls, this mighty struggle has brought a new life and soul and confidence into our party. . . . In this hard business, as never before in his life, . . . he not only commands the confidence of all the elements of his party . . ., but he has earned and won that affection which comes in the end to all statesmen who 'look forward, persevering to the last', an affection which forms their best reward.

It is difficult to credit that, by this stage, experienced political commentators of either persuasion could have seriously believed the rhetoric that they continued to spew forth. Whether they believed that it could affect electoral

---

[1] Sandars to Balfour, 19 January 1910, Balfour Papers.

behaviour in remaining contests is, of course, another matter. Although the *Daily Chronicle* (19 January) and the *Westminster Gazette* (20 January) were agreed that the Liberals stood to incur proportionately fewer losses in the counties, which the *Daily Telegraph* (20 January) hotly disputed, the prospects for an absolute Liberal majority were fast fading. Marlowe of the *Daily Mail* was proved correct in his assumption that the Liberals had been 'overdoing their confidence and that when the "silent voter" is heard from he may astonish them'; yet he had erred in supposing that the 'silent voter' would reveal a decided preference for Unionism.[1] The results were chequered and sufficiently ambiguous to allow both sides to claim a victory of sorts. The Liberals, shorn of their massive majority, emerged with 275 seats, two more than the Unionists; with backing from eighty-two Irish Nationalists and forty Labour MPs, their lease on office was renewed. One of the more surprising Liberal casualties was Norman, who had neglected his constituency at Blackburn to concentrate upon the Budget League and who had to wait until the next election to return to Westminster. The Unionists, having recovered so much of the ground they had lost in 1906, were curiously elated. 'The absolute majority is smashed, pulverised, annihilated,' trumpeted the *Observer* (23 January). 'Mr Asquith and his government must exist in subjection to Mr Redmond,' the Irish parliamentary leader, 'or they cannot exist at all.'

J. A. Spender quickly took the point. 'We shall go to smash', he predicted to Bryce, unless the militant Radicals accommodated themselves to the constraints of the new situation. On 25 January, the *Westminster Gazette* endorsed *The Times*'s proposal for a 'Round Table Conference between the leaders' to work out 'a policy of compromise upon some subjects, and abstention from others'. Spender appealed to Gardiner for assistance from the *Daily News*, telling him 'quite privately' that 'the Tory strategy' was 'to get in, to propose a hundred million loan for the navy, to dissolve again, & to make the election turn on this – in fact to hold a Khaki election'. There was no doubt in Spender's mind 'that we ought to prevent this at all costs ... for reasons of international & domestic politics alike'. He had not given up hope that Asquith would invoke 'Royal support for a Bill giving finance to the Commons', after which the Liberals could 'advance to the Second Chamber question more at leisure'. That the curtailment of aristocratic power should be the first order of business ('grievance before supply') struck him as impracticable. The King, like most Unionists and many Liberals, was disinclined to interpret the narrow election result as a mandate for drastic constitutional change, and could hardly be expected to 'give guarantees on the legislative veto Bill', yet to be drafted. To coerce him would 'be playing a very bad card'. Spender's advice was 'that we journalists should not make it too difficult for Asquith to hold on', lest 'we should not even get the Budget through'. Gardiner dismissed these arguments

---

[1] Marlowe to Northcliffe, 12 January 1910, Northcliffe Papers.

as 'full of timid alarms', and deplored the 'villainous' call for conciliation in the *Westminster Gazette*, which he took to be an 'evident reply to me'.¹

The difference between Spender and Gardiner was not so much doctrinal as one of professional self-perception. Temperament, perhaps reinforced by an awareness that his paper was funded by party sources, made Spender a ministerial apologist, if not quite a ministerial spokesman. Gardiner, while not oblivious to tactical considerations, shared with Scott and Massingham a Radical distrust of the ministerial mind. In recent months, his attitude towards Asquith had grown perceptibly cool. Soon after the January elections, he sent the Prime Minister a blunt reminder of campaign promises that had gone unredeemed since 1906, and he requested a reaffirmation of Liberal goals. Vaughan Nash, formerly his colleague on the *Daily News* and now serving in Downing Street, replied with assurances that Asquith 'realises all the difficulties of the situation & the danger of disheartening people'.² To Spender, the essential task was to keep the party in office. To Gardiner, it was to keep the party – in or out of office – on the path of Peace, Retrenchment, and Reform. So long as the House of Lords brandished its legislative veto, a Liberal government would be restricted to Tory-approved measures, and thus unworthy of its name.

Spender had better luck with Strachey, an addict of centrist politics, who lent the *Spectator* to the campaign for intra-party collaboration. 'Privately, I did not take counsel with anyone until I had committed myself,' Spender informed his ally. 'You state my view accurately & you are not wrong in thinking it to be the view of the steadiest men in the Cabinet,' he disclosed. For his part, Strachey was 'exceedingly glad' that Spender had 'liked my reference to the *Westminster*. I felt really very indignant at the way in which certain Liberal papers, notably the *Nation*, have treated you.' Massingham, who had condemned Spender's initiative as a sell-out, 'no doubt is a very clever fellow', Strachey supposed, 'but I am quite sure he loses far more supporters for his party than he ever gains'. Spender was a shade more charitable: 'Massingham is a very good fellow but he has a rooted idea that everyone who does not use violent language is a coward.'³

Accusations of cowardice flew in all directions, predicated on differing assessments of the mood of the electorate and the imperatives of the moment. Bonar Law, who was not usually characterized as a trimmer, infuriated hard-line Tariff Reformers by begging their indulgence 'if Mr Balfour decided that the chief amendment' to the King's Speech at the convocation of the new Parliament 'should be on Ireland'. Evincing a front-bench mentality, he was satisfied 'that Mr Balfour was now entirely with us' on the merits of protection,

---

¹ Spender to Bryce, 3 February 1910, Bryce Papers; Spender to Gardiner, 24 and 25 January 1910, and Gardiner's diary, 24 January 1910, Gardiner Papers.

² Nash to Gardiner, 17 February 1910, Gardiner Papers.

³ Spender to Strachey, 4 and 8 February 1910, and Strachey to Spender, 7 February 1910 (copy), Strachey Papers.

'& was as keen as we were in regarding it as the first constructive policy'. Whereupon Ware interjected: 'Why doesn't he put it first then?' Fortified by approval from Amery and others, Ware doubted 'whether I should in any way commit the *Morning Post* to their tactics'. It was not enough that, 'when the Budget comes on', the Unionist leaders were pledged 'to say all sorts of wonderful things about Tariff Reform. *Aren't* they fools?' he asked Lady Bathurst, whose views he claimed to have represented. 'Why they would have the country behind them & understanding them if they talked nothing *but* Tariff Reform on the Address, but just so as not to hurt the feelings of the Cecils it must be given second place.'[1]

The Liberals were on the horns of a comparable dilemma, procedural in form and ideological in content. Radical and Labour backbenchers favoured the immediate abolition of the Lords' veto, as did Redmond, who ominously threatened 'No Veto, No Budget'. The majority of Liberal journals weighed in on their side. 'We see no obstacle to the tactic of the Veto First,' avowed the *Nation* on 19 February. At Cabinet altitude, however, there was indecision and a countervailing preference for a more limited scheme of second chamber reform. Partly attributable to a failure of nerve, this retreat was accelerated by Asquith's embarrassed admission that he possessed no guarantee that the King would honour his request for an avalanche of Liberal peerages.

Divided over budget strategy, and specifically how far they should go to propitiate Redmond by tampering with the proposed liquor duties, the government was utterly paralysed by the question of the House of Lords. Harcourt and Lord Pentland proclaimed their intention to resign if Campbell-Bannerman's suspensory scheme of 1907 were not put directly into effect. Grey, diametrically opposed to them, intimated that he would 'go out' if the so-called unicameralists had their way; and Runciman, after consultation with McKenna, verified 'that Grey is not speaking or acting alone'. Morley, whom Asquith had bedecked with a viscountcy in 1908, would tolerate no further debasement of the coinage; as Harold Spender quipped, he 'really behaved (at the idea of creating peers) as an orthodox Christian might if it were proposed to add a fourth person to the Trinity'. Churchill, a Radical of headier vintage, swore to Masterman that he, too, 'would resign sooner than accept the Veto policy again', and that he would refuse to follow if Lloyd George 'goes back to that d----d Veto!' In the event, there were no resignations, and the backbench rebellion was headed off. Thanks to another of Haldane's ingenious compromises, whereby ministers agreed to differ, Asquith was able slowly to reassert his mastery. On 28 February, he announced plans to tackle the veto through the device of resolutions, framed by a Cabinet committee, with legislation – and possibly 'organic change' – to follow 'hereafter'. Massingham, in his 'Diary' for the *Nation* on 5 March, recorded that 'this week the Liberal

---

[1] Ware to Lady Bathurst, undated fragment [probably February 1910], Bathurst Papers.

Party has plucked its leaders from the pit'. By the Liberal Party, he meant the Liberal press.[1]

Three resolutions were carried by comfortable margins. Then, and only then, the budget was passed by a majority of ninety-three votes in the Commons, and without a division in the Lords. 'If a Veto Bill or Resolution passes the House of Commons it should be made a subject of a Referendum,' advised the *Nation* (26 February), which had shown periodic partiality for this expedient. In urging such an unconventional course, designed to obviate the mutual inconvenience of a second general election, Massingham was inspired by Churchill. The *Manchester Guardian*, similarly prodded by Lloyd George, echoed support, and Hobhouse approached Gardiner with a view to lining up the *Daily News* as well. The need for a referendum subsided, but the notion was kept alive by Massingham in the *Morning Leader* (21 March), the *Nation* (26 March), and in his correspondence with Cabinet members.[2]

A referendum or 'Poll of the People' also held obvious attractions for the Unionists, who craved a way out of the impasse over Tariff Reform. Strachey, for reasons of his own, dilated upon the advantages in successive issues of the *Spectator*. Garvin was mindful of Sandars's apprehension 'that either [Lloyd] George or Churchill will adopt sooner or later the tariff on manufacture – leaving us with nothing but the food tax', an electoral liability. His solution was to steal the Radicals' thunder before they stole the Unionists' clothes.[3]

In May, the death of King Edward 'completely transformed the political situation', as Asquith saw it. Through the summer and autumn, government and opposition leaders met furtively to explore various possibilities for breaking the constitutional stalemate through bi-partisan action. Against this muddled background, the referendum idea gained popularity in Unionist circles. Lord Lansdowne's cautious commendation in a speech on 23 November was a straw in the wind. Three days later, Garvin received a telegram from a Manchester journalist, who communicated explicit instructions from Bonar Law: it was 'vital' that Balfour should announce 'that Tariff on passing would be submitted for confirmation by referendum' before proceeding to legislation. Garvin, hitherto a sceptic, complied with a five-column spread in the final edition of the next day's *Observer*. He then waited nervously for the reaction of Balfour, whose approval he had had no time to solicit. On the 29th, Balfour told a packed and cheering audience at the Albert Hall that he had 'not the least objection to submitting the principles of Tariff Reform to a Referendum'. Blewett has ranked this as the 'greatest of the press initiatives' of the twin-election year: 'Garvin's appeal and the press response compelled a decision, when the time for decision had almost gone.'[4]

---

[1] See Koss, *Asquith* (London, 1976), pp. 119–21.
[2] Havighurst, *Radical Journalist*, pp. 199–200.
[3] Sandars to Garvin, 26 January 1910, Garvin Papers.
[4] Gollin, *Observer*, pp. 258–65; Blewett, p. 311.

By then, the Unionists were fighting another general election, and Balfour was fighting, after his fashion, to save his own political skin. During 1910, divisions within the party had widened, and his own relations with the press had deteriorated. Ware, returning to the *Morning Post* on 29 March after a sojourn in France, found it difficult 'to pick up the pieces again'. In his absence, the opposition seemed to have repudiated its sacred obligation to oppose. The Lords, seized by a Balfourite funk, made him 'ashamed of being an Englishman' by giving their 'vote for a Resolution that was only a sham'. Lacking firm leadership, they had played into the hands of the Liberals, who had only 'got up' the constitutional crisis as a means 'to burke Tariff Reform, and Cromer and all the Free Trade Unionists, with the same object, are anxious to get public opinion concentrated on this question and to make it the chief subject of discussion'. Resolved 'to press ahead boldly with our constructive policy', Ware would brook no diversions. 'The Tariff Reformers in the House are in a state of very healthy discontent,' he reported to Lady Bathurst,

> and I almost believe that Balfour will be forced to take the bold line, but of course things will never be right until the chariot comes for him, and this is beginning to be more and more the opinion among even those Tariff Reformers whom he has kept quiet with vague promises during the last five years.

If it provided any consolation: 'The Liberals seem in a terrible fright lest the Unionists should follow our advice, and so taunt them continually in the House with following the *Morning Post*'s directions.'[1]

The special object of Ware's distrust was Garvin, a mesmeric personality who 'unfortunately influences a lot of papers & has Balfour's confidence'. In neither respect did he exaggerate. Studiously briefed by Sandars, Garvin was Balfour's conduit to the Northcliffe press. Together with A. P. Nicholson, whose brother Reginald supplanted Moberly Bell as the '*real* manager' at Printing House Square, he contrived to exert an influence whereby Northcliffe's diverse 'papers might pull together in a time of political crisis'. Symbolically, 'at a late supper given by the Duke of Marlborough to Unionist journalists' on the evening of 28 April, 'Nicholson was on Balfour's right' and Garvin 'was on the Duke's'. More substantively, by issuing his clarion call for 'a truce of God' over the grave of Edward VII (8 May), Garvin set in motion the proceedings for inter-party conciliation. For that, he incurred the wrath of both the *Morning Post* and the *Daily News*. 'When the King died the Conference idea came to me in a flash with absolute conviction as the new policy for a wholly new situation,' Garvin subsequently explained to Northcliffe. 'It was my own idea and without consultation with anybody I made up my mind & moved at once.' Once the die was cast, however, 'I was in touch with Carlton

---

[1] Ware to Lady Bathurst, 29 March 1910, Bathurst Papers.

Gardens', Balfour's establishment, 'throughout. They did not discourage me to start with though thinking success unlikely. They approved in the end. They knew all I did – outside journalism.'[1]

As usual, Garvin was as active behind the scenes as in print. But, not for want of trying, he could not manage everything. The *Daily Mail* adhered to a more bellicose line than he must have wished. 'We are all greatly disquieted by reports coming from the Balfour circle that it is impossible to try the great coup,' Northcliffe was told by H. W. Wilson, who agreed with Ware that the Liberals had to be dislodged from office on the first available pretext. In the last resort, he contemplated, Balfour could carry on a minority administration by 'personally borrowing money in the City ... and ... expending this money without the sanction of Parliament'. The policies of official Unionism, which oscillated between decrying the Liberals and seeking to cooperate with them, stultified its political journals. 'Our press have positively done us harm,' protested J. H. Welsford, who ascribed his defeat in a spring by-election at Crewe to 'the attitude of the Unionist Press, particularly the *Daily Dispatch*, *The Times*, and the *Daily Mail*, all of which described from the beginning the contest as a walkover for the Radical Party'. Under ordinary circumstances, Garvin might have invigorated at least two of that trio. But, at this juncture, he was evidently holding back.[2]

At the same time, Garvin could do nothing to arrest further sniping against Balfour, which intensified as the result of his own equivocations. 'Why don't Winterton & F. E. Smith stop those attacks upon Mr B. in the *World* – which came out immediately after the General Election demanding the dropping of the food-tax altogether?' he asked Sanders. Winterton, dissociating himself from 'the supporters and admirers of Mr Balfour', retrospectively explained: 'The validity of his supporters' claim that his line of compromise was tactically sound is, in my judgment, open to grave doubt.' The following November, Winterton disposed of his controlling interest in the *World* for £1,500. As Tory MP for Horsham, he remained critical of Balfour's performance.[3]

The *Morning Post* lay far beyond Garvin's reach and was inveterately hostile to him. On the day it reported the King's death, it attained a 'record' circulation, '25% better' than when Queen Victoria died. The flag on its building flew at half-mast, the shutters were put up in mourning, and Wilkinson wrote a memorial tribute, which Ware confessed 'was not very good'. By drawing the shutters, the paper metaphorically closed out 'Garvin's line of

---

[1] Ware to Lady Bathurst, 29 March 1910, Bathurst Papers; Garvin to Sandars, 29 January 1910, Sandars Papers; Nicholson to Butes, 4 March 1910, and Garvin to Northcliffe, 20 and 29 April, and 13 June 1910, Northcliffe Papers; Grigg, *Lloyd George: The People's Champion*, pp. 259–60.

[2] Wilson to Northcliffe, 26 April 1910, Northcliffe Papers; Welsford to Sandars, 30 April and 2 May 1910, Sandars Papers.

[3] Garvin to Sandars, 5 May 1910, Sandars Papers; Winterton, *Pre-War*, pp. 16–17; Alan Houghton Brodrick, *Near to Greatness* (London, 1965), p. 126.

pleading for a political truce', which smacked to Ware of treachery. 'It is for the *aggressors* to propose that, not the Unionists on the defensive,' he insisted to Lady Bathurst; 'it will be construed as a sign of weakness.' Although many Unionists pretended that the late King had been hounded to his grave by importuning Liberals, Ware diagnosed the royal malady as the effect of too many cigars. 'If Garvin and the *Globe* will only remain quiet, I think we shall get our "truce" all right,' he concluded sullenly, 'but for them to shout about it and to ask for it is the surest way not to get it.' To his annoyance, the *Westminster Gazette* (10 May) responded to Garvin's broadside with the condescending statement that there could 'be no agreement to a truce of the character suggested by the Conservatives'. Thus, once again, the opposition was shown up as a band of beggarly fools.[1]

The *Observer*'s proposal for a 'Truce of God' received a more respectful hearing from *The Times*, where Alfred Austin extolled it in poetry. (Politically and aesthetically, the Poet Laureate gave a 'lamentable performance', thought Austen Chamberlain.) W. T. Stead, partly attracted by the psychic dimension, volunteered to help fulfil King Edward's imputed deathwish and told Garvin that Lloyd George, too, was 'much impressed'. Marlowe of the *Daily Mail* 'regretted very much the articles' Garvin wrote, but Lawson of the *Daily Telegraph* congratulated him on 'a stupendous thing'. Both Kennedy Jones and Leo Maxse put aside their misgivings, which were speedily to revive in Maxse's case. Writing as 'Pacificus' in *The Times*, F. S. Oliver took up Garvin's theme and demarcated the vast areas of public policy in which compromise might bring beneficial results. 'The idea of a conference on the Land Question much boomed in the papers,' Robert Sanders (later 1st Baron Bayford), the newly elected Conservative MP for Bridgwater, wrote in his diary on 8 June, when the third of Oliver's commissioned letters appeared. '*Times* especially keen on it,' he noted.[2]

To stave off another general election, which both sets of party leaders dreaded, the constitutional conference was given a chance. Journalists went along with it, some out of patriotism, some out of obligation, some out of sycophancy, and not a few out of a transparent desire to see the procedure discredited, once and for all. Lloyd George, one of the key Liberal participants at the ensuing clandestine sessions, was pumped by Harcourt and Pease for details of 'what was going on at the Conference'. At first, Lloyd George sanctimoniously 'deprecated the Cabinet knowing in case anything got into the Press'. That, coming from him, struck Pease as 'funny'. After his initial posturing, they were able to 'draw him', which was proof enough to Pease that 'Donald of the *Chronicle* could do so on other occasions'. With Lloyd George at the conference table, breaches of secrecy were inevitable. The architect of Welsh and English newspaper syndicates, he cultivated an array of press

[1] Ware to Lady Bathurst, 9 and 10 May 1910, Bathurst Papers.
[2] Gollin, *Observer*, pp. 186–87, 194–97; Sanders's diary, 8 June 1910, Bayford Papers.

contacts, and – as Herbert Lewis, his parliamentary crony, testified – never ventured to deliver a speech without first supplying a polished copy 'to one reporter on condition that a proof is sent' for final corrections.[1]

As the conference dragged on, it sprang leaks on every side. From the communications that passed between newspapermen, and between them and political figures of varying stature, it is clear that the deliberations were widely known, though stintingly publicized. It amused Northcliffe to see the 'newspaper quidnuncs ... completely out of their element' and stumbling in the dark, while he and Garvin knew every twist and turn. Harold Harmsworth, whom Northcliffe fraternally described as 'a particularly obstinate and determined man', worked in July to ensure that Buckle 'fully recognises the danger of the Conference breaking down' over the vexing Irish issue, for fear that resistance by *The Times* might precipitate a collapse. The difficulty, Harmsworth explained to the Master of Elibank, with whom he made common cause, was Buckle's blithe ignorance of electoral realities: 'he seems to entertain an incurable optimism in regard to the trend of domestic politics today ... and really convinces himself that we are living in what were for the Conservative party the halcyon days of 1895–1902'. Considering it futile to remonstrate with Buckle, 'an editor who offers to resign about twice every twelve months', Harmsworth turned to Garvin. 'I can always use influence there and it happens sometimes that Buckle follows Garvin's lead.' Accordingly, on the morning of 29 July, he 'spent two hours ... with Garvin ..., inducing him to comment favourably on Federalising the Constitution'. Garvin, having previously indicated a receptiveness to a federal approach to Home Rule, presumably did not require much inducement. In any case, his leading article in the *Observer* two days later was less an endorsement than a thoughtful consideration of the scheme. Ingeniously coupling devolution with Imperial Preference, so as to sweeten the medicine for the Unionist patient, Garvin continued to 'exert all his influence journalistically and otherwise to further the Conference', and appeared to Harold Harmsworth 'quite the most influential journalist qua journalist in the ranks of the Opposition'.[2]

---

[1] Pease's diary, 19 July 1910, Pease Papers; Herbert Lewis's diary, n.d., quoted in Grigg, *Lloyd George: The People's Champion*, p. 342. H. W. Wilson deduced that Lloyd George 'was probably K.J.'s informant' about the breakdown of the conference. Wilson to Northcliffe, 12 November 1910, Northcliffe Papers.

[2] Northcliffe to Garvin, 1 and 3 November 1910, Garvin papers; Northcliffe to Sandars, 22 November 1910 (copy), Northcliffe Papers; Harmsworth to Elibank, 27 and 29 July 1910, Elibank Papers 8802; Gollin, *Observer*, pp. 200–201. Garvin explained to Northcliffe: 'I didn't try to see Sandars because I get from him the extraordinary amount I do by never importuning and trusting him completely. He has never failed yet but his hour is not come to speak.' Revealing Smith as a collateral source, Garvin described 'a serious little row about leakage' in which Balfour and Lloyd George, neither 'unfriendly', verified that he 'knew everything' (Garvin to Northcliffe, 2 and 6 November 1910 [copies], Garvin Papers). Lord Esher's 'experience' was 'that Downing St. has been scrupulously discreet over the business', with the result that 'the Liberal papers were absolutely without knowledge of the last steps' of the conference, 'whereas

Arguably, however, Garvin's greater importance was as a journalist *qua* wirepuller, whose printed output was but the tip of an iceberg of propaganda. The constitutional conference, on which he pinned his hopes and – to a large extent – staked his reputation, achieved merely a delay, during which resentments welled up. As early as August, he and Goulding privately agreed that, subject to Lord Derby's approval, Bonar Law should vacate his safe seat at Dulwich to make a dramatic stand at North-West Manchester. Such a challenge, Goulding promised the potential candidate, 'would start the autumn campaign with a great bomb in the enemy's camp and with a press boom much would be done towards victory'. Garvin confirmed his enthusiasm on 10 August, when he asked Bonar Law's permission to announce the plan in the *Observer*. For the time being, though, he played down partisan antagonisms in public.[1]

The change came on 9 October, more than a month before the conference was finally given up as a failure. In that day's *Observer*, Garvin disowned his brainchild and summoned the Unionist troops to prepare for electoral combat. Ridiculing the 'malcontent manifestoes' promulgated by party dissidents, he pledged anew his fidelity to Balfour, whose leadership 'was in every respect decisive, statesmanlike and masterly'. Did he mean what he said? Admitting to Maxse that he was 'not happy about politics and never felt so isolated', Garvin pleaded with him to suspend disbelief in Balfour: 'I am as sensible as are you of his deficiencies but there is nobody else, . . . and it seems to me that to attack Balfour in the *Morning Post* manner simply makes the fortune of the Radical press, platform and cause and does more injury to tariff reform than other efforts make good.' Other Unionist editors were frankly bewildered. 'It seems now to be quite common knowledge that the Conference is in difficulties about the devolution scheme of Home Rule and that it may fail to find agreement upon that point,' Gwynne of the *Standard* wrote to Balfour on 28 October. Although 'such an ending due to such a contentious subject would not have greatly surprised or displeased the great mass of Unionists', Gwynne professed to 'regard the breakdown of the Conference as a national disaster', and therefore took the liberty of telling Balfour, 'in the most respectful way I can, that you must not count upon me to conceal my opinions if the Conference breaks down'. In reply to this threat, Balfour disputed Gwynne's 'common knowledge' as an 'utterly misleading compound of truth and falsehood' and promised clarification as soon as he returned to London after the weekend.[2]

Balfour and Garvin could depend upon each other, but they had both

---

The Times & the *Daily Mail* professed to know everything.' (Esher to Sandars, 14 November 1910, Sandars Papers).

[1] Goulding to Bonar Law, 4 August 1910, and Garvin to Bonar Law, 10 August 1910, Bonar Law Papers, 21/3/10, 12.

[2] Garvin to Maxse, 6 October 1910, Maxse Papers; Gwynne to Balfour, 28 October 1910, and Balfour to Gwynne, 29 October 1910 (copy), Sandars Papers.

become weak reeds. The former, in Maxse's opinion, was 'deeply and deservedly distrusted by the democracy.... He has shot his bolt and probably knows it.' Thirteen months later, after leading his party to a third demoralizing defeat, Balfour tendered his resignation in the face of a vituperative press clamour. Garvin himself was in desperate straits. He held on at the *Observer* through a change of régimes that temporarily impaired his political performance. At the beginning of August, Goulding recognized him to be deeply 'in trouble with his proprietor ... which I hope will be righted'. It was not until February 1911 that Northcliffe ordered the removal of his name from the list of the *Observer*'s directors and set about disposing of the property. Over the preceding six months his quarrels with his editor had grown more frequent and, on his side, more acrimonious. 'Either you get out or I do,' he wired to Garvin on one occasion. While this estrangement weighed as an important factor in the period preceding the December elections, it belongs more properly to the post-election period and will be considered in that context.[1]

In the hiatus between the two 1910 elections and again in their aftermath, there occurred numerous adjustments in the management of the political press. An outward quiescence, imposed by the 'Truce of God', masked a flurry of activity, much of it undertaken in the knowledge that a second appeal to the country was unavoidable. In April 1910, Pearson relinquished the *Standard* to Davison Dalziel, who perpetuated its party allegiance. Other transfers were not nearly so clear-cut. Since 1908, for example, the *Morning Leader* and the *Star* had been jointly controlled by the Rowntree Trust and the Cadburys' *Daily News* Company. What had seemed to be a logical partnership, rooted in a common religious background and commercial interest, foundered on the rocks of moral controversy. Joseph Rowntree, sensitive to criticisms from the Quaker community, regretted his connection with newspapers that derived their popular appeal from betting news. Moreover, the trust he had established in 1904 was explicitly non-partisan (as distinct from the journals it sustained) and non-profit-making, unlike the Cadburys' concern. As an outsider, Strachey inferred the tension from a conversation with Henry Cadbury,

> who is both director of the *Daily News* and of the *Star*.... I have little doubt that at heart he is quite a good young man, but he appeared to me to be wrapped up in a rhinoceros hide of self-righteousness which made him think he could do no wrong, and that he need not in the very least fear the charge of inconsistency as long as his own conscience told him he was doing right.

Strachey, a man of the world, was not opposed to gambling, but drew the line at the publication of 'tips'. He chided Henry Cadbury about 'the general vulgarity

---

[1] Maxse to Garvin, 8 October 1910, Garvin Papers; Goulding to Bonar Law, 4 August 1910, Bonar Law Papers, 21/3/10; Gollin (*Observer*, pp. 283–95) provides a fuller, less sentimental account of relations between Garvin and Northcliffe than Pound and Harmsworth (pp. 414–15).

of the *Star*. In that respect its standard is certainly as low as [any] London evening paper, if not lower.' The solution to this and related problems was a gradual tightening of the links between the two affiliated bodies, leading by steps to the absorption of the *Morning Leader* by the *Daily News* in 1912, and to the Cadburys' acquisition of exclusive custody over the *Star*.¹

Horatio Bottomley, fresh from defending his seat at South Hackney against a local Nonconformist minister, whom the *Daily News* had championed as the better Liberal, encountered a threat to his editorial chair. Writing in June to Goulding, a parliamentary adversary, he revealed that 'an influential section on "our side" of the House is desirous of securing a substantial interest in *John Bull*', which he crudely estimated to enjoy a 'circulation approximating half a million and . . . advertising income approximating a thousand a week'. All that was required of Bottomley was 'that I remain "sound" on the Land and Constitutional Questions, and that . . . I oppose any general system of "Protection"'. But even that, given the aberrant nature of his Liberalism, was asking too much. Impoverished after his latest bout of legal difficulties, he did 'not like the atmosphere of the proposed alliance', and told Goulding that 'I would infinitely rather enter into relations with some of *your* friends, being left with a free hand as an independent critic of the Liberal Party, unhampered by Cobdenite shibboleth and governed by Imperial ideas'. There is no evidence that Goulding or any of his Unionist friends took the bait. And the subsequent incorrigibility of *John Bull* suggests that the Liberal alliance never materialized.²

The Liberals were more successful at Bradford, where the *Yorkshire Observer* was taken over by two local activists, who 'feared . . . [it] was going to pass into doubtful hands, so they bought it'. Reporting the transaction to Scott, whom he invited to nominate an editor, Sir Robert Hudson identified these benefactors as James Hill ('in the wool trade: was Lord Mayor of Bradford last year: wealthy, generous & a keen Liberal') and Sir James Roberts ('head of the firm of Sir Titus Salt, himself one of the leading Free Traders of that district: created Baronet by our folk last year: I daresay even wealthier than Hill'). While the new owners of the morning *Observer* 'were prepared to lose money on it for some years if needs be', they 'ultimately . . . look[ed] to its becoming a property'.³

Reverting to nineteenth-century practice, the Liberals tended to the provincial press, while the Conservatives concentrated on the metropolis. On 1 November, in time for a crucial by-election at Walthamstow, the halfpenny *Evening Times* was launched. The choice of title gave irritation in Printing House Square, which feared possible confusion between its own august

---

¹ Strachey to Sir Edward Fry, 27 May 1910 (copy), Strachey Papers; Harris, *Life So Far*, p. 93; memorandum prepared for the author by A. P. Duncum, 16 August 1978.
² Bottomley to Goulding, 13 June 1910, Wargrave Papers.
³ Hudson to Scott, 5 July 1910, *Guardian* Archives.

product and 'a very low class paper which ... paid no attention whatever to foreign affairs'. The moving force behind the new venture was J. A. ('Archie') Morrison, Tory member for Wilton in the Parliament of 1900, who had recently made a comeback at Nottingham East. Balfour, according to Sandars, 'knows him & his great wealth'. Morrison's partners were Sir Samuel Scott, the Conservative MP for Marylebone West, and John Cowley. Assistant cashier on the *Evening News* when the Harmsworths had taken it over, Cowley went on to succeed Rothermere as chairman of the board of directors of the *Daily Mirror* and *Sunday Pictorial*. Joseph Chamberlain dictated a message of welcome to 'the Editor of the *Evening Times*', Charles T. Watney: 'I am glad to see that you propose to issue a new London evening paper to support the Unionist & Tariff Reform policy, and I do not doubt that there is much need of such a paper, as the policy is still without sufficient explanation to the working class.' Too late to affect the result at Walthamstow, where there was a slight swing to the Liberals, the *Evening Times* only briefly survived the general election. Before its demise, Watney was replaced as editor by Edgar Wallace, better known for other adventure stories.[1]

The established London Unionist dailies, few of which pretended to address the working class, gave greater cause for discomfort. The *Morning Post*, unquestionably the most snobbish of the lot, appalled Lord Esher by assisting 'an intrigue ... to dislodge McKenna from the Admiralty' on the part of 'Massingham and the *Daily News* and *Morning Leader* and *Manchester Guardian* group'. Marvelling at these strange bedfellows, Esher disclaimed any influence over the *Morning Post* ('It is a paper that has often attacked me personally'), and informed Spender of his intention to 'warn Sandars. *He* may have influence with the *M.P.*' Sandars was absolutely helpless in these quarters, where he was himself severely criticized for the decay of the party organization. To better purpose, he expended his energy in 'seeing the Ed. of the *Daily Telegraph* ... at Ld. Burnham's request'.[2]

The policies of the *Telegraph* needed steadying. Garvin, who tried in the *Observer* (23 October) 'to prepare Unionist opinion for the extent of change which we believe to be both inevitable and wise', saw support for the 'large settlement' slipping away. 'A little while ago, Burnham was not at all opposed in his heart to "federalism",' he reminded Sandars. 'He now talks of "something behind it" and pours forth views which I can only attribute in my own mind to Rosebery who would really hate being left out of any really great settlement.' The *Telegraph* was brought round, at least to the degree that, when the conference was abandoned, Garvin 'did my best' on its leader page to

---

[1] Sandars to Short, 24 October 1910, Balfour Papers; Chamberlain to 'the Editor of the *Evening Times*', 14 October 1910 (copy), Chamberlain Papers, L. Add. 329; Chirol to Northcliffe, 8 January 1911, Northcliffe Papers.

[2] Esher to Spender, 11 August 1910, Spender Papers, Add. MSS. 46,392, fol. 41; Esher to Balfour, 16 August 1910 (enclosing a copy of Spender to Esher, 10 August 1910), and Sandars to Short, 3 and 24 October 1910, Balfour Papers.

salvage Balfour and 'the unbroken and increasing power of the Unionist party' (9 November) from the wreckage.[1]

To steady Northcliffe was always a much bigger job. The *Daily Mail* adeptly attuned itself to Garvin's line. *The Times* ran another series of 'Pacificus' letters, but cautioned that 'any solution upon Federal lines would mean substituting a weaker for a stronger Constitution of the State' (2 November). To Northcliffe's outrage, Buckle balked at 'a quick change'. Defending him to Lady Northcliffe, whose husband was again too ill to receive direct correspondence, Wilson felt 'sure that it is wise for *The Times* to be extremely cautious in modifying its policy' or else it might ruin its reputation for prudence. 'With the *Mail*, too, extreme circumspection will be wise,' he added. 'The change proposed is a great one, and if the party is to be carried in support of it men's minds must be carefully prepared.' For this reason, Wilson enjoined consultation 'with Balfour, who, such as he is, is our only leader', in order to 'find out from him exactly what he is prepared to do and how far he is prepared to go'. Upon Northcliffe's recovery, Garvin also 'begged him' to give the party leadership the benefit of his wisdom 'about his papers and the Food Question'. Northcliffe had 'something interesting to say', Garvin alerted Sandars, based on the 'confirmed experience' of the *Evening News*, 'the ½d. paper more read by the working classes of London than any morning journal' and better equipped than the *Evening Times* to serve as 'our chief fighting agency in the Metropolis'. Hard as it tried, the *Evening News* could 'make no further way in the East end against the Food Taxers', who were anathema to working-class electors. Exactly the same lesson was to be learnt from Lancashire and spurred the adoption of the referendum as a safety valve.[2]

What, if anything, was the 'confirmed experience' of the *Observer*? The *Westminster Gazette* hesitated to assign one to a journal which 'leads us into a glowing Nirvana of politics in which all the positives and negatives of terrestrial parties become merged in a mystical absolute' (17 October). Still, Garvin's sudden lurches were themselves a commentary on the political dislocation of the times. For all its apparent consistency, the *Westminster Gazette* raised doubts about its own 'confirmed experience'. On 8 October, Spender angrily denied the *Spectator*'s imputations that the *Westminster* cut its opinions to the cloth of the Liberal administration, only to receive Strachey's private assurances that he had meant no disrespect:

> If I were the supporter of a Ministry – as I am sure you will be the first to admit the *Westminster* is – and an organ of a political party and not what the *Spectator* is owing to force of circumstances, something of an outcast, I should not in the least mind it being said that the decision of the Government

[1] Garvin to Sandars, 26 October and 9 November 1910, Sandars Papers.
[2] Wilson to Lady Northcliffe, 24 October 1910, Northcliffe Papers; Garvin to Sandars, 14 November 1910, Balfour Papers.

party in a matter like the Osborne judgment must affect my attitudes. For example, non-party man as I am to a great extent, if Balfour and the whole Unionist Party went in for payment of Members I should not, much as I detest payment of Members, feel justified in dying in the last ditch against it.

This exchange between Spender and Strachey, both avatars of a tradition that had largely – though not completely – ceased to apply, illuminated the predicament of the political press. The first general election of 1910 had shown, and the second was to confirm, the impossibility of political journalism to function effectively outside a parliamentary alliance. 'There is only one power tha[t] can save us,' Lord Robert Cecil declared to Northcliffe, 'and that is the Press.' Only a Cecil could have clung to the illusion that newspapers had either the resources or the inclination to repudiate a system in which they had struggled to achieve recognition as essential components.[1]

---

[1] Strachey to Spender, 11 October 1910 (copy), Strachey Papers; Cecil to Northcliffe, 18 November 1910, quoted in Pound and Harmsworth, p. 400.

Five

A CLIMACTERIC YEAR

The second election campaign of 1910, more narrowly focused than the first and – mercifully – half its duration, confirmed the verdict delivered eleven months before. The Liberal and Unionist parties emerged in a dead heat, each with 272 seats in the new Parliament. Having contested fewer seats, their percentages of the total vote none the less remained virtually unchanged on a slightly reduced proportional turnout. The vagaries of the electoral system must be taken into account. This time around, there were fewer triangular contests, owing to a restraint on the part of the Labour Party, which fielded fifty-six candidates (as compared with seventy-eight in January) and scored two gains. There were also fewer 'independent' contenders to litter the landscape.

The performance of the political press was much the same. Neal Blewett, on the basis of a random sampling, has calculated that the London morning papers allocated 'about one-quarter' of their editorial space to election coverage in December, a shade higher than the 'minimal figure' of one-fifth in the preceding campaign.[1] Quite obviously, the ardour of the press was undiminished and might even have intensified.

How could newspapers have afforded, twice within a single year, to lavish so much attention on an election? One might suppose that they would have exhausted their supplies of rhetoric and their readers' patience. To the contrary, being men of strong party allegiance, editors naturally assumed that their own obsessions were universal or, at any rate, that they should be. Their intimate connections with politicians, usually fortified by those of their proprietors, permitted them no pause for reflection and possible re-evaluation. Besides, by its very nature, the Edwardian political press automatically lent itself to partisan usage. At a time when many of its rivals were beginning to 'devote themselves mainly, if not wholly, to the collection of news, published with very little comment or criticism', *The Times* persisted in devoting 'quite as much space to criticism and comment as to news', with a disproportionate emphasis on political controversy. Moberly Bell explained this classic case to Northcliffe:

[1] Blewett, pp. 310 and 468 (n. 36).

In the old days when it had little competition news *came* to it – just as advertisements *came* to it – with the result that the critical side became more developed than the news side, and as competition increased *The Times* fell behind in its collection of news and became more and more an organ of comment and criticism.

That is the situation we have to correct and are gradually correcting.

To prove his point, Moberly Bell 'turned up *The Times* for this day fifty years ago – Thursday 1st November 1860', and measured '63 columns of advertisements' and only '33 columns of news and comment'.[1] That, to Northcliffe, seemed a proper balance. But others, who did not have to sustain the losses of political journalism, valued *The Times* – as they did the *Westminster Gazette* and other papers – precisely because of its preponderance of 'comment and criticism'.

The party organizers, who were often furtive investors in newspaper properties, had no cause for complaint on this score. Their objective was first to increase and then to exploit the potential of the press to provide electoral propaganda. Too late to assist the first Unionist campaign, S. J. Pryor had convinced Sandars, Balfour's private secretary, of the urgent need to orchestrate press opinion. There was scarcely time to attend to the problem before the second election was called, and an overhaul of the Central Office had to await the appointment of Arthur Steel-Maitland as party chairman the following spring. In the meantime, Unionist strategists, envious of ostensible Liberal successes in newspaper management, feared for their own prospects. 'If we come back from a General Election weakened by the loss even of ten, much less twenty seats,' Garvin gloomily reckoned, 'it would mean an absolute end to the [Lords'] Veto', followed by the enactment of 'Gladstonian Home Rule – plus pensions &c, Welsh Disestablishment and a crescendo of Socialist triumphs.' To avert such a catastrophe, he urged Balfour to shelve the unpopular food duties and promised that every Unionist organ – save for the *Morning Post* and the *Birmingham Daily Post* – would bow to necessity.[2]

Buckle, declaring himself a 'Preferentialist', strongly endorsed Garvin's suggestion. Burnham and Northcliffe, both Garvin's employers, were likewise eager to climb down from a seemingly indefensible position. Blumenfeld of the *Daily Express*, hitherto an apostle of pure protectionism, lent a wavering voice to the appeal. As a backslider, he was especially significant. Earlier that autumn, he had joined disaffected backbenchers in both Houses to found the 'Reveille' movement, designed to commit the Unionist leadership to 'a coherent and united plan of action' with Tariff Reform as its 'essential

[1] Moberly Bell to Northcliffe, 3 November 1910, Northcliffe Papers.
[2] Garvin to Sandars, 6 November 1910, Sandars Papers; Austen Chamberlain to Mrs Joseph Chamberlain, 13 and 16 November 1910, quoted in Austen Chamberlain, *Politics from Inside* (New Haven, 1937), p. 300.

element'. Sir Henry Page Croft (later 1st Baron Croft) led the group in the Commons, and Willoughby de Broke led it in the Lords. Notwithstanding protestations of loyalty, they posed an unmistakable challenge to the 'Old Gang', so tagged by Maxse, who promoted the 'Reveille' manifesto in the pages of the *National Review*. A tacit repudiation of Garvin's federalist approach, this document won unexpected support from Strachey, an inveterate anti-Home Ruler, who promised to 'back up the Reveille people in the *Spectator*'. F. S. Oliver felt obliged to defend 'Pacificus', his alter-ego, against charges of 'opportunism'.[1]

Although attentive to the movement, the *Morning Post* considered it too limited in its objectives and, one suspects, too undistinguished in its personnel. Certainly the group's 'backwoods' image counted mightily against it, as did its truculent avowal of last-ditch resistance to the Parliament Bill. In November, Blumenfeld withdrew from the executive committee, expressing particular disapproval of the contempt with which 'Reveille' spokesmen had responded to newspaper criticism. 'One thing I think you will admit and that is that our attack was not against you, but against the Unionist Press as a whole,' replied Page Croft, who regretted Blumenfeld's resignation as 'a great loss'. He told the committee 'that as far as the Reveille was concerned, we could expect to have no more help from the London press', and his followers were 'quite prepared for the consequences, and even hostile opposition'.[2] The effect was crippling and only added to the mood of backbench frustration. Without the support of metropolitan dailies, any political insurgency was doomed to failure.

The parliamentary Labour Party had come to realize as much. In the first of the 1910 elections, it had relied for publicity on Liberal facilities, most of them glad to serve the purpose. As much for doctrinal as electoral reasons, Labour came to crave its own voice. Keir Hardie, boasting considerable experience in journalism, stressed the efficacy of the printed word as a means of propounding the socialist creed. The weekly *Labour Leader*, which had slipped from his control in 1903, was inadequate to the task. Robert Blatchford reported the formation of a 'new company to take over' that declining property (estimated by Hardie to be running at a weekly loss of £5. 10s.), along with the *Huddersfield Worker*. 'Meanwhile,' Blatchford continued, 'Lady Warwick takes over *New Age* and *Woman Worker*, and very possibly will take over the *Clarion*.' The Countess of Warwick – Edward VII's 'Darling Daisy' – had been converted to socialism under Blatchford's influence. He offered to sell her his own journal, replete with his editorial services, for £20,000, calculating that, if she accepted, 'she will have three papers and I think will go straight for a

---

[1] *Morning Post*, 19 October 1910; Strachey to Maxse, 7 November 1910, and Oliver to Maxse, 9 November 1910, Maxse Papers. For the 'Reveille' movement, see Sykes, *Tariff Reform*, pp. 226–28, and Gregory Phillips, 'Lord Willoughby de Broke and the Politics of Radical Toryism,' *Journal of British Studies*, xx (1980), 207–208.

[2] Page Croft to Blumenfeld, 9 November 1910, Blumenfeld Papers.

Socialist Party'. Lady Warwick had the ambition, but not the capital resources to indulge either Blatchford's fantasies or her own. In any case, her three-link chain would not have been enough. Given the reading habits of the working classes, what was needed was nothing less than a mass-circulation evening paper. Blatchford, whose impulse was not strictly ideological, toyed with the idea of starting one: 'We should cause a national sensation and we should sell half a million of the first issue.'[1]

Hardie, less concerned with the mercantile aspects, saw the Labour Party 'sinking into flabby pragmatism of a particularly indeterminate kind', and therefore was moved 'to put forward one of his cherished ideals – that of a socialist daily newspaper'. His 'disaffection with parliamentary manoeuvres', as diagnosed by his biographer,[2] was no less acute than that of the 'Reveille' group or, for that matter, that of Radical pacifists; nor was his disaffection with the prevailing structure of the political press any less pronounced. In the later months of 1910, he formulated a series of proposals which he submitted to the Labour national executive. Receiving no satisfaction, he turned to the National Administrative Council of the ILP. 'What I had in mind,' he said subsequently, 'was a Socialist paper under the control of the ILP', and equidistant from the Labour Party executive and (except for incidental assistance in procuring advertisements) from the trade unions. His projected journal, with one edition each morning and another each evening, would require an investment of £25,000, which he hoped to collect from ILP members in ten-shilling driblets. There was to be an instalment plan for the purchase of shares in the venture, and home delivery was to be available to morning subscribers for the modest price of $3\frac{1}{2}$s. a week. Although unspecified, Hardie's editorial jurisdiction was presumed.

Distrustful of this 'Socialist Daily self-advertisement scheme', as Bruce Glasier labelled it in the privacy of his diary, Hardie's colleagues insisted upon the direct involvement of the parliamentary party. Indeed, an offer of £5,000 from a director of the National Labour Press in Manchester, which Hardie had taken as his corporate model, was contingent on dual ILP and PLP sponsorship. Throughout the spring of 1911, proposals shuttled back and forth. Hardie's intractability prompted insinuations about his motives, business competence, and fiscal rectitude. He gave some ground, but held out for a 'Committee of Management' dominated by the ILP and chaired by an NAC appointee, most logically himself, equipped with a casting vote. On 25 May, in defiance of his reiterated demands, the decision was taken to launch a daily newspaper 'in accord with the alliance of Trade Unionists and Socialists as embodied in the Labour Party'. This final recommendation, unacceptable to

[1] Blatchford to Thompson, undated letters [1910], Blatchford Papers. For Lady Warwick's press activities, see Margaret Blunden, *The Countess of Warwick* (London, 1967), pp. 202–205.
[2] Morgan, *Keir Hardie*, pp. 234–36; NAC minutes and reports, 15 March, 15 April, 3, 13, 25, and 31 May, and 26 June 1911.

Hardie, called for a board of nine directors, six of them to be elected at an annual joint session of the Labour Party executive and the NAC, two elected each year by subscribing trade unions, and one representing those private investors who held a minimum of one hundred £1 shares. The capital outlay was fixed more realistically at £100,000.

Hardie declined to serve on the directorate and sniffily blamed his estrangement on 'the NAC who have refused to co-operate further with me in bringing out a Socialist Daily paper'. Thus, he denied himself any connection with the *Daily Citizen*, which eventually appeared in October 1912. Nevertheless, he deserves credit not only for having pointed to 'a real gap in the armoury of the Labour movement', but also for having tried to fill it. For reasons of self-respect as much as for the promulgation of its nostrums, Labour required a daily newspaper at its command, not merely at its disposal. Hardie's troubles and his egotism, which was largely responsible for them, were alike typical of politicians who sought to utilize the press as a spur to party policy. It implies no disrespect to the quality of his socialism to observe that neither his ambition nor his problems set him apart from activists of other persuasions.

That Labour lacked an official organ was perceived as a mark of its continued parochialism. Judging from the returns, however, it still managed to put its message across. In the second election of 1910, the bonds between newspapers and party organizations were discernibly stronger than they had been the previous January. Yet the results were virtually unaffected. The single contest that generated the most excitement in the press was Bonar Law's unsuccessful bid to capture North-West Manchester. Garvin, one of the instigators of this dramatic candidacy, applauded to the point of exaggeration the sacrifice made by Bonar Law in relinquishing a safe seat in the Home Counties to rally the Lancashire Unionists. Blumenfeld showered praise in the *Daily Express*. Gwynne, now editing the *Standard* under new auspices, congratulated Bonar Law for speaking 'splendidly' at the outset of the campaign: 'Go on and prosper. You have a splendid future before you.' Gwynne added that Garvin, who had been seated nearby, considered the performance comparable to 'Bright at his very best'.[1] It did not occur to them that Bright, at the height of his oratorical powers and newspaper influence, had been soundly defeated at Manchester.

Northcliffe, who resisted historical analogies, gave hearty support. Bonar Law thanked him for having 'taken so much trouble about my candidature', and, at the risk of 'asking too much', requested one additional favour. 'From what I can see the result in my division is at least very doubtful,' he admitted on 22 November, 'and I think it extremely likely, as it gets nearer the time, [that] the representative of *The Times* will have good reason to think that I am not likely to win.' Such a prognosis 'would do a good deal of harm if ...

---

[1] Gwynne to Bonar Law, 14 November 1910, Bonar Law Papers, 18/6/133; Blewett, pp. 223–24.

published before the election, and if you could prevent it I should be much obliged'.[1]

Firm in the belief that suppression was one of the legitimate functions of political journalism, Northcliffe could take no offence. On the other hand, although disposed to accommodate his petitioner, he could do little more vis-à-vis *The Times* than to drop hints to Buckle or, better still, Nicholson. His other papers, more directly under his control, were more malleable and more beholden to the party. The *Observer*, for example, was offered £1,000 from Unionist funds to produce an extra million copies of a special edition for provincial distribution; the plan proved unworkable, but the serious consideration it received was testimony to the intimacy that existed. The *Manchester Courier*, closer to Bonar Law's prospective constituency, engaged in strident electioneering. From Percival Hughes, the principal agent at Unionist headquarters, Dunn negotiated another subvention of £500. A mutually profitable arrangement, it inspired Sutton with the hope that 'the paper will drag on for a few years', despite the fact that its 'circulation (about 12,000) is slowly declining all the time'.[2]

As always, newspapers flourished in the heady atmosphere of a general election. Their sales picked up, and their editorial services were gratifyingly in demand. Kennedy Jones, looking back on the trends he had helped to set, cited the campaign in December 1910 as both a minor landmark and a major portent. It was then, he recalled, that 'the idea of using the advertising columns of daily newspapers, irrespective of their politics, for propaganda purposes began in this country'. As practised at the time, the operation was admittedly small-scale, 'but it opened up new possibilities, which were highly developed during the Great War'. To Jones, 'with my inside knowledge of newspaper offices', it seemed 'ridiculous to suppose' that any sum, however 'considerable', was ever 'sufficient to influence or modify the policy of even the financially weak dailies, still less of those which are in a strong position'.[3] The performance of the *Manchester Courier* must weigh as evidence to the contrary. In most instances, the degree of reciprocity was less explicit, and the subtle shift in the allocation of party patronage was not yet obvious.

In the long run, newspapers could bank on a share of the revenues from political advertising whether or not they toed the appropriate party line. On 10 February 1978, Shirley Williams stated that the Labour government, in which she served as Secretary of State for Education and Science, 'would not dream of following' the example of a private company, which had cancelled an advertising contract in retaliation against criticism: 'Indeed, there would not be much government advertising if we withdrew it from newspapers that said

---

[1] Bonar Law to Northcliffe, 22 November 1910, Northcliffe Papers.
[2] Garvin to Sandars, 26 November 1910, Balfour Papers; Gollin, *Observer*, p. 256; Sutton to Northcliffe, 23 November 1910, Northcliffe Papers.
[3] Jones, *Fleet Street and Downing Street*, pp. 301–302.

unkind things about us.' Leaving aside other pressures that might be brought to bear on journalistic offenders, including exclusion from ministerial briefings, it is safe to say that early twentieth-century governments and oppositions showed considerably less forbearance. They expected fidelity and, when they failed to receive it, took their revenge.

For all their authority, their discipline was slack and growing more so. The recent conferment of a baronetcy on Harold Harmsworth did nothing to curb him maverick tendencies. Sandars, the recipient of angry complaints from Scottish Unionists about the alleged perfidy of the Glasgow *Daily Record and Mail*, pleaded in vain with 'Sir Harold to moderate the tone of that paper, and to give directions for an impartial attitude at least to be taken upon the Constitutional questions which are now agitating the public mind'. In desperation, he wrote to Northcliffe, 'venturing to ask you whether you could possibly, in whatever way you thought best, add the weight of your influence to the representations we have already made'. The elder Harmsworth 'telegraphed as delicately as I could', but promised no results. 'My brother and I are great personal friends,' he replied to Sandars, 'but I have nothing to do with his political career, and I never see his beastly paper.'[1]

For his own part, Northcliffe was more dependable. Leo Amery solicited support for his underdog candidacy at Bow and Bromley: 'I rang up K.J. the other day and asked him to let the *Mail* help me as much as possible, and they are giving me very good paragraphs, a matter of no small importance considering that I am entirely unknown in the district.' More effectively than *The Times*, the *Evening News* might draw votes in this working-class constituency, where George Lansbury was a formidable Labour opponent. Sympathetic, Northcliffe vowed to do his best. 'To be unknown by the democracy is to be damned by them,' he reflected. 'I have told my people to do everything possible to send a cinematograph to the district, and as the Poll approaches to see that the *Evening News* whips up the readers.'[2]

Speaking to Amery as one Fleet Street professional to another, Northcliffe plainly recognized the countervailing strengths and weaknesses of the tradition to which they both belonged: 'Perhaps the papers may not . . . altogether please you in what they do, but believe me, they are very old hands at electioneering.' In fact, some of the oldest hands caused the greatest exasperation. The *Morning Post* drew an invidious – and fallacious – distinction between Balfour and Bonar Law: the former was portrayed as a cynic, whose referendum pledge was 'a dodge to "sweep Lancashire" and win the election' at any cost; the latter, 'when he is returned to Parliament', could be expected to 'give his whole-hearted support to the first constructive policy of the Party', unadul-

---

[1] Sandars to Northcliffe, 21 November 1910, and Northcliffe to Sandars, 22 November 1910 (copy), Northcliffe Papers.
[2] Amery to Northcliffe, 26 November 1910, and Northcliffe to Amery, 29 November 1910 (copy), Northcliffe Papers.

terated Tariff Reform (26 and 28 November). It infuriated Garvin to see that paper, 'with its own supreme fatuity', so shamelessly misrepresent 'what is necessary to save its hero, Bonar Law'. He bristled still more when the *Manchester Guardian* (15 December), quoting extensively and 'delightedly' from the *Morning Post*, asked its readers: 'Is the Opposition breaking up?'[1]

That was a valid question, if mischievously put. Unionist leaders, with publicists trailing at their heels, were openly contradicting each other. Austen Chamberlain took no pains in his public speeches to mask his displeasure with what *The Times* dignified as Balfour's 'higher logic' (30 November). Literally his father's public voice, he was fawned upon by Ware, the Bathursts, and Maxse. 'Damn those Chamberlains,' exclaimed Lord Derby. 'They are the curse of our party – & of the country.' Garvin was 'alarmed' to see F. E. Smith, whom Sandars ranked as second only to Balfour as a platform performer, 'wobbling and inclined to follow Austen's disastrous lead. It will never be followed,' he warned Goulding, whom he knew to be in contact with Ware, '... by *The Times*, *Telegraph*, *Daily Express*, *Daily Mail*, or the *Observer*'. To his relief, the leading article in the *Globe* on 15 December was 'perfectly admirable', evincing the 'sort of "perceptive imagination" ... of which Austen is utterly devoid. In no case,' Garvin maintained, 'will the bulk of the Unionist press back down.' The solecisms of the *Morning Post* struck Garvin as the more reprehensible because he had personally informed Ware that the adoption of the referendum scheme, far from being a Balfourian deviation, 'came about from Bonar Law's wish'. When Ware disregarded this message, Garvin considered him to have 'behaved disgracefully.... I am through with him absolutely. He is now a curse to the cause in my opinion.' Blumenfeld was of the same mind and unforgivingly noted how 'Fabian Ware, naturally, fans the flame'.[2]

These disputes surfaced midway through the campaign, after it had become clear that Balfour's Garvinian strategy had not paid off. Lord Cromer and Harold Cox, a renegade Liberal who had quit Parliament and was to edit the *Edinburgh Review* as 'an organ of what may be called sane, individualist, Liberalism', had forecast that the provision for a referendum 'means 30 seats in the North'. The returns did not bear them out. There was the irresistible temptation to blame meddlesome newspapers for the party's disappointments. 'The *Daily Mail* stated that the Unionist peers stated that

[1] Northcliffe to Amery, 29 November 1910 (copy), Northcliffe Papers; Garvin to Sandars, 28 November and 15 December 1910, Balfour Papers; Goulding to Bonar Law [1910], Bonar Law Papers, 18/5/85, 87.

[2] Derby to Sandars, 15 December 1910, Balfour Papers; Garvin to Goulding, 16 December 1910, Wargrave Papers; Blumenfeld to Sandars, 17 December 1910 (copy), Blumenfeld Papers. Garvin's message to Ware was carried by Maurice Woods, an unsuccessful challenger in January at Bristol North, who was briefly attached to the *Morning Post* as a leader-writer; for his subsequent significance, see p. 357 below.

they would rather be abolished by the country than by the Conference,' recalled Robert Sanders, soon to be appointed an opposition junior whip.

> *The Times* had a series of articles saying that the real difficulty was Home Rule and suggesting that the Unionists should agree to some form of it.... Subsequently at the Albert Hall [Balfour] declared for a Referendum on Tariff Reform. That upset the *Morning Post* gang. Sowler of the *Manchester Courier* told me beforehand that such a declaration would carry Manchester. It did not.

Austen Chamberlain, mentor to 'the *Morning Post* gang', saw his qualms justified. 'Garvin and others, in the hope of conciliating so-called "moderate" opinion, raised the cry for the extension of the Referendum to Tariff Reform,' he icily reminded Lansdowne, whom he asked, 'Was it worth while? What evidence is there that we have gained any real strength in the constituencies by this new policy?' Conceding that it was 'of course impossible to *prove* one way or the other what the effect of the pledge has been', he himself was 'profoundly convinced' that the tactic had miscarried: 'It encouraged people everywhere to put Tariff Reform in the background and the House of Lords in the forefront and that played straight into the hands of the Government.'[1]

The Unionists marginally increased their share of the vote, but the Liberals kept office. Under the circumstances, Amery's defeat left Joseph Chamberlain 'sorry but not surprised'. Bonar Law's failure, though its effect was ironically to enhance his reputation, was more serious, and one that Northcliffe deplored for special reasons. 'The Unionist Party has been accustomed always to regard the Newspapers as a sort of doormat,' he wrote by way of commiseration;

> but they have just awakened to the fact that the Newspapers are of increasing importance as part of the machine.... It is notorious that the Unionist Press is more efficient than the Liberal Press. It is equally true that our organizations are not as efficient as the Liberal organizations.

H. W. Wilson, who had worked the *Daily Mail* for all it was worth, shared Northcliffe's regrets that 'the elections have not gone better'. At least, he consoled his chief, 'we have fought our hardest, and defeat after that brings no dishonour'. Sounding remarkably like a party agent, which was exactly how he saw himself, Wilson concluded that, 'if only we reorganize, next time we should really bring them down'. To that end, he suggested that Northcliffe

---

[1] Cox to Rosebery, 30 March 1912, Rosebery Papers, Vol. 10,123, fol. 309; Sanders to Garvin, 27 November 1910, Garvin Papers; Sanders's diary, 8 February 1911, Bayford Papers; Austen Chamberlain to Lansdowne, 9 and 18 December 1910, quoted in Chamberlain, *Politics from Inside*, pp. 310–12.

might personally 'undertake the work of reorganization or turn K.J. on to it, but I suppose this is quite out of the question'.[1]

But was it? Opposition journalists, smarting under the impact of a third defeat within five years, doubted the capacity of the parliamentary 'Old Guard' to put their ramshackle house in order. Provided that Northcliffe's health permitted, no one was more conspicuously endowed with the requisite managerial skills and ruthlessness. His anomalous position commended him for the assignment, for – according to Gwynne – the politicians 'all hate Northcliffe, but fear him'. While not oblivious to Northcliffe's positive and negative qualifications, Amery nominated Aitken, Bonar Law's friend and financial adviser, as 'someone who will lick this thing into shape, sack superfluous people, knock heads together and make the machine run'. It is noteworthy that, amid the post-mortems, these two names should have been put forward. Northcliffe derived his reputation, as Aitken (the future Lord Beaverbrook) was to gain his, from a mastery of the press. At the time, the common denominator between them was a stake in the Rolls-Royce company.[2]

The two general elections of 1910 served to strengthen the links between journalism and party organization, primarily by heightening the awareness of persistent deficiencies. Impelled by professional as well as partisan considerations, newspapermen unleashed a campaign to rebuild the Unionist structure; not a few saw it as a means of removing the man at the top. This agitation could not be ignored, least of all by those whom it threatened. Sandars, hoping to keep it within bounds, implored Balfour to come to terms with his overmighty subjects in Fleet Street. One way was for the Conservative Central Office to cooperate more efficiently with the press. Another was to advance those within the party who excelled in the arts of propaganda. Whether one liked him or not, Smith had definitely 'arrived in the very front rank' and deserved front-bench status. 'He is modern in his methods – especially with the Press,' acknowledged Sandars; 'but he is only à la mode, and we have to accept the fashion.'[3] More than a straw in the wind, Smith figured as a hurricane. He and Garvin were portrayed by Harold Begbie in the *Daily Chronicle* (5 December) as the real 'Masters of Conservatism', without whom 'the party would perish'.

*   *   *

The Master of Elibank, said to have been 'probably the greatest Chief Whip of his generation', could not 'allow this Election to conclude without sending' Gardiner a message of 'sincere thanks for all the help which you have extended

---

[1] Joseph Chamberlain to Amery, 12 December 1910, Amery Papers; Northcliffe to Bonar Law, 6 December 1910, Bonar Law Papers, 18/6/139; Wilson to Northcliffe, 13 December 1910, Northcliffe Papers.

[2] Gwynne to Lady Bathurst, 19 December 1911, Bathurst Papers; Amery to Bonar Law, 16 December 1910, Bonar Law Papers, 18/6/146; Taylor, *Beaverbrook*, p. 43.

[3] Memorandum by Sandars [December 1910], Balfour Papers.

to me during my somewhat difficult year of office'. Apart from the valuable function that the *Daily News* had performed in Lancashire through its popular northern edition, that paper had given yeoman's service in the metropolitan constituencies, where the swing to Unionism seemed to have been checked and the Labour advance had been contained. 'I feel that the results in London are largely attributable to the stimulus of your leading articles, and the care and tact with which you have dealt with delicate situations,' he told Gardiner. 'You have no idea of the difference it makes to me here to feel that one has a friend directing a great Liberal journal. It is so much easier to discuss matters freely and frankly.'[1]

Acland Hood, his Unionist counterpart and a man of inferior talents, could not have written to any editor – not even Garvin – in this vein. His accomplices in Fleet Street had shown purpose and initiative, but rarely 'care and tact', with the result that they had created many of the 'delicate situations' in which party officials found themselves. During the previous year, there had been mounting newspaper criticism of Unionist procedures. It came not only from such predictable quarters as the *Morning Post* and the *National Review*, but also from such mainstream organs as the *Daily Telegraph*, which had called upon its political leaders to 'scrap the existing party machinery and . . . instal new plant' (2 February 1910). In the wake of the second election, *The Times* ran a three-part series (16, 23, and 30 January 1911) on the shortcomings of Unionist operations. To be fair, Acland Hood appreciated these problems. But he was hopelessly overburdened, inaccessible, and increasingly irascible.

Under the strain of the December campaign, the gears creaked more and more audibly. Amery's 'only conclusion' – widely held – was 'that we must at all costs, and whatever the row and friction, reconstruct the whole party organisation'. In a lengthy critique, significantly addressed to Bonar Law, he decried 'the utter badness of the Conservative Central Office', an institution as Dickensian in its 'housing arrangements' as in its habits of circumlocution. Acland Hood's offer to retire as whip was not taken up, leaving Amery to despair that 'till he is poisoned or pensioned we shall not get a step forward'. Press relations were among the disparate responsibilities of Percival Hughes, an amiable aesthete who had not allowed the first election to interfere with his plans for an extended Christmas holiday. On the job, he tended to be closeted with Acland Hood or, euphemistically, otherwise engaged. From personal experience, Amery knew that 'newspaper men wishing to interview Percival Hughes . . . are shoved into a little coal hole which is also a main thoroughfare for clerks, and kept waiting by the hour'.[2]

[1] Blewett, p. 277; Murray to Gardiner, 17 December 1910, Gardiner Papers. Henry Cadbury later recalled these exciting times 'in the thick of political controversy, with the Master of Elibank . . . trying to dragoon the *Daily News* and to bring pressure on our editorial and political policy'. It had not been easy to withstand 'the crack of the Liberal Party Whip'. Autobiographical note by H. T. Cadbury, 13 August 1946, courtesy of E. C. Hambly.

[2] Amery to Bonar Law, 16 December 1910, Bonar Law Papers, 18/6/146; Blewett, p. 275.

A Climacteric Year 163

To improve the amenities, which Amery compared unfavourably with those provided by 'the ordinary dentist', was relatively easy. It would require more than money, however, to achieve the degree of centralization that had come to be regarded as imperative. The Central Office worked independently of, and sometimes at cross purposes with, the National Union, itself pent up in premises described by *The Times* as 'squalid, small and uncomfortable' (30 January 1911). Since 1903, the principal agent had not sat *ex officio* on the National Union executive, thus removing the linchpin. 'The reports that the National Union is to be put into thorough order do not satisfy me,' proclaimed H. W. Wilson, who apprehended that token concessions would forestall fundamental decisions. Amery, another root-and-branch reformer, cited the additional 'anachronism' of the Liberal Unionist Council, which perpetuated a division that 'is nowadays pure fiction', with deleterious effects in many constituencies.[1]

Publicists, considering their own efficiency to have been impaired, were impatient for drastic changes. The schemes that they promulgated in private correspondence were often constructive; but, put into print, they hamstrung the politicians who might implement them. On 13 December, Sandars 'had a talk . . . with Garvin and . . . begged him, and I think with success, to persuade his friends in the press to abstain from a hostile campaign against the Central Office', at least until such time as Balfour 'had inaugurated the tripartite agreement', recently outlined. Balfour concurred that Sandars's 'advice to Garvin was undoubtedly right. Nothing will more embarrass any scheme for party reorganisation', he was convinced, 'than a press crusade against the Central Office.' Yet that crusade was already under way, and Balfour could not oppose it without further loss of credibility.[2]

To Garvin, nearly as vulnerable as himself, Balfour confided his 'secret attitude' on constitutional prospects on 15 December, twelve days before he communicated with Lord Lansdowne and almost a month before he met the King's emissaries – Lords Esher and Knollys – and laid his 'cards upon the table'. A. M. Gollin, reviewing this unusual chronology, has ascribed 'this dependence on Garvin' partly to an eagerness 'to have his views on the proposed new course . . . planned for the party', partly to 'the fear that he might oppose' anything that took him unawares, and partly to the hope 'that the Editor could influence Northcliffe to do what he could, through his Press, to nullify the intrigues of Highbury'. Because the Balfourites assumed the agitation to be fomented by the Chamberlain entourage, they grievously underestimated its scope and depth. A glance at the *Daily Mail* would have dispelled the illusion that Carmelite House, where Northcliffe presided, was a

[1] Wilson to Northcliffe, 13 December 1910, Northcliffe Papers; Amery to Bonar Law, 16 December 1910, Bonar Law Papers, 18/6/146.
[2] Sandars to Balfour, 14 December 1910, and Balfour to Sandars, 17 December 1910, Balfour Papers.

potential counterpoise to Highbury: its leading articles were tinctured with Wilson's resentment. Nor was Northcliffe any longer susceptible to the influence of Garvin who, in any case, was growling fiercely in the *Observer* at the pusillanimity of official Unionism.[1]

For the time being, Garvin retained his status as one of Northcliffe's henchmen, also preserving a working relationship – through Sandars – with Balfour. Nevertheless, his ties in both directions were weakening. Esher, yet to hear directly from Balfour, saw Kennedy Jones shortly before Christmas and found him 'calm, but not in high spirits'. Recounting their conversation to Sandars, Esher quoted Jones's remark, half boast and half apology: 'I am afraid we (i.e. the Northcliffe gang) have temporarily smashed the Party.' That struck Esher as 'an exaggeration, but I think Garvin's violence is not a source of strength'. Sandars was inclined to agree on both scores. He reported the dialogue to Balfour, omitting the unflattering reference to Garvin, whom he curiously chose to identify as his informant. Conceivably he wished to shield Garvin, or possibly Garvin had corroborated Esher's account of Jones, who had a lifelong tendency to repeat himself. Whatever Sandars's motive, he was perplexed by Jones's statement: 'I don't know what he means: unless it be he recognizes that the *Daily Mail*, after all, has limitations & that party politics cannot be commanded on the same methods as a commercial venture.' His interpretation was far too optimistic.[2]

Balfour could not deny that there was 'a very great deal to be said' for Garvin's arguments, though he regarded them as 'somewhat overcharged'. Compared with others, however, Garvin was the very soul of moderation. Disturbed by an inflammatory article in the *Globe* on 16 December, which they saw as 'part and parcel of the scheme ... to create disruption' in Unionist ranks, Blumenfeld and Gwynne dispatched a 'joint telegram to Mr Balfour'. To Sandars, who was recuperating from the election ordeal at Torquay, Blumenfeld explained their intention. 'We simply face disaster if there is to be internecine strife,' he argued. 'I know, we all know, that our system, or rather the rusty old machine, has not done what it should or what it could but nothing is going to be gained by public attacks on persons.' As if to shed light on Jones's allusive comment, he saw evidence of a conspiracy based not at Highbury, but in Fleet Street: 'A certain influence not unknown to either of us is at work on a scheme to "capture the organisation" and substitute its own plan of campaign.' The *Globe*'s 'manoeuvre' ostensibly confirmed what he had 'heard a dozen times this week', namely 'that in future the party is to be "run on *Daily Mail* lines".' Along with Gwynne, who had just departed for Egypt, he condemned 'schemes of reformation being put forward by another newspaper or its proprietors with a view to Tammanyising the organisation'. Not only was the

[1] Gollin, *Observer*, pp. 309–12.
[2] Gollin, *Observer*, p. 321; Esher to Sandars, 27 December 1910, Sandars Papers; Sandars to Balfour, 28 December 1910, Balfour Papers.

idea preposterous, it was also 'bound to fail because its sponsors will not command the obedience of the greater section of the party. I am not exaggerating when I say that almost the entire provincial press with three or four of the London dailies would decline to follow.' Adamant that 'the time for doctoring up the machine is not yet and when it comes it should be left to those responsible to the party', Blumenfeld offered no alternative proposals: 'That is out of my province and the *Express* does not desire to enter into competition' for the custody of Unionism.[1]

Blumenfeld's 'excellent letter' made 'excellent sense' to Sandars, who accepted the fact that the party 'might have done better had the machine been more modern & efficient'. He shared the hope 'that we shall set our house in order at an early date', and that the necessary work 'must be done by men whose business it is and who are appointed to do it by the Party Leader'. In reply, he wrote 'a long & ill expressed letter', acknowledging the 'difficulty' with regard to food taxes, but insisting that it was 'a gross misrepresentation of the Chief to say that he has dropped, or proposes to drop, the Imperial side of the Tariff case'. Like Blumenfeld, he judged the strength of the party by the performance of its newspapers:

> No one recognizes more than I do the excellent service rendered by the Unionist Press. It has been splendid: but a newspaper can no more run a party than a party can run a newspaper. They have a common denominator ... and I pray that a responsible Press which has done such good work will not encourage any divergence of views.

Austen Chamberlain's 'break away', with Smith following at a distance, was to be deplored: 'See how the *Manchester Guardian* exulted over the manoeuvre.' Admitting that 'I may be wrong', Sandars had 'much difficulty in believing that the *Daily Mail* & *The Times* are going to abandon the general scheme of Tariff Reform'. What he believed instead was 'that the Party will remain intact, that men will see the folly of rival camps', and that the areas of controversy would gradually be 'reduced to the smallest limits, with the *M[orning] P[ost]* as the only organ of the minority!'[2]

That, indeed, was wishful thinking. Momentarily, however, the Christmas spirit was so pervasive that not even the Scrooge-like *Morning Post* could entirely resist it. On 9 January, Lord and Lady Bathurst dined with Austen Chamberlain, to whom they deferred. Ten days later, Lady Bathurst heard from her brother-in-law that Chamberlain 'disapproves of the line the *Post* has taken & has said so to the Editor on several occasions'. Reproaching the paper for his own transgressions, now repented, Chamberlain ventured the recon-

---

[1] Balfour to Sandars, 28 December 1910, Sandars Papers; Blumenfeld to Sandars, 17 December 1910 (copy), Blumenfeld Papers.
[2] Sandars to Blumenfeld [December 1910], Blumenfeld Papers.

sidered opinion that 'the way to promote Tariff Reform is to back up the leader of the party & to do what the *Westminster Gazette* did' in the early years of the century, when the Liberals had been savagely divided: the *Westminster*'s 'one aim was to re-unite the Party & bring it back to power; & they succeeded'. He faulted the *Morning Post* for being 'obsessed with the idea that it was always Mr Balfour who was to blame whenever anything happened with which it did not agree'. In short, he was prepared to give Balfour another chance, and he appealed to the *Morning Post* to do the same.[1]

Northcliffe, for one, was not nearly so considerate. He was experiencing renewed difficulties with *The Times*, where Moberly Bell and Buckle (who reportedly had the directors on his side) clashed over the editorial policy to be pursued with respect to the constitutional struggle. Sir Edward Tennant, Asquith's brother-in-law and 'a large shareholder' in the company, 'confirmed' that John Walter IV was anxious to dispose of '*all* his interests in the publication of *The Times* on condition that his "printing" bill, which was overdue and unpaid, should be met without question. This amounted to over £300,000', which Northcliffe would have been hard put to raise. He could draw no further capital from Sir John Ellerman, the shipping magnate and a silent partner in numerous newspaper ventures, who complained that, in the 'three years since we bought' *The Times*, 'the results, as you know, have not been up to our expectations. I cannot help thinking that the expenses are unduly heavy....' In the event, young Walter was persuaded to retain the shares and the titular chairmanship he had inherited on his father's death the previous February, and he survived Northcliffe to become co-proprietor.[2]

Invigorated by electoral combat and accepting the inconclusive result as a renewed challenge, Northcliffe threw himself into the task of directing his various properties in order to effect greater co-ordination among them. His own inconsistencies rebounded against him. 'Now that you have had your annual outburst against Churchill,' he berated Marlowe,

> I trust you will leave him alone for a time. As a result of the *Daily Mail*'s action, the *Evening News*, without any orders, joined it. The *Daily Mirror* also began but was stopped, and *The Times* people took up the cry.... They naturally think the *Daily Mail* represents my views, and they immediately start to 'please the governor'.

More unwilling than ever to brook insubordination, he refused to allow Buckle to pontificate 'about the "independence" of *The Times*'. He had had his fill of 'that sort of nonsense', he told Reginald Nicholson, his employee since 1903 and now manager at Printing House Square. 'Would indeed that *The Times*

---

[1] Austen Chamberlain to Mrs Joseph Chamberlain, 9 January 1911, Chamberlain Papers, AC 4/1/609; L. J. Bathurst to Lady Bathurst, 19 January 1911, Bathurst Papers.

[2] Hobhouse's diary, 6 December 1910, quoted in *Inside Asquith's Cabinet*, p. 83; *History of The Times*, III, ch. xxiv; Ellerman to Northcliffe, 23 January 1911, Northcliffe Papers.

were independent. . . . It has about as much independence on certain matters as has the hall porter at the Foreign Office or a Bond Street picture dealer's assistant.' He could not say the same about the *Observer*, which had led rather than followed official opinion, most recently into a blind alley, and which now incurred his proprietorial wrath.[1]

Always erratic in his adherence to Tariff Reform, Northcliffe concluded on the basis of 'twenty years' personal experience of Canada and [the] United States' that the negotiation of a reciprocity treaty between them would deal a mortal blow to the British movement for protectionism. With the announcement in late January 1911 that such an agreement had been provisionally reached, he hastily pronounced the cause to be dead and, with indecent glee, danced on its shallow grave. 'Exit Imperial Preference,' marked the leading article in the *Daily Mail* on 30 January. Calling it to Garvin's attention, as if that were necessary, Northcliffe did not so much express the hope as deliver the injunction that 'you will agree'.[2]

It went without saying that Garvin did not agree, and it remained only to be seen how far – and how publicly – he meant to carry his dissent. For the *Daily Mail* to have spoken in terms of a 'banged barred and bolted door' seemed to him 'as bad as bad can be'. He pleaded with Northcliffe not to reverse his stand, but merely to permit the *Observer* the latitude to distance itself. 'You know my record and my character,' he protested:

> I, of all men, would be left without a rag of the world's respect – & without a vestige of self-respect – if I were to throw over the cause to which I have given the best years of my life; and if I were now to echo the *Daily Mail* in views which you well know me to believe disastrous & wrong.

Though 'a bit sick at heart to see joy given to the enemy', Garvin continued to address Northcliffe as 'My dear Chief' and professed 'I love you all the same'. But Northcliffe, at his most imperious, demanded absolute compliance, as stipulated in the fifth clause of the 1905 articles of agreement, which reserved to him the right 'to direct and control all articles or comments of a political character . . . and to dictate what matter of political character shall or shall not be inserted'. Risking the consequences, the *Observer* on 5 February repudiated the 'somewhat gigantic assertions' of its sibling, the *Daily Mail*. Clutching at literary straws, the sure sign of an autodidact under duress, Garvin vowed that he would neither 'mumble like King Lear in his dotage' nor 'stake the fate of an Empire upon a hope, like Mr Micawber's, that something will turn up'.[3]

Austen Chamberlain, touched by the *Observer*'s tribute to his father's sacrifice, congratulated Garvin for having stood firm. 'What is the secret of the

[1] Northcliffe to Marlowe, 19 January 1911 (copy), and Northcliffe to Reginald Nicholson, 6 March 1911 (copy), Northcliffe Papers.
[2] Gollin, *Observer*, pp. 287–93.
[3] Garvin to Northcliffe, 1 and 2 February 1911 (copies), Garvin Papers.

Daily Mail's desertion?' he wondered. Actually, there was no secret. Northcliffe, propelled by his own volatility, was resolved to assert his authority over his newspapers so that their unity would set an example to the party and, in the process, demonstrate his overarching power. That he should have been contradicted in the columns of one of his own papers was therefore doubly intolerable. Continued collaboration with Garvin was out of the question. 'So far as I am concerned, the *Observer* is nothing,' he informed Aitken, who was trying to patch over differences. 'It is everything to Garvin', whom he gave the option to buy him out.[1]

Garvin had three weeks to find a benefactor who would meet Northcliffe's price of £40,000 with the understanding that editorial arrangements would not be disturbed. Aitken sounded out Goulding, and Lord Roberts applied to C. S. Goldman, for whom Garvin had worked on the *Outlook*. Now a Conservative MP, Goldman assembled a syndicate that included several South African financiers, Arthur Steel-Maitland, and Waldorf Astor. Meanwhile, Garvin entered into direct negotiations with Astor, the newly elected Conservative member for Plymouth whose father owned the *Pall Mall Gazette*. Time was running out for Garvin, who nursed the bruises from his previous collision with Goldman. 'I fear that a week may elapse before I am able to approach any one of the four or five people or sets of people willing to support me, with a definite & final proposition,' he wrote to John Coode Adams, the Astors' legal and business adviser, after a preliminary interview on 8 February. 'Then there are, in party interests, suggestions of compromise which of course I cannot repulse off-hand though I don't see how they are to come to anything,' he confessed.[2]

By 22 February, Garvin had sorted through 'the simultaneous enquiries made in other quarters' and was ready to offer Adams 'a definite proposition'. The *Observer*, with a circulation of 'practically 60,000', was available 'lock, stock & barrel' for £48,000, an amount immediately knocked down to £45,000. Even so, it exceeded Northcliffe's price by the estimated value of Garvin's shareholding. Cognizant of W. W. Astor's primary desire to secure a capable political editor for the *Pall Mall Gazette*, which had lost sales and reputation, Garvin pledged that, 'if that price were paid, I should be prepared to take over within seven or eight months' the control of that evening journal as well. The delay, he pointed out, would inflict no hardship, as 'early November or early February are the best times for starting or reorganising newspapers'. Garvin, as he himself studiously phrased it, was 'prepared to accept to begin with £1,500 on the *Pall Mall*', provided that he continued to draw an annual salary of £2,000 from the *Observer*. He 'would of course have then to give up the *Daily Telegraph*', which paid him '£2,000 a year for about ten hours' work a week'. Finally, he would decline the editorship of the *Globe*, temptingly offered by

---

[1] Austen Chamberlain to Garvin, 5 February 1911, Garvin Papers; Northcliffe to Aitken, 21 February 1911 (copy?), Northcliffe Papers.
[2] Garvin to Adams [February 1911], Astor Papers; Gollin, *Observer*, pp. 297–98.

Armstrong and Madge. 'The intending purchasers of the *Globe* have an absolute option; but are unlikely to complete unless I join them,' he mistakenly supposed. Convinced that the reincarnated Armstrong-Madge 'proprietorship would not last long', he prematurely anticipated the amalgamation of the *Globe* and the *Pall Mall Gazette*.[1]

The elder Astor, inconveniently abroad, required assurances from Adams that the *Observer*'s accounts were in order, that Garvin (a Roman Catholic by birth) was a sound Protestant who raised his children in the reformed faith, and that the political chiefs gave their assent. 'The support of the leaders of the Unionist party is absolutely assured,' declared Garvin, who furnished 'two letters' – one of them from Lord Roberts – 'typical of others that I have received'. The crucial endorsement came from Austen Chamberlain, who 'spoke highly of Garvin & urged our securing his services'. A few months earlier, he would have been less enthusiastic. Northcliffe posed no obstacle and, on 21 March, 'fully agreed ... not to be connected with any Sunday paper for 5 years'. On 5 April, the transaction was complete. The bone of contention having been removed, Garvin and Northcliffe were soon again companions on the golf links.[2]

The ministerial press was understandably reluctant to treat the matter so lightly. To the *Daily News* (6 February), the confrontation between Garvin and Northcliffe had qualified as 'not the least remarkable of the series of dissolving views' over Tariff Reform. *Truth* (12 April) considered the transfer of the *Observer* a subject 'of some public interest'. Northcliffe, incongruously cast as a hero, had been shrewd enough to recognize that it was 'not good business for a newspaper to devote itself to flogging a dead horse', as Imperial Preference had apparently become: 'Wise men and fools alike make mistakes, but only wise men see their mistakes and retrieve them.' Garvin, who 'was not disposed to toe the new line', survived – as he had often accused Redmond of doing – by recourse to 'American Gold'. The immediate conflict over public policy was held to be incidental to rival conceptions of the political press, its attributes, and its functions:

> To read the signs of the times aright is one of the essentials of conducting newspapers successfully – at any rate newspapers which seek to please a large public and aspire to be regarded as 'influential'. As a matter of fact, the influence which newspapers can exercise on public opinion has very definite limits, and is much stronger in stimulating opinion than in reversing it. Editors who conceive themselves to be prophets with a mission to convert the world from this or that error have generally come to grief. The most

[1] Garvin to Adams, 22 and 24 February 1911, and Adams's memorandum of 23 February 1911, Astor Papers.

[2] Garvin to Adams, 24 February 1911, and Adams's memoranda of 23 February and 30 April 1911, Astor Papers; Gollin, *Observer*, pp. 303–306. Garvin's second wife was a convert to Roman Catholicism, and his daughter Viola followed suit.

successful of them have been experts in the art of foreseeing which way the wind is likely to blow, and shaping their course accordingly. Some of them – John Delane, for instance – have been so successful in this that they have been able to persuade the public that they make the wind blow. This is the highest form of journalistic art.

By his own admission, Garvin was not an artist of Delane's school. Asked by a fellow journalist to 'summarise his policy', he enunciated

> three principles, all of which had stood the test of time. (1) To give the paper, above all, 'character'. (2) To restore in an age of tabloid journalism the full treatment of important subjects. (3) to give the public at need what it, at first, did not want – the only real path to moral influence.[1]

Because the test of time never produced clearcut results, Garvin was as much entitled to his view as were his critics. Nevertheless, his interpretation of tradition was distinctly more valid than his response to contemporary circumstances. Its partisan motive notwithstanding, *Truth* did not misrepresent Northcliffe, who replied in virtually identical terms to an entreaty from Leo Maxse. The editor of a monthly journal, Maxse petitioned Northcliffe to start a new political daily, aggressively Unionist in all respects. There were already 'two such newspapers – the *Morning Post* and the *Daily Express*', rejoined Northcliffe. 'Wild horses would not persuade' the management of either property to divulge 'how many copies they printed yesterday – or any day. I happen to know.' Nor had he 'seen either of them accomplish anything successful in the way of influencing public opinion in the right direction'. Labelling Maxse's proposal a formula for commercial suicide, Northcliffe argued that, invariably, 'such a newspaper as you suggest ... gives the impression of nagging, wearies the public, and loses readers. ... A nagging paper is like a nagging woman.'[2]

That Maxse should have approached Northcliffe at this juncture, while the transfer of the *Observer* was still in progress and so soon after the rupture with Garvin, was perhaps surprising. It implied that the Unionist hard-liners were desperate for allies in Fleet Street and that Northcliffe's apostasy was not expected to last. More profoundly, it indicated a decisive change of attitude on the part of many newspapermen, who were reacting to developments within their respective parties and concomitant adjustments in the structure of the press.

In 1911, after a year of frenetic electoral activity, both major parties – and the Labour Party as well – underwent a process of internal reorganization and reorientation. The results were most far-reaching among the Unionists, cul-

---

[1] Simonis, *Street of Ink*, p. 127.
[2] Northcliffe to Maxse, 11 March 1911, Maxse Papers.

minating in Balfour's surrender of the leadership. But the same forces were at work across the broad spectrum of party politics. Newspapers, serving simultaneously as catalysts and conduits, were directly affected. For them, 1911 was pre-eminently a year of transformations, some conducted more discreetly than others.

Astor's purchase of the *Observer* was but the first in a spate of editorial and proprietorial reshuffles. Coincident with the retrieval of the *Globe* from Hildebrand Harmsworth, and setting the stage for the remodelling of the *Pall Mall Gazette*, it was – by dint of the personalities involved – the most controversial, and therefore demands the extensive treatment it has received here. All the same, it illustrated the general tendency by achieving a measured distance between editorial policy and party requirements. The effect was obvious as early as 5 March, when Garvin issued a 'Demand for a Plain Policy' and said: 'Reluctant as we are to criticise Opposition leadership in any way at this moment, this is no hour for conventional echoes of official sentiments. . . .' Northcliffe was vindicated, at least in principle. Even the *Westminster Gazette*, respected by Austen Chamberlain for its prudent partisanship, was emboldened to rub against the ministerial grain. 'The position of an editor with a soul of his own would be more difficult than it is, if every criticism that he made of a public man was to be taken as evidence of unfriendliness,' insisted Spender, obliged to defend himself to Runciman.[1]

This marked retreat from the idea of editorial fealty, carried in a few extreme cases to the point of open rebellion, occurred against a background of intra-party turbulence and, more pointedly, in the face of intensified efforts to impose journalistic conformity. Writing at exactly this time, Hilaire Belloc and Cecil Chesterton warned of the dangers posed to the foundations of a free press by 'the pressures of party-machinery'. Unable to separate cause and effect, they found it difficult to say whether the press had been 'grossly and even ludicrously warped' by its subordination to the party system, or whether 'the motive force is the other way', with the press functioning as 'a voluntary agent freely supporting the Party System and its hypocrisies'. Partners in evil, the press and the party system were depicted as mutual pollutants. In retrospect, this fear may be discounted, but cannot be dismissed. To account for its intensity, one must investigate what Belloc and Chesteron called 'the dreadful antagonisms which separate the Siamese Twins of politics'.[2]

*   *   *

Although economic considerations were never absent, the various attempts made in 1911 to consolidate Fleet Street operations were, as a rule, politically inspired. Newspapers were to be made more efficient not only as commercial

---
[1] Spender to Runciman, 22 March 1911 (copy), Spender Papers, Add. MSS. 46,392, fol. 58.
[2] *The Party System* (London, 1911), pp. 218–26.

enterprises, but also as party instruments. Politicians and proprietors generally accepted this premiss, though they occasionally differed sharply with respect to its application. Editors, to the extent that circumstances allowed them any choice, went along. Most often, the essential effect was to accelerate a trend in post-Victorian journalism. Occasionally, however, it introduced new elements of conflict.

The availability of capital set the boundaries for what was practicable, without in itself ensuring the success of any particular property. Within those fixed lines of demarcation, there remained ample scope for the exercise of discretion. The task of party managers was first to stimulate newspaper investment and then to see to it that proper value was obtained for their supporters' money; in both areas, their interventions grew more direct as well as more frequent. Proprietors, while grateful for financial assistance in one form or another, were inclined to resist certain demands that inevitably followed from it. For the sake of mutual convenience, these interacting relationships were deliberately obscured and, when necessary, disingenuously denied. Nevertheless, they affected a widening segment of the political press.

The old model survived in those isolated instances where commerce and ideology jointly favoured it. Even here, however, the same patterns of contraction and accountability may be discerned. During the summer of 1910, the Cadburys and the Rowntrees conferred to arrange the complete amalgamation of their respective metropolitan dailies. The Rowntrees' controlling interest in the company that ran the *Morning Leader* and the *Star* was consequently 'handed over without consideration to the Cadburys', who 'agreed that the time had come for the *Morning Leader* to be incorporated with the *Daily News* and for the *Daily News* to acquire the *Star* newspaper which would be printed on *Daily News* machines', modernized for double duty. Joseph Rowntree was said to be 'particularly pleased' at the thought that at least two of these three 'leading Progressive newspapers' would survive to uphold tradition: that was something he deemed 'of vital importance for the future of British Liberalism'. He and his fellow shareholders settled for 'a much smaller price than they could have obtained from a purchaser taking over the concern for a commercial reason without any pledge as to continuity of policy'.[1]

The terms of the Cadbury-Rowntree agreement were ratified in April 1911 and took effect at the end of the year. The merger of the two morning papers resulted in staff redundancies. E. T. ('Ted') Scott 'survived the massacre', but decided anyway to relocate to the *Manchester Guardian*, where he was to succeed his father as editor in 1929. R. C. K. Ensor, one of the less fortunate, was given notice after two years as a leader-writer for the *Daily News*; it was 'an ugly business' for a man 'with two or three children & no other work & hardly any but Conservative papers in London', thought C. E. Montague, a *Guardian*

[1] 'The Star and Morning Leader (1909) Ltd.,' memorandum of 15 October 1929, Cowdray Papers.

director.¹ Ensor soon found employment on the *Daily Chronicle*, where he remained until 1930, the year that the *Daily Chronicle* and the *Daily News* came together as the *News Chronicle*.

'The new combined Liberal paper, the *Daily News and Leader*', as Harold Spender grandly touted it to John Burns, made its delayed debut on 8 May 1912. Lloyd George and Haldane were among the party notables who granted interviews for the first number, which was dominated by reports of the recent sinking of the *Titanic*. Ramsay MacDonald, too 'filled up at the moment' to contribute an article, considered it 'very unfortunate that the *Titanic* incident overshadowed what after all is the very much more important matter of the continued depression of labour'. Burns was likewise too busy to supply a piece on the Local Government Board: 'Apart from this the *D.N.* cannot be interested in anything I say or my Dept. does.' He was neither unusual nor mistaken in his presumption that the 'new' paper was a recast version of the *Daily News*. Gardiner, without a seat on the reconstructed board, stayed on as editor. Ernest Parke, relieved of his editorship, was compensated with a directorship. Scott duly surmised that Parke was 'in command at the *Daily News*, ... with Gardiner late editor now hardly more than chief leader writer'. As time would show, it was not a satisfactory arrangement.²

Effected without direct party tutelage, this amalgamation – broached in 1910, plotted in 1911, and implemented in 1912 – was none the less governed by political factors. It was ordained that the *Daily News* should absorb the *Morning Leader*, and not *vice versa*. The more vigorous of the two halfpenny journals, the *Daily News* was acknowledged by Lloyd George to have lent a 'powerful influence' to the enactment of his National Insurance scheme. 'I can see evidence of that in all the papers today,' he wrote with 'many thanks' to Gardiner on 29 March 1911, two days after the *Daily News* had boomed its support. 'Vested interests in this as in all reforms are potent & pernicious. They can be successfully fought in one way – by rousing the public conscience to the wickedness of exploiting human distress to satiate greed.'³ The *Daily News* excelled as a conscience-rouser, endearing itself to Lloyd George, Mac-Donald, and the Webbs, at the cost of alienating Burns.

It would be wrong to suppose that the Liberals practised *laissez-faire* in their dealings with the press. The active participation of successive chief whips in the financial affairs of the *Westminster Gazette* has been noted. During 1911, when the business side was temporarily running smoothly, collaboration between that paper and the government was maintained informally. Spender was warmly received at the Foreign Office by Grey and, in October, he was the

¹ Montague to Dodd, 19 December 1911, Montague-Dodd Correspondence, Add. MSS. 45,910, fol. 67.
² Spender to Burns, 6 May 1912 (with Burns's comments), Burns Papers, Add. MSS. 46,302, fol. 147; MacDonald to Gardiner, 8 May 1912, Gardiner Papers; Scott's diary, 19 September 1912, *Guardian* Archives.
³ Lloyd George to Gardiner, 29 March 1911, Gardiner Papers.

Asquiths' holiday guest at Archerfield in East Lothian. There, on 'neutral ground', he had the 'rare ... chance for the Liberal journalist' to converse for 'a delightful hour' with Balfour, who had motored over from Whittinghame. The Prime Minister not only spoke candidly to Spender, but also 'permitted McKenna to take me into his confidence – not as a journalist but as an old friend – so that we might consult together as to what was best and wisest for him to do' about the situation at the Admiralty. Lord Loreburn thought it was 'monstrous' that Spender, 'a mere journalist, should know things that were unknown to him, Cabinet Minister and Lord Chancellor'. But, however constitutionally unsound, that was the most convenient ministerial method for newspaper management.[1]

The *Manchester Guardian* was handled in much the same way, though by other elements within the Cabinet. Scott, having paid off his massive overdraft, was now securely in control. Lloyd George's job was to see to it that the editor's pacifist conscience did not get the better of him. The morning after the Chancellor delivered a bellicose speech at the Mansion House on the second Moroccan crisis, he invited Scott to breakfast. Churchill and the Master of Elibank joined in the 'endeavour to inculcate a little common-sense and patriotism into the head of Scott', who provided an account of their efforts:

> Lloyd George rather laid it on about *Manchester Guardian* – it would smash party if we and Government were at odds. *Manchester Guardian* he had found much more considered in Germany than any other Liberal paper and if we let Government down in international controversy it would be inferred that they had no sufficient backing in the country and give a dangerously false impression of their actual determination which up to a certain point was fixed and practically unanimous, Loreburn being the only exception.

Although not wholly convinced by Lloyd George, who seemed 'not immune from the microbe of Germanophobia', Scott was doubtless flattered by the attention he received. To dissociate himself or his paper from Lloyd George was always too painful to contemplate.[2]

Lloyd George also commanded the devotion of Sir Henry Dalziel, the proprietor of *Reynolds's Weekly*. But, in the case of this popular Sunday journal, more than verbal reinforcement was required. On 9 January 1911, the company that published *Reynolds's* – John Dicks Press Ltd. – was refloated. Four blocks of 10,000 one-pound common shares were issued over Dalziel's signature to individuals who were apparently designated by the Master of Elibank, the actual purchaser. That the certificates and relevant correspondence were retained among the Asquith papers would indicate that party funds

[1] Spender, *Life, Journalism and Politics*, I, 240–41.
[2] A. C. Murray's diary, 22 July 1911, and Scott's diary, 22 July 1911, quoted in *Political Diaries of C. P. Scott*, pp. 46–48; *also see* Ayerst, *Guardian*, pp. 365–68, where Scott is described as having 'been misled, not converted'.

A Climacteric Year 175

were used. Fourteen years later, an official of the Liberal Central Association sought information about the investment. Lord Dalziel of Kirkcaldy (as he had since become) replied that the John Dicks shares 'were valueless. The purposes for which they had been bought had been served,' he explained, 'but he would continue to help the Party in such ways as were within his power.'[1] A speculator in Marconi shares, along with Lloyd George and Isaacs, the Master of Elibank was a past master at concealed investments.

So, too, was Steel-Maitland, appointed in June 1911 as Unionist party chairman. At the same time, Lord Balcarres replaced Acland Hood as opposition chief whip in the House of Commons. Robert Sanders was one backbencher who was dismayed to see 'Steel-Maitland much puffed in Press on taking over his Central Office duties. Rather a pity for him to go in for that style of advertisement.' On the contrary, it was greatly to Steel-Maitland's advantage – and the party's – that he appreciated the value of newspaper publicity. He promptly pushed aside Percival Hughes, who had 'completely broken down and was absolutely useless', and brought in J. Malcolm Fraser 'to deal with Press matters'. Fraser was superbly qualified: a general utility man for Pearson, he had been assistant editor of the *Standard*, editor of the *Evening Standard* and the *St James's Gazette*, day editor of the *Daily Express*, and, most recently, editor of the *Birmingham Gazette*. The press department at Unionist headquarters, Steel-Maitland further informed Bonar Law, 'is being enlarged so as to feed provincial papers'. In keeping with the new spirit, Balcarres issued a set of instructions for the guidance of the perfect parliamentary private secretary: 'He must hold off the interviewer and flatter the bore; he will constantly be required to inspire or baffle the journalist.'[2]

Steel-Maitland, his work cut out for him, cunningly exploited the fluidity of the situation he inherited. The *Observer*, in which he had nearly become a shareholder, was feeling its way under the Astor family's ownership. Steel-Maitland could not pretend to enjoy the same degree of intimacy that had existed between Garvin and Jack Sanders, but relied on Waldorf Astor to keep Garvin in line. For the moment, Garvin was preoccupied by 'a thousand distractions connected with the transfer of the *Observer* and other projected changes'. Among them was the impending overhaul of the *Pall Mall Gazette*. F. J. Higginbottom, who had edited that paper since April 1909, had delivered his 'humble opinion' in favour of Garvin's continuation at the *Observer* and now had to pay the price. Without a reduction in salary,

[1] Certificates dated 9 January 1911, and Murray to Dalziel, 6 April 1911, Asquith Papers; a 'secret' memorandum by R. Humphrey Davies [1926] reports a meeting with Dalziel on 18 August 1925, Asquith Papers.
[2] Sanders's diary, 28 June 1911, Bayford Papers; memoranda by Steel-Maitland and Balcarres [July 1911], Bonar Law Papers, 41/I/1c, 2.

he was demoted to 'special parliamentary representative' at the turn of the year, when Garvin succeeded him.[1]

Garvin arrived at the *Pall Mall Gazette* office with a sense of history, heightened by a 'private letter' from Cook, who modestly reminded him of the paper's 'greatness in the days' when Stead was editor. He also carried with him a list of 'Thoughts and Ideas' for revitalizing the property. There was to be a 'Definite policy for politics', coupled with a 'Definite scheme for headlines'. More specifically, he envisioned a 'special series of articles giving the truth about things': for example, '*The Evolution of Germany*', with an emphasis on her 'offensive aims'. Consular reports were to be featured. 'There should be a good woman reporter.' The tone of the new *Pall Mall* was to be one not of 'optimism but reassurance'. Political coverage should always include 'something that the other side will want to read'. One proposed subject for inquiry was the 'State of the Unionist Press'.[2]

It took time for Garvin to put his ideas into practice. 'Five weeks hence the remodelled *P.M.G.* will be an organ to be reckoned with,' he promised Bonar Law on 4 January 1912; meanwhile, he implored him not to 'judge by the present form'. Two weeks later, he was still 'getting the new thing in order, and preparing for the final model to appear on January 29th'. It was an arduous undertaking. 'I now have to get up at 5.30 every morning for the *Pall Mall Gazette* and must turn in before 10 at night to get proper sleep,' he told Bonar Law.

> Otherwise one could not go on, and the *Observer* added means that the last two days of the week are wholly mortgaged. This must continue for a few months, though things will be easier afterwards. Meantime, I have stopped going out, and a pledge to dine with Aitken if he likes before the opening of Parliament is the last standing engagement I have got. Political friends with important things to tell me are coming to me a good deal at home for short dinners and talks.

Consumed by the 'grim business' of daily deadlines and profoundly aware that 'there is still vast room for improvement', he began to see the emergence of 'a thing that the best kind of supporters will delight in, and the best kind of opponents will respect'. Not every change was for the better, and he admitted to second thoughts about the decision to move the leading article to an inside page. 'As for the leader, I don't think any man on earth attaches more importance to it than I do,' he replied to a remonstrance from Stead; 'but that having been done, I could not, for many reasons, put it back.' By mid-February, he was able to relax his pace. 'Do knock on the head the silly story

---

[1] Garvin to Stead, 15 May 1911, Stead Papers; Higginbottom to Adams, 29 March 1911, and Adams's memorandum of 4 December 1911, Astor Papers.

[2] Garvin to Stead, 19 January 1912, Stead Papers; notes for reorganizing the *Pall Mall Gazette* [1911], Garvin Papers.

about my working seven days a week,' he urged Stead. 'The thing is going so well now that I can get away from London Sundays and Mondays, and put all my labour into five days – though as regards those, I confess to a certain amount of activity!'[1]

Writing to Waldorf Astor on 20 March, Garvin was 'happy to be able to say that everything has so far succeeded clean beyond our utmost expectation'. The sale of the *Pall Mall Gazette* had 'more than doubled and the increase has been solidly held, at least, the numbers we have average twenty-five thousand a night'. That, he estimated, was 'practically equal' to the circulation of the *Westminster Gazette*, and he hoped that, when he next wrote, 'it will be to report that we have left that journal behind once and for all. Then nothing will remain in front of us but the *Evening Standard*.'[2]

The two *Standards*, which had been taken over in 1910 by Davison Dalziel, were a source of worry to Steel-Maitland and the party chiefs. Like Astor, Dalziel was an obliging backbencher with more money than experience. He had renewed the editorial contracts of Woodward and Gwynne, both appointed by Pearson. Gwynne, by far the stronger willed, was the first to go. 'I feel that I owe it to your uniform kindness and courtesy ... to tell you that I am about to sever my connection with the *Standard*,' he wrote on 6 May to Balfour, whom he was soon to show less consideration. 'I have struggled hard,' he maintained, 'to sink my personal likes and dislikes in order to retain control of a paper in which I might do useful work for the party and the Empire but there are differences of journalistic principles so wide between my present proprietor and myself that I am afraid they are quite insuperable.' In the light of Davison Dalziel's antecedents, Gwynne wished it to be known that he entertained 'no objections whatever to Jews, nor have I any great dislike for financiers'. Nevertheless, 'the combination of Jew, finance and shady methods is too much for me' and led to his 'determination to fight as a private – since it is no longer permitted to me to fight as a captain'.[3]

A month later, Gwynne was still tottering on the brink of resignation; but it was Bonar Law rather than Balfour to whom he expressed anxiety 'that you should not think that I have been petulant or unreasonable in the matter'. This shift of loyalty was portentous. 'There are unreconcilable differences of principle involved which no sort of compromise could bridge over for any time,' repeated Gwynne. 'I have been willing to meet Dalziel reasonably, but when I found that we were fundamentally opposed in our views as to the proper conduct of a paper I thought it only right and just both for him & myself to retire.' The formal announcement appeared in the *Standard* on 9 June. Gwynne alerted Garvin to be on the look-out for it and begged him not to

---

[1] Garvin to Bonar Law, 4 January [1912], Bonar Law Papers, 12/4/3; Garvin to Bonar Law, 8 January 1912 (copy), and Garvin to Cook, 2 February 1912 (copy), Garvin Papers; Garvin to Stead, 19 and 30 January, and 16 February 1912, Stead Papers.

[2] Garvin to Astor, 20 March 1912 (copy), Garvin Papers.

[3] Gwynne to Balfour, 6 May 1911, Balfour Papers.

misconstrue its meaning. 'I look upon a paper as a very sacred trust,' he explained. 'Dalziel regards it as a money making machine and must therefore ruin it. His plan of campaign is to push his dirty little financial and commercial interests under my name, as it were, and naturally I couldn't stand this.'[1]

To add to the turmoil, Ware lost the confidence of Lady Bathurst and, scarcely a week after Gwynne's resignation, was summarily dismissed from the editorship of the *Morning Post*. He fixed the blame on Harcourt, Lady Bathurst's cousin, 'who had never hitherto taken any interest in the paper', but who now, as Colonial Secretary, 'used all his influence' against Jebb's stand on Canadian-American relations. (Harcourt was to resign his directorship in April 1914, when it became 'increasingly difficult to maintain even a nominal connection with a paper which showed such inveterate personal hostility to me on administrative as apart from personal matters'.) Jebb, whose own departure soon followed, confided that Ware had 'retired ... under circumstances very discreditable to others but in no wise to himself'. In retrospect, he tried to dignify the episode. 'The ultimate cause of the trouble,' he reminded Ware, 'was that we were running a Radical policy in the name of Conservatism, trying to twist the principles of Conservatism ... to suit our purpose, which was Liberal Unionist.' To accept this abstraction, one would have to suppose that Garvin and Gwynne were the victims of similar ideological contortions. In point of fact, all three of them experienced the same fate, owing to the unresolved – and perhaps intrinsically unresolvable – conflicts that existed between editorial and proprietorial authority.[2]

Rudyard Kipling noted the conjunction between Ware's exit from the *Morning Post* and Gwynne's from the *Standard*. 'Have you ever thought of Gwynne as a successor to Ware?' he asked Lady Bathurst. She was evidently not enthusiastic, for Kipling endeavoured to persuade her:

> I quite see your point in not wishing to take a man from one of the other papers but Gwynne is by no means the type of man one finds in London journalism.... As I see it, his seven years on the *Standard* has simply given him further knowledge ..., but it has in no way blunted him nor weakened his convictions; and, as you know, he is a good fighter.

Upon reflection, there was no one with better credentials. Sidney Low 'thought somebody might have suggested to Lady Bathurst that she ought to get me to edit the *Morning Post*; but nobody did', presumably because he was unacceptable to militant Tariff Reformers. On 7 July, Lady Bathurst offered Gwynne the editor's chair at £2,000 a year 'to start with', a hundred pounds less

---

[1] Gwynne to Bonar Law, 7 June 1911, Bonar Law Papers, 18/7/176; Gwynne to Garvin, 8 June 1911, Garvin Papers.

[2] Ware to Bonar Law, 3 May 1912, Bonar Law Papers, 26/3/8; Harcourt to Lady Bathurst, 2 April 1914, Bathurst Papers; Jebb to Hannon, 21 June 1911, Hannon Papers; Jebb to Ware, 30 July 1912 (copy), Jebb Papers.

than she had paid Ware. Ivor Maxse was delighted by her choice: 'We Unionists now at last have one daily London paper of repute under the editor[ship] of a *white* man of character. It is what we have lacked all these last few years.' Lord Roberts, too, was tremendously pleased. But Gwynne's greatest debt of gratitude was to Kipling, and his most treasured keepsake in later years was a pencil given to him by the poet's widow.[1]

'I want the Lords to be urged to resist at all costs,' Lady Bathurst, the wife of a diehard peer, instructed Gwynne at the very outset. She referred to the Parliament Bill, which had thrown Unionism into a deepening crisis. To the *Observer* (5 March), there was 'only one path of safety, as of honour, for the Unionist Party, and it is straight and plain. Surrender to the Parliament Bill is the unthinkable course combining the maximum of folly with that of disgrace.' Leo Maxse had 'rarely ... read the *Observer* with greater enjoyment'. The instigator of the 'Balfour Must Go' movement, he took it upon himself to co-ordinate a last-ditch press resistance to the Liberals' constitutional reform. Applauding Higginbottom's resolute stand in the *Pall Mall Gazette*, Maxse railed against Strachey's call for acquiescence in the *Spectator*, a journal 'more Iscariot than the Iscariots'. Blumenfeld's moderation was a disappointment. 'As a constant reader of the *Daily Express* and as an admirer of its combativeness in many good causes in which I am glad to say we are at one', Maxse expressed his 'deep concern' that any compromise would be tantamount to 'a total and unconditional surrender to the demagogue Government which would kill Unionism and Tariff Reform for many years to come, and would instal the present blackguards permanently in office'. To his agitated mind, the *Daily Mail* was no better, and *The Times* ('long ... a snake in the grass') was worst of all.[2]

Garvin, whom Balfour had consulted with such alacrity after the general election, was no longer favoured with official confidences. Perhaps his growing intransigence disqualified him, and perhaps his break with Northcliffe was seen to have diminished his usefulness. Along with Gwynne and Blumenfeld, he became more dependent upon Bonar Law, who undertook to supervise his personal investments. That brought him into closer contact with Aitken, Bonar Law's financial wizard, about whom he had mixed feelings. 'I like Aitken and am immensely impressed by his direct and sure ability,' Garvin told Bonar Law;

> but in my moral position it is most inadvisable to contract peculiar obligations towards anyone whose political career is quite unlike in its conditions

[1] Kipling to Lady Bathurst, 15 and 20 June 1911, Henry Peacock to Lady Bathurst, 27 June 1910 (fixing Ware's salary), Ivor Maxse to Lady Bathurst, 9 July 1911, and Lady Bathurst to Gwynne, 7 July 1911 (copy), Bathurst Papers; Low to Lady Stanley, 29 July 1911, quoted in Chapman-Huston, *Lost Historian*, pp. 243–44.
[2] Maxse to Garvin, 6 March 1911, Garvin Papers; Maxse to Higginbottom, 18 July 1911, quoted in F. J. Higginbottom, *The Vivid Life* (London, 1934), pp. 243–44; Maxse to Strachey, 27

what yours was when we first became acquainted in our great cause. My real friendship towards Aitken and admiration of his powers would be far more effective if I could say that it was perfectly disinterested.

Aitken's surprising election at Ashton-under-Lyne was widely ascribed to corrupt practices, and his protectionist principles were less consistent than he retrospectively made out. His clandestine activities with the press were not restricted to those properties for which he had assumed obligations. 'Don't get too much for the insurgent wing,' he counselled Gwynne in the summer of 1911. 'The country won't over-appreciate their conduct. It is good business for the *Express* and bad business for the *Post*.'[1]

Contrary to Aitken's advice, Gwynne joined Garvin in demanding the outright rejection of the Parliament Bill. No longer inhibited by Davison Dalziel, he wrote joyfully to Garvin 'that you and I are both now independent of what, for lack of a better term, I may call "professional newspaper proprietors"'. But Lady Bathurst did not permit him as much editorial autonomy as Garvin enjoyed under Astor. Both editors tried to distinguish between their brand of resistance and Maxse's, which seemed to them too extreme and potentially counter-productive. 'Your point of view, I take it,' Gwynne wrote disapprovingly to Maxse, 'is that by strenuous and frequent criticisms and attacks on Balfour you will at last force him to leave the Party. There I confess I do not agree with you at all.' Gwynne recalled having taken that tack 'in 1906, and found that if I had continued I should have split up the Party hopelessly'. His present strategy, therefore, was to strengthen Balfour, not to drive him from the leadership. Garvin, equally short-sighted in his objectives, insisted that, 'when we are out of this', Sandars would 'only have to lift [a] hand' to command the *Observer*'s resumed loyalty on Balfour's behalf.[2]

Yet, to all intents and purposes, Gwynne and Garvin served Maxse's divisive purpose. On 9 July, the *Observer* weighed the alternatives and concluded: 'It would be better that the Unionist Party should temporarily break up ... than that it should be hopelessly devitalised by endless disappointment, dissension and perplexity.' Like the Unionist majority in the House of Lords, the Unionist press was split between 'hedgers' and 'ditchers'. Garvin was enraged to see

---

April 1911, Strachey Papers; Maxse to Blumenfeld, 10 July 1911, Blumenfeld Papers; *National Review*, September 1911.

[1] Garvin to Bonar Law, 4 January and 11 May 1911, Bonar Law Papers, 12/4/3 ff.; Aitken to Gwynne, 26 July 1911 (copy), Beaverbrook Papers, C/148. For Aitken as a Tariff Reformer, compare Gollin, *Observer*, pp. 291–92, with Beaverbrook, *Politicians and the Press* (London, 1925?), pp. 120–21. For J. C. C. Davidson's view that Aitken was 'amoral' and had run a 'corrupt' campaign, see Robert Rhodes James, *Memoirs of a Conservative* (London, 1969), pp. 26–29.

[2] Gwynne to Garvin, 29 September 1911, Garvin Papers; Gwynne to Maxse, 19 July 1911, Maxse Papers; Garvin to Sandars, 12 July 1911, Balfour Papers.

almost the whole brass band of the Unionist morning newspapers... leading the noble movement to the rear, with the *Daily Telegraph* well in front, banging the big drum of scuttle. *The Times* follows the lead of its contemporary of Peterborough-court, though successfully reduced by that organ to a secondary part in the valiant procession.

The next morning, the *Telegraph* reiterated its 'judgment' that the time had not come 'for desperate expedients, or for plunging against the odds'. Garvin detected the sinister influence of Walter Long, who had 'tried ... to get at the Astors in order to have me muzzled .... These are the conditions under which Unionist journalism is expected to retain its vigour,' he complained. Austen Chamberlain provided him with 'a counterblast' against Long to be shown to the Astors if the need arose. Without Long's prodding, *The Times* was as timid as the *Telegraph*, and Garvin did not hesitate to say so in print on the very 'Sunday we were due at Northcliffe's!' Fortunately, his host took no offence. It was not that Northcliffe had mellowed, but rather that, now that the *Observer* was outside his stable, he was able to shrug off its pinpricks.[1]

Alliances in Fleet Street had altered drastically since the beginning of the year, when Garvin had been associated – tactically and remuneratively – with Northcliffe and Burnham. By summer, he was making common cause with Lady Bathurst, who thanked him for his 'kind remarks about the *Morning Post*' and anticipated 'that under our new Editor we may do even better work than in the past'. Admittedly, Garvin found it easier to collaborate with Gwynne than with Ware. But the shift in his own position, as yet only half acknowledged, was more decisive than the change of editorship at the *Morning Post*. It must have given him pause when Lady Bathurst welcomed him to the camp of reaction, expressing certainty 'that such papers as the *Observer*, the *Pall Mall*, the *Globe*, the *Morning Post* and the *National Review* who are *opposed* to Social Revolutions and the tyranny of the demagogue should unite to do their best to convert the country to sanity'.[2] Justifiably proud of his reputation as a social reformer, and perennially attracted to Lloyd George, Garvin was keeping strange company.

At *The Times*, Buckle resolved to 'defeat Garvin & his Wild Peers' after the *Observer* (23 July) warned Balfour that, in the event of surrender, 'he will never command a united party again'. As an antidote to the letters Amery and Smith had published in the *Observer*, Buckle and Northcliffe simultaneously sought a rebuttal from Curzon, who tendered sober 'advice' on 'the duty of the peers' (24 July). Buckle 'tried also to get St Aldwyn' to write as an elder statesman, 'but he was out of town'.[3] The ordinary reader would not have

---

[1] Garvin to Sandars, 12 July 1911, Balfour Papers; Austen Chamberlain to Garvin, 14 July 1911, Garvin Papers.
[2] Lady Bathurst to Garvin, 20 July [1911], Garvin Papers.
[3] Buckle to Northcliffe, 23 July 1911, Northcliffe Papers; Amery, *My Political Life*, I (London, 1953), 378.

suspected that politicians' letters in *The Times*, as in the *Observer* and other journals, were not only planted, but also solicited.

Awaiting the delivery of Curzon's bespoken goods, Northcliffe made 'a communication by telephone' with Sandars, who knew – if anyone did – Balfour's mind. Sandars was clearly taken aback by this direct approach:

> Lord Northcliffe begged to be advised as to a line for his Press. I temporized; but ultimately I was spared an interview, as Lord Curzon got into communication with Lord Northcliffe, squared his Press and wrote a long letter that evening to *The Times*. This settled the policy of Lord Northcliffe's newspapers.[1]

Balfour was in accord with Curzon's view that a policy of 'No Surrender' would lead to the debasement of the peerage and the prostitution of the royal prerogative. In a public letter to Lord Newton, he proclaimed his readiness to 'stand ... [and], if need be, to fall' with Lord Lansdowne, who enjoined his noble followers to withdraw their amendments for the sake of their chamber and the Crown. The *Morning Post* was sceptical, but polite. On the one hand, it defended those who 'feel that duty and regard for their principles compel them to oppose the passage of the Parliament Bill to the bitter end'; on the other, it considered it 'absurd to suggest that the party is torn in twain or that there is a revolt against the recognized leaders' (26 July).

Better than Garvin, who was rebuked by Waldorf Astor for his intemperate rhetoric, Gwynne maintained a posture of loyalty to Balfour and Lansdowne. In spite of its implicit contradictions, or possibly because of them, the *Morning Post*'s leading article on the 26th had 'saved a disaster not only to our cause but to the party. When honest men join together for a definite purpose,' Gwynne explained to Lady Bathurst, 'there are always rogues who follow in the rear trying to pick up things for themselves.' More 'by instinct than reason', he had 'decided on the lines of the leader' not so much to bolster Balfour as to safeguard 'the movement' from Smith, who was 'looking for his dirty little opportunity' to seize control. 'The effect has been to strengthen our followers and to weaken F.E.'s little plan.' Thus, the *Morning Post*'s disclaimer of any anti-Balfour designs was not to be taken seriously. On Monday, 7 August, Gwynne '*very, very privately*' promised Lady Bathurst 'a first class chance of victory on Wednesday', when the Parliament Bill was to have a final reading. 'Always remember,' he urged her, 'that the defeat of the Bill means the political death of A.J.B. Therefore the struggle has to be kept up with full strength.' His prognosis proved wrong, for the Bill was carried through the Lords with the help of 'ratters' and abstainers. Afterwards, Gwynne grimly

---

[1] Sandars, 'Diary of the Events and Transactions in connection with the passage of the Parliament Bill of 1911 through the House of Lords,' 12 August 1911, Balfour Papers.

vowed to resume the fight against Balfour he had begun in 1906 at the *Standard*.[1]

Buckle, by contrast, was satisfied by the result. 'I think we may congratulate ourselves,' he wrote to Northcliffe. 'It was a narrow margin, but it was not the right side.... All has now come out right for the Paper.' Northcliffe reciprocated his sentiments:

> I can truly say that I have never been so pleased with *The Times* as during the Parliament Bill discussion. You laboured against very heavy odds....
>
> Unfortunately our leaders do not understand newspapers and pay very much more attention to those of their enemies than to those of their friends.

True to form, Northcliffe divided the political world into enemies and friends, assuming that what went on in newspaper offices was more important than divisions in the lobbies at Westminster. He was particularly pleased with the battle that *The Times* had waged 'against the Forwards', backed by Amery and Smith. 'If an attempt is made, as is threatened by Garvin and others, to keep going the Forward organization for future use', Buckle predicted that it would 'not hold together, and the new party will consist almost entirely of those who want to pull down Balfour and Lansdowne'. Events proved him only partially correct.[2]

Gwynne, as we have seen, deserved a modicum of credit for heading off the Forwards. Marlowe unwittingly lent himself to their campaign. On 8 August, the *Daily Mail* published a letter from Strachey, who deplored the 'appeal to force' promulgated by Smith and other diehards; a leading article underscored Strachey's point. Northcliffe took Marlowe to task for giving such 'extraordinary prominence' to 'a movement which will die by itself at the end of this week if left alone'. Ever 'since the days of the establishment of Christianity', history had taught the lesson that the 'way of making a movement successful' was to 'attack the leader'. To liken Smith to the Redeemer was not so much to err as to blaspheme; but Fleet Street was inured to that.[3]

Edward Goulding, who had kept Garvin informed of front-bench deliberations, paid higher tribute to Blumenfeld's 'A-1' work in the *Daily Express*. 'I am sick of A.J.B. and the Lords,' he declared on the day of the showdown, when he hoped that Blumenfeld would proceed to 'go bald headed for an elected 2nd chamber'. Within the week, Northcliffe had come to share Goulding's weariness. Regretfully, he could no longer 'be so optimistic ... about the state of our party', nor so confident that the Forwards were played out. 'We are dealing with accomplished politicians,' he reminded Buckle and,

---

[1] Astor to Garvin, 4 August 1911, Garvin Papers; Gwynne to Lady Bathurst, 26 July and 7 August 1911, and 'Sunday' [1911], Bathurst Papers.

[2] Buckle to Northcliffe, 10 and 14 August 1911, and Northcliffe to Buckle, 12 August 1911 (copy), Northcliffe Papers.

[3] Northcliffe to Marlowe, 8 August 1911 (copy), Northcliffe Papers.

in the process, himself. 'At present they are engaged in trying to capture the organisation, of which they already control a considerable part.' Did Balfour possess either the resources or the stamina to resist them?[1]

* * *

Finding politics 'quite unusually odious', Balfour decamped for a Continental holiday on 10 August. Before leaving London, he unburdened himself to Sandars, who had 'rarely heard him speak with more vigour or with more intensity of feeling'. Soon afterwards, Sandars had 'a most interesting talk' with Gwynne, who in turn passed on word to Austen Chamberlain: Sandars 'thinks it quite possible that A.J.B. may give up his leadership owing to the feeling against him in the country'.[2]

It is noteworthy that Gwynne imparted this information to Austen Chamberlain on the 21st, two days before he got round to telling Lady Bathurst. Typically, he put his political obligations above those to his proprietor. 'Jack Sandars is such a liar that I never know what to believe,' he admitted to her. Nevertheless, he had replaced Garvin as Sandars's Fleet Street confidant. A month later, Sandars thought that Balfour might 'care to see what Gwynne writes to me' about the constitutional settlement. 'He has certain sources of information which are not without value.' Sandars, too, was playing a double game.[3]

Austen Chamberlain, spurred on by his invalid father, was hoping to succeed Balfour. His most formidable rival was Long. Smith was a dark horse: Aitken and Goulding, travelling together to America abroad the *Lusitania*, agreed that he 'had no chance at all'. Steel-Maitland and Balcarres, summoned to Whittinghame on 30 September, dissuaded Balfour from his intention to announce his resignation at Edinburgh, where he was scheduled to speak on 21 October. But a stinging letter from Long, to whom Balfour sardonically referred as 'my professed friend', promptly fixed his resolve. The deferred announcement was to be made in November, when the National Union convened at Leeds.[4]

How did Balfour measure 'the feeling against him in the country' to which he sacrificed himself? The Liberal press extolled him – perhaps misguidedly – as a voice of reason in a party that had gone mad. The Unionist press, on the whole, was no more antagonistic than it had been throughout the previous year. 'The

[1] Goulding to Blumenfeld, 10 August 1911, Blumenfeld Papers; Northcliffe to Buckle, 16 August 1911 (copy), Northcliffe Papers.

[2] Balfour to Lady Elcho, 10 August 1911, quoted in Max Egremont, *Balfour* (London, 1980), p. 238; Sandars, 'A Note on the Events leading to Mr Balfour's Resignation,' Sandars Papers; Gwynne to Austen Chamberlain, 21 August 1911, Chamberlain Papers, AC 4/1/675.

[3] Gwynne to Lady Bathurst, 23 August 1911, Bathurst Papers; Sandars to Balfour, 21 September 1911, Balfour Papers.

[4] Aitken to Bonar Law [October 1911], quoted in Robert Blake, *The Unknown Prime Minister* (London, 1955), p. 74; Sykes, *Tariff Reform*, pp. 249–50.

Observer under my editorship has taken the same independent tone right through,' Garvin justly insisted to Waldorf Astor, arguing that, if the *Pall Mall Gazette* was denied the same freedom to 'criticise Unionist leadership when that rôle obviously needs to be criticised, its support will not be very valuable when it thinks the leaders ought to be supported'. Northcliffe was behaving with (for him) remarkable restraint, even generosity. The *Daily Express* and the *Standard*, possibly owing to internal weaknesses, were also muted. The single exception was the *National Review*, where Maxse stepped up his 'Balfour Must Go' – 'B.M.G.' – campaign. Hard as he tried, however, he could not link his 'buffoonery' (as the *Daily Chronicle* called it on 1 November) with the *Observer*, which avoided vindictiveness and dreaded polarization.[1]

Balfour was less ruffled by what newspapermen published than by what they threatened behind the scenes. On 7 October, the Halsbury Club was founded. Named for the venerable peer who had rallied the diehards, it signalled the perpetuation of the Forward movement. The members included Austen Chamberlain, Milner, Amery, and Smith, with Lord Bathurst and Waldorf Astor among the lesser luminaries. Steel-Maitland dismissed the idea that the aim of the group was to overthrow Balfour and offered to prove his point by joining. In the *Observer* on 15 October, Garvin similarly insisted that 'there will be nothing in its spirit or constitution to exclude ... any Unionist who is earnest'. His sincerity was credited by Buckle, who agreed 'that in a short time, granted loyalty & luck, the wounds in the Unionist party may be healed', and who could not resist 'adding that, if you Diehards had won, these wounds would have now been gaping!!'[2]

Was Garvin deceiving his readers or himself? Astor, who understood that 'the logical consequence as well as the professed object' of the Halsbury Club 'was not to say B.M.G.', reported 'a somewhat heated and lengthy discussion' generated by 'an Anti-Balfour amendment'. Moved by Lord Winterton and seconded by Gwynne, it 'was supported apparently by a majority of those present', but withdrawn after 'Halsbury & Austen threatened to resign'. Was that not proof enough of the Club's mood, if not its avowed purpose? It was foolhardy for Lord St Aldwyn to doubt whether 'the strength of this movement goes much beyond the Birmingham gang, and those who are fools enough to be led by Maxse & the *Morning Post*'.[3]

Invited by Austen Chamberlain to 'meet and talk over the situation' at lunch on the 26th, Garvin described 'the last two or three weeks' as 'the most depressing he had ever known. He despaired of Balfour, hated the attacks on him and the manner of them and in fact found comfort nowhere.' As a dress rehearsal, Chamberlain had 'had a long talk' with Gwynne on the evening of

[1] Garvin to Astor, 2 August 1911 (copy), Garvin Papers; *also see* Gollin, *Observer*, pp. 351–52.
[2] Buckle to Garvin, 27 October 1911, Garvin Papers.
[3] Astor to Garvin [October 1911], Garvin Papers; St Aldwyn to Curzon, 19 October 1911, Curzon Papers, India Office Library Eur F 112/18/1–2.

the 23rd. 'He had been afraid that the Halsbury Club might stifle Tariff Reform; said we must fight on everything but could only win on that,' Chamberlain recorded in a memorandum. Gwynne was assured that 'he need not fear that the H.C. would burke T.R.' The editor professed to be in favour of an elected second chamber, 'but could not take that line in the *M.P.* because of Bathurst', who 'talked "as if he had promised his father on his deathbed to stand by the hereditary principle"'. (Chamberlain volunteered that he 'might be able to help with B.' in this regard.) The two men agreed on the shortcomings of Haldane's army reforms and the necessity for compulsory National Service. Finally, Chamberlain 'told Gwynne that I thought a good deal of the criticism against Balfour was wrong' and that the party 'had work enough in hand' without propounding a comprehensive legislative programme. Gwynne was satisfied, 'especially if you emphasise the fact that T.R. is at the root of all social reform'.[1]

On their own, journalists might nettle Balfour, but gave him no cause for fear. As Halsbury Clubmen, however, they developed connections that made them distinctly more menacing. Maxse's monthly outpourings in the *National Review*, puerile and repetitious, only became dangerous in the light of a resolution which he put on the agenda for the November meeting of the National Union. Ostensibly a commendation of Lord Halsbury ('our Grand Old Man') and other diehard peers, it was implicitly a vote of no-confidence in Balfour. Steel-Maitland sighted it among the 'many danger points in the autumn', and Lord Midleton recognized that, 'assuredly, if the leaders are to remain, Maxse must somehow be defeated or modified'. No one realized this better than Balfour, who advanced his resignation to 8 November so as to anticipate the National Union conference. 'I really think I must ask Leo Maxse to dinner tonight,' he supposedly remarked afterwards, 'for we are probably the two happiest men in London.'[2]

The idea of dinner with Maxse, with whom he had played tennis at Crabbet in happier days, was – of course – a Balfourian flippancy. Still, on 8 November, between his afternoon address to the City of London Conservative Association and his evening visit to the King, Balfour did find time for an interview with Gwynne. 'Isn't it funny he should send for me of all people at this juncture?' Gwynne wrote breathlessly to Lady Bathurst from the Carlton Club, where he had 'run in ... from seeing A.J.B.' As courtesy required, Gwynne said he 'was sorry for the reasons which made his resignation imperative – i.e. his health', yet 'could not resist asking him why he had sent for me', especially when

---

[1] Austen Chamberlain to Garvin, 23 October 1911, and Austen Chamberlain to Joseph Chamberlain, 27 October 1911, quoted in Austen Chamberlain, *Politics from Inside*, p. 370; memorandum by Austen Chamberlain, 23 October 1911 (10.00 p.m.), Chamberlain Papers, AC 4/1/718.

[2] Memorandum by Steel-Maitland, 20 September 1911, Balfour Papers; Midleton to Balcarres, 1 September 1911, quoted in Sykes, *Tariff Reform*, p. 248; Blanche Dugdale, *Arthur James Balfour* (New York, 1937), II, 86.

A Climacteric Year

Sandars interrupted with messages 'that Buckle of *The Times*, Northcliffe and a host of other people wanted to see him'. Balfour 'refused them all' and replied that he had selected Gwynne 'because you have always fought fair and ... because I look upon the *M.P.* as the only honest journal left in England'. Gwynne was surprised and flattered. 'Of course one must be prepared for tricks and dodges,' he told Lady Bathurst, 'but I will say this of Balfour that he never bears malice to persons. He wants Austen to be his successor and doesn't like Walter Long.'[1]

The succession was not in Balfour's gift, however. Over the next few days, the two leading contenders cancelled each other out, and Sir Edward Carson declined to step forward as a candidate. Prodded by Aitken, Bonar Law emerged as the new Unionist leader. As early as October, Aitken had promised him 'that if Garvin and Smith now came out or came out at the critical moment for you, that you would win'. Goulding used his influence, which was considerable, to convert Smith and to drain support from the Chamberlainites; he also cultivated Garvin, 'my dear Jim', who persisted in his adherence to Chamberlain. The two men returned from their transatlantic voyage in time for Balfour's resignation. In anticipation of the announcement, Aitken fixed a meeting between Bonar Law and Northcliffe. 'I was trying to persuade Bonar Law to allow his name to be brought forward as leader in the event of certain contingencies which could even then be foreseen,' he obliquely recalled. 'But if this move was to succeed it was of the utmost importance to secure Northcliffe's assistance or at least his benevolent neutrality.' Though Northcliffe withheld 'active assistance', he ensured Bonar Law 'a fair field for his candidature for the Conservative leadership'.[2]

A meeting was called for 13 November to select the new party leader. Balfour's secretary had no trouble believing that Bonar Law was being 'run by Max Aitken, the little Canadian adventurer who sits for Ashton-under-Lyne, introduced into that seat by him. Aitken practically owns the *Daily Express*,' he observed, 'and the *Daily Express* has run Bonar Law for the last two days for all it is worth.' Robert Sanders was also struck by this journalistic volte-face and pondered its significance. 'Goulding had been very keen for Austen & did not want Bonar Law to compete,' he wrote in his diary on the 12th. Then, 'on Friday morning the *Express* came all out for Bonar Law'.[3]

The performance of the *Daily Express* was easily explained. The previous January, at Bonar Law's recommendation, Aitken had written a generous cheque as a loan to Blumenfeld. The gross profits showed a slight improvement (£25,667 in the period from 1 July 1910 to 30 June 1911), but production costs

[1] Gwynne to Lady Bathurst, 8 November 1911, Bathurst Papers.
[2] Aitken to Bonar Law [October 1911], quoted in Blake, *Unknown Prime Minister*, p. 74; Goulding to Garvin, n.d., and 12 October 1911, Garvin Papers; Beaverbrook, *Politicians and the Press*, pp. 105–106.
[3] Sanders to Balfour, 10 November 1911, Balfour Papers; Sanders's diary, 12 November 1911, Bayford Papers.

increased with the installation of new machinery. By September, Blumenfeld was again in trouble. Unable to draw further from his shareholders, he turned to Steel-Maitland for party patronage, which Aitken's loan had been intended to obviate. Steel-Maitland attempted to wring additional money from Henderson, citing 'the disadvantage that the Party might suffer' if the paper 'passed into the hands of people who cannot be relied upon'. Henderson 'turned the proposal down ... because he did not wish to touch another paper', leaving Steel-Maitland to contemplate the benefits if the *Express* were 'entirely under Central Office control'. For this purpose, he requested Sandars to get Balfour to write 'a personal letter to some friend', possibly Lord Rothschild, whose name would attract other subscribers: '*Could not you get it done by hook or crook. And it needs to be done quick before it is collared.*' There is no evidence that Balfour, who had other things on his mind, obliged him. Aitken, already the party's 'trustee' for the *Globe* to the tune of £40,000, was ready to take a mortgage on the *Express* for the same amount. Although he did not take up shares until the following year, when the company was reconstructed, his influence was keenly felt from July 1911, when Goulding hawked the news that 'Sir Max has got the *Express*'.[1]

Unlike Blumenfeld, Garvin stayed loyal to Chamberlain until the evening of 10 November, when he heard the 'amazing words' from Chamberlain himself: 'I'm out of it. Long's out of it. Law is in.' His 'duty being now done, and fidelity kept staunch to the end', Garvin thereupon wrote to Bonar Law, pledging his support 'through thick and thin'. Receiving a blow-by-blow account of the episode from Goulding, Garvin furnished a detailed report to the readers of the *Observer*. 'Isn't Garvin too bad to give away the "inside" of the recent crisis?' Gwynne asked Lady Bathurst. 'There seems to be no restraint in the press now.' For his own part, Gwynne was 'personally a very great private-friend of Bonar Law but I backed Austen. Now ... that it is all over', he was prepared 'to believe from the chagrin of the Radicals that we have blundered on the right man'. There was the consolation that 'Bonar Law would as soon sacrifice his children as his belief in Tariff Reform', which no one could say for Long. Lady Bathurst took longer to reconcile herself to the outcome, but Gwynne implored her to 'remember that I am doing a lot privately among politicians to prove that we are the only paper that counts, and I think that I am succeeding'.[2]

---

[1] Steel-Maitland to Henderson, 20 September 1911 (copy), and Steel-Maitland to Sandars, 20 September 1911, Sandars Papers; 'Mr Locker Lampson's Scheme,' memorandum [1912], Steel-Maitland Papers; Goulding to Garvin, 1 July 1911, Garvin Papers.

[2] Garvin to Astor, 10 November 1911, Astor Papers; Gwynne to Lady Bathurst, 11, 12, and 20 November, and 19 December 1911, Bathurst Papers. Lady Bathurst was appalled when George Smalley, the London correspondent for the *New York Tribune*, ascribed the *Morning Post*'s vendetta against Balfour to 'a woman's impulses and emotions'. No feminist, she countered by invoking her father and brother who, 'for 20 years and more' before her advent to the proprietorship,

Fabian Ware, who had conducted the *Morning Post* through the early battles, was totally forgotten. A self-professed 'extreme Chamberlain man', he offered Bonar Law his support, for what it was worth; in return, he requested 'a short confidential talk' to discuss 'my own plans'. Buckle sent the new leader 'earnest good wishes for your success' without any strings attached. 'I feel the passing of Arthur Balfour very deeply,' he wrote a bit funereally, 'as I have been on terms of personal friendship with him for five & twenty years.' A. P. Nicholson, a younger denizen of Printing House Square, could not 'but feel pleasure in thinking that I have had a humble share in what I have written in *The Times* and in the influence I have asserted there, in forwarding the result' of the Carlton Club meeting on the 13th. Rewarded with praise from Aitken, the next best thing to praise from Bonar Law himself, Nicholson claimed to 'have given proofs of discretion, and, though my rôle is that of a news-getter, I have the interests of the party at heart'. Last and certainly least, Horatio Bottomley gratified Bonar Law with 'a specimen of many letters which come to me' at *John Bull*.[1]

After years of discord and discomfiture, the struggle over the Unionist leadership – the War of the Cecilian Succession – had apparently ended. Conflicts within and between newspaper offices continued apace. These were generational as well as ideological, personal as well as professional. Writing to Bonar Law on 19 November, Nicholson asked him not to divulge to Buckle, due to call the next day, 'that I had met you today at Sutton Place', Northcliffe's house. 'He would, I fear, think it very lacking in me not to have mentioned it to him first.' Buckle survived on borrowed time as editor of *The Times*: his resignation was delivered upon request the following July. Chirol was also to retire as foreign editor in 1912, after lodging a stiff protest that 'the traditions and prestige of the paper' had been 'steadily and grievously impaired by Lord N's interference, direct and indirect'. He was replaced by Wickham Steed, previously *The Times*'s correspondent in various European capitals, whom John Walter recalled as being 'completely under Northcliffe's thumb'. Moberly Bell, mourned by Chirol as 'poor old Bell', died in 1911. The old order gave way to the new.[2]

Everywhere along Fleet Street, the events of 1912 were to unfold as a

---

were opposed to Mr Balfour, not from personal dislike in any way but because they ... disliked his weakness, his feeling for party which apparently was stronger in him than principles & ideals, his avowed belief that a leader should follow his party instead of leading it, etc., etc., etc.

Smalley, *Anglo-American Memories*, 2nd ser., p. 47; and Lady Bathurst to Smalley, 26 April 1912 (copy), Bathurst Papers.

[1] Ware to Bonar Law, 11 and 20 November 1911, Buckle to Bonar Law, 13 November 1911, Nicholson to Bonar Law, 13 November 1911, and Bottomley to Bonar Law, 21 November 1911, Bonar Law Papers, 24/3/10, 25, 29, and 66, 12/2/4.

[2] Nicholson to Bonar Law, 19 November 1911, Bonar Law Papers, 24/3/61; Chirol to Buckle, 8 August 1911 (copy), *Times* Archives; notes by A. P. Ryan of an interview with Walter, 23 May 1968, Woods Papers.

dénouement to those of 1911, which stands out as a climacteric year. The *Pall Mall Gazette* faced a major reorganization under Garvin, who was too hard pressed to accept Hamilton Fyfe's invitation to run the *World* 'in support of the advance guard'. The *Daily News* and the *Morning Leader* completed the unfinished business of amalgamation, with the *Star* in tow. The *Daily Express* and the *Westminster Gazette* were both refloated with the assistance of party officials. Keir Hardie's quixotic campaign of 1910–11 bore fruit in the appearance of two Labour journals, the *Daily Citizen* and George Lansbury's *Daily Herald*.[1]

A final postscript was the growing apprehension of Aitken's power as a manipulator of the press and of politicians through the press. Garvin did not have to name names when he wrote to Astor that 'Law will do exceedingly well if some influences can be held in check'. If nothing else had occurred that year, the emergence of Aitken in 1911 would alone qualify as a landmark in the history of British political journalism. A financier first and foremost, though never pure and simple, he convinced himself – and tried to convince others – that he only 'went into the *Express* investment to please Blumenfeld'. Yet neither his genius for friendship nor his genius for profit was ever paramount. 'A newspaper is not an entity to him, nor has journalism a responsibility and a duty,' Collin Brooks and Arthur Mann subsequently agreed. 'A paper to him is an instrument of personal advancement as a "power" and journalism but a means of impressing the Beaverbrook brand upon the British political cattle.' That was soon to become evident. Meanwhile, a rival to Northcliffe was at hand.[2]

---

[1] Fyfe to Garvin, 2 November 1911, and Garvin to Fyfe, 4 November 1911 (copy), Garvin Papers. In the aftermath of the 1906 election, Ramsay MacDonald was already pursuing the idea of a new daily which would 'represent the views of the Labour Party' and 'should be run on strict Trades Union principles in all respects'. I am grateful to Dr Deian Hopkin for copies of MacDonald's correspondence with H. J. Whigham, who was expected to 'find the capital'.

[2] Garvin to Astor [November 1911], Astor Papers; Beaverbrook to Wargrave [1920s], Wargrave Papers; Collin Brooks's diary, 20 December 1925. Alan Watkins has included a pungent assessment of Beaverbrook among his *Brief Lives* (London, 1982), pp. 9–19.

Six

CANDID FRIENDS

At a meeting of the Cabinet, Asquith was overheard to remark that 'the Liberal press was written by boobies for boobies'.[1] While there can be no doubt that this complaint accurately reflected the Prime Minister's private sentiments, it would not have done for him to proclaim his disdain publicly. The exigencies of party politics required him to patronize newspaper ventures and, after his fashion, to consort with select journalists.

Fortunately for the Liberal Party, Asquith's colleagues did not share either his affectation or his inhibitions. Alexander Murray, the Master of Elibank, concluded his tenure as chief whip in the summer of 1912 by repeating to Gardiner 'how deeply I have appreciated all the personal kindness which I have invariably received at your hands & how great is my sense of the value of the services you render to Liberalism'. Doubtless he wrote bread-and-butter letters to other Liberal editors in the same vein, for that was one of his official duties. Poised to 'hand over my responsibilities to my successor', Percy Illingworth, Murray made a final attempt to come up with an 'arrangement for placing the *Westminster Gazette* on a firmer foundation'.[2]

Alone among the major Liberal dailies, the *Westminster* depended for its survival upon party or party-negotiated subsidies. The syndicate, which Murray's predecessor had cobbled together in 1908, began to fall apart in the early weeks of 1912. Sir Frank Newnes, no longer an MP, wanted to dispose of his shares in the paper that his father had founded, 'provided I can get a fair price for them'. The figure he had in mind was a mere £2,500. Donald Maclean, who acted as secretary to the directorate, brought Newnes's notice of sale to the attention of the board, which included such party benefactors as Lord Cowdray (formerly, as W. D. Pearson, MP for Colchester), Lord Allendale, Sir Alfred Mond, and Sir Charles Henry, MP for Wellington. Newnes, whose considerations appear to have been strictly financial, rescinded his notice upon the promise of a loan from Henry and Oswald Partington. Latterly MP for

---

[1] Hobhouse's diary, 17 July 1912, *Inside Asquith's Cabinet*, p. 118.
[2] Murray to Gardiner, 9 August 1912, Gardiner Papers; Murray to Sir Archibald Williamson, 8 August 1912 (copy), Asquith Papers; in the original draft, Murray described 'arrangements for the resuscitation of the *Westminster Gazette*, which has fallen upon serious days'.

High Peak and Junior Lord of the Treasury, eventually MP for Shipley, and ultimately 2nd Baron Doverdale, Partington counted among his credentials the fact that he was the chief whip's brother-in-law. In the event, however, he reneged, leaving Henry to advance Newnes the entire amount.[1] Having overcome this hurdle, the proprietors encountered more fundamental problems.

The directors of the *Westminster Gazette* were wealthy Liberals of varying hues and contrasting ambitions. Some, like Allendale and Henry, belonged to an older tradition. Others, like Cowdray and Newnes, had commercial expectations or, at least, commercial incentives. Mond was involved chiefly for the sake of promoting his claims for party preferment: 'I must say frankly,' he told Lloyd George, 'that if I don't get ahead in the political fighting line there is little attraction to me in being merely one of those rich men who are called on to supply funds and then forgotten.'[2] The task of the chief whip was to regulate, if not reconcile, these potentially conflicting interests.

On 6 June, the shareholders met in Murray's 'private room downstairs' at the House of Commons. The venue was deliberately chosen in order to 'emphasize the fact' that the whip's office had been 'the prime mover in the rescue of the paper three or four years ago'. There followed an 'extraordinary general meeting' of shareholders on 4 July, again held by request under Murray's auspices. Henry, who took the chair, announced plans to overhaul the company and to realize sufficient working capital by issuing new 5 per cent preference shares. Five directors – himself, Cowdray, Allendale, Mond, and Henry Webb, MP for the Forest of Dean – each pledged 'to find a further £10,000', provided that the party could raise double their total investment from other sources. Murray promptly issued an appeal to 'two or three friends of high standing in the Party', from whom he hoped 'to secure £100,000 . . ., the sum that is considered requisite for effectively carrying on the paper'. In fact, he approached four likely subscribers: Sir Archibald Williamson, MP for Moray and Nairn (and later 1st Baron Forres), who had made a fortune in Argentine railways and Californian oil companies; Sir Arthur Haworth, MP for Manchester South and a prosperous local businessman; Sir Edgar Speyer, the New York-born Anglo-German financier and philanthropist; and Sir Edward Partington, Oswald's father and the director of the Manchester and Liverpool District Bank. 'I have the full authority of the Prime Minister for the course I am taking,' Murray informed them, 'and he is keenly interested in the success of my endeavours.'[3]

Thereafter, 'with the full knowledge of my successor', Murray continued to

[1] Newnes to Maclean, 13 January 1912 (copy), Maclean to Newnes, 16 January 1912 (copy), Newnes to Maclean, 18 and 20 February 1912, Maclean Papers.

[2] Mond to Lloyd George [1911?], Lloyd George Papers, C/9/2/6.

[3] [Maclean] to Murray, 28 May 1912, printed circular announcing meeting of 4 July 1912, Murray to Williamson, Haworth, Speyer, and Partington, 8 August 1912 (copies), Asquith Papers.

devote himself 'to carrying out the arrangement in respect of the *Westminster Gazette* which I undertook to attempt to do when I was Chief Whip'. On 20 September, he sought to add the name of Lord Glenconner (formerly Sir Edward Tennant, MP for Salisbury) to a list of proprietors amended to include Lord Aberconway (formerly Sir Charles McLaren, MP for Bosworth), Lord St Davids (formerly J. W. Philipps, MP for Pembrokeshire), J. F. L. Brunner (now MP for Northwich), and Sir Francis Layland-Barratt (until recently MP for Torquay). He reiterated that Cowdray, Allendale, Mond, Henry, and Webb 'have agreed to subscribe the necessary £10,000 apiece, provided that at least £90,000 is raised', a tenth less than was initially stipulated. A certain 'friend of mine who desires to be nameless' had promised £10,000, which 'will appear in my name. J. A. Spender can make himself responsible to find £10,000.' That left a balance of £20,000, and Murray ventured that, if Glenconner 'were willing to come in', Oswald Partington could be persuaded 'to again cooperate'. Although neither Glenconner nor Partington delivered, Murray was able to report to Maclean on 14 October that £70,000 was in hand, and '80,000 is really assured. I do not anticipate difficulty in respect of the remaining 10,000.' His success was confirmed by Illingworth, who accepted the trusteeship 'for myself and my successor or successors in the office of Chief Whip of the Liberal Party' for 1,000 preference shares, each bearing a face value of £10, in the *Westminster Gazette* company.[1]

The Unionists, now led by Bonar Law, were involved more extensively in the same sort of activities. As party chairman, Arthur Steel-Maitland assumed responsibilities for newspaper management that were handled by the chief whip on the Liberal side. The techniques employed were as various as the properties in question. In February, Northcliffe advised Bonar Law that the *Manchester Courier* was again 'in extremis'. All that was needed in this case, however, was 'a handshake and a few words of thanks from the Leader' to W. T. Rothwell, 'a local alderman ..., who ladles out money by the hatful on very slight security, without asking for anything'. That seemed too good to be true. Northcliffe had consented to remain 'a director of the company merely for the sake of the party', notwithstanding that 'there is no possibility of its ever paying, and I am not fond of journeys to Manchester'. Over the past few years, he had 'contributed five thousand pounds to the *Courier*', and 'Mr Balfour personally invested a considerable sum', presumably during the time he was a Manchester MP. To ensure Rothwell's largesse, Northcliffe proposed to bring that 'unobtrusive gentleman' to Bonar Law's house for an informal discussion. That Aitken depended upon Rothwell's 'public service' to furnish him with publicity in his nearby constituency was further inducement for Bonar Law to comply.[2]

[1] Murray to Glenconner, 20 September 1912, Asquith Papers; Murray to Maclean, 14 October 1912, and Illingworth to Maclean, 16 June 1913, Maclean Papers.
[2] Northcliffe to Bonar Law, 13 and 15 February 1912, Bonar Law Papers, 25/2/16, 20; Aitken to Rothwell, 5 July and 12 November 1911, and Aitken to J. C. Buckley (his agent), 21 November 1912, Beaverbrook Papers, B/37, B/46.

Not all of the Unionists' press support could be procured so cheaply. The affairs of the *Daily Express* were analogous to those of the *Westminster Gazette* and required comparable mediation and financial outlays. Under Steel-Maitland's tutelage, a scheme was drawn up by Oliver Locker Lampson, MP for Huntingdonshire North, 'for a reconstruction of the business management, and the foundation of the paper upon a proper basis'. It was estimated that a minimum of £50,000 was urgently required 'to retain the only half-penny paper the Party possesses in London, and no less a sum than £700,000 to £1,000,000 would be necessary to start a similar paper, if the *Daily Express* were allowed to go'. Locker Lampson was prepared to buy a block of 101,000 ordinary shares, thus obtaining a controlling interest, for £25,000; in addition, he undertook to supply £30,000 towards the partial payment of interest on two earlier sets of debentures. With stringent economies, including the reduction of the managing director's annual salary from £5,000 to £1,000, there was the prospect that, *'at the very worst,* the paper would continue as it is for $2\frac{1}{2}$ to 3 years'.[1]

Assuming that Locker Lampson could make good his promise with the help of friends who made him their surrogate, his scheme faced an array of obstacles: Arthur Pearson, who held on as managing director, would either have to accept a token salary or else resign with a pension; the debenture holders would have to agree to forgo further payments of interest until the paper was turning a profit; and Blumenfeld, the editor, would have to submit to a new managerial structure. There was strong resistance in all three quarters, with Aitken stoking the fires of Blumenfeld's resentment. Locker Lampson was able to 'come to terms' quickly with Pearson, whose blindness really left him no choice. He thereupon 'saw Bonar Law', who was 'evidently anxious to be quit of *D.E.* affairs & ... obviously afraid of being expected to take sides' in what he perceived to be a 'competition' between Locker Lampson and Aitken. 'I said merely this,' Locker Lampson recounted to Steel-Maitland:

> That negotiations of a private character had taken place between Max & myself, but that we had come to no cooperation. I then stated myself ready to do without official Central Office support & left the matter at that. Bonar Law expressed the wish that you should give private support if you liked but had seen some newspaper dignitary recently who had asked him if the Central Office was moving to buy the *D.E.* This frightened him & he feels no official support should be given but leaves you to do as you like privately.

As the meeting to consider the scheme was held at the Central Office, with Steel-Maitland present, the line between 'official' and 'private' was very thin indeed.[2]

---

[1] Memorandum, 'Mr Locker Lampson's Scheme' [May ? 1912], Steel-Maitland Papers.
[2] Locker Lampson to Steel-Maitland, 9 May 1912, Steel-Maitland Papers.

To complicate matters further, Locker Lampson sought backing from Gray Buchanan, the head of William Jacks and Company of London, iron and steel merchants. Bonar Law was a partner in the parent firm in Glasgow. To soothe Buchanan's tender conscience, Bonar Law armed Locker Lampson with a letter, explicitly devised as window dressing: in it, he disclaimed 'any responsibility in connection with what is done' about the *Daily Express*, 'as I am equally interested in the success of all the papers which support us'. This stratagem assisted Locker Lampson 'in rehabilitating my position with Mr Buchanan & his friends', whose participation was essential. Claude Lowther, MP for Cumberland North, was similarly the conduit for Lord Leconfield, whose landed estates yielded extra income from mineral deposits. The list of other individuals who were canvassed for support – in many instances renewed support – reads like a *Who's Who* of Tory peers, backbenchers, and businessmen: among them were the Dukes of Westminster and Portland, the Marquess of Camden, the Earl of Iveagh, Lord Howard de Walden, Sir Hildred Carlile, George Lawson Johnston (later 1st Baron Luke and heir to the chairmanship of Bovril, Ltd.), John Waddington, Dudley Docker (the Birmingham industrialist who was to buy the *Globe* in 1914), Sir William Bull (chairman of the London Unionist MPs), and Sir Alexander Henderson. By late August, Locker Lampson had collected a total of £47,500 from Buchanan, Westminster, Howard de Walden, Carlile, Sir George Cooper, and John Mix. Steel-Maitland weighed in with the largest single investment of £20,000. In addition, Locker Lampson had 'got Sir Alexander Henderson to purchase £53,000 second Debentures for £14,000'. Other subscriptions, including Lawson Johnston's, were probably arranged by Lowther.[1]

Blumenfeld tried in vain to float an alternative scheme, which he entrusted Aitken to commend to Bonar Law. 'I need not tell you how grateful I shall be to you if I have your sympathy and support in this vital matter and I beg of you to stand by me,' he wrote beseechingly on 31 May to the Unionist leader, who could only have been embarrassed. To stave off Locker Lampson, an implicit threat to his editorial sovereignty, Blumenfeld proposed to 'purchase £101,000 of shares, being the control, for £20,000', which he could expect to borrow from Aitken; his further hope was 'that the Central Office shall induce the investment of £40,000 of new money in Income Bonds or Debentures'. Thus, making a stand for independent control, he banked on party patronage. Understandably, he was 'determined not to enter on a new phase' in his editorship 'unless I am placed in such a position that my experience in journalism and my knowledge of the paper shall have free and untrammelled scope'. To Henderson, he proclaimed his unwillingness to affiliate with Locker

---

[1] Locker Lampson to Steel-Maitland, 23 May 1912, and R. E. Prothero to Steel-Maitland, 25 May 1912, Steel-Maitland Papers; Bonar Law to Locker Lampson, 22 May 1912, and Locker Lampson to Bonar Law, 4 and 8 June 1912, Bonar Law Papers, 26/4/5, 14; Locker Lampson to Lowther, 28 August 1912 (copy), Beaverbrook Papers, H/15. For the link between Bonar Law and Buchanan, see Blake, *Unknown Prime Minister*, pp. 33–34.

Lampson: 'recent experiences in that connection are such that it is quite impossible for me to view with anything but apprehension any circumstance by which he could even in the most remote way have any voice in the destinies of myself or this business'. Steel-Maitland, to whom Henderson forwarded this manifesto, girded himself to 'have one more word with Blumenfeld and see whether I can arrange some common ground. If not, I feel inclined to wash my hands of the whole concern.'[1]

All the while, Locker Lampson kept 'moving' in conjunction with Steel-Maitland. 'Blumenfeld is suspicious,' he well knew, 'and I think it would be much the best for us to approach nobody now except together.' Postponing difficult decisions with regard to 'the questions of managership and Chairmanship', he deputed Henderson ('the most helpful man we could have got') to contend with irate creditors, who – as Sir Joseph Lawrence put it – were likely to 'marvel where all the money represented by the *D.E.* Debenture debt has gone'. To propitiate Blumenfeld and possibly Bonar Law as well, Locker Lampson strove to come to terms with Aitken. Pointedly telling him that he had already recruited 'sufficient assistance' to purchase the *Daily Express* 'without the help of any more money', he welcomed a contribution of £20,000, which would permit him to 'absolve my friends to that extent'. Aitken seems to have intended to sink not his own funds, but rather those of Otto Kahn, his Wall Street friend. With Steel-Maitland's approval (and editorial guidance), he wrote to Kahn, whose 'generous offer' was 'appreciated by Mr Bonar Law', but not taken up.[2]

'The man on whose shoulders both S-M and O.L.L. have apparently shifted the responsibility of dealing with me is Sir A.H.,' intuited Blumenfeld, who logically identified Henderson as the 'obvious man to get hold of' if Locker Lampson were to be stopped. Pearson's silent partner, Henderson was said to have 'found about £350,000 amongst his friends for the *Standard*', before it was sold to Davison Dalziel 'over Henderson's head'. Might he now draw on the same sources to pre-empt Locker Lampson's bid?[3]

There was hardly time to find out. On 9 July, it was announced that, three days hence, the directors of the *Daily Express* were to convene in order

> to receive the resignation of Mr C. Arthur Pearson as Managing Director and as a Director of the Company.... To elect Mr Oliver Locker Lampson

---

[1] Blumenfeld to Bonar Law, 31 May 1912, Bonar Law Papers, 26/3/44; Blumenfeld to Steel-Maitland, 3 June 1912, Blumenfeld to Henderson, 31 July 1912 (copy), and Steel-Maitland to Henderson, 1 August 1912 (copy?), Steel-Maitland Papers.

[2] Locker Lampson to Steel-Maitland, 21 June 1912, Lawrence to Steel-Maitland, 12 May 1912, Locker Lampson to Aitken, 11 June 1912 (copy), Steel-Maitland Papers; Taylor, *Beaverbrook*, p. 44; Steel-Maitland to Aitken, 4 July 1912, and Aitken to Kahn, 6 July 1912 (copy), Beaverbrook Papers, H/15.

[3] Blumenfeld to Aitken, 6 July 1912, Beaverbrook Papers, H/15; Lawrence to Steel-Maitland, 12 May 1912, Steel-Maitland Papers.

as a Director of the Company. ... To pass the Transfer of 110,000 Shares from ... Pearson to ... Locker Lampson.

On the day that this circular was posted, Locker Lampson addressed a stern letter of reproof to Blumenfeld:

> I have long found, & now I understand that although you gave me your solemn word that you would not communicate again with Aitken, you have seen him constantly since his interference in our affairs; that you have gone to him for advice against me, and that you have shown him our correspondence. I am absolutely at a loss to understand this action – I cannot explain it to myself. But it releases me from any further obligation to consider your feelings in this matter.

He went on to accuse Blumenfeld of having, through the *Daily Express*, 'embroiled me with the Tariff Reform League and Sir Joseph Lawrence first of all, secondly with the Conservative Central Office, and finally with Max Aitken', whom he could 'honestly say that I liked as much as any man in the House', but with whom it was consequently 'impossible ... to be such friends again'. Revealing on good authority 'that Aitken never intended to give you absolute control of the *Daily Express* if either he or his friend had purchased it', Locker Lampson unkindly suggested that Aitken's ulterior motive had been 'to control the *Daily Express* through you'. While he had 'never wanted to have to fight Max Aitken', he gloated at having prevented the paper from becoming 'his property by such scandalously underhand means. I am taking instant steps, openly and frankly, to have my name registered as the holder of 110,000 shares', 9,000 more than the number technically required to effect control. 'This I am doing immediately, and nothing you can do, and no threat you can urge, can alter this decision.'[1]

It looked as though Blumenfeld would directly be sent packing. Yet, contrary to expectation, he continued to edit the *Daily Express* until 1929 and stayed on as titular chairman of the company from 1915 until his death in 1948. What had happened? On 9 September, Blumenfeld received congratulations from J. S. Wood, a 'brother journalist' who was then attached to the *Daily Graphic*, on having 'completed the control of the *Daily Express*'. Three days later, Steel-Maitland 'heard from Oliver Locker Lampson that he has unconditionally resigned any claims as to being a director or as to work on the *Express*, leaving it altogether in Henderson's and my hands'. The fierce antagonism of Blumenfeld, who was justly regarded as irreplaceable, was plainly too much for him. Steel-Maitland drafted a letter for Bonar Law to send to the loser ('though perhaps it's a little too flowery'), and declared:

---

[1] Circular dated 9 July 1912, and Locker Lampson to Blumenfeld, 9 July 1912, Beaverbrook Papers, H/15.

I think that both he and Blumenfeld made mistakes, but when all is said and done Locker Lampson has been instrumental in saving the paper, and in spite of any mistakes he may have made or any excitability of which he may have been guilty, I think he is a really good fellow.

Locker Lampson remained an MP until 1945, shifting his seat to the Handsworth division of Birmingham in 1922. True to his word, he played no further part in the affairs of the *Daily Express*.[1]

By contrast, Aitken's part had barely begun. Already a power behind Blumenfeld's editorial throne, he steadily enlarged his shareholding until midway through the First World War, when he acquired an outright control. He achieved his hegemony by steps that remain to be charted. It would suffice at this point to observe that his movements, like his objectives, were shrouded in mystery. In all of his assorted transactions, political no less than commercial, he adeptly covered his traces so that they cannot be delineated with any degree of precision. According to his own studiously vague recollection, he had had 'for a number of years a considerable connection with the *Daily Express* of an indefinite character' before he assumed the proprietorship 'towards the end of the war'.[2]

Aitken's stealthiness, coupled with his propinquity to Bonar Law, made him intensely feared. Gwynne leapt to the conclusion that he was plotting to combine with Northcliffe in the custody of *The Times* and had to apologize for his unfounded suspicions: 'My excuse must be my zeal for the *M.P.* I have to fight the monopoly of *The Times* every day in my life.' To be sure, Northcliffe could have used Aitken's assistance in his constant struggle with the mandarins of Printing House Square. He trusted that competition from the revitalized *Pall Mall Gazette* would not only improve the *Evening News*, but also 'indirectly bear upon the *Daily Mail*', which he faulted for leading articles that 'carry no weight, despite our vast circulation'. *The Times*, however, was insensitive to outside stimuli. A. P. Nicholson, who had supplied Bonar Law with ammunition for a speech on 'the Expenditure of Exchequer monies on Insurance', proposed to back him up in print with 'some definite statements on the subject'. He had 'the courage to act on my information, especially as I feel some responsibility', but Buckle put the issue off-limits to him. Northcliffe would have preferred a more robustly partisan spirit. 'By the way,' he chided Churchill, whose naval estimates (like Lloyd George's insurance proposals) earned *The Times*'s qualified approval, 'your colleagues are not particularly able in their management of newspapers. My *Times*, *Daily Mail* and *Evening News* have been really helping them the last two or three days

---

[1] Wood to Blumenfeld, 9 September 1912, Blumenfeld Papers; Steel-Maitland to Bonar Law, 12 September 1912, Bonar Law Papers, 27/2/13.
[2] Beaverbrook, *Politicians and the Press*, pp. 10–11.

almost against their wish.' The joke, of course, was on himself.[1]

It took time for the *Pall Mall Gazette* to exercise the salutary influence that Northcliffe had in mind. Contending with difficulties of production and – from all indications – with an impatient proprietor, Garvin reflected upon the differences between himself and his predecessors in Northumberland Street. He was 'not a bit like Mr [Henry] Cust . . ., a brilliant man', whom W. W. Astor had dismissed in 1894. 'Your present editor,' he wrote to Waldorf Astor, 'is only a very earnest man who has had a practical training and who has proved his ability to "make" papers.' The circulation, which had risen 'to an average of just under a steady 30,000 a night before the Easter drop', bore him out. But obsolete 'mechanical facilities' confined the *Pall Mall* to sixteen pages, with the result that editorial content was 'hopelessly inadequate' and advertisements had to be turned away: 'net loss therefore heavy'. Nor was Garvin a bit like W. T. Stead, who had gone down with the *Titanic*. 'How grim a thing it is that he should have vanished in a sensation indeed,' mused Garvin, and especially 'in so huge a one as to make the fate of one of the most remarkable men in the world seem as nothing by comparison'. It was a relief for Garvin to return on weekends to the *Observer*. 'For the passing moment,' he confessed to Northcliffe one Saturday night that spring, 'I am sick of the *P.M.G.* and feel there is no joy in being a journalist. Not one twentieth of my ideas and hopes' went into the *Pall Mall*, where he performed 'the work of a diligent greengrocer'.[2]

Waldorf Astor, less imperious than his father, was more tolerant of editorial eccentricities. 'My own personal object and hope in life (including politics) is to be able to help to get certain things done with, through or under the right people,' he candidly told Garvin. Although he had no 'wish to spend time hunting for or shaping a career', his wife Nancy nursed strong ambitions for the two of them. In 1919, when he succeeded to his father's peerage, Nancy replaced him as Conservative MP for Plymouth and thereby became the first woman to sit in the House of Commons. A less spectacular parliamentary figure, Waldorf Astor was an active member of the Round Table group, which clustered around Lord Milner. His associates, who often gathered under his roof in St James's Square or at Cliveden, included Lionel Curtis, Philip Kerr (later 11th Marquess of Lothian), Grigg, Amery, and Geoffrey Robinson (later Dawson), editor-designate of *The Times*. Garvin was critical of 'the "Round Table" lot'.[3]

Like his father, Waldorf Astor contributed on a lavish scale to the Unionist cause. Herbert Praed, a Central Office fund-raiser, attempted to assuage

[1] Gwynne to Aitken, 21 March 1912 (copy), Gwynne Papers; Northcliffe to Marlowe, 16 January and 29 February 1912 (copies), and Northcliffe to Churchill, 1 August 1912 (copy), Northcliffe Papers; Nicholson to Bonar Law, 15 February 1912, Bonar Law Papers, 25/2/21.
[2] Garvin to Astor, 16 April 1912 (copy), Garvin Papers; Garvin to Northcliffe, 17 April 1912 and 'Saturday night' [1912], Northcliffe Papers.
[3] Astor to Garvin, 27 December 1912, Garvin Papers; Garvin to Astor, 27 December 1912, Astor Papers; Gollin, *Observer*, pp. 303, 364–65.

Astor's feelings that 'he has been neglected by the Party' by arranging for him to lunch with Bonar Law and to dine with Lord Lansdowne. 'In addition to the large sums he has given me for the Party Fund,' Praed revealed, 'he has subscribed most generously to oppose Communism & in other ways, amongst others he gave me £4,000 for the development of Conservative Clubs.' But Astor's most notable service was the maintenance of the *Pall Mall Gazette* and the *Observer*, 'both of which Papers are edited by Mr Garvin'. It did not escape Praed's scrutiny 'that on *some points* he does not see quite "eye to eye" with Mr Garvin'.[1]

Whatever their differences of emphasis or opinion, Astor and Garvin were united in the belief – as Garvin put it – 'that Bonar is not going to budge' from his position as a full-scale Tariff Reformer. For this reason, they flatly rejected Steel-Maitland's plea that the contentious question should be 'allowed to drop for a bit'. Astor's view was that 'the trouble has arisen' from the 'rot ... spread' by the *Daily Mail* ('although I don't think that paper has an enormous political influence, still it has a very big circulation'), obliging the *Observer* and the *Pall Mall* to retaliate with 'a fighting policy'. Garvin inferred Bonar Law's support not only from 'a very friendly letter from him, only personal but in the circumstances suggestive', but also from 'an enthusiastic Imperialist telegram ... from Max Aitken', who was presumed to speak with authority. In addition, a leading article in the *Morning Post* on 27 December denoted 'firmness. Gwynne is so intimate with B.L. that he would have never written it unless sure of his ground,' Garvin supposed.[2]

He and Astor were sadly mistaken. 'The Tory split on food taxes', which the *Nation* (4 January 1913) depicted as 'a furious newspaper war, with Mr Garvin and Lord Northcliffe as rival generalissimos', impelled Bonar Law to retreat to a Balfourian stance. Early in 1913, he contemplated resigning from the Unionist leadership until Garvin and others convinced him 'of the serious disadvantages of a change'. Still, Garvin could not forgive Bonar Law for dropping the controversial food taxes, seemingly in deference to Northcliffe. 'Morally – that is in respect of will and decision – there is no B.L., but only a receptacle which must always be inhabited by another personality,' he asserted picturesquely to Astor. In this instance, the 'Hermit Crab' was 'Aitken, always putting himself into the other man's ear, and swaying in his sinister, insistent way as he likes that strange unfixed feeble mass of timidity and ambition'. That Aitken had Bonar Law 'absolutely in his grip', financially and otherwise, was all the more disquieting in the light of suspicions that he was acting in collusion with Northcliffe. 'If only we could be sure that the Northcliffe-Aitken relationship was not simply playing

---

[1] Praed to Bonar Law, 5 June 1912, Bonar Law Papers, 26/4/9.
[2] Garvin to Astor, 27 December 1912, and Astor to [Steel-Maitland], 4 January 1913 (draft copy), Astor Papers; Steel-Maitland to Garvin, 23 December 1912, Garvin Papers.

with us all behind the scenes: the doubt gnaws,' brooded Garvin. 'But we can do nothing.'[1]

The blow to Imperial Preference was attended by the other disappointments at Bonar Law's unsteady hand. In February 1912, when the Liberal Government promulgated a third Home Rule measure, passions exploded into hysteria. Bonar Law, however intransigent he may have appeared to his ministerial adversaries, was – in the words of his biographer – 'much more moderate over the Home Rule question than many of the right-wing Conservatives', who sensed as much. The passage of the Parliament Act had shorn the House of Lords of its ancient prerogative to veto legislation, which Unionists were resolved to obstruct by other means. Gwynne, acutely conscious of the Lords' impotence ('The House of Lords cut its own throat and I am afraid that you can't resuscitate a man who has committed suicide'), was initially inclined to tread more cautiously than his proprietor saw fit. 'Bonar Law's pronouncement, I felt sure would displease you,' he wrote on 21 March 1912 to Lady Bathurst, whose diehard husband had cast his lot with the British League for the Support of Ulster and the Union.

> I wish that I could give you the comfort of thinking that your policy will be followed, but I am afraid it will not be. . . . In this matter, as you know, I do not see eye to eye with you, not so much as regards the theoretical but in regard to the practical side. . . . However the *M.P.* shall put forward your views when the time comes for discussion.

Garvin, equally reluctant to sanction an appeal to force at this juncture, called upon the Opposition to disrupt the normal conduct of parliamentary business in order to precipitate a general election. As late as 28 April, the *Observer*'s 'attitude' remained 'untouched by the spirit of hatred . . . or despair', but that was not to last long. Meanwhile, the *World* took it upon itself 'to get up a petition to the King about Home Rule', imploring recourse to the royal veto. Steel-Maitland, fearful that the situation was getting out of hand, thoroughly disapproved of this initiative. 'The King is not the proper person to petition,' he told Bonar Law. 'A petition also at the present moment is rather premature.' Significantly, he did not wish to dampen the ardour of party militants, but rather – like Gwynne and Garvin – to hold such expedients in reserve.[2]

The more extreme Bonar Law waxed in support of Ulster's resistance to Home Rule, the more he endeared himself to the *enragés* of his party and its press, including some who condemned his betrayal of protectionism. 'The ordinary political speech does not interest me at all,' admitted Harcourt

---

[1] Bonar Law to Garvin, 8 January 1913, Garvin Papers; Garvin to Astor, 9 January 1913 and [13 January 1913], Astor Papers.

[2] Blake, *Unknown Prime Minister*, p. 136; Gwynne to Lady Bathurst, 21 March 1912, Bathurst Papers; Gollin, *Observer*, p. 394; Steel-Maitland to Bonar Law, 12 April 1912, Bonar Law Papers, 39/1/3.

Kitchin, editor of the *Glasgow Herald*, 'but the last two of yours I have listened to have given me real artistic pleasure. It is not easy to interest a hardened newspaper man but you have done it – twice.' Gwynne 'was delighted to hear' that the Bathursts' gardener at Cirencester 'had B-L's photograph. It shows that he is gradually getting the people with him.' Addressing a rally at Blenheim Palace on 29 July, Bonar Law gave license to civil war in Ireland: 'I can imagine no length of resistance to which Ulster can go in which I should not be prepared to support them.' His incendiary remarks satisfied the *Observer*'s criteria for 'a policy of combat' (16 June). Gwynne, at last seeing eye to eye with his proprietor (as was Garvin with Astor), took 'some pains to put in its right light the question of Ulster'. From the livid response of the *Westminster Gazette*, he found it 'quite easy to see that the attitude ... the Ulstermen have taken up has altogether shaken the Govt.' The bounden duty of the *Morning Post* was to keep them shaken. *The Times*, however, was decidedly equivocal. Sympathetic to Bonar Law's statement at Blenheim that Ulster should not 'be robbed of her birthright', it warned on 13 August that physical force could only invalidate the Unionist case. 'I liked the leader better this morning,' commented Northcliffe. 'I have not cared for the violent Ulster language of Bonar Law, Carson, and others.'[1]

The editor to whom Northcliffe addressed this compliment was Geoffrey ('Robin') Robinson, who had recently taken over from Buckle. After more than twenty-eight years in the chair and a total of thirty-two years on the staff, Buckle retired, aged fifty-eight. He boasted to Sir Edward Cook (knighted the previous June) that he had served 'longer than any of my predecessors except Delane. Editing *The Times* killed Barnes at 56, Chenery at 58, and broke Delane down at 60, so that he only lived two years after retiring.' Buckle, who was to enjoy an active retirement of twenty-two years, looked forward to completing W. F. Monypenny's multi-volume biography of Disraeli and to editing Queen Victoria's correspondence. He had only the highest praise for his successor. 'You are quite right in expecting much of Geoffrey Robinson,' he assured Garvin. 'He should do great things.' Hardly a surprise, Robinson's appointment attracted widespread enthusiasm. Even Leo Maxse, writing in the September number of the *National Review*, was backhandedly polite: 'Although a fellow of All Souls there is no touch of the prig about a man who has seen too much of the world to imagine himself omniscient and infallible, or to regard Balliol as the hub of the universe.'[2]

[1] Harcourt Kitchin to Bonar Law, 21 May 1912, and Gwynne to Bonar Law, 25 August 1912, Bonar Law Papers, 26/3/33, 27/1/55; Gwynne to Lady Bathurst, 5 August 1912, Bathurst Papers; Northcliffe to Robinson, 13 August 1912 (copy), Northcliffe Papers.

[2] Buckle to Cook, 4 August 1912, Cook Papers; Buckle to Garvin, 9 August 1912, Garvin Papers. Meeting Buckle at the Athenaeum in 1930, Barrington-Ward found him 'fairly fit at 76'. Five years later, when Buckle died, Barrington-Ward recalled him as 'too conservative in thought. He made *The Times* a party organ, though he had the Irish issue and the formation of Unionism to compel him that way.' Barrington-Ward's diary, 23 January 1930 and 12 March 1935.

To Bonar Law, Buckle jested that he had 'caught Arthur Balfour's complaint' and had grown 'too old for this particular form of slavery'. He would 'not watch the fray from so close as before', but promised 'to cheer you on to a victory which cannot now be far off'. In a 'kind letter' of farewell, Bonar Law 'intimated some surprise' that Buckle had not remained at his 'post until after the next Election', assuming that Northcliffe would have permitted it. 'In some ways I should have liked to do so,' Buckle confessed. 'But the actual moment of my resignation, which has been impending for more than a year & a half, was determined by the convenience of the office & had no relation to public affairs. I should like you to know this.' Had Buckle delayed his retirement until after the next general election, he would have had to wait until 1918. By then, issues and alignments had changed in ways that neither he nor Bonar Law dared to anticipate.[1]

* * *

In preparation for the next electoral campaign, which kept receding in its imminence, there was a determined effort to tighten the bolts of the political press. Because newspapers were attentively read for intimations of party strategies or dissensions, it was more necessary than ever to effect control at all levels. Politicians, fearful of disclosures that might reverberate against them, attempted to restrain their journalistic cohorts. Proprietors, under mounting pressure to satisfy – or, at least, not to jeopardize – party interests, reined in their editors. Leading articles and even ordinary news reports were carefully vetted to ensure that they gave no hostages to fortune either explicitly or between the lines.

That this heavy-handed exercise of authority challenged the concept of newspaper independence, much less that it affronted professional self-respect, was deemed a small price to pay. Issues of momentous import were at stake: the sanctity of the Anglo-Irish Union, and the fate of Ulster loyalism; the fundamentals of social welfare, and the financial sources for its attainment; the exclusivism of the franchise; the survival of the Anglican establishment in Wales; and the defence of the Empire, menaced by growing autonomy in the dominions and by the rising threat of German expansionism. On any of these emotive subjects, and others besides, an editorial indiscretion could lead to serious embarrassment and, by extension, to political disrepute.

While not unthinkable, the idea of muzzling the press was recognized to be impossible. Party chiefs and their agents therefore depended upon newspapermen to act as their own censors. By and large, the system worked. Acutely conscious of their partisan responsibilities, often reinforced by a compromising reliance on party or party-induced funding, the custodians of

[1] Buckle to Bonar Law, 30 July and 14 September 1912, Bonar Law Papers, 26/5/52, 27/2/14.

the national press resisted the temptation to speculate about the policies of their respective sides. Instead they largely confined themselves to diatribes against their parliamentary antagonists, usually in the form of attacks on prominent personalities. Their pent-up frustration helps to account for the exceptionally vindictive nature of political journalism as practised in the years immediately before the First World War. Occasionally, unable to hold back, newspapermen fulminated against all manner of politicians. Yet their dread of the alternative invariably revived their partisan spirit.

It was easier, of course, to maintain discipline in the lower echelons, where communication was more frequent and contractual relations were more binding. However bitterly they might grumble, leader-writers were obliged to do the bidding of editors, and editors of proprietors. At the *Daily Mail*, H. W. Wilson was technically responsible to Marlowe, and both of them were beholden to Northcliffe, who was sensitive to Unionist imperatives. Spender and Garvin, who wrote the leaders for the papers they edited, were effectively guided by the politicians who employed them, and Blumenfeld was directed by Aitken, who qualified alternately as Bonar Law's servant and Svengali. 'Possibly, on occasions,' Donald of the *Daily Chronicle* 'was too meticulous, and withheld from his news department information which might properly have been used; but it was better to err on the side of discretion than to impair the confidence he enjoyed.'[1] The inventory here, though hardly exhaustive, points up a common predicament. With the notable exception of Scott, who both owned and edited the *Manchester Guardian* and whose intimacy with certain politicians derived from his earlier years at Westminster, the men who actually filled the columns of the political dailies stood on the bottom rung of a three-tiered ladder. Their subordination did not prevent them from enjoying direct and sometimes close contact with political leaders, which often required elaborate circumventions. Nevertheless, there existed intervening barriers, varying from case to case, but never to be discounted.

Lloyd George's campaign to change the face of land ownership furnishes a case in point. His comprehensive programme, delayed in its promulgation by ministerial qualms and conceivably by his complicity in the Marconi scandal, proposed to break up ancestral estates into small tenant holdings, with a revaluation of property taxes and the enforcement of a minimum wage for farm labourers. The pattern of urban landlordship was also earmarked for drastic reform as a means of alleviating slum conditions. Newspaper propaganda was considered essential to the success of this vast enterprise. 'Your articles on the rural problem are simply first-rate and you are rendering enormous help by preparing the ground so effectively,' Lloyd George wrote gratefully to Donald, whom he did not hesitate to send suggestions for further articles in the *Daily Chronicle*. 'You are exposing the scandalous treatment of the English agricultural labourer in a way which has hardly yet been done in our papers.' That was

[1] H. A. Taylor, *Donald*, p. 53.

patently unfair to other Liberal editors. While Spender had never disguised his reservations, Massingham 'accompanied Lloyd George all the way'. Scott was emphatically supportive, and Gardiner had long advocated the adoption of 'collective methods which have revolutionised agriculture on the Continent'. But Lloyd George, annoyed with Gardiner for other reasons, amused his Cabinet colleagues by insisting that 'I never read the *Daily News* now'.[1]

To borrow the useful classifications improvised by J. Malcolm Fraser, press supervisor at the Conservative Central Office, Gardiner's relationship to Lloyd George was that of a 'Candid Friend', favourably disposed, but variable. Donald, by contrast, was a 'Friend in Need', discreet to the point of dissemblance and loyal to the point of laudation. This distinction helps to explain why Donald's wartime break with Lloyd George, though less rancorous than Gardiner's, created the greater stir. Before the war, Donald was virtually Lloyd George's alter ego. When a rival paper 'scored a "scoop"' with the bizarre story of a plot to poison the Chancellor, Donald blandly remarked: 'Oh, yes; L.G. told me all about it at breakfast two days ago.' The collaboration had its unsavoury side. Burns believed – not illogically – that the *Daily Chronicle* disparaged him at Lloyd George's instigation. As a hatchet-man, Donald was indispensable. As a land reformer, he was able to invoke the old-time panacea of 'three acres and a cow', a slogan from bygone days when Chamberlain was a Liberal known as Radical Joe. He was sustained by the compliant attitude of Frank Lloyd, his proprietor, who saw the *Chronicle*'s progressivism justified by its healthy circulation.[2]

Gwynne, seeking to do what was expedient and, at the same time, what was 'right', had a harder task. He had regular interviews with Bonar Law to plot the course to be followed by the *Morning Post*, only to meet stiff objections from Lady Bathurst. Torn in his loyalties, he professed to be 'in perfect agreement' with her opposition to small holdings, but disagreed 'in the matter of tactics', where she favoured a more truculent response. 'I do not like the tone of the leader on small ownership in towns,' she bluntly informed him on 15 July 1912:

> We apparently approve of & bless the idea. I am too busy & too tired to write you long reasons for my objections to all forms of small ownership except the yeoman farmer, but I thought you quite understood this. I want to impress on you that I mean to have my way in this matter. That not only do I wish the *Morning Post* to refrain from approval but I want to have a campaign against small ownership, this autumn or late summer. I do not often interfere with the paper now but when there is a question upon which I feel very strongly you will remember that you admitted that my wish should prevail.

[1] Lloyd George to Donald, 20 September 1912 (copy), Lloyd George Papers, C/4/8/2; Koss, *Fleet Street Radical*, pp. 74–75; Havighurst, *Radical Journalist*, pp. 211–12; Lloyd George to Spender, 16 July 1909 (copy), Spender Papers, Add. MSS. 46, 388, fol. 201; Hobhouse's diary, 27 November 1912, *Inside Asquith's Cabinet*, p. 125.

[2] H. A. Taylor, *Donald*, pp. 21, 55; Cook's diary, 18 June 1914, Cook Papers.

Gwynne, primed by Bonar Law, tried to calm her down:

> I am the most reckless of men in my ordinary private-life but when I am entrusted with the editing of a paper like the *M.P.* I am cautious to a degree – perhaps over cautious. We are faced with a new wave of socialism and the statesmen of the party (by this I mean the thinkers and not the mere politicians) feel that something drastic has to be done to prevent the wave of discontent and rebellion which has permeated the industrial masses from spreading to the agricultural labourer.

When the Unionists finally took up cudgels (eventually sanctioning full-scale resistance to 'Radical Land Robbery'), Gwynne gave Lady Bathurst 'all the credit'. She did not want any acknowledgment, however, save for that of her proprietorial rights. 'I know ... that you cannot possibly let me know about everything,' she told Gwynne, 'but what I wish always to know are those things ... involving big expenses or any question of policy.'[1]

By laying down the law in no uncertain terms, Lady Bathurst not only ensured that she would have her way, but also defined the chain of command that prevailed along Fleet Street. She assured Gwynne 'that *you* are the Editor ... and that the paper's success is due to you', and she subsequently denied having any 'illusions about my position. I may sometimes supply ideas; often they fall flat.' Nevertheless, she boasted of her 'obstinacy', which was real enough. She prided herself on having 'very little to do with the paper', not because she was 'afraid', but 'because from my other duties it is impossible that I should do much'.[2] Yet her interventions, though intermittent, were always decisive. The same could be said to a greater or lesser extent about every newspaper owner.

Of Northcliffe, it could be said without the slightest qualification. He was the piper who called the tune, which his editors then played exactly to his specification. Their obligations to him took precedence over any principles or attachments they might have had. Walter J. Evans owed his longevity at the *Evening News*, where his editorship lasted from 1896 to 1921, to his self-effacing qualities. Marlowe weathered successive storms at the *Daily Mail* by accepting his status as a hireling. Neither of them was burdened with a strong political conscience, and neither aspired to direct influence in party councils. Northcliffe, leaving no doubt who was boss, addressed them brusquely. 'Are we getting middle-aged, or what has happened that we cannot make changes as we used [?],' he wrote reprovingly to Marlowe. 'The *Daily News* is four days out of six a better paper as regards news than we are, and has a guaranteed

---

[1] Gwynne to Lady Bathurst, 23 September and 15 October 1912, Bathurst Papers; Lady Bathurst to Gwynne, 15 July and 21 November 1912, Gwynne Papers; Bonar Law Papers, 32/3/13 and 40/5/4; *also see* H. V. Emy, 'The Land Campaign,' in *Lloyd George: Twelve Essays* (ed. A. J. P. Taylor; London, 1971), pp. 35–68.

[2] Lady Bathurst to Gwynne [March, 1914] Gwynne Papers.

circulation of 500,000 copies a day as a result.' Marlowe, perpetually on the defensive, could only apologize. Though less of a yes-man than Evans, he rarely presumed to say no. He had been in Fleet Street for fourteen years when Steel-Maitland asked Bonar Law: 'Do you by any chance know Marlowe, the editor of the *Daily Mail*? Even though Northcliffe rules this paper in considerable detail himself, it might be worthwhile your knowing Marlowe, in case you do not.'[1]

The effect of Buckle's departure from Printing House Square was to strengthen Northcliffe's hand vis-à-vis *The Times*. For all his Milnerite connections, Robinson was an unknown quantity to the parliamentary Unionist leadership. Unlike Buckle's or, for that matter, Nicholson's, his 'personal' correspondence with Bonar Law was punctiliously formal: on 13 November 1912, he was 'impertinent enough' to tender advice, along with an invitation to join himself and Grigg at lunch 'some day ... in my house at Westminster – it is only five minutes from the House of Commons – when business calls you in that direction in the middle of the day'.[2] Twice editor, from 1912 to 1919 and again – after Northcliffe's death – from 1922 to 1941, it was during his second innings that he established the rapport with Whitehall and Downing Street for which he became famous and, in some circles, infamous.

At the outset of his initial tenure, Robinson routinely acquiesced in Northcliffe's views and prejudices, confining his protests to the pages of his diary. His previous editorial experience on the Johannesburg *Star* and his Oxford laurels commanded respect; and, to be sure, *The Times* conferred a unique distinction upon him. Still, when it came to matters of political controversy, his policies ran according to Northcliffe's writ. 'Whether *The Times* ought to give attention to the internal wreckers of the Unionist Party ... is for you to judge,' conceded Northcliffe, whose stated preference was dead against it. Robinson was a man after his own heart. 'I have tried, since I have been in charge, to keep clear in the leading articles of all the small change of party politics,' he promptly affirmed, 'and I think it is best to continue this course, though I most heartily agree that the younger Unionist members are making asses of themselves.' To no avail, Buckle pleaded with him to stand up to the Chief: 'The independence of *The Times* is the basis of its authority; if it is to be regarded as a mere mouthpiece of Northcliffe, or a more respectable echo of the *D.M.*, who will regard it?' But Robinson was an appeaser long before he helped that word to acquire a pejorative connotation.[3]

In the words of Northcliffe's biographers, *The Times* was once 'again an

---

[1] Northcliffe to Marlowe, 30 November [1912] (copy), Northcliffe Papers; Steel-Maitland to Bonar Law, 28 July 1913, Bonar Law Papers, 29/6/32.
[2] Robinson to Bonar Law, 13 November 1912. Bonar Law Papers, 27/4/27.
[3] Northcliffe to Robinson, 13 December 1912 (copy), and Robinson to Northcliffe, 13 December 1912, Northcliffe Papers; Buckle to Robinson, 23 December 1912, *Times* Archives.

inflammatory focal point of his attention'.[1] That was to put it mildly. His aim was to attract a new class of readers without alienating the old ones and thus forfeiting prestige. On 5 May 1913, after sales had dipped below 41,000, the price was reduced by a third to twopence; the net gain, no higher than 6,000 copies, was barely sufficient to offset the expenses of an extensive promotional campaign. Then, on 16 March 1914, the price was halved to a penny. Back in 1858, Mowbray Morris had calculated that it would be 'impossible to produce a first-class paper at that price', and subsequent managers had held to this opinion out of a determination to maintain historic standards. Their fears might have been allayed had they known that the Faculty of Literae Humaniores at Oxford would set '*The Times* for a penny' as a topic for the next scholarship examination in Greek. More to the point, the average sale soared to 145,000, exceeding Northcliffe's hopes.

Northcliffe did not stop here. He introduced pictorial (i.e. block) advertisements, which the *Morning Post* rejected as beneath its dignity, and he issued directives that the typography was to be enlivened, with long articles 'boiled down' for easier digestion. In his struggle to 'save the paper from extinction', as he dramatized it to impress John Walter, he adjusted the proportions between domestic and foreign coverage, purged 'inefficient people' from the staff, discounted advertising and subscription rates, and proscribed weather reports from Continental resorts ('a waste of space, ink and composition'). That some of these economies were relatively piddling seems to have mattered less than that they cumulatively ruffled the 'dullardes', as Northcliffe mocked them in medieval spelling. Robinson, whose 'days and nights have been so occupied in trying to keep other people from complete despondency and resignation that I literally have not had time to think very much of what the paper should say', offered to work at half-salary to obviate 'still further reductions'. In his diary, he complained of the 'fearful worry and chaos in the office' caused by Northcliffe's 'contradictory orders, ... lunatic raging and nagging'. In fact, he learnt of most of these changes after they were effected. To implement his policy of retrenchment, Northcliffe relied on Hugh Chisholm, formerly editor of the *St James's Gazette*, who was made 'day editor' in June 1913 and a director the following August. A Scotsman by birth and bearing, Chisholm supposedly possessed a natural aptitude for penny-pinching.

Scotsmen and Jews, interchangeable to Northcliffe, were the butts of what Hamilton Fyfe described as his 'mischievous schoolboy humour'. A believer in racial stereotypes, he credited them with an instinctive acumen in business affairs. Although Jews on his payroll suffered his insults, which drove the

---

[1] The following paragraphs are based upon discussions and quoted sources in Pound and Harmsworth, pp. 434, 447–50, and *History of The Times*, IV, part 1, ch. iv; also Gwynne to Lady Bathurst, 2 June 1914, Bathurst Papers, and Northcliffe to Ellerman, 27 October 1913 (copy), Northcliffe Papers.

acting editor of the *Weekly Dispatch* to resign in a rage, there were many among their co-religionists with whom he got on famously. Isaacs, his counsel in the 1907 litigation with Lever, was forgiven for his part in the Marconi scandal, his Jewish lineage, and his Liberal enthusiasms. The Lawsons, Lord Burnham and his son Harry, were esteemed as worthy rivals, whom the *Daily Mail* – in an article 'obviously from the pen of Northcliffe' – wished 'well in [their] forthcoming ordeal' of competing against a cut-price *Times*. In the midst of his 'attack on the *D.T.*', intended to capture readers and advertisers from Peterborough Court, Northcliffe promoted the idea of commemorating the eightieth birthday of Burnham, 'a very delightful old man who is always kind to his workers, and is, even today, one of the ablest of our craft'.

Healthy competition was one thing Northcliffe never feared, and his piracy was pursued in a spirit of fraternalism, not without chivalry. At a time when the *Morning Post* was 'having a ding-dong fight with *The Times*', he took the readers of the *Daily Mail* 'behind the scenes in the newspaper war' (16 March 1914) and portrayed the Countess Bathurst as 'a young and beautiful woman of the world [who] revealed the inherited brains of two generations, and made the *Post* the goodly paper it is to-day'. By the same token, he did not permit political differences to cloud his personal relations with Spender and Donald, though he found Scott incomprehensible and Gardiner offensive. He could even bring himself to welcome the appearance of the socialist *Daily Citizen*. 'I think it very essential to the welfare of this Empire that Labour should have a proper newspaper,' he told Frank Dilnot, its editor, who had worked for a decade on the *Daily Mail*. 'We have the only representative Parliament in the world. I should like a really representative Press.'

It was ironic that he should have extolled the representative character of Parliament at a time when critics at both ends of the political spectrum were heatedly disputing it. Tory disaffection knew no bounds. On 13 November 1912, the Prime Minister was shouted down in the House of Commons, and Ronald McNeill – another former editor of the *St James's* and now Conservative member for East Kent – hurled a book from the Speaker's table at the head of Churchill, who had to be escorted – dazed and bloodied – from the chamber. The 'disciplined storm', which Garvin had helped to whip up in the *Observer* on 16 June, quickly assumed hurricane proportions. Along with the collapse of parliamentary decorum, there was the growing threat of insurrection in Ireland, which Protestant army officers could not be depended upon to suppress. Gwynne predicted that the Government would back down or, better still, fall. 'I agree with you about Home Rule,' he wrote to Bonar Law, who had made good his promise to be 'very vicious' on the subject. 'Even Massingham (the Radical Stead) seems to have chucked up the sponge.' But Gwynne, and possibly Bonar Law too, underestimated the indignation of Liberal backbenchers, further provoked by the Lords' untimely rejection of the Welsh Disestablishment Bill; and, as yet, he misjudged the blind intransigence of Ulstermen, goaded by extremist elements at Westminster.[1]

Left-wing Liberals had their own resentments against a system that denied them legislative gratification and effectively excluded them from power. The Cabinet, which they saw to be dominated by unreconstructed Liberal Imperialists, had failed in its feeble attempts to redress Nonconformist grievances over education, licensing laws, and the Welsh Church. It had dealt more leniently with seditious Unionists than with suffragettes. Most culpably, it had embarked on a costly programme for naval construction, deflecting revenues from social reconstruction and fuelling Anglo-German antagonism.

Within the parliamentary Liberal Party, a Foreign Policy Committee agitated for the assertion of democratic control over the diplomatic process, conducted by faceless individuals behind closed doors. Its efforts were complemented by an assortment of *ad hoc* bodies, professional and civic societies, chambers of commerce, and, not least, by the National Liberal Federation. In 1911, a year after he had retired from the Commons, Sir John Brunner was chosen president of the Federation, founded in 1877 by Joseph Chamberlain as 'a real Liberal parliament outside the Imperial Legislature'. In his new capacity, Brunner continued to campaign for the limitation of expenditure on armaments and improved relations with Germany. Lloyd George and Churchill, on whom he had previously relied for ministerial support, dissociated themselves from the 'economists' as a consequence of the 1911 Agadir crisis. Loreburn's resignation from the Cabinet ('Always remember that this is a Liberal League Government,' he wrote 'gravely and warningly' to Scott) reduced the 'pacifist' component to Morley, Burns, and Harcourt. Though weakly represented on the front bench, the Cobdenite tradition ran strong in the party as a whole and, especially, in its press.[2]

The *Nation*, which celebrated Brunner's election as 'a powerful and enthusiastic demonstration in favor of an understanding with Germany' (25 November 1911), was searchingly critical of foreign and defence policies. Scott and Herbert Sidebotham, his leader-writer, rekindled the moral fervour of the *Manchester Guardian*. The *Daily News* hankered likewise to re-fight the issues of the Boer War and, once and for all, to defeat the forces of jingoism. Visiting London on 19 September 1912, Scott 'lunched with Massingham ... & dined with Gardiner'. He found them 'almost equally strong in feeling against Grey's dependence on Russia & antagonism to Germany & ... prepared to go to all lengths in opposition'. Gardiner was restrained by Parke, who was a shade 'more cautious', preferring to work 'in concert with ... (if possible) the

---

[1] Randolph S. Churchill, *Winston S. Churchill*, II (Boston, 1967), p. 457; Gwynne to Bonar Law, 2 October 1912, Bonar Law Papers, 27/3/3; Koss, *Asquith*, pp. 134–35.

[2] Loreburn to Scott, 20 July 1911, Scott Papers, Add. MSS. 50, 901, fol. 21; Koss, *Sir John Brunner* (Cambridge, 1970), pp. 238–39.

Chronicle'. That was recognized by F. W. Hirst to be impossible. Representing 'official policy', the *Daily Chronicle* and the *Westminster Gazette* contrived 'to lie low and say nothing'.[1]

Hirst, editor of the weekly *Economist* since 1907, embodied the creed of mid-Victorian Manchester Radicalism. He had assisted Morley in the research for his three-volume life of Gladstone, and the assignment made an indelible impression upon him. In addition to restoring a partisan glow to the grey complexion of *The Economist*, he undertook to counteract the scaremongerings of yellow journalists – the tools of 'the Armour plate press' – who poisoned the atmosphere between nations. With an allowance from Brunner and Ernest Schuster, a Liberal financier, he dispatched Dudley Ward ('an honest journalist' and 'a real lover of peace') to Berlin, where he was to 'act as press-correspondent with the object of promoting friendly relations between Germany and England'. Brunner gave a lunch at the National Liberal Club to introduce Ward to representatives of the *Liverpool Post*, the *Yorkshire Observer*, the *Sheffield Independent*, the *Darlington Echo*, the *South Wales Daily News*, the *Aberdeen Free Press*, and the *Dundee Advertiser*. Hirst, who planned the event, considered it 'likely' that other papers – including the *Western Daily Mercury*, the *Eastern Morning News*, the *Manchester Guardian*, the *Daily News*, and the *Daily Chronicle* – would avail themselves of Ward's service.[2]

Brunner, once a major benefactor of Liberal newspaper enterprises, retained his faith in the efficacy of the published word, but was himself no stylist. Hirst helped him to draft circular letters to constituency associations, resolutions that were 'carried with perfect unanimity' by the Federation, and arguments for the consideration of sympathetic editors. 'The Liberal Press and the opinion of the rank and file are powerful agencies,' Hirst insisted in a letter – signed 'Political Economy', but acknowledged to be his handiwork – in the *Nation* on 30 December 1911. A leading article in the *Manchester Guardian* on 13 January 1912 reflected his inspiration. In March, when Churchill announced increased naval estimates, the Radical press howled in protest; in July, when he requested three additional ships for the Mediterranean fleet, the outcry was still greater. The *Nation*, appalled by the evolution of 'a virtual naval alliance between France and ourselves with Russia as a third (and slippery) partner', called on 13 July for 'an emergency meeting of the Federation . . . [to] act for the menaced cause of peace and Liberalism'. Massingham informed Hirst, who promptly relayed word to Brunner, that 'Ll. George is almost on the point of resignation, and a break up of the Cabinet is threatened on Churchill's

[1] Scott's diary, 19 September 1912, *Guardian* Archives; Hirst to Brunner, 16 October 1912, Brunner Papers; *also see* A. J. A. Morris, *Radicalism Against War, 1906–1914* (London, 1972), pp. 259–81.

[2] Hirst to Brunner, 5 and 19 December 1911, Brunner Papers; for the role of the press in 'the impulse and orchestration of patriotism', see Paul Kennedy, *The Rise of the Anglo-German Antagonism 1860–1914* (London, 1980), ch. 18.

proposal'. From talks with Morley and Harold Spender, Hirst ascertained that Lloyd George, Harcourt, Morley, and McKenna were 'sharply against' admiralty policy, while Grey, Haldane, and Asquith were 'mildly for Winston'.[1]

Impressive in itself, this manifestation of newspaper discontent drew its significance from divergences within the government. Conversely, its effects were vitiated by differences of perspective among editors, among politicians, and between the two groups. Lloyd George could cooperate no more effectively with McKenna (or Morley with Harcourt) than Scott with Massingham or Gardiner. Sustained collaboration between politicians and journalists proved more elusive still; Scott, for example, was 'at a certain disadvantage in depending on [Loreburn] for a knowledge of Grey's foreign policy'. Asquith, glancing in Lloyd George's direction at a Cabinet on 27 November, 'said that he thought it a pity that those who gave M[assingham] his information did not see that he took care to use the information accurately'. Lloyd George

> said that he had had Massingham to lunch and spoken to him about it, but that he couldn't lock him up in a room till he promised to sin no more. Thereupon Grey said 'Well if the Cabinet will authorise me to lock myself up with Massingham until he repents, I will take on the job willingly.'[2]

Massingham took hints but never dictation. Working at cross purposes with other participants in the anti-armaments movement, he attenuated its impact.

In anticipation of the autumn session of the National Liberal Federation, Brunner addressed a manifesto (ghost written by Hirst) to the chairman of every Liberal association in the kingdom. Asserting that the Government had listened more attentively to the 'Jingo press' than to its own editorial counsellors, it urged the passage of two resolutions, the first in favour of widening the Entente to embrace Germany, and the second for an international agreement 'for the purpose of securing all peaceful shipping and merchandise from capture or destruction in time of war'; if realized, the second objective would lessen the need for naval patrols and thus curtail provocative expenditure in peace-time.[3]

Hirst, who expected 'at least two millions of people' to read Brunner's appeal and agree with it, waited for the newspaper reaction. Disappointingly, the *Liverpool Post* 'had no article', whereas the local 'Tory rag' spoke briefly and slightingly. 'The *Manchester Guardian*'s article was a really splendid one,' as was the *Nottingham Express*'s. 'The *Yorkshire Post* had a curious article and

---

[1] Hirst to Brunner, 12 and 15 July 1912, Brunner Papers.
[2] J. L. Hammond, *C. P. Scott of the Manchester Guardian* (London, 1934), p. 152; Hobhouse's diary, 27 November 1912, *Inside Asquith's Cabinet*, p. 125.
[3] Koss, *Brunner*, pp. 256–59 and Appendix II.

I am glad to see that the *Scotsman* slated you. An attack by the *Scotsman* is about the highest praise that a public man can receive.' The *Nation* (19 October) accorded unqualified approval to Brunner's initiative and, moreover, credited the sense of party loyalty that motivated him. The *Westminster Gazette* and the *Daily Chronicle* were predictably silent. 'I am glad you are keeping the ball rolling in the *Daily News*,' Hirst told Brunner on the 21st. 'It seems to me to be wise to assume that Grey will endorse the resolutions' sooner than face censure by the Federation. 'I doubt myself whether he is really (like his clerks) Anti-German.' The belief that the Foreign Secretary was the prisoner of his Germanophobic and anti-democratic permanent officials, while not wholly without substance, enabled Radical dissidents to conceive of themselves as constructive critics.[1]

By the time the National Liberal Federation met at Nottingham on 21 November, the Government had worked out a compromise formula on shipbuilding and the crisis had subsided. The *Nation* (23 November) reported that Brunner had put his case 'with great power, and apparently with the entire assent of his audience', but it could no longer pretend that the party leaders were listening. An extra-parliamentary agitation, however vociferously backed by the press, was doomed without connivance at a higher level. Thus Brunner's follow-up missive on New Year's Day 1914 – warmly commended by the *Daily News*, the *Manchester Guardian*, and the *Nation* – would have fallen flat but for the fact that, on the same day, Lloyd George decried the 'organised insanity' of renewed naval competition in an interview with the *Daily Chronicle*. Donald, taking his cue, joined the onslaught. As F. E. Smith remarked sneeringly in a speech at Liverpool on 8 January, 'it did not matter so long' as Churchill was arraigned 'by Sir John Brunner and the old whining brigade of the same class'; only when Lloyd George 'expressed the view that the psychological moment had come for us to reduce our naval armaments' did the implications become serious.

It is conceivable that Lloyd George was coaxed from his tent by the public and private exhortations of his newspaper friends. T. P. O'Connor, who had been on holiday with him in Algiers, testified to Lloyd George's determination 'to break with Churchill on the Navy Estimates'. Though Scott begged him to resign rather than acquiesce 'in the face of the enormous liabilities incurred by Churchill without authority', it was Churchill's departure that Lloyd George contemplated. Reluctant to topple the Government, he had his ambitions as well as his convictions to consider and concluded that neither would be served by carrying his opposition too far. 'Winston has sent in revised figures,' he sheepishly informed Scott on 23 January. 'A swelling expenditure without any prospect or hope of reduction would have justified such a course' as Scott had

---

[1] Hirst to Brunner, 16 and 21 October 1912, Brunner Papers; *also see* Zara S. Steiner, *Britain and the Origins of the First World War* (New York, 1977), pp. 187–89.

advised; 'so would a mere nominal or colourable reduction. But what about this offer?' The answer he solicited was obvious.[1]

On platforms, in committee rooms, and especially in the Radical press, the disarmament campaign flickered until August 1914, when it was extinguished by events. Occasionally, too, it flared in ministerial precincts, where an ethic of collective responsibility prevailed against it. Full of sound and fury, these sporadic bursts of outraged emotion signified a good deal, yet accomplished nothing. For them to have succeeded, for better or worse, would have required a degree of cohesion between Liberal politicians and publicists that survived only as a dim memory.

* * *

Upholding the sacred tenets of 'Peace, Retrenchment, and Reform', Liberal critics of official Liberal policy – 'true fanatics' like Hirst – were painfully estranged from their party leaders. Since 1874, when Morley had eloquently inveighed against 'Compromise', he had repeatedly exhibited that proclivity. Lloyd George, younger and more vigorous, was generally unreliable as an ally; his very strength as a political operator counted as a disadvantage to the campaign that he sometimes encouraged, but always from a safe distance.

The agents of Unionist fanaticism had fewer disabilities. For one thing, they enjoyed the benefit of more direct access to their frontbench spokesmen who, being in opposition, were relatively free to prescribe drastic remedies; for another, they were less scrupulous in their efforts to excite popular passions. Thus, Garvin, Gwynne, and Maxse were empowered to act more boldly than Scott, Gardiner, and Massingham. Donald, waiting for periodic signals from Lloyd George, was more inhibited than Blumenfeld, the henchman of Aitken, who was in turn the henchman of Bonar Law.

The transcendent importance of the Irish question, especially as it affected the fate of Protestant Ulster, gave solidarity to Unionism in the years before the First World War. Bonar Law 'felt more strongly about the Ulster question than anything else in politics at this time'.[2] His militant stand, if incompatible with the conventions of parliamentary democracy, was applauded by his supporters. His approach to the vexing question of Tariff Reform was, by contrast, more pragmatic and therefore divisive. Many of the same people who celebrated his all-out resistance to Home Rule regarded him as a traitor to the protectionist cause.

It was a moot point whether the referendum pledge, ambiguously given to the electorate in the second general election of 1910 by Balfour, was binding upon his successor. Bonar Law, after initial hesitation, decided in April 1912

---

[1] O'Connor to Dillon, 13 January 1914, quoted in F. S. L. Lyons, *John Dillon* (London, 1968), pp. 344–45; Scott to Lloyd George, 18 January 1914 (copy), and Lloyd George to Scott, 23 January 1914, *Guardian* Archives.

[2] Blake, *Unknown Prime Minister*, p. 125.

that it was not. The following November, when the National Union met at the Albert Hall, Lansdowne publicly announced the recantation. There was a fierce protest from Free Fooders within the party, who assumed that they had buried the dreaded 'stomach taxes'. They pointed to recent Unionist by-election gains in Free Trade Lancashire, which would now be at risk. Ten days later, their fears were seen to be justified when the Liberals comfortably held Bolton, a seat that the Unionists had hoped to capture. 'I don't think you realize the apathy of the Conservatives up here,' Stephenson of the *Manchester Courier* wrote to Northcliffe after the poll at Bolton was declared. 'This is the kind of thing the *M.C.* has always had to contend with.'[1]

It was incumbent upon Bonar Law to reaffirm and, in some respects, to clarify Lansdowne's statement. He did so in a major speech on 16 December at Ashton-under-Lyne, Aitken's strategically situated constituency. There was no time to lose. Gershom Stewart, Unionist MP for the Wirral and a Tariff Reformer *faute de mieux* ('I would rather have Mr Bonar Law with the food taxes than any other leader without them'), was convinced that if Bonar Law would promptly 'reply to our log-rolling opponents by a little of the "same", ... we can secure the "wobblers" of our party'. Smith remitted dire warnings: 'Things in Lancashire are on the verge of a smash,' led by Lord Derby, with a powerful assist from Archibald Salvidge, the veteran party boss in Liverpool. With Derby in the chair, the Lancashire Conservative Association was set to meet on the 21st to consider an agenda of hostile resolutions. The *Manchester Courier* was openly antagonistic, and the *Liverpool Courier* (12 December) pleaded with Bonar Law to rescind his decision. J. M. W. Morison, Aitken's lieutenant in Ashton, apprehended that the sentiments of the *Liverpool Courier* 'will have an enormous effect in Lancashire'. Salvidge, implying that he was ordinarily able to guarantee satisfaction, hastened to assure Bonar Law 'that I knew nothing of this article until I read it in the paper, nor was I consulted in any way as to its publication'. While optimistic that 'an amicable solution' might yet be achieved 'without resorting to the columns of the public press', he informed Smith that he had 'received protests from numbers of business men who have votes in both Exchange and Wirral and who intend to abstain at the next election unless the Referendum pledge is restored. That is the way the wind blows,' reported Salvidge, the weather-cock of Merseyside.[2]

Bonar Law modestly concluded that his 'speech at Ashton did some good', but recognized it to have been quickly negated 'by two things; first by

[1] Stephenson to Northcliffe, 28 November 1912, Northcliffe Papers; for the Bolton by-election, see Clarke, *Lancashire and the New Liberalism*, pp. 388–89.

[2] Stewart to Bonar Law, 13 December 1912, Salvidge to Bonar Law, 13 December 1912, and Smith to Bonar Law, 18 December 1912, Bonar Law Papers, 28/1/32, 34, 53; Morison (president, Working Men's Unionist Association, Ashton) to Aitken, 12 December 1912, Beaverbrook Papers, B/68; Salvidge to Smith, 24 December 1912, quoted in Stanley Salvidge, *Salvidge of Liverpool* (London, 1934), pp. 125–26; for Salvidge as a power broker, see P. J. Waller, *Democracy and Sectarianism: a political and social history of Liverpool, 1868–1937* (Liverpool, 1981), ch. 14.

Northcliffe with his Papers and second, I am sorry to say, by Derby through the position he holds in Lancashire and the use he is making of it'. More helpfully than Bonar Law credited, Derby staved off a vote (which would have overwhelmingly rebuked the party leadership) by moving a three-week adjournment of the Lancashire Conservative Association for the ostensible purpose of surveying the electoral ramifications. He promised to 'condemn in as strong language as I can the line taken by the *Liverpool Courier*, for though I agree with what it preaches I am very much opposed to the methods it has used'. Moreover, as 'an obvious proof of my wish to pour oil on the troubled waters', Derby extracted an editorial 'assurance that they will close the discussion, ... now that the position in Lancashire and Yorkshire is thoroughly realised by the Party'.[1]

For Northcliffe, there was no defence. *The Times* and the *Daily Mail* (which Garvin nicknamed the 'Rag Times') did not so much denounce as belittle the Ashton speech. The following morning, the *Daily Mail* could only 'calmly wonder, as we read Mr Bonar Law's promises, what can have induced Lord Lansdowne to make the Albert Hall speech which has given rise to so much unnecessary discussion'. In that day's *Times*, Robinson – trying his hand as a leader-writer on a domestic topic – asked whether duties on imported food made economic sense in a period of rising prices. Lansdowne did not suppose that Bonar Law 'could have handled a difficult situation more tactfully', and shrugged off *The Times*'s leader as 'a singularly feeble production'. Henry (later 1st Viscount) Chaplin, an ardent Tariff Reformer, told Bonar Law that he found it difficult to 'understand some of the criticisms of your speech except in *The Times*. That is Northcliffe!! He is always trying to trip us up on Food Taxes.' Austen Chamberlain, fully supportive of Bonar Law's intentions (though mildly critical of his phraseology), foresaw 'a bad quarter of an hour to go through. The disaffection of *The Times* is serious and I do not under-rate it,' he admitted.[2]

These rumblings of northern discontent were amplified by Northcliffe's metropolitan dailies, which were not alone. Strachey prepared Bonar Law for an agnostic response in the *Spectator*: 'I think when you read it, though you will of course disagree, you will not consider it a criticism which will do any harm to the essential cause we have at heart, the cause of the Union.' Like many Unionists, Strachey's greatest fear was that an avoidable split over tariffs would impair the party's capacity to withstand the danger of Home Rule. Garvin sensed this most acutely. 'Unless dissensions are to damn us all some one had to speak out about the Carmelite House-Printing House Square performance', which he discerned to be more the cause than the effect of

---

[1] Bonar Law to Lansdowne, 25 December 1912 (copy), and Derby to Bonar Law, 20 December 1912, Bonar Law Papers, 33/4/83, 28/1/65.

[2] Lansdowne to Bonar Law, 18 December 1912, Chaplin to Bonar Law, 18 December 1912, and Austen Chamberlain to Bonar Law, 24 December 1912, Bonar Law Papers, 28/1/54, 55, 86.

Unionist discord. Resigned to the fact that 'the Unionist party is most likely to be out for years', he maintained that the future of the Union depended on the vigilance of a unified opposition. If Bonar Law's speech at Ashton left something to be desired, Northcliffe's public breach was gross insubordination. In the *Observer* on 22 December, Garvin said as much.[1]

Austen Chamberlain, whose maxim was 'Steady is the word', spoke 'fully & frankly' to Garvin the previous afternoon in an attempt to soothe him. His intervention was 'the kind of thing that makes one almost despair of Austen', complained Garvin. 'He has treated us quite badly as nearly all politicians do the newspapers to which they owe most.' Steel-Maitland, who professed to 'feel just as strongly about the line taken by *The Times*', counselled Garvin 'that silence on the subject of differences in the Party is extremely valuable just now'. Anticipating Garvin's recalcitrance, Steel-Maitland went over the editor's head to Waldorf Astor, whom he beseeched to exercise a restraining influence. Garvin, with as little success, went over Austen Chamberlain's head by journeying to see Joseph Chamberlain at Highbury. His mission, he disclosed to Astor, was undertaken 'in the hope of convincing' the younger Chamberlain that 'something must be done'. As if to add insult to injury, Austen Chamberlain ignored the *Observer* and the *Pall Mall Gazette*; instead, on the 28th, he chose the *Globe* 'to publish his important though rigid and not very wise letter on policy'. Garvin described it thus to Astor, whom he directed:

> Look at the *Daily Telegraph* today. Austen does not see, will not see that the weakening among the Unionist newspapers and in the House of Commons is such as he has never yet had to cope with. . . . He by his letter in the *Globe* thinks nothing need be done.

To rouse the country, it was first necessary to rouse the politicians.[2]

Chamberlain was not the only newspaper correspondent on the opposition front bench. Gwynne 'buttered . . . up' Walter Long, who agreed to write 'a letter for publication' in the *Morning Post* 'which will tend to calm the ruffled feelings of the party'. Gwynne himself was 'going down to see Joe and Austen' at Highbury and hoped 'to come back with some good tips'. Fortified by 'Joe's' approval, he published a hard-hitting article on the 27th, and 'had an immediate response. There were hundreds of letters, thanking us for the clear lead and damning the Free Fooders most cordially.' Among the letters that the *Morning Post* saw fit to publish was one rejected by *The Times*. It was written by Sir Roper Lethbridge, who claimed to 'have been a public advocate of Imperial Preference for nearly half-a-century & . . . one of the oldest "Parliamentary

---

[1] Strachey to Bonar Law, 19 December 1912, Bonar Law Papers, 28/1/63; Garvin to Astor, 19 [December] 1912, Astor Papers.
[2] Austen Chamberlain to Astor, 22 December 1912, and Garvin to Astor, 28 December 1912, Astor Papers; Steel-Maitland to Garvin, 23 December 1912, Garvin Papers.

hands" in the Party', though never an MP. Slow to grasp the situation, Lethbridge prayed to 'God that all this does not mean serious defection from our cause on the part of *The Times*, for that would be a great disaster'.[1]

He prayed to the wrong Lord, the one who moved in less mysterious ways. 'I really don't know what Northcliffe's game is,' confessed Gwynne, who was afraid that Bonar Law and Tariff Reform stood mutually discredited. Northcliffe, he told Lady Bathurst, 'is a villain anyway – has done more harm than any one man in England. . . . Derby is a fool – weak.' From a different vantage point, Lansdowne was inclined to rate 'Derby's propaganda' as 'the more serious of the two. *The Times*'s articles are very poor stuff, a mere reflection of the ill-informed criticism which one encounters in London Clubs and drawing rooms,' he wrote with Gladstonian logic to Bonar Law. 'If the hysterics become less violent, *The Times* will moderate its tone, & gradually drop into line, for it is not likely to cross the floor.' Garvin shared Gwynne's perspective rather than Lansdowne's. 'Our only real trouble is that by comparison with the Radicals we have not a reliable party press fighting on day by day,' he declaimed with a twinge of envy,

> and owing to the nature of Northcliffe's system we can never have one. The difficulty is not on this or that question. He lets us down in every question in every crisis; and likes letting us down to show his power – that is the Puckish element which makes him delightful in private life and a deadly danger in politics.

Amery chuckled to see 'Garvin belabouring "Uncle Five Heads" in *P.M.G.* and taking daily tea with Lady Northcliffe afterwards!' The *Daily Express* joined in making Northcliffe a moving target: by 'boxing the compass on Tariff Reform', it asserted on 7 January 1913, he had 'brought Unionism to the brink of ruin'.[2]

Yet, in the last analysis, Lansdowne was basically right. There were definite limits to Northcliffe's misconduct. 'The Harmsworth Press is doing all the harm it can, no one quite knows why,' Robert Sanders recorded in his diary on 29 December. But that harm was neither extensive nor permanent. A week later, Sanders wrote that 'the party is becoming almost unanimous in favour of the policy advocated by the *Daily Telegraph* viz "No food tax til after a second election".' That, he estimated, would satisfy 'about 70%' of his backbench associates. 'The press continues atrocious' despite this emerging consensus or possibly because of it. 'The *Morning Post & Express* make violent attacks on

---

[1] Gwynne to Aitken, 23 December 1912, Beaverbrook Papers, C/148; Gwynne to Bonar Law, 29 December 1912, and Lethbridge to Bonar Law, 23 December 1912, Bonar Law Papers, 28/1/84, 99.

[2] Gwynne to Lady Bathurst, 23 December 1912, Bathurst Papers; Lansdowne to Bonar Law, 27 December 1912, and Garvin to Bonar Law, 27 December 1912, Bonar Law Papers, 28/1/94, 95; Amery's diary, 2 January 1913, Amery Papers.

Lord Northcliffe & Garvin takes the same line in the *Pall Mall*. The real difficulty now,' thought Sanders, 'is for Bonar Law to find a dignified line of retreat.'[1]

Newspapermen, afflicted with a professional predisposition to magnify Northcliffe's responsibility, lacked the objectivity shown by Sanders and Lansdowne. In particular, they failed to appreciate that Northcliffe's power was far more absolute at the centre of his press empire than at the periphery. Colonel Harry Sowler, one of the five directors of the *Manchester Courier* and (like his forbears) a Tory activist in that city, acknowledged with embarrassment that this 'keen T.R. and Imperial Preference paper' had lost its way 'for one day this week'. Upon 'the receipt of a private note from a man of high standing', who intimated that Bonar Law had changed his mind, the *Courier* was 'induced to join in the advice that the so called Food Taxes should be made subject to a second general election'. Sowler, who went along, wanted Bonar Law to understand 'that Lord Northcliffe, although a director, has not interfered at all in this matter'. Harcourt Kitchin, still further removed, pledged the support of the *Glasgow Herald* to Bonar Law: 'The newspaper controversy in London is due largely to jealousy of the Harmsworths,' he declared, 'but the real division on the subject of "food taxes" is very deep, as you know.'[2]

Northcliffe revelled in the controversy, interpreting the squeals of his opponents as proof of his own importance and the enhanced prestige of *The Times*. 'I think the Paper is scoring heavily over the food duties business,' John Walter told him, 'in spite of the rather damaging legend put about by our rivals that *The Times* is forced to take its policies from the *Daily Mail*.' To Northcliffe, that legend was a compliment. On 13 January, Robinson cautiously confirmed that *The Times* was 'coming out of the "food tax" business all right, I think'. At that stage, Bonar Law's status was somewhat more problematical. The previous week, for the sake of party unity, he had reluctantly accepted a memorial that dictated a major modification of his Tariff Reform blueprint. Garvin and Astor considered that it would have been more honourable for him to resign, as he had previously threatened. Austen Chamberlain, downcast but 'deeply sensible of the difficulties', defended Bonar Law's unhappy decision. His reward was 'a tribute' on the 14th from Robinson, who – just as Lansdowne had predicted – thereupon moderated the tone of his paper. Confident that 'B.L.'s position will be quite unimpaired', Robinson had been to see Balfour, whom he found 'frankly delighted with the way things have gone'. Garvin, infuriated by the *Daily Mail*'s ecstatic placards ('Death of the Food Taxes'), put on a brave face in the *Observer* and the *Pall Mall Gazette*. Privately, as Robinson was

[1] Sanders's diary, 29 December 1912 and 5 January 1913, Bayford Papers.
[2] Sowler to Bonar Law, 2 January 1913, and Harcourt Kitchin to Bonar Law, 3 January 1913, Bonar Law Papers, 28/2/11, 14.

aware, 'G. still rampages ..., but he is doing himself more harm than anyone else'.[1]

Aitken, one of six Unionist MPs who had declined to sign the memorial to Bonar Law (Amery was another), supplanted Northcliffe as Garvin's scapegoat. Gwynne pinned the blame more squarely on Bonar Law, who had allowed the party to be stampeded 'into a surrender of their considered and declared principles'. He trusted that Bonar Law would 'have understood my attitude on the present situation', which he found difficult to spell out in print. 'I don't know what you feel,' he wrote dolefully on the 14th to Lady Bathurst, 'but as far as I am concerned all the interest seems to have gone out of my political life.' Not only had Bonar Law torpedoed the Chamberlainite cause, but also Austen Chamberlain had first privately affirmed and then publicly retracted his support for the Ashton policy. 'All I can presume is that in his splendid loyalty – before the catastrophe – he did not mean to give his leader away even to an old friend like myself,' sulked Gwynne, who wondered whether politicians owed loyalty to editors as well as to each other. To write the next day's leading article was a formidable task, but one he could not shirk. In it, he eschewed 'reproaches and recriminations', concluding that Lansdowne and Bonar Law deserved gratitude for having 'sacrificed their own interests in order to avert the break-up of the party', which would have rendered the Unionists 'incapable of resisting the destructive tendencies of the Government'. After acquitting himself, Gwynne poured out his grief to Lady Bathurst:

> ... Between ourselves, Bonar Law and I have been very devoted friends.... To go against him has cost me more than I can adequately describe.... Yesterday I felt it my duty to tell him that I may have to attack him and, to tell you the truth, I was pretty miserable all day long after it.

Resentments aside, the episode was over. 'Thus ended the first important crisis in Bonar Law's leadership,' Robert Blake has written; 'the policy of Imperial Preference received a set-back from which it took many years to recover – some would say that it never did recover from this blow.' In the process, the relations between Unionist politicians and their newspaper allies suffered a comparable set-back.[2]

* * *

---

[1] Walter to Northcliffe, 6 January [1913], and Robinson to Northcliffe, 13 January [1913], Northcliffe Papers; Austen Chamberlain to Bonar Law, 8 January 1913, quoted in Sir Charles Petrie, *Life and Letters of Austen Chamberlain* (London, 1939), I, 334–35; Gollin, *Observer*, pp. 380–85.
[2] Gwynne to Bonar Law, 10 January 1913, Bonar Law Papers, 28/2/46; Gwynne to Lady Bathurst, 14 and 15 January 1913, Bathurst Papers; Blake, *Unknown Prime Minister*, p. 116.

In the months remaining before the outbreak of war, party organizers worked to shore up a system that could no longer be expected to operate out of mutual trust, much less unquestioned loyalty. Liberal journals, engaged in sniping at their official leaders, gave gratuitous – and insidious – support to the Unionist hierarchy in its *volte-face* over protectionism. Unionist journals, dedicated to 'Big Navy' principles, gave Churchill the encouragement that the bulk of the Liberal press denied him. (Robinson, more guarded than most, hoped that Northcliffe would 'agree with me that it is far better *not* to do for Winston ... what his colleagues ... have very properly refused to allow him to do for himself'.[1]) It was, of course, vastly more satisfying for journalists to prey upon the disputes among their opponents than upon those in their own camp. That, however, only partly explains the tangle of party lines, which mirrored the instability of the times.

Methods of formal and informal control were applied in turn. Percy Illingworth, the Liberal chief whip, nominated Donald Maclean as an official shareholder in the *Birmingham Daily Gazette*, a relic of Pearson's provincial empire: Maclean and Robertson Lawson were each allocated 8,750 shares – 2,500 ordinary and 6,250 preference – in the renovated company, for which Maclean paid with party funds. Steel-Maitland, the Unionist party chairman, deployed the same techniques on a larger scale. He has been identified as a member of the 'mysterious quartet' that owned the *Sunday Times* during these 'shabby and boring years', when the circulation never exceeded 30,000 copies; the other investors were Hermann Schmidt, a German financier, Sir Basil Zaharoff, the 'notorious ... international munitions agent', and Dr Leander Starr Jameson, who had perpetrated the abortive raid on the Transvaal in 1895. In his official capacity, Steel-Maitland kept more respectable company.[2]

A chronic invalid, the *Daily Express* required a further dose of strong medicine in February 1913. Although the circulation had risen to around 295,000, the property groaned under the 'dead weight of debentures' and had incurred 'very heavy expenses of flotation'; interest payments were again in arrears, and there were outstanding debts for the supply of newsprint and the installation of new machinery. Blumenfeld was sanguine 'that things may gradually pull round', but Steel-Maitland was doubtful and estimated that £36,000 was necessary 'if the paper is to be given a clean start'. There was no thought of displacing Blumenfeld, for whom Steel-Maitland professed 'a real feeling .... I think he is a very loyal fellow, and should be safeguarded, but I think his sphere is editing – not managing.' What he prescribed was 'that the

[1] Robinson to Northcliffe, 13 January [1913], Northcliffe Papers.
[2] Birdsall and Cross, solicitors, to Maclean, 9 November 1912, Maclean Papers; H. Hobson *et al.*, *The Pearl of Days* (London, 1972), p. xv. No mention of Maclean's involvement in the Starmer-Morrell purchase of the *Birmingham Gazette* appears in H. R. G. Whates, *The Birmingham Post* (Birmingham, 1957), a 'centenary retrospect' of the paper which had absorbed the *Gazette* the previous year. Lawson was probably one of Maclean's wealthy constituents at Peebles.

paper should be really reconstructed', which could 'be done by getting hold of the control of the second debentures', held by Lawson Johnston. The first debentures were controlled by the estate of Lord Furness and by Davison Dalziel, who 'has played up well with the *Standard* of late and has some reason to continue to do so'. The Conservative Central Office already had 'control of the ordinary shares' and a promise from Sir Alexander Henderson that, 'within a year', he would turn over his substantial minority holding of second debentures at the low price he had initially paid for them.[1]

Considering all eventualities, apart from 'the risk of war', Steel-Maitland reckoned that, in the event of a foreclosure, the *Daily Express* would neither disappear nor 'change its politics. What might happen,' he warned Bonar Law, 'would be that it might become a less strong party organ.' At a time when other Unionist dailies were behaving erratically, even offensively, that was not a risk to be taken lightly. J. Malcolm Fraser, who supplied the figures for Steel-Maitland's analysis, concurred 'that if the Party lost control of the *Daily Express*, it would sooner or later regret having done so'. While he saw little chance that the paper would turn Liberal, it might 'be run on the more damaging lines of the Candid Friend. If cleverly done,' reasoned Fraser, 'this will do incalculable harm to Unionists, and will not hurt circulation', for experience had proved that there was always a 'good circulation to be got in running counter to the Leaders' Policy'. The party had a surfeit of Candid Friends; what it 'badly wanted' was – to repeat Fraser's dictum – a 'Friend in Need ... to arrest a stampede in the Press'.[2]

Fraser fitted the case into a wider context. In the event that the 'Unionists are returned to power, they will need more than ever a powerful Press to help them introduce Tariff Reform', and that was by no means assured. According to the survey he prepared for Bonar Law, *The Times* and the *Daily Mail* were 'Against Food Duties – Far from Warm on Tariff Reform'; the *Standard* could not be considered 'safe for reasons which need not be given here'; the *Daily Telegraph* was 'Fairly Safe'; the *Morning Post* was absolutely 'Safe'; and the *Morning Advertiser*, the *Daily Graphic*, the *Daily Mirror*, and the *Daily Sketch* were all 'Unsafe' to a greater or lesser degree. By his computation, the aggregate 'Daily Circulation of Safe & Fairly Safe' metropolitan morning papers '(including *Times & Standard*)' was '440,000 at most', whereas those in the 'most Unsafe' classification totalled '1,900,000 at least'. The circulation of the *Daily Express* was therefore not to be discounted.[3]

To preserve the *Express* as a 'Friend in Need' or at least to prevent it from slipping into the guise of a 'Candid Friend', Steel-Maitland marshalled all the

[1] 'Memorandum Re *Daily Express*' by Steel-Maitland [10 February 1913], Bonar Law Papers, 41/K/2.
[2] 'Memorandum Re *Daily Express*' by Steel-Maitland [10 February 1913], 'Memorandum Re *Daily Express*' by Fraser, 13 February 1913, and Fraser to Bonar Law, 13 February 1913, Bonar Law Papers, 41/K/1-2, 29/1/17.
[3] 'Memorandum Re *Daily Express*' by Fraser, 13 February 1913, Bonar Law Papers, 41/K/1.

influence at his command. On 18 April, Blumenfeld wired that he had 'decided to accept all of Sir Alexander Henderson's conditions' and was proceeding to buy out Lawson Johnston's block of second debentures. Aitken's cheque-book was apparently at his disposal. The following July, Northcliffe knowingly referred to the *Express* as 'Steel-Maitland's paper' on the grounds that 'it was he, with Aitken, who financed it'. Nevertheless, the final deal had yet to be ratified in January 1914, when Aitken proclaimed himself 'sure Lawson Johnston ["a sane man"] will sell out . . . at £15,000', and instructed Blumenfeld to let him know as soon as a 'firm offer' was in hand. In 1916, when the time ultimately came, Aitken completed the purchase in his own name. Only then was the property established on a solid financial base, though – as Stanley Baldwin was subsequently to learn – its party allegiance was far from safe.[1]

Northcliffe, the quintessential Candid Friend, continued to exhibit his candour. The transfer of the *Daily Mirror* to the hands of his brother Harold allowed him to devote his full energies to the *Daily Mail*, the *Evening News*, and *The Times*, which echoed one another in suitably different accents. To Maxse's satisfaction, expressed in the May 1913 number of the *National Review*, these journals accorded strong support to Lord Roberts and his movement for National Service. On 28 February, the *Evening News* featured an interview with Repington, 'the Military Correspondent of *The Times*', who condemned the inadequacy of Haldane's Territorial Army for purposes of resisting invasion. Unlike Steel-Maitland, Northcliffe did not rule out the possibility of war and believed that neither his countrymen nor his newspapers were 'sufficiently alive to the fact that Europe is getting on a war-footing'. Robinson acknowledged that the foreign situation had grown 'definitely serious', yet found it 'very difficult to handle without inflaming popular excitement and passion and frustrating all our efforts to set our military defences in order'.[2]

That Haldane had exchanged the War Office for the Lord Chancellorship did nothing to deflect attacks. He offered no rebuttal to his critics. 'To take any notice – publicly – of Repington would be disastrous,' he told Esher. 'The press always gets the last word.' On no account would he condescend to reply to Maxse's vituperation. The *National Review*, with libellous assistance from Belloc and Cecil Chesterton in the *New Witness*, waged a calumnious campaign against the Liberal ministry in general and those members in particular who were caught up in the Marconi scandal. Northcliffe, being 'neither a rabid party man nor an anti-Semite', refused to join the hue and cry. At his brother Harold's recommendation, he rode a 'soft pedal in *The Times* and the *Daily Mail*', thus keeping his promise to Churchill, who had begged him 'to treat the

[1] Blumenfeld to Steel-Maitland, 18 April 1913 (telegram), and Aitken to Blumenfeld, 12 January 1914 (copy), Beaverbrook Papers, C/239, H/13; Northcliffe to Robinson, 1 July 1913 (copy), Northcliffe Papers; Taylor, *Beaverbrook*, pp. 99–100.
[2] Northcliffe to Robinson, 3 March 1913, and Robinson to Northcliffe, 8 March 1913, quoted in *History of The Times*, IV, part 1, 97–98.

Marconi matter on non-Party lines'. Isaacs thanked Northcliffe for 'your generous treatment of the ... incident', and Lloyd George was grateful for 'the chivalrous manner in which you have treated [Isaacs] and myself, ... for I know the power you wield'.[1]

Lloyd George knew better than Haldane that press agitations had to be answered in kind. For that reason, he never forgave Massingham 'for deserting him' when his career had hung in the balance. The Liberal dailies, led by the *Daily Chronicle* and the *Manchester Guardian*, came to his rescue. And Gardiner obliged him with a 'tip top' article in the *Daily News*: 'It was a triumph of tact & judgment', prized as a token of 'warm & loyal friendship'. That these journals would exonerate Lloyd George was more or less predictable. Northcliffe's generosity, because it could not have been taken for granted, had a more pronounced effect. Behind the scenes, Sir Harold Harmsworth was remarkably active as a champion of the People's Champion and remonstrated with Aitken when further Marconi allegations were aired in the *Globe* and the *Daily Express*. 'The newspaper world of London is like a great telephone exchange,' he argued picturesquely. 'All interested know who is behind each paper and in case of personal attacks it is not the editor who gets blamed but the proprietor or controller.'[2]

A lingering dissatisfaction with the Unionist leadership may have softened Northcliffe's attitude towards the Liberal malfeasants. 'I confess I do not understand why the Unionist Party has never rallied round the *Courier*,' he complained to Stephenson in Manchester, 'either now or in the days of Nicol Dunn, who ... expressed, on leaving England' for South Africa, 'his great disgust at the manner in which the paper had been treated by local Conservatives,' particularly Lord Derby. 'The *M.C.* was thanked by all for what it did towards the Altrincham result' in a May by-election, but none of its admirers saw fit to help shoulder the burden. The last straw was broken in March 1914 when, 'without warning', the Conservative Central Office hired away the manager of the *Manchester Courier*. In the light of this 'scandalous action', Northcliffe blustered that he and Alderman Rothwell had come 'to the conclusion that neither of us was desirous of continuing to expend large sums of money on behalf of the Party', and that, 'in future, the *Courier* will be issued weekly'. He did not carry out this threat.[3]

---

[1] Haldane to Esher, 13 October 1913 (copy), Haldane Papers, Vol. 5910, fol. 137; Northcliffe to Lloyd George, 24 March 1913, Sir Harold Harmsworth to Northcliffe, 10 March 1913, and Isaacs to Northcliffe, 21 March 1913, quoted in Pound and Harmsworth, pp. 441–42; Lloyd George to Northcliffe, 21 March 1913 (copy), and Northcliffe to Churchill, n.d. (copies), Lloyd George Papers, C/6/8/2, C/3/15/20–21.

[2] Entries of 30 November 1914 and 25 January 1915, in *Lloyd George: A Diary by Frances Stevenson* (ed. A. J. P. Taylor; London, 1971), pp. 14, 24; Lloyd George to Gardiner, 26 March 1913, Gardiner Papers; Sir Harold Harmsworth to Aitken, 28 January 1914, Beaverbrook Papers, C/287.

[3] Northcliffe to Stephenson, 8 April 1913 (copy), Stephenson to Northcliffe, 30 May 1913, and Northcliffe to Sowler [March 1914] (copy), Northcliffe Papers. Stephenson reported a meeting

Northcliffe was himself the victim of persistent newspaper attacks for which he held Aitken responsible and Bonar Law accountable. The 'marked hostility' of the *Daily Express*, 'a notoriously imitative organ', provoked him to write from Paris on 24 May 1913 to Bonar Law, who had presumably heard rumours connected with the matter. More than he cared to reveal, he felt a mounting sense of isolation as other Unionist newspapermen began to close ranks. Neither he nor any of his deputies was present at a Tariff Reform banquet at the House of Commons on 15 April. Blumenfeld was invited by Sir Henry Page Croft, who promised that 'Gwynne, Garvin & Maxse are also putting in an appearance'. On such an occasion, Northcliffe would have been *persona non grata*, and Robinson would have been out of his element. Gwynne considered that 'Northcliffe was a fool' to have substituted Robinson for Buckle, 'a very able and sane journalist' who 'held the confidence of a vast number of public men. Indeed,' Gwynne suggested to Lady Bathurst, 'if I am run over by a taxi-cab or you want a change, he is in my opinion ... an ideal editor of the *M.P.*'[1]

Confident of his position, Gwynne could afford to banter. Truth to tell, he was 'worrying a little about our standing still in circulation', but did not 'really think that *The Times*'s reduction in price' had done more than lose the *Morning Post* 'a reader ... here and there'. His prophecy of 'victory over *The Times* was based on

> very simple reasoning: *The Times* is now in the hands of a halfpenny paper man who believes that the right rôle of *The Times* should be that of a rather better & fuller *Daily Mail*. We on the other hand are the *Morning Post* with all its fine traditions unchanged.

This optimism was 'borne out' by a comment made by 'Harmsworth's brother Harold (now Lord Something or other)' that Northcliffe 'wouldn't have a paper left in five years'. And, Gwynne heard, Northcliffe was 'losing his head too. He has furnished some rooms at *The Times* and sleeps there, appearing at odd moments in the night in a most gaudily-coloured dressing gown'. Consequently, Gwynne had 'no intention of allowing the *M.P.* to enter into the arena of vulgar squabbles and bitter quarrellings'. Not 'even in a third paper', volunteered by Garvin, would he 'enter into the slinging contest that Harmsworth has inaugurated'.[2]

---

on the afternoon of 23 April 1914 to consider the *Manchester Courier*'s finances. Seventy notices were sent out to local MPs, prospective candidates, and party officials. 'There were 20 apologies for non attendance & 8 people turned up.' Stephenson to Northcliffe, 23 April 1914, Northcliffe Papers.

[1] Northcliffe to Bonar Law, 24 May 1913, Bonar Law Papers, 29/4/20; Page Croft to Blumenfeld, 7 April 1913, Blumenfeld Papers; Gwynne to Lady Bathurst, 9 July 1913, Bathurst Papers.

[2] Gwynne to Lady Bathurst, 8 May 1913, 14 March and 2 June 1914, Bathurst Papers; Gwynne to Garvin, 16 March 1914, Garvin Papers.

Gwynne enjoyed a harmonious relationship with Lady Bathurst. 'I hold that a Proprietor, Manager and Editor of a paper are something like a Cabinet,' he philosophized. 'They may have internal differences of opinion – indeed they should have them – but to the outside world they should always show a united front.' While perfectly valid with respect to newspaper administration, this theory was belied by constitutional practice. The Cabinet and the Shadow Cabinet were both deeply divided across a range of issues, and their respective divergences were glaringly publicized. The Irish issue fixed the gulf between parties and generated tensions between them. On 11 September 1913, Loreburn, now untrammelled by office, sought to break the deadlock by writing a letter to *The Times* in which he urged the convocation of an all-party conference. It was published in the absence of Robinson and in contravention of his rule that the 'first object must be to kill the [Home Rule] Bill, and we shall distract and confuse people if we make overtures for peace before that is accomplished'. The letter was Loreburn's personal initiative, but it was written after preliminary consultation with John Walter and the King.[1]

The *Observer* (14 September) was responsive to Loreburn's appeal, which offered a 'last opportunity... to escape from the chains of... mechanical party warfare'. Gwynne was the first editor to see Bonar Law, who had been staying at Balmoral, and furnished Garvin with a full report. Churchill, another of the royal guests, had delivered a letter from Asquith and, as was his wont, spoke freely. Consequently, Gwynne recounted, Bonar Law and Carson were optimistic that a compromise could be worked out to exclude Ulster from the provisions of the impending legislation. Garvin gleaned a few more details in early October, when he visited Bonar Law at Margate. With unexpected cordiality, which betokened that bygones were bygones, Bonar Law said that his first impulse had been to suspect that 'Loreburn was acting in collusion with the Cabinet'. The King convinced him otherwise.[2]

Garvin scanned the ministerial press for signs of 'a change of wind on the Liberal side. The Asquith-Grey mind seems to be reflected by the *Westminster Gazette*'s friendly tone towards Conference,' he pointed out to Astor. 'Massingham & the *Manchester Guardian* are also for it. But the moment Lloyd George came back all the papers standing nearest to him began to pooh-pooh the idea.' In the Unionist camp, press opinion was equally mixed and mercurial. Inter-party collaboration came naturally to Garvin, but was a strain for Gwynne. Lansdowne, his own scepticism notwithstanding, was appalled by the truculence of the *Scotsman*, which looked to Smith as the party spokesman on Ulster. 'The newspapers are rather hard to keep in line over the Irish question – i.e. to keep a stiff upper lip and yet not wholly long-bolt the door,' observed

[1] Gwynne to Lady Bathurst, 6 November 1913, Bathurst Papers; *History of The Times*, IV, part 2, 537.
[2] Garvin to Astor [September 1913] and 7 October 1913, Astor Papers; Birrell to Asquith, 3 October 1913, Asquith Papers; *also see* Patricia Jalland, *The Liberals and Ireland* (Brighton, 1980), pp. 145 ff.

Steel-Maitland, who requested Bonar Law to keep him abreast of 'developments as they occur... so as to prevent any of our big papers taking the bit in its teeth'. Maxse, who boasted his own sources of information, was elated when the conference eventually failed. To him as to other extremists on both sides, compromise was futile and confrontation was unavoidable.[1]

Lloyd George's lack of enthusiasm may be explained by his exclusion from the secret conversations between Bonar Law and Asquith that took place at Cherkley, Aitken's country house near Leatherhead. Not that channels of communication were closed to him: on 29 September, he and Harcourt Kitchin 'discussed the political situation with all the cards on the table', and the editor of the *Glasgow Herald* was entrusted to relay word to Bonar Law. More legitimately, Lloyd George may have regarded these dialogues as a tacit threat to the reform schemes that he was hoping to implement in the face of Unionist resistance. From the summer of 1913, Sir Henry Norman was arranging with regional Liberal federations 'for propaganda work' on behalf of new housing proposals. In October, advance copies of the Land Enquiry report were distributed among representatives of the *Liverpool Post*, the *South Wales Daily News*, the *Lancashire Daily Post*, the *Northern Echo*, the *Manchester Guardian*, the *Daily News*, and the *Daily Chronicle*. Along with publicity in the journals managed by his Social Service Trust, Joseph Rowntree provided a total of £10,000 towards the administrative expenses of Lloyd George's land campaign. A comparable subvention had been expected from George Cadbury, who limited his service to the pages of the *Daily News* and the *Star*. 'My family only know – and it is well that this should be the case – the gigantic sacrifices I have made to firmly establish both papers, with a combined circulation of about 900,000 per day,' revealed Cadbury, who explained that this expenditure 'largely prevented my doing what I would like to have done on behalf of Land-Housing Reform, &c., but one cannot well do both'. The *Manchester Guardian* contributed a series by Hobhouse on 'Land and Labour'. Scott considered the idea of reprinting these articles in pamphlet form, but decided against it.[2]

Sir George Riddell, Lloyd George's golfing companion and the proprietor of the *News of the World*, commended the Nonconformist *British Weekly* for its attention to the land question. 'The Chancellor... asked me to tell you that your leader was the only [one] in which the true inwardness of the situation had been indicated', Riddell wrote to Robertson Nicoll, the editor-proprietor, whom he offered further material to be inserted anonymously. Determined to realize a maximum impact, Lloyd George religiously cultivated his friends and

---

[1] Garvin to Astor, 7 October 1913, Astor Papers; Lansdowne to Bonar Law, 23 September 1913, and Steel-Maitland to Bonar Law, 25 September 1913, Bonar Law Papers, 30/2/21, 26.

[2] Harcourt Kitchin to Bonar Law, 30 September 1913, Bonar Law Papers, 30/2/35; T. P. Ritzema (*Northern Daily Telegraph*) to Illingworth, 10 July 1913 (copy), B. S. Rowntree to Lloyd George, 3 and 6 October 1913, Cadbury to Lloyd George, 18 October 1913, and Scott to Lloyd George, 9 October 1913, Lloyd George Papers, C/5/4/2, C/2/3/13–26, C/8/1/11.

abused his enemies. In another speech at Holloway on 20 November, he castigated *The Times* for 'arrogating to itself the airs of Royalty' by taking scant notice of the land campaign. To Massingham, that speech 'seemed . . . as good as Limehouse, & it is hard to praise it higher than that'. But, for precisely the same reason, the King took offence, and Lloyd George formally apologized that he had meant to imply no disrespect to the Crown.[1]

Pulling out all stops, Lloyd George was as much concerned with the quality of press coverage as with its quantity. 'It is not enough to carry "the crowd" with you in a great campaign like this: you must convince the thoughtful men in the Party,' he insisted to Scott, whose paper he perceived to carry greatest weight among Liberal 'intellectuals'. In January 1914, he returned from a holiday with a plan to launch a London edition of the *Manchester Guardian*. Sir Charles Henry, who had accompanied him on his travels, was 'prepared to raise [a] quarter of a million' for this purpose. Scott and his son John, who tended to business affairs, came to London on the 14th and met Lloyd George and Henry at the Treasury. Henry first 'proposed to buy *M.G.* & amalgamate it' with the *Westminster Gazette*, of which he was part-owner. Scott replied that this was 'out of the question', though he did not rule out the possibility of joint production. The discussion then turned to problems of nomenclature. The existence of a Church weekly, *The Guardian*, precluded the dropping of a territorial designation from the banner. Henry 'suggested "London & M[anches]ter" or "M[anches]ter & London" Guardian, with small type for the "London" & the "M[anches]ter" alternately in the two places'. The Scotts agreed to 'consider [this] proposal' on the understanding that 'all special matter to be common & cost shared by the two issues'; 'in any case', they 'must have complete control'.[2]

Scott returned to Manchester to await concrete proposals and to seek advice from Hobhouse. Matters were still pending on 25 January, when Scott came to Walton Heath for a Sunday lunch with Lloyd George. There, he solicited additional information about Henry, and his host's response (as communicated to Hobhouse) was not entirely reassuring:

> He is a very rich man, lazily interested in the America copper syndicate and along with Mond is one of the people responsible for the *Westminster* which he would have liked us to take over. He is a Jew and probably the other people acting with him in the matter would also, some of them, be Jews. . . . Henry's politics, I gather, were rather of the *Westminster* type, but George says he is coming on and would give no trouble. Still one would prefer people

---
[1] Riddell to Nicoll, 27 October 1913, Nicoll Papers; Massingham to Lloyd George, 1 December [1913], and Lloyd George to Stamfordham, 19 December 1913 (copy), Lloyd George Papers, C/5/14/2, C/5/6/4.

[2] Lloyd George to Scott, 4 September 1914 (copy), Lloyd George Papers, C/8/1/9; memorandum by Scott, 16 January 1914, *Guardian* Archives.

of a different kidney. He might be all right about general politics, but what about Labour?

Scott, admitting that he would 'greatly prefer to have a portion of the capital held by a tried Liberal, thoroughly in sympathy with the *Guardian*'s politics', authorized Hobhouse to initiate 'informal negotiations with Brunner' – possibly Sir John, but more probably J.F.L. – who would be a counterbalance to Henry. Yet the idea was soon abandoned, despite the serious consideration it received. Three years later, Lloyd George tried again, but it was not until half a century later that the *Guardian* acquired a metropolitan base.[1]

Like all prominent politicians, Lloyd George was as keen to blot out criticism as to obtain affirmative support. Sir Edward Russell apologized to him for some 'disagreeable' references that had crept into the *Liverpool Post*, a paper 'which is always proud of your warm adhesion'. The problem, he explained, was that 'a newspaper tradition has undoubtedly grown up that you are the most interesting personality of the day and that everything about you is welcome to the general reader'. How was the public appetite to be satisfied without transgressing the conventions of clientage? Bonar Law, no less sensitive on this score, summoned Lord Faber 'and spoke to him about the hostile leaders in the *Yorkshire Post*'. Armed with a letter from Lansdowne, Bonar Law extracted a definite promise that Faber 'would put an end to them. Whether he will keep the promise or not I do not know,' Bonar Law told Austen Chamberlain.[2]

Sir H. L. W. ('Harry') Lawson and Sir Savile Crossley, who had entered the House of Commons together in 1885, offered a suggestion more redolent of the past than applicable to the present. Too often, they argued, 'large sums of money have been expended from the Party funds, with very indifferent results' and without 'permanent success'. Their solution was to dispense Central Office grants contingent 'on proper reorganisation' of the property involved. 'A Fund of £100,000 should be created' to 'be administered either by a species of Syndicate, or frankly by a Private Company with an efficient Board', and subject to the overriding jurisdiction of the party chairman. Under this 'scheme of Central Amalgamation and Control', assorted economies could be effected, capital could be allocated 'in a businesslike way', advertising revenues could be augmented and distributed more evenly, and, not least, the Central Office would possess the leverage 'to exert full control' over editorial aberrations. There was nothing particularly new in the Lawson-Crossley scheme, which was typically Victorian in its assumptions and procedures. To say the least, the

---

[1] Scott to Hobhouse, 28 January 1914, quoted in Ayerst, *Guardian*, pp. 354–55.
[2] Russell to Lloyd George, 28 January 1914, Lloyd George Papers, C/7/6/8; Bonar Law to Austen Chamberlain, 2 December 1913 (copy), Bonar Law Papers, 33/6/104. Russell asked Lloyd George to recommend a knighthood for Alexander Grigor, his partner and the business manager of the *Liverpool Post*. Russell to Lloyd George, 22 May 1914, Lloyd George Papers, C/7/6/11.

chances were slim that Bonar Law and Steel-Maitland would be able to succeed where Disraeli and J. E. Gorst had failed.[1]

Front-rank politicians had to make do with the opportunities available to them, which led the more adventurous among them to traffic with editors on the opposing side. Churchill, a specialist at the game, was advised by Garvin 'that it was very unwise to allow all the Ministerial news to appear first in *The Times* and the *Pall Mall Gazette* and much better to "feed" the Radical journals also from time to time'; according to Garvin, the 'anti-Winston attitude' of the *Daily Chronicle* was 'largely caused by personal jealousies', easily appeased. Morley, claiming to have had 'the P.M.'s assent', discussed Cabinet proceedings with Robinson; but his colleagues agreed that any 'indiscretion' on his part was, unlike Churchill's, 'unintentional'. Bonar Law followed the traditional pattern, with the result that Charles Palmer of the *Globe* was 'greatly indebted' to him 'for so kindly directing attention' to chinks in the Liberal armour. In his 'Comments of the Day' on 3 January 1914, Palmer duly attacked McKenna's Home Office policies and applauded Churchill's 'spirit of national duty' at the Admiralty. 'Recently I devoted a special article and a leaderette to exposing the latest instance of Ministerial insincerity,' he proudly informed Bonar Law. 'I need hardly say how greatly I appreciate your interest and how grateful I shall be to receive at any time any suggestion you may be good enough to offer.'[2]

Not every editor was as obsequious as Palmer, who – for five months longer – had Aitken standing behind him. When Bonar Law dealt with Northcliffe's men, the rôles were reversed. 'I can assure you that I always appreciated the friendly spirit which you showed to me,' he wrote punctiliously (and in the past tense) to A. P. Nicholson on the question of amending the Army Act. 'I am indeed sorry to find that your views are in direct conflict with mine, but I am not naturally intolerant, and am ready to give others credit for sincere conviction even on a subject in regard to which I feel so strongly.' To Lord Hugh Cecil, who sanctioned this drastic tactic to force a dissolution, Bonar Law cited the 'great difficulty' of working with a press that was 'both unreliable and dangerous'. His first imperative was to ascertain the constitutional procedure; his second was to overcome objections from Lansdowne and certain other colleagues. 'As soon as we have definitely decided to take this step,' he told Cecil,

> I think I must try to get in touch with our Press, not only from the point of view of preventing them discussing it in advance, which I agree with you in

[1] Memorandum by Crossley and Lawson, 'Newspaper Scheme', 27 November 1913, Bonar Law Papers, 41/K/3. Lawson (who became the 2nd Baron Burnham in 1916 and the 1st Viscount Burnham in 1919) was then MP for Mile End. Crossley (later 1st Baron Somerleyton) had retired from Parliament in 1906.

[2] Garvin to Astor, 13 December 1913, Astor Papers; Hobhouse's diary, 18 November 1913, *Inside Asquith's Cabinet*, p. 150; Palmer to Bonar Law, 2 January 1914, Bonar Law Papers, 31/2/9.

thinking would be a great disadvantage, but also in order to make sure that they will thoroughly support us when the policy is announced. The difficulty in all such cases, as you know, is Northcliffe.

In fact, the difficulty was not so much Northcliffe himself as a prevailing tendency that he was held to personify.[1]

For, in the final months of peacetime, there was a last scramble to acquire or develop journals, marked by a general awareness that the customary terms of trade no longer applied, at least not to the same degree. Sir Harold Harmsworth, after 'one or two talks about mutual newspaper arrangements' with Aitken, invited Blumenfeld 'to muse over' the possibility of 'interworking' the *Daily Express* with the *Daily Mirror*: 'Of course I would not have anything to do with the politics.' *The Times*, reduced in price to a penny (Tom Clarke heard that Northcliffe had wanted to make it 'a halfpenny and had literally to be "physically restrained"'), was better equipped than ever to withstand party pressure. 'So far as regards its political direction,' Buckle wrote approvingly to Robinson on the day that the revolution was announced, 'the Paper is worthy of its best traditions. It is madness, however, to try to confine the Editor to political directions.' Of course, Robinson's definition of politics differed profoundly from Buckle's. Comparing *The Times* to its leading rivals, he gave the *Morning Post* credit for having 'a definite policy, which it is trying hard to represent as a national policy, whereas the D[aily] T[elegraph] has none to speak of. But,' he accurately predicted, 'the *Morning Post* will find it difficult to shake off the shackles of party, from which I think we are gradually emerging, and I think there is going to be a great reaction against party within the next few years.'[2]

No editor found it easy to adapt to these evolving circumstances. 'G. Robinson almost in despair,' Spender told Cook over lunch at the Reform Club on 6 February. He added that the *Pall Mall Gazette* was 'in crisis also. Garvin lost £50,000 a year!' The *Westminster Gazette*, with a trifling circulation of 22,000, 'didn't pay. But the Board didn't interfere,' except for Henry, whom Spender called 'his worst' nuisance. Garvin confirmed that the *Pall Mall* was 'more trouble than it is worth' and 'about as harassing and difficult job as there can be in journalism'. He had managed to trim 'very nearly £20,000 a year' from the operating expenses. 'This year, if Heaven spares me, I shall either make it just pay or bring it as near paying point as any man could,' he declared to Northcliffe; 'and [I] don't care what happens afterwards.'[3]

[1] Bonar Law to Nicholson, 27 January 1914 (copy), and Bonar Law to Cecil, 3 February 1914 (copy), Bonar Law Papers, 34/1/19, 29. On 20 March, Bonar Law communicated his change of mind to J. P. Croal of the *Scotsman* (copy; Bonar Law Papers, 34/2/44).

[2] Sir Harold Harmsworth to Blumenfeld, 29 January 1914, Beaverbrook Papers, C/287; Clarke, *Northcliffe Diary*, p. 57; Buckle to Robinson, 11 March 1914, *Times* Archives; Robinson to Northcliffe, 2 March 1914, Northcliffe Papers.

[3] Cook's diary, 6 February 1914, Cook Papers; Garvin to Northcliffe, 3 February 1914, Northcliffe Papers.

This statement of indifference was not to be taken literally. Only recently, Garvin was furious to learn that the senior Astor, weary of the *Pall Mall* and the *Observer*, had given a purchase option to William Gardner Sinclair, a politically active businessman. Garvin was 'convinced ... from the first' that the Conservative Central Office was behind Sinclair's bid

> with the idea of getting a muzzle on the papers somehow. My strong belief is that Steel-Maitland is the nigger in the woodpile.... My reason for thinking so is that he so strongly suggested the other day Malcolm Fraser of the Unionist News Bureau as general manager of the papers. Now when party money was last found for the *Express* it was proposed to put in Malcolm Fraser in the same or somewhat similar manner.

Garvin continued to perform his editorial duties with no idea how this 'whole wretched situation' would be resolved. He had 'no personal complaint to make at all' about Sinclair, who was 'as hearty and amicable as possible'. Nevertheless, he insisted on the insertion of a clause in any final agreement 'stipulating for reasonable independence adequately guaranteed and if I cannot get that of course I shall not go on'.[1]

On 8 July, Gardner Sinclair ('purchaser') and William Waldorf Astor ('vendor') initialled a draft contract. The *Pall Mall* and the *Observer*, 'with subsidiary publications', were to be sold for £100,000, the details yet to be fixed. Garvin was soon resigned to seeing the papers

> in the hands of Gardner Sinclair, a vigorous Scottish Unionist whom I like, interest[ed] in many things, printing, oil, brewers, what not – inclined to work the *Observer* for the great business possibilities he sees and to give me a sufficiently free political hand. If he does not go on in the long run, Northcliffe may get the paper after all. Nothing would surprise me, but Sinclair is most positive and determined at present about going right forward himself.

So far as Garvin was concerned, anything was 'better than being kept in the dark after the scandalous manner of the last few months'. The younger Astors, Waldorf and his wife Nancy, were said to be 'heartbroken', but Garvin decided that he could not 'throw away my life and my children's interest'. He would have had second thoughts had he known that Fraser 'actually did the preliminary negotiations for Gardner Sinclair'. Steel-Maitland divulged these manipulations to Bonar Law, whom he invited to 'see Gardner Sinclair at lunch

---

[1] Garvin to Astor, 11 January 1914, Astor Papers. In the General Election of 1929, Gardner Sinclair offered motor transport to bring Lady Astor's voters to the poll at Plymouth. 'I have taken a great interest in politics for the last 40 years and had been Hon. Treasurer of the Party for so long, and I still feel it is the duty of everyone to work hard to keep this Socialist crowd out.' Gardner Sinclair to Lady Astor, 23 May 1929, Astor Papers.

with me as suggested', and whom Garvin unsuspectingly invited to lunch for the same purpose. 'We might at any time have difficulty with Garvin having full political control,' Steel-Maitland frankly warned. 'At the same time Garvin is a person to be careful of, so that he may not take a spite.' All of this cloak-and-dagger activity came to nothing. In February 1915, before Gardner Sinclair's option had run out, his health broke down, and the Astor family was left holding its newspaper parcels.[1]

Fraser and Steel-Maitland had better luck with the *Globe*, which Aitken had kept going at a compounded loss. On 26 May 1914, Fraser 'finally arranged ... that the Docker group', led by Dudley Docker, a Birmingham industrialist, would 'buy the *Globe* for £5,000, taking over its present staff. Max Aitken has behaved remarkably well,' Fraser informed Bonar Law, who would have expected as much. 'He has released the debentures & will pay Madge £4,000 on condition that the latter pays off at least £7,000 of the creditors. Madge says he will try & pay off *all* the creditors.' Rumours were rife. Goulding heard from Henderson that R. W. Holt 'had bought the *Globe*', possibly in Northcliffe's interest, but Madge told him 'that Docker was in it'. Blumenfeld understood that, if it had not been for Madge's 'exceptional good luck in securing a purchaser, ... the creditors would not have received a penny'. Aitken's version, perhaps apocryphal, was that he received no money, but instead paid £5,000 to Docker on condition that publication continued for at least six months. If true, he cut his losses by safely betting Docker £500 that he would not, in that time, turn a profit.[2]

While these proprietorial shuffles were going on, the Irish crisis reached its climax at the Curragh, where senior army officers preferred to accept dismissal rather than to carry out orders for what they construed as military operations to coerce Ulster. The *Morning Post* detected a 'Hellish Plot', which Churchill rejected as a 'hellish insinuation', and the *National Review* conjured up lurid visions of a Polish-style 'pogrom'. The *Daily Express* showed relative restraint: 'We cannot believe that Mr Asquith, Lord Haldane, and Lord Morley deliberately deceived Parliament,' it stated on 25 March: 'They were themselves fooled and deceived throughout.' Garvin stood apart, deploring the incident not so much as another example of Liberal perfidy or incompetence, but as a pretext for abandoning the Tory strategy to amend the Army Act. Gwynne, who could have had only a vague notion of Garvin's predicament, faulted his response in the course of defending his own. 'About news and views Garvin and

---

[1] Draft memorandum, 8 July 1914, Astor Papers; Garvin to Goulding [20] July 1914, Wargrave Papers; Steel-Maitland to Bonar Law, 9 August 1914, and Garvin to Bonar Law, 31 July 1914, Bonar Law Papers, 34/3/27, 33/1/36.

[2] Fraser to Bonar Law, 26 May 1914, Bonar Law Papers, 32/3/53; Goulding to Aitken, 10 June [1914], and Blumenfeld to Aitken, 22 June 1914, Beaverbrook Papers, C/318, H/13; Taylor, *Beaverbrook*, p. 79. J. B. Wilson, in a memorandum prepared for Tom Driberg (8 July 1954), recorded Beaverbrook's claim that 'I had to pay a man £5,000 in cash to take' the *Globe*. Driberg Papers.

I are at one,' he told Lady Bathurst, who had accused the *Morning Post* of being 'too spread eagle' in its coverage; 'but when there is a crisis such as we have really had, all rules-regulations go by the board. Garvin as a matter of fact preaches one thing, practises the other, for he has been putting views in the place of news in both his papers.'[1]

More than a question of proportions, it was one of basic definition. Proprietors and politicians constantly emphasized the superior value of news content, the former in order to build circulations (on the premiss that the reader wanted facts, not opinions) and the latter in order to restrict the areas of dissension. Editors, true to an older tradition, conceived of themselves primarily as the purveyors of views formulated on the basis of rigorous inquiry and intense political involvement. Not content merely to chronicle events, they aimed to influence them. Because the presentation of news could always be slanted or selective, the distinction existed more in theory than in practice. Nevertheless, the balance had begun to shift as the concept of objectivity was paid greater homage or, as some would say, lip-service.

The rise of a fledgling Labour press, hitherto unnoted for the simple reason that it went largely unnoticed, added to the confusion by evincing the same tensions.[2] The *Daily Citizen*, with trade unionist funding that had to be replenished within six months, was first off the mark. Originating in Manchester in October 1912, it soon extended its operations to London and claimed a circulation of 220,000. Its socialism, as distinguished from its preoccupation with industrial affairs, was nebulous; and its relations with the parliamentary Labour Party were mutually uncomfortable. The *Daily Herald*, which appeared almost simultaneously, had similar problems, but – as it proved – greater durability. It grew out of the *Worker*, a halfpenny monthly organ of the local branch of the Labour Representation Committee at Bow in the East End, where George Lansbury was elected MP 'in the year of Grace 1911'. The following year, 'over a cup of tea in the House of Commons', Ben Tillett, the maverick labour organizer, asked Lansbury to join the *Daily Herald* committee, then being formed. Although the *Herald* came to be known as Lansbury's paper, its first editor was actually Charles Lapworth, who served capably, but whose syndicalist enthusiasms provoked animosity. The initial sale, estimated at 230,000 copies, dropped off, and the financial base was shaky: at a meeting in Manchester in 1913, Lapworth and Tillett described how the furniture in the editorial office had to be bolted to the floor to prevent its removal by debt collectors.

[1] Gwynne to Lady Bathurst, 29 March 1914, Bathurst Papers.
[2] These paragraphs are based on the following sources to the extent that they corroborate each other: Lansbury, *Miracle of Fleet Street*, passim; Stanley Harrison, *Poor Men's Guardians*, pp. 173–77; George Slocombe, *The Tumult and the Shouting* (New York, 1936), ch. III; Keighley Snowden, 'The Rise of the Labour Press,' *Sells* (1914), pp. 29–32; letter to the editor of the *Guardian* by Maurice Gordon, 11 October 1979; Maurice Gordon to the author, 2 August 1981;

Lansbury, as chairman of the company, embroiled the *Herald* in his crusade for women's suffrage and reportedly recruited capital from benefactors of that cause. To publicize his commitment, he resigned his seat in the Commons and fought another by-election in November 1912. His defeat excluded him from Parliament for the next decade, but enhanced his reputation and the *Herald*'s. The party leaders sternly disavowed his tactic, and he replied with a prepared statement that received full coverage in the national press. H. R. Stockman, managing director of the Labour Press Agency, also 'sent a copy to the *Citizen* and was half afraid that they would suppress it under orders from the caucus', but Dilnot published a truncated version along with a disapproving leader and a derisive cartoon. Stockman, like Lansbury, lamented 'the way in which attempts are made to transform the Labour members into voting and talking machines that would only act when Mr Ramsay MacDonald pressed the particular button'. Another supporter rejoiced that Lansbury was now free to lead 'a Movement rather than a party centering round the *Daily Herald*'. Later to revive, the paper 'dwindled to a daily pamphlet' – a weekly pamphlet during wartime – that spoke for 'a lively Propagandist League' in defiance of official strictures. Lansbury and Dilnot were as hard put as any Liberal or Unionist editor to satisfy party requirements.

There had been a few editors (like Delane and Stead) who made a personal political imprint during the nineteenth century. There were also a few (like Garvin to a steadily diminishing extent) who did so after the war. But in the Edwardian period, often celebrated as the Golden Age of Editors, unseen participation in public affairs was a professional hallmark. Donald, for example, 'criticized the editors of the 'eighties for their lack of contact with the world', by which he meant the world of high politics, and considered that 'the role most appropriate to the editor of a daily newspaper' was that of a *deus ex machina*.[1] This criterion continued to the very end.

On 13 April 1914, Robinson 'motored over from some place in Yorkshire' (probably Settle) to Keswick, where Scott was staying. His brief, 'not stated' beforehand, 'proved to be [the] Ulster question. . . . He wanted to find a way out & said it was useless to see London Liberal editors; they were so unfair & so partizan.' Scott had 'no idea whether the visit was spontaneous' and suspected that Northcliffe was behind it. In any case, further conversations ensued in London. 'I am glad to hear . . . from Geoffrey Robinson that you are sympathetic with regard to reason in Ireland,' Northcliffe wrote to Scott a month later. On 23 June, Scott 'lunched with Garvin', whom he knew to be 'in intimate association with Carson'. It was Garvin's surmise that Carson and Asquith were already engaged in negotiations. 'Such secrets have been well kept

---

Stockman to Lansbury, 28 November 1912, and C. Stuart Smith to Lansbury, 28 November 1912, Lansbury Papers.

[1] H. A. Taylor, *Donald*, pp. 53–54.

before,' commented Scott. Harold Harmsworth, now Baron (and later Viscount) Rothermere, and the Master of Elibank, now Baron Murray of Elibank, were working towards the same end. The way was paved for another all-party conference which opened on 21 July at Buckingham Palace.[1]

In this last, desperate attempt to strike an Irish settlement, statesmen and political journalists alike were on trial. Party leaders had to take account of their principles and, more practically, the electoral forces they represented. Newspapermen were bound by comparable obligations. Both were fiduciaries, though the similarity was increasingly more apparent than real. Readers and voters were hypothetically one and the same, but a disjunction could be perceived between them. Was the ultimate responsibility of the publicist to a particular faction within the parliamentary community, insulated and remote, or to broad sections of the public at large? Was the national interest better served by maintaining secrecy, as the politicians enjoined, or by disseminating information, as journalists alone were then equipped to do?

Donald, who kept the *Daily Chronicle* under a strict embargo, was annoyed to discover 'the announcement of the conference in *The Times* and *Daily Mail*, for the reason that this premature publication has, I think, at once created a bad atmosphere'. He ascribed the misdemeanour to 'a lack of confidence' on the part of 'the Tory newspapers', to which he imputed a desire to wreck the proceedings. In retaliation, the *Daily Chronicle* 'trounced Bonar Law rather severely ... because we knew that he told the *Morning Post* and, presumably, *The Times*, also. The news was very discreetly dealt with in the *Morning Post*,' Donald had to admit; 'but it was there all the same.' The revelations were equally disturbing to Carson, who assured Blumenfeld that 'so far as I know' they had originated 'through no fault of the leaders of our Party.... You know how much I appreciate all that you do for us,' he went on, 'and I am not sure in the long run that you do not gain "kudos" by not publishing a matter which can only have been procured by someone getting information which it was treacherous to disclose.' That Carson, who was to bring down Asquith's wartime coalition by means of a press leak, should talk of treachery was not half so odd as that he should have supposed that such 'kudos' were prized more highly than either popular sales or the sensation of breaking a big story. On the 30th, after the conference had ended inconclusively, *The Times* delivered a detailed – and, in some respects, erroneous – summary. Lloyd George ventured that Donald 'could not have been angrier than the Prime Minister and I were when we read it. It is the most disgraceful breach of confidence which I have ever seen.' That, too, was saying a good deal. The distortions, which he took pains to correct,

---

[1] Scott's diary, 13 April and 30 June 1914, and Northcliffe to Scott, 12 May 1914, *Guardian* Archives.

left him in 'absolutely no doubt ... that the leakage must have occurred on the other side'.[1]

Yet, by implication, Lloyd George was himself guilty of a breach of confidence. And so were various others: Carson, who pleaded with Blumenfeld and tacitly verified his suspicions; Bonar Law, who spoke to Gwynne and sounded out Rothermere; and Rothermere, who communicated obliquely with Garvin and, one may assume, explicitly with Northcliffe. There was obviously a double standard: politicians were permitted to confide, but journalists were not permitted to disclose. Friends in Need were expected to abide by this antiquated procedure, Candid Friends to ignore it out of perversity or self-aggrandizement. Whether or not the double standard was consonant with the ideals and expectations of a modern democracy, it rocked the foundations of the political press. 'It is always a hard question to decide as to whether the publication of news is permissible or desirable in the public interest,' ruminated Beaverbrook, seemingly oblivious of the implicit irony.[2] That, like so many other questions of professional conscience, was to be raised all the more forcefully by the experience of war.

---

[1] Donald to Lloyd George, 21 July 1914, and Lloyd George to Donald, 30 July 1914 (copy), Lloyd George Papers, C/4/8/6–7; Carson to Blumenfeld, 21 July 1914, Blumenfeld Papers; *also see* Gollin, *Observer*, pp. 428–29.

[2] *Politicians and the Press*, p. 92.

Seven

DECLARATIONS OF WAR

The period that immediately preceded the outbreak of the First World War, as J. A. Spender recalled it, 'was a time of extraordinary bitterness' in British public life, 'when the most venerable institutions seemed to be tottering .... There was no peace for all editors, whatever line they took.' Spender, whom the American ambassador recognized as being 'in the Government's confidence to an unusual degree', was surely less exceptional than he later cared to contemplate.[1] It might well be asked whether he and his fellow editors deserved the pre-war peace that they consistently denied to others. By the lines of advocacy they adopted, they themselves intensified the bitterness and so abetted the various forces of destruction.

The declaration of war on 4 August 1914, followed by the proclamation of a party truce, clamped a lid on disputes within and, more emphatically, between parties. Nevertheless, passions continued to boil underneath. 'The appearance of national unity was deceptive,' A. J. P. Taylor has argued. 'There were still deep cleavages in the party outlooks', which the conduct of the war tended to widen. Suppressed in Parliament, where an 'unspoken Coalition between the front benches' created an 'increasingly artificial' atmosphere,[2] antagonisms were vented in the political press. To an extent that demands investigation, this relentless activity was pursued with the connivance of top-ranking parliamentarians and often at their instigation.

Outwardly, journalism acquired a new collective responsibility, more easily fulfilled in theory than in practice. In a memorable phrase, Élie Halévy called it 'the organization of enthusiasm'. Although Balfour had anticipated that 'the Press had better keep quiet in war-time', his unthinking advice to the delegates at the 1909 Imperial Press Conference was to prove hardly more desirable than feasible. The British government, like every other combatant power, quickly 'discovered that the Press was going to play a vital part' in keeping up civilian morale, in appealing to neutral opinion overseas, and ultimately, in undermining the self-confidence of the enemy. Spender, who counted himself

---

[1] Spender, *Life, Journalism and Politics*, II, 2–3; Page to President Wilson, 28 February 1914, quoted in *The Life and Letters of Walter H. Page*, III (New York, 1925), 110.
[2] Taylor, *Politics in Wartime* (London, 1964), pp. 13–14.

'slower than most' in succumbing to the war fever, testified that, 'so far from ceasing when the guns began to speak, the war of tongue and pen became more clamorous than ever, and something called "propaganda" was said to be as important as munitions'. As a patriot, he bowed to necessity. Yet, as a veteran publicist whose professional ethics rested on the eroding foundations of an old-style Liberalism, he retrospectively confessed to profound misgivings. In the last analysis, the wartime experience 'was corrupting to the Press, and a fatal snare to politicians' who led it into temptation. Inevitably, 'truth went deeper into her well while it lasted, and only painfully emerged when it was over.... At all events,' concluded Spender, 'the last thing that the Press was expected to do in the Great War was to keep quiet.'[1]

Then, as since, the distinction between publicity and propaganda – the latter remaining a nebulous concept which had yet to take on its modern stigma – was difficult to draw. Under the circumstances, both were regarded as legitimate extensions of diplomacy, born of the same impulse, and differing mainly in the levels at which they were pitched. Indispensable to each other's success, they were commodities that were packaged as much for domestic as foreign consumption. Newspapers, as the purveyors of national publicity, qualified automatically as instruments of propaganda.

The press was initially directed to carry on with 'business as usual', logically interpreted to mean the traditional task of imparting information, accompanied by comment. 'If the service rendered by the Press could be measured at all,' R. A. Scott-James had insisted only recently, 'it would be measured by the extent to which it enables the world to share knowledge and ideas – by the extent to which it is *communicative*.'[2] Always a vexing question, lately resolved according to the contradictory dictates of editorial and proprietorial consciences, what – or exactly how much – the press should communicate became a matter of vital controversy during wartime, when normal criteria no longer seemed to apply. A dwindling number of idealists upheld freedom of expression out of an ingrained belief that the unrestricted flow of fact and opinion would inspire faith in the righteousness of the British cause, certain inconveniences notwithstanding. Others, however, reckoned that the risks were too great. Mindful of the potential disadvantages of *laissez-faire* in journalism as in other spheres, these critics sought to institute official controls of varying stringency. They feared not only what newspapers might unwittingly divulge about military operations, but also – and perhaps more acutely – what they might reveal about latent tensions within society. In either case, they held that democracy required protection against the transgressions of its press, just as the press required protection against its own probing instincts.

A series of three Defence of the Realm Acts enabled the government to

---

[1] Halévy, 'The Era of Tyrannies' (1936), reprinted in *The Era of Tyrannies* (ed. R. K. Webb; Garden City, N.Y., 1965), p. 266; Spender, *Life, Journalism and Politics*, II, 21–22.

[2] Scott-James, *The Influence of the Press*, p. 27.

encroach upon economic activity and individual liberties within circumscribed spheres. The first and most vacuous was enacted on 8 August 1914; the third and arguably the most Draconian did not follow until March 1915. These acts were specifically directed at industrial production, involving the allocation of raw materials, the requisition of factories, the deployment of labour, and the distribution of profits. Their implementation was often haphazard and the results were uneven. With respect to newspaper production, the effect was essentially tangential. 'DORA,' anthropomorphized into a meddlesome woman, did not lack teeth so much as any real need to bite.

The early days of the war saw the improvisation of two governmental agencies: the Press Bureau, headed by Sir Stanley (later 1st Viscount) Buckmaster, the Solicitor-General; and the Foreign Office News Department, with responsibility for press relations. 'Thus,' one historian has ventured, 'from the very outset of the conflict, censorship and propaganda became the twin pillars upon which the British government waged its war of words against the Central Powers.'[1] In fact, neither regulatory body proved as effective as the authorities had intended or, conversely, as menacing as its opponents maintained.

Given the Foreign Office's deserved reputation for secrecy, its *ad hoc* News Department was a marked departure from custom and something of a contradiction in terms. Linked to the Press Bureau, though an autonomous unit, its function was more to justify than to explain policy, its disclosures were fitful and selectively addressed, and the bulk of its production went for export. That its procedures provoked irritation on the part of British newspapermen ought not to be weighed as evidence that their work was seriously impeded, much less that they suffered harassment in the line of duty. On balance, journalists probably gained more than they lost in the exchange. By the mere fact of its existence, the Foreign Office News Department opened certain channels of communication, admittedly narrow ones, which had been tightly shut.

The Press Bureau was a more formidable apparatus, established with an aim to guide rather than to restrict newspaper coverage of the war. To the greatest extent possible, it undertook to act in accordance with 'the underlying principles upon which popular government in this country must repose', as these were interpreted by Lord Robert Cecil. The Bureau was, so to speak, the funnel through which 'all information relating to the War which any of the Departments of State think right to issue is communicated to the Press'. At least in theory, then, its purpose was primarily one of coordination. Buckmaster, responding to questions in the House, stressed that this 'offspring of the War' possessed 'no means of collecting news and no power to compel its publication'; subject to the consent of the relevant service department, 'everything that can be made public without danger to the State' was suitable for publication. Under the direction of a Liberal jurist, assisted by a staff of some fifty 'skilled officers of the Army and Navy' and trained journalists who were

[1] Philip M. Taylor, *The Projection of Britain* (London, 1981), p. 12.

either brought back from retirement (like Sir Edward Cook) or else seconded from Fleet Street offices (like Harold Spender), the Press Bureau could be expected to deal sensitively with conflicts of interest. Whether it was equipped to satisfy the daily needs of its clients was another matter.[1]

There was no dearth of complaints about the system, however lenient it might appear by comparison with Continental models. Newspapers naturally resented constraints as a nuisance and, worse, a slur upon their patriotism. In particular, they fiercely objected to the makeshift arrangements at the front, where, as Lord Burnham angrily put it, 'war correspondents were locked up in stalls by a corporal's guard' and their reports were emasculated. *The Times*, like Burnham's *Daily Telegraph*, felt oppressed by 'a vigorous censorship on all newspaper material bearing on service affairs' and was compelled to deflect 'some part of its energies ... into a struggle with officials' whose 'incompetence' exceeded their 'common sense'. As the result of this 'troublesome business between the Press Bureau & the London papers', the Prime Minister was eventually obliged to endure a 'prayer-meeting' with 'no less than 25 editors of "leading" London papers: such a cohort of possible mischief-makers has rarely been assembled under the same roof'. Although 'not fond of the Press', he had to admit that 'there is some truth' to their allegations 'of news & particularly bad news being kept back or mutilated'.[2]

In the fourth week of hostilities, Cook noted in his diary 'a loud press outcry on the complete absence of news; and it is certainly hard to see,' he privately admitted, 'why there shd. be none of the Battle of Mons, which the Germans fought' amid the glare of full publicity. British journals had no choice but to rely on the version from Berlin. A week later, Cook recorded one newspaperman's fulmination against 'the absurdities of [a] Press Bureau run by halfpenny Colonels', superior in rank, but not intelligence, to Burnham's metaphorical corporals.[3] In the same disgruntled spirit, the *Nation* (22 August 1914) proclaimed itself

> willing to make allowances for the Government, but we do not think they are treating the Press fairly. We do not in the least mourn the eclipse of the war correspondent.... But it seems to us an unnecessarily strong measure to (a) establish an official Press Bureau, (b) set up a strict censorship, and (c) forbid the entry of British correspondents into the lines of the British Expeditionary Force.

[1] Lord Robert Cecil, quoted in Sir Edward Cook, *The Press in War-Time* (London, 1920), p. 31; Buckmaster, statement of 26 November 1914, *Parliamentary Debates* (Commons), 5th ser., lxviii, cols 1310–11. One of Buckmaster's interrogators was Sir C. Kinloch Cooke, a former editor of the *Pall Mall Gazette*.

[2] Burnham, speech at the Newspaper Proprietors' Conference, 2 July 1919, quoted in Cook, *Press in War-Time*, p. 178; *History of the Times*, IV, part 1, 220; *H. H. Asquith: Letters to Venetia Stanley* (eds M. and E. Brock; Oxford, 1982), pp. 514, 526; also see Sir Henry Lucy's letter to the editor of *The Times*, 25 November 1914.

[3] Cook's diary, 27 August and 2 September 1914, Cook Papers.

As a rule, opposition to the system was less doctrinaire and focused upon the anomalies. 'Liberals who are inclined to wax warm (as we notice some are) on behalf of the abstract freedom of the Press,' said the *Daily Chronicle* (9 November 1915), 'would do well to ask themselves whether the way to make Liberalism and democracy triumph in the world is to impose on Liberal democracies in war-time such a gigantic military handicap as an uncensored Press would be.' Not all of the opposition, of course, emanated from Liberal quarters. Arnold White, 'Looking Round' in the pages of the *Daily Express* (13 October 1914), asserted as strongly as Massingham that 'the suppression of legitimate comment is undesirable and will lead to dangers. If we emerge successfully from this war, but under the yoke of a vigorous censorship of opinion,' he predicted, 'we shall only have exchanged the haunting menace of Potsdam for the very tyranny against which Milton protested in 1644.'

For the press to allege unfair treatment was a conditioned reflex. The government, knowing as much, replied dismissively. Lord Haldane reminded the House of Lords on 31 August 'that there is no existing legislation by which Parliament has control over the Press, and, on the whole, it has not been necessary'. With certain 'slight exceptions', newspapers had 'acted very loyally in carrying out arrangements' laid down by the Committee of Imperial Defence before the war, thus obviating any need to seek 'exceptional powers' over them. Granted, 'direct information from the seat of war ... has not been given up to now'; but these unfortunate delays were ascribed to tactical exigencies and did not reflect a predetermined policy. As the victim of a notorious press agitation, Haldane demonstrated the degree to which newspapers remained unfettered.[1]

Much of the friction could have been tempered, if not avoided, by a constructive suggestion from either side. Instead there were recriminations, occasioned by frequent clashes between the appointed custodians of national security, as they defined it, and the guardians of the press, whose liberties were circumscribed. The grounds for protest cannot be denied; at the same time, they must not be exaggerated. Harold Spender, J.A.'s brother, recited a lengthy list of official infractions, culminating in the suppression of *The Times*'s dispatch from the battlefield at Mons: 'a most regrettable incident' in Haldane's opinion. 'We at once realised that a new thing had happened,' declared the younger and more tempestuous Spender, then employed on the *Daily News*. 'The country was in danger; and the country being in danger it was not going to allow a free press. That was the situation we were faced with.' Oliver Woods, later commissioned to write a compact history of *The Times* after nearly half a century on that paper, was astounded to read Spender's melodramatic account of the episode. 'What

---

[1] *Parliamentary Debates* (Lords), 5th ser., xvii, col. 561.

balls! The opposite was the case,' Woods annotated his copy of Spender's memoirs.[1]

Censorship, administered with a heavy though unsteady hand, had a discernible effect on the reporting of diplomatic initiatives, troop movements, and maritime losses. Whether it had as dire an effect as Harold Spender suggested is, at best, problematical. With respect to questions of political controversy, which came to impinge upon those of strategy, it was arguably less inhibiting than other factors. Chief among them was an editorial determination to maintain national solidarity – or, failing that, its semblance – in the face of a world crisis. Strong popular pressures were exerted in this direction. When the *Daily Mail* stepped out of line to denounce Lord Kitchener's latest 'tragic blunder' at the War Office (21 May 1915), copies were ceremonially set alight at the London Stock Exchange and banished from the premises of the Service clubs in Pall Mall, with a total estimated loss in subscriptions of 'a hundred thousand at least'. The *Daily News*'s subsequent attacks on Lloyd George, whom the *Daily Mail* had since befriended, had no adverse effect on circulation, but incurred more subtle penalties, including the exclusion of its lobby correspondent from ministerial briefings. The *Daily Telegraph* met with polite disapproval for publishing Lord Lansdowne's letter in support of a negotiated peace (29 November 1917), which *The Times* had rejected on the pretext that it 'believed it to reflect no responsible phase of British opinion' (30 November 1917). More formally, the *Nation* suffered a ban on its overseas distribution.[2]

In addition, there were practical considerations in favour of conformity. Fighting for their very survival, newspapers hesitated to assume further liabilities. At the *Westminster Gazette*, for example, J.A. Spender encountered 'mechanical difficulties' which mounted 'as the war went on'. Broken-down plant was difficult to repair and impossible to replace. Newsprint grew more costly as stocks ran low, forcing most journals to double their prices at the same time that they reduced the size of issues and, in some cases, even the size of pages. There was less space available for advertisements which, in any event, were cut back. Newspapers were supposed to help in recruiting, and their employees practised with a vengeance what they preached. 'The *Westminster* Staff was, as newspaper staffs go, a small one,' Spender reminisced, 'but it sent ninety men to the war from its various departments, too many of them never to return.'[3] By no means was this unusual.

By its own lights, the Press Bureau was administered without political bias. F. E. Smith, who took charge at the outset, made this point to Lloyd George.

---

[1] Spender, *Fire of Life*, pp. 204 ff.; marginal comment by Oliver Woods, n.d., Woods Papers; for a balanced view, see K. G. Robbins, 'Foreign policy, Government structure, and public opinion,' in F. H. Hinsley, ed., *British Foreign Policy Under Sir Edward Grey* (Cambridge, 1977), pp. 532–46.
[2] Pound and Harmsworth, pp. 478–79; Koss, *Fleet Street Radical*, pp. 227, 245; Havighurst, *Radical Journalist*, pp. 250–56.
[3] Spender, *Life, Journalism and Politics*, II, 23.

'Winston tells me you thought the constitution of our Bureau unduly Tory,' he recounted. 'You know about & (I know) don't object to Harold [Spender] & me', and there was hardly reason to fear a team of bureaucrats who 'do absolutely nothing except *gratuitously* answer a voluminous correspondence'. Putting aside his devotion to party, Smith professed not to 'care in work like this whether men are (or were) Tories or Radicals.... You know me too well to suppose I want party capital out of this damn office', which he had assumed as a stopgap. 'In fact,' he revealed, '*all our rows without exception* have been with Tory papers.' Northcliffe confirmed Smith's view with the opinion that, 'in certain instances, ... treatment has been meted out with particular severity to newspapers that took a prominent part in the anti-Home Rule agitation'.[1]

The *Morning Post* caused no difficulty at first. So obstreperous before the war, it was now happy to toe the official line. For its good behaviour, which was not to last long, it was informally 'exempted from censorship. That is a great tribute to all connected with the paper,' Gwynne told his proprietor. 'It is, of course, confidential for if it was made public the Chief Censor's life would not be worth living.' Gwynne explained how this exemption worked: 'Of course all telegrams and cables are censored in the ordinary way, but we, alone of all the papers in England, have not to submit our articles and descriptive accounts before publication.' Such concessions were bound to attract attention and, when they did, to be rescinded. Bonar Law counselled 'Harry' Lawson of the *Daily Telegraph* that comment about 'the Antwerp muddle', for which Churchill bore the blame, had to be handled 'guardedly, but I don't think that the newspapers should allow it to pass in silence; and I notice a letter in the *Morning Post* to-day which is apparently put in without consulting the censor'.[2]

Northcliffe's *Times* and *Daily Mail* were doubtless the worst offenders, with their unfounded (yet blurrily illustrated) reports of snow-encrusted Russian soldiers speeding by night down the length of Britain to join their allies on the western front. Against his better judgment, Gwynne was 'almost beginning to believe in the story of Russians passing through England. I hear it corroborated from so many sources, although officially it is denied.' On 14 September, after a fortnight's speculation, Cook attended a meeting at the Home Office, where McKenna presided. 'Donald begged McK to kill the Cossack story (which was done next morning).' Smith, on Kitchener's authority, countered that the fabrication 'does no harm' and might do good if the Germans credited it; but Lawson agreed with McKenna that there was 'no use in such lies'. At the close of the year, *The Times* retaliated with an

---

[1] Smith to Lloyd George, 9 September 1914, Lloyd George Papers, C/3/7/5; Northcliffe to Bonar Law, 4 February 1915 (copy), Northcliffe Papers; *also see* Northcliffe to Elibank, n.d., quoted in Pound and Harmsworth, p. 470. Harold Smith, F.E.'s brother and the Conservative MP for Warrington, was secretary to the Bureau.

[2] Gwynne to Lady Bathurst, 2 and 6 October 1914, Bathurst Papers; Bonar Law to Lawson, 16 October 1914 (copy), Bonar Law Papers, 37/4/24.

emphatic 'contradiction of [the] Press Bureau', which struck Cook as 'very unpatriotic'.[1]

The general tendency in the press, as in the country at large, was one of submission. Yet, for those with sufficient will and a modicum of ingenuity, it was possible to defy the system with impunity. To be sure, it also helped to have friends in power. Buckmaster, who relieved Smith of his 'damn office' on 30 September, continued as 'sole director of the Press Bureau' until 26 May 1915, when he replaced Haldane on the Woolsack. During his tenure, he discovered that 'many of the more powerful newspapers' enjoyed the advantages of a backstairs patronage 'which rendered the proper execution of my duties extremely difficult. On more than one occasion,' he minuted, 'when strong measures should have been taken with papers like *The Times* and the *Daily Mail*, my efforts to exercise against them the powers conferred by the Defence of the Realm Act were defeated from within' the administration. He 'could never assign exactly to any person the responsibility for this disastrous consequence', but took it as 'plain that there were people anxious to secure newspaper support who, in return for press favours, were friends of the newspapers when difficulties arose'.[2] The formation of a coalition, in which politicians of different persuasions jostled for influence, expanded the opportunities for collusion. The rise of Lloyd George, whom Buckmaster presumably had in mind as a culprit, was another catalyst. As opposed to most wartime controls, which steadily tightened, those governing the press were loosened at the end of 1915, when legal responsibility was shifted to the newspapers themselves. A high proportion of censorship operated on a voluntary basis in order to save time, money, and face for all concerned.

Collusion, if it could be obtained, was always preferable to collision, which exposed journalists and politicians alike to public criticism. The major newspapers were better able than the smaller fry to exploit the ambiguities of a situation in which costs rose at a faster rate than profits. The *Daily Herald* switched to weekly publication and, none the less, endured a penury which itself imposed a stern discipline. The *Manchester Courier*, which Northcliffe had threatened to turn into a weekly, tried an assortment of commercial expedients before it was extinguished in January 1916. The *Daily Mirror* sacrificed its Manchester edition, while the *Daily Citizen* retreated to Manchester on its way to oblivion. The *Daily Mail*, though never in jeopardy, soon curtailed its impromptu Sunday appearances. 'Some of our Scots subs,' Tom

[1] Gwynne to Lady Bathurst, 3 September 1914, Bathurst Papers; Cook's diary, 14 September and 31 December 1914, Cook Papers.
[2] Memorandum by Buckmaster [1916], quoted in R. F. V. Heuston, *The Lives of the Lord Chancellors, 1885–1940* (Oxford, 1964), p. 263; Cook, *Press in War-Time*, p. 46n. Charles Hobhouse confirmed that, at a Cabinet on 6 February 1914, 'we discussed the advisability of court-martialling *The Times* and *Daily Mail* for giving, no doubt merely to spite the Govt., information criticising our preparations'. But Kitchener and Churchill, 'who has an eye on future political movements, have no intention of offending these rags and they refused to take any action at present'. *Inside Asquith's Cabinet*, pp. 205–206.

Clarke wrote in his diary, were 'very gloomy' that, if the war continued until Christmas, 'we shall certainly be on half salaries, and a few weeks after that we shall have to close down'. Himself no Scotsman, Clarke worried that the *Mail*'s 'advertisements have come down wallop', and that 'all our small advertisements have been "scrapped"' to clear the back page of each eight-page issue for pictures, 'an innovation by the Chief'.[1]

Advertising revenues had to be increased to meet rising expenses. On 23 March 1915, the *Daily Chronicle* introduced an *Echo and Evening Chronicle* in a vain attempt to enter a lucrative market to which the *Daily News* already had access through the *Star*; it delivered its 'funeral card' on 3 May, after running up a deficit variously estimated at £60,000 to £100,000. The *Daily News* had less space to lavish in its six or eight-page issues on fiction, and its back-page photographs appeared irregularly. In Manchester, A. F. Stephenson hoped against hope that a link with the *Evening Mail* would help to defray the heavy losses of the *Courier*. Later on, in search of the same eldorado, the *Manchester Guardian* was to amalgamate with the *Manchester Evening News*. Meanwhile, as C. P. Scott boasted to his sister on the occasion of his seventieth birthday: 'The *M.G.* has held on wonderfully on the material side during the whole period of the war and is one of the few papers in England, I think, which is not losing money.' Circulation and advertising had edged upwards, and the paper's finances were further assisted by the agreement of its editor and staff to accept 'considerably reduced' wages. Reasoning that it was 'better to spread the influence and widen the basis of the paper than to grasp at profits', Scott staved off any rise in price or diminution in size. Eventually, he had no choice on either score, and a smaller *Guardian* sold for twopence first on Saturdays and then throughout the week. *The Times*, adopting a different philosophy, deliberately raised its price to cut its circulation, and thereby retained its full complement of pages without exceeding its allocation of newsprint.[2]

One of the earliest wartime casualties in Fleet Street was the *London Budget*, an inconsequential outlet of William Randolph Hearst's transatlantic empire. By contrast, other Sunday journals fared spectacularly well. The pack was led by the *News of the World*, which perversely understated its circulation, estimated to stand comfortably above a million. Its owner was Sir George Riddell, whose 'zeal was such that he always carried in his car a number of handbills advertising the paper' which he let fly 'out of the window ... when motoring through a village'. Using more conventional techniques of promotion, *Reynolds's Weekly* thrived as *Reynolds's Illustrated News*, and the *People* (later the *Sunday People*) kept going. In 1915, the *Sunday Pictorial* began as a spur-of-the-moment offshoot of Rothermere's *Daily Mirror*, and the *Sunday*

---

[1] Clarke, *Northcliffe Diary* (17 August 1914), p. 67.
[2] Stephenson to Northcliffe, 5 September 1914, Northcliffe Papers; C. P. Scott to his sister Isabella, 23 March 1917, quoted in Ayerst, *Guardian*, pp. 392–93; *Newspaper Press Directory* (London, 1917), p. 16.

Herald (soon to become the *Illustrated Sunday Herald* and later the *Sunday Graphic*) was spawned by the Hultons' *Daily Sketch*. T. P. O'Connor, never too old for a fling, launched *T.P.'s Weekly* in the same year. All of them put a high premium on pictorial content, which was not exclusively Northcliffe's innovation. Predominantly devoted to entertainment, they did not exclude the odd column of commentary on public events. The 'quality' *Sunday Times*, doing little to earn that designation, had a stagnant circulation of approximately 20,000 until 1915, when the Berry family took control. The *Observer*, the most explicitly political of the Sunday prints, averaged ten times that sale during wartime. Occasionally, when important items of news warranted, there were special seventh-day editions of the *Daily Mail* and the *Daily Telegraph* (both of which had briefly experimented with sabbath publication in 1899) and *The Times*. 'In the 1914–18 war,' Lord Camrose later observed, 'the anxiety for news overcame religious scruples and Sunday papers acquired for the first time an odour of respectability.'[1]

What they did not acquire, apart from the *Observer*, was any substantial claim to political influence. That was reserved for the metropolitan dailies, in company with a few provincials and such respectable weeklies as the *Spectator*, the *Nation*, and the *New Statesman*, founded in 1913 as the organ of the Fabian Society. For all the controversy he fomented in the monthly *National Review*, Maxse would 'sometimes regret that I have not control during the War of a daily newspaper such as the *Globe* or *Pall Mall Gazette*', better equipped 'to make the public "sit up"'. In terms of aggregate circulation, the relative status of the political press was declining; but properties within this charmed circle had never depended upon sales for either reputation or a sense of responsibility. Nor could it be denied that their managerial structures had become commercialized: Donald emphasized this 'far-reaching change' in his presidential address to the Institute of Journalists on 18 August 1913; J. A. Spender ('in the presence of Sir Alfred Mond & I hope in the hearing of Sir Frank Newnes') minimized its dangers at the twenty-first anniversary dinner of the *Westminster Gazette* on 31 January 1914; and Gardiner deplored the 'capitalistic encroachments' upon 'newspaper independence' in a speech at Glasgow on 29 October 1921. Conservative and even socialist editors were equally aware of the phenomenon and unsettled by it. Nevertheless, for the time being, the extent to which newspapers were 'tending to become more and more the mere vehicles of great business interests' (to quote Gardiner) did not rob them of authority. Paradoxically, the war gave political journalism a new lease on life by assigning it new partisan functions.[2]

Again, the two Spender brothers propounded contrasting, but not irrecon-

[1] Camrose, *British Newspapers and their Controllers*, p. 83.
[2] Maxse to Northcliffe, 8 July 1915, Northcliffe Papers; Donald's address appears as an appendix in H. A. Taylor, *Donald*, pp. 265–70; the notes for Spender's speech are among the Spender Papers, Add. MSS. 46,392, fols. 122 ff.; and Gardiner's remarks were reported in the *Journal* of the Institute of Journalists, January 1922.

cilable, views. 'Working on the *Daily News* before the Great War', Harold and his colleagues had 'never allowed the result of an important by-election to be known throughout the country without effective and immediate comment – even if we had to start our leaders at midnight. That,' he maintained, 'was the way to keep the Party spirit alive.' The party truce, negotiated by the whips to avoid awkward confrontations at the polls, put an end to this activity. It did not follow, however, that the party spirit was thereupon left to die. 'The virtual suspension of Parliament gave newspapers a power which they do not exercise in normal times,' J. A. Spender was grieved to point out, 'and the atmosphere of war furnished a unique opportunity of playing upon popular alarms and prejudices.'[1]

Party militancy, far from disappearing, resided largely with the press, which was not bound by the whips' compact and was inveterately hostile to its implications. Political animosities went underground at Westminster, only to surface in Fleet Street. There was a causal relationship between the two developments. Newspapers expanded their facilities for partisanship (while symptomatically condensing their parliamentary coverage) in order to fill a vacuum. 'Silence in high places cleared the way for demagogues,' A. J. P. Taylor has written in partial accord with J. A. Spender. 'Still more,' he goes on, 'it cleared the way for the masters of the press. The public wanted news, and could only find it in the newspapers. . . . Soon too the public wanted leadership, and again only the newspapers provided it.' Consequently, the so-called press lords 'did not snatch at influence and power; these were thrust on them by the abdication of the politicians'.[2]

For all its plausibility, Taylor's neatly schematic approach admits to certain qualifications. It achieves clarity at the cost of simplification by dividing politicians from newspapermen, positing that these were static categories and ignoring the ways in which they worked through each other to reach a wider community. In reality, the dichotomy was never so clear cut and was subject to adjustment under the impact of events. Newspapermen were not without political ambitions, which sometimes ran to fantasy: Northcliffe and Bottomley were asymmetrical cases in point. Politicians, no less diverse in stature and assumptions, did not lack a countervailing ambition to effect an outright control over newspapers: Aitken and Lloyd George were most conspicuous in that they actually succeeded; and Lansbury, between parliamentary innings, was a journalist *malgré lui*. Thus, the line between those who occupied 'high places' and those who variously qualified as 'masters of the press' was blurred by the traffic across it.

Had the formula been so elementary and, for that matter, the outcome so

---

[1] Harold Spender, *Fire of Life*, p. 316; J. A. Spender, *The Public Life* (London, 1925), II, 122.
[2] Taylor, *Politics in Wartime*, p. 16. Taylor echoes Lloyd George's view – expressed to Riddell on 23 June 1916 and quoted in Riddell's *War Diary* (London, 1933), p. 151 – and restricts his choice of 'press lords' to Lloyd George's adherents.

predictable, there would be little reason to proceed with this inquiry. Clearly, the situation was vastly more complicated. Just as some politicians abdicated more willingly and completely than others, some newspaper figures snatched at power and influence before the thrust came. What may be seen from a distance as an adversary relationship becomes, upon closer inspection, a network of uneasy and transitory alliances.

The imperatives of total war did not divert newspapers from their established loyalties or diminish their ardour. Agitations were not abandoned, but merely rechannelled. From the mounting tension, the press – or specifically that segment of it with an attuned political consciousness – gathered new momentum. Where it had previously followed, sometimes erratically, it was now deputed to lead. In so far as guidance and encouragement were needed, journalists received both in bountiful measure from frustrated politicians, who furtively adopted them as surrogates. Newspapers, permitted to broach topics that were proscribed within the parliamentary arena, were willingly used to circumvent a system that party spokesmen were formally pledged to uphold. In Fleet Street as at the front, the tactical manoeuvres were incessant and the savagery was unprecedented.

*   *   *

The popular response to the prospect of Britain's entry into the war was not, as legend would have it, unanimous. Within the Cabinet and the parliamentary Liberal and Labour parties, there were strong currents against intervention which had to be isolated, if not overcome. Not necessarily following along strict party lines, the same equivocations were present in the financial, commercial, and academic communities. On a day-to-day basis, the press articulated these early differences of emphasis and perception with an urgency that shaped the political controversies which rumbled throughout the wartime period and influenced parliamentary alignments thereafter.

The ministerial press, and especially that portion previously opposed to the government's foreign and defence policies, exemplified the Liberal dilemma and, more than that, subjected it to public scrutiny. Scott, Massingham, and Gardiner were compromised by having vouched for Germany's pacific intentions and by having disavowed successive programmes for national preparedness. Donald and, more conspicuously, J. A. Spender had distanced themselves from the extreme radical position, but insufficiently to escape either the moral responsibility or the subsequent indictment of guilt by association. 'The task of the Liberal journalist was one of extraordinary difficulty,' Spender later recalled.

An Opposition journalist might go ahead, declare boldly that this was a fighting business, and urge the Government to take all risks. A ministerial journalist supposed to be in touch with the Government . . . could only have done this at the risk of contributing to the thing he most feared, the shattering of the national unity and the break-up of the Government.

As events unfolded, Spender's 'letter-bag' at the *Westminster Gazette* office was 'daily . . . filled with letters declaring it to be the supreme duty of the Government to keep out of this quarrel' on the Continent. These appeals, he insisted, 'came from Conservatives as well as Liberals, and I knew that there was a strong party in the Cabinet which was of the same opinion'. To keep a clear mind and a free hand, he 'entered into none of the groups of journalists or politicians who were preparing to act together for war or against war'. Furthermore, 'not wishing to be bombarded with conflicting opinions', he went so far as to avoid the precincts of Westminster.[1] It was a high price to pay.

Unlike Lord Courtney, a veteran opponent of the Boer War and of more recent disarmament campaigns, editors were not permitted to 'choose the moment for speech or writing even at the risk of being too late'. They had columns to fill and readers to persuade. Courtney, waiting for issues to clarify, was 'afraid the *Daily News* must be left to fight a good fight much alone'.[2] He underestimated, of course, the quantity (if not the quality) of anti-war opinion in the Liberal and Labour press. Nevertheless, the *Daily News* did not disappoint him. On Saturday, 1 August, its leading article, 'Keep the Peace', was buttressed by Gardiner's enumeration of the reasons 'Why We Must Not Fight'. ('Your article is superb,' J. L. Hammond privately complimented Gardiner. 'Miles and away the best thing that has been written on it.') On Monday, the 3rd, the correspondence columns were filled with endorsements from like-minded readers, including G. M. Trevelyan and Gilbert Murray. Next morning, the last of peacetime, P. J. Baker (later better known as Philip Noel-Baker) put the case for 'Belgian Neutrality: Why England is not Bound to Fight'.[3]

That afternoon, Sir Edward Grey delivered his historic address to Parliament, and the *Daily News* was obliged to adjust to a new and fearful reality. Gardiner, who had previously gloried in his reputation as a 'pro-German', was quickly transformed into a 'Holy Warrior' against the menace of an ubiquitous 'Prussianism'. Lloyd George, pointedly and perhaps uncharitably, cited the painful conversion of the *Daily News* as evidence 'of the change which came over public opinion' during the first week of August and, in addition, a palpable demonstration of the process by which Liberal fundamentalists 'came tardily to the conclusion that war was justifiable'. Others

[1] Spender, *Life, Journalism and Politics*, II, 13–14.
[2] Courtney to Gardiner, 30 July 1914, Gardiner Papers.
[3] Hammond to Gardiner, 2 August 1914 (postmark), Gardiner Papers; Koss, *Fleet Street Radical*, pp. 148–50.

held up Gardiner and his paper to similar effect. Yet the tendency was a good deal more widespread than that, and Lloyd George himself may be taken to personify it.[1]

On 27 July, Lloyd George had placated Scott with assurances that 'there could be no question of our taking part in any war in the first instance', and he castigated *The Times* for having suggested that the entente with France constituted a full-scale alliance. Three days later, deploring the way '*The Times* is regarded in Europe as speaking with the voice of the British Foreign Office', the *Manchester Guardian* reminded the government that 'Englishmen are not the guardians ... of the peace of Europe. Their first duty is to England and to the peace of England.' For its own part, the paper was momentarily convinced that British involvement, real or implied, would be 'both a crime and an act of supreme and gratuitous folly'.[2]

Warmly approving, Arnold Rowntree hoped 'to proclaim to the world that the *Manchester Guardian* and not *The Times* represents the industrialism of the north and the wisdom of the north'. The *Nation*, in which he held an attenuated family interest, preached that message. So too, is more modulated tones, did the *Daily Chronicle*, which berated *The Times* for 'dictating to Sir Edward Grey' and attempting 'to usurp his functions ... in articles as ill-calculated to assist the peacemakers as any could be' (1 August). Over that anguished weekend, Donald's guest at Walton was Ramsay MacDonald, an avowed pacifist, who was introduced by his host to two neighbours, Lloyd George and Riddell. When war was finally declared, the *Chronicle* complied with 'An Appeal to the British People'. It was written not by Donald, who 'rarely wrote a leader', but by Ensor, whose affiliation with the Labour Party was no deterrent to a *de facto* bellicosity.[3]

The *Daily Citizen*, explicitly committed to socialism, lacked MacDonald's consistency, on the one hand, and Ensor's agility, on the other. Before Grey's critical speech, it had been indistinguishable from Radical journals in its Little Englandism. As late as the morning of 4 August, it rejected intervention in the 'wretched international intrigue', which it fashionably characterized as a 'Diplomat's War'. Even so, it had already began to accommodate its ideals to expediency: 'While fighting for peace, we must do what we can by organised effort, and in conjunction with the Trade Unions and the Co-operative Societies, to relieve some of the worst horrors of war.' The next day, it commented bleakly – and evasively – on the 'terrible news' and 'tragic madness'. Labour's task, the *Citizen* argued on 7 August, was to 'work for an

---

[1] Lloyd George, *War Memoirs* (London, 1934?), I, 41; Irene Cooper Willis, a wartime convert to Labour and an official of the Union of Democratic Control, also depicted Gardiner (who 'ought not, I am well aware, to stand alone') as the prototypical 'enlightened Liberal'. *England's Holy War* (London, 1928).

[2] Entry of 27 July 1914, in Scott, *Political Diaries*, pp. 91–92; Ayerst, *Guardian*, pp. 374–75; *History of The Times*, IV, part 1, 200–201.

[3] Pound and Harmsworth, p. 463; H. A. Taylor, *Donald*, pp. 23–24, 28.

early and honourable peace'. In the process, it added on the 22nd, Labour should participate in every 'co-ordinated national and local effort' to achieve victory. There was an implicit contradiction here that was to prove fatal to the *Daily Citizen* in particular and to socialist resistance in general. Perhaps it was naïve to expect that Frank Dilnot, its editor, had emancipated himself from the chauvinist attitudes of the *Daily Mail*, whence he came.

Boasting from its masthead to be 'the paper that foretold the war', the *Daily Mail* suffered no such scruples. No sooner had Northcliffe finished attacking his 'Know Nothing' rivals, who had misled the public over Irish affairs (20 July), than he furiously turned upon them for having ignored the threat of German aggression. 'The Ulster crisis looks like taking a back seat pretty quick,' Clarke wrote in his diary on 26 July,[1] and Northcliffe was never a man to be left behind. His critics tried to discredit him by recalling 'pro-German' sentiments in the *Daily Mail* and its sister publications: the *Evening News*, for example, had embraced 'the Kaiser as a very gallant gentleman, whose word is better than many another's bond' (17 October 1913); and, to Massingham's best recollection, 'it was not Germany, but France, of which the *Daily Mail* wrote that the time might come for rolling her in "mud and blood"' (*Nation*, 28 November 1914). But these accusations did not stick, and Northcliffe was more commonly condemned for poisoning the atmosphere with self-fulfilling prophecies.

'Your claim to be the true prophet of war does not call for dispute,' Gardiner addressed Northcliffe in an open letter in the *Daily News* on 5 December 1914; together with a follow-up in the *Star*, it was reprinted as a penny pamphlet. 'It had always been your part to prophesy war and cultivate hate,' he conceded to his adversary, whom he labelled 'the most sinister influence that has ever corrupted the soul of English journalism'. Northcliffe, who had had the effrontery to catalogue his 'scaremongerings' in a recent 'book of newspaper scraps', was said to pursue his incendiary mission 'not because of any faith that was in you, not because of any principle you cherished', but as a 'short cut to success – that success which is the only thing you reverence amidst all the mysteries and sanctities of life'. Robert Blatchford, whom Gardiner dismissed as an 'eccentric Socialist', rallied to Northcliffe's defence in the *Daily Mail* a week later. His response gave Gardiner the excuse for a front-page 'rejoinder' in the *Daily News*. 'There is not an audience in the country, of any party whatsoever, that does not receive your name or the name of the *Daily Mail* with a shout of derisive laughter,' Northcliffe was told. 'The people read you; but they despise you' (14 December).

Had Northcliffe mattered so little, Gardiner would not have wasted his invective. Northcliffe's official biographers have brushed aside the episode as 'a scathing polemical exercise which produced back-patting approval at the Reform Club'. But the official historians of *The Times* have acknowledged

[1] Clarke, *Northcliffe Diary*, p. 59.

more objectively 'that a considerable section of impartial opinion', including 'an influential group of Conservatives', shared Gardiner's disgust with Northcliffe's displays of 'vulgar personal self-advertisement'. Besides, like his friend Bernard Shaw, Gardiner recognized an alarming tendency, even among men whose 'own experience . . . reduced to utter absurdity the ravings and maunderings of . . . [their] daily paper', to 'echo the opinions of that paper like a parrot'. One could ignore Northcliffe only at one's peril. 'We all hate personalities,' George Cadbury wrote to Gardiner, 'but there are times in the interest of truth, and certainly in the interests of the paper, when they seem necessary, [for] only by attacking Lord Northcliffe himself can we attack *The Times, Daily Mail, Evening News, Weekly Dispatch*, &c.'[1]

On Saturday, 1 August, while most Liberal journalists were publicly and privately entreating the government to hold aloof, if only to be able to mediate in the deepening European conflict, Northcliffe summoned his troops to a four o'clock conclave at Printing House Square. There, he plotted his own strategy. Through George (later 1st Baron) Lloyd, a young Tory MP, Sir Henry Wilson had conveyed 'trustworthy information that the Government are going to "rat"' in their commitments to France and, indirectly, Russia. Several ministers, Lloyd George reportedly among them, were contemplating resignation in the event of war, and Liberal opinion in Parliament and outside was disposed towards neutrality at this juncture. Wickham Steed, who could always be counted upon to say what his chief wanted to hear, took the view that, if the government held back, *The Times* should 'go bald-headed against it'. When asked whether he was prepared to 'attack the Government at a moment of national crisis', Steed replied, 'Certainly.' Marlowe, expected to steer the *Daily Mail* in the wake of *The Times*, 'spoke against attacking the Government. The country would never forgive us.' Robinson supported him, urging the postponement of any decision until after the weekend. Events moved quickly and to Northcliffe's satisfaction. On Sunday evening, Amery called at Printing House Square and learnt 'that the rotten element in the Cabinet had been largely talked round', increasing the probability of intervention; he 'went on to the *Daily Express* and saw Blumenfeld and then Gwynne at the *Morning Post*, both of whom confirmed the better turn of affairs'. On Monday afternoon, after Grey's speech, an assistant librarian at *The Times* overheard an exchange in Steed's room. 'Well, it's come,' Northcliffe exclaimed with unconcealed relief. 'Yes, thank God!' rejoined Steed.[2]

Like J. A. Spender, who 'had been brought up that the British army should not be transported over sea until its communications were assured and the risk of invasion eliminated', Northcliffe was in no hurry to dispatch the British

---
[1] Pound and Harmsworth, pp. 470–71; *History of The Times*, IV, part 1, p. 270; Shaw, preface to *Heartbreak House*; Cadbury to Gardiner, 21 December 1914, Gardiner Papers.
[2] Pound and Harmsworth, pp. 463–64; *History of The Times*, IV, part 1, 210–11; Amery's diary, 2 August 1914, Amery Papers.

Expeditionary Force. At the *Daily Mail*'s editorial conference on 5 August, he 'made quite a scene' by decreeing that 'not a soldier of ours shall leave these shores!' Marlowe's contrary arguments prevailed, but not until the first edition of the next day's paper was delayed by a full two hours. At last, Marlowe had come into his own at Carmelite House, and he sometimes attended policy-making sessions at Printing House Square as well. At both locations, Northcliffe usually took the chair when vital questions were on the agenda. 'The Chief is at our evening editorial conference almost every day,' Clarke noted in early September with a hint of exasperation. Functioning as a liaison between his various properties, Northcliffe fashioned his proprietorship into a super-editorship. His ambitions, however, did not stop there.[1]

Deprived of any claim to have forced the government into war, and thwarted in his designs for the BEF, Northcliffe took credit for catapulting Kitchener into the War Office. Ironically, he was later to regret this supposed accomplishment. Since the previous March, the Prime Minister had been doubling as War Secretary. His instinct was to continue nominally in that capacity, 'delegating the work' of mobilization to Haldane, who had created and best understood the military machine. Meanwhile, Kitchener was requested to stand by for an undisclosed purpose. By the 5th, Haldane was convinced that Kitchener's presence in the War Cabinet would inspire a 'public confidence' that far outweighed the potential disadvantages. Accordingly, he 'pressed the P.M. to resign the war secretaryship and to appoint K., [who] ... was best for the nation'. Asquith later insisted that he had required no prodding from Haldane, much less from 'our intelligent and prescient Press' which was demanding the appointment of Kitchener, 'the only person whom I ever thought of as my successor' at the War Office.[2]

Until Kitchener proved himself a hopeless failure, everyone wanted a share of the glory for bringing him into office; afterwards, they were all eager to forget their complicity. Kitchener's official biographer stated that 'the Prime Minister's mind was largely made up for him by the persistence of Lord Northcliffe and the insistence of the public'; and Northcliffe's official biographers have admitted that, at least for a time, 'Kitchener's appointment ... was held to be a triumph of Northcliffe's publicity'. But Northcliffe had important allies, without whom he could not have prevailed: Milner, Austen Chamberlain, and Balfour among other politicians; and Blumenfeld, Maxse, and Gwynne among other newspapermen. Gwynne was particularly delighted by the result. 'I am in the happy position of being able to write directly to a Cabinet Minister and I am told by him that most of my letters are read to the Cabinet,' he informed Lady

---

[1] Spender, *Life, Journalism and Politics*, II, 14; Pound and Harmsworth, p. 464; Clarke, *Northcliffe Diary* (5 September 1914), p. 70.

[2] Haldane to his sister, 3 August 1914, and Haldane to his mother, 5 August 1914, Haldane Papers, Vol. 6012, fol. 49, and Vol. 5992, fol. 8; Asquith, *Memories and Reflections* (London, 1928), II, 81.

Bathurst. 'This affords me opportunities of putting forward some suggestions based on my practical knowledge of tactics.'[1]

For better or worse, Unionist politicians and publicists had worked in concert to exert pressure on a seemingly vacillating government. That was to set a pattern, though it was not to efface differences that carried over from peacetime. Two members of the Liberal Cabinet had made good their threats to resign. Instead of certifying the resolve of those who remained, their departure was taken to imply the intrinsic pacifism of the Liberal creed. In the September number of the *National Review*, Maxse nominated five other ministers who ought to have followed suit. His objective, like that of other self-appointed spokesmen for the opposition, was to spur the government to prosecute the war effort with full vigour, and with maximum expense to its personnel and principles.

United by their presumption of Liberal incapacity, the controllers of the Unionist press were continually divided over the methods to be deployed. Lawson, Robinson, and (to the extent that circumstances permitted) Marlowe were inclined towards moderation. 'One thing' Robinson had 'learnt very clearly, and that is that ... an article in *The Times* runs the risk of achieving rather more than it intended'. Blumenfeld, Gwynne, and Palmer of the *Globe*, each directly inspired by other elements within the party, were usually more outspoken. Garvin, boasting the widest range of confidential sources, played them off against each other. Northcliffe was a law unto himself. Maxse, who edited a monthly and intrigued every day, was recognized by Gwynne to be 'a fine fellow of whose absolute integrity and splendid patriotism I have the warmest admiration but I don't think half so much for his judgment. You see,' Gwynne had instructed Lady Bathurst, 'in politics as in tree-felling, there is a right moment to strike. To strike before or after the proper time is a waste of effort.' The *National Review* delivered its hammer-blows incessantly and with a numbing effect. Other Unionist journals, while sharing its concerns and pursuing many of the same vendettas, struck more selectively.[2]

All of them were in contact with parliamentary activists, though seldom with the same ones. This, no less than the different reading publics at which they aimed, accounted for variations in performance. The *Telegraph* nursed a tender regard for Balfour, as did Northcliffe in his odd way. Robinson, a graduate of Milner's South African Kindergarten, kept in touch with his mentor. Blumenfeld, through Aitken, was linked to Bonar Law. Arnold White, who wrote a regular column for the *Express* and contributed to the *National Review*, consulted Bonar Law, Carson, and Long, who allegedly sanctioned his tirades. Maxse and Gwynne were perhaps closest to Austen

[1] Sir George Arthur, *Life of Lord Kitchener* (London, 1920), III, 3; Pound and Harmsworth, p. 464; Gwynne to Lady Bathurst, 3 September 1914, Bathurst Papers.
[2] Robinson to Milner, 3 November 1914, Milner Papers; Gwynne to Lady Bathurst, 7 February 1914, Bathurst Papers.

Chamberlain, but were susceptible to influence from other front-bench figures and from military lobbyists, often back-bench MPs or backwoods peers. (Gwynne carried his deference to the military authorities to such extravagant lengths that he eventually conspired with the Asquithians to defend the generals against Lloyd George.) For reasons of convenience as well as conviction, certain Unionist newspapermen were more determined than others to discern and follow the official party line.[1]

The party chiefs, varying in their degrees of public support for the government and private dissent from its policies, had to tread cautiously. Aware of competing loyalties and overlapping areas of jurisdiction, they could ill afford to ignore the jealousies that persisted between publications, especially – but not exclusively – those on opposing sides. At the start of the war, Bonar Law paid a statesmanlike tribute to the awakened patriotism of the *Manchester Guardian*. His gesture brought down the wrath of the *Manchester Courier* which, having 'fought for the Conservative cause in this City for over 50 years', had 'never . . . been favoured with such an advertisement as you have . . . given to its Radical rival – the *Guardian*'. Bonar Law could only apologize that he had not 'considered that my reference to the attitude of the *Manchester Guardian* would be useful to that paper as an advertisement'; nor had he supposed that his friendly words could 'possibly have done any harm to any other newspaper' in the district. 'At the time I spoke,' he explained, 'I was thinking only of the best way of serving the country, not of party differences. . . .'[2] Publicists, as a rule, were incapable of similar detachment. And, come to that, few politicians could sustain it.

To rouse the country, newspapers waged a hysterical campaign against anything and anyone contaminated by German associations, which they took to denote German sympathies. The Tory press concentrated its fire upon cosmopolitan Liberals with German antecedents, educations, or investments. The *Daily News* deplored the witch-hunts conducted by the *Daily Mail*, yet stooped to inquire whether Milner's father had been christened Charles or Karl. Prince Louis of Battenberg, compromised by his kinship to the Kaiser, was hounded from his post as First Sea Lord. Haldane, who had studied philosophy at Göttingen, was mercilessly pilloried for having once sentimentalized Germany as his 'spiritual home'. In *John Bull*, Bottomley denounced public men who had the misfortune to be of German extraction and kept a running list of those who had anglicized their names. Blumenfeld, not without a vested interest (his father had fled from Nuremberg after the 1848 revolutions), protested that 'it was low down' for Bottomley to 'attack people with German names who had commissions in the Army'.[3] By implication,

[1] Chamberlain to Maxse, 1 February 1915, and White to Maxse, 4 February 1915, Maxse Papers.

[2] Editor of the *Manchester Courier* to Bonar Law, 6 August 1914, and Bonar Law to Editor, *Manchester Courier*, 10 August 1914 (copy), Bonar Law Papers, 37/3/10, 37/4/11.

[3] Note by Blumenfeld on a letter of apology from Bottomley, n.d., Blumenfeld Papers.

however, financiers (like Sir Ernest Cassel and Sir Edgar Speyer), novelists (like Ford Madox Hueffer and D. H. Lawrence, who had married a German), and especially political adversaries qualified as fair game.

Blumenfeld's sense of personal vulnerability impelled him to reiterate assurances to his readers (21 and 22 August 1914) on the front page of his paper:

> The Chairman and Editor of the *Daily Express* is not and never has been a German.
> The paper on which the *Daily Express* is printed is not and to our certain knowledge has never been made in Germany.
> There is not one German on the staff of the *Daily Express*.

These guarantees were preposterous but, under the circumstances, were felt to be necessary. Until Blumenfeld had cleared his own name, which his son was later to anglicize at Lord Beaverbrook's advice, he lacked the credentials to vilify others.

The Liberals, though they themselves were not blameless, got the worst of it. Their opponents, better versed in the arts of innuendo, could easily accuse them of having failed to prepare the nation for war and of a half-heartedness in rising to the challenge. Moreover, their private lives often lent themselves to caricature and their statements to misconstruction. Haldane, whose utterances and actions seemed almost to invite abuse, observed to the Lords 'that at a time of public excitement like the present fiction and truth are very liberally inter-mixed'.[1] The pages of the *Daily Express* bore him out, alternating the lurid adventures of 'The Beautiful Spy' with the injunction 'DO NOT BELIEVE RUMOURS'. By design or by default, newspapers fed the public a diet of fabricated news, including horrifying accounts of 'Hunnish' atrocities upon the women, children, and art treasures of valiant Belgium. At times, it was even too much for Bottomley. 'For shame, Lord Northcliffe,' he headed a column in *John Bull* (5 September 1914), in which he questioned the authenticity of reports in *The Times* and the *Daily Mail* about those peripatetic cossacks.

Rumours, which passed for 'scoops', sold papers. The more fantastic, the more attention they attracted and the greater their power to inflame. Sir John Simon ascribed mob attacks on German-owned bakeshops in London and Liverpool to 'the sort of thing which is published by Harmsworth, and which he and his like have instigated' by fomenting fears of enemy aliens. 'It must be a great satisfaction to him,' Simon supposed, 'to feel that he has sold his country for $\frac{1}{2}$d.'[2] In addition, rumours circulated by the press could be used to create a political effect, distinctly prejudicial to Liberal ideals of justice that were seen to hamstring the war effort. Opposition leaders did not scruple to capitalize on

---

[1] *Parliamentary Debates* (Lords), 5th ser., xviii, col. 67 (18 November 1914).
[2] Simon to Scott, 14 May 1915, Scott Papers, Add. MSS. 50,908, fols. 86–87.

the situation, sometimes as a means of hectoring the government into action, but also of avenging earlier slights and grievances. By remaining silent, when they might have issued retractions or rebukes, they gave tacit licence to their henchmen in the press. More culpably, they passed along hints to kindle editorial passions. On the one hand, they were eager to ensure that newspapers did not relent in their agitations; on the other, they took precautions against the possibility that those agitations might backfire against themselves. For both purposes, they intervened directly or through their deputies in the management of newspaper affairs. But that was no longer easy.

* * *

The outbreak of war did not disrupt the Unionist chain of command, though the enlistment of back-bench MPs restricted potential sources of newspaper investment. Bonar Law delegated responsibility for press arrangements to Steel-Maitland, who continued as party chairman until 1916. Steel-Maitland collaborated with Malcolm Fraser, the head of the Unionist News Bureau at the Conservative Central Office, who was later to become principal agent.

As if to signal how little had changed, Steel-Maitland and Fraser again turned to Oliver Locker Lampson, whom they had prompted to make an unsuccessful bid for the *Daily Express* in 1912. Despite that mortifying experience, Locker Lampson remained eager to set up shop in Fleet Street. In September 1914, he attempted to buy the *People*, which Madge and Armstrong had launched in 1881 to utilize premises vacated by the *Globe*. 'Certain difficulties' quickly arose between the would-be purchaser and the original proprietors and, at the recommendation of party officials, these were submitted to arbitration by a panel consisting of Gwynne, Goulding, and Long. The inclusion of Goulding, Aitken's friend and associate, portended another failure for Locker Lampson. Madge, outfitted with a knighthood, assumed sole custody for the *People*, which he ran for the next eight years.[1]

Determined to serve his party leaders, Locker Lampson was also 'rather anxious to see the problem of German atrocities settled upon a solid basis'. To this effect, he helped to form and endowed an Anglo-French committee, directed to collect sworn testimony from Belgian victims. In a circular letter to thirteen London editors, he appealed for cooperation.[2] This cause gave him an added incentive to control a newspaper of his own.

No more successful with the *People* than he had been with the *Daily Express*, he now intruded upon the pending transfer of the Astor papers to William Gardner Sinclair. Bearing 'an introduction ... through a friend', almost certainly Steel-Maitland, Locker Lampson called upon Sinclair at the Hotel

---

[1] Locker Lampson to Gwynne, 30 September 1914 (copy), and Gwynne to Locker Lampson, 8 October 1914, Locker Lampson Papers.

[2] Circular letter by Locker Lampson, 24 October 1914 (copy), Locker Lampson Papers.

Metropole on the morning of 21 October. Sinclair, yet to take up his option on the Astor properties, was 'quite prepared to sell the *Pall Mall Gazette*' to Locker Lampson, 'but on no account will I sell the *Observer*, as I intend to carry on this paper under my own proprietorship'. Garvin, whom he urged Locker Lampson to consult, reportedly accepted the 'probability' that he would be serving two masters in the event that Gardner Sinclair got 'a pretty good price'; but it was to be clearly understood that 'it is only the *P.M.G.* that we are discussing'. Locker Lampson deliberated until 3 November, then withdrew. 'The conditions of the war are such as to render it very difficult for me to think of anything but certain military work which I have got,' he replied with 'apologies' for the delay. One may infer that, as he had recently aimed to acquire another Sunday journal, it was really the *Observer* he was after, not its money-losing evening stable-mate.[1]

It would have been a relief to Steel-Maitland had Locker Lampson realized his ambition. Gardner Sinclair's procrastination threatened to put both papers at risk and made it still more difficult to handle Garvin. The two men were engaged in 'a fierce row as perhaps you know', Steel-Maitland wrote to Bonar Law on 17 October. He had advised Gardner Sinclair 'on the telephone' and planned to 'see him either in Edinburgh or in London. I went to see Garvin too.' Nine days later, he was disturbed to 'hear that Garvin has been breakfasting and lunching with Lloyd George and Winston Churchill', which led him to conclude 'that I am not called upon to try and act as mediator any longer'. To repay ministerial hospitality, the *Pall Mall Gazette* condemned (22 October) 'indiscriminate attacks upon the Government for its alleged failure to deal with what is called the "spy danger"'.[2]

On 2 December, Steel-Maitland 'had a talk with Gardner Sinclair', who confirmed the reasons for his heel-dragging; 'the money he needs is not less than £45,000, or perhaps £40,000', which he hoped to raise through second debentures, covered by a party guarantee. In return, Gardner Sinclair would agree 'to any stipulation to retain ownership of the papers and to run them in the Party interest', though Steel-Maitland sensibly doubted 'how far any such stipulation can be made of practical binding value'. Steel-Maitland proposed to see Bonar Law in order 'to discuss the advisability of helping him out on such terms' to meet the Astors' fixed purchase price of £100,000. Needless to say, he would have much preferred to shift that burden to Locker Lampson.[3]

From all indications, the party was prepared to grant Gardner Sinclair's request, and with a routineness that betokened that it was not unusual. On the last day of the year. W. W. Astor received a letter 'from Gardiner [*sic*]

---

[1] Gardner Sinclair to Locker Lampson, 21 October and 11 November 1914, and Locker Lampson to Gardner Sinclair, 3 November 1914 (copy), Locker Lampson Papers.

[2] Steel-Maitland to Bonar Law, 17 and 26 October 1914 (enclosing cuttings from the *Pall Mall Gazette*), Bonar Law Papers, 35/1/23, 33.

[3] Steel-Maitland to Bonar Law, 2 December 1914, and Steel-Maitland to Gardner Sinclair, 2 December 1914 (copy), Bonar Law Papers, 35/4/3.

Sinclair's Solicitors saying that he will complete the purchase of the Newton Street Building & take over the *Observer* & *Pall Mall Gazette* on January 31 according to contract'. Conveying the news to his son, now Major Waldorf Astor, he expressed sorrow 'if this brings you a disappointment' and enclosed a cheque for consolation. 'The *Observer* is a good property,' he acknowledged, 'but I regard the *Gazette* as brother to the Biblical ox in a pit. In my hands it has been a ponderous failure, & the incessant worries & squabbles connected with its management have brought me to regard it with deep disgust.'[1] At last, the long transaction seemed over. But the ox, true to its nature, refused to go away.

On 17 February, the younger Astor was apprised of 'an important development' in the final negotiations. Gardner Sinclair had taken 'very seriously ill & has been removed to Edinburgh in the charge of his Wife & two nurses. His condition is such as to necessitate the constant administration of narcotics & he is therefore quite unable to attend to business.' Before his collapse, Gardner Sinclair had been hard pressed by Rothermere to sell him the *Observer* for 'a definite sum of £60,000. . . . This offer has been put into the form of a Contract which has not yet however been signed.' A separate 'offer has been received' from an unspecified 'Radical Peer', who was seeking to 'purchase the *name* & goodwill of the *P.M.G.* for a small sum', and Dudley Docker was believed to be taken with the notion of amalgamating the *Pall Mall* with the *Globe*. Gardner Sinclair's solicitors advised him to cash in his chips: detaching the *Observer* from the *Pall Mall*, he could sell the first and unload the second; 'the freehold premises will fetch at least £35,000 on an immediate sale'; the machinery and office fittings, 'valued at £25,000, . . . would fetch at least £10,000 . . . in a *break-up* sale'; and their disabled client would see 'his way to get out of the deal not only without loss but at a small profit after paying all expenses'. As a businessman, Gardner Sinclair must have been sorely tempted. Yet, as a party loyalist, he would sooner incur 'a small loss' than commit a flagrant betrayal. It was therefore casually intimated 'that if Mr Astor would be willing to release him from the Contract', Gardner Sinclair would gladly 'consent to forfeit his deposit of £2,000'. Ownership of both papers would then revert to Astor who, according to his business agent, was likely to bestow them on his son.[2]

As the weeks passed, Steel-Maitland had begun to distrust Gardner Sinclair's intentions and, for this reason, did not know what to make of his physical breakdown. That the *Pall Mall Gazette* might revert to Radical hands was, paradoxically, less worrisome than that the *Observer* might fall into the clutches of Rothermere, whose brother had sold it to Astor in 1911. Garvin, 'naturally playing for his own hand', was known to have 'been in close touch with Rothermere from the beginning'. And Rothermere, with Harmsworthian

---

[1] W. W. Astor to Waldorf Astor, 1 January 1915, Astor Papers.
[2] J. Coode Adams to Waldorf Astor, 17 February 1915, Astor Papers.

bravado, proclaimed that the prize was within his reach. 'I expect to become the proprietor of the *Observer* next week,' he informed Bonar Law. 'Mr Sinclair has promised to transfer formally next Monday. I have however found him rather evasive.' Steel-Maitland banked on Gardner Sinclair's evasiveness along with Aitken's strong assurances that, for all his talk, 'H. Harmsworth would not think of buying the *Observer*', Northcliffe's cast-off. While Steel-Maitland had 'no doubt Aitken knows his man', he himself was 'not quite sure' that Rothermere was bluffing. Aitken was asked 'to keep a look-out . . . just in case of accidents', so that Bonar Law could 'get an early talk with Harmsworth if by any chance' a deal 'should materialise'. In early 1915, Aitken gave the signal and Bonar Law swung into action. Rather too fulsomely to carry conviction, he proclaimed to Rothermere that as soon as Aitken had

> told me that you intended that the paper should continue to support our Party I was personally well pleased that it should fall into your hands, for I have had myself sufficient experience of the way in which you do things to know that you always do what you promise.

It was a false alarm. On 9 March, Waldorf Astor pre-empted Rothermere; he was to retain the *Pall Mall Gazette* for only a few months; but he held the *Observer* through the next thirty years and then passed it along to his own son.[1]

Rothermere was feared as much for his fraternal connections as for his own instability. Northcliffe was the bane of all politicians, not merely Liberal ones. His metropolitan papers delivered constant blows. His involvement in Manchester journalism, more explicitly partisan, created problems of another order. The *Manchester Courier*, perpetually a losing proposition, 'was threatened with extinction' no fewer than 'three times' during the first six months of the war. On one of these occasions, Bonar Law saved the day by expressing 'great concern' that 'such a result would be a calamity to the party'. To remove this overhanging threat, local activists proposed to harness the *Courier* to the *Manchester Evening Mail* which, after a dormancy of a dozen years, had resumed publication on 29 August 1914. The financial incentives were as evident as the 'urgent need for an up-to-date Unionist Evening paper that will counteract the gross misstatements which have passed unchallenged, and put before the working man elector the striking facts and arguments in favour of the Unionist policy'.[2]

Bonar Law again looked to Alderman Rothwell to underwrite the joint enterprise. Initially, however, Rothwell stipulated that he would only 'finance

---

[1] Adams to Waldorf Astor, 17 February 1915, Astor Papers; Rothermere to Bonar Law, n.d., Steel-Maitland to Bonar Law, 2 February 1915, and Bonar Law to Rothermere, 3 March 1915 (copy), Bonar Law Papers, 36/5/3, 36/3/4, and 37/5/13.

[2] Edward Foster to Stephenson, 8 October 1914, and Foster to H. G. Price, 4 March 1915, Northcliffe Papers; Bonar Law to Northcliffe, 30 November 1914 (draft copy), Bonar Law Papers, 37/4/33.

one of the papers, morning or evening', and that only 'until the Unionists of the Manchester district have been given an opportunity to consider whether they will assist'. Faced with this choice, opinion divided between those who wanted an evening journal more authentically Unionist than the Hultons' *Evening Chronicle* and those who upheld the traditional view that 'the prestige of morning papers is paramount'. Northcliffe and Rothwell sided with the enthusiasts for an evening paper; but, moved by an appeal by Bonar Law, they 'agreed to share equally ... the loss of the *Manchester Courier* during the war', and saved it from impending bankruptcy. 'The loss at present is £10,000 a year,' calculated Northcliffe. At the same time, Rothwell was 'also paying for the whole loss on the *Manchester Evening Mail*'. Attempts to persuade Lord Derby to recruit backing, much less to subscribe personally, proved unavailing.[1]

A better prospect for the ailing *Courier* was a lifeline to the *Manchester Weekly Times*, a survival from the wreckage of the old daily *Examiner*. Colonel Harry Sowler, who had inherited a stake in the *Courier*, was one of the three directors of this once prosperous weekly: his partners were Amery and McNeill, both Unionist MPs who represented the Imperial Fund. Amery was away at the front, and McNeill – to Sowler's distress – announced that he could no longer recommend the expenditure of capital from the Fund for 'the continuance of the paper under present conditions'. Because McNeill did 'not know many wealthy people, and I am a very bad hand at asking for money for enterprises in which I am interested', he called upon Bonar Law to bring influence to bear upon Viscount Ridley and the Duke of Westminster. 'I have myself written to Sam Storey, but have had no reply as yet.' Soon afterwards, McNeill sent word that Lord Leconfield had 'generously consented to come to the assistance of the *Manchester Weekly Times* to the extent of £2,000, which at all events removed the necessity for immediate liquidation'. Thus, in the second city of British journalism, the Unionist press was kept alive by philanthropy.[2]

The war increased the operating expenses of newspapers and, at the same time, generally curtailed advertising profits. According to Gwynne, who 'steadily refused ... to be panicked into gross expenditure', *The Times* had hired twelve special correspondents, the *Daily Telegraph* 'about the same', and the *Daily Chronicle* even more. The *Morning Post*, 'really more economical than any other paper', managed with a roving team of four, all previously 'members of the staff or working on a small weekly salary. I think I can reduce that number by two,' Gwynne told Lady Bathurst. By the third week of November 1914, her 'anxiety' had reached the point that she was contem-

[1] Sowler to Northcliffe, 28 October 1914 and 26 March 1915, Northcliffe Papers; Northcliffe to Bonar Law, 3 December 1914, Bonar Law Papers, 35/4/9.
[2] Sowler to Northcliffe, 1 December 1914, Northcliffe Papers; McNeill to Bonar Law, 29 December 1914 and 9 January 1915, Bonar Law Papers, 35/5/62, 36/1/11.

plating the disposal of her family property. Gwynne tried to mollify her: 'The war is hitting everybody very hard, but I honestly think that we are feeling the rub as little if not less than any other paper.' The *Morning Post* now enjoyed 'a bigger circulation than we ever had'. To make ends meet, it would be better to raise a modest loan – 'Personally I think that our advertisements will go on increasing and that a large loan will be unnecessary' – than to resort to 'such drastic alterations as would result in deterioration of the paper and its value to you'.[1]

Like Gwynne, who confidentially communicated Lady Bathurst's disquiet, the Unionist leaders feared for the future of the *Morning Post*. That problem, one among several, might be resolved within a wider framework. 'It looks as though the *Standard*, with the *Evening Standard*, is coming to grief,' noted Steel-Maitland, who rated 'the *Evening Standard* . . . a good property and the morning *Standard* a bad one'. Davison Dalziel had taken control of this dual concern in 1910 with a heavy investment from Sir Alexander Henderson. Since then, Henderson had been kept at arm's length and had grown 'very sore'. In December 1914, Dalziel found himself 'in the strait', and his silent partner was disinclined to bail him out. Instead, 'Henderson has discussed the whole position' with Steel-Maitland, who told Bonar Law on the 18th: 'He is on very good terms with Gwynne and is going to have a talk to him if possible when Gwynne returns from France.' Steel-Maitland thought 'it would be an advantage' if Bonar Law 'could have a word with Gwynne also'. There were 'traditional jealousies between the *Standard* and the *Morning Post*', which had intensified in 1911, when Gwynne moved from one to the other. Nevertheless, 'from the Party point of view', it was desirable to work out an accommodation.[2]

A few days later, Steel-Maitland affirmed to Bonar Law that his overriding political 'object is to keep the *Evening Standard* in your hands. The morning *Standard* can be dropped without loss,' he reasoned, and the sacrifice would remove an obstacle. For, on the assumption that 'a good evening is a strength to a morning paper', Lady Bathurst might be induced to run the *Evening Standard* in tandem with the *Morning Post*. Gwynne's assignment was to press the suit, but not too strongly. Without his intercession, 'Lady Bathurst's tendency would be to turn down anything connected with the *Standard* without much consideration'. Primed by Bonar Law, Gwynne did his best. In late December, he 'had a talk' with Henderson, who expected to 'come into control of the *Standard*' on New Year's Day, owing to Dalziel's 'default in the payment of the debentures'. Gwynne then submitted to Lady Bathurst Henderson's 'suggestion (He was careful that it shd. be called a suggestion and not a proposal) that the morning *Standard* shd. be allowed to die but that the *Evening Standard* which is a first class paying property should be taken over by you and run by you as an evening paper'. She must have been gratified to hear

[1] Gwynne to Lady Bathurst, 25 November 1914, Bathurst Papers.
[2] Steel-Maitland to Bonar Law, 18 December 1914, Bonar Law Papers, 35/5/48.

that Henderson's 'chief reason' for coming to her 'was that he was afraid it might fall to Harmsworth'. Bonar Law, who had his own reasons to dread that prospect, had authorized Gwynne to say 'that he thought the idea worth considering and that he would be glad to talk it over with you or Lord Bathurst'.[1]

It was not clear which Harmsworth they wished to head off: at this stage, Harold was the more acquisitive, but Alfred was the greater menace. Nor, for that matter, was there solid evidence that either of them was planning to tender a bid. Possibly Lady Bathurst's well-known detestation of Northcliffe was conjured up to overcome her aversion to the *Standard*. In any case, the strategem failed. Dalziel was delivered from his creditors by the Hultons, who snatched the *Evening Standard* as a metropolitan launching pad. That transaction left him with the *Standard*, which he maintained at a loss until 1917, and gave him some surplus capital to waste upon the short-lived *Daily Call*.

Although Steel-Maitland and Bonar Law had not had their way, they could not have been seriously disappointed. The important thing was to avoid 'the appearance of a Unionist newspaper actually ceasing to exist' and, in this respect, they were successful. The *Observer* (with Garvin in place) and the *Pall Mall Gazette* were in the capable hands of a younger Astor, and the *Morning Post* was soon again secure in Lady Bathurst's grip. The *Standard* limped along as before. In the *Evening Standard*, now sundered from it, the Hultons purveyed a diluted Unionism, but that was preferable to the Harmsworths' fizzy brand. Under Madge's proprietorship, the *People* remained 'a weekly newspaper for all classes'. Its parent, the *Globe*, was safely entrusted to the care of Docker. Palmer, the editor of the *Globe*, combined with Bonar Law to defend 'the right of fair criticism of Ministers' which the Home Office had seemingly challenged; later in the war, denied Bonar Law's support, he was to resign on this very issue. Among other developments, the ownership of the *Daily Mirror* passed from Rothermere to a company under his control; and, upon the death of Alexander Kinealy, E. F. Flynn was appointed editor. Neither change registered an impact upon the *Mirror*'s 'decided political views', notable more for generating heat than light.[2]

No sooner did one difficulty recede than another came to the fore. Through the autumn of 1914, the *Daily Express* functioned smoothly, with a bold display of vigilance: 'We have martial law for journalists, but not for German spies,' taunted a banner headline on 28 November. At the turn of the year, its voice suddenly became muffled. 'Blumenfeld understands as well as anybody alive what the situation is,' Arnold White assured Maxse, 'but he has his paper to think of and after all that to an Editor must be the dominant factor in political

---

[1] Steel-Maitland to Bonar Law, 23 December 1914, Bonar Law Papers, 35/5/54; Gwynne to Lady Bathurst, 31 December 1914, Bathurst Papers.

[2] Steel-Maitland to Bonar Law, 26 January 1915, and Palmer to Bonar Law, 24 November 1914, Bonar Law Papers, 36/2/43, 35/3/54; *Daily Mail*, 25 November 1914; Maurice Edelman, *The Mirror: A Political History* (London, 1966), pp. 14–15; Simonis, *Street of Ink*, p. 105.

controversy.' Gwynne, too, recognized the restraints upon Blumenfeld, who had not lost the courage of his convictions so much as the authority to promulgate them: 'Just now the *Express* has got more masters than one.'[1]

Behind the scenes in Shoe Lane, the tug-of-war had resumed. On 26 January 1915, Steel-Maitland was startled to receive an 'extraordinary letter and memorandum', drafted (ostensibly) by Aitken and countersigned by Blumenfeld.[2] With 'great urgency' and considerable acrimony, Aitken reviewed the discussions that he had had 'last year' with Steel-Maitland, when it became apparent that the company could neither 'meet the sinking fund' nor pay interest on debentures. If Steel-Maitland wished 'to retain the organ for the Party', he could either accept responsibility for these accumulated debts 'or obtain the appointment of a friendly Receiver'. Aitken recommended the second course as the prelude to a complete 're-organisation with preferred shares for the First Debenture holders, and ordinary shares for the Second Debenture holders', contingent upon the guaranteed continuation of 'Mr Blumenfeld as Manager in absolute control for ten years'. He further proposed that Steel-Maitland should commit the Unionist Central Office 'to take up £10,000 of preferred shares to provide working capital'. The bulk of this allocation would go to settle an account with Frank Lloyd, 'the paper manufacturer and a creditor for £9,000', who was 'in a position to cut off all supplies of paper at a moment's notice'. As proprietor of the *Daily Chronicle*, Lloyd would have stood to gain from a foreclosure. According to Aitken's recollection, Steel-Maitland agreed 'to consider the plan' and – after consulting Henderson and presumably others – 'accordingly . . . telegraphed his consent'.

On 16 January, relying 'entirely on Mr Steel-Maitland's good faith', Aitken and Blumenfeld came to terms with Lloyd. The next day, Aitken tried to collect 'the sum of £10,000' that Steel-Maitland was understood to have promised. Instead, he received a visit from a solicitor, who obviously 'was not instructed as to Mr Steel-Maitland's agreement with me', and who took particular exception to the designated appointment of Blumenfeld to a receivership. Contacted on the 19th, Steel-Maitland reportedly confirmed: 'You shall have the money.' But Henderson, who was to advance it, proved to be 'in ignorance of the facts'. After a spate of angry letters and telephone conversations, Aitken was moved 'to request an investigation by persons in authority over the Central Office'; and, to show he meant business, he proposed to invite Gwynne and Garvin 'to join me in protesting against the conduct of the Central Office to Unionist newspapers and newspaper Editors'.

While Steel-Maitland was 'prefectly content' to allow Bonar Law and Lansdowne to 'judge the whole affair', he regarded any 'communication to

[1] White to Maxse, 4 February 1915, and Gwynne to Maxse, 4 March 1915, Maxse Papers.
[2] S. W. Alexander, Aitken's financial secretary, to Steel-Maitland, 26 January 1915, accompanying Aitken's memorandum 're *Daily Express*', Bonar Law Papers, 36/2/44. A duplicate copy of this memorandum, signed by Blumenfeld, implies that it was his handiwork. Beaverbrook Papers, H/15.

Gwynne or Garvin' as 'quite indefensible'. The goodwill – or, failing that, the acquiescence – of both editors was needed if other deals were to be put through. Gwynne was then in a benign mood and had to be kept that way. Garvin, his nerves jangled by the prolonged uncertainty at the *Observer* and *Pall Mall Gazette*, was an unguided missile. Absolving Bonar Law of the blame, he grumbled that 'an infinity of friction and misunderstanding might have been saved if the Central Office had approached me in the first instance directly' instead of negotiating with Gardner Sinclair behind his back. The *Observer* would survive under one management or another; but the *Pall Mall Gazette*, where the printers were threatening industrial action, give him 'serious anxiety.... It ought to be maintained by the Unionist Party on high-class lines as the Ministerialists maintain the *Westminster*.' The 'real sad part', however, was that 'our party's only ideal of a subsidised journal is the *Daily Express*'. Garvin, whose grievances were real enough, ascribed his difficulties to a Central Office 'intrigue [that] required a lot of fighting down'. Aitken would have found him a natural ally.[1]

Addressed to Steel-Maitland, Aitken's manifesto was really intended for the information of Bonar Law, who responded immediately. 'I am sorry to find that there is some trouble about the *Express*,' he calmly wrote to 'my dear S.M.' on the 27th:

> Of course, I would rather keep out of it altogether; but the danger of the arrangement falling through seems to me so serious that I think I must write to you about it ....
>
> If the *Express* is to be kept alive at all I am convinced that the arrangement described to us is the cheapest for the Central Office and the best for the continued life of the paper; and it would certainly be a very grave misfortune if this arrangement fell to pieces, and the whole thing had to be begun again.

Without delay, Steel-Maitland 'saw both Henderson and Aitken, and was prepared to have the money found, provided that the share of the Party in it could be kept private'. The method he adopted was 'to offer to lend it through Henderson on behalf of the ordinary shareholders', who included Locker Lampson: 'When all is said and done they are all members of the Party who act out of Party loyalty.' On Saturday, the 30th, he reached a verbal understanding with Aitken and, three days later, transferred it to paper. 'Your memo does not suit me and I return it herewith,' Aitken shot back.[2]

The financial provisions were acceptable to Aitken, who was empowered to

[1] Steel-Maitland to Bonar Law, 27 January 1915, and Garvin to Bonar Law, 1 March 1915, Bonar Law Papers, 36/2/44, and 36/5/2; Garvin to Waldorf Astor, 4 and 7 March 1915, Astor Papers; Garvin to Scott, 25 March 1915, *Guardian* Archives.

[2] Bonar Law to Steel-Maitland, 27 January 1915 (copy), and Steel-Maitland to Bonar Law, 26 January 1915, Bonar Law Papers, 37/5/5, and 36/2/43–44; Aitken to Steel-Maitland, 3 February 1915 (copy), Beaverbrook Papers, H/15.

'carry on negotiations with a free hand'. Although shorter than requested, it was satisfactory that Blumenfeld's managerial tenure should be extended for eight years, subject to his 'support of the Conservative Party as defined and led by Mr Bonar Law'. What Aitken stuck at – and demanded to have deleted from the document – was the statement that he 'disclaimed any wish to get control of the *Express*'. Steel-Maitland was 'quite mistaken in supposing' anything of the sort, Aitken declared. 'There is no reason why I should disclaim or intimate to you or anybody else for the present or the future.'[1]

Instead of deterring Aitken, Steel-Maitland goaded him on. Aitken was not yet the dominant power at the *Express* in March, when the paper – to his disapproval and Maxse's delight – resumed its attacks upon Haldane. Events moved swiftly thereafter. In May, Lawson Johnston saw Fraser at the Central Office and indicated his readiness to dispose of his second debentures. The self-constituted 'Voting Trustees' – Henderson, Blumenfeld, and Aitken – proceeded with a 're-organisation of the existing Company' by which each of them was allocated a larger block of ordinary shares. On 9 July, Aitken submitted the scheme to Steel-Maitland, from whom he requested the second instalment on the Central Office's appropriation. Despite 'another talk with Henderson', Steel-Maitland retained misgivings and a desire to substitute another name for Blumenfeld's. 'I still think it is not a good proposal,' he wrote on 3 August to Bonar Law, 'but, if you wish it, I do not want to hold out further about the question of the 3 Trustees, and I will not therefore do so.' A fortnight later, he remitted his 'cheque without further question'. For it, 'it is understood that Mr Steel-Maitland receives £10,000 of Preference Shares' and, in principle, the adherence of the *Daily Express* to Bonar Law. Given that those shares were 'in all respects similar to the other Preference Shares of the Company' and that Lawson Johnston's second debentures had been converted into ordinary shares for Aitken, the Central Office forfeited all security on its investment.[2]

More than ever, the finances of political journalism were complicated by the politics of fiscal control. The Labour press was far from exempt from prevailing pressures. On 24 February 1915, 'representatives of over 100 Trade Unions drawn from all parts of the kingdom' met at the Memorial Hall in Farringdon Street, London, and laid plans 'to make the *Daily Citizen* secure amid the difficulties and dangers inseparable from newspaper enterprise during

[1] Steel-Maitland to Aitken, 2 February 1915, accompanying 'Terms of Understanding,' 30 January 1915, and Aitken to Steel-Maitland, 15 February 1915 (copy), Beaverbrook Papers, H/15.

[2] Maxse to Blumenfeld, 3 March 1915, Blumenfeld Papers; Aitken to Haldane, 26 May 1915, Haldane Papers, Vol. 5911, fol. 95; Steel-Maitland to Aitken, 21 May 1915, copy of indenture dated 30 June 1915, Aitken to Steel-Maitland, 9 July 1915 (copy), and Anne B. Page (private secretary, Unionist Central Office) to S. W. Alexander (Aitken's financial secretary), 21 August 1915, Beaverbrook Papers, H/15; Steel-Maitland to Bonar Law, 3 and 17 August 1915 (enclosing copies of Steel-Maitland to Henderson, 12 August 1915, and Henderson to Steel-Maitland, 13 August 1915), Bonar Law Papers, 51/2/2, 14.

wartime'. A 'Shilling Fund' was launched to raise £5,000, the minimum required to carry on. Ramsay MacDonald's opening pledge of twenty shillings was matched by Frank Dilnot, Arthur Henderson, J. H. Thomas, J. R. Clynes, and Clifford Allen, among others, with a total of 625 shillings and sixpence raised 'in the space of 10 minutes'. Readers of the *Citizen*, implored to spare a shilling or two from their pay-packets, were less forthcoming. Although the second week of the appeal was more successful than the first, the paper was forced to shutter its office in Tudor Street on 13 March, when it published for the last time in London. On 5 June, it ceased its Manchester operations and disappeared entirely. Meanwhile, the weekly *Clarion*, having stayed put in Manchester, was 'doing ... very badly'. Blatchford, whose principal income derived from the *Daily Mail* in London, philosophized that the journal had 'seldom done anything else. But it has never died, and I don't think it will,' he remarked to 'Alec' Thompson, whom he left in charge.

> We could not sell it, you know. It would not be worth five pounds to anyone but us. It would hardly be honest to sell it. Besides who would be mad enough to buy it? ... If we changed the name of the *Clarion*, made it a Sunday paper, made it larger, dropped the Socialism and agnosticism, boomed it, and put our best work into it – it might succeed. But only a few of our own sort want the *Clarion*.[1]

Blatchford's candid appraisal, coincident with the pitiable response to the *Citizen*'s 'Shilling Fund', reveals that it was not exclusively for want of advertising revenues that socialist journals foundered and failed.

In fact, much to its humiliation, the Labour press was patronized as an advertising medium for its capitalist rivals. In the same issue of the *Daily Citizen* in which Dilnot bade farewell to London, there was a large paid announcement that the *Sunday Pictorial* would appear the following morning with contributions from Arnold Bennett and Horatio Bottomley, both talents-for-hire. In his own *John Bull*, which had boasted a prewar readership above a million, Bottomley spewed forth a venomous chauvinism and castigated the Liberals among whom he had once sat in Parliament. An incorrigible self-publicist, he was also a swindler who peddled insurance against zeppelin raids and shares in a non-existent co-operative bank. Nevertheless, Rothermere was an admirer of Bottomley's 'tonic-some utterances', which he believed to 'give inspiration and comfort to the most lugubrious souls'. On 25 July 1915, he went so far as to suggest in the *Pictorial* that Bottomley's 'services should be utilized more and more by the Government'. That motion was seconded by Bottomley himself, who had called in *John Bull* as early as 3 August 1912 'for the abolition of the musty, rusty, idiotic and corrupt system of Party, and the substitution of a Business Government' in which he was prepared to take a leading part.

[1] Blatchford to Thompson [March 1915], Blatchford Papers.

Although Rothermere may have been commercially astute in exploiting Bottomley's talent for sensationalism, his recommendation was proof of a warped judgment. It was ludicrous to think that Liberal ministers, themselves the victims of Bottomley's 'disgraceful and poisonous' diatribes, would consent to employ his 'misdirected zeal' in any capacity. That Rothermere could make such a suggestion was confirmation, as if any were needed, of his unfitness to direct the affairs of the *Observer*, notwithstanding the telephoned assurances of his representative that he would not tamper with its politics. The Harmsworth brothers were temperamentally incapable of holding to any self-denying ordinance. The Unionist chiefs had only to look beyond Rothermere to Northcliffe to see the dangers.[1]

'None of the great campaigns, events and resultant controversies of 1915 restored Northcliffe's reputation with politicians,' the official historians of *The Times* have written. 'Public men dreaded him and his newspapers.' On 3 March, while Rothermere's bid for the *Observer* was still pending, Steel-Maitland sent Bonar Law 'a line in haste to put you on your guard with regard to Northcliffe and the *Manchester Courier*'. Once again, Northcliffe was 'up in arms, or I fancy pretends to be, for ulterior purposes'. Reports 'that Lord Northcliffe would be glad to be released from any understanding he had entered into' were lent verisimilitude by a rumour – circulated by Docker – 'that the whole of the *Manchester Courier*'s staff were under a week's notice to leave at any time'. Steel-Maitland and Fraser promptly intervened with promises of local subventions. Neither the *Daily Mail* nor *The Times* could be handled so expeditiously.[2]

The government's decision to proceed with the legislation of Home Rule, then delay its implementation for the duration of the war, strained Liberal relations with front-bench Unionists. More profoundly, it embittered Unionist newspapermen, who felt betrayed by their enemies and let down by their friends. Unlike the politicians, whose mandate had grown stale, journalists were eager to carry the issue directly to the polls. Austen Chamberlain, for one, 'did not seem very hopeful' when Robinson of *The Times* and Wilson of the *Daily Mail* bearded him at a dinner in December 1914. 'He was not at all sure that we should win if there was a general election,' Wilson informed Northcliffe, 'and he was quite sure that the difficulties in the way of an Irish settlement are much greater than most people think.'[3]

Churchill, whom Northcliffe held personally responsible for obstructing the flow of news from the Admiralty, tried to convince Asquith that the way 'to check Northcliffe's power to check the Government' was to commandeer *The Times* and run it as an official organ. But Asquith's Liberal principles militated

[1] Simon to Scott, 14 May 1915, Scott Papers, Add. MSS. 50,908, fols. 86–87; Garvin to Waldorf Astor, 4 March 1915, Astor Papers.
[2] *History of The Times*, IV, part 1, 271; Steel-Maitland to Bonar Law, 3 and 4 March 1915, and Foster to Fraser, 4 March 1915 (copy), Bonar Law Papers, 36/5/4, 11–12.
[3] Wilson to Northcliffe, 14 December 1914, Northcliffe Papers.

against so high-handed a step, as they did against compulsory service and the other authoritarian measures that *The Times* saw as essential for winning the war. Robinson walked an editorial tightrope between his party leader and his proprietor: on the one side, Bonar Law was 'uncomfortable' with proposals for a full-scale coalition mooted in *The Times*; on the other, Northcliffe dissented from their view 'that useful criticism could perfectly well be made without opposing the war, or, indeed, discrediting the Government'. If the opposition was too timorous to oppose, Northcliffe stood ready to do the job for them.[1]

After serious discussions with public men – including Fisher, Curzon, Milner, and Esher – 'and probably as a result of reading E. T. Cook's biography of Delane', Robinson was driven to assert his editorial prerogatives. Lovat Fraser, who thought that the editor was 'trying to do too much' of the leader-writing, invoked the precedent of Buckle, who had carried his '*executive* responsibility . . . much too far, especially towards the end'. But Buckle, with whom Robinson was also in touch, encouraged him to take a strong stand for patriotic as well as professional reasons. There were recurrent disputes with Northcliffe who, at one point, requested Robinson's resignation. John Walter, who still had a say in the matter, refused to accept this 'fait accompli' on the grounds that 'the appointment of the Editor is vested by the Articles of Association in the Directors of the Company'. Consequently, Robinson kept his chair and, with it, the opportunity to win over Northcliffe by his increasing militancy.[2]

What Robinson and Northcliffe had in common was the fear of a compromise settlement, imposed by the Liberals' inability to take steps that were ideologically repugnant or electorally unpopular. '*We cannot possibly accept an unsatisfactory peace*, whatever happens,' Robinson insisted to Esher, 'though I quite agree that the autocracy of the last eight months has brought the risk appreciably nearer.'[3] Press censorship, which the *Morning Post* had gingerly defended on the premiss that 'over-careful precaution is a fault upon the right side' (9 February 1915), was suspected as a device to mask the government's defeatist intentions. In the *National Review* (March and April), Maxse featured releases from his own 'Unofficial Press Bureau', which specialized in anti-ministerial intelligence. 'Ministers, whose motto is or used to be "Trust the People", are maintaining a very curious attitude in this war,' observed the *Daily Mail* (24 March), which came to 'believe that this Government, which did not see the war coming, does not now understand the terrific nature of the struggle before it' (3 May). The secrecy that enveloped the Dardanelles offensive was certainly exasperating, but easier to bear than the

---

[1] Churchill, *The World Crisis*, III (London, 1927), part 1, 246; Robinson's notes of a meeting with Bonar Law, 29 December 1914, quoted in J. E. Wrench, *Geoffrey Dawson and Our Times* (London, 1955), pp. 114–15.

[2] Wrench, *Dawson*, p. 120; Fraser to Robinson [April 1915], *Times* Archives; Walter to Northcliffe, 22 March 1915, Northcliffe Papers.

[3] Robinson to Esher, 23 March 1915, Esher Papers.

apprehension that failure would result in a negotiated peace, inimical to British interests.

Dissatisfaction with the conduct of the war was widespread, and the quality of Asquith's leadership was debated less and less tactfully. Newspapers articulated the misgivings that politicians were bound to suppress. From their visits to the front, editors knew the extent of the muddle, though perhaps mistook its causes. The *Morning Post*, traditionally the forum of the military establishment, had close links with the generals. The *Daily Mail*, the self-advertised 'soldiers' friend', was inundated with letters from a 'hospital reading public', literally scarred by war. Northcliffe, who brandished them at an editorial meeting, paid three visits to France and twice interviewed General Sir John French, the Commander-in-Chief. 'The whole war is being unduly prolonged' by British ineptitude, he complained to Lovat Fraser, who had unpardonably written an optimistic leading article in *The Times* on 12 April. 'It must be obvious to everybody that something is wrong . . . . Why should we not peer closely into the scandal of the Dardanelles?'[1]

Gwynne sent the Prime Minister an unsolicited, fifteen-page typewritten memorandum 'on the subject of the Dardanelles Expedition and some other matters'. He received, for his pains, a patronizing reply: 'It is perhaps hardly necessary to assure you that all the considerations, political & strategic, to which you advert, have been present to the minds of, and been carefully weighed by, His Majesty's Government and their expert advisers.' Rebuffed, Gwynne put his case in print, appending to it a demand for Churchill's removal from the Admiralty. 'I see the *Post* has gone for the Dardanelles question, and, as usual, has done it both indiscreetly and inaccurately, and put itself in the wrong,' Lovat Fraser wrote to Robinson on 23 April, the day after Gwynne had been brushed aside by Asquith. 'The *Post*'s indiscretion seems to lie in attacking the whole scheme, root and branch, at the very moment that, as we understand it, another attack is impending.' Moreover, it occurred to Fraser, 'the *Post* does not say who can replace Winston.' Robinson probably agreed with Fraser, but Northcliffe's sympathies were with Gwynne.[2]

Not confined to the Tory side, these controversies unsettled the Cabinet and poured over into the Liberal press. On 29 March, the *Daily Chronicle* responded to 'the anti-Ministerial pin-pricks' that had appeared 'for the last month or so' in such papers as *The Times*, the *Observer*, and the *Morning Post*. Discerning an 'Intrigue against the Prime Minister', whose 'serene cheerfulness' was taken for Panglossian myopia, Donald acknowledged that 'it is Mr Lloyd George whom the Unionist press seem inclined to exalt as a luminary eclipsing his chief'. Though there was nothing in the article to suggest that Lloyd George was a party to these machinations, he considered his loyalty to

[1] Pound and Harmsworth, p. 473.
[2] Asquith to Gwynne, 22 April 1915 (copy), Asquith Papers; Fraser to Robinson, 23 April 1915, *Times* Archives.

have been impugned and 'vehemently disclaimed having anything to do with the affair', which he saw as McKenna's handiwork. McKenna, questioned by Asquith, 'has hotly denied that he had ever said or suggested to Donald that L.G. was in the plot, while admitting that he had had a talk with him on the subject of the attacks in the Tory Press'. That Donald's anodyne should have caused such a row was an indication of the tensions that were building up. By attempting to allay them, Donald had inadvertently brought them into focus.[1]

The *Chronicle*'s blunder was forgiven, if not forgotten. Three weeks later, Donald attended a small dinner to hear Lloyd George's proposals to curb excessive drinking (especially among munitions workers) by a system of state controls. McKenna was also present, as were Scott, Gardiner, Spender, and Massingham. Asquith, described by his biographers as being 'wholly sceptical as to the value of either agitation or imprecation in winning the War', stayed away. His own contribution to the government's press relations was to receive a deputation of metropolitan newspaper owners and editors at noon on 1 April. Churchill and Kitchener, who were feuding as bitterly as Lloyd George and McKenna, were ornaments to the occasion. Although Asquith's brief was to unveil the Press Bureau's revised guidelines, Cook recorded that the 'P.M. had apparently looked at none of our papers & said O about the circular' to be distributed. Instead, Asquith 'buttered up the Press no end (but not more than Lawson buttered himself & co.', thought Cook, who caught Riddell's 'eye & smiled when L. was expatiating on self-sacrifice of Press)'. In a rambling fashion, Asquith 'talked platitudes on true & false patriotism; but ended with caution on importance of sense of proportion'. Afterwards, Cook 'lunched with Spender', who 'said [that the] recent press outcry agst. P.M. was engineered by Ll. G. & Winston & Garvin. . . . Real foundation for it,' Spender admitted, 'is A's laziness & lack of ideas.'[2]

Cook and Spender had been followers of Asquith since Liberal Imperialist days; and Spender, a lifelong Asquithian, was to co-author Asquith's official biography. Their disenchantment was therefore doubly significant. For, as it was emerging, the fundamental division in political journalism was not so much between the Prime Minister's defenders and detractors as between those who articulated their criticisms and those who stifled them. This held true for Liberals as well as Unionists. Scott restricted his condemnations to private correspondence. 'Really,' he exploded to L. T. Hobouse, 'Asquith gets worse as he gets older and it is time he were dead and buried – politically!' Gardiner, who clung to Asquith with increasing tenacity, put aside his doubts and celebrated the Dardanelles invasion as a revival of the Gladstonian crusade against the Unspeakable Turk; his 'most admirable article' in the *Daily News* (1 May) won plaudits from McKenna, who considered it 'much needed and . . .

[1] H. A. Taylor, *Donald*, pp. 78–81; Asquith, *Memories and Reflections*, II, 70–71.
[2] Spender and Asquith, *Life of Lord Oxford and Asquith* (London, 1932), II, 122; Cook's diary, 1 and 3 April 1915, Cook Papers.

very opportune'. The following Saturday, 'A.G.G.' came out still more strongly. Conceding that the government had made mistakes ('What war has ever been conducted without mistakes?'), he insisted that 'no Ministry ever met an unexampled emergency with more efficiency, more capacity, or more success'.[1]

Gardiner was responding to a barrage of intensified newspaper atttacks: the *Morning Post*, 'unfalteringly hostile' to Churchill, was 'trying to drive a wedge in between him and Lord Fisher'; and the Northcliffe papers struck at random ministerial targets, though 'it is against Mr Asquith that the thunder in *The Times* is chiefly directed'. More 'regrettable' than the distress to individuals was the impression given to the Germans 'that the purpose of this country is weakening'. Yet interference with freedom of expression would pose a greater danger: 'That right is the very breath of Liberalism, and a challenge to it would be a precedent that would be used ruthlessly against democracy in the future.' Gardiner convinced himself that the more responsible Tory spokesmen appreciated the government's dilemma. Massingham, writing his 'London Diary' for the *Nation* the same day, shared his impression. The *Observer* and the *Pall Mall Gazette*, he was pleased to note,

> have rather markedly retired from the anti-Prime Minister movement, while *The Times*, retiring perhaps in order to jump back again, pleads that it is only out for the right of criticism. Who hinders? The door of criticism has never been shut since the door of war was opened. The only question is as to spirit and intent. The intent of *The Times* is obviously to change horses at the point and moment that the stream is running its fiercest.

Massingham and Gardiner correctly gauged Northcliffe's destructive tendencies, but erred in supposing – at least for the sake of argument – that he was an exception to the rule. Within days, the voices of Fleet Street were raised in a cacophonous din. By the time it abated, the Liberal government had been superseded by a coalition, and Gardiner, for one, had had second thoughts. On 22 May, exactly a fortnight after he had averred that nothing was more sacred to Liberalism than a free press, he decided that nothing was potentially more deleterious: 'There comes a time when even the freedom of the Press must give place to the safety of the State. That time has come with us.' To account for his recantation, we must evaluate the way in which newspapers helped to shape events and, more directly, the popular perception of events during the May crisis.

---

[1] Scott to Hobhouse, 23 April 1915, quoted in Scott, *Political Diaries*, p. 122; McKenna to Gardiner, 1 May 1915, Gardiner Papers.

Eight

FROM COALITION TO COALITION

From the very moment of its occurrence, the Cabinet crisis of May 1915 has stimulated a vehement debate. Gardiner's view that it was 'as obscure in its origins as it was sudden' was flatly contradicted by Garvin as being 'wrong in every way'. If contemporaries were unable to agree on so much as the sequence of events, what hope can there be for historians?[1]

To an extent that was no less real for its ostentation, the press played a vital role in these tangled proceedings, which marked a watershed in its long-term political development. According to Garvin (*Observer*, 23 May 1915), 'the great majority of British journals, irrespective of party', had hitherto 'played the game'. The time had come when they could no longer be expected to abide by the rules: 'The bulk of the Press in its own urgent interests may be driven to take common action apart from anything which the Government may have to do.' This clash of 'urgent interests' was one of the reverberating themes of wartime experience.

The influence of newspapers was continually manifest in either – or, some would say, both – of two ways. As free agencies, they brought a welter of pressures to bear, many of which cancelled each other out; in this respect, they pretended to power, whether or not they actually contrived to wield it. More fundamentally, though no less disruptively, newspapers were signally responsible for moulding opinion within the concentric circles of political society; this, by definition, was an indirect process. As much by default as by custom, newspapers were the purveyors of fact or at least what, under the circumstances, passed for fact. The truth, besides being extraordinarily difficult for anyone to establish, arguably counted for less than what was commonly held to be true. To all intents and purposes, therefore, credulity imposed its own potent reality.

If, as Churchill sardonically alleged, his 'Tory friends ... do not know except

[1] Gardiner, *The War Lords* (London, 1915), p. 79; *Observer*, 23 May 1915; *also see* A. M. Gollin, *Proconsul in Politics* (London, 1964), ch. xi, and 'The Unmaking of a Prime Minister,' *Spectator*, 28 May 1965; Cameron Hazlehurst, *Politicians at War* (London, 1971), part iii; M. D. Pugh, 'Asquith, Bonar Law and the First Coalition,' *Historical Journal*, xvii (1974), 813–36; Peter Fraser, 'British War Policy and the Crisis of Liberalism in May 1915,' *Journal of Modern History*, liv (1982), 1–26; and Koss, *Lord Haldane* (New York, 1969), ch. vii.

what they have read in the newspapers', how little else must the ordinary citizen have comprehended?[1] Public opinion, always malleable during wartime, was then largely manufactured by the press. And, while no longer quite so malleable as before, the press was itself largely the creation of the party system. Conflicts of loyalty, already pronounced in the pre-war years, were exacerbated by the struggle. As a sentiment, partisanship prevailed; but, as a governing principle, it was less binding. Even where party attachments were underpinned by financial arrangements, they worked with diminished stringency. Impatient with events, which had culminated in stalemate, newspapermen were more and more tempted to seize the initiative. The same conditions that served to make party leaders more reticent, owing to their determination to foster a spirit of unity, made journalists more anxious, more presumptuous, and more reckless.

The gruelling winter of 1914–15 left the party truce in tatters. From the sidelines, an assortment of public figures was demanding the abandonment of Liberal niceties and, specifically, a repudiation of voluntary service, which was regarded as an impediment to effective national organization. Since 20 April, when Asquith (on Kitchener's weighty authority) had denied rumours of a serious munitions shortage, his critics had been building a case against him. The press amplified their criticisms into a clamour. The climax came on 7 May, when the torpedoing of the passenger liner *Lusitania* was held to exemplify German criminality, fortuitously confirmed by the publication of the Bryce Commission's report of reputed enemy outrages in Belgium. Anti-German riots raged in the East End of London, Liverpool, and Southend, the target of a zeppelin raid. Inflamed by German ruthlessness, the British public was all too receptive to Bottomley's hateful appeals in *John Bull* for 'a vendetta against every German in Britain, whether "naturalised" or not. . . . You cannot naturalise an unnatural Beast – a human abortion – a hellish freak. But you *can* exterminate it.'

By the second week of May, the emphasis had shifted: the objective was no longer simply to galvanize the government, but to transform it. On the day that the *Lusitania* was sunk, the *Morning Post* opened its campaign for a 'Cabinet of Talents', capable of halting 'the waste involved in improvised methods'. The loss of civilian lives at sea, without warning, 'marks the end of the first phase of the war', declared the *Post* on the 12th, for this shocking incident had created 'a new conviction . . . that the German must be broken in pieces before there can ever again be peace and safety'. At the same time that Germany had forfeited any 'right to make peace on terms', an alternative that the Liberals were feared to favour, the lesson for the British was clear: 'The state should at once requisition the entire male population.' The *Daily Express* promptly chimed in. 'The Only Way – *Conscription!*' screamed its banner headline on the 11th;

---

[1] Churchill to Asquith, 21 May 1915, Asquith Papers.

and, two days later, above provocative photographs of anti-German demonstrations, it proclaimed that, 'The People demand a leader from their leaders.'

Throughout the week, the agitation grew. The *Globe* and the two *Standards* stepped up their advocacy of military compulsion, known to be anathema to Liberal fundamentalists. But the greatest material assistance came from the Northcliffe papers, which had never slackened. 'If you read *The Times* and the *Daily Mail* leading articles you will see very plainly what my views are,' Northcliffe informed Hamilton Fyfe, covering the war in Russia. 'I write most of the *Daily Mail* articles myself,' he revealed, 'and have a good deal to do with the concoction of those in *The Times*.'[1] None of his concoctions proved more damaging to the government than a dispatch from Colonel Charles à Court Repington, *The Times*'s military correspondent. Published on Friday, 14 May, it ascribed the costly failure of the British offensive in France to 'the want of unlimited supply of high explosive' and thereby cast into doubt not only Kitchener's competence at the War Office, but also Asquith's suitability as a war leader.

Repington's documented exposé of a shells scandal, followed up by investigations of inefficiency in the munitions works at Glasgow, gave substance to earlier allegations and so confirmed the worst suspicions of the Unionist Business Committee, a group of vigilant backbenchers who were badgering Bonar Law to take a stronger stand. 'Repington has put the Government very neatly between devil and deep sea,' J. A. Spender remarked to Lord Esher. There are those who have argued that, whatever his intention, Repington had plunged the Unionist leadership into similar straits.[2]

Scarcely twenty-four hours after Repington's dispatch, the waters were further muddied by the announcement that Lord Fisher had resigned as First Sea Lord owing to persistent differences with Churchill over the Dardanelles offensive. In the opinion of many informed observers, the Admiralty crisis quickly overtook the munitions crisis and was more directly responsible for Asquith's subsequent actions. 'The Liberal Government fell from a set of causes wholly unconnected with Shells,' Beaverbrook declaimed with typical certitude. Others, however, were equally adamant that *The Times*'s authoritative (and perhaps engineered) disclosures had registered the greater impact, though it was more convenient to fasten upon the Fisher-Churchill dispute as a public pretext for reshuffling the government. 'Crisis made by Repington's article in *The Times*,' Arnold Bennett wrote in his diary on the 21st, after a conversation with McKenna, who was well placed to know. Furthermore, McKenna suggested, 'Rep's article' had been 'arranged' by Churchill. Cook, whose principal source was Buckmaster, agreed that 'the explosives telegram fixed the mine' and that the 'Govt. might have survived

[1] Northcliffe to Fyfe, 11 May 1915 (copy), Northcliffe Papers.
[2] Spender to Esher, 17 May 1915, Esher Papers; Taylor, 'Politics in the First World War,' in *Politics in Wartime*, p. 19.

the Winny row' on its own. Although Buckmaster 'put all this bitterly as party game', Cook was inclined to 'another view', namely that Churchill and Lloyd George were among Repington's accomplices.[1]

It was not uncommon for bystanders to suppose that *The Times* had been worked by certain politicians: according to Beaverbrook, for example, Lloyd George 'inspired Lord Northcliffe to take up the question' so that 'he would be powerfully aided in enforcing his own munitions policy on the reluctant soldiers'. Nor was it the least unusual for contemporaries, especially bemused Liberals, to postulate the existence of a plot in which various politicians and publicists, credited with various motives, were implicated. The consensus was that the major culprit was Churchill, whose clash with Fisher was less important, and certainly less reprehensible, than his reported dalliance with Repington at Sir John French's headquarters. To assess the validity of these charges would be redundant and, on the whole, irrelevant to the purpose of the present narrative. Suffice it to say that if there was smoke without fire, it was inhaled by a sufficient number of prominent people – including the King – to compromise Asquith's position.[2]

Whichever crisis took precedence, the effect of the two together was immense. In fact, Asquith did not attempt to separate them in the memorandum he sent on Monday, the 17th, to his Liberal colleagues, whose resignations he solicited as the prelude to the formation of a coalition. The *Pall Mall Gazette* broke the story in its last edition the following evening and was acknowleged by the *Manchester Guardian* (19 May) to have scored 'the big journalist "scoop" of the year, although its details are purely a matter of surmise'. (The *Pall Mall* declined to return the compliment and instead praised the *Daily Chronicle* as 'the most fully and accurately informed among the morning's newspapers' on the 19th.) Garvin, soon to depart from the *Pall Mall* to concentrate exclusively on the *Observer*, was believed in some quarters to have derived his advantage from complicity in the intrigue.

In the *Pall Mall*'s account of the 'Great Political Crisis', as in the 'reminiscences' he furnished to Beaverbrook four years later,[3] Garvin gave pride of place to the Admiralty crisis. 'The whole method and temper of Cabinet administration in wartime is the question at stake,' he advised his readers on the 18th. At this juncture, he anticipated that Fisher ('not merely a man – he is a force of nature') might be retained at the Admiralty by substituting Balfour for

[1] Beaverbrook, *Politicians and the War*, pp. 88–89; Bennett's journals, 21 May 1915; Cook's diary, 19 May 1915, Cook Papers.
[2] Beaverbrook, *Politicians*, p. 88; Koss, *Haldane*, ch. vii.
[3] Memorandum by Garvin, 'The Admiralty Crisis of 1915 and the Crash of the Government,' 6 October 1919, Beaverbrook Papers, Box 3/IV. In the *Observer* on 23 May, Garvin gave an inconsistent account of this 'extraordinary episode': 'To suppose that Lord Fisher's coup alone could cause the transformation is as futile as ascribing the appearance of Goodwin Sands to the fall of Tenterdon steeple,' he stated archly. 'The fall of the late Cabinet could not have been brought about by Admiralty difficulties alone. The latter were the most obvious cause. They were not the most serious.'

Churchill, who was nominated for the India Office. Unable to ignore the munitions shortage, however categorically he denied its centrality, Garvin went on to nominate Lloyd George as 'Minister for War Supplies', who would create and superintend 'a colossal and vital department'. Such an arrangement, it went without saying, would reduce Kitchener to a figurehead. That was Garvin's intention, but he knew better than to press too hard at once. The War Office had become 'even more industrial than military', he explained the next day. 'Events have heaped on Lord Kitchener's shoulders a burthen that a super-Napoleon could not sustain. Decentralisation is imperative' and would be assisted by Kitchener's transfer.

Northcliffe saw matters differently and his own intervention – through Repington – as crucial. He arrived at Printing House Square on the 17th in a 'rather truculent mood', which lasted through the week. Determined at the very least to remove Kitchener, which Repington confirmed to be his own limited objective, he was as ready to override his editors as to defy his readers. 'I mean to tell the people the truth and I don't care what it costs,' he bellowed to his chauffeur. Robinson, convinced that Northcliffe's methods were 'mischievous and unnecessary', was able to head him off. Marlowe was less successful. On the afternoon of the 20th, he was shown a proof of the leading article that Northcliffe had composed for the next day's *Mail*, and tried to reason with him. 'You realize, I suppose, that you are smashing the people's idol?' Without disputing that Northcliffe's arguments were 'quite true', he pointed out that they 'will make the public very angry. Are you prepared for the consequences?' Undaunted, Northcliffe rejoined: 'I don't care twopence for the consequences. That man is losing the war!'[1]

After venting his indignation in print, Northcliffe lapsed into a playful mood. On the morning of the 21st, 'when his leader attacking Kitchener fell like a bombshell on amazed England', his comment to Clarke 'was that the verbose author of the leading article looked like getting the paper into trouble. He certainly does,' Clarke nodded in his diary. 'All day the telephones have been buzzing with protests from readers, and intimations that they will never buy our "damned rag" again.' Out of fears 'that public feeling may boil over', the gates around Carmelite House were locked and 'a special police guard' patrolled outside.[2] Led by the *Star*, the evening papers responded in a hostile chorus to Northcliffe's impudence, which no one regretted more than Garvin, who basically shared Northcliffe's sentiments. Aware that Kitchener's hand had been strengthened by the vitriolic campaign against him over the preceding two days, the *Pall Mall* concluded on the 21st that he 'must remain'. On the 22nd, the *Manchester Guardian* discerned 'a great popular rally to Lord Kitchener', who was upheld by the insistence of the *Daily Express* that an

[1] Wrench, *Dawson*, p. 125; Robinson to G. Campbell, 21 May 1915, quoted in *History of The Times*, IV, part 1, 275; Pound and Harmsworth, pp. 477–78.
[2] Clarke, *Northcliffe Diary*, pp. 78–79.

'Attack on Lord Kitchener Helps Germany'. Here, as elsewhere, Kitchener's patriotism was extolled at the expense of Northcliffe, decried in the *Daily News* as 'an unscrupulous adventurer' whose 'whole career has been a record of vulgar sensationalism'. The furore had yet to die down on the 29th, when *John Bull* warned belatedly of 'a movement on foot to crush Kitchener. ... If Kitchener goes, the Germans will come in.'

Northcliffe, far from minding this abuse, positively revelled in it. He was stung, however, by the relatively mild rebukes delivered in the *Pall Mall Gazette* and the *Observer*, papers that might have supported him, but instead faulted his tactical sense. 'I hope you will speak to Mr Astor about the way he spends his money in attacking me,' he wrote sniffily to Robinson, whose friendship with Waldorf Astor did not endear him to his own proprietor. 'I shall certainly retaliate on the Astor family in *The Times* and the *Daily Mail*.'[1] More seriously, Northcliffe was distressed to be denied the results that he and others had expected to follow logically from Asquith's decision to broaden the ministerial base.

Bonar Law, summoned to Downing Street on 17 May, had come away with the distinct impression that Asquith and Lloyd George were agreed that it was 'absolutely necessary to get rid of Kitchener'. Nevertheless, as Fisher picturesquely complained after the dust had settled: 'Kitchener, who can't get a thing right, gets the Order of the Garter, and I get the order of the boot.'[2] In the coalition that emerged, Asquith's dominance was secured, perhaps even reinforced. Kitchener retained the War Office, though a number of its major functions were hived off to Lloyd George at the newly created Ministry of Munitions. (It was implausibly suggested that, but for Northcliffe's misbehaviour, the first Minister for Munitions would have been Rothermere.) McKenna was elevated to fill the vacancy at the Exchequer, and Simon took over the Home Office, contrary to gleeful prognostications that both of them would be sent packing. Grey, Birrell, and Harcourt, three other candidates for displacement, were left undisturbed. Churchill was demoted, and Haldane was dropped. Apart from Balfour, who went to the Admiralty, the incoming Unionists and the lone Labour representative were relegated to comparatively minor posts.

Small wonder, therefore, that Northcliffe felt cheated. Margot Asquith reported that he went 'about saying that he made the Coalition and can smash it whenever he likes', but his official biographers have conceded that he 'had little cause to plume himself at the result'. Gwynne, too, was bitterly disappointed by an outcome that bore only a remote resemblance to the 'Cabinet of Talents' he had envisaged. The former ministry had 'shortcomings', he had noted the previous March, but at the same time it had certain advantages: 'with a

---

[1] Northcliffe to Robinson, 20 May 1915 (copy), Northcliffe Papers.
[2] Memorandum by Chamberlain, 17 May 1915, Chamberlain Papers, AC/2/2/25; Lucy Masterman, *C. F. G. Masterman*, p. 289.

Unionist Opposition we can stir them up – and stir them up with some effect, but given a Coalition Government we should get callous and careless'. As Asquith assembled the pieces, the new régime afforded him – and Bonar Law – a large degree of insulation from external pressures. 'Like yourself, I dislike it very much,' Gwynne confided to Lady Bathurst,

> but it is the last thing that England can do – at any rate, in the way of politicians, and we shall have to stand by it until it proves a failure, which I hope to God it will not, for we cannot afford to have any more failures. . . . But you may depend on our not giving up our independence, for Press and Parliamentary suggestion is all that is left to us.

Garvin was moved to repent of his past enthusiasm. 'I wanted a coalition but never dreamed of one like this,' he told Haldane, who he had 'hoped . . . would remain as Minister for Education'. Maxse signified his disdain by paying scant attention to the matter; by his criteria, any national government headed by Asquith belied its name.[1]

The Liberal press was not only dismayed but baffled. The *Westminster Gazette* trusted that Asquith had acted for the best, and the *Manchester Guardian* saw the advantages of Lloyd George's enhanced authority. 'No one, I think, looking at the new Government with a knowledge of real values, will feel that the position of this country has been strengthened,' Gardiner lamented in the *Daily News* on 5 June. The elder statesmen of the party were frankly appalled. Loreburn, mourning the demise of what was to prove Britain's last Liberal administration, was 'not surprised to hear this change of Government' was the product of 'a Press intrigue. Nor am I surprised,' he told Bryce, another quondam minister, 'that for the first time in our history a Press intrigue had succeeded.' Bryce was likewise convinced that there had been 'an intrigue worked through the Harmsworth press', which he viewed as 'a thing of evil omen'. That Northcliffe had precipitated the calamity, either single-handedly or – more probably – in league with other conspirators, was too widely assumed to be dismissed out of hand. Sir Frederick Pollock, the eminent jurist, wrote to Haldane: 'After the war, we must deport Northcliffe and Co. to Berlin, making it one of the terms of peace that it will be considered an act of war if we ever hear of them again.' Margot Asquith, whose histrionic opinions did not necessarily reflect those of her husband, vowed to wreak vengeance on *The Times* and the *Morning Post* ('and I can do a great deal') for having driven the Prime Minister to take such drastic action. Again, neither her effusions nor the suppositions entertained by others can be regarded as conclusive. But 'the general impression' at the National Liberal Club, as Burns described it in his

---

[1] Margot Asquith to Kitchener, 12 June 1915, Kitchener Papers, PRO 30/57/106; Pound and Harmsworth, p. 480; memorandum by Gwynne, 26 March 1915, Bonar Law Papers, 36/6/36; Gwynne to Lady Bathurst, 26 May 1915, Bathurst Papers; Garvin to Haldane, 26 May 1915, Haldane Papers, Vol. 5911, fol. 104.

diary, was that Asquith had capitulated to an agitation led by '*The Times* and the society Anarchist Journals like the *D. Mail*', which had 'stampeded' him into exchanging his Liberal government for a coalition that 'cannot work and will not last'.[1]

Whatever factors had induced Asquith to offer a coalition and Bonar Law to assent to it on terms that they were less than generous to himself and his party, there can be no denying the existence of powerful undercurrents of discontent. The press had revealed its capacity for disruption, whether real or potential, and somehow had to be controlled. For, if 'the general impression' at the National Liberal Club and elsewhere was to be dispelled, the all-party experiment had to be given the chance to prove its merit. That would be impossible, of course, if newspapers continued their disparagement. Asquith and his new colleagues promptly 'agreed that a fresh announcement should be made to the Press as to its duties in relation to war news and criticism. . . . For the future,' they decided, 'the institutions and conduct of proceedings should be in the hands of the Director of Public Prosecutions, and . . . power should be taken to suppress by executive action offending newspapers without previous prosecution.'[2] A significant departure from Liberal precedent, this procedure hardly betokened a sense of ministerial gratitude to a vigilant press. In any case, it was inadequate to achieve its purpose unless the newspapers themselves adopted a spirit of conciliation.

Some journalists, principally Liberal ones, were eager to rise to the occasion. A. P. Nicholson, who had left *The Times* to become lobby correspondent for the *Daily News*, presumed that 'as far as the news columns are concerned (and I hope editorially) a Coalition Government should be able to count on journals on both sides being fair'. To guarantee this result, he suggested to John Baird, then Conservative MP for Rugby and later 1st Viscount Stonehaven, 'that the new conditions might reasonably open up relations between Unionist leaders and the Liberal Press'. Baird proved sufficiently sympathetic for Nicholson, whose family straddled party lines, to broach the topic with Bonar Law. An erstwhile Unionist, Nicholson reminded Bonar Law that he had 'left the . . . party . . . with warm feelings towards yourself and since I have been on the *Daily News* I have always endeavoured, and sometimes succeeded, in moderating their tone of acerbity to you'.[3]

Others were fully determined to resist Nicholson's model, not to emulate it. They included his own editor as well as Gwynne, whose vow to maintain the independence of the *Morning Post* signified a rejection of front-bench con-

[1] Loreburn to Bryce, 24 May 1915, Bryce Papers; Bryce to Scott, 26 May 1915, Scott Papers, Add. MSS. 50, 908, fols. 95–96; Pollock to Haldane [26 May] 1915, and Margot Asquith to Haldane's mother, 24 May 1915, Haldane Papers, Vol. 5911, fol. 129, and Vol. 6082, fol. 8; Burns's diaries, 22 and 26 May 1915, Burns Papers, Add. MSS. 46, 337, fols. 97, 99.
[2] Asquith to the Sovereign, 28 May 1915, Cab. 37/128/25, fols. 110–11.
[3] Nicholson to Bonar Law, 22 May 1915, Bonar Law Papers, 50/3/33. 'At this time', Baird had replaced Aitken as 'Law's political adviser'. Taylor, *Beaverbrook*, p. 108.

trivances. It was clear enough that the coalition merely incorporated party differences without resolving them, thereby accentuating intra-party rifts. From the start, the new government was riddled with internal contradictions, and its cohesion was, at best, tenuous. The smouldering controversy over conscription provides the most telling case in point. While one component justified the resort to coalition as a means to tackle a problem that no single party dared to tackle alone, another accepted coalition as the price to be paid for keeping that vexing problem at bay.

Beneath a veneer of collaboration, there was profound mistrust. Transcending party lines, it indicated the increasing extent to which Liberals were divided from Liberals, and Tories from Tories. (Divisions within the Labour fold had been evident since the declaration of war.) F. W. Hirst, true to his Cobdenite faith, denounced the coalition as a deal between 'the Liberal imperialists and the Tory imperialists', who had banded together to rivet the chains of 'military slavery'. Except for his own articles in *The Economist*, the press could not be relied upon to help safeguard liberties. 'I fear that nearly all the Liberal journalists and newspaper proprietors can easily be got at and persuaded,' he told Sir John Brunner, from whom he solicited – and received – money to produce 'a good strong well argued pamphlet' against compulsion. Simultaneously, the pro-conscriptionists scented a whiff of treachery from the Unionist press, which seemed disposed to relent in its agitation in order to spare the feelings of Unionist ministers. Ronald McNeill, for example, wished to make certain that the coalition did not furnish an excuse for prolonged indecision. For that reason, he suggested to Bonar Law that Hugh Chisholm should be seconded from *The Times* to replace Steel-Maitland 'at the head of our Central Office'. Chisholm was known to be 'a keen believer in the political principles of our party'; his 'organising power' was legendary in Fleet Street, where it was urgently needed.[1]

Steel-Maitland stayed on until the close of 1916, when he was followed as party chairman by Sir George Younger (later 1st Viscount Younger of Leckie). Meanwhile, the fortunes of the Unionist press continued to dissipate. Although Garvin had employed the *Pall Mall Gazette* to superb advantage during the May crisis, he looked forward to emancipating himself from that daily burden. Through the early summer, he nursed the expectation that the *Pall Mall* would be saved from 'an unmitigated tragedy' by Dudley Docker, who would merge it with the *Globe*. However, Docker's offer, when finally tendered, was altogether too 'miserable'. Instead, the *Pall Mall* was acquired on 31 August by Davison Dalziel, who brought D. M. Sutherland from the *Evening Standard* to serve as editor. Without displacing Sutherland, Sir Henry Dalziel took over in 1917. Of greater concern to Garvin was the fate of the *Observer*. First of all, he agreed with Waldorf Astor, it 'should be independent

[1] Hirst to Brunner, 31 May 1915, Brunner Papers; McNeill to Bonar Law, 31 May 1915, Bonar Law Papers, 50/3/71.

of all other newspapers in this country'; secondly, it 'should continue, during this time of trouble which is coming, its National Policy'. Neither was easily managed. 'Northcliffe has so queered the pitch for honest critics,' complained Garvin, 'that it is difficult to open heavy guns without having one's motives and results confused with those of his mischievous games.'[1]

It was hard to say who had the greater grievance against Northcliffe, those whom he had opposed or those whom he had maladroitly tried to assist. Ousted from the Cabinet, Charles Hobhouse could have no better balm than Henry Chaplin's estimate that the circulations of *The Times* and the *Daily Mail* had plunged to 60 per cent. Oswald Partington, a retailer of newsprint, confirmed that those papers not only cancelled an order for 'special supplies', but also 'reduced their ordinary requirements'. Lord Hugh Cecil, a leading Tory proponent of coalition, reasoned that 'the papers do harm when they are wrong but much more harm when they are partly in the right', as in Northcliffe's case. 'One cannot help suspecting that the incessant jeremiads of (e.g.) *The Times* are unwholesome reading in Roumania & Bulgaria', where the allies were striving to sway neutral opinion. 'But at home the papers are certainly doing harm.' While 'some measure of compulsion may some time be necessary, the propaganda in its favour has been so inept & unskilful that opposition has been stirred up & strengthened', complained Cecil; to the detriment of the cause, there had been 'an attempt rather to agitate than to argue'. Bonar Law, closer to Army opinion, did not require persuasion. Continued attacks on the conduct of the War Office left him with 'no sympathy whatever with the Press as represented by the *Mail*. It is all Northcliffe, who is one of the most jumpy of men and rushes at everything, without any consideration, and really without any regard to anything except his own vanity.'[2]

Lord Milner, outside the government and a senior official of the National Service League, was at once less vulnerable and more disheartened. 'A great deal of fuss has been made about the "Northcliffe" agitation,' he observed in a memorandum written at Windsor, probably for the information of his royal host.

> Personally I discouraged it for all I was worth, foreseeing that, as Northcliffe is a 'red rag to a bull' not only to the Liberal but to a large section of the Unionist press, the fact of his making himself prominent in the agitation for National Service would create a reaction against it.

What Milner dreaded was 'just what has happened. Almost the whole Press – the *Morning Post* is almost the only exception – has joined in the hue and cry

---

[1] Waldorf Astor to Garvin [6 June 1915], 13 and 14 August 1915 (copies), and Garvin to Astor, 27 May 1915, 22 and 25 June 1915, Astor Papers; the details concerning the transfer of the *Pall Mall*, garbled in most accounts, are correct in Simonis, *Street of Ink*, pp. 108–109.
[2] Hobhouse's diary, 17 June 1915, *Inside Asquith's Cabinet*, p. 248; Cecil to Bonar Law, 25 June 1915, and Bonar Law to Sir J. Maclay, 14 June 1915, (copy), Bonar Law Papers, 50/4/45, 53/6/32.

against Northcliffe.' Nevertheless, it was possible to differentiate between the responses: on the one hand, 'a great many papers, while denouncing Northcliffe & declining to press the Govt., yet make it clear that they would support National Service', provided that the government – '& especially Lord Kitchener' – recommended it; 'on the other hand, some papers like the *Daily News*, the *Daily Chronicle*, the *Nation*, & the *Star* have thrown themselves furiously into the anti-Northcliffe agitation with the obvious intention of using the unpopularity of Northcliffe to damage the cause of National Service.'[1]

Milner did not exaggerate on either score. Northcliffe was indeed a liability to the conscriptionists and a boon to the voluntarists. On 31 July, the *Daily News* featured 'some reflections' by Gardiner on the first year of the war: 'In Germany, whose methods *The Times* and the *Daily Mail* seek to impose on this country, Lord Northcliffe would long ago have been dealt with as a public danger.' By contrast, the *Morning Post* tried to dissociate the movement for conscription from Northcliffe's compromising patronage. Commended by John Buchan of *The Times* as 'the only clean and patriotic paper in England', the *Post* shared Milner's apprehension that the issue would be decided not on its own merits, but rather on Northcliffe's demerits. And, Gwynne further suspected, the Liberal journals were doing their 'dirty work' at the instigation of 'certain Ministers', who would stop at nothing to thwart conscription. 'I admit all the folly of the Harmsworth propaganda,' he wrote to Kitchener's private secretary, 'but I see evil in the Radical press propaganda.'[2]

Perceptions of evil were reciprocal and uniformly predicated on the assumption that politicians were pulling strings. 'Lord Northcliffe and his friends are running an agitation here for conscription,' Harcourt advised Lord Liverpool in New Zealand, 'not because we are not getting sufficient men but because they think that it will damage the two men they hate most – Kitchener and the Prime Minister.' Frances Stevenson, Lloyd George's exceptionally devoted secretary, inferred that 'someone has bn. supplying the *Daily News* with information, and that someone is no doubt McKenna', who differed from Lloyd George (and resembled Harcourt) by adhering to the system of voluntary recruitment. Within the Cabinet as outside, the lines were jaggedly drawn.[3]

Kitchener was recognized, by virtue of his past valour and present non-party stance, to be pivotal. As early as 18 August, Margot Asquith had warned him of a plot to introduce compulsion, and begged him to stand by her husband, 'Grey, Crewe, Arthur Balfour, McKenna and Runciman' in order to 'beat Curzon, F. E. Smith, Winston and Ll. George'. The longer that Kitchener took to declare himself, the greater the tendency of both sides to bank on him.

[1] Memorandum by Milner, 29 August 1915, Milner Papers.
[2] Gwynne to Lady Bathurst, 26 August 1915, and Gwynne to Lt.-Col. O. A. G. Fitzgerald, 12 September 1915 (copy), Bathurst Papers.
[3] Harcourt to Liverpool, 4 September 1915 (copy), Harcourt Papers; entry of 17 September 1915, in Stevenson, *Lloyd George*, p. 60.

Gwynne fancied that, by 23 September, Kitchener had already 'made up his mind about Conscription, and we must not be too impatient for the announcement because he is preparing his figures so that they will be absolutely incontrovertible even by such despicable creatures as the *Daily News* and those who support it'. To Lady Bathurst, he professed renewed confidence that 'we shall both live to see National Service and Tariff Reform – Tariff Reform for certain'. Asquith, however, drew the opposite conclusion. Finding himself 'in a most critical situation' in mid-October, after Carson had resigned the attorney-generalship, he reminded Kitchener that 'so long as you and I stand together, we carry the whole country with us. Otherwise, the Deluge!' Obviously, either Gwynne or Asquith was mistaken.[1]

The immediate reason for Carson's resignation was the decision to evacuate British troops from the Dardanelles. Lloyd George and Bonar Law, without going to the same lengths, issued stiff protests. Although Carson was embraced by Northcliffe as 'a stout-hearted fellow', he forged more intimate links with Gwynne, Waldorf Astor, and Robinson. All of them agreed that Kitchener was useless, except as a prop to Asquith's waning authority. Yet they could not readily agree on an alternative. 'I have my doubts about L.G.,' Gwynne privately confessed. 'Indeed, who has not who knows him? But as sure as we are alive we shall come to some appalling disaster if we go on under the present man.' Gradually, Gwynne put aside his fears and intimated his preference for a Lloyd George premiership on the understanding that the Unionists were in no position to seize the helm. His only stipulation was that the substitution had to occur without a general election, 'for I consider this to be impossible in wartime'. No longer stigmatized as a Radical scourge, Lloyd George had come to impress his former adversaries as the most adaptive of Liberals and by far the most dynamic. Conversely, he gave disquiet to some of his old friends. Garvin 'blamed him for quarrelling with his own party' and asked Scott: 'What was the use of Ll.G. breaking with the *Daily Chronicle* & *Daily News* & cultivating the *Daily Mail* & *The Times*?'[2]

The 'balance', which Asquith had achieved in May, seemed to be tipping against him in early November. His first impulse was to dismiss Kitchener and (as in March 1914) annex the War Office to Downing Street, but Bonar Law sensibly cautioned against so drastic a step. Asquith then proposed to get Kitchener out of the way by dispatching him on a trumped-up mission to the Near East. In Kitchener's absence, Asquith intended to assume informal custody of the War Office with a view to putting its affairs in order. Maxse suspected that the ulterior purpose was to reinstate Haldane, and various

---

[1] Margot Asquith to Kitchener, 18 August 1915, and Asquith to Kitchener, 17 October 1915, Kitchener Papers, PRO 30/57/106, 76; Gwynne to Lady Bathurst, 23 September 1915, Bathurst Papers.

[2] *History of The Times*, IV, part 1, 281; Riddell, *War Diary* (21 October 1915), pp. 127–28; Gwynne to Sandars, 21 October 1915, Sandars Papers; memorandum by Scott, 13 and 14 November 1915, Scott Papers, Add. MSS. 50, 902, fols. 48–49.

Unionist dailies leapt to the same conclusion. On Saturday, 8 November, Haldane was astonished to read 'that Lord Kitchener had resigned & that I was to be put into his place', which was 'all very stupid'. He learnt that there had been 'a furious row', after which 'the Govt. plucked up courage & suppressed the *Globe*, which was one of the offenders'. For baldly stating that Kitchener had departed as the result of an altercation with his civilian colleagues, that paper was banned for a fortnight. Beaverbrook, withholding the incriminating fact that he had been one of the editor's informants, later recalled that 'when the errant newspaper was closed down the plan to change War Secretaries was closed down with it'. Kitchener remained in Whitehall, but Palmer quit his editorial office in the Strand. Bitterly resentful, he threatened a lawsuit against Docker, the proprietor, who had allegedly counselled him to attack Lloyd George on Kitchener's behalf. Thereafter, Palmer became assistant editor of *John Bull* and, from February 1920 until his death the following October, sat in Parliament as a Bottomley-style independent.[1]

The opportunity to refurbish the War Office was lost. Northcliffe, who felt 'particularly guilty' as one of the inventors of 'the K. myth', believed that the politicians could have outfaced their newspaper critics without engendering the 'disaffection' they feared. 'The public impression is that Mr Asquith has paralysed the efforts of Lord K. My opinion is that Lord K. was the Cabinet's old man of the sea,' Northcliffe told Lord Murray of Elibank: 'If the Government knew about newspapers and advertising – which they do not – they would realize that Lord K. is purely the creation of publicity, and as soon as his poster is off the hoardings and he is "kept out of the news", as the Americans say, he will cease to trammel action.' Always attracted to American methods, Northcliffe instructed his editors to delete from the columns of *The Times* and the *Daily Mail* all references that might be construed as 'puffing' Kitchener or 'booming' Churchill, his principal ally at this stage. Yet, apart from skewing the news coverage, Northcliffe's policy had little effect.[2]

For the time being, Northcliffe had to content himself with the increasingly sympathetic response he elicited from certain unlikely quarters. Lloyd George acknowledged the crippling effect of Kitchener's ineptitude. Massingham, diametrically opposed to Northcliffe on the issue of compulsion, none the less felt obliged 'to say that I think you have not had justice done you in respect of your general motives, considering all the facts you have known'. The 4th Earl

---

[1] Memorandum by Samuel, 26 May 1915, Samuel Papers; Lloyd George, *War Memoirs*, I, 311; Maxse to Chamberlain, 18 October 1915, Chamberlain Papers, AC/13/3/65; Haldane to his mother, 8 November 1915, Haldane Papers, Vol. 5994, fols. 149–50; Beaverbrook, *Politicians*, pp. 193–94; Sutherland to Lloyd George, 7 December [1915], Lloyd George Papers, D/1/1/10; *also see* Blake, *Unknown Prime Minister*, pp. 269–77. Simon, Home Secretary at the time of the *Globe*'s suppression, recalled that incident in an exchange with Lord Camrose, 27 March 1942, Simon Papers.

[2] Northcliffe to Murray, 8 November 1915, Northcliffe to Marlowe, 7 December 1915, and Northcliffe to Robinson, 30 December 1915 (copies), Northcliffe Papers; Northcliffe to Maxse, 29 October 1915, Maxse Papers.

Grey, Sir Edward's Tory cousin, refused to join 'the outcry against the Northcliffe Press. I admit it has sometimes given a wrong impression abroad, but Asquith's Govt. has never acted except in response to public opinion, and I am most grateful to *The Times* and *Daily Mail.*' The American ambassador, no longer quite so sure that Asquith qualified as 'a great man', spared a kindly thought on Christmas Day for 'poor Northcliffe. He thinks he's saved the nation from its miserable government, and the government now openly abuses him in the House of Commons.' That evening, Ambassador Page dined 'with a member of the Cabinet and he told me so much bad military news, which they prevent the papers from publishing or even hearing', that he was ready to believe 'that the war will last till 1918. That isn't impossible.' Northcliffe had always recognized this fearful possibility and continued to flail against it.[1]

* * *

'The question of conscription would indeed be a tedious topic to pursue through all its ramifications,' wrote Robert Blake, who thereby absolved himself of that laborious obligation. Following his artful precedent, this narrative will 'only notice a few salient points'.[2]

Kitchener survived the turmoil of November 1915 with undimmed popularity in the country, yet with diminished respect from his Cabinet colleagues, voluntarists and conscriptionists alike. His departmental responsibilities, already eroded by Lloyd George's control over munitions, were further circumscribed by the appointment of Lord Derby as Director-General of Recruiting. A keen advocate of National Service, Derby was – on the face of things – a curious choice. His brief was still more curious. Under his auspices, the system of voluntary recruiting was to be given a final chance to prove its efficacy and, if it failed, some form of military compulsion would be introduced. The implications were clear, although it was impolitic to dwell upon them.

On 23 May, when the coalition was in the process of formation, Garvin had predicted in the *Observer* that 'a scheme of compulsion, wisely and considerately framed, . . . will be accepted by the nation as a whole with relief and enthusiasm'. Disclaiming a devotion to 'compulsion for its own sake', he constructively argued that, if 'the new government' resolved to proceed with 'the registration of all able-bodied males between the ages of 18 and 55, to be called up as needed, that will be a complete system of National Service which could be made to work perfectly without compulsion'. It took much longer than Garvin and others had anticipated for the Asquith coalition to address the question of manpower. Ultimately, Derby promulgated a modified version of

---

[1] Massingham to Northcliffe, 23 December 1915, quoted in Havighurst, *Radical Journalist*, p. 241; Grey to Novar, 1 December 1915, quoted in Koss, *Haldane*, p. 156; Page to F. N. Doubleday and others, 25 December 1915, quoted in *Page*, II, 116. Page was doubtless referring to the seven-hour debate in the Commons on 30 November, when the Northcliffe press was castigated.

[2] Blake, *Unknown Prime Minister*, p. 282.

Garvin's scheme, restricted to unmarried men between the ages of eighteen and forty-one.

To most Liberals, Derby's proposals constituted an exercise in hair-splitting: without discarding the old procedures, they effectively discredited them and so paved the way for universal compulsion. Only Sir John Simon, however, made good his threat to resign in protest, thus depriving Northcliffe of the 'rare old bust-up' to which he had looked forward. 'Compulsion is near,' Northcliffe exulted on 28 December.[1] To more orthodox Unionists, it was not near enough. Lloyd George emphatically agreed with them.

From his vantage point at the *Daily Mail*, Tom Clarke detected 'a great liveliness now in Fleet Street', contrasting with the deadlock in the Cabinet. Lasting through the winter, it produced a new polarization within the political press, and prefigured the realignments of the following December. The *Manchester Guardian*, esteemed by Garvin as 'a daily newspaper second to none in the world for character and ability', was a straw in the wind. On 11 December, Scott journeyed to London 'primarily on Garvin's invitation to meet his proprietor Major Waldorf Astor MP – a charming person, quite young and full of enthusiasm and good-will'. During his four-day visit, Scott saw a good deal of Garvin, who preached 'that nothing could at present be done except to "create an atmosphere" by cautious but ... more significant criticism of the conduct of the war'. In addition, Scott held a series of interviews with Balfour, Bonar Law, Asquith, and, of course, Lloyd George. Invited to lunch with Lloyd George at Walton Heath, he had a chance encounter with Northcliffe, 'who had arrived unexpectedly'. Donald, who lived nearby, was not invited, but Scott called upon him and tried to reconcile him with Lloyd George. All in all, Scott was disappointed by the overwhelming pessimism of the politicians, Lloyd George included. Less than convinced by 'the case for compulsion', which he feared would provoke 'bloodshed at home as well as abroad and very grave labour troubles besides', he subsequently mystified Bonar Law – and irritated Lloyd George – by committing the *Manchester Guardian* to the line of 'being perfectly willing to accept compulsion on adequate evidence of its military necessity ... and total unwillingness to accept it without that'. For Scott, however, that was a major concession.[2]

The Liberal voluntarists were resigned to failure. 'Evidently there is no solid resistance anywhere to the George-Northcliffe influence,' lamented L. T. Hobhouse, 'and we may take it that the Cabinet will be more and more run by *The Times*.' Gardiner refrained from speaking out, sharing Scott's dread that the rejection of the Derby plan would bring the resignation of Asquith, followed ineluctably by the annihilation of Liberalism in a 'khaki' election, the

---

[1] Clarke, *Northcliffe Diary* (28 and 29 December 1915), pp. 85–87.
[2] Clarke, *Northcliffe Diary* (29 December 1915), p. 87; *Observer*, 23 May 1915; entries of 11–15 December 1915, 10–11 January and 28 (?) January 1916, Scott, *Political Diaries*, pp. 159–65, 169, 176.

accession of a Unionist dictatorship that would go straight for full-scale military and industrial compulsion, and the enactment of tariffs, which even the *Spectator* now approved as a wartime expedient. This reticence dismayed those who relied on the *Daily News* to resist 'this historic reversal of Liberalism and democracy', which the *Nation* (1 January 1916) saw to be 'led and promoted by Mr Lloyd George'. 'What has become of the *D.N.* these days?' demanded W. Llewelyn Williams, the Liberal MP for Carmarthen who had lost faith in his fellow Welshman:

> We are 'at the parting of the ways,' & no clear note in the Radical organ! I had a talk with A. P. N[icholson] on Wednesday. Indeed his article on Thursday was a pale reflection of my lurid talk! But I thought I detected a marked falling-off in his ardour against compulsion. I hope it isn't symptomatic of the paper's policy. Believe me, 'compulsion of single men' will be used by Ll.G. to justify all-round compulsion later on. That poor weakling of a P.M.! It is too pitiful. How can you make an invertebrate stand up?

Gardiner did not dispute this assessment, but declined to protest publicly for fear of undermining Asquith's position. Unlike Williams, who voted with the minority against the Military Service Bill on 5 January, he lamely reasoned on the 8th that it was better 'to accept this dangerous innovation in our national life' from Asquith's 'rather than from any other hand, for we know that he has come to his decision unwillingly, that he has yielded to considerations which are above suspicion, and that he will limit the operation of the system strictly to its present military needs'. In effect, he was praising the Prime Minister with faint damns.[1]

Asquith's supreme virtue, Gardiner implied, was his familiarity. To others, on both sides of the conscription issue, familiarity bred contempt. 'There is, unfortunately, no Prime Minister,' Northcliffe grumbled to Massingham. He adamantly denied the *Nation*'s assertion that he was acting out of 'some personal vendetta' against Asquith. That interpretation 'was invented by the oriental Donald of the *Chronicle*. I distrust Mr Asquith because he obviously distrusts himself.' Massingham, despite the pangs of sympathy he felt for Asquith, was no less severe in his printed judgments and still more caustic in his private communications. Asquith could expect no defence from him. Scott was scarcely more forthcoming in his support, Donald's eleventh-hour Asquithianism was transparently intended to show up Lloyd George, and Spender's dogged adherence was far too predictable to count for much. As if to compensate, Gardiner went overboard. Paying tribute to Asquith's 'patient wisdom and large statesmanship', he backhandedly extolled him as someone

---

[1] Hobhouse to Scott, 30 December 1915, quoted in Scott, *Political Diaries*, p. 166; Williams to Gardiner, 29 December 1915, Gardiner Papers; *also see* Williams's letter to the editor, *Daily News*, 18 November 1915.

who 'was big enough to do a base thing when he believed that something greater than his own honour was at stake'. Gardiner's hyperbole kept pace with the mounting pressures. Likening Asquith first to the noble Pitt and then to the nobler Abraham Lincoln, he marvelled at the Prime Minister's 'magnanimous calm' in the face of 'all the sneers and slanders' from the 'Dalziels, the McNeills and the Carsons, the Northcliffes and the Bathursts'.[1]

In his *Daily News* column on 1 April, Gardiner went out of his way to scorn the suggestion in the right-wing press that Carson would make a splendid war leader. Gwynne had been promoting this idea not only in the pages of the *Morning Post*, but also behind the scenes. 'Everything is prepared and I am only waiting for him to take the lead,' Gwynne stated on 20 March, after three months of intense effort on Carson's behalf. 'I have over 160 MPs of both sides sworn to stand by him, I have arranged the debates, got the facts together, got his private secretaries, his whips, in fact everything.' What Gwynne did not have, however, was the sanction of Bonar Law or Lloyd George or, preferably, the two together. 'The whole political situation is as bad as it can be; so bad indeed that it seems to me very doubtful if the present condition of things can continue,' Bonar Law revealed that same week to Croal of the *Scotsman*; 'but on the other hand I do not see the possibility of any change which would be an improvement.' His attitude, reportedly shared by Lloyd George, foredoomed Gwynne's designs for a Carsonite insurrection.[2]

Walking a tightrope, politicians risked being pushed to a fall by their newspaper cohorts. It was presumably for this reason that Bonar Law took Croal into his confidence. The adulation Carson enjoyed in the *Morning Post* was vitiated by the excesses of the *Daily Express*, which 'for the good of my health' he had 'given up reading, as it looks so like the *Daily News!*' Lord Derby was seriously embarrassed by an anti-ministerial blast in the *Liverpool Courier*, a paper that was assumed to represent his conscriptionist views. He 'definitely' assured Percy Woodhouse, one of the kingpins of Lancashire Unionism, 'that he knew nothing of the ... article until he read it, and that after it appeared, he asked the Editor to drop the matter without success'. Derby had more satisfactory results in Manchester with the *Daily Dispatch* and the *Evening Chronicle*, 'which he controls'. In the metropolitan press, he received particularly rough handling from the Northcliffe papers, possibly because he had declined to assist in the rescue of the *Manchester Courier*, which finally disappeared on 28 January 1916. Derby

---

[1] Northcliffe to Massingham, 17 and 26 January 1916 (copies), Northcliffe Papers; *Nation*, 20 April 1916; *Star*, 11 November 1915; *Daily News*, 29 January and 1 April 1916.
[2] Gwynne to Lady Bathurst, 20 March 1916, Bathurst Papers; Bonar Law to Croal, 25 March 1916, Bonar Law Papers, 53/6/66; Riddell, *War Diary* (19 March and 24 April 1916), pp. 165, 178; *also see* Churchill, *World Crisis*, III, 253–54.

was at a loss to understand Northcliffe, who 'has been pressing for my resignation in the *D. Mail* and in *The Times* has been urging me to stay'.[1]

Derby's bafflement was not usual. Northcliffe, whom Robinson diagnosed to be going through 'a bad bout' in the spring of 1916, was hitting out at politicians, right and left. Professing 'no anxiety to enter the Government', not that anyone had asked, he gave early notice of his ambition 'to take part in the final Peace Conference'. The presence in London of Colonel Edward M. House, special assistant to President Wilson, gave rise to 'talk' about peace aims which Northcliffe found unsettling. House, on his recurrent visits, avoided Northcliffe's company and consorted instead with Radical journalists, particularly Gardiner and Massingham.[2]

The vociferations of Northcliffe made lively reading, but bad politics. Massingham had a conversation with Morley, who remarked of *The Times*: 'It's very wicked, but (with a smile) it's very well done. I can't read any other paper.' The King, whom no one could mistake for an intellectual, was said to be one of the 'constant readers' of the *Daily Mail*. Not content with such a distinguished clientele, Northcliffe ventured vicariously into electoral combat. He threw his newspapers' support to Kennedy Jones, his old friend and business partner, who challenged the party truce by standing independently at an April by-election at Wimbledon. A calculated affront to both sets of party leaders, Jones's candidacy was condemned in the *Daily News*, where Gardiner deplored the lunacy of plunging 'the country back into the vortex of party politics' (15 April). Strachey deprecated Jones's bid in the *Spectator*, and privately expressed to Bonar Law and Steel-Maitland his 'indignation in regard to the way in which the Coalition Government is being treated by the Harmsworth Press'. Although a 'very keen Compulsionist' with 'a good many criticisms of the Government to make', Strachey pledged to support the coalition 'for all I am worth'. He was 'prepared if necessary to go further' than mere editorial service and would accept adoption 'as a Coalition candidate, pure and simple', in opposition to any maverick run by *The Times*. On the 19th, Jones was defeated at Wimbledon by 1,811 votes. Gardiner's reward was a joint message of 'thanks' from the Liberal and Unionist whips. Northcliffe reaped Jones's gratitude: 'Carmelite House helped me wonderfully. ... I shall have another "go" somewhere in the hope of further helping to get A[squith] out of his seat.' Printing House Square, where the pundits had rated his chances to be low (12 April), obliged him chiefly by issuing an appeal for motor cars to transport suburban electors to the polls (18 April). Soon to have better luck at Hornsey, Jones

---

[1] Carson to Blumenfeld, 18 May 1916, Blumenfeld Papers; Woodhouse to Bonar Law, 22 December 1915, Bonar Law Papers, 28/1/75; R. Hazel to Northcliffe, 16 November 1915, Northcliffe Papers; Derby to Esher, 25 March 1916, Esher Papers.

[2] Memorandum by Robinson, 14 May 1916, quoted in *History of The Times*, IV, part 1, 316–17; Northcliffe to Sir John Willison, 22 April 1916, quoted in Pound and Harmsworth, p. 498; Koss, *Fleet Street Radical*, pp. 212–14; Havighurst, *Radical Journalist*, pp. 244–45, 258.

meanwhile basked in Northcliffe's praise: 'Everyone thought you did wonderfully.'[1]

Jones, Northcliffe's satellite, was vaguely linked to Carson, who lurked in the shadows. With his defeat at Wimbledon, the Carsonite threat seemed to recede, only to revive with a vengeance in November. In the interim, Gardiner resumed his campaign against Lloyd George. It had been initiated late the previous summer, when Lloyd George was accused of coquetting with 'antidemocratic' elements and allowing his 'virtues' to be 'exalted to throw your chief and your colleagues into deeper disrepute' (18 September 1915). On 22 April, Gardiner published a second 'Letter to Mr Lloyd George,' whose virtues were no longer conceded. 'Your friends have been silent long.... They have pretended not to know what they know only too well,' Lloyd George was told in that morning's *Daily News* and again in that evening's *Star*. 'You have escaped not only insult; you have escaped exposure. You will escape no longer. If you are determined that the country shall choose between you and Mr Asquith it shall not make its choice in ignorance of you.' Lloyd George was branded 'one of the chief architects of the fall of the Liberal Government and of the establishment of the Coalition', who had since worked 'in close intimacy' with the 'chief assailants' of his own colleagues.

Gardiner wrote in anticipation of a second and tougher Military Service Bill, for which Lloyd George was strongly agitating. The government seemed on the brink of collapse and, within days, was further afflicted by disorders in Ireland. More a *cri de coeur* than a manifesto, Gardiner's 'attack' was put down to 'political causes' by Bonar Law, who considered it 'vicious and uncalled for'. Far from shattered by the blow, Lloyd George jauntily told Riddell 'that the *Daily News* article had really served him a good turn. It had rallied the Conservatives around him and also a number of people who dislike personal attacks.' Yet the incident must have rankled, for Lloyd George returned to it the next day, when he relished Bonar Law's comment that had he 'paid Gardiner to attack him in the *Daily News*, the result could not have been more in his favour. The effect has been to show the public that he (L.G.) was the only Minister not responsible for the recruiting muddle.'[2]

Among Radicals, Gardiner's tirade met a mixed reception. 'Some of it was sound enough,' thought Dr Christopher (later Viscount) Addison, 'but Gardiner missed the point of what is necessary to beat the Germans.' Old Joseph Rowntree read 'with pain ... Mr Gardiner's letter', which was 'evidently

---

[1] Massingham to Northcliffe, 28 April [1916], Jones to Northcliffe, 25 April 1916, and Northcliffe to Jones, 27 April 1916 (copy), Northcliffe Papers; Clarke, *Northcliffe Diary* (September, n.d., 1916), p. 101; Strachey to Bonar Law, 17 April 1916, Bonar Law Papers, 53/1/13; Strachey to Steel-Maitland, 17 April 1916 (copy), Strachey Papers; Gulland to Gardiner, 25 April 1916, Gardiner Papers.

[2] Riddell, *War Diary* (24, 28, and 29 April 1916), pp. 176, 179, 180. The following November, Lloyd George 'referred incidentally to Gardiner's earlier attack' at breakfast with Scott. Memorandum by Scott, 20–22 November 1916, Scott Papers, Add. MSS. 50, 903, fols. 83–84.

written under great irritation, and in lamentable forgetfulness of the splendid service to freedom which Lloyd George has given in the past'. There was no denying that Lloyd George had lately allied himself with those who had 'opposed his great measures of reform' and who now abused other Liberals. On that score, Rowntree was inclined to 'think Gardiner's words . . . will meet with general response from thoughtful people'. However many 'thoughtful people' Gardiner may have aroused, he knew that he made a slight impact on the public at large. 'Alpha of the Plough', his alter ego in the *Star*, exchanged a few 'Words at the Pig and Whistle' with 'Mr Higgins', who mindlessly parroted the *Daily Mail*'s litany of 'muddle, muddle, muddle, and wobble, wobble, wobble' on the part of a government allegedly in the pay of Berlin.[1]

Lloyd George was not primarily concerned with the likes of 'Mr Higgins', who followed opinion, and only at a distance. More important to him were the opinion-makers. As Beaverbrook shrewdly discerned, Lloyd George accepted newspaper comment 'as one of the most important presentations of the national mind'. Leading articles were 'the straws' that he used to determine 'which way the wind is blowing'. If they were critical, he would not be deflected, but would 'spare no pains' to ' "wangle" the critic round to a favourable view of his policy'. Many a wangle turned into a wrench. 'Mr Lloyd George likes praise – but not from a delight in flattery,' insisted Beaverbrook. 'He likes a good Press as a shopkeeper likes a good customer.'[2]

To satisfy those customers, Lloyd George employed William ('Bronco Bill') Sutherland, one of his secretaries at the Ministry of Munitions, as a press officer. Sutherland's dual responsibility, which expanded elastically through the war, was to keep Lloyd George abreast of what the papers were saying and to keep them from saying anything too harshly critical about Lloyd George. His 'egregious reputation for rumbustious intriguing only serves to confirm Lloyd George's own doubtful character in the minds of those who did not or could not compete in the same race for popularity,' one historian has observed. 'Although but few instances of his methods are documented', these are amply sufficient to justify the impression 'that Sutherland regularly, and crudely, manipulated the public account of events to enhance Lloyd George's personal popularity'. Or, as it was maliciously put into rhyme:

> When dirty Mr George desired to soothe
> The still more dirty Mr Handel Booth,
> He found convenient to his dirty hand
> The really filthy William Sutherland.[3]

---

[1] Addison's diary, 28 April 1916, quoted in Addison, *Politics from Within* (London, 1924), I, 251; Rowntree to E. R. Cross, 26 April 1916, Lloyd George Papers, D/20/2/90; *Star*, 4 May 1916.
[2] Beaverbrook, *Politicians*, pp. 108–109.
[3] John Turner, *Lloyd George's Secretariat* (Cambridge, 1980), p. 168; Belloc's verse (referring to Sutherland and F. Handel Booth, the 'ginger' Liberal MP for Pontefract) was given by R. H. Davies to Roger Fulford, who quoted it in the *Times Literary Supplement* (12 March 1971) and

On 3 May, the *Daily News* characterized the 'compulsion campaign', now nearing its climax, as 'only a means to an end': its underlying purpose was to discredit Asquith and to smash Liberalism for ever. Sutherland, after studying this article, concluded that the paper had 'so much overdone its attack' that a reply would be gratuitous. Lloyd George could dispose of the controversy 'by mentioning incidentally' that it was irresponsible journalism 'to stir up strife ... after an agreement has been arrived at by the Government on the questions at issue'.[1] Lloyd George would probably have taken this suggestion, but for a renewed onslaught by Gardiner three days later. Mocking the Minister for Munitions as nothing more than a Harmsworth hero, he recalled Lloyd George's earlier and more modest estimates of Britain's manpower capability and warned that the nation would ruin itself if it 'tried, at Mr George's inspiration, to do what Mr George said we could not do'.

Provoked beyond endurance, Lloyd George delivered a speech that day to his constituents at Conway, where he alluded with contempt 'to a cloudy discharge of poison gas' released by an 'assassin' in Fleet Street. 'I seek neither his friendship nor his support,' Lloyd George 'hissed out', according to the *Daily News*'s reporter. Gardiner replied on Monday, the 8th, that he was happy to be 'dismissed ... from the charmed circle of your friendship'; but, friend or foe, Lloyd George was not permitted to ignore 'an accusation which you know to be true and to which you have no answer. ... The charge against you,' Gardiner reiterated, 'is not that you have had disagreements with Mr Asquith, but that you have had agreements with Mr Asquith's declared enemies and the enemies of the Government.' Lloyd George was told that he could not 'walk in step with Mr Asquith and Lord Northcliffe at the same time'. It was not too late to 'make a wise choice', and, if he did, it might yet be possible 'to win the war with you and not without you'. Gardiner's condescension portended an unwitting irony.

Lloyd George was in no mood for penitence. He and Churchill 'got to talking' over breakfast on 14 June 'about ... the London Liberal papers'. Scott listened to their conversation with rapt attention:

> They had nothing to say about the *Westminster* except that you always knew what it was going to say. The one thing about which Spender was really interesting was Education. The *Chronicle* was fairly good but you never knew where you wd. have it. The *Daily News* was a poor thing. 'I dislike its mentality,' said Ch. Then with enthusiasm 'There's only one Liberal paper – the *M.G.*'

On recent occasions, Lloyd George had been 'rather cross' with the *Manchester Guardian*, which he found 'unnecessarily offensive' with respect to

---

identified it in a letter to the author, 26 July 1982. Sutherland, knighted in 1919, was Coalition Liberal MP for Argyll, 1918–24.

[1] Memorandum by Sutherland, 3 May 1916, Lloyd George Papers, D/1/1/17.

himself. But this stickiness was conveniently forgotten. Lloyd George and Churchill 'discussed the old theme' of bringing the *Guardian* to London, where it might exert a more direct influence. 'What wd. it cost?' Lloyd George asked Scott, who 'said £20,000 a year'. 'That's not much,' declared Lloyd George. 'All the same it is,' Scott reflected silently.[1]

At this moment, Lloyd George was especially susceptible to newspaper opinion. Eight days earlier, Kitchener was drowned, when the ship taking him to Russia struck a mine. ('Providence is on the side of the British Empire after all,' Northcliffe gleefully told his sister.) Scott saw Lloyd George as 'the natural person ... to succeed Kitchener as Secretary of State'; but Lloyd George was unwilling to take the post without the full jurisdiction over strategy and appointments that Kitchener had surrendered (in writing) to Sir William Robertson, Chief of the Imperial General Staff. On 17 June, Lloyd George drafted a lengthy memorandum in which he put the case for 'a Secretary of State for War who, apart from possessing personality, will possess real power and influence'. That day, he was furious to read in the *Daily Chronicle* a leading article which urged the next War Secretary to be content to 'shine in his own orbit, without infringing on the orbit of the Chief of the General Staff'. This editorial argument, Lloyd George contended, was really 'most harmful: it will prejudice the negotiations with Robertson. . . . And it is by no means certain that I shall go to the War Office.' Yet neither this mishap nor Margot Asquith's qualms about Lloyd George's suitability ('Was he not too much of a pressman – too mixed up with the press – the Northcliffe press?') prevented Lloyd George's terms from being met.[2]

Soon after his arrival at the War Office, Lloyd George issued instructions for the 'compulsory acquisition' of the National Liberal Club; a gathering place for disgruntled Radicals, it was commandeered for war purposes, specifically the compilation of a national register. This edict, protested the *Nation* (9 September) and the *Daily News* (9 and 12 September), added insult to injury. 'Massingham and Gardiner have been bitter,' minuted Sutherland, 'but they have a very small following.' The *Morning Post*, with a larger following among the military-minded, savagely berated Lloyd George on 28 September for spending too much time across the Channel, where he was said to have 'spoken very freely about the shortcomings of our generals' to their French counterparts. Such accusations were 'the invention of an ill-conditioned mind in search of mischief,' Lloyd George replied publicly. Scott, repelled by Lloyd George's

---

[1] Memorandum by Scott, 12–17 June 1916, Scott Papers, Add. MSS. 50, 903, fol. 53; for instances of their dissension, see memorandum of 28 (?) January 1916, and Lloyd George to Scott, 20 April 1916, in Scott, *Political Diaries*, pp. 176, 202.

[2] Scott, *Political Diaries*, p. 221; H. A. Taylor, *Donald*, pp. 92–93; Lloyd George, *War Memoirs*, I, 457. According to Donald's biographer, the offending 'article ... was not forgotten': from the time of its publication in June until Lloyd George's elevation to the premiership in December, he and Donald 'did not meet, although they spent most of their week-ends as near neighbours at Walton Heath, and played golf on the same course'.

jingo rhetoric about ending the war with nothing less than a 'knock-out blow', did not call at the War Office when he came to London in October and instead 'saw McKenna by appointment at the Treasury'. The War Office was now off-limits to Donald, who compensated by an intimacy with Robertson and Bonar Law. Though he 'was not in the habit of seeing the Prime Minister', Donald went so far as to telephone Downing Street for an appointment.[1]

One of the few newspapermen who crossed Lloyd George's new threshold, easily and repeatedly, was Northcliffe. Lloyd George was 'a shirt-sleeve politician', he told Sir Douglas Haig, who had replaced French as the British Commander in Chief, who 'does whatever he, N., advises!' On 6 October, Northcliffe lunched secretly with Lloyd George at Milner's house in Westminster. 'A great deal of important information was elicited which you ought to know,' he wrote afterwards to their host, who had not been present. Edmund Gosse, a student of political affairs since his librarianship in the House of Lords, recalled Rothermere's description of Northcliffe as 'a perpetual weathercock' and volunteered his 'impression – for what it is worth –' that Northcliffe 'thinks that Grey and Asquith ... cannot last much longer'. Scott suspected something much more sinister: 'There is a rumour going about – I shd. hope quite unfounded – that Northcliffe has some information', perhaps about the Marconi scandal, 'which he holds over Lloyd George in terrorem'.[2]

Despite the reproaches that conscience occasionally forced him to deliver, Scott continued to credit Lloyd George with a residual Liberalism. If Asquith were to step aside, as events seemed to warrant, his successor 'must almost inevitably be Lloyd George', Scott wrote to Hobhouse on 28 November. Northcliffe stumbled towards the same conclusion from the opposite direction, ascribing Lloyd George's effectiveness to his emancipation from Liberal restraints. In this vein, *The Times* hailed the War Secretary on 7 November as 'a great driving force and an invaluable leader of democracy in war'. One could hardly expect, however, that the relationship between two such highly egocentric personalities as Lloyd George and Northcliffe would be devoid of friction. Aitken, whose favourite recreation was to undo his own mischief, disclosed to one of Lloyd George's private secretaries – who informed the other and thence Lloyd George – 'how Northcliffe had been to him & told him that he was out to destroy Ll.G. "I want your help, too,"' Northcliffe was quoted as saying. 'I am going to get as many newspapers as possible to help me.' Afterwards, Beaverbrook described how he had pleaded 'in vain' to

---

[1] Notes by Sutherland, n.d., with cuttings, Lloyd George Papers, E/1/4/7; entry of 2–3 October 1916, Scott, *Political Diaries*, p. 227; memorandum by Donald, 24 November 1916, quoted in H. A. Taylor, *Donald*, pp. 110–11.

[2] Haig to his wife, 11 September 1916, quoted in *The Private Papers of Douglas Haig, 1914–1919* (ed. R. Blake; London, 1952), p. 166; Northcliffe to Milner, 6 October 1916, quoted in Pound and Harmsworth, p. 507; Gosse to Haldane, 31 October 1916, Haldane Papers, Vol. 5913, fols. 75–76; memorandum by Scott, 20–22 November 1916, Scott Papers, Add. MSS. 50, 903, fol. 85.

temper the hostility of Lloyd George, who retorted that he 'would as soon go for a sunny evening stroll round Walton Heath with a grasshopper as try and work with Northcliffe'.[1]

Both at the time and in retrospect, it suited Aitken to emphasize the discord between Lloyd George and Northcliffe. His image of himself as the perpetrator of the 'honest intrigue' that brought down the Asquith government compelled him to discount the influence of his rival for that coveted distinction. Northcliffe, in turn, took to celebrating the December upheaval as his own victory. 'Who killed Cock Robin?' the *Morning Post* impudently asked on 4 December. 'You did,' Cecil Harmsworth told his eldest brother, who did not demur. Whether, in fact, Northcliffe or Aitken was as instrumental as either made out remains a moot point.[2]

To adjudicate between these – and other – conflicting claims would be a taxing and ultimately pointless exercise. 'It would take a combination of Meredith, Browning, & Henry James to give you the story of our change of Govt.,' J. A. Spender wrote to a friend after the event. 'The old P.M. – bless his memory – never could see that by neglecting the art of advertisement he was handing himself over body & soul to the Northcliffe Press & its hero,' he went on. His brother Harold offered a contrasting interpretation. 'It was certainly not the fault of Mr Lloyd George,' he dutifully protested, if he happened to attract admiration from certain 'friends of the Press . . . [who] stood honestly and boldly for a more active prosecution of the war. . . . It was preposterous to expect that he should reject their help.' While the younger Spender dismissed the 'mean and unworthy insinuations' that Lloyd George had contracted 'a working alliance' with Northcliffe, he acknowledged that the two men had reached 'a fortuitous temporary agreement in regard to the conduct of the war'. That, both Spenders could agree, was the prologue to the drama that unfolded in early December. About the climax, however, neither they nor anyone else could pretend to certainty.[3]

*   *   *

In late October 1916, W. H. Mudford died. More than fifteen years earlier, he had retired as editor of the *Standard*, a venerable morning paper that now stood on the brink of collapse. He was a forgotten figure, whose obituaries 'surprise[d] the public with information that a few days ago he was still alive'. Sir Henry Lucy, who remembered him from their prime, recollected how Mudford 'withdrew into his shell with increasing persistency, . . . never lunched or dined out', and 'neither granted nor sought interviews with political

---

[1] Entry of 18 November 1916 in Stevenson, *Lloyd George*, p. 125; Beaverbrook, *Politicians*, pp. 360–61.
[2] Taylor, *Beaverbrook*, p. 102; Pound and Harmsworth, p. 513.
[3] Spender to ? [December 1916] (copy), Spender Papers, Add. MSS. 46, 392, fol. 251; H. Spender, *The Prime Minister* (London, 1920), pp. 239–43.

personages'. Yet, in equally large measure, his success in Fleet Street and his weight in party councils had gained from this elusiveness. The paradox of Mudford's career was especially irresistible during the First World War. Then, as Gardiner observed, newspapermen were conspicuous 'amongst the very greatest of mankind. They rank with Prime Ministers, peers, and princes of the Church: *primus inter pares.*'[1]

The story of the December upheaval has been told many times. To a greater or lesser extent, the participation of journalists, either individually or collectively, has figured in each narration. Interpretations have varied strikingly with regard to emphasis and moral judgment. Some would have it that the press manufactured the crisis, others that the press merely brought it to culmination. In any case, newspapers have received credit - or blame - for an unusual degree of public activism. 'Could Lloyd George have become prime minister without the aid of the press?' one scholar has asked. 'It is doubtful. Or at least not at that time and not in that way,' he has replied to his own question. 'The press caught and reflected Britain's mood in late 1916. Lloyd George rode to Downing Street on the crest of that wave.'[2]

That, so far as it goes, is a compelling argument. At least for present purposes, however, it does not go quite far enough. For, without begging the issues, it adeptly circumvents some of them by positing a false antithesis between editorial and political currents and, moreover, by suggesting that a national 'mood' could have existed independently of either, much less of both. In fact, the preceding weeks had witnessed an intensified convergence of interests, with the result that professional and party lines became hopelessly entangled. It was difficult to ascertain who was prompting whom, on whose behalf, and in what capacity. Aitken, for example, was as yet better known as a parliamentary promoter than as a newspaper proprietor; but his 'notes' reveal that he schemed complementarily in different spheres, ignoring considerations of conventional partisanship.[3] Northcliffe was first and foremost a press magnate, though no less a political powerhouse for that. Sir George Riddell and Sir Henry Dalziel were newspaper-owning members of Lloyd George's entourage, the first outside Parliament and the second within. Better than a seat at Westminster, Gwynne boasted an intimacy with Carson, who also communicated with Blumenfeld and, most decisively, with Robinson. Through Aitken, Blumenfeld was linked to Bonar Law, who was oddly accessible to Donald as well. Garvin exploited Astor's contacts in addition to his own. Marlowe's impressions were filtered through Northcliffe, and Scott's through a haze of wishful thinking. That Gardiner and J. A. Spender functioned with relative autonomy reflected not so much their own inclinations as

---

[1] Entry of 30 October 1916, Lucy, *The Diary of a Journalist* (London, 1923), III, 286-87; interview with Gardiner, *Christian Commonwealth*, 3 March 1915.
[2] J. M. McEwen, 'The Press and the Fall of Asquith,' *Historical Journal*, xxi (1978), 882-83.
[3] Taylor, *Beaverbrook*, pp. 106-107.

the growing impotence of the Asquithian cause. Within the universe of political journalism, these and other orbits constantly intersected. If, therefore, the press 'caught and reflected' a general 'mood', it was one that newspapers had helped materially to create.

Ostensibly of minor significance, the parliamentary debate on 8 November over the disposal of confiscated enemy property in Nigeria sounded the death knell of the Asquith coalition. Bonar Law, as Colonial Secretary, was obliged to defend ministerial policy against Carson, who proved to command substantial and passionate Unionist support. There emerged the twin threat that Carson might wrest the Unionist leadership from Bonar Law, ignominiously shackled to the Liberals, or that Asquith might opt for a dissolution, potentially devastating to Unionist prospects. To guard against either eventuality, Aitken – who 'had practically fallen out of British politics' in recent months – brought Bonar Law into contact with Carson and Lloyd George. Though he later obscured the fact, he was seeing Lloyd George almost daily at the War Office and must have known that Lloyd George and Carson were both disaffected. Gradually, Bonar Law's reservations were overcome, and 'the Triumvirate' took shape. On the 25th, Aitken drafted a proposal for the appointment of a small and select War Council, over which Lloyd George would preside. Bonar Law, after honing the prose, was deputized to convey the document to Asquith, who was requested to promulgate it as his own communiqué. Apprised of the basic terms beforehand, Asquith did not seem 'altogether opposed to the idea', which he agreed to consider over the weekend. His reply, delivered to Bonar Law on Monday morning, the 27th, was unexpectedly negative. To retrieve the situation, which was fast disintegrating, Bonar Law prevailed upon Asquith 'to have a frank talk with Lloyd George' on Friday, 1 December. Meanwhile, he set about mollifying his Unionist lieutenants, whose distrust of Lloyd George was second only to their resentment of Carson.[1]

Intentionally or not, the newspapers forced the pace of events. On the 23rd, the *Morning Post* signalled Carson's concordat with Lloyd George, whom that paper recognized as 'a force to which the nation may adhere, which the nation may follow'. Gardiner, writing two days later in the *Daily News*, preached that Lloyd George would 'do well to refuse the proffered crown of the *Morning Post* and to beware of those who go about with lists of new Cabinets in their pockets'. Yet few editors, even on the Liberal side, could resist the mounting temptation to draw up such lists. Scott, guided by talks with Lloyd George on the 21st and 22nd, came to contemplate the likelihood of a Lloyd George premiership 'with Asquith possibly as Lord Chancellor and Balfour in some purely honorary office'. While he restricted these nominations to his private correspondence, Donald rushed into print on

---

[1] Blake, *Unknown Prime Minister*, pp. 305–307; Taylor, *Beaverbrook*, pp. 108–13.

2 December with a roster identical to the one that Aitken had fed to the *Daily Express*.[1]

Donald's performance in the *Daily Chronicle* was especially important in view of the controversy it sparked. By his own testimony, he lunched on the 24th with Robertson, who proclaimed himself 'in favour of some arrangement which gave Mr Lloyd George greater power'. Afterwards, he 'called on Mr Bonar Law at the Colonial Office' and found him 'rather despondent' about the clumsiness of the existing War Council, but with 'no scheme to propose just then'. Bonar Law planned to broach the subject with Asquith and urged Donald to do the same. 'As a matter of fact', Donald did telephone Downing Street for an appointment, but decided that 'it would be inadvisable' to interview the Prime Minister 'before we published an article'.[2]

The article in question, entitled 'The Trials of the Coalition', appeared on Wednesday morning, the 29th. 'The Ministry's arch-defect,' it maintained, 'is inability to make up its mind', and 'mere changes of personnel' would not suffice to provide the 'firmer methods needed'. The severity of tone, no less than the explicit demand for reconstruction, 'created an immense sensation in political circles', recalled Harry Jones, the paper's lobby correspondent. 'My dear Harry,' Jones was greeted that afternoon by Geoffrey Howard, one of the Liberal whips, 'there is a dirty intrigue on against the P.M. I hope that the *Chronicle* is not in it.' In spite of Howard's fears that this 'article coming now will encourage the plotters', he credited Jones's innocence more readily than one of Asquith's biographers, who has unconvincingly ascribed the episode to a campaign by Carson and Aitken to intensify 'the newspaper pressure upon Asquith'.[3]

J. A. Spender, another of Asquith's biographers, knew better. Unlike Donald, who had been fended off, Spender was always welcome at Number Ten. Days earlier, he had discussed the problem with Asquith, who 'said he was sick of all this gossiping and whispering and was determined to take no notice of it'. But notice had to be taken and, on the afternoon of the 29th, Spender took it in the *Westminster Gazette*. His front-page leader deplored 'an appearance of delay and indecision, which may belie the fact, but none the less makes an unhappy impression' that critics did not hesitate to exploit. Donald marvelled at the coincidence. 'Some of our friends,' he subsequently wrote to Spender, 'thought there was collusion between us, which, as you know, was not the case.' Spender confirmed that he had 'had no prompting except my own unaided wits'. Just as Donald had intended his article as 'friendly criticism, although I believe it was not accepted as such', Spender defended 'the right of friendly journalists to say what the consequences would be ... unless the old

[1] Scott to Hobhouse, 28 November 1916, quoted in Scott, *Political Diaries*, p. 235; Donald to Blumenfeld, 27 February 1917, Blumenfeld Papers.
[2] Memorandum by Donald, 24 November 1916, quoted in H. A. Taylor, *Donald*, pp. 110–11.
[3] Memorandum by Jones, n.d., Beaverbrook Papers, Box IV/5; Jenkins, *Asquith* (London, 1964), p. 426.

Government could shake itself loose and get out of the trap'. As it proved, friendship betrayed their purpose.[1]

By the time of this remorseful exchange, the trap had been sprung, and 'the old Government' was no more. Donald and Spender ought to have realized that their separate warnings on the 29th would be wilfully construed as indictments. Neither, however, had been able to gauge the imminence of the crisis, much less the scale of impending changes. In a sense, each unwittingly served as an accessary to a movement which gathered strength throughout that week.

On Monday, the 27th, Robinson recorded in his diary 'an immense series of interviews at the Office', followed by 'an important dinner' at the home of F. S. Oliver. There, he, Milner, Astor, and Sir Henry Wilson 'definitely counselled the much harassed Carson to pull L.G. out' of the government 'rather than go on w[ith] the present indecision about everything'. Lloyd George's resignation was known to be a distinct possibility, though Unionist antagonism was expected to weigh heavily against him. For him to join Carson in opposition would certainly weaken the ministry, but not necessarily bring it down. On Thursday, when Northcliffe paid 'his weekly visit to London', Robinson 'impressed him with the importance of having no minor squabble w[ith] L.G. at a moment when it was really necessary to reconstruct the Govt. and only L.G. cd. do it'. Northcliffe, as eager to get back into the picture as to lend a hand, 'undertook to see' Lloyd George the next day. *The Times*, fulminating against 'Weak Methods and Weak Men', was his calling card.[2]

Friday was an unusually busy day for Lloyd George. He breakfasted at Riddell's with Lord Burnham, who had succeeded the previous January to his father's barony and the ownership of the *Daily Telegraph*. Angling for increased press support, Lloyd George remarked to Burnham 'that Northcliffe has deserted me'. Later that morning, Lloyd George saw Aitken, who urged him to resign if his full demands were not met and conceivably helped to draft the statement in which those demands were stiffened by the outright exclusion of Asquith from the projected War Council. Lord Derby dropped in and approved the document. Bonar Law, who was shown it after delivery, was less enthusiastic. Statement in hand, Lloyd George crossed Downing Street to keep the appointment with Asquith that Bonar Law had fixed. He returned in time to receive Northcliffe, who 'turned up' at his doorstep, 'grovelling, and trying to be friends'. According to Frances Stevenson: 'He (N.) acknowledges that D. is the only man who can save the country, & N. will back him.' Aitken, too, vowed 'to put his money on Ll.G. and will give him the backing of the *Express*', the closest he yet had come to admitting the fact of his proprietorship. In preparation for a negative response from Asquith, who had promised a

---

[1] Spender and Asquith, II, 244; McEwen, 874; Donald to Spender, n.d., and Spender to Donald, n.d., quoted in H. A. Taylor, *Donald*, p. 113.
[2] Robinson's diary, 27 and 30 November 1916, Dawson Papers.

'definite answer' at eleven o'clock on Saturday morning, Lloyd George was 'rallying all his forces around him'. He did not conceal from Northcliffe that his 'ultimatum was apparently unsatisfactory to the P.M.'[1]

Before nightfall, the *Evening Standard* appeared on the newsstands with 'An Appeal' to Lloyd George, who was implored to 'do your part without counting the cost, without calculation as to personal results'. Harry Jones had 'no doubt' that this message was inspired, if not actually written, by J. W. Pratt, MP for Linlithgow and secretary of the Liberal War Committee, a Lloyd George ginger group. The 'important political changes' demanded by Lloyd George were now widely broadcast. Not to be outdone, Aitken telephoned Blumenfeld with instructions to headline Lloyd George's scheme ('Coalition Crisis – New War Control') in Saturday's *Express*. More deviously, he set to work to ensnare Donald, who simultaneously aired these revelations in the *Chronicle*. Whereas Aitken dealt directly with Blumenfeld, he was careful to approach Donald circuitously. The story was first planted with Edward Price Bell, the London correspondent of the *Chicago Daily News*, who was advised to attribute it to War Office sources. Bell imparted the information to Donald, who checked with the War Office, where Lloyd George's underlings were poised to verify the details. How much Lloyd George knew – or wished to know – about this manoeuvre is difficult to say. 'No one knew better than Aitken how to keep a secret,' A. J. P. Taylor has testified, 'and also no one knew better how to run a publicity campaign.'[2]

Maximum publicity was vital to Lloyd George, who aimed to extract concessions from Asquith or, failing that, to resign in a blaze of public adulation. It was equally vital to Aitken, who sought to rule out an accommodation. The Saturday papers, led by the *Express* and the *Chronicle*, obliged them both in ample measure. In possession of fewer details, most of the others pounded away at the government, but exempted Lloyd George from their condemnations. The *Daily Telegraph* accorded him notable solicitude, while *The Times* and the *Morning Post* focused upon the defects of his colleagues. The *Daily Mail* directed its fire at Asquith, Grey, Balfour, and – as something of an afterthought – Haldane. Clarke, sent to Northcliffe's house in St James's Place to fetch the copy for Saturday's leading article, returned to Carmelite House with explicit instructions. 'I want the word "Government" in quotes all the way through the article,' said Northcliffe. 'And I want it extra leaded' for emphasis. 'The heading is to be "The Slackers: A National Danger". And the contents bill is to be "Asquith A National Danger".' Marlowe accepted the text without the trappings. Applying an editorial 'brake on the Chief's

---

[1] Riddell, *War Diary* (1 December 1916), p. 225; Frances Stevenson's diary, 1 and 2 December 1916, quoted in *Lloyd George*, pp. 130–31; Robinson's diary, 'Saturday' [2 December 1916], Dawson Papers.
[2] Memorandum by Jones, n.d., Beaverbrook Papers, Box IV/5; Taylor, *Beaverbrook*, pp. 113–14.

impetuosity', he headed the article 'The Limpets: A National Danger' and repeated this catch-phrase on the contents bills.[1]

Ignoring Lloyd George and seemingly unaware of his ultimatum, Gardiner addressed 'A Letter to a Critic' in the columns of Saturday's *Daily News*. Insisting that he did not 'regard Mr Asquith as a godlike person', he none the less refused to 'be among the mongrel pack that yelps at his heels'. Wide of the mark, he identified the leader of the pack as Northcliffe, a creature of 'fickle emotions', whom Robertson Nicoll had had the audacity to condone in the current issue of the *British Weekly*. Northcliffe was incapable of providing the type of criticism that gave 'helpful advice and stimulus' to any administration; instead he specialized in 'the ignorant hysteria fomented by a sensational and irresponsible Press'. Gardiner had said all this before. This time, however, his prose was elegiac and his mood was unmistakably defeatist. He was sadly 'prepared to admit that Mr Asquith failed to deal with the menace' by securing adequate 'newspaper advertisement'. The implication was that this failure was irrevocable.

No one could have faulted Lloyd George on that score. On Saturday, he wired Scott, inviting him to Sunday lunch at Walton Heath. Before Scott's arrival, *Reynolds's Newspaper* broke the sabbath calm with a scoop, which Beaverbrook took to be 'an interview with Lloyd George written in the third person'. Given Lloyd George's intimacy with Sir Henry Dalziel, the authenticity of *Reynolds*'s information was automatically assumed. 'Grave Cabinet Crisis,' proclaimed the headline: 'Lloyd George to Resign,' with the threat of a 'Campaign in the Country' to follow. *Reynolds*'s, which did not normally attend to affairs of state, explained that 'the final step' was being 'delayed at the request of several of Mr Lloyd George's colleagues in the Cabinet', but might be expected that very day. The issues were delineated with startling clarity and, not the least coincidentally, Lloyd George's concerns were phrased in much the same way as they appeared in the letter of resignation he had drafted.[2]

Accompanied by Scott, Lloyd George hurried back to town in response to a summons from Asquith, who had painfully interrupted his own country weekend. Bonar Law had stayed behind in London, spending an arduous Sunday morning with the Unionist ministers, who were incensed by this latest example of Lloyd George's 'trafficking with the Press' and disposed to advise 'the immediate resignation of the whole Government'. In mid-afternoon, he went to see Asquith. What passed between them, along with what remained unsaid on both sides, has been the subject of a vast and inconclusive literature. However he managed it and whatever his motives, Bonar Law persuaded Asquith to compromise with Lloyd George, who was waiting at the War Office (with Aitken at his elbow) for his turn to confront the Prime Minister. At five o'clock, Bonar Law was called to a second meeting with Asquith, this time with

[1] Clarke, *Northcliffe Diary* (2 December 1916), pp. 104–105.
[2] Beaverbrook, *Politicians*, pp. 410–11; McEwen, 879–80.

Lloyd George present. Although certain questions of personnel had yet to be settled, it was cordially agreed that Lloyd George would chair the new War Council and that he would furnish daily reports to Asquith, who would retain the premiership. The day and – so it seemed – the dispute ended with an announcement to the press that the government was in the process of reconstruction.[1]

Certain newspapers were not prepared to leave it at that, with the result that Sunday's ministerial accord was destroyed by Monday morning's headlines. The *Morning Post* gloatingly pronounced 'Cock Robin' to be dead, presumably at the instigation of Carson, who knew of Asquith's objection to his membership on the War Council. The *Manchester Guardian* spoke in terms of the humiliation of Asquith, whose 'most natural constitutional course would be either to resist the demand for a War Council, which would partly supersede him as Premier, or alternatively himself to resign'. By prior arrangement, these remarks were quoted with approval in *The Times*, where Robinson struck the fatal blow. Applauding Lloyd George's 'stand against the present cumbrous methods of directing the war', it endorsed his scheme for 'organising victory', and at once recognized 'the inclusion of Sir Edward Carson' to be as 'essential' as the ostracism of Asquith, who was temperamentally unfit for the task.

Clearly, Robinson was determined to rub salt in Asquith's wounds. He succeeded, Beaverbrook recalled in an unpublished memorandum, not so much by 'what he said but [by] the nasty sort of way he said it'. As Austen Chamberlain informed the Viceroy of India, *The Times* implied 'a complete surrender by the Prime Minister, who was to be left in his position only on condition that the whole conduct of affairs was placed in Lloyd George's hands'. Worse than a loss of face, Asquith lost the confidence of his Cabinet subordinates, Liberal and Unionist alike, who were jolted by the morning papers. Perhaps fortified by their testimony to his indispensability or perhaps looking for a pretext to retract his concessions, he wrote accusingly to Lloyd George:

> Such productions as the first leading article in today's *Times*, showing the infinite possibilities for misunderstanding & misrepresentation of such an agreement as we considered yesterday, make me at least doubtful as to its feasibility. Unless the impression is at once corrected that I am being relegated to the position of an irresponsible spectator of the War, I cannot possibly go on.

Lloyd George replied, all too improbably, that he had 'not seen *The Times* article', but that he hoped Asquith would 'not attach undue importance to these effusions'. Failure to implement 'the suggested arrangement' would

---

[1] Beaverbrook, *Politicians*, p. 423; for an incisive biographical discussion as well as a dependable narrative, see Blake, *Unknown Prime Minister*, ch. xx.

serve no better purpose than to reward Northcliffe, who 'frankly wants a smash'.[1]

Not unreasonably, Asquith believed that Lloyd George had intrigued with – or through – Northcliffe to inspire *The Times*'s disclosures, which were far too graphic to have been the product of guesswork. It had not gone unnoticed that Northcliffe and Lloyd George were together on the 3rd. That day, Cecil Harmsworth confided to his diary that his brother 'Alfred has been actively at work with Ll.G. with a view to bringing about a change'. Northcliffe's biographers have suggested that they met to discuss the literary projects on which Lloyd George intended to embark in the then likely event of his departure from office; but they add that discourse was not confined to non-political topics. 'The London Liberal daily papers,' Cecil Harmsworth noted on the 6th, 'are full of denunciations of Northcliffe, whom they regard as the arch-wrecker of the Asquith Govt. There is truth in this, of course, but not the whole truth.' All the same, there was truth enough for the Prime Minister and his wife. Nothing that was said or, for that matter, subsequently written could alter their conviction that Lloyd George and Northcliffe had plotted their downfall. Years later, Margot Asquith read Beaverbrook's account, serialized in the *Evening Standard*. 'It's no use Ld. B., or Winston, or anyone else saying that Ll.G. did not inspire *The Times* leader on Monday Dec. 4th', she declared, as Edwin Montagu had told her stepdaughter 'that Ll.G. was *with* Northcliffe & they wrote it together'.[2]

Contrary to these natural suspicions, Lloyd George stated in all truthfulness that he 'had not communicated any information ... to the proprietor or editor' of *The Times*. Although Northcliffe was 'very pleased' by the *Globe*'s encomium (12 December) that he 'alone' had 'just brought down the Asquith Cabinet', Robinson regarded it as an 'outrageous and (as N. knew) most dishonest puff'. Nor did Aitken, by his own humble admission, deserve the telegram of 'Hearty Congratulations' that he received from Northcliffe on 4 December. In fact, Robinson had acted quite independently of the two obvious culprits. His principal source was Carson, the triumvir with the least to lose and the most to gain from a breach of confidentiality. On Saturday, the 2nd, Robinson arrived at Cliveden, where he began to compose his leading article for Monday. His host, Waldorf Astor, supplied details that had surfaced too late for use in Sunday's *Observer*. Robinson also had 'a talk w[ith] Ld. Milner', another guest, 'to whom Asquith was now almost affectionate in his appeals for

[1] Beaverbrook, 'Report on Cabinet Crisis 1916,' Beaverbrook Papers, Box IV/24; Chamberlain to Chelmsford, 8 December 1916, quoted in Chamberlain, *Down the Years* (London, 1935), p. 121; Asquith to Lloyd George, 4 December 1916, and Lloyd George to Asquith, 4 December 1916 (copy), Lloyd George Papers, E/2/23/12–13; *also see* Spender and Asquith, II, 262–64.
[2] Cecil Harmsworth diary, 3 and 6 December 1916, quoted in Pound and Harmsworth, pp. 513–14; Pound and Harmsworth, pp. 514–15; Margot Asquith to Wickham Steed, 29 June 1931, *Times* Archives; *also see* Tom Clarke, *My Lloyd George Diary* (London, 1939), pp. 225–30, *and* J. M. McEwen, 'Northcliffe and Lloyd George At War, 1914–1918,' *Historical Journal*, xxiv (1981), 651–72.

help'. They encouraged him to sound out Carson, whose views were vividly reflected in the second, more truculent half of the text. After meeting Carson, late on Sunday afternoon, Robinson dined with Northcliffe, who was fresh from seeing Lloyd George. Only on Tuesday, the 5th, and then at his own request, did Robinson consult Lloyd George. Scott, on the other hand, saw Lloyd George twice on Monday and twice again on Tuesday, but never obtained the amplitude of information vouchsafed to Robinson.[1]

Early on the evening of the 5th, Asquith tendered his resignation to the King. Bonar Law, invited to form a new government, deferred to Lloyd George, who succeeded beyond all expectations, most notably Asquith's. The *Daily Mail* ('The Paper that is Combing Them Out') rejoiced at the nation's deliverance from 'The Haldane Gang'. At Northcliffe's insistence, it printed the 'worst possible picture' of the outgoing Prime Minister. The *Daily News* was not alone in forecasting that Northcliffe would occupy a seat in the new ministry. 'Ah-h, wouldn't they like to get me out of Fleet Street!' he remarked. 'I prefer to sit in Printing House Square and Carmelite House.' To scotch the rumours and to placate certain top-ranking Unionists, Lloyd George went on record that he had 'no intention of asking' either Northcliffe or Churchill, Rothermere's leading candidate, 'to join the Administration'. Yet prudence required at least a gesture of goodwill. Upon taking the helm, he bade Aitken to telephone the message that 'the Prime Minister would like to see Lord Northcliffe at No. 10 Downing Street'. The reply, after minutes of pregnant silence at the other end, was that 'Lord Northcliffe sees no advantage of any interview between him and the Prime Minister at this juncture'. The grasshopper had spoken.[2]

---

[1] Memorandum by Robinson, n.d., quoted in Wrench, *Dawson*, p. 141; Beaverbrook to Morison, 20 September 1949 (quoting telegram of 4 December 1916 to which he replied 'I think you exaggerate the share I have taken in recent events'), *Times* Archives; Lloyd George, *War Memoirs*, II, 998; *History of The Times*, IV, part 1, 297–300; Robinson's diary, 'Saturday' [2 December 1916] and 3 December 1916, Dawson Papers; Scott, *Political Diaries*, pp. 245–48.

[2] Clarke, *Northcliffe Diary*, pp. 20 (introduction) and 108 (8 December 1916); Pound and Harmsworth, p. 515; Beaverbrook, *Politicians*, p. 544.

Nine

SQUARING AND SQUASHING

One of the first problems of Lloyd George's premiership concerned the creation of a press lord. Sir Max Aitken, convinced that he was destined for the presidency of the Board of Trade in the new administration, prepared to defend his seat at Ashton-under-Lyne in a mandatory by-election. But Lloyd George forgot his promise, if indeed he had ever made one. Aitken was faced with 'an acute dilemma', largely of his own fabrication. The easiest solution was to elevate him to the peerage as Baron Beaverbrook. Despite the personal reservations he subsequently professed, he seemed delighted at the time to ascend to the constitutional altitudes of Northcliffe and Rothermere. A few years later, he congratulated 'Bill' Berry (the future Viscount Camrose) on being 'made a Baronet but you ought to go to the House of Lords which is the real and rightful Newspaper Proprietors Association'.[1]

There were strong objections to Aitken's ennoblement, viewed as typical of Lloyd George's methods and style of dispensing patronage. Lord Derby protested that other Lancashire MPs were worthier of the honour, and Bonar Law was reportedly reluctant 'to see a peerage conferred on an intimate friend of his'. At first, the King could not 'see his way' to agree that the 'public services of Sir Max Aitken called for such special recognition'; but he relented in order to remove his Prime Minister from 'a position of great embarrassment'. The fiercest opposition, however, came from practising journalists, who did not mistake Aitken's peerage as a tribute to their profession. 'We are all terrified of having men like Max Aitken . . . thrust upon us,' Leo Maxse wrote candidly to Bonar Law. Gwynne 'didn't make any comment' about 'Aitken's dirty peerage' in the *Morning Post* 'because I did not want to foul the nest of the new Govt. just when they were starting. I'm not sure I've done right,' he confessed to Edward Goulding, 'for it was one of the worst jobs ever perpetrated and I am ashamed of it all.' In fact, the *Morning Post* could not resist the unkind suggestion that Aitken might call himself 'Lord Bunty', after the title character in a West End comedy, *Bunty Pulls the Strings*. The Liberal papers were less

---

[1] Beaverbrook, *Politicians*, pp. 531–33, and *The Decline and Fall of Lloyd George* (London, 1963), p. 305, as corrected by Taylor, *Beaverbrook*, pp. 121–27; Beaverbrook to Berry, telegram [1921] (undated copy), Beaverbrook Papers, C/78.

frivolous. In the *Daily News* (9 February 1918), Gardiner neither forgot nor forgave 'how an obscure Canadian financier [was] exalted from Sir Max Aitken into Lord Beaverbrook for arranging the dinners and breakfasts at which Mr George and Sir Edward Carson intrigued for the fall of the Coalition'.[1]

The apotheosis of Aitken contrasted with the self-effacement of J. A. Spender, who declined a baronetcy in Asquith's farewell honours list. Still more, it contrasted with Spender's dejection. Counting 'twenty-one years' – it was actually twenty-two – since he 'took hold in Tudor Street', Spender reckoned that the days of his editorship were numbered. ' "Time he went" will, I expect, be the comment of Downing Street & Carmelite House & others of our hustlers,' he told Cook, his predecessor at the *Westminster Gazette*. 'All the same I shall do my best to beat them for a year or two longer & then to my farm.' Again, he miscalculated, though not by much. He fought his losing battle until November 1921, when the *Westminster* was converted to morning publication.[2]

For Beaverbrook, journalism offered limitless political and commercial opportunities. No longer inhibited by membership in the Commons, he at last felt free to acknowledge 'that he owns a majority of the shares of the *Express*', which he characterized to Scott as 'B.L.'s organ'. He had obtained them by acquiring the 'non-dividend-bearing Ordinary Shares' of Lawson Johnston, who happily traded them for 'dividend-bearing Preference Shares' without voting rights. This transfer was effected well in advance of the December 1916 crisis; yet it was only in September 1918 that Beaverbrook proclaimed himself 'a full-blooded journalist' and accepted formal designation as 'Chairman at the head of affairs' at the *Daily Express*.[3]

Owing as much to sentiment as to financial considerations, Beaverbrook may have genuinely conceived of his paper as Bonar Law's representative in Fleet Street. Nevertheless, it was Lloyd George who drew the principal advantages. In any case, relations between Bonar Law and Lloyd George were remarkably close. Whereas Bonar Law was served by J. C. C. Davidson and Stanley Baldwin, men who were to cause problems for Beaverbrook (and vice versa) later on, Lloyd George dealt with Beaverbrook directly, occasionally using him as an intermediary. Beaverbrook was particularly useful in negotiating on the government's behalf with his fellow press lords. With Northcliffe's support, he initiated a publicity campaign to raise a public loan. Northcliffe proved even more sticky than the Governor of the Bank of

---

[1] Nicholson, *King George V* (London, 1952), pp. 511–12; Blake, *Unknown Prime Minister*, p. 347; Maxse to Bonar Law, 7 December 1915, quoted in Taylor, *Beaverbrook*, p. 123; Gwynne to Goulding, 19 December 1916, Wargrave Papers.

[2] Spender to Asquith, 20 December 1916 (copy), Spender Papers, Add. MSS. 46, 388, fol. 100; Spender to Cook, 1 February 1917, Cook Papers. According to Riddell (*War Diary*, p. 233), Donald declined first a knighthood, then a baronetcy.

[3] Memorandum by Scott, 9–11 August 1917, Scott Papers, Add MSS. 50, 904, fol. 95; text of speech by Lawson Johnston, 25 September 1918, Beaverbrook Papers, H/13. Lawson Johnston was knighted in 1920.

England. On the grounds that 'newspapers need leadership', he nominated successive individuals – including Kennedy Jones – to take charge of the drive. Beaverbrook resisted the idea, just as he refused an offer of 'some newsprint' from Northcliffe 'if I will increase the price of the *Daily Express*'. He got his newsprint anyway, and the public loan netted a million pounds.[1]

Beaverbrook and Lloyd George admired each other for the courage and cunning that each saw mirrored in himself. 'His temperament responds as ever to the spur of danger,' Beaverbrook wrote of Lloyd George, whose maxim for dealing with the press was bluntly put: 'If they can't be squared they shall be squashed!' It gave no discomfort to Beaverbrook to implement this policy, much less to contemplate it.[2]

Whatever their past differences and future rivalries, they shared a mystical belief in the power of the press as well as an avowed determination to manipulate it for purposes of political propaganda. Yet, for all Lloyd George's ingenuity and Beaverbrook's deviousness, there were certain tasks they could not accomplish. Moreover, in various instances, Beaverbrook counted as an impediment. As the leader of a faction of the parliamentary Liberal Party, Lloyd George craved the benediction of at least one respected Liberal daily. The *Manchester Guardian*, which came closest to obliging him, held back partly out of principle and partly out of mistrust of the company he was keeping. The *Westminster Gazette*, the *Daily News*, and the *Star* were plainly hostile out of a spirit of outraged Asquithianism. The *Daily Chronicle*, once a staunch ally, gravitated in their direction. As the leader of a broad-based coalition, Lloyd George hoped to compensate with Unionist newspaper support, which had buoyed him in November and early December 1916. It quickly subsided, however, leaving him temporarily isolated and, to his mind, vulnerable.

Predictably, Northcliffe was the first to flaunt his unpredictability. When the ministerial appointments were announced, he bristled at the retention of Balfour and Lord Robert Cecil, both of whom he branded 'failures'. The *Daily Mail* indulged in diatribes against them. Balfour, needless to say, took it in his stride, but Cecil sent word to Lloyd George 'that my resignation is now, and always, at his disposal', after a wounding reference in *The Times* (9 December) and 'similar attacks, only much more violently worded, in the other papers which have supported Lloyd George, such as the *Daily Mail* and the *Morning Post*'. More acceptably, the *Weekly Dispatch* (10 December) featured a flattering profile of Lloyd George written by Northcliffe, who ensured it the widest possible attention: transmitted by cable to an estimated 'eighty million readers' in North America and Australia, it was reprinted in Monday's *Times*

---

[1] Beaverbrook to Morison, 20 September 1949 (quoting communications from Northcliffe dated 22 January, 19 February, and 2 March 1917), *Times* Archives; Taylor, *Beaverbrook*, p. 129.
[2] Beaverbrook, *Politicians*, pp. 544–45.

and *Daily Mail*. Was this celebration of the Prime Minister designed to show up his colleagues? Balfour and Cecil, among others, must have wondered. They could not have known that Gwynne was not only in communication with Robinson, but also the recipient of 'two letters . . . [which] have been extremely useful to me in this crisis' from Jack Sandars, who had turned savagely against Balfour and the Cecil connection.[1]

Northcliffe, too big to squash, had to be squared, and in a hurry. On Sunday, the 10th, Sir Maurice Hankey 'motored down to lunch with Lloyd George at Walton Heath', where they defined Hankey's responsibilities as secretary of the War Cabinet. In his presence, 'Lloyd George had a long talk on the telephone with Lord Northcliffe, whom he seems to funk'. Afterwards, Hankey travelled back to London 'with an odious fellow called Sutherland, some sort of political parasite of Ll.G.'s'. An astute observer of the political scene, Hankey regarded the appointment of Amery as political secretary of the War Cabinet as proof of Northcliffe's baleful influence. On 10 January 1917, Walter Long, the Colonial Secretary, 'was full of complaints of Amery, who, he said, was quite untrustworthy and ought not to be present at meetings, particularly owing to his intimate association with *The Times*'. Annoyed by 'the infernal Press', with its 'misleading paragraphs' about his work, Hankey rejected Amery's 'methods and told him so flat. He is a scheming little devil and his connection with *The Times* would make it possible for him to oust me, so the position is delicate.' For Lloyd George, the position was more delicate still.[2]

Northcliffe soon felt that Lloyd George was avoiding him, which was probably the case. To Riddell, who surely saw 'the Prime Minister more often than I do, which is about once a fortnight', he wrote on 18 February to warn about the incompetence of Neville Chamberlain, making his ministerial debut as Director-General of National Service. Only the previous day, Northcliffe had been thwarted in his move to incite Lord Fisher to deliver an anti-government speech in the House of Lords. Fisher was dissuaded from this course by Donald, signifying that the Liberal press could not be written off. Lloyd George now turned in that direction, attempting to mend fences before he grabbed at the properties on which they stood.[3]

Already, and without effect, Lloyd George had tried to come to an understanding with Gardiner, whom he summoned to Downing Street on 21 December. They had not met since the previous April, when Gardiner had accused Lloyd George of treachery and Lloyd George had publicly referred to Gardiner as 'an assassin'. Bygones being bygones, Lloyd George 'was extremely agreeable, & having produced cigars, sat down before a document'

[1] Cecil to Bonar Law, 9 December 1916, Bonar Law Papers, 81/1/31; Clarke, *Northcliffe Diary* (11 December 1916), pp. 108–109; Gwynne to Sandars, 11 December 1916, Sandars Papers.

[2] Hankey's diary, 10 December 1916 and 10 January 1917, quoted in Stephen Roskill, *Hankey, Man of Secrets*, I (London, 1970), 329, 352.

[3] Northcliffe to Riddell, 18 February 1917 (copy), Northcliffe Papers; Fisher to Donald, 17 February 1917, quoted in H. A. Taylor, *Donald*, pp. 66–67.

that he wished to discuss. It was from President Wilson, who asked each belligerent power to state its war aims. Implying 'that there is no difference between us', the note struck Lloyd George as being tantamount to 'a pro-German declaration'. Gardiner disagreed with that interpretation: 'It seems to me a natural inquiry. He is a neutral addressing both sides.' Neither of them able to convince the other, they agreed to differ. 'Well, I hope you will not support an appeal worded in these terms,' concluded Lloyd George. Gardiner, declaring himself 'not anxious for a quarrel with America', promised only to 'bear in mind what you have said when I write on the subject tonight'. Meanwhile, given the opportunity, he offered 'a suggestion from another point of view'. Although he did not believe that Wilson's phraseology was unfriendly, he recognized 'that there are newspapers in London which will use it for offensive attacks on America', and he entreated Lloyd George 'to warn them against unnecessary & provocative language'. A few hours later, back at his editorial desk, Gardiner received 'a message ... from the Press Bureau requesting editors in their comments on the American note to avoid personal attacks on the President'. The directive seemed to hint that, short of character assassination, attacks were entirely permissible. The Tory papers had no difficulty in reading between the lines, and the *Daily Chronicle* particularly 'showed how well this message was understood'. Interviewed by the *New York Times* (2 December), Northcliffe stated that 'the suggestion that Great Britain should consider peace can only be regarded as hostile'. Denied the 'respectful attention' advocated by the *Daily News*, Wilson was puzzled 'how his note could have been so "widely misread"' by the British press. Gardiner knew the answer. 'How many editors,' he asked himself, 'did Mr Lloyd George speak to that evening in the tones he employed with me?'[1]

Waiting for his interview with the Prime Minister, Gardiner struck Riddell as looking 'worn. All his ideals have been shattered.' On Christmas Day, Riddell reported to Lloyd George that Gardiner had 'asked Donald to join him in urging discussion of peace terms'; but Donald, married to a patriotic Frenchwoman and consequently 'sound on the war', was said to have refused. Thereafter, Gardiner heard from T. P. O'Connor and 'another henchman of Ll.G.' that the Prime Minister would be glad to renew old ties. These overtures meant less to him than to George Cadbury, his elderly proprietor, who did not object to a slashing attack on Carson so long as Gardiner 'dealt tenderly with Lloyd George, who has done much for the country by his finance bills and in other ways, and I do earnestly hope he may not be led astray, as Joseph Chamberlain was'.[2]

[1] Memorandum by Gardiner on 'a conversation with Ll.G. on the American note of December 20, 1916', Gardiner Papers; in a letter to the editor of the *Nation* (12 March 1921), Gardiner shed 'some light on this interesting theme'.
[2] Riddell, *War Diary* (21 and 25 December 1916), p. 233; entry of 4 January 1917, *Journals of Arnold Bennett*, II (ed. N. Flower; London, 1932), 182; Cadbury to Gardiner, 17 April 1917, Gardiner Papers.

To the extent that Lloyd George exercised any lingering appeal to the *Daily News*, it was through the imagination of its owner, and against the better judgment of its editor. At the *Manchester Guardian*, Scott bore dual responsibility. On 2 May, he 'breakfasted with Lloyd George', who complained of the paper's failure to support the government's agriculture schemes. 'Nobody cared what the *Daily News* & the *Nation* said because they made it their business to find fault,' Lloyd George told Scott. 'The *Chronicle* was better, but still did not carry much weight. But people did think a lot of what the *M.G.* said.' Lloyd George had the habit of repeating himself in conversations with newspapermen. Not only that, but he sometimes paid the same compliments to different people. To Spender, he averred that the *Westminster Gazette* stood second to *The Times* in its reputation abroad, which was why he allegedly shrank from its censure.[1]

The split in the Liberal Party was replicated at every stage in the proprietorship of the *Westminster*. In June 1916, Spender got wind of a plan for 'getting me out of the *W.G.*', though it was unclear whether the instigators – Sir Alfred Mond and Sir Charles Henry – were acting 'with or without Ll.G.'s connivance'. Lord Murray of Elibank took the *W.G.* matter in hand ... pretty strongly', guaranteeing Spender's sovereignty subject to an understanding that he would desist from criticisms of Lloyd George. Within six months, Lloyd George was no longer Asquith's colleague, and Mond and Lord Cowdray were among the lesser luminaries in Lloyd George's coalition. The other shareholders were divided in their loyalties, with Murray struggling to keep a balance between them as much for the survival of the paper as for the dim prospect of Liberal reunion. Lloyd George called Murray's attention to the latest abusive item in the *Westminster*. Had 'this kind of hitting below the belt' appeared elsewhere, Lloyd George insisted that he 'should never have complained'. But he wanted to show Murray 'another example of the kind of offensive attack which you and Cowdray are subsidizing against your friends'. His assertion that he had 'never heard of another case where a member of a Govt. financed a paper to attack his own colleagues' almost sounded as if he had appointed Cowdray to the Air Ministry in order to square the *Westminster Gazette*.[2]

According to one account, Lloyd George had no sooner arrived in the premiership than David Davies, his parliamentary private secretary and a man of means, approached one of the Asquithians on the *Westminster* board with a view to obtaining control. More probably, however, the attempt was not made until the following March, when Davies (later 1st Baron Davies of Llandinam) ascertained the names of the shareholders. Dr Thomas ('Tom') Jones, the assistant secretary of the War Cabinet and yet another of Lloyd George's

---

[1] Memorandum by Scott, 30 April–4 May 1917, Scott Papers, Add. MSS. 50, 904, fols. 7–8; Spender to Asquith, 4 October 1917, Asquith Papers.

[2] Spender to Murray, 6 June 1916, Murray to Spender, 7 June 1916 (copy), Murray to Lloyd George, 18 July 1916 (copy), and Lloyd George to Murray, 17 September 1917, Elibank Papers.

Welsh cronies, understood that Davies was acting on his own initiative. 'There is no doubt that a man with a paper in his pocket has a big leverage in political circles here,' Jones wrote to his wife. 'The P.M. particularly "studies" and "humours" such people.'[1]

Davies, who had shifted political ground by then, was not responsible for a second, more serious assault. On 6 October 1917, Lord Crewe alerted Asquith to the fact that Spender's case was 'both grave and urgent'. Murray and Cowdray were taking steps to curtail editorial freedom. In the face of a threatened libel action by the Prime Minister and the demand of 'hostile shareholders' that he should 'refrain from all criticism of the Government or Ll.G. in the future', Spender prepared to resign. It would then be 'open to the shareholders to elect a new board and change the direction of the paper by a bare majority', with the likelihood that backers of Lloyd George would take over 'before the end of the year'.[2]

Unexpectedly, the end of 1917 found Spender in firm control. He owed his reprieve to Northcliffe, of all people. On 15 November, Lloyd George loosely dangled the possibility that Northcliffe, who took an avid interest in air power, might assume ministerial jurisdiction in that vital sphere. The next morning, Northcliffe peremptorily announced in *The Times* that, after 'anxious consideration', he had decided to refuse the 'great honour and responsibility' he had been offered at Cowdray's expense. 'I feel that in the present circumstances,' he told the Prime Minister in cold print, 'I can do better work if I maintain my independence and am not gagged by a loyalty that I do not feel towards the whole of your Administration.' Cowdray was too mortified either to continue in office or ever to forgive Lloyd George. Hastening to Spender's rescue, he augmented his shareholding to become 'the good Angel of the W.G.'[3]

The *Westminster Gazette*, then, slipped from Lloyd George's net. By default, he revived the idea of purchasing the *Daily Chronicle* from Frank Lloyd. A businessman out to make a profit, Lloyd was not bound by Scott's devotion to Radical tradition, by Cadbury's Quaker piety, or by Cowdray's vengeful partisanship. He knew the value of his product, however, and fixed a purchase price of a million and a half pounds. Clearly, it was more economical to square the *Chronicle* than to buy it, and Lloyd George made reasonable progress in this direction. Through 1917, he enjoyed reassuringly cordial contacts with Donald, whose aversion to a negotiated peace was in accord with his own policy. The Milnerites grumbled that Buchan, one of their number,

---

[1] Joseph Davies, *The Prime Minister's Secretariat 1916–1920* (Newport, Monmouthshire, 1951), p. 56; Jones to his wife, March, n.d., 1917, quoted in Jones, *Whitehall Diary*, I (ed. K. Middlemas; London, 1969), 26.
[2] Crewe to Asquith, 6 October 1917, Spender to Asquith, 4 October 1917, and memorandum by Spender [October 1917], Asquith Papers.
[3] Pound and Harmsworth, pp. 592–93; Spender to Murray, 6 September 1918, Elibank Papers; *also see* Wilson, *Downfall*, pp. 116–17.

could 'never get access to Lloyd George, who on the other hand continually sees that ruffian Donald of the *Chronicle*'. To the feigned 'astonishment' of an anonymous critic in the *Saturday Review* (2 March 1918), Donald was 'the latest and most distinguished' recruit to 'the Press Gang' which, in effect, ran the country. Nevertheless, this intimacy was a good deal more apparent than real. 'Our attitude towards Mr Lloyd George's Government is precisely that of Mr Asquith,' Donald wrote testily in the spring of 1917; 'we give it support in prosecuting the war, but, unlike Mr Asquith, we occasionally criticise some of its actions.' In the second half of 1918, when the Asquithians grew more outspoken, Donald stepped up his criticisms. Having failed to square him, Lloyd George proceeded to squash him. It was, as we shall see, an especially unsavoury incident in the history of the modern political press.[1]

* * *

'It is no good omen for the future of England or democracy,' thought Lord Bryce, 'that the press of one man, speaking with many voices to the mob of the streets and that of the clubs, should play the part of Kingmaker.' He reminded Sir George Otto Trevelyan, a fellow survivor of mid-Victorian Liberalism, 'how in the sixties & seventies we used to complain of Delane for infinitely less!'[2]

Bryce wrote with greater poignancy than accuracy. However many voices were at Northcliffe's command, it was a delusion – common enough – to suppose that Fleet Street chanted in unison. Conversely, it was idle to pretend that Lloyd George was wafted to power by some irresistible force, euphemistically known as public or popular opinion. As concepts, public and popular had never been synonymous, though the gap between them had narrowed since Delane's day and was virtually to close with the extension of the franchise in 1918. Strictly speaking, neither was to be confused with newspaper opinion, which existed separately and informed them both in unequal proportions.

Early wartime experience had underscored the disparity between those journals that aspired to political influence and those that settled for the benefits of a mass circulation. While the press as a whole was utilized to attract volunteers for the army and subscribers to the war loan, ministerial confidences were reserved for a privileged few. The break came in December 1916. Lloyd George, by the alliances he struck and the favours he bestowed, did not so much obliterate the accepted categories as bring them into collision. His exploitation of *Reynolds's Newspaper* on 3 December presaged his disregard for convention, based upon a shrewd regard for dramatic effect. Of all the

---

[1] Riddell, *War Diary* (26 September 1917), p. 278; Amery's diary, 20 August 1917, Amery Papers; H. A. Taylor, *Donald*, p. 161; Donald to W. E. Evans (secretary, Ilford Liberal and Radical Assn.), 17 April 1917 (copy), Beaverbrook Papers.

[2] Bryce to Trevelyan, 22 January 1917 (copy), Bryce Papers.

properties he tried to control, it was fittingly the *Daily Chronicle*, the least ideological of the major Liberal dailies, that fell into his clutches. By the end of the war, he had helped to dispel the nineteenth-century myth that editors were priests, that newspapers were pulpits, and that leading articles were scripture.

'Opinion has had its day in the daily Press,' declared Kennedy Jones in 1919. 'For the past twenty years its intrinsic value has steadily depreciated.'[1] As one who had debased the coinage of penny and halfpenny journalism over the past two decades, he was well placed to know. Certain subtleties, however, eluded him. If, as he maintained, the mass of the population did not credit or necessarily comprehend editorial casuistries, it did not follow that press opinion had lost any significant degree of intrinsic value; on the contrary, it meant that the press was forced to surrender its pretension to an extrinsic authority it had probably never possessed. Newspapers were certainly read more widely, but for their war news, which eclipsed their editorial comment. So far as one can tell, they changed few minds that were not predisposed to change.

For all that, they continued to manifest a distinct influence. Image-conscious politicians were inordinately sensitive to the impressions created by adverse publicity: Lord Robert Cecil was a case in point. The fluidity of parliamentary alignments invested journals with the functions of beacons, which signalled the febrile responses of key individuals. Politicians pored over the daily press for intimations about one another: Lloyd George, for example, measured Cowdray's fidelity by the *Westminster Gazette*, until Cowdray discovered Lloyd George's duplicity from *The Times*. For the *Morning Post* (12 February 1918), usually a reliable index to Carson's intentions, 'the lot of a newspaper in these times is not a happy one'. The inconveniences inflicted by 'Dora, that fearful servitress of the cause of Freedom', were less onerous than attendant moral obligations. A responsible editor had 'a choice': he could 'bow down and worship the idols of Democracy'; or he could incur disapprobation (and risk sales) by 'saying not what is pleasant to hear but what is of service to the country'. Even Northcliffe, when he flew at Kitchener, had accepted unpopularity as a penalty for patriotism. Commercialism and conviction were often at odds.

Jones, who should have known better from the experience of his own candidacies, mistook the deflection of newspaper opinion for desuetude. Wartime exigencies sometimes compelled journals to speak obliquely, but always with due confidence that any clues they dropped would be picked up. More conventionally, newspapers acted as watchdogs in the constituencies, where the party truce played havoc with traditional loyalties. Arthur Mann, editor of the *Evening Standard*, assured Derby that the Hulton properties in Manchester would be 'all right with regard to the Cotton Duties', proposed for the protection of Indian manufactures. While some Lancashire MPs might

---

[1] *Fleet Street and Downing Street*, p. 182.

resist, it could be assumed that 'they should decline to vote against the Government'. In any event, Mann undertook to keep Derby 'informed with regard to any information he may get'. Derby also depended upon the local press to support his twenty-two-year-old son, Captain Lord Edward Stanley, who fought a June by-election in the Abercromby division of Liverpool. From a strictly provincial perspective, not much seemed to have changed.[1]

The transformation was more visible in London. Whereas the first coalition had been formed in such a way as to emphasize party affiliations, the effect of the second coalition was to cut across them. The major metropolitan dailies found it difficult to adjust to Lloyd George's requirements, and some refused to try. The strain was evident at Printing House Square, where Northcliffe and Robinson disagreed in their definitions of newspaper independence. Northcliffe adhered to a policy of vigilance, which gave him licence to discriminate between members of the administration. By contrast, Robinson considered the coalition as a whole to have met his basic criteria, and he was loath to distress the Milnerites who studded its ranks.

'It is the wisdom of successful government,' Lloyd George later remarked, 'that it should harness powerful but unruly natural elements to some beneficent task.' Accordingly, he prevailed upon Northcliffe to follow up Balfour's special mission to the United States by going there as a grandly styled Minister Plenipotentiary. When the invitation was first extended in April 1917, Northcliffe turned it down. But on the evening of 30 May, finding the Prime Minister 'very emphatic', he accepted 'the post with more regret and reluctance than I can express' or that Lloyd George could recall. Northcliffe had already sailed by 7 June, when his appointment was simultaneously announced on both sides of the Atlantic. That morning, his instructions were pinned to the notice board at Carmelite House: 'I am leaving to take over Mr Balfour's American Mission and it is essential that not one line of criticism of the United States, men, books, or anything else, should appear in the *Daily Mail* ... or any other publication associated with the *Daily Mail*.' At a stroke, Lloyd George had turned the poacher into a gamekeeper. 'The acute criticism which Lord Northcliffe's appointment called forth' from professional diplomats and scandalized Asquithians was a small price to pay for a five-month respite.[2]

'Upon matters political I suppose the Editor would have kept you fully informed,' Wickham Steed wrote to Northcliffe, who had arrived safely in New York. Thoughtfully, Steed supplied his 'own impression ... that Lloyd George and the War Cabinet are losing ground, mainly through their own fault'. His complaints were vacuously metaphorical: 'They have allowed themselves to be swamped by detail and are now unable to see wood for trees.' But the

---

[1] Derby to Bonar Law, 10 March 1917, Bonar Law Papers, 81/4/13; Sir Robert Hudson to Northcliffe, 27 June [1917] (copy), Northcliffe Papers; Waller, *Democracy and Sectarianism*, p. 280.

[2] Lloyd George, *War Memoirs*, I, 1005; Pound and Harmsworth, pp. 528–31.

government's torpidity that summer was real enough. 'Men who are devoted to Lloyd George and his colleagues,' reported Steed, 'say despondingly that the only way to make them act is to frighten them by agitation from outside.'[1] Northcliffe, for better or worse, was too far removed to lend a hand.

Asquith was no more willing than Lloyd George to formalize the breach in Liberal Party ranks. Contemptuous of Lloyd George's 'crazy adventure', he trusted that it would fail, leaving him to pick up the pieces with clean hands. His associates, eager to seize the initiative, worked through the constituency organizations and the press to counteract their leader's immobility. W. M. R. Pringle and J. M. Hogge, a pair of Young Turks, broke ranks to champion an independent contender at Abercromby. Walter Runciman, an older Turk, furnished Gardiner with 'scribblings' for editorial guidance. 'I wish there had been more time for me to collect the material you wanted,' he explained, 'but I expect in any case to see an illuminating article in today's *Daily News* when it reaches me.' From all indications, the vehement anti-coalitionism of the *Westminster Gazette*, which plunged Spender into conflict with the proprietorship that summer and autumn, derived from a similar determination to stiffen the party's backbone.[2]

Along with this growing restiveness on the part of certain Liberals, anxious to translate their passive independence into aggressive opposition, Lloyd George was encountering difficulties with Labour. In May, he dispatched Arthur Henderson, a minister without portfolio in the War Cabinet, to investigate the turmoil in Russia. Henderson returned, as Lloyd George crudely described him, 'magnetised by his experiences' and infected by 'more than a touch of the revolutionary malaria'. He soon received an invitation from the Soviet in Petrograd (as St Petersburg had temporarily become) to send delegates from the British Labour Party to a meeting of the International in Stockholm. Before summoning a special party conclave to consider the matter, he slipped across to Paris to discuss the agenda with French and Russian comrades. His Cabinet colleagues were furious. Without informing them, Henderson had taken leave, and in the company of Ramsay MacDonald, a notorious opponent of the war effort. Moreover, any British workers who ventured to Stockholm at his recommendation would rub shoulders with foreign pacifists and possibly enemy agents. On 1 August, while Henderson was kept waiting on the 'doormat' outside the Cabinet office, his conduct was debated and censured. Ten days later, he resigned from the War Cabinet, where his place as Labour spokesman was filled by George Barnes.[3]

It was about this time that Geoffrey Robinson changed his name to Dawson by deed-poll to comply with the terms of entail of his aunt's estate. 'The line I

[1] Steed to Northcliffe, 11 July 1917, Northcliffe Papers.
[2] Memorandum by Asquith, 28 May 1917, Asquith Papers; Runciman to Gardiner, 28 July 1917, Gardiner Papers; Wilson, *Downfall*, pp. 120–25.
[3] Lloyd George, *War Memoirs*, II, 1127; *also see* David Marquand, *Ramsay MacDonald* (London, 1977), pp. 218–20.

have taken in *The Times*,' he informed Northcliffe, 'is to encourage as far as possible those robust Labour elements which are opposed to touching Stockholm with a barge-pole.' It seemed to him 'far better to admit that there is a certain patriotic section of Labour which is genuinely, if mistakenly, convinced of the value of a conference' than to indict the entire Labour movement for subversion. The *Morning Post* was 'doing infinite harm by shouting for repression', insisted Dawson, who noted that 'its circulation among the working classes is probably minute'. No less predictably, the Liberal journals took Henderson's part with varying degrees of commitment. At breakfast with Lloyd George on the 11th, Scott 'represented that Henderson was one of the most muddle-headed of men and that a good deal might be set down to that', but his host 'would hear of no excuse'. The controversy simmered through August, as did the Prime Minister's temper. Both were brought to a boil on the 29th, when the *Daily Express* assailed Henderson in particular and socialism in general. 'Have you seen the leader in today's *Express*?' Lloyd George asked Bonar Law. 'It explains why no man in any party trusts Max.'[1]

The fissure on the left, which was to have profound repercussions, was immediately counterbalanced by one on the right. The latter took the form of a National Party, which promulgated its manifesto at the end of August. It was ill-timed. 'The bulk of mankind and of the newspapers preferred to concentrate on the President's reply to the Pope,' Dawson observed with amusement. The *Morning Post*, an exception to the rule, 'extravagantly boomed' the enterprise and commented facetiously on the slighting attitudes of its rivals: 'At first most of them thought it judicious to boycott the movement altogether; but they are now devoting columns to prove that they were right in saying nothing about it.' The *Daily Telegraph*, for example, discountenanced what it took to be a ruse 'to attack or weaken the Government'. Far from that, retorted the *Morning Post*, the National Party was a 'little group of earnest and patriotic men', who provided 'a nucleus' for 'a great, a noble, and an honest cause, and it deserves the support of a nation which has long floundered in the political slough of despond'.[2]

The immediate target was Bonar Law. 'There was not a single adventure against which Union stood, from Home Rule in Ireland to Home Rule in India, in which he has not acquiesced.' He had seen the storm brewing and told Croal

---

[1] Robinson to Northcliffe, 7 August 1917, Northcliffe Papers; entry of 9–11 August 1917, and Scott to Hobhouse, 28 August 1917, in Scott, *Political Diaries*, pp. 298, 300–301; Lloyd George to Bonar Law, 29 August 1917, Bonar Law Papers, 82/3/24. A. J. P. Taylor (*Beaverbrook*, p. 159) dates Lloyd George's letter as 29 August 1918, when the *Daily Express* engaged in yet another 'mean piece of treachery'; but the item has been catalogued as 1917, which – allowing for the spidery penmanship – appears the more probable.

[2] These paragraphs are based on the following sources; Dawson to Northcliffe, 1 September 1917, Northcliffe Papers; Bonar Law to Croal, 3 August 1917 (copy), Bonar Law Papers, 84/6/99; and the *Morning Post*, the *Daily Telegraph*, and *The Times* for August and September 1917. *Also see* W. D. Rubinstein, 'Henry Croft and the National Party 1917–22,' *Journal of Contemporary History*, ix (1974), 129–48.

of the *Scotsman* that there was 'no doubt that our Party is very seriously disaffected at the moment, mainly on account of Churchill', whose restoration to office stuck in Tory throats, 'but as regards the Government as a whole, and especially as regards the Prime Minister'. Dawson, who delighted in pouring 'a little tepid water on them in *The Times*', privately identified the malcontents as Lord Leith of Fyvie, 'Brigadier-General' Page Croft, Lord Bathurst ('the Prince Consort of the *Morning Post*'), and Sir Richard Cooper ('of the "sheep dip" '), the Independent Unionist MP for Walsall. Page Croft, who sat for Christchurch from 1910 to 1940, was an ardent imperialist who returned to the mainstream in 1922, after Lloyd George was deposed, and (as 1st Baron Croft) held office under Churchill during the Second World War. Convinced that the leading lights of the National Party lacked voltage, Dawson declined 'to print their nightly reports of swollen letter bags and widespread enthusiasm'. But the *Morning Post* ran daily lists of 'assentors', among whom unenfranchised women figured 'in large numbers'.

In the long run, of course, the alienation of Page Croft counted as a minor ripple, while that of Henderson caused a tidal wave. To Lloyd George, always a man of the moment, the Tory die-hards posed the greater threat. If Bonar Law were forced to withdraw either from the Unionist leadership or the War Cabinet, he could not be replaced as Henderson had been. For safety's sake, Lloyd George sought to ingratiate himself among Liberal editors. Scott 'congratulated him on his appointment of Churchill', who served 'to strengthen his Government on the Liberal side where it was far too weak'. In the interests of 'truth & justice', which happily coincided with the goal of Liberal *rapprochement*, the *Manchester Guardian* published a series of articles to exonerate Haldane, who was 'very glad this powerful paper has brought them out'. Haldane's pre-war record was also favourably re-examined by the *Glasgow Herald*, 'which divides Scotland with the *Scotsman*'; and, to Haldane's further surprise, 'Donald of the *Chronicle* has joined in off his own bat'. Was it coincidental that Scott met Robert Bruce, the editor of the *Glasgow Herald*, at breakfast in Downing Street on 20 October, and that 'Donald turned up' at Walton Heath the next day, seeming 'to act ... as a kind of scout for Lloyd George'?[1]

Lord Fisher learnt from Gardiner, whom he touted as '*The Ablest Living Journalist*', that 'Lloyd George had been *tête-à-tête* with him'. Gardiner, drawing the 'conclusion ... that Lloyd George was in a tight place, and in the complete grip of the Tories, ... was very sad and hopeless accordingly'. All the same, Gardiner did not use his influence with James Douglas to prevent the publication of a 'gross attack' in the *Star*, against which Lloyd George brought a suit for libel. Rothermere, whom Lloyd George might have hoped to appease by promoting Churchill, mounted an autumn offensive in the *Sunday Pictorial*

---

[1] Entries of 28 September, and 20 and 21 October 1917, in Scott, *Political Diaries*, pp. 305, 307, 309; Haldane to Gosse, 4 September and 8 October 1917, Gosse Papers.

which did not abate until the third week in November, when Rothermere himself was named Minister for Air. At exactly that time, Lloyd George's attentions to the *Westminster* yielded bitter fruit. His knack for squaring seemed to have deserted him. Steed judged it 'one of the ill effects' of Northcliffe's distance from the scene that 'the P.M. gets surrounded by unwholesome influences like that of Donald; on the other hand,' Steed told 'the Chief', Lloyd George's well-known 'fear of press criticism is much decreased because he imagines that as you are not there to bite him, public opinion as revealed in the Press is a more negligible quantity'. It was not clear whom Steed conceived to be the more gullible.[1]

Although it was doubtful that Northcliffe's absence had much to do with it, relations between Downing Street and Fleet Street were badly strained in the autumn of 1917. The reasons were sometimes no less quixotic than obscure. Waldorf Astor, who had been appointed to Lloyd George's secretariat at Garvin's suggestion, confounded his editor by issuing a threat that he would 'only give the Prime Minister one more chance' to satisfy his demand for tighter liquor controls. 'I can only say that by a course so out of proportion in a war like this you would only wreck your career and your paper on that line,' protested Garvin, who 'could not possibly follow it. Many bigger things are to be remembered and the *Observer* has stood for them.' The field of Sunday journalism had grown more crowded, most recently by the boisterous intrusion of Bottomley, who acquired the *National News* from Odhams Press and ran it in conjunction with the *Sunday Evening Telegram*. (The *National* outlived the *Telegram* to become the *Sunday Illustrated* in 1921.) 'It is of course ten times easier to start new Sunday papers than new dailies,' Garvin pointed out to Astor, 'because the expense is ten times less and the novel possibilities more numerous.' But none of their competitors, he was pleased to say, duplicated the *Observer*'s winning 'combination ... of acquiring public influence and making money'.[2]

Hearing that Northcliffe was due back within weeks, Steed wrote to him on 14 October that his influence was urgently needed. The *Globe* had inexplicably turned against Lloyd George, going so far as to moot the possibility that Asquith might resume power. Robertson, the Chief of the Imperial General Staff, was rumoured to bear responsibility. It remained a mystery, however, why and how the *Globe* had lent itself to his purpose. The explanation, known to a select few, was that Leo Maxse was playing games. Branching out from the *National Review*, where Haldane sarcastically rated his October performance as 'magnificent', he made a furtive entry into daily journalism by assuming the

---

[1] Fisher to Lord Ranksborough, 2 September 1917, quoted in A. J. Marder, ed., *Fear God and Dread Nought*, III (London, 1959), 479; entry of 28 September 1917, in Scott, *Political Diaries*, p. 306; Steed to Northcliffe, 20 September 1917, Northcliffe Papers. For a terse account of Lloyd George's lawsuit, see *The Times*, 28 September 1917.

[2] Garvin to Astor, 21 and 24 September 1917 (copies), Garvin Papers. For Bottomley's Sunday activity, see R. J. Minney, *Viscount Southwood* (London, 1954), pp. 151–52.

editorship of the *Globe* on a trial basis. By his own logic, he lacked the qualification of gender. 'If Lady Burnham edited the *D.T.* it would be a vastly different paper,' he told Lady Bathurst, whom he encouraged to participate more actively in the affairs of the *Morning Post*; 'and if Mrs Waldorf ran the *Observer*, there would be less of this sickening booming of Winston Churchill, while Lady Northcliffe has sound opinions on nine questions out of ten.' His disability notwithstanding, Maxse scored a notable success. Anonymity contributed to it by keeping the professionals guessing. Strachey conceded that the *Globe* 'has been, from the journalistic point of view, quite good of late', and he wondered whether it had a new owner. John Buchan, belying his title of Director of Information, was unable to enlighten him. 'It is curious that you, who know so many things about the press, should not know who is really in control of the *Globe*,' Strachey replied to Buchan's plea of ignorance. 'I still think it must be Northcliffe, under an alias.'[1]

For once, Northcliffe was not even tangentially involved. He returned to London on 12 November, the same day that Lloyd George delivered a speech in Paris full of exasperation with the military command. 'A careful study' of the text confirmed the *Morning Post*'s 'worst fears. He really intends that his new Political Council – this great experiment, as he calls it – is to direct the strategy of the Allied Armies,' the paper stated with mock incredulity on the 14th. 'Mr Lloyd George has discovered strategy as M. Jourdain discovered prose, and now he moves in it as if it were his native element.' The leading article in that morning's *Daily News* was equally hostile, and Gardiner's Saturday column on the 17th was positively scathing. Loulou (now Viscount) Harcourt, who deprecated the Paris speech as 'International Limehouse', applauded Gardiner's 'splendid articles on Ll.G. I suppose the man is mad with megalomania.' But others considered Gardiner to have done him an injustice. On the evening of the 16th, Tom Jones dined with Nancy and Waldorf Astor, Balfour, Dawson, Philip Kerr, and some lesser celebrities. They talked 'about Northcliffe' (whom Nancy damned 'with all the curses' she could muster), 'Rothermere, Hulton, Bottomley, and other irresponsible controllers of the Press'. Kerr, who served as private secretary to Lloyd George,

> charged the Press with 'doctoring' the news. This roused Dawson to maintain that *The Times*, the *Telegraph*, and the *Morning Post* and possibly the *Chronicle*, were scrupulously careful to give the news honestly and in due proportion, which is more than ... can be said of the *Daily News*, which published the P.M.'s Paris speech and completely distorted it.

Dawson went on to reveal 'that a few hours earlier Leo Maxse had begged him to publish a three-column attack on the P.M. in *The Times*'. Dawson had

[1] Steed to Northcliffe, 14 October 1917, Northcliffe Papers; Haldane to Gosse, 5 October 1917, Gosse Papers; correspondence between Maxse and Docker, September-October 1917,

refused and predicted that the piece would 'probably appear in the *Morning Post* or the *Globe*'.¹

Weeks later, the episode continued to haunt Lloyd George. There had been 'a conspiracy to defeat him on his Paris speech, . . . an unholy alliance of the Generals' press and the partizan Liberals', he told Scott, who was surprised to learn that Lloyd George 'considered himself in danger'. On a subsequent occasion, Lloyd George repeated that, when 'the *Daily News & Nation* joined hands with the *Morning Post & Spectator*', they had 'very nearly succeeded in upsetting him'. The Prime Minister was not exaggerating either the panic he had felt or the store he had set by the *Manchester Guardian*. While the practical value of Scott's defence was problematical, his defection would have been a crushing blow under those circumstances. As Amery pithily noted in his diary: 'L.G. full of gratitude to Scott because the *Guardian* had not joined the Cocoa and Old Port cabal against him.'²

It was out of desperation that Lloyd George informally offered a ministerial appointment to Northcliffe, and that desperation was intensified by the condescension of Northcliffe's refusal. 'As to the Northcliffe business,' the deputy editor of the *Morning Post* wrote (while Gwynne was at the front) to Lady Bathurst, 'I do not pretend to understand it thoroughly, or the Cowdray sequel either. But I know . . . that there is more in it than meets the eye.'³ Although Northcliffe spurned office, his papers were mildly supportive of the Paris speech. Perhaps, after all, Lloyd George achieved his purpose. Just for good measure, Northcliffe was elevated to a viscountcy in the new year's honours list.

Garvin, for one, took the view that an accommodation between Lloyd George and Northcliffe would be 'better for the Country, better for journalism'. He recited his reasons to Scott, who was perplexed by the *Observer*'s revised opinion: 'It is a changed situation now that [Northcliffe] has discharged a big political mission & that Cabinet Office has been pressed upon him. . . . I don't want him to break with L.G. in this emergency.' More typically, Strachey dreaded the prospect of such a partnership. 'Dangerous as I think Northcliffe, I would rather have him in the open than see him behind a Prime Minister whom he can "politically blackmail" to any extent,' he declared to Buchan, who could not shake his conviction 'that Northcliffe means, when the pear is ripe, to claim the Premiership'.⁴

Maxse Papers; Maxse to Lady Bathurst, 6 October 1917, Bathurst Papers; Strachey to Buchan, 14 and 18 December 1917 (copies), Strachey Papers.

¹ Harcourt to Gardiner, 18 November 1917, Gardiner Papers; Jones, *Whitehall Diary* (16 November 1917), I, 39.

² Entries of 16–19 and 28 December 1917, in Scott, *Political Diaries*, pp. 319, 325; Amery's diary, 16 December 1917, Amery Papers.

³ Robert Hield to Lady Bathurst, 19 November 1917, Bathurst Papers.

⁴ Garvin to Scott, 20 November 1917, *Guardian* Archives; Strachey to Buchan, 14 and 18 December 1917 (copies), Strachey Papers.

In spite of appearances, it was Dawson rather than Northcliffe who propitiated the Prime Minister by denying space in *The Times* to Lord Lansdowne's cautious appeal for an elucidation of war aims. Northcliffe, to whom the credit and blame personally accrued, was in Paris on 27 November, when Dawson unilaterally decided 'that the general effect of its publication would be thoroughly bad'. By the time he returned, it was too late except to fault Dawson's judgment. 'The Editor used to say in after years that his difference of opinion with Northcliffe over this matter was the sharpest they ever had,' which was saying a good deal indeed. On the 29th, the *Daily Telegraph* did the gentlemanly thing and published the Lansdowne letter. 'We do not say that Lord Lansdowne ... does not take some of the ground which many thinking and patriotic men may disapprove,' it declared with conscientious convolution.[1]

The *Manchester Guardian* combined resolute backing for Lansdowne with stern reproaches to *The Times*, whose 'Last Word' on 12 December was virtually its first word as well. The *Westminster Gazette* gave a cordial reception. The *Daily News* (1 December), welcoming Lansdowne's statement as 'a torch in the darkness', was not surprised to see it depicted by the *Daily Mail* as a 'White Flag' and by the *Morning Post* as 'a surrender cloaked in the camouflage of hypocrisy'. The *Daily Chronicle*, no admirer of President Wilson in the past, called upon him to rebuke Lansdowne and, implicitly (Gardiner thought), himself. The *Evening Standard*, like the gallant *Telegraph*, demurred only on the specific point about 'Freedom of the Seas'. All in all, reckoned the *Daily News*, 'the cleavage between reason and unreason follows the lines that we might have anticipated'. What no one could have anticipated, however, was the anomalous behaviour of the *Sunday Pictorial*, which sent Arnold Bennett 'a long wire asking me to write an article defending Lansdowne's letter ... as an antidote to the "knock-out-blow" speechifying' of Lloyd George. 'I have written on war topics for the *S.P.* before,' Bennett informed Gardiner, who gave him free rein in the *Daily News*, 'but this is the first time they have asked me to write on war politics, & I hope you will agree with me in regarding it as a distinct sign of grace.'[2]

Gardiner was too much of a doubting Thomas to partake of Bennett's euphoria, and his cynicism again proved justified. 'You know how Lord Northcliffe's brother, Lord Rothermere, starts a "stunt" against Mr George one week in the *Sunday Pictorial*,' he stated in an open 'Letter to the Liberal Whip' on 9 February 1918, 'how the services of the invaluable Lord Beaverbrook are invoked to silence that gun, how next week the *Sunday Pictorial* proclaims Mr George to be the "Only Man," and how in the following week Lord Rothermere is appointed Air Minister and commandeers the British Museum.' In other words, Rothermere had been squared, with

[1] *History of The Times*, IV, part 1, 336–40; Wrench, *Dawson*, pp. 156–57.
[2] Bennett to Gardiner, 6 December 1917, Gardiner Papers.

the delayed result that Bennett's foray into 'war politics' was neatly squashed.

* * *

The new year eventually brought peace, enshrined in diplomatic treaties that redrew the map of Europe. During the preceding months, a series of seismic shifts altered the topography of British journalism. Outwardly, it was a hiatus between periods of expansion and contraction. No new metropolitan dailies or weeklies were established in the concluding phase of the war, and the sixty-year-old *Standard* was the single noteworthy fatality. Nevertheless, momentous changes were taking place, most of which escaped detection.

An inescapable problem was the increasingly acute shortage of imported newsprint. Many of the quality journals raised their prices, partly as a means of limiting sales: the *Daily News*, followed by the *Star* and the *Evening News*, cost a penny from January; the *Manchester Guardian* paused at a penny-halfpenny on 28 January before going on to end the war at twopence; in March, the *Daily Telegraph* proceeded directly to twopence, while *The Times* – having gone from three halfpennies to twopence in February 1917 – took a further jump to threepence; by April, the circulation of the twopenny *Westminster Gazette* was 'creeping up again' so that it was only 20 per cent below the sale 'at a penny twelve months ago'.[1] Such actions could not have failed to affect patterns of newspaper consumption within different social classes and income groups; in that sense, they carried broad implications. Yet any changes in distribution were less politically significant than a succession of internal adjustments.

In the closing weeks of 1917, Buchan was able to satisfy Strachey's curiosity by confirming 'that Beaverbrook now owns and runs the *Express*', though he was sceptical of Strachey's further deduction 'that Beaverbrook is in working agreement with Northcliffe'. Beyond that, Buchan knew nothing. Incredibly, neither did Sir George Younger, who had replaced Steel-Maitland as Unionist Party chairman. 'By the way,' Younger asked Beaverbrook from party headquarters, 'what is the position of this Office with respect to the *Daily Express*?' From the files he had inherited, it was clear that 'we have a considerable sum invested in its Preference Shares but there doesn't appear to be any evidence, so far as I can see, that they give us a say in the running of the paper'. In due course, Younger was to have his answer in print: the *Express* was accountable exclusively to Beaverbrook, who was himself uncontrollable. He was no more indulgent towards party officials than towards other investors, including the underwriters whom he coerced into becoming preference shareholders. Goulding, who helped him to twist arms and raid pockets, reported that Oliver Hoare, the Tory banker, threatened 'troubles in front unless you adopt a different attitude and took them more into your confidence'. But Beaverbrook

---

[1] *Newspaper Press Directory 1918* (London, 1919), p. 22; A. H. Watson to Maclean, 27 April 1918, Asquith Papers.

had the wherewithal to keep his own counsel. His political kindnesses were usually acts of commercial expediency. 'It is not good business to attack Lord Rothermere even by implication,' he advised Blumenfeld, his trusty editor. 'We are in the middle of complex paper deals with him, and he has always been generous in these matters.'[1]

The nation's economy, like Beaverbrook's, was suffering from the effects of German submarine warfare. At a Cabinet on 11 January, Lloyd George was 'very annoyed with the headlines in the *Evening News* and *Evening Standard* of the night before'. By emphasizing the scarcity of food supplies, they threatened to incite panic and, at the same time, provided 'most excellent propaganda for use against us by the enemy'. The Prime Minister delivered an admonition to Dawson, and Derby spoke stiffly to Hulton, 'who, with Northcliffe, as the P.M. said, were becoming a most menacing and powerful combination'. Their jeremiads were regarded as especially dangerous in the light of Russia's withdrawal from the war and the sympathy it aroused in pacifist circles. Lord Robert Cecil 'produced a copy of the *Herald*', George Lansbury's weekly, where the 'Plenipotentiary for Great Britain of the Russian People's Government' urged British workers to follow the Bolshevik example. 'At once,' within the Cabinet, 'there was a desire to suppress the *Herald*.' Cecil dampened enthusiasm by posing a stark choice between 'complete liberty of the Press or rigorous all-round suppression of offenders, the *Morning Post* not less than the *Herald*'. Lloyd George pointed out that 'the evening papers, with their sensational headlines' and huge sales, 'did more damage to the morale of the nation than did the *Herald*, with its limited circulation of 40,000 or 50,000'. He could not convince Milner, who argued 'that these *Herald* articles were a direct attempt to upset the War Cabinet and that the effect of the suppression of the *Nation* had been very good for it. This the P.M. doubted.' Going back to the initial proposition, 'Carson wanted to know whether some paper could not be got to go for Northcliffe', to which Lloyd George replied wistfully, 'only the *Daily News*, and it is always girding at him'.[2]

Lloyd George was able to depend on the press lords, if not the Lib-Lab sentimentalists, to stand firm against Bolshevism. The *Daily Express*, for example, shrieked that Litvinov's feeble remarks to a Labour conference on 23 January qualified as 'the most menacing speech ever delivered by the Ambassador of a friendly country'. It was less certain that he could count on sustained newspaper support in his running battle with the military chiefs. Writing from Edinburgh on the 25th, Younger noted 'great indignation up here

---

[1] Strachey to Buchan, 14 December 1917 (copy), Strachey Papers; Younger to Beaverbrook, 19 October 1917, and Goulding to Beaverbrook, 20 December [1917], Beaverbrook Papers, H/15 and C/318; Beaverbrook to Blumenfeld, 20 December 1917, quoted in Taylor, *Beaverbrook*, p. 133. Goulding joined the board of the *Express* in September 1918 'so as to be associated' with Beaverbrook. Beaverbrook to Goulding, 25 September 1918 (telegram), and Goulding to Beaverbrook, 30 October [1920], Beaverbrook Papers, C/318.

[2] Jones, *Whitehall Diary* (11 January 1918), I, 44; *Herald*, 12 January 1918.

over the attacks on Haig and Robertson', both native sons: 'the unfairness of the newspaper ramp against men who can't defend themselves is causing the strength of feeling'. Younger met an MP who 'had been asked to write a strong article against Haig' according to specifications that 'emanated from 10 Downing Street. ... Sutherland is said to be in it as usual.' Haig understood that Lovat Fraser, who started 'the attack on the War Office' in the *Daily Mail*, had recently 'spent a Sunday with L.G.'[1]

Tucked into the ministry, Rothermere gave faithful service. The Scottish reaction probably had been triggered by his properties in Glasgow. Lloyd George used the same technique with Beaverbrook, whom he appointed Minister of Information and Chancellor of the Duchy of Lancaster. That left Northcliffe, whose various obsessions – including his health – did not permit him to return to America. Through an ingenious arrangement, 'the entire direction of foreign propaganda' was delegated to him, and he delegated back to Beaverbrook the responsibility for contacts with allied and neutral states. Beaverbrook was as pleased to attain ministerial status as was Northcliffe to avoid it. 'The people would never tolerate a newspaper man being a member of the Government,' Northcliffe had previously told Repington. Holding to this shibboleth, he corrected *The Times*'s inaccuracy 'that I have been appointed MINISTER of Propaganda in Enemy Countries. Such an appointment would place *The Times* in a very difficult position,' he maintained. 'I am DIRECTOR, not Minister. I shall accept no position under the Government that would harass *The Times*, and I have lately again refused Cabinet office.' (According to Steed, the war secretaryship was the post in question.) Northcliffe's appointment was announced on 7 February, the same day that the Cabinet decided to remove Robertson. His papers – including the *Daily Mail*, which had alliterated that 'Ministerial Meddling Means Military Muddling' (13 October 1916) – looked the other way.[2]

The Prime Minister braved a hurricane of criticism. 'There really is more stir about this than I have yet known in any of these purely domestic rows,' wrote Milner, who advised Lloyd George that 'the number of people, who are your friends, ... but are nevertheless seriously upset about the relations of Government and Press, is not negligible'. His recommendation was 'to lie low till the storm blows over, and *to keep the friendly Press off the war path* as far as possible. The less people hear or see of Northcliffe, Beaverbrook (certainly the most unpopular name of all) etc. for the next few weeks the better.' It was not easy, however, to keep under wraps personalities who paraded daily with such ostentation. Robert Sanders commented that the backbenchers around him were 'down on the Press men who have been given places in the Government.

[1] Younger to Bonar Law, 25 January 1918, Bonar Law Papers, 82/8/5; Haig to his wife, 26 January 1918, in Haig, *Private Papers*, p. 280.
[2] Taylor, *Beaverbrook*, pp. 138–41; Northcliffe to Repington, 18 October 1916 (copy), Northcliffe Papers; memorandum by Northcliffe, 19 February 1918, quoted in *History of The Times*, IV, part 1, 350; Steed, *Through Thirty Years* (Garden City, N.Y., 1924), II, 186.

Unionists are very angry at Beaverbrook's appointment.' Austen Chamberlain came to Carson's dinner-table on 4 March 'full of infamy of L.G. in appointing these Press magnates . . . and confident that if he and Carson liked to combine in a resolution on the subject, the Government would collapse'. Milner 'told him that he was barking up the wrong tree', and Kerr 'expanded by pointing out that as long as L.G. had no properly organised backing in the House or the country . . ., he was naturally tempted to create a Press following of his own'. Amery added 'that the putting of great newspaper proprietors into a Government was no more heinous an offence than putting in great landed proprietors for the sake of their local influence'.[1]

Amery's analogy would have cut no ice with Scott, who plainly told Lloyd George at lunch that day 'what I thought about his recent appointment of pressmen'. Showing no repentance, Lloyd George praised Beaverbrook as 'extremely clever' and knew of no evidence that he had engaged in financial improprieties. 'As for Northcliffe,' Lloyd George went on,

> he was safe as long as he was occupied and *The Times* had been quite reasonable during the 7 [*sic*] months he had been in America. It was necessary to find occupation for his abounding energies if they were not to run into mischief. Neither he nor Beaverbrook would allow their propaganda work to be determined by their personal political views – indeed he doubted if they had any considered views. . . .

That was a far cry from the weighty reasons that Lloyd George had improvised to overcome resistance from the King. In conversation with Scott, Lloyd George was rehearsing the 'masterpiece of adroitness' that he presented the next day in the House of Commons, where Amery heard him demolish 'the whole ponderous attack'. Still, the controversy refused to subside. On 11 March, Chamberlain lodged a second parliamentary protest and was discomforted to receive hearty Asquithian support. 'They and I do not act from the same motives or pursue the same objects,' he icily insisted.[2]

There were even stranger bedfellows. In January, Repington had resigned from *The Times*, where his military despatches had been laundered to conform with editorial vacillations. He promptly shifted to the *Morning Post*, an intrepid opponent of Lloyd George's 'strategical and military interventions' (12 February), which did not share Chamberlain's qualms at making common cause with the Asquithians. 'Rumour says that Repington & McKenna have been seen together!' Sanders exclaimed in his diary. All signs pointed to the fact that 'Asquith & Repington were playing the same game', the latter with

---

[1] Milner to Lloyd George, 27 February 1918, quoted in Beaverbrook, *Men and Power* (London, 1956), p. 284; Sanders's diary, 3 March 1918, Bayford Papers; Amery's diary, 4 March 1918, Amery Papers.

[2] Entry of 4 March 1918, in Scott, *Political Diaries*, p. 336; Amery's diary, 5 March 1918, Amery Papers; *Parliamentary Debates (Commons)*, 5th ser., civ, col. 77.

conspicuously more daring. Gwynne was determined to uphold the generals at all costs. 'We are now governed by a Junta of Press magnates with a bit of a scoundrel on top, and no man is safe in these days,' he wrote to his lady proprietor on 18 February. From the sidelines, Haldane saw 'a grand political row' taking shape. 'Margot is up to her elbows in intrigues and actually (do not mention this) had Gwynne . . . at Cavendish Square today!' he revealed to his sister in the early hours of the same morning. 'But,' Haldane predicted, 'the Liberals are too pacifist to get a vote of no confidence in Ll.G.' Gwynne soon realized as much. 'We are not agitating in the *Morning Post* for a change of Government,' he assured Lady Bathurst on 5 March, 'but . . . we cannot be accused of following the Northcliffe Press example.'[1]

Gwynne's purpose, as it evolved, was 'to let the people from time to time get accustomed to the idea that the alternatives are not necessarily Lloyd George or Asquith. There might be somebody else.' But who? In the *Daily News* (2 February), Gardiner advanced the 'democratic' idea of 'a Labour administration . . . with additions from sympathetic quarters from outside Labour's ranks'. Sir G. O. Trevelyan, 'most disagreeably impressed' by this suggestion, changed the reading habits of a lifetime: 'I now take the *Chronicle*, and like it well.' In the *Spectator* (16 February), Strachey renewed his plea for 'a National Ministry representing all the solid elements in the country'; but J. S. R. Phillips of the *Yorkshire Post* doubted whether anyone but Henderson would go along. Garvin feared that 'if L.G. is much further harassed he may determine to make B.L. Prime Minister'. Lloyd George 'could do it', and Beaverbrook would then 'take full measures to satisfy Northcliffe', Garvin was 'quite certain'.[2]

To placate his diverse critics, Lloyd George would have had 'to dismiss Rothermere, Beaverbrook and Northcliffe, as none of them will resign'. That harsh reality was put to him by Captain F. E. ('Freddy') Guest, the coalition's chief whip. Mindful of the dire consequences of such a purge, Guest urged Lloyd George 'to stand to your guns'. Long-term interests were at stake. Sustained in office, 'Beaverbrook would continue to support you and your Government up to, and through, the next General Election. I think Rothermere would feel inclined to do the same. Northcliffe may do anything,' but there was no hurry to find out. Guest was 'almost sure that within two or three months at the latest both Rothermere and Beaverbrook' would amicably take leave: 'Rothermere on account of ill-health, and Beaverbrook . . . to regain his

---

[1] Sanders's diary, 13 February 1918, Bayford Papers; Gwynne to Lady Bathurst, 18 February and 5 March 1918, Bathurst Papers; Haldane to his sister, 18 February 1918 (1.15 a.m.), Haldane Papers, Vol. 6013, fols. 13–14. Gwynne subsequently defended Repington as 'a valuable asset. . . . The publishing people tell me that when he joined us, our circulation gave a bump upwards.' Gwynne to Lady Bathurst, 16 October 1918, Bathurst Papers.

[2] Gwynne to Lady Bathurst, 5 March 1918, Bathurst Papers; Trevelyan to Bryce, 9 February 1918, Bryce Papers; Phillips to Strachey, 8 and 13 March 1918, Strachey Papers; Garvin to Astor, 11 March 1918, Astor Papers.

liberty.' Surely it was better not to incur their wrath. In the meantime, he advised that Sutherland 'should be instructed to curtail his activities', which had too often rebounded. 'When I first took over, last May, I agreed to leave all connection with the London Press entirely in his hands,' recalled Guest, who had gradually come to 'believe it would be wise that the Whips' Office should resume its traditional function of being the chief repository of information suitable for the Press'.[1]

Lloyd George withstood the pressure by waiting it out. Before long, his opponents began to quarrel among themselves. Or else, they were distracted by their own concerns. The *Observer*, torn between Garvin's ardent ministerialism and Astor's disquietude, was 'half-paralysed in the midst of the war' by a labour dispute that threatened to be 'disastrous'; in addition, Garvin complained that the 'paper we print on is shabby'. He hoped that Astor, after three years of collaboration, 'would see differently and give me a partnership. . . . That may have been an erroneous speculation,' he admitted, 'but it was neither unnatural nor unworthy.' Although he was 'sure Waldorf doesn't want to treat me like a journalist he might pick out of the street', Garvin was driven to consider resignation. 'I had an immense influence before I knew him and I am certain that if I parted from the *Observer* I would have it again.' The Duke of Sutherland, 'itching to get into some newspaper trouble', inquired of Northcliffe whether the *Observer* was for sale. A change of ownership might have afforded Garvin better terms. But he communicated that Astor did not have 'the remotest idea of selling'.[2]

That was more than one could say with certainty about Lady Bathurst. Aggrieved by her estrangement from Chamberlain, who disapproved of Gwynne's deviations, she intimated an intention to dispose of the *Morning Post*. E. R. Peacock, a Canadian financier (and later a governor of the Bank of England), was said to have raised sufficient capital 'to negotiate purchase of said daily'; and John Pilling, the railway contractor, was 'also . . . seeing someone with a view to sharing control'. Davidson, Bonar Law's private secretary, could ascertain no 'connection between the two P's' and asked Beaverbrook to investigate. In the event, Lady Bathurst reconsidered. 'So you wouldn't sell the *M.P.* to Lascelles, how curious!' Peacock teased her. He was presumably alluding to Edward Lascelles, the second son of the 5th Earl of Harewood, whose Balfourite connections would have disqualified him. In July, Lady Bathurst rejected Gwynne's request for a salary increase with a proclamation that 'I do not intend to sell the *Morning Post*, but neither do I

---

[1] Guest to Lloyd George, 26 February 1918, Lloyd George Papers, F/21/2/13; Cecil Harmsworth claimed to have been offered 'the post of Chief Whip of the Coalition' in November 1917 (Pound and Harmsworth, p. 594).
[2] Garvin to Astor, 11 March 1918, Astor Papers; Garvin's 'Night Thoughts' [written between January and May 1918], Garvin Papers; Northcliffe to Garvin, 15 April 1918 (copy), and Garvin to Northcliffe, 17 April 1918, Northcliffe Papers.

intend to bear all the worry & anxiety & trouble ... in order to run it entirely for the benefit of the Staff'.[1]

Over-estimating Lady Bathurst's commitment and possibly her assets as well, Maxse appealed to her on behalf of the *Globe*, which had 'done remarkably well during the past nine months' under his supervision. Besides nearly doubling its sale ('which, considering the immense difficulties in the way of production, scarcity of paper, etc., etc., is somewhat surprising'), the *Globe* has turned 'a big weekly loss ... into a substantial weekly profit'. Most of all, it had gained in political stature. 'Just as the *Morning Post* is the only independent morning paper, so we claim to be the only independent evening paper,' wrote Maxse, who confessed that he 'sometimes wondered, as we are so much in harmony, whether we could not have linked up in some way or another and mutually supported each other'. Lady Bathurst, he promised, would find it easy to cooperate with Dudley Docker: 'The politicians have made great and wholly unsuccessful efforts to "nobble" him.'[2] But she was clearly not interested in any further 'worry & expense & trouble', and the *Globe* was left to resume its slide towards extinction.

The Liberal press experienced a comparable number of false alarms, but also some decisive changes. By January, the struggle at the *Westminster Gazette* had been resolved, though perhaps not entirely to Spender's satisfaction. 'I understand all the difficulties,' Lord Esher assured him. 'I only wish you and I had complete control of the *W.G.* . . . You would have been more comfortable and independent.' Cowdray took the largest single block of new preference shares; his fellow subscribers included David Davies (on the rebound from Lloyd George), Sir Walter Runciman (father of the ex-minister), Oswald Partington, Sir Henry Webb (MP for the Forest of Dean), Lord Forteviot (formerly, as Sir John Dewar, MP for Inverness), J. F. L. Brunner, Donald Maclean, and Spender himself.[3]

With ramifications for the future of the *Westminster*, there were concurrent developments within the Starmer-Morrell provincial empire. Out for a Sunday stroll, Goulding 'ran across Hamar Greenwood', the Coalition Liberal MP for Sunderland, whom he directed to see Beaverbrook 'at once'. As Greenwood understood it, 'the Starmer ... syndicate of papers at Birmingham Sheffield & district ... are for sale – they are short of cash'. In fact, the Starmer-Morrell chain was in the process of acquiring an additional link at Nottingham, where Sir Jesse Boot, the retail chemist, required assistance in maintaining the morning *Express* (afterwards the *Journal*) and the *Evening News*. 'The ques-

---

[1] Davidson to Beaverbrook [1918], Beaverbrook Papers, C/203; Peacock to Lady Bathurst, 13 March [1918], and Lady Bathurst to Gwynne, 18 July 1918 (copy?), Bathurst Papers.

[2] Maxse to Lady Bathurst, 5 June 1918, Bathurst Papers.

[3] Esher to Spender, 13 January 1918, Spender Papers, Add. MSS. 46, 392, fol. 267. Sir Walter Runciman eventually declined to incur the full liability, which did not jeopardize control (W. Runciman, his son, to Maclean, 11 August 1918, Asquith Papers). There is no evidence here or in the Esher Papers that Esher took any part.

tion of control' inevitably arose in negotiations. Morrell entertained 'no objection' to the designation of either Boot or his wife as chairman, provided that there were adequate guarantees that the Nottingham papers 'could not ultimately get into the hands of the opposite party', by which he apparently meant the coalition. 'You will agree with me,' he wrote to John Gulland, the independent Liberal whip, 'that there could be no greater calamity for the party than that their only Organ in this large area should be allowed to stop.' At Boot's suggestion, the chief whip was named 'Arbitrator in case of any dispute'. That was only fitting, as Boot's investment of £5,000 in preference shares was matched by the party, half in the name of Maclean and half in the name of A. D. Fairbairn, a chartered accountant. When Boot was relieved of his entire holding in 1921, the Maclean and Fairbairn shares (since transferred to Sir Robert Hudson) were jointly assigned to Cowdray's son. In the process, Cowdray's Westminster Press Ltd. was set on the foundations of the interlocking Starmer and Rowntree Trust properties.[1]

The axe that had hung over Spender's head now began to swing more widely, though the actual executions were delayed. Gardiner's contract at the *Daily News* was renewed in March 1918 with no hint of the fate that was to befall him fifteen months later. George Cadbury admired his articles on temperance and looked forward to peacetime, when both the *Daily News* and the *Star* could return to a halfpenny, preferably equal in size and 'without advertisements'. Politically, too, he was prepared to take risks. For the *Daily News* 'to go in for a large Labour Party in the House of Commons' would not be 'a popular thing to do among our middle-class readers'; but, he reminded his son, 'we have always gone in for what we believed to be right, rather than for what pays'. The Cadburys appreciated Gardiner's impatience with Asquith, but not his inveterate hostility towards Lloyd George, which was the source of friction between them.[2]

It was the reverse for Dawson, whose first editorship at *The Times* ended in February 1919. From the spring of 1918, Northcliffe grew more unruly and, some said, unhinged. Incensed by the appointment of Chamberlain to the War Cabinet, he served notice that 'I shall not ... be able to continue to give the great support of my newspapers to the Government which I now do – often with a twinge of conscience'. On 4 May, after 'carefully reflecting upon the attitude of *The Times* towards the Prime Minister', he concluded 'that the Paper ... lacks independence'. The government's 'flabbiness' was somehow Dawson's fault. 'So long as Sutherland continues to tell Lloyd George that *The Times* will dance to any tune he plays,' Northcliffe told his editor on 5 July, 'so long will he continue his covert negotiations' with left-wingers and Lansdown-

---

[1] Goulding to Beaverbrook, 'Sunday' [1918], Beaverbrook Papers, C/318; Morrell to Gulland, 17 January 1918, and memorandum by Hudson, 22 March 1922, Asquith Papers.
[2] Contract dated 21 March 1918, George Cadbury to Henry Cadbury, 8 February, 16 March, and 29 April 1918, Edward Cadbury to Gardiner, 13 April 1918, and George Cadbury to Gardiner, 10 June 1918, Gardiner Papers.

ites. Northcliffe's 'own belief is that the Prime Minister is not a free man' and required constant jogging from *The Times* to loosen his shackles. 'He is oblique, evasive and Welsh.'[1]

On 18 July, *The Times* echoed criticisms of Bonar Law from the *Observer* (23 June) and the *Globe* (11 July). Dawson was obviously building up for his assault on 'The Prime Minister's Position', five days later. While there was no doubt that Lloyd George was 'out to win the war', he was said to be hampered by faint-hearted 'men who should never have been his colleagues at all'. That was more to the liking of Northcliffe, who considered this leading article an accurate 'statement of my views on the general question, and those views admit of no compromise'. As he intended, members of the government were incensed. Long, who had 'reason to know Northcliffe wants me & other "worn-out old Tories" out', suspected that this attack and a 'further effort' on 19 August were 'inspired' by 'some underling at No. 10', probably the egregious Sutherland. '*The Times* article was very nasty and if anyone connected with the P.M. had anything to do with it it would be quite intolerable,' agreed Bonar Law, who thought he could 'say with certainty that not only would L.G. himself resent such an article but that no one from No. 10 has any influence at present with N.' That point was emphatically made by the *Daily Mail*'s violent attacks on Milner, whose eleventh-hour advocacy of a negotiated peace had been made known in the *Evening Standard* on 17 October. 'How can *The Times* keep pace w. these personal squabbles?' Dawson asked in his diary, after Northcliffe 'said he'd served notice on L.G. that he could no longer support him'. Dawson recoiled from Northcliffe's enmities, and the tension between them became mutually unbearable.[2]

To all appearances, Gwynne was the most vulnerable. His leading articles were saturated with a sullen discontent. 'There will be a change ... sooner or later,' the *Morning Post* foretold on 26 April, 'because the Prime Minister, by his preoccupation with party politics and political manoeuvres, has brought himself into a position which has ensured the downfall of better men than Mr Lloyd George.' Gwynne also betrayed symptoms of paranoia. 'We have arrayed against us the cleverest, the most unscrupulous scoundrels in England,' he told Lady Bathurst. The most dangerous was Beaverbrook, 'who governs England. ... Everywhere he goes he drops poison against the *M.P.*' The only trustworthy politician was 'Carson, and against him there is a

---

[1] Notice by Northcliffe, 16 April 1918, quoted in *History of The Times*, IV, part 1, 357; Northcliffe to Dawson, 4 May and 5 July 1918 (copies), Northcliffe Papers. Clifford Sharp, the bibulous editor of the *New Statesman*, informed Northcliffe via Steed that Lloyd George had conversed with Haldane and the Webbs about 'a negotiated peace with Germany at Russia's expense'. Lansdowne and Milner were implicated. Sharp to Steed, 13 June 1918 (copy), Northcliffe Papers.

[2] Northcliffe to Stuart, 26 July 1918, quoted in *History of The Times*, IV, part 1, 364n.; Long to Bonar Law, 19 August 1918, and Bonar Law to Long, 20 August 1918 (copy), Bonar Law Papers, 83/6/30, and 84/7/64; Gollin, *Proconsul*, pp. 571–72; Amery's diary, 6 November 1918, Amery Papers; Dawson's diary, 4, 6 and 14 November 1918, Dawson Papers.

conspiracy in the Press – especially the Northcliffe Press – which makes it almost impossible for him to be able to do anything'. Denied a higher salary, when Dawson had received a derisory rise of seven pounds a week, Gwynne was 'hurt to the quick' to receive instead a formal injunction. 'I should be very much obliged if you would edit the paper more carefully and devote less of your time to seeing politicians and to all sorts of cabals and intrigues,' Lady Bathurst wrote to him in July. 'I have never intrigued. I don't know how to,' he protested. 'As for "colloguing" with politicians, have you not realised that they won't speak to me? For we have been frank about their absolute failures and have forfeited their sympathy.' Gwynne's survival would have been difficult to predict.[1]

So, for a time, was Garvin's future at the *Observer*. That he and Astor were driven to frame a formal agreement was testimony to the uneasiness between them. Following Lloyd George's example, there was to be 'a small Cabinet dealing with policy . . . in all its aspects and on all matters'. Astor would be chairman, and Garvin would be one of 'three to five members'. In case of any 'difference or dispute' between Garvin and Astor (or either of them and the collective council), it would be submitted to a three-man tribunal, consisting of Goulding, F. S. Oliver, and Lionel Hichens, who had graduated from Milner's Kindergarten to a successful career in business. 'The decision of the said Tribunal', it was laid down, 'shall be final and conclusively binding', and might include the 'terms and conditions upon which the said James Louis Garvin shall if possible continue to contribute literary or other matter to the said paper during the remainder of the said period of six years'. A legal protection for both editor and proprietor, this agreement provided a mechanism for Garvin's displacement. Yet his editorship continued until 1942, five years longer than Gwynne's at the *Morning Post*.[2]

The first of the editorial casualties was one of the least expected. Robert Donald was the victim of Lloyd George's revenge. The breaking-point came in May, when Donald compounded his offences by appointing Major-General Sir Frederick Maurice as the *Daily Chronicle*'s military correspondent. On 7 May, Maurice asserted in a letter to *The Times* that the Prime Minister had misled Parliament with regard to the number of troops deployed in France. Two days later, in the stormy 'Maurice debate', Asquith moved for a select committee to ascertain the validity of Maurice's allegations. For the first and last time during the war, the opposition divided the House – unsuccessfully – against the government. The *Star* (9 May) did not require the verdict of a select committee to indict Lloyd George as 'the grand old camouflager'. To Scott, however, there 'really seemed to be no case worth enquiring into, unless it were one

---

[1] Gwynne to Lady Bathurst, 27 April, 27 May, 18 June, 17 and 26 July 1918, Bathurst Papers.
[2] Astor to Hichens, 2 August 1918 (copy), Astor Papers; *also see* John Stubbs, 'Appearance and Reality, a case study of the *Observer* and J. L. Garvin, 1914–42,' in Boyce, Curran, and Wingate, eds., *Newspaper History*, p. 324.

against Maurice' for insubordination. Lloyd George, 'whatever his faults', had 'proved himself right exactly on the vital matter of unity of command as to which the *Daily News* and the *Morning Post* – singular alliance! – have been perpetually nagging at or attacking him'.[1] Henceforth, the *Daily Chronicle* was to nag and attack with them.

Like Repington's earlier appointment to the *Morning Post*, Maurice's employment by the *Chronicle* was a calculated provocation. Donald, having previously irked Lloyd George by siding with Robertson, was renewing his reputation as the generals' friend. In that capacity, he cast his lot with the Asquithians, now roused from their lethargy. On 13 September, after the Prime Minister paid tribute to France's General Foch without mentioning Haig, the *Chronicle* remarked that it was 'a small mind that petulantly refuses to acknowledge the services of a great soldier'. Eight days later, it challenged an official decision to withhold publication of Haig's spring despatch. Its attacks were not restricted to military affairs, however. Long was disturbed by references to 'graft' in a report about pensions. 'The P.M. tells me he thinks it might be well for me to write to Editor of *D. Chronicle* & ask him for his authority for his statements', but Long feared that that 'wd. be playing into the impudent rascal's hands'. Bonar Law, to whom Lloyd George showed the article, was likewise 'doubtful about the wisdom of writing a letter'. More decisive remedies were at hand.[2]

Throughout the preceding year, Lloyd George had been making desultory efforts to obtain custody of the *Daily Chronicle*, paired with the best-selling *Lloyd's Weekly News*. These negotiations had involved Donald and implied no threat to his tenure. Early in 1917, Lloyd George had hoped that Lord Leverhulme, the millionaire soap manufacturer and (as W. H. Lever) former Liberal M.P., would buy out Frank Lloyd. But Lloyd's price of £900,000 for the ordinary shares alone was too high even for so well-endowed a philanthropist as Leverhulme. Besides, 'he knew nothing about newspapers'. Beaverbrook, believed by Donald to have been using Leverhulme as a front-man, 'revealed himself' the following March: 'He saw himself controlling proprietor of the papers and said he was going to make a hell of a lot of money out of the business.' Beaverbrook's offer of £500,000 was not taken seriously by Lloyd, who 'by this time ... was suspicious of the methods adopted and intensely annoyed at the publicity and gossip which had arisen over the matter'. At lunch on the 21st, when Donald questioned Beaverbrook's motives, Lloyd George unconvincingly professed ignorance. Donald then approached some affluent Asquithians – Cowdray, the elder Runciman, Partington, and McKenna – with whom he claimed to have come within an ace of success. These counter-moves must have been known to – and resented by

[1] Scott to Courtney, 10 May 1918, Courtney Papers.
[2] Beaverbrook, *Men and Power*, p. 55; Long to Bonar Law, 1 September 1918, and Bonar Law to Long, 2 September 1918 (copy), Bonar Law Papers, 84/1/1, and 84/7/76.

– Lloyd George. In turn, Donald was disgusted that Guest, as Coalition Liberal chief whip, should engage in 'a very dirty business' with Beaverbrook.[1]

It was against this background that the *Daily Chronicle* hired Maurice and sharpened its criticisms of the government. The bidding then entered a new and more rancorous phase. According to Beaverbrook's undated account, he had no sooner declined an improbable invitation to combine with Donald (possibly when they met at the Ministry of Information on 17 April) than he was approached by Sir Henry Dalziel, who 'asked me to join forces with ... friends' of Lloyd George. Beaverbrook 'agreed to do so ... on the basis of my paying £200,000 & securing the weekly paper'. Keen to enter the lucrative Sunday market (he was to launch the *Sunday Express* before the year was out), he would have been happy with either *Lloyd's Weekly* or the *Sunday Times*, merged by the Berry brothers into a giant syndicate of indeterminate shape. While 'waiting for the result of H.D.'s negotiations' with Lloyd, he 'heard strange rumours of proposals for my exclusion'.[2]

Prodded by Lloyd George's complaint that matters had 'now been drifting for a whole year', Guest formulated a 'scheme' that shut out both Beaverbrook (whose ambitions may have been too grandiose) and Donald (whose loyalty was suspect). There was to be a new holding company with Dalziel as chairman and 'absolute political controller (subject only to retirement by the Prime Minister acting through Capt. Guest as holder of the Political Control shares)'. As Guest conceived of the arrangements, 'complete commercial control' would reside with the Berrys, 'a stipulation enforced by my largest subscriber'; at least for the time being, they would not avail themselves of the 'opportunity of selling the *Sunday Times* to Max Beaverbrook'. That Dalziel was 'professionally' opposed to them was probably responsible for their dropping out. For, though he incurred 'no financial liability whatsoever', Dalziel was the linchpin. 'The P.M. can now, with his influence with H.D., close and achieve a very great & vital coup in his own interest,' rejoiced Guest. So it proved. 'The *Daily Chronicle* purchase has been completed,' Riddell wrote in his diary on 1 October. 'L.G. is to have full control of the editorial policy through Sir H. Dalziel, who will in effect be his agent.'[3]

E. A. Perris, the news editor, heard of the sale from Riddell on 3 October. He informed Donald, who laughed scornfully. (According to the recollection of Mildred Canivet, who had edited the women's pages, 'Perris had known all along' and was kept quiet with the promise of the editorship under Dalziel.) On

---

[1] Donald, '*Daily Chronicle* Negotiations, 1917–1918,' and Jones, 'Sale of the *Daily Chronicle*,' Donald Papers; Riddell, *War Diary* (23 June 1918), p. 334.

[2] Beaverbrook to Lloyd George, n.d. [1918], Beaverbrook Papers, E/10/269. Beaverbrook afterwards told Arnold Bennett that he had tried to buy the *Chronicle*. 'Deal didn't work. Ll.G. was cross with him,' leaving unclear whether that was cause or effect. Bennett's journal, 5 October 1918.

[3] Lloyd George to Guest, n.d. [August 1918], and Guest to J. T. Davies, 'Saturday' [24 August 1918], Lloyd George Papers, F/21/2/32, 34; Riddell, *War Diary* (1 October 1918), p. 365.

the 4th, Donald 'saw Mr Lloyd a little before lunch' and 'was about to ask him to allow me to issue a contradiction to settle the rumours when, to my astonishment, he told me that the statement was true'. Dalziel, Lloyd revealed, had made him an offer in July. Then, in September, Guest and Lloyd George had paid him a visit. Lloyd

> said that Mr Lloyd George complained of the criticisms which had appeared in the *Daily Chronicle*, and said, 'We cannot trust Donald.' He said that Mr Lloyd George did not resent ordinary criticism, but complained very bitterly of the articles which had appeared about Haig, more particularly with one in which the Prime Minister was said to have a small mind. Mr Lloyd said that that was more than he could stand.

(Mrs Canivet confirmed that 'Ll.G. had been bothering Frank Lloyd for some time' and that the 'small mind' gibe – which was Harry Jones's – 'was the last straw'.) Donald, who had not expected Lloyd to sell before the war was over, had until six o'clock the next evening to empty his desk.[1]

'No one believed that Lloyd's price (£1,600,000) could possibly be found,' wrote J. A. Spender, who seemed to forget Lloyd George's talent for fund-raising. He informed Maclean on the 8th that 'the names of the subscribers except Andrew Weir & James White are still in doubt'. Grant Morden, a Canadian financier, '& some other of Beaverbrook's rascals are suspected', but Spender was inclined to 'doubt if Ll.G. could have commanded them, unless he too has paid the price – which is total submission to Tories, tariff-reformers & grafters'. Weir, a Scottish shipper, was to become 1st Baron Inverforth and Minister of Munitions the following January. Guest had heard of him from Sir Charles Sykes, soon to be elected Coalition Liberal MP for Huddersfield, and verified 'that Lloyd could not possibly take exception to him as a principal on the grounds of politics'. White has been identified as a 'notorious Lancashire company promoter who committed suicide in 1927' without the knighthood he had been promised. His investment, like Weir's, qualified as a contribution to the Lloyd George Fund, which realized a windfall profit in 1926, when the *Chronicle* again changed hands.[2]

The *Morning Post* broke the news to the public on the 7th, tartly commenting that it was 'at least a coincidence' that the purchase was effected just when 'the journal was developing into an outspoken critic of Lloyd-Georgian politics'. On the 15th, during question time in the Commons, Pringle asked

> whether the attention of the Chancellor of the Exchequer had been called to the recent purchase of London newspapers for the purpose of changing their

[1] Donald, '*Daily Chronicle* Negotiations', Donald Papers; H. A. Taylor, *Donald*, pp. 178–79; memorandum by Mildred Canivet, 5 May 1933, Donald Papers.
[2] Spender to Maclean, 8 October 1918, Asquith Papers; Guest to Lloyd George, 7 September 1918, Lloyd George Papers, F/21/2/36; H. A. Taylor, *Donald*, p. 181; Herd, *March of Journalism*, p. 257.

political policy, whether the Government would set up a Committee to inquire into the tendencies towards monopolistic control of the Press, and whether a supply of paper would be granted for new newspapers to promote the policy of the newspapers purchased.

Dalziel, whose 'sole ewe lamb was *Reynolds's Newspaper*' when the war began, had since 'increased his flock' by acquiring managerial control of the *Pall Mall Gazette* and the Lloyd group. 'With the greatest reluctance', he rose to respond to this 'base agitation', which he alleged to have been 'provoked and encouraged ... by a committee of three Liberal editors'. The facts, as he presented them, were that Lloyd, with whom 'I have been doing business ... for thirty years', had decided on account of 'failing health ... that he would have to release himself from the vast responsibility of carrying on that large undertaking'. (Hardly the invalid that Dalziel made out, Lloyd was aged sixty-three and led an active life until 1927.) Only after others tried and failed had Dalziel mercifully come to Lloyd's relief. 'The suggestion ... that because the *Daily Chronicle* appeared to criticise the Prime Minister therefore I rushed in ... is entirely incorrect.' A report of this debate was the first acknowledgment in the *Chronicle* that changes had occurred. '*Chronicle* never announced Donald's resignation,' remarked Gwynne, who published a letter from Donald in the *Morning Post* on the 17th. Moreover, the *Chronicle* had 'mangled Pringle's speech in reference to Lloyd George's interference' (Pringle had specifically credited Dalziel with 'the powerful aid of the Prime Minister') and 'contained nothing of Carson's speech about Northcliffe'. As late as the first week of November, according to Gwynne, 'the old proprietors of the *D.C.* did not know the names of the new purchasers'.[1]

The *Daily Chronicle* continued as a self-professed 'liberal and democratic organ'. Perris assumed the editorship 'subject to the approval of the managing director', namely Dalziel, who in turn was subject to the approval of Lloyd George. Spender put down Perris as 'merely a news-gatherer without politics or writing capacity ..., the sort of man loved by the newspaper bosses'. Maurice retreated to the *Daily News*, where Harry Jones soon followed. Ensor remained as chief leader writer. Notwithstanding some seven years of 'close collaboration' with Donald, he declined an invitation to a lunch in Donald's honour on 14 November: 'If the lunch were simply a friendly mtg. to celebrate the success of your past brilliant editorship, I should of course go to hold up both hands'; but 'I feel I can't run the risk of an attendance wh. mt. be misconstrued'. The event was more a wake than a celebration, for Donald was never to recover editorial prominence. Lloyd had been squared and Donald squashed.[2]

* * *

[1] *Parliamentary Debates (Commons)*, 5th ser., cxviii, cols. 78–94; *Daily Chronicle*, 16 October 1918; *Morning Post*, 17 October 1918; notes by Gwynne, 11 November 1918, Gwynne Papers.
[2] A. Rhys Roberts (solicitor) to Ensor, 16 November 1918, and Ensor to Donald, 13 November 1918 (copy), Ensor Papers; Spender to Maclean, 8 October 1918, Asquith Papers; H. A. Taylor, *Donald*, p. 185; Jones, 'Sale of the *Daily Chronicle*,' Donald Papers.

The seizure of the *Chronicle*, Spender lamented to Maclean, was 'a very serious business for the "old gang"', in that it equipped the coalition with dependable support from a metropolitan Liberal daily. Anxious to retaliate, David Davies was heard to be 'seething with vague ideas about a morning *W.G.*' Spender, aware of the obstacles, proposed 'a meeting the moment Parliament assembled [to] see whether we can bring out a morning sheet at all events for the election, if there is to be one'.[1]

Lloyd George was known to favour an autumn appeal to the electorate, whether or not the war was over. For that reason, he had been in such a hurry to wrap up his negotiations with Lloyd. It was not that he expected that the *Chronicle* would help him win so much as he wished to be spared the inconvenience of its mounting opposition. The voters, vastly more numerous and heterogeneous than when they last went to the polls in 1910, were an unknown quantity. No one, least of all the newspapermen, knew how much weight editorial opinion would carry. Long trembled at the putative influence on 'the working man' of *John Bull*, a journal he mistakenly believed to enjoy 'a circulation of 6,000,000 & ... it is going up'. Lloyd George was certainly more sophisticated than that. Yet, as the *National Review* put it, he had 'a positive craze for the Press, being convinced that, given sufficient journalistic backing, nothing else matters'.[2]

The keepers of Lloyd George's 'myrmidon Press', as Gwynne derided them, catered to his craving out of their own self-interest. Rothermere invited Sutherland to lunch on 27 September and passed along a message. 'The press crowd, he says, are by no means insistent on conscription for Ireland', and he, Northcliffe, and Hulton had agreed among themselves that they 'did not care very much what was done' about Home Rule. Like Lloyd George, Rothermere was 'breast high for an election. He is anxious to give any help in the way of influencing newspapers,' and indicated 'that Northcliffe is willing to go to Paris to work the *Daily Mail* among the soldiers so as to explain the matter to them'. Writing a few days later to Riddell, Northcliffe stipulated certain conditions. He would 'be very happy to help' Lloyd George, 'and my Paris *Daily Mail*, which now has a daily circulation of 320,000 among the soldiers, could, I think, win the election, if I go there and work'. But he was 'not going to work for the return of the Old Gang': Chamberlain, Long, and possibly Asquith, who was mentioned as a post-war Lord Chancellor. 'My exact position may be summed up in the following words', carefully chosen: 'I do not propose to use my newspapers and personal influence ... unless I know definitely, and in writing, and can consciously approve, the personal constitution of the Government.' Riddell lost no time in showing 'the letter to

---

[1] Spender to Maclean, 8 October 1918, Asquith Papers.
[2] Long to Bonar Law, 19 August 1918, Bonar Law Papers, 83/6/30; *National Review*, n.d., quoted in Pound and Harmsworth, p. 667.

L.G., who said that he ... would not dream' of complying.[1]

Lloyd George's refusal was less remarkable than Northcliffe's presumption. A matter of common knowledge, it demonstrated to George Cadbury how far the Prime Minister had allowed himself to become 'a mere tool of Lord Northcliffe, who through *The Times* and *Daily Mail* largely rules England'. Cadbury had taken Gardiner to task for being too severe. He now apologized: 'I had a strong presentiment that if he adhered to his radical views it might save a revolution and would absolutely dish! the Tory papers. But your policy may have been right. You are on the spot.'[2] Lloyd George must have sensed the danger that he himself might be dished. He could neither count on Northcliffe's goodwill nor rule out the possibility that Northcliffe would resort to wrecking tactics.

With the expert assistance of Sir Henry Norman, Guest took soundings and reported 'that generally speaking the *Press* remains about the same as hitherto', predominantly opposed to an early election. Lloyd George, putting quality above quantity, was undeterred. On 22 October, Amery 'went to a meeting at 12 Downing Street', the chief whip's office, where Charles Higham (subsequently knighted for his efforts) 'expounded his advertisement scheme with great enthusiasm and vigour'. Sanders, Guest, and Norman were also present. Amery 'was quite at one' with Higham, 'a professional advertiser, ... that advertising in the Press on modern lines is much better political propaganda than the old business of leaflets and posters'. It was 'finally decided' that, instead of articles which purported to 'be amiable generalisations issued as by a group of citizens', there should be press releases which would 'directly and frankly appear over the name of the Coalition Publicity Committee and so be able gradually to take on a more definitely political character'. Norman tried his hand at writing one ('Persons or Policy?'), which he was 'ready to insert over his own name in the *Manchester Guardian*' if Lloyd George 'thought it useful'. Apparently he did not, or else Scott proved unaccommodating, for the article never appeared. Northcliffe declined to see Higham and telephoned Riddell to complain 'in strong terms about the scheme'. Riddell agreed that 'the advertisements ... would create a wrong impression'. Using his 'influence', as Northcliffe enjoined, he stated his objections with the result that 'ultimately the advertisements ... were withdrawn'.[3]

Riddell was the intermediary between Lloyd George and Northcliffe, whose relations were at a nadir. On 12 November, nine days after the Prime Minister had told him to 'Go to Hades', Northcliffe resigned as director of

[1] Gwynne to Lady Bathurst, 11 September 1918, Bathurst Papers; memorandum by Sutherland, 27 September 1918, Lloyd George Papers, F/93/2/9; Northcliffe to Riddell, 3 October 1918 (copy), Northcliffe Papers; Riddell, *War Diary* (3 October 1918), p. 366.
[2] George Cadbury to Gardiner, 10 June and 16 October 1918, Gardiner Papers.
[3] Amery's diary, 22 October 1918, Amery Papers; Guest to Lloyd George, 17 and 29 October 1918, Lloyd George Papers, F/21/2/42, 46; Riddell, *War Diary* (30 October 1918), pp. 376–77.

enemy propaganda. The previous day's armistice robbed the announcement of its intended impact. Lloyd George publicly expressed 'gratitude for the great services you have rendered to the Allied cause' and politely stated that Northcliffe had seen his job to completion. Beaverbrook, after recurrent battles with the Foreign Office and several threatened resignations, had relinquished office on 21 October. 'You may take it from me that there is no political significance whatever in Beaverbrook's resignation,' Bennett informed Gardiner. Beaverbrook was suffering from a throat ailment, which required an operation. 'He didn't want to resign, but his specialists refuse to take responsibility for his recovery if he doesn't, & that is all there is to it.' Nevertheless, the appearance created by these two departures was ominous.[1]

The swift collapse of Germany at the beginning of November heightened the imminence of an election. On the 4th, Northcliffe published a signed article, 'From War to Peace', in *The Times* and the *Daily Mail*. At his own expense, it was cabled to newspapers abroad. A highly egotistical statement, it signified its author's bid for a seat at the approaching peace conference. Edward Cadbury's thoughts that day were more altruistic. 'We must keep emphasising the world point of view, otherwise we shall never get a League of Nations,' he wrote to Gardiner, 'and it is important for the *Daily News* to keep putting forward the view of a world state.' Especially for this reason, he felt 'very strongly about the underhand methods that are being used to give the Government a blank cheque' at the polls.[2]

Lloyd George unveiled his plans for an election to an assembly of Liberals on the 12th. Four days earlier, Guest gave a luncheon at the Ritz to float 'an idea of his for a committee of Unionist and Liberal proprietors to try and strike the same note' during the campaign. Amery and Sanders, the only Unionists who turned up, provided detailed accounts in their diaries. Rothermere, Dalziel, and Riddell, all classified as Liberals, were present. Norman 'completed the party'. Amery 'felt I was in a real den of thieves when they once started talking and realised more than ever that the political strength of the Liberal Party has lain not in its principles but in the thorough-going unscrupulousness of its wire-pullers'. Sanders, equally censorious, reported that 'the dominant note of the conversation was the insistence by all these Liberals of the danger of Tory dominance in the Coalition'. Rothermere struck him 'as more of a bounder than I imagined'. It was the first time that Amery had 'met or even seen' Rothermere 'at close quarters ... : a more perfect specimen of the plutocratic cad it would be hard to imagine'. When Guest suggested consultation with editors, Rothermere boasted that he had

[1] Pound and Harmsworth, p. 670; *History of The Times*, IV, part 1, 386–87; Clarke, *Northcliffe Diary* (notes on November 1918), p. 117; Taylor, *Beaverbrook*, pp. 155–56; Bennett to Gardiner, 29 October 1918, Gardiner Papers.
[2] *History of The Times*, IV, part 1, 390–91; Edward Cadbury to Gardiner, 4 November 1918, Gardiner Papers.

'six editors and if any one of them dared to say something I disapproved of I should have him on the pavement in half-an-hour. My brother would do the same to any of his editors.' Amery, a professional journalist, considered 'this kind of creature ... one of the biggest dangers we have got to fight in future'.[1]

More immediately, however, the Prime Minister needed 'this kind of creature' in his fight with other politicians. 'Your Administration has been sustained by a Coalition of the Press, a section of the Liberal Party, and the Conservative Party,' Rothermere reminded him on the 14th. 'Without the aid of the Press, it is a fair thing to say that the present Coalition Government could not have survived the storms of the last eighteen months.' Rothermere reiterated his promise to 'do all I can to help your candidates'; but, moving into line with Northcliffe (who demanded in that morning's *Mail* a separation of 'the Sheep from the Goats'), he stated that 'I must reserve for myself the full liberty of telling the readers of my papers what they must expect if they are so foolish as to return an increased number of Conservative members to the next House of Commons'. That, of course, was unacceptable to Lloyd George. He and Bonar Law were drafting a joint manifesto and dispensing their 'coupons' expressly to efface tribal differences within the coalition.[2]

Beaverbrook, refreshed by a month's convalescence, was ready to use his influence. Invited by Churchill to canvass press support for Lloyd George, he escorted Rothermere and Hulton to a dinner in Downing Street. Bonar Law, whose presence would have been awkward, wisely stayed away. Rothermere left with the promise of a viscountcy and Hulton with that of a barony. The King grudgingly complied in Rothermere's case, but would not confer anything above a baronetcy on Hulton. (Royal misgivings further obliged Lloyd George to 'postpone the fulfilment' of his 'definite promise' to Dalziel, who exchanged his knighthood for a baronetcy in 1918, but who had to wait 'faithfully and patiently' until 1921 to become Baron Dalziel of Kirkcaldy.) Asking nothing for himself, at least not explicitly, Beaverbrook also delivered the unequivocal support of the *Daily Express*, with a circulation that he estimated to be edging towards half a million. While not to be despised, its importance was not to be exaggerated. One day the previous summer, Blumenfeld met

> George Ulick Browne, FSA, FZS, FRGS, 6th Marquess of Sligo, who is also Baron Mount Eagle, Viscount Westport and Earl of Altamont. Educated Harrow. Formerly captain in the Army. His Majesty's Lieutenant for the County of Mayo and Custos Rotulorum. He owns 125,000 acres, has a house in Mayo, another in Surrey, another in Upper Belgrave Street. ...

[1] Amery's diary, 8 November 1918, Amery Papers; Sanders's diary, 10 November 1918, Bayford Papers.
[2] Rothermere to Lloyd George, 14 November 1918 (copy), Beaverbrook Papers, C/282. Rothermere had resigned office in April, having exhausted his 'stock of health'. Rothermere to Lloyd George, 23 April 1918, quoted in Beaverbrook, *Men and Power*, p. 380.

His clubs are the Carlton, Travellers', Burlington Fine Arts and Kildare Street, Dublin. He is a wide-awake, intelligent man of the world.

Blumenfeld recounted their conversation:

> 'You are a journalist, aren't you?'
> I admitted the soft impeachment.
> 'What's your paper?'
> 'The *Daily Express*.'
> 'Dublin?'
> 'No, London *Daily Express*.'
> 'Hm. I cannot say I have ever seen it.'
> Then, putting his finger to his lips, he said:
> 'What are you, political or commercial?'
> 'No, we are in the interest of the Wool Trade.'
> 'Oh, I see.'

Not every editor would have enjoyed a joke at his paper's expense. But, then, not every editor would have found himself in this situation.[1]

'Unfortunately', as Gwynne had discerned in September, 'the Press of this country is all tied to one Party or another, or to one personality or another.' This tendency extended to the religious weeklies, where the *Baptist Times* (13 December) offered 'no apology' for its pledge of denominational loyalty to 'Mr Lloyd George and the Coalition'. That left the *Morning Post* to 'stand alone in protesting against dishonesty and stupidity, whether it comes from those with whom we have worked in the past, or from those who have been opposed to us'. Northcliffe usurped this position, which Gwynne was forced to abandon upon the discovery that he belonged among 'those who wish to retain, against those who wish to break up, the present social system'. By an overwhelming vote, the Labour Party decided on 14 November to leave the coalition and confront the electorate on its own. Fears of Bolshevism at home and abroad were rampant and not entirely spontaneous. On the 20th, only eight days after Lloyd George had proclaimed himself unafraid of revolution, Lord Robert Cecil saw Riddell 'about the anti-Bolshevist campaign ... in pursuance of the Cabinet instructions'. Cecil undertook to 'instruct someone in the Foreign Office to get together all the facts on the subject', which Riddell would distribute 'to the more important popular papers, such as some of the Sunday papers and the provincial press'. On the grounds that 'something ought to be done with some of the London papers',

---

[1] Taylor, *Beaverbrook*, p. 160; Stamfordham to Bonar Law, 19 April 1919, Bonar Law Papers, 97/2/11; Guest to Lloyd George, 17 May 1920, quoted in Beaverbrook, *Men and Power*, p. 245; Beaverbrook, *Politicians and the Press*, pp. 15–16; Blumenfeld to Beaverbrook, 24 July [1918] (containing a more or less accurate transcription from *Who's Who*), Beaverbrook Papers, H/13.

Alfred Harmsworth (1st Viscount Northcliffe) by Max Beerbohm (circa 1903)

Sir Edward Levy Lawson (1st Baron Burnham), proprietor of the *Daily Telegraph,* as caricatured by Max Beerbohm (Thomas Photos, Oxford)

J. L. Garvin, editor of the *Observer* from 1908 to 1942 and the *Pall Mall Gazette* from 1912 to 1915. (Cartoon by Cleaver, published by arrangement with the librarian,

H. A. ('Taffy') Gwynne, editor of the *Standard* from 1904 to 1911 and the *Morning Post* from 1911 to 1937. – *Punch*, 11 September 1929

C. P. ('Great') Scott, editor of the *Manchester Guardian* from 1872 to 1929, as depicted by 'Matt' in the *Manchester Evening Chronicle*

With Lord Birkenhead holding the lantern, Lords Rothermere ('Mutt') and Beaverbrook ('Jeff') dig to disinter the Lloyd George coalition. – David Low in the *Star*, 14 December 1923

The Political Body-Snatchers.

Lords Rothermere and Beaverbrook (lower right) as uninvited guests at an 'Eve-of-the-Session Party at the Borgias'. – David Low in the *Evening Standard*, 21 November 1933

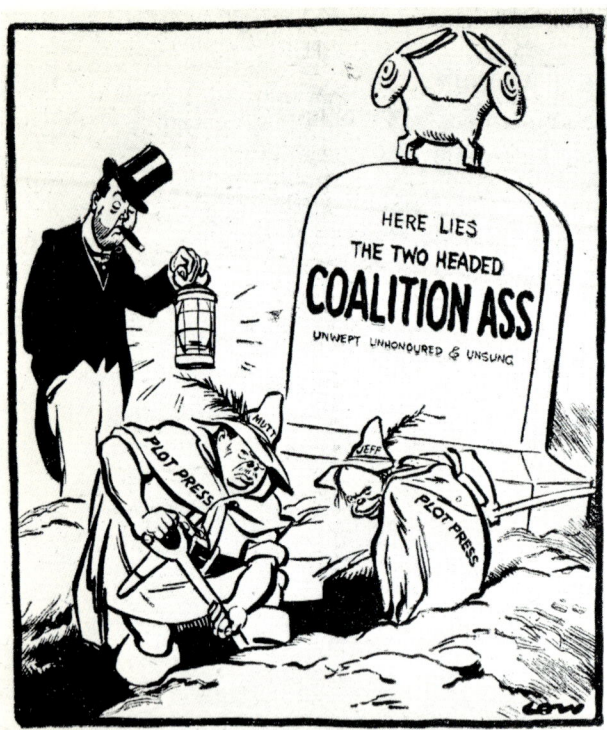

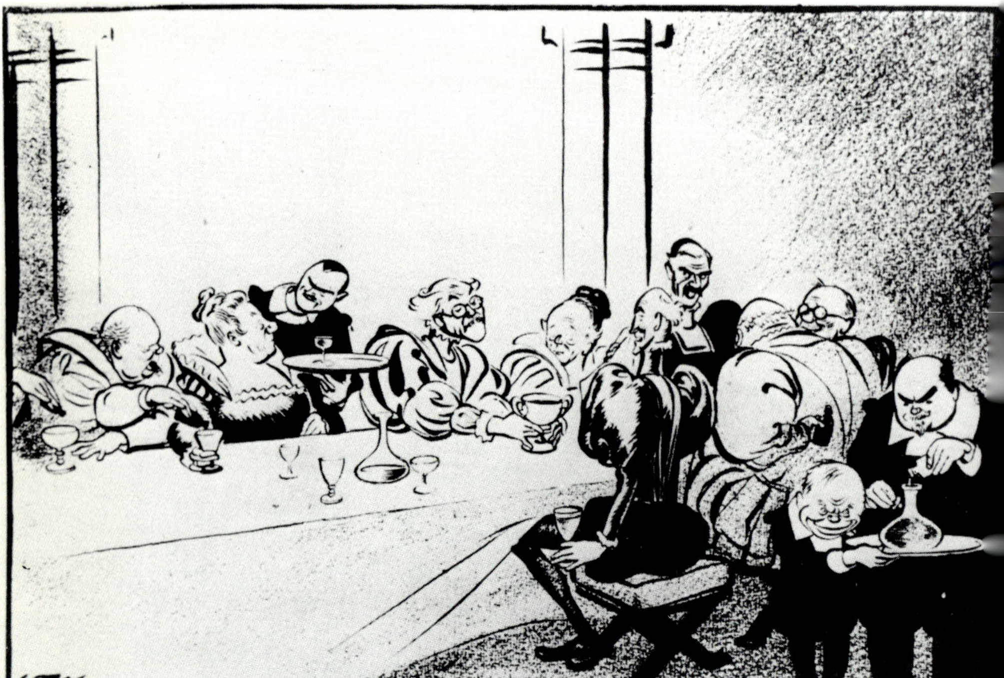

EVE-OF-THE-SESSION PARTY AT THE BORGIAS'. (Copyright in all countries)

Lord Beaverbrook, depicted in *Punch* during the week that Stanley Baldwin accused him of seeking 'the prerogative of the harlot'. — *Punch*, 18 March 1931

Lord Beaverbrook, celebrating a Conservative victory, as portrayed by Michael Cummings

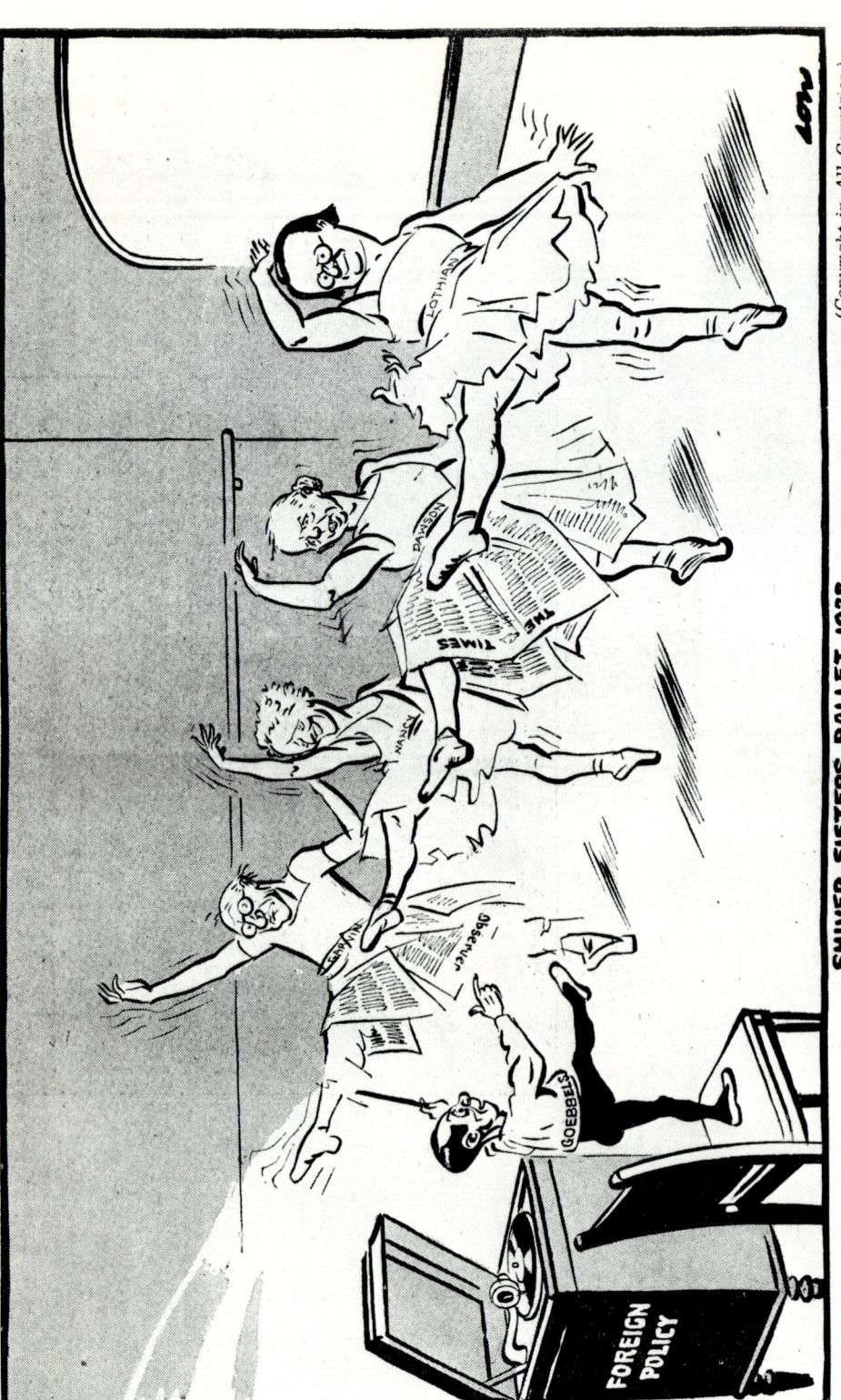

David Low's cartoon of the 'Shiver Sisters' – *left to right*, J. L. Garvin, Lady Astor, Geoffrey Dawson, and Lord Lothian – *Evening Standard*, 3 January 1938.

Philip Zec's controversial cartoon in the *Daily Mirror*, 6 March 1942, which provoked a stormy debate in Parliament and nearly led to the banning of that paper.

A commentary on Fleet Street prospects. – Heath in the *Sunday Times*, 21 March 1976

Overleaf: Rupert Murdoch, the new owner of Times Newspapers, with William Rees-Mogg, then editor of *The Times*.

PRIVATE EYE

No. 499
Friday
23 Jan. '81
30p

"What do you think, Sport?"

"Frightfully good, Sir!"

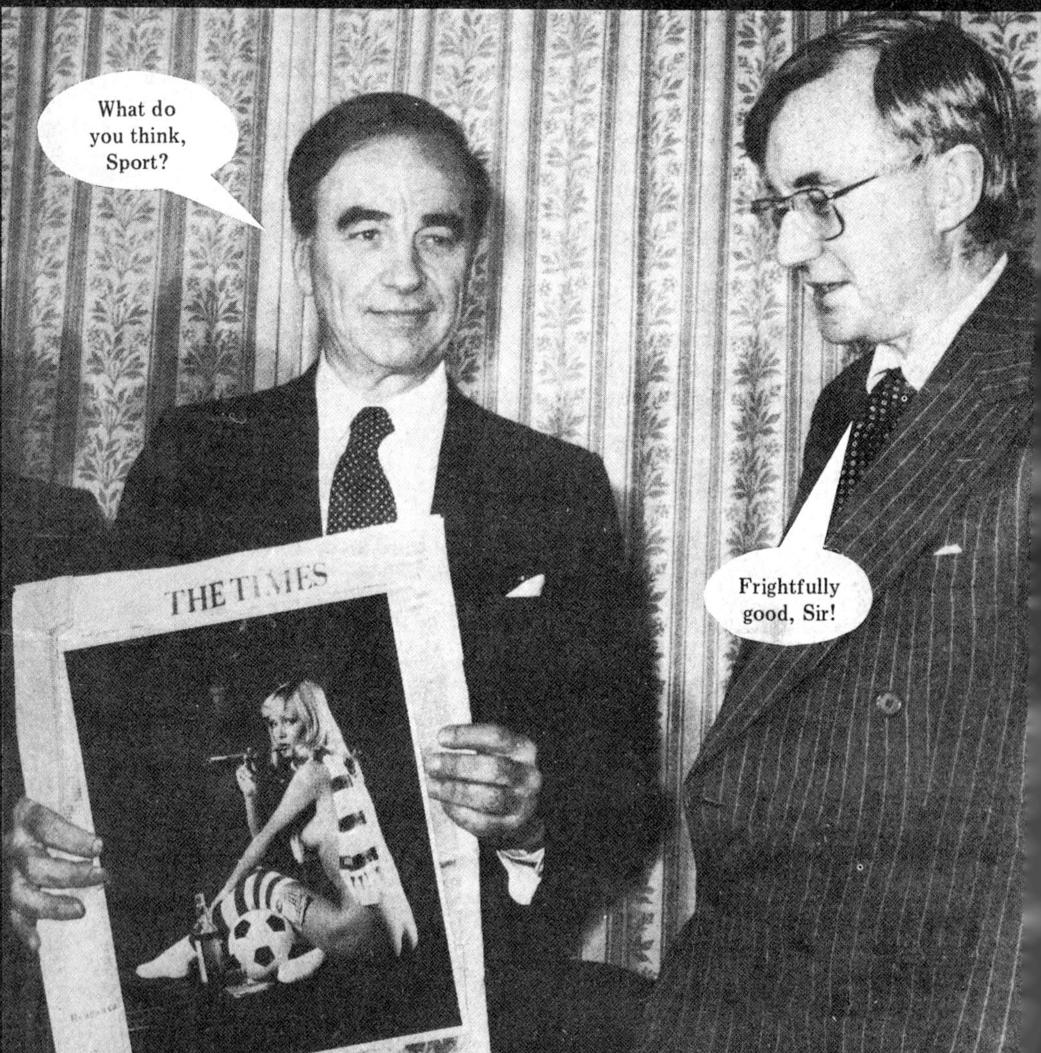

NEW LOOK FOR TIMES

Cecil 'had already got two articles into the *Daily Telegraph*', a natural outlet for them.¹

Philip Snowden, after failing to hold Blackburn for Labour, 'fully realised ... the serious disadvantage' inflicted upon his party 'through the lack of newspapers to present its policy to the public'. The *Daily Citizen*, which had 'lacked definiteness and vigour', was beyond resuscitation. The *Herald*, which Robert Blatchford credited with a midsummer 'sale of 100,000', did not resume daily publication until the new year. None of the other three pro-Labour weeklies was suited to electioneering. The *New Age*, brilliantly edited by Orage until 1922, moved on an elevated plane from Guild Socialism to Social Credit. The *New Statesman* preached a more doctrinaire collectivism to the same intelligentsia. The *Clarion* addressed its homilies to an entirely different readership. Blatchford found 'something comically tragic in the situation of the Old Perisher', as he called his journal. 'She has kept her flag flying and her nose clean and she has hardly any friends.' Alec Thompson suggested that they start a Labour daily that would appropriate 'the name of the *Clarion*', but Blatchford's 'idea was a paper that would have a national appeal' rather than a sectarian one. 'The *Clarion* is as good a name as another for a Labour or Socialist paper,' he supposed, 'but no Labour or Socialist organ will get the ear of the people.' Snowden might have disagreed with his intention, but not with his conclusion.²

On the surface, Labour's plight was desperate. Its enemies were saying that socialism, besides being unpatriotic, was synonymous with Bolshevism. Yet, all things considered, Labour did not fare badly. The *Daily Mail* chivalrously offered Henderson a full column each morning so that Labour's 'views may be properly and promptly put before the country'. *The Times*, too, gave 'full attention to labour matters', which Northcliffe declared 'much to my liking'. In part, he was trying to rattle Lloyd George. But Hamilton Fyfe, later editor of the *Daily Herald*, impressed upon him 'that if the *Daily Mail* will give Labour a fair show, it can be kept on constitutional lines'. On the premiss that the Liberal Party had been laid flat by Lloyd George's 'knock-out blow', Massingham exhorted the readers of the *Nation* (23 November) to vote for Labour candidates in this 'Sinister Election'. More calmly, the *Daily News* emphasized that there was 'no essential difference' between its own brand of progressivism and that of the Labour Party, 'a confession' that the *Morning Post* (30 November) expected to 'simplify the task of the elector con-

¹ Gwynne to Lady Bathurst, 5 September 1918, Bathurst Papers; Cecil to Lloyd George, 20 November 1918, Lloyd George Papers, F/6/5/47.
² Snowden, 'Why Labour Papers Fail,' in *Sells* (1919), pp. 23 ff.; Blatchford to Thompson, 12 July and 3 August 1918, Blatchford Papers. With a weekly sale of approximately 3,000, the *New Statesman* commanded less influence than the *Nation* or the *Spectator*, and had more in common with the *Saturday Review* and the *Outlook*: 'the average Englishman is indifferent to them; they do not strike the popular note' (Scott-James, *Influence of the Press*, p. 303). The loss of Shaw as a contributor diminished its wartime appeal (Hyams, *New Statesman*, pp. 61-63).

siderably'. Snowden expressed gratitude for Gardiner's 'valuable help' and 'great admiration of the present stand of the *D.N.*' Henderson, on behalf of the party executive, afterwards sent 'thanks for the sympathetic treatment and prominent display ... which the *Daily News* has shown towards the Labour cause'. He wrote in almost identical terms to Northcliffe. Although regarded as no substitute for a press of its own, it was no mean feat to attract simultaneous patronage from such disparate quarters.[1]

The Asquithians were not in much better shape. With Dalziel in charge of the *Daily Chronicle* and Scott (despite his distaste for a 'khaki' election) in Lloyd George's corner, they were reduced to minority representation in the national press. Massingham's tergiversation left them without a weekly forum. On Sundays, they were voiceless. Their chief resources were the *Westminster Gazette* and the *Daily News*, with the *Star* as its appendage. Spender and Gardiner were different types, who had previously tended to stand apart. Spender was renowned for his reasoned eloquence. 'Your leader in last night's *W.G.* is most powerful & moving,' Cowdray could not 'refrain from advising' him after the armistice was proclaimed. Gardiner had come to specialize in declamatory invective. 'The nation is in the presence not of an election, but a conspiracy,' he raged on the 23rd. Harcourt, deputizing at independent Liberal headquarters 'in the absence of the Whips', applauded 'your admirable article. ... I hope you are reprinting this by the 10,000's: it ought to go everywhere.' Gulland, when he returned to Parliament Street from a tour of the constituencies, concurred. 'All your Election stuff is excellent,' he told Gardiner, whom he did not hesitate to offer 'suggestions on several points'. McKenna implied no disrespect to the *Westminster* when he remarked that, 'almost single-handed in the London press', the *Daily News* had 'kept our flag flying'.[2]

One of the weighty charges that Gardiner hurled against Lloyd George on the 23rd was that he had perverted the nature of political journalism. 'A dinner table for six will seat all the men who control nine-tenths of the Press opinion of the country': Northcliffe, Rothermere, Beaverbrook, Riddell, Dalziel, and Hulton. ('Perhaps Mr Hulton may be excluded for he has had no title or office from Mr George,' Gardiner added unsuspectingly.) These men were 'Mr Lloyd George's Press Agency', his 'bodyguard', his 'instrument' as he was 'their instrument'. Day after day, they exalted him. 'Ten million papers' poured from the presses 'in London last Sunday. There was not one that did not sing the praises of Lloyd George. Yet all that vast chorus proceeded from only four or five men, the intimates of Mr George.'

[1] Fyfe to Northcliffe, 27 November 1918, Northcliffe Papers; *History of The Times*, IV, part 1, 447–48; Snowden to Gardiner, 10 December 1918, and Henderson to Gardiner, 3 January 1919, Gardiner Papers; Henderson to Northcliffe, 3 January 1919, quoted in Pound and Harmsworth, pp. 688–89.
[2] Cowdray to Spender, 12 November 1918, Spender Papers, Add. MSS. 46, 392, fol. 277; Harcourt to Gardiner, 26 November 1918, Gulland to Gardiner, 5 December 1918, and McKenna to Gardiner, 19 December 1918, Gardiner Papers.

More than 'Election stuff', as Gulland called it, this was what Gardiner sincerely believed and what he helped to teach others. His arguments were powerful, but were they true? Guest tried to bring the major newspaper proprietors together around a table at the Ritz. Beaverbrook tried at Number 10. On both occasions, only three of the six places were filled (counting Beaverbrook, who invited himself). If, as Gardiner insisted on 14 December, Lloyd George had *'won the Press'* (not really the war), he never permitted himself to take that victory for granted. Through the campaign, he feared that the press would be his undoing. Its agitations threatened to divide him alternatively from the Conservatives, on whom he depended for a parliamentary majority, and from the Liberalism that he held to sustain him.

On 25 November, the day that Parliament was dissolved, Lloyd George sent for Sanders. He 'wanted to know what reports we had' about newspaper attitudes. 'He is evidently a little uneasy. He is anxious to know if anyone could get at Northcliffe. I was afraid not.' Polling was fixed for Saturday, 14 December, with ballots to be counted a fortnight later to allow for the collection of the service vote. The coalition's seal of approval, taking the form of a letter co-signed by Lloyd George and Bonar Law, was bestowed on one candidate – and, equally to the point, denied to all others – in each contest. The *Daily Mail* (26 November) jeered that the Coalition Liberals had struck 'A Very Bad Bargain': the 'machinations of the caucus' would result in the return of 'a multitude of mediocre candidates', mostly Tory reactionaries. 'The Press is attacking all Caucus arrangements,' Sanders noted on the 27th, 'and the Liberal portion of it is trying to make out that the Unionists have got the best of the deal.'[1] Extracts from the *Daily Mail* and the *Weekly Dispatch* served the purpose of the *Manchester Guardian* (2 and 3 December).

Lloyd George would not permit either Beaverbrook or Lord Reading (formerly Sir Rufus Isaacs) to play at 'peace-maker' between himself and Northcliffe. Dawson advised him, through Milner, that 'it would be a great mistake to ... make advances to him, as it would only feed the restless vanity, now almost a disease, wh. is at the bottom of his attacks'. Nevertheless, Lloyd George could hold back only so long. 'The *Daily Mail* on "wobbling" amused me somewhat,' J. C. C. Davidson wrote to Beaverbrook on 30 November. 'It reminded me of the famous heading "wobble, wobble, wobble" just before the last Government came down. N. seems to be nibbling but lacks the courage to bite.' Lloyd George was too superstitious to be amused. That day, Cecil Harmsworth received 'a message from Downing Street saying that the P.M. wants to see me urgently. Ll.G.,' he reported to his diary, 'discusses with me the reasons for Northcliffe's unfriendly attitude to him and his Govt.' As Cecil Harmsworth had 'not seen N. for many weeks', he could 'only

---

[1] Sanders's diary, 27 November 1918, Bayford Papers. For the vagaries of the 'coupon', including its award to David Davies, who neither deserved nor wanted it, see Wilson, *Downfall*, ch. 6.

surmise' the obvious. But he did observe that Lloyd George seemed 'low-spirited about the Election. ... He paces up and down the Cabinet room more agitated in his manner than I have ever seen him during the war, save on one or two very critical occasions.'[1]

Baited by the Hun-haters in Fleet Street, including Northcliffe, who described himself as being 'determined to bring pressure to bear', Lloyd George began to emit growling noises about a punitive settlement with Germany. In ways he would quickly come to regret, the campaign brought out the worst in him. Even the *Manchester Guardian* had to admit (11 December) that, rather than restraining 'the cheap violence of his followers, ... he has played up to it'. Too much for some, his vow to make Germany pay 'up to the limit of her capacity' was hardly enough for others. Northcliffe wired him at Leeds, where he was scheduled to deliver a speech, and demanded a militant stand on reparations. 'Don't always be making mischief,' Lloyd George telegraphed in reply. *The Times* (9 December) was not alone in charging him with obfuscation. 'Has Mr Lloyd George come to you and told you honestly what he means on any of the great questions on which he claims your mandate?' the *Daily News* asked its readers on election day.[2]

The voters did not seem to care. The couponed coalitionists, predominantly Tory, won a massive majority. 'In the feverish state of national opinion,' A. J. P. Taylor has written, 'the triumph needed little support from the press.' Maybe so, but the government and its friends were taking as few chances as possible. Unable to trust the Paris edition of the *Daily Mail* to deliver the military vote, they ordered the shipment of fifty tons (or 800,000 copies) of London newspapers on each of three successive nights in December. Milner arranged with Riddell that 'these would be copies of 3 papers': Beaverbrook's *Express*, Rothermere's *Mirror*, and Dalziel's *Chronicle*. Owing to paper shortages and transport problems, however, only 100,000 copies of the *Express* actually crossed the Channel. They probably contributed less to the election result than to that paper's post-war popularity.[3]

In the last analysis, Lloyd George did not derive his phenomenal appeal from the press, but merely used the press to diversify that appeal. Doubtless, he overdid things, as did various acolytes on his behalf. That, under the circumstances, was better politics than the opposite extreme. Asquith, campaigning at East Fife, was surprised to 'hear ... that the London papers have been publishing a tissue of absurdities' about his reception among his con-

---

[1] Beaverbrook, *Politicians and the Press*, pp. 15-16; Milner to Lloyd George, 26 November 1918, quoted in *History of The Times*, IV, part 1, 448-49; Davidson to Beaverbrook, 30 November 1918, Beaverbrook Papers, C/203; Cecil Harmsworth's diary, 30 November 1918, quoted in Pound and Harmsworth, p. 676.

[2] Northcliffe to Dawson, 30 November 1918 (copy), Northcliffe Papers; Pound and Harmsworth, p. 682.

[3] Taylor, *Beaverbrook*, p. 161; Milner to Lloyd George, 4, 7, and 16 December 1918, Lloyd George Papers, F/38/4/30-32.

stituents. 'I have never had more enthusiastic & crowded gatherings', and the newly enfranchised women 'were even more friendly & demonstrative than the men'. In his opinion, 'the Press had ceased to a large extent to be in any trustworthy sense a news-agency'.[1] The outcome at East Fife, where he lost the seat he had held since 1886, disproved his judgment. Newspaper opinion, always more than the sum of its parts, generally proved a reliable guide to the electoral psychology of the nation. Those who prided themselves on ignoring it were doomed to be squashed in the 'khaki' avalanche.

---

[1] Asquith to Gardiner, 16 December 1918, Gardiner Papers.

Ten

THE EMERGENCY PERIOD

Peace was restored, and a new Parliament was expeditiously elected on a new register. But a return to normal party politics was postponed, perhaps indefinitely. With an aura of impregnability, the coalition incorporated the dominant forces of official Unionism, a phalanx of Liberals who had ridden on Lloyd George's coat-tails, and a token Labour presence. Its opponents at Westminster consisted of a scattering of renegade Tories, some sixty Labour MPs, and a rump of thirty-three independent ('Wee Free') Liberals. (Representatives of Sinn Fein, who had swept aside the Irish Nationalists, chose not to take their seats.) The statistics barely conveyed the gravity of the result, for the Liberal and Labour frontbenches were equally bereft of experience. Asquith, Henderson, and many of their respective lieutenants were among the casualties, some never to resume their parliamentary careers.

'The Prime Minister has an immense opportunity, but I doubt whether he will take it,' Northcliffe wrote to Rothermere when the results were known. Having predicted to Dawson that the 'Old Gangsters' would preserve their stranglehold 'unless *The Times* takes a very strong stand regarding the selection of the next Cabinet', he now turned furiously upon his recalcitrant editor. 'I am not given to saying, as most people do, "I told you so"', declared Northcliffe, who none the less reminded Dawson how he had seen 'the possibilities of the present deplorable Cabinet when I asked you to begin that campaign last summer'. While most of Lloyd George's appointments were foregone conclusions, Robert Sanders (himself a junior minister) observed that his fellow 'Conservatives are very angry about Winston' (who combined the secretaryships of state for war and air), 'while the Northcliffe Press is making a dead set at Austen' (who landed the Exchequer). Northcliffe, trusting that he might yet 'be able to change the Government and avert a semi-revolution in England', vowed that the appointment of his brother Cecil to a paltry under-secretaryship at the Foreign Office 'will not move me to the extent of a single colon or comma'.[1]

---

[1] Northcliffe to Rothermere, 31 December 1918, quoted in Pound and Harmsworth, p. 688; Northcliffe to Dawson, 30 November 1918 and 12 January 1919 (copies), Northcliffe Papers; Sanders's diary, 9 February 1919, Bayford Papers.

The punctuation in the *Daily Mail* was considerably more barbed than that in *The Times*, which adhered to its own house style. On 14 January, for example, the former denounced Churchill's 'grotesque arrangement', whereas the latter politely questioned the logic of ministerial pluralism without impugning Churchill's credentials. Marlowe, the pliant editor of the *Mail*, was made chairman of Associated Newspapers. 'It does not mean any extra work,' he was assured by Northcliffe, who wished to enhance Marlowe's claims to 'some titular distinction ... from this or the next Government'. It was Dawson, however, who received (and declined) the offer of a title, presumably a baronetcy.[1]

To the irritation of Northcliffe, who was 'not a believer in the dining-out theory of the editorship of *The Times*', Dawson not only subscribed to it, but also was reported to dine out on stories about his proprietor's private life. The conflict between them was as much one of style as substance. Then, as later on, Dawson frequented high table at All Souls and mingled in high society at Cliveden. His favourite milieu was the 'interesting little dinner', such as the one he had attended on New Year's Day 1918 'with the Prime Minister in Downing Street', where Milner and the Milnerites had met 'for the purpose of pressing on L.G. the need for certain changes of personnel'. Northcliffe, whom Beaverbrook recognized as having 'no talent for the kind of argument which impresses the politician at a private meeting', preferred to deploy 'heavy artillery' from a distance. By the early weeks of 1919, Northcliffe was determined to dismiss Dawson, who spiked his biggest gun.[2]

Garvin, an editor with whom Northcliffe had previously parted company, knew that 'Robin was likely to go and gathered from him that Steed would wear the giant's robe'. Whether Steed fitted that garment was a matter of sartorial judgment. Educated at Continental universities, he had spent a quarter of a century on the staff of *The Times*, which he had represented as a correspondent in most of the major European capitals. In the process, he had acquired a devotion to Balkan nationalisms, a calming acquaintance with socialist intellectuals, a mistress who fanned his ardent francophilia, and a disfiguring streak of anti-Semitism. All of these traits, combined with a detestation of Lloyd George, endeared him to Northcliffe, whom he had assisted with war propaganda and whom he accompanied on his extensive travels. It hardly seemed necessary, therefore, for Sir Campbell Stuart to verify that Steed had 'the right perspective', namely Northcliffe's. On 6 February, when Stuart conveyed Northcliffe's invitation, Steed

---

[1] Northcliffe to Marlowe, 1 January 1919, quoted in Pound and Harmsworth, p. 688; Wrench, *Dawson*, p. 461.

[2] Northcliffe to G. S. Freeman (deputy editor), n.d., quoted in Pound and Harmsworth, p. 694; Dawson's diary, 1 January 1918, quoted in Wrench, *Dawson*, p. 161; Beaverbrook, *Politicians and the Press*, p. 46.

asked me to say to you 'that he most gratefully accepts, and that you know him well enough to be sure that he will do his best and that he knows your chief wish is to promote good of country and Empire. He would regard himself as your trustee as far as the policy of *The Times* was concerned, and would do everything in his power to safeguard and develop your property and especially to guard and increase your reputation.'

In short, Steed's obsequiousness left nothing to be desired. Disclaiming 'the functions of ... a journalistic autocrat', he celebrated the hidden virtues of Northcliffe, 'in his way a genius, a large-hearted man, intensely intuitive and full of a faith which, despite the peculiarity of its modes of expression, was real and deep'.[1]

According to Steed's slightly faulty recollection, it was not until the 7th that he heard that Dawson, 'my friend and immediate chief', had resigned, and that the succession was open to him. 'There never was any question' in Dawson's mind 'of Steed's readiness to accept'. Steed pretended otherwise, at least in retrospect. Conveniently based in Paris, where he was covering the peace conference, he journeyed to the south of France, where Northcliffe had gone to combat 'the inertia of ill-health'. They met on the 9th at Avignon. There, 'seated in the ferry boat that plies to and fro across the Rhône', Steed 'agreed to accept the editorship on certain conditions'. The principal one, which indicated the triviality of the others, was that, 'after placing the facts of a situation before Northcliffe, and suggesting a policy in regard to them', Steed – subject, of course, to Northcliffe's approval – would 'be as free to carry it out as I had been in carrying out the policies I had suggested for propaganda against the enemy'. Northcliffe could hardly object to either the stipulation or the analogy. In return, he asked Steed to coordinate the editorial policies of the Northcliffe papers 'and thus consolidate their influence. This was a complication for which I had not bargained,' reflected Steed, who grasped at the opportunity to become a sort of editorial major-domo.[2]

After a delay to consult John Walter, who grudgingly accepted the *fait accompli*, the announcement appeared in *The Times* on 25 February. Dawson composed his own letter, from which he was persuaded to delete a reference to Northcliffe's 'taking a more active part', and gave it 'to the Press Association, together with separate copies for the *Morning Post*, *Daily Telegraph*, and *Yorkshire Post*, all of whom I asked to refrain from comment while just giving the facts'. In the words of G. S. Freeman, the deputy editor, the response was 'not ... worse ... than was to be expected'. In private correspondence, newspapermen comforted Dawson by venting their indignation with North-

---

[1] Garvin to Northcliffe, 26 February 1919, Northcliffe Papers; Stuart to Northcliffe, 7 February 1919, quoted in *History of The Times*, IV, part 1, 475; Steed, *Through Thirty Years*, II, 340.

[2] Steed, *Through Thirty Years*, II, 286–87; Dawson's memorandum [March 1919], and Northcliffe to Dawson, 29 January 1919, quoted in Wrench, *Dawson*, pp. 181–84.

cliffe. Strachey congratulated him 'most heartily upon . . . an act of which every working journalist, of whom I count myself one in spite of my proprietorship' of the *Spectator*, 'ought to be proud'. Buchan was 'astounded at the news', which he took personally as 'a tremendous blow'. Chirol had cushioned the shock for Moberly Bell's widow, who considered Dawson's dismissal 'the worst day's work Lord N. ever did'. Northcliffe subsequently tried to allay her fears with the explanation that he had had 'no personal quarrel with Geoffrey Dawson. . . . He and I did not agree about the vacillations of our present Government in the face of the enemy – that is what it amounted to.' His defensiveness betrayed a certain ambivalence. 'Parting with dear Robin is a personal grief to me,' he told Steed. Nevertheless, 'after pondering the sad business' for months, he was convinced that Dawson was 'a child in the hands of skilled intriguers', whose influence had to be broken for the sake of *The Times*'s independence.[1]

More accurately, Northcliffe had acted out of frustration. Unable to strike at the politicians who closed ranks against him, he moved to assert his mastership within his own sphere. The magnitude of the coalition's parliamentary majority temporarily put Lloyd George beyond reach. An article in the *Daily Mail* (25 February), critical of the government's response to a threatened miners' strike, 'made a good deal of talk', reported Hamilton Fyfe. Yet, as he recognized, the Prime Minister remained 'in a strong position for the only Opposition that counts is the Labour Party, who have not the political experience or acumen to show him up'. Northcliffe's post-war sympathy for Labour, variously ascribed to social conscience or a sense of fair play, was primarily inspired by an antagonism to Lloyd George. Under Steed, *The Times* was better suited to go along. Garvin considered it 'far and away the best morning paper', but not wholly by virtue of its intrinsic qualities. 'You are still fortunate,' he told Northcliffe, 'first in yourself, next in your competitors. The *Telegraph* is thick lumpy porridge just now and the *Morning Post* cheap brandy.'[2]

Before long, the Labour Party was less dependent upon Northcliffe's expedient patronage. On 31 March, the *Herald* resumed daily publication, which had been suspended at the outbreak of war. Its policy, promulgated that day, was 'truth in news and honesty in propaganda. We shall try to voice the aspirations of Labour. We shall work unceasingly for a revolution, peaceful but complete, which shall destroy the present system of competition and force and replace it by the rule of cooperation.' The conversion had been delayed by the

---

[1] Freeman to Steed, 26 February 1919, quoted in *History of The Times*, IV, part 1, 486; Strachey to Dawson, 5 March 1919 (copy), Strachey Papers; Ethel Moberly Bell to Dawson, 25 February 1919, and Buchan to Dawson, 25 February 1919, quoted in Wrench, *Dawson*, pp. 188–89; Northcliffe to Ethel Moberly Bell, 16 June 1919 (copy), Northcliffe Papers; Northcliffe to Steed, 25 February 1919, quoted in *History of The Times*, IV, part 1, 486.

[2] Fyfe to Northcliffe, 25 February 1919, and Garvin to Northcliffe, 26 February 1919, Northcliffe Papers.

difficulty of procuring adequate paper supplies, which eased only under the threat of industrial action against the mill-owners. 'People who talk of the tyranny of Trade Unionism,' George Lansbury later insisted, 'have very little conception of the open and secret tyranny exercised by the capitalist against those he wishes to destroy.'[1]

For his part, Lansbury had little conception of financial necessities. He estimated that £400,000 would be required to effect the transformation and confessed to have made 'a mistake in asking for this apart from the Trades Union Congress and the National Labour Party'. Some of the individual unions, most notably the Miners' Federation, subscribed generously, and shares were also taken by co-operative societies and private benefactors. The total raised, however, met less than half Lansbury's amount, and the company had to float debentures. 'Looking back, and in the light of after events', Lansbury saw 'that had we asked the Movement officially to become responsible, and had the request been acceded to, many things which have injured us would not have happened'. He was referring especially to damaging allegations that the paper was sustained by Bolshevik funds. In the early post-war years, before Labour staked its claim to being the party of loyal opposition, its leaders were likely to regard the formal accreditation of the *Herald* as too mutually entangling. Besides, how was Labour to reconcile its anti-capitalist ethic to the realities of newspaper management? There was no easy solution to the problem, which engaged more erudite minds than Lansbury's. At the 225th meeting of the Rainbow Circle on 8 May 1918, twenty progressive intellectuals heard J. A. Hobson expatiate on the ways to 'make feasible a free newspaper run co-operative lines as an organ for the new democratic movement'. In the ensuing discussion, various 'remedies' were debated and discounted: 'Past experience has shown that a collectively-run newspaper is not practicable.... Labour papers are as bad as others.'[2]

However revolutionary its rhetoric, Labour conducted its political journalism strictly according to the rules that the older parties had long since begun to bend or even break. The *Daily Herald* paid greater fealty to the parliamentary socialists than the coalition Liberals could exact from the *Manchester Guardian* (though not the *Daily Chronicle*), the independent Liberals from the *Daily News* (though not the *Westminster Gazette*), or the Conservatives from any of their newspaper satellites. Anxious to make up for lost time, Lansbury instead recaptured it. The *Daily Herald*, which he continued to edit until his return to the House of Commons in 1922, followed an atavistic course set by nineteenth-century journals. Its ideology did not disturb the preconceived pattern and, ironically, may have reinforced it.

---

[1] Lansbury, *Miracle of Fleet Street*, pp. 16–17; Harrison, *Poor Men's Guardians*, p. 185.
[2] Lansbury, *Miracle*, pp. 17–18; minutes of the Rainbow Circle, 8 May 1918. On 31 March, the *Daily Herald* offered the self-fulfilling prophecy: 'We shall be accused of being – in the vulgar term of abuse, used so constantly – "Bolsheviks".'

Like other managers of party publicity (Younger, Guest, and Maclean), Lansbury assumed that the press would gradually revert to pre-war procedures whereby ownership dictated partisanship. No one could then have anticipated the development of other mass media, which, by the time of the 1926 General Strike, were beginning to challenge the hegemony of the printed word. Few, as yet, perceived the inherent defects of the Victorian model. Lloyd George set the pace by commandeering the *Daily Chronicle*. Not since 1892, when the *Pall Mall Gazette* was surreptitiously bought by W. W. Astor in the Conservative interest, had Fleet Street witnessed so daring an act of political brigandage. (Pearson's efforts on behalf of the Tariff Reform League were concentrated in the provinces, and Northcliffe had wrested control of *The Times* on his own initiative and without perceptibly changing its orientation.) Lloyd George, an innovator in practically every other respect, was a hidebound traditionalist when it came to dealing with the press. His object was not only to secure a measure of editorial support for himself, but also to shut out his detractors. For that reason, he took notice when Donald soon aquired 'a large part' of Sir James Hill's holding in the *Yorkshire Observer* and the *Bradford Daily Telegraph*.[1]

But Lloyd George did not confine his publicity operations to the select journals at his immediate disposal. As Prime Minister and the foremost maker of news, he enjoyed incomparable advantages as well as the facilities to exploit them. An underling provided Guest with a progress report 'After Nine Weeks' Working' of the press: a daily news 'summary' was distributed among 250 ministers, MPs (including 'almost every' Coalition Liberal and a 'few Unionist members'), and civil servants; 'Labour papers' had been 'found especially useful' in disseminating the contents; articles were planted 'continuously in "friendly" papers like the *Daily Chronicle, Pall Mall Gazette, Observer*, and (occasionally) *The Times*'; the 'hostile press is reached, sometimes effectively, by personal contact, letters to the editors and by other means'; and, finally, there had been 'steady headway' in serving the needs of the provincial press 'either in the form of special articles, letters or notes, explanations and a defence of the Government's action' in matters of legislation.[2]

The Asquithian Liberals were known to resent this activity as prejudicial to their electoral prospects. Under the supervision of Maclean and Hudson, they maintained a skeletal publicity apparatus in Abingdon Street, largely for the convenience of those enterprises to which they were financially committed. A statement of their post-war assets listed 'shares in newspapers held in the names of leading Liberals who act as nominees and give blank transfers': small-scale Dalziels, as it were. Walter Runciman, whose father counted among them, was said by 'an unimpeachable source' to have 'acquired a controlling interest in *Land and Water*, the *Field*, the *Law Times* & some 25

[1] Guest to Lloyd George, 21 March 1919, Lloyd George Papers, F/21/3/12.
[2] Wallis Myers to Guest, 4 April 1919, Lloyd George Papers, F/21/3/15b.

other periodicals' in an ostensible bid 'to regain some of his lost political influence'. Assuming (as did Steed) that the story was true, it was a roundabout way for Runciman to achieve his purpose and was more probably a straightforward commercial speculation. Labour's *ad hoc* provisions were still more meagre and disparate. Lansbury gamely offered, provided that his Liberal and Tory counterparts followed suit, to do his 'best to supply the names of all the people who have subscribed sums from 6d. to £1,000 towards the upkeep of the *Daily Herald*'. Admittedly, he was glad to be spared that obligation, 'because, like Nicodemus of old', many of his benefactors had done 'good without being known or wanting to be known'.[1]

On the face of things, the Conservatives were the most enviably endowed. Yet their publicity was inhibited by their membership in the coalition and by the unpredictability of the press lords on whom they heavily relied. For a combination of mercantile and political reasons, both likely to prove misguided, party functionaries continued to invest in newspaper ventures. Oliver Locker Lampson, retired from the navy, resumed his proprietorial dabbling by purchasing 'some local weeklies with a circulation of only 5,000' in his Huntingdonshire constituency.[2] Rescue missions of this type were nothing new and, at best, gestures of goodwill. Inspired by a diffused ethic of *noblesse oblige*, they were insufficient to register a discernible electoral impact, much less to arrest the precipitous decline of provincial journalism.

To an extent unappreciated by the Royal Commission on the Press, deliberating in the aftermath of the next world war, the events of 1914–18 had accelerated pre-existing trends. In spite of their short-sightedness, however, the commissioners accurately gauged the situation. In 1919, they reported, the provincial press was in utter disarray. The national dailies siphoned off circulation and advertisements at a time of soaring production costs. Through expanded northern and Scottish editions, the metropolitan aggressors were

> able considerably to reduce the advantage in terms of time and space hitherto enjoyed by the provincial dailies and to invade what, until their coming, had been a sheltered market. The provincial morning papers found themselves faced for the first time with competitors whose resources, both financial and journalistic, enabled them to give their readers a more extensive service of foreign news and a greater variety of features. They found also – and this applied to the evening papers as well – that their own readers were coming to expect the livelier style and appearance that characterised the London papers.[3]

[1] 'Statement on Structure of the Liberal Party' [1919], Asquith Papers; Steed to Northcliffe, 21 June 1919, Northcliffe Papers; Lansbury, *Miracle*, pp. 18–19.
[2] Locker Lampson to Editor, the *Metropolitan*, 17 January 1919, and Locker Lampson to A. Weigall, 7 February 1919 (copies), Locker Lampson Papers.
[3] Report, Royal Commission on the Press, 1947–49, ch. vii.

As any student of newspaper history will know, the actual process was not nearly so abrupt; but these conclusions were none the less irrefutable.

Confronted with falling revenues and mounting expenditures, provincial papers either closed down or banded into chains. Economically, but also politically, they had lost their former value. Sir Edward Hulton, whose empire predated the war, pondered – not too seriously – 'a proposition to purchase a number of Provincial newspapers at four times what they are worth'. The Starmer-Morrell syndicate negotiated better terms by tapping a residue of political loyalty. Party allegiance, formerly responsible for stimulating the growth of the provincial press, now contributed to its subsidence. Liberal journals, which had traditionally predominated outside London, experienced a numbing perplexity that split their directorates and muddled their editorial views. Their Tory rivals had difficulty in adjusting to new alignments, more viable at Westminster than in the constituencies. 'The party political spirit,' A. P. Wadsworth observed from a vantage point in Manchester, 'was less keen than it had been when every large town had to have its Tory and its Liberal papers who fought and scratched each other like the papers of Eatanswill.' The post-war contraction of the provincial press was equally the cause and effect of this atmospheric change.[1]

It had suited W. E. Gladstone to contend that the provincial newspapers spoke with the true voice of the nation, whereas Fleet Street slavishly articulated the conceits of contiguous Clubland. Given that the *Pall Mall Gazette*, the *Globe*, the *Westminster Gazette*, and other staples of West End readership were on their last legs, it was not clear who would fill the vacuum. To be sure, there was no shortage of candidates. Bottomley added a seat in Parliament to his assorted platforms in the weekly press. Bonar Law credited him with 'a great gift of interpreting the thoughts of the man in the street'.[2] Beaverbrook, who had relinquished a seat in the Commons, asserted his own claims, no less disruptive to the conventions of the political press.

The two cases invite comparison. A dozen years earlier, Bottomley had sat for South Hackney as a nominal Liberal; this time, symptomatically, he was elected for the same constituency as an independent, defeating a Coalition Liberal by a plurality of over 8,000. Beaverbrook, who had been a machine-made Unionist during his six-year parliamentary fling, 'also liked independence', according to his biographer. 'It was of course independence within safe limits', unlike Bottomley's. 'His unconscious ideal was a Conservative government always in power, with himself attacking it on almost every detailed item in its programme.' More through evasiveness than by blatancy, Beaverbrook posed by far the greater challenge. The *Daily*

---

[1] Hulton to Beaverbrook, 30 May 1919, Beaverbrook Papers, C/180; Starmer to Maclean, 25 November 1919, Asquith Papers; Wadsworth, *Newspaper Circulations*, pp. 27–28.
[2] Sanders's diary, 23 February 1919, Bayford Papers.

Express, which he legitimately held to represent 'a particular kind of mind in every class', refused to satisfy party expectations.[1]

On 26 February, its coverage of an impending by-election at Leyton West caused 'a very great deal of comment, and ... some annoyance', particularly in the way that the Tory candidate was 'made the subject of an attack by a recognised Unionist organ'. Sir George Younger, 'from the point of view' of the Unionist Central Office, regarded Blumenfeld's 'action as rather serious'. After consulting Beaverbrook, Blumenfeld issued a stiff rejoinder. 'The *Daily Express* is a free and independent journal,' he maintained, 'giving a general support to the Unionist Party because in the main it subscribes to Unionist principles, but that by no means implies that we are a Unionist Party organ.' With apologies for his 'lack of brevity', Blumenfeld went on to dispute that party officials had

> a right to participate in directing the policy of the paper. You are holders of a certain number of Shares and you have a voting voice to the extent of that holding and no more. It would be fatal to the prospects of the paper if I were to admit the suggestion of even a part-control of policy by shareholders, and particularly by a political organisation; and I for my part would never permit it.... I would not remain Editor of this paper for one hour if I had to become the servant of any political organisation, nor would the prestige of the paper last over night.

Younger was forced to back down. Writing on 1 March, the same day that an independent Liberal wiped out the coalition's huge majority at Leyton West, he lamely pleaded that his strictures had been 'wholly misunderstood.... I wrote to you rather hurriedly and didn't make it clear that, when I spoke of the *Express* being a recognised Unionist organ, I intended to convey that it was recognised by the public' as such. Younger pretended to feel 'perfectly certain that your general support of the Party is strengthened by occasional criticisms of an independent kind'. Nevertheless, the *Express*'s criticisms were more than occasional; and the contest at Leyton, the first in a string of reverses, was no minor incident. Beaverbrook, sheltering behind Blumenfeld, was stretching the limits of journalistic independence.[2]

His behaviour was all the more audacious in that he had arrived in Fleet Street as a commissioned trustee of his party, who gradually established control over a company in which that party retained a substantial investment. Yet deference was alien to his nature, and he delighted in playing the system against itself. Other proprietors, while they did not escape reproach, could defy party directives without laying themselves open to the charge of

---

[1] Taylor, *Beaverbrook*, p. 175.
[2] Younger to Blumenfeld, 26 February and 1 March 1919, and Blumenfeld to Younger, 28 February 1919 (copies), Beaverbrook Papers, H/15.

ingratitude. Even after Beaverbrook had begun to pay his own way, and handsomely, the fact remained that he was biting the hand that had once fed him. Consequently, his divergence from party lines struck at the very heart of the old political press.

What was one to make of Beaverbrook? A powerhouse of contradictory impulses, he perpetually vacillated between mawkish sentimentality and savage vindictiveness. The lengths – or depths – to which he was prepared to carry his machinations were illustrated at this time by his poisoned relations with Garvin. Maurice Woods, a former leader writer for the *Morning Post* and a failed politician, was employed as Beaverbrook's amanuensis; in that capacity, he ghosted the drafts of Beaverbrook's highly personalized political histories. His chronic alcoholism, aggravated by the bibulous company of Lord Birkenhead (as F. E. Smith had become upon his elevation to the lord chancellorship), had got him cashiered from two regiments during the war and led to the breakdown of his marriage. In 1910, his wife Viola had first met Garvin, who commissioned her to write occasional pieces in the *Observer* and to whom she turned for emotional support. The unexpected death of Christina, Garvin's first wife, raised the possibility that they might marry. Beaverbrook, however, stood in the way. By forbidding Woods to admit adultery, he held Garvin – and indirectly the *Observer* – in thrall. Viola, of course, could have purchased her freedom by pleading her own guilt, but by doing that she would have risked losing the custody of her son and would certainly have exacerbated tensions between Garvin and the puritanical Astors. For more than a year, Beaverbrook held firm. Finally, Birkenhead prevailed upon him to stand aside and Viola obtained her divorce. In the summer of 1921, she married Garvin, who adopted her son Oliver – later a distinguished journalist in his own right – as a substitute for the son he had lost in the war. Eight years later, Maurice Woods was fatally injured in a motor accident, from which Beaverbrook emerged shaken but unharmed, as was his wont.[1]

Younger would not have dared to reprove Gwynne or Garvin, to cite two examples among many, for – unlike Blumenfeld – they were not the recipients of funds from the Unionist Central Office. And he surely knew better than to waste his time with editors who held their positions on the sufferance of Rothermere or Northcliffe. By denying Northcliffe first a veto over Cabinet appointments and then a seat at the peace conference, Lloyd George had ensured his enmity. There were rumours that Northcliffe might be bought off by naming him ambassador to Washington, but Steed implored him to resist: 'If you were out of England and tied up in any official job during the next few years, I should pretty well despair of our pulling the country round the nasty

---

[1] Several dozen letters from Garvin to his prospective second wife, dated between March 1919 and their wedding in August 1921, survive among the Woods Papers. They document his mental distraction, physical torment, and 'difficulties on the *Observer*' with the Astors, with whom he hoped to 'go on together without breaking with the P.M.', Beaverbrook's putative objective (25 March 1920).

corners that lie ahead of it.' There was another rumour, better founded, that Curzon had been tapped to succeed Balfour at the Foreign Office. 'The idea... fills me with disgust & I feel strongly inclined to torpedo it,' Steed wrote to Northcliffe. 'What do you think?'[1] Whatever Northcliffe thought, that appointment was made the following autumn.

That Northcliffe's wishes were ignored, and with impunity, greatly intensified his disaffection. Steed, Iago-like, preyed upon it. 'It is important that we should maintain our independence of any and every government and of any and every individual Minister,' he set forth in a secret 'Memorandum on Policy', drafted in mid-April. 'This independence may be friendly, neutral, or hostile', accorded on the basis of 'what we regard as national interests'. Backed up by 'careful propanda', the effect 'should be that politicians whom our support may have placed in office will never feel so sure of the unconditional continuance of that support as to keep us outside their counsels, or to cease to seek our guidance and advice'.[2] Neither Northcliffe nor, for that matter, Beaverbrook could have put it better.

The men around Northcliffe nourished his fantasies. Steed, besides imagining that he could destroy Curzon, religiously proclaimed Northcliffe's unique qualifications for the premiership. H. W. Wilson of the *Daily Mail* meanwhile puzzled over the 'question whether Winston would not make a better Prime Minister than Lloyd George.... Slippery though he is, he is less slippery than Lloyd George whom no one trusts.' The *Mail* did not go so far as to advocate this change, and instead contented itself by misprizing politicians in general and Lloyd George in particular. Its pettiness was symbolized by a refusal to celebrate the marriage of Asquith's younger daughter to a titled Romanian diplomat. 'Please do not boom the forthcoming Asquith wedding,' Northcliffe instructed W. G. Fish, the news editor. 'Keep it down.' Not all of the restrictions, however, were imposed by the proprietor. Appropriately ensconced at Fontainebleau, Northcliffe was unsettled to hear 'from two successive visitors that the *Daily Express* is constantly beating us in political news.... The only men who get the news,' he complained to Marlowe, 'are those that the Government are afraid of,' and the *Mail* seemed to have lost its terror. Fish, replying on Marlowe's behalf, acknowledged 'that the *Express* has succeeded in getting a few political "scoops"', which he detected 'from internal evidence to come direct from Bonar Law'. The *Daily Mail* was paying the price of its vaunted independence. 'Our chief weakness is at present that most of the Ministers and ex-Ministers are not sufficiently friendly with us to go out of their way to give us tips.'[3]

The Northcliffe press could expect no consideration from Lloyd George,

---

[1] Steed to Northcliffe, 15 March 1919, Northcliffe Papers.
[2] 'Memorandum on Policy' [April 1919], quoted in *History of The Times*, IV, part 1, 498–99.
[3] Wilson to Northcliffe, 3 April 1919, Northcliffe to Fish, 5 April 1919 (copy), Northcliffe to Marlowe, 11 April 1919 (copy), and Fish to Northcliffe, 5 May 1919, Northcliffe Papers.

whose diplomacy at Paris was arousing anxiety at home. On 8 April, some 370 MPs telegraphed to remind him of his campaign pledge to 'Make the Huns Pay'. It was easy as well as convenient to fasten responsibility on Northcliffe, whose papers decried any sign of leniency towards the defeated enemy. On the 14th, Lloyd George 'left for London in excellent spirits', having 'made up his mind to attack Northcliffe & declare war to the knife'. Two days later, he delivered a slashing speech in Parliament to exactly this effect. Frances Stevenson, who attended a private rehearsal, had to 'say it is very clever & amusing, & will make N. very sorry for himself'. Lloyd George returned to her and the peace conference on the 17th, 'very pleased with himself'. He described how he had treated the House 'to an amusing skit on Northcliffe, which pleased them hugely, & which will make N. squirm'. Tapping his forehead as if to cast doubt on Northcliffe's sanity, Lloyd George had proceeded to pity the delusions of a man who waited in vain 'for the clamour of the multitude that is going to demand his presence ... to direct the destinies of the world'. Bonar Law, a spectator at the performance, thought it 'wonderfully well done'. Sanders was not present, knowing 'beforehand that he was going to disclose nothing and to attack Northcliffe'. Not that he disapproved of Lloyd George's action. 'Part of his code', observed Sanders, 'is that when a newspaper goes for you persistently it pays to attack it in public. Then anything it says in the future is discounted. The Northcliffe story,' truth to tell, 'is pretty dirty.'[1]

Rothermere, who had been clinging to Lloyd George as a shield against Bolshevism, 'was not quite sure how to take' this denunciation of his brother. His son Esmond, with a stronger sense of family honour, 'did not like it at all' and stalked back to London. Miss Stevenson inferred that he hoped 'to inherit *The Times* one day & therefore will not wish to incur his uncle's displeasure'. Northcliffe himself responded with uncharacteristic restraint. 'We must be careful not to involve ourselves in *wrong* quarrels with the Prime Minister,' he minuted to the staff at Printing House Square, where he noted 'a tendency ... to hit back when the Prime Minister makes foolish remarks about me.... Silence is a more effective and dignified weapon,' he insisted. Renewed medical problems, necessitating throat surgery in June, distracted and possibly humbled him. More probably, he knew that he had been bested and was waiting for the storm to blow over.[2]

By July, Northcliffe had the satisfaction of informing Marlowe that, again, 'Downing Street is desperately anxious for our support. They approach me in every kind of way.' That was not surprising, he reasoned vaingloriously, for

---

[1] Entries of 14 and 17 April 1919, Stevenson, *Lloyd George*, pp. 179–80; Steed, *Through Thirty Years*, II, 320; *History of The Times*, IV, part 1, 499–501; *Parliamentary Debates* (Commons), 5th ser., cxiv, cols. 2952–53; Bonar Law to Carson, 17 April 1919 (copy), Bonar Law Papers, 101/3/47; Sanders's diary, 8 May 1919, Bayford Papers.

[2] Entry of 17 April 1919, Stevenson, *Lloyd George*, p. 180; memorandum by Northcliffe, 22 April 1919, quoted in *History of The Times*, IV, part 1, 501–502.

'my attitude is not a personal one. When the Prime Minister does what I think right I say so; when he does what I think wrong I equally say so.' At the nursing home where he was slowly recuperating, he claimed to be 'pestered by politicians', including Birkenhead, who allegedly applied for an interview. 'I greatly dislike these politicians trying to see me over the heads of my Editors,' he rambled to Marlowe. 'Moreover I never allow them into my house and never go into theirs.'[1]

Apart from Birkenhead's get-well message, which mentioned looking forward to 'a long talk about public affairs' (a strange sentiment to express to someone who had had a throat operation), these contacts were mostly figments of Northcliffe's imagination. Beaverbrook, who diagnosed the symptoms better than any physician, wrote that a 'night of gloom' had already descended. Although Northcliffe still 'gave much attention to his newspapers', it often took an odd form. From his sick-bed, he ordered 'a big flag' with *The Times* 'in very large letters' to be flown from the flagpost at Printing House Square, and also 'a very large sign covering the whole of the building with gilt letters from four to six feet high' so that 'the taxi-drivers will know the place when they see it'. A sense of proportion had never been Northcliffe's strongest suit. He lived until 1922, continuing to direct and misdirect his newspapers. But, as Beaverbrook put it, 'his shadow was no longer lengthening across the land', and his 'hatred for Lloyd George dominated him' to the end.[2]

* * *

During the troubled summer of 1919, the coalition suffered its own share of ailments. Humiliated by a steady stream of by-election losses, it was internally divided over Irish policy, intervention in the Russian civil war, and fundamental questions of social reform. Preliminary proposals for a centre party, which might have brought together Lord (formerly Sir Edward) Grey and Lord Robert Cecil (who had withdrawn from the government in defence of the Welsh Church), were generating considerable 'newspaper excitement', if little else. The peace treaty, a momentary glory, was condemned alternately as too generous and too vindictive. Frances Stevenson attended the historic ceremony in the Hall of Mirrors at Versailles, thronged 'with representatives of the Press. The Press is reducing everything that is noblest and impressive in modern life into terms of Press photographs and Press interviews,' she peevishly complained. 'In fact they try to dominate everything.'[3]

Lloyd George's honeymoon with Fleet Street had degenerated, like most of his extra-marital affairs, into a love-hate relationship. Even his shotgun

---

[1] Northcliffe to Marlowe, 8 and 17 July 1919 (copies), Northcliffe Papers.

[2] Beaverbrook, *Men and Power*, pp. 88–89; Northcliffe to William Lints Smith (assistant manager), 15 and 25 July 1919, quoted in Pound and Harmsworth, p. 742.

[3] Sanders's diary, 19 July 1919, Bayford Papers; entry of 28 June 1919, Stevenson, *Lloyd George*, p. 187.

marriage with the *Daily Chronicle* seemed to be headed for the rocks. Guest informed him that Lord Inverforth (as Andrew Weir had become) thought that 'there is not very much use in his staying on much longer' at the Ministry of Supply (as the Ministry of Munitions had become). 'I think, in his heart, he is anxious to retire from politics and to return to business,' reported Guest. 'Inverforth thinks that he could put real life into the *Chronicle*, which certainly is much needed.'[1] His ambition portended a conflict of interests with Dalziel.

The changes hovering at the *Chronicle* were preceded by an upheaval, distinctly to Lloyd George's advantage, at the *Daily News*. Following in the wake of Donald and Dawson, Gardiner was relieved of his editorship. This decision had been long in coming. The results of the general election had demonstrated to George Cadbury that the paper had 'lost influence in the country because it has never acknowledged the good work that Lloyd George has done.... Constant nagging at an individual,' he protested, 'very largely diminishes the influence of a paper – it makes it too one-sided.' Gardiner offered no 'defence or argument', save for a denial 'that the influence of the *D.N.* has enormously lessened'. Although he considered 'the issues of the time ... far too grave to permit me to barter' his principles 'for any consideration whatever', his attitude towards Lloyd George was thereafter less relentlessly hostile. On 12 April, he cited 'welcome evidence of late that Mr Lloyd George has been working in complete accord with President Wilson' and only wished that the Prime Minister were not 'hampered by the reckless promises with which he baited his hook last December'.[2]

The following month, however, Gardiner reverted to type. The economic and territorial provisions of the draft treaty drove him to distraction. 'If the Peace Terms are the last word we have to say to Germany, let us make up our minds for the inevitable consequence,' he wrote for publication on 10 May. 'Let us decently bury the Covenant and prepare for the next war in whatever quarter it may break.' On a proof copy, preserved among his private papers, he inscribed: 'This is the article wh. led to my resignation of the editorship of the *Daily News*.' But it did not lead immediately to that conclusion. On 29 May, Henry Cadbury suggested that it was one thing for a signed contributor to rail at the Prime Minister, but quite another thing for the editor to do so. Taking his cue, Edward Cadbury proposed that Gardiner should, without financial sacrifice, resign the 'actual Editorship and Executive Control', while continuing his weekly columns in the *Daily News* and the *Star*. In addition, his opinion was to 'have weight' in the selection of a successor who would not 'make the fulfilment of the conditions difficult'. The formal announcement was delayed until 10 September to give the Cadburys time to scout for a replacement. 'Personal circumstances' did not permit J. L. Hammond, their first

[1] Guest to Lloyd George, 7 June 1919, Lloyd George Papers, F/21/3/28.
[2] Cadbury to Gardiner, 30 December 1918, and Gardiner to Cadbury, 2 January 1919 (copy), Gardiner Papers.

choice, to accept. Arthur Greenwood, then a featured columnist on the *Observer*, 'wouldn't touch the *D.N.* with a long stick'. Clifford Sharp reportedly declined to leave the *New Statesman*, and W. P. Crozier could not be lured from the news editorship of the *Manchester Guardian*, where his fidelity was rewarded with a directorship and, in due course, with the editorship. It was finally decided to allow Stuart Hodgson to preside at the *Daily News* 'in loco editoris'.[1]

Lloyd George, without soiling his hands or opening his pocket-book, was thus rid of a serious nuisance. And Gardiner's removal stood as an object lesson to other editorial trouble-makers. All the same, Lloyd George was far from satisfied. In early September, Waldorf Astor 'spent 3 or 4 days' with him in Brittany, where he found the Prime Minister overwhelmed by 'lassitude and general worry.... He was much perturbed by Rothermere's attack on Bonar,' Astor told Garvin. 'I think his main anxiety at the moment is to prevent the Coalition being smashed, but he certainly does not intend being guided by reactionaries.'[2]

Since the election, Lloyd George had ingeniously played off Rothermere against Northcliffe by appealing to Rothermere's professed liberalism and to their spirit of fraternal rivalry. Suddenly, Rothermere lurched out of control, taking a path that was to culminate in the Anti-Waste League, which he founded early in 1921 as a brake on 'Squandermania'. On 16 September, Davidson, Bonar Law's parliamentary secretary, saw Sutherland, who 'at once explained that he was very annoyed with Lord Rothermere's articles'. At a recent lunch, Sutherland revealed, 'Rothermere had ... stated the lines of his proposed attack' to himself and Lloyd George. 'Sutherland said that the Prime Minister had tried to persuade Rothermere not to attack Mr Bonar Law personally on the ground that it would not be right to attack a man who had lost two sons in the war.' As Rothermere, too, 'had lost sons in the war', that 'argument was subtle', yet singularly ineffective. Despite Sutherland's 'impression that Rothermere had decided not to attack Mr Bonar Law', the campaign went ahead. Davidson was left to 'wonder what the real truth of the situation is'. Goulding had his suspicions. 'I am anxious as to the way Rothermere is attacking Bonar – his papers in Glasgow can do much harm – and I have reason *to know* the whole thing is personal,' he wrote to Beaverbrook. 'You must stop the attack. Get Rothermere again in the Government as sec. to the Treasury or a post ... where he can ruthlessly cut down expenditure.'[3]

---

[1] Edward Cadbury to Gardiner, 2 June 1919, Hammond to Gardiner, 25 July 1919, Greenwood to Gardiner, 4 August 1919, Henry Cadbury to Gardiner, 9 September 1919, Gardiner Papers; Scott to Hobhouse, 9 and 27 September, and 14 October 1919, *Guardian* Archives; Wilson Harris, *Life So Far* (London, 1954), pp. 198–99.

[2] Astor to Garvin, 4 September 1919 (copy), Astor Papers.

[3] Memorandum by Davidson, 16 September 1919 (copy), enclosed in Davidson to Beaverbrook, 16 September 1919 (copy?), Bonar Law Papers, 101/3/47; Goulding to Beaverbrook, 19 September [1919], Beaverbrook Papers, C/318.

The Emergency Period 363

To meet the challenge, Lloyd George clutched at straws. Presumably for a modest subvention, he got the English-Speaking Union to publish a special number of its monthly journal, the *Future*, as a 'Government statement of national needs'. The normal circulation doubled to three million, but the venture failed to impress the Prime Minister's wife. 'Why should you object to the *Future*?' he asked her. 'Is it your notion that Ministers should stand to be shot at & spat upon . . . & that they should never reply? I have just had enough of that & I mean to put up a fight.' In fact, as he must have realized, the *Future* was hardly an arena for political pugilism. He got relatively better value from the *Outlook*, managed by Lord Lee of Fareham to enable his rich American sister-in-law 'to make use of her money as an influence for good or in support of patriotic causes'. Deeply devoted to Lloyd George, who appointed him Minister of Agriculture in August, Lee claimed to have negotiated the purchase of that weekly from Beaverbrook, who 'was not unwilling to be relieved of the responsibility and expense, provided that the paper passed into the hands of someone whose political views were not antagonistic to his own'. E. R. Thompson, chief leader-writer of the *Evening Standard*, was appointed to the editorial chair that Garvin had once occupied. For 'one wild moment', Lee and his sister-in-law 'indulged in the "pipe-dream" of trying to secure control of a group of papers – including the *Morning Post* which was perennially short of finance'. At precisely that moment, he would have been most attractive to Lloyd George.[1]

Along with their American wives and private fortunes, Lee and Astor had a good deal in common. Both were single-minded politicians, earnest but somewhat naïve, whose loyalty to the coalition outweighed their attachment to party. Lee was elevated to the peerage by a sleight-of-hand; Astor, by the death of his father in October. His unwelcome inheritance occasioned a by-election in the Sutton division of Plymouth. Beaverbrook telephoned on 27 October to test Northcliffe's reaction to the idea that Lady Astor might defend her husband's former seat. According to Beaverbrook's inside information, 'Sir George Younger and Company would be only too glad to have an opportunity of looking unkindly upon her candidature'. It was not that Younger doubted her capacity to ward off a challenge from Labour: 'the worst of it is the woman is sure to get in,' he was said to have remarked. Rather, he had reason to doubt the content of her Conservatism. 'If you want a party hack

[1] Lloyd George to his wife, 15 September 1919, quoted in *Lloyd George, Family Letters*, p. 190; *The Times*, 18 September 1919; Lee, *A Good Innings*, pp. 187–88. Without mentioning Northcliffe by name, the *Outlook* (18 December 1920) criticized the pretensions of 'the New Press-Gang'. Northcliffe thereupon rescinded an invitation to Lee, a 'parasite [who] attacks me in this journal, kept by his wife's money'. Lee maintained that 'he had had no interest whatever' in the *Outlook* 'since August 1919, either financially or editorially'; but Northcliffe ascertained from the registry at Somerset House that Faith Moore, Lee's sister-in-law, held the 'controlling interest. Lady Lee also Shareholder. Lee Director.' Northcliffe to Hudson, 20 December 1920, and 28 December 1920 (telegram; copy), and R. Montague Smith to Marlowe, 7 April 1921, Northcliffe Papers.

don't elect me,' Nancy Astor declared in her adoption speech. 'Surely we have outgrown party ties. I have.' So, too, had Lloyd George, who endorsed her in a letter drafted by Philip Kerr. That was the least he owed to the wife of the proprietor of the *Observer*. After her victory, he welcomed her to Westminster as the first woman MP.[1]

With half as many votes as her husband had polled in the general election, Lady Astor did far better than others who fought by-elections in defence of the coalition. The next contest, called for 20 December, was a three-cornered fight at Spen Valley, where a Coalition Liberal MP had died. Sir John Simon was attempting a comeback there in the Asquithian interest. A procession of Labour spokesmen – 'Thomas, Henderson, Clynes, etc.' – expressed justifiable confidence to Sutherland that their standard-bearer would win, despite the galling fact that 'the newspapers have been particularly bad in ignoring completely the Labour Candidate', and 'the Wee Free papers have been the worst offenders'. Unlike Labour, which had learnt to make a virtue of necessity, Lloyd George made a necessity of necessity itself. Sutherland's agenda included a meeting with the Berry brothers, William and Gomer, whom he sought to keep 'personally very friendly to the Prime Minister'. Inconveniently, they were 'in the habit of talking a bit about the need of new men in the Government, the desirability of dropping Walter Long, Austen Chamberlain, etc.' But that was to be tolerated as they had 'considerable newspaper ambitions and intend, if they can, to rival Northcliffe. They are spending a lot of money on the *Sunday Times* and intend to make a big thing of the *Graphic*, etc., newspapers which they recently acquired.' Sutherland considered the Berrys 'men to be reckoned with seriously' and understood that 'their public ambitions at the moment are to become JPs', something he had already requested the Lord Chancellor to arrange. 'With a little effort,' he told Lloyd George, 'I am sure we can keep them substantially in hand.'[2]

Had the *Sunday Express* sustained its momentum and faithful service, Lloyd George could have dispensed with the *Sunday Times*, especially as the *Observer* catered handily to the same market. However, as Goulding pointed out to Beaverbrook, the *Sunday Express* was proving 'a terrible drain and going back I fear steadily in circulation'. Recalling those early years, before his 'folly' began to pay, Beaverbrook described how 'I sometimes used to go out into my garden and shake myself like a dog. . . . I always wrote off the very considerable sums I had invested in, or advanced to, the *Sunday Express* as a potential total loss.' Slow to break through the sales barrier, the paper meanwhile failed to command serious attention. The royal household, a

---

[1] Lee, *A Good Innings*, p. 4; Stuart to Northcliffe, 28 October 1919, Northcliffe Papers; Kenneth O. Morgan, *Consensus and Disunity* (Oxford, 1979), p. 154; John Grigg, *Nancy Astor* (Boston, 1980), p. 74; entry of 1 December 1919, Stevenson, *Lloyd George*, p. 190.

[2] Memorandum by Sutherland, 14 December [1919], Lloyd George Papers, F/93/2/18. For the extensive 'capitalist interests' of all three Berry brothers, see the Labour Research Department, *The Press* (London, 1923), pp. 21–29.

voracious consumer of weekend newsprint, received a dozen copies of five different Sunday journals: six of the *Observer*, three of the *Sunday Pictorial*, and one each of the *Sunday Times* (read by the King), the *Weekly Dispatch* (also read by the King), and the *People* (read by the Serjeant Footman). The Prince of Wales took the *Observer* and the *Sunday Pictorial*. No copies of the *Sunday Express* were in the pile.[1]

Insolvent newspapers, struggling to enlarge their audiences, could not afford to go out on a political limb. Prosperous ones could afford not to. Lloyd George stood high and dry on the shrinking ground in between. The *Globe*, after its wartime revival, was again slipping, this time irredeemably. Docker told Goulding that Maxse had departed from the editorship as stealthily as he had arrived, refusing 'to take 1d. of remuneration of any kind', although 'he worked like a black'. The *Globe* quickly passed from Docker to Robert Donald (who paid £40,000) to Laurance Lyon, the Canadian-born Conservative member for Hastings, who 'burnt his fingers badly', went bankrupt, and resigned his parliamentary seat. It ended up in the hands of Clarence Hatry, a commercial banker who 'conceived the idea that he would like to be a baronet'. In 1921, the oldest evening journal was amalgamated with the *Pall Mall Gazette*, which, two years later, merged with the *Evening Standard*.[2]

Early in 1920, still smarting from Labour's triumph at Spen Valley, Sutherland grimly surveyed the scene. By neglecting intellectual opinion, the coalition had allowed itself to be tagged as 'a capitalists' party. Even the journalists who support us . . . regard our party in this way and none of them believe we are ballasted for a long journey.' The independent Liberals suffered a comparable plight. The *Daily News* chastised them for failing to conclude an electoral pact with Labour. On 16 January, Henry Cadbury made sure that they understood completely what was meant by his family's proclamation 'that the *Daily News*, under their proprietorship, was an independent organ'. Maclean, speaking for Asquith (as he officially did in the Commons), replied that his colleagues 'had never regarded the *Daily News* as a thick and thin supporter of the Party, in the sense that [they] might look upon the *Westminster Gazette*'; yet he hoped that, 'with all its independence', the paper might still be 'reckoned as the leading exponent of Liberalism in the London press, and one of the mainstays of the Liberal Party'. Cadbury disabused him – just as Blumenfeld and Beaverbrook had disabused Younger – of the illusion. Glad 'to clear the ground', Maclean logically inquired whether 'it would be wise for us to assume that the *Daily News* was to be regarded in the future as a Labour organ'. Cadbury 'did not dissent . . . except in so far as to reiterate that they were an independent organ', now committed to the proposition 'that Labour should as early as possible be

---

[1] Goulding to Beaverbrook, 19 September [1919], Beaverbrook Papers, C/318; Taylor, *Beaverbrook*, p. 228; J. M. Blanch (business manager) to Astor, 18 March 1921, Astor Papers.
[2] Goulding to Beaverbrook, 19 September [1919], Beaverbrook Papers, C/318; memorandum by Sutherland, 6 July 1920, Lloyd George Papers, F/22/2/3; *also see* H. A. Taylor, *Donald*, ch. xii.

given responsibility'. He 'was quite impervious' to Maclean's argument that, by 'endeavouring to crush out the Liberal Party at by-elections', the paper was precluding the possibility of a Lib-Lab accord. Gardiner received a transcript of this interview, which he took to show 'what the Liberal party is face to face with in regard to the Press. . . . It seems to me to invite the question whether the party is to remain an effective organisation or go under.'[1]

In addition to a nominal directorship, Gardiner retained his Saturday column in the *Daily News*, in which he celebrated Asquith's return at Paisley in a February by-election. Back in Parliament, where he performed depressingly, Asquith displayed a new awareness of press opinion. 'With much admiration', he 'read the whole' of Gardiner's article of 21 February, a belated castigation of Labour for its snub to the Liberals at Spen Valley. Encouraged by these few words, Gardiner called on successive Saturdays for a 'Liberal-Labour entente' – not 'a fusion', which was 'not possible even if it were desirable' – to 'sweep the Coalition and all its works out of existence'. Concurrently, Scott collected Lloyd George's gratitude for a rather ambiguous article in the *Manchester Guardian* on 16 March. 'Don't desert me,' the Prime Minister appealed poignantly to Scott at the close of 'a very useful conversation' the next day. 'Come and see me sometimes and correct my faults. . . . Or help my best self.' Scott was moved, as he was intended to be.[2]

If Northcliffe was to be believed, he too was being courted. 'In case I do not see you to-day,' he wrote to Steed on 12 January, 'I hope you will realise that the Prime Minister is making advances to *The Times* through Churchill, and to my other papers *via* the Lord Chancellor.' The former was an unlikely emissary. 'I cannot accept Mr Churchill's view that Labour is incapable of governing,' Northcliffe told the staff at Carmelite House; at any rate, 'it could not govern worse than he does'. Birkenhead's so-called advances were probably related to the three-part series he was writing for the *Weekly Dispatch* (11 and 25 January, and 1 February) on the lessons of Spen Valley. Sanders noted that 'F.E.'s letters to a Sunday paper have not helped him' except materially: 'He got £100 a piece for them.' For certain, Northcliffe received no overtures from or through Carson, who amused Bonar Law with a blasphemy entitled 'The Northcliffe Creed':

> ... So Northcliffe is *The Times*, Northcliffe is the *Daily Mail*, and Northcliffe is the *Evening News*.
> And in this trinity neither is before or behind; and there is not top or bottom.

[1] Memorandum by Sutherland, 5 January 1920, Lloyd George Papers, F/93/2/19; memorandum by Maclean, 16 January 1920, and Gardiner to Maclean [18] January 1920, Asquith Papers. On the crucial importance of Spen Valley, see Maurice Cowling, *The Impact of Labour 1920–1924* (Cambridge, 1971), pp. 1–2.

[2] Asquith to Gardiner, 21 February 1920, Gardiner Papers; entry of 16–17 March 1920, Scott, *Political Diaries*, pp. 383–84.

So that in all things as is aforesaid: Northcliffe in three papers and three papers in Northcliffe must be worshipped.

Lloyd George knelt at other shrines.[1]

Steed, a more reliable source than his proprietor, reported a visit from Lord Robert Cecil, who miscalculated that Asquith would be beaten at Paisley. 'Have you ever thought of the possibility that Grey might accept the Premiership?' he asked Steed, who found Stuart and Freeman receptive to the idea. But Asquith held back the Labour tide at Paisley for another four years. To all practical purposes, his resumption of the Liberal parliamentary leadership put an end to the movement for a centre party. Lloyd George saw him as 'a great boulder, blocking the way' to a rapprochement with Labour, for which he himself claimed to have 'far greater sympathy'. That was not the impression that Lloyd George created, however, in a ninety-minute speech to the Coalition Liberals on 18 March. The parliamentary correspondent of the *Westminster Gazette* concluded the following day that 'our political Merlin' was 'headed ... away from Labour' and in the direction of a 'stronger alliance' with the Tories. That morning's *Times* agreed: drawing a distinction between Labour and socialism, it scolded Lloyd George for seeking 'to win personal and political advantage out of the exploitation of ignorant fear' of a red peril.[2]

Left, right, and centre, all minds were fixed on the emergence of Labour as an elemental power. Through any number of kaleidoscopic combinations, the challenge could be met by cooperation or confrontation. Either tactic put a premium on publicity. For all its disadvantages, Labour came to be envied for the enterprise and solidity of its press support. Granville Wheler, the Conservative member for Faversham, complained to Younger that the *Daily Herald* was the only morning paper on sale at the underground station in the Strand in time to get 'into the hands of the working man early'. Younger forwarded this communication to Beaverbrook on 14 February. 'We certainly can't claim the *Express* as *our* paper,' he teased, 'but you are after all a shade better than the *Daily Herald*, & you may wish to catch the early worm at the tube stations.' Beaverbrook promised to have a word with his circulation manager. 'I do not think you ought to speak harshly of the *Daily Express*,' he replied to Younger's Valentine. 'We give you splendid support. . . . You and I agree on almost all political subjects. Also we agree as to personalities. There is no reason for any difference between us.'[3]

---

[1] Northcliffe to Steed, 12 January 1920 (copy), Northcliffe Papers; memorandum by Northcliffe, 31 January 1920, quoted in Pound and Harmsworth, p. 763; Sanders's diary, 15 February 1920, Bayford Papers; Lord Birkenhead, '*F.E.*,' *the Life of F. E. Smith* (London, 1959), pp. 344–46; 'The Northcliffe Creed,' enclosed in Carson to Bonar Law, 31 January 1920, Bonar Law Papers, 98/6/6.

[2] Steed to Northcliffe [February 1920], Northcliffe Papers; entry of 16–17 March 1920, Scott, *Political Diaries*, p. 383.

[3] Wheler to Younger, 12 February 1920, enclosed in Younger to Beaverbrook, 14 February 1920, and Beaverbrook to Younger, 18 February 1920 (copy), Beaverbrook Papers, C/334.

More valuable to Labour than the efficiency with which the *Herald* distributed its copies in central London was the effort of other dailies to kill Labour with kindness. The Asquithian and Lloyd Georgian journals vied for the distinction of extending their patronage to a comprehensive progressivism. This obliged them to stress the reasonableness of Labour doctrines and the patriotism of Labour statesmen. To the *Daily News* and the *Manchester Guardian*, conciliation came naturally. Northcliffe continuously enjoined his editors to take a 'moderate tone', as circumstances required: 'By attacking Labour as a whole we should antagonise them.' There were, of course, certain notable exceptions. In the *Morning Post* on 4 August, the Duke of Northumberland published the first of three pieces in which he undertook 'to trace and define the path of revolution' as plotted by foreign agents. The key words in his lexicon were 'menace', 'betrayal', 'conspiracy', and 'danger'. Strachey wrote to tell him 'how very much impressed I was by your articles', a decided improvement on the *Morning Post*'s usual tirades, 'which are often at once too irritable and too irritating and therefore serve as non-conductors of public sympathy'. As always, moderation was a relative concept.[1]

That held true on the Labour side as well. According to Ross McKibbin, who has charted the party's evolution, the *Daily Herald* 'had one indispensable quality – it was the only paper Labour had'. This state of affairs had its mutual drawbacks. However tempting, it was surely invalid to judge Labour's objectives – as opposed to its militant mood – from the *Herald*'s persistently crude and strident rhetoric of class conflict. The authorities were at a loss to make this distinction and consequently overreacted. In the summer of 1919, amid fears that troops would resist orders to break strikes or bear arms against the Russian revolutionaries, the War Office issued instructions for copies of the *Herald* to be seized at railway sidings and destroyed 'with as little publicity as possible'. Such heavy-handedness diminished neither the *Herald*'s sale – audited at a peak of nearly 330,000 in October 1920 – nor its sympathy for the Bolshevik cause. Lansbury, who made a detour to Russia without a passport the following March on a shopping expedition for Scandinavian newsprint, was pilloried as the recipient of Soviet subsidies, supposedly derived from the sale of the Tsarist crown jewels. He retaliated by inveighing against the iniquities of a 'master class' that 'intended to provoke a bloody revolution in order that the workers may be ... shot down like dogs'. At its most hysterical, the *Herald* assailed Lloyd George, 'the bondservant of moneybags', for cancelling the construction of four warships; instead of rejoicing at a step towards disarmament, it denounced an 'economy for the taxpayer' that aggravated conditions of 'unemployment for the worker'.[2]

---

[1] Northcliffe to H. G. Price, 12 April 1921 (telegram; copy), Northcliffe Papers; Strachey to Northumberland, 19 August 1920 (copy), Strachey Papers.

[2] Ross McKibbin, *The Evolution of the Labour Party 1910–1924* (Oxford, 1974), p. 222; Harrison, *Poor Men's Guardians*, p. 185; Lansbury, *Miracle*, pp. 140–47; *Daily Herald*, 19 October 1919, 28 August and 19 November 1921.

At the very least, Maurice Cowling has argued, the *Daily Herald* 'created an attitude towards government which made it difficult for trades unionist leaders to collaborate openly. The result was a heightening of language even when they did not mean it.' Representing that section of the Labour movement which urged the pursuit of industrial 'Direct Action' for political ends, the paper helped 'to establish a body of prejudices' that was taken to characterize the movement as a whole.[1] Thus, to the discomfort of the Webbs and other Labour moderates, the *Herald*'s propaganda projected an image of extremism that provided politicians of antithetical persuasions with a provocation and a pretext.

Whether Lansbury, a Christian socialist and lifelong pacifist, took seriously his own bombast is much to be doubted. His five fellow directors – Ernest Bevin, Frank Hodges, Ben Turner, Robert Williams, and Francis Meynell – varied in their degrees of enthusiasm in proportion to their degrees of revolutionary zeal. Some of them had served on an unofficial committee of the TUC that raised funds for the reactivated daily after the war. By the autumn of 1920, those modest reserves were exhausted. Claiming to be the victim of an advertisers' 'boycott' (9 October), the *Herald* was forced two days later to raise its price to twopence. Lansbury threw himself on the mercy of the party conference, which responded with pious resolutions, yet disclaimed any intention of 'taking over' the stricken property. Henderson, a parliamentarian first and foremost, went no further than to accept a shareholding as a 'trustee', forgoing a directorship. He was not to be let off so easily. On 2 March 1922, the board resigned *en bloc*, after electing Henderson and C. W. Bowerman, secretary of the TUC and MP for Deptford, to 'assume the responsibility of continuing and developing the *Daily Herald*, and place it in the front rank of Labour newspapers in the world'. Furious at Lansbury's precipitous action, Henderson really had no choice. He did not require Tom Shaw, another trade-unionist MP, to point out 'the danger of the Labour Movement finding the money and a few individuals directing the policy of the paper, possibly in a spirit contrary to that of the decisions of the Party itself'. From the embarrassments of other party leaders, Liberal and Conservative alike, he knew full well what to expect.[2]

*   *   *

Labour, still a cumbrous movement that enveloped a party, backed into custody of a daily journal, with results that remain to be investigated. The *Herald* was neither a profitable enterprise nor, except for Will Dyson's

[1] Cowling, *Impact of Labour*, p. 39.
[2] *Report*, Labour Party Conference, 1920; Lansbury to Henderson, 2 March 1922, and Shaw to Henderson, 7 March 1922, quoted in McKibbin, *Evolution*, pp. 223–24; *also see* Alan Bullock, *The Life and Times of Ernest Bevin*, I (London, 1960), 112–13.

haunting cartoons, a particularly distinguished one. Nevertheless, it fulfilled one of the rites of political passage.

By the time that Henderson and his parliamentary associates were making their quasi-official entry into political journalism, the leaders of the older parties were facing eviction from their accustomed places. The opposition Liberals, under Asquith's desultory command, epitomized the process, which they struggled to arrest. The *Daily News*, hitherto their morning voice in the metropolis, now inclined towards Labour with a disconcerting detachment. It gave 'more space and prominence to some remarks made in Welsh by Ll.G. to a lot of Calvinist parsons,' Asquith sulked on 16 June 1921, than to his own weighty address the previous day to the Eighty Club.[1] The *Star* accompanied its sister paper on its migration, leaving only the *Westminster Gazette* to represent the Asquithian view in the national press.

In desperation, the 'Wee Free' Liberals retreated to their provincial strongholds, only to find them weakened by economic pressures and years of neglect. J. B. Morrell and Sir Charles Starmer were ardent champions of the cause, which Starmer was to represent as MP for Cleveland in the short-lived 1923 Parliament. Since entering into partnership in 1903, they had acquired four morning and four evening papers, along with 'fourteen weekly papers published from fourteen provincial towns'. Most recently, they had added the *Sunday Mercury* at Birmingham, which boasted 'a rapidly growing sale'. The losses incurred by many of these ventures were offset by the profits from a pair of non-political 'sporting papers' and especially from Starmer's lucrative interest in the *Advertising World*, 'one of the main reasons that has enabled him to put vitality into one derelict paper after another'.[2]

Writing to Maclean in the spring of 1920, Morrell stressed the impediments to future progress. 'As I mentioned to you the other day there are a large number of Newspapers in the market at the present time', when the provincial order was fast crumbling. These included no fewer than a dozen weeklies, which Morrell had rejected for purchase and expected to 'be bought by their more enterprising local competitors unless there is some local politician who is anxious to keep the papers for their political value'. The Starmer-Morrell chain, forged largely from the cast-offs of local activists, had 'absorbed all the available capital . . . at our disposal' and was no longer in a position to expand. 'A newspaper investment does not interest the ordinary business man and the

---

[1] Asquith to [Hilda Harrisson], 16 June 1921, in *H.H.A.: Letters to a Friend* (ed. D. MacCarthy; London, 1933), I, 188.

[2] The following paragraphs are based on Morrell to Maclean, 22 June 1920, Asquith Papers. An undated memorandum among the Cowdray papers listed the principal Starmer-Morrell holdings as the Midland Express Company at Birmingham, acquired at public auction in 1912; the North of England Newspaper Company at Darlington, formed in 1903; the Nottingham Daily Express Company, acquired from Sir Jesse Boot; the *Sheffield Independent*, taken over from H. J. Wilson in 1909; the Hereford Press and Printing Company, bought by the Birmingham concern in 1919; the *Islington Gazette*; and weeklies at Chesterfield, Norwich, Durham, and Swindon.

money required is too great for the working journalist', with the result that publications either perished or 'grouped together under the same proprietor'. Although some of the Fleet Street giants – Hulton and Rothermere, for example – extended their networks beyond London, the provinces constituted a separate domain. 'With regard to provincial papers', Morrell considered his own group to be 'far the most important, but Donald has papers both in Bradford and Hull' and Samuel Storey 'controls papers in Sunderland, Hartlepool, Newcastle and Portsmouth'.

In view of 'this tendency for the formation of groups ... not only amongst daily papers but amongst weeklies', Morrell recommended that 'those responsible for the Party organisation should' devise 'some machinery whereby these papers could be saved or at any rate explored before they are either stopped or pass into unsympathetic hands'. A typically Victorian request, coming from a man with typically Victorian incentives, it was inspired by the perception of a distinctly new danger. 'The Liberal Party has an immense advantage over the Labour Party in its Provincial and weekly Press,' Morrell told Maclean, 'and whilst leaders appear to be losing their influence, I am firmly convinced that the tone of a paper is of enormous political value.' After generations of battling against the Tories for journalistic terrain, the Liberals trained their rusty weapons on Labour, which was overtaking them in the industrial constituencies. They did so with the traditional notion that newspaper strength on the periphery could redress parliamentary weakness at the centre.

Incapable of extending their newspaper operations, the independent Liberals decided instead to consolidate them for greater effectiveness. The idea was to couple the money-losing *Westminster Gazette* with the Starmer-Morrell syndicate and, in the process, to weed out the followers of Lloyd George from among its shareholders. Sir Charles Henry was known to have 'been anxious for some time to rid himself of the liability of his shares' in a paper that contradicted his beliefs; and Lord St Davids, another of the infiltrators, seemed equally amenable to the proposal. The Westminster Press group therefore emerged in the summer of 1920 as a structure of unalloyed Asquithianism. It was constructed by Morrell's 'splendid and self-sacrificing work', as Maclean paid tribute to it, and by Lord Cowdray's financial generosity. Cowdray's initial impulse was to launch a morning paper to fill a conspicuous gap. He calculated that £325,000 would be required as working capital, allowing 'for an estimated annual loss of £50,000 for 3 years – the paper to be self-supporting afterwards'. Offering to contribute £100,0000 from his own resources, he reasoned that 'a morning paper would certainly give us a good chance of establishing a paying Liberal paper, whereas if we continue as we are the life of the *Westminster Gazette* must necessarily expire within the next year or year and a half'.[1]

[1] Maclean to Cowdray, 16 April 1919 (copy), and memorandum by Cowdray, 30 June 1920, Cowdray Papers; Maclean to Morrell, 27 July 1921 (copy), Asquith Papers.

While that project hung fire, the partners engaged in a byzantine process of share-swapping. At a meeting on 10 February 1921, Cowdray 'agreed that the Westminster Press should be the holding company into which the Whitehall Securities Ltd. (all owned by himself and his family) would put the new capital'. The Rowntree Trust exchanged its shares in the *Northern Echo* and *Sheffield Independent* for Westminster Press shares, with the understanding that Starmer and Morrell would follow suit. Acting as trustees for the chief whip, Maclean, Hudson, and Geoffrey Howard accepted Morrell's 'most kind and generous offer' of shares in Starmer's Birmingham company, which were then converted into Westminster Press shares. 'Nottingham was put on the side for the time being', but plans were made to lease the Sheffield and Darlington properties to the Birmingham subsidiary, 'thus saving Income Tax' for the outside shareholders. Hudson confessed to being 'a little mystified by the business. I have signed applications for shares in a company without any intention of paying for them' and with the realization that, as the registered owner, he would 'rightly be held responsible if I dispose of them'; moreover, 'if a blank transfer signed by me were stolen & got into wrongful hands', he would have some awkward explaining to do. But, as Maclean 'says it is all right for me to do these things', Hudson was 'content' to hold 25,000 shares jointly with Howard. His qualms were an indication that the system was breaking down.[1]

Hudson was also symptomatic in another respect. Without tempering his hostility to Lloyd George, he had grown impatient with Asquith and susceptible to the notion of a centre party led by Grey and/or Cecil. Friendly with Northcliffe, whose widow he was to marry, Hudson drafted a commendatory leading article on the subject for *The Times*, though he did not imagine that 'Bob Cecil will ever cut much ice with the British Public' on his own. Cowdray, presumably ignorant of this exercise, harboured similar tendencies. In July 1920, he had a guarded discussion with Northcliffe, whom he found 'prepared to do everything he can to further Grey being the leader of the Liberal Party', but unwilling to 'lift a finger for Asquith'. Raising the tantalizing possibility that the Asquithians might persevere without Asquith, Cowdray ventured 'that if Grey would come back to politics the Liberals stood a very good chance of driving Lloyd George out at the next election'. In that eventuality, Northcliffe promised Cowdray that material sent by Liberal headquarters to *The Times* would 'readily secure all the prominence you wished'.[2]

Asquith, however, was seemingly oblivious to the despair of his friends and

---

[1] Memorandum [by Morrell] of a meeting on 10 February 1921, Cowdray Papers; Maclean to Morrell, 27 July 1921 (copy), Hudson to [Maclean?], 5 October 1921, and Hudson to R. H. Davies, 18 October 1921, Asquith Papers. A 'memorandum for Major Pearson on the position of Whitehall [Securities Ltd.] with regard to the control of Westminster Press Limited,' prepared on 4 June 1923, showed these 25,000 shares to be held 'for Abingdon Street' by Maclean, Howard, and Viscount Gladstone. Whitehall, headed by Major Pearson, held a majority of voting shares.

[2] Hudson to Northcliffe [1921], Northcliffe Papers; Cowdray to Maclean, 19 July 1920, Maclean Papers.

the derision of his enemies. Rothermere, whose papers at Glasgow had endorsed him at nearby Paisley as a lesser evil, told Lord Murray on 1 April that his 'editors and political writers are astounded at Mr A's obvious inadequacy for the position he is expected to fill'. The *British Weekly* (25 May) waspishly demanded to know 'Who is the leader of the Independent Liberals?' On the morning of 13 July, Scott called at the *Daily News* office to see Henry Cadbury, who 'had written to say "he would like to talk over the present position of Liberalism and its Leadership"', but who 'really had nothing to say beyond reporting that his father thought ill of Asquith as a leader and wanted to know what I thought'. Scott, of course, 'was entirely of his opinion', as 'was practically every Liberal' he knew. Even so, 'it was an extremely difficult thing to dispossess an ex-Prime Minister from the leadership of a party except with his own good-will which at present appeared in Asquith's case to be not forthcoming'.[1]

It was under this cloud that the Westminster Press company got started. Not surprisingly, the response was less enthusiastic than anticipated. Partington declined to take up the shares earmarked for him. 'I am very sorry to have to alter my decision but it is only after the most careful consideration,' he explained to Cowdray. Like 'many . . . old supporters', he had been alienated by 'recent events', including the publication of Margot Asquith's indiscreet memoirs, and doubted whether there was any 'future for the Liberal Party'. J. F. L. Brunner, who had succeeded to his father's baronetcy, proclaimed himself 'more disposed to give the uncalled capital to the party than for the *Westminster Gazette* to be continued, but he fell into line' and subscribed for 1,000 new preference shares. The blueprint for a new metropolitan morning paper was shelved, and the fate of the *Westminster Gazette* was uncertain. 'We are coming to a point at which a decision about the *W.G.* is urgent,' Spender wrote to Cowdray on 22 October. As he understood it, the proprietors had 'definitely' decided that 'the paper shall not continue *as an evening paper*', but had not spelt out whether they meant 'to convert it into a morning paper or to wind up & sell to the highest bidder'. If the latter, the property would 'almost certainly' fall to some 'nominee of Ll. George. Two efforts from that quarter have been made this year,' and, only the previous week, Downing Street had 'captured the *Edinburgh Evening News*'. Spender gloomily predicted that 'the process will go on', for Lloyd George 'has apparently a bottomless purse to draw on for these operations & a full-blown syndicate, with the *Daily Chronicle* for its base, to work them in unison'.[2]

After months of delay, damaging to staff morale and advertising accounts, a

[1] Rothermere to Murray, 1 April [1920], Elibank Papers; entry of 13 July 1921, Scott, *Political Diaries*, p. 390.

[2] Partington to Cowdray, 9 November 1920, Cowdray to H. Pearson, 20 January 1921, and Spender to Cowdray, 22 October 1920, Cowdray Papers. *The Times* (23 October) confirmed the purchase of the *Edinburgh Evening News*, which had 'hitherto supported the cause of the Independent Liberal Party'.

decision was finally made. On 14 July 1921, Starmer and Morrell met Major Harold Pearson, Cowdray's son, at Liberal Party offices in Parliament Street. 'The improvement of the Evening Paper was ruled out as being impracticable owing to the heavy cost and severe competition. Altogether about 1,700,000 Evening Papers are sold in London every day', it was reckoned, and the market seemed to be saturated. 'It was considered that it would be far more to the advantage of the Liberal Party' – and to Westminster Press Ltd. as well – 'to publish a Morning Paper which could be bought by leading Liberals throughout the country, and provide excellent propaganda for the Party.'[1] The logic was not only faulty, but also quaint. Could any paper, morning or evening, succeed on this basis?

On Saturday, 5 November, the *Westminster Gazette* appeared for the last time in its nocturnal guise. Two days later, it surfaced on the morning news-stands. On the day of its reincarnation, Spender slipped away to cover the naval conference at Washington in the improvised capacity of 'political editor'. It was better for all concerned, he thought, for him to be 'out of the way for a few weeks'. No one 'could have been more generous' than Cowdray and Starmer, he assured Maclean. 'Of course I can't pretend not to feel the vulgarisation of something that we have tried to keep clear of that kind of taint for these thirty years.' Set in his ways, Spender found it difficult to adapt to a new routine, which would have kept him at his desk through the long evenings. More to the point, the paper had altered its format and perspective in ways that he could not abide. Lord Camrose, a newspaperman of a different breed, later ridiculed as 'almost pathetic' Spender's 'extraordinary admission' that the old *Westminster* had gone 'to press with our last edition about half an hour earlier than most of our competitors', possibly to the inconvenience of 'journalists relying on the last editions of the evening papers for the very latest news, but of advantage to our kind of reader who wanted papers delivered to his house by six o'clock'. The new *Westminister* did not afford an opportunity for the unhurried, reflective journalism that Spender proudly practised.[2]

Across the Atlantic, he was spared the grief of seeing the deterioration, day by day. Sir Campbell Stuart was 'not much impressed with the morning *Westminster Gazette*', hardly the rival to *The Times* that Spender had once contemplated. To Clifford Sharp, filling in as chief leader-writer, it seemed 'an outrage – the *Westminster* transformed into a third-rate provincial sheet and offered at 2d.' Spender returned in late January and intimated his intention to resign. Grey, Gladstone, and Harcourt 'begged him, for the sake of the party & liberalism, to remain. Their appeal & his obligation & friendship to me is weighing on him,' Cowdray was happy to hear from Mrs Spender. Nevertheless, her husband kept his resolve, and the *Westminster* made the appropriate

[1] Memorandum of a meeting of 14 July 1921, Cowdray Papers.
[2] Spender to Maclean, 4 November 1921, Maclean Papers; Camrose, *British Newspapers*, pp. 7–8.

announcement in mid-February. 'Stripped of all sentiment and personal feeling, the bare outstanding fact', as Cowdray saw it, was 'that Spender, after his generation of absolute control of the *W.G.*, cannot work with others who have to produce a paper at the minimum cost consistent with it wielding all the political power that is possible on commercial lines'. To Spender, 'the short point' was that 'a first-class serious paper' could not be produced on the basis of Starmer's formula of giving 'news like the *Daily Mail* only more of it'. Nor would he serve as second-in-command to J. B. Hobman, a rank provincial who had accompanied Starmer from Sheffield to Birmingham and thence to London.[1]

Spender did not exaggerate the sadness of his leave-taking, which was 'entirely my own act' and without political overtones. That could not be said about Gardiner's departure from the *Daily News*, where he had tenuously held on as a weekly contributor. His column for 12 February 1921 ('What is Wrong with Parliament?') was set into type, but withheld from publication at the last minute. The previous weekend, Lloyd George came to Birmingham to receive the freedom of the city and an honorary degree from the university. Dame Margaret Lloyd George, who accompanied him on select ceremonial occasions, was known to have 'paid a visit to George Cadbury at the Manor House, Northfield'. Gardiner's natural surmise was that he had been the main topic of conversation. The circumstantial evidence, impossible to corroborate, was reminiscent of the visit that Lloyd George and Dalziel had paid to Frank Lloyd in the summer of 1918. The upshot was a letter from Hodgson, wearily informing Gardiner of the directors' decision 'that frontal attacks ... on L.G. are definitely to be discontinued'. Gardiner preferred to terminate his contract rather than submit to the injunction that he should 'write non-politically just now'. Writing in the *Nation* on 26 March, Massingham inferred that the 'rather rueful pages' of the *Daily News* 'will lack in future the one pen that seemed to have a definite political creed and force of conviction behind it'. It struck him as 'extraordinary ... that a newspaper with such a past should drop its missionary side as if it were a stale sandwich thrown out of a railway carriage'.[2]

'The slow seepage in the standing of Asquithean [*sic*] Liberalism cannot be explained by asserting a simple correlation between its journalism and its failure,' Maurice Cowling has insisted. There is no assertion here that the correlation was simple, much less direct. Yet it cannot be denied that the two phenomena were related, and not merely in the agitated minds of contemporaries. If, as Cowling has suggested, 'most of the best journalism' was being

---

[1] Stuart to Northcliffe, 30 November 1921, Northcliffe Papers; Sharp to Spender, n.d., quoted in Wilson Harris, *J. A. Spender* (London, 1946), p. 220; Cowdray to H. Pearson, 1 February 1922, Spender to Cowdray, 4 February 1922, and Cowdray to Maclean, 13 February 1922 (copy), Cowdray Papers. Hobman was to stand three times unsuccessfully as a Liberal candidate.

[2] Spender, *Life, Journalism and Politics*, II, 140; Hodgson to Gardiner [13 February 1921], Henry Cadbury to Gardiner, 6 March [1921], and Gardiner to Henry Cadbury, 7 March 1921 (copy), Gardiner Papers.

produced on the Asquithian side, it was strikingly apparent that 'journalistic capability' was finding it increasingly difficult to express itself. Those who adhered to the cause were being driven from their wobbly platforms. Their successors, who did not presume to qualify as full-fledged replacements, were invariably lacklustre and probably picked for that very quality: Perris at the *Daily Chronicle*; Hodgson at the *Daily News*; and Hobman at the *Westminster Gazette*. Massingham survived a bit longer at the weekly *Nation*, where his resignation was accepted 'with regret' on 13 December 1922 and took effect the following May. The reconstructed board of directors – including John Maynard Keynes, Walter Layton, and Ramsay Muir – was truly a constellation of 'formidable intellectual assets'. But the new editor, H. D. Henderson, was no match for Massingham as a controversialist.[1]

The spirit and much of the talent had gone out of the Liberal press, mirroring – though not, in itself, causing – the party's parliamentary distress. The politicians habitually complained that they were poorly served. 'A Liberal Journalist', in a letter to the *Nation* (9 October 1920), countered that they themselves were to blame: 'Owing chiefly to disloyalty and weakness on the part of Liberal leaders, the path of a Liberal newspaper in these days is not a flowery one.' Clearly, as the Liberals lost ground, they suffered an analogous erosion of their journalistic base. The morning *Westminster Gazette* was absorbed by the *Daily News* in 1928. Two years later, this amalgam merged with the *Daily Chronicle* to become the *News Chronicle*. The *Nation* succumbed to the embrace of the *New Statesman* in 1931. Each of these successive contractions was a response to worsening market conditions. At the same time, each reflected the shifting realities of political alignment. Arguably, a stronger press might have given direction to an enfeebled party. True to its nature, however, the Liberal press accentuated that enfeeblement.

Lloyd George, a disruptive force in every arena, was the captive of the monsters he had created. His fitful attempts to seek an accommodation with moderate Labour, like his efforts to restore Liberal unity on his own terms, were continuously thwarted by the antagonisms he aroused in and through the press. His desperate bid to weld the two wings of the coalition into a permanent electoral alliance was similarly subverted by newspapermen who refused to attune their loyalties at a wave of the wizard's wand. Not so much devoted to party tradition as distrustful of his motives, they stymied him by denying him publicity when he wanted it and heaping it upon him when he sought to escape from surveillance. On the evening of 18 March 1920, he addressed the Coalition Liberal members on the imperative need for fusion with the

[1] Cowling, *Impact of Labour*, pp. 98–99; Havighurst, *Radical Journalist*, pp. 296–302; Peter Clarke, *Liberals and Social Democrats* (Cambridge, 1978), pp. 215–16. C. P. Scott was 'awfully sorry about the trouble as to the *Nation*, both for Massingham's sake & for the *Nation*'s.... Nothing which the new "group" can contribute,' he insisted, 'is likely in the least to compensate for what we shall lose of a fine & courageous Liberal initiative'. Scott to Hammond, 8 January 1923, Hammond Papers.

Unionists. 'All were bound to secrecy', and, as an extra precaution, Guest and Sir William Edge were stationed 'at the door to impress on each men as he went out that there must be no word to the Press. Next morning,' Sanders was amused to note, '*The Times* had a full account and the *Glasgow Herald* further still.' Steed, who had been 'anxious not to give ... unnecessary advertisement' to the Prime Minister, 'sat down and smote him as shrewdly as I knew' in a leader entitled 'What is a Liberal?' (19 March), which the *Manchester Guardian* described as being 'bitter with exactly the bitterness of a Liberal, to whom intellectual principles are everything' (20 March). Marlowe drafted a rejoinder for the *Daily Mail* that went so far that 'it appeared to be running after Labour' and had to be toned down. The *Evening News*, on the heels of 'a sensational interview' with Churchill ('Why I support Mr Lloyd George'), recalled on the 20th that the Prime Minister had 'had no hard words for Labour when it consented to join the Coalition. One cannot help suspecting that his real grievance against it now is that it does not support Mr Lloyd George.'[1]

It was idle to expect any journal owned by one of the Harmsworth brothers to sacrifice a 'scoop' out of consideration for Lloyd George. Northcliffe, the eldest of the brood, expended his waning energies in dogging the coalition. In spite of his awareness that *The Times*'s 'sometimes tactless pin-pricking of the Prime Minister ... has created the impression – especially in clubs – that we have a vendetta against him', he decreed 'that we must maintain all our policies. They are right.' His siblings heeded his advice. The antagonism of the *Western Daily Mercury* at Plymouth, owned by Sir Leicester Harmsworth, prompted Lord Astor to angle for control 'as an insurance on the constituency', now represented by Lady Astor. 'I have no confidence in Harmsworth as I know he has deliberately avoided meeting me,' Astor wrote uneasily to Garvin. (In 1921, the *Mercury* was subsumed by the *Western Morning News*, which Sir Leicester had recently bought, 'eventually' as a gift 'for my boys'.) Rothermere was the brother who pricked with the sharpest pin. 'The House of Commons must listen to the irresistible cry of the people,' he declaimed in his *Daily Mirror* on 4 October 1920. To amplify that cry, he founded the Anti-Waste League, which won a by-election at Dover in January and a pair of contests in June. Dr Christopher Addison, attacked as a spendthrift for his plans to build 'homes for heroes', was hounded from the Ministry of Health by a backbench agitation 'stirred up by the anti-Wasters and the Northcliffe press'.[2]

The Irish question, even more than social welfare, was an obstacle to fusion.

---

[1] Sanders's diary, 21 March 1920, Bayford Papers (where Lloyd George's speech is postdated); Steed to Northcliffe, 21 March 1920, and Stuart to Northcliffe, 18 March 1920, Northcliffe Papers. For a superb discussion of Lloyd George's pursuit of 'fusion', see Morgan, *Consensus and Disunity*, pp. 180–90.

[2] Memorandum by Northcliffe, 1 January 1921, and Sir Leicester Harmsworth to Northcliffe [1921], quoted in Pound and Harmsworth, pp. 781, 773; Astor to Garvin, 10 August 1920 (copy), Astor Papers; Addison to his wife, 15 June 1921, Addison Papers.

Politicians may have pretended otherwise, but the newspapers saw to it that fundamental differences were kept in the forefront. Lloyd George appalled his Liberal followers by his ruthless recourse to repression, administered by the infamous 'Black and Tans'. Scott 'wrote him a heart to heart letter on the subject' in May 1921 and received a polite acknowledgment, 'which no doubt is as much as one could expect'. That summer, they were 'so hopelessly at variance ... over Irish affairs' that, as Lloyd George nervously remarked, it would have been 'difficult ... to meet without coming to blows!' The government appeased Scott, only to incur the wrath of the diehard Unionists, by proceeding to implement a modified version of Home Rule. Outraged by the censure of General Dyer, who had suppressed Indian turbulence with unconscionable brutality, these higher-than-High Tories organized in the press and the constituencies to defend imperial values in the face of nationalist aspirations.[1]

As before, the *Morning Post* and the *Spectator* were particularly imbued with Orange fanaticism. *The Times*, torn between Steed's sympathy for subject nationalities and the Ulster loyalism of Northcliffe's mother ('the Old Lady of Totteridge'), could not resist the temptation to stir the cauldron of inter-party discord. John Walter disapproved. 'Is not the present a favourable opportunity for the Paper to reconsider its attitude towards Ireland?' he asked Northcliffe on the eve of the treaty-signing. 'I allude not so much to its policy as to its tone, which has been creating an impression for some time past that we are more anxious to damage L.G. than to see his Government achieve a settlement with the Irish.' Walter was convinced 'that this attitude is losing the Paper its authority as well as its readers'. Steed, professing solidarity with Northcliffe, warned him that Walter 'has lately been working steadily against you, the Paper and me'. *The Times* established contact with Lord Derby, who agreed 'to write a long and "chatty" letter under the heading "From a Former Correspondent"'. Having declined the Lord Lieutenancy of Ireland, that 'fat gentleman' cheered Stuart with the prophecy 'that the great Welshman will have a breakdown in three months, and will retire from public life'. H. W. Wilson trusted that Northcliffe would then seize the chance 'to lead and reconstruct a new Unionist party – or rather a party which shall work for the regeneration of our country and for national interests', which Lloyd George was alleged to have betrayed. Northcliffe perpetually invited such flattery for the pleasure of brushing it aside. 'Do you realise the fact that, if I enter political life, I have to abandon all connection with the Press, which is my sole source of power?' he replied to Wilson. 'Mine is a new kind of position in the world,' he proclaimed, by now pathetically. 'I have been more or less forced into it, but I prefer it to any other as a means of getting things done.'[2]

---

[1] Scott to Hammond, 11 May 1921, Hammond Papers; Lloyd George to Scott, 23 July 1921, quoted in Scott, *Political Diaries*, p. 394.

[2] Walter to Northcliffe, 1 December [1920], Steed to Northcliffe, 5 December 1920, Stuart to Northcliffe, 12 January 1921, Wilson to Northcliffe, 26 January 1921, and Northcliffe to Wilson, 27 January 1921 (copy), Northcliffe Papers. Stuart, unlike his chief, delighted in extending

The strategy of *The Times* was to hasten an appeal to the country in which the cohesion and credibility of the coalition might be destroyed. As neither Bonar Law nor certainly Chamberlain was likely to break loose, the paper's device was to turn Derby against Lloyd George. No matter that Derby, an early proponent of fusion, did not willingly lend himself to the purpose. That he was working hard to head off the threat of diehard separatism in Lancashire did not prevent *The Times* from harnessing him to its own stationary bandwagon. 'Note *The Times* again this morning on our window cheering for an Election,' Younger instructed Bonar Law on 29 January 1921. Younger knew that its editorial interpretation of Derby's remarks at Manchester the previous day was 'thoroughly unjustified, that Derby made a good Coalition speech, & there wasn't a hint of criticism'.[1] For a variety of motives, other journals likewise harped on the internal contradictions of the coalition and did not scruple to put words into politicians' mouths.

Despite its successes at Westminster and, for that matter, at international conferences, the coalition failed to take root in the constituencies, where newspapers helped to keep alive a countervailing spirit of sectional partisanship. At every level, the press impeded fusion by asserting the superficial and transitory nature of parliamentary arrangement. The effect, in the minds of voters and backbench MPs alike, was to expose differences that the coalition tended to cloak. The editor of the *Strathspey Herald*, for example, applied to Younger for financial assistance 'in supporting Unionist principles' as distinct from coalition ones. Strictly speaking, this remote Scottish journal – with a circulation 'somewhat under 1300' – did not qualify as a bona fide party organ as it did not even subscribe to the Central Office's lobby press service. In ordinary times, it might have looked to the local MP, whom it had backed for election. But Sir Archibald Williamson, who sat for the surrounding district, was a Coalition Liberal and consequently 'of little use' to the *Herald*.[2] This distinction could be ignored at Westminster, but not in the country at large.

Only the *Daily Chronicle*, directly subservient to Lloyd George, was an unequivocal advocate of fusion. It received intermittent support from the *Observer* and from such isolated provincial journals as the *South Wales Daily News* at Cardiff. The *Chronicle*, which had maintained circulation but lost pungency, was in the throes of reorganization. Inverforth, bringing to bear his business know-how, agreed with Guest that Perris could be left to edit, subject to supervision 'by some tactful person with good common sense. The matter is

---

hospitality to politicians. 'For example – I had Lord Reading, Hamar Greenwood and Mr Edward Shortt, among others, to lunch the other day, ... and as a result *The Times* published the most important column of exclusive Irish news that I think has appeared for some time in any newspaper.' Stuart to Northcliffe, 12 January 1921, Northcliffe Papers.

[1] Younger to Bonar Law, 29 January 1921, Bonar Law Papers, 100/1/51.

[2] R. D. Waterhouse (Bonar Law's private secretary) to Younger, 8 December 1920, and Younger to Waterhouse, 13 December 1920, Bonar Law Papers, 101/4/111, 99/8/10. For Williamson's classification as a Lloyd George Liberal, see Wilson, *Downfall*, p. 161.

now therefore ripe for your decision and action,' Guest told Lloyd George in September 1920. Within weeks, Philip Kerr left his desk in Downing Street for 'other fields', specifically the political directorship of the *Chronicle*. Although 'his relations with all his colleagues' in Fleet Street were 'said to have been of the happiest', he was determined not to remain there indefinitely. 'I don't want to take on the Chairmanship, or Managing Directorship,' he informed Lloyd George at the turn of the year, when 'the six months temporary agreement with Dalziel' was nearing an end. 'Indeed, so far from wanting to increase my responsibilities ..., I want to relinquish them,' he declared. To do the job 'properly I ought to settle down to it for ten years & go into Parliament so as to get the proper political contacts. That I'm simply not prepared to do.' For the time being, however, his presence ensured that 'things are much better in the office now. The *D.C.* is better & will be better still in the next few weeks as you will see. And if there is an immediate General Election I will, of course, see it through.'[1]

Kerr evidently warmed to the task. On 8 July 1921, he 'had another talk with Dalziel', who revealed that the Board was 'still sticky about entering into any agreement about the chairmanship, but are perfectly willing to appoint me nominated Director with editorial control'. After a transitional period, Dalziel would step down. 'Do you see any objection to this plan?' Kerr asked Lloyd George. The delay would afford him 'an opportunity to size things up, and find out if I can really carry the Board, though in the meanwhile my hands will be a good deal tied, except for purely editorial policy'. Nothing could have suited Lloyd George better. Kerr remained on duty to receive credit for the paper's panegyrics when the Prime Minister sweepingly extended unemployment insurance. 'The line you have taken in the *Chronicle* has been most helpful,' Edward Grigg told him. 'You have held the fort splendidly, and I would have written or telegraphed if I had felt there was anything I could suggest in addition to what you were doing already.' Lloyd George's requirements were more easily met than those of Kerr, whose authority went without formal recognition. His connection terminated before his departure for America the following March, nine months in advance of the next election. His experience justified Wadsworth's opinion that the *Chronicle* ultimately 'died not from any of its defects as a newspaper but from the financial entanglements into which a succession of owning syndicates had landed it'.[2]

Its solvency notwithstanding, the *Daily Chronicle* was almost as great a trial

---

[1] Guest to Lloyd George, 16 September 1920, and Kerr to Lloyd George, 1 January 1921, Lloyd George Papers, F/22/2/13, F/34/2/10; J. R. M. Butler, *Lord Lothian* (London, 1960), pp. 81–82.

[2] Kerr to Lloyd George, 8 July 1921, Lloyd George Papers, F/34/2/3; Grigg to Kerr, 23 September 1921, Grigg Papers; Wadsworth, *Newspaper Circulations*, p. 26. Geoffrey Dawson later entertained a vague 'recollection ... that Philip [Kerr] very soon found out that he liked neither the people nor their methods and got out of it [the *Daily Chronicle*] very quickly'. Dawson to Grigg, 11 February [1941], Grigg Papers.

for the Lloyd George Liberals as the *Westminster Gazette* for the Asquithians or the *Daily Herald* for the parliamentary Labour Party. By the same token, the *Daily Express* was a perturbation for the Conservatives. In February 1921, it violently opposed Sir Arthur Griffith-Boscawen, whose ministerial appointment obliged him to stand for re-election at Dudley. The candidate's grievous offence was to have sanctioned an embargo against the importation of cattle from Canada. Beaverbrook, a self-commissioned guardian of Canadian interest, did not permit personal acquaintance or party loyalty to inhibit him. 'Can you do anything to stop this ramp?' Younger appealed to Bonar Law. 'It is a disgraceful as well as an unfair one & it is no use my trying to interfere.' Boscawen explained that 'because I refused to be stampeded into giving a definite pledge on a most difficult & delicate subject', Beaverbrook 'placarded the whole town that I was in favour of dear meat & his paper has practically gone over to the Labour party'. On 3 March, the seat fell to Labour. 'The party is furious with Beaverbrook over the defeat of Boscawen at Dudley,' Sanders wrote in his diary ten days later. 'Coming just after our sensational victory at Woolwich,' where Ramsay MacDonald was repulsed, 'it was particularly annoying.'[1]

A fortnight after the Dudley result, Bonar Law resigned from the Cabinet and the leadership of the Unionist Party on medical grounds. Younger, 'stating a fact within my own knowledge', maintained that the *Express*'s 'recent attitude in the Dudley Election had, in my opinion, much to do in finally breaking down the health of my Leader', who was suffering from high blood pressure. With Bonar Law's retirement, the party suddenly lost what little influence it had had over Beaverbrook, whose capacity for treachery was exceeded only by his presumption. No sooner had the *Express* inflicted this humiliation than it applied to Younger for a further subvention. 'I think your letter ... must have been addressed to me by mistake,' he replied icily. 'The *Daily Express* has recently made itself particularly prominent in most unfairly attacking a Member of the Government, and I deeply regret that any money belonging to my Party is embarked in the newspaper. So far from becoming a Guarantor as you suggest, my desire would be to get out of all responsibility whatever in connection with the newspaper.'[2]

If the request was difficult to believe, it was easy to understand. Blumenfeld, saying that he would 'be very sorry if a quarrel on this particular issue was to develop into a permanent severance', reminded Younger of the party's long involvement with the enterprise, which was 'only kept going by the guarantees given by Lord Beaverbrook and myself'. Commercial logic compelled him to 'point out ... that if we manage to pull through, the shares of your friends

---

[1] Younger to Bonar Law, 23 February 1921, and Boscawen to Bonar Law, 27 February 1921, Bonar Law Papers, 100/2/28–29, 36; Sanders's diary, 13 March 1921, Bayford Papers.

[2] Younger to the Secretary, *Daily Express*, 1 April 1921, and Younger to Blumenfeld, 18 April 1921 (copy), Beaverbrook Papers, H/15. For Beaverbrook's retrospective view, see *Politicians and the Press*, pp. 35–36.

would regain their value as the result of the sacrifices of other people'. Surely, therefore, it was not unreasonable to expect them to share the liability in 'these bad times'. Otherwise, Blumenfeld darkly hinted, Beaverbrook 'could foreclose on the Company at any moment and give all the minority shareholders, including myself, short shrift'.[1]

The gossip in Fleet Street confirmed the gravity of the situation. Earlier that year, Stuart heard from Lord Burnham 'that the *Daily Express* was losing £3,000 a week'. Northcliffe, before he 'left London' in July on a round-the-world voyage, 'was told that they were in a desperate state, and were trying to borrow quarter of a million from the Conservative Party, and lots of rubbish which I did not believe'. For once, the rumours were essentially true. But the *Daily Express* was not the only invalid. The *Morning Post* was also said to be 'in a bad way', and receiving money from the Duke of Northumberland. Stuart undertook to see Lord Apsley, Lady Bathurst's son, to ascertain the facts. Gwynne subsequently assured his proprietor that the *Morning Post* was not so 'badly hit' as the *Daily Telegraph*, admitted by its official historian to have faced a 'prospect of continued independent existence after the end of the First World War [that] was far from reassuring'. *The Times* was again going through a bad patch. 'Something is urgently needed to peg down the sale,' Northcliffe wrote to Stuart on 25 February. He had 'sent Steed an analysis of the figures yesterday – a steady diminution'. Still, he was 'not the least afraid of the position. I wish that I were as sure about the cure of my throat as I am about the cure of *The Times*.'[2]

Northcliffe had the supreme advantage of being able to bank on other newspaper assets. 'The *Daily Mail* circulation is now 1,345,000 and apparently is increasing quite fast', with the expectation of a rise to 'a million and a half before the end of the summer', Rothermere informed an envious Beaverbrook. The *Mail* was also 'doing extraordinarily well in the matter of advertisements. They must be scooping the pool.' Rothermere's own *Daily Mirror* was feeling the pinch. 'Thanks to the *Sunday Pictorial* I can go on for quite a long time,' he boasted to Beaverbrook, whose *Sunday Express* provided no comparable protection. 'I am wondering how Fleet Street is paying its weekly bills,' Rothermere went on cruelly.

> There must be much searching of pockets. Some of the weaker brethren will be hard put to it before long. . . . There should be a rare raking round of the whips' offices this year for newspaper subsidies, but if there is a general election in view, I imagine there will be a certain amount of shyness in

[1] Blumenfeld to Younger, 13 May 1921 (copy), Beaverbrook Papers, H/15.
[2] Stuart to Northcliffe, 28 January 1921, and Northcliffe to Stuart, 15 March [1922] (copy), Northcliffe Papers; Gwynne to Lady Bathurst, 23 March 1922, Bathurst Papers; Burnham, *Peterborough Court*, pp. 169–70, and 172 (where it is stated that the general belief that the *Telegraph* 'was in serious financial straits' was 'completely inaccurate'); Northcliffe to Stuart, 25 March 1921, quoted in *History of The Times*, IV, part 2, 586.

The Emergency Period

making prompt payments. I cannot imagine how the *News* and *Chronicle* can continue to go on. They must be right up against it. Neither of them have [*sic*] behind them a millionaire like yourself, who takes much more interest in politics than he does in the finances of the newspaper.[1]

That was really putting the boot in.

The press was generally in as distressed a state as the coalition, which Rothermere recognized to be incapable of surviving much longer. 'There is a suicidal war going on in Birmingham, Newcastle and the north-east of England, where the newspapers have all come down to a penny,' Northcliffe observed that spring. 'That means extinction of half of them. It also entails the eventual increase in the price of the remainder of them.' Although his political judgment was impaired, his commercial sense was unerring. 'Newspapers are going [to go] through Hell for the next year or two,' he warned. 'A great many must inevitably disappear. *The Times* will not be one of them for many reasons. Those which remain will share a prosperity not hitherto known in Newspaperdom.' He did not live to see the recovery of which Beaverbrook and Rothermere were the principal beneficiaries. A quarter of a century later, the clarity of his vision was confirmed by the first Royal Commission on the Press, which adopted 1921 as 'a convenient starting point for a history of the chains' that dominated the next phase of newspaper activity. 'The emergency period which succeeded the first World War had just been declared at an end and the way was open to new developments', to which we shall now turn.[2]

---

[1] Rothermere to Beaverbrook, 10 February 1921 (copy), Beaverbrook Papers, C/282a.
[2] Northcliffe to Stuart, 5 April 1921 (copy), Northcliffe Papers; Report, Royal Commission on the Press, 1947–1949, p. 57.

Eleven

INTERESTING COINCIDENCES

Northcliffe, who had come to exceed even his own standards of abnormality, was rapidly approaching a bizarre end, variously ascribed to ulcerative endocarditis, syphilis, Indian jungle fever, and a delayed reaction to poisoned ice cream. Too delirious to notice, he spent his last days in a wooden shelter atop a neighbour's roof in Carlton Gardens, ventilated to allow maximum exposure to the salubrious summer breeze.[1] His death, in stark contrast with his lifetime of fifty-seven years, was 'perfectly peaceful', and came on the morning of 14 August 1922. At the same time, though with less apparent finality, Lloyd George's ministerial career was drawing to a close. On 19 October, the Conservatives retracted their support, and he tumbled from office, never again to rise.

Northcliffe's removal from Fleet Street and Lloyd George's eviction from Downing Street rank as twin landmarks in newspaper history. Though two months apart, these events left a single vacuum. Long-standing tensions between the two men, intensified by mounting desperation, tended to obscure similarities of style and perspective. Each, in his way, had played havoc with the political press, defying its conventions, encouraging its presumptions, exploiting its tactical and commercial advantages, and – incidentally – accentuating its paradoxes. Constantly impinging on each other, they belonged to a world that was not big enough for both of them and that was diminished by their almost simultaneous departures.

Alike in many of their assumptions about the power of the press, Northcliffe and Lloyd George inadvertently collaborated to perpetuate certain traditions of late-Victorian political journalism at the expense of others. An obsession with *The Times* was, in effect, one of the bonds between them. Both had shaken themselves loose from the trammels of party as a means of obtaining greater personal leverage. Both remained instinctively political animals, anxious to widen – if not to deepen – the nature of political discourse and public participation. Lloyd George, in dispensing honours to newspapermen on an unprecedented scale, was as frankly cynical (and arguably as pragmatically

[1] Pound and Harmsworth quote the medical bulletin, pp. 881–82; Paul Ferris, *The House of Northcliffe* (London, 1971), pp. 273–76, disputes it.

democratic) as was Northcliffe in allocating news space. 'We must not let politics dominate the paper, but we must get the *news* in politics and give it all,' Northcliffe instructed Tom Clarke at the *Daily Mail*. 'But, please, no long-winded columns of mere words and hackneyed speeches of corrupt solemnity,' he pleaded. 'Treat politics as you would treat all other news – on its merits. It has no "divine right" on newspaper space.'[1] Lloyd George, whose corruption had the saving grace of never being solemn, was no less contemptuous of any divine-right theory. By force of personality, he made politics newsworthy, and therefore succeeded brilliantly at the game.

Whether by design or default, the two men were categorically independent, though independency – as a formal designation – was appropriated by Lloyd George's Liberal rivals on the one hand and by a smaller group of diehard Tories on the other. In the press as in Parliament, the label covered a multitude of sins and not a few virtues as well. Kennedy Jones, usually no stickler for nomenclature, noted 'an extraordinary recrudescence in Fleet Street of the claim to be "independent". This term was intelligible in mid-Victorian times, when most papers were the recognized mouthpieces of a political party,' commented Jones, who found it out of place in the twentieth century, when a journal's political line was 'thought to be its proprietor's own affair'. Besides underestimating the Victorians' capacity for diversity and self-delusion, Jones ignored the recent tendency for newspapers to function as unrecognized mouthpieces. Assuming his own professional experience to be the norm and romanticizing it to suit his purpose, Jones was astounded by the near universality of the claim. 'Almost every paper puts it forward', none more preposterously than the *Morning Post*, which, 'in alluding the other day to the *Globe* passing under the control of Mr Robert Donald, said that the *Globe*'s political policy in the future would be "tenaciously independent", as though there were varying degrees of independency'.[2]

In fact, there were varying degrees, and fluctuating ones at that. As yet more a slogan than a principle, the concept meant different things to different people, and frequently to the same people at different junctures. It was routinely invoked to show up competitors, not as a brake on partisanship. Henry Cadbury's definition was not synonymous with Scott's or Cowdray's, much less with Dalziel's or Kerr's, Astor's or Garvin's. Rothermere, Northcliffe, Hulton, and the Berry brothers indulged in the same fashionable rhetoric, but without agreement as to its implications. Laurence Cadbury marked the centenary of the *Daily News*, which he had helped to transform into the *News Chronicle*, with a statement that that 'paper has always been, and still continues to be, independent and under no obligations to any political party'.[3] That, of course, was hyperbole.

[1] Clarke, *Northcliffe Diary* (31 March 1921), p. 197.
[2] Jones, *Fleet Street and Downing Street*, p. 344; Beaverbrook, *Politicians and the Press*, p. 10.
[3] L. J. Cadbury to Layton, 16 December 1946, Layton Papers.

There was, then, overwhelming agreement with Beaverbrook's 'own view
... that the normal attitude of the Press towards the politicians must be one of
complete independence'. Few would have conceded, however, that Beaverbrook practised what he preached. With him and Rothermere in mind,
Gwynne delivered the 1930 presidential address to the Institute of Journalists,
taking the press to task for 'assuming a paramount and almost dominating
position in public affairs, even attempting to create political parties'. He urged
the membership to safeguard independence by 'limit[ing] their activities to
their proper functions, which are to keep watch and ward, to inform, advise and
instruct. To go beyond that is to invite disaster.' He forgot, of course, his own
recurrent trespasses. Gwynne and Jones included, newspapermen rested their
claims to independence on the shortness of memory.[1]

So it continued through the inter-war decades. Contradictorily interpreted as
the right to ignore politicians and to dictate to them, to assist them across party
lines and to supersede them, independence was more easily flaunted than
strictly observed. No self-respecting editor or proprietor could afford to
disclaim it; at least in that respect, the situation had changed since the
nineteenth century, when journals had often affixed party labels to their
mastheads. Yet, on balance, the 'independent' newspapermen of the inter-war
period were closer to their Victorian forbears than to their twentieth-century
descendants with regard to actual political performance. Consonant with the
spirit of the age, they conceived of themselves as a distinctly new breed,
rejecting the past that had created not only their problems, but also their
opportunities for advancement. It took another generation, demarcated by
another world war, for those opportunities to be fully grasped. Only then did
newspaper independence acquire its modern connotation.

Displaced journalists, along with those like Jones who had turned their backs
on Fleet Street, naturally exaggerated the extent of post-war dislocations,
which they attributed – for better or worse – to commercial factors. Gardiner
and Spender deplored the general process of 'trustification', which allegedly
transformed a craft into an industry. Sir Sidney Low, put out to pasture in 1897,
complained of newspaper-owners who were 'not really interested in anything
but carrying on a kind of journalistic Harrod's or Selfridge's. It is hard to preach
the gospel in that sort of tabernacle.' By then, Low and his brand of Conservatism were both too stale to qualify for a pulpit. Gardiner had the experience
of a brief flirtation with the *Sunday Express*, and Spender enjoyed a longer
affiliation with the *Sunday Times*, where 'a subject was sometimes suggested to
him, but his treatment of it was his own'. Most significantly, Garvin soldiered
on at the *Observer*. The appeal of a particular gospel, more than any other
single factor, determined the availability of a tabernacle.[2]

[1] Beaverbrook, *Politicians and the Press*, p. 10; Hindle, *Morning Post*, p. 244.
[2] Low to Henry Curtis, 16 January 1922, quoted in Chapman-Huston, *Lost Historian*, p. 304;
Koss, *Fleet Street Radical*, pp. 291–92; Harris, *Spender*, pp. 226–27.

There is no denying that major alterations were occurring in the contours of the national press. Increasingly fewer properties were clustered in increasingly fewer hands and engaged in a struggle for ever larger mass circulations. Nevertheless, what contemporaries saw to be unique was, more accurately, the acceleration of a trend. Wartime experience, prolonged at Westminster by the durability of the Lloyd George coalition, speeded up all sorts of processes, few of which it could legitimately be said to have created. Economic and structural developments in journalism counted among them. Capital intensification, with its primary emphasis on advertising revenues, was certainly nothing new. The formation of syndicates had disquieted the Victorians, let alone the Edwardians, and the decline of the provincial dailies was already pronounced before 1914. The condition of metropolitan morning papers was outwardly stable, with the conversion of the *Westminster Gazette* compensating for the wartime closure of the *Standard*. Among metropolitan evening papers, however, only three of the ten titles that had existed in 1900 were publishing at the end of 1923. The rate of attrition was highest among morning provincial papers, invariably more politically oriented and less commercially secure than their evening counterparts: of the forty-one that survived in 1921, twenty-eight remained in 1937. What was left of political journalism in the provinces, never as flourishing a field as some made out, was successively subordinated, eclipsed, and destroyed. Colin Seymour-Ure has pungently summed up the matter: 'In general, . . . the twinkling shoal of provincial papers was trawled by the press barons and neatly parcelled on the slab.'[1]

Arthur Mann was brought by Sir Edward Hulton from Manchester in 1916 to take charge of the *Evening Standard*. Three years later, going against the tide and his personal inclinations – 'I would rather live in London than Leeds,' he told his father – he accepted the editorship of the *Yorkshire Post*. His talent and courage were to make it a leading light in the dark days of the 1930s. Yet he started out under somewhat false pretences on the advice of Gervase Beckett, then Conservative MP for Whitby and co-proprietor with his brother Rupert. 'If I may make a suggestion I should not at your interview lay too much stress on development at the London end,' Beckett told him. 'This can & will (I hope) follow in due course, but the majority of the Board, & the majority of the readers of the *Y.P.* are local business men more interested in commerce than in politics.' With encouragement from Geoffrey Dawson, intermittently resident in the vicinity, Mann expanded the horizons of the *Yorkshire Post*. He was congratulated 'heartily on the ever-increasing interest of the paper' by Beckett, who switched to a Leeds constituency in 1923. Eventually, Mann struck a close alliance with Anthony Eden, Gervase Beckett's son-in-law. Criticized for

---

[1] Alan Lee, 'The structure, ownership and control of the press, 1855–1914,' in Boyce *et al.*, eds., *Newspaper History*, pp. 128–29; *Report*, Royal Commission on the Press, 1947–1949, p. 188; Wadsworth, *Newspaper Circulations*, pp. 27–28; Seymour-Ure, 'The Press and the Party System,' in G. Peele and C. Cook, eds., *The Politics of Reappraisal 1918–1939* (London, 1975), p. 236.

putting 'judgments on Foreign Policy . . . above Party loyalties' in his vehement attacks on appeasement, Mann held on until November 1939. The merger of the *Yorkshire Post* with Rothermere's *Leeds Mercury* furnished the pretext for his dismissal. Equally to his detriment, he had exceeded the boundaries of provincial journalism and taken seriously the idea of independence.[1]

Soon after Mann went to Leeds, A. J. Cummings left the *Yorkshire Post* to take up a position as a principal leader-writer for the *Daily News*. It has been suggested that 'no other journalist did as much as Cummings to keep the spirit of Liberalism alive in the country during this unhappy period' between the wars.[2] Whether or not one is prepared to accord him this pre-eminence, his contribution was substantial, and it could only have emanated from an office in Fleet Street. The *Yorkshire Post*, like the *Manchester Guardian* and a handful of other provincial dailies (using that term elastically to embrace the Scottish and Welsh press), might sometimes bear upon the national debate, but lacked the authority to shape it. The spirit of Liberalism, in so far as it informed party strategies and electoral responses, had to be kindled in the metropolis. The same held true for the spirit of the Labour Party, which had long since outgrown its journalistic breeding grounds in Manchester. The spirit of Conservatism, on the other hand, had always preponderated in the London press, with provincial papers serving more or less as sounding boards. Once considered a serious weakness, this concentricity came to be valued – perhaps too late – as an intrinsic strength.

By the early 1920s, at least with regard to political affairs, the national press was overwhelmingly the London press, distributed throughout the country. The time had passed when one could pretend otherwise; and the time was fast approaching when Oliver Woods could observe that Sir William Haley, the editor of *The Times*, would sooner 'spend large sums' to send his senior staff 'roving all over the world' than to let them 'see their own country. I think it may be a manifestation of his provincialism,' Woods remarked of Haley, who had served his apprenticeship in Manchester. 'He once said to me that only London mattered. Nothing in the North signified.'[3] Bluntly stated, Haley's attitude was rather the manifestation of an astute professionalism.

We shall return to Haley, who epitomized the outlook and ethics of a later age. Before his style of editorship was possible, and indeed common, vast transformations had to occur in the topography of the political press. Apart from a contraction of its dimensions, though not entirely unrelated to it, there was a modification of expectations.

As newspapermen came to conceive of themselves as being better equipped than elected politicians to defend essential party interests, they generated a

---

[1] Mann to his father, 10 December 1919, G. Beckett to Mann, 7 December [1919], and 12 March [1920], Dawson to Mann, 2 September 1920, Mann to R. Beckett, 15 December 1938 (copy), Mann Papers.
[2] *Journal*, Institute of Journalists, xl (November 1952), 128.
[3] Diary note, 5 September 1963, Woods Papers.

spirit of partisanship which continuously clashed with the requirements laid down by their parliamentary mentors. These tensions, manifest before the war, led to altercations afterwards. Ultimately, after the next war, they were accepted with a mixture of grateful relief and bitter resignation as an index to political vitality. For the time being, however, they provoked resentment and recrimination.

Relations between and within national newspapers, signalled by transfers of ownership and replacements of personnel, invariably affected the procedures of party support. Simultaneously, changes of balance within and between parties had far-reaching consequences in the conduct of political journalism. Each set of conditions influenced the other and, in the process, evolved a new framework. That, of course, had always been the case. What was different, beginning in the so-called post-war emergency period, was the degree of volatility.

Without going so far as to dismiss commercial, technological, and ideological challenges, it is easy enough to discount them at this early stage. The establishment of giant chains did not necessarily deflect, much less inhibit, political expression. Nor, in itself, did the rise of the Labour Party: the socialist *Daily Herald* canvassed for readers with the same crass commercialism as the unabashedly capitalistic *Daily Mail* and *Daily Express*; and the tendency to grovel to advertisers was another characteristic of the age, not the monopoly of any type of journal. Likewise, a willingness to suppress unpalatable truths was all too universal. Norman Angell held it to be

> one of the disillusionments of a purely 'political' democracy that the 'free Press' – the unfettered and abundant production of cheap newspapers to which our grandfathers looked as the means of popular freedom and enlightenment – has become one of the worst obstacles to the development of a capacity for real self-government, perhaps the worst of all the menaces to modern democracy.[1]

But Angell, best known as the author of *The Great Illusion* (1910), was invariably suffering from disillusionment and mistaking its causes.

According to legend, the advent of broadcasting in 1922 registered a 'notable impact' on the responsibilities of the press. In fact, the intrusion was regarded in most precincts with quizzical indifference. If, as H. A. Taylor has argued, 'the loss by the newspapers of their monopoly of news dissemination was an unprecedented event', it was not yet perceived as anything quite so cataclysmic. Popular habits, much as Angell deplored them, ensured the continued supremacy of the written word, if only to corroborate and interpret what was

[1] Angell, *The Press and the Organisation of Society* (London, 1922), pp. 16–17. For Angell's earlier connections with the Harmsworth press, see K. Robbins, 'Public Opinion, the Press and Pressure Groups,' in F. H. Hinsley, ed., *British Foreign Policy Under Sir Edward Grey* (Cambridge, 1977), p. 76.

fleetingly heard over the wireless. 'So far as the present generation is concerned,' Lord Riddell declared in the *Radio Times* (21 December 1923), 'I believe that those accustomed to read and who like reading will continue to read whether they use the radio or not.' More puzzling still is Taylor's conjecture that broadcasting was especially 'important politically in changing the relationship of authority generally towards the Press', with 'political consequences [that] were underrated'.[1] The BBC, which changed from a company to a corporation in 1926 without altering its initials, posed no greater threat to the conventions of political journalism than to its commercial foundations. Paradoxically, by arousing public interest, broadcasting may have had the immediate effect of conferring a wider indispensability on published comment. Its long-term effect, obvious during and after the Second World War, is another matter, not to be projected backwards.

'In terms of the history of the "mass media"', Asa Briggs has noted the 'interesting coincidence that Lord Northcliffe bought the *Daily Mail* in 1896, the year when Marconi first demonstrated his wireless inventions to a leading Post Office engineer, and died in 1922, the year when the BBC was founded'.[2] The annals of media history are indeed littered with interesting coincidences: broadcasting was introduced within weeks of the collapse of the coalition, and scored a *coup* in its coverage of the 1922 election returns; the BBC was licensed by the Post Office in time to report Labour's gains in the general election of 1923; and it was chartered as a public body in the wake of the General Strike, which had demonstrated its utility and relative impartiality.

Nevertheless, contingency must not be confused with causality. The disembodied voices that floated over the airwaves did not, even figuratively, pronounce a death sentence on written journalism. The political press, already reeling, was to fall of its own accord. Only after the event did radio sound the knell. It remained for television, decades later, to supply a visual alternative to the printed page. Furthermore, to the extent that an adversary relationship slowly developed between the old and newer media, it was undercut by reciprocal interests. Revenues from commercial broadcasting were eventually deployed to shore up select newspaper enterprises. And, as we shall see, politicians habitually failed to discriminate when they alleged that they were victimized by the media.

More decisive than any new external pressures was the intensification of familiar internal ones. With so many intersecting crises at hand, the controllers of the political press did not have time to contemplate future dangers. At any rate, those dangers were too amorphous. Garvin was more fearful of the deleterious effects of the telephone, which spared a reporter the necessary

---

[1] H. A. Taylor, *The British Press* (London, 1961), p. 163.
[2] Briggs, *The Birth of Broadcasting* (London, 1961), p. 21. Northcliffe did not, of course, buy the *Daily Mail*; he created it.

inconvenience 'of going to see things for himself'.[1] Like others who pursued journalism as a political vocation, he was compelled by a sudden convergence of events to adapt his aims and methods. Yet he survived, as did the tradition to which he belonged.

In an attempt to acquaint journalism students at the University of London with 'the actual processes of making a newspaper', Wickham Steed professed himself 'a believer in "views"'. Earlier in 1921, during a visit to the United States, he had been 'struck by the disproportion between the space given to "news stories" and the space given to "editorials"'. To him, as to Garvin, that distinction was untenable. 'Newspapers that merely provide attractive episodal reading,' he told his audience,

> are apt to exercise a debilitating influence on the public and to give their readers a perpetual indigestion. There must be reasoned comment, enlightened by some principle, some general creed, social, political or economic. After all, what makes a newspaper 'bite', apart from the excellence of its news, is the faith, the energy, the determination with which it is written.[2]

Steed was promulgating a time-honoured formula, but one that was becoming impossible to implement.

For, to Steed's own disadvantage, general creeds were fast crumbling into parochial concerns. Social priorities, political allegiances, and economic precepts were in a state of flux. The upheaval began that spring. 'You had hardly left England when Bonar Law fell out of office,' Steed wrote to Northcliffe, who had gone to France. Austen Chamberlain sent an emissary to Printing House Square 'within half-an-hour of the announcement about Bonar Law to say that Austen hoped to be elected leader of the party, and to ask whether *The Times* would support him'. Steed pontificated that '*The Times* never supported any persons on personal grounds but that there seemed . . . to be no one else in the running, and that Austen was entitled to the job, if he wanted it'. Holding no brief for Chamberlain, he consoled himself with the knowledge 'that L.G. had really been a good deal upset by the Bonar episode, and that he is not at all happy at the idea of having to work closely with Austen'.[3] The Prime Minister's discomfort was *The Times*'s best reward.

Bonar Law's departure, all the more for the abruptness with which it came, weakened the coalition. The result in Fleet Street was to release centrifugal forces that had been building up. Beaverbrook now felt free to commit the

---

[1] Diary note, 5 September 1963, Woods Papers.
[2] Steed, *The Making of a Newspaper* (London, 1921), pp. 10–11. According to Stephen Leacock, 'the greatest difference' between British and American newspapers was one of 'atmosphere', as the Abdication crisis was to demonstrate: 'With us in America the great thing is to get the news and shout it at the reader; in England they get the news and then break it to him as gently as possible.' *My Discovery of England* (New York, 1922), p. 120.
[3] Steed to Northcliffe, 22 March 1921, Northcliffe Papers.

Daily Express to 'a position of complete independence of the Coalition Government', notwithstanding his intimacy with several of its leading members. Following suit, Blumenfeld served notice that he considered himself 'a Unionist in the sense that I agree with the fundamental doctrines of the Unionist creed, even if I do not always accept the detailed measures of a Coalition Government'. Despite his Welsh background, or possibly because of it, Gwynne was especially keen to disown the coalition. Balfour absent-mindedly asked Bonar Law, who came to tea at Cannes, if he had heard of Gwynne, whose name was invoked by an importunate correspondent. 'It must be the Editor of the *Morning Post*, one of the greatest enemies of the Government,' replied Bonar Law. There was no longer any reason to mince words.[1]

Anticipating moves within the parliamentary Unionist Party, and thus inciting them, the majority of Unionist journals sought to dismember the coalition in order to seek an independent Unionist majority at an early election. Steed was of the mind that Lloyd George had outstayed his welcome. Gwynne had never consented to extend one. Rothermere blew hot and cold, often at the same time. 'The recent bye elections have been a blow to the Government,' Sir Robert Sanders admitted after reverses in the St George's division of Westminster and at Heywood, where 'the Bottomley & *Daily Mirror* machine [had been] going strong'.[2] So as to have his cake and eat it, too, Rothermere backed the coalition, while condemning its wasteful excesses, in his *Sunday Pictorial*. Beaverbrook was coming to the conclusion, articulated in the *Sunday Express* on 19 November 1922, that it was imperative to 'recreate the party system on an understandable basis'. The *Spectator* and the *National Review* could agree on that score, if about little else.

With lessening degrees of tenacity, other Unionist newspapers dutifully adhered to the coalition arrangements. The two quality Sundays were among them: the *Observer* piously reiterated its belief in Lloyd George's 'destiny', and the *Sunday Times* declined to print a book review in which Desmond Mac-Carthy made sport of the beleaguered Prime Minister. The *Daily Telegraph*, derided by Gwynne as so much 'a subservient admirer of Lloyd George' that it was unworthy of its 'reputation of being a Conservative paper', featured appeals from prominent statesmen for 'Unity and Coalition' and pleaded with 'members of the Unionist wing of the Coalition to back up their leaders in the assurances of continued loyalty and support recently given to Mr Lloyd George' (13 March 1922). Gwynne detected that Lloyd George had dispensed 'the usual bribe' of privileged information to get the *Telegraph* to maintain the 'attitude ... that his disappearance will be a national disaster'. His suspicions

---

[1] Beaverbrook, *Politicians and the Press*, pp. 35–36; Blumenfeld to Younger, 13 May 1921 (copy), Beaverbrook Papers, H/15; Lady Sykes (Bonar Law's daughter) to her husband, 2 April 1921, quoted in Blake, *Unknown Prime Minister*, p. 425.

[2] Sanders's diary, 19 June 1921, Bayford Papers.

were well founded. M. A. Gerothwohl, a rusticated academic who wrote leading articles for the *Telegraph*, sent regrets from Peterborough Court to Downing Street 'that my Chief, Lord Burnham, was unable to breakfast with the P.M. today. It is one reason the more why' Gerothwohl wished to see Grigg directly 'after the Cabinet meeting, in order that the P.M.'s desiderata may be reflected in tomorrow's leader'.[1]

By lending itself to Lloyd George's purposes, the *Telegraph* was complying with directives from the Unionist Central Office. Sir Malcolm Fraser, now functioning as principal agent, complimented Mann on the *Yorkshire Post*'s arguments in favour of 'the continued need for the Coalition' as a means of alleviating class tensions. From his 'own inner knowledge from confidential sources', Fraser could confirm 'the grave danger from Socialist work which holds sway at the moment'. Mann suggested that, in order to withstand the red peril, the Coalition Liberals and Unionists should wrap themselves in a 'Liberal Unionist' mantle, made fashionable by Chamberlain's ascent. Fraser took soundings. 'While many regard it with favour,' he reported, 'there are others who take the line of the Prime Minister, that neither side wishes to wear the colours of the other. Though probably it would be distasteful to very few if they changed into khaki, instead of changing into one another's clothes!'[2]

The remarkable thing was how quickly both Mann and Fraser changed not their clothes, but their tune. Forsaking all attempts at assimilation, they opted for separatism. By the start of 1922, the *Yorkshire Post* stood implacably opposed to the continuation of the coalition experiment; it subsequently claimed a measure of the credit for influencing those northern Unionist MPs who voted to abandon Lloyd George the following October. Similarly disposed, Fraser resisted pressure for an early election, which would have bound the Unionists to Lloyd George and thereby exposed divisions within the party. 'Downing Street had been working the Press as usual,' Sanders noted in his diary on 6 January; 'now Malcolm Fraser is working it in the opposite direction', with results that persuaded him that 'the Conservatives could get a majority on their own'. That was what the *Morning Post* had insisted all along, and what others came gradually to believe. 'Of course I am in favour of freedom of Labour and very strongly in favour of it,' Gwynne assured Lady Bathurst, who had unfairly rebuked him for sliding towards the centre. 'But I also know that if the Conservative party went to the country with that cry, it would be defeated at the polls, for the cry would be raised "Trades Unionism is in danger" and on that cry the working men would vote as a man.' The task,

[1] Hobson *et al.*, *Pearl of Days*, p. 174; Gwynne to Strachey, 13 March 1922, Strachey Papers; *Daily Telegraph*, 7, 8, and 13 March 1922; Gerothwohl to Grigg [1922], Grigg Papers. Professor Gerothwohl, born in London and a specialist in Romance languages and literature, was described as 'by far the ablest and best informed commentator on foreign affairs of his age and standing'. Grigg to Dawson, 10 July 1924, Grigg Papers.
[2] Fraser to Mann, 9 May 1921, Mann Papers.

as he saw it, was to emancipate Conservatism without damaging its electoral appeal.[1]

Newspapermen, who had been all too conspicuous among the pillars of the coalition, reverted to their former allegiances when it became apparent that Lloyd George could not be expected – or perhaps even trusted – to negate the political effects of class conflict. That realization, more than his miscalculations in foreign policy or his scandalous debasement of honours, cost him press support. Some, like Riddell, parted company on personal grounds. In most cases, however, the defectors were Unionists who saw no further rewards and an assortment of dangers from continued dependency on Lloyd George. While their journals remained nominally independent, they themselves enlisted as party activists, anxious to restore the paradigm of two-party government. Mann and Gwynne separately attested to the recrudescence of partisanship among editors. Hulton, with encouragement from Beaverbrook, accepted the chairmanship of the Unionist Party in the Epsom division of Surrey: 'A beastly article in the *Evening Standard*' on 30 May 1921 'rather upset' Lloyd George, who had made a point of 'being very kind to Hulton'.[2] Rothermere, an erstwhile Liberal of sorts, was also promoting Unionist disengagement. For a time, owing to the physical incapacity of his brother Northcliffe, he threatened to qualify as the foremost agent of destruction.

* * *

In 1897, H. G. Wells wrote 'A Story of the Days to Come', which opened with a nostalgic recollection of 'the excellent Mr Morris', a fictional 'Englishman ... [who] lived in the days of Queen Victoria the Good' and who – as befitting his nationality and social station – always 'read *The Times*'. Countless generations later, when the plot unfolds, Mr Morris's descendants 'did not even know that there ever had been a *Times* – that institution had foundered somewhere in the intervening gulf of years'.[3] Wells, for all his fertility of imagination, could think of no better way to evoke the passage of time.

It is a commonplace to observe that, within Wells's own lifetime, many of his most outlandish fantasies proved to be unwelcome realities. Although *The Times* has not yet met extinction, it has faced that threat so often that its immortality can no longer be playfully presumed. When the paper changed hands in 1908, its survival was guaranteed by one or another potential

---

[1] Sanders's diary, 6 January and 18 February 1922, Bayford Papers; Gwynne to Lady Bathurst, 11 November 1921, Bathurst Papers.

[2] G. Rowland Blades to Beaverbrook, 'Thursday', and Beaverbrook to Blades, 23 January 1922 (copy), Beaverbrook Papers, B/16; Stevenson, *Lloyd George* (31 May 1921), p. 219.

[3] Reprinted in *The Short Stories of H. G. Wells* (Garden City, N.Y., 1929), pp. 701–702. The demise of *The Times*, regarded as unthinkable, served equally well for purposes of 'woomanship' as for science fiction. 'Good heavens, I thought *The Times* had ceased publication' was a sure-fire way to spark a conversation with an attractive stranger in a railway carriage. Stephen Potter, *Three-Upmanship* (New York, 1962), p. 181n.

ownership. Since then, at increasingly shorter intervals, its fate has hung in the balance. The first of these periodic crises occurred in 1921–22, when Northcliffe went on his final rampage.

Sent into exile by his doctors, who tended to his inexhaustible exhaustions, Northcliffe had plenty of time to brood. He came to curse *The Times* as a drain on his flagging energies. Its failure to turn a profit, which he had cavalierly proclaimed not to dismay him, now rankled as proof of his inability to exercise effective control. 'Trying to improve *The Times* is like biting a rusty file,' he complained to his secretary. Trying to improve it from abroad, where he was grimly resigned to live out his days, was still more futile. Ensconced in 'the little story-book village of Roquebrune' on the Riviera, he dilated on the shortcomings of Steed, whom he nicknamed 'Pinhead' and plotted to cashier.[1]

Within three years of his appointment, Steed's position had become precarious. The likely candidate to replace him was Sir Campbell Stuart, who stoked the fires of Northcliffe's resentment by remitting regular reports of *The Times*'s commercial and political decrepitude. 'The only safe rule about Stuart is that he will have been looking after No. 1, first, last and all the time,' Steed later asserted. 'N. understood this perfectly well but he liked to utilise Stuart as a Wangler – without always realising that Stuart might be wangling him.' A harsh but not unfair judgment. What Steed perhaps failed to appreciate, however, was Northcliffe's emotional dependence on Stuart, whom he embraced as a younger version of himself. Northcliffe, childless in wedlock though not outside, had found an adopted son. According to Steed's further recollection, 'in 1919 or early in 1920 N. swelled the Wangler's head by promising to make him heir to the whole Carmelite House property (*Daily Mail*, *Evening News*, *Weekly Dispatch*)': Stuart's 'high glee' ultimately turned into 'rage on finding that N. had left him only £500 as a special legacy'. In addition, Stuart was one of three people whom Northcliffe vested with power of attorney. He was not the only gilded youth to win Northcliffe's favour. Another visitor at Roquebrune was Keith Murdoch, the Australian journalist who had made his mark with a celebrated wartime dispatch from Gallipoli. 'Northcliffe ... has developed a warm personal regard for him which augurs well for Murdoch's future,' commented Clarke. Not even Wells could have prophesied that Murdoch's son would eventually own *The Times*.[2]

In the tug of war between Steed and Stuart, Rothermere soon weighed in on Stuart's side. His motives were typically unclear. Before departing for France,

---

[1] Northcliffe to Price, n.d., quoted in Pound and Harmsworth, p. 782.

[2] Clarke, *Northcliffe Diary* (24 March 1921), p. 187; Steed to Morison, 4 August 1939, *Times* Archives. Murdoch modelled his Sydney *Evening News* on the *Daily Mail*. 'When we have built circulation we will begin to make Australia talk,' he told Northcliffe. 'Great political influence ... will come in time. And part at least will be yours. That is a certain amount of return for you, isn't it?' Murdoch to Northcliffe, 23 April 1922, Northcliffe Papers. For an incisive treatment of Keith Murdoch's professional origins, see Murray Sayle, 'Rupert Murdoch's Gallipoli,' in *Spectator*, 10 October 1981.

Northcliffe had hinted at a readiness to unload *The Times*. Garvin's explanation, as good as any, was that Northcliffe 'doesn't care for anything once he gets it'. The articles of association stipulated that it was possible for 'a shareholder to sell to his brother without offering his shares to the other shareholders', and Northcliffe confessed 'that there never was a question of anybody but Rothermere' replacing him. Early in 1921, when Northcliffe was preoccupied with redrafting his will, Rothermere 'turned up' in the south of France. He arrived 'in an old Ford car' and (as recounted to Steed by Sir Robert Hudson) 'explained that Bolshevism was coming, that they would all be reduced to beggary, that he was trying to get used to it in advance, and had therefore sold his Rolls-Royce, dismissed his valet, and reduced his expenses to the lowest limit. He wanted N. to do the same.' Without too much difficulty, Rothermere persuaded his elder brother to save his strength by cutting his losses. Steed and Stuart were duly advised that Northcliffe meant to relinquish his base at Printing House Square and to restrict his future operations to Carmelite House, where his control was absolute. The homecoming, so to speak, was to be announced on 1 May at a dinner to commemorate the twenty-fifth anniversary of the *Daily Mail*.[1]

Intended to cause a sensation, these plans were delayed and finally defeated by a combination of legal and family factors. John Walter and Sir John Ellerman, as minority shareholders, could not have blocked the transfer; but their opposition would have posed a serious embarrassment. During April, Walter was beyond reach in South America. More to the point, Northcliffe's mother, aged eighty-three, thoroughly disapproved: Alfred was her favourite son and the only one she deemed worthy of responsibility for *The Times*. Her misgivings were justified by Rothermere's infantile behaviour. '... There is quite a prominent London daily awaiting an immediate sale,' he alerted Beaverbrook, whose *Daily Express* divulged that 'a great historic newspaper' was on the verge of transfer. The *Morning Post* and the *Daily News* denied that this reference was to themselves. Lloyd George, knowing *The Times* to be the paper in question, mistakenly suspected the long arm of Lord Cowdray, extended on behalf of the Asquithians. Others expected a move by Lords Inverforth and Pirrie on behalf of Lloyd George himself. All disavowals notwithstanding, such suspicions persisted through the spring. 'Some people take an inordinate interest in the proprietorship of newspapers, and rumours have been flying about that you had bought out the Walters and Ellerman or that they had bought you out,' Riddell wrote to Northcliffe on 4 June. Boasting 'a legal mind of sorts', Riddell 'regarded them as lies', but remained perplexed. 'The people at Downing Street deny all knowledge of having purchased a London morning paper,' he went on, 'and while I don't place too much reliance on

---

[1] Garvin to Viola Woods, 16 June 1920, Woods Papers; *History of The Times*, IV, part 2, 596–97; Steed to Morison, 4 August 1939, *Times* Archives.

official denials, for the life of me I can't see what paper they can have bought.'¹

Rothermere had lost the battle, but not yet the war. Northcliffe held him partly to blame for *The Times*'s economic difficulties. On Rothermere's advice, the paper had purchased huge stocks of its 'special white newsprint ... at any price', only to see prices tumble. 'Not while my mother lives, but as soon as the old lady is gone, I'll get level with that bugger Harold!' Northcliffe vowed to Steed, who suddenly found himself back in his employer's good graces. Possibly, too, Northcliffe was annoyed with the political shilly-shallying of his brother, who resolved 'not ... to do anything at the present juncture to embarass [sic] the Government'. Preparing to embark on a world tour, which was an effective way to scotch rumours, Northcliffe proposed that Steed should accompany him as far as the United States. It was not so much an invitation as a command. On 16 July, the two men sailed from Southampton aboard the *Aquitania*. They were photographed on deck, Northcliffe's arm wrapped protectively around Steed's stooped shoulders. The *Daily Mail* and *The Times* received instructions to publish the picture, 'not less than 4 1/4 inches square'.²

The second honeymoon did not last long. Speaking 'off the record' to a *New York Times* interviewer, Steed told an indiscreet anecdote about the Prime Minister's relations with the King. The text of the interview, replete with the peccant passage, was then cabled to London with an attribution to Northcliffe. The effect of this 'extraordinary *contretemps*' was twofold: Northcliffe was convinced that Steed had made him look a fool; Steed concluded 'that N. was really off his chump at times' and that Rothermere – who demanded Steed's resignation – 'was desperately anxious to get rid of me as the chief obstacle to R's plans to get hold of T[he] T[imes]. Until then', it had not yet dawned on Steed 'that N. was bound to go mad'. Now, confronted by Northcliffe's irrationality, he became 'determined not to irritate him and, above all, to prevent him from wrecking the Paper'.³

At Vancouver, Steed took leave of Northcliffe, who continued across the Pacific to Australia, New Zealand, and the Orient, then through the Suez Canal to Palestine, 'the country of Christ'. Pausing in the south of France to 'get used to the cold', he received a political briefing from Steed:

> The Lloyd George Cabinet may be down within a month; or it may hold on until a General Election; or Grey, who is gaining ground, may win the confidence of the country; or there may be a Grey-Balfour Coalition; or again there may be a Tory revolt under Bonar Law or Derby. In short,

---

[1] Rothermere to Beaverbrook, 3 May [1921] (copy), Beaverbrook Papers, C/282a; Riddell to Northcliffe, 4 June 1921, Northcliffe Papers.

[2] Steed to Morison, 4 August 1939, *Times* Archives; Rothermere to Beaverbrook, 3 May [1921] (copy), Beaverbrook Papers, C/282a; *History of The Times*, IV, part 2, 606.

[3] Steed to Morison, 4 August 1939, *Times* Archives; Steed, *Through Thirty Years*, II, 366–69. While Steed had his own reputation to defend, Stuart considered him 'too intelligent to be inaccurate'. Stuart to Morison, 4 January 1951, *Times* Archives.

anything may happen, though one thing certain is that the country is now much nearer the lines of policy we have consistently advocated for the last three years than it has been since the war; and your papers are becoming the true organs of public opinion.

There could have been no better welcome for Northcliffe.[1]

Proximity to London quickly brought back all the old aches and pains. He complained of the *Daily Mail*'s 'priggish nonsense', the *Evening News*'s 'vulgar tone', and *The Times*'s editorial 'blunders' and 'fatuous optimism' over fiscal accounts. On 22 February 1922, upon receipt of 'appalling gross figures' from his business manager, he telegraphed that he would return to Fleet Street 'within seven days'. On his way, he stopped at the Paris office of the *Continental Daily Mail* to meet a representative of the compositors, 'a damned ungrateful swine' who asked for higher wages. Northcliffe literally kicked him out of the room. He then crossed the Channel to administer a kick to 'the editorial troglodytes of Printing House Square'.[2]

In between consultations with some thirty medical specialists, Northcliffe agonized over the direction of *The Times*. 'I am a little concerned about the position of newspapers and the anomalous situation whereby my *Daily Mail* is rapidly approaching two million copies net per morning and my *Times* is practically stagnant as regards net sale,' he wrote to Lord Burnham on 2 March. That was to put it mildly. In the 'belief... that a newspaper either goes forward or backward – it never stays still', Northcliffe ordered a reduction in price to take effect on Monday, the 6th. Only Stuart had known of this change beforehand, and it fell to him to revoke it after Northcliffe's death. Ignoring Steed, who took legal advice in the expectation that his contract might be broken at any moment, Northcliffe made Stuart his deputy. 'We shall only hold our readers if we are a better paper than the *Daily Telegraph*; and in many ways we are not so good,' he told his managing director. *The Times*'s 'political information', in particular, was 'not nearly so good', and its leaders suffered by comparison with those in the *Morning Post*. It was Stuart's mission to 'let [the] staff know plainly' that they had to 'fight for their lives'. By the end of March, he claimed credit for a degree of improvement. At his dictation, the paper had dropped an article 'on Churchill and his views on Russia which everybody knows', and had substituted one entitled 'Chamberlain Challenges Premier' (29 March), which had the added virtue of an anti-ministerial slant. 'I know that our articles on politics are getting *The Times* talked about because we are getting news,' he proudly reported.[3]

---

[1] Pound and Harmsworth, pp. 826–29; Steed to Northcliffe, 14 February 1922, Northcliffe Papers.

[2] Pound and Harmsworth, pp. 829–31; *History of The Times*, IV, part 2, 624–26.

[3] Newman Flower, *Just As It Happened* (London, 1950), p. 36; *History of The Times*, IV, part 2, 628; Northcliffe to Burnham, 2 March 1922 (copy), Northcliffe to Stuart, 25 March and (telegram) 26 March (copies), and Stuart to Northcliffe, 31 March 1922, Northcliffe Papers. The

That spring, Steed was packed off to a series of international conferences, leaving Stuart to function as managing editor in all but name. 'As to politics,' he informed Northcliffe, 'I am keeping in the closest touch with Hudson who is, as usual, invaluable.' With one foot in the Asquithian camp and a finger in every pie, Hudson affectionately confirmed that he was seeing 'Campbell daily. He seems happier if he has had a jaw with me on the kaleidoscopic happenings of the hour. He is a shrewd observer, with an old head on his young shoulders.' Stuart also had periodic meetings with Lord Derby, then ambassador to Paris, whom he told 'very definitely' on the evening of 14 March that Northcliffe 'would not support this Government' on any conditions. Not content merely to influence political decisions, Stuart aimed to turn them to journalistic advantage. It was 'all very well to go and see these statesmen and discuss high politics with them', he reckoned, 'but if you cannot get any news to publish, it is rather a waste of time'. Derby rewarded him with the admission 'that he expected the Prime Minister to leave office within a fortnight and that Mr Chamberlain would be called upon to form a government, and then the struggle for supremacy would follow'. A week later, after some preliminary 'leg-pulling . . . about making friends' between Northcliffe and Lloyd George, Derby tendered 'advice on how we could conduct the campaign against the Government'. Stuart 'listened very politely', if not altogether credulously, and immediately communed with the political correspondents of the various Northcliffe dailies. 'These men cannot have too much guidance in difficult times like these.'[1]

After a few weeks of jerky wire pulling, Northcliffe left for France with a strengthened resolve to retain *The Times* as a weapon to destroy the coalition. Day after day, it proclaimed the imminence of an upheaval. Derby proved a disappointment, a lightweight despite his corpulence. By 15 March, Northcliffe had come 'to the conclusion that he cannot make up his mind. He evidently wants to be Prime Minister,' despite his fervent disclaimers to Stuart, 'but he is frightened of the criticism of Lloyd George's newspapers, and of Birkenhead and Winston.' Hudson confirmed that 'the Fat Man was sorely tempted for 48 hours, but considerations of personal safety finally triumphed'. A leader was needed to stir the backbench Unionists to active rebellion. Stuart set no store by Chamberlain, who would have to be forced 'to take a strong stand against the P.M. At the moment he is putty in his hands.' Nevertheless, there were signs that the coalition was crumbling. 'The Welshman's friends have been putting out feelers to *my lot!*' Hudson revealed, and had 'had the door very forcibly slammed in their faces'. Hudson did not doubt that, by 'steering a wise & safe course', Northcliffe's papers would 'break up the

---

article to which Stuart referred was actually headed: 'New Tory Vote/ Mr Chamberlain's Challenge/ Prime Minister Over ruled.'
[1] Stuart to Northcliffe, 15 and 21 March 1922, and Hudson to Northcliffe, 19 March [1922], Northcliffe Papers.

Coalition, but *when* the final bust-up will come, I can't say'. Massingham, equally confident that Lloyd George's days in Downing Street were numbered, urged Northcliffe to consider the 'prospect which many people are furthering' of an alternative combination led by Cecil and Grey. As there was not a single 'Liberal paper that's worth a damn' for the purpose of resisting the 'constant campaign of suggestion' that Lloyd George should be welcomed back to the Liberal fold, Massingham solicited outside assistance. 'I will ask my newspapers to make a point of reporting Lord Robert,' replied Northcliffe. 'Many thanks for the hint.'[1]

For Lloyd George, as for Northcliffe, it was a race against time. Each man engaged in complicated transactions to fortify his personal position. Lloyd George, endowed with greater psychological and physical resources, was slightly more successful in staving off the inevitable. Although his premiership did not survive the year, it lasted long enough to deprive Northcliffe of the satisfaction of seeing it fall.

In the months that remained to him, Northcliffe settled old scores. His boldest stroke was to rid himself of a symbolic encumbrance by purchasing John Walter's shares in June. He had had 'very little personal feeling' towards the Walter family apart from a belief that, in the clandestine negotiations of 1908, they had 'behaved like petty hucksters' who treated him 'badly and meanly'. While he owed them no gratitude, he was sufficiently respectful of their prestige to indicate that, if the fourth John Walter showed 'any desire to regain *The Times* for his family, I should certainly feel disposed to leave my interest to him on very easy terms'. In 1913, a revised agreement had accorded Walter the option to buy Northcliffe's majority shareholding in the event that the chief proprietor either died or decided to divest. Thereafter, Walter found 'cooperation between N. and myself' increasingly 'difficult'. He 'got on best with Northcliffe when he was at a distance or on paper' and therefore 'had as few dealings with him & interfered as little in the affairs of the Paper as possible'. Walter regretted Dawson's dismissal, feared for Steed's security, and took exception to 'heavy items' of recent expenditure, which may have been concocted to frighten him off. It came as a relief when Northcliffe offered generous terms to terminate the connection. Surrendering the right to have first call on Northcliffe's ordinary shares in the then unlikely event that they came on the market, Walter also declined to continue the charade of his chairmanship.[2]

Except to Walter, who thought him no more eccentric than usual, it was

---

[1] Northcliffe to his mother, 15 March 1922, quoted in Pound and Harmsworth, p. 837; Hudson to Northcliffe, 19 March [1922], Massingham to Northcliffe, 27 March [1922], and Northcliffe to Massingham, 1 April 1922 (copy), Northcliffe Papers.

[2] Northcliffe to Buckle, 14 August 1908 (copy), Northcliffe to Moberly Bell, 13 March 1909, and memorandum by John Walter, 26 September [1921], *Times* Archives; notes by A. P. Ryan of an interview with John Walter, 23 May 1968, Woods Papers; *History of The Times*, IV, part 2, 632 ff.

obvious that Northcliffe was deranged. From 25 May until 18 June, he roamed about the Continent, behaving more and more scandalously. Steed, summoned to his side, described his ravings as frequently obscene, yet punctuated by 'intervals of uncanny lucidity'. Brought home to die, Northcliffe ingeniously evaded quarantine to telephone his offices with distraught messages, accusations, and harangues. In July, he pencilled a new will, obligingly witnessed by one of his male nurses. On 14 August, the end came. Before it did, Northcliffe had caused the confusion that lingered on after him.

One of his many deathbed obsessions was that, 'now Northcliffe's gone, *The Times* will be squared'. This fear was not entirely due to delirium. Walter understood from Steed that, the previous year, Northcliffe had tried to sell the paper after being 'worked upon by various people who wished to get it out of his hands & into [the] hands of [the] Govt.' Supposedly, Northcliffe 'saw through the plot', to which Rothermere was an accessary. News of Northcliffe's breakdown again set the gears in motion. The pivotal figure was Sir Edward Grigg, formerly colonial editor of *The Times* and now private secretary to Lloyd George. On the evening of 16 June, after an approach from the Walters, Grigg had 'a discreet word with the Prime Minister', who was 'deeply impressed' by the scheme laid before him. On the understanding that Lloyd George and his friends would cooperate to resurrect Walter as chief proprietor, *The Times* would undertake to 'be mildly Liberal Imperialist in tone, independent in home issues, and in foreign relations give reasonable support to the Government'. Furthermore, Grigg 'had reason to think that Lloyd George would like to resign, after the settlement of the Irish crisis, and might himself be ready to edit *The Times*'. That eventuality might precede a general election or follow upon it. In either case, it would have been extraordinary. 'Editors of *The Times* have often believed that they were more important than prime ministers,' A. J. P. Taylor has observed. 'Lloyd George was the only prime minister who apparently agreed with them.'[1]

Within days, the Walters brought Dawson into the picture, and Lloyd George widened the discussions to include Rothermere. So far as one can tell, Lloyd George was playing a double – or possibly a triple – game, keeping each of his potential partners in the dark about the others. At any rate, he was too shrewd to put all his friends' eggs in one basket. Sir Howard Frank, one of his henchmen, was negotiating with Ellerman 'to put up the money' (estimated at £650,000) in order to 'run *The Times* ... upon absolutely impartial lines in the interests of the nation. The last four words however can be variously construed,' Frank cautioned Lloyd George, whom he envisaged as 'putting your head into the lion's mouth, not an enviable position if acute divergence of views arise'. A second scheme, elaborately formulated by David Davies (now

---

[1] Memorandum by George Beer (news editor) of a telephone conversation with Northcliffe [31 July or 7 August 1922], *Times* Archives; *History of The Times*, IV, part 2, 683 ff.; Taylor, 'Lloyd George: Rise and Fall,' in *Politics in Wartime*, p. 132.

apparently back in good grace), was to raise £900,000 for Lloyd George 'to become Managing Director and Editor of *The Times* within six months of relinquishing his position as Minister of the Crown'. Yet, while the political implications were more clear-cut, the budget was inadequate. Last, but certainly not least, there was Rothermere, who enjoyed an easy access to capital as well as an unearned reputation for electoral sagacity. Unlike the others, he was prepared to dispense with the hereditary tradition of the Walters and all that it entailed. 'If Lord Rothermere had secured *The Times*,' Beaverbrook later testified, 'it was his intention to put Lloyd George in as the Editor and with control of the policy separate from the authority of Lord Rothermere.' That 'would be a great stroke and an exciting political event'. Who can dispute him?[1]

The solicitors were busy even before Northcliffe was dead. Their advice was to delay until the legal position was clarified. Accordingly, Lloyd George rejected Grigg's plea, made during a round of golf on 8 August, to plunge ahead. He reiterated the opinion that *The Times* 'should go back to John Walter', but declined to specify with whose pecuniary assistance. On the 19th, five days after Northcliffe's demise, Birkenhead wrote urgently to Lloyd George in apparent ignorance of what was afoot. Urging that '*no time* should be wasted', he expressed 'little doubt that all the money required ... can be obtained from an unimpeachable source (not H.)', who may be safely assumed to have been Harold Harmsworth, Viscount Rothermere. Lloyd George countered that 'nothing can happen until N.'s Will is proved. ... It will take at least a fortnight from his death.' Meanwhile, he promised an opportunity to 'interchange views on this and many other topics' when they met the next weekend under Beaverbrook's roof at Cherkley. Any discussions there would still have been premature, and serious deliberations were delayed until mid-September, pending 'the result of [a] very careful enquiry' by W. S. Chilcott, Tory MP for the Walton division of Liverpool and a fervent coalitionist. By then it was too late.[2]

According to the provisions of Northcliffe's final will, made after Walter had forfeited his option, Northcliffe's widow was to inherit *The Times*. This document, anachronistically signed 'Harmsworth', was successfully challenged by one of the lesser beneficiaries. By agreement among the executors and legatees, the will that Northcliffe had drawn up in March 1919 was recognized as binding. Among its clauses, it encapsulated Walter's option and thus spared

[1] Frank to Lloyd George, 8 September 1922, Lloyd George Papers, F/17/4/9; memorandum by Davies, 'Suggested Heads of Agreement re *The Times*,' 21 September 1922, quoted in *History of The Times*, IV, part 2, 718–19; Beaverbrook to Morison, 30 September 1949, *Times* Archives. Contrary to the impression of Garvin and others, Beaverbrook was never in the running, but watched attentively from the sidelines, where Rothermere 'always ... brought his personal issues to me'.

[2] Birkenhead to Lloyd George, 19 August and 14 September 1922 (enclosing memorandum by Chilcott, 9 September 1922), and Lloyd George to Birkenhead, 20 August 1922, Lloyd George Papers, F/4/7/39–41.

him – and *The Times* – the ruinous consequences of his recent impetuosity. 'It is a miracle to see that chance again,' gasped Garvin.[1]

It remained to be seen whether Walter, within the three-month limit, could secure the means. Stuart, having hurried back from a visit to Canada, was at his service. His first move was to procure Ellerman's block of shares on behalf of Major John Jacob Astor (later 1st Baron Astor of Hever), who lent his immense fortune to Walter's purpose. 'All other possibilities of saving the paper were dropped when Astor came along and offered to underwrite the whole thing,' recalled Walter. 'Apart from the Duke of Devonshire,' whom Buckle tried to enlist, 'Henderson, who became Lord Somebody-or-other, and Lansdowne (whom my father knew well) were potential backers.' None of them had a purse as large as that of young Astor. The second son of William Waldorf (1st Viscount) Astor, who had handed over the *Observer* to his firstborn, John Jacob was soon to join his sister-in-law Nancy in Parliament as the Conservative member for Dover. With his secret patronage, Walter was able to match Rothermere's 'best price', which rose in October to £1,350,000. When costs were counted, Astor had paid £1,580,000, which was roughly double what he knew the property to be worth.[2]

Walter was thereupon installed alongside Astor as co-chief proprietor for life. The Carmelite House properties, which Stuart had been promised as a bequest, went to Rothermere for £1,600,000. Nor did Stuart collect the peerage that Lloyd George allegedly dangled as a bribe. Instead, for his invaluable work as a go-between, he was made a director of *The Times* for life. However, at the insistence of Dawson, who returned as editor, Stuart was swiftly relieved of the managing directorship. Steed, marked out as a casualty in any case, stayed through the general election, which may be said to have put a seal on the vast changes that had occurred in public life. Failure to gain control of *The Times* was but one sign among many that Lloyd George was losing his grip. 'What happened in the autumn of 1922,' reflected Buckle, the senior ex-editor of the paper, 'was an absolutely necessary rescue.' He was referring specifically to events at Printing House Square, but might just as well have been describing developments at Westminster.[3]

*   *   *

Lloyd George, who dabbled in journalism for fun and substantial profit, considered newspaper support to be essential if he was to fight the impending

---

[1] Garvin to Walter, 9 September 1922, *Times* Archives. Garvin was 'unalterably fond' of Northcliffe, 'though we never could agree about principles and methods in politics nor even about the conduct of journalism'.

[2] Ferris, *House of Northcliffe*, pp. 278–79; *History of The Times*, IV, part 2, 717–19, 740–42; notes by Ryan of an interview with Walter, 23 May 1968, Woods Papers.

[3] Steed, *The Press* (Harmondsworth, 1938), pp. 92–96; Buckle to Lints Smith, 24 January 1932, Wood Papers; Frank Waters's diary, 1 April 1952 (after Sir Campbell Stuart, 'an evil man', had published his memoirs, *Opportunity Knocks Once*).

election with the Conservatives at his side, still more if they stood against him. That accounts for his covert intervention in the struggle for custody of *The Times*. Thwarted in the attempt, he commanded less devotion in Fleet Street than at any other time in his long ministerial career. The *Daily Chronicle* won gratitude for standing by him, as if it had any choice. From left and right, however, editorial opinion converged against the coalition and its palliatives. Gwynne of the *Morning Post* was unappeased by the Geddes Report, which lowered an 'axe' on government spending without going so far as to abolish those 'doubtful' ministries, 'established since the war' to provide the Prime Minister 'with unlimited opportunities for exercising patronage'. The *Daily News*, from the opposite standpoint, deplored cuts in housing and other social programmes: 'Big business is accustomed to controlling the Tory Party: when Liberals coalesce with Tories it necessarily controls them too' (29 March).[1]

It was in the area of foreign affairs, where Lloyd George aspired to redeem himself, that his vulnerability was most acute. Garvin, who cleaved to him longer than most, 'said our whole say in the *Observer* on Sunday', 19 March, when he urged his hero 'to assert his position at any cost and go to an immediate General Election as Premier with the Conservative leaders or without them'. Privately, Garvin contemplated that Lloyd George 'would peg out firm his claim in the future' by boldly resigning 'after the Irish Bill and after one great testamentary speech on the Genoa policy'. The Irish settlement, however, alienated more support than it attracted; and, owing largely to a volte-face in French foreign policy, the carefully planned international conference at Genoa in April and May came off as a damp squib. 'As you know I had practically no hope of any good resulting from the Genoa Conference,' Bonar Law wrote to Mann, who hankered after a clean break with the Prime Minister. While Bonar Law conceded that Lloyd George 'must have some loss of prestige as the result of Genoa', he declined as yet to condone 'any definite action in connection with it'.[2]

Lloyd George was politically bankrupt. Garvin sadly realized as much: 'The Conservative party will never come back effectively to the P.M. and both the others just now are moving further away from him.' Nevertheless, Lloyd George's Unionist creditors were strangely reluctant to foreclose on him. The longer they equivocated, the greater the indignation of Tory publicists. Gwynne had 'an hour's talk with Austen Chamberlain' and was so 'very little impressed by what he said ... that I think there is nothing for the Diehards to do but to go on fighting' in order 'to get hold of the party "machine" and, in time, be the control party'.[3]

[1] Grigg to Perris, 30 March 1922, Grigg Papers; Gwynne to Lady Bathurst, 17 February 1922, Bathurst Papers.
[2] Garvin to Grigg, 21 March 1922, Grigg Papers; Mann to Bonar Law, 27 April 1922, Bonar Law Papers, 107/2/32; Bonar Law to Mann, 28 April 1922, Mann Papers.
[3] Garvin to Grigg, 21 March 1922, Grigg Papers; Gwynne to Lady Bathurst, 23 March 1922, Bathurst Papers. At Cliveden, Garvin had met Lloyd George, whose 'hair [was] coming to be

Chamberlain, whose misplaced sense of loyalty estranged him from his backbench followers, did not wish to be seen as taking dictation from disaffected newspapermen. Similarly, Grigg's 'efforts to get the P.M. to retire into private life and collect his forces for another period of power' were defeated by Lloyd George's disinclination 'to throw up the sponge' ostensibly in response 'to the howls of enemies like Northcliffe, who stab him in the back and never meet him face to face'. Dawson, between innings as editor of *The Times*, could appreciate the situation. On holiday at Avignon, he had 'seen nothing for 10 days but rather emotional French papers & a rag called the *Continental Daily Mail*'; those were sufficient to indicate that his friends in Downing Street were 'having a pretty damnable time, largely on account of these rags. My blood boils,' he wrote to Grigg,

> when I see an extract from some self-advertising pronouncement of *The Times* solemnly proclaiming that it is above all party politics. . . . The truth is that, for the first time for many years, *The Times* has become a mere one-sided party organ. . . . Why cannot this 'organized hypocrisy' be exposed – preferably not by the P.M., who has too many other critics? I wish I could think of a plan!

Colonel Clive (later 1st Baron) Wigram, private secretary to the King, was no less incensed. Grigg's 'most interesting . . . account of events at Genoa' persuaded him that 'the P.M. must be a wonderful fellow. The poisonous attacks on him by the Northcliffe Press are a disgrace,' concluded Wigram, 'and Wickham Steed's articles are not those of an Englishman.'[1]

The Genoa conference, then, was a gamble that Lloyd George lost. Sir Robert Sanders took the superficial view that 'in spite of much newspaper writing the country seems to care little about it'. The press and the politicians, however, cared a great deal. Tom Clarke was sent to Victoria Station to see 'how the crowd received the Prime Minister' upon his return. 'Don't attack Lloyd George,' Northcliffe instructed him by telephone. 'There's no need. He is going downhill fast enough without it.' The *Daily Mail* also received prompting from Locker Lampson, now 'righthand man' to Churchill, whose misgivings he freely communicated. 'Winston felt that he could not see Mr Marlowe because of his feeling that he must remain loyal to the Prime Minister while he is abroad; had he seen Mr Marlowe he would have been bound to have unburdened himself.' Instead, Locker Lampson did the job for him, enabling

---

nearer white than grey', and pleaded with him to 'retire for a time. . . . No one dares to stand up to him as I do – no one,' Garvin told Viola Woods (9 February 1920, Woods Papers); 'but he knows I am an honest and seeing person.' On 1 May 1921, Garvin wrote 'a centenary study' of Napoleon, whose predicament and 'biological problem' strikingly resembled Lloyd George's.

[1] Grigg to R. H. Brand, 30 March 1922 (copy), Dawson to Grigg, 27 April 1922, and Wigram to Grigg, 6 May 1922, Grigg Papers.

the *Daily Mail* to exploit divergences within the ministerial team. Curzon found it 'distressing and even humiliating' to read on 5 July that he was due to retire from the Foreign Office. Grigg, trying to calm him down, described the statement as 'one of the unceasing attempts of the Northcliffe Press to discredit the Government by sowing unwarranted doubts of the loyalty of its members to each other'. In fact, Grigg attested, 'no member of the *Daily Mail*' had been received at Downing Street 'during the last three weeks, and only two visits have been made on behalf of that paper during the previous three months'. By denying complicity, Grigg was tacitly admitting to a growing weakness.[1]

Northcliffe's death relieved Lloyd George of an anxiety, yet occurred too late to affect the government's cohesion or electoral prospects. Months passed before that event was reflected in the political orientations of *The Times*, the *Daily Mail*, and the *Evening News*, which meanwhile persisted in sullen opposition. Before *The Times* finally eluded his grasp, Lloyd George shopped around for other sources of newspaper support. One possibility was a modest investment in the *Democrat*, the self-proclaimed 'organ of constitutional trade unionism', with a weekly sale of fewer than 10,000 copies. If Lloyd George was resolved to make overtures to the left, as Churchill feared and others second-guessed, this prefabricated platform might assist his purpose. Founded in April 1919 'to represent the views and aims and policy of the moderate anti-revolutionary labour wing', the *Democrat* borrowed its name from a defunct and distinguished exponent of Victorian progressivism. Percy Creed, soliciting capital to keep it going, pointed out that the extreme socialists boasted 'a large number of weekly papers and one daily one', the *Herald*, none of them 'self-supporting, except perhaps the Glasgow *Forward*, but they all get money from somewhere and carry on'. He estimated that it would require 'no great effort' for the *Democrat* to build 'a circulation of, say, 60,000 copies weekly' among industrial workers. That would confer 'a great – perhaps a predominant – influence' at the polls. Mond, now Minister of Health, was said to have given his approval – and possibly his financial support – to the venture, but without practical effect. 'This is not a party paper,' the editor of the *Democrat* insisted to his readers on 21 October 1922, 'and the present state of party politics inspires no desire to become one.'[2]

There was the further prospect that the *Spectator*, an older and more respected weekly, might change hands. St Loe Strachey, its owner-editor since 1898, was feeling his age and the economic pinch. A few years earlier, he had proposed that Lord Astor should join him 'on the business and general side'. Had that partnership materialized, John Buchan, who exemplified Strachey's

[1] Sanders's diary, 16 May 1922, Bayford Papers; Clarke, *Northcliffe Diary* (21 May 1922), pp. 281–82; memorandum by Douglas Crawford, 8 May 1922, enclosed in Marlowe to Northcliffe, 9 May 1922, Northcliffe Papers; Curzon to Grigg, 6 July 1922, and Grigg to Curzon, 7 July 1922 (copy?), Grigg Papers.
[2] Creed to Strachey, 27 February 1922, Strachey Papers; Creed to Grigg, 21 August 1922, Grigg Papers.

'ideal of judicial journalism', would have been called upon to serve as a sort of 'understudy director'. In the spring of 1922, Strachey opened negotiations with Runciman and his 'people', who shared his aversion to Lloyd George. The idea was for Runciman, who had diversified his mercantile holdings to include a string of non-political periodicals, to purchase 'a large share in the *Spectator*'. But the impending general election, which raised false hopes of an Asquithian revival, made Runciman 'reluctant to add to my publisher investments just now'. Otherwise, 'I would have been proud to have been connected with your unique journal, the views & tone of which attract me intensely,' he told Strachey. Deciding not to sell, Strachey first appointed Evelyn Wrench as managing director and then, in 1925 (the same year that the *Democrat* folded), conveyed 'a considerable amount of the Ordinary Shares of the *Spectator* to him – enough to give him control'. By then, expenditure had been 'cut down ... by three or four thousand a year' and the revenue was 'not only good, but better than ever'. There was no longer any question of keeping the journal in the family. Strachey's son John, a regular contributor, had the requisite literary skills; but, in the light of his conversion to socialism, he agreed with his father that 'it would have been an absurd position for him to inherit control of the *Spectator*, though he could quite well receive dividends on my shares'.[1]

In at least two other cases, transfers of ownership were neither so protracted nor so politically inconclusive. In September 1922, the *People* was bought by Colonel Grant Morden, the Canadian-born Conservative MP for Brentford and Chiswick. A daredevil speculator in Klondike gold-mines and other far-flung fields, Morden was rumoured to have been linked through Beaverbrook with several newspaper enterprises, though the only title registered in his own name was *Coming Fashions*. He reportedly paid £160,000 – a trifling sum for him – for the *People*, using Robert Donald as his agent and decoy. Donald himself had recently taken over the *Referee*, another desecrator of the sabbath; for a time, he edited the two papers in tandem. Both remained vaguely Conservative in their political bias, which was not allowed to intrude upon their popular features. In 1924, Donald was replaced at the *People* by Hannen Swaffer, who began under Northcliffe on the *Weekly Dispatch* and ended up under Beaverbrook on the *Express*. Swaffer's efforts to lift the moral tone came to grief the following year, when Morden paid off his printing bills by presenting the *People* to Julius Elias (later 1st Viscount Southwood) at Odhams Press, already in possession of *John Bull*. Swaffer, who lost his editorial chair to Harry Ainsworth (who held it until 1958), complained that Morden had treated 'me and my men as though we were a tin mine somewhere in Uganda'. Thereafter, the *People* reverted to sensationalism and revived to

---

[1] Strachey to Buchan, 26 November 1920 and 11 September 1922 (copies), Strachey to Runciman, 10 May 1922 (copy), Runciman to Strachey, 17 May and 11 June 1922, and Strachey to Bernard Mallet, 21 January and 13 August 1925 (copies), Strachey Papers; *also see* Hugh Thomas, *John Strachey* (London, 1973), pp. 35–37.

enjoy new prosperity as the *Sunday People*, ultimately attached to the *Daily Mirror* group. The *Referee* eventually became the *Sunday Referee*, but without comparable success.¹

On 5 September 1922, while Morden was quietly concluding his misguided purchase, the Trades Union Congress voted overwhelmingly to legitimate the *Daily Herald* by acquiring the shares and assuming the liabilities of the Victoria House Printing Company, in which ownership was hitherto vested. 'This vote,' its front page proclaimed the following morning, 'means that the *Daily Herald* now belongs to and is under the control of the Organised Labour Movement.' By raising its 'affiliation fees from one penny to threepence per member', the TUC made it possible to reduce the price of the paper to a penny with the 'immediate aim' of 'securing 500,000 readers'. Lansbury ('entirely on my own initiative') relinquished the editorship to Fyfe, but continued his connection as one of the ten directors. Having once 'told Lenin that the Bolshevik doctrine of discipline was abhorrent to me', he did not feel that he 'could ... put my mind into someone else's keeping'. During the preceding 'eleven years of almost superhuman effort', he and his associates had 'succeeded in keeping the paper alive, maintaining all the time a spirit of rebellious adventure'. Now, in return for 'a much greater claim on official and non-official support', the *Herald* was obliged to make a sacrifice. 'Some of us regret the loss of freedom which this change of ownership and control involves,' admitted Lansbury, who bowed humbly to 'a rule of life'. The essential problem, one that the *Herald* was never to resolve, was 'that all such movements as ours need the stimulus which independent thought and expression alone can give', but could rarely afford that luxury. 'Officialism always dries up initiative and expression.' But what was the alternative? The argument 'that the paper is no longer free' was admittedly true, if 'only in part'. For it would be 'folly to imagine that any executive committee will pay people to destroy its influence and power in the columns of a paper they find the money to support'. Lansbury had the consolation of knowing 'that at long last the despised and rejected of Fleet Street is paying its way, and so bids fair to become one of the chief cornerstones of present day journalism', designedly to the advantage of Labour as a social movement and a parliamentary force.²

'How can we restore Democracy as our form of Government?' Gardiner asked rhetorically in the new *John Bull*. 'An awakened public can alone break the power that controls them,' he answered. 'They must mistrust the great commercialised press that has enslaved them.' The *Daily Herald*, echoing his indictment (15 September), accepted the challenge 'to present the truth' for the benefit of 'all the workers whether by hand or brain'. So, in due course, did *The Times*, released from bondage to a 'press gang'. J. J. Astor, mindful that he

---

¹ *Morning Post*, 18 September 1922, Minney, *Southwood*, pp. 178–86; *The Times*, 17 October 1981.

² *Daily Herald*, 6 and 11 September 1922; Lansbury, *Miracle*, pp. 1–2, 41.

had 'only recently become acquainted with his subject', projected 'The Future of *The Times*' in the pages of the *Empire Review*. Declaring that his objective had been 'to secure as far as possible the continued independence of one great journal, and through it the perpetuation of the highest standards of British journalism', he pregnantly stated that 'the function of a newspaper like *The Times* is not to enter into rivalry with the Government of the day, . . . be it Tory, Liberal, or Labour'. Gardiner welcomed this assurance, contrasting it with the way that Rothermere, for one, operated as 'an irresponsible power working through the passions of the mob'. Nevertheless, Astor's 'enlightened conservatism' was bound to colour the presentation of news no less than the socialism of the *Daily Herald*, the diehard toryism of the *Morning Post*, or the discordant liberalisms of the *Daily Chronicle*, the *Daily News*, and the *Westminster Gazette*. There remained, as Astor observed, a 'plain tendency to partisanship. No political party is nowadays content unless some important organ of the Press is enslaved in its service.'[1]

Although Astor simplified the issues, particularly as they weighed upon his double life as an MP and newspaper proprietor, he was correct in his inference that the balance between supply and demand had shifted. 'Officialism', accepted by Lansbury as a cruel necessity, was generally in retreat. The editorial service that the Conservative and Liberal parties expected was no longer theirs to command. Only the Labour Party, in defiance of its libertarian principles, exercised a sufficient control over its journalistic resources – slender though they were – for them to preach what the party aimed to practise.

If the *Daily Herald* was the most conspicuous case in point, the *Labour Leader* emphatically proved it. Since Keir Hardie's pioneer days, this weekly journal had stagnated under successive editorships until it was little more than an ILP newsletter. In 1922, Clifford Allen (later 1st Baron Allen of Hurtwood) became party treasurer and Ramsay MacDonald returned from the electoral wilderness to the party leadership. At the behest of the National Administrative Council, the two men formulated plans to bring the *Labour Leader* from Manchester to London, there to revitalize it under NAC auspices. MacDonald, whose primary goal was to subordinate the ILP, had his own pronounced views about newspaper management. He had got his start as a journalist and edited the *Socialist Review* until his first premiership in 1924. Reluctant to duplicate the *New Statesman*, which nettled him by its erudite heterodoxies, he wished to transform the *Labour Leader* into a chatty digest, congenial to an expanded readership of 'a gentlemanly, democratic &, on the whole, amateur kind'. Allen thought otherwise and proposed H. N. Brailsford to wield editorial power. A thoroughgoing professional with fifteen years' membership in the ILP to his credit, Brailsford struck MacDonald as an unsuitable choice. MacDonald unconvincingly recounted that he had asked a mutual friend how

[1] Astor, 'The Future of The Times,' *Empire Review*, xxxviii (1923), 944–51; Gardiner, 'The Press and the State,' *Nation*, 15 September 1923.

Brailsford 'would do as editor of a paper that was actively propagandist, and the answer was swift and prompt: "He would not do at all; that's not his line; he would either destroy such a paper or resign within six months."' Allen did not so much overcome as circumvent MacDonald's objections, and Brailsford was appointed.[1]

With a subsidy from the ILP to enlarge the *Labour Leader* to sixteen pages and to remunerate contributors, Brailsford began his tenure in September 1922, at the same time that the TUC assumed responsibility for the *Daily Herald*. To MacDonald's further disapproval, the name was changed to the *New Leader*, and it gave the 'impression of a magazine with special highbrowed contents', not one to which 'the active people in the party are to contribute regularly'. The talents on display – including Bertrand Russell, Keynes, Shaw, Hobson, Angell, Wells, and Nevinson – both justified MacDonald's misgivings and met Brailsford's standards for eclecticism. 'I want to tell you something of our plans for the *Leader*,' Brailsford wrote to Wells, from whom he extracted an article for the inaugural number. 'I have no doubt that it can be a creditable and useful weekly. But my ambition goes further. It must try to lead and inspire the Labour movement.' That, surely, was MacDonald's job, or ought to have been. The trick was to reconcile Brailsford's private aspiration with the *New Leader*'s public assertion (24 November 1922) that 'in initiative, in speech, in tactics, ... MacDonald will infallibly become the symbol, the personification, which we have hitherto lacked'.[2]

MacDonald was far too vain and insecure to ignore the implicit contradiction. 'The *New Leader* troubles me,' he told Allen in the summer of 1923. 'It will not do, and wherever I go, I find people are dissatisfied with it', usually on the grounds that its heady intellectualism made it difficult to distribute through the ILP branches. 'H.N.B. unfortunately seems to grow more rather than less detached from us,' complained MacDonald. Distracted for a time by the unanticipated burdens of office, he soon had all the more reason to resent Brailsford's unsolicited advice on questions of foreign policy and unemployment. Writing to Allen on 16 September 1924, he inveighed against the 'nasty small spirit' that infected the party: 'As to the *New Leader*, frankly I have lost all interest in it. It is not the kind of paper that does any good to anybody. It has neither weight nor place and its egotistical aloofness would kill any movement.' Six days later, Allen read this letter aloud at a *New Leader* lunch and implored the Labour press to abate its criticisms, but Brailsford and Fyfe scorned the appeal.[3]

After Labour tumbled from office, soiled and bruised, relations predictably

[1] NAC minutes, 18 April, 12 May, and 25 June 1922; memorandum by MacDonald, 'My Ideas of the *Leader*,' 11 May 1922, and MacDonald to Allen, 13 May 1922, Allen Papers.

[2] MacDonald to Allen, 5 September 1922, Allen Papers; Brailsford to Wells, n.d. [1922], Wells Papers.

[3] MacDonald to Allen, 17 August 1923 and 16 September 1924, Allen Papers; Nevinson's diary, 22 September 1924.

worsened between the party leadership and the *New Leader*, its very title implying an affront. MacDonald, irritated by Brailsford's spirited campaign for a 'living wage', commented tartly in the *Socialist Review* (March 1926): 'I suppose it is hard for an editor with no executive responsibility to refrain from telling us how he would act if he were King, Lords and Commons combined, the head of every Department of State and all the Under-Secretaries as well.' To which Brailsford rejoined (26 February): 'It is not great leadership which seeks to check the initiative and arrest the thinking of a democratic party.' Almost word for word, this debate had been rehearsed by Lansbury, now back in business as the editor of *Lansbury's Labour Weekly*, a colloquial rival to the *New Leader*. In June 1926, after a further clash over the handling of the General Strike, Brailsford offered his resignation, which the NAC voted to accept in October. His departure was variously ascribed to his exorbitant demands for salary and 'complete autocratic control'. Those were distortions. Brailsford's offence was to have stood firm for editorial sovereignty, incompatible with 'officialism' of any denomination.[1]

* * *

Late in life, Lord Beaverbrook wrote a disarming account of Lloyd George's 'decline and fall' which, forty-one years earlier, he had contrived to bring about. His initial impulse was to entitle the book 'And Great Was the Fall Thereof', but an apprehensive publisher prevailed upon him to relegate that allusive phrase to the subtitle. Still, the implication remained the same. As a witness to the events he chronicled, Beaverbrook knew how decisive they had been.[2]

In August 1922, Beaverbrook took a holiday at Deauville, where a conversation with the Aga Khan awakened him to 'the dangerous character' of British involvement in the armed conflict between Greece and Turkey. He returned to London with the 'conviction ... that for Britain to fight Turkey, in pursuance of the exploded policy of supporting Greek Imperialism, would be a monstrous error, which must be avoided at all costs'. Curzon, the Foreign Secretary, took exception to Beaverbrook's efforts at private diplomacy. Lloyd George was 'indefinite and evasive'. Churchill and Birkenhead, who had been disposed towards conciliation, now 'astonished' Beaverbrook by expressing 'complete agreement with the Prime Minister's Near Eastern policy' to the extent that Birkenhead contemplated the probability of war with France.

After further 'discussion proved unavailing', Beaverbrook went to see Bonar Law, who had relinquished the leadership of the parliamentary Con-

[1] *Report*, ILP annual conference, 1927; *also see* Marquand, *MacDonald*, pp. 453–54.
[2] These paragraphs are based on Beaverbrook, *Politicians and the Press*, pp. 48–51, and *The Decline and Fall of Lloyd George*, pp. 160–61; Michael Kinnear, *The Fall of Lloyd George* (London, 1973), ch. 5; and Blake, *Unknown Prime Minister*, ch. xxviii.

servative Party, but not his moral authority within it. 'These men mean war,' Beaverbrook warned his friend, and thereby – in his own estimation – gave 'the signal for the overthrow of the Coalition Government'. Bonar Law, a non-interventionist in every sense, was moved only so far as to write an open letter, published in *The Times* and elsewhere on 7 October, in which he protested that 'we cannot alone act as the policemen of the world'. Beaverbrook proudly recalled that 'only the *Daily Express* perceived that this was a root and branch condemnation of the Chanak policy', by which British troops were pledged to resist the Turkish advance on the Straits, and furthermore 'that a new potential Premier had taken the field, and that an alternative administration had at last become possible'. Certainly Bonar Law himself had no such perception as yet.

With his captivating gift for self-dramatization, Beaverbrook held that, by prompting 'Bonar Law's letter opposing war with Turkey', he had triggered the Tory rebellion: 'After that Toryism simply slid like an avalanche in the direction of its natural leader.' In fact, the slide was neither simple nor direct. The coalition had been faltering for many months, and the standard of Tory revolt was already hoisted when Bonar Law finally rallied to it. Derby, who first intimated his misgivings to Chamberlain in early September, was among those anxiously awaiting a showdown. 'Seriously, I am very much interested in the line the *Daily Express* has taken ... and I think it is absolutely the right one,' he told Blumenfeld on 3 October. While he was loath to 'criticise the Government now, when at any moment it is a case of peace or war', he confessed that he could not 'trust Lloyd George any longer'. Derby was typical in that he had a grievance without a strategy. He reasoned on the 9th that 'if one said bluntly that one would not have Lloyd George as Prime Minister it would be extremely difficult from a loyal point of view for any of his followers not to resent it and so they would only follow him. We must do it however somehow.'[1]

To say that Beaverbrook was not as singularly responsible as he retrospectively suggested is not to deny his importance, particularly as an actor behind the scenes. Other newspapermen, acting in their professional capacities, were also active in bringing the crisis to a head. A letter to the editor of *The Times* (4 October) from Eleutherios Venizelos, the Anglophile Greek premier, elicited a hostile retort from Major-General Sir Frederick Maurice, ever ready to impugn Lloyd George's veracity. 'Unfortunately we do not take the *Daily News*, and so I did not see Maurice's telegram,' Lord Stamfordham wrote from the Palace, where Grigg's word was accepted that Maurice had ventured to 'misrepresent the relations between the Cabinet and the Military Authorities on the spot'.[2] The *Daily News*, contrary to its Gladstonian tradition, recoiled from a confrontation with the Unspeakable Turk. The *Daily Telegraph* reverted to a Disraelian posture, the *Morning Post* to a Palmerstonian one.

[1] Derby to Blumenfeld, 3 and 9 October 1922, Blumenfeld Papers.
[2] Stamfordham to Grigg, 5 October 1922, Grigg Papers.

On 8 October, the *Observer* swung round. Its leading article enumerated the reasons 'Why the Premier should Retire'. In an accompanying signed column, Garvin issued a 'Call for New Men and New Minds', imploring readers to 'face the brutal fact. Irredeemably, miserably, the British Government four years afterwards has lost the Great War in the East.' Grigg was more perplexed than angry. 'I am not sure ... that yesterday's *Observer* will have contributed greatly to the chances of peace,' he wrote on the 9th to Lady Astor.

> I am not quarrelling with old Garvin's views, though I regard his handling of the Eastern Question as very superficial ..., but a personal attack upon the chief representative of the nation at such a fateful moment ... is hard to understand from one of his deep patriotism and profound understanding of affairs.

As usual, 'old Garvin' followed his own logic. 'The *Observer* will be found quite well able to take care of itself in all circumstances,' he bluffly assured Grigg. 'It expects the Premier to become in due time the leader of the Left. A General Election will do more than anything else to restore efficient politics.'[1]

Conservative MPs were summoned to a meeting at the Carlton Club at 11 o'clock on the morning of the 19th. Although the event appeared to be a capitulation to dissident elements, historians have shown it to be 'a counteratttack on the part of the Coalitionists who were ... confident of winning the day'. In anticipation of this conclave, *The Times* pinned its hopes on Bonar Law, who alone had the capacity 'to restore something like stability to the political life of the country'. Steed, in the twilight of his editorship, saw the former Conservative leader on three successive evenings and promised him 'whatever influence *The Times* possesses'. Admittedly 'without knowledge of all the circumstances', Steed later supposed that he and his paper had been 'instrumental ... in persuading Mr Bonar Law that it was his duty to overthrow the discredited Coalition and to restore Party Government'. Describing himself as 'an outsider', he had 'some reason to think that Mr Bonar Law might not have been willing to become Prime Minister and to face the General Election' unless 'the support of *The Times*' was guaranteed. With it, Steed projected that the Conservatives would amass a clear majority of seventy-five seats in the next Parliament. That was three times the number envisaged by the most sanguine party managers.[2]

As Robert Blake has remarked, 'Bonar Law had one important asset on his side – the Press.' Rothermere clambered aboard the moving bandwagon. 'Stick your toes in today,' he advised Bonar Law on the morning of the Carlton Club gathering. 'George & Chamberlain haven't one chance in a thousand of

[1] Grigg to Lady Astor, 9 October (copy), and Garvin to Grigg, 11 October 1922, Grigg Papers.
[2] Blake, *Unknown Prime Minister*, p. 453; Steed to Bonar Law, 17 October 1922 (1 a.m.), Bonar Law Papers, 117/2/1; Steed, *Through Thirty Years*, II, 285.

winning an election whilst the Conservative party might and I think would.' It amused Bonar Law to receive such encouragement. 'You are a queer creature,' he replied to Rothermere with undeserved kindness. 'You abuse me like a pickpocket, forget all about it & then write a most friendly letter for which, notwithstanding, I am obliged.' He was still more obliged for Rothermere's published encomia.[1]

Backbench and editorial voices were raised in unison, investing each with a heightened resonance. G. R. Lane-Fox (later 1st Baron Bingley), the Conservative member for Barkston Ash and party chairman in Yorkshire, entreated Bonar Law to return. His plea was alleged to carry special weight. 'My own view corresponds very closely with the view that you have regularly put forward,' Lane-Fox told Mann of the *Yorkshire Post*. 'I don't want to see the identity & tradition of the Conservative party sunk in perpetuity in a Coalition party without tradition or principle behind it – & meaning nothing except all that is conveyed by the words Lloyd George.' It was Lane-Fox, Mann noted approvingly, who 'seconded the resolution of revolt at the Carlton Club'. The *Yorkshire Post* had not put him up to it, but was said to have strengthened his resolve. Transparently 'as a recognition of political services', Mann was soon offered a knighthood, which he declined out of prudence.[2]

There was, then, no shortage of candidates for the distinction of having lured Bonar Law out of retirement and back into the leadership. Beaverbrook and Steed lodged separate claims. Curzon, Amery, and Sir Samuel Hoare all assumed or had assigned to them a modicum of credit. Sir George Younger, arriving to escort Bonar Law to the Carlton, helped him to put on his boots for the occasion. A reluctant Prime Minister as well as an unknown one, Bonar Law maintained that no one had influenced his decision half so much as 'my own family – my sister and children'. In any case, he was greeted at the Carlton by a tremendous ovation. Earlier that morning, it was announced that an independent Conservative candidate had trounced a Coalition Liberal in a by-election at Newport, and that was a powerful stimulus. Bonar Law, looking 'very nervous and unhappy', listened as Stanley Baldwin denounced Lloyd George, 'a dynamic force' who had shattered one party and threatened to shatter another. Then, beginning 'almost inaudibly', Bonar Law supported the resolution 'against the continuation of the Coalition'.[3]

The *Morning Post* had erroneously supposed (19 October) that nothing of

[1] Rothermere to Bonar Law [19 October 1922], and Bonar Law to Rothermere, 19 October 1922 (copy), Bonar Law Papers, 107/2/70.

[2] Lane-Fox to Mann, 17 October 1922 (with Mann's comments), and Mann to Baldwin, 27 December 1923 (copy), Mann Papers. Mann declined a second time in February 1929, but accepted the Companionship of Honour – in company with Garvin – from Churchill in December 1940.

[3] Bonar Law to Sir Robert Borden, n.d., quoted in Blake, *Unknown Prime Minister*, p. 456; Kinnear, pp. 127–28; H. A. Taylor, *Jix* (London, 1933), p. 161. The full account in *The Times* was furnished by 'a correspondent', in fact Hoare. J. A. Cross, *Sir Samuel Hoare* (London, 1977), p. 79.

consequence would occur at the Carlton Club meeting, evidently contrived by a tactician 'less honest and more cunning' than Chamberlain. Gwynne was therefore embarrassed to receive a 'charming letter' from Lord Selborne, who congratulated him on the outcome. 'You have put altogether too high a value on the little I have been able to contribute to yesterday's great success,' Gwynne replied with due modesty. Having been caught napping, Gwynne was all the more eager to proclaim his devotion. 'You and I have been estranged and the fault was mine,' he wrote on the 23rd to Bonar Law, who that day was unanimously elected party leader and appointed Prime Minister. 'I am sorry and apologise to you privately as I have already expressed my regret publicly,' Gwynne went on. 'I feel that the country is in such a desperate state that any man who attempts to clean up the mess deserves the thanks and support of his fellow-countrymen.' Bonar Law was happy to 'consider the incident closed. . . . Your letter is everything I could have wished for.'[1]

It had been a trying week for Bonar Law. Shunned by the top-ranking Conservative ministerialists, with the notable exception of Curzon, he constructed his Cabinet in anticipation of an appeal to the country. This 'Government of the second eleven', as Churchill tagged it, recruited an unusually high proportion of its members from the back-benches. F. Stanley Jackson hesitated before settling into a junior ministry. For twenty years, he had been a 'sleeping partner' in the *Yorkshire Post*, 'a purely Conservative paper' in which 'the shareholders are limited to people of our views'. Was it mandatory, he wondered, for him to resign this directorship? Bonar Law, determined to signal a break with his predecessor's habit of 'trafficking with the press', insisted upon Jackson's severing that family connection. 'Of all the directorships,' Davidson replied on the Prime Minister's behalf, 'he feels that that of a newspaper is most open to criticism when held by a Member of the Government, and he is of the opinion that in these circumstances you ought to resign it.' Hoare, on becoming Secretary for Air, was said to have divested himself of a seat on the board of an unspecified newspaper.[2]

Although Bonar Law had explicitly discounted electoral considerations in his Carlton Club speech, these could not be ignored. Steed, with apologies for 'butting in', begged him not to take office as a caretaker: 'Were it announced that you agreed to act only for a year, there would inevitably be some decrease of enthusiasm in the immediate future and a considerable increase of uncertainty as to the position a year hence.' Bonar Law's essential task was to provide a viable alternative to the late coalition without destroying the chances

---

[1] Gwynne to Selborne, 20 October 1922, Selborne Papers; Gwynne to Bonar Law, 23 October 1922, and Bonar Law to Gwynne, 23 October 1922 (copy), Bonar Law Papers, 107/2/74, 107/4/37.

[2] Jackson to Davidson, 26 December 1922, and Davidson to Jackson, 28 December 1922 (copy), Bonar Law Papers, 111/15/83–84. Hoare's connection was almost certainly with the *Express*, although *The Directory of Directors* (1920–22) selectively listed Goulding and not him as a member of that board.

of eventual reunion with those senior Conservatives who stubbornly identified with it. To accomplish this dual mission, he relied on the press not only to celebrate the virtues of an independent conservatism, but also to refrain from salting wounds. Derby, who accepted the war secretaryship in the new administration, accordingly reminded Blumenfeld that there was 'nothing ... that would prevent' Chamberlain and the others from 'coming back and I do hope that in the *Daily Express* you will do everything you can during the Election to encourage them to do so. One also wants to get all the moderate liberals of the McKenna type,' added Derby, 'as in fighting Communism we shall want all the help we can get.'[1]

Amid the prevailing disorder, it was anyone's guess what constellations would emerge. The Liberals might overcome their mutual antipathies, or Labour might exploit the divisions within the older parties to break through. Least of all could the possibility of a Lloyd Georgian restoration be ruled out. Rothermere was struck by second thoughts on this score. On the pretext that he was too 'much pre-occupied' with legal affairs, he declined an invitation to meet Bonar Law on the evening of the 23rd. Instead, he proposed to 'await your declaration of policy on Saturday ..., as I shall then be able to decide what measure of support I can accord you in the coming election.' Sanders, now Minister of Agriculture, ascribed this reversal to the fact that 'Rothermere is trying to get a step in the Peerage as the price of his support'. Reportedly, Rothermere also demanded – in vain – a Cabinet appointment for his son Esmond.[2]

Yet, at least in other instances, there were solid motives for equivocation. The *Glasgow Herald*, having miscalculated on the 18th that the demise of the coalition was not to be 'seriously apprehended', strove to come to terms with a situation it had not foreseen. Robert Bruce, its editor, promised to welcome Bonar Law to Glasgow, 'your own City', at the climax of the campaign. 'We have had a difference of opinion as to the ways and means of keeping moderate opinion together,' he acknowledged unrepentantly. In Scotland, to a far greater extent than elsewhere, the coalition had welded its Liberal and Unionist elements into a single machine. Bruce, 'perturbed by the thought of what may happen in Scotland if the compact is broken', trusted Bonar Law to 'say something which would help us to keep to the electoral arrangements already made with the National Liberals'. Croal of the *Scotsman* concurred that 'the immediate future' depended on 'the Coalition ... holding together in Scotland. That is vital for us.' How, if at all, were these constituency requirements to be satisfied? The *Glasgow Herald* resorted to obfuscation. 'Our election slogan from the beginning has been "Keep Together". We have all got

[1] Steed to Bonar Law, 19 October 1922, Bonar Law Papers, 117/2/2; Derby to Blumenfeld, 25 October 1922, Blumenfeld Papers.
[2] Rothermere to Bonar Law, 23 October 1922, Bonar Law Papers, 107/2/75; Sanders's diary, 25 October 1922, Bayford Papers; Blake, *Unknown Prime Minister*, p. 472; Davidson, *Memoirs*, p. 135.

together,' it declared on 1 November: 'Our new slogan is "Fight Together stoutly", so that the King's Government in Mr Bonar Law's hands will get the chance, to which it is entitled, of proving that it can interpret the will of moderate-minded people in sound administration and, where needful, sound legislation.' The argument, put with greater force than logic, was that togetherness had become a uniquely Conservative attribute, making Bonar Law the spiritual heir to the coalition. Aware of the incongruity, Bonar Law was willing to be cast in that peculiar light. 'Many thanks for your letter enclosing the copy of the leader which I had already read with much pleasure,' he wrote to Bruce.[1]

The lines of battle were blurred even in the minds of prominent politicians, and newspapers purposefully added to the confusion. 'Never perhaps has a general election been held where the issues were less clear and the electors received less guidance,' asserted the *Manchester Guardian* (13 November). Bonar Law collected press support on different grounds from disparate sources. Riddell unexpectedly endorsed him in the *News of the World* out of pique with Lloyd George. Hulton's *Evening Standard* was swayed by an appeal from Derby. Donald, a temporary presence in Sunday journalism, supplied three pages of 'notes' on how to deal with Lloyd George ('Tell him he is a liar and that he knows it'), which Bonar Law found 'admirable'. Donald was also in touch with 'Max' Beaverbrook who, at the cost of 'more than one old friendship', decreed that the party could have no truck with those 'ex-Ministers and members who followed Mr Chamberlain and Lord Birkenhead'. His militancy, over which Bonar Law professed to have no control, was something of a mixed blessing. Sir Archibald Salvidge, whom Bonar Law could not afford to alienate, suffered a 'venomous' attack in the *Daily Express*. Beaverbrook dealt more sympathetically with Griffith-Boscawen, whose ministerial career was cut short when he lost his seat at Taunton. Bonar Law promptly arranged for him to stand in a by-election at Mitcham, where the candidate mistakenly assumed that Beaverbrook's 'help ... would be invaluable'.[2]

The *Daily Mail*, the *Evening News*, the *Daily Mirror*, and the *Sunday Pictorial* all fell into line after Bonar Law threatened to expose Rothermere's attempted extortion. Until then, according to Beaverbrook, 'Lord Rothermere appeared to be holding the scales. He regarded himself as a timekeeper or referee, giving equal space to Lloyd George and his colleagues, along with Bonar Law and his friends.' At the wind-up, however, Rothermere was delivering 'timely and valuable support'. To ensure that the *Morning Post*

---

[1] Bruce to Bonar Law, 25 October 1922, Croal to Bonar Law, 31 October 1922, Bonar Law to Croal, 2 November 1922 (copy), and Bonar Law to Bruce, 3 November 1922 (copy), Bonar Law Papers, 108/1/15, 112/14/1–2, 112/7/1.

[2] Donald to Bonar Law, and Bonar Law to Donald (copy), 30 October 1922, and Salvidge to Bonar Law, 24 October 1922, Bonar Law Papers, 108/9/12, 108/1/9, 25; Beaverbrook, *Politicians and the Press*, p. 55; Beaverbrook to Boscawen, 18 November 1922 (telegram; copy), and Boscawen to Beaverbrook, 18 November 1922, Beaverbrook Papers, B/16. For the defeat at Mitcham of Boscawen by an independent Conservative, financed by Locker Lampson and backed by Rothermere, see Cowling, *Impact of Labour*, p. 257.

would remain on its best behaviour, particularly with regard to pending Irish constitutional legislation, Ronald McNeill undertook to have a word with 'our friend Taffy'. He reported that Gwynne 'was impressed by my pointing out that we did not want to carry the Irish Bill in alliance with the opposition groups *against* a Conservative minority', and that Gwynne had 'promised to drop the question' in the interests of Tory unity. That Allen Algernon Bathurst, better known as Lord Apsley, was standing as the Conservative candidate at Southampton was yet another reason for the *Morning Post* to mind its manners. 'Allen's victory drove us all wild with delight & the Conservative return to power has made us feel that we have not laboured in vain,' Gwynne told Lady Bathurst, his proprietor and Apsley's mother.[1]

Had the custody of *The Times* been settled more quickly, Dawson might have modified, if not repudiated, its tone of anti-coalitionism. But Steed held on through the interregnum, availing himself of a last chance to smite Lloyd George. The new régime at Printing House Square and the new Cabinet were formed within the same week: another interesting coincidence. Walter affirmed that he and Astor had no plans 'to turn the Paper definitely into a Conservative organ. ... The Paper would remain entirely independent of Party.' As such, it might well have lent itself to Lloyd George's purpose. Dawson was offered a return engagement as editor on 27 October, at the height of the campaign, but delayed his decision until his demands were met in full. Milner urged him to accept, provided that the co-proprietors were 'prepared to give him good enough terms', which Milner helped to draft. On 4 December, Chirol heard from an inside source that, at last, Dawson had agreed. 'I believe Dawson has imposed conditions which will enable him to be really Editor which of course he never could be under the incubus of Lord N.,' remarked Chirol, who looked forward to 'a speedy return to old standards with the touch of youthful vigour & freshness they by no means exclude'. Strachey, too, was confident that Dawson 'will make *The Times* once more a great organ of public opinion, and also one which is alive and of our own, and not another age. ... Nobody,' he was sure, 'could have rocked the boat worse than poor Lord Northcliffe did in the last four years of his life, and yet he never managed to upset it. That is the best of omens.' On New Year's Day, 1923, Dawson 'put into the paper a short formal note of my return'.[2]

Lloyd George, by contrast, was denied a second coming. Although C. P. Scott had predicted that the election would leave him 'holding the balance', the size of the Conservative majority obviated any need for renewed coalition.

---

[1] Beaverbrook, *Decline and Fall*, p. 217; McNeill to Bonar Law, 20 November 1922, Bonar Law Papers, 108/2/15; Gwynne to Lady Bathurst, 20 November 1922, Bathurst Papers.

[2] Dawson's diary, 27 and 28 October, and 31 December 1922, quoted in Wrench, *Dawson*, pp. 208, 212; memorandum by Walter, 24 October 1922, quoted in *History of The Times*, IV, part 2, 769; Milner to Grigg, 17 November 1922, Grigg Papers; Chirol to A. L. Kennedy (leader-writer and special foreign correspondent), 4 December 1922, *Times* Archives; Strachey to Dawson, 7 December 1922 (copy), Strachey Papers.

Alone among the major metropolitan journals, the *Daily Telegraph* had waved the coalition banner from the Conservative side. Grigg praised it for exerting 'a remarkably steadying influence during these days of political confusion', true 'to the principles which it has always proclaimed'. Nevertheless, like Chamberlain, it stood in stark isolation. What had first seemed a set-back for Lloyd George was now visibly a defeat.[1]

The Asquithian Liberals, whom Scott expected to draw votes from the Tories, emerged with fifty-four seats, eight fewer than Lloyd George's National Liberals. They had relied chiefly on the Westminster Press group for electoral publicity, and it proved inadequate to their needs. The *Westminster Gazette*, unsure where to hit or how hard, allowed Lloyd George to testify against himself: in 1918, he had proclaimed it 'our task ... to make Britain a country fit for heroes to live in'; now, he implored 'the working man ... not [to] go down the wrong avenue seeking a paradise that is not there' (8 November).

A correlation was posited between the operations of the Westminster Press and the results in certain provincial constituencies. The previous March, against Hudson's advice ('We can't disturb matters on this side of the General Elect^n.'), the *Nottingham Journal* was annexed to the Pearson empire. The secretary of the Midland Liberal Federation, who spoke to 'its merits as a newspaper', advocated the transfer: 'It backs the local Liberals to the fullest extent, and does it wisely.' With 'a good candidate in the Central Division' of Nottingham, that morning journal could spell the difference between failure and success. In the event, the Asquithians won the seat by twenty-two votes. After the election, they found it more difficult to keep up their spirits and their newspaper properties. Partington gave notice of his intention to withdraw the amount he had invested in Westminster Press debentures. Starmer, who could not have been surprised, remonstrated that 'the success of the *Westminster Gazette* is regarded in newspaper circles as little short of a miracle, and the Provincial Group is now going to benefit from many years of hard work'. A perennial optimist, as his party allegiance required, Starmer insisted that 'the influence of these papers cannot be over-estimated and to anyone with the time to spare, they will not only prove interesting but remunerative'. His message, however, did not carry conviction.[2]

The Labour Party, which netted 142 seats on 29.4 per cent of the poll, consolidated its position as the party of opposition. At the outset of the campaign, Arthur Henderson, as party secretary, addressed a circular letter to editors throughout the country:

---

[1] Scott to Hobhouse, 30 October 1922, quoted in Scott, *Political Diaries*, p. 431; Grigg to Burnham, 23 October 1922 (copy), Grigg Papers.

[2] William Finnemore (secretary, Midland Liberal Federation) to Geoffrey Howard, 18 March 1922, note by Hudson, 22 March 1922, and Starmer to Partington, 4 and 20 December 1922, Asquith Papers.

At the last General Election, and later, during industrial disputes, several of the London and provincial daily and weekly newspapers provided facilities for the statement of Labour's case by placing a column or some other amount of space at the disposal of the Labour headquarters. The newspapers made it quite clear that they did not necessarily agree with the views set out in the Labour column. ... Labour has no vast press resources of its own whereby it can present a daily statement of its case to the electors during the forthcoming General Election, and it will have to rely to no small extent upon the good will of non-Labour newspapers.

This time, such good will was not so readily forthcoming. Under Rothermere, who equated Labour with Bolshevism, the *Daily Mail* did not renew its hospitality. The *Daily News*, anxious to promote a Liberal revival, declined to commit itself. For much the same reason, Scott was 'afraid' that the *Manchester Guardian* could not 'spare a daily column for the purpose you suggest. But,' he informed Henderson, 'we always do our best to give Labour a fair share of publicity in the usual way.'[1]

Henderson's request implied a want of confidence in the *Daily Herald*, recently subordinated to party control, and less surprisingly a tendency to dismiss the array of Labour weeklies. For him to go begging, cloth cap in hand, was symbolic of an immaturity that his party was speedily to outgrow. If Labour operated under a journalistic handicap, it was hardly evident at the polls. There, as indirectly in the press, Liberal weakness worked to its advantage. Arthur Shadwell, editor of the 'moderate' *Democrat*, was too 'intensely relieved at the removal of Mr Lloyd George' to pay much heed to Labour's programme: 'The country needs a quieter, steadier, and more normal conduct of its affairs; and this means turning to the Right, not to the Left' (4 and 11 November). Garvin, too, recognized the reality of polarization. Writing to Grigg, just elected at Oldham on the National Liberal ticket, he ventured that 'either Unionism or Socialism ... will have to be the basis of Government in the future. Each will get accretions from the middle things.'[2]

Labour politicians, especially those with part-time backgrounds in journalism, paid homage to the nineteenth-century belief that newspaper coverage was the functional equivalent of electoral support. They were seldom dissuaded, even when the parliamentary advance of their party haltingly showed otherwise. Full-time newspapermen, who came more directly into contact with the predilections of democracy through a market that consistently expanded at a faster rate than the franchise, took a clearer and indeed a more cynical view of what people read, why they read it, and with what practical effect. 'Oh, the

---

[1] Henderson to 'Dear Mr Editor,' 20 October 1922, and Scott to Henderson, 26 October 1922 (copy), *Guardian* Archives.
[2] Garvin to Grigg, 20 November 1922, Grigg Papers. As Conservative MP for Altrincham (1933–45), Grigg was one such accretion.

Great British Public,' exclaimed Blatchford, who had 'just been looking at the *Daily Sketch*', so hot a property that it was quickly to pass from Hulton to Rothermere to the Berrys, who merged it with the *Daily Graphic* in 1926. In the racy pages of the *Sketch*, Blatchford found 'a portrait of a "beautiful" film actress, who is to marry the son of a multi-millionaire, "the salad-dressing King"'. One of the founding fathers of socialist journalism, Blatchford ruefully compared the mass circulation of the *Sketch* with the precipitous decline of the *Clarion*, a child which he was soon forced to abandon. 'The Perisher does not pay and is it any wonder. Look at the *Daily Mail*,' he told a friend. 'It is a rotten rag. But ----?'[1]

The *Clarion*, needless to say, lacked the resources to compete with the *Sketch*, much less the *Mail*. More tellingly, it lacked the essential frivolity. Its folksy and discursive quality, which had seemed refreshing to the late Victorians, was an anachronism; its audacity had paled; and its gift for proselytizing had deserted it. Blatchford, who never lost his penchant for nautical metaphors, watched from the shore as the *Clarion* 'trimmed sails and goes down gallantly without a squeal. She was the cleanest thing in journalism and won the respect of her opponents.'[2] By then, cleanliness was no asset and to claim the respect of one's opponents was tantamount to an admission of defeat.

---

[1] Blatchford to William Palmer, 30 December 1922 and 6 March 1923, Blatchford Papers.
[2] Blatchford to Palmer, 15 July 1923, Blatchford Papers.

Twelve

TROUBLEMAKERS

The magnitude of the Conservative majority in the 1922 General Election promised to usher in an era of calm. In fact, the ensuing period saw nothing of the sort. Two further elections were called in short order, allowing no repose either in Fleet Street or at Westminster. In response, the political press continued its contortions, which quickened to resemble the movements of St Vitus's Dance.

As parties changed hands and directions, broke apart and came together, so did the newspaper properties that attached to them. More often than not, however, the journalistic ramifications were delayed. The *Daily Telegraph*, having gone out on a coalitionist limb, was now cut off. In the early weeks of 1923, Gwynne repeatedly 'heard ... on very good authority that the *Daily Telegraph* is for sale'. But five years and two managing editorships were to pass before Lord Burnham finally sold his family heirloom to the Berrys, who have since retained it as their own. For the first few months of Dawson's second editorship, until foreign and imperial controversies arose, *The Times* betrayed no sign of change, 'except in respect of tone', and even that was arguable.[1]

In the spring of 1923, when normalcy had seemingly returned, the Liberals engaged in serious attempts to put their publishing houses in order, usually with a view to facilitating the rapprochement that was to come of necessity. Massingham departed in April from the *Nation*, where the new management alarmed Scott by evincing a tendency 'to emphasize the differences between Liberalism & Labour, instead of interpreting their essential unity of spirit & aim'. For his own part, Scott worked to implement 'a scheme of amalgamation' along progressive lines. His spirit of conciliation during the election campaign had not been reciprocated by the *Daily Herald* (7 November 1922), which mocked the way that 'the *Manchester Guardian* ... still goes on talking about Liberals and Tories as if there were a difference between them'.[2]

Antagonisms between the rival Liberal camps were more personal than

---

[1] Gwynne to Lady Bathurst, 22 January 1923, Bathurst Papers; *History of the Times*, IV, part 2, 794–95.
[2] Scott to Hammond, 24 January 1923, Hammond Papers; entries for 8–9 March 1923, Scott, *Political Diaries*, pp. 437–39.

ideological, but no easier to efface. The *Manchester Guardian*, having just concluded an agreement to purchase the *Manchester Evening News* and absorb its profits, was enviably equipped to take a lead. The Westminster Press group, its counterpart on the Asquithian side, was mired in financial difficulties. Sir Donald Maclean, defeated at the polls by a Conservative who carried Lloyd George's informal endorsement, was informed that payments on the pre-preference shares had to be met before 'a further loan from the Bankers' could be negotiated. Although an outright majority of Westminster voting shares were held by Whitehall Securities, owned by Lord Cowdray and managed by his son, Major Harold Pearson, sizeable blocks were divided between the Rowntree Charitable Trust, the nominees of Liberal headquarters in Abingdon Street, and a number of 'outside shareholders', some of whom were partial to Lloyd George. These complicated affairs demanded urgent attention that proved a distraction from ordinary politics.[1]

One of the strongest proponents of Liberal reunification and Lib-Lab accord was Beaverbrook, whose aim – as discerned by his biographer – 'was to destroy the electoral relics of Coalition'. While he would have preferred a firm pledge to pursue Imperial Preference, 'Beaverbrook had good reason to be content with the government which he had helped to create', at least until his advice was ignored over the question of the British war debt to the United States. Rothermere, a press lord of far wider commercial girth, hungered after a slice of Beaverbrook's reputed influence. *The Times* had eluded him, but his brother's death had left him master of the *Daily Mail*, the *Evening News*, the *Weekly Dispatch*, the *Daily Mirror*, the *Sunday Pictorial*, a trio of papers in Glasgow, and a host of magazines. Writing to Beaverbrook from Paris on 26 April 1923, Rothermere proposed that 'sometime early in June ... you, Bonar and myself' should get together for

> a discussion as to how his administration can be made one of the most successful of modern times .... If Bonar places himself in my hands I will hand him down to posterity at the end of three years as one of the most successful Prime Ministers in history, and if there is a general election I will get him returned again. This may sound boastful but I know exactly how it can be done.

Rothermere never had his chance. Within weeks, Bonar Law fell fatally ill and terminated his premiership. 'I am out of politics now,' he wrote to Rothermere ('My dear Harold') on 21 May, 'and wish to tell you how very grateful I am to you for the support which you gave me when I needed it

---

[1] Ayerst, *Guardian*, p. 484; statements of 6 April and 4 June 1923, and J. H. Macdonald to Maclean, 21 March 1923, Cowdray Papers.

most .... The part your papers have taken in making it easy for me to resign has been splendid.'¹

Beaverbrook, whose moment of glory had been brief, weighed the alternatives and relished none of them. The leading contenders were Curzon, 'handicapped by his personal unpopularity', and Baldwin, who was 'closer in touch with the machine and the constituencies', but who would have to learn to 'work the Press in his own interest – an art for which apparently he has no inclination or talent'. Derby was a 'dark horse ... who would bring Austen Chamberlain back to the Government as his contribution'. On the grounds 'that if you back a man for the Premiership, you are more or less obliged to support him afterwards', Beaverbrook stayed his hand in the hope 'of regaining a complete independence for my own policies'.²

The Times boosted Baldwin's stock by dwelling upon the problems that would confront any government led from the House of Lords. The *Morning Post* did not stick at constitutional proprieties. Gwynne could 'entirely agree' with Lady Bathurst's opinion 'that a peerage should not be a bar – even in these days – to the Premiership', but considered Baldwin 'immeasurably superior' to Curzon, 'a bad and wicked man', who 'would have ruined the Party and brought the Labour people in'. The *Daily Telegraph*, hopelessly out of step, plumped for Curzon and sent a team of photographers to Paddington Station on Whit Monday, the 22nd, to greet him; they recorded an expression of patrician confidence that did not last out the day. 'The King's Choice', as *The Times* called it, was Baldwin, under whom Curzon consented to serve. Among the major Conservative papers, only the *Telegraph* confessed to regrets. The *Manchester Guardian* broke rank to praise the appointment, which the *Daily Chronicle* and the *Westminster Gazette* joined to belittle.³

Baldwin, whose ascent had been remarkably swift, had the extra asset of being relatively unfamiliar. Retaining the Exchequer, which he intended to keep warm for McKenna, he kept his ministerial adjustments to a minimum. Hopeful of mending the rift within the party, he discussed his plans with Dawson, who came to Downing Street on the 23rd. The relationship between them was to be a close one. Baldwin did not inherit his predecessor's rapport with Beaverbrook, whom he believed – perhaps mistakenly – to have intrigued against him, and his relations with Rothermere were poisoned from the start. According to Amery, Rothermere made the mistake of trying 'with Baldwin what he had done with Bonar', bargaining his 'support for a place in the Cabinet for himself and an under-secretaryship for Esmond'. Asked whether 'there was

---

¹ *Sunday Express*, 19 November 1922; Taylor, *Beaverbrook*, pp. 201–202; Rothermere to Beaverbrook, 26 April 1923, Beaverbrook Papers, C/282a; Bonar Law to Rothermere, 21 May 1923 (copy), Bonar Law Papers, 108/9/63.
² Beaverbrook to Borden, 10 May 1923, quoted in Taylor, *Beaverbrook*, p. 207. For a conflicting view, see Davidson, *Memoirs*, pp. 158–65.
³ Gwynne to Lady Bathurst, 28 May 1923, Bathurst Papers; *also see* Keith Middlemas and John Barnes, *Baldwin* (London, 1969), pp. 166–70.

anything else', Rothermere said 'that he would also appreciate a further step up in the Peerage, and then Baldwin replied that there was no question of him getting any of the things he wanted'.[1]

Acclaimed by *The Times* as being 'singularly free from self-advertisement' (23 May), Baldwin nevertheless appreciated the value of publicity. F. Stanley Jackson, who had assumed the party chairmanship in March, was particularly useful in this regard. By and large, the newspapermen themselves saw to Baldwin's needs. Strachey, who had hailed his advent as 'inevitable', promised 'to make certain changes' in the *Spectator* to their mutual advantage. Beginning in October, that journal would go to press 'a day earlier' so as to ensure distribution in 'all parts of Great Britain by Friday morning'. Its editorial content would 'emphasize very strongly ... that the Unionist & Constitutional party must not be afraid of being & also proclaiming itself as, the most truly democratic party in the State'. Strachey did not 'of course suggest for a moment' that the Prime Minister 'should give us a blank cheque but merely that you should bless our endeavour in this direction' in the form of a signed article. From long experience, he knew that Baldwin had 'to be very careful about the Press and its jealousies'. Moreover, he did not wish it to be said that the *Spectator* had become '*the* party organ or even *a* party organ'. It was precisely because the journal occupied a 'kind of independent-non-partizan position' that Strachey thought that it 'would help'.[2] His logic was quaint and, in any case, his timing was wrong. By October, Baldwin was committed to a programme of tariffs that the *Spectator* could hardly be expected to swallow, much less champion. 'Protection is the evil genius of the Unionist Party,' it declaimed with a certainty that Conservative Free Fooders were 'not going to vote down one set of economic fallacies [*i.e.* socialism] in order to secure the triumph of another set, which they regard with even greater aversion' (3 and 10 November).

In the meantime, Beaverbrook and Rothermere turned from political to corporate mergers. Sir Edward Hulton was known to be dying and anxious to dispose of his newspaper interests, concentrated in Manchester and London. The Berry brothers were definitely interested, and Beaverbrook moved to pre-empt their bid. 'Will the Midland Bank honour my cheque for one million pounds?' he asked McKenna, its chairman. With McKenna's assurances, Beaverbrook remitted this amount with five times more to follow within the week. Before the balance was due, he had transferred the package to Rothermere for six million pounds. As his brokerage fee, he deducted the *Evening Standard*, swollen by its concurrent absorption of the *Pall Mall Gazette*. To be strictly accurate, Beaverbrook traded a 49 per cent interest in Express Newspapers for a 51 per cent controlling interest in the *Evening Standard*, which he

---

[1] Entry of 17 July 1923, *The Amery Diaries*, I (eds. J. Barnes and D. Nicholson; London, 1980), 334.
[2] Strachey to Baldwin, 21 August 1923 (copy), Strachey Papers.

coveted for reasons best known to himself. The result was to make him and Rothermere minority partners in each other's enterprises, an arrangement that lasted until 1933. Rothermere sold the Hulton provincial titles – with the *Glasgow Daily Record* thrown in for good measure – to the Berrys in 1924, and disgorged the *Daily Sketch* the following year. His total profit was estimated at £1,800,000. The Berry brothers (later Lords Camrose and Kemsley) and their confederate, Sir Edward Iliffe (Conservative MP for Tamworth and later 1st Baron Iliffe), eventually auctioned off these properties (excluding the *Sketch*) for £2,400,000 more than they had paid Rothermere for them. Thus, everyone did exceedingly well. As Francis Williams has remarked: 'The mounting profits from newspaper production at this period provided ample commercial justification for such profitable buying and selling – if commercial justification were the only test'. For these men, it was the crucial one.[1]

On the afternoon of 3 October 1923, Gwynne heard 'on good authority' – as usual – 'that Beaverbrook is in with Rothermere in the purchase of the Hulton concerns'. (A report to this effect in that day's *Yorkshire Post* was flatly contradicted by Lancelot Storr, Davidson's personal assistant and soon-to-be head of the Conservative Policy Secretariat, who had 'information' that 'ascribes the purchase to others'.) On less good authority, Gwynne told Baldwin 'that L.G. is behind the deal, with ample promises'. The threat of a challenge from Lloyd George, backed by the press lords, was perpetually rumoured. Baldwin, who never ceased to quake at the prospect, was disquieted to learn that, before Lloyd George embarked on an American tour in September, he had 'declared that he was coming back to sweep the country on an Empire policy. So [we] will have to hustle with ours,' advised Gwynne. Hustle is exactly what Baldwin did. In a speech at Plymouth on 25 October, he embraced imperial protection as a cure for unemployment and, coincidentally, internal party ailments. Neville Chamberlain, then Chancellor of the Exchequer, later recalled that 'if we had not gone for T.R. in 1923, Ll.G. would have done so', and others were similarly convinced. That, along with inexperience, helps to account for what Baldwin's biographers have described as his 'illogical haste to appeal to the country' at the earliest opportunity.[2]

Lloyd George was across the Atlantic when Baldwin delivered his Plymouth speech. The *Daily Chronicle* anticipated his reply on the 29th in a leading article written by C. A. McCurdy, the National Liberal member for Northampton and chairman of the *Chronicle* board. Baldwin had created a 'great divide', declared McCurdy, who did not doubt that 'all Liberals will be on the Free

[1] Taylor, *Beaverbrook*, pp. 214–15; Williams, *Dangerous Estate* (London, 1957), pp. 174–75, and *The Right to Know* (London, 1969), pp. 98–102. In consecutive leading articles on 13 October, the *Yorkshire Post* deplored 'A Malicious Attack' in the *Sunday Express*, intended 'to undermine the personal standing of Mr Baldwin', and also 'the regrouping of the English Press' under Rothermere, with Beaverbrook's assistance.

[2] Gwynne to Baldwin, 3 October 1923 (copy), Gwynne Papers; Storr to Vice-Admiral Sir W. R. Hall, 3 October 1923, Davidson Papers; Middlemas and Barnes, p. 220.

Trade side'. On 9 November, when Lloyd George's ship docked at Southampton, Mond rushed abroad 'for fear Beaverbrook should capture him' by getting there first. His reward was a ringing 'Free Trade pronouncement'. Baldwin had inadvertently accomplished what no intermediary during the past seven years had been able to do. Lloyd George and Asquith joined to wage a concerted campaign from a makeshift platform. Lansbury, speaking as much for Labour as for the *Daily Herald*, was equally grateful for that 'famous Plymouth speech, which led to the General Election and our salvation'.[1]

The Conservative organization was scarcely ready for the conflict. The 'Outline of a Scheme for Conservative Propaganda' was prepared by D. M. Sutherland, whose credentials consisted of eight years as editor of the *Pall Mall Gazette*, preceded by two years at the *Evening Standard* and three years at the *Sheffield Daily Telegraph*. He urged the establishment of a Research Department to produce propaganda which

> would be circulated mainly through the morning, evening and Sunday newspapers .... Generally the purpose of the Propaganda would be for insertion primarily and mainly in those papers which are read chiefly by the people it is intended to reach and not as now in those organs which are already devoted to the interests of the Party and are read by its supporters .... For the purpose of political propaganda for the working classes the evening papers, especially in the provinces, and the Sunday newspapers provide the best media.

Only after the 'tariff election' of 1923, when 'the Party settled down to make use of its time in opposition constructively', was an appropriate apparatus devised, and with considerably more sophistication than Sutherland had recommended.[2]

In the short run, the Conservatives managed as best they could. *The Times*, unusually well informed at every turn, enjoyed direct access to the Prime Minister. The *Yorkshire Post* received intelligence from Jackson, who did not require a directorship to remind him of his family obligation, and from Admiral Sir Reginald Hall, now principal party agent. Beaverbrook scarcely exaggerated, however, when he recorded:

> On the expediency of this election the Conservative Press and Conservative headquarters were utterly at variance. Hardly more than one responsible Conservative organ thought a precipitate General Election on this issue advisable. The others were only dragged in by the hair of their heads.

---

[1] H. A. L. Fisher's diary, 9 November 1923, Fisher Papers; Lansbury, *Miracle*, p. 165.
[2] Memorandum by Sutherland, n.d. [1923], Baldwin Papers; John Ramsden, *The Making of Conservative Party Policy* (London, 1980), pp. 22–23.

Still later, he recalled that Baldwin's 'anger against me was much increased by my hostile attitude during the Election of 1923', which justified his predictions of disaster. 'The *Observer*, the *Morning Post* and the *Yorkshire Post* all declared that I was responsible for his defeat on that occasion,' though Beaverbrook himself 'held no such opinion'. There was no gainsaying that 'the verdict of those newspapers was not calculated to make him love me the more'.[1]

What Beaverbrook and Rothermere wanted was a good deal less clear than what they wanted to avert, namely a 'rushed' election in which 'Bonar Law's carefully constructed majority would be wantonly squandered'. When the *Daily Mail* called on 2 October for 'a serious plan of action', it did not have a dissolution in mind. At that point, neither did Baldwin, who dismissed the prospect one day only to revive it the next. Before proceeding to the polls, he made a desperate effort to bring Austen Chamberlain and Birkenhead into line, and possibly into the government. His failure to win them over made it all the more imperative to persevere, but at what pace? Opinion in the constituencies, communicated directly and through the press, was overwhelmingly negative. Neville Chamberlain noted that 'the *Sunday Times* backs the *Spectator* in its proposals for a referendum in lieu of a general election. I must say I think the idea is worth serious consideration.' Lord Younger forwarded a leading article from the *Scotsman* (7 November), which 'very accurately expresses the prevailing feeling up here' in favour of postponement. Apart from Garvin, who counselled Baldwin to 'act lively', few journalists were able to muster any degree of enthusiasm. The best that *The Times* could manage was to credit 'the sincerity of [Baldwin's] conviction ..., shown by the readiness with which he is prepared to risk the highest position in the State' (13 November).[2]

Rothermere and Beaverbrook – 'Harold' and 'Max' – exchanged information and advice in a series of telegrams, which document their transition from scepticism to hostility.[3] On 1 November, Rothermere announced that he had 'given my newspapers strict instructions not to commit themselves ... until I can judge whether Baldwin understands the subject and has the imagination and energy to go through with it'. Beaverbrook, 'very glad to know that you are delaying decisions about protection until Baldwin develops his plan', also pledged to 'make no commitment'. Two days later, he reported 'many Conservative members and candidates dreadfully upset by Baldwin's declaration at Manchester for general tariff and election. They say last election decided for five years of tranquillity and recuperation and Baldwin gives

---

[1] Mann to Hall, 12 October 1923 (copy), Davidson Papers; Beaverbrook, *Politicians and the Press*, p. 76, and *The Abdication of Edward VIII* (London, 1966), p. 25.

[2] Beaverbrook, *Politicians and the Press*, pp. 76–77; Neville Chamberlain to Baldwin, 4 November 1923, Younger to Baldwin, 7 November 1923, and Amery to Baldwin (quoting letters from Garvin), 10 November 1923, Baldwin Papers.

[3] Telegrams exchanged between Beaverbrook and Rothermere (copies as dated), Beaverbrook Papers, C/282a.

instead disturbance and uncertainty.' Yet it was futile, he admitted two days later, to resist on narrow 'grounds of tranquillity'. To Rothermere's query on the 5th whether there was 'any truth in the statement that General Election will be held November thirtieth', Beaverbrook wired that he saw 'no possibility'. A conversation with Baldwin that evening left him 'quite convinced that he is not contemplating election until early next year'.

The 'opposition' was still 'growing rapidly' on the 7th, when Beaverbrook heard 'many Conservative members say that they will decline to stand again if Baldwin insists on going to country now. Please let me know what policy you want ... to take in your Hulton newspapers,' he asked Rothermere, who refused 'to commit papers'. His fear, reiterated in telegrams on the 8th and 9th, was 'that divided tariffists will be smashed' in a December contest, 'and Labour will win many seats'. Beaverbrook, refreshed by a weekend at Cherkley with Lloyd George, Churchill, Birkenhead, and Austen Chamberlain as his guests, was full of gossip on the 14th. By then, Baldwin had fixed 6 December as the polling date, and Beaverbrook ventured to 'think Baldwin will be defeated and George strengthened if political tactics adopted'. To this end, he requested Rothermere to 'let me on your behalf run policy of Hulton Manchester newspapers on Conservative Free Trade lines'. From the south of France, far enough away to 'laugh consumedly at the political situation', Rothermere declined to play along. 'Being of no party I have no intention of committing the papers until I see a Government and policy entirely to my liking,' he proclaimed on the 14th. 'As you know I am a convinced protectionist. Cannot speak with different voices [in] London and Manchester,' he went on the next day. His considered judgment, however, was that the 'cause of protection will be best served' if he undertook to 'advise electors to vote for Liberal candidate if there is no downright tariff candidate' on the ballot.

It was fanciful to suggest, as Amery did, that Baldwin might have conciliated Beaverbrook and Rothermere by dealing with them personally rather than through intermediaries. Their disaffection was much too deeply rooted, and separately rooted besides. Beaverbrook, sly and sprightly, was an Ariel who no longer had a Prospero to direct him. Rothermere, whose 'mind ... had a stodgy texture', had the bearing of a Caliban. Crude and heavy-handed, he lacked 'the redeeming virtue which Beaverbrook shared with Churchill, a naive delight in his own machinations'. Whereas Beaverbrook revelled in the contradictions of his impulses, Rothermere was brutally insensitive to his own. For example, on 20 November, the lunchtime edition of his *Evening News* advertised 'An Article by Lord Rothermere, "My Plea for Tariffs", ... in next Sunday's *Sunday Pictorial*'. In the 6.30 edition that day, the text was altered to portend 'An article by Lord Rothermere, "Should Free Trade Have One More Chance?"' The ultimate appearance of the article did little to clarify its author's ideas or intentions. 'It is because I feel that Mr Baldwin's tariff proposals do not go half far enough,' he lamely reasoned, 'that I ask: Should we give Free Trade one more chance?' In other words, half a cheap loaf was worse than none at all.[1]

'There were times,' Paul Addison has written, 'when Rothermere appeared to have a vested interest in prophesying doom', and this was certainly one of them. As he saw it, the nation, the empire, and the press were collectively headed for the rocks. 'Tariffs or no tariffs *there is a bad time coming*,' he warned Beaverbrook, whom he advised: 'Make as much as you can now . . . . If I were you I should cut down your expenditure to the bone, then float the *Express* with the *Standard*. You could get a million & still control the business thro' deferred shares.' His business transactions, inseparable from his attempts at statesmanship, were carried out *avant le déluge*.[2]

Such pessimism was a common attitude on the political right, where the spread of socialism was variously apprehended as a threat to the social order, a challenge to the constitution, a rejection of imperial values, a danger to national security, and a death-blow to capitalism. Lady Bathurst, for one, saw the writing on the wall in ten-foot-high crimson letters. Gwynne, 'doing my best under the most difficult circumstances to make the *M.P.* strong & flourishing', had offered to resign the previous February, when he knew he had 'quite lost your confidence'. In May, Lady Bathurst indicated – not for the first time – that she was willing to be bought out. 'The fact that the paper is up for sale, if generally known, will adversely affect its value' as a political organ, Gwynne told her. Then, midway through the November campaign, she suddenly announced her impending departure. Perhaps, like another countess who rang up Philip Snowden to ask 'frantically . . . if it were true that the first thing the Labour Party would do would be to cut the throats of every aristocrat and steal all their property', she actually believed what she read in the *Morning Post*. More probably, she shared Rothermere's foreboding that the days of prosperity were numbered. In any case, Gwynne thought it 'appropriate perhaps but very distressing to us all' that she should choose to 'end your proprietorship in a great fight for protection', a cause dear to the hearts of her father and grandfather.[3]

Gwynne did not allow either the uncertainty at the *Morning Post* or the vexation within Conservative ranks to prevent him from extolling Baldwin as a second Joe Chamberlain. But the newspapers that supported Baldwinian protectionism were few and far between. 'The only whole-hearted backers of the adventure were the *Morning Post* and the *Yorkshire Post* – and they were

---

[1] Amery, *My Political Life*, II (London, 1953), 283; Middlemas and Barnes, p. 257; Paul Addison, 'Patriotism Under Pressure,' in Peele and Cook, eds., *Politics of Reappraisal*, p. 190; *Evening News*, 20 November 1923, quoted in A. G. Gardiner, *Certain People of Importance* (London, 1929 ed.), p. 237.

[2] Addison, 'Patriotism Under Pressure,' p. 192; Rothermere to Beaverbrook [15] November 1923 (copy), Beaverbrook Papers, C/282a.

[3] Gwynne to Lady Bathurst, 8 February, 28 May, and 21 November 1923, Bathurst Papers; Snowden, *An Autobiography* (London, 1934), II, 607–608.

mouthpieces of the Chief Whip's office,' commented the *Fortnightly Review* (February 1924). The *Saturday Review* (24 November 1923) added itself, *The Times*, and the *Daily Telegraph* to that list; along with Liberal and Labour journals, the *Daily Mail* and the *Evening News* were counted as archopponents; and the *Spectator*, the *Daily Express*, the *Daily Graphic*, the *Daily Mirror*, and the *Daily Sketch* were classified as 'Laodicean in attitude, or else non-committal'. This inventory was corroborated by the *Manchester Guardian* (28 November), which detailed a 'Civil War in the Tory Press' that pitted newspapers against Baldwin and each other:

> The indignation and perplexity of London Conservatives over the antics of the main part of the Conservative Press in London moves even Liberals to sympathy. Nothing remotely resembling the present state of things has ever been known in London before. No evening paper is supporting the Government .... How different from the days when the newspaper posters and caricatures of the popular Tory Press furnished the chief ammunition of the party!

To the *Guardian*, 'the spectacle of the Tory Press vigorously whacking one another on the head every morning is a healthy stimulant'. The *Daily Mail* and the *Daily Express* were busily attacking *The Times*, the *Express* (ignoring Blumenfeld's antecedents) 'not scrupling to bring in the fact of Major Astor's American birth, while the *Morning Post* pours broadsides into both of them, and they accuse the high Tory organ of inconsistency'.

That the Conservatives would lose ground was a foregone conclusion. The results on 6 December gave them 258 seats, 87 fewer than they had won under Bonar Law's command. Although still the largest party in Parliament, they lost their majority. Baldwin, held to blame, withstood a movement to displace him. 'Above all things', Gwynne 'most earnestly' begged him 'not to do anything in a hurry. Do take plenty of time.' He was relieved to discover that Lady Bathurst agreed 'that Baldwin should remain. I think that he is the only man whose character and statesmanship can avert a great disaster in the future.' Most emphatically, Rothermere did not agree and vowed 'unrelenting opposition if Baldwin stays on'. Convinced that the parliamentary deadlock made a 'new election certain in or before May', he gave the Tories a last chance to pick a leader who met with his approval before the 'turn of year', when he intended to 'start campaign [to] give Liberals a chance'.[1]

With or without Rothermere's blessing, the Liberals were in no shape to seize the initiative. With 158 MPs, they occupied a quarter of the seats in the new House of Commons, and needed time for their wounds to heal. Although Lloyd

---

[1] Gwynne to Baldwin, 7 December 1923, Baldwin Papers; Gwynne to Lady Bathurst, 10 December 1923, Bathurst Papers; Rothermere to Beaverbrook, 10 December 1923 (telegram; copy), Beaverbrook Papers, C 282a.

George had contributed generously towards election expenses, and wound up his *Lloyd George Liberal Magazine* as a further gesture, he balked at handing over – or indeed accounting for – the total funds at his disposal. Maclean gave him the benefit of the doubt: Lloyd George 'had very heavy newspaper commitments – particularly with regard to the *Chronicle* – which, while productive of good revenue, required liquid capital to be held in reserve'. In further negotiations that summer, Hudson and Maclean learnt that Lloyd George 'had a very large sum invested in newspaper properties bringing in a substantial income, which we gathered to be round about £50,000 a year'.[1]

The Liberal press, therefore, was one of the stumbling-blocks. It also worked against full-scale Liberal reunion in other, more subtle ways. The *Westminster Gazette* inclined to the view that, if the Liberals could not form a minority administration, they should explore the possibilities of collaboration with the Conservatives. The *Daily News*, with the *Star* following suit, favoured 'a Coalition Cabinet of Liberals and Labour men' who, together, would overpower the Tories. George Armstrong, 'for a good many years assistant editor of the *Daily News*' and manager 'of their Northern (Manchester) edition while it lasted', fell out with Stuart Hodgson over this issue. Armstrong remonstrated 'that there was no possibility of that course being adopted' and, contrary to editorial instructions, wrote a leader (8 December) 'advocating instead a purely Labour Government with Liberal support as far as the respective programmes agreed – which was very far!' Soon afterwards, Armstrong informed Scott 'that he is leaving the *News*' and that he had applied to Perris for a position on the *Chronicle*. Scott put in a good word with Lloyd George on behalf of Armstrong: 'His views are pretty much those of the *M.G.* and he has I believe done a great deal of late years to keep the *D.N.* sane and straight.' However adamantly Liberals maintained that reunification was complete, their newspaper properties signified otherwise.[2]

Asquith, with the 'hearty concurrence' of Lloyd George and Simon, was prepared to try the experiment of permitting Labour to take office. It is difficult to see what else he could have done. His pragmatism, disguised as magnanimity, was to rebound against him. With 191 seats, 33 more than the Liberals, Labour resented its dependence on Liberal patronage and especially the condescension of the Liberal press. The *Daily Herald*, aware that its own circulation of roughly 400,000 did not suffice, complained on 14 November that other journals had universally slighted one of Ramsay MacDonald's major campaign addresses: as opposed to fifty-four column inches in the *Herald*, the speech occupied ten inches in the *Daily Mail*, five and three-quarter inches in the *Daily News*, four and three-quarter inches in the

---

[1] Maclean to Gladstone, 10 January 1924 (copy), and memorandum of 1 July 1924, Maclean Papers.

[2] Armstrong, *Memories* (London, 1944), p. 195; Scott to Lloyd George, 21 December 1923 (copy), *Guardian* Archives.

Daily Chronicle, three and a half inches in the *Daily Express*, and a mere two and a half inches in the *Westminster Gazette*. Scott wrote sympathetically to MacDonald:

> I gather that you and your party feel that they have been unfairly treated by the press in the matter of reports during the election and we ourselves received a strong letter of protest ... from one of your supporters. I looked into the matter and found indeed that for several days together no report of your speeches had appeared in the paper. That was not our fault, unless it be a fault that we relied on the Press Assn., as we relied upon them for practically all election speeches outside our own area. As they sent no reports on these days we could publish none .... In any case I hope you will understand that there was no intentional ignoring on our part – far from it.

It suited MacDonald, however, to construe the general neglect as a boycott. 'Liberal papers like the *Daily News* have never been more dishonest nor more gleeful in their gloating over the prospects of a Labour defeat,' he declared in the *New Leader*. Willing to absolve the *Manchester Guardian*, he continued to 'think ... that the way that the *Daily News* and the *Westminster Gazette* behaved was contemptible. We expect nothing better from the *Daily Mail* and such miserable products.'[1]

MacDonald began to form his Cabinet ('the most horrible job of my life'), but did not become Prime Minister until 22 January 1924, the day after the Liberals had combined with Labour to turn out Baldwin. Prepared for the worst, Rothermere calculated that, within 'two months', the first 'Labour Government will shake economic structure to its foundations', with newspapers bound to suffer a 'loss probably fifty per cent advertisement revenue for long period'. On the contrary, Beaverbrook celebrated 1924 as a bumper year for advertising receipts. The *Daily Express* profited at the expense of the *Morning Post*, which frightened away customers by drastic cut-backs and rumours of 'its projected sale'. In Fleet Street as in Parliament, the Liberals were caught in a squeeze. Starmer advised Cowdray that they could not expect that any 'paper produced to promote the *Westminster Gazette* policy will ever be a great financial success because, strange as it may appear, Conservative papers appeal a great deal more to advertisers than do papers which support Liberal Principles'.[2]

The advent of Labour held the promise of a fillip to the circulation of the

---

[1] Scott to MacDonald, 9 December 1923 (copy), *Guardian* Archives; MacDonald, 'The Task Before the Party,' *New Leader*, 14 December 1923; MacDonald to Scott, 11 December 1923, quoted in Scott, *Political Diaries*, p. 448. R. W. Lyman has tabulated that, 'in a sample seven successive days in November', *The Times* announced 'twenty-three Labour meetings as against 212 for Liberals and Conservatives'. *The First Labour Government* (London, 1957), p. 66.

[2] Rothermere to Beaverbrook, 19 December 1923 (telegram; copy), Beaverbrook Papers, C/282a; Beaverbrook, *Politicians and the Press*, p. 82; Gwynne to Lady Bathurst, 6 January 1924, and Peacock to Lady Bathurst, 7 January 1924, Bathurst Papers; Starmer to Cowdray, 6 March 1924 (draft), Cowdray Papers.

Daily Herald, which barely 'paid our way from advertisements and sales revenue'. Thus, the paper had commercial as well as partisan reasons to rejoice. 'To-day begins the most difficult and dangerous period in the history of the British Labour Movement,' it intoned with due solemnity on 23 January. 'Up to now its political representatives have been critics. . . . Now the great Movement which they have behind them waits eagerly for its leaders to justify the confidence and loyalty that have placed them where they are.' Not every Labour journalist was so reverent. Brailsford had doubts about certain ministerial appointments, and Blatchford went further to regret the presence of MacDonald at the helm. 'And don't you feel proud and elated when you see that our *Clarion* hardships and sacrifices have resulted in making "Ramsay and Macdonald" prime minister of England?' he remarked wryly. 'Talk about the irony of fate. What?' Nevertheless, Blatchford was sufficiently a loyalist to forgo the '40 quid a week' he was getting from Rothermere, whose diatribes were intolerable. 'Glory to God. I have sacked Lord Rothermere,' he announced after breaking his contract with the *Daily Mail*. 'I really could not stand him any longer: his bloated syndicate, his contemptible panic, his stupidity and his impudent attempts to down Mr Baldwin and boss the Government. So I sacked him. It was a point of honour. . . . I didn't feel clean.'[1]

Beaverbrook pointed up yet another irony. 'Heretofore no British Ministry for a hundred years had been without considerable newspaper backing,' he argued with reasonable accuracy. 'The Socialists' – as he and his editors made it a practice to refer to the Labour Party – 'could claim only one organ with a small circulation, and this newspaper could not be depended on by the new Prime Minister, for it really represented the extreme Left of his own supporters.' As a captain of 'the so-called "Capitalist Press"', Beaverbrook went out of his way to compensate for this deficiency by according 'the new Ministry a considerate welcome on the whole'. Its foreign policy, directed by MacDonald, inspired 'great expectations'. Baldwin stood lower down 'in the descending scale of values', Beaverbrook wrote in the *Sunday Express* (17 February). 'Now that he is stripped of power and *patronage* he must rely on his own capabilities', which had 'so far proved of second rank'. Lord Astor would not have disputed this assessment, though he would not have wished to see it stated in the *Observer*. 'The real strength of Baldwin is *not* his honesty (the electors begin to get bored with that) or his "grip" (which so far has been conspicuous by its absence . . .) or his imagination in framing policy,' he told Strachey. 'His strength lies in the absence of any outstanding personality to take his place.' Strachey could not help but 'agree with what you say about Baldwin. Still, I cannot believe that the Unionist Party is so hopelessly devoid of leadership that we must put up with a man who has proved so incapable of understanding the country and the party.'[2]

[1] Lansbury, *Miracle*, p. 165; Blatchford to Palmer, 2 and 22 January 1924, Blatchford Papers.
[2] Beaverbrook, *Politicians and the Press*, p. 83; Beaverbrook to Arthur Brisbane, n.d., quoted in Taylor, *Beaverbrook*, p. 220; Astor to Strachey, 18 February 1924, and Strachey to Astor, 21

Momentarily, Beaverbrook and Rothermere assumed that they had found an alternative in Churchill, whom they encouraged to stand – with 'the full support of their press' – as an independent Constitutionalist in an upcoming by-election in the Abbey division of Westminster. Twice defeated as a Liberal, Churchill was ready to mute his colours as a prelude to changing them back to Tory blue. His wife, always more cautious, implored him not to 'let the Tories get you too cheap'. She was particularly anxious about press relations. '*The Times* I feel sure is against you at present or at any rate not helping – Couldn't we cultivate John Astor gradually? I feel that though no genius he would be quite as much help as Beaverbrook. *The Times* can really do more than the *Daily Express.*' With Baldwinian rhetoric, *The Times* condemned Churchill as 'an essentially disruptive force' (6 March). Despite the fulsome assurances of the *Evening Standard* that support for Churchill 'was increasing' (1 March) to the point that volunteers were ringing up 'so numerously that the Paddington telephone exchange operators wish he had a dozen lines' (6 March), the local constituency organization declined to adopt him. 'Churchill Wins,' exulted the *Evening Standard* on 20 March, only to admit the next day that a recount had given a 43-vote edge to the official Conservative candidate.[1]

Gwynne warned Baldwin that Churchill had to be stopped in the Abbey division, 'your "Jena or Austerlitz" – make no mistake'. At the *Morning Post*, Gwynne seemed to be facing his Waterloo. Amid bitter recriminations, which threatened to wreck the paper, its transfer went ahead. Gwynne appealed to Sir Walter Preston, one of the joint trustees and an occasional Conservative MP, 'to do all you can for Lady Bathurst', who had to be made to consider more than the financial side. 'Up to the present, Lady Bathurst has been and is today a shining example of disinterested patriotism,' he contended. But if it were true that she was negotiating with either Beaverbrook or Rothermere, 'she would be loathed and hated by the very people she now holds in respect. It would simply kill her if people turned their backs on her, it would ruin Apsley's political career', and it would discredit the *Morning Post*. 'If fishy people take it over it would die.'[2]

With Labour in office, if not exactly in power, Lady Bathurst became

---

February 1924 (copy), Strachey Papers. The Labour Government did not seem to affect Astor's style of life. R. M. Barrington-Ward, then with the *Observer*, lunched on 6 May 1924 with Astor, 'who was off for a temperance meeting after and then Newmarket for the 2000 Guineas tomorrow – two of his main interests'. Barrington-Ward's diary.

[1] Churchill to his wife [24] February 1924, and Clementine Churchill to her husband, 24 February 1924, quoted in Martin Gilbert, *Churchill*, V (London, 1976), 29–30; *also see* Chris Cook, 'By-Elections of the First Labour Government,' in *By-Elections in British Politics* (eds. C. Cook and J. Ramsden; London, 1973), pp. 53–61.

[2] Gwynne to Baldwin, 7 March 1924, Baldwin Papers; Gwynne to Preston, 21 January 1924 (copy), Gwynne Papers. The assumption that Sir Walter was the 'Preston' whom Gwynne addressed as co-trustee rests upon the recollection of Sir Kenneth Preston, who confirmed (letter to the author, 25 May 1982) that his father '*was* friendly with Lord and Lady Bathurst, who lived at Cirencester, some nine miles away', and shared his political views.

fatalistic. Politics afforded her no incentives, and the financial prospects were bleak. 'We are paying £130,000 a year more in wages than we did in my father's day, in order to produce a greatly inferior paper,' she complained to Gwynne. 'I could have made the paper pay but I should have had to give my whole life to it & I should even then have been met by unsurmountable Trades Union obstacles. If journalists wish to kill newspapers they are going the right way.' To no avail, her business manager tried to explain that 'the whole business of the production of a newspaper has changed since 1907'. New methods of distribution 'and the immense extension in the field of news activities, home and foreign, have increased editorial costs greatly. Competition for circulation regardless of cost is at the root of half the troubles from which Fleet Street is suffering.' Gwynne defended his subordinates: 'Nearly every one of the staff, who has done good and signal service, has been offered much larger salaries to leave us and, since I have been editor, not a single one has accepted these offers .... That there have been increases in salaries' was a fact he would 'frankly admit, but that was forced upon us by the National Union of Journalists, whose terms the Newspaper Proprietors Association accepted towards the end of the war'.[1]

In late February, the Unionist Central Office intervened through the party chairman to see that the *Morning Post* did not come to grief. 'I can assure you that I am most anxious to find a way of putting the *M.P.* project through satisfactorily to all,' Gwynne heard from Jackson, who added 'that S.B. is very keen'. With difficulty, Jackson assembled a consortium with the Duke of Northumberland at its head. Other investors included the Duke of Buccleuch (who was 'not sure that it would be to the advantage of the future that the Duke of Northumberland's name should be too prominent'), Lords Leconfield and Banbury, Sir Percy Bates, Sir Henry Page Croft, John (later 1st Baron) Gretton, and Sir James Craig as a possible conduit for 'Ulster money'. That spring, the *Morning Post* was handed over 'for £470,000, of which £100,000 was paid in cash and the remainder in debentures'. The return was predictably disappointing. By November 1925, the expenditure had 'not only not earned' a profit, but further 'heavy losses [had] been made'.[2]

Gwynne's editorship and partisan attachments were happily undisturbed. Ian Colvin, who had worked under him for a dozen years, told Lady Bathurst that it was 'a consolation to us all that you are selling ... to the Duke of Northumberland: he is the man I should trust of all others to carry on the great traditions of the paper'. And Lady Bathurst herself was 'of course glad that the *Morning Post* will be owned by men of right principles & whose ideas are the same as ours'. Still, she harboured 'a slight resentment at the *way* the

---

[1] Lady Bathurst to Gwynne, 18 April 1924, Gwynne Papers; Peacock to Lady Bathurst, 1 February 1924, and Gwynne to Lady Bathurst, 4 February 1924, Bathurst Papers.
[2] Jackson to Gwynne, 29 February 1924, Buccleuch to Gwynne, 13 April 1924, and memorandum of 19 November 1925 (copy), Gwynne Papers.

transaction was carried out', specifically the motives imputed to her. 'Of course had the buyers been other than Die-hards I should have broken off negotiations even after the trustees had accepted the terms,' she disclosed. It pained her to think that Gwynne had 'believed that I would sell the *Morning Post* to Rothermere or the Jews or anyone – just as you were afraid before the war that the German Ambassador might influence me by flattery'. Lady Bathurst wanted to set the record straight; she was a businesswoman, but also a Borthwick.[1]

Gwynne, too, was concerned with the record. In the *Evening Standard* of 14 May, the 'Londoner's Diary' contained 'a mass of mis-statements' that he hastened to contradict. 'You say: "The *Morning Post* has for some time past been considered practically the official organ of the Conservative Party, and certainly has close relations with the Conservative Central Office."' In fact, he protested to Beaverbrook, 'I rescued the *Morning Post* from the Central Office. And as for the close relations', party officials would not hesitate to say 'that they regard the *Morning Post* as a thorn in their side'. Furthermore, Gwynne wished it to be known 'that I have never had any pressure of any kind put upon me by any single Director in this Company . . . . So if I have sinned, I have sinned on my own.'[2] That he reacted so strenuously to gossip was not surprising. Because that gossip contained more than a grain of truth, professional honour demanded that he at least dispute what he could not possibly disprove.

* * *

Sir Edward Grigg, now a Liberal MP without a 'National' prefix and later a Conservative MP with one, took a consistently shrewd approach to the relationship between politics and the press. Early in 1924, he recommended the rejection of a tirade that H. W. Massingham had submitted for publication in *The Round Table*, 'A Quarterly Review of the Politics of the British Empire' begun in 1910 under Milnerite auspices. Massingham's indictment struck Grigg as 'bad in tone and extremely confused in its criticism . . . . Let us have a first-rate article and leave the functions of the revivalist pulpit to other people,' he urged John Dove, the editor. From his own experience in Fleet Street and Downing Street, Grigg recognized the existence of a 'general problem presented by the whole press, good or bad, in the modern world – namely, political power and responsibility inextricably interwoven with the need for commercial success, and irresponsibility in the sense that the public cannot turn it out'. Culpability, however, was more diffuse than Massingham had allowed. Grigg 'could quote examples of misrepresentation from the *Daily Herald* which

---

[1] Colvin to Lady Bathurst, 13 April 1924, Bathurst Papers; Lady Bathurst to Gwynne, 18 April 1924, Gwynne papers.
[2] Gwynne to Beaverbrook, 14 May 1924, Beaverbrook Papers, C/148.

would do no discredit to the *Daily Mail*', and knew 'of even more august organs which pervert and suppress' the news. 'That is simply human nature, which seldom feels strongly without being partisan.'[1]

Although rarely so clearly perceived, the point had been reached at which journalistic and party political interests had diverged. Many politicians and a few editors worked to resist the trend, even occasionally to reverse it. Yet there was no mistaking the fact that, across the spectrum, old patterns of reciprocity no longer held to any meaningful extent. During the nine-month lifetime of the first Labour government, the leaders of each of the three parliamentary groups were more vulnerable to attack from the newspapers nominally behind them than from those avowedly against them. Baldwin's survival was a triumph over the disruptionist forces in Conservative journalism. Asquith led the Liberals until 1926 in the face of a debilitating estrangement from refractory elements in the Liberal press, who underlined the untenability of his position. MacDonald feuded with Labour editors, whose deviations he blamed for his reverses. Their respective predicaments, illustrative of a process of formal disengagement, require scrutiny.

Having led his party to defeat, thereby allegedly opening the floodgates to socialism, Baldwin could not escape censure. The 'pack of ravening wolves', described by his cousin as 'snarling at his heels', included Rothermere's 'Trust Press hovering round like a malevolent imp'. It did not go unnoticed by the *Evening Standard* (30 November 1923) that Baldwin's son, Oliver, had campaigned on Labour platforms. As indicated by the Abbey by-election, the attacks did not so much subside as assume a different form. To Strachey, who found it 'horrible ... to see the Press prostituted ... and used as the medium of a private vendetta', he postured that he was 'indifferent to Beaverbrook's attacks .... He lowers everything he touches .... He was spoiled by my predecessors.' Despite this air of unconcern, Baldwin suffered deeply.[2]

A conspicuous example of Baldwin's problem with press relations, and perhaps evidence of his ineptitude as well, was an interview he gave to F. W. Wilson, a reporter from the *People* who had requested 'further information as regards his statements of policy contained in his recent speeches'. Baldwin neglected to demand a proof copy of the article, which appeared on 17 May and purported to be Baldwin's 'reply to alleged intrigues' by Churchill and others. 'I hope you will treat the article in the *People* with the contempt it deserves,' Baldwin wrote to Churchill, 'and accept my assurance that the offensive remarks were never uttered by me.' That the *People* was owned by Grant Morden, a feckless Tory backbencher, compounded Baldwin's embarrassment. His threat of an injunction was one of the factors that drove Morden to

---

[1] Grigg to Dove, 19 January 1924, Grigg Papers. For the origins and intentions of *The Round Table*, see Walter Nimocks, *Milner's Young Men* (Durham, N.C., 1968), pp. 187–96.

[2] Philip Burne-Jones, quoted in Middlemas and Barnes, p. 257; Strachey to Baldwin, 7 May 1924 (copy), and Baldwin to Strachey, 9 May 1924, Strachey Papers.

abandon the property and did little credit to Swaffer's editorship. Wilson's reward was to become chief sub-editor on Beaverbrook's *Sunday Express*.[1]

The incident could have been averted had there existed the publicity apparatus that Baldwin had recently begun to create. His shadow cabinet, fortified by the membership of Austen Chamberlain and other ex-Coalitionists, set up a network of policy committees, each chaired by a shadow minister and all coordinated by a policy secretariat annexed to the Central Office. One of the ways in which this structure was to assist in the formulation and dissemination of policy was to secure greater and more reliable coverage for the speeches of 'Ministers', as Baldwin and his colleagues presumptuously designated themselves. 'Owing to the fact that practically the whole of the so-called popular press is closed to us', it was considered 'very important that we should give the amplest facilities to those papers which are prepared to report Ministers' speeches adequately', if possible by circulating typescript copies in advance. The use of film propaganda was explored, and the National Union was directed to overhaul its literature and publicity department under the command of someone 'with definite Conservative convictions and with an instinctive *flair* for politics'. John Ramsden has concluded 'that the policy exercise of 1924 played a part in the Conservative recovery of that year, if only by helping the Conservative leaders to recover their belief in their own ability to govern effectively'. An additional effect was to strengthen Baldwin's hand in dealing with the press lords, then and thereafter. Still, bolts had been loosened which could not easily be screwed tight. On the evening of 7 November 1925, Brooks 'wrote a leader lashing out at the Party system', which saw print in the next day's *Yorkshire Post*, reckoned to be 'the second most influential Tory paper in the kingdom, and perhaps the first, since the *Morning Post* is something now of a coterie sheet'.[2]

MacDonald and his associates, being ministers in the full sense, lacked the time – and arguably the administrative talent – to construct a comparable machinery. They relied by default on instruments that they found not only insufficient, but also treacherous. The *New Leader* and the *New Statesman* were both self-consciously intellectual and increasingly censorious. The Glasgow *Forward*, though it made room for the Prime Minister's weekly pronouncements, was tinged with the red dye of Clydeside. The *Daily Herald*, he complained in July (nine months after Raymond Postgate and other sympathizers with the Third International had been purged from its staff), was 'fast becoming a Communist organ'. At the same time that MacDonald publicly

[1] Statement by the Central Office, n.d., quoted in Middlemas and Barnes, p. 267; Baldwin to Churchill, 20 May 1924 (copy), Baldwin Papers; Arthur Christiansen, *Headlines All My Life* (New York, 1961), p. 35.

[2] Ramsden, *Conservative Party Policy*, pp. 23–24; memorandum by Sir Patrick Gower to 'The Chairman' [Jackson], 8 May 1924, Lord Stonehaven (formerly Sir John Baird) to Baldwin, 10 May 1924, and McNeill to Jackson, 19 May 1924 (copy), Baldwin Papers; Brooks's diary, 7 November 1925.

dismissed charges that the Labour Party was infiltrated by Communists, he privately condemned their disproportionate prominence in the Labour press. 'If Communists are to enjoy the luxury of a daily paper,' he told Henderson, 'they ought to find the money and the patronage for themselves, and not play the cuckoo game.'[1]

Hamilton Fyfe, the editor of the *Herald*, was infuriated by MacDonald's accusation that the paper had become 'a dumping-ground for rubbish which would be put in the waste-paper basket for anyone who knew his business or who was not out for mischief'. After thirty years in the trade, Fyfe was outraged to be told that 'I do not know my business as editor.... I have had to do with so many Prime Ministers,' he replied with warranted insolence,

> that I am not surprised by the petulant tone of your letter.... The *Herald* is the organ, not of your government, not of a Party, but of the Labour Movement. In that Movement there are many currents of opinion. It would be foolish to aim at making the policy of the *Herald* fit in with all these currents of opinion, but it is very important that no section should feel resentment at not being allowed to express its own views in its own newspaper.... It should help for a Prime Minister to keep in touch with the sentiments and convictions, the reactions and perplexities of those who have put him where he is.... You have been Prime Minister for eight months.... Isn't it just possible that you have something to learn too?

Fyfe would have stood on safer ground if the *Herald*'s circulation had increased, as did the *New Leader*'s, during Labour's tenure of office. Instead it declined from 419,000 at the time of the previous election to 354,000 the following October; and Lansbury, as general manager, regarded its critical stance as a contributing factor.[2]

MacDonald suffered a more direct blow from a peripheral source. Or, at any rate, he chose to treat it as one. On 25 July, the *Workers' Weekly* (which became the *Sunday Worker* in 1925, the *Daily Worker* in 1930, and the *Morning Star* in 1966) called upon British soldiers to 'let it be known that, neither in the class war nor in a military war, will you turn your guns on your fellow workers'. This 'incitement to mutiny', so classified by the director of public prosecutions, would have attracted little attention but for the controversial negotiations then in progress for an Anglo-Soviet treaty. Pursuant to MacDonald's skilful mediation to devise a more equitable plan for the payment of German reparations, the *Workers' Weekly* advocated the cancellation of Russia's pre-revolutionary debts and the appointment of a trade unionist as ambassador to Moscow. Inadvisedly, the Attorney-General (with Cabinet approval) took

[1] Rose Rosenberg (MacDonald's secretary) to J. S. Middleton, 28 July 1924, and MacDonald to Henderson, 11 August 1924, quoted in McKibbin, *Evolution*, p. 230.
[2] MacDonald to Fyfe, and Fyfe to MacDonald [August 1924], quoted in Fyfe, *My Seven Selves* (London, 1935), pp. 258–59; McKibbin, *Evolution*, pp. 231–32.

steps to prosecute J. R. Campbell, acting editor of the offending journal and – as it proved – a disabled veteran of the last war. Still more inadvisedly, the case was dropped and Cabinet complicity was denied after an outcry from Labour's rank and file. Simon helped the Conservatives to draft a censure motion, which Asquith tried to head off by moving for an investigation by a select committee. The Conservatives joined the Liberals to defeat the government, and MacDonald grasped at this opportunity to dissolve Parliament.[1]

It had been a trial for MacDonald to govern on the sufferance of the Liberals, whom he repaid by depicting as senescent and expendable. The *Manchester Guardian* thought it strange that 'the Prime Minister, who can be so sweet to the foreigner from whom he differs most widely, has nothing but unconcealed dislike and exaggerated suspicion for those who in this country stand nearest to him in politics' (3 October). The *New Statesman*, too, faulted him for ingratitude: 'If he had treated his Liberal allies with even common courtesy he might have remained in power not merely until 1925, but for some years to come, possibly even for a decade' (11 October). Neither could appreciate that MacDonald had no appetite for 'power' on such restrictive and humiliating terms. His strategy was to smite the Liberals, not to befriend them. As the *Daily Chronicle* commented on 21 October, eight days before the third poll in as many years, the Liberals' 'disinclination to enter upon an early struggle was well-known to all politicians' and to none more than MacDonald, who sought to exploit it.

'General Election and a busy time now in prospect, if the Campbell trial and the Russian Treaty together bring the Govt. down,' R. M. Barrington-Ward wrote in his diary on 2 October. 'I hope to God I don't have to go down to Plymouth' to campaign for Lady Astor. 'It is not my place: the *Observer* is my place.' For want of a good excuse, he 'spoke for 30 or 40 minutes' on the North Quay at Plymouth on the 19th. 'The rest of the two hours was heckling, question and answer.'[2] Political journalists were often obliged to do double duty.

The Conservatives blamed the Liberals for having put Labour into office. Labour blamed the Liberals for having cast them out. Caught in the middle, the Liberals offered no effective rejoinder. The *British Weekly*, stricken by the death of Robertson Nicoll and the enfeebled pangs of the Nonconformist Conscience, affirmed its 'position ... as a Liberal paper', but declared itself 'willing to give the idea of Liberalism a broad and inclusive interpretation' (16 October). That, in essence, was to define the Liberal dilemma in the 1924 campaign. Liberalism had been elasticized to stretch in either direction. The *Daily News* instructed its readers 'to vote against Tory candidates without exception' and, beyond that, to vote Labour in those 'rare cases' where a

---

[1] A. J. P. Taylor, *English History 1914–1945* (Oxford, 1965), pp. 218, 225; Lyman, *First Labour Government*, pp. 237–38.
[2] Barrington-Ward's diary, 2 and 19 October 1924.

wasted Liberal vote would benefit the protectionists (11 October). The *Daily Chronicle*, sensing that Conservatism posed 'a less immediate danger than Labourism', urged 'mutual support' between the older parties, with Liberals to vote for Conservative candidates where no Liberal was standing (29 October). As the Liberals fielded 113 fewer candidates than the previous year, those contingencies arose with fatal frequency.

At the eleventh hour, the campaign was enlivened by a release from the Foreign Office, which claimed to have intercepted a letter from Grigori Zinoviev, president of the Communist International, to his British comrades. Containing instructions for the organization of seditious activity, this document was taken as evidence that Labour politicians were either the knowing accomplices or the unwitting dupes of the Communists. A copy of the 'Red letter' mysteriously arrived at the office of the *Daily Mail*, which gave it full exposure. Conservative Party officials, including Jackson and Hall, were certainly 'implicated in its publication'. Davidson, who was not, had 'no doubt that the result of the election was affected by the Zinoviev Letter .... We would have got in in 1924,' he later recalled, 'but we would have had a smaller majority .... You will always find that it is when the country is scared of wild-cat schemes and wants safety that it turns to the Conservative Party.' Victor Cazalet, to whom the electors at Chippenham turned for safety, welcomed the Zinoviev letter as 'a regular bombshell to the Socialists. The *Daily Mail* and other Conservative papers have played up magnificently,' he declared, 'and the result on Wednesday [the] 29th was stupendous when the first seven gains were found all to be Conservative.'[1]

With 419 seats, the Conservatives more than retrieved the majority that Baldwin had squandered ten months earlier. They triumphed chiefly at the expense of the Liberals, who were reduced to a rump of 40. Asquith lost at Paisley to a Labour challenger, took a peerage, and retained the titular leadership. Lloyd George easily survived the onslaught to become the ranking Liberal in the House of Commons. The Labour Party, having lost 64 seats and picked up 24, was marginally stronger than it had been in the 1922 Parliament. It was also vastly more experienced and could ascribe its misfortunes – in part justly – to Tory trickery.

Baldwin proceeded to form his second administration, which was to last for nearly five years. Dawson told him that the Cabinet contained 'some daring rather good appointments, some duds, and some deplorable blots', and (on 7

---

[1] Recorded conversation of 5 July 1961, quoted in Davidson, *Memoirs*, p. 199; Cazalet's diary, 24–30 October 1924, quoted in Robert Rhodes James, *Victor Cazalet* (London, 1976), p. 96. In his edition of the Davidson 'memoirs', Rhodes James describes the Zinoviev letter as 'a forgery'; in his subsequent biography of Cazalet, he calls it 'almost certainly a forgery'. The case – seemingly closed by L. Chester, S. Fay, and H. Young, *The Zinoviev Letter* (London, 1976) – has been reopened by Christopher Andrew in the *Historical Journal*, xx (1977), 673–706, and xxii (1979), 211–14. Writing to Dawson from Monte Carlo on 18 March 1930, Marlowe described how the *Daily Mail* had obtained its copy of the document (Dawson Papers).

November) said as much in *The Times*.¹ The choice of Churchill, now Conservative MP for Epping, as Chancellor of the Exchequer struck Dawson as commendable, but irritated the *Morning Post* and others. Nevertheless, Baldwin's success entitled him to a free hand.

'The Press, on the whole, has done yeoman service, particularly the *Daily Mail* and the *Morning Post*,' John Gretton, the Tory member for Burton, wrote to Baldwin; 'but little thanks are owing to the *Express*. Plainly they have been swept on the flowing tide and not too willingly.' That, in every respect, was a valid assessment. Baldwin could not bring himself to thank Rothermere, who never forgave him. Birkenhead considered it a major error on Baldwin's part:

> After the help which the *Daily Mail* had given in the election, the statement that the election had not been won by the Stunt Press was taken as a gratuitous insult by Rothermere, who had worked very hard to win the election. R never ceases to refer to this in conversation.

Baldwin dealt more generously with Gwynne, who hailed him as 'the master of the destinies of England' and – overstepping his bounds – supplied 'suggestions for a Cabinet' that would exclude 'men like Curzon, Horne, Churchill and Birkenhead' and include Grey at the Foreign Office and possibly J. H. Thomas at the Colonial Office. Instead of taking umbrage, as he would have done with Rothermere, Baldwin genially ignored this advice. On 27 December, he felt 'an impulse to send' Gwynne 'a line to wish you all good for the coming year, but particularly to tell you how I appreciate and value the unswerving support you have always given me. Your friendship has been as a rock.' Knowing exactly how to appeal to Gwynne's emotions, the Prime Minister added that his cousin, Rudyard Kipling, joined 'in all my good wishes and affectionate greetings .... He is seated by me in a big chair, working away at a book of cross word puzzles.' Significantly, Baldwin did not try this tack with Beaverbrook, whose son was Kipling's godchild.²

If the election had not been won by the 'Stunt Press', neither had it been lost by the socialist press, which behaved more responsibly than angry Labour politicians were prepared to concede. 'Reaction for the moment triumphs,' the *Daily Herald* dutifully stated on 31 October, 'but Labour will consolidate, regain, extend, and, in the end, win its way to the Co-operative Commonwealth.' Yet, in the mind of Tom Shaw, a minister under MacDonald, the *Herald* was 'the worst informed paper in Europe so far as the Socialist Movement is concerned', and its receptiveness to 'Communist or minority opposition' could not be brooked. At the end of the year, a committee of inquiry was appointed. Before its first meeting, Lansbury resigned as general

¹ Dawson's diary, 6 November 1924, quoted in Wrench, *Dawson*, p. 233.
² Gretton to Baldwin, 1 November 1924, and Gwynne to Baldwin, 30 October 1924, Baldwin Papers; 'Very Secret' memorandum by Davidson [1927], quoted in Davidson, *Memoirs*, p. 201; Baldwin to Gwynne, 27 December 1924, Gwynne Papers.

manager. 'We have a great abundance of critics in high places,' against whom he was powerless to contend. His replacement was Robert Williams, one of the ten members of the investigatory body and a staunch trade unionist. Philip Millwood, a Quaker pacifist with ILP credentials, relinquished the secretaryship of the *Herald* in March 1925. That, as Ross McKibbin has incisively argued, completed 'the departure of the old guard' as well as the 'second phase in the *Herald*'s life .... In the event, the *Herald* was not official enough to satisfy the people who paid its bills, but too heavily encumbered with political reporting to gain a mass circulation.'[1]

It took longer to dislodge Brailsford from the *New Leader*. Scott, who met him on 27 November 1924, found him 'overworked and much depressed' by the recent election. 'For 10 months', Brailsford 'had not seen ... or had any communication with MacDonald ... because early on Brailsford had made ... not any criticism of MacDonald, but merely some suggestions on policy. That had been regarded as an even greater offence.' At the same time that MacDonald 'boycotted the *New Leader*, he was furious with the *Herald* which perhaps was not wonderful', Brailsford was quoted as saying, 'as its editor was a Communist and perhaps hated MacDonald more than any other person in the world'. Had Scott heard and reported Brailsford correctly? If so, the misconceptions among Labour journalists were as far-fetched as those among outsiders and far more damaging.[2]

The mutual misconceptions among Liberal newspapermen were no less striking. Mainly, though not exclusively, they involved questions of finance. The Asquithians, reluctantly reconciled with Lloyd George, believed him to have a bottomless purse, selfishly withheld from their control. They would have used it not only to defray election costs, which had emptied their 'war chest', but also to bail out the Westminster Press group. Its provincial properties were at least moderately successful; but the *Westminster Gazette*, after three years of morning publication, was running aground. Sir Leicester Harmsworth, who had sat in Parliament as a Liberal from 1900 to 1922, was offered an interest in the ailing concern. Apart from being Rothermere's brother, which could not be held against him, he was principal owner of the *Western Morning News* and the *Western Evening Herald* at Plymouth. After 'considerable thought', he refused:

> It has always seemed to us that Propaganda by newspaper should follow rather than precede the attainment of the mammoth circulation (in which endeavour a strong Propagandist policy is rather a deterrent than an aid as a rule) which is necessary to the financial success of a London newspaper

[1] Shaw to Norman Ewer, 11 February 1925, and Lansbury to Ben Turner, 3 January 1925, quoted in McKibbin, *Evolution*, pp. 231–33.

[2] Entry of 27–30 November 1924, Scott, *Political Diaries*, p. 470. Brailsford, who would have known better than to call Fyfe a Communist, was probably referring to Norman Ewer, the *Herald*'s foreign editor, or to William Mellor, the assistant editor. See F. M. Leventhal, 'H. N. Brailsford and the *New Leader*.' *Journal of Contemporary History*, ix (1974), 91–113.

now-a-days; and which also is necessary if it is to be of great service in leading large bodies of voters in the right direction. The *W.G.* in the old days professedly appealed to a limited number whom it rightly held in high repute; who indeed regarded it frankly as an exponent – a brilliant exponent – of Liberalism rather than as a newspaper. As such, however, it was obviously a financial failure; and, if I may be permitted to offer an opinion, this will, I think, continue to be the case so long as it is primarily a Propagandist organ rather than a newspaper.

The next step was for Starmer to meet Sir Stanley Holmes (later 1st Baron Dovercourt), a Liberal in the 1918 Parliament who was to return to Westminster as a Liberal National in 1935 and retire as a Conservative in 1954. Asked 'to disclose his hand', Holmes 'said that if he became a buyer he would have the assistance of the Berrys & added that the Berrys could no more run a Liberal paper than the *W.G.* could run a Conservative paper'. Moreover, the Berrys were more interested in parts of the provincial group, which Starmer was unwilling to detach.[1]

On 13 January 1925, Scott was invited to breakfast at the Reform Club with Maclean, who 'would only talk about the *Westminster Gazette*'. The paper was 'losing heavily': Maclean estimated 'sixty or seventy thousand a year, but Ld. Cowdray, who finds the money afterwards, put it at a much higher figure'. Recently, Cowdray had discussed the situation with Maclean and 'told him frankly that, as at present run, he did not think the paper as a political instrum^t. was worth the money. At the same time', Cowdray was reluctant 'to see the paper die or be transferred to one of the great syndicates'. The suggestion was made that the *Manchester Guardian* might 'run it', but Scott demurred that 'the connected questions of control & finance would probably present an insuperable difficulty'. Later that morning, Scott and Maclean 'went on to see Lord Cowdray', who 'evidently had thought very little about the quest^n. which Sir D.M. h^d. raised, but sent for the "dossier" of the *Westminster*'. The contents revealed that circulation had 'gone up to 250,000 (by aid of the generous free insurance coupon system)', that advertisements 'were doubling year by year', but that 'the loss, without allowing for depreciat^n., was over £2000 a week. This was largely compensated by the profits of the "Starmer" group of provincial newspapers (which Lord C. finances).'[2]

Cowdray's proposed solution to the problem was for the *Westminster Gazette* to be taken over by the *Daily Chronicle*. That would serve a dual purpose, for the directors of the *Chronicle* appeared dangerously to 'aspire to become serious rivals to the *Daily Mail*. They can only do that, as Maclean remarked, by becoming a "stunt" paper & that w^d. not be very useful to Liberalism.' It did

---

[1] Harmsworth to Major Harold Pearson, 15 December 1924, and Starmer to Pearson, 6 January 1925, Cowdray Papers.
[2] Scott's diary, 13 January 1925, *Guardian* Archives.

not seem to cross Cowdray's mind that Lloyd George might have neither the inclination nor the available capital to take on the burden. In any case, Harold Pearson, who chaired the Westminster Press, soon decided 'definitely' to hold on. 'Under these circumstances,' Cowdray informed Scott, 'you will appreciate that the preliminary talk I had the pleasure of having with you cannot be carried further.' Scott must have been puzzled by Pearson's optimism, but hardly disappointed.[1]

Just as the *Westminster Gazette* was the metropolitan linchpin for the sprawling Westminster Press syndicate, the *Daily Chronicle* was the mainstay of United Newspapers Ltd., which also published papers at Edinburgh and Leeds. The *Chronicle* was commonly regarded as Lloyd George's personal property. He never sat on the board, where McCurdy had succeeded Dalziel as chairman; but one of its six members was his son Gwilym (later 1st Viscount Tenby), who lost his seat for Pembrokeshire in 1924 and recaptured it in 1929. The enterprise was reconstituted as a public company in 1925, when new preference shares were issued. The staff was said to have subscribed £25,000 of the £550,000 that was raised, the amounts for their purchases advanced by the proprietors and repaid by deductions from salary.[2]

Still, Lloyd George was dissatisfied. He was eager to launch another land campaign and 'had money enough to carry it on at full blast for 4 or 5 years'. But some of his parliamentary colleagues, most notably Maclean, would have preferred to receive direct and unlimited access to his fabled resources. 'He was supposed to have a million of party funds at his disposal with which he refused to part,' Scott was led to understand. Lloyd George denied, however, that either he or 'the trustees of the fund' had anything on that scale. What they had, he explained to Scott, was 'a controlling share in several newspapers – the *Daily Chronicle*, the *Sunday News* (formerly *Lloyd's Weekly*), the *Edinburgh Evening News*', and the *Yorkshire Evening News*, which Scott mistook for 'a Leeds Weekly'. Lloyd George said that he would 'like to sell the *Chronicle*', and Scott deduced that he 'meant the other papers too. He was not a newspaper man,' Lloyd George maintained, 'but a politician & found the newspaper business troublesome. His difficulty' with respect to the *Chronicle* 'was to save its political character', which would be compromised in 'the hands of a Beaverbrook or a Rothermere'. The paper was 'making £50,000 a year. Even after starting their Leeds Office' to facilitate distribution through the north of England and into Scotland, the paper cleared £20,000. 'The *Edinburgh Evening News* was incredibly profitable, making £50,000 a year.' But what use were these revenues if they brought constant recrimination or if they had to be handed over to the

---

[1] Scott's diary, 13 January 1925, *Guardian* Archives; Cowdray to Scott, 26 March 1925 (copy), enclosed in Cowdray to Maclean, 26 March 1925, Maclean Papers.
[2] H. A. Taylor, *Donald*, pp. 239–41.

Liberal Central Association, which Scott had to agree was 'wholly incompetent'?[1]

On 22 September 1926, Lloyd George was 'up in town trying to put a little spunk into the *Chronicle & Sunday News*'. It worried him that 'the *Express* had passed us in circulation', and at the tense moment when he was passing by Asquith as Liberal leader. With a lawyer to advise 'what my powers were', he 'gave a fairly plain intimation that unless immediate steps were taken to put things right I should reconstruct the Board – that is sack the lot,' he told his wife. 'McCurdy is lazy & flabby, Gwilym indolent . . . . Perris spends too many of his evenings at the Kit Kat Club', instead of at his desk. 'The property is a good one but it requires ceaseless activity & watchfulness . . . . I mean to keep at it.'[2]

Within two months, United Newspapers Ltd. was sold to a pair of wealthy baronets, Sir David Yule and Sir Thomas (later 1st Baron) Catto, both Scotsmen who had made their fortunes in the India trade. Lord Reading, who had just stepped down as Governor-General of India and up to a marquessate, accepted the chairmanship of the reconstructed company 'at the urgent request of Lloyd George'. The purchase price was said to be in the region of three million pounds. 'Mr Lloyd George had the ha'pence, and the cake was transferred to friendly hands,' quipped H. A. Taylor, who continued the story to its bitter end. Yule died in July 1928, and Reading promptly bowed out. The *Daily Chronicle* and the *Sunday News* were bought by William Harrison, a practising solicitor who had assembled a collection of interlocking newsprint and publishing operations. According to the gossip-mongers in Fleet Street, his Inveresk Paper Company sank between £1,500,000 and £2,000,000. Little, if any, was saved in June 1930, when the *Daily Chronicle* merged with the *Daily News* to form the *News Chronicle*. At the time of the *Chronicle*'s overnight demise, its circulation hovered slightly below the million mark, but its coffers were empty and its spirit was broken. The next year, 'with a much attenuated sale', the *Sunday News* was enfolded by Kemsley's *Sunday Graphic*. The house of cards had tumbled to reveal Lloyd George as the joker in the pack.[3]

*   *   *

Newspapers, whether struggling or solvent, were a threat to political reputations. Politicians, whether shaky or secure, were unsettled by the press and its controllers. Each side expected a return on its investment that the other was either unwilling or unable to deliver.

[1] Scott's diary, 13 November 1925, *Guardian* Archives.
[2] Lloyd George to his wife, 22 September 1926, *Lloyd George Family Letters*, pp. 206–207.
[3] H. A. Taylor, *Donald*, pp. 241–45; Hyde, *Reading*, pp. 395–96; note by Blumenfeld, 5 July [1928], Beaverbrook Papers, H/16; Camrose, *British Newspapers*, pp. 90–91. The *Morning Post* published a series of seven articles (7–14 November 1927) on the Lloyd George Fund, which it had 'reason to believe' had been augmented by the sale of the *Daily Chronicle* 'and allied newspapers for the enormous sum in cash and shares of £2,900,000.'

Lloyd George's undercover – and underhand – direction of the *Daily Chronicle* was financially rewarding, but politically damaging. It gave ammunition to his enemies and disquietude to his friends. His problems began earlier, in the aftermath of the 1924 electoral *débâcle*, when it became evident that his ascent to the Liberal leadership was only a matter of time. His avowals of loyalty to Asquith, though genuine enough under the circumstances, were unaccompanied by the monetary payments that would have carried greater conviction. At the same time, he sensed and protested against a 'persistent and growing hostility' on the part of the *Manchester Guardian* which, to his nostrils, 'reeks of Labour'. If Scott had transferred his allegiance, it was not apparent to MacDonald, who 'complained very bitterly' that the *Guardian* 'had not kept in touch with him during the latter part of his administration and had consequently misunderstood the situation'. Scott tried to mollify both men, but their egos clashed with his policy of 'plain speaking'. There was 'no Liberal paper in England', said Lloyd George, 'which treats me with less courtesy and fairness than the *Manchester Guardian*'.[1]

That, of course, was a blatant distortion. The *Daily News* was at least as tenderly disposed towards the aspirations of Labour as distinct from its tactics, and the *Westminster Gazette* nursed a consuming suspicion of Lloyd George. Cowdray, scarred by Lloyd George's treachery in 1917, was determined that the vast sums he had poured into the Liberal press should not benefit his old adversary. Maclean, Hudson, and other party managers in Abingdon Street shared his mistrust and probably intensified it. As a symbolic concession to Cowdray, whose 'immense sacrifices' were acknowledged, the party trustees handed over their 25,000 shares in Westminster Press Ltd. 'We are aware that the shares have only a nominal value, and that the transfer can be no more than a gesture of appreciation of the generosity and devotion of Lord Cowdray to Liberalism,' Maclean wrote to Cowdray's son, whose 'own hard and unselfish labours' were duly noted. 'These shares today have little or no value,' confirmed the recipient, who expressed 'every hope that in time the *Westminster Gazette* will make good, and if it does the shares will be of value. This, however, can only be achieved by continuing to find capital.' Cowdray was essential to the purpose, and therefore his views could not be disregarded. It was at his house that Asquith and his acolytes met on 25 November 1925 and plotted 'to break with Ll.G. on the financial opening'. Weeks later, after the National Liberal Federation meetings had passed without a showdown, Maclean reported that Cowdray was 'roused to rage ... & vows that if a clear issue between Ll.G. and Headquarters is not defined by *Asquith*, he will close his support & allow things to take their course as far as he is concerned'. Cowdray's commitment to the *Westminster Gazette* was

---

[1] Lloyd George to Scott, 30 January 1925, and entries of 4 March and 30 June–1 July 1925, in Scott, *Political Diaries*, pp. 474–75, 481.

linked to the primacy of Asquith. It was no coincidence that one did not long survive the other.[1]

Rummaging through the strong-boxes in Abingdon Street, the party agents discovered certificates for shares in John Dicks and Company, publishers of *Reynolds's Illustrated News*. (The 'Illustrated' had been added to the masthead the previous year, and the possessive was dropped in 1936.) The party, it appeared, had another clandestine investment on its hands. In an interview on 18 August 1925, Lord Dalziel of Kirkcaldy provided an explanation, but dashed any hopes of profit. As calls beyond the initial payment of five shillings per share 'had not been met, the rights of the holders . . . had been forfeited' and the shares 'were valueless. The purposes for which they had been bought had been served,' confirmed Dalziel, who said 'he would continue to help the Party in such ways as were within his power'. Adept at covering his tracks, as his testimony to Parliament with respect to his involvement in the *Daily Chronicle* had shown, Dalziel offered assurances that 'if the paper were sold, . . . the books recording this transaction would not be at the disposal of the purchaser'. He added 'that the current stories of the sale of the paper to the Labour Party had no foundation in fact'. That was something of a consolation.[2]

Labour was known to be in the market for new properties. Eventually, its National Co-operative Press company acquired *Reynolds News* (as its title had since been further simplified) and coupled it with the *Sunday Citizen*. MacDonald was not prepared to wait. 'The iniquity of the socialist press had been one of MacDonald's chief preoccupations since before the election', according to his biographer, 'and for some months he had devoted an inordinate amount of time and energy' to a scheme that would have put the *New Statesman* under the control of 'a very fine band of young men down from Oxford'. Nothing came of this project, however.[3] Nor, for the time being, was he successful in his efforts to remove Brailsford from the *New Leader*. The changes at the *Daily Herald*, left incomplete by Fyfe's retention of the editorship, were more to his liking, but not entirely to his advantage.

Through 1925 and well into 1926, Baldwin's position *vis-à-vis* the press was comparatively satisfactory. The Liberal and even the Labour papers addressed him respectfully. Burnham was the model of docility. 'Berry', insinuated Beaverbrook, who did not specify which brother he meant, acted as 'the door-keeper at Downing Street'. The Prime Minister's Tory critics were unusually restrained. 'Some of the young lions on my papers wish to open long range fire on the Baldwin Govt. now,' Rothermere told Beaverbrook on 3 February 1925, 'but I am holding them back. I make a prophecy. The Baldwin Govt. will look sick before March is out.' Events, or rather the utter paucity of

---

[1] Maclean to Pearson, 1 August 1925, and Pearson to Maclean, 6 August 1925, Asquith Papers; Koss, *Asquith*, pp. 273–74.
[2] 'Secret' memorandum by R. Humphrey Davies [1926], Asquith Papers.
[3] Marquand, *MacDonald*, pp. 419–20. Sidney Webb, on taking office in MacDonald's government, resigned from the board of the *New Statesman*.

them, forced Rothermere to perform as lion-tamer much longer than he had expected. On 9 March, Churchill lunched with him and obtained his promise to glorify the budget 'what ever it was. If I took off taxes good – if not – he wd. applaud the courage of stern finance.' By summer, Rothermere had revised his timetable in the 'belief that the present Administration will come to grief early or later in 1927'. His prophecies kept exceeding the deadlines he set for them.[1]

Beaverbrook accepted the situation with a realism born of resignation. 'So long as the Conservative Government do nothing', he knew that 'they can go on for a very long time'. Churchill had taken to keeping more respectable company, depriving Beaverbrook of his companionship and disclosures. Beaverbrook faulted his judgment on economic policy, but not sufficiently to assail him at Birkenhead's instigation. He was 'now completely severed from the inside world of politics' to the extent that 'he ceased to write political articles in his newspapers or to retail political news to his correspondents'. His attraction to Lloyd George lay behind; his campaign for Empire Free Trade lay ahead. As 1925 drew to a close, Beaverbrook – the 'hermit crab' – drew further into his shell. 'The hostility of the Tory Party to Rothermere and myself – principally, I fear, myself', convinced him that anything 'we curse ..., however wrong and distasteful', was guaranteed to win the blessing of 'the rank and file .... This hostility is likely to continue until the election draws nigh,' he predicted. 'Then, of course, the Conservative Party will want our support very badly – and we shall not hear any more about the Platform being able to beat or do without the Popular Press.' The press lords were much addicted to prophecy.[2]

The Times concurred in Beaverbrook's estimate of Baldwin's 'miraculous success', but put it down 'to his own qualities, and in particular to that broad instinctive sanity – sometimes verging on sentiment, but never on pettiness – which always directs his outlook on national affairs' (7 March 1925). In turn, Beaverbrook looked upon Printing House Square and Downing Street as twin dependencies of Washington. '*The Times* has now become simply a great propaganda organ directed, as far as transatlantic affairs are concerned, by Jack Astor, its proprietor, to further some vague idea of Anglo-Saxon union,' he told Sir Robert Borden, the Canadian statesman. Dawson, despite his imperial tutelage as 'one of Milner's young men, ... cannot counteract this tendency. His job is to please Astor – which he does remarkably well – on points about which Astor cares such as kow-towing to the United States.' Thus, Baldwin's fawning support for the American debt settlement and Churchill's reckless return to the gold standard ('in order to mobilize the

---

[1] Beaverbrook to Rothermere, 28 November 1925, quoted in Taylor, *Beaverbrook*, p. 225; Rothermere to Beaverbrook, 3 February 1925, Beaverbrook Papers, C/282a; Churchill to his wife, 10 March 1925, and Rothermere to Churchill, 27 July 1925, quoted in Gilbert, *Churchill*, V, 106, 130.

[2] Beaverbrook to Borden, 28 January 1925, and Beaverbrook to Mackenzie King, 28 December 1925, quoted in Taylor, *Beaverbrook*, pp. 225–28.

useless gold hordes of the United States') were certain to earn *The Times*'s approval.[1]

Only one ripple disturbed the calm of the government's press relations that year. Birkenhead, now Secretary of State for India, resumed his sideline in journalism to keep him in the style to which he had grown accustomed. When Baldwin took him to task, he defended his right and professed his need. That July, the question was raised in the Commons. 'Strong feeling was expressed on all sides that a Cabinet Minister should not, whilst holding high office, write articles for the Press, for which it was assumed he received remuneration,' minuted Jackson. 'The matter was considered by the Cabinet, & it was decided that the practice should cease.' Yet Birkenhead was not to be penalized. After all, he had given up a lucrative career at the bar along with an annual pension of £5,000, due him as a former Lord Chancellor, in order to serve at the India Office. Baldwin asked Jackson 'as Chairman if it could be arranged that the approximate amount of the pension . . . could be found out of Party Funds' so as to indemnify Birkenhead for his loss of income. With two payments, totalling £10,000, Birkenhead's pen was laid aside until 1930, when MacDonald had reason to complain of his articles in the *Daily Telegraph*. Baldwin's other colleagues managed to subsist on their ministerial salaries, supplemented by private resources. Hoare, who received no fees for the secrets he continuously leaked, admitted that a piece 'signed by me' in *John Bull* was 'in point of fact nothing more than a verbatim reproduction of the monthly letter that I send round to the members of my Conservative Association'. In most cases, the temptation did not arise. Derby, outside the government and therefore free to scribble, declined an invitation to contribute to the *Daily Express*: 'I have never written an article in my life, and for the very simple reason that I do not believe that I am competent to do so.' That, in a backhanded way, was a compliment to journalism as a profession.[2]

As Dawson told a friend on 10 February 1926, 'Baldwin and his Government are in a more than ever impregnable position for the moment'. Amery's Middle Eastern policies were subject to a degree of journalistic sniping that he tended to exaggerate in retrospect. Hoare's reduced air estimates suffered 'the combined attacks of the *Daily Mail* and the *Morning Post*', which were repulsed by Blumenfeld's 'most helpful article in the *Express*'. These small exceptions proved Dawson's rule that 'on the whole the Cabinet is very popular and unprovocative'.[3]

---

[1] Beaverbrook to Borden, 16 July 1925, quoted in Taylor, *Beaverbrook*, p. 227.
[2] Birkenhead to Baldwin, 16 July 1925, Hoare to Baldwin, 18 June 1925, and MacDonald to Baldwin, 10 July 1930, Baldwin Papers; 'confidential and secret' memorandum by Jackson, n.d., Davidson Papers; Davidson, *Memoirs*, pp. 276–77; Birkenhead, *'F.E.'*, p. 544; Derby to Blumenfeld, 21 September 1925, Blumenfeld Papers.
[3] Dawson to Drummond Chaplin, 10 February 1926, quoted in Wrench, *Dawson*, p. 245; Amery, *My Political Life*, II, 328; Hoare to Blumenfeld, 25 and 26 February 1926, Blumenfeld Papers.

All the while, a storm was brewing in the coal industry, which led to the outbreak of a General Strike in May. The antecedents have been charted too often and too well to require recapitulation here. But the participation of the political press, no less than the effects upon it, provides a subject unto itself.

In support of the miners' claim for higher wages and reduced working hours, the general council of the TUC called out the forces of organized labour. By including printers, they 'evidently intended a complete closure of the national press' that would embrace even the *Daily Herald*. Fyfe, leading a delegation from his staff, successfully appealed this illogical decision. But a police raid on the *Herald*'s offices, followed by the government's steps to requisition the *Herald*'s stock of newsprint, knocked that paper more or less out of commission. In 'the struggle for dominance in the field of communications', as G. A. Phillips has called it, both sides resorted to improvised weapons.[1]

Fleet Street would have preferred to remain a safety zone, but quickly found itself a strategic battleground. On Saturday, 1 May, against a background of tense negotiations between the government and the TUC to avert the stoppage set for midnight on the 2nd, Beaverbrook was called to an urgent meeting at the *Sunday Express*. The compositors took strong exception to a government-paid advertisement, designed to recruit strike-breakers. Beaverbrook, whose 'main concern was to get his papers published', telephoned Birkenhead, who advised him to compromise. He then rang up Churchill, who growled: 'Close down; you can afford it.' Beaverbrook, 'perfectly prepared to go on publishing at almost any cost', agreed to delete a few objectionable words from the advertisement, thus allowing the *Sunday Express* to reach the news-stands. His hope that Monday's *Daily Express* and *Evening Standard* would not be impeded was dashed by actions taken elsewhere.[2]

At Rothermere's *Daily Mail*, Marlowe insisted upon the inclusion of a bellicose leading article, 'For King and Country', which the printers refused to set into type. On this pretext, Baldwin broke off his dialogue with the TUC, and the strike was declared. It could have been avoided, Beaverbrook believed, had the government exhibited more of Birkenhead's moderation and less of Churchill's 'old Gallipoli spirit ... and excessive excitement'. For, at this moment, Churchill came forward to conduct publicity operations. 'The idea of representing a strike which arose entirely out of industrial conditions and had entirely industrial aims as a revolutionary movement was mainly Mr Churchill's,' insisted the *British Worker* (10 May), the TUC's riposte to the government's *British Gazette*. Churchill was 'super-editor' of the *Gazette* and hankered after the command of the BBC as well. Davidson, who later recalled that his own 'most difficult task was to blue-pencil some of the remarks' that Churchill planned to insert in the columns of the *Gazette*, pointedly recollected

---

[1] G. A. Phillips, *The General Strike* (London, 1976), pp. 167–68; *also see* Patrick Renshaw, *The General Strike* (London, 1975), chapter 21.

[2] Taylor, *Beaverbrook*, p. 231.

that Baldwin had burdened Churchill with this assignment to 'keep him busy, stop him from doing worse things'. Fyfe was quicker to perceive the implicit danger. Churchill 'sees the whole affair as a film producer would see it – with this difference,' he observed in his 'rough diary' on the first day of the strike: 'Film producers do not act; Winston intends to appear as the hero of the story himself.'[1]

Only after Davidson put the government's case to Lord Burnham, president of the Newspaper Proprietors Association, and had found that 'the leaders of the newspaper fraternity' were infected with 'mugwumpishness', was Churchill mobilized. His initial strategy was to stake his campaign headquarters at Carmelite House. That would have been ideologically appropriate, but geographically unsound. Instead, he commandeered the *Morning Post* at its own invitation. Its plant, an island fortress along the Strand, was bounded by Wellington Street (204 feet wide) to the west, Aldwych (222 feet wide) to the east, and Exeter Street (132 feet wide) to the north. 'If any *Emergency Protection* became necessary, 3 strands of barbed wire should be run round the exterior of pavement at once. A 6 ft. wooden palisade could be erected later,' it was suggested. 'For *really serious business*, the Gaiety Theatre could be garrisoned, and the Lyceum occupied with a detachment' of troops. Gwynne, gripped by Churchill's siege mentality, alerted the local police that, as the *Morning Post* had 'for some considerable time taken a strong line on the subject of the Bolshevik intrigue', it was to be 'expected that attempts will be made by the extremists to damage or injure the building or machinery'.[2]

The outworn premises of the *Morning Post* were on the verge of being vacated when they were put to this last, spectacular purpose. Its proprietors, fighting a losing battle that was to end a decade later in amalgamation with the *Daily Telegraph*, had nothing to lose and possibly something to gain from their compliance. Adversity helps to account for the paper's desperation, and therefore deserves documentation. On 9 July 1925, Rupert Beckett, co-proprietor of the *Yorkshire Post*, had 'had an interesting call ... from the Duke of Northumberland and Sir Percy Bates', respectively chairman and vice-chairman of the *Morning Post* board. 'They are losing money, and without fresh and considerable funds cannot carry on for more than another month,' Beckett told Arthur Mann. 'They & their friends are not inclined to find more money, but do not wish that the property should be acquired by any of the London groups or individuals (Berrys Rothermere Beaverbrook). They came to enquire whether the *Y.P.* would take them.' Beckett's answer was 'nothing doing'. The *Yorkshire Post*, with its 'advt. revenue ... decreasing ... and ...

[1] Taylor, *Beaverbrook*, p. 232; Graham Norton, 'The Nine-Day Wonder,' *Sunday Times Magazine*, 10 April 1966; Davidson, *Memoirs*, pp. 238–39; Fyfe, *Behind the Scenes of the General Strike* (London, 1926), p. 25.

[2] Hindle, *Morning Post*, p. 239; Davidson, *Memoirs*, p. 236; Gwynne and Ivor Fraser (Manager) to the Chief Inspector, Bow Street Police Station, 1 May 1926, and diagram (copies), Gwynne Papers. Ivor Fraser was Sir Malcolm's brother.

likely to go worse', was not prepared to 'look on anything with that weight of Debenture debt'. The trouble with the *Morning Post*, in Beckett's opinion, was that its 'Board possesses no newspaper man': Northumberland held vast estates, littered with coal mines; Bates was deputy chairman (and later chairman) of the Cunard Line; Lord Apsley, who represented 'the Glenesk debenture holders', was a lightweight among diehards; and the others were an assortment of distillers, City financiers, backbenchers, and backwoodsmen.[1]

For all these afflictions and others besides, the *Morning Post* kept going. Its directors apparently overcame their disinclination to increase their outlays. On the afternoon of 3 November 1925, Lane-Fox had no sooner brought Leo Amery 'tales of the imminent collapse of the *Morning Post* and its being taken over by Beaverbrook' than Gwynne arrived at the Dominions and Colonial Office 'not to tell me that the *M.P.* is collapsing', but to mention that 'it was going very strong and had stolen away some of Beaverbrook's best men'. Whom was Amery to believe? Elias, who understood the paper to be 'experiencing a serious decline in its fortunes', recommended its purchase by Odhams, where the expensive machines that printed the *People* stood idle six days a week. Moreover, if the *Morning Post* shifted its operations to the Odhams premises in Long Acre, its 'impressive island site' in the Strand could be profitably developed. After consulting his associates, whose responses ranged from 'doubtful' to 'strongly against', Elias decided not to persevere. On 14 May 1926, when its circulation had dropped to 80,000, the *Morning Post* slashed its price to a penny to undercut *The Times* and the *Telegraph*. Soon thereafter, it moved to more economical quarters in Tudor Street.[2]

The General Strike provided the paper with an opportunity to arrest its decline, reassert its political importance, and use its facilities to dramatic effect. There were problems, however. The first issue of the *British Gazette* was delayed until 5 May, owing to a walkout on the part of the *Morning Post*'s regular typographers. Davidson was appalled. 'I do think that the men engaged in the production of Newspapers might volunteer to help the Govt. to produce what they can't produce themselves,' he wrote pettishly to Gwynne on the afternoon of the 3rd. Churchill refused to accept that 'the resources of the whole country' would fail to yield two hundred men trained to operate high-speed rotary presses. 'Don't they teach printing in the universities?' he demanded to know. 'Cannot we got volunteers to do this job from the universities?' Sir Andrew Caird, the managing director of the *Daily Mail* and 'the greatest authority present', responded 'that it would take months to

---

[1] Beckett to Mann, 9 July 1925, Mann Papers.
[2] Entry of 3 November 1925, *Amery Diaries*, I, 425; Minney, *Southwood*, pp. 220–21. Two years later, Brooks heard 'that the position of the *Morning Post* is precarious'; the Duke of Northumberland, 'rich as he is, ... cannot afford to lock away an unproductive half million'. Brooks's diary, 6 June 1927.

train an amateur staff ... in adequate numbers without damaging the machines irretrievably'.[1]

Gwynne was 'positively ashamed of my colleagues .... 95% of our compositors, stereotype hands and machine men are dead against the strike,' he reckoned, 'and I have not the slightest doubt that in this office I could get volunteers to turn out a Government four-page number to the extent of our machinery. But,' he cautioned, 'it would have to be accompanied by a definite promise from the Government that the men would not suffer for their patriotism.' Such a promise, initialled by Churchill, was promulgated on the 6th: 'No man who does his duty loyally to the country in the present crisis will be left unprotected by the State for subsequent reprisals.' Beaverbrook sent over reinforcements from the *Express*, and Sir Malcolm Fraser rounded up technical staff from other shuttered offices. It was not necessary, therefore, for Gwynne to avail himself of an offer from Harold Macmillan. The Conservative MP for Stockton-on-Tees, a publisher by trade and a progressive by reputation, kept a confidential directory of blackleg printers whom Macmillan and Company had used to break a strike.[2]

A set of more formidable obstacles was posed by Churchill, whose designs were characteristically grandiose and imprecise. When he addressed the *Morning Post* board on 3 May, he had not yet settled on a name for the journal ('? "The London Gazette"'), but had already formulated elaborate plans for 'a large free distribution' with the help of the Air Ministry. 'The Government is considering the issue of regulations forbidding any newspaper to appear without a licence,' he stated. 'Licences will however be granted to all well-disposed newspapers, which should do their best to appear, however abridged.'[3] His own intrusions made that extremely difficult.

At five o'clock on the morning of the 5th, Fyfe 'was roused from sleep' by an unknown caller, who stood on his doorstep and 'held out ... a copy of the *British Gazette*, No. 1'. Delivery was not usually so expeditious. So far as Fyfe was able to 'observe or discover, ... no copies were on sale in the streets or at the newsagents' shops'. Of the 232,000 printed that day, huge bundles were reportedly left to moulder unwrapped in urban alley-ways and (dropped by the RAF) in open fields. A print run of 2,209,000 on the 12th entitled the *British Gazette* to claim 'an unexampled achievement in journalism' (13 May); but, to the end, copies were still not reaching Scotland and arriving erratically at most provincial depots. From all indications, the surplus vastly exceeded the number

[1] Davidson to Gwynne, 3 May 1926 (2.30 p.m.), Gwynne Papers; memorandum by Bertram Crosfield, courtesy of John Crosfield.

[2] Gwynne to Davidson, 3 May 1926 (copy), 'Notice to the Printing Trade – Official,' initialled 'W. S. C., 6.5', Macmillan to Gwynne, 5 May 1926, and Gwynne to Macmillan, 6 May 1926 (copy), Gwynne Papers. Brendan Bracken, director of Eyre and Spottiswoode and later a Conservative MP, supplied 'blockmaking resources' to the *British Gazette* 'without any cost to the State'. Bracken to Gwynne, 11 May 1926, Gwynne Papers.

[3] Draft of Churchill's statement 'read at a meeting of the *Morning Post* Board, Monday, 3 May 1926' (copy), Gwynne Papers.

of copies that actually found their way into the hands of paying readers, who were requested to pass them along.[1]

The same problems of distribution plagued the *British Worker*, issued by the TUC as an antidote to the 'Cabinet's Own Newspaper', as it branded the *Gazette* (5 May). It printed 320,000 copies in London that morning and widened its circulation during the ensuing week by launching simultaneous production in Manchester, Cardiff, Sunderland, Glasgow (as the *Scottish Worker*), and, briefly, Leicester. Although 'at best a qualified success, serving the purposes of [the TUC Publicity Committee in] Eccleston Square better than those of local strike organizations', the *British Worker* has been judged as 'no less propagandist in character than the *British Gazette*, but in the circumstances of the strike it was less tempted to falsification'. Certainly both emergency organs were subject to comparable degrees of censorship. 'The only news that need be included in the *British Worker* is such as to show the spirit of our own people, the unity of our own action, and the enthusiasm and loyalty with which the General Council's instructions are being carried out,' Fyfe was instructed by the secretary of the Publicity Committee. The *British Gazette*, especially in the first few days before Davidson sharpened his blue pencil, aggressively denounced the strike as unconstitutional and the strikers as frustrated incendiaries, rejected by the mass of British society.[2]

Reflecting its editorial environment, the *British Gazette* was a condensed version of the *Morning Post* and dipped into the pigeon-holes of that office to fill its hastily assembled pages. One of its less prudent borrowings, given the sacrifices that the miners were being called upon to make, was an item on the 5th to the effect that W. E. Pease, the late Tory MP for Darlington and an owner of collieries in the north east, had left a sizeable estate. Whether by oversight or necessity, a varying proportion of each day's contents was duplicated the next. 'Many false rumours are current,' the paper warned its readers. 'Believe nothing until you see it in the *British Gazette*.' Those who heeded this injunction were led to believe that, apart from temporary inconveniences, matters were safely in hand. 'Vital Services Better Each Day,' proclaimed a headline on Monday, the 10th. 'Cricket in Full Swing' proved the point. Foreign opinion, whenever critical of the strike, was extensively quoted. Suitable appeals from national leaders were prominently featured.

The *Gazette* was limited to four pages. The *Worker* was reduced to half its customary size on the 7th because 'the Cabinet has stopped our supply of paper'. Neither filled the vacuum. A panoply of local strike bulletins sprang up. 'Don't take any notice of rumours,' the halfpenny one at Islington retaliated on the 7th. 'The only authentic information direct from the TUC will be put in the *Bulletin*.' On the 12th, it reported the discovery by Fred Montague (later 1st Baron Amwell), Labour MP for Islington West, 'that at the Gillespie Road

[1] Fyfe, *Behind the Scenes*, pp. 27–29; Phillips, p. 179.
[2] Phillips, pp. 171, 179; Fyfe, *Behind the Scenes*, pp. 83–84.

School the children had Sir John Simon's speech [derived from the *Gazette*] read to them instead of the usual scripture lesson!' The *Nottingham Strike Bulletin*, available for a penny, contained an extract from the Paris edition of the *Daily Mail* (5 May) which 'shows that the Government and its supporters mean to try to smash the Trade Unions' (8 May). The official bulletin of the Newport Industrial Council Central Strike Committee (9 May) disputed an assertion in the *British Gazette* 'that the National Council of Evangelical Free Churches had handed over the whole of its organisation to the Government', whatever that could have meant. 'Our Strike Bulletin goes like hotcakes,' the secretary of the Edinburgh and District Strike Committee informed TUC headquarters on the 8th. 'We can only get out 5000 to 7000 per day' of a one-page broadsheet for which a penny was asked, 'but we could easily dispose of several times as many. Our supplies of paper & ink are running down however.'[1]

The established newspapers were not much better off than these multifarious strike bulletins. 'The strike proceeds,' Barrington-Ward grimly recorded in his diary on Sunday, the 2nd. Representing the *Observer* in Garvin's untimely absence, he 'went round to see Sir William Berry and J. Gomer Berry at the *Sunday Times*', who 'agreed to act together in anything our papers could do in the way of publishing'. The next week's *Observer*, reproduced by Roneo and delivered by private motor cars within a sixty-mile radius, was a two-sided sheet that measured 16½ by 12 inches. Beaverbrook 'struggled to keep the *Daily Express* going, at first only in a rudimentary form', with his wife taking charge of the staff canteen and his girlfriend manning the switchboard. Arthur Christiansen, who subsequently took over as editor, had 'a vivid memory of working on a "scab" or "black" edition of the *Sunday Express* on 8 May 1926' that contained 'only twenty-two items' arranged in 'three miserable columns . . . on one side of the sheet only'. The *Daily Mail* imported quantities of its Continental edition, but its Fleet Street product was similarly limited in size, if not in tone. All of the other metropolitan dailies, regardless of political orientation, were drastically cut back. Wednesday's miniature edition of *The Times*, fondly nicknamed 'Little Sister', was printed by multigraph and measured 13 by 8 inches. That afternoon, a fire was set in the unguarded machine-room at Printing House Square.[2]

Dawson, who had been suffering from a fever of a medical sort, returned to London on Friday, the 7th, to find the office 'picketed and policed but full of good people carrying on with increasing success'. He 'lunched at the House of Commons . . . and had a long talk there afterwards with the Prime Minister mainly on my own subject of publicity which in my view (and he agreed) was

---

[1] G. W. (?) Crawford to Mr Simmons, 8 May 1926, TUC HD 5366. Sample copies of these strike bulletins are to be found in the General Strike collection, TUC Library.

[2] Barrington-Ward's diary, 2 May 1926; Donald McLachlan, *In the Chair* (London, 1971), p. 62; Christiansen, *Headlines*, p. 43; Taylor, *Beaverbrook*, pp. 231–32; Fyfe, *Behind the Scenes*, p. 29.

being mishandled by Winston'. At Baldwin's request, Dawson wrote 'a letter for the Cabinet', which plunged him into 'a correspondence with Winston'. Dawson professed that he could 'most fully appreciate the reasons for starting the *British Gazette*', though its truculence dismayed him. 'All I urge is that the Government should encourage and not handicap, still less prevent altogether, the gradual establishment of the regular independent newspapers.' Nevertheless, 'Winston's wild commandeering raids' continued, culminating on the 11th 'by the seizure (in the interests of Winston's *Gazette*) of about a quarter of our available paper stocks'. The *New Statesman* (15 May) considered it 'scandalous that *The Times* should have been deprived of its paper supplies in order to enable Mr Churchill to poison public opinion'. Beaverbrook, threatened with the confiscation of the *Express*'s newsprint, persuaded the Home Secretary to delay the order, and the strike was over before it could be executed.[1]

Outside London, the pressures were applied unevenly. The *Yorkshire Post* significantly expanded its sale with relatively slight injury to its format. Brooks, its assistant editor, boasted in his diary that 'the paper has appeared daily and has been taken from Leeds to London and Leeds to Carlisle nightly. It has gained tremendously in prestige, for it gave a four page paper when organs like the *Mail* and the *Telegraph* were reduced to miserable sheets.' In Glasgow, four dailies banded together to produce the *Emergency Press*. In Edinburgh, the *Scotsman* continued independently, and more remote Scottish journals received cooperation from the printing unions. 'The *Manchester Guardian* was the only one of the great national newspapers to make a moderate and liberal voice heard,' according to Phillips; 'and even its four-page emergency edition was largely restricted to straightforward reporting.' In fact, the *Guardian*'s 'moderate and liberal voice' was inaudible under these circumstances. Scott, expressing solidarity with Sir William Joynson-Hicks, the notoriously right-wing Home Secretary, saw 'that this strike, which is really an attack upon Constitutional and Parliamentary Government, must be met and fought'. Accordingly, his son Ted wrote a leading article on the 6th that condoned most – if not all – of the regulations introduced under the Emergency Powers Act: 'Once a conflict of this kind has broken out the Government must use all its powers to maintain the major public services,' declared the *Guardian*. 'The technical branches of the army and navy are available .... There is no reason why, if necessary, they should not be used.'[2]

That put the *Manchester Guardian* at odds with Lloyd George who, alone among the major politicians, declined to condemn the strike action. Indeed, in the column he wrote for the Hearst syndicate in America, he took what many prominent Liberals regarded as 'a much too pro Labour line .... But I did it

[1] Dawson's diary entries for 7, 8, 9, and 11 May 1926, quoted in Wrench, *Dawson*, pp. 248–49; Dawson to Churchill, 8 May 1926 (copy), Woods Papers; *also see* entries of 8 and 9 May 1926, *Amery Diaries*, I, 453–54.

[2] Phillips, p. 181; Brooks's diary, 16 May 1926; Scott to Joynson-Hicks, 8 May 1926, quoted in Ayerst, *Guardian*, pp. 462–63.

deliberately,' he told his wife on 18 May, '& I mean to stick to it.' Asquith, Grey, and Simon contributed anti-strike manifestoes to the *British Gazette*, virtually indistinguishable from the ones supplied by Tory elder statesmen. 'After poor old Asquith, poor old Arthur Balfour has been persuaded by Churchill to write an article,' Fyfe noted on the 10th. 'It is even sillier than Asquith's. People are saying that Churchill wrote them both.'[1]

Lloyd George was not content, however, to preach from a transatlantic pulpit. On 5 May, he put forward a scheme for collaboration by the *Daily News*, the *Westminster Gazette*, and the *Daily Chronicle*. George Armstrong was summoned by Colonel Thomas Tweed, Lloyd George's 'henchman', to a meeting at Queen Anne's Gate. There it was suggested that Armstrong 'should take the editorship' of a news-sheet to be printed at a non-union shop 'outside the metropolis'. The editors of the *Daily News* and the *Westminster Gazette* had visited Lloyd George at Churt over the previous weekend and had given their approval; that of the *Daily Chronicle* was naturally assumed. With assurances 'that the three Liberal London newspapers were officially backing the proposed paper', which was to be called 'the Independent News', Armstrong accompanied W. M. Eagar, yet another of Lloyd George's assistants, on an expedition to Luton on the 10th. 'The financial arrangements were discussed quite clearly and definitely on the basis that the financial guarantee would have to come from Mr Lloyd George.' Hodgson of the *Daily News* went so far as to compose a leading article for the inaugural issue. The managers of the printing plant at Luton 'took strong exception' to Hodgson's conciliatory tone, which 'confirmed [their] worst fears ... of the policy which the Independent News might pursue'. Immediately, they began to raise awkward questions. Had the boards of the three London papers formally approved the venture? (Eager 'had made perfectly clear ... that the Boards ... could not meet before the paper was started'.) Was the *Daily News* empowered to pledge the backing of its sister paper, the *Star*, 'which had not come into the picture at all' in preliminary discussions? Did Sir Charles Starmer endorse the project? Would it be open to misconstruction as an 'attempt to make Party capital out of the present position'? Not least, would the paper's 'editorial freedom to criticise the Government' extend to support of militant trade unionism? The collapse of Lloyd George's scheme on the 10th anticipated the collapse of the General Strike by two days. If nothing else, Tweed saw to it that Armstrong 'was well paid for my pains'.[2]

---

[1] *Lloyd George Family Letters*, p. 206; Fyfe, *Behind the Scenes*, p. 69. A letter from Balfour to Churchill, 8 May 1926, requesting 'two very trifling alterations' in his proofs, confirms his authorship. Gwynne Papers.

[2] Armstrong, *Memories*, p. 201; memorandum by Eagar, 10 May 1926, Lloyd George Papers, G/20/2/15. The *Daily News's Strike Fortnight* (London, 1926), describes (p. 14) the suppression of Lloyd George's appeal by the *British Gazette*. Bertram Crosfield, the managing director of the *Daily News*, left a different account of these negotiations with Messrs. Hudson and Stacey, who were prepared to print at their plant in Luton. A. A. Gibbs of the *Luton News* demanded assurances that Crosfield 'was acting on behalf of the Daily News Ltd. and not on behalf of Mr

For the nine days that it lasted, the adventure had been great fun. Beaverbrook was 'almost inclined to favour the idea of having a General Strike every year by law'. Gwynne enjoyed the *frisson* of quasi-ministerial status. 'Since the beginning of the strike,' he told Lord Eustace Percy at the Board of Education, 'I sit in my office with the Treasury telephone at my elbow and am a kind of liaison officer between the Government and the paper.' Jackson, Fraser, and Davidson were on hand to fetch and carry. Admiral Hall saw to security arrangements. 'Winston has been my most frequent visitor,' Gwynne reported, 'and, between ourselves, he has been a bit of a nuisance, for he is constantly coming in and dictating articles, some of which I have to cut out.' On the night of the 9th, 'Baldwin paid us a visit . . . and excited tremendous enthusiasm. He is quite firm, and you need have no fear of a weakening on his side.'[1]

In the happy expectation that the carnival would go on indefinitely, Churchill laid long-term plans for an advertising drive and improved methods of distribution. But the *British Gazette* made its ultimate appearance on Thursday morning, 13 May. The farewell number, an exercise in self-congratulation, paid generous tribute to the *Morning Post*, which 'had but once intermitted its daily issue' during the preceding century and a half, yet selflessly allowed 'its very name . . . to disappear'. Davidson sent Gwynne a 'very delightful official letter of thanks', followed by a personal message 'to let you know officially that my end of the show were grateful & proud of what you & your stout crew did' during the 'wonderful nightmare'. Hall reciprocated Gwynne's 'flattering document' of gratitude with praise for the editor's 'right royal help . . . . When the next edition of the *Gazette* is to be published,' he concluded, 'I hope to be at call.' Not everyone was so complimentary. Lord Burnham and Sir Andrew Caird were 'horrified at the action of the *Morning Post* in using the National paper, the *British Gazette*, to which all the newspaper proprietors have contributed so loyally during the week, to announce' that on Friday, the 14th, the *Post* would resume publication at the reduced price of a penny. 'It is possible that the Chancellor of the Exchequer will have an embarrassing volley of questions in the House tomorrow,' Caird warned Gwynne on the evening of the 12th, 'and it is certain that the *Morning Post* will be expelled from the NPA' for having unilaterally 'upset all hope of an agreement' between the proprietors and the unions.[2]

Consequently, Gwynne and Sir Percy Bates recognized 'that it would be lack of tact, if not of something worse' for the *Morning Post* to publish the 'nice

---

Lloyd George's group, which he had definitely turned down'. Memorandum by Crosfield, courtesy of John Crosfield.

[1] Beaverbrook to Tim Healy, n.d., quoted in Taylor, *Beaverbrook*, p. 232; Gwynne to Percy, 10 May 1926 ('the first day that there has been comparative quiet in this office') (copy), Gwynne Papers.

[2] Gwynne to Davidson, 18 May 1926 (copy), Davidson to Gwynne, 18 May 1926, Hall to Gwynne, 29 July 1926, transcript of a 'message . . . received at 10 p.m. . . . from Sir Andrew Caird,' 12 May 1926, Gwynne Papers.

things' that Churchill said in a letter on the 12th. Churchill agreed that his remarks should be withheld 'while any conflict between the *Morning Post* & the Newspaper Proprietors Association is still proceeding', as they might be interpreted 'to commit the Government to taking sides in what is essentially a trade question'. Gwynne expected official assistance in resolving the difficulty, and not merely in recognition of the paper's service to the national cause. 'The recent crisis has proved that the *Morning Post* has given the present Government very considerable support,' he stated with undisguised partisanship. 'I realise that the sacrifice the proprietors are making will be appreciated by the ranks of the Conservative Party.' Owing to 'the tireless efforts' of Esmond Harmsworth, 'peace in the NPA' was speedily restored. 'Newspaper jealousies are proverbially strong,' Gwynne wrote to him, 'but if I may say so, you have risen above them all and shown great statesmanship and courage.' Whether Harmsworth's diplomacy had ministerial impetus must remain a matter for surmise.[1]

Caird was appointed 'an honorary member of the *Morning Post* staff', and Davidson treasured his purple pass to the building as a souvenir. At Churchill's suggestion, a dinner was held in honour 'of all who took part in the production of the *British Gazette*', some of whom were rewarded in next year's honours list. There were annual *British Gazette* luncheons to commemorate 'those extraordinary ten days', which Churchill looked back upon as 'one of the most vivid experiences of my somewhat variegated life'. Gwynne asked to keep as 'a very tangible and palpable momento of the *British Gazette* .... a telephone instrument' left behind in his room 'which connects me with the Treasury and with other Government offices .... Of course,' he assured Churchill, 'you understand this would be a private privilege not to be divulged to the public.' It is not clear whether his wish was granted and, if so, whether this momento moved with the *Morning Post* from the Strand to Tudor Street. In any case, it would have been disconnected when the Conservatives left office.[2]

Gwynne's personal connections did not depend on this channel of communication. The appointment of Davidson as party chairman in November afforded his easier access to Baldwin. Churchill, 'glad to think' that the events of May 1926 'have left behind them a better understanding between us', invited Gwynne to 'come & see me some time, & let us have a talk. I am much in the House of Commons in the afternoon, & nearly always free,' he wrote wistfully in the spring of 1927, when he merely had budgetary matters to keep

[1] Gwynne to Churchill, 13 May 1926 (copy), Churchill to Gwynne, 13 May 1926, memorandum by Gwynne [13 May 1926], Gwynne to E. Harmsworth, 13 May 1926 (copy), E. Harmsworth to Gwynne, 17 May 1926, and 'Agreement ... between the Newspaper Proprietors Association and the undermentioned Unions', 17 May 1926, Gwynne Papers.

[2] Caird to Gwynne, 17 May 1926, memorandum to the General Manager from the Editor, 12 May 1926, Gwynne to Churchill, 14 May 1926 (copy), and Churchill to Gwynne, 10 June 1927, Gwynne Papers.

him occupied.[1] The coal strike, which had dragged on long after the General Strike was defeated, was at last settled. To the disgust of Beaverbrook and Rothermere, Baldwin was more firmly entrenched than ever. The political press, which had suffered more than an interruption, was now forced to adjust to the 'Changed Values' that *The Times* so presciently discerned on 21 May 1926. That process was to prove painful and, in some instances, fatal.

---

[1] Churchill to Gwynne, 10 June 1927, Gwynne Papers.

Thirteen

THE WAGES OF HARLOTRY

The General Strike was followed by a flurry of activity, nearly all of it anticlimactic. Politically as well as professionally, newspapermen were compelled to adjust to situations that finally caught up with them. Nowhere was this more apparent than in the redefinition of editorial responsibility.

The annual conference of the TUC, held in Bournemouth in September, inevitably proved to be an inquest. Arthur Horner, speaking for the humiliated membership of the Miners' Federation, condemned the transgressions of Hamilton Fyfe in the *Daily Herald*. Ernest Bevin, all too aware of the anaemia of trade unionism, sought to avert a further bloodletting. 'Is the *Daily Herald* to become purely a stereotyped paper and avoid criticism?' he asked rhetorically. 'Unless the editor and the staff can express their thoughts and are prepared at times to face even your hostility if they believe they are right, then the paper is not worth its salt in developing thought and in moulding public opinion.' In fact, these lofty principles were soon betrayed by Bevin himself. Behind closed doors, where he always operated with fewer scruples and overweening authority, Bevin secured Fyfe's dismissal. The other directors were 'surprised, but they always did whatever Bevin told them to do,' recalled Fyfe, who accepted a settlement of £750 in lieu of a year's wages and who left as soon as William Mellor was ready to take over.[1]

Brailsford, subject to comparable recrimination, told Scott 'in confidence' of his own impending departure from the *New Leader*: 'The explanation is that, though I was continually compromising in an effort to please a mixed public, the inner governing circles of the party had never liked the paper.' That the weekly 'circulation had nearly trebled' ought to have eased his difficulties, but 'most of the new circulation was outside the party, & therefore was powerless to influence it'. His departure, delayed until October, fortuitously coincided with Fyfe's from the *Herald*.[2]

H. W. Nevinson reflected that 'all the very best editors' of his lifetime were 'deposed on account of their excellence': Ernest Parke, Donald, Gardiner, Spender, Massingham (twice), and Brailsford. It is not to detract from the

---

[1] TUC, *Report*, 1926, pp. 454–55; Fyfe, *My Seven Selves*, p. 279.
[2] Brailsford to Scott, 23 July 1926, *Guardian* Archives.

excellence of any of these individuals to suggest that party allegiances and professional attitudes counted still more strongly against them. The 2nd Viscount Burnham, whose closest connection with the *Daily Telegraph* was as its 'honest biographer', observed in 1955 that, through the period of the First World War, 'the Editor's function was very different from what it is in newspaper offices to-day or even from what it was in most newspaper offices in the late nineteenth century'. The *Telegraph* held to a tradition of faceless editors, informally designated as managers or heads of staff. Arthur Watson served for three years under the *ancien régime*, then for a quarter of a century under the Berrys, who changed neither the chauffeur nor the route. *The Times*, which had made it a point of honour in earlier days not to disclose the identity of its editor, alternated between those who primarily wrote and those who primarily managed. As elsewhere, the distinction was most clear-cut in the minds of the men involved. 'I'm not an editor, you know,' Gardiner told Robert Lynd, who interpreted that to mean that Gardiner 'was not greatly interested in the organising side of a newspaper, and that it was the political and literary features that alone engaged his whole heart'. Others would have said that Gardiner qualified for editorial distinction for those very reasons.[1]

During the inter-war decades, the practice at Peterborough Court became more and more prevalent, extending across the political spectrum. Lord Rothermere, who set the tone and forced the pace, professed little use for editors, whom he regarded as expendable. His son, inheriting his aversion with his peerage, later appointed an 'acting' editor of the *Daily Mail* so as to signpost the precariousness of that position. At the *Daily Express*, where Blumenfeld was first elbowed aside and then kicked upstairs, Beverley Baxter lasted for the better part of four years before 1933, when Arthur Christiansen began his long tenure. There, according to Christiansen, the 'form of wastage was in Assistant Editors, or Managing Editors as they are now called, American style'. Repeating, if only to disavow, Hannen Swaffer's 'slick ... crack' that 'a Managing Editor is a man who just manages to edit', Christiansen recited his own formula for editorial success:

> A newspaper editor is three people.
>
> He is a behind-the-scenes observer of great men and great events, who often knows as much about the nation's business as the men who conduct it and who can, directly or indirectly, wield great power through his newspaper.
>
> Next, he is a dedicated technician for whom the blank columns of tomorrow's newspaper are an ever-renewed challenge and excitement.
>
> Finally, he is an ordinary man, with his average share of success and

---

[1] Nevinson, *Last Changes, Last Chances* (New York, 1929), p. 273 n.; Burnham, *Peterborough Court*, pp. 161, 187–89; *News Chronicle*, 4 March 1946.

failure, remembering events great and small with the random selection of fallible human memory.

Taken in reverse order, the last of these attributes was especially obvious when Christiansen came to write his memoirs, four years after his retirement in 1957. With respect to the second property, technical competence, he was amply endowed. Yet, as the first of these 'three people', the one who moved in high circles and exercised influence, Christiansen hardly existed. 'The policies were Lord Beaverbrook's job, the presentation mine,' he candidly admitted.[1]

Personal factors entwined with institutional ones to dictate a fundamental change in editorial functions. C. P. Scott relinquished his chair at the *Manchester Guardian* in July 1929, though he remained governing director and, in that capacity, an increasingly embarrassing presence in the office. Collin Brooks, who bade him farewell in the *Financial News*, heard afterwards 'that the day after the retirement the old man forgot all about it and blue pencilled Ted Scott's leader as usual'.[2] Scott died on New Year's Day 1932, and his son, aged forty-nine, at last came fully into his own. Four months later, Ted Scott was drowned in a boating accident on Lake Windermere. The dynastic line was then broken.

'The prestige of the *Manchester Guardian* is one of the miracles of our time,' thought Brooks, who – like many people – had long wondered 'what will happen ... when Scott goes'. A migrant from the *Liverpool Courier* to the *Yorkshire Post*, Brooks anticipated that his own paper 'would become the dominating influence' in the north 'after the death of Scott, either from his loss or from the decline of the importance of Liberalism or from the decline of the importance of Lancashire – or from a combination of any or all of these'. Accustomed to hear the *Yorkshire Post* 'described as "the *Manchester Guardian* of Conservatism"', he looked forward to the day when the *Manchester Guardian* would be known as 'the *Yorkshire Post* of Liberalism'.[3]

Brooks waited in vain. W. P. Crozier, who had joined the *Manchester Guardian* in 1904 and had served as news editor since 1912, was appointed to fill the sudden vacancy. 'Thanks to him,' A. J. P. Taylor has written, 'the *Manchester Guardian* was transformed from a provincial organ of opinion into a national newspaper pre-eminent also for its news. . . . No English editor stood up to the impact of Hitler more firmly than he did.' As Taylor implies, however, this transformation was gradual. For all his solid virtues, including a schoolmasterly attention to syntax, 'Crozier was a stranger to London and its political world'. Following in C. P. Scott's footsteps, he made regular pilgrimages to the capital, where he interviewed public figures. Again, like his

---

[1] Christiansen, *Headlines*, pp. ix, 144, 274; *also see* Williams, *Dangerous Estate*, p. 83. In a letter to the editor of *The Times* on 22 April 1983, Lord Cudlipp listed editors of the *Daily Express* as an 'endangered species': there had been six of them within the previous six years.
[2] Brooks's diary, 19 July 1929.
[3] Brooks's diary, 27 July 1925.

illustrious predecessor, he recorded these conversations in lengthy memoranda, circulated among top-ranking members of the staff in order to inform – though not necessarily to form – the *Guardian*'s views. Of the men who received his visits, only Amery (possibly from his days on *The Times*) was a prior acquaintance. Crozier, lacking the intimacy with major politicians to which Scott made such insufferable pretence, did not presume to dispense advice. Instead, he 'listened, asked questions and departed', preserving his ability to recognize an evasive or disingenuous response.[1]

Whether by disposition or design, this new generation of editors was a self-effacing lot who mingled less frequently and certainly less freely with the panjandrums of Westminster and Whitehall. Garvin, a survivor from the so-called golden age, was something of an exception; but he edited a weekly and did so with increasing remoteness. Gwynne, another old-timer, found his closest contacts on the fringes of political society, which tended to skew the perspective of the *Morning Post*. Dawson, of course, consorted with statesmen at All Souls and Cliveden, but strictly in a private capacity that ultimately worked to the discredit of *The Times*. Regarding his friends' confidences as sacrosanct, he deliberately suppressed information about worsening conditions in Germany: 'I do my utmost, night after night, to keep out of the paper anything that might hurt their susceptibilities.' His negative example was partly responsible for promoting an ethic of disengagement, yet was also a justification for an attenuation that was already the norm. The rule was for editors to be neither seen nor heard, but merely read. A model editor, Oliver Woods subsequently explained to his wife, 'should meet people of Cabinet level once or twice a year' and should otherwise rely on subordinates 'whose judgment is recognised', for 'it is bad for an editor to be his own reporter. Social grace is necessary when on the climb – when there it should be unnecessary.' Just as Vernon Bartlett admirably served successive editors of the *News Chronicle* in this regard, Woods served Sir William Haley, an editor of *The Times* who 'did not mix much with Cabinet ministers', thus patterning himself on Barnes rather than Delane or Dawson.[2]

On the political side, the stock of social grace was conspicuously depleted by the withdrawal of Asquith in October 1926. J. A. Spender, always his admirer, paid him tribute: 'As he goes along, the journalist comes to class public men into those with whom he can & those with whom he cannot have self-respecting relations,' and Asquith – indisputably one of the former – had 'helped to smooth the path & lighten the work of a Liberal editor'. Garvin, who had long since adapted to the rough and tumble, took a less pious view. 'So your news

---

[1] W. P. Crozier, *Off the Record: Political Interviews 1933–43* (ed. A. J. P. Taylor; London, 1973), pp. xix–xx, xxiv (where Taylor reveals that Crozier was 'the first editor for whom I wrote'); *also see* Ayerst, *Guardian*, pp. 494–500.

[2] Dawson to H. G. Daniels (special correspondent), 23 May 1937 (copy), Dawson Papers; journal entry by Joan Woods [1960s], Woods Papers; Anthony Sampson, *Anatomy of Britain* (New York, 1962), pp. 125–26.

was right indeed about poor Squiffy,' he told Waldorf Astor when the announcement came. 'His lachrymose exit could hardly have been less effective in itself: nor will he go down as a great man. . . . On the other hand,' Garvin was obliged to concede, 'he was a fine personality in various ways & one does not remember anyone more free from the small petty vices of politics.' That was more than Garvin was prepared to say for Baldwin, 'a weak and morally-timid person with fits of intermittent obstinacy like all weak persons. He will never be a leader, a captain, in this world.' Acknowledging that 'moral leadership' was in abeyance, Garvin promised Astor that it would 'come someday back to your *Observer* – probably before 1927 is out'. In the meantime, however, the most portentous event in Fleet Street was the arrival of Cecil Harmsworth King at the *Daily Mirror*, then a paper with neither style nor ideology, which Northcliffe – King's uncle – had 'always regarded . . . as a sort of bastard child [and] protected without pride'.[1]

Other comings and goings were relatively routine. At a party that summer for Lady Astor, Dawson asked Barrington-Ward why he had ever left *The Times*, where he had worked in 1913–14. Had he remained, he would 'have been "high in the hierarchy" now'. Barrington-Ward 'reminded him that I didn't go back' after the war because Dawson 'himself was parting with Northcliffe and leaving his job and advised me to go to the *Observer* – where indeed I have been v. well treated'. The following year, Barrington-Ward returned to *The Times*, where he was to succeed Dawson as editor in 1941. Fyfe, at the cost of forfeiting the support of the trade unionists who ran the *Daily Herald*, impressed Lloyd George, who suggested he should 'go to see McCurdy' for a job as features editor on the *Daily Chronicle*. With an understanding that matters were set, Fyfe went on holiday and returned to find that McCurdy was no longer in a position to fulfil his promise. Fyfe thereafter freelanced for the *Spectator* as well as the *Chronicle* and other journals. He was too poor to pay heed to their politics.[2]

Beaverbrook, without loss of antipathy, emerged from his apathy. Under the general management of E. J. Robertson, 'the business side' of the *Daily Express* was showing a marked improvement. 'The paper is capable of earning £3000 or £4000 a week once the goodwill is thoroughly established,' Beaverbrook told Lord Wargrave (as Goulding had become). 'After all it has not been a long fight, for when you joined the Board the concern . . . was barely managing to keep going from month to month. Now it is certainly as strong as any popular London paper, with the exception of the *Daily Mail*.' Robertson's contribution was not merely administrative. Ignoring Blumenfeld, who was too much inclined to credit Baldwin with saving graces, Beaverbrook reported that Robertson had 'behaved with splendid judgment throughout the Strike

---

[1] Spender to Asquith, 7 October 1926, Asquith Papers; Garvin to Astor, 18 October 1926, Astor Papers; Edelman, *Daily Mirror*, pp. 1, 11.
[2] Barrington-Ward's diary, 23 July 1926; Fyfe, *My Seven Selves*, pp. 281–88.

and showed force of character and vigour in decision which convinces me that he is the foremost young figure in Fleet Street'.[1]

That was high praise indeed, coming as it did from a man who did not hesitate to damn. In November 1926, Beaverbrook wrote a signed, 'exclusive' article for the *Sunday Pictorial*. He offered it 'without price', save for a 'promise to advertise it extensively ... in the daily Press'. Entitled 'Has the Press Any Power?', this triple-column sermon dealt with 'the chief accusation raised by the politicians against the Press, and particularly against the popular Press', namely 'that it has power without responsibility. . . . The truth is exactly the opposite of this calculation,' argued Beaverbrook. 'The proprietor of a popular newspaper has responsibility without power, and he stands at the bar of popular opinion, not once every five years, but every morning of every day.' To illustrate his point, Beaverbrook hazarded that, if Rothermere 'had committed a third of the blunders in judgment and national policy which have been perpetrated by Mr Baldwin and Mr Churchill in the last fifteen months, he would have been punished in an unmistakable manner.' In the letter that accompanied his 'rough draft', Beaverbrook expressed confidence that Rothermere would not 'consider the attack on Baldwin ... too severe'. Either he miscalculated or the sight of a proof copy prompted his own second thoughts. The article was peremptorily 'cancelled'.[2]

The single minister to enjoy Beaverbrook's unequivocal favour was Hoare, whose brother had invested in – and, not inconceivably, still held – *Express* shares. When the Air Minister landed at Paris on the last leg of a return flight to India, he 'refused to give any interviews of any kind whatever ... to any but Max's papers'. He patronized the *Evening Standard*, 'much to the annoyance of other reporters', on the grounds that he and Beaverbrook 'were particular friends'. Furthermore, 'if an *Express* man had turned up, I should have done for him what I did for the *Evening Standard*'. Davidson, whom Beaverbrook denounced in his 'rough draft' for the *Sunday Pictorial* as the pivot of a 'small reactionary clique', did not approve of such reciprocal selectivity. He suspected that Beaverbrook was behind Rothermere and that Lloyd George was behind both of them. 'During the last few weeks it has become clear that Rothermere is definitely backing Lloyd George,' Davidson wrote on 17 August 1927 to Lord Irwin (formerly Edward Wood and later successively 3rd Viscount and 1st Earl of Halifax). 'The reason, of course, is perfectly obvious. He wants troubled and somewhat dirty water to fish in', instead of 'the smooth and crystal stream of the Baldwin Government. . . . It would be most amusing to know,' thought Davidson, 'whether Lloyd George has agreed to the same

---

[1] Beaverbrook to Wargrave, 31 May 1926, Wargrave Papers. Beaverbrook was moved to 'rejoice' at Wargrave's decision 'to stay in the *Daily Express*' at this time. 'You and two or three other shareholders stand out in my memory as having given me unswerving support,' he told Wargrave on 6 December 1928 (Wargrave Papers).

[2] Beaverbrook to W. McWhirter (editor, *Sunday Pictorial*), 15 November 1926, and proof copy, Beaverbrook Papers, G/15/111.

terms which Bonar rejected in '23 in return for Rothermere's support in his newspapers. Nearer the election it may be necessary to tell the truth but not yet.'[1]

On the afternoon of 24 September, Davidson 'had a two hours conversation' with Thomas Marlowe, 'an emphatic and patriotic Tory' who had left the *Daily Mail* after twenty-seven years as editor 'solely because R. has decided to espouse the cause of Ll.G.' By Marlowe's account, Rothermere 'was completely dominated by the Beaver, who had in his possession enough information to blackmail R. successfully', probably concerning the circumstances of Rothermere's ennoblement. 'The game is for R. and Max to give half-hearted support to the Conservative Party before and during the early part of the Election,' still two years in the offing, 'and at the critical moment to stab Baldwin in the back and run in Ll.G. Beaverbrook is the master mind,' Marlowe was convinced, and he, in turn, easily convinced Davidson. For Baldwin's enlightenment, Davidson provided an 'analysis of the *Daily Mail* covering $2\frac{1}{2}$ years' and culminating in a leading article (4 October) alleged to constitute 'an attack on the Conservative Party of a very violent nature'. (On the contrary, the item in question was a platitudinous plea to the delegates of the National Union, who were to assemble the next day at Cardiff: 'The country is in no condition for constitutional revolution. Its urgent needs are the revival of industry and the decrease of taxation.') Detecting hidden meanings, Davidson expected Baldwin to see that this piece 'obviously was dictated by Lloyd George himself'. He appended a list of 'nearly 150 leading articles attacking the Govt.' between 12 May 1925 ('Let Insurance Scheme Wait') and 16 September 1927, when the criticisms came full circle. The most explicitly hostile of them preposterously branded Baldwin 'A Socialist Prime Minister' (29 September 1925).[2]

Confronted with evidence of this nature, Rothermere replied in a signed article in the *Daily Mail* (19 October): 'As in the time of Lord Northcliffe so to-day, neither the *Daily Mail* nor any of its associated newspapers is attached to any party or to any party leader.' Roused to greater fury, he followed this pronouncement with a tirade against a bill to equalize voting qualifications between the sexes: 'With this destruction of the Conservative Party Mr Baldwin's name will be for ever associated.' Lloyd George would never have dictated that one.

Rothermere rebelled against Beaverbrook before, together, they launched a

---

[1] Hoare to Blumenfeld, 24 February 1927, Blumenfeld Papers; Davidson to Irwin, 17 August 1927 (copy), Davidson Papers.

[2] Memorandum by Davidson, 24 September 1927, Davidson Papers; Davidson to Baldwin, 4 October 1927, Baldwin Papers. 'The *Daily Mail* has been running a great agricultural stunt all the summer,' noted Sir Robert Sanders, who heard from Marlowe that 'it was being done in the interest of L.G.' In December, Baldwin delivered an after-dinner speech 'to the Central Office Staff ... & impressed on us' the dangers of 'the L.G. & Rothermere alliance'. Sanders's diary, 10 November and 9 December 1927, Bayford Papers.

full-scale offensive against Baldwin. The incitement was financial, not political. 'He was paying Beaverbrook large sums from the profits of the *Daily Mail*,' yet his own Daily Mail Trust 'was receiving very little from its holding in the *Daily Express*, which instead was being built up as the deadly rival of the *Daily Mail*'. In other words, Rothermere was subsidizing an assault by Beaverbrook, who vowed to Davidson: 'I shall go back to New Brunswick and retire a failure if I don't succeed in killing the *Daily Mail*.' In October 1927, Rothermere offered two and a half million pounds for Beaverbrook's majority shareholding, with the proviso that Beaverbrook would desist from further newspaper activity. Without that assurance, he would pay only a million pounds. 'Beaverbrook turned smartly round and offered to buy the Daily Mail Trust's 49% at that price.' From Beaverbrook's standpoint, there was really no reason to terminate the pre-existing arrangements. By the end of 1928, though 'not quite sure of these figures', he ventured that Wargrave would 'receive about £100,000 in cash' from the projected sale of the *Evening Standard*, realizing £80,000 profit'. Those negotiations were not consummated and, five years later, Beaverbrook instead paid Rothermere £275,483. 8s. for his minority interest in the *Standard*, which thereupon became part of London Express Newspapers.[1]

Along Fleet Street and extending through the provinces, this was a period of consolidation. *The Times* was quietly putting its house in order. The *Morning Post* was trying to live down its reputation for being 'too extreme'. The Duke of Buccleuch, aware that 'silly fools' were saying that 'the Duke of Northumberland makes more Bolshies than anyone else', called upon Gwynne 'to make the *M.P.* a popular newspaper without pandering like those with the largest circulations. ... Personally I think you will succeed, but there will be a lot of wirepulling to stop it,' he warned. 'The *Daily Telegraph* might have done a lot of good,' he continued with dukely disdain, 'if the proprietor was not obsessed with steps in the Peerage; in fact, the only honest title now is Mr.' The Berrys, who had yet to acquire the *Telegraph* or ascend to the peerage, were an anxiety to Garvin, who safeguarded his own honesty as a commoner. 'The *Sunday Times* had been giving trouble,' he told his noble proprietor. 'We are always fighting the *S.T.*' Owing to 'the stagnation of politics', the *Observer* found itself in 'a very difficult phase of management. No high-class journal can keep up a circulation on politics in the party sense,' and the *Observer*'s 'situation is exceptionally difficult. ... To act with judgment & spirit in such a fog, not to be dull yet not to be rash, is not easy.' Garvin accepted the prospect that the next administration 'will be of sorts a Coalition Government. That is, either a Labour-Liberal combination. Or a Liberal-Unionist one.' He was pleased to see that, on the morning of 8 November 1927, *The Times* reverted to the

---

[1] Taylor, *Beaverbrook*, pp. 248–49; memorandum by Davidson, 30 October 1928, quoted in Davidson, *Memoirs*, p. 316; Beaverbrook to Wargrave, 3 December 1928, Wargrave Papers.

practice of calling the Conservatives by their 'proper name of the "Unionist Party"', a more attractive appellation than 'Conservatism', a 'dull, dull word' that implied 'not enough!' Ever the prophet, he now foretold that 'Liberalism & Unionism together will prevent the triumph, not necessarily in 1929, but in a very few years, of Socialism and the surtax method.'[1]

Many of the familiar standard-bearers disappeared or, at the very least, reduced their commitments. Lord Riddell held on to the *News of the World*, but retrenched elsewhere. He informed Beaverbrook that 'since I sold the major portion of my interest in the *Western Mail* some years ago, I do not take much part in directing its policy. ... Lord Buckland is now principal shareholder.'[2] H. Seymour Berry, created 1st Baron Buckland in 1926 and soon to die, was the eldest and least prominent of the brothers, better known as a coal-owner than a press magnate. Lord Cowdray, whose fortune derived from oil, died in 1927 and was succeeded by his son Harold, a businessman of greater flexibility and a Liberal of greater pragmatism. Although the new Lord Cowdray had sat as MP for the Eye division of Suffolk from 1906 to 1918, Lloyd George 'never knew him very well' and gathered that he only 'kept up the feud out of loyalty to the father' and without much conviction.[3] This generational change registered a marked effect on the Liberal press, where morale was low and rapidly sinking lower.

On 18 January 1928, Cowdray met Henry Cadbury and Sir Walter (later 1st Baron) Layton to attempt a comprehensive salvage operation. The original objective was to create a triple alliance of Liberal morning papers: the *Daily News*, the *Westminster Gazette*, and the *Daily Chronicle*. Cowdray, taking the initiative, 'reported that I had written to Spender asking his support' and promising him 'an entirely free hand' in setting up 'a Political Committee' to consist of Spender himself, Layton, and an undesignated editor. Layton, part-time financial adviser to the *Daily News* board since the previous year, when he had turned down the offer of its editorship in order to continue at *The Economist*, contacted Catto in the hope of drawing in the *Chronicle*. Committed to Harrison, who had refinanced that paper with loans from Lloyd's Bank, the *Chronicle*'s owners were not interested. That left the *Daily News* and the *Westminster* to move bilaterally, at least for the time being. 'I am truly sorry we shall not be working together – but it cannot be helped,' Lord Reading wrote to Cowdray on 1 February, the day of fusion; 'we are now competing for Liberal & other readers as I suppose we were before. However good fortune to

---

[1] Buccleuch to Gwynne, 17 April 1927, Gwynne Papers; Garvin to Astor, 26 October and 8 November 1927, Astor Papers. 'Under the Coalition,' Garvin wrote to Scott on 17 December 1929 (*Guardian* Archives), 'I refused handles of superior brass and suffixes too. Last week I did it again without a moment's hesitation. ... A journalist *on active service* must go plain.'

[2] Riddell to Beaverbrook, 30 November 1927, Beaverbrook Papers, C/276.

[3] Clarke, *Lloyd George Diary* (2 October 1933), p. 239. One of the 1st Viscount Cowdray's last public acts was to sign a letter to *The Times* (2 June 1926) critical of Lloyd George's response to the General Strike.

both is not inconsistent with wishing that one may succeed better than the other.'[1]

Maclean, for one, was relieved to learn that the *Chronicle* had dropped from the package. 'I'm sure it will be better for the Party,' he assured Cowdray, whom he consequently expected to 'have more power in moderating the Ll.G. complex of the editor', Stuart Hodgson, 'and/or some of his staff'. Maclean was also 'sure Spender would have found it very difficult, if not impossible', to work in conjunction with certain elements on the *Chronicle*. And Spender's participation was deemed vital. Nevertheless, upon his return from an American lecture tour, Spender was 'a good deal perplexed by the newspaper change in my absence & the part in it attributed to me'. He decided to hold aloof: 'In the present state of the press there is positively no other choice.'[2]

The provincial properties of the Westminster Press group were not included in the transaction. Nor was the profit-making *Star*, where Wilson Pope had been editor since 1920. With a cash advance of £100,000 from Cowdray, the *Daily News* proceeded to resurrect its northern edition, shut down in March 1921. Fundamental questions, however, remained to be resolved. Henry Cadbury posed some of them in a memorandum on 5 March:

1. Is it our intention or desire to obtain a circulation of at least a million? If that is so, our appeal must be to the largest possible body of readers.
2. Are there a million people in this country who are Liberal in interest, and who would therefore wish to read a Liberal paper?
3. Is our appeal to be made so as to interest the woman reader, equally with the man reader?
4. Are we to give the kind of political news service which would satisfy those who are interested in the political organisations of the Liberal Party, or is our Liberal appeal to be so based as to swing a considerable part of the doubtful votes. ... In other words, how far should the *Daily News & Westminster* be a journal of opinion, or how far should we administer the Liberal point of view in such well-coated pills that we may affect the vote of a considerable number of waverers at the time of a General Election?

The alternatives were visible that morning on the news-stands, where the *Daily News* provided a 'short summary' of the fierce by-election battle at St Ives, while the *Chronicle* lavished space 'for political purposes'. Which format was to be adopted? Recognizing 'that it was very essential that our news service was entirely unbiased as between one section and another of the Liberal Party', Cadbury wondered 'how far we are to become interested in the internal difficulties and struggles of the two sections of the Party'. To ignore these

---

[1] Memorandum by Cowdray, 18 January 1928, and Reading to Cowdray, 1 February 1928, Cowdray Papers; draft memoir and H. T. Cadbury to Layton [March 1927], Layton Papers.

[2] Maclean to Cowdray, 2 February 1928, Cowdray Papers; Spender to Lady Oxford and Asquith, 12 February 1928, Asquith Papers.

divisions, which was tantamount to denying them, would be a breach of duty. Yet to parade them 'before the public does the cause of Liberalism as a whole real dis-service'.[1]

What was left of the Liberal press was a microcosm of a microcosmic Liberal Party. Harcourt Johnstone, an undying Asquithian, complained to Cowdray that 'certain members of the *D.N.* staff – to put it no more definitely' – had been heard to 'boast that they are out to help L.G. & down us – tho' they may do it more or less unobtrusively'. Johnstone 'earnestly hope[d] you'll get your million circulation & I agree that too much politics wd. be fatal to that end. All I pray,' he concluded, 'is that the political items may be selected without too much prejudice by the gentleman in charge.' Cowdray was by no means oblivious to the problem. 'Disunity is very harmful for the Party,' he declared on 7 March, 'but the harm is nothing compared to what it would be if the Party were to come under the dominion of a "Boss" ', even one with the 'enthusiasm, eloquence and drive' of Lloyd George. Johnstone and others seemed in danger of 'going off the deep end' in the opposite direction. 'With some of you,' Cowdray replied tartly, 'it is becoming a positive hobby to credit L.G. [with] all the ills that happen, and you are losing your sense of proportion.' True, the new *Daily News* had declined to print a letter from the Liberal Candidates Association; but that was 'a stupid mistake' and not, as Johnstone imagined, an act of censorship. The old *Westminster Gazette* had made it a policy to 'place politics first, and the cost to us was about £1 in dead loss for each working minute of its six years as a morning paper'. Its successor was not to be weighed down by party burdens. 'This means that Political organisations will of necessity continue to think that their views are unduly suppressed,' supposed Cowdray, 'but let it be recognised that the driving force is "filthy lucre" and not "filthy L.G."!'[2]

After a month of further haggling, Cowdray completely lost patience. Vivian Phillipps, one of the most demonstrative Asquithians and arguably the most devious, alleged that the *Daily News* had slighted a resolution passed by the executive committee of the Liberal Council, a congregation of Asquithian recusants. That resolution was prominently featured in the *Manchester Guar-*

---

[1] Memorandum by H. T. Cadbury, 5 March 1928, Cowdray Papers. 'To take ... Cadbury's memorandum ... seriatim', Cowdray answered as follows:

(1) Yes.
(2) Yes.
(3) Yes, but I have never found out how you can differentiate between what is interesting to a man and a woman. ...
(4) I agree that with a million as our objective we cannot cater with the idea of satisfying political organisations – certainly not in quantity, but we can always be striving to improve the quality.

Memorandum by Cowdray, 7 March 1928, Cowdray Papers.

[2] Johnstone to Cowdray [March, 1928], Cowdray to Johnstone, 15 March 1928 (copy), and memorandum by Cowdray, 7 March 1928, Cowdray Papers. Johnstone was Liberal MP for Willesden East in 1923–24, for South Shields from 1931 to 1935, and for Middlesbrough West from 1940 to 1945.

dian and *The Times*, 'whilst even the *Chronicle*, which does not look with too favourable an eye perhaps upon the Council, finds space for a reference to it'. Phillipps therefore found it 'little short of outrageous that a paper claiming to be a Liberal organ should ignore a pronouncement of this kind which has behind it the authority not merely of a body of prominent Liberals, but of a statesman of such world reputation as Lord Grey'. That was more than Cowdray could bear. He returned Phillipps's letter, which had not been 'worded ... so as to produce a feeling of sympathy'. Its effect was to make Cowdray doubt whether the game of political journalism was worth the candle. Soon afterwards, he asked Sir Herbert Samuel to evaluate the consequences of a potential sale to Rothermere. Samuel, who had recently succeeded Phillipps as head of the party organization, had 'no hesitation in saying that such an event would be a very severe blow to all our hopes for a Liberal revival'. Cowdray was probably referring to the disposal of certain provincial holdings, but he would have had strong reasons – political as well as commercial – to relieve himself of the vice-chairmanship of the reconstructed *Daily News*.[1]

Predictably, the circulation of the amalgamated morning journal was less than the sum of its previously separate parts. The *Daily Chronicle* was an obvious beneficiary, but other rivals got their share of the custom. The *Express*'s 'sales are still running very high', Beaverbrook was informed on 11 February. Returns, too, were 'naturally very high because of the increased print we have put out for several days in order to catch the *Westminster Gazette* readers', shopping for a substitute.[2] The *Daily Telegraph* and *The Times*, by virtue of their membership in the 'quality' league, were most likely to attract the *Westminster*'s former clientele, who would have been put off by the strident Toryism of the *Morning Post*.

Beaverbrook took the liberty of 'making a few observations – as a fellow professional or, at least, would-be professional' – to Sir William ('Bill') Berry, who had taken over the *Telegraph* on 9 January: 'I think it shows an immense improvement. The leader columns now deal with the topic of the day and not with one about a day old, as under the previous regime.' Still, there was 'one suggestion' that Beaverbrook presumed to 'put forward' for Berry's consideration:

> Why don't you make representations to the Conservative party as such that all the Cabinet Ministers' letters should not be confined to *The Times*? It is a most unfair arrangement. I would ask Ministers and the party managers that letters should be addressed *both* to the *Daily Telegraph* and *The Times*.

[1] Phillipps to Cowdray, 19 and 20 April 1928, Cowdray to Phillipps, 19 and 21 April 1928 (copies, including draft versions), and Samuel to Cowdray, 31 May 1928, Cowdray Papers. Phillipps had been Liberal MP for Edinburgh West from 1922 to 1924. For an account of the Liberal Council, a body of 'distinguished Liberals' whose 'history ... was not to prove very distinguished', see Wilson, *Downfall*, pp. 339–41.

[2] Robertson to Beaverbrook, 11 February 1928, Beaverbrook Papers, H/17.

No doubt *The Times* would refuse to print, but that would put their newspaper hopelessly in the wrong.

Once Bonar Law decided to advise his colleagues not to send any more party letters to *The Times*, and I was commissioned to take this news to Northcliffe in the form of an ultimatum. He gave way at once when faced with the prospect of the loss of the official letters. At that time it was proposed to take the *Morning Post* as a substitute vehicle for publication.

Beaverbrook admitted an ulterior motive: 'I don't like *The Times*. It is too hypocritical for my taste.' At the same time, he disclaimed any ambition for personal gain: 'I am not interested in my own newspapers. So this letter indicates a restless and meddlesome mind.'[1]

If uncharitable, the suspicion is none the less inescapable that Beaverbrook was seeking to embroil Berry with the government on the one hand and with *The Times* on the other. He later celebrated his friend and future biographer as 'The Man Who Likes to Stir Things Up', and the same may be said of him. Having cut loose from party entanglements, he was artfully encouraging Berry to become ensnared. Perhaps the most striking example of Beaverbrook's emancipation was the patronage he extended to David Low, whose cartoons were featured in the *Evening Standard*. Often insidiously left-wing, Low tilted at the Tory leaders and drove them to outrage. George Gilliat, raised to the editorship of the *Standard* when E. R. Thompson died in 1928, revealed that Low's work was difficult to syndicate. Gilliat had approached 'some 25 papers, and... found that in the main the Conservative firms were rather afraid', with 'most of the acceptances coming from the Liberal papers'. That was not surprising. Low made a specialty of depicting the pomposities of the Blimps in power. Birkenhead, stung by the Tory defeat in the 1929 election, blamed Beaverbrook for having added insult to injury: 'Your Cartoonist over a long period of time published filthy and disgusting cartoons of me. ....' But Beaverbrook always staunchly defended Low, who had licence to caricature his employer as a pint-sized mischief-maker and, as an Empire Crusader, an Imperial-pint-sized one at that. Only Rothermere, a caricature of himself, was out of bounds to Low's pen.[2]

During the long imminence of the general election, Rothermere was out of bounds in numerous areas. Despondent and disgruntled, he refused to subscribe to the Institute of Journalists. 'I can never forget that this Association,

[1] Beaverbrook to Berry, 6 February 1928 (copy), Beaverbrook Papers, C/78. 'Something more than an event in the world of journalism', as *The Times* called it in a leading article on 9 January, the transfer of the *Daily Telegraph* was 'a difficult and delicate topic' for Dawson to address. Financial report of *The Times*, February 1931 (copy), Dawson Papers.

[2] Beaverbrook, 'The Man Who Likes to Stir Things Up,' in M. Gilbert, ed., *A Century of Conflict* (London, 1966), p. 3; Gilliat to Beaverbrook, 3 March 1928, Beaverbrook Papers, H/1; Birkenhead to Beaverbrook, 6 June 1929, quoted in Taylor, *Beaverbrook*, p. 261. There were occasions when Low did portray 'Fat Rother' and 'Little Beaver'; see his *Autobiography* (London, 1956), p. 180 and the illustrations herewith.

for years, identified itself with unfair criticisms of Northcliffe,' he told Blumenfeld. 'I would suggest that you endeavour to induce those immensely wealthy new comers unto journalism, like the Astors, to provide you with a sufficient sum of money.' More brusquely, he refused to serve the publicity needs of the Conservative Party. 'Rothermere has definitely thrown in his lot with Lloyd George at the next election,' Davidson wrote to Lord Irwin in the spring of 1928. Paradoxically, that situation 'has made it almost impossible for Beaverbrook to avoid supporting us. The Berrys, who control a great proportion of the provincial press, are fighting Rothermere in almost every city in the United Kingdom for the possession of local papers, and so far have been winning,' reported Davidson. 'They I think can be definitely relied on to support us when the time comes.'[1]

Davidson may have exaggerated Rothermere's commitment to Lloyd George, but neither the depth of his bitterness nor the ferocity of his struggle with the Berrys. Through the agency of Allied Newspapers Ltd., the Berrys had already obtained control from Rothermere over the erstwhile Hulton newspapers. They went on to form a separate company, Allied Northern Newspapers Ltd., to extend their dominance. The 'head-on clash' with Rothermere, as Francis Williams has called it, 'found ... a sordid if dramatic expression ... in three cities, Bristol, Newcastle and Derby'. In the course of battle, 'several formerly independent local papers were driven to the wall while the invading giants spent money with wanton recklessness on trying to force each other out of business'. Lord Camrose, perhaps not the most impartial source, later calculated that Rothermere's costs at Newcastle alone exceeded a million pounds. By the end of 1929, the Berry brothers claimed a total of twenty-five daily and Sunday newspapers, not counting the *Midland Daily Telegraph*, which they held in association with Iliffe, and the profusion of periodicals published by their Amalgamated Press. Rothermere controlled fourteen daily and Sunday newspapers, and had a substantial interest in three others. The following year, the Berrys picked up the *Sunday News* (which they merged with the *Sunday Graphic*) and the *Independent* and *Mail* at Sheffield (which they merged with their local *Star*). Rothermere acquired papers at Leicester, Hull, and Grimsby as links in his Northcliffe Newspapers chain. At that point, a truce was called: Rothermere agreed to stay out of Cardiff, Sheffield, and Aberdeen; in return, the Berrys recognized south-western Wales as his fiefdom. Under the terms of the final treaty, concluded in 1932, Rothermere exchanged his evening paper at Newcastle for the Berrys' evening papers at Bristol and Derby, leaving the morning *Bristol Times* to the mercy of a local entrepreneur. By then, Rothermere had disposed of his majority shareholding in the *Daily Mirror* and the *Sunday Pictorial*, though they remained within his

---

[1] Rothermere to Blumenfeld, 23 May 1928, Blumenfeld Papers; Davidson to Irwin, 7 June 1928 (copy), Davidson Papers.

orbit. He was soon to sell his minority interest in Beaverbrook's enterprise as well.¹

With so many transactions to engage his attention, it was remarkable that Rothermere should have found time to expend on domestic and international politics. But, in a typically reckless way, he did. Since the mid-'20s, he had championed the improbable cause of Hungarian irredentism, demanding 'justice for Hungary' in the pages of the *Daily Mail* on nearly every morning in June 1927. Paul Addison has detected the heady influence of Princess Stefanie Hohenlohe-Waldenburg, the Jewish-born divorced wife of a Magyar nobleman; but the idea of a romance between them was remote, as Rothermere preferred his 'yum yums' to be of slighter proportions. His interest may well have been awakened – though it was certainly not encouraged – by F. A. Szarvasy, chairman of the British Foreign and Colonial Corporation, whom he drew upon for financial advice and allegedly for funds. In all likelihood, an agreeable visit to Budapest was all that Rothermere required to launch him on this bizarre mission. On numerous occasions thereafter, he was petitioned by Hungarian admirers who proposed to restore the monarchy with him as king. That would have been a sure way for them to sustain his interest, notoriously quick to flag, and thereby ensure themselves outlets for international propaganda. Flattered, Rothermere was more taken with the prospect for his son Esmond, who 'paid a quasi-royal visit in 1928 and was acclaimed almost like Bonnie Prince Charlie'. The project was kept alive by Lajos Lederer, a young Hungarian journalist employed as Rothermere's 'Hungarian secretary'. Yet, in the end, neither Rothermere nor Esmond would 'throw his hat (or rather his crown) into the ring'.²

The Conservative Party chiefs would have been delighted to have Rothermere remove himself to some castle along the Danube. Instead, keeping them guessing, he wandered no further than the south of France. Szarvasy, who spent five hours with him there in early September 1928, came back with the astounding news that Rothermere 'had made up his mind definitely to support the Labour Party between now and the next election'. Anything was possible where Rothermere was concerned. Szarvasy told Davidson that he had 'struggled with him' on this score and finally worked out a compromise. If Baldwin, in his speech to the party conference at Yarmouth, would include 'a

---

¹ Williams, *Dangerous Estate*, pp. 178–79; Steed, *The Press*, pp. 98–100; Camrose, *British Newspapers*, pp. 67–68; Report, Royal Commission on the Press, 1947–49, pp. 58–60; Labour Research Dept., *The Press* (1923 ed.), pp. 21–29.

² Addison, 'Patriotism Under Pressure,' in Peele and Cook, eds., *Politics of Reappraisal*, p. 193; Rothermere, *My Campaign for Hungary* (London, 1939). Beaverbrook recalled that Rothermere, in bidding for *The Times*, had 'depended upon a gentleman in the City named Mr Szarvasy, who had a flair for the capitalisation of good businesses. But the bad fairies gave Mr Szarvasy at the time an extra mixture of bad judgment, coupled with bad conduct whenever he got into a corner.' Beaverbrook to Morison, 30 September 1929, *Times* Archives. Lajos Lederer has described his own connections with Rothermere in the *Observer* (9 August 1981), and in conversations with the author.

sentence ... of sympathy with Hungary', Rothermere 'would be prepared to give unqualified support to the Conservative Party (which he would really much rather do) during the next general election. This is a promise,' Davidson wrote to Baldwin, 'which Szarvasy says you can get confirmed from Rothermere's own lips as soon as you like,' as Baldwin was then staying at Nîmes. As an extra token, Rothermere hoped that the Prime Minister would see fit to devote 'one sentence or possibly two in your speech' to the praise of Esmond, who was to announce 'his resignation from Parliament next week'.[1]

In a postscript to this letter, Davidson proposed to 'talk things over with Van' – Robert (later 1st Baron) Vansittart, then Baldwin's principal private secretary and subsequently permanent under-secretary at the Foreign Office – 'to get [the] F.O. view secretly'. He had presumably done so before the afternoon of the 24th, when Vansittart joined him for an hour-and-a-half-long interview with Esmond, a 'conceited but ... on the other hand quite a decent sort of fellow', whose parliamentary career was impaired by his Hungarian escapade. Vansittart decreed that foreign questions were inappropriate for discussion at a party conference and saw a danger of affronting the French. As if on cue, he then asked whether 'a chance reference to Hungary' would pave the way for a reconciliation between Baldwin and Rothermere. 'Harmsworth gave the whole show away very nicely,' recorded Davidson, 'by saying that Rothermere was terribly hurt and offended by the series of snubs and open rebuffs from Baldwin, and that he was prepared to have a bridge built as easily as possible from Baldwin's point of view.' After probing the origins of the estrangement, Davidson had 'no doubt' that Esmond 'will report faithfully all that passed to his father', along with a recommendation that any endorsement of Labour should be withheld, pending a sweeping review of foreign affairs.[2]

Sir William Berry took 'the view that Rothermere was gradually going mad': perhaps not 'mad in fact', but 'undoubtedly mad in action'. Over lunch with Davidson on 6 March 1929, Berry also waxed 'very anti-Lloyd George' and was nearly as hostile to Churchill and Joynson-Hicks, 'pinning his faith on Neville as the first Lieutenant to the Prime Minister'. As the meal ended, he sheepishly 'asked ... whether now his brother [Lord Buckland] is dead it would be possible for him to be considered for a peerage'. Davidson assured him 'that it was more than possible', but 'felt that it would be better if it were after the election rather than before'.[3] Thus, Sir William was kept dangling until 1929, when he was created Baron Camrose. That was a year after his younger brother had been made a baronet.

Newspapermen awaited the general election with a variety of expectations.

[1] Davidson to Baldwin, 13 September 1928, Davidson Papers. In a separate memorandum that day, Davidson concluded: 'The support of the Rothermere press is important, and if the purchase price is a platitudinous utterance, then I feel it should be paid.'

[2] Davidson to Baldwin, 13 September 1928, and memorandum by Davidson, 24 September 1928, Davidson Papers.

[3] Notes of Interviews with Chairman, 13 December 1928 and 6 March 1929, Davidson Papers.

The most common one was the boost that the campaign would inevitably give to circulations. No less important in many minds were the opportunities that would be afforded for the exercise of journalistic influence. The growing independence of the press, whether real or simulated, meant that bouts of partisanship were increasingly confined to election periods.

Davidson 'had originally contemplated an election in November 1928', but the Cabinet favoured postponement until the following spring. Lloyd George began to prepare for combat as early as June 1928, when the *Sunday Express* (24 June) disclosed that he was giving up his syndicated American column – and the £20,000 a year he earned from it – in order to apply his full time and energies to the Liberal effort. On its own behalf, the *Sunday Express* commissioned Leslie (later 1st Baron) Hore-Belisha, Liberal MP for Devonport and one of Lloyd George's zealots, to contribute 'Political Notes'. Contrary to 'the intention of Lord Beaverbrook', Hore-Belisha indulged in sarcasm that upset the 'pretty balance' between Churchill and Joynson-Hicks, not the two most compatible Cabinet colleagues. 'The explanation' was offered 'that Mr Blumenfeld thought some expressions too strong and altered them' for the worse: 'All this comes from want of Editorial direction on the part of somebody who sits soft.' Beaverbrook perceived otherwise and told Robertson that 'however hard I try, I cannot get Hore-Belisha out of the attitude of consistent and persistent hostility to the Cabinet'. Thus, Hore-Belisha had 'proved himself quite incapable of that kind of detachment of view which alone can give a political journalist a big position in Fleet Street'. The same deficiency was evident in 1942, when Hore-Belisha, driven from office, raised troublesome questions about Beaverbrook's wartime mission to the United States.[1]

The readers of the two *Express*es had no way of knowing the misgivings that Beaverbrook privately entertained. Beverley Baxter made 'a careful study of all letters addressed to the Editor' and considered it 'worth noting that the trend ... over the last three or four weeks is rather antagonistic'. One correspondent after another had faulted 'our defence of the police' in civil disorders, 'constant criticism of Joynson-Hicks, unfriendly attitude towards France', and so on. Baxter did 'not offer any comment ... except to wonder if perhaps in our general policy we are a little sparing of praise, and too prone to attack'. Baldwin and his ministerial colleagues would have been disposed to agree. As the election approached and Conservative weakness became apparent, Baxter proposed that 'the *Daily Express* should begin to constitute itself as the guide, counsellor and friend of that unhappy party'. Beaverbrook would have none of that.[2]

---

[1] Davidson, *Memoirs*, pp. 298–99; A. A. Whelan to Robertson, 6 August 1928 (copy), and Beaverbrook to Robertson, 30 September 1928 (copy), Beaverbrook Papers, H/17; Taylor, *Beaverbrook*, p. 524; *also see* Crozier's interview with Hore-Belisha, 20 February 1942, in *Off the Record*, pp. 288–92.

[2] Baxter to Beaverbrook, 20 August 1928 and 12 September 1929, Beaverbrook Papers, H/16, H/18.

Introspection was an editorial and proprietorial pastime during this lull before the storm. Prolonged political uncertainty, coupled with the shakiness of finances, encouraged the general tendency of newspapers to temporize. It also accounted for the rapt attention that they paid to one another. A leading article ('No Coalition') in the *Star* on 2 October 1928 implied to Baxter 'that the Liberals at least are willing for an understanding with the Socialists which might well extend to many constituencies where there would normally be a three-cornered fight'. Beaverbrook inferred the contrary: 'Notwithstanding what the *Star* says, Lord Beaverbrook's opinion is that there will be no Coalition between Liberal and Labour.' His electoral experts had forecast that 'Lloyd George should be in a position to dictate his terms to put either party in power', and the *Express* comported itself on that premiss. Not so *The Times*, which expected Baldwin's return with a diminished majority. Barrington-Ward, who had transferred his services from the Cliveden Astors to the Hever Astors, lunched with the former on 2 November. Nancy ('just back from America' and 'not quite so sparkly as sometimes'), Waldorf, Philip Kerr, and Tom Jones all pounced upon him for 'the shortcomings of *The Times*'s editorial policy' in foreign affairs. He had to admit – if only in the privacy of his diary – that the paper was 'much too subservient to the Foreign Office, Admiralty (especially) and conventional club view', but he neither exercised authority in these matters nor felt free to 'criticise ... to people outside'.[1]

There were logical reasons for this exceptional degree of self-consciousness. In the autumn of 1928, the Institute of Journalists sponsored a series of lectures, delivered by senior members: Gardiner gave the first on 10 October ('The public will ultimately lose its respect for the press and return contempt for contempt'); Donald, the second on 24 October (making the dire prediction that 'in the near future there will be three fewer morning newspapers in London'); and Gwynne, president-elect of the Institute, the third on 7 November. For present purposes, Gwynne's was the most instructive. It began with a recollection of 'the old days when – at least in politics – the leader writer was only allowed "to think of it" in one way'. Under that system, any 'speech made by a front-bench politician was "admirable", "clear and unmistakable", "a statesmanlike pronouncement", etc., etc.', provided of course that the politician and the newspaper belonged to the same party. If not, 'whatever might be the nature of the speech', the editorial response 'never varied from wholesale condemnation of it'. Although Gwynne identified himself as 'a warm admirer of late Victorian journalism', he gave his own generation credit for having 'adopted a better and altogether more sensible method in political commentary. Indeed, the change has been so thorough that we have perhaps run into the other extreme,' he told his audience of novices. 'Independence of political thought is now so widely spread that it has almost become confusing,

---

[1] Baxter to Beaverbrook, 2 October 1928, and Beaverbrook to Baxter, 3 October 1928 (copy?), Beaverbrook Papers, H/16; Barrington-Ward's diary, 2 November 1928.

and it is difficult, if not impossible, at times to give the correct political label to any newspaper.'[1]

That may have been to stretch the point. Nevertheless, the point was there. For a larger proportion of a dwindling number of newspapers, there existed an unprecedented array of options. Over the next quarter of a century, that range was to widen as the ranks of newspapers were to thin, until such time as the political press was no more than a shadow of its Victorian self. Gwynne's lecture was more an augury than an inventory, but no less significant for that.

Rothermere, the freest of free agents, immediately gave substance to Gwynne's hypothesis. His pro-Labour manifesto, which his son had persuaded him to delay, was delivered on 9 December. It took the unconventional form of a personal letter 'to a correspondent', published that day in the *Sunday Dispatch*. 'I have little or no hope from any political party in this country,' Rothermere informed his unnamed – and, in all likelihood, non-existent – interrogator. 'I do, however, think something may be gained by bringing the electorate sharply up against reality' and, for this purpose, a socialist majority might prove salutary. The *Daily Herald* reprinted and derided Rothermere's 'latest lucubration' the next morning. The *Morning Post* (10 December) denounced the 'conversion to Socialism', which Rothermere (11 December) denied having made.

Once Lloyd George's campaign got under way, promising an alternative to Baldwinism on the one side and socialism on the other, Rothermere moved from obstructionism to enthusiasm. 'George has got a sudden accession of strength & it appears likely that Rothermere will support him,' Beaverbrook wrote to an American friend on 24 March 1929, after Lloyd George had promulgated a set of 'categorical, definite, detailed, practical proposals' to conquer unemployment. 'If George gets consistent support he will win a great many seats & so no doubt hold the balance of power in the next Parliament,' predicted Beaverbrook. 'The Conservative party stands no chance of coming back with a majority.' Sharing this vision, Rothermere sent a telegram four days later to Gwynne and probably to others as well. 'There is only one way to fight the Socialist Party and that is a "Get Together" Movement,' he proclaimed. 'Under the magnetic personality of Mr Lloyd George Victory is certain. Without it there is nothing but disaster ahead.' Gwynne's telling response was to forward a copy of this wire to Davidson at party headquarters, thereby sparing himself and the *Morning Post* the confusion that attended what he had prematurely celebrated as the 'independence of political thought'.[2]

*   *   *

[1] Institute of Journalists, *Journal*, November and December 1928; *also see* H. A. Taylor, *Donald*, p. 238 and appendix.

[2] Beaverbrook to J. M. Patterson, 24 March 1929, quoted in Taylor, *Beaverbrook*, p. 259; Lloyd George's speech of 1 March 1929, quoted in Wilson, *Downfall*, p. 345; Rothermere to Gwynne, 28 March 1929 (telegram; copy), Davidson Papers.

The *Daily Herald*, with a mission not to fight socialism but to propagate it, was not permitted the luxury of equivocation. 'Bevin's biggest contribution to the Labour movement in 1929–30 lay outside the sphere of government,' according to his biographer. Deciding in the autumn of 1928 'that the time had come to take a direct hand' (as if to suggest that Bevin had hitherto held back), he undertook to raise sufficient capital – possibly as much as a million pounds – to put the paper on a par with its mass-circulation rivals. Negotiations with the Prudential Assurance Company for a loan of £300,000 fell through, as did other projected arrangements. Thereupon, Bevin turned to Elias, 'a simple, unassuming character with great business ability' who was still 'looking for a daily paper with which to occupy the silent presses of the *People* during the week'.[1]

Bevin did not offer the *Daily Herald* for sale, but rather for lease and in such a way as to preserve editorial jurisdiction for the trade unions. He and Elias, 'the presiding genius of Odhams', understood perfectly each other's requirements. Bevin urgently needed an increase in circulation and advertising revenues to plug the drain on TUC finances, restricted by the punitive Trade Disputes Act of 1927. Elias, with a commercial mentality ahead of his time, 'had no interest in newspapers as vehicles of ideas, neither his own nor anyone else's', but 'was concerned with them simply as merchandise'. Possibly, too, he entertained certain personal aspirations. 'We have no party creed or bias. We want a peerage for Elias,' sang the *Herald* angels after he took over.[2]

The agreement between the TUC and Odhams was not ratified until 30 August 1929, exactly three months after the general election. It established a new company with a fixed capital of £100,000. Shares to the value of £49,000 were assigned free of charge to the TUC in exchange for the paper's goodwill and copyright. The remaining £51,000 was vested in Odhams, which subscribed in cash. Four 'A' directors, who alone commanded voting rights with respect to political and industrial questions, were appointed to represent the TUC; along with Bevin, they were Walter Citrine, Ben Tillett, and Arthur Pugh. Five 'B' directors were appointed to represent Odhams. Elias was named chairman, and Bevin vice-chairman. 'No one was invited to join the Board from the National Executive of the Labour Party or from the Parliamentary Labour Party,' Alan Bullock has pointed out. 'The political policy of the party was defined in the articles of association as that laid down from time to time by the Labour Party Conference; its industrial policy as that laid down by the TUC.' In the event of a dispute between directors over these ambiguous categories, an outside arbitrator was to be called in. Lord Sankey, who occupied the Woolsack in the second Labour government, was named 'first referee'; Sir William (later 1st Earl) Jowitt, the Attorney-General, was next on tap. 'The surprising thing is that this partnership between the TUC and a commercial, profit-making firm of publishers worked,' Bullock has remarked

[1] Bullock, *Bevin*, I. 420.
[2] Williams, *Right to Know*, pp. 107–10, and *Dangerous Estate*, pp. 188–89, 192–93.

with restrained incredulity, 'largely thanks to the mutual confidence of Elias and Bevin.' While it cannot be said that the two men saw eye-to-eye, they contrived to overlook each other in reasonable amity.[1]

By the time that this complex machinery was set in place, MacDonald had returned to the premiership at the head of a second minority Labour administration. The *Daily Herald*, with a circulation of about 250,000 and a penchant for words like 'lucubration', could have provided the Labour Party with but slight electoral assistance. Soon afterwards, owing to Bevin's indefatigability and Odhams's lavish offers of free gifts and insurance schemes, circulation rose above the million mark with the help of a Manchester edition. Even so, there was no correlation between the paper's sales and the turn-out of Labour voters. In 1929, when the *Herald* was still struggling for survival, Labour polled over eight million to elect 288 MPs on 39.3 per cent of the average vote. (The Conservatives returned 260 MPs on a fractionally higher percentage.) In 1931, when the *Herald* was a redoubtable success, the total Labour vote fell by a million.

The Liberals, backed by massive funding from Lloyd George, fought their last great battle in 1929. Like Labour, they sought to maximize their inferior resources for publicity. William Harrison, however, was no Elias. 'With the *Chronicle* under the control of proprietors who are not enthusiastic Liberals', Henry Cadbury and Cowdray agreed that the time had come 'to gain additional political followers for the *Daily News*. In order to make the most of this possibility,' Cowdray advised, 'we ought to give considerable thought as to how we can best produce in the news columns sound political teaching without losing the present pleasant reading but rather superficial matter.' That marked something of a climb-down. The Westminster Press company, which sustained 27 per cent of the 'trading losses' on the *Daily News*, met a deficit of £90,066 in the eleven-month period following incorporation (1 February to 31 December 1928) and a further £37,454 in the first quarter of 1929. A 'very satisfactory increase in sale', though not immediately apparent, 'as well as almost a 50% increase in Advertising Revenue' had somehow failed to achieve a breakthrough.[2]

Other Liberal newspapermen were similarly anxious, but mutually suspicious. On 17 January, Sir Robert Donald wrote to request an interview with Cowdray, who saw him five days later. Sensing the 2nd viscount to be of different stuff from his father, Donald 'started by asking whether we were still interested in newspapers and, if so, whether I was tired of the business'. Tartly, Cowdray 'replied ... that I needed some occupation but, at the same time, I repeated words I heard my father use ..., namely, we were always prepared to sell at the right price'. He hastened to add, 'however, that in the case of

[1] Bullock, *Bevin*, I. 421.
[2] Memorandum by Cowdray, 14 December 1928, and annual report, Westminster Press Ltd., 30 March 1929, Cowdray Papers.

newspapers politics entered into the matter and I was not entirely free'. For example, six months before, he had turned down an offer that did not contain the necessary political safeguards. Donald presumed – and Cowdray did not deny – that that offer had emanated from Sir Leicester Harmsworth. 'Politically, he was as good a Liberal or better than Harmsworth,' remonstrated Donald, who described how he had dissuaded Rothermere from starting an evening journal in Birmingham. That, it emerged, had been largely in Donald's own interest. For he 'was not thinking of the *Daily News*', but rather of the Birmingham *Sunday Mercury*, which he was angling to acquire on behalf of Anglo-Foreign Newspapers Ltd., a new company chaired by H. S. Horne, 'who is a Liberal. Their policy at the moment,' Donald stated, 'is to collect profitable trade journals and the foreign element is limited to a share in the Paris *Daily Mail*.' His parting words were for Cowdray to 'be thinking it over and let me know', but exactly what it was that Cowdray was being asked to ponder was 'not very clear'.[1]

Despite Donald's aspersion and the fruitlessness of previous discussions, the Westminster group resumed its desultory negotiations with Sir Leicester Harmsworth. J. B. Morrell spent the afternoon of 4 April listening to him 'in a very pleasant room – with some interesting Constables on the wall' to provide visual distraction. In this civilized atmosphere, Harmsworth engaged in 'a general talk', giving not 'very much to report' to Cowdray. He proffered assurances 'that, whilst he wishes to see the Liberal Press in the country maintained and strengthened, he is very anxious to protect his own considerable business interest in the West, which was bringing him in £95,000 a year'. Among other things, Harmsworth mentioned that he had received 'more than one offer from Harrison, and if Harrison came up to his figure, he would have to give it serious consideration' without mind to politics. He briefed Morrell on the latest skirmishes in the provincial war between Rothermere and the Berrys, anticipated that the *Daily Express* would outstrip the *Daily Mail*, and mooted 'a combination of the *Daily News* and our Group with his own papers'. Morrell cited the Cadburys as an obstacle: 'apart from their dislike of being associated with other papers, [there] was the clause in the Cadbury Trust which said they must have control'. To probe Harmsworth's intentions, Morrell 'asked him whether he was still of the opinion that the Harrison Group ought to be included' in any larger amalgamation. Harmsworth saw the advantage, but 'thought it would be difficult to combine' the *Chronicle* and the *Daily News* 'in the same way as was done with the *Daily News* and the *Westminster Gazette*'. From all indications, the *Chronicle*'s 'circulation was going down', although its advertising receipts were holding up. The high price that Harrison had recently paid as well as his plans to spend £240,000 on the installation of new machinery did not suggest that he conceived of himself as a bird of passage, much less that

---

[1] Memorandum by Cowdray, 22 January 1929, Cowdray Papers.

his plumage would soon be plucked. Morrell departed with 'no doubt that Sir Leicester Harmsworth is more interested in a *Daily News & Westminster* combine with his own papers than with the Harrison Group'. Yet the conversation moved him to give 'some further thought to the idea of attempting to amalgamate the *Chronicle* with the *Daily News*', which seemed the easiest and most politically desirable way to 'convert the *Daily News* liability into an asset'.[1]

Before this tack could be pursued, the election intervened. The warm-up began long before Parliament was dissolved. Sir William Berry volunteered his services to direct 'a two months' campaign of an intensive nature' to counteract Lloyd George's onslaught. Davidson implored Baldwin to rescind 'the rule against Cabinet ministers writing articles' as it imposed a handicap on the Tory side. Would it not be sufficient, he asked, if ministers were not allowed to accept fees? That would never have satisfied Birkenhead, who had quit the India Office with a wish 'in any case to go into Berry's business after this Parliament'. When the contest was over, both Birkenhead and Churchill accepted remunerative commissions from the *Daily Telegraph*. Churchill's contribution consisted of a series of vivid dispatches from North America. 'From our window we can see at night the Rothermere paper mills all lit up,' wrote his son, aged eighteen, who accompanied him to Canada. 'Papa said apropos of them, "Fancy cutting down those beautiful trees we saw this afternoon to make pulp for those bloody newspapers, and calling it civilisation." '[2]

With ministerial pens kept under wraps, the Conservatives depended on a cohort of professional publicists. 'The coming election is, to my mind, the most important of all that have occurred in the history of England,' Gwynne told Baldwin. 'If you fail to get a majority in the next Parliament the failure of democracy in England is assured. If you succeed I believe it is safe for a century, if not for all time.' The Labour Party, which Gwynne interpreted as 'the negation of democracy', appeared relatively less menacing to Rothermere, whom the *Morning Post* accused of having turned socialist out of revenge. 'Wrong as usual,' Rothermere replied to Gwynne with a shrug.

> You are telling your readers that I am angry. On the contrary I am thoroughly amused in exposing your political game. Like my brother the late Lord Northcliffe I relish and thrive on controversy.
>
> Having consolidated the Liberal Party by your sinister attack on Mr Lloyd George you now seem in full flight but the mischief you have done to the Conservative Party cannot be repaired. Within three months of the start of this unscrupulous campaign of yours, the Liberal Party began to make

[1] Morrell to Cowdray, 5 April 1929 (with note by Morrell dated 24 April 1929) and memorandum by Morrell, 5 April 1929, Cowdray Papers.

[2] Note of Interview with Chairman, 18 December 1928, Davidson Papers; Davidson to Baldwin, 18 March 1929, Baldwin Papers; entry of 20 March 1928, *Amery Diaries*, I, 539; Gilbert, *Churchill*, V, 341, 344 n.

spectacular progress culminating in the wonderful bye-elections of three weeks ago,

when seats at Eddisbury and Holland were captured from the Conservatives. At the time, the *Observer* (24 March) credited the Liberals with 'their very best week since the war'. Yet Rothermere did not go so far as to suppose that a full-scale Liberal revival was at hand. Rather, he predicted with startling accuracy that 'the Socialist Party will win the election in the sense that it will be the largest party in the new House'. The *Morning Post* had misrepresented him, he insisted, by asserting that he was working towards that end. 'Rapprochement between the two anti Socialist parties under the circumstances is all to the advantage of the Conservative Party. It is a course I have strongly urged and I shall continue to do so.'[1]

Small wonder that Rothermere was misunderstood. Depending upon the truculence of his mood, his statements could be construed as endorsements of any party or as a plague on all political houses. Labour dared neither to embrace nor to offend him. Conservative officials were in no hurry to write him off. The Liberals deigned to count him as one of themselves, if only to the extent that Maclean momentarily fantasized that Rothermere might join his brother Leicester 'in finding the cash ... for a Liberal Press to grow and expand'.[2]

This, indeed, was a time of Liberal self-delusion. Lloyd George had money, ideas, an unaccustomed deference from Liberal elder statesmen, and a grip on the public imagination. To those old enough to remember it, the magical spirit of 1906 seemed to have been reignited. Walter (later 1st Baron) Rea, a veteran of those halcyon days who was trying for a second comeback, was distressed to observe that the *Daily News* was taking a more casual approach than it had done under George Cadbury's stewardship. 'Unfortunately these days we have to run Elections not on the fundamental issues of policy, but on issues which will be understood by the big majority of the 25 million voters,' explained Henry Cadbury, who recalled that, even in 1906, the 'minor issue' of Chinese Slavery had been magnified out of all proportion. For that reason, the *Daily News* paid less attention to Grey's sober speech at Taunton than to Lloyd George's antics. 'Personally I would rather read one of Grey's speeches than a dozen of Lloyd George's,' Cowdray confessed to Rea, 'but for vote catching and selling a popular newspaper, I am afraid that there is no question but that "L.G. has it".'[3]

[1] Gwynne to Baldwin, 5 April 1929, Baldwin Papers; Rothermere to Gwynne, 11 April 1929 (copy), Gwynne Papers. For a spirited account of Rothermere's campaign activity, including the Albert Hall meeting his *Evening News* arranged for Lloyd George on 26 March, see John Campbell, *Lloyd George, The Goat in the Wilderness 1922–1931* (London, 1977), ch. 8.

[2] Memorandum of an 'Interview with Donald Maclean, 1st May 1929,' Cowdray Papers.

[3] Cadbury to Cowdray, 23 May 1929, and Cowdray to Rea, 22 May 1929 (copy), Cowdray Papers. Rea was Liberal MP for Scarborough 1906–18, for Bradford North 1923–24, and for Dewsbury 1931–35.

Whatever Lloyd George had, he did not keep it long enough to benefit at the polls. F. W. Doidge took time off from covering the 'hustings' for the *Evening Standard* to report privately to Beaverbrook. 'The Labour candidates have been almost invariably the best platform speakers. The Conservative candidates have been the worst,' he communicated on 6 May. 'If these meetings are to be accepted as any criterion of the public mind, then it would seem that there exists a strong enmity towards Lloyd George', whose name elicited 'real hostility' whenever it was mentioned. ' "Where are the Homes for Heroes?" "Who promised to hang the Kaiser?" "What about squeezing Germany till the pips squeak?" All the old wartime cries are now used to confound the Liberal candidates.' Labour contenders were particularly adept at being able 'to destroy the Liberal Leader's prestige out of the mouths of old enemies in his own party'. Each Labour candidate was asked by telegram to make a platform reference to the *Daily Herald*. Doidge found it 'rather amusing at Portsmouth on Thursday night to hear the Labour candidate declare that he got more material for his speeches out of the *Daily Express* leaders than from almost any other source'.[1]

Perhaps Lloyd George's challenge had peaked too soon. Perhaps it had never really existed. Garvin, 'doing my best in this horrible contest' to ensure that the *Observer* kept the respect of 'its Liberal readers and the Labour readers too', was in 'a moral pinch'. He regarded Davidson's direction of the Conservative effort as 'the most miserable show of my lifetime. Baldwin never will have the vision or drive enough,' Garvin told his proprietor on 23 May. 'He might easily have roused a magnificent fight', but seemed too obsessed with the Liberals to perceive the greater threat from Labour. Garvin's advice, tendered six days later on the eve of balloting, was diametrically opposed to Baldwin's policy: 'Fight Socialism; respect Liberalism, for it is undying; tell Liberals that they *cannot* be more than third & that your programme is far wider in itself than theirs and *more practically progressive*.'[2]

The results gave the Liberals fifty-nine seats, few of them in the industrial areas of high unemployment to which their appeal had been addressed. They had lost heavily to Labour; but, then, so had the Conservatives, who emerged with 260 seats. That was exactly the number Beaverbrook had projected as their maximum in a telegram to Rothermere on 12 May. Always glad to be proved a pundit, Beaverbrook saw no reason to regret the tepidity of his support. 'I wanted the defeat of the Government because I believe it was bad,' he replied on 7 June to a rebuke from Birkenhead. Nor did Rothermere have any misgivings about his own, more aggressive antagonism. Gwynne, however, lamented Baldwin's failure 'to save democracy in England. . . . This is the moment for courage, courage and more courage,' he counselled his chief on the 31st. 'In the permutations and combinations of the future I hope only . . .

[1] Doidge to Beaverbrook, 6 May 1929, Beaverbrook Papers, H/18.
[2] Garvin to Astor, 23 and 29 May 1929, Astor Papers.

that you will not have anything to do with the Liberals as long as L.G. is their leader.' Baldwin, whose chances would have been improved had he followed Garvin's advice rather than Gwynne's, received further commiseration from Asquith's widow. 'The boosting in the Press of Ll.G. shows how *very* little power it has,' she added with mordant logic.[1]

Remarkably few politicians grasped that salient point. Birkenhead, for example, heaped the blame for the Tories' defeat on the perfidious press lords. On 4 June, Amery attended a Derby Eve dinner at the Ambassadors Club: 'F.E. made the usual amusing speech in which he described how he had been sent for to form a government by Lord Rothermere but that Lord Beaverbrook had insisted on coming round as having equally contributed to the destruction of the Unionist Government.' At a lower level, the unsuccessful Tory candidate at Swansea West expressed disappointment at his poor showing, which he ascribed to the fact that 'the Rothermere Press has purchased our two local evening papers – the *South Wales Post* and the *Cambria Daily Leader*' – which had split the Conservative vote by plumping for the Liberals. Such excuses did not carry conviction. Barrington-Ward, responsible for editing *The Times* in Dawson's absence, saw matters more clearly. 'Baldwin resigned today,' he noted in his diary on 4 June: 'I wrote a leader, on the whole complimentary to his Administration. It has been surprisingly good at home though not dramatic enough for democratic needs. Abroad it has been slow and unimaginative.... The Labour Govt. will probably prove the converse of this judgment.' Two days later, Barrington-Ward dined at the Astors', where he met Terence O'Connor and Harold Macmillan, two of the Conservative casualties with whom he 'discussed the late election and present prospects. The main agreement was that the progressive part of the party must capture and liberalise the machine, and that someone of Cabinet rank (e.g. Neville Chamberlain) should head the organization.' These recommendations were more to the point than other people's recriminations.[2]

It was exceedingly difficult for party spokesmen, especially those tangentially connected with newspaper management, to appreciate the limitations of journalistic influence. 'Driving up to town on Friday from Burton', where he had defended his seat, John Gretton saw 'everyone ... reading newspapers: there must have been a record amount of paper printed' during the campaign, he remarked to Baldwin.

> Our Press would appear to need strengthening and a careful revision of the whole Press situation is suggested. We want newspapers which do not leave out a part of the news but set out the news of the day in due proportion, a

[1] Taylor, *Beaverbrook*, pp. 261–62; Gwynne to Baldwin, 31 May 1929, and Lady Oxford and Asquith to Baldwin, 2 June 1929, Baldwin Papers.
[2] Entry of 4 June 1929, *Amery Diaries*, I, 597 (Taylor, *Beaverbrook*, p. 261, dates this dinner as 5 June and includes Beaverbrook's witty rejoinder); A. W. E. Wynne to Baldwin, 4 June 1929, Baldwin Papers; Barrington-Ward's diary, 4 and 6 June 1929.

very difficult thing to secure. The interpretation of the news or the propaganda in the leading articles, etc., is secondary. The majority of the popular newspapers are no longer news-sheets but they are 'headline mongers' and they leave out generally, or hide in an obscure place, the news which does not suit their propaganda.

Gretton's arguments were essentially valid, yet utterly impracticable. How was 'the whole Press situation' to be defined, and under what – or whose – auspices was it to be carefully revised? Who was to legislate the allocation of column space, and to whose satisfaction? Furthermore, on what grounds was it to be assumed that the consumption of newsprint either reflected the prevalence of propaganda or materially affected voting patterns? Beaverbrook, with a humility that belied each of Gretton's preconceptions, congratulated Lord Derby on the Conservative showing in Manchester and Liverpool. In his opinion, 'the Conservatives would have done better' throughout the country if only their policies had been clarified and the Central Office had operated with reasonable efficiency. 'I am sure there is no obstacle to the support of the Conservative Party by the independent newspapers,' he assured Derby. 'On the other hand, the Party may not care for the support of these papers, in which case it is not worth bothering about.'[1]

Baldwin evidently considered certain newspapers more 'worth bothering about' than others and made his choice on the basis of their compliance. His letter of appreciation to Lord Camrose (as Sir William Berry had just become) gave both Berry brothers

> real pleasure. We have had the satisfaction of giving our assistance to somebody for whom we have the greatest respect and in whose honesty of purpose and singleminded devotion to the welfare of the community one could only have the most unbounded confidence. . . . You had inspired in my brother Buckland a great affection and there is not the smallest doubt that had he been living the result would have been different in at least three seats in South Wales.

To Beaverbrook, who imagined that his name and Rothermere's were inscribed on 'a list of "Untouchables" ', Baldwin extended no overtures. Rothermere, proud to bear that label, vowed 'that if the Conservative party wants an alliance with the Rothermere Press, the terms will be of a most exemplary character', bearing 'a direct relationship' to questions of policy and personnel. 'You and I have the situation entirely in our hands,' Rothermere told Beaverbrook. 'Without our active support, there is not the remotest chance of the ex-Premier and his group of intimates returning to office.' Believing another

---

[1] Gretton to Baldwin, 4 June 1929, Baldwin Papers; Beaverbrook to Derby, 6 June 1929 (copy), Beaverbrook Papers, C/113.

election to be 'inevitable next year', Rothermere expected with 'complete certainty that a considerable proportion of the 5,000,000 odd Liberal voters will go Labour', thus according 'Ramsay the clear majority for which he will appeal'. More immediately, in the *Sunday Express* on 7 July, Beaverbrook struck out on his Empire Crusade, 'independent of all parties'.[1]

That newspapermen, including Camrose along with Beaverbrook and Rothermere, advanced claims for political potency was not half so surprising as that Baldwin continued to accept them at face value. But none of them was unusual in this respect. 'It may seem difficult at the present moment to estimate the influence of the Press upon public opinion and it is never easy to see very far ahead,' Morrell acknowledged in a letter to Cowdray, 'but I am convinced as ever that your father was right in the view he expressed when he interested himself in our papers, that the future good government of the country will depend to a very large extent upon the existence of a sane Press.' Fearing the dismemberment of the provincial syndicate that he and Starmer had built up, Morrell reiterated his hope that, 'in the near future', some means could be found to effect an amalgamation between the *Daily News* and the *Daily Chronicle*. An association with Sir Leicester Harmsworth, whose newspapers had vigorously expounded Liberal tenets in the recent election, 'might be a half way house which would lead to a complete fusion in the future'. Preferably it would not be so complete as to include the participation of H. S. Horne, whom Morrell considered to be 'only out to make a large sum of money & has no political interest'.[2]

Serious negotiations were renewed on 19 June, when Cowdray spent the morning with Maclean, now back in Parliament as member for Cornwall North. That afternoon, the two of them met Harmsworth and Morrell. Cowdray, 'without being in a position in any way to commit the Cadburys', conveyed his 'impression ... that their attitude towards their own isolated control of the *Daily News* was considerably modified compared with a few months ago'. In the light of these altered circumstances, Cowdray 'had been wondering whether it would be possible for L.H. to secure the *Chronicle* and *Sunday News*' from Harrison's Inveresk Paper Company, 'and then a Combine might be formed in which he would put his assets (i.e. *Daily Chronicle* plus West of England newspapers)' in return for a 50 per cent shareholding, the remainder to be divided evenly between the Cadbury Trust and the Westminster Press. Harmsworth 'said he would see Harrison', but 'did not anticipate that Harrison could put a sale price on the *Chronicle* sufficiently low to be of any interest to the Combine, and that his view was that it was better for the *Chronicle* to stew for a bit and go along without it'. Harmsworth's main

---

[1] Camrose to Baldwin, 29 June 1929, Baldwin Papers; Beaverbrook to Rothermere, 3 July 1929 (copy), and Rothermere to Beaverbrook, 5 July 1929, Beaverbrook Papers, C/282a.

[2] Morrell to Cowdray, 15 June 1929 (enclosing 'memorandum of Interview with Sir Robert Donald and Mr [H.S.] Horne, 13th June 1929'), Cowdray Papers.

worry was that the Cadburys would decline to cooperate. In that event, declared Cowdray, he and Harmsworth could enter into a fifty-fifty partnership. Cowdray, who recounted these conversations in a detailed memorandum, took the precaution of deleting his dismissal of the Cadburys from the copy he sent to Layton.[1]

Harrison proved as unaccommodating as Harmsworth had predicted. He was too busy gobbling up properties to beware of the acute indigestion that would soon incapacitate him. Several months earlier, 'by pure chance', Garvin had encountered him 'at dinner and he said astonishing things'. The *Observer*, intimated Harrison, was the next course on his menu. Negotiations were already in progress and it was 'only a question of price' so far as the Astors were concerned. That was something Garvin refused to believe, although he drafted a letter to Astor (which he perhaps did not send) in order to allay those doubts he denied having:

> However loose we sit to party as independent Unionist thinkers and advanced Progressives with regard to both social and international policy, it would be a terrible thing, to say no worse, to sell the *Observer* to the Lloyd George interest in plain view of the General Election. It would blast the political credit of everyone concerned.

In fact, the only change to occur in the structure of the *Observer* was the substitution of Sir Henry Craik, Conservative MP for the Scottish Universities, for F. S. Oliver as one of the three members of the tribunal. During the spring campaign, the lethargic performances of the *Daily Chronicle* and the *Sunday News* effectively dispelled any impression that Harrison was running his papers in Lloyd George's interest. 'The *Daily Chronicle* cannot be regarded, properly speaking, as a Liberal Organ at the present time,' Harmsworth declared the following October. 'It is under the control of a gentleman who I believe to be a member of the Conservative Party: who certainly has prominent Conservatives on the Board of his Provincial Newspapers Company.'[2]

By then, the *Daily News* and the *Daily Chronicle* were experiencing similar difficulties. J. A. Spender, whom Cadbury had persuaded to supply the *Daily News* with old-style Asquithian political commentaries, clashed bitterly with Tom Clarke, a Lloyd Georgite imported from the *Daily Mail*. The chairman and vice-chairman divided in their sympathies, creating a tension that unsettled their partnership. The *Star*'s falling profits went less far towards offsetting the losses of the *Daily News*, which was taking an uncomfortably long time to come 'out of the wood'. Cowdray was 'asked . . . to take a greater

[1] Memorandum by Cowdray, 19 June 1929, Cowdray Papers.
[2] Garvin to Astor, 22 November 1928 (draft), Garvin papers; memoranda of March 1929, Astor Papers; Harmsworth to Cowdray, 9 October 1929, Cowdray Papers.

interest in the business and put up some capital' towards the £150,000 that was needed.[1]

About this time, rumours began to circulate that Harrison's bubble had burst. 'The talk in the Street,' Collin Brooks noted in his diary on 6 August, 'is that William Harrison is going crazy.' With the pride that proverbially comes before a fall, Harrison had reportedly 'appointed Beverley Baxter to be managing editor of all his papers at a remuneration of ten thousand a year, and made the appointment without so much as warning Perris, who is managing editor of the *Chronicle*'. In mid-October, Brendan Bracken 'was full of exciting news ... that Cadbury had bought the *Daily Chronicle*'. A director of the *Financial News*, among his other publishing commitments, Bracken was vying with Rothermere 'to buy in Harrison's illustrated papers'. Bracken was misinformed, however. 'The *Chronicle* story is all wrong tho' given to us by H's own bankers,' he informed Garvin. 'The position is obscure but one thing seems certain. The Cadburys are not buyers.' The *Financial News* had been set 'to publish the tale ..., but by good fortune ... cut it out in time'. There was no mistaking the fact that Harrison had landed himself 'in a rare mess', but Bracken gave him credit for being 'wise in one respect. He has piled so much upon his bankers that they dare not break his interest. The newspaper business is passing thro' odd times.'[2]

On the contrary, it was Harrison who was trapped. Reported to be 'in a very nervy state due to great personal worry', he 'lost 1½ stones in weight' and it became 'difficult to carry on a coherent conversation with him'. By early November, his Inveresk shares, originally priced 'round about £4', had 'sunk to something like 30/'. Among those hardest hit was Lloyd George, whose Fund held substantial amounts of second preference and ordinary shares in United Newspapers, interlocked with Inveresk. '*Daily Chronicle* – a tremendous mess,' he wrote in disgust to his wife on 3 January 1930. Lord St Davids, chairman of the Lloyd George Fund trustees, was 'putting his back into it' in an effort to save the investment. Apparently, he achieved some success, for the shares retained a considerable value four years later.[3]

Under the circumstances, there was 'great uncertainty as to who really controlled United Newspapers'.[4] The Cadburys, far from being eager pur-

---

[1] Memoranda and correspondence, September 1929, and memorandum by Cowdray entitled 'History of *Daily News* Negotiations,' 23 March 1930, Cowdray Papers.

[2] Brooks's diary, 6 August and 20 October 1929; Bracken to Garvin, 'Monday' [October 1929], Garvin Papers.

[3] Memorandum [by B. F. Crosfield] of his conversation with Layton and Catto, 5 November 1929, Layton Papers; *Lloyd George Family Letters*, p. 210; Stevenson, *Lloyd George* (10 March 1934), p. 260.

[4] The following paragraphs are based upon: memorandum by Cowdray, 'History of *Daily News* Negotiations,' 23 March 1930, heads of agreement, 27 February 1930 (with attached copy of George Cadbury's memorandum, 'written in 1911'), annual reports of the Westminster Press Ltd., 28 March 1931 and 26 March 1932, Harmsworth to Cowdray, 20 January 1930, L. J. Cadbury to Cowdray, 2 March 1930, and Morrell to Cowdray, 1 July 1931, Cowdray Papers;

chasers as initial reports suggested, were ultimately to step in as virtual receivers after other expedients had failed. Cowdray and Harmsworth, having come together to raise fresh capital for the *Daily News*, now aimed to 'pull off an amalgamation with the *Daily Chronicle*' to boot. Harmsworth urged quick action so as to pre-empt the restyled *Daily Herald*, which threatened to 'make a serious inroad into the *D.C.* circulation'. Delay would render the *Chronicle* as worthless as the *Sunday News*, whose chances for becoming 'a real great weekly paper' were rated as 'very little removed from nil'. On behalf of their hastily improvised 'Z Company' (soon superseded by a 'Y Company'), Cowdray and Harmsworth entered into tortuous negotiations with Catto, who indicated on 15 January 'that he was not prepared to father a scheme of amalgamation under which he and his colleagues would not have at least 50% control'. Catto was playing off Cowdray and Harmsworth against the Cadbury trustees, with whom he was negotiating separately. In addition, he had Harrison and his creditors at Lloyd's Bank to satisfy.

Who would be the first to call whose bluff? Various schemes were floated only to be torpedoed by one or another of the principals. On 27 February, the heads of agreement were drawn up for a 'proposed amalgamation between the *Daily News* and the *Daily Chronicle*', with Cowdray and Harmsworth designated as 'partners'. A forthcoming statement would elaborate 'generally the future policy of the proposed amalgamated journal'. That document, it was clearly stipulated, would 'not make any specific reference to the term "Liberal"', but would 'broadly be in accordance with the policy' laid down by George Cadbury for the Daily News Trust 'and the maintenance of Free Trade'. There was a studied vagueness to the phraseology. In any case, according to Cowdray's recollection, 'this tentative agreement fell down because Harrison attacked Catto and Catto withdrew'. That may have been part of the story, but cannot have been the whole. No longer a pivotal figure, Harrison was already at odds with Catto, who did not have much to offer. Layton, negotiating with him directly on behalf of the Cadbury trustees, did not think him 'the least likely to find any cash to help the *Daily News* with any of its pension or compensation arrangements' because 'he and his friends have lost heavily in the slump of Inveresk shares and are going to be very chary of throwing good money after bad'.

Had Cowdray and Harmsworth succeeded, the two morning papers would have been merged as the *News and Chronicle*, and the *Star* would have obtained greater autonomy. Instead, without a conjunction, the *News Chronicle* was born on 2 June, with the *Star* remaining an appendant. At the eleventh hour, there had been a change of heart among members of the Cadbury

---

memorandum by H. T. Cadbury, 15 December 1929, Layton to Clive Pearson, 2 August 1934 (copy), and Layton to L. J. Cadbury, 24 December 1929 (copy), Layton Papers; Evidence, Royal Commission on the Press, 1947–49, Cd. 7409, q. 8191; memorandum prepared by A. P. Duncum, 16 July 1982.

family, who decided to increase their burdens rather than reduce them. Suffering from weak eyesight, Henry Cadbury was eager to retire 'after nearly twenty-three years in Fleet Street'. His elder brother Edward and Ernest Parke were set to depart with him. But Laurence, the youngest of George Cadbury's sons, stepped forward in collaboration with Layton, his tutor at Cambridge before the war.

In May, a revised scheme was rushed through whereby Laurence Cadbury and Layton assumed 'technically complete final control' over operations. It was agreed that Cowdray's Westminster Press 'would continue to exercise the influence due to a friendly minority', but there was no room for Harmsworth, who took his exclusion in good grace. Morrell, who considered him deserving of a 'commission' for his pains, was left to wonder why someone so 'very shrewd' and 'in poor health' should have wished 'to add to his worries'.

What emerged was a multi-tiered structure, dominated by Layton and heavily populated by the Cadburys and their kin. The board of the Westminster Press was reconstructed to include nominees of the Daily News Ltd., who also occupied a majority of the seats on the board of the *News Chronicle*, appointed by the voting trustees. Two of the directorships were reserved for representatives of United Newspapers. Political credentials no longer counted as much or, at least, as obviously. 'None of my four colleagues in the five-man Trust of the *News Chronicle* could be described as red hot radicals,' remarked Layton, whose own Liberalism was unimpeachable. Over the next few years, the board was infiltrated by Conservative businessmen, linked to the United Newspapers interest. These arrangements obtained until 1936, when the Daily News Ltd. established an exclusive control.

During the final month of their separate existences, the *Daily News* had sold 765,000 copies a day, and the *Daily Chronicle* 828,000. In July, four weeks after merger, the net daily sale was 1,480,122. Given that the *Daily News*'s circulation had remained virtually static after its absorption of the *Westminster Gazette*, the result was heartening. Between July and December, there was a dip in sales, attributable partly to 'seasonal losses normally experienced by both papers' and partly 'to amalgamation wastage, and to competition', especially from the revitalized *Daily Herald*. By the end of 1931, the decline had been 'checked and ... the paper appeared to be about holding its own in spite of the heavy competition to which it was subjected'. The total loss that year to the parent company had been reduced to £27,215 and was easily offset by the profits from its subsidiaries.[1]

In terms of personnel, the transformation was considerably less happy. 'Beyond question the most disastrous event of the journalistic year was the sudden and sensational collapse of the *Daily Chronicle* and its amalgamation with the *Daily News*,' mourned the *Newspaper Press Directory*: 'Few people

---

[1] Annual reports, Westminster Press Ltd., 28 March 1931 and 26 March 1932, Cowdray Papers.

had anticipated so complete a *débâcle* as the disappearance of the paper associated for so many years with the Lloyd family and certainly at one time one of the best properties in Fleet Street.' The ranks of the unemployed – and politically unemployable – were swelled by the announcement 'that a third of the *Daily News* staff were to be dismissed in order to make room for a corresponding number of the *Chronicle* men'. (The same formula had been adopted in 1912, when the *Daily News* merged with the *Morning Leader*.) R. C. K. Ensor, preferring not to wait for the axe to fall, left the *Chronicle* in March 'on entirely amicable terms' and with the realization that 'the change had grown inevitable'. His own leader-writing talents were sadly wasted, as the paper had already 'reached the stage of ... almost confining itself to popular news and light (mainly feminine) articles. So the ground that I stood on had disappeared.' Ted Scott passed along this information to J. L. Hammond, a mutual friend: 'Ensor ... has given up the *Chronicle* at last: its latest phase has proved too much for him,' and he had offered 'to write occasional leaders' for the *Manchester Guardian* from his home in High Wycombe.[1]

The *Sunday News* perished still more ignominiously. Unwanted by the proprietors of the *News Chronicle*, it was shunted to the Berrys, who used its remains to fertilize the *Daily Graphic*. When Robert Blatchford 'saw what Edgar Wallace', its ultimate editor, 'had done to it' under Harrison's control, he 'gave the paper six weeks to live' under its new ownership. In fact, he noted on 17 August 1931, it had 'only lasted five'.[2] For once, Blatchford had erred on the side of optimism.

* * *

'Now that we have a Labour Govt. in power,' C. P. Scott wrote in July 1929 to Arthur Henderson, the Foreign Secretary, 'anything is possible. We ought never again to see a bad Tory Government like the last, sitting on the back of the nation like an old man of the sea,' assumed Scott, who 'felt as if the world had suddenly become a hopeful place when they disappeared'.[3]

Needless to say, Scott's first choice would have been for Lloyd George to resume command. But a second Labour administration, dependent on Liberal support without being contemptuous of it, was a satisfactory alternative. With Labour just twenty seats shy of an absolute majority, neither its claims nor its prospects could be denied. The *Nation* (8 June 1929) conceded the 'serious possibility' of eventual Labour predominance, and tacitly foretold its own absorption by the *New Statesman* two years later.

With greater agility than Asquith had shown in 1924, Lloyd George gave

[1] *Newspaper Press Directory* (London, 1931), pp. 55–56; Ensor to E. T. Scott, 28 March 1930, *Guardian* Archives; E. T. Scott to Hammond, 16 April 1930, Hammond Papers.
[2] Blatchford to Palmer, 17 August 1931, Blatchford Papers.
[3] Scott to Henderson, 3 July 1929 (copy), *Guardian* Archives. For initial misunderstandings between 'Ministers and the Press', see *The Times*, 20 June 1929.

constructive parliamentary support to MacDonald, whose policies sometimes did not go far enough to satisfy the Liberals' criteria for progress. Beyond Westminster, however, the party was drained of energy and financially impoverished. Although Lloyd George's primacy was undisputed, his private resources remained separate and continued to provide a bone of contention. 'Scrap the Fund,' demanded the *Daily News* (1 November) on the grounds that Liberals had become 'absolutely sick to death of the squalid interminable controversy which has raged about this subject for years'. However problematic the 'strange death' that had befallen the Liberals before 1914, they were quite obviously 'sick to death' after 1929, when their façade of unity began to crack.

During his second premiership, MacDonald dealt more assuredly with the press, enjoying a larger proportion of journals to deal with. He earned the respect of the Institute of Journalists by following Baldwin's precedent 'in instructing the members of the Government not to write for the Press on current political problems while they hold office under the Crown'. Improving upon another of Baldwin's techniques, he employed a press officer to maintain contact with the Lobby. On 16 March 1930, he paid a ceremonial visit to the Odhams plant in Long Acre to see the new *Daily Herald* roll from the presses. 'You are a very courageous man, Mr Elias,' the Prime Minister genially declared. 'You're taking a great risk you know, running a daily paper.' There were geographical limits to these gestures, for he declined to journey to Manchester on 28 June to help launch the *Herald*'s northern edition and instead attended the air display at Farnborough.[1]

To minimize his risk, Elias replaced Mellor, a survivor from Lansbury's days, and appointed a procession of editors. Francis Williams, who held the job from 1937 to 1940, recalled how Elias 'ordered the use of more and more pictures, producing from a disgruntled wit the comment that the only way to get any socialism into the official Labour paper was to write it on the back of a bathing beauty'. Blatchford disapprovingly noted this general trend towards triviality: 'The great Air Pageant; the Wimbledon Tournaments; The Test Match; Great Speech by Lord [*sic*] George – where do *we* come in?' he asked in exasperation. 'Newspapers want *news*,' even if readers evidently did not. 'And there's the boom in sex stuff. Tripe about love and marriage and the rest; nearly always done by women writers, who must hate the job, poor things. The fact is,' he told 'Whiffley' Palmer, 'this is not the same world as the world of the nineties when the *Clarion* was going strong.' Nevertheless, the *Daily Herald* went from strength to strength by making politics as inconspicuous as possible. With an army of paid canvassers, laden with a battery of free gifts (including the sixteen-volume Odhams edition of Dickens's collected works), the *Herald*

---

[1] Motion moved by Alan Pitt Robbins of *The Times*, reported in Institute of Journalists, *Journal*, September 1929; Colin Seymour-Ure, *The Press, Politics and the Public* (London, 1968), p. 232; Minney, *Southwood*, pp. 236–37; Bullock, *Bevin*, I, 423.

edged past the *News Chronicle*, then the *Daily Mail*, and finally – for a few glorious days in mid-decade – pulled ahead of the *Daily Express*. Its readership increased eightfold to stabilize at around two million.[1]

Designed for profitability rather than propaganda, the *Herald* neither served nor thwarted MacDonald's purpose. The Liberal press, reflecting the conciliatory attitude of its parliamentary leaders and its own uncertainties, held him in better stead. Clarke, who took over from Hodgson as editor of the *News Chronicle*, was certainly no doctrinaire. Edward Chattaway, who simultaneously replaced Wilson Pope as editor of the *Star*, did not cut much of a figure, and it was not until 1936, when Robin Cruikshank replaced him, that the *Star* recovered its partisan thrust. Both Chattaway and Cruikshank were particularly attracted to Herbert Morrison, then Labour MP for Hackney South, whom they popularized as 'Mr London' in exchange for his confidences. More specifically, A. J. Cummings, the *News Chronicle*'s chief leader writer, displeased Cowdray by being 'entirely intolerant of anything except the most Labour point of view'.[2]

At the *Manchester Guardian*, Ted Scott avowedly pursued a policy of 'Keeping Labour In' (8 August 1931). Leader-writing duties passed from Arthur Ransome – whose political bent was so indistinct that Hammond had reason to inform his wife that 'Ransome by the way is Liberal not Labour' – to Malcolm Muggeridge. Aged twenty-eight, Muggeridge was the son of the Labour MP for Romford and a relation of the Webbs, yet 'as completely devoid of party or other political prejudices as anyone intensely interested in politics could be. And a pretty writer,' added the younger Scott, who found him 'altogether a swan'. The venerable C. P. Scott, 'afraid I am but a feeble help to my dear Ted in these days', was equally taken with Muggeridge, who has since repaid the Scotts' compliments with withering acerbity. Among other services, Muggeridge made it easier to dispense with Kingsley Martin, who left to become editor of the *New Statesman*-cum-*Nation* after three unhappy years on the *Guardian*. 'It seems a good move & I think Kingsley Martin will do the job well,' wrote C.P. to Hammond. 'He will be much more at home than on a daily. He needs time & he needs space.' Martin later memorialized the 1930s as 'the great age of the weeklies', which furnished 'the natural place' for 'all the younger writers who wished to make a reputation as literary figures or even as budding politicians'. From then until the early 1960s, when they experienced a generic decline, these journals of opinion – the *New Statesman*, the *Spectator*, *Truth* (1877–1956), *Time and Tide* (1920–62), Claud Cockburn's *The Week* (1933–46), and latterly *Tribune* and

[1] 'The New "Daily Herald",' *The Times*, 17 March 1930; Williams, *Dangerous Estate*, pp. 198–205; Blatchford to Palmer, 28 June 1930, Blatchford Papers. In 1932, Bevin arranged for the Victoria Printing House Company to produce a twopenny *New Clarion*, which was one of Elias's acquisitions the next year.
[2] B. Donoughue and G. W. Jones, *Herbert Morrison* (London, 1973), pp. 358–59; Cowdray to Layton, 20 May 1931 (copy), Cowdray Papers.

The Economist – appropriated many of the critical functions of the political press.[1]

Like Martin, Cummings was a commentator on the press as well as a distinguished contributor to it. He saw the world of journalism, like political society around it, evolving 'into a simple dichotomy of Socialists and anti-Socialists'. Fearing the curtailment of precious freedoms, he decided that – the growls of G. D. H. Cole notwithstanding – there was less danger from the perpetually fragmented left than from the right, where 'a reaction of perfect unanimity' was bound to occur in the face of any 'real crisis'.[2] That, at any rate, was the lesson he learnt from events on the Continent. Although such analogies were to prove happily inapposite, they had enough verisimilitude to be drawn with mounting frequency and will be considered in the next chapter.

For the time being, the notion that the right-wing press would band together to resist socialism or for any other purpose was fanciful, to say the least. Many of its controllers were barely on speaking terms with each other. Beaverbrook, having dropped his Empire Free Trade bombshell in early July 1929, thereafter embarked on a Baltic cruise (which included a visit to Russia) and did not persevere until the autumn. Perhaps, had Baldwin been more responsive, the offensive might have been called off. On 4 November, Beaverbrook indicated to Neville Chamberlain that he was willing 'to do a deal' and that his 'personal feelings about S.B. would not stand in the way'. A week later, appropriately enough on Armistice Day, Beaverbrook was invited to Baldwin's house, where he was gently persuaded to put his case to Parliament. On the 19th, he delivered one of his rare speeches in the House of Lords, where he was outflanked and outwitted. The effect was to drive him back to newspaper propaganda. Rothermere, with 'no underlying tug of loyalty towards the Conservative party', stood ready to assist him. Benefiting from the support of Rothermere's multifarious journals, Beaverbrook was alternately prodded and constrained by Rothermere's 'wooden-headed obstinacy'.[3]

On 10 December, full-page advertisements in most of the principal dailies proclaimed the launching of the Crusade. Beaverbrook subscribed £25,000 towards a campaign chest of £100,000. Rothermere added £5,000 'to be specially earmarked [for] candidates' expenses'. From the beginning, therefore, the venture had all of the qualities of a breakaway political movement. In addition to editorial space, the *Daily Express* and its sister papers provided personnel. Doidge was chief organizer, and Bruce Lockhart wrote pamphlets

---

[1] J. L. Hammond to Barbara Hammond, 11 August 1929, E. T. Scott to Hammond [November 1930], C. P. Scott to Hammond, 24 January and 22 December 1931, Hammond Papers; Kingsley Martin, *Editor* (London, 1968), p. 12; Muggeridge, *Chronicles of Wasted Time*, I (London, 1972), 50. For 'The rise and peaceful fall of the weeklies,' see Anthony Howard in *The Times*, 22 July 1978, a slightly 'abridged' version of his article in the previous month's *Journalism Studies Review*, pp. 12–15.

[2] Cummings, *The Press* (London, 1936), pp. 19, 79–80.

[3] Feiling, *Neville Chamberlain*, p. 173; Taylor, *Beaverbrook*, pp. 267–69.

and collected the statistics for Beaverbrook's speeches. Beverley Baxter ('that infernal fellow') complained that the 'concentration which I have been forced to give to Empire Crusade matters has undoubtedly injured the paper', which had to consider the sensibilities of 'a million Conservative readers'. Beaverbrook apologized to Amery, whose friendly speech at Glasgow was 'crowded out' of the *Express*: 'The truth is that an Editor . . . is only useful so long as he works honestly and earnestly in furtherance of the political programme. The moment he shows the slightest tendency to "stall" he can do incredible injury.' But he offered no apologies to Sir William Bull, whose sneers went intentionally unreported: 'It is impossible to open the columns of the *Daily Express* to those who are against us. . . . Our space is limited and we need every inch of it for the purpose of putting forward the views of our supporters.' Whatever had become of those lofty principles Beaverbrook had once enunciated?[1]

The rest of Fleet Street looked upon the activities of Beaverbrook and Rothermere with cynical bemusement. For 'a little bit of fun and malice', Barrington-Ward (with Dawson's approval) contrived in *The Times* (2 February 1930) to juxtapose an announcement 'about the formation of their new party' with a report about two monkeys that had escaped from the London zoo. Decades afterwards, Kingsley Martin still chuckled at this 'riotous editorial joke. . . . But the incident had its more serious side,' he recalled more vividly than accurately. 'It was in fact part of a determined effort, by men whose only claim to public leadership was that they were millionaires and press owners, to oust the Prime Minister and remodel the Conservative Party to suit their own personal whims.' Contrary to Martin's recollection, Baldwin was not Prime Minister at that time. Nor was it incontrovertible that Beaverbrook had channelled his Empire Crusade into the United Empire Party in a bid for supreme power. 'The reason why I could never lead a political party, even if any other than the United Empire Party would be willing to take me, is because I cannot be bothered with tosh,' he asserted to Amery, whose superior 'mental process' commended him for the Tory leadership.[2]

Lord Bayford (as Sir Robert Sanders had recently become) observed 'a great deal of dissatisfaction with [Baldwin's] leadership just now. Besides that, Rothermere & Beaverbrook are running a very vigorous Protection campaign which always makes trouble in the party.' Significantly, Bayford viewed these two phenomena as separate, which – to Beaverbrook's and Rothermere's disappointment – was how they remained. On 5 February, Bayford heard

[1] Baxter to Beaverbrook, 21 January and 14 February 1930, Beaverbrook to Amery, 1 October 1930, and Beaverbrook to Bull, 19 December 1929, quoted in Taylor, *Beaverbrook*, pp. 273–74. 'As the result of long experience in journalism here & in the USA', William F. Blood was convinced that 'Beaverbrook's great and sorely needed campaign is not being *100%* furthered by his Press. There's a "yellow streak" or *two* in his camp.' Blood to P. J. Hannon, 13 April 1930, Hannon Papers.

[2] Barrington-Ward's diary, 2 February 1930; Martin, *The Press the Public Wants* (London, 1947), p. 73; Beaverbrook to Amery, 24 September 1930, quoted in Taylor, *Beaverbrook*, pp. 275–76.

Baldwin 'let go against Rothermere at a dinner of the 1922 Club'. Those remarks were a reprise of a speech that morning at the Coliseum, where Baldwin, 'after a good deal of deliberation', had 'decided not to make any allusion' to Beaverbrook. He and Beaverbrook were then each trying to convert the other to his cause. It would have required relatively little to bring them together. Gwynne volunteered to try. Remonstrating with Beaverbrook that 'your United Empire Party cannot be a permanent thing', and warning that 'Rothermere will kill you, not wittingly but by his appalling personality', he concluded that 'a bridge must be found for you and the Conservative Party. I am optimist enough to think that I am not far off providing such a bridge.'[1]

Beaverbrook demanded from Baldwin the right to run Empire Free Trade Conservative candidates, or at least to place them in nomination before selection committees in appropriate constituencies. Rebuffed, he issued a manifesto on the 17th on behalf of the United Empire Party. 'You have gone and done it this time!' Gwynne scolded 'My dear Max' the next day. 'The game was in your hands and you have thrown it away simply because you could not wait a bit,' he declared. 'The Conservative Party which practically goes the whole of the way with Rothermere and a long distance with you is to be disrupted by you both. And for what? ... Baldwin's Coliseum speech went further along all our paths than we could have hoped.' (To Amery, Beaverbrook revealed that his hand had been forced by Rothermere, who would have stood no further delay: 'I wanted his support more than I can tell you.') Gwynne declined to publish an advertisement designed to raise funds for the United Empire electoral effort: 'After careful consideration I have come to the conclusion that it would be inconsistent for the *Morning Post* to condemn the new Party in one part of the paper and in another part to publish an advertisement in its favour.'[2]

In order to assert his own loyalty, Gwynne denied to Davidson that the *Morning Post* had criticized the performance of the Conservative Central Office in the previous election. The only mistake, he admitted 'between ourselves' on 8 May, had been 'not jumping Beaverbrook's claim' for imperial preference 'before he was ready.... It would have put Beaverbrook in his place ..., while as things are at present he seems to have taken the lead and we seem to be following meekly after him.' Gwynne was wasting his words for, before the month was out, Davidson was removed and Neville Chamberlain had taken

---

[1] Bayford's diary, 7 February 1930, Bayford Papers; Baldwin to Beaverbrook, 5 February 1930, quoted in Taylor, *Beaverbrook*, p. 281; Gwynne to Beaverbrook ('Between Ourselves'), 22 February 1930 (copy), Gwynne Papers. Gwynne had previously stated that the 'one mistake I think both you and Rothermere are making ... is the idea of starting a separate organisation to carry out your ideas'; nevertheless, he hoped that Beaverbrook would 'always remember that I am at your service in any matter where my peculiar position in regard to the Party and its leaders may be of use to you'. Gwynne to Beaverbrook, 7 and 29 January 1930, Beaverbrook Papers, C/149.

[2] Gwynne to Beaverbrook, 18 and 19 February 1930 (copies), Gwynne Papers; Beaverbrook to Amery, 22 February 1930, quoted in Taylor, *Beaverbrook*, p. 282.

over as party chairman. On the surface, this was a victory for Beaverbrook, who was emboldened to cancel plans to share a platform with Baldwin at the Crystal Palace on the 24th. Gwynne's fears of the press lords were not limited, however, to their rending effect on the party. On the morning of 24 August, he received a telephone call from G. Ward Price, Rothermere's agent, who proposed to open negotiations for the purchase of the *Morning Post*. Following the death of the Duke of Northumberland, a major – though not majority – shareholder, Rothermere aspired to become principal owner 'with the intention of maintaining the *M.P.* as a high class paper, definitely anti-Socialist, strongly Conservative, a defender of the Church and State, in fact to be conducted on its present lines'. Gwynne declined to quote 'figures' without the consent of the board, but promised to 'pass on the suggestion and proposal' with a fervent hope that nothing would come of it. To his immense relief, nothing did.[1]

Camrose, who was eventually to succeed where Rothermere had failed, was playing the middle against both ends. The *Daily Telegraph*, its circulation inching upwards, projected an image of impartial concern. On the one hand, Camrose politely refused an article by Beaverbrook on 'new markets for British Anthracite Coal' – hardly a contentious theme – for fear 'that its publication in our papers would lead at the present moment to a great deal of misunderstanding as to our position, and particularly as to my own motives'; on the other, lest it be thought that he was a kept man, he served notice that if Baldwin 'promised anything in regard to papers he might be able to influence, it would not necessarily have applied to ours'. Churchill tried in vain to use the *Telegraph* and the *Sunday Times* as platforms for his extreme Indian views. Baldwin 'knew of this' and counted on Camrose 'to start at once a London evening paper to counter the *News* and *Standard*' instead. As Camrose was temporarily short of ready capital, Davidson went to Bristol on 11 March to raise £400,000 from the Wills brothers, directors of the Imperial Tobacco Company. He evidently returned empty-handed, for the scheme was abandoned. Even so, Camrose had demonstrated his commitment, not that it prevented the *Telegraph* from presenting a 'fair point of view' on Empire Free Trade. 'I must say that you give me a better deal than I get from *The Times*,' Beaverbrook wrote gratefully to him that summer. 'Occasionally the *Morning Post* praises me. Once in a while I become a favourite, but mostly the paper knocks me to bits.' Like Baldwin, he was more susceptible than contemporaries suspected or even than most historians have allowed.[2]

Baldwin, whom Beaverbrook accused of wanting 'all the assets of Empire

---

[1] Gwynne to Davidson, 8 May 1930 (copy), and memorandum by Gwynne, 24 August 1930, Gwynne Papers; Taylor, *Beaverbrook*, p. 288.

[2] Camrose to Beaverbrook, 14 January and 14 March 1930, Beaverbrook to Camrose, 12 July 1930 (copy), Beaverbrook Papers, C/78; Thomas Jones's account of a conversation with Baldwin, 11 March 1930, quoted in Barnes and Middlemas, pp. 592–93.

Free Trade without taking on the liabilities', was ready to take on Beaverbrook. Ignoring the consistent advice of Tom Jones, who 'begged him to make no public reference to Beaverbrook and Rothermere, to ignore them completely' and allow them to go on 'boring their readers and lowering their circulation', he hit out in a speech on 24 June. Bracketing his foes with Hearst across the Atlantic, he declared that nothing was

> more curious in modern evolution than the effect of an enormous fortune rapidly made, and the control of newspapers of your own.... It goes to the head like wine, and you find in all these cases attempts have been made outside the province of journalism to dictate, to domineer, to blackmail.

It was a dress rehearsal for his more spectacular performance the following March. All that was lacking was a biblical allusion.[1]

Beaverbrook's retort was to intervene at Norfolk North, where a by-election was occasioned by the elevation of Noel Buxton to a peerage. Labour held the seat on a reduced poll, leaving Beaverbrook to crave 'the opportunity ... of contesting a seat against a Conservative Office candidate' so as to 'show whether we are stronger'. Meanwhile, he traded compliments with Cummings, who calculated that, had Beaverbrook 'been on the other side', he 'would have added two thousand votes to the Labour majority'. Beaverbrook reciprocated by professing the belief that Cummings's 'b---- paper (I hope a member of the staff of the *Daily News* knows what that means)' did the Conservative challenger 'more harm than all the rest put together.... The *Daily Herald* does not know how to fight a battle, and I hope you will not teach them.'[2]

That Beaverbrook would sponsor an insurgent candidate loomed as a nightmare for Chamberlain, who met him on 18 July and proposed a truce. Beaverbrook (according to Chamberlain's version) was asked to

> call off his attacks on Baldwin and the Party, cease to include offensive cartoons and paragraphs in the *Evening Standard*, and stop inviting Conservatives to direct subscriptions to him in order that they might be used to run candidates against official Conservatives. In return, Central Office would support any Conservative who accepted the official policy, even though he expressed personal agreement with Beaverbrook, and tried to persuade his local association to adopt these views.

The terms, as Beaverbrook understood them, were significantly different, but equally unacceptable. A collision was narrowly averted in another by-election at Bromley, where Rothermere intended that his son Esmond should force the issue. But at Paddington South, on 30 October, an Empire Free Trader took

---

[1] Jones, *Whitehall Diary* (31 October 1930), II (ed. K. Middlemas; London, 1969), 277; Taylor, *Beaverbrook*, p. 289.
[2] Taylor, *Beaverbrook*, p. 290; Cummings to Beaverbrook, 11 July 1930, and Beaverbrook to Cummings, 12 July 1930 (copy), Beaverbrook Papers, C/104.

the field against an official Conservative candidate and won handily. 'I am going out entirely for by-elections this year, and shall exclude all other forms of propaganda,' trumpeted Beaverbrook in a private letter on 13 January 1931. Churchill regretted these tactics as a diversion from his own Indian mutiny, which he was waging 'à outrance' in the pages of the *Morning Post*. 'Merely nagging the party and hampering them at by-elections unites all its solid loyalties against Max,' he counselled Rothermere.[1]

The showdown came in March, when the last in this series of by-elections was held in the safe Tory constituency of St George's, Westminster. Alfred Duff Cooper (later 1st Viscount Norwich), who had written to congratulate Beaverbrook on the result at Paddington South, was chosen to stand in the official Conservative interest. Sir Ernest Petter, an industrialist who was 'really more Rothermere's man than Beaverbrook's', carried the banner of Empire Free Trade. 'If we win this fight the Conservatives will select a new leader and take up our policy and we'll all live happily ever after,' dreamt Beaverbrook, who incongruously denied having 'a personal vendetta against Mr Stanley Baldwin'. If not quite so above-board as he made himself out, he was no more underhanded than Chamberlain, who gave Barrington-Ward lunch, followed by 'some flattering observations ... about recent *Times* leaders on Beaverbrook – author unacknowledged, of course, but evidently (and rightly) assumed to be me'. Camrose, prepared to credit Beaverbrook's relative innocence, pointed out that 'Rothermere has all along acted as though he has a vendetta. ... You and he are linked together so closely politically that it is difficult to separate you in the references' that appeared in the *Daily Telegraph*. 'We are doing our best to be fair,' insisted Camrose, 'but you people make it very difficult.'[2]

Gwynne's 'reading of both Rothermere and Beaverbrook is that they are living in a world of their own ..., both unscrupulous and having enormous *powers of suppression* as well as of publicity'. Thomas Marlowe 'never had any doubt that R was under the influence of B.' After all, 'Northcliffe used to say "Max A. hypnotises Harold."' Chamberlain undertook to make 'some inquiries' to ascertain 'which was top-dog'. To Baldwin, that hardly mattered.[3]

On 17 March, two days before polling, Baldwin brought the campaign to a climax with a speech at the Queen's Hall. He did not discriminate between Rothermere's properties, which had stooped to the level of mocking him for having dissipated his father's fortune, and Beaverbrook's. None, in his estim-

---

[1] Taylor, *Beaverbrook*, pp. 290–91, 297–98, 302; Churchill to Randolph Churchill, 8 January 1931, and Churchill to Rothermere, 3 February 1931, quoted in Gilbert, *Churchill*, V, 379, 386.

[2] Beaverbrook to L. W. Dent, 8 March 1931, and Beaverbrook to Clifford Turner, 14 March 1931, quoted in Taylor, *Beaverbrook*, p. 305; Barrington-Ward's diary, 25 February 1931; Beaverbrook to Camrose, 9 March 1931 (copy), and Camrose to Beaverbrook, 12 March 1931, Beaverbrook Papers, C/78.

[3] Gwynne to Marlowe, 23 March 1931 (copy), and Marlowe to Gwynne, 24 March 1931, Gwynne Papers.

ation, qualified as 'newspapers in the ordinary acceptance of the term. They are engines of propaganda for the constantly changing policies, desires, personal wishes, personal likes and dislikes of two men.' Then, with a rhetorical flourish that has been identified as Kipling's handiwork, Baldwin went on to accuse 'the proprietorship of these papers' of 'aiming at ... power without responsibility – the prerogative of the harlot throughout the ages'. Kingsley Martin called this statement 'the most remarkable of Lord Baldwin's career' and gave it credit for winning the day.[1] Yet, apart from its Kiplingesque interpolation, it contained nothing that Baldwin (among others) had not said – or that Beaverbrook had not disclaimed – on numerous occasions.

Dawson, the recipient of Baldwin's thanks 'for the consistent support you have given me through a very difficult time', spent the morning after the by-election in bed with the papers. 'You wouldn't have known fr. the *D.M.* that there'd been an election at all!' he remarked in his diary with some amusement. Given the lacklustre quality of the rebel candidate, the strength of the local Tory machine, and the social complexion of the constituency, Duff Cooper – and Baldwin – would have triumphed at St George's in any event. Baldwin's singular achievement was to have retailed a phrase, not of his own coinage, which was to echo emptily down the decades. Soon enough, it was to rebound against him. For, worse than giving harlotry a bad name, he had inadvisedly dignified a privilege as a prerogative. He had also stigmatized the political press, with which – like it or not – he was obliged to deal. As soon as there was 'a lull in the storm', Chamberlain seized the 'opportunity to make contact again' with Beaverbrook. Party interests demanded as much. There is a name, too, for those who live off the earnings of harlots.[2]

---

[1] Martin, *The Press the Public Wants*, p. 74. For a balanced account, see Gillian Peele, 'St George's and the Empire Crusade,' in Cook and Ramsden, eds., *By-Elections in British Politics*, pp. 79–108.

[2] Baldwin to Dawson, 20 March 1931, and Dawson's diary, 20 March 1931, Dawson Papers; Chamberlain to Beaverbrook, 23 March 1931, quoted in Taylor, *Beaverbrook*, p. 306.

Fourteen

'IN QUEER STREET'

That the 1930s constituted a decade of heightened political consciousness, though propounded as an orthodoxy by literary critics, would be hard to infer from the day-to-day contents of the national press, much less from the behind-the-scenes activity of its controllers. The economic issues and foreign policy questions that overshadowed public debate did not readily lend themselves to distinctly partisan approaches, which, in any event, few major newspapers were disposed to take. Instead of clarifying party lines, these controversies tended to blur them. Fissures within each of the parliamentary groupings, counteracted by a series of practical accommodations between them, plunged editorial offices deeper into confusion. The wayward impulses of certain proprietors, attended by widening differences of opinion within other corporate managements, played havoc with traditional alignments. Not least, straitened circumstances militated against the flaunting of party colours.

Inevitably, too, the conduct of old-style political journalism was undermined by the belief that Westminster was a mausoleum, devoid of creative energies and therefore unworthy of respectful attention. This assumption, no longer confined to malcontents on either the radical left or right, was pervasive. Among the voices raised to this effect, perhaps none was more symbolic than that of Stephen Spender, the son and nephew of 'classical' Liberal publicists, who joined in pursuing 'the goal of an unpolitical age' with the trumpet-call that the 'great parliamentary era is over'.[1]

Stripped of its rhetoric, Spender's argument did not imply a negation of politics so much as a reorientation: a recasting of moulds. Democracy, if it was to survive, was said to require the surgical removal of its diseased organs, including mislabelled organs of opinion. Without going so far as to sacrifice their points of view, newspapers prudently sought to distance themselves from a system that was seen to have fallen into decay and disrepute. At first, the trend was most pronounced in the provinces, and there among evening prints, but it spread quickly and broadly. Careful to establish chronology, the editor of the *Edinburgh Evening News* recalled how his paper had proclaimed its independence in 1931, after the crack-up of Harrison's empire, in order to obtain 'more

---

[1] Spender, *Forward from Liberalism* (London, 1937), pp. 16–17.

scope'.¹ Beyond the pale of the political press, yet not exempt from its conventions, John Lehmann launched *New Writing* in the spring of 1936 with a manifesto that encapsulated prevailing attitudes: while that journal, primarily devoted to literature, did 'not intend to open its pages to writers of reactionary or Fascist sentiments, it is independent of any political party'. Whatever their self-imposed restrictions and however cautiously they couched their avowals, the vast majority of publications took sanctuary behind similar walls.

The rise of fascist movements on the Continent, attracting apologists and emulators in domestic circles, was itself sufficient cause for concern. Mussolini, whose wartime propaganda in support of Italian interventionism was modestly funded by British official sources, had since excelled in the art of press manipulation. 'His sort of fascism could never have appeared before the days of popular journalism,' Denis Mack Smith has insisted; at the same time that it brutally succeeded 'in gagging criticism' at home, it projected a flattering image abroad. To be sure, Britain was 'a more literate and politically more sophisticated society' than Italy, but neither the similarities nor the effects were negligible.²

Mussolini's ingenious use – and abuse – of journalistic techniques served to ensure him a sympathetic response from many quarters in Fleet Street. John Walter, 'invited to meet him at tea' during a visit to Rome in 1926, instructed Dawson that *The Times* 'cannot do better than maintain an attitude of friendly benevolence towards Mussolini and his policy'. Barrington-Ward, who functioned as 'the virtual "Foreign Editor"' at Printing House Square and in that nebulous capacity wrote the bulk of the leading articles on diplomatic affairs, required little persuasion that the territorial provisions of the Versailles Treaty stood urgently in need of revision. For Hungary's sake, but also out of sympathy with Italian and German claims, Rothermere leapt to the same conclusion. To him, if not to most other advocates of appeasement, the vacuous ideology and strong-arm tactics of fascism were inherently congenial. Long before his collusion with Sir Oswald Mosley, Rothermere was already viewed – and may well have esteemed himself – as Mussolini's British counterpart.³

After 1929, when Ramsay MacDonald formed his second minority Labour administration, the debility of parliamentary institutions grew painfully obvious in the light of mounting social distress. The collapse of Wall Street, precipitating a world-wide depression, intensified the mood of desperation. S. K. Ratcliffe, back on the staff of the *New Statesman* after a roving commission in America, was convinced that 'the Govt. can do nothing but limp on to resignation and defeat, leaving no chance for another Labour Govt. for ten years provided of course that Baldwin or another can stave off the Beaverbrook

---

¹ Evidence of J. J. Seager, Royal Commission on the Press, 1947–49, Cd. 7448, qq. 9769–79.
² Mack Smith, *Mussolini* (New York, 1982), pp. 67–68. For the subventions channelled to the 'future Italian dictator' in 1917–18 by Sir Samuel Hoare, a 'future Foreign Secretary', see Cross, *Hoare*, pp. 55–56.
³ Walter to Dawson, 22 March 1926, *Times* Archives; *History of The Times*, IV, part 2, 931.

menace'. His own grim prediction, ventured in May 1930, was that 'a Government of National Safety, a British Fascismo', would be in power 'within a year'. That summer, Garvin was equally 'anxious to the core' about national prospects. Despite his view that 'Labour, for want of intellectual calibre (apart from a few) and genuine unity, will likely come to the most appalling crash', he decided that 'the only safe course is to keep it in as long as possible'.[1]

Mosley, one of the few ministers who satisfied Garvin's criteria for intellectual vigour, resigned his junior office in May 1930, after his colleagues had brushed aside his proposals for combating unemployment. The following February, he led a small band of dissidents into his New Party, a halfway house along his steep descent into fascism. 'The Socialists and the Government are disintegrating,' gloated Beaverbrook, who regretted that Mosley had 'done a foolish thing. He should not have detached himself from the Labour Party', but 'should have stayed inside it and bombarded it from within, as we have done to the Conservatives'. For the time being, however, Beaverbrook's guns were silent. 'There is peace between Baldwin and myself' on the understanding that Baldwin would 'ask for a mandate for food taxes' at the next election. 'If Baldwin betrays us,' he told Arthur Brisbane, the veteran New York editor, 'we will start out on the trail once more.'[2]

It suited Baldwin's convenience to prolong Labour's tenure so as to avert an appeal to the electorate, the likelihood of renewed hostilities with Beaverbrook, and the unwelcome responsibility for an array of imperial and defence questions that threatened the cohesion of the Conservative Party. The Liberals, beset by internal divisions and financial worries, were likewise inclined to shore up the crumbling Labour edifice. Yet, on 5 August 1931, the worsening crisis within the international financial community forced the *Manchester Guardian* to concede 'that the situation cannot be tackled comprehensively and courageously by any Government whose measures', bound to incur unpopularity, would be 'liable to exploitation by other parties' at the polls. 'Is it entirely out of the question,' that paper therefore asked, 'that a common basis could be found for dealing with an emergency so far beyond the normal range of party politics?'

Dawson, holding to Disraeli's dictum that 'England does not love coalitions', was dead set against any such expedient. His opinion, tendered privately to Baldwin and publicly to the readers of *The Times*, was that it remained exclusively MacDonald's 'business to get the country out of the mess', simplistically attributed to Labour's 'policy of extravagance'.[3] But the firm backing

---

[1] Ratcliffe to Gardiner, 25 May 1930, Gardiner Papers; Garvin to C. P. Scott, 11 August 1930, *Guardian* Archives.

[2] Beaverbrook to Brisbane, 3 March and 23 April 1931 (copies), Beaverbrook Papers, C/64. Brisbane got his start in 1896 on Pulitzer's *World* and, the next year, established a working relationship with Hearst comparable to Blumenfeld's with Beaverbrook. See Piers Brendon, *The Life and Death of the Press Barons* (London, 1982), pp. 137–38.

[3] Memorandum by Dawson, 23 August 1931, quoted in Wrench, *Dawson*, pp. 291–92.

that MacDonald required to implement swingeing economies, starting with a cut in the unemployment benefit, was not forthcoming from the Labour side. Resisting a momentary temptation to resign, the Prime Minister was moved by royal entreaties to head a National Government with Conservative, Liberal, and token Labour support. Whether his action was a shameful betrayal of his party, which split in the process, or a shining act of patriotism has been long and passionately debated. More germane to the present inquiry is the complicity of the press in these momentous proceedings.

Dawson, perhaps second only to the King in his opportunities to dispense advice, quickly overcame his own antipathy to the idea of coalition and thereafter worked assiduously to overcome Baldwin's. Sequestered at Dawson's house on the fateful morning of Sunday, 23 August, Baldwin 'could not be located' by Palace officials and consequently lost his chance to have the first word with the King. He and Dawson were engrossed in a discussion of personnel matters, which – Dawson proudly recorded – Baldwin said were 'easier for him to talk . . . over with me than with any of his political colleagues'. The National Government, as it took shape on the 24th, was to be 'a co-operation of individuals to cope with the emergency'; as soon as it had fulfilled its purpose of restoring public confidence (and relieving the pressure on the Bank of England), party politics would supposedly resume their normal course. That these makeshift arrangements would persist through any future election was hardly contemplated. Indeed, as Dawson and Arthur Mann 'entirely agreed' on 7 September, one of the incidental benefits of the National Government was to emphasize 'the undesirability of an early General Election'. For the Liberals, holding out against the protectionist tide, this deferral was a powerful inducement. For Beaverbrook and the Empire Free Traders, it was a provocation.[1]

With Baldwin's blessing, Dawson was soon on intimate terms with MacDonald. As early as 10 September, Dawson began to modify his stand and to anticipate 'the importance of going to the country as a National Government and not in three parties'. Baldwin, recognizing an improvement upon his original design, was 'very receptive' during 'a long talk' that day, and urged him to put his case to the Prime Minister. Invited to lunch at Chequers on the 13th, Dawson 'had a couple of hours heart to heart w. Ramsay, who gave me his whole story of the crisis'. Dawson was surprised to find him 'quite prepared for a National Govt. appeal & to serve under Baldwin subsequently'. Thus, *The Times*'s proclamation on the 15th that 'even a premature appeal to the country would hardly be more mischievous than protracted uncertainty' carried the sanction of both MacDonald and Baldwin, with the latter strongly in favour of 'urging an appeal to the country by the Natl. Govt. & not by a party'. Barrington-Ward, who 'contributed some minor suggestions' to Dawson's

---

[1] Davidson, *Memoirs*, p. 370; Wrench, *Dawson*, pp. 291–92; Nicolson, *George V*, p. 461.

'excellent leader', was gratified to see how it 'set Press and politicians going' the next day.[1]

Fraught with ironies, *The Times*'s belated discovery of MacDonald's supreme statesmanship underscored the isolation of his position. Certainly it was no substitute for the backing of the *Daily Herald*, which had been wrenched from him. On the afternoon of 24 August, when his intentions became known, a 'council of war' was convened in 'Uncle' Arthur Henderson's room at Transport House. Ernest Bevin, George Lansbury, Walter Citrine, and Hugh Dalton were among the stalwarts who gathered, 'full of fight', to deal with the imminence of MacDonald's apostasy. 'This is like the General Strike,' declared Bevin, who professed himself 'prepared to put everything in', even TUC money. The first step was to send for W. H. Stevenson, who had recently risen to the editorship of the *Herald*. Suspected of being 'still under the influence' of MacDonald and Philip Snowden, who were 'working on him very hard' to soften any attacks upon themselves, Stevenson revealed that he proposed to preface his remarks in the *Herald* 'by paying tribute to the courage of those who are staying in' office. 'And what about the courage of those who are coming out?' growled Henderson, who was set to evacuate the Foreign Office the next day. With this unavuncular outburst, wrote Dalton, 'the whole emphasis ... changed. The *Herald* in the days that followed, under Bevin's influence, gave a fine lead.' Robert Skidelsky has interpreted this to mean that the paper, having 'consistently sought to minimize the crisis' during the preceding week, even to the extent of suppressing certain 'true facts' that it was peculiarly well placed to know, now struck 'attitudes' that reflected 'unmistakably the guiding intelligence of Ernest Bevin' and the intransigence of the TUC's general council. For example, it declared on the 27th that there had 'never been any doubt from the moment the political crisis began that those who took a line opposed to that of Mr MacDonald were representing accurately the mind of those from whom they derived their power'.[2]

'No public man can run the risk of earning the disapproval of journalists, which will always tell against him in the long run,' Stevenson had once preached to Herbert Morrison. MacDonald, no stranger to obloquy, was concerned not so much with the long run as with the short. The *Herald*'s courteous acknowledgement of his sincerity was outweighed by its crude taunt that the reconstruction of the government marked a 'surrender to the City' (25 August). Obviously, he would have to enlist other defenders, whose affiliations did not much matter. To keep in touch with opinion at Westminster, and possibly to deflect it, he posted 'at least one Lobby man' to stand on duty through the long night of the 24th. Then, as soon as the dust had settled, Sir Robert Donald was

[1] Dawson's diary, 10, 13, and 15 September 1931, Dawson Papers; Barrington-Ward's diary, 15 and 16 September 1931.

[2] Dalton's diary, 24 August 1931, quoted in Dalton, *Call Back Yesterday* (London, 1953), pp. 273–74, and (more completely) in Marquand, *MacDonald*, p. 646; Skidelsky, *Politicians and the Slump* (London, 1967), pp. 364, 369.

deputized to arrange a private dinner at the Reform Club for 'the Prime Minister ... to meet the Editors of Liberal newspapers' on 15 September. Donald, besides being an old friend who owed his G.B.E. to MacDonald, was fittingly antagonistic to Lloyd George, whom a fortuitous illness had excluded from membership in the National Government. After MacDonald was expelled from the Labour Party on the 28th, he formed a National Labour Party and Donald agreed to chair its publicity committee. 'The friendly aid of Conservative and Liberal newspapers was not enough, and would be misrepresented,' Donald's biographer has reckoned. 'Small as it was, the party needed a Press of its own.' In addition to running a fortnightly *News-Letter*, Donald acquired custody of the weekly *Everyman*, which was diverted from its literary pursuits to cater to the propaganda needs of National Labour. 'You know even better than I do,' MacDonald wrote to him in the wake of the October campaign, 'what the difficulties were with which our hurriedly improvised organization had to contend, and I simply do not know how they would have been surmounted without your experience and whole-hearted help.'[1]

To say that those difficulties were surmounted was something of an exaggeration. National Labour, the newer new party, ran twenty candidates, of whom thirteen were returned with Tory connivance. The New Party, robbed of its eponymous distinction, failed in all twenty-four of its contests, although its publicity resources were comparatively better. Under the editorship of Harold Nicolson, who was pirated from the staff of the *Evening Standard*, and amply endowed by Sir William Morris (later 1st Viscount Nuffield), *Action* hurriedly began weekly publication on 8 October. Priced at twopence, it boasted an immediate sale of 160,000 copies. As a showcase for *avant-garde* intellectualism, the journal had redoubtable merit; 'as an attempt to raise recruits for a new party', however, Blatchford judged it 'the most opaque and feeble production I can remember, though the manifesto of the anti-British Labour Party', as he referred to National Labour, 'runs it close. How few officials or politicians know how to use the King's English,' he complained superciliously.[2]

If nothing else, one would have expected a high level of literary craftsmanship from Nicolson, who took responsibility for the 'Notes of the Week' and the book reviews. But the bombast of Mosley's leading articles withered his blue pencil. Conjuring up his 'vision splendid', the Leader harangued the readers of the inaugural number that 'the fundamental task of new creation ... is far more relevant to the modern age than the transient labours of a nineteenth century Parliament'. By 2 November, Nicolson was painfully aware 'that I am not ... well suited to be a man who runs a weekly. I see both sides of every question', a particular disqualification when trying to satisfy Mosley's demands for mili-

[1] Stevenson to Morrison, 21 December 1929, quoted in Donoughue and Jones, *Morrison*, p. 143; Seymour-Ure, *The Press, Politics and the Public*, p. 232; Donald to E. T. Scott, 9 September 1931, *Guardian* Archives; H. A. Taylor, *Donald*, pp. 258–59.

[2] Skidelsky, *Oswald Mosley* (London, 1975), pp. 264, 280; Blatchford to Palmer, 29 October 1931, Blatchford Papers.

tancy. Still, Nicolson aspired 'to make something of this paper. The difficulty is that I am backed and financed by a political party. And even then it is not a party but a rather sly little movement.' The circulation had tumbled to 'barely 15,000' on 31 December, when *Action* was discontinued. Mosley, who made a habit of pouring new wine into old bottles until they finally broke, affixed the same title to the journal he founded later in the decade under the auspices of the British Union of Fascists. By then, Nicolson had parted company with him and had entered Parliament as National Labour member for Leicester West. In its second, 'low-brow' incarnation, *Action* was edited by John Beckett, the renegade Labour MP for Peckham.[1]

Contrary to the original blueprints, the National Government went to the country on 27 October 1931 as a collective entity with a request for 'a doctor's mandate' to cure the ills of the nation. (Beaverbrook suggested that if MacDonald went 'on in his present course much longer he will get an ultimatum from his own doctor'.) Anything more specific would have alienated the Liberals, whose adherence gave the semblance of a 'National' dimension. Ten days before polling, Barrington-Ward 'held a conference' with representatives of the *Daily Telegraph* and the *Morning Post* 'to decide upon the nomenclature of parties in this strange General Election that is coming'. The Beaverbrook and Rothermere papers, denied the satisfaction of a pledge to introduce tariffs, grudgingly fell into line. It was to be assumed, A. J. Cummings commented afterwards, 'that when a Government of the Right is faced with a real crisis, or is in the throes of a General Election, the recalcitrant Conservative newspapers will shed their differences in a single revolution of the globe and re-form themselves on the united front'. By holding the vexing issue of protectionism at bay, the leaders of the National Government were able to draw upon the Liberal press for varying degrees of support. The *News Chronicle*, against Cummings's better judgment, was among those that willingly suspended disbelief. That was to leave the *Daily Herald* as the only London daily to warn that 'every vote for a "National" candidate is a vote for Tariffs, for higher prices and for food taxes' (24 October). The *Manchester Guardian*, where Ted Scott was 'getting more and more' into 'a socialist way of thinking (or rather feeling)', also refused to play the game. 'This sham unity, this temporary and embarrassing alliance of tigers and sheep, is worth less than nothing,' it fulminated on 6 October. 'Taking as it does increasingly every day the form of an alliance against Labour, it is perhaps the greatest threat to national unity that we have.' Cobdenism and socialism, long regarded as antithetical, had somehow grown mutually dependent.[2]

Supporters of the National Government, the overwhelming number of

---

[1] Nicolson, *Diaries and Letters, 1930–1939*, I (London, 1966), 96–97.
[2] Beaverbrook to Sir John Jarvis, 29 September 1931, quoted in Taylor, *Beaverbrook*, p. 319; Barrington-Ward's diary, 19 October 1931; Cummings, *The Press*, p. 79; Scott to Hammond, 16 November [1931], Hammond Papers.

whom were unreconstructed Conservatives, occupied 554 seats in the new House of Commons. The opposition consisted of a rump of fifty-two Labour MPs, along with the four members of Lloyd George's family entourage. Within the National fold, the Liberal flock divided almost evenly between two shepherds: Sir Herbert Samuel, who held the Home Office, led those Liberals who eschewed either prefixes or suffixes; Sir John Simon, soon to arrive at the Foreign Office, led the Liberal Nationals, a breed that proved increasingly indistinguishable from mainstream Conservatives. As a self-styled 'group', reluctant to formalize their divergence, the Liberal Nationals did not set up an independent publicity apparatus. In the opinion of Geoffrey Shakespeare, one of their number, they consequently suffered 'serious misrepresentation in certain quarters of the Liberal Press', partial either to Samuel or to Lloyd George.[1]

Newspapers were bound to reflect these dislocations and, on the face of things, capitalized upon them. *The Times*, Barrington-Ward noted in September, 'is being bought much: this crisis is as nourishing to circulation as a war, though I want neither'. In anticipation of electioneering, that paper 'decided to postpone our circulation campaign and new type ... probably until January'. (In the event, *The Times* did not get its facelift, including the landmark substitution of Roman lettering for ornamental Gothic script in its masthead, until October 1932.) *The Times*'s financial statements belied Barrington-Ward's sanguine impressions, however. The twelve-month period that ended in June 1929 had been 'extraordinarily prosperous', leaving a surplus for building renovations. But the accounts for the ensuing fiscal year 'reflected only too faithfully the beginning of the depression in the financial and industrial world' that was to become 'even more acute' as 1930 wore on.[2]

Unlike the *Daily Telegraph*, which dropped its price to a penny in December 1930, *The Times* continued to sell for twopence. It was thus more expensive than any of its metropolitan rivals, though as costly as the leading provincial dailies. The house historian of the *Telegraph*, preferring to stress the benefits of 'editorial ... improvements', celebrated a gain in circulation, which 'was over 175,000' at the end of 1930 'and steadily increasing'. Dawson, not nearly so impressed, maintained that the *Telegraph* had achieved 'to some extent a bogus circulation, a very large number of copies being distributed free with the object of reaching *The Times* figure and having a case for raising advertisement rates'. Eventually, the authorities at Printing House Square were obliged to take the lively competition from Peterborough Court more seriously, but they looked upon 'the semi-popular *DT*' as a mechanism for 'weaning readers from the purely popular press and preparing them for *TT*';

---

[1] Memorandum by Geoffrey Shakespeare, then Liberal National MP for Norwich, 12 February 1932, Simon Papers.

[2] Barrington-Ward's diary, 16 and 21 September 1931; financial report of *The Times*, February 1931 (copy), Dawson Papers.

Barrington-Ward expected to 'skim the cream of these new readers' in due course.[1]

More than ever, advertising revenues were of crucial importance. The twopenny *Manchester Guardian*, despite 'the letters of abuse' it received and 'a lot of cancellations of orders' from newsagents in select middle-class residential areas, experienced (so far as Ted Scott could tell) 'a rise in circulation. But a severe hit in advertising on top of everything else' more than offset it. The advertising manager 'had actually to withdraw the whole of his canvassing staff at one time – they were practically kicked downstairs,' Scott informed J. L. Hammond in mid-November. 'Boots withdrew the whole of their Xmas advertising and gave it extra to the *D[aily] Dispatch*. There have been other cases.' Although 'the resentment is dying down and some cancellations have been recancelled', the editor foresaw 'a period of isolation for the *M.G.*' that did not portend 'very good business'. Early in 1932, Oscar Hobson of the *Financial News* returned to Manchester, where he had been city editor of the *Guardian*, to attend the funeral of C. P. Scott. He found Ted pessimistic about the future of the paper: 'Of course, they're in Queer Street like all the rest of us.'[2]

To be sure, there were different addresses in Queer Street, some better situated than others. Beaverbrook, once again 'the leader of the hobgoblins' within the Tory Party, reported an increase in the retail trade accounts of both the *Daily Express* and the *Daily Mail* during the first three-quarters of 1932, and that was before the normal Christmas boom. 'All the important papers are up,' he proclaimed subjectively. 'But *The Times* suffers terribly. Its profits are £3,000 on a capital of several millions.' For essentially non-political reasons, contrasting with certain other cases, *The Times* was forced to economize by pegging its salaries to the NUJ minimum. Consequently, it lost a good deal of literary and managerial talent. Among the departures was that of J. C. Akerman, who had joined Harrison in 1928 as vice-chairman of the *Daily Chronicle* and its provincial affiliates. 'His motives were probably mixed,' as his erstwhile employers reasonably deduced. After Harrison's 'meteoric rise' and 'equally spectacular fall', Akerman was invited to resume at Printing House Square, but opted for the vice-chairmanship of the *News Chronicle* board. There, he had to contend with exactly the same problems. In the twelve-month period that followed incorporation, the amalgamated company incurred a trading loss of £39,980, which was held not to indicate its 'real position and prospects' on the grounds that an 'abnormally heavy expenditure' had been necessary 'in the early months of the fusion'. The fact remained, however, that 'advertisements were not yielding the economic return justified

[1] Burnham, *Peterborough Court*, pp. 206–207; memorandum by Dawson, appended to financial report of *The Times*, February 1931 (copy), Dawson Papers; Barrington-Ward's diary, 15 March 1935.
[2] Scott to Hammond, 16 November [1931], Hammond Papers; Brooks's diary, 6 January 1932.

by the sales', which dipped to 1,336,512 in January 1931 and then improved slightly.[1]

'Anxious to reduce expenditure', even though they were relatively prosperous, Rothermere and Beaverbrook invited Bertram Crosfield, the managing director of the *News Chronicle*, to tea at Rothermere's flat on 16 February 1932. 'We discussed all sorts of schemes over hot buttered toast and large chunks of seed cake,' wrote Crosfield, who returned the next day 'to discuss further details' at 'another larger tea party', this one distinguished by 'a nice plum cake'. The two press lords struck Crosfield as 'apt rather to overdo their dolefulness in order to get me into a suitable frame of mind for accepting suggestions which might not all of them in the long run be to our advantage'. Nevertheless, they 'managed to come to an amicable understanding with regard to free gifts, insurance, etc., that in the end will save us all a good deal of money and worry'.[2]

The convulsions in Fleet Street and at Westminster were, in many ways, analogous. Just as parties came together in the face of economic adversity, sometimes changing their leaders and directions in the process, so too did journals. It was not so much the survival of the fittest as the survival of the relatively least unfit. The *New Statesman*, where Kingsley Martin's appointment was kept under wraps for a time, merged in 1931 with the *Nation*; the former was showing a small profit, drained away by the legal battles of Clifford Sharp, the outgoing editor; the latter was recognized by Keynes, who had more important things to do than to chair its board, as being 'no longer viable'. Reflecting the discrepancy in assets, the staff of the *Nation* was obliged to make the greater sacrifice.[3]

At the beginning of the following year, a merger between the *Financial News* and the *Financial Times* was rumoured to be 'in active shaping'. The moving force was reportedly Lord Camrose, whose family had purchased the *Financial Times* from the reclusive Sir John Ellerman in 1919. Both financial dailies took nominally 'independent' political stances, and each persistently accused the other of kow-towing to advertisers, for whom they feverishly competed. Founded in 1884 by H. H. Marks, who subsequently entered Parliament on the Conservative side, the *Financial News* was the more blatantly partisan. During the 1920s, its Tory coloration had grown more pronounced under the ownership of Sir John Jarvis and the successive editorships of Sir Laming Worthington-Evans and Sir Edward Hilton Young (a recent convert from Liberalism and later 1st Baron Kennet), all of whom saw service as Conservative MPs. Brendan Bracken, a ginger-haired youth of twenty-seven whose firm of Eyre and Spottiswoode already published the *Banker*, acquired dominant

---

[1] Beaverbrook to Brisbane, 20 October 1932 (copy), Beaverbrook Papers, C/64; News Chronicle Ltd., directors' report for the year ending 3 June 1931, Cowdray Papers.
[2] Crosfield to ?, 18 February 1932, copy courtesy of John Crosfield.
[3] Hyams, *New Statesman*, pp. 119–23.

control in 1928, the year before his election as Conservative member for Paddington North. Major John Hills, one of his principal associates in the venture, was also his companion on the Tory backbenches. To cope with the ravages of the Depression, Bracken cut his own salary by a third and expected the staff to follow his example. Such voluntary economies hardly sufficed. On 29 February 1932, Collin Brooks described 'the office ... astir with the impending dissolution of the paper and Bracken's rat-like rushing from one expedient to another'. That June, the immediate crisis was overcome by massive lay-offs. 'There are so many excellent journalists thrown out now,' lamented Brooks, 'that one can do nothing to help and little to sustain their courage.' With a new lease of life, the *Financial News* continued until 25 July 1945, the very day that the Labour victory was announced. Then, with questionable symbolism, it was absorbed by the pink-hued *Financial Times*.[1]

Rothermere, who had been prophesying doom year in and year out since the war, was proved a sage at last. Travelling on the Continent in the summer of 1929, he pointed to a group of affluent American tourists and told his 'Hungarian secretary' that the luxury hotels would be empty next season. The crash came that winter, and he had protected himself by 'going liquid'. Bracken regaled Hobson and Brooks with the story (probably misdated) of how 'Rothermere cleared nearly £3,000,000 by bearing Wall Street at the end of December [1931] and that he (literally) neither knows how much he is worth or where his investments are'. Too late to make a difference, Rothermere advised Beaverbrook to do the same. 'For ten or fifteen thousand a year in directorships you can certainly get twenty "trustys" ' to carry the burdens of newspaper management without forfeiting an overriding influence. That was the 'policy' that Rothermere had implemented at the *Daily Mirror*, where he parcelled out control among individual shareholders. McWhirter, the former editor of the *Sunday Pictorial* and a kingpin of the Rothermere organization, subsequently described to Brooks 'the various divisions and groups within the board of Associated Newspapers'. Although Rothermere no longer controlled the business, 'he behaves as if he did and nobody challenges him'.[2]

Admittedly, the *Mirror* (with the *Sunday Pictorial* tethered to it) was not worth the investment it had locked up. In 1931, when Rothermere executed his scheme of divestiture, its circulation 'had begun to stagnate at the low level of

[1] *Financial Times*, 12 November 1969, and information conveyed to the author by Christopher Johnson, then managing editor; Brooks's diary, 25 and 31 January, 29 February, and 20 June 1932. The difference between the *Financial Times* and the *Financial News* may be illustrated by their contrasting responses to the formation of the National Government in 1931: the former did not allow this event to usurp the front-page primacy of its stock market reports; the latter gave the political crisis a three-column spread and transposed its stock quotations to the inside pages.

[2] Rothermere to Beaverbrook, 2 February 1931, Beaverbrook Papers, C/287; Brooks's diary, 4 January 1932 and 6 November 1935. Ignoring Rothermere's advice, Beaverbrook took advantage of market conditions to purchase the Daily Mail Trust's minority shareholding in the *Express* for roughly £550,000, less than half the amount he had offered in better times. Taylor, *Beaverbrook*, p. 333.

800,000 to which it had slowly dropped'. Under the editorship of Leigh Brownlee, who took over at this juncture from Alexander Campbell, the sale sank to 700,000 within three years. By 1935, it was a paper with a predominantly female readership that belonged largely to a lower income group, but it seemed 'to have no clear impression of who those readers were, of how they located themselves socially or politically'. A step removed from Rothermere, the *Mirror* was now subject only to his 'occasional intervention', usually transmitted through John Cowley, who began as his secretary and became chairman of the *Mirror* and *Pictorial* companies. The *Daily Mail*, on the other hand, remained Rothermere's personal sounding-board through the decade.[1]

By Bracken's calculation, which wholly disregarded political factors, 'the *Manchester Guardian*, the *Yorkshire Post* and the *Liverpool Post* can stand the strain as only those properties are really vulnerable which have been over-financed by the banks'. Taking a political view, Ted Scott was not so sure. 'What I feel,' he confessed to Hammond, 'is that we cannot live much longer as a twopenny paper and we can't afford to come down to a penny.' With 'politics ... getting into an ugly shape', it was inevitable that the *Guardian* would 'be driven more and more to take an anti-property line. And that is fatal to a 2d. paper', not to say a Liberal one. Taking 'a critical view of the pretensions of the National Government' (as opposed to Crozier, who 'takes a purely National view'), Scott considered it 'impossible to sit, or appear to sit, on the fence', leaving the *Guardian* no choice but 'to side more and more with people' of a moderate Labour disposition. Though ignored by Bracken, this 'limiting factor' was recognized in retrospect by the historian of the *Daily Telegraph*:

> The Parliamentary system of this country is a two-party one and any newspaper which hopes to be constructive must generally align itself with the policy of one of them and so deny itself the readership of the most ardent supporters of the other. This argument does not presume that all the readers of the *Daily Telegraph* are Tories any more than that all the readers of the *Daily Mirror* [in 1955] are Socialists, but the effect of party loyalty on circulation is sensible.

How sensible? That was something else the argument did not presume to stipulate.[2]

From the standpoint of leading journalists, the political press might have lost its commercial viability, but neither its mission nor its gratification. Barrington-Ward, writing in his diary on 15 November 1931, expressed a reluctance 'to lose my direct touch with politics, which is, after all, the largest thing in our kind of journalism and gives the writer the feeling that he is doing something worth-

---

[1] Edelman, *Daily Mirror*, pp. 20, 26–27; A. C. H. Smith, *Paper Voices* (London, 1975), p. 83.
[2] Brooks's diary, 4 January 1932; Scott to Hammond, 16 November [1931], Hammond Papers; Burnham, *Peterborough Court*, p. 207.

while'. Dawson, basking in the afterglow of the 1931 election, recalled 'floating the idea' for a National appeal to the electors 'in an article which I wrote myself, which was received with howls of execration by the *Daily Mail*, by all the Liberals and most of the nervous Conservatives and above all by the City. However most of them came round to it in the end – with the result that you know.' *The Times* was singularly equipped by reputation to cover political issues and to comment upon them extensively. For it to desist would have been a dereliction of duty. But to what degree, if any, could other newspapers afford to indulge a political commitment that was notably more binding among writers than readers?[1]

Going above the editor's head to Lord Cowdray, Mrs J. A. Spender deplored the curtailment of her husband's opportunities to contribute signed columns to the *News Chronicle*. Tom Clarke had reportedly decreed 'that the paper had been getting too heavy, that they wanted less politics, not more', although that may have been an excuse for getting rid of an Asquithian incubus. Given that the *News Chronicle* was 'the only Liberal paper there is', Mrs Spender considered it 'absurd to damp down Politics, indeed it is wicked'. But wickedness, as she defined it, was seen to pay; or, at any rate, old-fashioned virtues no longer paid as well. That was epitomized by the predicament of the *Manchester Guardian*, which was rewarded for the courage of its convictions by the undergraduates at Balliol College, Oxford, where the junior common room took four copies in May 1932 'compared with a single copy a year ago, chiefly as the result of the policy of the paper in the last nine months'. Yet, as Spender must have remembered from his youth, Balliol was far from typical. At the Oxford and Cambridge University Club in London, the library committee voted to reduce that year's newspaper consumption. Two fewer copies of *The Times* (for a total of sixteen) were taken from Tuesday to Friday, with an identical order for the final edition of the *Evening Standard* on weekdays. Along with two copies of the *Daily Sketch* (down from three), the club subscribed to various weeklies, but to none of the provincial dailies. Clubland was obviously not only feeling the pinch, but also reflecting a devaluation of the political coinage that had nothing to do with the abandonment of the gold standard.[2]

What was true of the educated mind was still more palpably true in the 'real world', which Bernard Shaw observed to be populated by 'cinema poisoned ignorant romantic duffers who read the *Daily Mail* when they read at all, except the serial in the *Daily Herald*'. He neglected to mention the *Daily Express*, where Arthur Christiansen soon began to strive with spectacular success 'to simplify news in such a way that it would be interesting to the permanent

---

[1] Barrington-Ward's diary, 15 November 1931; Dawson to Sir Francis Lindley, ambassador to Japan, 19 November 1931 (copy), Dawson Papers.
[2] Mary Spender to Cowdray, 9 December 1931, Cowdray Papers; Ayerst, *Guardian*, p. 474n.; minutes, library committee, Oxford and Cambridge University Club, 12 December 1932.

Secretary of the Foreign Office and to the charwoman who brushed his office floor in the morning'. Blumenfeld, one of the perpetrators of the so-called Northcliffe revolution, was dismayed by its belated effects. 'The truth of the matter is that from devoting too much attention to the sayings and doings of our legislators, the Press has now gone to the other extreme, and devotes too little,' he argued in 1933. For that, Blumenfeld insisted,

> Parliament has itself to blame. Since the War it has degenerated into an assembly of talkers and do-nothings. All reality has departed from party politics, and the shadow-fights at Westminster have ceased to interest anybody. Never in my long experience as a journalist has Parliament been so lacking in forcible and picturesque personalities, or so out of touch with the feeling of the nation, as at the present time. It is not surprising, therefore, that the national newspapers have ceased to treat its manoeuvres seriously, and prefer to concentrate on the few political issues which seem to them to touch the realities of the moment.

Obviously, the situation was more complicated and the blame, so to speak, was more diffuse.[1]

Judging from the aggregate circulation figure, the public was getting, if not the press it deserved, then at least the press it wanted. Lady Rhondda, the wealthy owner of *Time and Tide* ('Independent Non-Party'), held no brief for Rothermere, yet bristled at G. D. H. Cole's suggestion that governmental authorities should rescue the mass readership of the *Daily Mail* from his pernicious influence. By advocating the exercise of 'power to decide what the readers of the *Daily Mail* should read', Cole was actually proposing 'to spoon-feed the public against its will, since its will is to read the *Daily Mail* as it is now'.[2] Beyond that, it remained an open question whether the newspapers (including the *Daily Mail*) materially abetted the shift from party political concerns or merely expressed the re-ordering of popular preferences.

In either case, the creation and perpetuation of a National administration was widely taken to denote, for better or worse, a repudiation of partisanship. The spirit of the 1930s, inimical to the customary postures and procedures of political journalism, demanded the adaptation of old models at the same time that public taste dictated the adoption of new images. Needless to say, neither political activity nor that already shrunken portion of the press that attended to it was obliterated. Both were inhibited, however, and had to

---

[1] Beatrice Webb's diary, 30 November 1930, Passfield Papers; text of a television interview in January 1960, quoted in Christiansen, *Headlines*, p. 147; Blumenfeld, *Press in My Time*, p. 124.

[2] Cummings, who quoted Lady Rhondda's retort to Cole, agreed with her that Rothermere, 'in so far as he is a monster at all, ... must be taken as a gigantic monster image of the average *Daily Mail* reader'. *The Press*, pp. 81–83.

adjust their boundaries, which editors were to find especially restrictive and difficult to defend.

* * *

The declension of the political press, signalled by the thinning of its ranks and the vitiation of its historic functions, continued apace through the decade. The process affected each of the major parties as well as those 'sly little movements' that splintered from them. Mosley's New Party might have been saved by 'brilliant journalistic support', contended Beaverbrook, who ascribed its misfortunes to 'a conspiracy of silence in the newspapers, except for the particular newspapers I am connected with'.[1] Those who suffered most acutely, however, were the parliamentary Liberals, whose forbears had been the progenitors of a system that now claimed them as victims.

By this time, as one historian has pointed out, the *News Chronicle* was virtually all that 'remained for the whole party whose philosophy made a virtue of diversity and argument'.[2] The last citadel of Liberalism in the metropolitan morning press, this paper felt an obligation to accommodate growing divergences that further weakened its foundations. These tensions were reflected within its management and staff, in its relations with feuding politicians, and in its appeal to a volatile readership. As spelt out in the press, pre-eminently both the repository and the exponent of nineteenth-century Liberal ideals, the story of the Liberal decline – or downfall – was largely the story of the *News Chronicle*.

Liberal journalists, deprived of employment elsewhere, had no other refuge unless they were prepared to transplant themselves to Manchester or else were sufficiently distinguished (like Ensor) to contribute to the *Guardian* by post. Relieved of his command at the *Financial News* in 1934, 'partly because he was too Liberal for Bracken's liking', Oscar Hobson became city editor of the *News Chronicle* and eventually earned a knighthood. Paul Bareau (later editor of the *Statist*) followed Hobson's choice, as did numerous dispossessed Liberals.[3] While they enriched the *News Chronicle* by their talents, they intensified its problems by the mutual resentments they carried with them.

Seeking to make a virtue of necessity, the amalgamation of the hybrid *Daily News* and the stricken *Daily Chronicle* had been predicated on an agreement 'that consistent support should be given to the promotion of unity in the Liberal Party'.[4] That was more easily said than done. Without overcoming previous conflicts of personality and principle, the Liberal leadership proceeded to

[1] Beaverbrook to Nicolson, 25 June 1931, quoted in Nicolson, *Diaries*, I, 79–80.
[2] Seymour-Ure, 'The Press and the Party System,' in Peele and Cook, eds., *Politics of Reappraisal*, p. 239, which adds that 'the *Manchester Guardian* had a national reputation but remained essentially a provincial paper with a circulation of 40,000'.
[3] *Financial Times*, 12 November 1969.
[4] Heads of Agreement, 2 June 1930, Cowdray Papers.

splinter under pressure of events. Each of the sectional groups demanded even-handed support from the *News Chronicle*, which could not conceivably serve them all and consequently satisfied none of them.

Clarke, appointed editor at the time of fusion, was a warm admirer of Lloyd George. With a firmer grasp of Radical doctrines and an evangelical zeal, so was Cummings, the chief leader-writer. Sharing their hero's antipathy to the National Government, they ran foul of the neo-Asquithian or Whiggish elements, who accused them of a left-wing bias. 'It does seem to me to be a pity to do anything to help drive people out of the Party just because they venture to disagree with L.G.,' Lord Cowdray complained to Sir Walter Layton, 'and Cummings's attitude all along has been to be entirely intolerant of anything except the most Labour point of view.' Cowdray, who gratefully accepted the National Government as a bulwark against socialism, was distressed by persistent allegations that the *News Chronicle* was being used by Lloyd George to carry on a flirtation with Labour behind the back of Sir Herbert Samuel, the accredited custodian of parliamentary Liberalism. Harcourt Johnstone, who held his seat in the Commons as a Samuelite Liberal, protested that, except on those occasions when Layton 'personally intervened', the paper took 'a line calculated not to help the Party as a whole, but to damage one leading Liberal for the benefit of another'. Easily persuaded by such arguments, Cowdray committed his 'ruminations' to paper: 'This is the only London daily newspaper which puts forward the Liberal point of view. Its politics for the last year or two have been consistent and have taken a definite line,' but the paper was 'still apt to stir up troubled waters by not allowing L.G. to be forgotten'.[1]

Cummings saw the Liberal predicament much more clearly and better understood the practical alternatives. Reviewing the 'prospects for reconstituting the Liberal party' in November 1931, he recognized that it was idle to suppose that Lloyd George would disappear and idler still for the party organizers to bank upon his continued pecuniary assistance. 'L.G. remains a disturbing factor, and may be more so in the future, largely because there is no one of sufficient calibre to take his place & focus party enthusiasm,' Cummings told Layton. A crypto-Conservative brand of Liberalism, 'recognised in the country as such, would probably be the final catastrophe', he warned. Such emphatic views frightened Cowdray, who considered it 'a mistake to allow Cummings to write any of the articles in the "Notes of the Day" ' section, where a 'judicial atmosphere' had to be preserved. Cummings 'is amazingly good in what he writes', conceded Cowdray, 'but the whole essence of his style is to be controversial'. Exactly that quality commended Cummings to Beaverbrook, who tried to lure him to the *Daily Express*. Cummings thought it best not to put his friendship with Beaverbrook to the test. He stayed put on the *News Chronicle* 'in spite of inadequate pay, Nonconformist Chadbands and worse

[1] Cowdray to Layton, 20 May 1931 (copy), Johnstone to Layton, 30 May 1932 (copy), and memorandum by Cowdray, 6 October 1932 (copy), Cowdray Papers.

irritations', enjoying 'on the whole the opportunity to write what I wanted to write', thanks to Layton and Clarke.[1]

By granting Cummings a licence to praise Lloyd George, the *News Chronicle* did not endear itself to those Liberals who variously attached themselves to the National superstructure. As Foreign Secretary, Simon was stung by criticisms of his feeble handling of the Manchurian crisis. 'The temptation of saying something unpleasant to me in order to please Lloyd George was too much for the Liberal Press,' he wrote peevishly, 'but this sort of partisanship has entirely destroyed their influence.' Spender again 'protested ... without result' that Grey's 'name is never ... mentioned without a disparaging epithet' while the *News Chronicle* favoured Lloyd George with an 'attitude ... of admiring complacency at his worst gaffes'. Spender wrote an article partly to redress the balance and partly as 'a test case of my position on the staff', where Clarke 'hardly disguises that he thinks me a nuisance & a burden'. To his surprise, it was printed on 4 April 1932. That month, meeting at Clacton, the National Liberal Federation absolved its parliamentary spokesmen of 'any obligation to support the policy of the present Government', unmistakably set on a course of protectionism. Samuel and his Free Trade followers departed from office in August, leaving the Simonites behind. Cowdray weighed the commercial implications: for more than a year, the *Daily Herald* had been 'the only popular London paper which has been appealing to that large number of readers who disagree with the Government'; now that the Liberals had withdrawn (though not yet returned to the opposition benches), it was 'possible that ... this advantage', hitherto the monopoly of the *Herald*, 'will be shared by the *News Chronicle*'.[2]

In fact, whatever the journalistic or electoral benefits of opposition, the Liberals failed to collect them. 'From a party point of view Liberalism is in an almost hopeless position,' Lord Lothian (formerly Philip Kerr) observed in September 1933. The following month, Clarke was 'an editor no longer'. He resigned on 2 October, after 'Layton hinted that it might be better if we parted company'. Although sad to leave Fleet Street, he looked forward to 'freedom from the machinations of rival Liberals ready to eat each other (and me possibly) up'. His immediate reward was a farewell lunch with Lloyd George, who 'said the Radical tradition had now passed to the Labour moderates who bought the *Daily Herald*' and who professed to have 'no use for, and little interest in, any of the political parties'.[3]

---

[1] Memorandum by Cummings, 13 November 1931, Layton Papers; Cowdray to Layton, 9 February 1933 (copy), Cowdray Papers; Cummings to Beaverbrook, 17 June 1931, Beaverbrook Papers, C/104.

[2] Simon to Mrs V. R. Carruthers, 22 March 1932 (copy), Simon Papers; Spender to Cowdray, 3 and 4 April 1932, and memorandum by Cowdray, 6 October 1932, Cowdray Papers; Roy Douglas, *History of the Liberal Party 1895–1970* (London, 1971), pp. 227–29.

[3] Memorandum by Lothian, 7 September 1933, Lothian Papers; Clarke, *Lloyd George Diary* (2, 4, and 5 October 1933), pp. 236, 239–40.

Within days of Clarke's dismissal, Cowdray died. Towards the end, he had come to appreciate Clarke's 'difficulties as a journalist trying to make a success of a popular newspaper with the political handicap of a divided party'. His successors were to prove less empathetic. The editorial vacancy was promptly filled by the elevation of Aylmer Vallance, whom Layton had brought from *The Economist*. Henry Cadbury, who retained a seat on the six-member Daily News & Westminster board, which appointed three of the five voting trustees, found it 'a great comfort' that Vallance was already 'in charge' on the 16th; otherwise, the paper might have been disposed 'to take a Jingo view' in response to Hitler's ominous decision to boycott the disarmament conference at Geneva. 'Personally,' he admitted, 'I am not so anxious about party politics – I think they can take care of themselves.'[1]

It was more difficult to obtain a suitable replacement for Cowdray, who had doubled as a director of the Daily News & Westminster Ltd. and a voting trustee of the overall company. His son, who inherited his peerage and fortune, was then aged twenty-three and, by his own recollection, 'never took any direct part in the newspaper side' of his family's far-flung commercial empire. Later to become a 'legendary personality' and 'one of the richest and most formidable men in Britain', the 3rd Viscount was to make a single incursion into politics (if indeed it qualified as such) by serving as principal private secretary to the Under-Secretary of State for Air in 1941–42. Given his youth and inexperience, his newspaper-owning responsibilities were assumed by his uncle, Clive Pearson, who was already in charge of the general operations of S. Pearson & Son. Lady Denman, the 3rd Viscount's aunt and Clive Pearson's sister, helped to defend family interests, which J. B. Morrell now represented among the trustees.[2]

Morrell, Layton, and Laurence Cadbury sought to vitalize the concern by appointing Lothian to the Westminster board and making him 'what might be called a political Director of the News and Westminster Ltd., in the interests of independent Liberalism'. How that would have fit with Layton's functions was left ambiguous. Lothian replied to Pearson, who extended the invitation, that, if the proposed position was 'to carry effective weight, indeed to be tolerable, it will only be because there is explicit agreement' between the minority and majority shareholders 'as to the policy of the *News Chronicle* on certain fundamentals'. So far as Lothian could tell from conversations with Layton and Vallance,

> the general policy of the *News Chronicle* is to try to create an effective opposition to the present National Government and its probably Conservative successor. While its general political philosophy may be called Liberal or

[1] Clarke, *Lloyd George Diary* (17 March 1932), p. 143; Henry Cadbury to Layton, 16 October 1933, Layton Papers.
[2] Sampson, *Anatomy of Britain*, p. 384; Lord Cowdray to the author, 27 October 1982.

perhaps radical and not Socialist, it regards the Labour Party as the natural nucleus of such an opposition and will support its candidates as against National Government or Conservative candidates, unless the candidate is an advocate of Communist or revolutionary methods. At a General Election it would, I think, support the Labour Party, while opposing the more extreme elements in its policy, as against the Government.

Fearing that his role as a Liberal watchdog 'would rapidly be confined to that of making ineffectual protests', Lothian thought it

> true to say that while the present direction of the *News Chronicle* has no particular criticism to make of Sir Herbert Samuel's declaration of policy, it does not think that such a programme alone can be made the basis for an effective appeal by a left opposition party, or for holding circulation for the *News Chronicle* itself, or that the independent Liberal Party can be made, under present circumstances, into an effective rival either to the Government or the Labour Parties.

While he did not quarrel with these assumptions, he anticipated that they would result in 'perpetual complaint and frustration' for anyone who undertook, 'as a political director, to ensure that the *News Chronicle* supported the Liberal Party'. Pearson allayed some of these misgivings by releasing documents that Layton had reportedly withheld, but Lothian noted uneasily that, by implication, 'the Heads of Agreement gave to circulation a priority over politics'. To the extent that 'the paper continued to be anti-Samuel and pro-Labour, . . . his position as a member of the official Liberal Party would be an impossible one'.[1]

On 13 February 1934, Lothian met Pearson 'to talk the matter over'. The next day, he formally declined. Refusing to accept his decision as final, Pearson and Lady Denman conferred on the 21st with Layton in the 'unfortunate' absence of Laurence Cadbury, 'away in Africa'. Each of them affirmed 'that Lord Lothian would be an excellent appointment to the News & Westminster Board (or to the trusteeship) if he saw his way to accept the position', his gloomy appraisal of Liberal prospects notwithstanding. At Pearson's suggestion, they proceeded to concentrate on 'questions of policy & principle' in an attempt to iron out the differences that Lothian had seized upon. Layton graciously recalled that, in the ministerial crisis of August 1931, the previous Lord Cowdray had helped to map an editorial line 'that worked out to the reasonable satisfaction of both the majority and minority interests'. Confident that harmony could be restored, he reiterated 'the desirability that the *News Chronicle* should not be tied to any Party' by its owners. Pearson, no proponent of laissez-faire in this context, 'remarked that even recently there had been

---

[1] Pearson to Layton, 18 January and 14 February 1934, Layton Papers; Lothian to Pearson, 7 February 1934, and Pearson's 'reminder of a conversation with Lord Lothian, 13 February 1934,' Cowdray Papers.

some examples of naughtiness' which had escaped neither his attention nor Lothian's. He and Lady Denman 'enquired whether the Cadbury side and Sir Walter himself continue to be in agreement with the policy laid down in the Heads of Agreement; or, if no longer in sympathy with that policy, whether they are heading away from the Liberal faith to some new Labour policy'. Speaking for themselves, they were prepared to recognize

> that there may be occasions when Liberal and Labour should work together; and we realised that it is of no avail for a newspaper requiring circulation to be preaching unpopular or old-fashioned lectures. On the other hand, we continue to have a faith in broad Liberalism and we consider that the paper has a higher responsibility than to support the Labour policy which is so often sloshy and ill-conceived.

Layton was requested to 'set forth' a comparable 'definition of his faith' in the form of 'a draft of the instructions relating to policy such as might be given to the Editorial side'. He complied on 14 June with a statement that carried the endorsement of Vallance and Laurence Cadbury. It struck Pearson not as 'a fair declaration of Liberalism but rather as a declaration of Socialism'.[1]

The pages of the *News Chronicle* bore witness to these strains, which were emblematic of the Liberal dilemma. Vallance, who lasted until Gerald Barry took over in 1936, compounded the difficulties by divorcing public from private morality. Outwardly more high-minded than his predecessor, whose reputation had been sullied by prior association with Northcliffe, he was incongruously addicted to the low life. Tongues were set wagging by his debaucheries, which took place after working hours and left the premises littered with empty bottles and occasionally pieces of ladies' apparel. Years later, Collin Brooks savoured 'the story of the Aylmer Vallance episode at the *News Chronicle*, when the austere Quaker newspaper office became a veritable brothel'. The editor and his companions were said to have fornicated 'all over the place!! Even Arthur Cummings's sacred desk was violated.' Such scandals were particularly shocking in Bouverie Street, where – as Elie Halévy noted – the traditional atmosphere 'was Puritan as well as Radical'.[2]

Lloyd George, who practised promiscuity with greater discretion, received from Vallance 'a hint of combination & understanding with the *Herald* on a progressive policy', which promised a realignment of the political left. That was corroborated by 'a young friend', hired to write leaders for the *News Chronicle* with instructions that his stand was to be 'half way between Maxton and Samuel'. Eager to insinuate himself, Lloyd George invited Sir Walter and Lady Layton to dinner on 10 March 1934. Afterwards, they had 'a long talk on the

---

[1] Pearson's 'reminder of a conversation with Sir Walter Layton and Lady Denman, 21 February 1934,' Cowdray Papers; Pearson to Layton, 14 June 1934, Layton Papers.

[2] Brooks's diary, 15 November 1945; Halévy, *History of the English People in the Nineteenth Century*, Epilogue, I (New York, 1961), 108.

political situation' and agreed 'that Liberalism (or rather the Liberal party) had missed the boat and was a complete washout'. Lloyd George gathered that 'Layton & all the management of the *News Chronicle* are inclined to go Labour'. Soliciting an investment from his host, who had profitably disposed of his Inveresk shares, Layton 'outlined a scheme for extending the *News Chronicle-Star* group into a much larger group of papers' by purchasing at least a controlling interest in the provincial Starmer syndicate and by starting 'a Sunday paper on the lines of the *Observer*'. The proposed chain 'would operate on an advanced progressive policy', and Layton 'had evidently broached the subject to Elias', who was offered 'a large share in the management'. Volunteering to 'put money into the scheme', Lloyd George was to be 'kept informed of the progress of Layton's plans'.[1] That nothing came of this initiative deprived it of impact, but not of significance.

Perhaps Elias and his TUC associates felt strong enough to spurn a grandiose alliance, which Lloyd George's participation would have made unattractive to them. On the day that the Laytons dined with Lloyd George, Labour won a spectacular victory at the Liberals' expense in the London County Council elections. 'The Labour sweep of London does not surprise me,' declared Garvin, who persisted in interpreting politics as an outgrowth of journalism. 'The meaning of the *Daily Herald* is not realised by one Conservative in 10,000' he told Lord Astor. 'A few years ago Labour had no big daily – an immense handicap. Now the *Daily Herald* had more readers than the *Daily Mail* and never ceases a relentless propaganda.' By the same logic, the devastation of the Liberals was even more predictable. So it seemed to Margot Asquith. 'How sad it is that we have no really good Liberal newspaper,' she commiserated with A. G. Gardiner, '& *what* a state of chaos & Hate we see all over the world.'[2]

Had the *News Chronicle* ceased to function as a Liberal organ? Not even its voting trustees could agree on an answer. Morrell drew Layton's attention to a paragraph in the *Observer* (6 May) that bracketed the *News Chronicle* and the *Herald* 'together with the Socialist Opposition'. He regarded that impression as 'rather unfortunate but not without justification', for the *News Chronicle* provided a platform for G. D. H. Cole's 'advocacy of the Socialist state' at the same time that it gave short shrift to the proceedings of the National Liberal Federation. Similarly, the paper featured a column by 'Red' Ellen Wilkinson, soon to return to Parliament as Labour MP for Jarrow, 'who has nothing particular to say, and is not even interesting, whilst no room can be found for an article by Spender'. Meeting at Newcastle on 28 April, the Northern Liberal Federation passed a resolution condemning 'the persistent advocacy of an understanding with the Labour Party which has become the policy of the *News*

[1] Stevenson, *Lloyd George* (10 March 1934), p. 260. James Maxton, Labour MP for the Bridgeton division of Glasgow and chairman of the ILP, was too much the symbol of extremism for this remark to have been meant literally.

[2] Garvin to Astor, 10 March 1934, Astor Papers; Lady Oxford and Asquith to Gardiner, 15 March 1934, Gardiner Papers.

Chronicle', an 'illiberal and undemocratic policy' at that. Letters from readers expressed comparable indignation.¹

Laurence Cadbury, whose investment accorded him primacy among the five voting trustees, tried to adjudicate. On 11 May, he visited Bouverie Street and heard from Layton that Morrell had written in forthright terms. 'I am glad you have done so as I agree with you in disliking the Socialist tone of the paper,' confided Cadbury, who explained that Layton was 'so obsessed with the importance of non-industrial matters, in particular international peace, that he has strong opinions which it is difficult to change'. Cadbury undertook to exert a countervailing influence and anticipated 'a reversal of policy' before long. As a start, he proposed to commission Hartley Withers to pen a rejoinder to Cole. Then, as soon as Clive Pearson recovered from a bout of medical mishaps, they could all 'have another discussion together. I am most anxious that he and you should join me in keeping up pressure from the right direction.'²

Like the proverbial bull in the china shop, Pearson returned to London on 20 June, when he railed against the 'general impression that the *News Chronicle* has abandoned Liberalism and is going or has gone Labour'. The following morning, Layton telephoned to relay Cadbury's suggestion that it would be 'highly desirable' for Pearson to 'discuss affairs with the Editor', but that was rejected as a pointless exercise: 'Our demand that the *News Chronicle* shall be run on Liberal lines' was not to be made 'dependent upon a debate between me and the Editor'. To stave off 'a somewhat theoretical conference on principles' and allow time for Pearson's anger to cool, Cadbury proposed an alternative procedure. For 'the next two or three weeks', Pearson was directed to 'blue pencil anything in the paper which you felt was pro-Labour Party and anti-Liberal'; these annotations would then be submitted to Layton and Vallance, whose comments would be delivered ('preferably orally') as 'definite points for discussion' by the assembled trustees. Once more, Pearson refused to be fobbed off with anything so open-ended. What he demanded were explicit 'assurances that the *N.C.* shall undoubtedly support Liberals and not Labour in by-elections and in a general election', not the belated consideration of 'blue pencillings on my part such as suggest a continuance of my grumbles'. As an immediate demonstration of 'good faith on the part of the management', he called for Spender 'to renew his contributions' with 'a far fuller freedom than had been afforded to him' in the recent past. Pearson received no satisfaction on this score, but eventually discerned that either Cadbury or Layton was 'endeavouring to influence the paper towards Liberalism and away from an unqualified support of Labour'. While not 'unappreciative of the effort' they were expending, he did not yet 'consider that a satisfactory result has been achieved. Has it not got to be recognised when there is something funda-

[1] Morrell to Layton, 10 May 1934, and F. K. Watson (secretary, Northern Liberal Federation) to Layton, 8 May 1934, Layton Papers.
[2] Cadbury to Morrell, 12 May 1934 (copy), Cowdray Papers.

mentally wrong that drastic changes are needed and that modifications or adjustments are insufficient?' For this purpose, he asked to be informed of the precise 'nature of the contract with the editor, Mr Vallance', whom he was anxious to displace.[1]

The oil that Cadbury attempted to pour on these troubled waters was ignited by the *Evening Standard*, which stated on 26 July that the *News Chronicle* had finally 'gone Socialist. It has been engaged in breaking the tidings gently to its readers for some time past.' This hyperbolic conclusion was inferred from a report that Major H. L. (later 1st Baron) Nathan, the Liberal MP for Bethnal Green (where his wife had been defeated in the LCC elections), was poised to defect to Labour. Instead of rebuking Nathan, the *News Chronicle* that morning had seemingly sympathized with him by asking: 'Where is the effective focal point of progressive Radicalism to be found?' Layton 'realised at once' that these words, hastily drafted by Vallance, 'might be read to imply advice to Liberals to join Labour', and he issued instructions that 'this impression must be corrected editorially in the next day's paper'. By then, however, the damage was done.

Layton tried to make light of the episode. The item in the *Evening Standard*, which he interpreted as 'a vicious attack on myself' by Beaverbrook, had had the effect of making 'the *N.C.* the subject of general talk in Parliament and in Clubs for two days'. On the principle that all publicity was good publicity, this attention did 'no harm'. In any case, there were mitigating circumstances. Forewarned of Nathan's intention, Layton had 'twice discussed with Cummings what we should say when it happened' and they had decided to express regrets in 'a friendly tone'. Unfortunately and inexplicably, the announcement was delayed until late on the evening of the 25th, when 'the office was completely absorbed in following the news of the Austrian coup d'état'. Vallance, subject to distraction, was left to deal with Nathan on his own.[2]

Aware that 'the Nathan incident has led to a good deal of discussion', Cadbury agreed that a full-scale meeting of the trustees could no longer be postponed. He fixed it for mid-afternoon on 1 August, and made certain that B. H. Binder would be present to represent the United Newspapers minority interest. A chartered accountant, without any strong party loyalties to cloud his commercial judgment, Binder was expected to side with the majority in favour of editorial independence. Although Cadbury did 'not think that the comments of the *Evening Standard* can be entirely dismissed', he understood that Layton would be put into 'an impossible position if the Liberal outlook of the paper is dependent on your seeing every word that is written day by day. We must be able to depend upon the discretion of the editorial staff.' That was what Pearson

---

[1] Pearson to Cadbury, 21 June, 7 and 26 July 1934 (copies), and Cadbury to Pearson, 25 June 1934, Cowdray Papers.
[2] Layton to Cadbury, 27 July 1934 (copy), enclosed in Cadbury to Pearson, 28 July 1934, Cowdray Papers.

feared most. Spender, who primed him with arguments, thought it 'more than ever necessary to discover the nature of Vallance's contract. Who is in control – Layton, Vallance (the editor) or the Trustees? Why should Cummings', whose acerbic portrait of Runciman on 14 April continued to rankle, 'be brought in?'[1]

The trustees' meeting neither restored peace nor provoked a blood-letting. Cadbury and Layton evidently held firm in the face of an attack that was more broadly based than they had anticipated. Sir Thomas Catto, who stood behind United Newspapers as the person to whom 'ultimate control ... might revert', was no less opposed than Pearson to the conduct of the *News Chronicle*. 'We cannot allow Pearson and Catto to form a united front against us,' Layton advised Cadbury. But how were they to be stopped? Lloyd George spoke to Layton 'of taking a hand', but Layton 'made it quite clear that there can be no sort of interference from that quarter either'. In September, Cadbury broached with Morrell the possibility that he might buy out one or both of the minority interests. Pearson, they agreed, had 'become far more politically minded of recent months than he ever was before, while Lady Denman and other members of the family are equally keen'. Morrell's opinion was that the existing arrangements would hold unless the *News Chronicle* went 'too immoderately against Pearson's views'.[2]

The 'united front' that Layton rightly dreaded took shape on the evening of 1 November, when Catto invited Pearson and Morrell to dine at Claridge's. His other guests were Binder and Akerman, United's voting trustees, and Sir Herbert Grotrian, the chairman of that company and a former Conservative MP. According to the minutes taken by Morrell:

> Mr Pearson expressed the view that was shared by everyone present, that the editorial policy of the paper was not only not in accord with the policy laid down at the time of the fusion, but was not in the best interests of the paper. He pointed out that whilst the Daily News controlled the voting Trust, if both the United Newspapers and the Westminster Press were agreed that the policy laid down at the time of fusion was not being carried out, he thought their opinion could not be overlooked.

The ironies were explicit. In his desperate attempt to defend Liberal purity, Pearson was recruiting allies who were avowedly indifferent – or even opposed – to his cause. Catto professed himself 'quite satisfied to leave the management' of his properties 'in the hands of Sir Herbert Grotrian and Mr Akerman', but 'felt that as 50% of the capital in the *News Chronicle* belonged to United Newspapers' he had a right to make his voice heard. Akerman, who paid closer attention to the balance sheets than to the leading articles, registered the

---

[1] Cadbury to Pearson, 28 July 1934, and memorandum by Spender, n.d., enclosed in Spender to Pearson, 31 July 1934, Cowdray Papers.

[2] Layton to Cadbury, 15 August 1934 (copy), and Cadbury to Layton, 21 September 1934, Layton Papers.

complaint that 'the expenses were ... increasing to a very considerable extent'. Binder 'disclaimed belonging to any political party' and therefore was all the more 'emphatic that the paper was making a mistake in losing [its] appeal to the mass of Liberals in this country'. As a Conservative, Grotrian proclaimed that it was 'no concern' to him 'whether or not the opinions expressed in the *News Chronicle*' were consistent with the agreement of 1930, 'but his shareholders were very materially interested in the financial success of the paper', which had been jeopardized by making it 'a feeble imitation of the *Daily Herald*'. Moreover, 'from the advertising point of view, the Socialist readers' attracted to the *News Chronicle* 'were not nearly so valuable as the old body of *Daily News* readers', who were supposedly being alienated.[1]

Although equally vehement in their opposition to the ostensible drift of the *News Chronicle* towards the Labour Party, the two dissident groups were fundamentally incompatible. Pearson's views, had they been translated into editorial policy, would have been likely to inflict greater hardships on circulation. Lloyd George saw as much. In 'a long talk' with Cummings on 2 November, the day after the dinner at Claridge's, he warned that fraternization with Labour 'would be a profound mistake and would ultimately kill the *N.C.* ... On the other hand he pointed out that a still more certain way of killing the paper would be for it to turn Whig.' Vallance, increasingly under fire, remonstrated that he had only 'accepted the editorship' on the firm 'understanding that I should be free to run the paper as an independent radical organ – opposed, naturally, to revolutionary socialism but not tied to any of the groups which once formed the Liberal Party and – a fortiori – hostile to Toryism'. It was not his fault that the Liberal consensus had since further eroded, with the unforeseen result that 'moderate-minded "gradualist" Labour leaders' most nearly approximated 'the spirit of philanthropic radicalism' that George Cadbury had enshrined in his memorandum of 1911. Denying that the paper had lost 'a soul of its own', Vallance castigated 'the elderly Reform Club Whigs', whose 'bitter hostility' threatened to swing the paper 'unmistakably to the Right'.[2]

Layton took the point, but kept it within limits. Sensing that there existed 'a practical policy for Liberals to enter, with a view to capturing the Labour Party intellectually', he put the case for 'a free association of independent political organisations uniting on an agreed and defined objective'. As an economist, he was bound to admit that Free Trade lay beyond the realm of practicality. As an armchair strategist, he ruefully acknowledged that the party had 'been terribly weakened by split after split and by personal quarrels, ... with the result that it has forfeited prestige and confidence'. Nevertheless, Liberalism survived as an idea, 'deep-rooted and persistent'; its doctrines had 'permeated all parties in

[1] Memorandum by Morrell of a dinner on 1 November 1934, Cowdray Papers.
[2] Memorandum by Cummings, 2 November 1934, and Vallance to Henry Cadbury, 27 November 1934 (copy), Layton Papers.

this country and [were] more in the minds of thoughtful people and statesmen all over the world than at any time in history'. What, then, was the justification for Liberals to persevere on their own? The 'tactical problem', as Layton tautologically defined it, was that the creed had 'lost force in becoming diffused'. The *News Chronicle*, with its 'solid core' of Liberal readers, had the mission to clarify and thereby reinvigorate the Liberal inheritance. The way 'to do this effectively' was for the paper to 'keep before the public the points of difference between it and Labour policy', yet 'without in any way obscuring the view that the carrying out of any progressive policy will certainly require the co-operation of the moderate elements in the Labour Party'.[1]

In effect, Layton was stringing a tightrope, impossible for Vallance or any other editor to walk. Even before these subtleties proved unintelligible to the electors, they aroused the fury of Binder, who had eclipsed Pearson as the foremost proprietorial critic of editorial policy. Goaded by Garvin's insinuations in the *Observer* (17 March 1935), he deplored the 'attitude of the *News Chronicle* in exploiting the Peace question and attacking the Government' in a March by-election at Norwood. As no Liberal had entered that contest, the paper did not hesitate to endorse the Labour challenger, a trade unionist who fervently supported the Peace Ballot. The magnitude of the Conservative majority suggested that Liberal voters at Norwood had ignored the *News Chronicle*'s advice. Binder was 'very unhappy about the whole business. You know how I hate to differ from Layton,' he reminded Akerman. Yet, 'if the present policy persists', it would be only a matter of time before the paper lost its patriotic readers to its Tory rivals, while those 'readers who may like ultra "left-wing" politics' would surely take them from the *Herald*. In March, he privately informed Layton 'that silence from me over a period did not mean that I was satisfied with the paper's views'. Finally, on 2 April, he wrote with the consent of Akerman and Catto to demand a meeting of the trustees to consider 'the continued support of Labour politicians'. The previous day's paper, the first he had seen since returning from abroad, was more than he could bear. In its news pages, 'the star turn orators were two members of the Labour Party, including Major Nathan, for whom the newspaper appears to have developed increased affection since he joined the Labour Party'. In the literary section, 'there appeared a propaganda review of a book by a Labour politician'. Binder, who sent copies of his correspondence to Pearson, was ready 'to take legal advice on behalf of the interests I represent'.[2]

Before he and his allies were able to force a showdown, the general election intervened. Afterwards, Laurence Cadbury opened negotiations to buy out his disaffected partners, which was the only solution. Interestingly enough, amid all these acrimonies, there were conspicuously few references to the *Star*, which

---

[1] 'Notes on Policy' by Layton [December 1934], Cowdray Papers.
[2] Binder to Akerman, 20 March 1935 (copy), enclosed in Binder to Pearson, 2 April 1935, and Binder to Layton, 2 April 1935 (copy), Cowdray Papers.

had ceased to count as either a financial or political asset. Writing in 1934, a German commentator characterized it as an evening journal of 'modest claims', addressed to 'the harmless, pious, and humanitarian section of the lower middle classes, who have no taste for strong meat in matters of politics, culture, or sex'. This judgment was hardly too severe. In July 1935, Cummings was 'threatened with an urgent invitation to take hold of the falling *Star* for twelve months' with the purpose of injecting 'some stiff doses of nerve-tonic into its miserable body. But I am not much interested in the task of resuscitating this rather repulsive corpse-like object,' he told Beaverbrook, once a customer for the property. Before long, Lord Strabolgi (formerly, as J. M. Kenworthy, consecutively Liberal and Labour MP for Hull Central) ventured a tentative bid on behalf of 'people who would like the *Star* to become a Right Wing Labour paper'. Grateful for the assistance that the *Star* had recently given them at the polls, Strabolgi and his friends wanted 'to see the paper more definitely identified with the Party'.[1]

It was just as well that Cadbury and Layton rejected these overtures, which might have relieved them of an encumbrance, but which would have certainly confirmed the worst suspicions of Binder and Pearson. The *Star* remained affixed to the *News Chronicle*, and eventually came to share in its revival, which passed by the Liberal Party. What was notable at this juncture, when Liberal fortunes were at a nadir, was that Labour activists were better equipped in all essentials to mine the vestigial resources of the political press. Doubtless this was largely because they were vastly more confident of their own future. The *News Chronicle* and the *Star*, dependent upon non-Liberal minority shareholders to help stiffen their Liberal backbones, had necessarily abandoned the nineteenth-century presumption that effective political journalism had to be connected and subservient to party. In this respect as in others, Labour was the natural heir to the Liberal tradition.

* * *

Contrary to a lingering impression, Conservative Party leaders were scarcely better placed than their Liberal counterparts to regulate, much less command, newspaper support. Although pro-Tory journals were more numerous, few among them had taken warmly to the idea of a National Government, which struck them as incapable of restoring the vigour of the capitalist system, promoting a spirit of patriotism, or tending to the requirements of imperial defence. Certain publicists, including Beaverbrook, admittedly had old scores to settle. Others, drawing inspiration and occasional financial sustenance from refractory backbench elements, regarded Baldwin and his associates as traitors to the cause. Not even *The Times*, which acquired an unfortunate reputation as

---

[1] Karl von Stutterheim, *The Press in England* (London, 1934), p. 116; Cummings to Beaverbrook, 23 July 1935, Beaverbrook Papers, C/104; Layton to Cadbury, 17 December 1935 (copy), Layton Papers.

a quasi-official mouthpiece of the administration, particularly in the area of foreign affairs, was nearly so obedient as legend would have it.

In a broad sense, the whole of the national press could be classified as 'conservative' on the basis of the social values it upheld and aimed to inculcate. In the face of disruptionist movements, there was little to choose between the responses of *The Times*, the *Daily Telegraph*, the *News Chronicle*, the *Morning Post*, or even the *Daily Herald*, which was striving to assert its respectability.[1] Only the Communist *Daily Worker*, which had a limited circulation and a restricted influence, stood opposed to the predominant political culture, questioning the legitimacy of parliamentary institutions and sanctioning a resort to 'mass struggle in the streets' (18 February 1932). Its own party allegiance was far more rigid than that of any of the bourgeois newspapers it denounced.

Rothermere, not surprisingly, was something of a deviant. After the 1931 *débâcle*, Nicolson dined with 'Tom' Mosley, who asked him 'to arrive early as he has something to say. That something,' Mosley revealed, 'is that Rothermere wishes to place the whole of the Harmsworth Press at his disposal.' Taken aback, Mosley was uncharacteristically 'cautious'. But the collapse of the New Party, with *Action* as part of the wreckage, left him desperate for allies. Rothermere, guided by Ward Price, may well have accelerated Mosley's drift towards fascism; at any rate, Rothermere furnished a pretext. At this stage, Mosley was planning to delay his next move until the following autumn, when he expected a further deterioration in economic conditions to play into his hands. He realized, 'however, that the Harmsworths, being restless folk, cannot be kept on ice' and it might therefore be necessary 'to do something violent in the spring', just to propitiate them. 'It is a bore being thus dependent on the prima donnas of the Press,' said Nicolson.[2]

With his own lost causes to champion, Beaverbrook was not about to accompany Rothermere into Mosley's camp. On 17 July 1933, the *Daily Express* registered an unprecedented sale of 2,054,348 copies, and henceforth adorned its front page with the emblem of the 'Red Crusader'. No Bolshevik, this quixotic figure carried the lance of Empire Free Trade, the symbol of a revolution that sought to capture the Conservative Party and not to destroy it. Like Mosley's movement, the *Express* glorified itself as an 'achievement of

---

[1] John Stevenson has noted a striking similarity in newspaper responses on 1 November 1932, when the National Unemployed Workers Movement marched on Parliament to present their petition. 'Ninety per cent of the Marchers may well be dupes, pawns in a Communist game directed by the master-intriguers of Moscow,' calculated the *Daily Telegraph*. *The Times* urged the demonstrators to stop being 'the dupes of political propagandists who believe in violence as the proper instrument of policy'. The *Manchester Guardian* accused the Communists of 'exploiting the unemployed' ('The Politics of Violence,' in Peele and Cook, eds., *Politics of Reappraisal*, pp. 154–55). 'Against violence, against disorder as a reply to oppression' (30 September 1932), the *Daily Herald* averred that 'trade unionism ... has no use for violence and mob-rule' (2 February 1933).

[2] Nicolson, *Diaries* (11 December 1931 and 18 January 1932), I, 97–98, 107.

youth'. Christiansen, a twenty-nine-year-old 'eaglet' who epitomized this quality, recalled its boast: 'In Europe, the youth are giving the Fascist salute and hailing one Caesar or another. In Britain they are producing the *Express* and hailing themselves.'[1] That was obviously an exaggeration, but it implied an equal detestation of the 'tired old men' who held power at Westminster.

Although personal relations between Beaverbrook and Rothermere remained close, continued political collaboration was impossible. 'Hurrah for the Blackshirts!' cheered the *Daily Mail* on 8 January 1934, and a week later it celebrated Mosley's British Union of Fascists as 'a well-organised party of the Right ready to take over responsibility for national affairs with the same directness of purpose and energy of methods as Hitler and Mussolini have displayed'. Mosley recognized Beaverbrook as an antagonist and began to attack him. Convinced that 'politics thrive on personalities', Beaverbrook did not 'mind how much or how often Mosley dresses me down' in the *Daily Mail* and elsewhere, but Rothermere vowed 'to tell Mosley that if he attacks you I shall drop his Blackshirts. You are my greatest friend and this is the least I can do.'[2]

Apparently, that was also the most that Rothermere could do – or tried to do – to impose discipline. Arthur Cranfield, the assistant editor of the *Mail*, met Barrington-Ward at a dinner party on 16 May 1934 and was 'v. frank about Rothermere and how his whims and telephone calls' set the policies for the paper. That morning, for example, the *Mail* had contained a pair of leading articles: 'Keep Out of It,' advising the British to 'mind our own business' over the plebiscite in the Saar; and 'Fed Up,' a castigation of 'the apathetic sexagenarians of Downing Street' who lacked Mosleyite dynamism. According to Cranfield, Rothermere's habit was to ring the office at odd hours and specify 'to the inch the space to be given to Mosley and his absurd blackshirts, now under R's protection. And this is journalism and public opinion!' exclaimed Barrington-Ward, who considered it 'a misfortune that newspapers cannot be forbidden insurance and other props and promoters of an artificial circulation', for then 'proprietors would . . . have to fight to win the genuine thing and would have to study opinion. Newspapers would be cheaper to launch and journalism would be free again', or so he imagined.[3]

Vigour and experimentalism were not the exclusive attributes of the young, however. On 31 May, Cummings found Lloyd George 'simply bursting with vitality' and eager to exchange views. This septuagenarian, who had not resided in Downing Street for a dozen years, was 'a little puzzled' that Beaverbrook was 'not in with Lord Rothermere proclaiming the Fascist gospel'. Describing the interview to Beaverbrook, Cummings claimed to have 'replied that I had not

---

[1] Christiansen, *Headlines*, pp. 92–93.
[2] Beaverbrook to Rothermere, 7 and 9 May 1934, and Rothermere to Beaverbrook, 7 May 1934, quoted in Taylor, *Beaverbrook*, p. 330.
[3] Barrington-Ward's diary, 16 May 1934.

worried myself to go beyond the simple explanation of your superior political sagacity'. To Beaverbrook's embarrassment, Blumenfeld had enlisted as a charter member of the January Club, a 'front organisation' for the BUF that was founded 'to provide a platform for leaders of Fascist and Corporate State thought'. Blumenfeld was then 'Chairman of the *Daily Express* but takes no part in the editorial direction', Beaverbrook hastened to point out. 'Blumenfeld is of course a Jew', and it was 'strange indeed to see a Jew', even one so comfortably assimilated, 'in this company'. In any case, Beaverbrook insisted, 'the *Express* is strongly against Fascism'.[1]

Thereafter, the gulf between Beaverbrook and Rothermere widened. On 7 June 1934, Mosley held a monster meeting at Olympia, from which his stewards ejected hecklers (allegedly all Communists and Jews) with nauseating savagery. 'The Fascist technique is really the most brutal thing I have ever seen, which is saying something,' reported Brooks, repelled by the spectacle he had come to applaud. Rothermere, too, was said to have recoiled from the Fascists, whom he had previously romanticized as a militant branch of the Young Conservatives and whose revolutionary tendencies were now unmistakable. Yet his break with Mosley was not as clean as an exchange of public letters between them was meant to suggest. Brooks noted that 'Rothermere (who is quite certainly a maniac of a mild brand) filled the *Sunday Dispatch*' the following weekend 'with justifications for the Fascists – justifications which missed the whole point', namely 'that to answer Communist brutality by Fascist brutality in the middle of an orderly audience of peaceful citizens is to undermine the whole theory of the modern State'. By contrast, the *News Chronicle* and the *Daily Telegraph* were both 'exceedingly good in their descriptives' of an event that had 'probably done more to rally opinion to the National Government than anything since 1931'. A fortnight later, Brooks was 'still in a rather depressed mood'. He had been weighing an offer to write for the *Sunday Dispatch*, but its style of journalism was 'farcical – a purposeless buffooning.... The utter irresponsibility and ignorance of the paper's treatment of every topic,' he observed in August, 'is amusing but rather terrifying. And Rothermere telephoning leader instructions from North Scotland like a half-wit who has not comprehended the first thing about international commitments is equally terrifying but not so amusing.'[2]

Brooks took the job anyway, and

> found R more likeable and sane than ever I had anticipated. But the fact remains that with a dictator of this kind, on whose whim thousands of men depend for their livelihoods, a great business is conducted like a Byzantium

[1] Cummings to Beaverbrook, 1 June 1934, and Beaverbrook to Cummings, 3 June 1934 (copy), Beaverbrook Papers, C/104; *also see* Richard Griffiths, *Fellow Travellers of the Right* (London, 1980), pp. 50–51.

[2] Skidelsky, *Mosley*, pp. 322–23; Brooks's diary, 11 and 24 June, and 26 August 1934 (containing a copy of Brooks to Norman Watson, 10 June 1934).

Court and not an enterprise ... for the honest dissemination of news and views.

One of his first assignments was to ensure the paper's fulsome support for Randolph Churchill, who braved paternal displeasure to fight as a diehard insurgent in a February by-election in the Wavertree division of Liverpool. 'You're having a leader on Randolph again,' Rothermere informed William Brittain, the editor, who was given no choice. 'I've told Brooks to write it. He's to say Randolph Churchill has plenty of guts – understand that? – guts.' Brooks, a Liverpudlian by wartime adoption, was assigned to speak on behalf of Churchill, whose pre-emptive candidacy split the Conservative vote and handed the seat to Labour. The next by-election was at Norwood, and Rothermere proposed that Brooks himself should stand. 'Do it, my dear fellow, do it,' he implored, promising to contribute £250 towards Brooks's expenses. Additional funding was to be obtained from Lady Houston, the rabidly right-wing owner of the weekly *Saturday Review*, who adulated Mosley and was consumed by the belief that Ramsay MacDonald was a Soviet stooge. 'Lucy' Houston was annoyed with Rothermere for 'not keeping his word': he had 'promised to give co-operation to her patriotic efforts', but drew the line at allowing her to 'attack Ramsay in his papers, and that is all she cares for'. Brooks, having done his 'best to smooth her down', was rewarded with a pledge of backing 'to the tune of £1,000'. Chastened by the result at Wavertree, Rothermere decided not to proceed. 'We'll have to stand down,' he notified Brooks, whose challenge had been tipped in the *Evening News*; 'if we split the vote at Norwood the Socialist will get in and that will precipitate a crisis.' In the ensuing general election, Lady Houston tried to persuade Brooks to 'fight Sam Hoare in Chelsea, promising all the finance I might need', but he excused himself on the grounds that 'the moment was not yet, and that I was tied to the papers'.[1]

David (later 1st Viscount) Margesson, the Conservative chief whip, arranged a meeting with Brooks to discuss 'how to reconcile R to official Conservatism'. Brooks 'said from the first that I was very fond of R and would not in any way betray his confidence, but if I could help to re-cement the Party, I would like that'. Margesson, however, was at a loss for suggestions. 'What can we do?' he asked Brooks, to whom he confessed his own discomfort with the 'heart-rending' situation that 'the safe Conservative seats' were often 'held by these hopeless duds'. The problem was partly financial. 'I tell you, Brooks, that your City men will give us money for the National Government but they won't give a penny for the Tory Party alone.' Beyond that, it was one of personalities. 'We know Ramsay is a liability', but Baldwin had 'had to accept the Ramsay leadership because of Buckingham

---

[1] Brooks's diary, 10, 23, and 25 January, 3, 13, and 15 February 1935.

Palace' in 1931, 'and that same influence is potent in keeping Ramsay in office still'.[1]

MacDonald could not be propped up much longer, and Baldwin's ascent to the premiership – either in advance of a general election or in its immediate aftermath – was a foregone conclusion. This prospect made Beaverbrook (who had 'learnt one thing from father, and that was to hate! to hate!') all the more determined to bring the government down. 'You don't hate MacDonald?' Lloyd George asked him. 'No!' thundered Beaverbrook, 'with a diabolical look on his face'. The object of his hatred was '*Baldwin!*' Rothermere, whom Frances Stevenson credited with 'different motives', was less inclined 'to destroy the Gov. wholly' and prepared to settle for a major reshuffle. Winston Churchill, advocating 'a thorough reconstruction' so as to create an opening for himself, disapproved of Rothermere's tactics no less than of Rothermere's blatant pro-Germanism. 'Rothermere rings me up every day,' he told his wife on 13 April.

> His anxiety is pitiful. He thinks the Germans are all powerful and that the French are corrupt and useless, and the British hopeless and doomed. He proposes to meet this situation by grovelling to Germany. 'Dear Germany, do destroy us last!' I endeavour to inculcate a more robust spirit.

In this respect, Churchill was less of a tonic than the champagne that Rothermere drank – and poured for Brooks – to prevent them from 'being depressed by what we know'.[2]

Lloyd George, with whom Beaverbrook and Rothermere were back in contact, posed a threat to Baldwin in his own right. On 15 December 1934, he announced in a joint communiqué to the *News Chronicle* and the *Daily Herald* that he was preparing a New Deal for which he hoped to obtain non-party support. His plans were unveiled in a speech to his constituents at Bangor on 17 January 1935, his seventy-second birthday, and called for the drastic remodelling of the Cabinet along the lines of his own wartime administration. Discounting Lloyd George's statement that he was not intending 'to launch a party campaign', but not dismissive of his ideas for tackling unemployment, the next morning's *Times* logically deduced that he was trying for a comeback. Dawson had anticipated the bombshell with a leading article on the 11th that seemed to pave the way for an accommodation between Lloyd George and Baldwin, perhaps even for Lloyd George's return to office in a reconstituted National Government. 'The political situation is baffling,' admitted Sir Edward Grigg, who sent 'many congratulations' to Dawson. With a foot in each camp, Grigg was 'sure that S.B. wants to reconstruct and to prevent Ll.G. from developing

---

[1] Brooks's diary, 6 March 1935.
[2] Stevenson, *Lloyd George* (10 January 1935), pp. 296–97; Brooks's diary, 9 March and 28 May 1935; Churchill to his wife, 13 April 1935, quoted in Gilbert, *Churchill*, V, 636.

and exploiting a triangular situation. But this must mean coming to some understanding with Ll.G. on the lines of policy set out in your leader', which had acknowledged Neville Chamberlain to be the major stumbling-block. 'Rothermere (who, whatever his other failings, is not a bad authority on electoral prospects) has apparently made up his mind that the Government as it stands is faced with certain disaster,' Grigg added, 'and he has been urging Ll.G. to stand forth as the saviour of society.' In fact, although Lloyd George counted Rothermere as being 'with him over his new plan', he set greater store by other sources.[1]

Garvin, resolved 'to keep my heart as well as my head', limited coverage in that Sunday's *Observer* to 'only an introductory note or two. All impulses shall be filtered and set to cool,' he promised Grigg, with whom he shared the hope that Lloyd George would 'come into the National Government – dropping the feud with the PM like all other personal feuds'. Affirming that he had always 'hated "Party"', he was waiting for the Jubilee celebrations to pass before the *Observer* would 'strongly advocate reconstruction *with* Lloyd George – unless he himself queers our pitch in the interval. I devoutly hope not.' The 'supreme thing', Garvin maintained, was for Baldwin 'to avoid Ll.G. in opposition at the General Election', which could not be long deferred.[2]

It impressed Grigg as 'rather remarkable that the whole of the English Press, with the exception of the *Daily Herald*', greeted Lloyd George's initiative with at least qualified approval. His purview, needless to say, was limited to the mainstream and excluded the *Daily Worker* on one extreme and the *Morning Post* on the other. Both the *Manchester Guardian* and the *News Chronicle*, which were suspected of harbouring pro-Labour tendencies, evidently preferred the Lloyd George package 'to the possibility of a Socialist victory at the next election'. The *Herald*, while steadfastly loyal to Labour, was taken with the proposal to nationalize the Bank of England, which was the only item that Lord Snowden declined to endorse. Lloyd George was invited to submit his blueprints for consideration by a Cabinet committee, where there was no doubt that Chamberlain would resist them. These deliberations continued through the spring and culminated on 4 June, when Lloyd George testified for the ninth time and came away with the feeling that his interrogators 'knew in their hearts they were going to knife me'. Neither surprised nor perturbed, he assured Miss Stevenson 'that I too had a dagger in my sheath', which was the Council of Action he was forming 'to rouse public opinion on issues of peace and unemployment'.[3]

By then, he had lined up considerable support within the Nonconformist

[1] Grigg to Dawson, 11 January 1935 (copy?), Grigg Papers; Stevenson, *Lloyd George* (10 January 1935), p. 296.

[2] Garvin to Grigg, 17 and 30 January, and 18 February 1935, Grigg Papers; Garvin to Astor, n.d., enclosed in Lady Astor to Jones, 2 May 1935, Jones Papers.

[3] Grigg to Dawson, 19 January 1935 (copy?), Grigg Papers; Stevenson, *Lloyd George* (1 July 1935), p. 310.

communities, organized through the National Council of Evangelical Free Churches. Their pulpits and presses (including the *Baptist Times*, the *Methodist Times*, and the interdenominational *British Weekly*) were largely at his disposal.[1] Angus Watson, a Tyneside businessman who owned a controlling interest in the *Spectator*, was among his affiliates. The adherence of Layton, one of the thirty-two signatories of the 'Call to Action', guaranteed Lloyd George prominent attention in the *News Chronicle* and the *Star*. The *Manchester Guardian* was predictably sympathetic, while *The Times* jeered that it was just as well that Lloyd George was not asked to take office, as that would have obliged him to 'forego the delicious dream of leading a Nonconformist rally for Peace and Public Expenditure' (8 June).

Beaverbrook was persuaded neither by Cummings's testimonials to Lloyd George's 'wise & sagacious statesmanship', nor by the personal messages that Cummings was entrusted to deliver. 'He wants to meet you and loves you,' Cummings reported to Lloyd George after dining (with Garvin and others) at Beaverbrook's house. '*But he is cold about the New Deal.*' Rothermere was more susceptible to flattery. Brooks was engaged in a conversation with him one morning when 'his secretary flung open the door and ushered in Lloyd George'. From the adjoining room, where Brooks waited, he heard them talk 'in loud voices for about forty-five minutes. It was, I guessed, Lloyd George's hope to get support for his New Deal and Rothermere's insistence to get Lloyd George's support for a strong air force.' Rothermere never tired of describing how Lloyd George had come, hat in hand, to his house in Stratton Street. Yet the effect upon his newspapers was imperceptible.[2]

That Lloyd George should have taken the trouble to make such appeals was unfathomable. His dual campaign was anathema to both press lords. The National League of Airmen, whose alarmist propaganda was generously endowed by Rothermere and Lady Houston, was an affront to the internationalism of Lloyd George's backers. At Rothermere's dictation, Brooks attacked the League of Nations in the *Sunday Dispatch* (8 September) as an instrument for making 'our sons into the hired mercenaries of some unworthy race'. Beaverbrook had only contempt for the Peace Ballot, which he called the 'Blood Ballot'. In his opinion, the spread of pacifism was primarily due to Cummings at the *News Chronicle* 'and Mr Elias, who lunches at the Savoy Grill'. Of the two, Beaverbrook regarded Cummings as the more culpable because he was undoubtedly sincere. Elias, judging from his mid-day gourmandism, 'probably agrees with me'. On 18 October, Beaverbrook retaliated

---

[1] Koss, 'Lloyd George and Nonconformity: the Last Rally,' *English Historical Review*, lxxxix (1974), 77–108.

[2] Stevenson, *Lloyd George* (19 March 1935), p. 304; Brooks's diary, 23 January 1935. Lajos Lederer has recalled to the author an earlier occasion, probably in 1929, when Lloyd George arrived at Rothermere's suite at the Savoy to protest against an item in the *Daily Mail*'s 'London Diary'. Instead of firing the offending journalist, Rothermere raised his salary out of gratitude for the attention he had elicited.

in the *Daily Express* by releasing the results of a poll conducted among 80,000 'professional men', who indicated varying degrees of readiness to become involved in the festering Abyssinian crisis. To the question 'Am I my brother's keeper?' Beaverbrook ventured an equivocal reply. 'Well, of course. We have a responsibility.' But God had given the British people 'a special duty, a particular task', which was to attend to 'the countless races of the British Empire'. That put intervention, even in the mild form of economic sanctions, out of the question. During the election campaign, he privately proclaimed himself 'against the policy of "collective security" and the League of Nations. I am entirely in favour of Isolation. . . . I want Empire Free Trade, and cannot get it.' His instincts and, more egregiously, Rothermere's ran counter to Lloyd George's leftward tack.[1]

In late May, Baldwin traded places with MacDonald. As Prime Minister, he shuffled the cards in his ministerial pack, but did not include either Churchill or Lloyd George in the deal. 'Baldwin will get away with anything,' fumed Beaverbrook. 'I fear the British public likes hypocrisy.' Garvin likewise regretted the opportunities that were missed. 'Baldwin & I have not been intimate since the big row about Unionist leadership in 1922!' he recalled. 'But we have remained civil and he knows how often I have given him generous interpretation in complete disregard of small personal things.' Unlike Beaverbrook, Garvin had expected better of the new Premier. Knowing precisely what to expect, Dawson thought that the transfer of power was 'a very smooth and swift affair'. *The Times*'s leading article on 'Change-Over Day', 7 June, concluded with an encomium to 'Mr Baldwin's temperament and character, . . . which perhaps only Mr MacDonald can yet appreciate fully'.[2]

The election could come at any time and, if Cummings could 'have my say in it, the *NC* will fight . . . tooth & nail. The Tories will of course win comfortably,' he conceded in advance. 'But if they expect a comfortable time afterwards & another long term of office they will get some shocks.' It was not clear whom he expected to administer them, but surely he could not have had in mind the Liberals, who did not pretend to offer an alternative. With only 161 contenders in the field, Samuel reluctantly agreed to advise 'Liberal voters, in constituencies where there is no Liberal candidate, to vote for whichever candidate supported the policy of the Peace and Reconstruction movement', regardless of party label.[3]

If only in the short run, the *News Chronicle*'s editorial predicament was eased by Lloyd George, who provided a platform on which all Liberals (save for the

---

[1] Beaverbrook to Cummings, 1 October 1935 (copy), Beaverbrook Papers, C/104; Beaverbrook to S. Samuel, 2 November 1935, quoted in Taylor, *Beaverbrook*, p. 357.

[2] Beaverbrook to Brisbane, 27 May 1935 (copy), Beaverbrook Papers, C/64; Garvin to Grigg, 28 May 1935, Grigg Papers; Dawson's diary, 7 June 1935, quoted in Wrench, *Dawson*, p. 324.

[3] Cummings to Beaverbrook, 18 October 1935, Beaverbrook Papers, C/104; Stevenson, *Lloyd George* (23 October 1935), p. 319; *News Chronicle*, 26 October 1935.

irredeemable Simonites), many Labour spokesmen, and a sprinkling of dissident Tories could unite. 'Peace and Reconstruction Campaign Opens,' the paper announced in a banner headline on 21 October. That morning, a leading article showered praise upon this 'wise and far-sighted attempt to lay the foundations of better days in the field of international politics'; next day, the leader-writers turned to the concomitant 'national reconstruction proposals', which they esteemed as 'constructive and realistic'.

On the 25th, Parliament was dissolved, and Baldwin went to the country with a demand for 'all sanctions short of war' to halt Italian aggression in Abyssinia. That cry was shrewdly worded to take the wind from his opponents' sails, which thereafter never billowed. 'The Socialists want to fight Italy because they hate Fascism,' Beaverbrook observed, but Lansbury, the pious pacifist who led them, 'wants to pray' instead.[1] Lansbury chose this inconvenient moment to depart, and Major Clement Attlee assumed the leadership at short notice. Herbert Morrison, whom the *News Chronicle* (31 October) discerned to be a more powerful figure, wrote a series of twenty-one articles in the *Daily Herald*, where he comprehensively outlined 'What Every Voter Should Know'. If the Labour Party 'entered the fight with the necessary confidence and aggression', he reasoned, it remained 'quite possible for them to win a Parliamentary Majority'.[2] Under the circumstances, it was a major achievement for Labour to increase its representation to 154 seats, three times its total in 1931, but little better than a third of the massive Conservative majority. On 15 November, the day after polling, the *Herald* paid tribute to Attlee, 'whose leadership has earned him the warm gratitude of every section of the Labour movement'. Its own affection was understandably lavished upon Lansbury, its founding father, who was 'not only the most loved figure in the Labour movement, but perhaps in the whole of politics'.

A mere twenty-one Liberals were elected. They included the four members of the Lloyd George clan, but not Samuel, who lost his seat at Darwen to a Conservative challenger. Layton's election-night party in Bouverie Street turned into a wake, where the mournful silence was interrupted by Vallance's vindictive applause at the announcement of each Liberal lost deposit. The news of Samuel's defeat gave him special delight. Vallance was soon discharged from the editorship and fittingly joined the *New Statesman*.[3]

When the new Parliament assembled, Baldwin was firmly in control. But his mastery did not extend to the field of diplomacy, where a bungled response to the Abyssinian crisis promptly incurred criticisms. *The Times*, having stood by Baldwin during the election, was among the newspapers that turned furiously against him in this instance. As interpreters of 'public opinion', a concept that

---

[1] Beaverbrook to Paul Block, 1 October 1935, quoted in Taylor, *Beaverbrook*, p. 356.
[2] That, at any rate, was the inference that the *Morning Post* (21 October) presented to its readers as verbatim.
[3] Private information from interviews.

The Times legitimated by adoption on 16 December, editorial voices were fated to contradict one another as well as statesmen. The mounting preoccupation with foreign affairs made the press a battleground, strewn with controversies that continue to echo.

Fifteen

GENTLEMAN'S AGREEMENTS

It was one thing for the press to assert its political independence, which no one could seriously dispute, but quite another for it to act responsibly upon its claims. In the years that preceded the Second World War, newspapermen were usually left to their own devices, which were to prove more discreditable than any previously imposed upon them by party managers.

> You cannot hope to bribe or twist
> Thank God! the British journalist,

Humbert Wolfe cynically attested.

> But, seeing what the man will do
> Unbribed, there's no occasion to.[1]

The deformities of pre-war journalism, especially evident in the area of foreign affairs, invited subsequent accusations of collusion and censorship. Although magnified and possibly distorted in retrospect, these failings were real enough at the time.

As always, editors knew far more than they saw fit to communicate, perhaps even more than they themselves wished to know. Their circumspection, increasingly in defiance rather than in ignorance of the facts, was a misguided response to the growing threat of war and the dread of national defeat. Resolved to avoid – or, at least, not to hasten – the inevitable, they took it upon themselves to calm prevailing fears. In this way, they variously qualified as appeasers or the *de facto* accomplices of the statesmen who practised appeasement. Needless to say, there existed profound differences in their motives, incentives, and degrees of inadvertence. These discrepancies, no longer dictated by party allegiance to any significant extent, cannot be ignored. Yet neither can they be counted as more than extenuating circumstances. For by cumulative effect, if rarely by design, the press projected popular miscon-

---

[1] Wolfe, 'Over the Fire,' in *The Uncelestial City* (New York, 1930), pp. 30–31. In his testimony to the Royal Commission on the Press (Minutes of Evidence, Cd. 7318, q. 580), Hannen Swaffer quoted Wolfe's 'comment' and added: 'I do not agree with that, mind you.'

ceptions and thereby shared complicity. The events leading to the abdication of Edward VIII, which it treated with a complaisant silence, were but one of many evasions of responsibility in the late 1930s.

Culpability is extremely difficult to assign, given that contemporary ideologies were complex and never static. It would be erroneous to suppose that advocates of disarmament were necessarily sympathetic to – or unafraid of – Hitler's Germany, much less that proponents of rearmament were uniformly opposed to totalitarianism. Within both of these divided camps, there were some who were appalled by the 'excesses' of the fascist régimes, some who condoned them, and a great many who contrived to look the other way. There were right-wing enthusiasts for aerial defence who insisted upon Hitler's friendly intentions while others warned of impending German aggression, socialists who distrusted Soviet policy only slightly less than the sinister designs that they attributed to Baldwin and Chamberlain, pacifists who were prepared to contemplate military intervention under the auspices of the League of Nations, champions of the League who preached peace at any price, xenophobes who sought to revivify the Anglo-French alliance, detractors and defenders of Hitler who were equally responsive to his territorial grievances, and isolationists who trusted that problems would solve themselves. Ardent imperialists were to be found in every group. So, for that matter, were anti-Semites, churchmen and agnostics, trade unionists, aristocrats, and financiers. Opinion was much too kaleidoscopic to permit broad classifications.

Moreover, opinion was inherently volatile. Newspapermen had helped to make it so by their self-serving attempts to obtain personal recognition, political leverage, and especially commercial advantage. The Frankensteins now cowered before the monster they had created. Gripped by a pervasive apprehension of another world conflict, they did not know how much they could safely say without fulfilling their own dire prophecies. In certain cases, their inhibitions amounted to moral paralysis. They did not require either prompting from Whitehall or hints from Berlin, both in plentiful supply, to remind them that the press was uniquely equipped to exacerbate tensions, which statesmen on both sides were ostensibly striving to allay. Rightly or wrongly, inflammatory journalism was considered to have been one of the principal causes of the previous war. That harrowing experience cast as long a shadow in Fleet Street as in Downing Street, and no one wanted to repeat it.

The publication of unpleasant truths threatened other unfortunate consequences that few were willing to face. Circulations and advertising revenues would presumably suffer on the grounds that mass readerships would inevitably recoil from prognostications of gloom and destruction. Editors debated this point with foreign correspondents, who angrily protested when their dispatches were being watered down or suppressed, but who were regarded as tiresome and, frankly, often were. Proprietors and business managers had the last word and agreed that the public (whether it knew it or not) wanted nothing so much as distraction from harsh realities. Some journals were better suited than others to satisfy this apparent demand, but all of them made at least some effort to minimize the potential dangers. Consequently, the bright spots were made to glow and the areas of darkness were left unilluminated as they spread.

Newspapers, enjoying a 'golden age' that time was to tarnish, had collectively emerged from the Depression with 'a natural desire to foster' a general 'recovery by creating a good psychological atmosphere'. For this purpose, they tended to emphasize contentment at home and security abroad. 'Both financially and intellectually it was unwise or impossible for the British Press to adopt a strongly critical line towards Nazi Germany,' one historian has argued; 'the readers did not want to read it, and the intellectuals did not want to write it.'[1] Although not devoid of an essential validity, this explanation goes too far in trying to shift the blame and raises more questions than it answers. Were financial and intellectual factors weighted evenly, as implied? How can we judge the actual preferences of the reading public, which was permitted no real choice in the matter? Since when had newspapers depended upon the compliance of intellectuals, many of whom were denied opportunities to promulgate contrary views?

It is easier, of course, to diffuse responsibility than to fasten it, and patriotism is frequently a disguise for opportunism. In the last analysis, responsibility must reside with the select individuals who decided what was printed and what was not. Geoffrey Dawson's disinclination to antagonize German sensibilities has been noted, and awaits both explication and judgment. Despite the ignominy he has suffered as a key member of the so-called Cliveden Set, depicted by Low in the *Evening Standard* (3 January 1938) as performing 'the Shiver Sisters Ballet' under the direction of Goebbels, he was representative of a far wider phenomenon. If *The Times* under his editorship deliberately – and, as it proved, foolishly – minced words, it was merely doing what each of its rivals did to a greater or lesser extent. Its instincts were no worse and ironically may have been more honourable. In any case, *The Times* can be condemned no more for trading on its inflated reputation than for following standard editorial procedures.

Self-conscious of the embarrassments it might cause and increasingly wary of the anxieties it might foster, the press habitually committed sins of omission in its coverage of international affairs. In previous generations, its propensity to dispense advice to foreign powers had given grievous offence to Napoleon III, Abraham Lincoln, and Bismarck, among others. Mowbray Morris, manager of *The Times* during its Victorian heyday, had defended the practice:

> Many people say that we trouble ourselves too much about our neighbours on the continent; that their Governments are good enough for the mass of

[1] F. R. Gannon, *The British Press and Germany 1936–1939* (Oxford, 1971), p. 2.

the people, and that the only effect of our misplaced sympathy is to keep alive the flame of discontent and give undue importance to the discontented. *The Times* is particularly obnoxious to these people, and its conductors are advised to mind their own business,

he wrote to a friend in 1857. Undeterred by such arguments, Morris protested that

> we *do* mind our own business when we expose the evil systems of the continent. No doubt it would be easier to make things pleasant by false representations or by total silence; but if all men were to pursue this course, what would become of the world's progress?[1]

Over the decades, his successors lost this Palmerstonian presumption, which must have seemed terribly quaint in 1938, the year of Munich, when Morris's letter was published in the second volume of *The History of The Times*. By then, British values were not regarded as suitable commodities for export.

'"When in doubt leave out" is a golden rule prompted by an inward monitor,' Garvin told Grigg, whose article for the *Observer*'s coronation supplement required emendation. Suspicious of 'alarmist information ... that ... might be fatal to peace' (20 May 1938), that paper ignored the chilling report that Oliver Woods, Garvin's stepson, drafted after a visit to Dachau in September 1934. Beaverbrook, attentive to his own 'inward monitor', emblazoned the *Daily Express* with the assurance that 'There Will Be No War', a slogan that Christiansen took 'to suit the spirit of the time and the spirit of the people'. Did Beaverbrook and the dozen European correspondents whom he allegedly canvassed actually share this delusion? On 4 April 1935, Collin Brooks went to tea with him at Stornaway House, where they 'talked much of R[othermere]'s belief in an imminent war, and Beaverbrook was insistent that it be kept out of the papers'. Brooks agreed from the standpoint 'of selling ink and paper at a profit', but could not help feeling that Rothermere was right. 'Does it matter, Brooks?' asked Beaverbrook, who 'grinned impishly' at his guest's misgivings. 'A paper can't afford to prophesy disaster, can it?'[2]

The question, as Beaverbrook put it with typical bluntness, was therefore more one of commerce than one of conscience. Percy Cudlipp, whose job as night editor of the *Daily Herald* invested him with responsibility 'for the selection of front page news', later recalled the difficulties he and Francis Williams had had with Elias, the chairman of the financial directors. As the head of Odhams Press, which held 51 per cent of the shares, Elias 'very often thought that the choice of news ... showed a predisposition ... to choose depressing ... front-page stories'. It was not that he doubted the accuracy of

[1] Morris to Dr D. Lardner [1857], quoted in *History of The Times*, II, 281.
[2] Garvin to Grigg, 12 April 1937, Grigg Papers; memorandum by Woods, September 1934, Woods Papers; Christiansen, *Headlines*, p.145; Brooks's diary, 4 April 1935.

these accounts, but rather that he was 'alarmed' by their implications. Elias 'by temperament looked forward with great dread, as most of us did but he perhaps more than many, to war'. There was one occasion, Cudlipp vaguely remembered, when Elias had protested to the effect that 'the only idea our editorial people have is to depress and horrify our readers'. Cudlipp, who succeeded Williams as editor in 1940, 'did not regard that as pressure' and blithely remarked to his assistant that Elias was 'going to have a very gloomy paper again to-morrow'. Events permitted no alternative. Williams, whose resignation 'was the culmination of a clash' with the directors, offered a contrary recollection: 'There were numerous occasions on which the commercial proprietors of the paper felt sure that' the editorial tendency

> to emphasize increasingly the serious nature of international developments ... was likely to drive away some public support for the newspaper, and some advertising support and there were a number of occasions when leading articles, which had been written either by myself as editor or by the leader writer under my direction, were subsequently and without consultation ... sub-edited to the extent of a fair number of passages being cut out ... by the then chairman of the commercial board of directors (whose attention the editorial director had drawn to them) on the grounds that the expression of policy was too vigorous.

Because 'the system of control on the *Daily Herald*' was so unusually elaborate, proprietorial injunctions could be circumvented and sometimes even defied, with the result that the *Herald* was eventually 'rather more violent in its criticism of Chamberlain' – whom Elias insisted upon calling 'Mr Chamberlain' – 'than many newspapers'. Nevertheless, the overriding perception of what Kingsley Martin condescendingly described as 'first-rate selling-matter ... for the masses' was much the same here as elsewhere.[1]

Not even the *News Chronicle*, which prided itself on saying what had to be said, was immune from the epidemic of self-restraint. The paper was unusually resourceful in its pursuit of intelligence. Stanley Baron, a member of its features staff, had a sister who tutored Geoffrey Dawson's children, and she passed along scraps of Cliveden gossip that crept into Cummings's columns. In foreign capitals, the paper relied on a team of distinguished correspondents. Without being disregarded, warnings from these men on the spot were sometimes held back. Oscar Hobson extended (and perhaps exceeded) his authority as City Editor to suppress incriminating evidence that Ian Colvin had collected about the German economy. On the morning in 1938 that Chamberlain flew to Munich, William Forrest wrote an astringent leading article, which was set into type and fitted on the page. It received the editorial approval of Gerald Barry,

---

[1] Evidence, Royal Commission on the Press, 1947–49, Cds. 7318 and 7432, qq. 435–36, 9063–65; Martin, quoted in Cummings, *The Press*, p. 43.

whom Forrest later credited with at least 'the strength of other people's opinions'; but Layton stopped it at seven o'clock that evening, insisting that criticisms were inappropriate 'at such a desperately dangerous moment'. For the same reason, Layton again overruled Barry and declined to break the story of an Anglo-French sell-out that Vernon Bartlett telephoned from Munich. 'If that's the news,' Layton told Barry, 'it's too yellow to print.'[1]

Neither Garvin and Beaverbrook nor Elias and Layton were apologists for fascism, which all of them abhorred. Not even the Astors, who played host at Cliveden and eagerly promoted the cause of Anglo-German friendship, were oblivious to Nazi brutalities, which they (like countless others) expected to abate under the impact of British goodwill. There was general acceptance of the fact that Germany and Italy (and Hungary, Rothermere would add) had legitimate grievances against the punitive provisions of the Versailles settlement. The *Daily Herald* (25 November 1937) placed itself firmly on the side of the revisionists who favoured 'an agreement based on justice'. Nearly as widespread was a disapproval of French villainy, which W. P. Crozier was pleased to see 'expressed equally in *The Times*, the *News Chronicle*, and the *Manchester Guardian*', under his own editorial command.[2] Beyond that, assorted newspaper owners and editors welcomed the Nazi régime as a bulwark against Bolshevism, which they ranked as a greater tyranny and a more immediate danger to the British Empire. These sentiments came naturally to the *Morning Post* as well as to the *Daily Mail*, where Ward Price, Göring's favourite British correspondent, celebrated Hitler as the saviour of western civilization (21 September 1936). Price was one of the very few who espoused theories of Aryan racialism, which even Rothermere did not include among his personal prejudices.

Rothermere was a case unto himself and, as such, an obstacle to generalizations. 'There is nothing in modern politics – not even in German politics – to match the crude confusion of the Rothermere mentality as revealed in the Rothermere Press,' Cummings wrote in the *News Chronicle* on 31 August 1937. 'It blesses and encourages every swashbuckler who threatens the peace of Europe – not to mention direct British interests – and then clamours for more and more armaments with which to defend Britain, presumably against his lordship's pet foreign bully.' The contradictions were obvious, but Rothermere was too hysterical to notice them. On the one hand, he credited Hitler's protestations of partiality to Britain; on the other, he contended that those protestations would carry weight among German strategists only if the British

---

[1] Interview with Barry, quoted in Gannon, *British Press*, p. 39, as corroborated and supplemented by the author's interviews with Stanley Baron, William Forrest, and Tom Baistow, 20 August 1981. Vernon Bartlett recalled in a letter to the author (16 April 1982) that 'Walter found it difficult to make up his mind, and I remember how, one day in the early 1930s when we were together in Berlin, I timed his decision to telephone to Ribbentrop – a few minutes over an hour before he could pick up the telephone.'

[2] Crozier to Alexander Werth, 19 February 1935, *Guardian* Archives.

government measured up to its responsibilities. In other words, Britain had to earn German friendship by asserting her vigour and vigilance. With less romanticism and more consistency, Garvin made essentially the same point. 'There will be no war if Germany knows us strong enough to clinch the issue,' he told Grigg on 5 May 1935. 'Already the most satisfying chastening is felt there; but they respect nothing, and are checked by nothing, but equal practical force and nerve force.'[1]

To the point of obsession, Rothermere pleaded for massive air rearmament, a cause embraced by Mosley and Churchill from other points on the political spectrum. Not content to rely on his newspapers and the National League of Airmen, he tried to recruit parliamentary allies. Brooks was present on 18 April 1935, when 'Ned' Grigg and 'Freddie' Guest, both erstwhile followers of Lloyd George, came to Rothermere's house to discuss 'the menace of air war from Germany'. They reportedly concurred 'that Baldwin is now fully alive to the situation', which might hasten his advent to the premiership; at that time, 'Ll. George will be taken in, and by that means the semblance of a National Government will be preserved'. Heartened on both counts, Rothermere pointed out that *The Times*'s leading article that morning, ' "pro-German" in its denunciation of the Treaty of Versailles, had enormous significance'. Grigg ascribed it to Lord Halifax, whom he identified as 'the big influence on Geoffrey Dawson' and the man who 'leads the party in the Cabinet ... in favour of concessions and justice to Germany'. Weeks later, Baldwin replaced the faltering MacDonald (who 'no longer trusts himself ... to read a statement to the House') and presided over a reshuffle in which a place was allocated to Halifax (who thereafter rose higher), but not to Lloyd George.[2]

Through this period of political and diplomatic uncertainty, *The Times* pursued 'a policy of detachment and independence', reflected in successive articles on the Abyssinian crisis that Philip Snowden discerned to be 'having a profound influence on important opinion in this country, though they are probably not making you more popular in official quarters'. Dawson, who constantly strove 'to make the best I could of British policy, which could hardly have helped itself, but was clearly shaken' by events, confirmed that his friends in high places were 'absurdly touchy' and resentful. Any guidance he may have received from Halifax would have been gratuitous and possibly less important than his formal contacts with Anthony Eden, then minister without portfolio for League of Nations affairs. 'Different people tell me nearly every day that they have been warned by the Foreign Office to look to *The Times* no longer for the British point of view,' Dawson replied sulkily to Snowden. The editor could not have it both ways. Always quick to disclaim any official connection that would compromise his vaunted independence, he was none the less dismayed

[1] Garvin to Grigg, 5 May 1935, Grigg Papers.
[2] Brooks's diary, 18 April 1935. Neither as president of the Board of Education (1932–35) nor as Secretary of State for War (June–November 1935) did Halifax enjoy Cabinet rank.

whenever his quasi-ministerial credentials were called into question. At the end of the year, John Walter had 'no doubt that in moments of danger *The Times* still speaks with "the authentic voice of England", and what is more, still makes itself heard above all other voices in spite of the increasing din'. So it seemed to foreign dictators, who mistakenly interpreted that voice as an echo from Whitehall.[1]

The November elections resulted in a resounding triumph for Baldwin, whom Tom Jones ('not biassed by friendship') extolled for having 'avoided all trace of the *Daily Mail*'s lust to arm the nation to the teeth'. Rothermere was incensed by the Prime Minister's obvious restraint during a campaign that Beaverbrook saw as a calculated appeal to the Liberal sentimentalists: 'It was League, collective security and economic sanctions all the way.' The idea of applying sanctions against Italy was anathema to both press lords, who had 'a telephone talk' on 4 December. Beaverbrook was invited to contribute a 'special' to the *Sunday Dispatch*'s leader page. 'If we press now, we can kill sanctions and save the country from war,' Rothermere told him. In fact, once the election was over, the idea of sanctions was summarily abandoned. On the 7th, Sir Samuel Hoare crossed to Paris, where Beaverbrook was already in residence. The next day, the Foreign Secretary concluded an agreement with Pierre Laval, his French counterpart. Abyssinia was to be partitioned, its sovereignty to be confined to a mountainous area in the hinterlands, with access to the coast through what *The Times* derided as 'a corridor for camels' (16 December). The Hoare-Laval pact was accorded Cabinet approval on the 9th and provoked a public outcry that led to Hoare's removal from the Foreign Office. Beaverbrook looked upon the 'rejection of the Italian deal with consternation' and vowed 'to stand unswervingly in support' of Hoare, his old friend, who had been made a scapegoat. 'The Peace plan was sound and should have been pressed as a basis for negotiation,' insisted the *Daily Express* (20 December). 'The Government should never have given way and never allowed Sir Samuel Hoare to be sacrificed.'[2]

The sacrifice of remote Abyssinian territory mattered a good deal less to Beaverbrook and Rothermere, who regarded it as the price to be paid for Baldwin's electoral hypocrisy. Oscar Hobson accused Rothermere and Brooks 'of being responsible for changing Baldwin's policy', and Brooks took that as a compliment; Rothermere 'has steadily reiterated, with deadly effect, Baldwin's attack on sanctions of some months ago ("you cannot conceive an effective sanction that does not mean war") which has made everything Baldwin now says in support of sanctions sound like the utterings of a war

[1] Dawson's diary, 3 May 1936, Snowden to Dawson, 1 May 1935, Dawson to Snowden, 2 May 1935 (copy), Walter to Dawson, 23 December 1935, Dawson Papers.
[2] Jones to Abraham Flexner, 17 November 1935, quoted in Jones, *Diary with Letters*, p. 155; Beaverbrook to Doidge, 25 November 1935, Beaverbrook to Eden, 24 November 1942, and Beaverbrook to Hoare, 14 December 1935, quoted in Taylor, *Beaverbrook*, pp. 358–59; Brooks's diary, 4 December 1935.

monger'. If ruinous for purposes of diplomacy, the technique made for lively journalism. Beaverbrook, hoping for more spectacular results, took up the cry that 'Mr Baldwin Must Go' (*Daily Express*, 20 December), but privately conceded 'that the Government is so strong, it cannot even commit suicide'. Consequently, he soon lapsed into despondency.[1]

Dawson, though 'slightly sorry' to see Hoare 'made the victim of the public indignation', was thoroughly opposed to the 'unjust peace' that the British and French had sought to impose. *The Times* was applauded by the *New Statesman* for 'taking an unexpectedly strong line' on the Abyssinian question (21 December), and Barrington-Ward calculated that 'the effect of our intervention was enormously increased by the reputation for detachment, self-control and common sense – good judgment, in fact – which G.D. has won for the paper'. Admittedly, however, *The Times* was selective in the strong lines it took. Abyssinia, with its proximity to the Suez Canal, elicited far greater concern than the Japanese invasion of Manchuria, let alone the Chaco dispute between Bolivia and Paraguay. Conspicuously stinting in its criticisms of Germany, the paper would never have endorsed the view – expressed by Robert (later Baron) Boothby, the Conservative MP for Aberdeenshire East, in a letter to the *New Statesmen* on 4 January 1936 – that 'to abandon Abyssinia ... would be to destroy the League and to give the "All Clear" signal to Hitler for 1937'. Beaverbrook counted 'the editor of *The Times* newspaper' as 'the most important' of all the 'personages' in 'a pro-German ... sect' that worked assiduously to neutralize a body of pro-French opinion. 'The strange thing is that both these groups are actuated by the same motive,' he observed. 'They are both afraid of Germany.'[2]

Stranger still has been the tendency of many commentators to regard the press as part and parcel of the appeasement phenomenon, variously interpreted as a movement and an ethic. The differences among newspapers, if less pronounced than the affinities, were equally symptomatic of permutations within the larger political culture. To debate the efficacy of appeasement, a concept which has been recognized as embracing a diversity of meanings, would be redundant. To assess its morality would be otiose. To catalogue the responses of newspapers in chronological sequence would be a tedious exercise, more likely to obscure the major themes than to elucidate them. Instead, with more modest aims, the present study will continue to concentrate on the political performance and presumptions of the press in an effort to evoke the mood that influenced the policy-makers. This procedure may help to explain the evolution of new alignments within the parliamentary sphere and in the

---

[1] Brooks's diary, 11 December 1935; Beaverbrook to P. Block, 4 February 1936, quoted in Taylor, *Beaverbrook*, p. 362.

[2] Dawson to a member of the staff, 18 December 1935, quoted in *History of The Times*, IV, part 2, 898; Barrington-Ward's diary, 21 December 1935; Beaverbrook to J. M. Patterson, 8 August 1936, quoted in Taylor, *Beaverbrook*, p. 364.

electorate beyond. For, during the pre-war years of appeasement, the political press experienced a full share of the fears and humiliations that it documented in other sectors of public activity.

* * *

'Before the war, British journalism led the world,' recalled Hannen Swaffer with a chauvinism born of nostalgia. At the same time, journalists were alleged to have misled British opinion to the extent that 'MPs of all parties' were gripped by a 'growing resentment . . . against irresponsible newspaper criticism by the controllers of large circulations'.[1] How, if at all, can these implicit contradictions be reconciled?

Party managers, among the last to appreciate the realities of the situation, sought to restore the mechanisms for formal collaboration that newspapermen had been struggling to dismantle. Their recommendations, like their aspirations, were depressingly familiar. Joseph Ball, the director of the Conservative Research Department, wrote to Baldwin after the 1935 election to urge

> an intensive campaign of propaganda and education with the first priority being to acquire the control of a suitable weekly publication, and, secondly, to build up a staff of really good young writers capable of exposing effectively the fallacies upon which the public is being regularly fed.

Despite its recent victory at the polls, 'the National cause' was supposedly 'seriously handicapped also by the absence of a daily or evening newspaper with a wide circulation among the masses, and giving the Government regular and wholehearted support'. The Labour opposition boasted the *Daily Herald* and was expected imminently to acquire 'an evening paper run on similar lines'; on Sundays, it was represented by *Reynold's*, under the management of National Co-operative Press Ltd. Doubtless Ball overestimated the partisan utility of these organs, as he certainly exaggerated the subservience of the *News Chronicle* and the *Star* to the Liberals, who had 'many provincial papers' among their further assets. 'We have nothing at all comparable to these popular papers,' complained Ball,

> for the *Daily Mail* and the *Daily Express* attack us more frequently than they support us, while, although *The Times* and the *Daily Telegraph* are admirable newspapers and give us their full support, their circulations are so small in comparison with the others which I have mentioned that their influence among the masses is almost negligible. We ought to have a great popular paper devoted to our cause.[2]

---

[1] Evidence, Royal Commission on the Press, 1947–49, Cd. 7318, additional comments 79, 83.
[2] Ball to Baldwin, 6 December 1935, Baldwin Papers. Ball was knighted in the next honours list.

By his criteria, the *Morning Post* was not worth mentioning.

How valid were those criteria? Would Ball and his associates have traded their overwhelming parliamentary majority for more reliable representation in the mass circulation press? Had not the election returns clearly demonstrated, neither for the first time nor the last, that a party could triumph in the face of unfriendly journalism? Putting aside such considerations of logic, pre-war party strategists hankered after the kinds of partnerships that they imagined their predecessors to have enjoyed and, more importantly, that seemed to exist among their opponents. Any knowledgeable Liberal or Labour leader might have disabused Ball of his illusions. That, however, would not have mattered. Each party strove to keep up with the Joneses, ignoring the fact that the Joneses had long since fallen behind themselves.

Testifying in 1947 before the Royal Commission on the Press, Francis Williams outlined the arrangements for 'the political control' of the *Daily Herald* during his years as editor. In an *ex officio* capacity, Williams had

> attended meetings of the National Council of Labour (which is a joint body of the political Labour Party and the trade unions) and kept such contact as he felt was necessary with the political leaders and the trade unionists; but in the main the initiative for such contact ... would come from the editor. He would feel that it was necessary and desirable to have a talk with the leader of the Parliamentary Party or some other prominent person, or one of the trade unions, on a particular issue, and would approach them, and not be approached by the Party or the trade unions.

There was nothing to prevent other editors or correspondents, regardless of their political and professional attachments, from taking similar initiatives. The best of them regularly did. Labour spokesmen were accessible to Crozier, Layton, and Cummings, to name but three among many. Barrington-Ward, to a greater extent than Dawson, crossed party lines to take counsel from Labour and especially Liberal leaders; indeed, on the day he took over as editor of *The Times*, he lunched with Lloyd George and Clement Davies, receiving from the former 'a lecture which lasted for over an hour on how to run a paper'. Shortly afterwards, Colin Coote left *The Times* to take up leader-writing duties on the *Daily Telegraph*, where he eventually became editor. He had briefly served as a Liberal MP and, as one of his obituarists noted, 'his traditional Liberalism was a cogent influence in enabling that avowedly Conservative newspaper to maintain its vigorously independent judgment'.[1]

No paper, then, could claim a monopoly on the favours of any party and, conversely, no party could impose strict discipline on any paper. The *Daily Herald*, however closely bound to the Labour hierarchy by its managerial

---

[1] Evidence, Royal Commission on the Press, 1947–49, Cd. 7318, qq. 437–38, 557; *The Times*, 23 November 1979.

structure, frequently diverged from the official Labour position, which, in any case, was seldom firmly established. Such infractions brought 'quite stiff protests', usually taking the form of reprimands from Ernest Bevin, whose bullying tactics were not to be underestimated. Nevertheless, the paper retained its 'freedom to interpret the policy of the Labour Party and to print the speeches of the Labour Party's opponents'. Latitude was the price that had to be paid for a mass readership. That the *Herald* did not assert that freedom more pugnaciously, even to the extent that *The Times* distanced itself from official Conservatism or the *News Chronicle* from official Liberalism, was essentially due to the loyalty of its staff, who held to the rule of 'printing your own side'. This tendency was especially manifest in the disproportionate amount of space that the paper devoted to municipal politics, which its rivals tended to treat perfunctorily. The results were spectacularly reflected in the local elections of 1937, a vindication of Herbert Morrison's programme for 'good publicity'.[1]

Although, in retrospect, there were shades of disagreement about the degree of partisan fidelity required of the *Daily Herald* in the pre-war years, the consensus was that the paper's support for Labour – conceived as a movement that enveloped a party – had been voluntary and, as a rule, pragmatic. The envy of the Conservative Research Department, while understandable, was therefore misplaced. Had a band of younger talents been assembled to plead 'the National cause', there was absolutely no guarantee that they would have found outlets for their wares and still less likelihood that their commitments would have been immutable.

For the time had passed when journalists were expected, much less required, to adhere to the political viewpoints of their employers. Over the years, Swaffer drew salaries from Northcliffe, Hulton, the Berrys, Beaverbrook, and – 'simply because I was a Socialist' – the *Herald*. 'I liked all my proprietors because I liked the game,' he bantered. Others were less cavalier, but nearly as mobile. George Edinger resigned as a leader-writer for the *Sunday Express* in 1936, when he refused to condemn sanctions against Italy; he thereafter continued to write 'on less controversial subjects and even on controversial ones that did not conflict too openly with the paper's policy', until he moved to the *Herald*. Coote asked to be relieved of the obligation to write pro-appeasement leaders for *The Times* at the time of the Munich crisis, but remained at Printing House Square for the next four years. William Forrest, then a member of the Communist Party, found it easier to cover the Spanish Civil War for the *News Chronicle* than for the *Herald*, where he had put up with Bevin's intimidation and interference. The cases can be multiplied, and all of them signalled a broad retreat from a nineteenth-century ideal.[2]

[1] Evidence, Royal Commission on the Press, 1947–49, Cds. 7318 and 9432, qq. 569, 9060; Donoughue and Jones, *Morrison*, pp. 208–209.
[2] Tom Driberg, '*Swaff*' (London, 1974), pp. 230–31; memorandum by Edinger, Evidence, Royal Commission on the Press, 1947–49, Cd. 7325. Edinger's case that the *Herald* barred

If, not atypically, Joseph Ball misjudged the character of the Labour press, which did not expand its base as anticipated,[1] he failed utterly to grasp the complexities of Liberal journalism. Its provincial properties were mostly of negligible significance, more profitable – if at all – for advertising than electoral purposes. The *Manchester Guardian*, with a circulation that hovered around 50,000, was a prominent exception. Yet, in the bluff opinion of Swaffer, its influence was 'largely a fiction which exists in the minds of oldish people', who had known it in the legendary days of C. P. Scott. In 1936, following the precedents of *The Times* and the *Observer*, the proprietorship of the *Guardian* was reconstituted as a trust, with the ordinary shares apportioned among seven directors, three of whom were members of the Scott family. This manoeuvre was designed as a safeguard against the Inland Revenue, not as a means either to protect or promote a spirit of greater editorial independence. 'A Trust can be as repressive in effect as anything else,' Swaffer was to remind the Royal Commissioners who interrogated him.[2]

Concurrently and with more direct political implications, the *News Chronicle* underwent a complicated process of 'capital reorganisation', which was Laurence Cadbury's euphemism for the transfer that now occurred. This restructuring, like previous ones, grew more extensive as it proceeded. The initial proposal, worked out between Pearson and Layton in the summer of 1936, was for the Westminster Press and Daily News companies to join in buying out the preference shareholding of United Newspapers. The terms, as modified, would have assigned 86½ per cent of the equity to the Cadburys as against 13½ per cent to the Pearsons, with profits to be divided in proportion. In the event, Morrell did not find this scheme sufficiently 'attractive' to recommend its adoption. On 17 September, he and Pearson met Cadbury and Layton, and an agreement was reached whereby the Daily News Ltd. absorbed the Westminster as well as the United minority interests in order to effect an exclusive control. Estimating the copyright and goodwill of the *News Chronicle* (as distinct from the money-losing *Star*) to be worth approximately one million pounds, Layton turned to Lloyd's Bank for a loan, which was repaid over the ensuing decade. Sir Herbert Grotrian, chairman of United, gladly accepted £500,000 as reimbursement for half the share capital. According to Layton, a separate payment of £135,000 went to the Westminster Press, but Pearson quoted a much higher figure that presumably included the settlement of outstanding debts. 'Morrell and I sold our interest for a total of two twenty five

---

non-party contributors was weakened by the fact that he had been the Liberal candidate at Saffron Walden in 1935 before joining its staff.

[1] The abortive plans to launch an evening *Herald* are discussed in Minney, *Southwood*, pp. 316–17. The launching on 1 January 1937 of *Tribune*, a weekly platform for the militant Labour left, did not serve a comparable purpose.

[2] Evidence, Royal Commission on the Press, 1947–49, Cd. 7318, qq. 558–59, 642; Ayerst, *Guardian*, pp. 492–93.

thousand which is a reasonable price and is lovely as terminating the unsatisfactory political responsibility,' he informed his sister and other associates on 'the date of severance'.[1]

The Cadburys thus tightened their grip on the *News Chronicle*, where they no longer had to contend with cavils and challenges from the voting trustees, henceforth representing only the Daily News Trust. Layton, whose position was fortified, was relieved of the obligation to justify editorial policy to co-proprietors who had preached orthodox Liberalism for a combination of unorthodox reasons. The Daily News trustees, as executives of 'the parent or holding company', met twice a year to discuss the general principles that the respective editors of the *News Chronicle* and the *Star* were expected to 'apply ... in their day to day administration of the papers'. In addition, there were monthly board meetings, primarily concerned with business arrangements, where questions of editorial policy rarely arose. Laurence Cadbury chaired these sessions, and his older brothers, Edward and Henry, attended only 'three or four times a year', when the meetings were held in Birmingham for their convenience. Although Laurence claimed that he made it a practice to see the editor not fewer than 'three days a week', members of his staff have irreverently recalled that 'the Grocer' usually arrived in London late on Wednesdays or early on Thursdays to participate in editorial conferences on Thursday afternoons. (When required to stay the night, he put up at the Savoy, where he dispensed miserly gratuities.) Layton, whom he trusted implicitly, was a daily presence in Bouverie Street and began each day with a telephone call to the editor of the *News Chronicle*. Much as before, the topics and perspectives for leading articles were decided by '*ad hoc* discussions'. Layton did not have to pay comparable attention to the *Star*, given that its leaders were preponderantly 'in the nature of human interest which do not necessarily require a particular policy behind them'.[2]

As a rule, the policies of both papers were hammered out on the premises rather than imposed from above. Cadbury was susceptible to argument, and Layton actively encouraged it. There were, as they themselves told the Royal Commission, occasions when the *News Chronicle* 'deliberately tried to lead public interest', with the result that it 'too markedly' suffered 'a loss of popularity and sale'. In particular, the paper braved criticism for its loyalist stand during the Spanish conflict and for publishing 'an extremely lurid description of what was going on in concentration camps' in pre-war Germany.

---

[1] Morrell to Layton, 27 June 1936 (copy), Morrell to Pearson, 7 September 1936, notes of agreement, 17 September 1936, and text of a telephone message from Pearson to Lady Denman and others, 17 September 1936, Cowdray Papers; Layton to Cadbury, 15 July 1936 (copy), and Layton, draft memoir, Layton Papers; *Financial Times*, 4 November 1936; Evidence, Royal Commission on the Press, 1947–49, Cd. 7409, q. 8191.

[2] These paragraphs are based on evidence provided by Cadbury, Layton, A. L. Cranfield, and R. J. Cruikshank to the Royal Commission on the Press, 1947–49, Cd. 7407, qq. 8191 ff., as supplemented by the author's interviews.

But none of the few examples they cited could be construed as a narrowly partisan response. The *News Chronicle* retained a Liberal inclination, but with no delusions about the party or itself. 'We do not seem to have got many Liberal Members of Parliament,' Layton wryly observed, 'but on the other hand many of the policies that have been pursued, to some extent in advance of public opinion, have ultimately proved to be the line followed by the country.' However gratifying to contemplate in retrospect, those policies were impediments to political efficacy at the time. The *News Chronicle*, conducted with an awareness that it would take more than newspaper support to revitalize the Liberal Party, persistently gave umbrage to one Liberal faction or another. Far from being the dutiful party organ that outsiders took it for, it qualified as a sympathetic source of Labour news. 'Bevin controlled the *Daily Herald*,' noted Lloyd George, 'and one had to turn to the *News Chronicle* to know what the Labour Party was really up to.'[1]

The degree to which Liberal and Labour journals got caught up in internecine rivalries or simply retreated from political combat might well have afforded a measure of consolation to Conservative Party managers. Instead, obsessed by their own problems, Tory publicists pitied themselves as the victims of some peculiar deprivation. In fact, they still enjoyed a relative advantage over their competitors on the left, although it was decidedly less than that to which they had been accustomed. In qualitative terms, admittedly more difficult to gauge than quantitative ones, the Conservative leadership could depend upon steadfast backing from a group of distinguished dailies and weeklies. Moreover, these were the papers of heaviest political weight. The undeniable drawback was that this group, embracing none of the mass-circulation giants, showed signs of decrepitude and decay. The joke in Fleet Street was that the circulation of the *Morning Post* declined each day by the number of names in its death columns. *The Times*, while registering a modest improvement in sales, seemed to Grigg to have 'become the embodiment of all that is weak in the national spirit at this critical time. What *can* we do about it?' he asked Garvin, whose *Observer* was subject to similar criticism.[2]

The most dynamic papers on the right were invariably the most fractious. Whether that was cause or effect can be debated, but hardly mattered under the circumstances. Parliamentary opponents of the National administration were given platforms in the Beaverbrook and Rothermere press from which to disseminate their views. Patrick Donner, for example, who had switched his constituency from Islington West to Basingstoke and distinguished himself as 'the spearhead of the attack on the India Bill', was recruited as a contributor of political notes to the *Daily Mail*. On every conceivable issue, and sometimes where no genuine issue existed, the *Mail* and its sister papers strove to undermine Baldwin's authority. Taking care to mute his Mosleyite sentiments,

---
[1] Diary entry of 12–14 June 1937 in Jones, *Diary With Letters*, p. 351.
[2] Brendon, *Press Barons*, p. 166; Grigg to Garvin, 30 October 1936, Grigg Papers.

Rothermere by no means recanted them. On 8 June 1936, Brooks wrote a signed article that approvingly reported a Blackshirt meeting in London's East End, where 'organisation is triumphant'. He would have expressed himself much more emphatically, he revealed in his diary, but 'the real essence of the matter' was that 'Jewish advertisers would be offended' to the point of withdrawing their accounts. 'This is the freedom of the Press, and this is the power of the Jew. Herein ... is the justification of Fascism,' Brooks savagely concluded.[1]

The tactics employed by Beaverbrook and Rothermere were as different as the men themselves. Although no less intense, Beaverbrook's hostility was more clearly focussed and studiously better tempered. He yearned to topple Baldwin and laid out his 'top hat with mourning coat & black gloves' in readiness for the political funeral. But he shared neither Rothermere's apocalyptic vision nor his reverence for Nazi spirituality. Quite absurdly, Beaverbrook pinned his hopes to Hoare, who resumed his ministerial career in June 1936. Mosley, he recognized, had embarked on a 'path [that] ... can never lead him anywhere'. Churchill struck him as too much of an alarmist and francophile. Lloyd George, who delivered a glowing account of his interview with Hitler ('The Germans have definitely made up their minds never to quarrel with us again') in the pages of the *Daily Express* (17 September 1936), seemed to have lost all sense of proportion. Rothermere, refusing to allow differences of opinion to come between old friends, continued to be more intimately associated with both Lloyd George and Churchill. In 1935, the three of them enjoyed a Christmas holiday in Morocco, where Rothermere offered Churchill £2,000 if he 'went teetotal' through the next year. There were some things, however, that money could not buy.[2]

The *Daily Mail* was the heart of 'the most complete newspaper combine in Great Britain', but its circulation trailed behind that of the *Daily Express*. Sir Patrick Hannon, the Conservative MP for the Moseley division of Birmingham, offered Beaverbrook 'sincere congratulations on the amazing success, from the point of view of commercial achievement, of the *Daily Express* and the *Sunday Express*. At the same time', as one Empire Crusader to another, he joined 'in respectful sympathy ... that your Imperial propagandist efforts for consolidation and unity within the British Commonwealth of Nations and the detachment of this country from continental entanglements have not been successful'. To Hannon, it seemed an irony that Joseph Chamberlain's campaign for Tariff Reform, 'sustained by most leading newspapers in addition to your own', had worked only belatedly and partially.'You remind me that Protection came 29 years after Joe Chamber-

---

[1] Brooks's diary, 29 January, 7 February, and 7 June 1936.
[2] Beaverbrook to Bracken [April 1936], and Beaverbrook to E. H. Dennis, 27 October 1936, quoted in Taylor, *Beaverbrook*, pp. 364–66; Gilbert, *Churchill*, V, 648–49, 694–95, 933.

lain launched his policy,' replied Beaverbrook. 'It will be a bad business if Isolation takes as long as that.'[1]

Rothermere was disappointed by the sale of the *Daily Mail*, which slid from nearly two million at the start of the decade to 1,510,000 in 1939. He and his associates were even more worried by the *Sunday Dispatch*, which sank to 741,000 in 1937, when the *Sunday Express* was selling 1,350,000. As diagnosed by Brooks, 'the root trouble was that we spend in promotion about £300 a week whereas our massed rivals are spending £20,000'. Sir George Sutton, the managing director of Associated Newspapers, overheard Rothermere remark that the *Daily Mirror* owed its recent success to 'sensationalism and pornography', which inspired Sutton to maintain 'that that was what we needed' at the *Dispatch*. 'Even what is regarded as a normal popular paper is, of course, a medley of salacious and sordid items mixed with a little surface politics and the pursuance of personal feuds,' lamented Brooks, who saw 'the whole episode' as 'an interesting sidelight ... on how great newspapers are run, and what motives actuate their proprietors'.[2]

Beaverbrook, who could afford to resist temptations of this sort, deflected his imperial energies to the expansion of his own empire. He had been publishing separate editions of the *Daily* and the *Sunday Express* in Manchester since 1927 and in Glasgow since 1928. His *Evening Standard*, however, was confined to a London clientele as much by orientation as by distribution, and he wished to establish a foothold in the potentially lucrative Scottish evening market. Glasgow, the obvious site for such an enterprise, already accommodated three evening papers: the *Evening News*, part of the sprawling Kemsley chain; and the *Evening Times* and the *Evening Citizen*, both locally owned by the firm of George Outram & Company, who also published the morning *Glasgow Herald*.

After broadly hinting that he might add to the congestion, Beaverbrook decided to acquire a majority holding in the *Citizen*. Frank Waters, who was on the spot as general manager of the *Scottish Daily Express*, was deputed to open negotiations with the Outram directors. Despite their professed willingness 'to retain political & editorial control, leaving business & circulation side to *Express*', it proved difficult to devise a mutually acceptable formula. The talks started in the opening days of 1936, broke down in 1937, and resumed in the late summer of 1938, when Beaverbrook suddenly grew 'eager to purchase' and an agreement was finally ratified. Waters, who later tended in turn to the managerial requirements of *The Times* and the *News Chronicle*, now supervised both Glasgow operations as proconsul for E. J. Robertson, the general

---

[1] Gannon, *British Press*, p. 32; Hannon to Beaverbrook, 6 July 1936 (copy), and Beaverbrook to Hannon, 7 July 1936, Hannon Papers. Hannon entitled himself to close attention in the Beaverbrook press (see Taylor, *Beaverbrook*, p. 265) by being a director of the *Evening Standard*, as confirmed by Michael Wardell (chairman of the board) to Hannon, 6 April 1938, Hannon Papers.
[2] Brooks's diary, 14 March 1937.

manager of Express Newspapers in London. With 51 per cent of the control, Beaverbrook had got everything he wanted from the *Citizen* and, more to the point, little that he did not want.¹

Not the least of Beaverbrook's satisfactions was the fright he gave his fellow press barons. 'Lord Kemsley ... is in a panic about the immediate future of newspapers, as he may well be,' Brooks recorded in March 1938, after Kemsley had complained to Rothermere 'that little Beaverbrook, who does not take his money from Fleet Street, will force a pace that will ruin the other proprietors'. As war approached, the price of newsprint soared, profits diminished and, Brooks predicted, were 'likely to go lower – the outlook grim'. Still, Beaverbrook led a merry chase. At breakfast with Waters on 9 May 1939, he 'talked rapidly & zealously of buying a Sunday newspaper in Scotland, of taking over the *Scotsman* ("They're in low water, you know"), of ultimately absorbing Outrams ("If you want it, of course").' Their conversation was interrupted for five minutes so that 'My Lord B' could dictate 'over the 'phone two-thirds of today's *Evening Standard* Londoner's Diary'.²

Except for Beaverbrook, whose balance sheets were cause for jealousy, these were bleak times. The Royal Commission on the Press, reporting after the war, confirmed that of the 207 newspapers it investigated, thirty-eight – 'or 18 per cent' – had been operating at a deficit in 1937. 'As long as newspapers are sold to the public for less than they cost to produce, they will need a supplementary source of income,' the commissioners agreed. Some of the best-known properties were variously consigned to this category. An anonymous, but obviously well-informed commentator declared in *The Economist* on 2 January 1937 that no less than 'a sum of the order of £2,000,000' would be required to ensure the *Daily Herald* 'a self-supporting position. There are very few industries which impose an entrance fee as high as this.' The Berry brothers met the crisis by dividing their family interests in the Amalgamated Press. That year, Lord Camrose took custody of the *Daily Telegraph* and the *Financial Times*, leaving 'complete and undivided control' of the *Sunday Times* to Lord Kemsley, who acquired all but one of the group's provincial dailies as well. Kemsley promptly leased and soon sold the *Reading Gazette* to Lord Iliffe, a longtime family associate, who also relieved him of a string of minor periodicals. As a follow-up, Kemsley bought the *Newcastle Journal*, only to merge it with his *North Mail*.³

Fraternal combinations seemed particularly susceptible to economic pres-

---

¹ Waters's diary, 3 and 14 January 1936, 16 August 1938; Camrose, *British Newspapers*, pp. 138–39. In a letter to his wife, postmarked 24 January 1939, Waters reported further concessions from the Outram's board, which 'was as rigid as a piece of batter pudding. ... We are going to have a lot more fun with the *Citizen* than the *Express*,' he anticipated, 'because we shall have more personal control. And what we make it will be entirely up to us' (Waters Papers).
² Brooks's diary, 17 March 1938; Waters's diary, 9 May 1939.
³ Report, Royal Commission on the Press, 1947–49, Cd. 7700, pp. 60–61, 81, 143; Hobson *et al.*, *The Pearl of Days*, p. 209.

sure. Somewhat prematurely, Brenden Bracken rejoiced that Beaverbrook's *Scottish Daily Express* had

> made Camrose meet his Culloden. That nobleman has been wise in his decision to retire from what is called popular newspapers. Poor old R[othermere] – who is getting more & more like Lady Houston in his handling of controversies – has been encouraging his papers to make ponderous attacks on Layton. Your *Express* figures must have made R & his satraps wince. We shall witness the *N. Chronicle* beating the *Mail*'s circulation. Northcliffe's brothers are very like Napoleon's.

Other family concerns, including the *Manchester Guardian*, were badly hit. 'Hope best, prepare for worst' was the motto Garvin inscribed on a statement of 'Facts, Figures and Estimates' that he prepared for Lord Astor. In the previous fiscal year, the *Observer* had 'made over £37,000 absolutely net'. For the year due to end on 28 February 1938, 'we shall be lucky if we just pay our way'. Advertising revenues were suffering from 'the unprecedented uncertainty respecting peace and war; by Continental alarms; and by the feeling that the British position is weakened in every quarter of the globe by our simultaneous entanglements and risks'. So far as Garvin could foresee, 'the creeping paralysis of confidence' would continue, bringing 'rising costs' and decreased profitability.[1]

Astor's recommendation was 'for the *Observer* to be and look more like the *Sunday Times* – especially in the way of having more snippets of news and fewer news features. A policy more surely fatal could not be imagined,' protested Garvin. 'It ignored the character of the solid middle-class in the provinces who furnish 2/3 of the *Observer*'s circulation. Their mentality is as different as possible from that of the bright young things.'[2] True enough, the *Sunday Times* had surged ahead to a sale of 270,000, while the *Observer* sold 201,000 in 1930 and 207,000 in 1937. Nevertheless, Garvin was correct to recognize that different newspapers addressed different social and intellectual readerships, and that the *Observer* would probably lose more than it gained by a shift of orientation. Yet the general tendency, as Astor articulated it, was towards homogeneity. By de-emphasizing politics, devoting more space to entertainment features, and standardizing formats, newspapers were growing virtually indistinguishable from one another.

The exception to that rule was the *Morning Post*, the dowager of Fleet Street, and its fate served to reinforce the trend. For generations it had maintained the same style and the same prejudices, seemingly oblivious to the fact that the world was changing. H. A. Gwynne, the editor since 1911,

---

[1] Bracken to Beaverbrook, 14 January 1937 (copy), Beaverbrook Papers, C/56; memorandum by Garvin, 12 October 1937, Garvin Papers.

[2] Notes, n.d., on 'The *Observer*'s "features, character & form",' Garvin Papers.

solicited a column for the paper's 'What Next?' series from Bernard Shaw, who replied – not for publication – by directing that question at the *Morning Post* itself. The rectories and country houses of Old England were still inhabited, and the retired colonels and 'half-ennobled' plutocrats seemed to him as abundant and 'solid as ever'. But the 'literary appetites' of these atavistic classes no longer ran so predictably in the same 'old grooves', with the result that the paper lost its normal clientele. 'What Next,' wondered Shaw, for the *Morning Post*? Within months, that was exactly the question uppermost in Gwynne's mind.[1]

Before the end of 1936, Brooks was informed that Rothermere 'is contemplating buying the *Morning Post* and wanted to know what I thought, and would I edit it . . . as a strong Right Wing paper'. Nothing came of these plans, perhaps because the resignation from the board of Lord Apsley, who had perpetuated the Borthwick family connection, temporarily eased tensions. The following autumn, rumours again began 'accumulating about the demise of the *Morning Post*'. Dawson, who heard them, was stunned by the announcement on 29 September that, 'as from 1 October, the *Morning Post* will be amalgamated with the *Daily Telegraph*'. The editor of *The Times* 'had a desperate struggle with a leader about it' and, in a statesmanlike manner, confined his remarks to the daunting problems of producing a London daily. In the privacy of his diary, however, he admitted that 'the news didn't admit to anything v. distinctive' apart from the thought that it was mandatory for *The Times* 'to put together a good paper to compare with the amalgamated *Telegraph-Post*'.[2]

It was 'a sad day' for Gwynne, who assured Beaverbrook that 'Camrose has behaved with generosity both to the Staff and myself. One of these days I will come and tell you a little bit about the last year and a half of the *Morning Post*,' he promised. 'It would amuse you.' In addition to the purchase price, said to be around £150,000 for a property that had run up a loss of over £40,000 in the course of its last fiscal year, Camrose provided pensions as well as places for nearly half of the depleted editorial staff. Although 'both assured of jobs', two foreign correspondents came to see Dawson in the hope of transferring to *The Times*, which stood to gain in other ways. Its board authorized an expenditure of £10,000 for a campaign 'to help catch the old *Morning Post* readers', many of whom were expected to regard the *Telegraph* as too parvenu and frivolous. That was not so much a matter of political preference as one of social values. 'It is *terribly* sad that yr. fine old true blue Tory paper is going to those *rich* & colourless Camroses,' Margot Asquith, the widow of the Liberal Prime Minister, wrote to Gwynne. 'I never agree with a

---

[1] Shaw to Gwynne, 22 June 1936, Gwynne Papers.
[2] Brooks's diary, 20 December 1936; Dawson's diary, 29 and 30 September 1937; *The Times*, 30 September 1937; *World's Press News*, 29 July 1937.

word it says, but it has *character* – wh. few papers have, & above all *courage*, wh. no paper has.' As usual, her logic was problematic, but her instincts were sound.[1]

* * *

One did not have to agree with Winston Churchill, and conspicuously few of his contemporaries (including some who shared his aversion to doctrines of appeasement) did, to recognize that he, too, possessed a superabundance of character and courage. Of all the major politicians of the late 1930s, he was the most dependent upon the press both for income and propaganda. The *Evening Standard* was his principal outlet until the spring of 1938, when his contract was abruptly terminated and he shifted to the *Daily Telegraph*. His son, Randolph, perpetuated the family connection with the *Evening Standard* through the war, when he took a leave of absence with salary.[2]

Churchill's contacts in Fleet Street were not limited to those particular journals for which he wrote. Rothermere and Garvin were among the old friends with whom he kept in touch. Before delivering a speech in Paris on 24 September 1936, he sent a draft of his text to Dawson, asking 'if the Editor will let him know how it strikes him'. Barrington-Ward, who took charge of *The Times* in Dawson's absence, considered it an 'odd and slightly ingenuous request, since we have been by implication critics of his point of view'. Nevertheless, he complied by remitting his own 'opinion and some suggestions', which arrived too late to temper Churchill's appeal for closer Anglo-French collaboration. That hardly mattered. Churchill 'wanted us to understand his view', Barrington-Ward concluded from a 'very civil' telephone conversation after the event.[3]

Foreign affairs did not provide the only incentives for Churchill to traffic with the press. Out of office, he remained a privy councillor and, partly in that capacity, developed staunch sympathies for Edward VIII, who succeeded to the throne in January 1936. From the start of the new reign, there was gossip that the King was romantically involved with Wallis Simpson, twice married and (for the time being) once divorced. Like Beaverbrook, another of the King's protagonists, Churchill looked askance at Mrs Simpson's plans to file for a second divorce, which would pave the way for a royal marriage, 'morganatic or otherwise'. Although his advice was not heeded, his assistance was enlisted

---

[1] Gwynne to Beaverbrook, 29 September 1937, Beaverbrook Papers, C/149; *Morning Post*, 30 September 1937; Dawson's diary, 6 October 1937; Barrington-Ward's diary, 27 October 1937; Countess of Oxford and Asquith to Gwynne, 4 August 1937, Gwynne Papers.

[2] For 1937, Churchill 'contracted ... a total income ... of £13,630 from his books and articles alone: £2,880 from the *Evening Standard*, £4,200 from the *News of the World*' (Gilbert, *Churchill*, V, 785n., 933); Beaverbrook to Driberg, 24 November 1952, Driberg Papers.

[3] Barrington-Ward's diary, 22, 23, and 25 September 1936.

by those whom Tom Jones described as being 'not unwilling to use the marriage controversy as a means of pulling the P.M. down'.[1]

It was a peculiar controversy, which simmered under a tight lid for the better part of a year before coming to a boil. The foreign press, particularly in the United States where Mrs Simpson had been born and well bred, exploited the saga for all it was worth and possibly more besides. All the while, British newspapers maintained a stiff and increasingly awkward silence. 'There was "a gentleman's agreement" which kept the affair out of our Press while it was raging with you and elsewhere,' Jones reported to a transatlantic friend; even 'the *Daily Worker* was behaving properly'. As a result, Jones estimated that 'there must have been millions who had never heard of Mrs Simpson', much less of the constitutional crisis that took shape around her. Newspapermen who mingled in London society were quick to take sides, but sublimated their arguments so as to elude the comprehension of the general public. On 23 November, for example, Barrington-Ward read between the lines of a 'very bad and tendentious leader in the *Daily Mail*', which dealt with 'the King's visit to the Special Areas' and tried 'to draw a distinction between the King's "direct" approach to the problem' of poverty 'and the vacillations and delays of his Ministers'. He attributed this perspective to the fact that Esmond Harmsworth, Rothermere's son, 'has been seen dining lately with Mrs S.', whose cause was thereby circuitously championed.[2]

All pretences were finally abandoned on 2 December, when the King informed Baldwin of his resolve to proceed with the marriage. The next day, in a leading article that differentiated between 'King and Monarchy', *The Times* guardedly spoke out against a union 'incompatible with the Throne'. The King's surmise 'that this morning's comment has been organized' by Baldwin, Dawson, and the Archbishop of Canterbury was dismissed by Barrington-Ward as 'obviously fantastic nonsense'. Baldwin's approval went without saying, but he had not known 'what was going to appear in *The Times*' until the King, fearful that Mrs Simpson would be attacked by name, telephoned 'instructions' for him to vet a proof copy. Disclaiming any 'control over *The Times* or over any other newspaper', Baldwin ('full of apologies') asked to see the piece when it was already 'too late to stop or amend it'. Far from intending to denounce Mrs Simpson, Dawson 'hoped we should never have to mention her'.[3]

'The storm breaks,' Harold Nicolson wrote in his diary on the 3rd. He

---

[1] Jones to Flexner, 12 December 1936, quoted in Jones, *Diary with Letters*, p. 295. For accounts of the Abdication crisis from different points of view, see Gilbert, *Churchill*, V, ch. 41; Barnes and Middlemas, *Baldwin*, ch. 34; Frances Donaldson, *Edward VIII* (London, 1974), ch. 21; and Beaverbrook, *The Abdication of King Edward VIII* (London, 1966).

[2] Jones to Flexner, 12 December 1936, quoted in Jones, *Diary with Letters*, p. 295; Barrington-Ward's diary, 23 November 1936.

[3] Barrington-Ward's diary, 2 and 4 December 1936; Dawson's memorandum, quoted in Wrench, *Dawson*, p. 349.

contrasted 'a fine leading-article in the *Telegraph*' with the 'confused muddled jumble in *The Times*', which amounted to 'an amalgam of tortuous and pompous nothings. The other papers write in sorrow rather than in anger,' he was pleased to observe. Yet *The Times*'s 'amalgam' was crucial and, in most quarters, commanded respect. Walter Runciman, then president of the Board of Trade and a politician whom Dawson held in high esteem, sent congratulations on a leading article that was 'perfect in argument, temper, phraseology and historical sense' and one that would surely give 'a lead to the British Press for which all of us can be and are grateful'. Transmitted by telegraph, the editorial was reproduced in *The New York Times*, where Nicholas Murray Butler, the president of Columbia University, 'read it with a distinct thrill for it represents the old Thunderer at its best'. Cosmo Gordon Lang, who was alleged to have provided inspiration as archbishop, was among the many churchmen who responded with praise. 'I thank you for your admirable leader in *The Times* this morning,' he wrote to Dawson on the 3rd, thus implying that he had not been a party to its composition. 'I note that the *Daily Mail* has broken loose and ventilates the impossible compromise: also *News Chronicle*. I earnestly hope that the Government will stand firm.'[1]

One of the strongest endorsements came from Lady Violet Bonham Carter, Asquith's daughter and an influential Liberal in her own right. 'Thank heaven the forces of decency have routed Beaverbrook, Rothermere, Tom Mosley & Lady Houston,' she told Dawson, 'but that Winston shd. have played their game – just as he seemed to be qualifying to play a really useful part – is tragic & to me quite inexplicable.' Although that was to assign guilt by association, it did not exaggerate the damage to Churchill's credibility. At the outset, he had joined Beaverbrook in encouraging the King to broadcast directly to the nation, but Baldwin declared the idea to be 'thoroughly unconstitutional' and potentially divisive. 'Only three papers would be on your side,' the Prime Minister warned the Sovereign, 'the *News Chronicle*, the *Daily Mail*, and the *Daily Express*.'[2]

Beaverbrook, relentless 'in pursuit of ... a favourable Press for the King', saw Layton for a second time on the 3rd, the day that the *News Chronicle* attracted considerable attention by airing the possibility of a morganatic marriage, possibly – as Baldwin's biographers have deduced – because 'this was the only paper which did not realise that the morganatic scheme was dead' at this point. Beaverbrook also 'had an interview with Mr Elias of the *Daily Herald*', whom he found 'personally favourable to the royal suit', but who was promptly brought to heel by his Labour Party associates. Whether or not Beaverbrook professed that his aim was 'to bugger Baldwin', as Randolph

---

[1] Nicolson, *Diary and Letters*, I. 281; Runciman to Dawson, 3 December 1936, Butler to Dawson, 3 December 1936, and Lang to Dawson, 3 December 1936, Dawson Papers.

[2] Lady Violet Bonham Carter to Dawson, 9 December 1936, Dawson Papers; G. M. Young, *Stanley Baldwin* (London, 1952), pp. 239–40.

Churchill naughtily recounted, he did not deny that Baldwin's removal from Downing Street would have been 'a welcome by-product'. Perhaps, along with Churchill, he and Rothermere were genuinely stirred by the King's plight. It was not unreasonable, however, for Baldwin to assume ulterior motives on the part of the *Daily Mail* and the *Daily Express*, which he told his niece 'I always call the Devil's press'.[1]

On the basis of 'a very sound idea ... as to what line each important paper would take', Beaverbrook counted *The Times*, the *Morning Post*, the *Daily Telegraph*, and the *Daily Herald* among his – and the King's – antagonists. That the Kemsley papers, including the *Sunday Times*, would be hostile 'was only to be expected'. Jones confirmed this line-up and added the *Observer* to the list of ministerial supporters. Like others, he was perplexed by the position of the *News Chronicle*, which was shaken on the morning of the 4th, when Layton had 'an hour's talk' with Vincent Massey, the Canadian High Commissioner, who cited adverse sentiment in the dominions and 'rubbed in the case against the morganatic marriage which the foolish *N.C.* and *Star* have been running'. The *New Statesman*, too, gave serious consideration to the morganatic solution, which, as Baldwin explained to the House on Friday afternoon, the 4th, did not exist under English constitutional law. With this definitive statement, MPs (according to a first-hand account in the next morning's *Telegraph*) 'rose to a striking demonstration so prolonged that, for a while, Mr Baldwin could not continue'. Churchill, who had been expected to pose a supplementary question, sat stunned. Immediately thereafter, the members dispersed for the weekend, which many of them spent in their constituencies, where they discovered opinion to be 'very marked' against the King.[2]

On Saturday morning, Brooks was summoned to breakfast with Rothermere, 'who wanted me to write an article' to be entitled 'I support the King'. Significantly, Brooks shirked the assignment and Rothermere capitulated without so much as a murmur. Neither of them qualifying as constitutional experts, they easily 'agreed that the King might well send for his other advisers, on the precedent of Edward VII and George in 1910 and 1931'. That was a pipe-dream they shared with Churchill, who visualized himself coming to power after the government resigned and Labour declined to step into the breach. 'The King actually saw Winston last night,' revealed Rothermere, 'but the visit is secret.' In fact, Churchill and the King had dined together with Baldwin's permission, and both of them made contact with Beaverbrook afterwards. Rothermere, excluded from these deliberations, did not know what to make of them. Esmond was convinced that 'the line for us to run as a

---

[1] Beaverbrook, *Abdication*, p. 66; Barnes and Middlemas, *Baldwin*, p. 1005n.; Donaldson, *Edward VIII*, pp. 285, 275n.
[2] Beaverbrook, *Abdication*, p. 68; Jones to Flexner, 12 December 1936, quoted in Jones, *Diary with Letters*, p. 295; Barrington-Ward's diary, 4 December 1936.

newspaper group is that of "King's men but not Simpson's men"', and that seemed 'sound enough' to Brooks.[1]

While the Harmsworths were mapping their strategy and Churchill was pleading for time, the King conveyed word of his decision to abdicate. 'Our cock won't fight,' proclaimed Beaverbrook, who recognized the futility of perseverance. 'The responsibility,' he later contended,

> was the King's. Throughout all the days of public controversy he shackled the Press that was favourable to himself. He would allow us no liberty in expressing our views or in arguing for his cause. His chief desire was to secure a minimum of publicity for Mrs Simpson. He was also anxious to avoid any suggestion of conflict with Baldwin. As a result, the pro-Baldwin Press had the field all to itself.

Beaverbrook plainly misjudged both the quantity and the quality of newspaper support for the King. 'Whenever Max was involved in a battle like this he never pulled punches, and the truth was not in him,' wrote J. C. C. Davidson, who knew him well and resented him deeply. 'With a great newspaper', Beaverbrook might have 'had a very strong weapon ... to make a real breach'; but neither his *Daily Express* nor Rothermere's *Daily Mail* were 'siege weapons, for they have no real weight, and it was very striking how the British people refused absolutely to be stirred up by a pro-King hysteria at the behest of the old Rothermere-Beaverbrook Alliance'. To be sure, Davidson was not impartial in his evaluation of Beaverbrook's monarchical sentiments. But Beaverbrook, transparently less emotionally committed than Churchill, allowed room for doubt. Annoyed by Mrs Simpson, who contradicted his advice to the King and ultimately thwarted his campaign, he did not much care what title she adopted and quipped that she should marry Rothermere and become the Queen of Hungary.[2]

'The pro-Baldwin Press', as Beaverbrook called it, had 'had the field all to itself' because it naturally dominated the field. Davidson, who 'saw a great deal of Baldwin at that time', testified that 'SB believed very strongly in the freedom of the press' and did not resort to collusion in order to obtain support that came of its own accord. In dealing with *The Times*, 'all he did was to telephone Dawson and ask him what line he proposed to take'. The notion of a partnership between Baldwin and Dawson, sanctified by the Archbishop of Canterbury, was a fiction. 'For the first few days of the crisis', when Barrington-Ward was in the chair, the performance of *The Times* was rated as 'magnificent; but when Dawson came hastening back from Canada, the newspaper lost its character and even its information became about forty-eight

---

[1] Brooks's diary, 5 December 1936; Donaldson, *Edward VIII*, pp. 279–80.
[2] Taylor, *Beaverbrook*, p. 370; Beaverbrook, *Abdication*, p. 79; Davidson, *Memoirs*, p. 415; Brendon, *Press Barons*, p. 166.

hours out of date'. The feeling in Downing Street was 'that it was essential that one respected national newspaper should be properly informed so that it could give the nation a lead', and *The Times* was not chosen. After meeting Dawson on the afternoon of the 2nd and telephoning him twice that evening, Baldwin 'began to withdraw behind the formal front of the government' and had no further contacts with editors. Full responsibility for press relations devolved upon Davidson, whose special job was to ensure 'that the *Daily Telegraph* was completely informed of all developments'. He recalled that his confidence in Camrose 'was not misplaced; nothing secret was disclosed, and of course I made no attempt to influence the newspaper's attitude'. Consequently, as Frances Donaldson has concluded, 'it was the *Daily Telegraph* and not *The Times* which emerged with most credit from the crisis'.[1]

This protracted episode, which literally culminated in a nine days' wonder, was a distraction from international realities. 'Meanwhile,' H. N. Brailsford reminded the readers of *Reynolds News* (which had just dropped its cumbersome apostrophe), on 6 December, 'against the background of this sour comedy, looms up the tragedy of Madrid.' Tacitly, but no less tellingly for that, the crisis illustrated how diverse newspapers, by 'a gentleman's agreement', willingly suppressed information. In the United States, where libel laws weighed less heavily, such journalistic behaviour would have been regarded as a betrayal of public trust, let alone a dereliction of professional duty. To Colonel R. R. McCormick, the Anglophobic owner of the *Chicago Tribune*, the pusillanimity of the British press was proof that the country had gone Nazi.[2] That was a ludicrous distortion, but scarcely worse than the countervailing proposition that the British press effectively exercised its precious freedom during these pre-war years. With respect to foreign and domestic controversies alike, too little was said until too late. The problem was one of decorum, not dictatorship.

* * *

On 28 May 1937, having dislodged one King and seen through the coronation of another, Baldwin departed from the premiership at the height of his prestige. 'Let the audience not stint its applause,' Beaverbrook declared sardonically in the *Daily Express* the morning after 'the chief actor' had taken 'farewell of the political stage'. Neville Chamberlain, who stepped forward on cue, soon impressed Beaverbrook as 'the best P.M. we've had in half a century', not counting Bonar Law, 'who never got a chance'. Beaverbrook must have been flattered by the rumour that Chamberlain would have liked to appoint him as Colonial Secretary. Racked by asthma and eager to resume his travels, he was not a candidate for office. 'Lord Beaverbrook is done with

[1] Davidson, *Memoirs*, pp. 414–15; Barnes and Middlemas, *Baldwin*, p. 1004; Donaldson, *Edward VIII*, p. 269.
[2] Brendon, *Press Barons*, p. 195.

governments,' he wrote imperiously to Cummings. 'He will never be in any governments any more.' Churchill, who subsequently prevailed upon him to rescind this self-denying ordinance, would have been grateful for an invitation to join the reconstructed ministry. None was forthcoming.[1]

Rothermere was too besotted with Hitler to pay much regard to these changes of personnel at Westminster. Older than his years, he was in failing health and his fortune was wasting away. At the end of 1937, he relinquished the chairmanship of Associated Newspapers to Esmond, who announced that his father 'had no longer any interest in the management of the company or the conduct of its newspapers'. Esmond also replaced Rothermere as chairman of the Daily Mail and General Trust, which had expanded its name to indicate the breadth of its holdings. Finally, in November 1940, Rothermere died out of harm's way in Bermuda, where his doctors and Beaverbrook had contrived to send him, and Esmond inherited the viscountcy. 'Esmond Harmsworth does not really know anything about the newspaper business and probably cares less, although he works hard at it,' a friend told Brooks, who agreed that it was 'difficult to think of Esmond as Lord Rothermere'.[2]

The cast of characters had changed considerably. Baldwin and Samuel took peerages, leaving their parties to be led by Chamberlain and Sir Archibald Sinclair, respectively. Attlee continued at the helm of the Labour opposition, but with a diffidence that deflected attention. The withdrawal of the older press lords, which was only temporary in Beaverbrook's case, created openings into which Camrose and Kemsley quietly insinuated themselves. Yet the fundamental issues remained the same, however different the spirit in which they were approached.

In 1938, shortly before Mass-Observation initiated its inquiries and public opinion polls were introduced, PEP (Political and Economic Planning) undertook the first systematic survey of the relationship between British newspapers and their readers. 'A government in office exercises a twofold influence on the Press,' it reported, 'through office departmental channels and through party headquarters. This latter influence is shared with the Opposition parties.' That discovery was neither profound nor controversial. It was followed, however, by a set of three categories into which journals were 'roughly divided', and these proved altogether more problematical. The first of these groups encompassed 'non-political' organs, 'such as most provincial weeklies'. The second consisted of 'the avowed political organs', of which three – all located on the left – were designated. To the third classification belonged 'the more or less "independent"' papers, most of which were acknowledged to 'have strong

---

[1] Beaverbrook to R. B. Bennett, 9 March 1938, and Beaverbrook to Cummings, 27 March 1937, quoted in Taylor, *Beaverbrook*, pp. 373, 379.

[2] Addison, 'Patriotism Under Pressure,' in Peele and Cook, eds., *Politics of Reappraisal*, pp. 205–206; Camrose, *British Newspapers*, pp. 54–55; Hugh Cudlipp, *The Prerogative of the Harlot* (London, 1980), p. 176; Brooks's diary, 31 January 1941.

political convictions, even if they do not toe the party line'. Cutting across these classifications – with sufficient force to negate them – was the further admission that 'newspapers naturally reproduce the propaganda of the parties they support, and this in many cases strongly flavours their treatment of the news'.[1]

This report, given the rudimentary procedures of investigation and the agency of sponsorship, could no more have been expected to yield insights than to avoid a bias. Yet, in addition to evincing a disregard for antecedents, it betrayed a striking ignorance of current practices. The categories it postulated were far from discreet, each embracing as it did a wide range of contradictory impulses. Nor were the lines of communication either as clear or constant as was implied. To bracket the *Daily Herald* and *Reynolds News* with the *Daily Worker* as the mainstays of party journalism, and concurrently to accept *The Times* and the *Daily Telegraph* at face value as 'independent' (even between quotation marks), was not so much to engage in simplification as to pervert meanings. If, for whatever reason, the press delivered a distorted image of the world, it was equally true that the press itself was seriously misrepresented.

Without denying that successive Foreign Secretaries and their Cabinet colleagues continually attempted to 'inspire' *The Times* and other newspapers, usually as a safeguard against what Runciman condemned as 'adventurous speculations', Colin Seymour-Ure has trenchantly argued that allegations of impropriety can be considered 'valid only in an extremely narrow way'. Dawson, as much by his social proclivities as by his professional conduct, invited accusations that he had 'used improper *means* to achieve influence' and moreover 'sought influence towards improper *ends*'. Given the circumstantial nature of the evidence brought against him, he is not indictable on either count. His devotion to the cause of appeasement was obvious, but its effects may be exaggerated and its motives misconstrued. However grievously wrong his assumptions about foreign affairs, it did not follow correlatively that he betrayed 'journalistic values', whatever those might have been. In his 'exercise of editorial discretion', Dawson was merely using the resources at his disposal – as any of his counterparts would have done – to advance views to which he was genuinely committed. To single him out is to concede to *The Times* a pre-eminence that was no longer its due. Worse than that, it is to shift the burden of responsibility from Downing Street to Fleet Street.[2]

The failure of *The Times* to dissociate itself from government positions was a reflection of its own weakness. 'Like other Editors,' the historians of that paper have maintained, 'Dawson ... consulted his personal preferences among

[1] PEP, *Report on the British Press* (London, 1938), p. 206. Founded in 1931, PEP was a non-partisan body of businessmen, academics, and public officials who examined a variety of social and economic areas.
[2] Seymour-Ure, *The Political Impact of Mass Media* (London, 1974), pp. 81, 87–98. For a crude assertion of the contrary view, see Harrison, *Poor Men's Guardians*, p. 205, which says that 'it was the sheer fog generated and cast over events by a poisoned press that prevented a practical anti-war coalition emerging out of the many-sided anti-fascism of the later thirties'.

Conservative statesmen' (several of whom were actually Liberal Nationals) and gave 'no hint that he consulted statesmen, whether Conservative or not, who were known to oppose the policy of the party' as executed by its standard-bearers. Consultation was always a selective process and should not imply dictation. On both sides of the appeasement debate, politicians frequently complained that they had given their time and counsel only to see their stands challenged or compromised by supposedly friendly newspapers. Dawson, who 'would have argued that it is no use telling politicians to do what politicians had decided is utterly impossible', gave less offence than some of his contemporaries. There was no mistaking him for a lackey, however.[1]

Because opinion was sharply divided within each parliamentary encampment, journalists rarely had to abjure partisanship in order to register dissent. *The Times*, which Hazlitt had long ago described as 'ever strong upon the stronger side', identified not so much with the Conservative interest as with the ministerial mind. Even those papers that continued to profess explicit party allegiances tended to avail themselves of the increased opportunities to pick and choose. Out of sophistication or desperation, party leaders came to accept this situation. Sinclair, combining both attributes, thanked Crozier 'for the general publicity' that the *Manchester Guardian* gave to the Liberal effort. 'It is really an immense encouragement ... to know that we have the solid, but not indiscriminate, backing of your great newspaper.' That was the most that any party could have expected.[2]

At least until the Munich crisis, when fissures widened, Chamberlain enjoyed overlapping advantages for publicity as leader of the Conservative Party and head of a nominally National administration. Although complementary, each status was separate and the second clearly took precedence. In the event, Chamberlain proved more firmly entrenched as party chief than as premier. Yet, while they lasted, these parallel arrangements secured him 'a remarkably easy ride from the press'.[3]

Whereas Beaverbrook welcomed Chamberlain as an improvement upon Baldwin, Garvin was quick to decide that 'the best course of procedure' was to 'finish Chamberlain as soon as possible' so that the *Observer* 'should be as little interfered with as possible'. Through Sir Joseph Ball, who administered the Conservative Research Department, Chamberlain had ample means to interfere with the editorial process. By taking 'certain steps privately', Ball 'destroyed the cases of Eden and Cranborne', who resigned from the Foreign Office on 20 February 1938 in protest against the Prime Minister's exercises in personal diplomacy. But for Ball's efforts to square newspaper opinion, the sensation caused by Eden's departure would have been all the greater. Instead,

---

[1] *History of The Times*, IV, part 2, 1008.
[2] Sinclair to Crozier, 5 August 1937, *Guardian* Archives.
[3] Ramsden, *Conservative Party Policy*, p. 87. In addition, Chamberlain continued as chairman of the Conservative Research Department.

Eden was further isolated. According to the *Manchester Guardian* (24 February), whose castigation Ball apparently took as a tribute to his own skills, 'the Government press' presented a 'curiously distorted' picture of the incident and 'for the most part . . . preserved a unity of silence that could hardly be bettered in a totalitarian state'.[1]

Ball was one of Chamberlain's trusty servants in *pourparlers* with foreign dignitaries. His techniques for dealing with Fleet Street potentates were no less furtive. In neither sphere, however, did Chamberlain rely exclusively on intermediaries. The week before Eden's resignation, when hints of a Cabinet rift began to circulate, the Prime Minister planted an article in the *Sunday Times* to scotch 'rumours of differences between himself and Anthony'. Kemsley, the recipient of a direct approach from Downing Street, gladly complied on the 13th and must have shared the embarrassment when events promptly belied his rebuttal.[2]

The Berry brothers, Kemsley and Camrose, were especially devoted to Chamberlain and eager to do his bidding. They did not presume, as their Victorian predecessors perpetually had done, to offer their own recommendations with regard to policies and appointments. Nor, at this juncture, did Beaverbrook. 'I know you have influence with the P.M. & that it is likely to become as great as it was with Bonar Law,' Cummings wrote flatteringly to him. 'Why don't you persuade him to take in Winston, who would put into re-armament a snap and directive power it sorely needs?' Beaverbrook felt no such temptation. The cost of bringing Churchill into the government would be 'a guarantee to Czecho-Slovakia that we will fight in defence of that artificial nation', for which Beaverbrook felt as little sympathy as did Garvin or Dawson. 'Of all the alternatives offered to us', Beaverbrook considered Churchill, an anti-isolationist who preached collective security, to be 'the worst'. When Beaverbrook eventually turned against the Chamberlain administration, it was decidedly not in a Churchillian direction. 'How I hate them on account of their neglect of agriculture and the Colonial Empire,' he angrily declared the following summer.[3]

Beaverbrook was too preoccupied with financial transactions – and, for long stretches, too far removed from the nerve centre of political journalism – to pay sustained attention to international developments. Consequently, wishful thinking overwhelmed his judgment. 'Britain will not be involved in a European war this year, or next year either,' the *Daily Express* recklessly assured its

---

[1] Memorandum by Garvin, 12 October 1937, Garvin Papers; Ball to Chamberlain, 21 February 1938, quoted in Ramsden, *Conservative Party Policy*, p. 87.

[2] *The Diaries of Sir Alexander Cadogan, 1938–1945* (ed. D. Dilks; London, 1971), p. 47.

[3] Cummings to Beaverbrook, 14 March 1938, and Beaverbrook to Cummings, 16 March 1938 (copy), Beaverbrook Papers, C/104; Beaverbrook to Grigg, 20 June 1938, quoted in Taylor, *Beaverbrook*, p. 383; Beaverbrook to Waters, 12 August 1938, Waters Papers. Garvin and Beaverbrook were both in contact with Hoare, sometimes through Grigg. Grigg to Garvin, 25 January 1938 (copy?), Grigg Papers.

readers on 30 September 1938. The last four words of that notorious streamer headline were appended by the proprietor, who came to regret them. Although erratic, Beaverbrook's control over editorial performances remained absolute, though he would never admit as much. More candidly, Kemsley subsequently boasted to a delegation of Canadian journalists that, from his room at Kemsley House, 'I dictate all the leading articles printed in my papers'. With Rothermere out of commission, no one else was entitled to advance such a sweeping claim. Few would have wished to do so.[1]

Who, then, bore responsibility for what was published and, no less important, what was not? This question was posed with mounting urgency not only by the anti-appeasers, but also by certain fringe elements, who likewise saw themselves as the victims of an embargo. Historians, positing a black-and-white dichotomy between the government and its critics, have often ignored the shades of opinion on both sides. Divided among themselves, those who warned against the Nazi menace were not the only ones to complain of unfair treatment by the press and, in fact, were not nearly so disadvantaged as legend would have it. The columns of Liberal, Labour, and select Tory provincial journals (most notably the *Yorkshire Post*) were open to their views. If the editor of *The Times* refused to accommodate their letters, the *Daily Telegraph* (recalling its courtesy to Lord Lansdowne in 1917) was more gracious. The Communists had the *Daily Worker*, for what it was worth, and were not ignored elsewhere.

Truth to tell, it was the Mosleyites who suffered the greatest deprivation. With equal detriment to their flagging crusade, the wearing of political uniforms was proscribed by legislation and news of their activities was circumscribed by yet another 'gentleman's agreement'. Dorothy, Viscountess Downe, who was adopted at North Norfolk as the British Union candidate (a personal friend of Queen Mary, she abridged her party tag 'to eliminate the Fascist savour'), told Brooks that Mosley was 'extremely anxious to get reports of his meetings into the Press – not support editorially, but publicity'. At a private lunch with Brooks, whom he considered 'far more valuable to the Right outside his movement than in it', Mosley admitted that he was 'a little perturbed that nobody will report his meetings. He does not want support, but report.' Nicolson, who had once tended to his publicity needs, had disowned him. Rothermere, whom Mosley later described as having lacked 'the exceptional character necessary to take a strong line towards the end of a successful life', had been frightened away. Lady Houston reportedly withdrew her support when 'a paragraph in *Action*, or some other journal connected with us', suggested that 'she was a vain and silly old woman'. Thus Mosley could neither control the small and unruly weeklies he had spawned nor obtain coverage from the respectable press.

[1] Taylor, *Beaverbrook*, p. 384; Evidence, Royal Commission on the Press, 1947–49, Cd. 7318, q. 698.

His complaints were uniquely justified. Whether he deserved his fate is beside the point.[1]

Newspapermen, striving to second-guess the government and thereby to preserve an equilibrium at home and abroad, more or less conformed to their gentlemanly code. At the same time, they were increasingly taxed by problems of accountability. Whom did they represent? What interests did they serve? To which groups or individuals did they owe service or, at the very least, explanations? Barrington-Ward was shaken by a 'controversial talk on the telephone' with R.H. (later 1st Baron) Brand on 17 February 1938, the day after a leading article in *The Times* had ventured that strengthened defences were not incompatible with the intensified pursuance of an Anglo-German accord. 'Brand is always negative,' remarked Dawson, who had known him since Kindergarten days in South Africa. Barrington-Ward, more concerned with proprietorial proprieties, stiffly maintained that 'a director of the paper should not butt in with his views'. If that was the case, what were directors for? That issue was highlighted in early June, when Walter took strong exception to *The Times*'s proposals for satisfying the demands of the Sudeten Germans at the expense of Czechoslovakian integrity. Dawson replied by pitting his 'own experience' against the sentiments of the co-chief proprietor. Neither Walter's forbears nor – certainly – Northcliffe would ever have brooked such defiance.[2]

For better or worse, the editorial luminaries of the 1930s were self-consciously their own men. They effectively established their hegemonies by discountenancing directives from above and by manifesting an ambivalent solicitude towards their reading publics. Most obvious at *The Times*, this shift of gravity was replicated at the *News Chronicle*, where the removal of dissident members from the board had the passing effect of making it easier to hold the Cadburys at bay. Allowing for differences of personality and circumstances, the same patterns were visible at the *Manchester Guardian*, the *Yorkshire Post*, and the *New Statesman*. In each of these cases, and arguably several others, editorial dignity eclipsed competing influences.

Not every editorial office, of course, was tenanted by a luminary. More usually, proprietors kept a tight rein on editors, who were relegated to the shadows. Garvin, aware that his lustre had dimmed, redoubled his efforts to obtain a shareholding in the *Observer*. In rapid succession, Francis Williams and Percy Cudlipp learnt the hard way that the political directors of the *Daily Herald* had more than mere ornamental value. Christiansen survived at the *Daily Express*, like Watson at the *Daily Telegraph* and numerous others, by accepting the fact of his subservience. The Kemsley and Rothermere properties were edited – nominally, at any rate – by an assortment of nonentities who left no mark on their papers, much less on posterity. At the end of 1938,

[1] Brooks's diary, 21 February and 3 March 1938; Mosley, *My Life* (London, 1968), pp. 346–48.
[2] Barrington-Ward's diary, 17 February 1938; *History of The Times*, IV, part 2, 913, 921–22.

Brooks severed his 'formal attachment' with the *Daily Mail* and the *Sunday Dispatch*, continuing 'for a while' his 'not satisfactory ... position as a kind of adopted son' to Rothermere.[1]

To speak of editorial luminaries, therefore, may be to skew perspectives. Relatively few individuals aspired to this status and fewer still achieved it. The years before the Second World War did not qualify, like those before the First World War, as an age of great editors. Nevertheless, because so many contemporary polemics and historical assessments have emphasized the editorial contribution to appeasement, it is necessary to investigate the charges against those 'guilty men' who unmistakably wielded editorial power.

Barrington-Ward conveniently serves the purpose. In the spring of 1938, he declined a lucrative appointment at the BBC, convinced that 'I should have shirked something in giving up' the deputy editorship of *The Times*. He was not thinking selfishly about the succession to Dawson, which came his way in 1941, but rather about the superior opportunities at Printing House Square for 'having some hand in the events of one's day, and that is not, I hope, a contemptible ambition'. On the contrary, what may be regarded as contemptible was his failure to take a stronger hand. A. P. Ryan, who served successive editors of *The Times*, later speculated that things would have been different had Barrington-Ward taken over a decade earlier. Admittedly 'biased with the need to avoid almost at all costs a second world war', he was 'much more likely to have been influenced by the editorial staff at home and in continental posts. ... He would not have been got at by Halifax and co.', with the 'probability ... that, with him as editor, *The Times* would have been nearer to Duff Cooper and even Churchill than Halifax'.[2]

To say that *The Times* might have stood nearer to Duff Cooper, whose reputation as an anti-appeaser has been inflated, is not to say very much at all. In other respects, too, Ryan's interpretation is more notable for its generosity than for its substance. Barrington-Ward was less aloof from his colleagues than Dawson and certainly less snobbish. Yet he moved at the peripheries of the same circles and imbibed the same influences. Late in 1938, Wickham Steed published a book, *The Press*, in which a recriminatory 'postscript' (dated 14 October) had been hastily inserted. In his diary, Barrington-Ward took note of this 'v. characteristic effort' on the part of Dawson's predecessor:

> Quite good in the main (thanks to Stanley Morison's help) but containing some gratuitous, hostile references to *TT* and a postscript accusing, without evidence given, unnamed newspapers which do not share Steed's opinions on relations with Germany (i.e. his lifelong Germanophobia) of subservience to some clandestine Governmental organization and to pressure from

[1] Brooks's diary, 31 December 1938.
[2] Barrington-Ward's diary, 28 June 1938; memorandum by A. P. Ryan [*circa* 1970], Woods Papers.

large advertisers. ... The allegation, if it affects *TT*, is completely false. Obviously untrue in any case since every newspaper during the [Munich] crisis has taken the line it might have been expected to take.

More than any leading article he wrote or assigned to be written, this private remonstrance elucidates Barrington-Ward's position and, by extension, *The Times*'s.[1]

Steed's accusations, which Barrington-Ward paraphrased without prejudice, were specifically that the British press was acting 'partly in response to suggestions "confidentially" made by some clandestine organisation that represents, or pretends to represent, the views of official quarters' and partly out of intimidation by 'certain large advertising agents' who warned that to 'cause an alarm ... was "bad for trade"'. Both charges were eventually brought before the Royal Commission on the Press, which discounted the first and dismissed the second. Although it may have been 'a common impression among journalists at that time', the notion that advertisers (whom Mosley, among others, did not hesitate to characterize as Jewish activists) had held newspapers to ransom was not substantiated. Steed, whom the commissioners 'interviewed privately ... at his own request', could supply 'no precise information about newspapers' having succumbed to 'organised pressure ... by advertising interests.'[2]

Not surprisingly, it proved easier to instance attempts to sway editorial policy by members of the government, agents of the Conservative Central Office, and the director of the Conservative Research Department. Arthur Mann of the *Yorkshire Post* saw 'nothing unusual in that'. As he well knew, other parties as well as discordant factions within the Conservative fold behaved similarly, just as politicians had always done. The editor of the *Glasgow Herald* recalled an occasion when 'a senior member of the Cabinet' had 'made it quite clear that he and his colleagues thought that our shortcomings were due to lack of information'. Far from taking that as a threat, confidential or otherwise, the editor simply 'thanked him and said we took note of what he said'. There was no harm in trying, but also no guarantee that the effort would not serve to stiffen a paper's resistance. The *Glasgow Herald* was no more deflected from its course by this unidentified Cabinet minister than the *News Chronicle* was chastened by a disapprobatory message that Layton received from Goebbels. Again, Steed's cloak-and-dagger view does not hold.[3]

With lengthened hindsight, what conclusions can be drawn? While it would be futile to deny that external pressures were applied or, at least, vaguely sensed, it would be foolhardy to suppose that these particular influences were

---

[1] Taylor, *Beaverbrook*, pp. 385–86; Barrington-Ward's diary, 10 November 1938.
[2] Steed, *The Press*, pp. 249–50; Report, Royal Commission on the Press, 1947–49, Cd. 7700, pp. 136–37.
[3] Report, Royal Commission on the Press, 1947–49, Cd. 7700, p. 137.

the operative ones. So far as one can tell with any degree of certainty, official coercion was neither more widespread nor more intense during the late 1930s, when antithetical pressures were also being exerted. As Barrington-Ward rightly pointed out, newspapers invariably took the very lines that they could have been expected to take, with or without the 'evil counsel' that Steed alleged. For his own part, Barrington-Ward adamantly insisted that he had followed his own lights, and it would be unreasonable to dispute his claim. Nor is there any cause to dispute the fact that those lights blinded him. In both respects, he was typical of the pivotal figures in British journalism during that period of moral confusion. Whatever tutelage they may have received from whatever minatory power would have been superfluous, for they were resolved to commit their own mistakes.

Sixteen

THE SHIVER SISTERS BOW OUT

At the end of September 1938, Chamberlain met Hitler at Munich, where – with French and Italian complicity – he bartered Czechoslovakian territory for a flimsy assurance of 'peace in our time'. While easing the immediate diplomatic crisis, the Munich settlement intensified the crisis of conscience within British political society.

It has been suggested that Munich marked a departure in the conduct of British foreign policy: a shift from familiar concepts of appeasement, imbued with a spirit of magnanimity and predicated on moral considerations, to a bastardized version, born of weakness and implemented out of desperation. More usually, however, the episode has been seen as the culmination of pre-existing trends. In any case, Munich brought out the vital issues in full relief. No longer was there any serious doubt about Germany's readiness to resort to war or the lengths that British statesmen were prepared to go to avert that risk. Clusters of dissident Conservatives, who had hitherto stood apart from one another with pitiable ineffectuality, now moved towards a common ground. At the same time that Eden and his fellow 'glamour boys' (as they were known to their ministerial detractors) forged links with 'the Winston brigade' (which Nicolson had prudently hesitated to join), contacts were extended among Liberal and Labour activists, who likewise strove to subordinate their mutual suspicions and resentments. At last, an alliance of anti-appeasers was taking shape, embracing individuals of diverse persuasions and varying degrees of fortitude.[1]

With limited effects in the House of Commons, where Chamberlain was accorded a standing ovation upon his return from Munich, the government's critics assembled in the corridors and smoking-rooms at Westminster, at private luncheon and dinner parties, and, most prominently, in the columns of the opposition press. From their experience, it becomes clear that 'opposition' had expanded beyond its customary boundaries to acquire a new meaning. For, like the anti-appeasers themselves, the newspapers that supported them were recruited – to a greater or lesser extent – from all parties. To be sure, it was more

[1] Martin Gilbert, *The Roots of Appeasement* (London, 1966), epilogue; Neville Thompson, *The Anti-Appeasers* (Oxford, 1971), ch. 10.

natural for those with Liberal or Labour affiliations to engage in criticism of the National administration. Yet each of the journals that opposed appeasement found itself at odds with considerable segments of party and popular opinion.

In January 1938, the *News Chronicle* had instituted regular 'policy conferences', initially held at monthly intervals. The agendas were directly influenced by developments within the parliamentary community, where Eden's 'Group' soon began informal and somewhat desultory discussions of foreign problems. Simultaneously, comparable bodies emerged within the Liberal and Labour folds, where analogous dissensions were provoked by Continental events. These constellations moved in orbits that did not as yet intersect. To achieve concentricity, *Reynolds News* issued a call on 20 March for a 'united democratic alliance' against the forces of disruption abroad and capitulation at home. The board of the *News Chronicle* welcomed this overture 'as an indication that Labour may be modifying its policy and is coming to recognize that its chances of winning the next election single-handed are small'. As much out of concern for electoral prospects as for international imperatives, the *News Chronicle* resolved to work on behalf of a 'Peace Alliance', thus avoiding the Communist connotation of a 'Popular Front'.[1]

On the whole, newspapers were a good deal less constrained than parliamentarians, who had to contend with the demands of their respective whips and constituency associations. Journalists, provided that they did not jeopardize circulations and occasionally even if they did, had licence to sit on fences or straddle them. This greater latitude, which was not fully exploited in every instance, derived partly from commercial factors, partly from a breakdown in communications between editors and party officials, and, not least, from newspapermen's own awareness that their electoral influence had diminished. For all three reasons and probably others as well, Henry Cadbury had grown 'quite sure that ... the ordinary reader is not so politically minded as he was 30 years ago', before questions of gender had helped to complicate matters. 'Party politics, I think, are now almost a dead issue,' he told Layton, 'and indeed may actually put off some of our new readers obtained through the canvassing method.'[2] Amid the general confusion, it was easy for newspapers to back away from the controversies that divided parties, but still more tempting for them to side with one faction against another. The *News Chronicle* and the *Manchester Guardian* took advantage of Liberal disunity to speak their own minds. The *Daily Herald* finally broke with its pacifist tradition to espouse rearmament, much to the distress of certain Labour fundamentalists. With less impunity, the *Yorkshire Post* and the *Glasgow Herald* were among the most conspicuous of the Conservative dailies that stood opposed to the government's foreign policy.

Whether they promoted appeasement or deplored it, newspapers did not – of course – reflect the unanimous opinion of the people who produced them. This

[1] Notes, Policy Conference No. 3, 1 April 1938, Layton Papers.
[2] Henry Cadbury to Layton, 31 May 1938, Layton Papers.

fact, however elementary, cannot be over-emphasized. In addition, there is a second stereotype that must be challenged. Contrary to received opinion, newspapers rarely acted upon dictation from the public figures whom they supported in the heated debate over appeasement. That was equally true of the papers that defended the government's foreign policy and those that assailed it, all dependent on the same sources. Instructions were indeed issued, but whether they were accepted was more or less a matter of editorial discretion. Collusion was the journalist's prerogative and not the politician's due. 'I can call spirits from the vasty deep,' Glendower boasted to Hotspur in Shakespeare's *Henry IV*. 'Why, so can I, or so can any man,' retorted Hotspur. 'But will they come when you do call for them?'

After communicating with Vansittart and Halifax on 12 August 1938, John Tower, the chief leader-writer of the *Yorkshire Post*, advised his editor that the Foreign Office was providing 'information necessary for guidance' to four 'responsible' newspapers: *The Times*, the *Daily Telegraph*, the *Manchester Guardian*, and the *Yorkshire Post*. 'There is no desire whatever that the four papers mentioned ... should display a false optimism' about German intentions. 'But the desire is expressed that they will allow the information coming from Germany to reach the public gradually without giving it an immediately panic-character.' Significantly, no official attempt was made to discourage the 'popular' journals 'from talking rather more optimistically, the explanation ... being that if they were warned off that line they would immediately become sensationally pessimistic and might create in advance the very conditions of popular panic upon which Nazis are known to reckon as one of their weapons'. Thus, the Foreign Office operated both selectively and decorously in its relations with the press. Its reluctance to infringe editorial sovereignty was epitomized when Halifax 'caused to be suggested' to Tower 'that the next leader of the *Y.P.* dealing with the crisis might perhaps conveniently take the line' that Germany should desist from military 'measures ... calculated to be a stumbling block to her neighbours'. The Foreign Secretary could not have been more punctilious. Tower, 'after consulting the F.O.' and especially 'after hearing of the increasingly grave view taken by the French Government', drafted an article that 'accorded fully with Lord Halifax's views'.[1] The *Manchester Guardian* responded with similar speed and effect, but the *Daily Telegraph* took its time, and *The Times* remained flatulently optimistic.

The most notorious case in point was *The Times*'s *ballon d'essai* on 7 September, which put the case for the dismemberment of Czechoslovakia. Drafted by Leo Kennedy, the text was hurriedly revised by Dawson, who regarded it as 'a very mild suggestion, and one that has been consistently made before, that no avenue should be left unexplored which might lead to settlement' of the Sudeten question. Acknowledging that it was exceedingly 'difficult to predict anything in these days with events changing from hour to hour',

[1] Tower to Mann, 12 August 1938, Mann Papers.

Dawson believed that this leading article, 'which caused so much hubbub, did good rather than harm'. Admittedly, it did not go down well at the Foreign Office, which authorized its representative at Prague to disown *The Times*'s views. But Halifax 'did not seem at all to dissent' when Dawson kept an appointment to lunch with him at the Travellers' later that day. 'Halifax does not dissent, privately,' Barrington-Ward heard afterwards from Dawson, 'though the Foreign Office is in a high state of indignation about it.' Dawson further understood that Attlee and Eden were 'perfectly sensible' about *The Times*'s suggestions.[1]

Nevertheless, it was instantly assumed that Dawson had been 'inspired' by Halifax, presumably during the preceding weekend, which the two of them had spent in Yorkshire. In *The Week* (8 September), Claud Cockburn went so far as to allege that Halifax had conveyed a formal request from the Cabinet. Dawson considered such charges too absurd to warrant a contradiction, but his reticence seemed merely to confirm suspicions. The anti-appeasers were not alone in leaping to conclusions. Decades later, R.A. (by then Lord) Butler, who had been under-secretary at the Foreign Office at the time, was 'convinced that Halifax knew this article was to appear: the two Yorkshiremen were very close and I saw Dawson leaving the Office on the 6th after a long interview with the Foreign Secretary'. When Butler was asked for details to substantiate his claim, his memory grew vague: 'All I am certain about is that there was some contact between the two men, Halifax and Dawson.' There is no evidence that this contact occurred before the afternoon of the 7th, when the leader was already in print. Halifax may have welcomed its sentiments, but it is highly unlikely that he had assisted in formulating them.[2]

Through the commotion, Dawson remained sanguine. 'I am not myself apprehensive of a general war, though it is obviously a time of great anxiety and there is no knowing what results any "incidents" might produce,' he wrote to John Walter on 14 September. Over the next few weeks, as the Germans became more strident and the French more craven, anxieties deepened. 'Quite a number of people say there is no danger of war,' Frank Waters noted in his diary on the 26th. 'This is not due to any subtle reasoning or inspired political prevision. They say the war-talk is due to scaremongering by newspapers. Nothing more.' Two days later, trenches were dug in Regent's Park, virtually at the private doorsteps of Dawson and Barrington-Ward.[3]

The parallels with August 1914 were striking, if pointlessly belaboured. Resolved not to repeat history, which it interpreted to its own convenience, the press forbore from inciting popular opinion. Then, as *The Times* rhapsodized

---

[1] Dawson to Walter, 14 September 1938, quoted in *History of The Times*, IV, part 2, 934–35; Barrington-Ward's diary, 9 September 1938.
[2] Butler, *The Art of the Possible* (London, 1971), p. 69; Butler to Woods, 17 April 1972, Woods Papers.
[3] Dawson to Walter, 14 September 1938, quoted in *History of The Times*, IV, part 2, 934–35; Waters's diary, 26 September 1938.

(29 September), Chamberlain boldly went 'On to Munich'. At least 'for the moment', he had succeeded where Sir Edward Grey had failed twenty-four summers previously. 'It would be reckless to build high even upon the broad-based consultation which has now been achieved,' the paper conceded. The results 'may be no more than a respite', but an 'imminent war' had been averted and that itself was cause for gratitude. As Christmas approached, *The Times* offered its readers the opportunity to purchase special greeting cards bearing an exclusive souvenir photograph of the Prime Minister (just back from Munich), his wife, the King, and the Queen, waving to the crowd from the balcony of Buckingham Palace. Shakily, peace continued to prevail.

Duff Cooper resigned from the Cabinet in protest against the Munich agreement. *The Times* (suppressing an account of his speech by Anthony Winn, its lobby correspondent) rejected his criticisms as 'facile and false' (4 October); but other newspapers took them – and the betrayal of Czechoslovakia – more seriously. Anti-ministerial voices, hushed during the emergency, were again audible. They were quickly stilled, however, by calculations that Chamberlain, if pushed too far, might dissolve Parliament and appeal to the country, where his popularity was redoubtable. Except for a declaration of war, a general election was the most widely dreaded prospect. The government, though supremely confident of victory in the event, feared the divisive effects of a campaign at this juncture. Its assailants, divided between and within parties, faced the threat of annihilation at the polls.

On 5 October, Collin Brooks called at the Conservative Central Office to deliver Rothermere's 'plea for an immediate General Election', with a view to obliterating the fragmented opposition. That day, writing in his diary, Barrington-Ward reported a din of 'General Election talk. Election may be necessary if Neville is not given a chance,' he reasoned. 'But it will look like a too clever exploitation of the escape from war and might do much harm eventually.' Lady Chamberlain, Sir Austen's widow, shared these trepidations. In a conversation with Barrington-Ward on 10 November, she contemplated that her brother-in-law 'may be forced by the present critical clamour into a General Election, just when he wants to get on with further agreements' to stabilize European affairs. *The Times* and the *Daily Mail*, once Siamese twins in Northcliffe's nursery, now urged divergent courses: the former maintained that Chamberlain's purpose would best be served by shunning electoral combat; the latter, by precipitating it.[1]

Chamberlain's dilemma was as nothing compared to that of his adversaries, who could afford neither to keep silent nor to force the issue. The Liberal papers advocated a reshuffle that would bring Churchill into office. This method was intended to obtain what an election would certainly preclude. J. A.

---

[1] Barrington-Ward's diary, 5 October and 10 November 1938; Brooks's diary, 5 October 1938. Iain McLean has bewared of 'grandiose generalisations' in interpreting the post-Munich by-election returns at Oxford and Bridgwater, Cook and Ramsden, eds., *By-Elections*, ch. 6.

Spender, who had severed his link with the *News Chronicle* in 1935 and had since been writing for the 'nice, lively but decent and serious papers' of the Westminster provincial group, vehemently disapproved of the idea. In the curious company of Garvin, whose outstanding merit – according to Keynes – was 'that he makes the worse cause appear the worser', Spender applauded Simon's resolute defence of the government's foreign policy. 'It will be interesting some day,' he told Simon, 'to know what has been going on behind the scenes between Tory dissentients & left-wing Liberals & what made the *News Chronicle* suddenly proclaim Winston as its hero & leader.' As one 'Wee Free' to another, disregarding subsequent changes in nomenclature, Spender thought it 'a deplorable business to see the old Liberalism thus reduced'.[1]

It was understandable, if unreasonable, for Spender to resent the *News Chronicle*'s tactic as a repudiation of his editorial paternity and its own party heritage. Yet, in journalism as in other areas, Liberalism had completely lost coherence. The rancorous dispute over appeasement created yet another division that cut across pre-existing ones. Like the Asquiths and other prominent Liberal families, the Cadburys were deeply split. Outraged by attacks on Chamberlain, Paul Cadbury announced to his cousin, Laurence, that he was giving up the *News Chronicle* for the *Birmingham Post*, 'and I think that there must be many thousands of your readers who will feel the same'. With assurances to Layton 'that I am not in agreement with Paul's line of argument', Laurence Cadbury disclosed that he had met Eden on the evening of the 7th, which may help to account for the *News Chronicle*'s recommendations.[2] The *Manchester Guardian* braved comparable displeasure to promote an anti-appeasement alliance.

The 'left-wing Liberals' in Bouverie Street – among them Vernon Bartlett, who won a November by-election at Bridgwater as a self-styled Independent Progressive – were inveterately sceptical about the procedures and results at Munich. So, too, were the allegedly right-wing socialists at the *Daily Herald*, who insisted that Chamberlain's initiative did not 'in any way absolve us from the necessity of continued clear analysis of the facts' (29 September). It was more difficult for the *Herald* to accept Churchill, of all people, as a potential saviour. 'There is only one danger of Fascism, of censorship, the unification of parties, of national "discipline",' warned Robert Fraser, then a young leader-writer on the *Herald* and later chairman of Independent Television News, 'and that will come if Chamberlain is overthrown by the Jingoes in his own party, led by Winston, who will then settle down, with his lousy and reactionary friends, to organize the nation on Fascist principles for a war to settle scores with

---

[1] Spender to Clive Pearson, March [n.d.] 1935, quoted in Harris, *Spender*, p. 224; Spender to Simon, 6 October 1938, and Garvin to Simon, 11 October 1938, Simon Papers; Kingsley Martin, *Editor*, p. 244.

[2] L. J. Cadbury to Layton, 8 October 1938, enclosing Paul Cadbury to L. J. Cadbury, 7 October 1938 (copy), Layton Papers.

Hitler.'[1] The *Daily Telegraph*, which counted Churchill among its regular contributors, knew the difference between Conservatism and Fascism. 'Only the most blunt, plain, even brutal language will make its effect,' Churchill had proclaimed in his column on 15 September. The *Telegraph* came to heed this injunction. 'Great as is the debt we owe to Mr Chamberlain,' it declared on 3 October, 'it would be greater still if he had stood out more forcefully' in aid of Czechoslovakia.

In contrast to *The Times*, the *Observer*, and the *Sunday Times* (owned by Kemsley, the more dutiful Berry brother), Camrose's *Telegraph* paid increasingly studious attention to German moral transgressions. At most, it gave stinted praise to Chamberlain's diplomacy, and its comments were often doubled-edged. By 17 October, it was 'so obvious . . . that the *Daily Telegraph* is working to bring down Chamberlain and put in Eden, Duff Cooper & Churchill' that one self-styled 'old reader . . . dropped it in favor [sic] of the *The Times*'.[2] Dawson was happy to receive a flurry of private letters to this effect, but the government would have been happier if the *Telegraph* had clung to both its readers and its habitual loyalties. In terms of practical politics, the equivocations of the *Telegraph* were more damaging than abuse from predictable sources.

Exonerating Chamberlain and, by implication, Hitler as well, *The Times* held firmly to the view that, 'had there been a free settlement in the years after the war' instead of an allied *diktat* at Versailles, 'the political evolution in Germany would have been very different' (7 November). The *Observer*, owned by a collateral branch of the Astor family, slowly began to retreat from this position. After celebrating Munich as welcome proof of Hitler's capacity for 'healing statesmanship' (2 October), Garvin mounted a campaign for immediate conscription and full-scale rearmament. In these spheres, the *Observer* pushed ahead of the *News Chronicle* and the *Herald*, which shuddered at the thought of compulsion. Considering the befuddled policies of the opposition parties and the seeming hopelessness of Churchill, the *Observer* stuck to Chamberlain as the best available alternative. There was a certain logic in its illogic, just as there was a disturbing illogic in the logic of the *News Chronicle* and the *Herald*.

Of all the routinely Tory papers, metropolitan or provincial, the *Yorkshire Post* went furthest towards disowning Chamberlain. With its sister paper, the *Evening Post*, it belonged to the Yorkshire Conservative Newspaper Company, under the chairmanship of Rupert Beckett. His older and more politically active brother, Gervase, who had died the previous year, was Eden's father-in-law. Eden himself had briefly served on the staff and remained in close contact with Arthur Mann, the single-minded editor. Although Rupert Beckett later allowed it to be supposed that he deserved a measure of credit for

---

[1] Fraser to Hugh Dalton, 20 October 1938, Dalton Papers.
[2] Donald Macleod to Dawson, 17 October 1938 ('Not for publication'), Dawson Papers.

the paper's prescient heterodoxy, he was as much 'fed up' as were other directors with Mann's 'steady spate of personal criticism and recrimination' against the Prime Minister. 'Judgments on Foreign Policy should be exercised above Party loyalties,' Mann remonstrated with Beckett, whom he reminded: 'I am not merely Editor of the Y.P. I am one of the leaders of Journalism in England... through the Press Association and Reuter's, of which as you know I am a director.' Given his professional status, which was analogous to Garvin's, Mann could not be easily dislodged. That he drew his salary from the Yorkshire Conservative Newspaper Company, floated on the investments of local party benefactors, was a disconcerting irony.[1]

Henry ('Chips') Channon, the Tory MP for Southend-on-Sea and personal private secretary to Butler at the Foreign Office, took stock of newspaper allegiances in the aftermath of 'the Munich crisis and its sensible conclusion'. To his immense satisfaction, 'the Astor Dynasty not only had its way, but led the movement', with the Beaverbrook and Rothermere properties 'enthusiastically' backing 'the winning side'. At first, 'the powerful Berry clan and Press were ... opposed to Munich' and 'critical of Chamberlain'. But Kemsley, 'a realist' (and, like Channon, a social climber), was already showing signs of 'giving in; and Camrose, in all justice, has been ill'. Misconstruing the initial reaction of Kemsley and underestimating the tenacity of Camrose, Channon compared these alignments to those during the Abdication crisis, when 'the Astors and Berrys vied with each other in traducing Edward VIII and intrigued against him for months' out of a common puritanism. Now, with 'the Rothermere and Beaverbrook factions' to tilt the balance, the Astors had carried the day in favour of 'peace with Germany', a devotion that Channon glibly ascribed 'to Lothian's influence on Lady Astor'.[2]

These 'random reflections', offered by a contemporary whose acquaintance with social forces was limited to the ones he encountered in Belgravia drawing-rooms, are palpably superficial, yet not without significance. Channon typified a tendency to identify newspapers with particular personalities, whose whims and prejudices had ostensibly superseded ideology. There is no denying the effect of individuals on the ways that international events were interpreted in print and consequently perceived by the public at large. If Lord Lothian's influence on *The Times* was neither so direct nor so substantial as Channon assumed, the editorial policies of the *News Chronicle* might well have been

---

[1] Beckett to Mann, 14 December 1938, and Mann to Beckett, 15 December 1938 (copy), Mann Papers; Camrose, *British Newspapers*, p. 110.

[2] *Chips: The Diaries of Sir Henry Channon* (ed. R. R. James; London, 1967), p. 180. Henry Carr, who sub-edited the Manchester edition of Kemsley's *Daily Sketch*, recalled that, 'before the Munich agreement', instructions were telephoned from London 'that we were to put out a contents bill containing a reproduction of one of the more agreeable photographs of Hitler, with the one word "Peace". ... It was another instance of journalistic knowledge, experience and sense of responsibility to the public being overriden by the fiat of a Press Lord.' Evidence, Royal Commission on the Press, 1947–49, Cd. 7339.

different if, as Spender had wished, Lothian had consented to become a director in 1934. The 'left-wing Liberals' would then have been thwarted, and the appeasers would presumably have had an additional voice in Fleet Street. Nevertheless, the debate would have persisted, perhaps with other inflexions. For, in any case, 'peace in our time' was an illusion. To the extent that they ever existed, the newspaper alliances of late 1938 had crumbled by the following spring under renewed provocation from Berlin.

* * *

On 7 March 1939, Channon attended a dinner of the 1936 Club in the company of 'the Prime Minister, who was jolly, enjoying himself and amazingly open and confiding'. Responding to questions 'with humorous precision', Chamberlain declared that he foresaw 'no crisis on the horizon, all seems well; he thinks the . . . dangers of a German War less every day, as our re-armament expands'. Three days later, in an address to his constituents at Chelsea, Sir Samuel Hoare heralded the dawn of a 'Golden Age' in which 'five men in Europe, the three dictators and the Prime Ministers of England and France, . . . might in an incredibly short time transform the whole history of the world'. Then came the Ides of March, when German troops suddenly moved into Prague.[1]

The Times, shocked by Hitler's perfidy, took 'notice . . . that German policy no longer seeks the protection of a moral case' (16 March). But its words rang hollow and its endorsement of subsequent British guarantees to Poland were grudging, to say the least. It became fashionable to denigrate 'the gang at Printing House Square', as Hugh Dalton did in a stormy debate in the House of Commons on 3 April, for having whetted Hitler's appetite for conquest.[2] Writing in the *Spectator* (7 April), 'Janus' was not the least 'surprised that *The Times* figured so largely' in parliamentary acrimonies: 'No single factor contributed so much to the disasters of last September as *The Times*'s leader on the 7th of that month, suggesting that Czechoslovakia might be wise in her own interests to let the Sudeten-German areas go.' For *The Times* to quibble (1 April) that the British should safeguard Polish 'independence', but not explicitly Polish 'integrity', seemed like more of the same.

For their part, the members of the Printing House Square gang were neither surprised nor disheartened by such denunciations. 'Incidentally', Dawson acknowledged 'a certain amount of rather silly talk' by people who obviously 'do not read *The Times*', but who did not hesitate to assert that it was prepared to allow Poland to go the way of Czechoslovakia. Barrington-Ward was equally unperturbed, at least until Lord ('Eddie') Winterton, the newly appointed Chancellor of the Duchy of Lancaster, 'replied to some commonplace greeting

---

[1] *Chips*, p. 185; *The Times*, 11 March 1939.
[2] *Parliamentary Debates* (Commons), 5th ser., cccxlv, col. 2580. The official historians of *The Times* (IV, part 2, 962) changed Dalton's epithet to the 'Printing House Square crowd'.

... with a vicious and unexpected attack' on the paper 'for the harm he alleged it to be doing abroad'. Barrington-Ward retorted 'that the harm, if any, was being done by those partisans who tore statements by *T.T.* from their context and misrepresented its views'. In fact, by persisting in its forlorn appeals to German conscience, *The Times* invited misrepresentation and recrimination. Its influence had declined, but not yet its reputation. When Winterton taunted that the paper 'must be losing ... to the *Daily Telegraph*', Barrington-Ward stiffly informed him 'that the circulation of *T.T.* was never so high. I didn't lose my temper with him, however,' he was no less proud to reflect.[1]

The *News Chronicle*'s immediate response to the German invasion of Czechoslovakia, which thereupon ceased to exist, was to reprint lengthy extracts from *The Times*'s 'notorious' leader of 7 September 1938 together with a recapitulation of its own forebodings of 26 September. 'History has already judged between these views.' No grace was given to Chamberlain, who had gone to Munich in the belief that 'he was righting an injustice', but who 'instead ... opened the floodgates of injustice'. On the 18th, it was mooted that he should resign as 'the first step' towards national 'unity' and the creation of a 'peace front' against Nazi aggression:

> The present Prime Minister has identified himself so personally, so ostentatiously, with the policy of so-called 'appeasement', his misjudgment of the character of Nazism and of its leader has been so profound that while he remains in office nations that are our potential allies in a struggle and a large section of our own people will with difficulty be persuaded that the policy is dead.

Still, the *News Chronicle* found it easier to address international contingencies than to grapple with the perplexities of domestic politics. At a policy conference on 31 March, Layton advocated a commitment to a full-fledged National administration, incorporating representatives of every party and persuasion, but R. J. Cruikshank 'put up a strong case ... that it was essential in peace time as well as war time to have an opposition'.[2]

Compulsion remained a stumbling block, unacceptable to some in principle and to others under Chamberlainite auspices. Soon, however, other considerations began to weigh heavily. Ivor Bulmer-Thomas, who entered Parliament in 1942 on the Labour side and exited in 1950 as a Conservative, anticipated 'that if there were a General Election in the autumn, as was possible, ... the Liberal Party would be reduced to less than ten members in the House'. Furthermore, Thomas told the policy-makers of the *News Chronicle* on 8 June, 'the paper would incur the illwill of the Labour Party if it supported any

---

[1] Dawson to Stanley Washburn, 4 April 1939, quoted in *History of The Times*, IV, part 2, 963; Barrington-Ward's diary, 11 May 1939.
[2] Notes, Policy Conference No. 17, 31 March 1939, Layton Papers.

wrecking candidatures on the part of the Liberals'.[1] Either way, to force an election would be to dig a grave for Liberalism. Yet how else was Chamberlain to be moved, if not displaced? The question, a familiar one, was posed with mounting urgency.

Rothermere, out on his own limb, was above these mundane matters. On the 'historic day' of 28 June, the twentieth anniversary of the signing of the Versailles Treaty, he telegraphed to assure 'my dear Ribbentrop . . . that the British Government is not engaged in the policy of the encirclement of Germany' and was absolutely intent on peace. More pointedly, *The Times* stated on 3 July that 'war is not inevitable unless Germany makes it so'. The question of Danzig, 'already a self-governing German territory' though beyond the perimeters of the Reich, could 'be settled – and settled easily – by cooperation' (12 July). There was a world of difference, of course, between Rothermere (who affirmed that 'I have always been a fervent admirer of the Führer') and Dawson (who, on 4 April, saw 'for the first time' that the Nazis were implementing a 'full programme of Prussianism'). But, together, they fostered the strong suspicion that the 'Shiver Sisters' – as David Low billed them – had not stopped pirouetting. 'We all have the feeling that there is going to be another Munich over Danzig and that Chamberlain will then appear again as the Great Appeaser,' confided Nicolson, 'much depressed'.[2]

Amery shared Dawson's Milnerite upbringing, but rejected his prognosis. In his opinion, conveyed privately to Halifax and publicly to an audience at Birmingham, the only effective answer to the Danzig question would be the formation of a War Cabinet. Macmillan and Nicolson pooled their literary skills to compose a letter to this effect. With Eden in tow, they delivered it on 30 June to Peterborough Court, where Camrose was known to be sympathetic to the idea of an all-party coalition. 'The Berry cat', coached by these politicians, jumped 'out of the bag' on 3 July, when Channon spotted 'a full leader of a column and a half' in the *Telegraph*, 'demanding the inclusion of Winston Churchill in the Government. It is quite threatening, and the PM is taken aback by it,' Channon wrote in his diary. 'The Press Lords are to combine in an attempt to force the Prime Minister into inviting Winston into the Government. The Eden-ites have joined them, hoping to get a Cabinet seat for Anthony too.'[3]

The *Star*, on 1 July, was the first to speculate that 'Mr Chamberlain will shortly . . . invite Mr Churchill to enter the Government'. The following day, the *Sunday Graphic* tipped him for the Admiralty, while the *Observer* commented that Churchill's continued exclusion from office 'must be as bewildering to foreigners as it is regrettable to most of his own countrymen'. True to

---

[1] Notes, Policy Conference No. 25, 8 June 1939, Layton Papers.
[2] Rothermere to Ribbentrop, 28 June 1939 (copy, telegram), Simon Papers; Brooks's diary, 2 December 1939; Nicolson, *Diaries and Letters*, I, 405–406.
[3] Maurice Cowling, *The Impact of Hitler* (Cambridge, 1975), p. 252; *Chips*, entry of 3 (misprinted as 9, and corrected on the basis of internal evidence) July 1939, p. 204.

its name, the *Sunday Pictorial* made its point with a front-page portrait of Churchill, 'the man that Hitler fears'. On Monday, the 3rd, the *Yorkshire Post* earned the *New Statesman*'s encomium as 'the strongest new recruit' (8 July) by approvingly reporting an appeal by Sinclair, the Liberal chief, for the admission of Churchill and Eden to the 'inner counsels' of state. The *News Chronicle* and the *Manchester Guardian* put the same case in their own words. All of these journals reiterated their demands on the 4th, when they were joined by the *Daily Mirror*, the *Evening News* (which had embraced Churchill on 22 April), and the *Daily Worker*. With mixed feelings, blended in differing proportions, the *Daily Mail* accepted Churchill's emergence as an inevitability, the *Daily Express* as a near certainty. Yet, as always, quality mattered more than quantity, and tradition mattered most. 'I hope the *Daily Telegraph* push will result in your being brought in to the Government,' Churchill was told by Amery, who did not mistake that paper's strategic importance.[1]

Patrolling 'the lobby of the House of Commons', Channon overheard J. H. Thomas's remark to Eden that 'we cannot count on the *Evening Standard*. They will let us down.' The *Standard* was relatively exiguous, but a useful barometer. As such, it predicted that Chamberlain would 'stand fast' in the face of this 'terrific barrage from the newspaper artillery' (4 July). Colin Coote, having tried and failed to draw *The Times* into the agitation on behalf of Churchill, offered Robert Boothby 'a small bet that the other Mr C. won't listen to it for a moment'. That, hazarded the *New Statesman*, was a safe wager. Unruffled, Chamberlain wrote to his sister at the end of 'a comparatively quiet week enlivened only by the drive to put Winston into the government'. He regarded that incident as 'a regular conspiracy', hatched by Randolph Churchill and abetted by the Russian ambassador; hence, presumably, the complicity of the *Daily Worker*. Professing indifference to what had been scribbled in most papers, he admitted that he was

> vexed that Camrose who used to be such a firm supporter should now have committed himself. As soon as I saw the leader in the *Telegraph* I sent for him and explained just why I was not prepared to invite Winston. I did not convince him, but perhaps the interview was useful as at any rate there was no bitterness in his mind. But since his illness Camrose is a changed man.

Although Chamberlain mistook the origins of the campaign, he accurately perceived that his critics had 'as usual overplayed their hand', with the result that they had alienated not only the Conservative rank and file, but also the Edenites, 'who don't see why their hero should be given such a second place'.[2]

Channon, who confirmed the resentment caused 'by the fact that Winston is

---

[1] Amery to Churchill, 3 July 1939, quoted in Gilbert, *Churchill*, V, 1081.
[2] *Chips*, p. 204; Coote to Boothby, 6 July 1939, Chamberlain to his sister, 8 July 1939, and Camrose's memorandum, 3 July 1939, quoted in Gilbert, *Churchill*, V, 1081–82, 1084, 1086.

stealing all Anthony's thunder', was relieved to note on the 6th that 'the plot is finally dying down'. Holding to his old formula, he calculated that the ministerial forces 'could never defeat the Berrys combined with the Astors' and had only withstood the present onslaught because the Berrys were 'themselves divided; Camrose being pro-Churchill, but Kemsley anti. The Astors, surprisingly enough, take a strong pro-Churchill line,' continued Channon, who deduced that 'Lady Astor, frightened by anonymous letters and gossip about the so-called "Cliveden Set", has thrown over her principles' and upset her husband's. That was clearly a distortion of the situation at the *Observer*, where Garvin and his proprietor realized that they had been hoodwinked by Hitler. The scales fell from their eyes with a clatter. Garvin pleaded for full conscription and an Anglo-Russian alliance, while Lord Astor shuttled between Halifax and Churchill, striving to line up Liberal and Labour backing.[1]

When Channon spoke of the Astors, he meant the ones ensconced at Cliveden, not their cousins at Hever Castle, who controlled *The Times*. That paper remained faithful to Chamberlain and, accordingly, scorned the 'mischievous and futile' attempt (13 July) to foist Churchill upon the government. To Barrington-Ward, the transmogrification of Churchill into the 'saviour of the country' was 'a little ridiculous. Much better not to press too hard for his inclusion,' he reasoned. 'If P.M. did give way now it wd. look like abdication. And, if Winston did come in, the Cabinet wd. split. You can't have a War Government until there is a war.'[2]

Yet, despite strenuous efforts to hold aloof, *The Times* backed into the controversy. On 10 July, it published a letter from J. A. Spender, who dissociated himself – and the Liberal tradition – from Sinclair's recent utterances, intended 'to assail the Prime Minister ... and hold him up to odium as an incompetent man of infirm purpose'. Led by Lady Violet Bonham Carter, nine prominent Liberals rallied to Sinclair's defence, but *The Times* refused to print their rejoinder without significant modification. According to Barrington-Ward, the text 'tailed off into a demand for the immediate inclusion of Winston in the Cabinet', a topic that was barred from the correspondence columns lest it should give rise to 'a discussion pro and con of Winston's personal merits'. Lady Violet considered this excuse 'very thin' and, alleging censorship, declined to expunge the contentious peroration. The following evening, Barrington-Ward attended 'a small party' at the home of Sir Roderick Jones, the head of Reuters. In addition to Lord Lothian, who was set to depart for the embassy at Washington, and Joseph Kennedy, his opposite number, the guests included 'an assemblage of Press magnates': Lords Camrose, Kemsley, and Southwood (as Elias had become), Colonel Fred Lawson (who became the 4th Baron Burnham), Sir Campbell Stuart, and Layton. Barrington-Ward 'had a passage

---

[1] *Chips*, pp. 204–205; Garvin to Astor, 29 June 1939, Astor Papers; Cowling, *Impact of Hitler*, p. 252.
[2] Barrington-Ward's diary, 4 July 1939.

with Layton about V. Bonham Carter's letter', which Layton had signed and which he revealed to have been released 'to all the Press with an intimation that it had been "refused" by *T.T.*' out of hand. 'Nothing so dishonest as a "Wee Free" Liberal,' fumed Barrington-Ward, who, the next day, was appalled to see the letter featured in virtually every major newspaper along with condemnations of *The Times*'s double standard. 'Dog eats dog,' reported the *New Statesman* (15 July), which noticed that the *Daily Herald* was the only canine 'too polite to mention the matter'.[1]

This unedifying controversy was the dénouement to a drama that had never reached a climax. 'As for the Churchill episode,' Chamberlain jauntily informed his sister on 23 July, 'it has in Joe Kennedy's picturesque phrase "Fallen out of bed" and although I see Garvin in an insufferably dull and boring article tries to keep it alive it has lost all life and even Camrose has now dropped it in the *Telegraph*.' Churchill himself, 'in view of the assertions now so loudly made that I am concerned in an agitation to drive Mr Chamberlain from office', drew up a statement in which he protested his innocence. On second thought, he decided not to release it for publication, perhaps because he did not wish to call attention to his own isolation. Sequestered at Chartwell, where he took refuge in historical studies, he was easily discounted. One of the few who still paid serious attention to him was Hitler, who met Lord Kemsley at Bayreuth on 27 July 'and referred particularly to Mr Winston Churchill and his powers of expression'. Kemsley advised the Führer not to attach undue importance to any of Chamberlain's parliamentary opponents, 'and whilst giving every credit to Mr Winston Churchill for his ability as a writer and as a speaker, he reminded Herr Hitler that Mr Churchill had been unfortunate in his campaigns on at least four occasions in the past, starting with the Abdication of King Edward VIII'. Sooner than Kemsley imagined, Churchill had the opportunity to redeem himself.[2]

*   *   *

While Kemsley was enjoying an adventurous holiday in Germany, Beaverbrook was quietly making plans to return to Canada, perhaps for ever. Disembarking at Quebec on 11 August, he was anxiously asked about the state of European affairs. 'I would not be here if I did believe that war was imminent,'

---

[1] Barrington-Ward's diary, 10 and 11 July 1939; *History of The Times*, IV, part 2, 969–71; Lady Violet Bonham Carter to Gardiner, 18 July 1939, Gardiner Papers.

[2] Chamberlain to his sister, 23 July 1939, unpublished statement by Churchill, n.d., and memorandum by Kemsley of a conversation on 27 July 1939, quoted in Gilbert, *Churchill*, V, 1091, 1092, 1094. In a conversation on 7 January 1940, Adele Barrington-Ward 'found Kemsley full of the belief that, if it had been left to him, *he* could have managed Hitler and *he* could have stopped the war. The egotism of newspaper proprietors ... is prodigious,' remarked her husband, who made an exception of the Astors. 'It is an occupational disease.' Barrington-Ward's diary, 7 January 1940.

he replied, echoing the assertion in that morning's *Daily Express*. That was the eighth and final time in 1939 that the *Express* hazarded this brazen assurance.[1]

Contrary to the impressions of these peripatetic press barons, the threat of war increased from day to day. In many minds, the only question was whether an election would be held before hostilities broke out, for that would determine the effectiveness of Britain's response to the inevitability of German aggression. 'If before the autumn there were no war, it was likely that the P.M. would go to the country and in this case he would probably be returned with an overwhelming majority,' the editorial strategists at the *News Chronicle* concluded on 13 July. In the light of this distinct possibility, A. J. Cummings proposed 'a constituency agreement with Labour' to avoid splitting the anti-appeasement vote. 'It was agreed that nothing could be said about electoral co-operation with Labour in the paper since Labour had given no encouragement to the idea at its last Party Conference', but 'soundings' were to be taken privately while the *News Chronicle* persevered in giving 'full publicity to the activities of the Liberal party and to Sir Archibald Sinclair'.[2]

Labour attitudes, vague and contradictory, were difficult to gauge. Although it was clearly understood that the party leaders would never serve under Chamberlain, it was uncertain whether another pilot might command their allegiance. Under what circumstances and on what terms might Labour join a coalition? The events of July served as a litmus test.

The *Daily Herald* looked the other way when Churchill would have profited from its support. Continuing to inveigh against Chamberlain, it could not bring itself to back anyone who sported a Tory label. The *New Statesman*, willing to forgive Churchill's pro-Franco sentiments, lamented 'that the best leader of our ruling class has ... been granted no role except that of Cassandra' (1 July). Similarly, writing in *Time and Tide* (22 July), Harold Laski excused Churchill's 'sudden lapses from balance in judgement' and estimated that 'the great bulk of the Labour Party' recognized his indispensability. Yet the buzzings of these gadflies counted for less than the *Herald*'s stony silence, which betokened the implacable enmity of the TUC. The issues on which Labour would fight an autumn election were as problematic as the alliances it might forge either during a campaign or, more probably, afterwards.

Parliament was adjourned from 4 August until 3 October on a motion by the Prime Minister. Macmillan, among those who 'deeply resented this long period of absence from the scene', extracted the promise that members would be recalled to Westminster 'in the event of any change in the situation'. Besides their apprehension that any change would be for the worse, MPs were set on edge by recurrent rumours of a snap election. Churchill was not too preoccupied with the saga of the English-speaking Peoples to consider political prospects. 'I suppose if there is no war, Chamberlain will wish to have an

---

[1] Taylor, *Beaverbrook*, pp. 394-95.
[2] Notes, Policy Conference No. 30, 13 July 1939, Layton Papers.

Election on the "Munichites versus the rest",' he wrote on 13 August to Mann at the *Yorkshire Post*. 'You and I and Anthony will have to consult together upon the extremely difficult problems such an episode would present.'[1]

As it happened, other 'extremely difficult problems' intervened and took precedence. Parliament reassembled on 24 August in response to the startling announcement of a German-Soviet non-aggression pact, which – as Churchill told the readers of the *Daily Mirror* that morning – made it 'increasingly difficult to see how war can be averted'. Undeterred by Britain's pledge to Poland, formalized on the 25th, Hitler attacked that country on the morning of 1 September. That afternoon, Churchill was summoned to Downing Street, where he 'agreed ... without comment' to join a war administration. He was less elliptical in conversations with journalists, who promptly – 'to the great annoyance of many', revealed Lord Hankey – trumpeted the impending appointment. That may have been Churchill's way of holding Chamberlain to the bargain.[2]

For Chamberlain, so far as one could tell, required close watching and constant prodding. In the opening days of September, when Mussolini was dangling the possibility of another Munich-style conference, there were doubts as to how far the Prime Minister would go, how quickly, and – especially – with whom. Arthur Greenwood, deputed to 'speak for England' in Attlee's absence, pledged Labour's unequivocal dedication to the war effort. Nevertheless, Chamberlain sensed, and the *Daily Herald* corroborated, that the Labour Party was not disposed to affiliate with him. He entertained the vain hope, however, that the Liberals would be more forthcoming. On Sunday morning, the 3rd, after Germany had ignored the time-limit that the British had set, war was declared. Only then did Chamberlain form his nine-man War Cabinet, which contained Churchill as First Lord of the Admiralty. As Secretary of State for the Dominions, Eden returned to office at a lower level.

During the ensuing period of 'phoney war', when words were deployed as weapons, the British press was vested with heavy responsibility. According to a potent myth, which Hitler helped to propagate and apparently believed, propaganda had undermined Germany's fighting spirit during the First World War. Afterwards, the British authorities had dismantled their ramshackle apparatus, but soon improvised new agencies that employed the same standard techniques to cope with domestic disaffection and disorders. Apart from carrying occasional government advertisements, newspapers were not directly involved. The *British Gazette* during the 1926 General Strike was, as we have seen, the exception that proved the rule. The National Publicity Bureau, established in 1935, supposedly 'carried through the first modern, large-scale

---

[1] Macmillan, *Winds of Change* (New York, 1966), pp. 547–48; Churchill to Mann, 13 August 1939, Mann Papers.
[2] Gilbert, *Churchill*, V, 1109; Hankey to Lady Hankey, 3 September 1939, quoted in Stephen Roskill, *Hankey*, III (London, 1974), 419.

propaganda campaign on a national basis in the history of British politics', yet without any marked effect on editorial or (judging from by-elections) electoral preferences.[1]

The experiments undertaken by totalitarian régimes encouraged the British to resume the export of 'overseas publicity', which one anonymous official defined as 'propaganda with facts'. Through an expanding network of criss-crossing bureaucratic channels, including the BBC, attempts were made to project a flattering image of British culture, society, and politics. Other countries, most notably the dictatorships, were engaged in comparable activities, which were usually better funded and possibly more persuasive. The British, despite the genius that Hitler attributed to them, were amateurs by comparison.[2]

By September 1939, a skeletal structure was in place. Some of its components and most of its procedures were legacies from the First World War. At Electra House, along the Victoria Embankment, Sir Campbell Stuart was practising the arts of 'black' (i.e. covert) propaganda that he had learnt from Northcliffe at Crewe House. Elsewhere in Whitehall, at the instigation of Hoare, a special under-secretaryship for publicity was created at the Foreign Office. With the 'unforgivable acquiescence' of Halifax, Hoare secured the post for the 16th Earl of Perth. This appointment, which Oliver Harvey (later 1st Baron Harvey of Tasburgh) considered 'a real scandal', was defended by Chamberlain on the grounds that Perth (as Sir Eric Drummond) had amassed 'a great deal of experience with publicity' as secretary-general of the League of Nations and, subsequently, ambassador to Rome. At the outbreak of war, Perth's department was detached from the Foreign Office and reconstituted as the Ministry of Information. Baron Macmillan, the eminent jurist, was called upon to assume ministerial jurisdiction over the collection, regulation, and distribution of news. That, as in 1914, was not an easy assignment. The MoI, known still more familiarly as the 'Ministry of Aggravation', saw a succession of heads. Within months, Macmillan made way for Sir John Reith, whom Hoare had nominated in the first instance. Reith did not survive the advent of Churchill, who replaced him first with Duff Cooper and finally with Brendan Bracken, the first Minister of Information to enjoy the benefit of a familiarity with Fleet Street.[3]

Until the summer of 1941, when Bracken took charge, this 'misbegotten' ministry did not know its proper functions, much less how to fulfil them. As a central clearing-house, it bottled up intelligence from the service departments. Its recourse to censorship, chiefly by means of Defence ('D') Notices, was haphazard and singularly ineffective. 'Except for despatches going abroad,

---

[1] R. D. Casey, 'The National Publicity Bureau and British Party Propaganda,' *Public Opinion Quarterly*, iii (1939), 624.

[2] Philip M. Taylor, *Projection of Britain*, especially ch. 7.

[3] *The Diplomatic Diaries of Oliver Harvey, 1937–1940* (ed. J. Harvey; London, 1970), p. 292 (entry for 24 May 1939); *Parliamentary Debates* (Commons), 5th ser., cccxlviii, cols. 1499–1503 (14 June 1939); Cross, *Hoare*, pp. 304–306.

submission to censorship was voluntary,' one historian has explained. 'Any correspondent was free to write, and any editor to print, any story they got hold of', provided that national security was not infringed. 'The censorship system was thus based on bluff, goodwill (for no editor wanted to help the Germans) and the realisation that, if it broke down, a much more vexatious compulsory scheme would have to be substituted.'[1]

In order to exercise 'the creative function of providing a steady flow of facts and opinions calculated to further the policy of the Government in the prosecution of the war', the Ministry of Information was formally directed 'to preserve intimate and cordial relations with the newspapers through their proprietors, editors, and reporters'.[2] How could it preserve what had never existed? The ministry could count upon newspapermen's patriotism, but enthusiasm was asking too much.

'Information and Censorship were committing incredible follies,' Dawson recorded in his diary on 5 September. Three days later, he spent the 'morning, afternoon and night' at Printing House Square, locked in 'more struggles with the censorship, which develops new follies daily'. On the morning of the 9th, Ward Price telephoned Collin Brooks from Carmelite House and complained 'that the Ministry of Information is one glorious muddle'. Esmond Harmsworth, who had been installed as chairman of the newspaper section, was 'a decorative but useless person'. His deputy, Tom Clarke, was 'a good fellow, who has been out of practical journalism ... for a decade or so' and had lost his touch. 'The Ministry cannot understand that a newspaper has a time for going to press,' declared Price, who blamed the infuriating delays on the ineptitude of Lord Perth and the lack of adequate facilities for processing foreign reports.[3]

Newspapers, Lord Macmillan nervously observed on the 16th, were 'in a state of revolt'. Frustrated by the paucity of news, they filled their columns with condemnations of bureaucratic controls, especially those that they held responsible for their own vexations. The Ministry of Information, a closer target than the enemy, was prey to snipers. The *Daily Mail* and the *Daily Express* grumbled about its incompetence, while – at the other extreme – the *Daily Herald* cited its potential threat to personal freedom. Layton 'mentioned in passing' during a policy-planning session on 20 October 'that he thought the *N.C.* should not support the *Daily Herald*'s attack on the Ministry of Information'. His colleagues 'generally felt that internal propaganda should be reduced to a minimum, but that no necessary expense should be spared on foreign propaganda'. Given the fact that British newspapers circulated

---

[1] Michael Balfour, *Propaganda in War 1939–1945* (London, 1979), ch. 3; Angus Calder, *The People's War* (New York, 1969), p. 66.

[2] Memorandum signed by Churchill, 1941, quoted in Balfour, *Propaganda*, p. 64.

[3] Dawson's diary, 5 and 8 September 1939, Dawson Papers; Brooks's diary, 9 September 1939.

abroad, where they were studied as an index to civilian morale, this distinction broke down.[1]

Beaverbrook, unconvincingly adamant, denied that he nursed any ambition to become Minister of Information. 'The Ministry has now been stripped of its function and appears to me to be nothing more than a minor department, and a discredited one at that,' he told Hoare on 30 October. 'I would have been the best man for the job at the outset. I have the experience in journalism and propaganda' and, he might have added, the ability to differentiate between them. There were rumours that Chamberlain had him in mind for the assignment. Certainly, Chamberlain knew that a firmer hand was necessary. 'Campbell Stuart is carrying on something which is called Enemy Propaganda,' he wrote sardonically on 7 November. 'It appears to be directed to Attlee, Greenwood, Miss Ellen Wilkinson, any member of the Cabinet, and any Newspaper Proprietor who is prepared to lunch or dine with Campbell.' At the turn of the year, Chamberlain hit upon the idea of transferring Leslie Hore-Belisha from the War Office, where he had shown 'special qualifications', to the hot seat at the MoI. Attlee, Camrose, and W. W. Hadley, the editor of the *Sunday Times*, were among those who expressed positive reactions. But, at the last moment, Halifax demurred that 'it would have a bad effect on the neutrals both because H.B. was a Jew and because his methods would let down British prestige'.[2]

Instead of moving laterally to become overlord of the press, Hore-Belisha was sacked and became its pensioner. 'He was getting all kinds of offers to write or speak,' he told Crozier of the *Manchester Guardian* on 20 January 1940. One customer had 'offered £2,000 for four articles but he wasn't accepting it', though 'he had to make a living'. Eventually, he 'decided to write for the *News of the World* at £300 a time', which was double the rate proposed by the *Sunday Times* and a third higher than the *Daily Mirror*'s latest bid. Cecil King believed that Hore-Belisha had made a tactical blunder:

> Personally, if I had been he, I should have given my story to the *Sunday Express*, a good-class paper that had given him the staunchest of political support. Alternatively, to the *Sunday Times*, which would help impress the Colonel Blimps who are mostly anti-Belisha. The *Sunday Pic[torial]* has given him most support, the *Mail* crowd have been helpful, but by writing for the *News of the World* he is pleasing a paper which will not help him politically, which will not put him over at all, and which will not be quoted.

[1] Memorandum of 16 September 1939, quoted in Balfour, *Propaganda*, p. 57; notes, Policy Conference No. 37, 20 October [1939], Layton Papers.

[2] Beaverbrook to Hoare, 30 October 1939, and Chamberlain to Gladstone Murray, 7 November 1939, quoted in Taylor, *Beaverbrook*, p. 399; Chamberlain to his sister, 7 January 1940, quoted in Macleod, *Chamberlain*, p. 286.

'Chequebook journalism', as it was later called, did not yield political dividends.[1]

Political journalism, as practised according to custom, had its own disadvantages. In a conversation with Laurence Cadbury, Layton 'raised a very interesting point' when he boasted that the members of the *News Chronicle* 'staff were for the most part passionately devoted to the paper's policy'. While such devotion was gratifying, Cadbury feared that 'their ardent desires as crusaders may at times interfere with their professional capacity as journalists'. These qualms may account for his reluctance to acquire an interest in *Time and Tide*, which Lady Rhondda was having difficulty managing on her own. Cadbury was eager to ease his party commitments, not augment them. In particular, he objected to the way that Cummings continually spouted the idiosyncratic – and allegedly defeatist – views of Lloyd George. 'He has always been very much in Ll.G.'s pocket,' asserted Cadbury, who presumably did not mean to suggest any financial impropriety.[2]

Wartime conditions gave proprietors the incentives and, where necessary, the excuses to impose discipline. On 28 November 1939, Eden was 'deeply moved to hear' that Mann's 'connexion with the *Y.P.* is at an end'. The owners of the *Yorkshire Post* had been sorely tempted to request his resignation earlier, but relented in the knowledge that he would not have gone quietly. Now, there was no one to listen. Eden, laden with ministerial responsibilities, regretted his friend's departure as 'a great loss' to the paper, perhaps 'an irreparable one', but 'also a loss to the nation at this time', when independent voices were muffled. The occasion of Mann's dismissal was the merger of the *Yorkshire Post* with the *Leeds Mercury* into a new penny daily under the editorship of W. L. Andrews, who came with the *Mercury*. Mann, professing himself 'no devotee of a vague and out-of-date traditionalism', had initially supported the amalgamation out of 'political as well as financial considerations..., for a "popular" 1d paper expressing anti-Socialist opinion was certainly an asset to the Conservative Party, especially if it contributed to the exclusion of the Labour press' from the Leeds area. For a mixture of political and financial reasons, other provincial journals also fused at this time. The Conservative *North-Devon Herald* and the Liberal *North-Devon Journal* 'combined ... on a policy of entire impartiality as between the two Parties' under the direction of P.A. (later 1st Baron) Inman, a future Labour Cabinet minister, who recognized that 'the Labour Party had not risen to be a very important factor in the constituency then'.[3]

---

[1] Interview with Hore-Belisha, 20 January 1940, Crozier, *Off the Record*, pp. 127–33; diary entry of 2 February 1940, King, *With Malice Towards None* (London, 1970), p. 20.

[2] Cadbury to Layton, 31 July, 25 September, and 13 October 1939, Layton Papers.

[3] Eden to Mann, 28 November 1939, and memorandum by Mann, 2 October 1939, Mann Papers; *Time and Tide*, 2 December 1939; Evidence, Royal Commission on the Press, 1947–49, Cd. 7392, qq. 6332–34.

The following year, Mann was indemnified with the Companionship of Honour, which he accepted

> with unholy joy because it was a public recognition of the value to the State of the kind of journalism I tried to make the Y.P. stand for as against the type of newspaper that my late Directors fancied would bring them larger profits. I think, judging their decision even on a crude commercial basis, they were short-sighted & foolish.

In fact, the C.H. was little more than a glittering consolation prize. Garvin received the same honour in the same list. Having decined it twice before – once in 1918, when he 'thought it was going to be cheapened' by Lloyd George, and the second time in 1929, when MacDonald 'refused to give C. P. Scott the P.C. and O.M. as I had been urging' – he gratefully accepted it from Churchill. Barrington-Ward regarded Garvin, his mentor, as a worthier recipient than Mann, 'who has qualified merely as a heated partisan of Winston and bitter enemy of Neville in the "Munich" controversy', though he had been 'at least a successful editor before he lost his wits and temper'. In the course of 1941, Garvin was to lose his wits, temper, and chair at the *Observer*. These Companions of Honour then became companions in adversity.[1]

Less attention was paid to editorial dislocations in Leeds or Barnstaple, which were almost as remote as developments in Scottish journalism. In wartime, the centripetal force of London was stronger than ever. 'People talk in awe, almost in reverence, of the *Scotsman* and *Glasgow Herald*, especially in the South of England', but Frank Waters, the general manager of Beaverbrook's *Scottish Daily Express*, knew better. 'Ask some one whether he has read either, and he will say, as a rule, "No, but we know their reputation".' Beyond the metropolis, the tendency was for journals to 'trade on reputation'.[2]

In the jungle of London journalism, it was harder to make a reputation, harder still to keep one, and nearly impossible to live one down. On the afternoon of 6 February 1940, Cadbury tried an experiment. He 'summoned four of our leading Trades Unionists' to his office at the *News Chronicle* 'and asked them a series of questions', formulated to test their degree of political awareness. 'Who is the editor of the *Daily Herald*?' he began. 'None of them knew.' Who, then, was Francis Williams? This hint 'rang a bell in the brains of two of them', which Cadbury took as proof that there were 'distinct limitations on the reputation of Francis Williams in the Trades Union world'.[3] Proceeding

---

[1] Mann to Crozier, 3 January [1941], and Garvin to Crozier, 14 January 1941, *Guardian* Archives; Barrington-Ward's diary, 1 January 1941.

[2] Waters's diary, 9 November 1939. After four years in Beaverbrook's employment, Waters received a £5 increment. 'Friendship is about the last quality Lord B. would understand or encourage with his employees,' Waters wrote on 12 March 1940. 'A man who is a load of dynamite can't be friendly with anyone or anything.'

[3] Cadbury to Layton, 6 February 1939, Layton Papers.

less empirically, the directors of the *Daily Herald* soon removed Williams from the editorship and replaced him with Percy Cudlipp. The same year, Hugh (later Baron) Cudlipp left the *Sunday Pictorial*, where he was to return in 1946 for the second of three innings. (Reginald, a third Cudlipp brother, was to edit the *News of the World* from 1953 to 1959.)

The pace of editorial change quickened. During the First World War, when newspapers had been more plentiful, editors were frozen in place for the duration and demobilized afterwards. This time, the upheavals occurred earlier on. The *Financial Times*, *Reynolds*, the *News of the World*, and the *Daily Sketch* were among those affected. With the celebrated exception of the *Evening Standard*, where Michael Foot took over from Frank Owen, editors were usually too old to be called up for military service. Rather, they succumbed to other wartime exigencies. Dawson, who thoughtfully prescribed 'Relief for Ministers' in *The Times* (16 April 1940), was getting ready to lay down his own burdens; if peace had been preserved, he would have stepped down in 1939.

Ministerial changes, involving men of equally advanced years, came more slowly. On 3 April, Chamberlain rearranged his team to include Lord Woolton as Minister for Food, and to allow Hoare to trade places with Sir Kingsley Wood. These adjustments anticipated by five days the German invasion of Norway. Cummings pointed out to his colleagues at the *News Chronicle* that 'the *Herald*, *The Times*, the *Mirror* and the *Manchester Guardian* were all critical of the reshuffle' as a typically empty gesture. In the *Observer* (7 April), Garvin registered an 'accustomed disappointment which has become almost amusing by repetition'. The only consolation to *The Times*, which was keeping strange company, was the 'ground for still more confident hope that the co-ordination of defence will now pass in effect into the hands of Mr Churchill' (4 April). Dawson indicated to Amery that he intended 'to make a push for a proper War Cabinet', and Amery assisted by providing a confidential copy of a 'short memorandum which I drew up for the use of a few friends in both Houses. It might afford handy material for one of your leader-writers when you have to deal with the subject.' Before long, it did.[1]

The news from Norway grew more and more depressing. By Thursday, 2 May, 'Chips' Channon was 'beginning reluctantly to realise that Neville's days are, after all, numbered'. On the 5th, 'a storm of abuse of the PM in the Sunday Press' reinforced that impression. 'Rothermere has come out against the Government: Kemsley is pro it: the *Telegraph* and Beaverbrook are mildly critical, but stay their hand.' Characteristically, Channon muddled the details, but caught the drift of events. By 'Rothermere', he surely meant Esmond Harmsworth, who had delegated formal control to Cowley. The *Telegraph* did not, of course, publish on Sunday, and its criticism of Chamberlain that week

---

[1] Notes, Policy Conference No. 51, 4 April 1940, Layton Papers; Amery to Dawson, 16 April 1940, *Times* Archives.

was too superficial to wound. Beaverbrook was vastly more supportive than Channon allowed. 'What is the Damage?' he demanded rhetorically in the *Daily Express* on the 6th, making light of the Norwegian setback in a 'splendid article' – the last from his pen for five years – that Chamberlain applauded as 'a courageous and inspiring summons to a saner view'.[1]

To Dawson, however, the fall of Norway furnished 'A Warning and an Opportunity'. Under that sober heading, a leading article in *The Times* called on the 6th for 'a stock-taking both of the structure and of the personnel of the Government', each obviously deficient. J. L. Hammond, who had resumed leader-writing chores on the *Manchester Guardian*, asserted that morning: 'We are facing the greatest crisis in our history with a Government weaker than any Government that has made war since Addington faced Napoleon.' From 'the general agitation in the Press', Dawson inferred that he had been 'right to get my reflections on the direction of the war into the paper this morning and the article had many repercussions during the day'.[2] Not the least portentous was the announcement that, the following afternoon, the Prime Minister would open a two-day debate on the Norwegian campaign and related matters.

Dawson was in the press gallery on the 7th 'to hear the Prime Minister' give 'rather a lame performance'. Nicolson, seated on the benches below, listened to this 'very feeble speech' to which Amery forcefully replied by quoting the words of Oliver Cromwell to the Long Parliament: 'You have sat too long here for any good you have been doing. ... In the name of God, go.' Nicolson sauntered into the lobby, where he met Camrose, for whom he wrote a weekly book review in the *Telegraph*. 'Although a firm supporter of Chamberlain', Camrose was clearly 'much shaken'.[3]

When the debate resumed on the 8th, Herbert Morrison delivered 'a very damaging attack', culminating in a bold challenge. 'Until that moment the House had not really foreseen that the Opposition were to press for a Division,' wrote Nicolson, who thought 'that it was a mistake that they should do so, since it will create a bad impression in the country and leave much bitterness behind'. The Labour Party leaders were themselves uneasy, and the early editions of the *Daily Herald*, the *Manchester Guardian*, and *The Times* variously warned that throwing down the gauntlet might have the effect of mobilizing Chamberlain's supporters. Resigned to this likelihood, Dawson sent *The Times* to press at 9.30 that evening, then returned to Westminster at ten o'clock for the wind-up and the vote. 'Government majority was only 81 in a crowded and excited assembly and there was a general conviction that it meant a reconstruction at once,' he wrote breathlessly in his diary after he 'came back to Printing House Square to

---

[1] *Chips*, p. 244; Chamberlain to Beaverbrook, 6 May 1940, quoted in Taylor, *Beaverbrook*, p. 408.

[2] Dawson's diary, 6 May 1940, quoted in Wrench, *Dawson*, p. 414.

[3] Dawson's diary, 7 May 1940, quoted in Wrench, *Dawson*, p. 414; diary entry of 7 May 1940, Nicolson, *Diaries and Letters*, II (London, 1967), 76–77.

alter a few headlines'. In the event, forty-one National backbenchers had voted against the government and some sixty others had abstained. ('But for personal sympathy with Mr Chamberlain,' Garvin oddly supposed the following Sunday, the government's majority 'would have been below zero'.) 'I Say Get Out,' Morrison repeated in the *Daily Mirror* on the 9th. That, in short order, was just what Chamberlain did.[1]

Who was to take his place? There were isolated gusts of support for Lloyd George, whom the *Daily Mail* commended for his 'high thinking and modest living' (10 May) and whom Garvin and Lord Astor esteemed for more valid qualities. At an emergency meeting on the 9th to map the policy for the *News Chronicle*, Cummings expressed certainty that 'the Whitsun recess would not save the Government, and . . . that Chamberlain would have to go'. Gerald Barry 'said that only Hitler was able to save Chamberlain', and the German invasion of the Low Countries that night seemed to bring a stay of execution. It fell to Layton 'to decide which of the possibilities for the Premiership the paper should support. Although he had originally thought Halifax was a possibility, he now felt that the only two names which would command support were Churchill and Lloyd George.' Cummings 'definitely preferred Churchill as Premier', but Layton 'personally was not sure that Churchill was up to his last-war standard of efficiency' after the disastrous landings in Norway.[2]

Like Layton, Beaverbrook realized that the substitution of Halifax for Chamberlain 'would simply mean the continuance of the present Administration'. Nevertheless, Halifax was indisputably the front runner. As Beaverbrook later recited: Chamberlain, as soon as he knew that he could not continue, 'wanted Halifax. Labour wanted Halifax. Sinclair wanted Halifax. The Lords wanted Halifax. The King wanted Halifax. And Halifax wanted Halifax,' supposedly with reservations. The press, including Beaverbrook's own papers, was largely reconciled to the prospect of Halifax's ascent. Yet, when the dust had settled, Churchill emerged as the leader of a broad-based coalition. Beaverbrook offered him congratulations, advice on appointments, and the promise of some 'useful ideas on the publicity side'.[3]

Even in partnership with Labour, the Sinclair Liberals, and Beaverbrook (who became Minister for Aircraft Production), Churchill could not afford to dispense with key members of the old guard. Chamberlain became Lord President of the Council, Halifax stayed put as Foreign Secretary, and Simon was raised to the peerage and relegated to the Woolsack. The fatal blow to

---

[1] Diary entry of 8 May 1940, Nicolson, *Diaries and Letters*, II, 78; Dawson's diary, 8 May 1940, quoted in Wrench, *Dawson*, p. 414; Donoughue and Jones, *Morrison*, p. 271.

[2] Cowling, *Impact of Hitler*, p. 383; notes, Policy Conference No. 52, 9 May 1940, Layton Papers.

[3] Undated note by Beaverbrook [1940?], Beaverbrook's 'summary' of 1963, and Beaverbrook to Churchill, 12 May 1940, quoted in Taylor, *Beaverbrook*, pp. 409–11. For corroboration and clarification of Beaverbrook's assessment, see Paul Addison, *The Road to 1945* (London, 1975), pp. 98–102.

Chamberlain had been struck within the Conservative Party hierarchy, where pivotal figures had swung behind Churchill. Newspapermen had been bystanders, innocent or otherwise, who brought no pressure to bear because they had had none at their disposal.

J. A. Spender was astounded by 'the lack of support from which Chamberlain has suffered in his party & in the press. In the old days, when Gladstone or C.B. or Asquith was attacked, we all rushed to his defence, politicians & newspapers alike. Except for you & Halifax,' Spender wrote to Simon,

> scarcely any of his colleagues came openly to his support & his press has been deplorable. The popular press, with its eye for circulation, go for any man when they think the tide is setting ever so little against him, but hitherto this has been just the point where the serious press has stood firm. Instead of doing this in Chamberlain's case, the serious press has wobbled & wavered & finally joined the populars in the man-hunt.

Beaverbrook recalled 'the old days' differently. Appearances (and Beaverbrook's own previous testimony) to the contrary, Asquith had been toppled in 1916 and Lloyd George in 1922 by revolts against their governments that 'came from within. The same applies at this time,' he insisted. 'Those who do it from without are simply wasting their ammunition,' for a press agitation could never succeed of its own accord. Furthermore, in the dark days of May 1940, there was no ammunition to spare.[1]

* * *

As war leader, Churchill gloriously fulfilled and perhaps even exceeded all expectations. Domestic affairs were not permitted to deflect him from his essential purpose. For all his past connections with Fleet Street, he proved relatively indifferent to the problems that arose there. The Ministry of Information received only his fitful and grudging attention. Duff Cooper, whom he appointed to preside over its operations, recalled that 'when I appealed for support to the PM, I seldom got it. He was not interested in the subject. He knew that propaganda was not going to win the war.' Bracken, who thrived where his predecessor had languished, could not deny that 'it is very difficult to be a Minister of Information – or Propaganda'.[2]

---

[1] Spender to Simon, 16 May 1940, Simon Papers; Beaverbrook to Lord Davies, 7 May 1940, quoted in Taylor, *Beaverbrook*, p. 407.

[2] Duff Cooper, *Old Men Forget* (London, 1953), p. 288; *Parliamentary Debates* (Commons), 5th ser., cccci, col. 923 (29 June 1944). Duff Cooper's 'asinine ignorance of newspaper practice' was illustrated on Sunday afternoon, 29 June 1941, when he summoned a meeting of 'editors' to announce 'the new and unexpected Govt. changes'. It was an 'Editor's right not to attend handout conferences personally' and to send 'any trustworthy deputy'. On this occasion, 'only the editor of the *Daily Mirror* was personally present. Duff lost his temper', and 'refused to impart any "background" except to "editors". ... Duff must go,' concluded Barrington-Ward. A few weeks later, Duff went. Barrington-Ward's diary, 29 June 1941.

Churchill's idea was to leave newspapers free to get on with their business, while they left him free to get on with his. Unfortunately, Hitler did not make it easy for either of them. The German occupation of Norway had stemmed the flow of Scandinavian newsprint, which became 'rarer than gold. Sizes of papers have been further limited to 8 pages', four fewer than the reduction voluntarily adopted the previous autumn, and Waters was 'now actually embarrassed by extra sales', which depleted supplies. 'Like many other things newspaper life has become so standardised and stereotyped that originality will count for nought,' he wrote in his diary on 28 April 1940. 'That for a newspaper is pure hell.'[1]

In September, when the Luftwaffe began aerial bombardment, the hellfire was felt more directly. On the night of the 12th, 'the *Express* lost 1000 tons of newsprint by fire – £24,000 worth' at the wholesale price of £24 a ton. On the night of the 26th, the sky glowed crimson over London's dockland from uncontrollable fires that consumed 'more than 16,000 tons of newsprint', representing to the *Express* a loss of £370,000 or 'roughly ... a fortnight's consumption'. In the same nocturnal conflagration, *The Times* lost three hundred tons stored at Kitchin's Wharf, and other newspapers suffered heavily. *The Times*, however, claimed the distinction of being the first office to be hit. In the early hours of the 25th, a bomb fell on Printing House Square, where the underground presses (operating on a 'new and very early time-table') managed to produce 80,000 copies out of a normal print run of 189,000. The damage to the plant was severe, but there were no casualties. Ignored by the British press, including *The Times* itself, the incident was seized upon by enemy propagandists, who rejoiced that 'one of the workshops for the distortion of truth in London nearly disappeared from the surface of the globe'.[2]

Shortages of newsprint, coupled with the governmental regulations that they necessitated, restricted newspaper production. Disruptions in railway services impeded distribution. Domiciled at Passfield Corner, the Webbs did 'not see the *Manchester Guardian* now because owing to the absence of the second post during the war we cannot get it until the next morning when it is rather late to read it'. Despite these obstacles, aggregate sales were higher than before the war. In February 1943, when 4,320 tons of newsprint were used weekly, more copies circulated than in 1938, when 23,000 tons was the weekly consumption. Four men out of five and two women out of three were estimated to read at least one paper a day. Desperate for news, the public was willing to pay more for less. Shorn of its customary features, the press remained a recreation, a consolation,

---

[1] Waters's diary, 28 April 1940. On 14 September 1942, George Blake wrote to Waters, who was in the army, 'that increasing shortages of paper and manpower are rendering the editorial functions largely mechanical' (Waters Papers).

[2] Waters's diary, 12 and 26 September 1940; Dawson's diary, 24–25 September 1940, quoted in Wrench, *Dawson*, p. 429; minutes of *The Times* Board, 26 September 1940 (copy), Woods Papers; F. P. Bishop, 'When the Clocks all Stopped in Printing House Square,' *Times House Journal*, October 1940.

and a means of sharing in the communal experience. 'Well I must buy all the papers for the next few days,' vowed young Colin Perry, who was proud to be one of the 'Londoners under bombardment' in the Blitz and who peppered his diaries with quotations from the *Daily Express* and the *Evening Standard*. On 18 September 1940, after Glasgow was subjected to intensive raids, Waters reported that 'newspaper sales' were 'terrific. The *Citizen* sold over 31,000 extra' that evening.[1]

From an average daily size of twenty-one pages, the *News Chronicle* shrank to six pages in July 1940 and to four pages after the following March. *The Times*, priced at twopence, entered the war with a twelve-page format. In the spring of 1940, when most of its penny rivals opted for eight-page editions, it allowed itself the luxury of three ten-page appearances per week. Thereafter, its choice was either to 'conform to the 8-page size or increase its price' as a brake on circulation. To preserve the paper's historic character 'as a national register of news', the proprietors decided that, from 7 April 1941, the price would be raised to threepence. Yet, as Barrington-Ward was amazed to note, this increase 'in no way diminished the demand for the paper. Extraordinary. Beyond the most optimistic forecast.' The financial year that ended in July 1944 showed the largest profit in *The Times*'s history. 'The circulation of the paper is now bigger, at 3d., than it was a year or two before the war at 2d.,' remarked Barrington-Ward, who knew that 'too much store must not be set by those facts. War is notoriously good for newspapers.' The *Manchester Guardian* and the *Daily Telegraph* likewise deliberately sacrificed circulation for size and with gratifying results.[2]

Newspapers were prepared to submit to the rationing of precious newsprint supplies, and helpfully assisted in the process through the formation of the Newsprint Supply Company. They were less amenable to other controls, which they fought to ward off. The Ministry of Information, owing partly to its structural defects and partly to the excitements of the moment, caused unrest by its threats to extend censorship. Seldom clearly formulated, these Draconian proposals rarely came to anything. 'Just the same, Fleet Street was seething over the whole Ministry of Information set-up,' wrote Arthur Christiansen, who recalled 'an agitation to make me Minister of Information' in place of Duff Cooper. Cummings and Cruikshank, the editor of the *Star*, jointly appealed to Churchill, himself 'so great a journalist', to recognize 'that *journalism* demands above all things *journalists*, and news requires *news-*

[1] Calder, *People's War*, p. 504; Beatrice Webb to J. L. Hammond, 24 June 1941, *The Letters of Sidney and Beatrice Webb* (ed. N. MacKenzie; Cambridge, 1978), III, 449; diary for 10 September 1940, Perry, *Boy in the Blitz* (London, Corgi edn., 1974), pp. 125–26; Waters's diary, 18 September 1940.

[2] Memorandum by Layton, Documentary Evidence, Royal Commission on the Press, 1961–62, Cd. 1812, IV, 242; *History of The Times*, IV, part 2, 990–91; minutes of *The Times* Board, 2 May 1940 (copy), Woods Papers; Barrington-Ward's diary, 6 April 1941 and 6 July 1944; *Newspaper Press Directory* (1945), pp. 48 ff.; Ayerst, *Guardian*, p. 543.

papermen', not the well-connected amateurs who earned the Ministry the nickname of 'Minnie'.[1]

Like 'Dora', her older sister, 'Minnie' was a fusspot, dreaded not so much for what she did as for what she might do. Barrington-Ward, for example, was alarmed to hear on 27 May 'of projects circulating, unofficially as yet, in the Ministry of Information for the virtual reduction of the Press to the recorder of official news and views'. Convinced that such an arrangement, reminiscent of Churchill's escapade during the General Strike, 'would be disastrous for public morale', he fixed a meeting with Sir Walter (later 1st Viscount) Monckton at the Ministry. Monckton explained that the scheme in question was 'only intended, at most, to take powers' in the event of an 'emergency and that Duff knows the danger inherent in them and is in no way anxious to use them'. But Barrington-Ward suggested that a better procedure would be 'to tackle individually and severely' those particular papers that engaged in 'speculation on military intentions' or otherwise subverted the war effort.[2]

That, essentially, was what transpired. In May 1940, under pressure from the Foreign Office, the Ministry imposed a ban on the export of Fascist and Communist journals. The proscription of Fascist literature remained in effect through the war. Policy with respect to Communist publications followed the tortuous path of Anglo-Soviet relations. The *Daily Worker* was warned in July 1940 that its campaign for 'revolutionary defeatism' was in contravention of Defence Regulation 2D, which deemed it an offence 'systematically to publish matter calculated to foment opposition to the prosecution of the war to a successful issue. Nevertheless, its infractions continued. On the evening of 21 January 1941, Morrison, as Home Secretary, 'arranged with Scotland Yard to go along to the *Worker* offices . . . and stop the presses then and there'. At the same time, Cockburn's *The Week* was also suppressed indefinitely. Morrison, whose 'instinctive attitude to the press' has been described by his biographers as 'permissive', maintained that he had committed no 'attack on freedom'; on the contrary, these papers' 'slavish obedience to the Moscow line was a negation of freedom of the printed word'. The only significant protest came from Aneurin Bevan, the Labour MP for Ebbw Vale and then a member of the editorial board of *Tribune*, who held no brief for the *Daily Worker*, but believed that its editors were entitled to a court hearing. The ban was lifted only in August 1942, fourteen months after Hitler had broken his pact with Stalin.[3]

Other newspapers, untainted by foreign associations, were undeniably

---

[1] Camrose, *British Newspapers*, pp. 153–55; Christiansen, *Headlines*, pp. 186–87.

[2] Barrington-Ward's diary, 27 May and 4 June 1940.

[3] Balfour, *Propaganda*, p. 66; Morrison, *An Autobiography* (London, 1960), p. 225; Donoughue and Jones, *Morrison*, pp. 297–98; Michael Foot, *Aneurin Bevan*, I (London, 1962), 325–26. In a poll on 23 January, Mass-Observation (Report No. 552) ascertained that 32 per cent of its respondents were in favour of suppressing the *Daily Worker* as opposed to 37 per cent opposed. It was 'noticeable that plenty who said they were against suppression . . ., at the same time said they were against the *Daily Worker* itself'.

capable of causing greater mischief. The *Daily Mirror* and the *Sunday Pictorial*, which had swung sharply to the left during the 1930s, ran into difficulties by being more Churchillian than Churchill now saw fit. 'Throughout the disastrous midsummer of 1940', when public confidence was shaken by the evacuation from Dunkirk, these popular papers denounced those 'men at the top whom they considered inefficient or discredited survivors of the appeasement era'. The victims, arraigned by a pseudonymous trio of Beaverbrook journalists as 'Guilty Men', were known to readers of the *Mirror* as 'dope ministers', 'old blunderers', and 'the old loitering gang'. Chamberlain was the principal target, but Wood, Simon, and Halifax were all fair game. Lloyd George lent his authority to these attacks, which William Connor, writing as 'Cassandra', waged with blistering invective.[1]

Servicemen were attracted to the *Mirror* by its lively 'forces' column and, more probably, by the charms of 'Jane', its scantily attired comic-strip heroine. What they found elsewhere in its tabloid pages were criticisms of the 'brass-buttoned bone-heads' who commanded them and the 'Men of Munich' who lurked in high places. Churchill and his Cabinet reportedly suspected that 'various sinister figures', including that 'evil man Hearst', were behind the *Mirror*. 'Not a bit,' Cecil King claimed to have assured him. 'There are five executive directors. I am one of them. I'm more interested in politics than the others, so they leave politics largely to me.'[2]

Arriving at the office on 7 June, King was told that his cousin Esmond Harmsworth had delivered 'a message from Churchill', who was 'apparently aware that a storm is blowing up over Chamberlain and his friends'. In the last few days, the *Daily Herald* and the *Daily Mail* had begun to echo the *Mirror*'s grumblings, while the *News Chronicle* and the *Star* tactfully questioned the utility of certain veteran ministers and *Tribune* called for their impeachment. Churchill made it clear to King that, 'if Chamberlain is forced out, . . . he will have to resign as jointly responsible . . . for the policy of the Cabinet since the outbreak of war'. In other words, the Prime Minister would regard the prolongation of these attacks as a challenge to his own leadership. In view of this ultimatum, which King preferred to interpret as a 'request', the directors of the *Mirror* and the *Pictorial* 'agreed that we would not attack the Chamberlainite members of the Government' until Churchill had the opportunity 'to ease Chamberlain out on the grounds of ill-health'. Meanwhile, King gathered from Harmsworth that Churchill had squared the *Herald* through Ernest Bevin, the Minister of Labour, 'and the *News Chronicle* through Layton and probably Lloyd George direct'.[3]

The *Mirror* was forced to 'pipe down', but only for a season. By October, when Chamberlain resigned for genuine medical reasons, Churchill was

---

[1] King, *Malice*, pp. 46–47; *Daily Mirror*, 6 June 1940; Calder, *People's War*, pp. 287–88.
[2] Edelman, *Mirror*, p. 106.
[3] Addison, *Road to 1945*, pp. 107–108; King, *Malice*, pp. 47–49.

convinced that its renewed tirades 'stood for something ... dangerous and sinister, namely an attempt to bring about a situation in which the country would be ready for surrender'. Lloyd George, advocating a compromise peace with Germany, regretted that a 'reservoir of unreasoning optimism' was constantly 'replenished by the press and by other propaganda', with the result that 'anyone who calls attention to the realities is regarded as defeatist'. To Churchill, the level of optimism in that reservoir could never be too high. After Attlee tried to reason with King and H.G. ('Bart') Bartholomew, the editorial director, Churchill privately protested that the *Mirror*'s policy was 'just that which it would be most effective for a fifth-column newspaper to pursue'. Activated by 'a spirit of hatred and malice against the Government which is after all not a Party but a National Government', the paper was accused of generating an atmosphere 'of despondency and resentment, of bitterness and scorn', which could only work to Hitler's benefit. The last straw came on 26 October, when the *Sunday Pictorial* faulted Parliament for 'letting the people down' and argued that half of the Cabinet should join Chamberlain on 'a permanent rest-cure'. The Prime Minister wanted to retaliate with immediate suppression, but the Home Secretary declined to gratify his 'repressive instincts' on the grounds that 'the democratic principle of freedom for expression of opinion means taking the risk that harmful opinions may be propagated'.[1]

The attacks subsided, only to revive in March 1942, after the humiliating loss of Singapore. On the 6th, a cartoon by Philip Zec in the *Mirror* showed a half-drowned sailor, clinging to a raft in oily seas. 'The price of petrol has been increased by one penny – official,' ran the caption supplied by 'Cassandra'. That obscure message could be taken either of two ways: as a tribute to the heroism of merchant seamen; or as an innuendo that, with government connivance, lives were being risked to realize higher profits. Bevin waxed 'highly emotional' on the subject. 'How,' he demanded of Morrison, 'was he to "press" people almost into the merchant navy if they were then to see the suggestion (in the cartoon) that they were being "pressed" in order to put the price of petrol up for the owners?' Simon concurred that the cartoon was not only 'cruel and deplorable', but also – and more to the point – actionable. Prevailing over them and Churchill, who 'didn't at all like it at the time', Beaverbrook persuaded Morrison that a stern warning would suffice. Accordingly, on the 19th, Bartholomew and C. E. Thomas, the *Mirror*'s editor, were summoned to the Home Office, where Morrison 'cheerfully' threatened them with the fate that had befallen the *Daily Worker*. Bevan, who disdained the 'form of journalism' represented by the *Mirror* ('I do not like the strip-tease artists'), saw the irony of its being brought to heel by Morrison, who had 'taken its money' as a

[1] War Cabinet minutes, 7 October 1940 and 17 November 1941, quoted in Donoughue and Jones, *Morrison*, pp. 297, 299; Lloyd George to G. M. Ll. Davies, 31 October 1940, quoed in K. O. Morgan, 'Peace Movements in Wales, 1899–1945,' *Welsh History Review*, x (1981), 421; Churchill to King, 25 January 1941, quoted in Edelman, *Mirror*, pp. 104–105, and Hugh Cudlipp, *Publish and Be Damned* (London, 1953), p. 158, where the wording is different.

columnist. So, for that matter, had Churchill, who came to consider the *Mirror* 'the worst of all. . . . It makes me spit.'[1]

Whereas none of the Fleet Street dailies had expressed concern when the *Daily Worker* was shut down, the mere threat to invoke Defence Regulation 2D against the *Mirror* unleashed a storm of protest. The *Manchester Guardian*, the *News Chronicle*, and the *Daily Herald* professed varying degrees of outraged libertarianism. *The Times*, commenting on Morrison's statement to the Commons, insisted that 'yesterday's reminder to one newspaper will in no way deter the rest from the discharge of their duty' (20 March). Of the big guns, only Camrose's *Telegraph* and Kemsley's *Sketch* and *Sunday Times* took the government's part.

For the rest of the war, the *Daily Mirror* minded its ways without quite mending them. Morrison's admonition did its work and possibly served to chasten other would-be offenders. The government, too, learnt a lesson from this unedifying episode. And, not least, improved prospects for victory alleviated the tensions that had led to confrontation. There were further clashes between editorial and official opinion, but none of them had the same intensity or constitutional ramifications.

Regarding each other with wariness, the government and the press evolved a new relationship during wartime. Or, at any rate, they kicked over the traces of earlier relationships. George Orwell, in the 'London Letter' he addressed to the American readership of the *Partisan Review* on 15 April 1941, declared that British journalism had grown more homogeneous and, in the process, more radical. 'The tone of the popular press has improved out of recognition during the last year', to the point that it was barely distinguishable from that of the 'quality' press. 'All of them print articles which would have been considered hopelessly above their readers' heads a couple of years ago.' But the change was not simply one of intellectual standards. 'Nearly the whole of the press is now "left" compared with what it was before Dunkirk – even *The Times*', which Orwell had identified in his previous 'London Letter' as the organ of 'reactionaries'. Indeed, 'to find any straight-forward expression of reactionary opinions' that spring, one would 'have to go to obscure weekly and monthly papers, mostly Catholic papers'. Allegedly, this shift reflected 'the decline in the trade in consumption goods', which 'robbed the advertisers of much of their power over editorial policy'. More emphatically, it reflected a heightened commitment to objectivity ('I believe that this is the most truthful war that has been fought in modern times') and a retreat from partisan politics. 'Debates in

---

[1] Foot, *Bevan*, I, 354–55; *Parliamentary Debates* (Lords), 5th ser., cxxii, cols. 506–16 (26 March 1942); Donoughue and Jones, *Morrison*, pp. 299–300; Calder, *People's War*, pp. 288–89; interviews with Morrison (28 May 1942) and Churchill (26 March 1943), Crozier, *Off the Record*, pp. 324–25, 349–50. Lunching at the Reform Club on 23 March 1942, Brooks saw Morrison, 'who, after his attack on the *Daily Mirror*, is said to be virtually "finished"; for those who hate the *Mirror* say he should have suppressed it out of hand, and everybody else says he is menacing freedom of speech. Poor little bewildered 'erb.' Brooks's diary.

Parliament are probably not misrepresented in the press,' Orwell supposed, 'but with a House full of dead-heads they are growing less and less interesting and only about four newspapers now give them prominence.'[1]

The *Daily Mirror*, with its motto 'we are all in it together', was pugnaciously populist. The *Daily Herald* moved leftwards to recapture lost ground, the *News Chronicle* did so out of social concern, and *Picture Post* by the editorial dynamism of Tom Hopkinson. The Beaverbrook papers, especially the *Evening Standard* (which shared Orwell's services, and Bevan's with *Tribune*), followed suit. Perhaps their owner was too busy with affairs of state; perhaps, too, he harboured a latent radicalism. In either case, as Orwell observed, the *Standard* was the sounding-board for 'young journalists of left-wing views who are allowed to say what they like so long as they don't attack the boss directly'.

That summer, *The Times* was similarly invigorated by the advent to its editorial chair of Barrington-Ward, a self-styled 'Tory Radical', who entertained 'a belief in independence toward Ministers and in a strict sense of justice'. As the official historians of that paper have slyly put it: 'He had not his predecessor's instinct for politics without policy provided the Conservative party was in power.' The new editor was assisted by E. H. Carr, who came to Printing House Square with considerable experience in diplomacy and after a stint at the Ministry of Information and who left in 1946 to pursue a distinguished academic career. Carr, besides being 'very productive of leaders', proved 'very willing. . . . to listen to counsel on how to put advanced views in such a way that they will seem to our constituency the most normal and inevitable truths'. Put off by Dawson, who sheltered behind 'rather transparent conventions . . . to stave off discussion of political or social issues', Carr enjoyed greater latitude under Barrington-Ward, who was more 'inclined by temperament to accept in advance . . . the upheaval which this war is now creating and will create'. On 29 July, twelve days after he began his seven-year editorship, Barrington-Ward gave an impromptu after-dinner speech to the 1922 Club. 'Somewhat embarrassed', he chose the topic of reconstruction and, 'incidentally', pointed out to his audience of Tory backbenchers 'that *The Times* was not a Conservative paper and that we regarded it as essential to be free to consider proposals on their merits'. To Sir Herbert Williams, then Tory MP for Croydon South, *The Times* soon came to qualify as nothing more than 'the threepenny edition of the *Daily Worker*'.[2]

Of course, not everyone in Fleet Street was swept along by these strong currents. The *annus mirabilis* had opened with an honours list that struck Frank Waters as 'nice and Jane Austenish'. In addition to the dignities conferred on

---

[1] Orwell, 'London Letters' dated 3 January and 15 April 1941, reprinted in *Collected Essays, Journalism and Letters* (London, Penguin edn., 1970), II, 67, 137–39.

[2] Barrington-Ward's diary, 9 January, 13 February, 18 March, and 29 July 1941; *History of The Times*, IV, part 2, 1024–25; *Parliamentary Debates* (Commons), 5th ser., ccclxxxvi, col. 2017 (18 February 1943); *also see* A. C. H. Smith, *Paper Voices*, p. 90, and Addison, *Road to 1945*, pp. 151–53.

Mann and Garvin, Camrose managed 'to scramble up another rung of the social ladder with a viscountcy. The distinction's so important, don't you think?' Waters wrote facetiously to his wife. Camrose, he reckoned, was

> aiming at an earldom which he'll get if the war goes on long enough, by kow-towing to the Conservative Party. As Editor-in-Chief of the *Daily Telegraph* he's carefully suppressed every twinge of conscience that paper has had – and there have been many – over major issues of High Policy. The Conservatives now have him well and truly gagged.

Not for nothing did Camrose suffer derision in *Tribune* as the Tories' 'ever loyal yes-lord' (e.g. 21 March). His brother, Lord Kemsley, graduated to a viscountcy four years later. Channon described a scene at the Kemsley dinner-table, where a proof copy of the *Daily Sketch* was delivered: 'it contained a short, sharp leader story offensive to Mr Churchill', which was removed between courses. To displease the Prime Minister was to forego preferment. Craving further adornment, Baron Luke bought a controlling interest in *Truth*, which he hoped to use 'as a lever to a Viscountcy'. He was as unsuccessful as Collin Brooks, whom he hired to 'bring it back to the great days when Labby [Henry Labouchere] was its chief'.[1]

With Layton (who waited until 1947 to collect his peerage) seconded to the Ministry of Supply, Laurence Cadbury took charge of the *News Chronicle* and found it 'no easy job to keep his emotional team in order. He himself has broad opinions,' wrote Barrington-Ward, 'but none of the *News Chronicle*'s ideologies and prejudices.' Barrington-Ward also heard of difficulties at the *Observer*. On 6 March, he lunched with Dr Thomas Jones, now a member of the board, who reported that a search had begun 'for an eventual successor to Garvin. We discussed possibilities.' It was understood that the paper would 'one day belong to David Astor', born in 1912 and now serving with the Royal Marines, who saw 'the whole of my future in terms of the *Observer*'. In May, despite Garvin's known apprehensions, Astor assumed responsibility for 'organising regular contributions for the centre page', which Garvin considered his own 'sacred' sphere. 'I know you realize that I have no vainglorious desire to see my stuff in print,' he wrote disarmingly to the editor, born in 1868, 'but that I am acutely interested in drawing attention to conceptions which can help in the hellish situation we have arrived at'. David Astor prized his 'pupil-and-teacher relationship' with Garvin, whom he depended upon 'to instruct me in the profession of journalism so that eventually I may be a good servant of the paper you have done so much to create as a leading organ of intelligent thought'. Nevertheless, his youthful idealism posed a threat to Garvin's supremacy.[2]

---

[1] Waters to his wife, 1 January 1941, Waters Papers; *Chips* (entry of 4 February 1942), p. 320; Brooks's diary, 31 October and 12 December 1940.

[2] Barrington-Ward's diary, 6 and 27 March 1941; David Astor to Garvin, 26 May and 20 August 1941, Garvin Papers.

Having no wish to be reminded of his mortality, Garvin resented what he took as incursions upon his authority. His dispute with the Astor family, though of a professional nature, was shaped by political events and coloured by personal factors. In April 1941, when the war was going badly, mutterings against Churchill came briefly back into fashion. Oliver Harvey claimed to know for a fact that there was 'collusion' between the new Lord Rothermere – 'as bad as his father' – and Southwood of the *Daily Herald*, who had joined 'the remnants of the Chamberlainites . . . to raise their ugly heads at the first signs of trouble for which they can't be held directly responsible'. Churchill won a massive vote of confidence in the House of Commons on 7 May and, the next month, Russia was welcomed as an ally. Still, Garvin detected that David Astor and his 'set' were 'critical of Winston', which Astor rejected as 'an over simplification, if I may say so'.[1]

Unlike Gerald Barry, who bluntly exclaimed 'that he is tired of Winston's rhetoric', Garvin could not get his fill. Perhaps he was over-compensating. For, as Field Marshal Lord Gort asserted in a controversial dispatch, which Lord Astor took to heart and committed to memory, the *Observer* 'did not play its part in trying to remedy . . ., by timely constructive criticism', the 'many grave deficiencies and serious human inadequacies in Mr Chamberlain's administration'. Wary of Garvin's impetuosity and inconvenienced by his unconventional work habits, Lord Astor was eager for a clean break with the past. As stipulated in his agreement with Garvin, he submitted his grievances to a tribunal. Sir Edward Grigg and Dawson were appointed to arbitrate, along with Mann, Garvin's own nominee, who joined at Bracken's invitation. They considered the charges that 'the tone and attitude adopted by Mr Garvin' were prejudicial to the interests of the *Observer*, where matters of 'political controversy', offensive to the proprietor, had been 'unnecessarily raised'.[2]

A compromise was worked out, only to be upset on 22 February 1942, when Garvin published a signed article which seemed to render 'the new *Observer* contract impossible of execution'. Among other things, Garvin had written disapprovingly of Beaverbrook's release from office, which he trusted 'would be of brief duration'. Whether his intention was to buttress Churchill or to chivvy him was, to all intents and purposes, irrelevant. Garvin acknowledged that his article, by taking sides with Beaverbrook, 'brought about an absolute incompatibility of conviction' with the Astors and destroyed 'all hope of an honourable and workable settlement' with them. Grigg, as chairman of the tribunal, was 'obliged by circumstances' to recommend that 'My dear old

---

[1] Harvey's diary, 17 and 18 April 1941, Add. MSS. 56,397; David Astor to Garvin, 20 August 1941, Garvin Papers.

[2] Brooks's diary, 31 December 1941; Bracken to Mann, 5 September 1941, Mann Papers; memorandum by Mann, 5 October 1941, Grigg Papers; memorandum by Lord Astor, 28 October 1941, and Grigg to Garvin, December [n.d.] 1941, Garvin Papers.

Garve' should resign.[1]

His displacement followed with an urgency that surprised even those who had known it to be 'in the wind for some time'. A. G. Gardiner, who understood from personal experience 'how these things happen . . . – the slow smouldering & the sudden flame', reported that the view at the Reform Club 'is that it was the attitude to Churchill that brought it about'. Later, Gardiner heard from Wilson Harris, who was 'called in to tide the ship over the immediate weeks', that 'the immediate crash was over the attitude of Garvin to Beaverbrook'. That cast a different light on the matter. 'I can't pretend to support any judgment that believes in B.,' declared Gardiner, who wondered: 'What is Beaverbrook's game & where does J.L.G. stand in regard to it? B. is an intriguer first, last & always & he is the more dangerous because his intrigues are governed by no principle', merely 'by personal aims & an insane passion to pull strings'. It was natural for a Liberal journalist, embittered by memories of the last war, to scent a press conspiracy. But Sir Thomas Dugdale (later 1st Baron Crathorne), whom Brooks met at the Conservative Central Office, was likewise 'fearful of what Max Beaverbrook may do'. The new Tory chairman regarded Beaverbrook 'as a man utterly and completely untrustworthy, a crook of crooks, without principle or conscience'. He agreed with Brooks that, as the result of Garvin's divestiture, 'the Party has no Press at all – either daily or periodical – *Truth* being nearest to a dependable organ and that more Right than centre'. Dugdale thought that young Rothermere was behaving 'better now than before', but was 'apt to be drawn off by the dinner-table flattery of women. Kemsley was still unstable of opinion.' These suspicions were groundless. Yet how could one tell for sure?[2]

Lord Astor did not have time to worry about them. His first task was to find an editor who would serve until such time as his son was ready to take command. The obvious candidate was Mann, who put aside his misgivings and then fell ill with pneumonia. Harris and Geoffrey Crowther, on loan from the *Spectator* and *The Economist* respectively, 'helped out' in the interim. Astor was looking forward to the arrival of Mann, whom he respected for having 'worked closely with W.C. in the Neville days' and who was 'strong on winning the war'. Eden, whom Mann credited with a salutary influence over Churchill, was 'very glad to hear' from Grigg 'that Arthur Mann has agreed to take it over and I am sure he will do the job extremely well'. They were all disappointed when Mann, weakened by illness, withdrew. Astor then fell back upon Ivor Brown, hitherto best known as a drama critic, whom Gardiner did not consider

---

[1] Garvin to John Walter, 3 March 1942, *Times* Archives; Grigg to Garvin, 24 February 1942 (copy), Grigg Papers. Beaverbrook, in transferring from one ministry to another, was 'grateful for the most agreeable personal references' in the press. 'I owe so much to the generosity of the newspapers that I am now altogether the debtor of those who were my competitors in days gone by.' Beaverbrook to Crozier, 30 June 1941, *Guardian* Archives.

[2] Gardiner to Frank Swinnerton, 1 March, 25 April, and 11 May 1942, Swinnerton Papers; Brooks's diary, 12 March 1942.

'the man for such a salvage job', but who proved quietly effective as acting editor.[1]

Viola Garvin, the literary editor, left with her father, and several of the regular contributors accompanied them. Astor was sorry to learn that Kemsley had offered Grigg 'five times as much as we paid you' to write for the *Sunday Times*, for the *Observer* 'could not compete . . . on that sort of scale'. After all, as Grigg well knew, 'Kemsley has not a deadweight of a heavy weekly annuity to an ex-editor around his neck as well as an extra 6 months at full salary plus entertainment allowance'. That was the staggering price that Astor had paid to pension off Garvin and relieve him of his shareholding. Instead of showing gratitude, Garvin was reported – 'on what seems reliable authority' – as 'being naughty and creating unnecessary prejudice against us in Downing St. by saying that I am anti-Winston'. Such behaviour on Garvin's part was more than likely. Looking back upon 'the *Observer* earthquake', nothing less than 'a tragedy in journalism', he convinced himself that the Astors had 'wanted to change the thing into the *Cliveden Gazette*'. Borrowing his logic from Claud Cockburn, who had popularized the 'Cliveden Set' theory of contemporary history, he told his stepson that, after Lothian's death in December 1940, Lady Astor became determined to bring the paper 'under David's influence and Hers'. Supposedly, if 'Cliveden' had had its way, Garvin would have been forced 'to write under the direction of a committee'. Doubtless, he fervently believed it all. Yet it was absurd to suggest that David Astor's views were identical to his mother's. Besides, as one of the prancing 'Shiver Sisters', Garvin was in no position to throw stones at Cliveden.[2]

Lord Astor was not 'anti-Winston', but rather critical of parliamentary authority, which derived from an election that had seemingly taken place in a different world. 'I am disturbed by the feeling one encounters that one cannot expect to win a complete victory and so need not even make the attempt,' he wrote to Grigg. 'Our martial spirit has been dampened down and no one (except Cripps once) has given us a spiritual lead.' The phenomenon of Sir Stafford Cripps, who improbably emerged from the Labour sidelines as a serious contender for moral and political power, testified to the widespread disenchantment with official party leaderships. Newspapers, by articulating this malaise, heightened the estrangement. The *Herald*'s persistent carping at a government that contained Labour members drove Bevin to exchange sharp words and sharper silences with Southwood. Percy Cudlipp, its editor, in-

---

[1] Astor to Grigg, 26 June 1942, and Eden to Grigg, 1 July 1942, Grigg Papers; Gardiner to Swinnerton, 26 July 1942, Swinnerton Papers.

[2] Astor to Grigg, 8 and 31 May 1942, Grigg Papers; Garvin to Oliver Woods, 19 August and 14 October 1942, Woods Papers. 'This time last year you were struggling with J.L.G. and wondering what would happen to the *Observer* if he did not continue his association,' Lord Astor reminded Grigg on 8 December 1942 (Grigg Papers). He enclosed a manager's report that showed a 'really extraordinary' rise in sales over the past twelve months: 'the position is most satisfactory and gratifying'.

stanced 'three times when Ministers, besides Mr Churchill, tried to exert an influence on the *Daily Herald* in relation to comments on the news'. Sinclair felt compelled to defend his record at the Air Ministry to Crozier: 'You are my only staunch friend in the Press. Therefore, when I read any criticism in the *Manchester Guardian*, my first feeling is that I am probably in the wrong.' Under these concditions, no politician – not even Churchill – was beyond reproach.[1]

Beaverbrook, temporarily outside the charmed circle, had the perspective to see that 'a necessary result of a wartime coalition is a marked falling-off in Party allegiance'. That accounted for the by-election result on 25 June 1942 at Maldon, where Tom Driberg stood as an independent and captured a Tory seat. 'You are in the happy position of being both an MP & a columnist,' Christiansen reminded Driberg, whom he scolded for using the *Express* as a receptacle for 'what you cannot get rid of in Parliament'. Afterwards, Driberg tried 'so far as possible – though not always successfully – to keep my Parliamentary and journalistic activities separate'. It was not easy, however. Bound to one another by the ties of a coalition, party organizations lost contact with their press followers, who turned against them at will. 'My own view is that the political parties and particularly the Conservative Party must occupy the electors with political disputation,' Beaverbrook advised Sir Patrick Hannon. 'If they fail to do so, then the making of political propaganda will pass into other hands.' What Beaverbrook feared was already a reality.[2]

---

[1] Astor to Grigg, 11 March 1942, Grigg Papers; Minney, *Southwood*, pp. 334–35; Evidence, Royal Commission on the Press, 1947–49, Cd. 7432, q. 9120; Sinclair to Crozier, 6 March 1942, *Guardian* Archives.

[2] Beaverbrook to Blumenfeld, 6 July 1942, Blumenfeld Papers; Christiansen to Driberg, 28 April 1943, and Driberg to W. J. Brown, 31 October 1944 (copy), Driberg Papers; Beaverbrook to Hannon, 26 September 1942, Hannon Papers.

Seventeen

THE ROAD TO 1947 AND BEYOND

During the wartime years, when 'normal party politics were ... suspended in the interests of national unity'. British society was travelling along 'The Road to 1945'.[1] The press actively participated in this 'reformation of British politics' and, in turn, was transfigured by it. For newspapers, as for the country as a whole, the general election of 1945 was an unmistakable landmark. Two years later, it was followed by the appointment of the first Royal Commission on the Press, which measured the distance of the journey. In professional as distinct from strictly political terms, 1947 therefore qualifies as the ultimate destination.

The route was clearly signposted. On 11 September 1943, *The Economist* took stock of the relations between 'The Government and the Press', with a view towards post-war arrangements. 'On the one hand', the article noted 'a tendency to overstate the degree of wartime control over newspapers, ... which in fact operated very far from onerously'. On the other hand, too little attention was being paid to 'what the press itself must do, if it is to discharge fully its public responsibilities'. Looking forward to the time 'when the wartime grip of the Government, such as it has been, is removed', the anonymous author (perhaps Geoffrey Crowther) recommended the retention of select agencies to provide 'professional guidance' in the 'hard and unending ... struggle to maintain high standards, in the face of proprietorial pressures, financial considerations and the contemporary mistranslation of popularity to mean vulgarity'.[2] Those problems were hardly new, but a willingness to invoke state assistance as a means of solving them marked something of a departure, arguably more symptomatic than significant.

Various newspaper controllers could appreciate without difficulty the need for some degree of state intervention in the conduct of journalistic affairs, provided – of course – that it did not pertain to themselves. *The Economist*'s 'advice ... may be highly suitable where "the Beaver", Camrose or Cowley are concerned', Laurence Cadbury mused in a letter to Layton. Yet, he quickly added, 'even this depends on one's political or social point of view. Some

---

[1] Addison, *The Road to 1945*, pp. 13–14.
[2] *The Economist*, 11 September 1943.

people may, I suppose, object to Bevin and the Trades Unions controlling the policy of the *Daily Herald*, but such objection would I think carry little weight.' As for the *News Chronicle*, Cadbury could not 'see for the life of me' why any editorial functionary or external authority 'should be regarded as possessed of all the virtues and judgment while we presumably are asked to abdicate'.[1] For their part, the directors of the *Herald* would not have hesitated to prescribe *The Economist*'s remedy for their 'capitalist' rivals, each of whom would have considered it less appropriate for themselves than for the others. Later, testifying before the Royal Commission, a procession of witnesses aired an array of proposals along these lines.

Like other aspects of partisan activity, the trade in Fleet Street properties went into abeyance. That, however, did not preclude planning for future contingencies. On 2 June 1942, Collin Brooks was invited to lunch at the Sorcerer Room of the Savoy with J. C. Akerman, who proposed to renew his connection with the *News Chronicle*, this time as its owner. As managing director of the Provincial Newspapers group, Akerman aimed at buying the *News Chronicle* and its satellites from the Cadburys, with the *Financial News* as ballast. He visualized himself as chairman of the new amalgamation, with Brooks as editor-in-chief. Upon ascertaining that 'Laurence Cadbury will not sell any share in the *News Chronicle*', Akerman decided that 'we might go for the *Daily Mail*', which also proved unavailable. Evidently, political factors did not enter into his calculations. Nor, come to that, did they weigh so heavily as before upon the Cadbury brothers, who presently took the view that the *News Chronicle* would be compromised if Layton accepted the presidency of the Liberal Party Organisation.[2]

In the respected opinion of A. P. Wadsworth, who became editor of the *Manchester Guardian* in 1944 upon the sudden death of Crozier, the effect of the war was 'to lift newspaper circulations to higher levels than had ever been known'. Nevertheless, he hastened to point out, those gains were not spread evenly. Here, Wadsworth's graphs prove more instructive than the tables compiled for the Royal Commission; the latter, designed to compare average sales in 1947 with those a decade earlier, did not take account of fluctuations in between. The circulation of the *Daily Mail*, for example, continued to tumble until 1940, bottomed out from then until 1942, and thereafter began to creep upwards. Thus, the *Mail* looked a good deal healthier in 1947 than in 1937, but its percentage of the total market was still far less than it had been in 1930. The *News Chronicle* saw a modest recovery during the second half of 1942, with the *Daily Herald* following in 1943. The circulation of the *Daily Telegraph* peaked in 1940, then fell sharply until 1942, when the decline was arrested. The *Daily*

---

[1] Cadbury to Layton, 13 September 1943, Layton Papers.
[2] Brooks's diary, 2 and 8 June 1942; L. J. Cadbury to Layton, 7 January 1944, Layton Papers. Instead, Lady Violet Bonham Carter filled the vacancy created by the death of Lord Meston. Eventually, in 1952, Layton became deputy leader of the Liberal Party in the House of Lords.

Express and the *Daily Mirror* rose steadily throughout the entire period and surged ahead after 1943. 'The biggest gains among the mornings,' concluded Wadsworth, 'have been of those papers that have gone farthest towards becoming papers of entertainment.' The same held true among evening journals and in the Sunday arena, where the advances of the *Observer* and the *Sunday Times* were dwarfed by the *News of the World*. Restricted to a 'half page of stuff', the 'political articles' of the *News of the World* had no 'adverse effect on ... circulation', which 'was maintained in spite of them'.[1]

With newsprint in short supply, space was at a premium: the tonnage allocated to the *News Chronicle*, for example, was cut by 10 per cent in March 1942, raised by $11\frac{1}{2}$ per cent in September 1943, and raised again by 5 per cent in June 1945, but the size of the paper was four pages throughout this period and beyond. Fortuitously, there was less political news to report. *Ipso facto*, the political press lost its primary mission. That fate was happily accepted out of a determination to avoid entanglements. Barrington-Ward 'had to tone down Carr's leader somewhat' in *The Times* on 23 May 1943. 'The political effects of what he writes are not always plain to him,' reflected the editor, who shared the prevalent aversion to political effects in general.[2]

Nothing pleased Barrington-Ward more, not even healthy circulation reports, than to hear Churchill say that 'he read the papers every morning, *The Times* "last but one"', finishing up with the *Daily Telegraph* 'because I know that it will be all right!' Barrington-Ward would not have wanted the Prime Minister to save *The Times* for last, for that would have meant that he took it for granted, when its 'business ... was to see things on their merits' and without an 'axe to grind'. Needless to say, Churchill revised this sequence in conversations with other editors. 'Well, I like the *MG*. I always read it,' he declared the same week to Crozier, who spotted a copy 'lying spread out on the table' at Number Ten. The Prime Minister also spared a few good words for the *Yorkshire Post*. Crozier, 'to draw him', mentioned the *News Chronicle*. 'All over the place! Geese! Geese!' exploded Churchill.[3]

From Churchill's standpoint, the geese had apparently taken over the farmyards of Fleet Street. Of the major dailies, only the *Telegraph* adhered to a discernible party position. Writing to Beaverbrook 'merely as a close personal friend', Aneurin Bevan expressed concern that the vagaries of the *Daily Express* would have 'the most harmful effects on your political reputation.

[1] Report, Royal Commission on the Press, 1947–49, Cd. 7700, Appendix III; Evidence, Royal Commission on the Press, 1947–49, Cd. 7398, qq. 1720–22; Wadsworth, *Newspaper Circulations*, pp. 28–29, 35–37.

[2] Memorandum by Layton, Documentary Evidence, Royal Commission on the Press, 1961–62, Cd. 1812, IV, 242; Barrington-Ward's diary, 23 May 1943.

[3] Barrington-Ward's diary, 29 March 1943; interview of 26 March 1943, Crozier, *Off the Record*, p. 349. On a previous occasion, Churchill introduced Crozier as 'the Editor of our leading Liberal paper, no the only Liberal paper, for who would apply that great name to a paper which, like the *News Chronicle*, is moved only by nervous hysteria?' Crozier, *Off the Record*, p. 299.

They will give rise to the unwholesome impression that a straight political line is not being followed but rather a series of rather unpleasant intrigues are being set afoot.' Beaverbrook gave tit for tat by sending Bevan the same letter, with *Tribune* substituted for his own paper. Convinced that the existing coalition would not survive and that it presaged the splintering of the Labour Party, Beaverbrook wanted to keep his options – and Churchill's – open. 'For though I am a Conservative,' he professed, 'I am not of the Conservative Party.'[1]

Given the uncertainties with which they had to contend, newspapermen found it easier to rake over past political controversies. Morrison's decision to release Sir Oswald Mosley from prison in November 1943 was a case in point. Although the war was still being fought, Mosley was no longer regarded as a public danger and his health had broken down. Within the Labour movement and outside, there was a sharp outcry against Morrison's act of clemency, which rekindled the passions of the 1930s. Bevin's opposition notwithstanding, the *Daily Herald* applauded the move to forgive Mosley, a prodigal son, 'for a lapse of judgment which in his heart of hearts he probably regrets' (26 November). The *Daily Mail* welcomed the move as a vicarious vindication. But the *Daily Express* gave its benediction only after a clash between Beaverbrook and Christiansen. Informed by telephone that he 'was entitled' to advocate Mosley's release, the editor had mistakenly assumed that he was equally entitled not to do so. Holding 'no strong views about Mosley's continued imprisonment', Christiansen 'had a long memory of the disastrous effect which support of Mosley had had on the sales of the *Daily Mail* in the 1930s'. He and Beaverbrook 'quarrelled so violently' that Christiansen could 'well believe the story which reached me many years later that only the most persuasive pleadings by the managers saved me from dismissal'. Significantly, the issue at stake was commercial, not political, and the frame of reference was the previous decade.[2]

Churchill naturally disapproved when left-wing members of Beaverbrook's staff stood (like Driberg) – or threatened to stand (like Owen) – as independent candidates in wartime by-elections. By the early months of 1944, such challenges could no longer be ignored. On 14 February, Barrington-Ward was invited to lunch with Churchill and Eden. The purpose, it became clear, was to discuss 'home politics' and, in particular 'these by-elections. Was he to write a letter to every Govt. candidate?' asked Churchill, who 'said he wanted support' from *The Times*. Barrington-Ward replied that support would be forthcoming 'if Govt. candidates could run on a good reconstruction programme'. At that, Churchill sighed and said, 'Don't press me to your Christian communism.' Barrington-Ward found 'Winston explosive, but not bad tempered', yet 'appearing to take nothing in, no argument. Diehard and pugnacious,

---

[1] Bevan to Beaverbrook, 12 May 1942, Beaverbrook to Bevan, 14 May 1942, Beaverbrook to Arthur Sulzberger, 9 February 1942 and 20 March 1943, quoted in Taylor, *Beaverbrook*, pp. 531–32, 541, 555.
[2] Christiansen, *Headlines*, pp. 140–42.

evidently sore about these by-elections and probably under Max's influence at the moment.' It was common to regard Beaverbrook as a sinister master-mind, who did not so much stand as crouch behind the Prime Minister. 'Watch Beaverbrook,' Gardiner warned from the sidelines that May. 'He is deep in his intrigue again. . . . He's out for the Premiership. . . . No less an ambition than that.'[1]

As the war in Europe neared an end, political life began slowly to resume a familiar pattern. Most newspapers, however, were strikingly reluctant to pick up where they had left off in 1939, if not before. *The Times* joined the *Manchester Guardian* and assorted organs of the left (including the *Daily Worker*) in condemning British intervention in the Greek civil war. Churchill drafted a stinging letter of rebuke, replete with derisive references to the paper's handling of the Munich crisis, but Beaverbrook prevailed upon him not to send it. 'You told me your newspaper policy was – Square or Squash. That was a quarter of a century ago,' recalled Beaverbrook, who may have confused Churchill with Lloyd George. 'This letter to Barrington-Ward . . . does not make any effort to "Square" and it does not "Squash".' Bracken seconded Beaverbrook's advice. 'You can't berate an editor like that,' he reportedly told Churchill. 'He may be wrong and I think he is but he has his point of view as you have yours. Besides you can't tackle him on "Munich". That was Geoffrey Dawson's responsibility.'[2]

Perhaps it would have been better if Churchill had vented his spleen in private correspondence. Instead, he unburdened himself in a speech to Parliament on 18 January 1945:

> How can we wonder, still more how can we complain, of the attitude of hostile and indifferent newspapers in the United States when we have in this country witnessed such a melancholy exhibition as that provided by our most time-honoured and responsible journals [loud and prolonged cheers] and others to which such epithets would hardly apply [laughter]?

Bracken disclosed that Churchill had intended to be much more damning to *The Times*, but again 'Max restrained him'. Surely, argued Beaverbrook, the paper deserved some credit for 'its fine work in this war. And which paper,' he teased Churchill, 'gave you the best leader on your birthday?' All the same, Churchill said quite enough. Seated in the gallery, Barrington-Ward kept his eyes lowered ('I went on with my notes and did not inspect the demonstration') through the ordeal. He listened as Churchill's 'direct and obvious reference' to *The Times* 'immediately touched off the loudest, largest and most vicious –

[1] Barrington-Ward's diary, 14 February 1944; Gardiner to Swinnerton, 15 May 1944, Swinnerton Papers.

[2] Beaverbrook to Churchill [December 1944], quoted in Taylor, *Beaverbrook*, p. 562; Barrington-Ward's diary, 6 February 1945. On the 16th, Barrington-Ward gleaned from Stanley Morison 'the detail that it was shown to Eden too'.

even savage! – cheer that I have ever heard in the House'. There was no doubt in his mind that the clamour came from the direction of the Tory benches, where 'the pent-up passions of three years' had erupted. Churchill's impression was that the cheering, 'louder' than any 'since the last war', had come 'from all parts of the House'. MPs, aware of the editor's presence, 'looked up at him. The proprietor of *The Times* was also in the House.' Barrington-Ward's only worry was that the humiliation might 'put a strain on the support' he enjoyed from John Astor, the Conservative member for Dover until the next election. A fortnight later, Barrington-Ward heard through the grape-vine that *The Times* could expect no forgiveness until it had repented. 'Very well,' he decided, 'it will not be forgiven.'[1]

Such defiance was not to be undertaken lightly, for it came in the midst of an intensified debate over the political responsibilities of journalists. 'Keep clear of political parties,' G. Wagstaffe Simmons enjoined the London members of the Institute of Journalists. As president of the metropolitan chapter and a newspaperman for sixty years, he was 'prepared to co-operate with journalists of every political faith in the promotion of the best interests' of the profession, but he declined 'to be identified in any way with any organisation of journalists which is pledged to any political party or combination of parties'. Chartered in 1890, the Institute was seventeen years older than the National Union of Journalists and, as befitting its seniority, less aggressive in pushing for higher wages. Affiliated to the TUC, which the Institute considered beneath its corporate dignity, the NUJ had recently called upon its membership to 'make up its mind where it is going to stand politically – with the other trade unions in the Labour movement, or timidly aside'. In a further attempt to bring journalists 'under the umbrella of politics', the TUC had resolved that only card-carrying members of the NUJ would be permitted to cover its annual conference proceedings. Prizing its 'freedom from alignment with the TUC, whose finances support a particular brand of politics', the Institute of Journalists protested that, sooner than allow themselves 'to be marshalled into one political camp', self-respecting professionals should hold aloof.[2]

That made sense to Barrington-Ward, who found the 'NUJ becoming tiresome with a demand for the "closed shop" where it is wholly improper – on the editorial side of journalism'. Anticipating the time when this 'denial of editorial freedom ... will have to be resisted', he wondered whether newspaper managements would stand together and whether the government would

---

[1] *Parliamentary Debates* (Commons), 5th ser., cdvii, col. 400; Barrington-Ward's diary, 7 March 1944, 18 January, 1 and 6 February 1945; Lord Moran, *Churchill* (Boston, 1966), pp. 256–57.

[2] Institute of Journalists, *Journal*, February, April, and July 1944; National Union of Journalists, *The Journalist*, May and June 1944. For the founding of these organizations, see A. J. Lee, *Origins of the Popular Press*, pp. 88, 112–16. For the strife between them, see C. J. Bundock, *The National Union of Journalists* (Oxford, 1957), chs. 22–23, which projects 'the non-party character' Bundock had described to the Royal Commission. Cd. 7317, qq. 54–56.

come to their defence. Michael Foot, who was to provide answers to these questions as Minister for Employment in 1975, approached these issues from the perspectives of the NUJ and the Labour Party, which adopted him as candidate at Devonport. His editorship of the *Evening Standard* had terminated in 1943, but he continued to write leading articles until the following spring, when he announced his parliamentary aspirations. 'As far as this Socialist business is concerned my views are unshakable,' he informed Beaverbrook:

> The leaders which I now write are hardly worth writing since they are non-committal and from my point of view I am associated with a newspaper group against whose policies (but not against the proprietor) I am resolved to wage perpetual war. Somehow things were different before. The compromise worked and certainly greatly to my advantage. But I do not see how it could work very much longer. The business of maintaining allegiance to my own political ideas and to a newspaper which fundamentally must be opposed to them is too difficult.

Beaverbrook, who felt 'the urge for a return to party warfare', could be trusted to understand.[1]

'The movement of opinion during the war has been to the left,' Beaverbrook accurately perceived. His staff, 'chosen with complete disregard to their political opinions', accordingly contained 'a large majority of Labour supporters' and a sprinkling of Communists. 'Most journalists are Labour, the best ones anyway,' his general manager insisted provocatively. Beaverbrook erred, however, in assuming that this situation would fail to work to the electoral advantage of the Labour Party, which 'will never poll an effective majority of the Country's votes, while it is dominated by the Trade Union interests. For the electorate will prefer the straight conservatism of the Tory Party to the disguised conservatism of the Trade Union bosses.' According to Beaverbrook's calculus, 'Churchill will lead his party to victory at the polls. His immense prestige will be worth, of course, very many votes. The weakness and divided counsels of his opponents may prove an even more valuable asset.' Only when the returns proved him wrong did Beaverbrook pause to reconsider.[2]

Other press magnates, even if they shared his myopia, did not come close to matching his vengeful ardour. The *Daily Mail*, having failed to reap the whirlwind, was in too sorry a state to rouse itself, much less its readers. Baron (soon to become Viscount) Portal, who drew his income from industry and his

[1] Barrington-Ward's diary, 7 June 1944; Foot to Beaverbrook, June [n.d.] 1944, and Beaverbrook to A. A. Berle, 31 August 1944, quoted in Taylor, *Beaverbrook*, pp. 550, 560. For Foot's later involvement with the 'closed shop' issue, see the *Observer*, 16 February 1975.
[2] Beaverbrook to J. S. Knight, 9 September 1944, quoted in Taylor, *Beaverbrook*, pp. 560–61; Evidence, Royal Commission on the Press, 1947–49, Cd. 7364, q. 5052.

inspiration from ministerial service under Churchill, sought Barrington-Ward's advice about purchasing that property. He was told to consult Stanley Bell, who had just retired as general manager 'with compensation amounting to £65,000' after a falling-out with Rothermere. Barrington-Ward could not imagine how Rothermere, alleged to be nearly bankrupt, could have paid this settlement. He was still more surprised to hear from several informants that Rothermere had 'put a large sum into the Liberal Party'. It was not clear which was the more doubtful, Rothermere's motives or his solvency. On 6 October, Brooks was 'lunched by old Sir George Sutton at the Ritz, where we talked newspaper shop and politics'. Sutton, whose memories of Carmelite House stretched back to Northcliffe's heyday, confessed to 'a poor opinion of Esmond Rothermere, and says that Lady O'Neill's control of him is so well known in political circles the *Mail* has lost all real influence'. That was a simplification. But, then, the system of control at Associated Newspapers was an unusually simple one, relying as it did 'so much on personality and so little on form'.[1]

'I suppose we have now got to indulge once more in the old slogans of Party warfare,' Laurence Cadbury wrote without relish to Layton. 'It is not an exhilarating thought.' To a solicitor, who had requested biographical information, Layton confirmed that Laurence had 'not retained the close association with the Society of Friends which some other members of his family have done'. Nor was Laurence, whose son was elected to Parliament in 1979 as a Conservative, as steadfastly Liberal as his own lineage implied. More disturbed by the spread of socialism than by the lassitude of an entrenched Toryism, he regretted the *News Chronicle*'s progressive bias as a drain on circulation, always his primary concern. During the war, the paper had muted its party colours, which Laurence Cadbury would have been glad to leave indefinitely in storage.[2]

The *Observer* occupied an analogous position. There was no going back to its pre-war style and attitudes. As 'the basis for a statement' on 'future policy and purpose', Arthur Mann – appointed a trustee – extracted passages from various memoranda and from a statement that Ivor Brown had issued on 1 November 1942. Promulgated on 14 June 1944 as a 'moral code', this document outlined the goals to be pursued 'without distinction between political parties' and, if necessary, in resistance to them:

> Amid this chaos the transient nature of existing Parties and alignments becomes obvious, while the permanence of principles is plainer and more precious than ever. The *Observer* should not be a Party paper. It must be tied

---

[1] Barrington-Ward's diary, 18 September 1944; Brooks's diary, 6 October 1944; Report, Royal Commission on the Press, 1947–49, Cd. 7700, p. 43. Lady O'Neill, the widow of the 3rd Baron, married Rothermere in 1945 and Ian Fleming in 1952; she was the second of Rothermere's three wives.
[2] Cadbury to Layton, 19 March 1945, and Layton to S. Clench, 18 October 1944 (copy), Layton Papers.

to no group, no sect, no interest. It should belong to no combine of journals. Its independence must be absolute. But merely to stand alone, challenging and bracing as that attitude may be, is not enough. One must also stand for a system of ideas and for a pattern of constructive reform. Not to be bound by Party or personal ties makes allegiance to declared principles all the more necessary.

In the Brave New World that was coming, 'Christianity without dogma' was to have the concomitant of political journalism without parties.[1]

Not even *The Times* was impervious to such heady idealism. Frank Waters, discharged from the army and reluctant to return to Beaverbrook's outpost in Glasgow, received an offer to become assistant manager at Printing House Square. Waiting 'to see what are the terms and conditions', he assumed a mission of 'imposing upon the nation some of the radical ideas & reforms it so badly needs'. *The Times*, he knew, might serve 'as a potential weapon without comparison. Properly handled and adroitly developed it can be exploited as a remarkable instrument of power & persuasion.' On 21 December 1944, after a meeting with Astor and the board, Waters took on the assignment. Earlier that day, he had seen Ralph Assheton (later 1st Baron Clitheroe), the new chairman of the Conservative Party, who 'was keen that I should go forward as a candidate but considered it impossible to do both *The Times* job and parliamentary work as well'. In his Glasgow days, Waters had flirted with the National Labour Party, until he saw that its local operations were 'a political façade for plutocratic building contractors'. The notion that he might stand as a Conservative, coupled with his objectives for *The Times*, indicated how far the pendulum had swung.[2]

Barrington-Ward was also in touch with Assheton, who invited him to dine *à deux* on 8 January 1945. They discussed economic issues, Assheton evincing 'his desire to see *T.T.* "stronger" on these matters', with strength being a euphemism for orthodoxy. His guest, 'though I should not have invited the discussion', confessed that 'it was pleasantly conducted'. But, however congenial, the evening made no difference to *The Times*'s editorial position on the subject of post-war reconstruction. Without being removed from the party chairmanship, Assheton was soon elbowed aside, and his functions were usurped by a troika, consisting of Beaverbrook, Bracken, and James Stuart (later 1st Viscount Stuart of Findhorn), the chief whip. By dint of audacity, Beaverbrook 'became in effect the party manager' of a party to which he professed not to belong.[3]

In May, after the German surrender, Churchill proposed to extend the

---

[1] Memorandum of 14 June 1944, Mann Papers. The indented portion comes, word for word, from Brown's 'The New *Observer*, a Paper and a Policy,' 1 November 1942.
[2] Waters's diary, 1 February 1941, 16 and 21 December 1944, 5 January 1945.
[3] Barrington-Ward's diary, 8 January 1945; Taylor, *Beaverbrook*, p. 564.

lifetime of his coalition until Japan was defeated, with an election to follow the restoration of peace. His Labour colleagues, some more categorically than others, rejected this timetable. On the 23rd, Churchill summarily disbanded the coalition and formed a preponderantly Conservative 'caretaker' administration to carry on through the election, which was fixed for 5 July. Three weeks passed between the break-up of the coalition and the dissolution of Parliament, which marked the official opening of the campaign. Another three weeks lapsed between polling day and the declaration of the results, delayed for the collection of the overseas service vote. In the interim, the political press went through many of the old motions with a distinctly new spirit and a decidedly different effect.

* * *

The general election of 1945, the third 'khaki' election of the century, was bitterly fought between foes who, until recently, had been partners. That, in itself, created an atmosphere of unease and confusion. Many contenders, as well as a large section of newspaper opinion, wished that bipartisan collaboration had somehow continued into the post-war age. But, once the tocsin was rung, such sentiments were irrelevant. Beaverbrook, among others, saw to that.

On the evening of 4 June, Churchill jumped the gun by delivering an election appeal over the BBC. Brooks, who had tuned in, was inclined 'to think he overplayed the partizan leader a little.'[1] There can be no doubt that, by resorting to vituperation, which was to be the staple of his campaign, Churchill tarnished his image. Perhaps he felt the need to establish his credentials among Tory activists, who had not accepted his leadership with enthusiasm. In any case, he set the tone for what followed.

The next evening, Clement Attlee 'did his piece' on behalf of the Labour Party and, in the opinion of Lord Moran, Churchill's physician, 'did it well'. Repelled by Churchill's 'bluster', Moran was convinced 'that the P.M. is on the wrong tack: Max and Brendan are his advisers, and he will not learn from anyone else'. Beaverbrook's biographer has strenuously insisted that his subject was not responsible for 'inspiring the virulence which Churchill discharged against the Labour leaders' (who were accused of designs to establish a 'Gestapo') and, indeed, that the two men 'hardly met while the campaign was on. . . . Nor did Beaverbrook issue any direct orders to his newspapers', which were left to intuit his wishes and probably went overboard in the attempt. At the very least, that was not the recollection of R. A. Butler, who dined with Churchill on 5 June 'and listened to Attlee's sober but stinging answer ("The

[1] Brooks's diary, 5 June 1945. 'Good God!' exclaimed Nicolson at the heresy that Churchill might be considered 'a politician'. Entry of 7 February 1944, Nicolson, *Diaries and Letters*, II, 347.

voice we heard last night was that of Mr Churchill, but the mind was that of Lord Beaverbrook")' in the company of Beaverbrook, Stuart, and Oliver Lyttelton (later 1st Viscount Chandos). After the broadcast, Beaverbrook 'rushed from the table to the telephone to call *Daily Express* experts in various cities', who assured him that Attlee's remarks had fallen flat. With or without Beaverbrook's instructions, the *Express* said as much the following day.[1]

'I do not manage or control the *Daily Express*,' Beaverbrook wrote drily on the 12th to Sir John Anderson (later 1st Viscount Waverley), who took him to task for that paper's prediction that the next Conservative government would lower the income tax. Again, there is contradictory evidence. Christiansen recalled that Beaverbrook, who 'had the time of his life' during the campaign, was then living in Arlington House, not far from Christiansen's own residence. It was no great inconvenience, therefore, for 'Lord Christiansen' (as Beaverbrook dubbed him over the telephone) to deliver the early editions of the paper to his proprietor. 'One night around midnight', Christiansen met Bracken, 'the *éminence grise* of the Tory Party', at Beaverbrook's apartment. 'As we left ... together at 2.30 a.m., Brendan put his arm around my shoulder and said, "Chris, the Conservative Party will never forget what you have done for us."' That may have been the night that the *Daily Express*, in an infamous headline, branded the Labour Party 'The National Socialists'. Brian Chapman, who was on duty as assistant managing editor, resigned in disgust. If Beaverbrook disapproved, Christiansen neglected to mention it.[2]

In a content analysis of the *Daily Express* from 16 June to 5 July, A. C. H. Smith has calculated that 20 per cent of the space allotted to election coverage – or 241 column inches – was lavished upon Churchill's campaign tours, starting on 23 June. This figure does not include 'reports of what he said, and of his other activities during the period', which were classified separately. In the seventeen issues surveyed, the election consumed 31 per cent of the total editorial matter, distributed as follows: '56 per cent reported or discussed Conservative views and public appearances, 26 per cent those of Labour, and the remainder concerned the smaller parties and the election process; 11 per cent of it was visual matter, photographs and cartoons.' Given that the bulk of Labour's inferior share (including the only photograph of a Labour politician) was devoted to Harold Laski, whom the *Express* portrayed as the personification of socialist villainy, the balance was even more skewed. This lopsidedness 'created the impression that the *Express* was to some extent the reproduced voice of Churchill himself'.[3]

At the opposite pole stood the *Daily Mirror*. Morrison, who ran Labour's campaign from Transport House, found it more malleable than the *Daily*

[1] Moran, *Churchill*, pp. 271–72; Taylor, *Beaverbrook*, pp. 565–66; Butler, *Art of the Possible*, p. 127.

[2] Beaverbrook to Anderson, 12 June 1945, quoted in Taylor, *Beaverbrook*, p. 566; Christiansen, *Headlines*, pp. 240–41.

[3] Smith, *Paper Voices*, pp. 25–27.

Herald, which was beholden to Bevin, his rival within the party hierarchy. According to Hugh Cudlipp, 'the Labour Party enjoyed the support of the *Mirror* in the 1945 election because it incorporated or appeared to incorporate in its programme more of the aspirations of the *Mirror*'s readers and writers than any other political group'. That was true, but only part of the story. Morrison skilfully angled for the support of the *Mirror* and landed it by laying on the cockney charm. He relied on Sydney Elliott, the political editor and subsequently editor of the *Herald*, to bring him face to face with Bartholomew, whom he embraced as a 'six-ribboned cherub'. The two men had not met since 1942, when Morrison, as Home Secretary, had rapped Bartholomew over the knuckles. They now agreed to let bygones be bygones. Zec, who had been the cause of the earlier unpleasantness, was commissioned to advise on the design of Labour posters.[1]

Definitely more paternalist than socialist, the *Mirror* captured the mood of 1945 without trying to shape it. With a circulation and a rhetoric that kept pace with the *Express*, the *Mirror* rendered incalculable assistance to the Labour side both in print and, especially, behind the scenes. Without ever delivering a formal endorsement, which would have been beside the point, it diligently highlighted Tory injustices and seized upon Tory contradictions. Thus, strictly speaking, it could claim to stand independently. The paper's phenomenal popularity among servicemen (30.3 per cent of whom were regular readers in the autumn of 1941) led Harold Nicolson's Tory friends to 'feel that the Forces will all vote for Labour. . . . They say that the *Daily Mirror* is responsible for this, having pandered to the men in the ranks and given them a general mistrust of authority.' Garry Allighan, the columnist who dispensed advice to men and women in uniform on 'the citizen's rights you are fighting to preserve', was elected Labour MP for Gravesend.[2]

Maurice Edelman, a beneficiary of the *Mirror*'s support in his own contest at Coventry West, later wrote an official history of that avowedly unofficial paper. For the first time in electoral history, he argued, 'Labour was not overwhelmingly outweighed in the National Press by the Tories'. Edelman arrived at this odd conclusion by cribbing it from R. B. McCallum and Alison Readman, who had reckoned that the 'combined net sales for June 1945' of the three London morning papers supporting Labour 'totalled approximately 6,000,000', while the aggregate circulation of the four pro-Conservative morning papers was 'approximately 6,800,000'. Apart from the inexplicable exclusion of evening and weekly journals, neither Edelman nor McCallum and Readman differentiated between types and degrees of support, with the result that their figures are debatable. In the Tory camp, they located the *Express*, the *Mail*, the *Telegraph*, and the *Sketch* (which stopped short of declaring a

---

[1] Cudlipp, *Publish and Be Damned*, p. 236; Donoughue and Jones, *Morrison*, p. 335.
[2] P. Kimble, *Newspaper Reading in the Third Year of the War* (London, 1942), p. 6; entry of 13 June 1945, Nicolson, *Diaries and Letters*, II, 469; Smith, *Paper Voices*, pp. 117, 237.

preference), but not *The Times*. Still more impressionistically, they bracketed the *News Chronicle* with the *Herald* and the *Mirror* as Labour organs. True enough, the *News Chronicle* was outspokenly anti-Tory. Yet its controllers would have balked at Edelman's suggestion that this paper was instrumental 'in redressing the old imbalance between press support in favour of the Socialists and Tories'. Furthermore, the trade unionists in charge of the *Herald* disdained the counterfeit proletarianism of the *Mirror*, and preferred to quote from the *Manchester Guardian* (as they did extensively on 4 July).[1]

Of all the papers, the *Herald* was the most conventionally partisan and, perhaps for that reason, regarded as minimally effective. Lord Camrose 'heard prominent members of the Party, some of whom had been directors of the Daily Herald Ltd., say that the *Herald* was very little use to them as a political newspaper'. Until the campaign was well under way, 'it could fairly be said that the *Herald* was by no means as political as the *Express* or the *News Chronicle*'. Thereafter, the *Herald* went 'all out', boldly asserting that 'a vote for Churchill is a vote for Franco' (18 June) and that Tory 'Frauds, Cheats, Wrigglers Seek Power' (26 June). 'The main head-lines of the *Daily Herald* blazoned election news every day except six during the month preceding polling day.' Moreover, on four of those 'off-days', the election figured in the second headline. Imputing a not-so-latent fascism to the Conservatives, the paper held that Churchill was 'swayed by Isolationist Advisers', geared for war against Russia (19 June). Despite such vehemence, the *Herald*'s 'plain speaking' has been judged less persuasive than the double-entendres of the *Mirror*, which dwelled jocularly upon Churchill's self-diagnosed infirmities and virtually ignored his oratory.[2]

With two major exceptions, the *Daily Herald* on one side and the *Daily Telegraph* on the other, the leading dailies eschewed formal party attachments. To be sure, each of them had a clear political orientation, but it tended to run counter to party interests as defined by the whips. This was especially the case among the traditionally Liberal papers, which were conducted with a chastening awareness that their party – fielding candidates in fewer than half of the constituencies – offered no viable alternative. The *News Chronicle*, under Barry's editorship and Layton's guidance, fudged the differences between the contenders on the left and tried to speak for a bilateral progressivism. Edited by Wadsworth, who was not himself a Liberal, the *Manchester Guardian* was equally keen to blur distinctions. Wadsworth wrote eighteen of the twenty-one 'long' leaders dealing with the election, as well as a dozen of the 'shorts'. With a pungency that Crozier had kept under wraps, he sought to promote 'the chance of a Liberal-Labour majority' (5 July), the best that he could hope for, by

---

[1] Edelman, *Mirror*, pp. 147–48, 151; McCallum and Readman, *The British General Election of 1945* (Oxford, 1947), p. 181.
[2] Camrose, *British Newspapers*, p. 45; McCallum and Readman, *General Election*, p. 190; Smith, *Paper Voices*, pp. 116, 238.

urging readers to vote Labour where no Liberal was standing. 'His misjudgment of Labour's chances enabled him to take a line which did not differ widely from what the *Guardian* had been saying for a good many years,' the 'biographer' of that paper has shrewdly noted. Wadsworth's task was therefore lightened by his defeatism. 'Had he been a better prophet, he would have had a harder decision to make.'[1]

In stressing the affinity between Liberalism and Labour, the *News Chronicle*, the *Manchester Guardian*, and the *Star* endeavoured to separate Labour from socialism. To Wadsworth, writing on 7 June, it was as 'fantastic' a 'misuse of words' to refer to 'the Labour people' as socialists as to call them Communists or Bolsheviks. For reasons of convenience, it also suited the *Daily Mirror* to divorce Labour from any ideology. The *Observer* and *The Times* went along with this trend, which the *Daily Telegraph* and the *Sunday Times* worked to resist. Simultaneously, most of the traditionally Conservative papers took pains to proclaim themselves Churchillian rather than Tory. 'This is a Man,' the *Mail* said of the Prime Minister, whose 'undiminished vigour' demanded 'the fidelity of a people' (4 July). The *Sketch* and the *Express*, with considerably less subtlety than *The Times*, likewise strove to distance their hero from his discredited predecessors and even from his colleagues. By boosting Churchill at the expense of his party, they inadvertently helped to identify Toryism as a negative creed.

The situation was hopelessly complicated. Wadsworth, a non-Liberal at the helm of a distinguished Liberal paper, was reconciled to the seeming inevitability of a Churchill victory and aimed no higher than to restrict its magnitude. Beaverbrook, accused of clasping left-wing vipers to his bosom, was confident of 'at least a comfortable majority', which he, for one, would find more comfortable if the old guard failed to share in the bounty. His single venture into print was a signed article in the *Herald*, which also provided a showcase for the vagrant talents of Hannen Swaffer and Michael Foot. Ernest Bevin, on the other hand, wrote for the *Observer*, and Garvin found a haven on the *Telegraph*. At the *Sunday Times*, Hadley put aside his residual Liberalism and 'accepted Kemsley's unintelligent brand of Conservatism with a certain complacency'. Although the *Telegraph* exuded optimism, Camrose was taking no chances. 'Churchill or confusion is the choice,' stated Garvin's article on polling day. Fearful that the electorate might choose wrongly, Camrose was quietly engaged in negotiations to dispose of the *Financial News* in the belief that Labour's success would spell the end of financial journalism, if not of the capitalist system. On the assumption that Labour would lose, the *Mirror* condemned the calling of the election as an unconscionable infliction. On the same assumption, *The Times* treated the Labour challenge with patronizing magnanimity. Had Barrington-Ward suspected what was coming, he might

---

[1] Ayerst, *Guardian*, pp. 560–63.

have stopped hankering after 'some kind of resumed coalition Govt' and would probably have held Carr on a tighter rein.[1]

The *Observer* stood apart, self-consciously but portentously. To the incomprehension of Lady Astor, who wistfully recalled how her father-in-law had purchased the property in 1911 to maintain it as a Tory organ, the paper took a vow to pursue 'an independent policy' in political affairs. In three consecutive numbers (17 and 24 June, and 1 July), a spokesman from each party was allowed to put his case: Dingle Foot led off for the Liberals; Ernest Bevin followed for Labour; and Richard Law (later 1st Baron Coleraine) wound up for the Conservatives. 'Now our part is done,' the paper editorialized on the Sunday before polling:

> The voter's hour draws near. Our aim has been not to tell him how he should vote but to help him vote well. ... It is precisely here, we believe, that an independent newspaper can perform a valuable and necessary function during an election campaign. By refusing to take sides it is not evading responsibility: it is accepting the responsibility of giving its readers an impartial survey of what the election is about.

David Astor, whose twenty-seven-year editorship did not begin until 1948, was behind this 'unusual stance'. The retirement from Parliament of his mother, who did not so much stand down as have the rug pulled out from under her by Lord Astor's decision on her behalf, made it easier to break with tradition. The parliamentary ambitions of David Astor's three brothers, all Conservatives, did not deter him. Like his father, soon to transfer control of the *Observer* to a set of trustees, the editor-elect proposed to transcend the political fray. In effect, however, the *Observer*'s detachment may be seen to have operated to Labour's advantage. By bucking the system, David Astor tacitly allied himself with the forces of change. That was evident from his assemblage of contributors, who included Orwell ('perhaps the greatest political influence on me'), Bertrand Russell, John Strachey (who defeated Dingle Foot at Dundee and went on to hold successive offices in the post-war Labour governments), Arthur Koestler, and Isaac Deutscher.[2]

All in all, the sharpest differences among newspapers were ones of deportment, not party preference. 'Hit the cymbal, bang the drum!' hawked the *Daily Express* (7 June). 'Walk up, walk up to the greatest sales circus of all time, the biggest most important General Election in the history of mankind, or the British nation.' The *Daily Mirror*, as King recalled, was even more unabashedly 'sensational and sexy'. Barrington-Ward was appalled by the

---

[1] Assheton to Beaverbrook, 25 January 1946, quoted in Taylor, *Beaverbrook*, pp. 566–67; Hobson *et al.*, *Pearl of Days*, p. 230; *Financial Times*, 12 November 1969; Barrington-Ward's diary, 4 July 1945.

[2] *Observer*, 28 December 1975; Michael Astor, *Tribal Feeling* (London, 1963), p. 201; Grigg, *Nancy Astor*, pp. 168–69; interview with David Astor, 20 June 1978.

'cheap tone' that prevailed, and held Churchill personally responsible. 'How can I throw up my hat for Winston in his present temper or encourage people to vote for his Govt without the assurance that they are going to do as well as the late coalition or better, in fulfilment of its policy and pledges?' he asked plaintively in his diary.[1]

Instead of providing thoughtful assurances, Churchill indulged in scare-tactics and invective. His hucksters took their cue from him and invited retaliation in kind. It would have been 'ingenuous to expect that any party battle would exclude the art and craft of the ring', *The Times* reflected on polling day. 'But the most hardened electioneer might be astonished to find how the powerful constructive case which the successors to the coalition can present has fallen back' into mud-slinging, 'designed to impugn the Labour Party's right to be considered democratic'. The *Manchester Guardian* agreed that, by squandering 'all his magnificent gifts on a trumpery exercise in political falsification', Churchill had made 'a pathetic descent' (3 July). The campaign was over before the *Observer* could pass judgment. 'It has seldom been the fate of a Tory Prime Minister to receive from *The Times*, on polling day, a rebuke for his irresponsible conduct of an election campaign,' it remarked on the 8th. That rebuke, 'it must be said frankly', was deserved.

Denied ideological sustenance by the Conservative leaders, who used their platforms for less dignified purposes, *The Times* and other potential exponents of an advanced Toryism were unable to offer a cogent appeal. It was fanciful for Barrington-Ward to esteem the Conservatives as 'successors to the coalition' when they themselves – much to the relief of the *Daily Telegraph* – spurned that legacy. Newspapers could not create a policy where none existed or, at any rate, where politicians declined to articulate one. Nor, given Churchill's avoidance of social issues, could the Liberal and Labour papers shift the focus of popular attention. Perhaps they did not really try. Liberal publicists were inhibited by their party's weakness, Labour ones by their party's internal dissensions and their own vulgar propensities. The problem was no longer the distribution of newspaper support between parties, but rather the distribution of newspapers between categories. 'The Press provides for a sufficient variety of political opinion,' reported the Royal Commission on the basis of the 1945 experience, 'but not for a sufficient variety of intellectual levels.'[2] Commercial inducements were, of course, a powerful factor in the lowering of standards. Yet the politicians, Morrison as well as Churchill, encouraged tawdriness and triviality in the abused name of democracy.

The question remains: What, if anything, did all this sound and fury accomplish? Or, from a contemporary vantage point, what results were ascribed to it? On the standard premiss that every copy of a newspaper was

---

[1] Cecil King, *The Future of the Press* (London, 1967), p. 60; Barrington-Ward's diary, 1 and 4 July 1945.
[2] Report, Royal Commission on the Press, 1947–49, Cd. 7700, p. 176.

read by an average of three people, the overall readership of the *Daily Express* (9,900,000) duplicated almost exactly the total Conservative vote (9,988,306). To equate the two groups, however, would be to accept a false syllogism. A substantial proportion of *Express* readers presumably disregarded its histrionic advice, just as many readers of the *Mirror*, the *Herald*, and the *Mail* ignored – or were oblivious to – the editorial directives they received from those papers. There was a vague correlation between newspaper consumption and party predilections, but it varied from place to place and, more strikingly, from class to class. In a survey of four hundred electors at East Fulham, Mass-Observation discovered that 'about one-fifth of Conservatives ... read papers which adopted a Labour or Liberal policy', while 'nearly a third of those intending to vote Labour read Conservative papers, and half as many again read Liberal papers'. Those who declared their support for Labour 'were, in fact, almost equally divided between readers of Labour papers and readers of papers favouring another party'. A quarter of them read the *Herald*, which otherwise found few customers in the constituency. Conservative sympathizers 'read the *Mail* proportionally three times as much' as Labour or Liberal enthusiasts. Owing to the primitive techniques at its disposal, Mass-Observation did not determine which Liberal papers were read by whom. (One suspects that the *Star* enjoyed a wider distribution in East Fulham than the weightier *News Chronicle* or the *Manchester Guardian*, which would have been difficult to obtain.) More importantly, unlike later market surveys, Mass-Observation did not ascertain whether readers were conscious of the party loyalties of the papers they read. Nevertheless, these findings were significant, if isolated and incomplete. The triangular relationship between parties, newspapers, and voter-readers, always more isosceles than equilateral, was weakened by the First World War and destroyed by the Second.[1]

From a later, more systematic investigation, David Butler and Donald Stokes derived 'ample evidence that in Britain the more strongly partisan voter is indeed more likely to expose himself to political information' distributed through newspapers. 'Although a number of voters without very strong party attachment report following politics in the press, the link between exposure and party commitment is plain.' But not so plain as to signify the existence, much less the direction of a causal relationship, for it admittedly remained a moot point whether 'the partisan seeks out news of politics' or, conversely, extracted political intelligence out of news. It would be interesting, but impossible, to establish whether the 'strongly partisan voter' and the voter 'without very strong party attachment' read the same papers and with comparable acuity. Beyond that, there is the familiar problem of measuring degrees of commitment on the part of the voter and the newspaper alike. What will strike one reader as fair comment will invariably infuriate another as a wilful distortion. Bracken, as Minister of Information, could not escape this

[1] Mass-Observation Report No. 2270c.

problem. 'BBC news bulletins are wholly free from interference by the Government, or by any of the political parties,' he assured Driberg. 'A good testimony to their unbiased independence is the fact that we receive just as many complaints from the Right, who think that the BBC bulletins are too Left, as complaints from the Left.' Objectivity is itself a highly subjective concept.[1]

Newspapermen, even more vulnerable than broadcasters, realized as much, and waged the 1945 campaign accordingly. The more elevated their arguments, the smaller and more select the audiences that they stood to reach. On 2 July, Laurence Cadbury took strong exception to a remark in that morning's *News Chronicle* that 'the Liberal and Labour radio speakers have won all the honours' in the battle for the airwaves. 'All readers are not, of course, listeners to political radio broadcasts,' he told Layton, 'but neither do all our readers pay attention to the Leader column.' His impression was unhappily confirmed when Barrington-Ward eventually went to lunch with Churchill, who volunteered the 'astonishing confession' that, as much as he admired *The Times* of late, 'I never read the leaders'. Who, then, did read those leading articles, once the core of every respectable and responsible newspaper? From all indications, the ones in the quality papers were more usually skimmed than studied, while those in the popular prints were mainly decorative. The educated public could gauge a newspaper's attitude from its selection and display of news stories. Consequently, it mattered more how prominently a topic was featured – at what length? with what size headline? in what position on which page? – than what was said about it. Opinion, political or otherwise, insidiously crept in between or behind the lines. 'You always taught me not to let the paper's editorial views dominate the news columns,' Christiansen recalled to Beaverbrook; 'of course they often did by inference, but it was, nevertheless, against your teaching.'[2]

Over time, the leader-writers in the better papers (being those that employed better leader-writers) came to write for the edification of one another. Hammond, a past master of the craft, congratulated Wadsworth on the quality of his election leaders: 'You have proved even to your own doubting self that you are "*capax imperii*".' That was not to be confused with *vox populi*.

---

[1] Butler and Stokes, *Political Change in Britain* (London, 1969), p. 222; Bracken to Driberg, 26 February 1945, Driberg Papers.

[2] Cadbury to Layton, 2 July 1945, Layton Papers; Barrington-Ward's diary, 13 December 1946; Christiansen to Beaverbrook, 7 January 1961, Beaverbrook Papers, C/81. According to a Mass-Observation report, prepared for the Advertising Service Guild in 1949, a '"serious-minded" minority' of newspaper readers regarded the leading article with a 'sort of stable approval that seldom rises to enthusiasm'. As compared to 'more than half' of *The Times*'s readers who said that they read the editorial columns, 37 per cent of *Daily Telegraph*, 29 per cent of *News Chronicle*, 24 per cent of *Daily Express* and *Daily Mail*, 15 per cent of *Daily Herald*, and a mere 3 per cent of *Daily Mirror* readers said that they read this feature. Except in the case of the *Mirror*, the percentage of readers who 'particularly' liked this feature was dramatically lower in each instance. *The Press and Its Readers* (London, 1949), pp. 48–50.

Without having 'ventured to forecast' the 'silent revolution' that occurred at the polls on 5 July, Wadsworth responded 'with confidence' to the belated announcement of the Labour landslide (27 July). Barrington-Ward, too, was overwhelmed by 'election results pouring upon us in a grt. avalanche'. In the light of the upset, he 'pondered my leaders' – which was what a serious editor did – and arranged for Donald Tyerman to write one 'reminding Labour that it has not been returned to power by the Labour Party but by a mass of voters who are in no way dedicated to the principles of Socialism'. His logic was curious and his presumption extraordinary. If, as he soon discovered, Churchill 'never read the leaders', Attlee had even better justification for skipping directly to the crossword.[1]

* * *

In the general election of 1945, 'when only sound broadcasting existed and its impact was confined', though by no means negligible, newspapers were still relatively plentiful and identifiable in terms of a particular partisan slant. Afterwards, with the advent of television and the expansion of radio, the political influence of the press grew steadily more 'randomized', sporadic, and marginal. Within *The Changing British Party System*, as S. E. Finer has mapped its contracting boundaries, party organizations could no longer pretend to 'control the media, which have become increasingly independent of them since 1945'. By then, as we have seen, the press already exercised a considerable 'discretion on how to handle the campaign'. But it was only in the post-war period that the extent and effect of this transformation were fully appreciated.[2]

In the course of adjusting to the new situation at Westminster, political journalists were bound to reflect upon their own professional functions and obligations. Whereas a Conservative victory might have blunted the challenge, the triumph of the Labour Party symbolized a revolutionary spirit that demanded nothing less than a reappraisal of national institutions. The Royal Commission on the Press must be seen in exactly that light. Even before it began its inquiries, editors were compelled to ask themselves difficult questions. 'With a Labour Govt in office', Barrington-Ward resolved that the policy of *The Times* should be 'independent but not hostile' so as to be 'in a good position to bring some influence to bear'. At least that was his pious hope, inspired by a conviction that, over the next five years of Labour rule, 'the opportunities and the risks' would 'about match each other'. *The Times*'s flexibility was facilitated by assurances from Waters, with whom the editor saw

---

[1] Hammond to Wadsworth, 10 July 1945, quoted in Ayerst, *Guardian*, p. 563; Barrington-Ward's diary, 24 June 1947.

[2] Finer, *The Changing British Party System, 1945–1979* (Washington, D.C., 1980), pp. 128, 161.

'very much eye-to-eye', that the paper's 'financial position ... is so good that there is nothing to stop it going to town in whatever direction is decided'.[1]

The Liberal papers, on shakier ground financially and politically, underwent a similar process of disengagement. In a conversation with Frank (later Baron) Byers, one of the dozen successful Liberal candidates, Laurence Cadbury 'raised ... the question of how Liberals were to deal with their Labour opponents' in the House and especially outside. Unless the Liberals were 'able to put up as good a fight against them as against the Conservatives', there did not seem to Cadbury 'to be much hope for the Liberal Party'. Byers was a disappointment. 'It was difficult to get him down to concrete propositions suitable for a political campaign.' Egbert Cadbury, Laurence's cousin and a Liberal activist who had stood at Stroud in the recent election, succeeded Henry Cadbury as a trustee and was 'exceedingly annoyed at the lack of criticism of the Government' in the pages of the *News Chronicle*. He could only 'hope that the *N.C.* will endeavour to get a little punch into its leading articles', which he, for one, continued to read.[2]

The *Manchester Guardian* was striving to shed its parochialism and to assert a national identity. 'The submergence of the Liberal party' at the polls was 'a disappointment' (27 July), but also an opportunity. The paper 'did not, of course, formally dissociate itself from the Liberal Party – that would have been bad business and bad politics', but rather 'it let certain connections drop'. Wadsworth declined to follow his predecessors' practice of joining the Manchester Liberal Federation, which C. P. Scott had once headed. When he promised 'that the *Manchester Guardian* will always do the utmost in its power to uphold Liberal principles and to further the Liberal cause', he scrupulously refrained from specifying the Liberal Party and decided that, 'in the best interests of the paper in the present state of national affairs', any such assistance would have to be rendered 'without formal ties'. In case of any lingering doubt, Wadsworth subsequently refused to serve on a Liberal fund-raising committee or to attend a dinner of Liberal journalists in honour of Clement Davies, the party leader. Lastly and most explicitly, he revised the appropriate entry in the 1956 edition of *Everyman's Encyclopaedia* to state, with Delphic ambiguity, that the paper had been 'independently progressive' in its outlook 'since the decline of the Liberal Party'.[3]

Longer than most, Percy Cudlipp remained enrolled in the old school, from which his brother Hugh played truant. Having been editor of the *Evening Standard* from 1933 to 1938 ('No cause is really lost until we support it,' he had told Hugh), Percy withstood Beaverbrook's blandishments to lure him back from the *Daily Herald*. Although 'attracted to the prospect', as any editor 'fond

---

[1] Barrington-Ward's diary, 29 July 1945; Waters's diary, 15 October 1945.
[2] L. J. Cadbury to Layton, 14 September 1945, Henry Cadbury to Layton, 23 January 1946, and Egbert Cadbury to Layton, 4 July 1946, Layton Papers.
[3] Ayerst, *Guardian*, pp. 564–65.

of writing would be', he could not imagine 'taking steps which would be unfair to Odhams Press and to the Labour Party'. In July 1949, he turned down an invitation to visit Beaverbrook in Jamaica the following February. 'During that month the Labour Party will be celebrating its Jubilee,' he explained, and it was thought fitting 'that the editor of the *Herald* should be on hand at such a time'. Hugh Cudlipp, whom Richard Crossman did not regard as 'a serious-minded Socialist', would never have permitted a party obligation to stand in his way. Twice editor of the *Sunday Pictorial* and, in between, managing editor of the *Sunday Express*, he eventually found his *Mirror*-image in Cecil King, whom he advised, cajoled, and finally displaced. King, who 'declares himself to be no socialist', was not even a member of the Labour Party, though he flew a red flag from his Rolls Royce (registration mark CHK 44) in the 1964 election. 'His policies were as intuitive as they were intellectual,' Edelman has written. The corollary is that they were neither.[1]

An abjuration of party affliation was not to be construed as political disinterest and certainly not as uninterest. 'Politically, the most important papers are probably *The Times*, *Observer*, and *Manchester Guardian*,' Kingsley Martin estimated in 1947, when all three had broken loose from party moorings. None of them counted as a political journal in the classic sense. But, then, Attlee was not a Prime Minister in the classic mould. To Barrington-Ward, whom he entertained at lunch on 24 October 1945, he 'explained that he had brought in Francis Williams', formerly editor of the *Herald*, as his press relations officer 'because he himself ... knew nothing of newspapers'. Being, by his own admission, 'old fashioned', Attlee read *The Times* 'every morning at breakfast', and also cast a 'glance at the *Daily Herald*. Must I read the *Daily Mail?*' he wanted to know. He and Barrington-Ward 'talked of papers and of Winston's propensity for reading them'. Churchill 'used to get them all as soon as printed, the same night, and read them avidly, especially if he had been making a speech'. By contrast, the new tenant at Number Ten 'seemed innocent of all such sophistication'.[2]

Out of office, Churchill did not alter his habits. From Anthony (later Baron) Hurd, now Conservative member for Newbury, Barrington-Ward received a detailed account of a Tory conclave at which questions were raised about the behaviour of the press. Told that Churchill had classified only the Kemsley papers as 'reliable', Barrington-Ward was moved to wonder 'about the faithful *D.T.*', which seemed to go by the board. Asked about *The Times*, Churchill reportedly replied that 'it was "parlour Socialism", "willing to wound but afraid to strike" and so on'. Hurd confirmed a feeling of indignation among

---

[1] Hugh Cudlipp, *The Prerogative of the Harlot*, p. 256; Percy Cudlipp to Beaverbrook, 14 October 1945 and 10 July 1949, Beaverbrook Papers, C/103; entry of 20 March 1952, Crossman, *Backbench Diaries* (London, 1981), p. 96; Waters's diary, 1 January 1952; Brendon, *Press Barons*, pp. 211–13; Edelman, *Mirror*, p. 156.

[2] Martin, *The Press the Public Wants*, p. 54; Barrington-Ward's diary, 24 October 1945.

Tory MPs 'that the paper will not nail its colours to the mast on either side'. 'Why the devil should it?' responded the irate editor, who considered it ironic that 'people like an "independent Press" but hate an independent newspaper'. Six months later, Barrington-Ward again interrogated Hurd 'to get something of a Conservative Party reaction to the paper'. As before, the chief complaint was 'that the comment of *The Times* is often ambiguous', which was interpreted to mean 'that it fails to take a party line either way, and particularly the Conservative way. They will have to get used to that,' Barrington-Ward grimly concluded.[1]

Kemsley's loyalty, exhibited in the *Daily Sketch* (which masqueraded as the *Daily Graphic* from 1946 to 1952), the *Sunday Times*, and a gaggle of provincial daily and Sunday papers, was indeed unimpeachable. Predicated on personal devotion to Churchill, who had made certain to raise him to a viscountcy before departing from office, it was directed by William (later 1st Baron) Mabane. A National Liberal who had held minor posts in the coalition and caretaker administrations, Mabane lost his seat at Huddersfield in 1945 and thereupon became 'one of Kemsley's courtiers, an adviser whose counsel varied between the very good and the very bad' and who claimed credit for coining the phrase that politics was 'the art of the possible'. With Mabane's sense of practicality to fortify his own social prejudices, Kemsley was staunchly opposed to the 'revolutionary turbulence' (as the *Sunday Times* bewailed on 21 October 1945) that Labour threatened to unleash. Camrose was the more prudent of the Berry brothers and therefore disqualified himself as a contender for Churchill's gratitude. Bracken took the view that 'Camrose hasn't a nerve in his body and has always known just what he wanted', namely to make the *Telegraph* 'a sound, middle-class paper' with a circulation of not 'more than 1,400,000'. Still roughly 400,000 short of that putative goal, the *Telegraph* was described by Francis Williams as owing its solid success to that 'somewhat timorous type of middle-class reader who wants a non-committal and essentially respectable paper ...', but who cannot achieve the intellectual level of *The Times*'. As Williams quipped: 'To read the *Telegraph* is rather like carrying a neatly-rolled umbrella.'[2]

Bracken, who lost his seat at Paddington in the Labour floodtide and moved to higher ground at Bournemouth, was out of the Ministry of Information and back in the newspaper trade. Brooks heard from Hargreaves Parkinson, who was 'enjoying his editorial dictatorship' over the *Financial Times* (which had absorbed the *Financial News* on the day that Labour took office), that 'B.B. is active again in the concern but not visible'. In 1946, David Astor began a stint

[1] Barrington-Ward's diary, 20 December 1945 and 30 July 1946.
[2] Hobson *et al.*, *Pearl of Days*, p. 240; Barrington-Ward's diary, 15 April 1946; Williams, *Press, Parliament and People* (London, 1946), p. 178. In his testimony to the Royal Commission (Cd. 7351, qq. 4327–28), Michael Foot made 'quite clear' his distaste for Kemsley's 'systematic misrepresentation and distortion and unfairness to opponents', but allowed that the *Sunday Times* was 'a good deal better paper than any other in the Kemsley Chain'.

as foreign editor of the *Observer* in preparation for assuming the editorship. His cousin Gavin (later 2nd Baron Astor of Hever) was also 'desperately anxious to learn the newspaper business'. Barrington-Ward, who had attended Gavin's 'coming-of-age ball' on 18 July 1939 ('how long can these things last?'), was pleased to offer instruction to the son of the co-proprietor and the future chairman of *The Times*. Waters 'found him pleasant, shy, overmodest' and perhaps too much inclined 'to defer to seniority', which was apparently not one of Waters's own characteristics. 'Gerald Barry, after twelve years or so of editing the *News Chronicle*' (actually, it was barely ten), struck Waters as being 'bland, pompous and pontifically exuberant'. In 1948, Barry made way for Robin Cruikshank, a more diffident personality who lived in dread of 'the Birmingham Reaction', as Laurence Cadbury's temper was known to his employees in Bouverie Street. Cruikshank's transfer from the *Star* (where he was replaced by Arthur Cranfield) to the *News Chronicle* signalled a shift to the right in the editorial views of the morning paper, especially pronounced in the area of foreign affairs.[1]

The Parliament that assembled in 1945 contained a record number of journalists. The same had been said about the Parliament of 1906, which hitherto held the distinction of having the largest progressive majority, but the 'journalists' in its ranks had been mostly indigent Radical and Irish members who fell into that occupational category more or less by default. In 1945, however, a phalanx of full-fledged professionals was elected. Eric Harrison, a parliamentary reporter for *The Times* who failed in his own bid for a seat, counted some forty victors out of some ninety hopefuls. They included such veterans as Beverley Baxter, Vernon Bartlett, Ivor Bulmer-Thomas, F. J. Bellenger, Driberg, and Bevan, along with such newcomers as Michael Foot, Maurice Webb (who testitified before the Royal Commission as 'both a politician and a newspaperman'), Lord Broxbourne (who had briefly edited the *English Review*), Barbara Castle (housing correspondent for the *Daily Mirror*), J. P. W. Mallalieu (who 'worked on London newspapers, 1933–41'), R. H. S. Crossman (assistant editor and later editor of the *New Statesman*), Allighan, Edelman, and Hurd. Obviously, some were more active in journalism than others. Sir Alan (A.P.) Herbert, the Independent MP for Oxford University and a contributor to *Punch*, was not in the same league as Wilson Harris, the Independent MP for Cambridge University and editor of the *Spectator*. Moreover, Harrison's selection was – perhaps inevitably – haphazard. Christopher Hollis qualified by virtue of his memberships on the boards of *Punch* and the *Tablet*, but John Strachey was omitted. Yet there was no denying the 'influx of journalists', whom Harrison expected to use their

[1] Brooks's diary, 10 October 1945; McLachlan, *In the Chair*, pp. 232–33; Waters's diary, 8 October, 19 and 28 November 1946. William Forrest (interview of 20 August 1981) ascribed the differences between Barry and Cruikshank over foreign affairs to the fact that the former had a Russian-born wife, sensitive to criticisms of the USSR, while the latter's wife was an American.

'wide knowledge of politics and of public affairs generally' to improve the quality of parliamentary debates.[1]

The effects were predictably mixed. Despite their training, which had supposedly inculcated a respect for the 'economy of words', these journalist-MPs often proved windy and verbose. Nor did they always manage to separate their responsibilities in accordance with the conventions at Westminster. On 3 April 1947, Allighan published an explosive article in the *World's Press News*, 'the Fleet Street trade paper of the day', in which he breezily alleged that it was a common practice for MPs ('of whom 21 are ... in the NUJ') to accept 'bribes' in return for 'leaks' to the press. 'Every newspaper in the Street has anything up to half a dozen MPs on its "Contacts" list,' he asserted. 'Some of the "contacts" are on a retainer, some get paid for what they produce, some are content to accept "payment in kind" – personal publicity', and some settled for a drink at the bar. 'Herbert Morrison is not half the Party "boss" he's accused of being,' Allighan went on; 'if he were he'd put the bar out of bounds to Labour MPs, some of whom have succeeded in approaching the fringe of semi-sobriety' with the help of Beaverbrook's money.

The case came before the Committee on Privileges, which heard Allighan admit to having committed 'a grievous mistake', compounded by the fact that he himself had taken a fee for supplying confidential information to the *Evening Standard*. Guy Schofield, the editor of the *Evening News*, confirmed that he paid a weekly allowance of £5 to an unnamed Labour MP for reports of private Labour Party proceedings, and Evelyn Walkden stepped forward as the individual in question. Assorted penalties were meted out. Arthur Heighway, the editor of the *World's Press News*, was reprimanded by the Speaker for having published Allighan's accusations, notwithstanding their substance. Schofield and his lobby correspondent, Stanley Dobson, were found guilty of contempt of the House not for employing a 'contact', but for refusing to disclose his name upon request. On 30 October, after receiving Allighan's abject apology, the House voted by 187 to 75 to expel him. Morrison, as if to confirm that he was 'not half the Party "boss" he's accused of being', had recommended only a six-month suspension. Walkden got off with a stern rebuke and finished his parliamentary term.[2]

---

[1] Institute of Journalists, *Journal*, November 1945. In a letter to the author (28 February 1983), Sir Harold Wilson has recalled that his name would have appeared on this list had he accepted the job he had been offered on the *Manchester Guardian* instead of the Webb Medley Senior Research Scholarship at Oxford.

[2] *World's Press News*, 3 April 1947; Herd, *March of Journalism*, pp. 317–20; Charles Wintour, *Pressures on the Press* (London, 1972), pp. 142 ff. In the ensuing by-election at Gravesend, Sir Richard Acland held the seat for Labour in a contest 'where there was no Liberal candidate' and 'the newspapers on both sides attempted to suggest that the Liberals supported the party which the newspaper favoured'. The Royal Commission on the Press sitting at that time, concluded that, 'with the possible exception of *The Times*, there could be no doubt in the reader's mind as to which side the different newspapers supported'. Report, Royal Commission on the Press, 1947–49, Cd. 7700, p. 359.

Earlier that year, on 26 March, the Prime Minister appointed the first Royal Commission on the Press. According to Kingsley Martin, this step was another reflection of the presence at Westminster of 'a large number of Members who had worked inside newspaper offices'. To be precise, the ball was set rolling by the National Union of Journalists, which met at Liverpool on 19 April 1946 and passed a resolution calling for a public inquiry into the 'ownership, control and financing of national and provincial newspapers, news-agencies and periodicals'. Attlee's initial response was negative, but Churchill accepted the proposal, which he linked to the management of the BBC. Michael Foot and Haydn Davies, who had been education correspondent for the *News Chronicle* and industrial correspondent for the *Star*, then tabled a motion that had the backing of over a hundred of their fellow Labour MPs. Representatives of the NUJ had little difficulty in enlisting the support of Morrison, who perhaps wished to repent for his recent outburst at the *Daily Herald*'s coverage of his conference address. In fact, there were suspicions that Morrison had inspired not only the NUJ initiative, but also the backbench motion for a Royal Commission, which was passed on 29 October – after a six-and-a-half-hour debate – by a vote of 270 to 157. Five months passed before Attlee named the commissioners, who held sixty-one meetings, thirty-eight of them devoted to the collection of oral evidence from a total of 182 witnesses.[1]

'With the object of furthering the free expression of opinion through the Press and the greatest practicable accuracy in the presentation of news', the Commission was directed 'to inquire into the control, management and ownership of the newspaper and periodical Press and news-agencies including the financial structure and the monopolistic tendencies in control, and to make recommendations thereon'. It was an awesome brief. Under the chairmanship of Sir William David Ross, provost of Oriel College, Oxford, and formerly vice-chancellor of that university, the Commission was established with sixteen other members. Lord Simon of Wythenshawe – who, as Sir Ernest Simon, had been a Liberal MP – dropped out to become chairman of the governors of the BBC. Lady Violet Bonham Carter, who had just completed a five-year term as one of those governors, was one of the three women commissioners. Another was Barbara Wootton (later Baroness Wootton of Abinger), whose governorship of the BBC came later. The commissioner most directly involved with newspaper production was Sir George Waters, the long-time editor of the *Scotsman*. R. C. K. Ensor had been a leader-writer for nearly half a century and, with G. M. Young, was now a contributor to the *Sunday Times*. J. B. Priestley, as well as being a successful novelist and broadcaster, was a director of the *New Statesman*. Through the National Co-operative Society, Neil S. Beaton was remotely connected with the proprietorship of *Reynolds News*.

[1] Martin, *The Press the Public Wants*, p. 19; Donoughue and Jones, *Morrison*, p. 359; Camrose, *British Newspapers*, pp. 1–2; Report, Royal Commission on the Press, 1947–49, Cd. 7700, pp. 1–3.

The other commissioners included a solicitor, a trade union official, a civil servant, and a *de rigueur* clergyman.[1]

The appointment of the Royal Commission was not so much accompanied as anticipated by an outpouring of books and pamphlets about the press, its structure, and its psychology. Wilson Harris's *The Daily Press*, first published in 1943, was even more pertinent when it was reissued in 1946, for the intervening general election seemed to bear out its hypothesis that

> the fortunes of a paper are not made by the solid core of readers who can be counted on to stick to it whatever happens, but by the non-political mass who tend to prefer it for one reason or another, but with so loose an adhesion that a comparatively small inducement would divert them to a rival.

The Bureau of Current Affairs, listing Wilson's book among seven recommendations 'for further reading', issued Aylmer Vallance's tract, *Control of the Press*, on 21 September 1946. 'For once, in this discussion, let us make the Press our own head-line news,' Vallance proposed, though he himself was more inclined to dwell upon the larger imperfections of 'our social and economic system'. Francis Williams, from behind his desk in Downing Street, followed with an alliterative analysis of *Press, Parliament and People*, which concurred that 'most people buy daily papers for reasons which have nothing to do with politics', although 'some popular papers' could justifiably claim 'a certain political following'. However, 'speaking generally, the larger a newspaper's circulation the less evidence is there that it has any political influence, at any rate in domestic affairs'. His convoluted arguments, based not so much on negative evidence as on negative experience, pointed up the need for a Royal Commission.[2]

The announcement of an impending inquiry, 'which will have the effect of removing this subject from the theoretical to the practical sphere of politics', prompted Kingsley Martin to deliver a lecture on 'The Journalist in the Socialist State' at the Central Hall, Westminster, on 27 November 1946. With Percy Cudlipp in the chair, Martin took pains

> to emphasize that our serious newspapers with a comparatively small circulation have a political influence quite out of proportion. The vastly circulated Press has nothing like a political influence proportionately to its circulation. The last election was an obvious example of that. . . . The people

---

[1] Camrose, *British Newspapers*, pp. 2–3. Priestley also figured in the proceedings as the source of a 'misunderstanding'. In a 'service message' on 29 September 1947, the Kemsley provincial papers were instructed 'Please kill story of Priestley at Merthyr' not for suspected political reasons, but to ensure that the capsule report from the Press Association was not used in place of a fuller version. Report, Royal Commission on the Press, 1947–49, Cd. 7700, p. 47.

[2] Harris, *The Daily Press* (London, 1946), p.124; Vallance, *Control of the Press* (London, 1946), pp. 2, 19; Williams, *Press, Parliament and People*, pp. 162–63.

then acted and voted from their own experience, whatever the popular newspapers might say to them.

Within months, he developed these themes in a book, *The Press the Public Wants*, which more accurately described the press that he wanted the public to want. Camrose, lacking any such missionary zeal, compiled what was ostensibly a work of reference. Waters 'read Viscount Camrose's newly published & widely advertised book, *British Newspapers and their Controllers*', and logically took it to be 'an anticipatory reply to the Royal Commission on the Press'. Camrose had built his 'case largely of big fleas & little fleas', differentiating between them only by size. What Waters found 'particularly depressing is the "so on ad infiniteness" ' of Camrose's catalogue. 'The Press is now a vested interest involving the fate of many millions of pounds,' Waters wrote in his diary. 'A steady return, an unhesitating yield, in the view of the Viscount, justify the existence of the entire Press. ... I'm afraid I am not impressed.'[1]

For that matter, a great many people were not impressed by the eventual report of the Royal Commission on 26 July 1949. The commissioners were defeated by their own prodigious industry, which produced a mound of indigestible and sometimes contradictory material. They had asked most of the right questions, but did not know what to make of many of the answers. The statutory rationing of newsprint, which lasted with fluctuating intensity until 1956, made it difficult for them to discern which changes were temporary and which were permanent. Certain myths, especially those concerning the manipulation of the press in the 1930s, were effectively dispelled, while others were enshrined by repetition. Beaverbrook, who resented the proceedings as an exercise in socialist victimization ('I expected no better from that fellow Driberg, but I never thought Michael Foot would do this to me'), unexpectedly enjoyed the occasion of his testimony on 18 March 1948, when he locked horns with Lady Violet Bonham Carter and said a lot of things that he probably did not believe.[2] Whether the commissioners believed them is still more difficult to tell. In the event, they affirmed to no one's surprise that the problems were numerous, complex, and best left to the press itself for constructive solution.

The only substantive recommendation to emerge was one for the establishment of 'a General Council of the Press' under a paid chairman and with the

---

[1] Text of lecture delivered 27 November 1946, Martin Papers; Waters's diary, 20 September 1947.

[2] Taylor, *Beaverbrook*, pp. 584–86. E. J. Robertson, Beaverbrooks's general manager, shared his conspiratorial view. He came to lunch on 6 January 1948 (Waters's diary)

in an angry mood over the Royal Commission on the Press which is the outcome of malice & spleen of a bunch of politically prejudiced journalists & ex-journalists whose aim has been to gain control of the Press. He said the move dated back to 1943 when an attempt was made by the NUJ to impose the principle of the closed shop upon all editorial members. That was foiled.

'objects ... to safeguard the freedom of the Press; to encourage the growth of the sense of public responsibility and public service amongst all engaged in the profession ...; and to further the efficiency of the profession and the well-being of those who practise it'. When the House debated the report on 28 July, Morrison especially welcomed this proposal and cited a spate of irresponsible comments about the Royal Commission and its findings as conclusive proof that a Press Council was an urgent necessity. Nevertheless, four full years were to pass before the various proprietorial and professional bodies set up a voluntary regulatory agency as the Commons had unanimously requested.[1]

In this as in other respects, the Royal Commission was less important for what it directly accomplished than for what it symbolized. Its appointment in 1947 was an occasion to which its report two years later did not rise; but it was an occasion none the less. The deficiencies of that report were most glaring with respect to 'political considerations', which were either minimized or put aside. Holding tenaciously to the opinion that 'free enterprise in the production of newspapers is a prerequisite of a free press', the commissioners were blinded to the fact that one freedom could vitiate another. They conceded the existence of a 'political factor in the selection and presentation of news', but took the Panglossian view that disparities 'can often be accounted for by legitimate differences of opinion on news value'. In any case, it was comfortingly supposed that, even in those rare instances when 'excessive bias' was at work, 'it seldom produces the complete suppression of a fact or a topic whose importance of news admits to no doubt, and conversely, ... it seldom leads to the publishing of complete fabrications'. (At what point did a bias become 'excessive' or a fabrication become 'complete'?) The saving grace of any 'political bias' was that it operated 'neither constantly nor consistently, whether as between different papers or between different issues of the same paper', with the incidental effect that 'occasionally' what might 'appear at first sight to spring from undue bias' was, upon closer inspection, 'found ... to be equally attributable to other causes'.[2] If not a whitewash, the report of the first Royal Commission amounted to little more than a gloss on the subject.

Another Royal Commission deliberated on the entangled affairs of the press in 1961–62, and a third in the 1970s, when conditions had deteriorated still further. Chaired by Lord Shawcross (formerly Sir Hartley Shawcross and a Labour Cabinet minister), the second Commission covered much the same ground as its predecessor and offered many of the same general conclusions, replete with a warning against 'the dangers of governmental interference with

---

[1] Report, Royal Commission on the Press, Cd. 7700, pp. 164–79: *Parliamentary Debates* (Commons), 5th ser., cdlvii, cols. 2683–2794; Donoughue and Jones, *Morrison*, p. 359n.; H. A. Taylor, The *British Press*, pp. 100–101; Stuart Hood, *The Mass Media* (London, 1972), pp. 79–80.

[2] Report, Royal Commission on the Press, 1947–49, Cd. 7700, pp. 109, 155–56.

the Press which we think would follow from other artificial attempts to regulate the independence of market forces'.[1] The rhetoric was redolent of the nineteenth century, when Cobden and Bright had trusted implicitly to the purifying influences of *laissez-faire*. To contemplate state intervention, even to the circumscribed extent that the third Royal Commission permitted itself, was, in a way, to revive the debate of the 1850s over the 'taxes on knowledge'. The arguments of the mid-Victorians, who had developed the political press as an instrument of party government, died hard. Meanwhile, their creation continued to die softly.

* * *

Punctuated by Royal Commissions, the history of the British press since 1947 has been an unremitting story of crisis, closure, and complaint. Contrary to the optimistic assumptions of the 1949 report, metropolitan and especially provincial properties have continued to fold, and those that remain have been clustered in fewer and fewer hands. While this dispiriting and apparently irreversible process has undermined the commercial foundations and arguably the social functions of printed journalism, it has scarcely affected political patterns except, again and again, to confirm them.

Before proceeding to a final assessment, it may be useful to summarize the developments of recent decades, if only to justify the chronological and thematic limitations of the present study. By 1947, the party attachments of newspapers – as they had been understood to operate over the preceding hundred years – were effectively abandoned. In most cases, to repudiate them would have been redundant. Parliamentary preoccupations, which had survived even Northcliffe's vaunted 'revolution', were reduced in consequence.

Frank Waters spent a 'disillusioning ... evening in the Press Gallery' on 14 February 1946 and was appalled by the levity of the food debate. The following morning, none of the papers gave 'any real indication of the mood of the House last night', when the benches were 'less than half filled' by apathetic MPs, and several papers completely ignored the occasion. 'The failure of the Press correctly to reflect such a mood is, I think, wrong in that it misleads the public which is dependent to a large extent for its interpretation of politics upon a diet of cream, much of it journalistic titivation and titillation,' lamented Waters. 'Party feeling doesn't enter into it,' he added emphatically. It was too late for that. A year later, one of Waters's friends in the City had the 'cockeyed idea ... for raising a million pounds' to launch a Conservative weekly in which 'leading industrialists' would 'dissipate their excess profits by buying advertising space for no purpose other than to wish the Tory party "All the

---

[1] Report, Royal Commission on the Press, 1961–62, Cd. 1811, p. 98; James Curran, ed., *The British Press: a Manifesto* (London, 1978), pp. 1–11.

Best"'. That sort of enterprise was generations out of date.[1]

At the end of 1947, Barrington-Ward fell fatally ill. Aged fifty-seven, he was already contemplating retirement ('Barnes and Delane did not last beyond 58'), but his sudden departure came as a shock. 'The gossips about Fleet Street' saw A. P. Ryan and Donald Tyerman as rivals for the succession, and Donald McLachlan (who said nothing of the sort in his biography of Barrington-Ward) reportedly 'thought that the only possible qualifier for the post would be Geoffrey Crowther' of *The Economist*. William Casey, the *locum tenens*, was elevated despite his own advanced age and poor health. It was clearly a stopgap appointment. In October 1952, Sir William Haley took over. He had worked in Manchester journalism and had been a director of the Press Association and Reuters, but his outstanding credentials derived from his tenure as Director-General of the BBC. But for his commitments at Broadcasting House, he would have come to Printing House Square a year earlier, for he 'always regarded the Editor of *The Times* as the head of my profession'. Like his modern predecessors, Haley felt the hand of history upon his shoulder. Unlike them, however, he did not become its pawn. In Delane's day, he realized, 'it was the restricted field of the Press's impact which gave it its influence. For when in past times the influence of the Press was talked about it was almost entirely in terms of political influence', which no longer applied to the same extent or in the same form. To be sure, newspapers remained capable of exerting a 'deeper and ... subtler influence – and, I believe [a] healthier one compared with the old days', but from outside the 'monolithic blocks' of political parties, with their mass memberships 'recruited rather from an attitude of mind than from belief in a particular political philosophy, or Party programme'.[2]

As Casey was beginning an interregnum at *The Times*, Ivor Brown ended one at the *Observer*. Though hardly unexpected, David Astor's investiture 'raised many an eyebrow in Fleet St.', where 'not even the Berry dynasty has dared to appoint a younger son as editor in the highest meaning of the term'. And it was undoubtedly 'in the highest meaning of the term' that Astor meant to edit. Like Haley, he espoused a non-doctrinaire and studiously non-partisan liberalism (with a small 'l' as opposed to Wadsworth's) in an effort to encourage 'the two large parties ... to "liberalise" themselves in their urgent need to capture more centre votes'. In this connection, he had consulted Dingle Foot, who was to return to Westminster in 1957 as Labour MP for

[1] Waters's diary, 14 and 15 February 1946, 12 February 1947. The Royal Commission reported (Cd. 7700, p. 119) 'that all newspapers, whether of the right or of the left, normally give a greater proportion of space to the Government than to the Opposition. This reflects the fact that speakers who announce Government action and propound Government policy inevitably create more "news".'

[2] McLachlan, *In the Chair*, pp. 266–69; Waters's diary, 6 and 7 December 1947; Haley, 'The Public Influence of Broadcasting and the Press' (Clayton Memorial Lecture), *Memoirs and Proceedings of the Manchester Literary and Philosophical Society* (Manchester, 1954), xcv, 11–13; profile of Haley, *New Statesman*, 6 February 1954.

Ipswich, but who meanwhile agreed as 'an ardent, hereditary and very clear thinking Liberal' that 'in the long run it is of greater interest to the Liberal element in this country that both parties should develop in this way than that the Liberal Party should itself survive'. Laurence Cadbury had been saying as much for years.[1]

On 3 January 1949, newspapers were allowed to resume a 'free sale', this time permanently. Although the supply of newsprint remained subject to tonnage restrictions, there was a restoration of the competition that the Royal Commissioners had held out as a boon. 'In the free-for-all of the Fleet St. Stakes' the first morning, *The Times* increased its sale by 'a bare 20,000 copies, the *Telegraph* some 80,000, the *Express* 150,000', while the *Herald*'s circulation plunged by approximately 100,000 and the *News Chronicle* stood 'shakily about the same'. The *Daily Mirror*, a Prometheus unbound, 'swung leftward with another half-million copies', to the annoyance of Waters: 'Thereby may be judged the taste & intellectual standing of this democracy.' The quality dailies, previously protected by government controls, now took consolation where they could find it. E. J. Robertson soon cheered Waters by remarking that the *Telegraph* 'would lose to *The Times* one day anyway', even though that day kept receding. For his part, Cadbury professed 'no desire to emulate the 4 million of the *Express* or *Mirror*', but would not 'feel happy until we stop the rot and actually start putting on sales'. It was a point of honour, not economics, he wished Layton to understand. 'I hate being fourth in the race. We ought at least to be able to be ahead of the *Herald*, . . . with all the strings' that the TUC tied to it.[2]

Labour held a hairbreadth majority in the general election of 1950, but lost it in the next election the following year. The Liberal contingent in the House of Commons fell from twelve to nine and finally touched bottom at six, where it languished throughout the decade. During the 1945 campaign, the *News Chronicle* had pioneered in the publication of public opinion polls, which then took a week or longer to be tabulated. By 1950, polling techniques had improved and the *Daily Express* got in on the act. The Tactical Committee, established at the Conservative Research Department in 1948, had grave misgivings that these surveys of electoral opinion would create a bandwagon

[1] Waters's diary, 2 August 1948; Astor to Mann, 2 May 1950, Mann Papers. Over the objections of Lady Astor, who 'thinks we should have nothing to do with any members of the Foot family (apparently because she dislikes Michael Foot who stands for the Lab. party in the Devonport div. of Plymouth)', Dingle Foot became a trustee of the *Observer* in 1952. There was the further 'question of membership in the House of Commons'. Lord Astor knew 'by personal experience that it can be quite unpleasant for a Member of Parliament who is directly associated with a newspaper if that paper takes a line which is opposite to his party'. Accordingly, the *Observer*'s policy was 'that we should not elect a Member of Parliament as a Trustee while he was an MP, but that a Trustee who stood as a candidate need not resign unless he was elected'. David Astor to Mann [1950?], and Lord Astor to Mann, 4 January 1952, Mann Papers.

[2] Waters's diary, 2 January and 2 June 1949; Cadbury to Layton, 12 February 1949, Layton Papers.

effect which, so to speak, would decide the election before the votes were actually cast. The *News Chronicle* and the *Daily Express*, dissimilar in every other respect, were known to appeal to large numbers of floating voters, whose unconditioned reflexes might determine the outcome in a close contest. 'The *Daily Express* will almost certainly forecast a Conservative win, though perhaps a small one,' reckoned the Tory tacticians. 'The *News Chronicle* will forecast a victory for whichever Party the Gallup Poll expects to win.' To sway uncommitted voters, it was deemed necessary to sway the pollsters. If the Tactical Committee took 'no action, the *Mail* will probably not compete directly with the other two', but there were unspecified 'ways ... in which the *Mail* might be enabled to weigh in with a last minute poll favourable to the Conservatives'. In fact, the *Express* misleadingly projected a narrow Conservative lead, the *News Chronicle* accurately predicted the same for Labour, and the *Mail* – probably for want of time – engaged not in poll-taking, merely pole-axing.[1]

'General Election forecasters are all swinging to the Right for no apparent reason,' Waters noted three days before balloting. 'Hostility to a further dose of Socialism rather than any enthusiasm for Tory policy' seemed the only explanation. 'The *Express* & *News Chronicle* polls both reflect a trend in favour of the Conservatives', but Waters was 'impressed most of all by the first of the private estimates by *The Times* parliamentary staff who predict a cautious Tory lead of not less than 40 seats'. Still, however much he wanted to see Labour out, 'the return of the Tories to power does not thrill me. I cannot overlook the sorry record of 1935 to 1939. Tories en masse or in little cliques make my hackles rise.'[2] Apparently, a majority of the electors shared his memories and sentiments.

The Times took its cue from its lobby pundits, the *News Chronicle* from Dr Gallup, and the *Daily Herald* from Transport House, with the result that it 'judged its news by the test of whether it would help the party'. The *Daily Telegraph* was unmistakably pro-Conservative, but paid proportionate attention to Labour speeches and commented courteously on 17 February, after Morrison had given the same one twice. The *Daily Mail*, always on the look-out for a scapegoat, specialized in attacks on Aneurin Bevan, the embattled Minister of Health, who was not to be forgiven for his snarling reference to 'Tory vermin' and whose latest alleged offence was to charge that 'Churchill Starved the Babies' during wartime (4 February). The *Manchester Guardian* found it 'hard to be convinced that the Conservatives (even led by Mr Churchill with all his virtues) or Labour (with such an incumbrance as Mr Aneurin Bevan) can be whole-heartedly supported', and sadly concluded on

---

[1] Tactical Committee file, 1950 election, Conservative Research Department, quoted in Ramsden, *Conservative Party Policy*, pp. 144–45. The Labour Party had a corresponding Policy and Publicity Committee, which emerged in 1943 from the policy sub-committee of the NEC.
[2] Waters's diary, 20 February 1950.

polling day that the party most likely 'to achieve realism and courage first will be the one that is out of office tomorrow'. Beaverbrook, who enjoyed private friendships with both Churchill and Bevan, faced the same difficult choice. He rushed back from the Bahamas, expecting that 'I should have to go against Winston Churchill'. Instead his papers berated the Labour ministers without suggesting that the Conservatives were equipped to do much better. In the aftermath, the *Evening Standard* turned upon John Strachey, declaring that he had 'never disavowed Communism' and implicating him in the Soviet spy scandals (2 March). Shawcross, then Attorney-General, persuaded Strachey not to sue for criminal libel, and Michael Foot rallied to Strachey's defence in *Tribune* with an article – 'Lower than Kemsley' (10 March) – that led to other legal entanglements.[1]

Only one newspaper fought the 1950 campaign with anything like the old fervour. That was the *Daily Mirror*, which may well have been prodded by Gallup's discovery that the working-class electorate was more solidly behind the Labour Party than it had been in 1945. Tory statements were quoted, only to be derided as 'stunts'. By means of photographs, the mass unemployment of the 1930s was vividly brought to mind. On 21 February, to remove any vestige of uncertainty, the *Mirror* told its readers 'Where We Stand', firmly and explicitly in the Labour camp. 'We have made this decision after full and careful consideration of the claims of all the parties,' it insisted. 'We support the Labour Party because it has kept its promises and earned our trust.' Edelman, in his panegyrical history of the paper, saw this endorsement as crucial: 'No one can doubt but that the final heave of the *Mirror* in the last days of the campaign when support for Labour was running away like sand in an hour-glass made the difference between victory and defeat.'[2] More probably, however, the *Mirror* was preaching to the converted.

Following the *Observer*'s precedent, it became increasingly common for newspapers to feature signed contributions from representatives of each party. From 'the whole campaign' of 1945, McCallum could 'only recall one article by a Conservative leader, excluding Lord Beaverbrook', and that was the one that Richard Law had written for the *Observer*. Now such articles were standard fare in most journals, including the *Mirror*. This technique was especially attractive to the fence-sitters, such as the *News Chronicle*, which preferred to allow the politicians to speak for themselves. When the campaign was over, Henry Cadbury was 'very proud' of 'the level-headed attitude' that the *News Chronicle* had adopted. He was 'quite sure that now we must back the Labour Party in power', which could be done 'with every confidence', given that their minuscule majority would compel them 'to drop their nationalisation programme'. His hope was that the paper would 'drop purely Party politics' as

---

[1] H. G. Nicholas, *The British General Election of 1950* (London, 1951), p. 176; Taylor, *Beaverbrook*, p. 596; Thomas, *Strachey*, pp. 260–61.
[2] Edelman, *Mirror*, p. 177.

quickly as possible and 'get back to our general policy of six months ago', before the election had revived partisan spirits. 'Perhaps to elaborate this point a little further,' he instructed: 'Give all party news but refrain from Party propaganda.'[1]

Between the general elections of 1950 and 1951, important personnel changes occurred at the *News Chronicle* office. Waters left *The Times*, where his promotion had been impeded, 'to understudy Bertram Crosfield who is due to retire before the end of the year' as managing director and who never received half the credit he deserved from his Cadbury in-laws. 'The old-age problem in Bouverie St. is a little frightening,' Waters discovered upon arrival. Layton allegedly tried to remedy it by applying 'great pressure' on the Cadbury brothers to secure an appointment 'at a fairly high level' for his eldest son. In April 1950, Layton himself relinquished the chairmanship of the *News Chronicle* and the *Star* to Laurence Cadbury. He remained vice-chairman of the Daily News Trust and thereby capable of exercising his 'hypnotic influence'. The political effect, particularly in the vexing area of industrial relations, was to accelerate the paper's drift to the right. The typography seemed to reflect this turbulence. Waters compared notes with Stuart Maclean, his opposite number on the *Daily Mail*, who 'expressed concern over the changed appearance of the *News Chronicle* which, according to him, seemed uncertain in its role & character, looking some mornings more *Express*-like than the *Daily Express*, on others like the old *Daily News*'. Maclean admitted that he and his associates at the *Mail* were 'secretly rather pleased with what was happening', for they 'aimed to fill the gap between the *Times* & *Telegraph*' on the one side and the popular dailies on the other. In due course, the *Daily Mail* was to swallow the *News Chronicle* in that attempt.[2]

The 1951 election, in which the Liberal Party fielded a mere 109 candidates (as compared with 475 the previous year), plunged the *News Chronicle* into dejection. The *Manchester Guardian*, more entitled to speak for 'the Radically minded voter', concluded 'that the Labour Government has come to the end of its usefulness' and that 'a Churchill Government is ... the lesser evil' (22 October 1951), a view that Wadsworth himself did not share. In reaction to the general slide towards Toryism, the *Daily Mirror* tripped over its own feet in rushing to the defence of the Labour Party. Reducing the election to a single issue, that of atomic warfare, it persistently asked 'Whose Finger on the Trigger?' Churchill's finger, it was implied, itched to pull the trigger that would start a third world war.

This time, 'the final heave of the *Mirror*' made no difference and may have been counter-productive. Churchill, returned with an overall majority of

---

[1] Colin Seymour-Ure, *The Political Impact of Mass Media*, p. 229; McCallum and Readman, *General Election of 1945*, p. 203n.; H. Cadbury to Layton, 28 February 1950, Layton Papers.
[2] Waters's diary, 12 May, 7 July, and 31 October 1950, 11 January 1952; Layton, draft memoirs, Layton Papers.

seventeen, took legal action against the *Mirror*, and was awarded £1,500, which he donated to charity. Before the case was settled out of court, there were suggestions that 'a rapprochement should be effected between Churchill' and Cecil King, 'the writ withdrawn, and a peerage offered to boot if the present vitriolic policy of the *Mirror* is toned down'. That would have been to square rather than to squash. 'A peerage would be almost irresistible to any Harmsworth, and to have the ear of the Prime Minister would naturally be flattering & gratifying,' calculated Waters. 'But dramatically to change the *D. Mirror*'s policy would inevitably mean a loss of sale – probably a crippling loss, and that is more than King's colleagues & shareholders would stand for.'[1]

At least in the case of the *Mirror*, then, political acrimonies were important for selling papers. On the day that the ballots were counted, the suspenseful 'neck-and-neck' results proved exceptionally 'good for newspaper sales', with the *Star* adding an extra 500,000 to achieve a circulation of 1,753,000. Fleet Street would have found it beneficial to hold an election – and preferably a close one – every day. Although a continued system of rationing limited each paper to roughly half its pre-war level of newsprint consumption, with the price per ton more than double the pre-war rate, newspapers circulated more widely in Britain than in the United States: 'the scale of distribution there is 354 copies a thousand of population, compared with 596 in this country'.[2]

Needless to say, the levels of domestic distribution varied enormously and to the disadvantage of quality papers with smaller circulations, which had to lower their advertising rates accordingly. Laurence Scott, who estimated that a circulation of 250,000 'was the absolute minimum for commercial security', was mindful that the *Manchester Guardian* was competing for advertisers in 1950, when its sale was a humble 140,000 against *The Times* and the *Daily Telegraph*, which sold 270,000 and 970,000 respectively. He was 'convinced that our future depends largely on acquiring "national" status in the eyes of advertisers'. For the *News Chronicle*, which competed unsuccessfully in a different league, the problem was more acute. The paper expanded to forty-two pages a week in January 1950, only to contract to thirty-six pages in July. The price of newsprint and the paucity of advertisements allowed no choice.[3]

Beaverbrook, who had crossed swords with Layton in the past, wrote to him from the south of France in the summer of 1952, when the *News Chronicle* was poised to enlarge its weekly size to forty-eight pages. 'There is much comment in many directions about the *News Chronicle* and the *Star*,' he began, and knowing 'nothing of the facts', he offered that, 'if you want to buy these papers, I would be glad to provide money for you'. The proposed arrangements were reasonably straight-forward:

---

[1] Edelman, *Mirror*, pp. 177–79; Waters's diary, 1 January 1952.
[2] Waters's diary, 27 October 1951; *The Times*, 5 February 1952.
[3] Ayerst, *Guardian*, pp. 592–93; memorandum by Layton, Documentary Evidence, Royal Commission on the Press, 1961–62, Cd. 1812, IV, 242.

The policy of the paper and also the production of the news pages would be entirely your responsibility. And I would not interfere.

The business side would rest with me.

You would deal with the situation openly and frankly, leaving control in the keeping of yourself and your associates. We would make a community of interest between the *Express* and the *News Chronicle* which would be publicly declared.

There would be a similar community between the *Standard* and the *Star*.

But the community of interest would be for business and management only.

Layton, who later remarked that 'the difficulties were too many', replied with gratitude 'for the handsome offer' and cited 'only . . . two of the snags – one is that I am 68, not 58; the other is that the present holders have no wish to sell!' A precious opportunity was lost.[1]

Beaverbrook's motives, as always, remain open to speculation. Having left the *Daily Mail* in the shade, he was alarmed by the popularity of the *Daily Mirror*, which was pulling farther ahead of the *Daily Express*. Recognizing and perhaps overestimating the *News Chronicle*'s appeal to Nonconformists, with whom he perversely identified, he was finding it 'difficult to hold out against the pornographic competition', especially in the Sunday market.[2]

The *News Chronicle* could not have expected better terms. At the beginning of 1954, its circulation was 'still falling' and, Waters admitted, 'causing us much concern'. On 18 January, Laurence Cadbury telephoned, furious at the receipt of 'an hysterical letter' from Cruikshank 'about the state of alarm & depression in Bouverie St.' The 'Birmingham Reaction' was to order an 'immediate change of Editor'. The candidates included Tyerman, by then twice passed over at *The Times*, and Percy Cudlipp, whom Egbert Cadbury considered 'much too Labour inclined' to edit 'an independent paper not tied to either Party'. The ultimate choice was Michael Curtis, the deputy editor, who quit in 1957 to become personal aide to the Aga Khan.[3]

Waters was weighing an offer from King to join the *Mirror* group, 'the richest & most powerful publishing concern in the realm', if not the most prestigious. He discussed the pros and cons with Hugh Gaitskell, soon to become Labour Party leader, who came to lunch on 1 June. 'Hugh said Cecil King was a very strange man', the unlikely combination of 'a Northcliffe & a Wykehamist, . . . very able but . . . very isolated'. At the same time, Gaitskell was dismissive of the *News Chronicle*: its circulation had 'shrunk with the Liberal party' and 'under the present set-up it's hopeless'. His own anxiety was

---

[1] Beaverbrook to Layton, 20 August 1952 (copy), and Layton to Beaverbrook, 28 August 1952, Beaverbrook Papers, C/215; Layton, draft memoir, Layton Papers.
[2] Beaverbrook to Driberg, 13 May 1953, Driberg Papers.
[3] Waters's diary, 18 January 1954; E. Cadbury to Waters, 9 September 1954, Waters Papers.

in the field of weekly journalism, where he hoped to establish a rival to the *New Statesman* and *Tribune* on the grounds 'that these papers *are* harmful'.¹

Waters declined King's invitation, and instead – with Layton's guarded approval and Cadbury's knowledge – 'sounded King on the possibilities of a merger' between the two groups. King 'admittedly wants the *Star* but thinks the N/C too far gone to retrieve without putting in an awful amount of work' and, even then, 'it may not be possible to reconstruct'. However, if the Cadburys were willing 'to maintain a subsidized interest in order to spread the risks', the *News Chronicle* might be refashioned into 'a Daily Observer style of paper', ten pages in size and perhaps reverting to the title of the *Daily News*. Layton was sceptical, but did not 'produce any stronger argument against the merger than that it would cause a flight of readers through association with the *Mirror*'. Waters brushed aside these fears with a tart reminder that King's uncle Alfred had managed to run the *Daily Mail* and *The Times* simultaneously without material harm to either.²

The negotiations seemed to be going well. In September, Waters left for a holiday in Majorca, confident that the future of the *News Chronicle* was settled. Minor details would be sorted out at a meeting on 19 October, after his return. On holiday, he was stricken with polio. He was driven to Paris, where he died, aged forty-six, at the home of Geoffrey Hoare, the paper's correspondent there. The package he had worked out with King, perhaps never tied as tightly as he thought, fell apart. It was a private nightmare and a public misfortune.³

Before the custodians of the *News Chronicle* could deal with King or any other potential purchaser, they had to decide among themselves where they stood in the party political picture. To Cruikshank, the *News Chronicle* remained 'a paper of considerable political importance' with an ability to tap 'the liberal and middle-of-the-road sentiment in this country'; by his estimate, 'the largest number of our readers support Labour', but there was 'a fair slice of

---

¹ Waters's diary, 27 May 1954; Joan Waters's diary, 1 June 1954. Crossman (who described King as 'a nephew of Northcliffe and a great big, beefy, rather silly fellow, who lives in Chelsea, is a Wykehamist but is otherwise insignificant'), confirmed the party leaders' hatred of those 'vicious enemies', the *New Statesman* (where Martin 'will instinctively support any left-wing view which isn't getting a fair hearing or which is unpopular') and *Tribune*, which had resumed as a weekly in 1952. 'How can you take the *Tribune* seriously, with a genuine circulation of not more than 18,000?' Crossman demanded of Gaitskell. 'It's read everywhere in the constituencies,' Gaitskell replied. 'It's the single most important factor which our people on the Right complain of.' (Entries of 19 December 1951, 25 February 1952, 27 October 1954, and 24 March 1955, Crossman, *Backbench Diaries*, pp. 54, 80, 360, and 410.) The Gaitskellite antidote was the weekly *Forward*, edited in London by Francis Williams from 31 August 1956 to 25 March 1960. The involvement of Alma (later Baroness) Birk betokened a link with the King group.

² Waters's diary, 22 July, 3 and 7 August 1954.

³ *World's Press News*, 22 October 1954; private information from Joan Waters Wood (Waters's widow, who married Oliver Woods, his old friend, in 1956) and others. Cecil King (letter to the author, 23 February 1983) had only vague recollections of these 'events 40 years ago' and did not recall that negotiations had 'reached an advanced stage'. Pugnacious as always, he divulged his recipe for political journalism as 'olive oil ... laced with vinegar'.

... Liberal readers who now appear to be divided 6/4 between Conservatism and Labour as second choice'. Curtis, too, envisaged a renewed 'political appeal', which would have to wait upon events to obtain focus. Himself a paid-up member of the Labour Party, who had co-edited the *London Labour News* with Tom Baistow and who none the less helped Layton to draft the Liberal Party manifesto, he was a quintessential Gaitskellite. More hard-headedly, Waters had seen that the paper's 'chief handicap' was 'that the Leftish political *élan* of the prewar and immediate postwar periods had evaporated and some of our readers have evaporated with it. ... Our dilemma,' he had summed up, 'seems to be that we can neither embrace the radical wing – if it ever existed – of the Conservative Party, nor the radical wing of the Labour Party. ... In fact, it would seem almost impossible to foster a radical spirit in a welfare state.' Laurence Cadbury, in Waters's opinion, suffered from 'weakness & timidity, & lack of news instinct', while 'the aristocratic Layton' was the captive of 'his somewhat unworldly political aims'. Thus, the *News Chronicle* was the victim of an identity crisis, essentially political in nature.[1]

In the general election of 1955, the paper took an ambivalent stand, consonant with Egbert Cadbury's view that there could be 'no greater tragedy occurring as far as the future of this country is concerned than if a Labour Government were returned ... with a substantial majority'. The *Manchester Guardian*, driven to the conclusion that 'we do not want a Labour Government just now' (29 April), embraced the Conservative Party as 'a reformed sinner' (24 May). The *Daily Herald* held firm, but the *Daily Mirror* came unstuck. 'The *Mirror* might not be able to win you the next election but, if we turn against you, we can certainly lose it for you,' Hugh Cudlipp had threatened. Crossman, who regarded the election as lost six months before it was fought, later heard 'that Cecil King had wanted the *Mirror* group ... to adopt the slogan, "We are pro-Labour but not this time," meaning, of course, that the Labour Party was so divided and poorly led that the *Mirror*, its strong supporter, could not conscientiously recommend it as a Government'. In the actual campaign, as A. C. H. Smith has shown, the *Mirror* stood 'in striking contrast ... with itself ten years before. Hardly a trace remained of the confident exchange between the paper and its readers then', and the paper's enunciated 'Election Policy' was to 'Keep the Tories Tame' by denying them 'a bloated majority'.[2]

In substance, if not in style, the *News Chronicle* and the *Daily Mirror* were not far apart. But the possibility of an amalgamation did not survive Waters's death. Geoffrey Hoare, 'like most of the older members of the staff to whom I

---

[1] Memoranda by Cruikshank (9 September 1953), Curtis (3 August 1954), and Waters (7 September 1953 and 24 August 1954), Layton Papers; note by Waters [1954], Waters Papers; interviews with James Cameron (20 July 1982) and Tom Baistow (20 August 1981), who recalled how Cummings, 'shaking like a leaf', wrote an attack on Aneurin Bevan at Curtis's dictation.

[2] E. Cadbury to Waters, 9 September 1954, Waters Papers; entries of 26 December 1954 and 19 April 1955, Crossman, *Backbench Diaries*, pp. 377, 418; Smith, *Paper Voices*, pp. 153–56.

have talked', was 'immensely unhappy' about the way things were going. For all the 'energy, knowledge and experience' lavished upon it, no less than the nourishment obtained in November 1955 by swallowing the Manchester *Daily Dispatch*, the *News Chronicle* continued to founder. 'When I see the continual success of the *Daily Mirror* and, above all, the *Sketch*, of all papers, putting on circulation at a record rate, then I despair of the great British public and of British journalism,' he wrote to Waters's widow. 'The only tiny ray of hope seems to be the steady gain by the *M.G.*, still one of the world's best newspapers, and the *Daily Telegraph*, improved I feel by the presence of Donald McLachlan', who had transferred from *The Times* to become deputy editor of the *Telegraph* and later editor of the *Sunday Telegraph*. In comparison, the *News Chronicle* achieved 'strikingly little results'.[1]

Egbert Cadbury, the most realistic member of his family, saw the futility. On 4 December 1956, he outlined 'three possible courses that we can take', the first being 'to line up with the "Beaver"', the second to amalgamate with the *Daily Mail* and the third with the *Daily Herald*'. The last, he supposed, would provide the best chance of keeping the *Star* alive, but held other disadvantages. 'I must say that, personally, I think the *Daily Herald* is a terrible rag,' he told Layton. 'I see it most mornings and I also see the *Express*. I do not like the *Express* either.... I would have less apprehension in joining with the *Mail* than with any other paper.' Yet, as he was forced to admit, 'a sinking ship cannot always call upon the particular lifeboat crew it wants to save it'.[2]

Despite Egbert Cadbury's preferences, it was to the *Herald* that Layton turned for rescue. He opened 'private talks with the Chairman of Odhams' about 'whether it would be possible to create a composite journal of the left that would be independent of any party apparatus and in which the editor could be protected from party pressures'. The secretary of the TUC and the leader of the Labour Party, but not the leader of the Liberal Party, were brought into the discussions. Dora (later Baroness) Gaitskell rang up Oliver Woods of *The Times* 'in a tremendous flap' on 13 May, imploring him that no mention should be made of the fact that her husband had dined with Curtis. 'From what she said the negotiations were "hot" but far from conclusive.' The next week, hints of the negotiations leaked out, obliging Curtis to summon 'heads of departments', whom he told 'that there was some truth in the story', and whom 'he gave a strong impression that he himself was in the dark over it and that the move had been made by the Cadburys without his knowledge'. Layton and the Odhams directors, who controlled 51 per cent of the *Herald* shares, formulated a 'general directive on policy'. The TUC, however, would not accept any scheme that would release Odhams from its 'political tie to the Labour Party'. On 24 July 1957, its general council ratified a new pact with Odhams, permitting the *Herald* to boast that 'our future as Labour's daily newspaper is

[1] Hoare to Joan Waters, 19 January 1956, Waters Papers.
[2] E. Cadbury to Layton, 4 December 1956, Layton Papers.

assured'. Without alleviating the paper's financial distress, this agreement at least guaranteed its political identity, assuming (as some still did) that that was an asset. 'If the *Daily Herald* ever got loose,' Crossman ventured in 1958, 'Odhams would soon turn it into a Labour rag, like the *People*.' Two years later, when the *News Chronicle* finally disappeared, Gaitskell shed no tears. Unwilling to 'upset the *Daily Herald*, who are delighted ... and hoping to get the readers', he wrote off the *News Chronicle* as 'a bad paper, badly managed. That's all there is to it.'[1]

After his failure, Layton withdrew. 'Since 1950 my responsibility for the *News Chronicle* policy has greatly diminished; my public activity has increased,' he wrote to Laurence Cadbury on 27 September. His departure precluded the Beaverbrook option, just as Waters's death had foreclosed a deal with King. That left only Rothermere's Associated Newspapers group as a customer. On 17 October 1960, the paper's 'last splash' was to announce 'the improbable news that it was being "merged" with the true-blue *Mail*' the following morning. The *Observer*, detecting 'poison in the cocoa' (23 October), was amused to note that Laurence Cadbury had first put the purchase price at £1,500,000, then revised it to £1,925,000. Francis Williams, writing in the *New Statesman* on the 22nd, noted without amusement that £1,000,000 was the sum Cadbury was 'proposing to invest in a chocolate factory in Germany'. Rothermere, to whom Williams gave credit for acting 'with the utmost propriety and goodwill', got extra plant for the *Evening News*, which incorporated the *Star*. Cadbury's conduct has been judged less favourably.[2]

Murder or suicide? Either way, the result was fatal. 'Many papers have died over the years in Fleet Street,' Williams knew well enough. 'None has ever been buried so cynically as the *News Chronicle* and the *Star*.' On the afternoon of 'Black Monday', the 17th, Margaret Stewart was at her desk, 'half-finished' with a story, when her telephone rang at 5.20 and she was summoned to an emergency meeting of the NUJ chapel at seven o'clock that evening. That, at the shortest possible notice, was how she 'learned that the paper had folded and that 3,500 people were out of a job, in the biggest mass close-down in journalistic history'. The 'dominant reaction', as she described it and as others corroborated, was one of 'anger rather than self-pity':

> Anger that the *News Chronicle* should be sold like a cake of soap to Carmelite House; anger that the two papers, with their valuable sites,

---

[1] Woods to Maurice Green, 13 May 1957 (copy), and memorandum by Woods to the editor of *The Times*, 20 May 1957 (copy), Woods Papers; memorandum by Layton, Documentary Evidence, Royal Commission on the Press, 1961–62, Cd. 1812, IV, 243; entry of 28 February 1958, Crossman, *Backbench Diaries*, p. 668; P. M. Williams, *Hugh Gaitskell* (London, 1979), p. 667.

[2] Layton to Cadbury, 23 September 1957 (copy), Layton Papers; Baistow, 'Ten Years On and Down,' *New Statesman*, 16 October 1970; Williams, 'The Murder of the *News Chronicle*,' *New Statesman*, 22 October 1960.

combined circulations, printing plant, wharf, and other interests should have fetched so little as £1½ million; anger above all at the meanness of the compensation – the Cocoa handshake, as it was called. The proposed one week's pay for every year of service was described by Jim Bradley, the National Union of Journalists' General Secretary, as one of the worst offers ever made when a paper closed down.

The political implications, which did not seem to ruffle the Cadburys, were no less disturbing. 'A merger with the *Guardian* or the *Herald* would have been bearable', but a take-over by the *Mail*, 'the paper that at one time supported Mosley and Mussolini (though it is trying to forget it) hardly represents a marriage of true minds'.[1]

Christiansen, whom Beaverbrook had pensioned off with £3,000 a year and £35,000 in cash, was struck by 'the wave of revulsion against the Cadburys. In my cynical way, I had thought that every one was prepared for the ultimate demise of the *News Chronicle*. But not at all,' he wrote to his former chief. 'If the Cadburys had closed it down without finding compensation for their staffs, they could not have had a worse press than by associating themselves with the *Daily Mail*.' To those who persisted in equating newspaper support with electoral prospects, the treachery was all the greater in the light of the Liberals' by-election breakthrough at Torrington, followed by their token advance in the 1959 election. 'At the time', what most infuriated Geoffrey Hoare was that Laurence Cadbury, 'that silly little rabbit, should throw away the only popular Liberal newspaper, and at the birth of some sort of a Liberal revival, too'.[2]

The *News Chronicle*'s popularity had been more generic than real. It went to the grave with an average daily sale of 1,206,000 copies, some 300,000 less than its circulation in 1951, but by no means a negligible figure. The *Star* was selling 744,000, little better than half its circulation in 1951. Yet, in the interests of journalism and Liberalism alike, could not some way have been found to keep them going? Williams, who understood that Cadbury had seen Jo Grimond, the Liberal Party leader, 'only a day or two before the final announcement', wondered whether he had then or previously attempted 'to explore the possibility of direct Liberal support'.[3] That was to ignore the vast changes that

[1] Williams, 'Murder of the *News Chronicle*,' and Stewart, 'The Night the Blow Fell,' *New Statesman*, 22 October 1960; G. Glenton and W. Pattinson, *The Last Chronicle of Bouverie Street* (London, 1963); Documentary Evidence, Royal Commission on the Press, 1961–62, Cd. 1812, I, 150–53. The *Observer* used the wrong analogy when it said (5 February 1961) that the *New Chronicle* had been 'sold with its editor, staff and readers as a nineteenth-century Russian estate was bought and sold with its souls'. For Norman Cursley, the last editor of the *News Chronicle*, 'Black Monday' was a 'last day as a journalist' (*The Times*, 4 May 1972). Ralph McCarthy, the last editor of the *Star*, also left Fleet Street. Their staffs dispersed. As for the 'souls', the circulation of the *Daily Mail* was 2,084,000 before the merger and 1,917,000 a decade later.

[2] Taylor, *Beaverbrook*, p. 623; Christiansen to Beaverbrook, 22 October 1960, Beaverbrook Papers, C/81; Hoare to Joan Woods, 3 May 1961, Woods Papers.

[3] 'Murder of the *News Chronicle*,' *New Statesman*, 22 October 1960. Grimond (letter to the author, 23 February 1983) has recalled only a telephone conversation with Laurence Cadbury,

had occurred in newspaper ethics and party practices, which together put the idea of a subvention out of the question. What would have been automatic in 1880 and a not uncommon (though a clandestine) practice in 1910 was, by 1960, a mutual impracticality.

The experience of the *Daily Herald* soon proved that point. Persevering as a Labour Party organ, it lost circulation (1,412,414 copies in 1960 as against 1,465,994 in 1959) and, with it, an ability to attract advertising accounts. At a time when politicians were allegedly 'minuetting to-and-fro delivering vacillating speeches about nothing in particular', it was incumbent upon the *Herald* to publish them 'with a zeal which ushered away the readers in dazed droves'. Moreover, until August 1960, when a revised agreement between the TUC and Odhams conceded a greater measure of editorial discretion, the paper 'was obliged to appraise and advocate Labour policy in an entirely uncritical manner – a deadly dull mission'. In keeping with that agreement, John Beavan (later Baron Ardwick) was appointed editor. He worked smoothly and efficiently with Sir Christopher Chancellor, the new Odhams chairman. The following year, their partnership was interrupted after the *Mirror* group outbid Roy Thomson (later 1st Baron Thomson of Fleet) for control of Odhams. The TUC found itself in bondage to King. As the Labour politicians could not stop him, they resolved (in Gaitskell's words) not to 'bitch up our relations with him too badly'. In a 'public pledge', drafted by Hugh Cudlipp and signed by King, comforting assurances were given – and naïvely accepted – that the *Herald*'s 'future ... as a separate entity will be fought for with the utmost energy', and that Beavan, 'who has done so much to improve the *Herald* will continue his work as editor'. To that, Cudlipp personally added a 'promise ... that the *Herald* would be kept alive for a minimum of seven years whatever may happen'. In 1964, the TUC sold its 49 per cent shareholding in the *Herald* to the International Publishing Corporation, as King's conglomeration had been reconstituted, and Beavan was unseated. The umbilical cord between the *Sunday Mirror* (formerly the *Sunday Pictorial*) and the *Daily Mirror* was cut in 1970, when IPC sold its two Sunday papers – the *Mirror* and the *People* (afterwards the *Sunday People*) – to Reed International. More directly, on 15 September 1964, IPC transmuted the *Daily Herald* into the *Sun*. During the transitional editorship of Sydney (later Baron) Jacobson, it retained a Labour pigmentation, but its character had changed by the time that Rupert Murdoch acquired it in 1969, and it was to change still more dramatically thereafter.[1]

---

who 'would have been all too well aware that the Liberal Party has never had enough money to conduct its own affairs, let alone lending to anyone else'.

[1] Memorandum submitted by Daily Mirror Newspapers, Ltd., Documentary Evidence, Royal Commission on the Press, 1961–62, Cd. 1812, I, 73, 101–103; Williams, *The Right to Know*, pp. 147–52; Edelman, *Mirror*, pp. 188–89; P. M. Williams, *Gaitskell*, pp. 667–68; Butler and Stokes, *Political Change*, pp. 229–31; interviews with Sir Christopher Chancellor (11 July 1978) and Lord Ardwick (18 August 1978). At the time of its submergence, the *Herald* was estimated to have a circulation of 1,300,000.

Other proprietorial adjustments occurred in these years and in those that followed. The most important of them will be reviewed in the concluding chapter. None, however, was as relevant to the political history of the British press as either the overnight shut-down of the *News Chronicle* or the step-by-step capitulation of the *Daily Herald*. Both events obviously postdated the appointment of the first Royal Commission on the Press, the focal point of this chapter, yet each retrospectively served to illuminate some of the basic issues that had been left concealed or obscure. In that sense, they count as detours, contiguous to – but not conterminous with – the road to 1947. They confirmed, as if confirmation were necessary, that politicians, whether acting individually or through party agencies, had lost their power to control newspapers or even to sustain them. The political press, as the Victorians had improvised and nurtured it, was not only dead, but buried.

Eighteen

POSTSCRIPT AND POST-MORTEM

In 1952, when appendicitis confined him to hospital for almost a fortnight, Richard Crossman read the two-part fourth volume of *The History of The Times* (spanning the years from 1912 to 1939), then newly published. 'What struck me was the enormous power of the press in politics before 1918 and its steady decline since then,' he reflected in his diary.

> Northcliffe could really make and unmake Cabinet Ministers. He could get Lord Haldane sacked simply by attacking him, whereas today, if Lord Beaverbrook or Lord Kemsley launch a campaign against a Cabinet Minister, the effect is usually to strengthen his position. Of course, the main influence of *The Times* in its day was in foreign affairs, where its leading articles were really studied as semi-official statements of British policy. But even here I cannot believe that it is taken so seriously today as it was even as late as 1938, when just before Munich Dawson proposed the secession of the Sudeten areas.

Simplifying what he had read to accord with his preconceived notions, Crossman went on to propound his own tendentious theories. 'Part of the reason' for the curtailment of *The Times*'s influence in particular and that of journalism in general was, as he saw it,

> the rise to power of the Labour Party, which tends to write off all newspapers as capitalist. A Labour Cabinet ... is not nearly as open to newspaper influence as a Conservative Cabinet. But the basic reason for the change is the extension of the franchise in 1918 and the coming into being of a real thing called democratic public opinion, whereas, in the old days, political decisions were really taken by an oligarchy and a newspaper proprietor merely operated as a member of an oligarchy with a particularly loud voice. ... Today if you want to influence politics through the press you don't do it by running campaigns against certain politicians or for certain causes. Your aim is to educate or to stimulate opinion to bring the pressure on the politicians.[1]

[1] Entry of 20 May 1952, Crossman, *Backbench Diaries*, pp. 105-106.

In the next decade, when he graduated from being a backbench diarist to the candid chronicler of Cabinet proceedings, Crossman had persistent cause to modify those judgments.

The British press of the post-war age was indeed a different animal which, if not exactly tame, no longer functioned as a beast of prey. The change had taken place by the general election of 1945, but it took two – and possibly three – subsequent national campaigns to awaken politicians to the fact. Even then, some continued to think in terms of outmoded relationships, which they tried in vain to resurrect. By the time of the second Royal Commission on the Press in 1961-62, it was clear from the stinted and vacillating loyalties of the major newspapers that the old system had perished. It was not yet clear, however, by what process. 'Newspaper proprietors today behave rather better than they did in the first thirty years of the century, and fortunately possess a great deal less political power than in the bad old days,' testified Randolph Churchill, who begged the question whether less power had made for better behaviour or better behaviour had checked the abuse of power. 'The increasing power of radio and television has also tended to make newspapers less personally partisan and to encourage newspaper proprietors in the dissemination of the truth,' he added as another truism. Discerning, as some would not have done, 'a change in the characteristics of the newspaper proprietors', the younger Churchill did not specify whether it was cause or effect.[1]

The political press, its ranks depleted by the closure of the *News Chronicle* and the submergence of the *Daily Herald*, thereafter underwent further permutations. In the process, it indicated not only the distance it had travelled from nineteenth-century models, but also the forces that impelled it. Competition from broadcasting was more apparent than real. Instead of draining away readers or advertisers, television – as it profitably expanded into the commercial sphere – yielded revenues that went to shore up crumbling edifices in Fleet Street. The intensification of labour problems, resulting in periodic stoppages and shut-downs, weakened the economic foundations of the press without directly unravelling its political fabric. The invasion of the industry by multi-national consortia had similarly mixed effects, which, at one extreme, augured the revival of certain discarded practices. Nevertheless, the old contractual obligations were defunct and a new pattern was gradually emerging in their place.

Newspapers grew steadily more catholic and less partisan in their ordinary news coverage. When confronted by a general election, they usually expressed a party preference, but always with at least a gesture of pragmatism and often

---

[1] Memorandum by Randolph S. Churchill, Documentary Evidence, Royal Commission on the Press, 1961-62, Cd. 1812, V, 235. It was common to ascribe the waning of newspaper partisanship to competition from the younger, more impartial media. See a statement by Ness Edwards, a former Labour Postmaster-General, quoted in *The Times*, 5 October 1959; *also see* Butler and Stokes, *Political Change*, p. 267.

for a different party from the one they had previously endorsed. What had been routine now became a ritual, performed only occasionally and then with increasing agnosticism. Without necessarily forsaking politics, though that has sometimes followed suit, newspapers became less explicitly party political. Before proceeding to an analysis of these subtle adjustments, there are some significant events to take into account.

* * *

In 1945, realizing that 'to remain a provincial morning paper was to court slow death', the directors of the *Manchester Guardian* resolved 'to become national'. Seven years later, they announced plans to bring out a London edition, then 'quietly withdrew the intention', which was seen as 'a considerable gamble'. Instead, on 24 August 1959, the paper dropped its territorial prefix and began simultaneous publication in London and Manchester. With an improved sale of 'about 230,000', the *Guardian* was no longer losing money, but it had yet to attain a fully national status. Oliver Woods, celebrating the supremacy of *The Times* (its 'outstanding editorial achievement' that year was the coverage of the election campaign in the autumn), pointed out on 1 December 1959 that Printing House Square had no cause for alarm: 'Once again people of authority and standing in many fields are writing to *The Times*. The *Guardian*'s letters continue to have no significance. Five of the letters printed in the *Daily Telegraph* one day recently were *The Times*'s rejects.' Under the dextrous editorship of Alastair Hetherington, whose later partiality to Harold Wilson briefly recalled C. P. Scott's to Lloyd George, the *Guardian* was seen 'to have adopted a definite policy of swinging from news to features. We shall not follow,' decreed *The Times*. On 29 August 1970, the *Guardian* shuttered its offices in Cross Street, Manchester, and entered into a cohabitation with the *Sunday Times* in London. By 1974, it had leapfrogged ahead of *The Times* which had itself swung in the direction of features.[1]

Starting in 1958, to the embarrassment of Sir William Haley, *The Times* directed its appeal to the 'Top People'. The campaign was markedly successful. 'More MPs and senior civil servants read *The Times* than any other quality daily newspaper,' an independent survey confirmed in 1977. Among them were 89 per cent of Labour MPs (as opposed to 74 per cent who read the *Guardian* and 37 per cent who read the *Telegraph*), and 81 per cent of Conservative and Liberal MPs (as opposed to 26 per cent who read the *Guardian* and 68 per cent who read the *Telegraph*). Michael Foot, then Lord President of the Council and Leader of the House, admitted to reading *The Times* 'with due scepticism'; even so, he made sure to read it, knowing that

---

[1] Documentary Evidence, Royal Commission on the Press, 1961-62, Cd. 1812, I, 261; Ayerst, *Guardian*, pp. 627-29; minutes of assistant editors' meeting, 1 December 1959 (copy), Woods Papers.

any 'suspicion ... in the mind of *The Times* ... might flit across the minds of others'. It was the nature of 'Top People' to be critical.¹

Unfortunately, it was also their nature to be relatively few. At the instigation of Gavin Astor, who wanted to know what sort of inheritance to expect and who preferred not to judge the vitality of the enterprise by the lustre of its correspondence columns, a team of chartered accountants from the highly respected firm of Cooper Brothers was commissioned to provide a comprehensive stock-taking. This inquiry began in November 1957 and concluded the following February with a report that faulted *The Times* for its élitist image and archaic managerial structure. Many of the findings were fiercely resented, implying as they did that the paper had consistently sacrificed efficiency and profitability in order to bolster prestige. Yet most of the recommendations, which were fewer than the criticisms, were slowly implemented.²

None too soon, *The Times* set about to broaden its appeal among younger readers, women, and the less-than-top people beyond the environs of London. 'Home news', entrusted to John Grant, was expanded in scope to take account of social realities. Haley headed a committee of overseers to modernize procedures and increase circulation. His subsequent appointment as chief executive, deputed to preside over the 'complete reorganization of the management and of the capital structure', drew him away from normal editorial functions, which were informally assumed by Iverach McDonald and Woods, managing editor and deputy managing editor respectively. All the while, the underlying financial difficulties became more acute. In 1962, Lord Astor of Hever (as John Astor had become in 1956) emigrated to protect his family fortune in America from the lengthened arm of the British tax authorities. His son and heir, who had already replaced him as chairman of the company, was soon named a co-proprietor. Given the advanced age of John Walter, the fifth of his line, it was reasonably assumed that, before long, Gavin Astor would succeed to exclusive control over *The Times*.

His 'own finances ... inextricably interwoven with those of The Times Publishing Company', Gavin Astor struggled to make ends meet. The extensive renovation of Printing House Square proved far more costly than initially estimated. In 1963, the younger Astor went further into debt by paying £250,000 for the Walter family's minority shareholding, which might otherwise have fallen into the hands of a third party. Roy Thomson, the unprepossessing Canadian millionaire who had failed in a bid for Odhams, was known to be in the market for a piece of *The Times*. He had bought the *Scotsman* in 1953 and the *Sunday Times* in 1959. Beaverbrook commended his compatriot as 'a straight fellow' who, as such, 'will have his difficulties in attuning himself to

[1] *The Times*, 16 February 1977. Foot's words, as quoted in *The Times* on 23 February 1977, are softened from his statement in the House: *Parliamentary Debates* (Commons), 5th ser., cmxxvi, col. 1246.

[2] Sampson, *Anatomy of Britain*, pp. 467-69; interviews with John Grant (30 July 1982) and others.

production in Britain'. To the contrary, it now began to appear as if British production would have to attune itself to the 'acquisitive instinct' of Thomson, for whom newspaper ownership was not so much a vocation as an addiction. A new and somewhat implausible type of press magnate, who disclaimed the slightest interest in editorial policy and described balance sheets as his 'favourite reading', Thomson struck some people as too good to be true, others as too true to be good. In 1970, when he was seventy-five years old, a television interviewer asked him how many newspaper properties he owned. 'I think it's 182,' he answered tentatively, 'but we bought one the other day in North Carolina, that may make it 183.' Asked what 'remaining ambitions' he entertained, Thomson briskly replied: 'More newspapers – I'd like to have one newspaper for every day of the year – 365.' By then, he had collected his peerage and, among other prizes, *The Times*.[1]

On 3 May 1966, the paper was radically 'redesigned' to afford a 'keener selection and sense of news and its more extensive coverage'. Most conspicuously, news articles (still unsigned) pre-empted classified advertisements on the front page. Within six months, sales had risen by 20 per cent, though they remained below the fixed target. 'It was recognised that the successful achievement of the various objectives which were essential for strengthening the political and social influence of *The Times*', along with ensuring its solvency, 'would require an immediate infusion of management and marketing skills'. That, Gavin Astor cautiously estimated, 'would cost at least £2½ m. over the next five years, and would absorb most if not all of the anticipated annual profits until 1970', with the further likelihood 'that it would be necessary to invest still more development capital during the 1970-80 decade'.

His own 'liquid capital' had been eroded 'by heavy borrowing'. Where, then, was the necessary money to come from? 'It was becoming more and more urgent for *The Times* and for my family,' he explained, 'to extricate themselves from the increasingly vulnerable financial entanglement in which they both found themselves.' There were three possible alternatives: he could 'continue in the honour and privilege of sole ownership' while the paper, starved for investment, 'gradually declines and wilts'; he could 'sell out completely'; or he could 'seek a suitable partnership' as the Walters had done. Embarking on the third course, he had a limited range of options. The *Daily Telegraph* and the *Guardian* (despite hankerings on the part of Laurence Scott) were ruled out on the grounds that they were direct competitors. The *Observer* was an obvious possibility. Linked by family ties to *The Times*, it was moreover a paying guest at Printing House Square. But the *Observer* was saddled with its own deficit, and the provisions of its trust posed obstacles to amalgamation. The next

[1] Memorandum by Gavin Astor, 29 December 1966, *Times* Archives; Beaverbrook to Driberg, 13 July 1960, Driberg Papers; Anthony Howard, 'The Tycoon who was captured by *The Times*,' *Observer*, 8 August 1976; transcript of Lord Thomson's interview with Robin Day and Lord Francis-Williams, BBC-TV, 22 March 1970, Woods Papers; Thomson, 'The Next Ten Years,' in V. Brodsky, ed., *Fleet Street* (London, 1966), p.35.

candidate was the *Financial Times*, which was invited to enter a holding company under its own chairman, Lord Robbins. Although an elaborate formula was worked out to the satisfaction of the 11th Earl of Drogheda, then managing director of the *Financial Times*, Robbins and the Pearson dynasts feared that their property would be subsumed and probably impoverished by a merger. Lastly, there was the intriguing possibility that *The Times* could come to an arrangement with the 1st Baron Egremont, who has been identified as 'one of the richest (and most surprising) men in Britain'. Formerly (as John Wyndham), Egremont had been secretary to Harold Macmillan, the retired but hardly retiring Prime Minister, whose interests he was understood still to represent. He reportedly had amassed 'financial backing up to £5 m.', including 'a substantial sum of his own' for the purpose of buying *The Times*. The scheme was discussed at select dinner tables, but came to nothing. Otherwise, Macmillan might have succeeded where Lloyd George had failed nearly half a century earlier. That would have been to turn back the clock and, indeed, the calendar.[1]

Thomson was waiting with a handsome offer, which was accepted on 30 September 1966. *The Times* was to merge with the *Sunday Times* to form Times Newspapers Ltd., which Haley agreed to chair for the first three years. C. D. (later Sir Denis) Hamilton, Thomson's right-hand man, was appointed editor-in-chief of the combined operation, and the board was duly reconstructed. Exchanging his '98% interest in *The Times*' for 'a 15% share on an immensely richer business', Astor took the honorific title of Life President. Although 'inevitably . . . sorry to see the end of a long era in the history of *The Times*', he realized that 'to be the private owner of a "National Institution" . . . is an anachronism today', when 'the survival and prosperity of newspapers depend upon brilliant commercial and professional management'.

The proper assurances were given that the editorial freedom of both papers would continue to be respected. But, before the union could be consummated, approval had to be obtained from the Monopolies Commission. As Harold Wilson, the Prime Minister, had already intimated his assent, no serious difficulties were contemplated and none arose. Four 'public figures', two nominated by Astor and two by Thomson, were added to the board as guardians of the national interest. Upon Hamilton's eventual retirement, an 'editorial director' would take the place of the 'editor-in-chief'. Throughout these protracted deliberations, Wilson maintained 'a strictly non-interventionist view'. If the press was to be bailed out by corporate businessmen – and neither he nor his advisers could offer 'any practical proposals for preventing'

---

[1] Memorandum by Gavin Astor, 29 December 1966, *Times* Archives; various conversations with Lord Robbins and others; Lord Drogheda, *Double Harness* (London, 1978), pp. 189-94; Sampson, *Anatomy*, pp. 336-37; memoranda by A. P. Ryan, 3 and 18 December 1969, 9 January, 13 and 27 May, and 9 June 1970, Woods Papers. Harold Macmillan (letter to the author, 15 September 1982) did not recollect Egremont's moves and perhaps never knew of them.

that occurrence – it was surely preferable to have a businessman like Thomson, who took pride in allowing his editors the freedom to make political choices. 'I have said this and I mean it most sincerely,' Thomson later declared on television. 'I believe there should be more Labour papers in this country; and I am not a Labour man basically.' With respect to welfare services, he located himself 'to the right of the Tory party'. Nevertheless, on the premiss that 'half the people at least in this country are Labour supporters, ... I believe they ought to have more newspapers'.[1]

No one could have agreed more heartily than the Labour politicians, who perpetually felt at a cruel disadvantage in putting across their message to the electorate. 'The more the official leadership loses the support of the general public,' Crossman had observed in 1954, 'the more they lay the blame on wicked journalists', who were denounced as Tory scribes. In 1962, five years after the Conservatives first experimented with paid advertisements, the Labour publicity managers overcame their repugnance and resorted to the same techniques. That, however, smacked of paying tribute to the enemy and was regarded as no substitute for active editorial support. In 1964, after a heavy expenditure on newspaper display advertisements, Labour scraped back into office. The *Daily Herald* was refitted as the *Sun* just in time to favour the Labour challenge. No less predictably, so did the *People* and the *Sunday Citizen* (as *Reynolds News* had become). The *Daily Mirror*, which had recoiled from Labour in 1959 after the party's third successive defeat ('The *Mirror* did itself a great deal of damage by backing the Labour Party heavily up to the Election day and then going completely non-political two days later,' according to Crossman), now returned docilely to the fold. It was not a question of going 'Forward with the People', a slogan it had long since jettisoned, but rather a weary sense 'that it was time for a change'. The *Guardian* and the *Observer* adopted the same philosophy, which *The Times* thoughtfully understood, but could not bring itself to share. 'The Labour Party have always hated *The Times* deep down,' as Oliver Woods knew from his experience of having 'to some extent lived within the Establishment' of that party. Recently, Haley had 'antagonised the Tories as well, to a degree which they will I think never forgive. *The Times* has to stand on its own legs now.' In the past, it had 'derived a good deal of its power from being the premier paper in the most powerful capital of the world. Now,' Woods contemplated, 'it can at best look forward to being a sort of English-language *Journal de Genève.*'[2]

---

[1] Entry of 8 February 1967, Crossman, *Diaries of a Cabinet Minister*, II, 229-30; Francis Williams, *The Right to Know*, pp. 184-91 (Williams was one of three additional members of the Monopolies Commission on this occasion); transcript of Thomson's interview, BBC-TV, 22 March 1970, Woods Papers.

[2] Entries of 3 December 1954, and 13 November 1959, Crossman, *Backbench Diaries*, pp. 374, 798; Lord Windlesham, *Communications and Political Power* (London, 1966), pp. 35-37, 241; Richard Rose, *Influencing Voters* (London, 1967), pp. 168-71; Smith, *Paper Voices*, pp. 178-79; note by Woods [late 1963], Woods Papers.

In the 1964 campaign, which 66 per cent of the respondents in a major survey 'followed ... in the press' (compared with 59 per cent in 1966), the Labour Party enjoyed wide and often sympathetic attention. What it craved, however, was something more solid and dependable, unsusceptible to deviance. 'The press are contemptible and corrupt. Unbearable!' exclaimed Wilson, 'wild with fury' at the way his attack on Edward Heath had been reported. 'True,' agreed Crossman, 'but if you lambast the Tory leader you mustn't expect the Tory press to be wildly enthusiastic.' In March 1966, Wilson fought another election and increased his parliamentary majority. The line-up in Fleet Street was much the same: six dailies (with an aggregate circulation of about twenty-five million) sided to a greater or lesser degree with the Conservatives; four (with an aggregate circulation of about twenty-one million) sided with Labour. Although usually counted among the Tory half-dozen, *The Times* was so ambivalent on this occasion that David Butler and Anne Sloman, in their compilation of *British Political Facts*, sensibly listed it as '?/Lib'. In the field of Sunday journalism, Labour held the advantage with endorsements from four papers that sold close to thirty-three million copies, as opposed to the Conservatives' four (including the *News of the World*, which did not venture an explicit recommendation) that sold 382,000 less.[1]

How much were any – or all – of these endorsements worth? Even from 'a most generalised view', it was evident 'that readership preference and political attitude do not coincide exactly'. Colin Seymour-Ure, probing more deeply, was not surprised to discover that 'attitudes of readers are broadly in line with those of their newspapers, but not to such an extent that similarity of outlook is a prerequisite of readership'. Of the daily papers, the *Telegraph* and the *Mirror* each drew as many as two-thirds of their readers from the supporters of the parties with which they themselves identified. Of the Sunday papers, only the *Sunday Telegraph* (launched in 1961) matched this proportion. The *Daily Express* and the *Daily Mail* (the latter with a supposed residue of *News Chronicle* customers) probably had as many, if not more, non-Tory than Tory readers. The *Guardian*'s preference for Labour was shared by only 35 per cent of its readers. The same held true for the 'anti-Conservative' *Observer*, which was 'significantly more popular with *Guardian* readers than with readers of any of the Conservative Dailies'. Correspondingly, the pro-Conservative *Sunday Express* was 'less popular with *Guardian* readers than with the Conservative Quality Dailies and less popular as a Sunday companion to the anti-Conservative *Sun* and *Daily Mirror* than to any of the Popular Conservative Dailies'. Here, factors of 'education and social class' complicated the picture and might have outweighed political attitudes. For example, most of the readers of the pro-Conservative *Daily Sketch* were

---

[1] Butler and Stokes, *Political Change*, p. 219; entry of 9 December 1966, Crossman, *Diaries*, II, 155; Seymour-Ure, *The Press, Politics and the Public*, pp. 52-53; Butler and Sloman, *British Political Facts 1900-1979*, p. 449.

Labour or Liberal voters, 60 per cent of whom also read the pro-Labour *Mirror*.[1]

It was as difficult for newspaper writers as it was for newspaper readers to sort out the issues of the 1966 campaign. At *The Times*, A. P. Ryan grumbled that 'this ruddy election beats all records for dullness & lack of spirit. The efforts of all sides to make a live fight of it are, so far, as painful to follow as they are ineffective. Maybe,' he hoped against hope, 'a Zinoviev letter or something is about to pop out of the bag' to stir things up.[2] To Wilson's relief and Heath's frustration, the calm remained unbroken. For once, a general election failed to generate news.

Tom Driberg, whose continued friendship with Guy Burgess, the escaped spy, had once threatened to explode into another 'Zinoviev letter', took the lead in trying to launch a new Labour daily. For this purpose, the Labour Press Co-Operative Society was founded in the summer of 1965 to collect pledges of readership and subscriptions for shares, of which 20,000 were to be issued in £1 denominations. Among Driberg's associates were Vera Brittain and her husband, Professor George Catlin, Baron (formerly Ted) Willis, Lady Megan Lloyd George (now Labour MP for Carmarthen), and two parliamentary novices, Norman Buchan and Hugh Jenkins (later Baron Jenkins of Putney). The chairman was Ernest Kay, a provincial newspaperman who was then managing editor of *Time and Tide* and whose books include *The Wit of Harold Wilson* (1967). Innocuously entitled, the sixpenny 'Morning News' was to be 'not merely a political newspaper', but one that would 'soon rank among the great newspapers of the world'. On May Day 1966, it was announced that, from 3 October, the Labour 'movement will have – at last – its own influential national daily newspaper'. That was a mirage. On 9 June, Willis informed Kay that 'almost £20,000 has been raised and most of this has been ... swallowed up in promotion'. There was 'still no clear idea of the kind of paper that it is proposed to produce, or of its political policy'. Willis had an appointment to see the Prime Minister the next afternoon, and intended to 'put the situation to him as frankly as I can'. Two weeks later, Kay was obliged to state that, owing to insufficient support in Downing Street and elsewhere, the projected paper 'cannot now be published in the forseeable future'. In January 1967, the Society's affairs were put in the hands of a liquidator. Most of the subscriptions were never refunded, but a wealthy Labour MP, who was not affiliated with the Society and who preferred to remain anonymous, offered to reimburse necessitous investors.[3]

Labour's hopes were dashed, but not destroyed. After June 1967, when the

---

[1] Seymour-Ure, *The Press, Politics and the Public* pp. 54-57.

[2] Ryan to Woods, 18 March 1966, Woods Papers.

[3] Woods to Maurice Green, 20 March 1958 (copy), Woods Papers; various circulars of 1965-66, Willis to Kay, 9 June 1966 (copy), and other correspondence, Driberg Papers. Lord Willis (letter to the author, 25 February 1983) particularly recalled Robert Maxwell's strong negative advice on the basis of 'considerable research in this area'.

Sunday Citizen folded, the party felt more victimized than deprived. Wilson, 'a voracious newspaper reader' who 'felt jealous of anybody else having contacts in Fleet Street', contributed to the paranoia. In a television interview on 16 October 1972 (as reported in the next day's *Times*), he complained that the press, being 'overwhelmingly anti-Labour', would 'go to almost any lengths to discredit Labour's leader'. His Cabinet colleagues, sometimes at the cost of incurring his resentment, none the less made 'skilful use of press relations' to obtain favourable publicity for themselves and their departmental policies. For example, by giving dinner parties and picking up the telephone, Crossman managed to extract friendly coverage from such diverse (and, in some cases, improbable) sources as *Tribune*, the *New Statesman*, the *Financial Times*, *The Economist*, the *Guardian*, and the *Sunday Times*. Inevitably, some of them dispensed more satisfactory service than others. But that would have been true no matter who owned or edited them. Nor was Crossman unique in his efforts 'to put the Government in a decent light', where he might also display himself. He mentioned Barbara Castle and Roy Jenkins as but two members of the Cabinet who were particularly adept at cultivating the press. 'In fact,' he supposed, 'almost every Minister does a certain amount, every Minister is approached and airs his views.' The Prime Minister, naturally enough, did 'a great deal ... of steering' in this direction, using Gerald Kaufman (a former correspondent for the *Daily Mirror* and the *New Statesman*, and subsequently MP for the Ardwick division of Manchester) and Marcia Williams (later Baroness Falkender) 'extensively for this purpose'.[1]

On 17 July 1969, 'the big story in the morning papers was Hugh Cudlipp's announcement that next January the *Sun* would be wound up'. Just as King had displaced Bartholomew in a palace *coup*, Cudlipp had since displaced King after the latter's Harmsworthian 'all-out attack' on Wilson ('Enough is Enough') in the *Mirror* and the *Sun* on 10 May 1968. Cudlipp, but not the IPC directors, had approved King's outburst. 'In the light of future events,' Francis Williams tartly commented, 'Cudlipp's failure either to raise objections himself or to inform other directors of King's decision to issue such a statement ... has a somewhat inimical character.' Within the fortnight, King was dismissed and Cudlipp was raised to the chairmanship.[2]

Once there, Cudlipp 'found that running IPC wasn't exactly his kind of show'. To trim the trading losses, exacerbated by the devaluation of the pound, he soon entered into a partnership with Reed International, a conglomeration

---

[1] Entries of 30 April and 11 May 1967, 31 January, 2 February, and 20 July 1969, Crossman, *Diaries*, II, 344, 350, and III, 350, 353, 583; interview with David Wood, 21 August 1981; *also see* Alan Watkins in the *Observer*, 7 February 1982.

[2] Entry of 17 July 1969, Crossman, *Diaries*, III, 573; Williams, *The Right to Know*, pp. 158-65. King had made it clear that 'I, in discussions with Mr Hugh Cudlipp, the editorial director, lay down the broad policy. And I take public responsibility for it' (*Future of the Press*, p. 92). Allegations that his ulterior purpose was to topple Wilson and install a 'business administration' are investigated in Brendon, *Press Barons*, pp. 215-17.

of publishers and paper manufacturers. There was room under this umbrella for the magazines that King had purchased from Odhams and Rothermere, for the *Daily Mirror*, for the two Sunday papers, but not for the money-losing *Sun*. The Cabinet was divided as to whether the IPC-Reed merger had to be brought before the Monopolies Commission. Barbara Castle, as Minister for Employment, 'felt it her duty just to put the matter forward', and Anthony Wedgwood Benn weakly supported her. At that, Wilson 'launched into a great attack, saying this was political suicide. The *Daily Mirror* was the only paper likely to be loyal to us in the election, and we must be political people, not mere runners of Departments,' he reminded his colleagues. 'The merger was perfectly sensible,' he declared with Roy Jenkins's concurrence and with the result that there was not 'a single supporter for a reference' to the Commission.[1]

Robert Maxwell, a successful publisher and then Labour MP for Buckingham, had already made a bid for the *Sun*. 'His idea,' as Crossman understood it, 'is to turn it into a *Daily Worker* bought by the élite, with very little advertising, and he thinks that with half a million circulation and a rather higher price he can keep it going.' The previous year, Maxwell had also made an offer for the *News of the World*, which was snatched from him by Rupert Murdoch. That, Murdoch crowed, had been 'the biggest steal since the Great Train Robbery'. Now, in a still bigger steal, Murdoch acquired the *Sun*, which he promptly converted into a garish tabloid. As such, it fitted comfortably into what the *Sunday Times Magazine* (21 April 1974) was to describe (before Murdoch became its proprietor) as his 'bordello of papers'. From the remnants of his father's holdings, Murdoch built an empire that stretched from his native Australia to Britain and soon traversed North America.[2]

Aggressive, itinerant, and outwardly brash, Murdoch personified the new proprietorialism of the 1970s. He seemed as immune to the crises of the decade as he was indifferent to its political controversies. The politicians did not reciprocate his disregard and, especially when an election was impending, courted him all the more feverishly. Wherever he happened to be, there was always a telephone within his reach, and they used it to solicit his support. The point to be made is that, regularly and often personally, that support was solicited by politicians and never subject to their command. Murdoch declined the knighthoods they proffered, perhaps out of genuine humility or perhaps (like King) because he was holding out for something better. His reticence was not emulated by his subordinates. His papers, both in Britain and elsewhere, lurched from one party persuasion to another for reasons that were seldom articulated and manifestly more commercial than ideological. 'The *Sun* has a

---

[1] Entry of 10 February 1970, Crossman, *Diaries*, III, 810-11. Ted (later Baron Castle), the minister's husband and a former editor of *Picture Post*, was among those who lost jobs on the *Sun*.

[2] Entry of 17 July 1969, Crossman, *Diaries*, III, 573; Brendon, *Press Barons*, pp. 242-43.

mind of its own – like you,' that paper told its readers at the time of the 1970 election. Then, and again in the two campaigns of 1974, that mind was made up for Labour, but not so clearly as to prevent 57 per cent of those readers from misperceiving that the *Sun* stood above the fray. In 1979, a change of mind made the *Sun* emphatically Conservative. To what end? Over half of the paper's readers voted contrary to its specific advice, and a third of them were under the erroneous impression that the *Sun* had urged them to vote Labour.[1]

There was little risk that the sophisticated readership of the *Observer* would commit such a mistake, but there was a grave threat that the paper itself would soon fall silent. In June 1975, David Astor gave notice that, unless the trade unions agreed to substantial economies, he would be compelled to close down in September. Over the preceding ten years, while the *Sunday Times* and the *Sunday Telegraph* had bounded ahead, the *Observer*'s sale had scarcely budged. Unlike its rivals, appended to dailies, the *Observer* was 'a Sunday singleton' with no one 'to share what are the punishing overheads of overmanning' in the composing room. Thomson's decision to 'rationalise his own printing arrangements' by bringing *The Times* and the *Sunday Times* together in Gray's Inn Road, side by side if not quite under the same roof, left both the *Observer* and the *Guardian* out in the cold. The historic premises vacated by *The Times* were purchased by the *Observer*, a sitting tenant, for £5.5 million. It was a good property investment, but a heavy liability in terms of newspaper production. Rebuffed by Astor, who set his sights on dividing printing operations between the *Financial Times* in London and the *Yorkshire Post* in Leeds, the *Guardian* moved to Farringdon Street on its own. The unions vetoed Astor's novel scheme, with the result that the *Observer* stayed put as a solitary prisoner in its oversized and underused quarters. Small wonder, therefore, that its pages began to betray a 'growing lack of journalistic confidence'. To Tom Baistow, 'a former admirer' who remembered the paper's principled 'stand against Suez at the cost of circulation', it was depressing to see the *Observer* become 'increasingly right-wing on the domestic front, with a middle-aged yearning for the tidy order of a Centrist utopia that must have cost it many young potential readers'.[2]

On 24 August, after eight weeks of haggling with the unions, Astor was able to tell his readers that the *Observer* had 'come through a nasty time'. In return 'for redundancy payments at the higher rates usual in Fleet Street', the production staff had accepted 'a 30 per cent reduction in regular and casual jobs'. The lay-offs were fewer than requested by management, but still 'substantial by any standards'. The *Observer* had won a reprieve, which was not

[1] Conversation with Rupert Murdoch, 20 April 1978; John Whale, *Journalism and Government* (London, 1972), pp. 50-51; Royal Commission on the Press, 1977, *Attitudes to the Press*, Cds. 6810-13, pp. 54, 69; Robert Worcester and Peter Kellner, 'A Rival for Television,' New Statesman, 4 May 1979.
[2] Baistow, 'Anatomy of the *Observer* Crisis,' *New Statesman*, 27 June 1975.

to be mistaken for a new lease of life. 'I don't believe we will solve the problems of Fleet Street even if the newspapers paid no wages at all,' a trade union official was quoted as saying. Given the economic recession, coupled with the high cost of newsprint and labour, the outlook remained bleak.[1]

The speculation in Fleet Street was that, before very long, the *Observer* would drop into the lap of one speculator or another. For a time, Murdoch seemed the most likely to succeed. Sir James Goldsmith, the head of an Anglo-French food cartel and the owner of *L'Express* in Paris (which had obviously affected his syntax), was known to nurse ambitions to obtain a foothold in the British press, 'a perfectly remarkably good institution'. Later on, he claimed to have gone so far as to examine 'all the facts and figures' before inviting 'half a dozen leading editorial staff' to a dinner, where he proclaimed his candidacy. His bid, never seriously entertained, was predicated on the understanding that the *Observer* would be printed by Beaverbrook Newspapers, in which he had acquired a 35 per cent non-voting shareholding from Murdoch. Afterwards, when he lost out to Trafalgar House in the auction for the Beaverbrook properties, Goldsmith unloaded those shares. More to his subsequent humiliation, *Now!*, his weekly news-magazine, was to prove an expensive failure. Although he owed his knighthood to Wilson, Goldsmith was a staunch Tory who made it clear that, in any case, he would not be content as 'a passive investor'. His acquisition of the *Observer*, either on his own or in league with whatever partners, was a potential danger.[2]

Astor's hope was to ward it off with a subsidy or low-interest loan from the government or even the EEC. Instead, the *Observer* unexpectedly received an infusion of American capital, as in his grandfather's day. The source was Atlantic Richfield, a giant oil conglomerate with executive headquarters in Los Angeles. Fleet Street seemed to be floating on oil. Cowdray's Westminster group, which now controlled the *Financial Times*, had been built on oil profits, and the Thomson, Beaverbrook, and Associated chains were all lubricated by investments in the North Sea oilfields. (Murdoch's extensive holdings included 'minerals'.) The new owners of the *Observer*, who made the gesture of leaving ten shares in the possession of the paper's trustees, effected a minimum of changes. Robert O. Anderson, the chairman of Atlantic Richfield (which traded on the New York Stock Exchange as Arco), became chairman of the *Observer* as well. Donald Trelford, who succeeded Astor as editor in 1976 after a decade on the staff, retained his chair. In 1978, Conor Cruise O'Brien, an intellectual troubleshooter, was set above him as editor-in-chief. Now reduced

---

[1] Astor, 'A Letter to the Reader,' *Observer*, 24 August 1975; Stephen Fay and Roy Perrott, 'The Unravelling of a Fleet Street Crisis,' *Sunday Times*, 24 August 1975. For Fleet Street's worsening economic difficulties, see articles by Sheila Black in *The Times*, 21 February 1976, and Peter Wilsher in the *Sunday Times*, 21 March 1976.

[2] *The Times*, 14 November 1977, 26 and 30 June, 9 and 10 July 1981, as well as letters as noted in text; Lord Shawcross, 'Press Freedom for Whom?' *Spectator*, 18 July 1981.

to being one of three non-executive directors, Astor continued to take a keen interest in the affairs of the paper; 'after all', as Lord Goodman, his friend and counsellor, reasoned in a letter to *The Times* (9 July 1981), 'he had spent virtually the whole of his professional life working to maintain the independence and integrity of the *Observer*', which Arco had chivalrously volunteered to defend.

At least for a time, it appeared that, once again, the New World had been called into existence to redress the balance of the old. The arrangement lasted for nearly four years, and reportedly lost Arco £8 million beyond the token purchase price. In March 1981, Anderson suddenly disclosed his intention to sell out to Lonrho International, a company that Heath had ringingly denounced for having unveiled the 'unacceptable face of capitalism' and that the *Observer* had vigorously criticized for its conduct of African mining operations. In a letter to *The Times* (12 March), Astor, O'Brien, and Sir Hugh Greene asked for the terms of this 'secret deal ... to be publicly examined', thus allowing 'time for other possible purchasers to come forward'.

Whom did they have in mind? There was some talk that Michael Curtis might entice the Aga Khan to underwrite a new syndicate. Others spoke idealistically of some form of collective enterprise, possibly in collaboraton with certain high-minded commercial publishers. Murdoch and Goldsmith had receded as possibilities. Besides, both were as fully controversial as Roland ('Tiny') Rowland, the chairman of Lonrho.

After a thirteen-week inquiry, the Monopolies Commission reported in late June that, while Lonrho's control of the *Observer* 'might operate against the public interest', remedial terms could be imposed. Astor, brushing aside these precautions as 'little more than a farce', warned in another letter to *The Times* (4 July) that, if the government accepted the recommendations of the seven-to-one majority, the *Observer* would be either 'dead or unrecognisable within three years'. Edward du Cann, the Conservative MP for Taunton and a Lonrho director, accused Astor of being 'a bad loser .... His wild allegation that Lonrho's management of the *Observer* will be illiberal, or incompetent, or both, is as demonstrably silly as it is offensive' (*The Times*, 6 July). In replying to du Cann's 'travesty of interpretation', Goodman (9 July) conveyed 'sympathy to the courageous editor and talented journalistic staff upon whom the prevailing uncertainty must weigh heavily'.

That uncertainty was removed on the 9th, when the government consented to the proposed take-over, subject to 'an agreement on editorial safeguards acceptable to all sides'. Trelford, writing in anticipation of the verdict though not in any doubt of what it would be, did not blame John Biffen, the Secretary of State for Trade, whom *The Times* portrayed as 'sucking very hard at the lemon which was nearly a raspberry presented to him by the Monopolies Commission' (6 July). Nor did Trelford castigate the chairman and directors of Lonrho, 'who can hardly be blamed for wanting to own the *Observer* and accepting it when offered'. The culprit in his eyes was Anderson, who decided 'to dispose of the *Observer* without proper concern for its future or any reference to the people who entrusted it to him'. And the greatest blame of all lay 'with the Commission itself, which has produced a shoddy report'. Shirking any 'serious analysis of the central issues involved', the commissioners had arrived at a predetermined and 'specious solution'. *The Times*, like every other newspaper in Fleet Street, took a dim view of the outcome and could not help thinking that its own recent 'sale was conducted with more honour' (9 July).[1]

For, the previous winter, Times Newspapers had been sold to Murdoch. The company's difficulties, 'often the subject of ill-informed comment', were hitherto being tackled with modest success and with the hope that the introduction of new technology would 'make the company efficient and profitable for the future .... We will not succeed in the present challenge,' the executive committee of the board had recognized on 28 May 1976, 'if there is a negative approach from any minority or if there are wildcat disputes. That will undermine the future of everyone in the company.' Nevertheless, those disputes continued, occasioning periodic lost print runs and stoppages, and reaching a climax on 30 November 1978, when publication was suspended for more than eleven months. The following November, when the presses rolled again, the two papers and the three supplements had to scramble to win back readers, advertisers, contributors, and their own self-confidence. The support of the Thomson Organisation, now headed by Kenneth (the 2nd Baron) Thomson, was uncertain. On 22 October 1980, it was announced that Times Newspapers was for sale and would close permanently in March if no purchaser had been found. 'I do not quarrel with that decision,' William Rees-Mogg, the editor of *The Times*, wrote in his paper on the 23rd. 'Even if I did not owe a great deal to the Thomson family, ... it would be foolish to ask them for a further investment when £70m has been lost, and lost so wrongly and wastefully.'

Murdoch rushed in where angels might well have feared to tread. Despite his extensive holdings in Fleet Street (or, as some unkindly said, along its gutters), his bid was not submitted to the Monopolies Commission owing to Biffen's controversial decision that satisfactory guarantees had been tendered. On 11 February 1981, however, Murdoch appeared before the Commons' Select Committee on Education, Science, and the Arts to prove his fitness to take custody of the three weekly supplements. While the negotiations were pending, he responded courteously (unlike Thomson in 1966) and indeed disarmingly to all such inquiries. Asked whether, if he acquired *The Times* and the *Sunday Times*, he would alter their character, he protested: 'Oh no, no, [he] would not dream of changing them at all.' Among a 'series of specific

[1] Because the *Observer* lost most of its print run owing to an industrial dispute, *The Times* reprinted Trelford's leader of 5 July the following day. O'Brien now became a featured columnist, Trelford stayed on as editor, and Anthony Howard joined him as deputy editor. In the light of these developments, Trelford's 'The new deal that newspapers need' (*Observer*, 10 July 1977) makes especially poignant reading.

formal undertakings', he pledged to keep them as 'editorially independent newspapers of high quality, ... free from party political bias and from attachment to any sectional interests'.[1]

His critics, instancing numerous promises that Murdoch had made only to break, refused to believe that the leopard had changed his spots. Their 'rare excitement' struck Sir Larry Lamb, then editor of the *Sun*, as 'amusing. For 11 years I have enjoyed precisely the freedoms which your colleagues so eagerly sought and so easily won,' Lamb addressed the editor of *The Times* on 29 January. 'For the benefit of those MPs who think otherwise', Lamb explained 'that the *Sun*'s whole-hearted support for the Tories in the 1979 general election was not dictated by Mr Murdoch', but was instead 'decided by a 'consortium' of senior journalists who did not like what was happening to the Labour Party'. To credit that interpretation required a willing suspension of disbelief, which many found more palatable than the unwilling suspension of *The Times*.

Before the deadline that Thomson had set, Murdoch obtained his own guarantees from the trade unions and took control. Rees-Mogg, who had replaced Haley in 1967, ended his fourteen-year editorship in March 1981. 'The two ideas on which I have edited this newspaper have been stability and openness,' he wrote in a valedictory article on the 7th. '*The Times* is clearly not the newspaper of a party, but it is not even the newspaper of a single opinion.' Harold Evans, who had been editing the *Sunday Times* with great flair since 1967, succeeded Rees-Mogg. He described himself and Murdoch as 'two relatively impulsive people restraining each other'. A year later, he could not restrain Murdoch from demanding his resignation. There were allegations that Murdoch's move, which defied the spirit if not quite the letter of his agreement, was prompted not by the typographical and editorial innovations that Evans had introduced, but by fundamental political differences. Evans was supposedly too critical of Margaret Thatcher's brand of Conservatism and too supportive of the incipient Social Democratic Party. 'Mr Murdoch wants leaders extremely right-wing on such issues as race in this country, domestic politics, the domestic economy,' asserted Anthony Holden, who resigned as features editor out of sympathy with Evans. Charles Douglas-Home, the new editor, dismissed these charges as nonsense. A member of the hierarchy, whom Evans had driven to the point of resignation, he knew of 'absolutely no instruction or vestige of an instruction to the editor to publish or not to publish any political article'. Douglas-Home, although the nephew of a Conservative Prime Minister, claimed to 'hold no party card' and to have 'voted three ways in the past five elections. I can't imagine why Murdoch's chosen me,' he told an interviewer. 'I'm everything he's said to abhor – double-barrelled name, been to Eton, and I'm not an obedient man.' Thereafter, *The Times* tapered

---

[1] Bruce Page, 'Going for Broke,' *New Statesman*, 2 October 1981; *The Times*, 12 and 23 January 1981.

off in its enthusiasm for the Social Democrats, but so did most major newspapers.[1]

Evans's dismissal at the whim of his proprietor illustrated the point made by Paul Johnson, a former editor of the *New Statesman*, after 'Biffen's Baleful Benediction' for Lonrho's take-over of the *Observer*. 'The truth is, the moment you try to define the concept of ... "editorial traditions", you realise the whole thing is a nonsense, fit only for a Weekend Competition,' Johnson wrote bluntly in the *Spectator* on 18 July 1981. Undertakings of the sort that Rowland and Murdoch provided were 'largely unworkable, except on a basis of compromise which must, in practice, allow authority to drift to where the money is'. Johnson's logic was irrefutable, and grist for the mill of those whom he had left behind in the Labour Party.

The controllers of the British press, who loomed disproportionately large in socialist demonology, were ever fewer, more impersonal, and vastly more gargantuan in scale. As their respective enterprises grew more capital-intensive, they themselves appeared more intensively capitalist, fulfilling the Marxist stereotype. 'Since the end of the 1960s, we have seen the transfer of much newspaper ownership to highly diversified corporations with industrial and financial interests of all imaginable kinds,' Neal Ascherson observed in 1978, before the process had gone still further. 'Newspapers are becoming one division of a diverse portfolio, and often the least profitable division.' True enough, but hardly anything new. In 1921, strolling on the Riviera, Northcliffe had introduced Tom Clarke to the proprietor of the *Westminster Gazette*: 'This is Lord Cowdray, Tom. He finds it easier to make money out of oil than newspapers.'[2]

In retrospect, it was possible to romanticize 'the sometimes crazy plutocrat who ran newspapers and only newspapers'. In fact, such a creature probably never existed. Beaverbrook, for whom newspapers were initially a political sideline and always part of a larger portfolio, had died in 1964. His properties were inherited by his son, who modestly disclaimed the peerage that went with them. Two years later, asked his opinion of Fleet Street's prospects, Sir Max Aitken gurgled: 'Why, I think the present is fine and the future is glorious.' Thereafter, his legacy trickled through his fingers. Trafalgar House, a property development and transport conglomerate under the chairmanship of Victor (later Baron) Matthews, bought Beaverbrook Newspapers in 1977 and, three years later, merged the *Evening Standard* with Associated's *Evening News*.

---

[1] *Daily Mail*, 13 March 1982; *Observer*, 14 March 1982; *Sunday Times*, 14 March 1982. For the waxing and waning of press support for the SDP, see David Wood in *The Times*, 15 February 1982, and Alan Watkins in the *Observer*, 21 February 1982. Neither more successful nor less obstinate in their craving for old-style journalistic resources, the SDP and its Liberal allies launched an *Alliance* magazine (edited by Christopher Layton) and a fortnightly *Democrat*, both superseded in May 1983 by a monthly *New Democrat*.

[2] Ascherson, 'Newspapers in Internal Democracy,' in Curran, ed., *The British Press*, p. 131; Clarke, *Northcliffe Diary* (26 March 1921), p. 191.

After Thomson's eventual retreat and before Lonrho renounced its intention to enter the evening market, the big three – Trafalgar House, Reed International, and Murdoch's News International – monopolized about 75 per cent of national daily sales and 90 per cent of national Sunday sales in the country.[1]

Like the 3rd Viscount Rothermere (Vere, whose father had abdicated the chairmanship of Associated in his favour back in January 1971), Matthews is a Tory by instinct, but a businessman first and foremost. Since the autumn of 1982, he has headed Fleet Holdings, which was hived off from Trafalgar House, where its major shareholders came from. 'The modern model', as he embodies it, has 'no political as distinct from honorific ambitions of his own and no wish to tell his papers what political tune to play, apart from keeping clear of "subversive" tendencies. None has a *party* affiliation,' Donald Tyerman mused in some 'vilely desultory thoughts' to the author, 'though, of course, most have a clear leaning.'[2] It would be naïve to expect otherwise, yet even more naïve to suppose that such leanings would be allowed to jeopardize profits. Nor, as the election campaign of 1983 made still more clear, were they temperamentally disposed to be found on the losing side.

'Who is to own the British press?' Sir Denis Hamilton asked in his 1976 Haldane Memorial Lecture, as if to imply that there existed an open choice in the matter. Like Cecil King, in his Granada Northern Lectures nine years earlier, he did not have a constructive answer. In different ways, both of them recognized that 'the left did not have a clear enough voice in the national press'. That was to assume that the left had a clear voice to project, which has not necessarily proved the case. Nor was there any assurance that such a voice would resonate with greater force and conviction from the columns of an avowedly Labour organ. Employing nineteenth-century logic, which had not worked to Labour's advantage in the twentieth century, Hamilton proposed that the TUC should 'try once more to run a newspaper; it might be a new one or an ailing daily or Sunday paper revived'. In either case, 'it would be complying with the classic commercial maxim: find a gap in the market and fill it'.[3]

For the leaders of the amorphous 'left' to compete with their 'capitalist' adversaries on their own ground was neither congruous nor feasible. Nevertheless, support was canvassed in the spring and summer of 1976 for 'a new daily newspaper committed to trade union and Labour views but independent of the party and the TUC'. These qualifications, if taken seriously, posed a contradiction in terms. 'The prime mover' was identified as William Keys, general secretary of the Society of Graphical and Allied Trades (Sogat) and also

---

[1] Ascherson, 'Newspapers,' p. 131; Aitken, 'Today and Tomorrow,' in Brodzky, ed., *Fleet Street*, p. 31; Brendon, *Press Barons*, p. 218.
[2] Tyerman to the author, 18 July 1978.
[3] *The Times*, 4 February 1976. Hamilton's lecture was published as *Who Is to Own the British Press?* (London, 1976), King's as *The Future of the Press* (London, 1967).

chairman of the TUC's printing industry committee, who pointed to 'a growing concentration towards the right in the press over the last decade' that had to be counteracted. Accordingly, he sought to enlist TUC funds for 'an independent daily of the labour movement, able to present the news without the political bias of private ownership, yet free to criticize the TUC or the Party'.[1] That formula had been tried before and, as this study has attempted to show, had worked less well each time.

Still, what Hamilton saw as 'a gap in the market' continued to rankle as a foreshortening of the spectrum. Keys was again involved in 1979, when the Campaign for Press Freedom was founded, with 'the establishment of a new newspaper of the Left' as one of its priorities. 'We do not accept that the British press of today represents the last word in press freedom,' declared a spokesman for the group. 'Nor do we accept that railing about the press is sufficient. We want to see action.' Tony Benn (formerly Anthony Wedgwood Benn) was among the parliamentary sponsors. Jacob ('Jake') Ecclestone, the president of the NUJ, was chairman, and James Curran was an academic consultant. They worked out that 'the cost of launching and running' a Labour daily 'could be answered by a weekly levy of TUC-affiliated unions to produce a fund' of £18 million over the next three years. Hamilton's admission that the views of the left were under-represented was approvingly quoted, along with Stanley Baldwin's less germane condemnation of newspaper harlotry as 'power without responsibility'.[2]

That autumn, the annual Labour Party conference considered concrete proposals after hearing 'vehement attacks on a press "highly biased" against the Labour movement and against private ownership of an industry which had failed to provide "genuine press freedom, diversity, or access" '. In referring the question to the NEC, Lady (formerly Lena) Jeger, the chairman-elect of the party, expressed the hope of seeing a new paper before the next general election: 'I can assure you that the spirit is willing but the flesh is harder to find.' As time passed and the flesh failed to materialize, Benn urged direct action: 'The workers, and I do not mean just the journalists, in every newspaper should band themselves together and demand from their proprietors that one page every week be available to them to say what they want on behalf of the Labour Party.' Far from being the 'tremendous advance' that Benn imagined, that would have been a modest throwback to the arrangements that Northcliffe had generously catered in 1918. Left-wing critics of the media were never more hopelessly old-fashioned than when they were posturing as revolutionaries.

[1] *The Times*, 10 August 1976.
[2] *Guardian*, 27 August 1979. Ecclestone and Curran replied in *The Times* on 13 March 1981, ten days after Bernard Levin had had a 'bit of fun at the expense of the Campaign' and its objectives. What they were proposing, they solemnly proclaimed, was not 'a notionally balanced and uniform press, but rather a range of schemes to bring about more diverse ownership and a greater variety of views. Is that unhealthy?'

Their grievances have frequently been incontestable, but their proposed remedies have tended to reveal a curious ignorance of historical precedent.[1]

To be sure, neither indignation nor impracticality – which, more often than not, went hand in hand – was the monopoly of any particular political denomination. 'Emotional revulsion at some of Fleet Street's activities runs deep on the Left and Right,' Charles Wintour, twice editor of the *Evening Standard* (under different régimes) wrote in the *Observer* on 20 February 1983. His comments were inspired by the fierce 'anti-media sentiments' expressed two days earlier, when the House of Commons had debated (and denied a second reading to) a private member's Bill to provide a legal right of reply to any individual or group of individuals who had 'reasonable grounds for considering' that reports about them were 'factually inaccurate or distorted'. Introduced by Frank Allaun, the Labour MP for East Salford and a member of the NUJ, who conceded that 'Conservative Members too can be misrepresented in the media', this Bill drew the support of ninety MPs, including several 'Tory worthies'. The *Daily Mail* protested that such a law would be 'liberty-filching', and Wintour saw it as a dangerous precedent. After all, he reasoned, 'once a Press-bashing Parliament begins to legislate on what the Press can and cannot do, it may never know where to stop'. Yet, clearly, some means of redress was needed beyond that provided by the Press Council, which acted slowly and lacked compulsory powers. Within days of this debate, the Queen took legal action against the *Sun* for its series of 'astonishing inside secrets of the fun-loving royals'. It was the first time that a sovereign (employing a Palace official as plaintiff) sought not only an injunction, but also damages. Her uncle, Edward VIII, did not have to contend with the likes of Rupert Murdoch.[2]

The story goes on, repeating itself beyond redundancy to the point of parody. Each further instalment, in addition to confirming the inutility of the press for traditional purposes of partisan combat, had intensified the economic gloom. Lonrho, which boasted a willingness to sacrifice £2 million a year on the *Observer*, has not been pleasantly surprised to the contrary. Times Newspapers, which lost £15 million in its first year under Murdoch's stewardship, forecast a second-year loss of £5 million that had to be revised to £13 million. Associated's *Mail on Sunday*, launched with tremendous fanfare in 1982, was

---

[1] *Guardian*, 6 October 1979; *The Times*, 16 March 1981. At the end of 1982, a relatively minor incident cast serious doubt upon the ability of Labour activists to practise as they preached. A power struggle erupted at *Tribune* between John Silkin, a senior Labour politician and the controlling shareholder, and Chris Mullin, the editor and a fervent exponent of 'Bennite' views. 'I believe in editorial freedom,' averred Silkin, 'but I believe in it within certain limits', which Mullin was held to have exceeded. The episode seemed to the *Observer* (12 December) a 'perfect parable of the double standards that too often lurk at the heart of left-wing politics'.

[2] *Parliamentary Debates* (Commons), 6th ser., v, cols. 792-94 (2 June 1981); Wintour, 'A Warning Shot from the House of Commons,' *Observer*, 20 February 1983; *New York Times*, 24 February 1983; *U.K. Press Gazette*, 28 February and 7 March 1983. Out of court, the *Sun* agreed to pay £4,000 to the Newspaper Press Fund and to discontinue the series, based on materials obtained by breach of confidence.

said to be running at a loss of £20 million. The *Guardian* and, for a time, the *Express* group were operating at yawning deficits, and the pink-tinctured *Financial Times* unexpectedly ran into the red. The *Telegraph*, long presumed to be securely solvent, was said to be 'facing current annual losses of £3 million'; that was denied, but not with sufficient finality to scotch rumours that the Berry family might soon dispose of it, possibly to Maxwell.[1] All in all, economic circumstances were hardly propitious for the establishment of any new journals, left, right or centre.

None too happily, the politicians had to make do with the depleted resources available to them, ever more captious and defensive. Some, having been journalists, managed effectively enough on their own behalf. Others struck an assortment of informal relationships with editors and political correspondents. The best publicized, though not the most directly useful, was doubtless the golfing companionship between Denis Thatcher, the Prime Minister's husband, and William ('Dear Bill') Deedes, a former Tory MP and Cabinet minister who had been editor of the *Telegraph* since 1974. 'It is fashionable on the Left, even the moderate Left, to dislike the *Daily Telegraph*. It is regarded as sinfully to the Right,' Patrick O'Donovan wrote in the *Observer* on 29 June 1980 to mark the occasion of the *Telegraph*'s 125th birthday. Yet, he reminded his readers, the *Telegraph* 'can and does criticise the Conservative Party from the pinnacle of its own orthodoxy'. In that special sense, even 'the house magazine of the Right in Britain' testified to the change that had occurred in the conventions of the political press over the hundred years since Disraeli had mocked the Gladstonian *Daily Telegraph* as the Delirium Tremens.

There remains one further difference to be noted. Whereas Victorians of all political persuasions had invariably invested the Press with a capital letter, a practice that lingered through the next generation, the participants in recent debates have usually demoted it to a small 'p'. On the other hand, in a decidedly un-Victorian manner, they have taken to referring to Left, Right and Centre with deferential capitals. There can be no better illustration of the decline of the British political press, even in its own eyes.

* * *

In his intelligent survey, *The Political Impact of Mass Media* (1974), Colin Seymour-Ure asked 'the question why the relationship between newspapers and parties may be thought worth studying anyway'. As he enumerated them, the reasons may be taken to justify both the concept and methodology of this two-volume investigation. 'First, there have been very obvious historical

---

[1] Wintour, 'Nought for Fleet Street's Comfort,' *Observer*, 28 November 1982; Steven Rattner, 'Bad News at the Financial Times,' *New York Times*, 8 November 1981; *The Times*, 24 November 1982; conversation with Lord Marsh (chairman, Newspaper Publishers Association), 14 July 1982.

associations between press and party systems', the experience of each being shaped by the other. 'In the second place, the press in widely varying types of political system is given a role explicitly or implicitly that connects it to party', as dictated by public attitudes and electoral necessities. 'A third reason for expecting a connection between press and party systems is that the functions of parties are highly compatible with the capabilities of newspapers', at least traditionally. 'Where competing parties exist, one might expect to find a connection not only between individual papers and parties but also a correspondence, or parallelism, between the *range* of papers and the *range* of parties.' In certain Continental democracies, this 'parallelism' has been artificially preserved by means of subsidies, allocated on the basis of registered electoral support. In Britain, where (according to S. E. Finer's thesis) the 'range' and popular appeal of parties have jointly diminished, this 'parallelism' has been allowed to lapse. 'To explore the connection between press and party systems fully requires a much more elaborate study' than Seymour-Ure saw fit to undertake. The present work, indebted to his insights, has taken up the challenge.[1]

Admittedly, that challenge has been accepted only in part. For, to obtain a complete sense of the transformation that has occurred within the British structure, it would be helpful to compare post-war developments not only with their domestic antecedents, but also with foreign practices. The *Dangerous Estate*, as Francis Williams (1967) styled the British press, differs strikingly from *The Fourth Branch of Government*, as Douglass Cater (1959) dignified the press in the United States. The Prime Minister's appearances during Question Time in the House of Commons are not, for better or worse, the equivalent of presidential news conferences. The Watergate investigations, regretfully cited as an impossibility under the British system, dramatically illustrated these transatlantic differences, which have been variously ascribed to a 'traditional lack of openness in British politics', tighter legal restrictions, and contrasting professional functions.[2]

In the United States, where many newspapers are now owned by the same people as those in other English-speaking societies, the press never approached the same degree of ironclad partisan attatchment. In that respect, British newspapers have become more Americanized. Owing to the compartmentalized nature of American party politics, it was always common for newspapers to endorse candidates of different persuasions at the local, state, and national levels. In Britain, where party ideologies were stronger and party organizations more centralized, such discrepancies were rare. Moreover,

---

[1] Seymour-Ure, *The Political Impact of Mass Media*, pp. 157-59; *also see* A. H. Halsey, *Change in British Society* (Oxford, 1978), p. 79.

[2] Ian Waller, 'The "Lobby" and Beyond,' *Encounter*, xxiv (June 1965), 73-80; Jeremy Tunstall, *Westminster Lobby Correspondents* (London, 1970), pp. 94-95; Cater, *The Fourth Branch of Government* (Boston, 1959), ch. 8. Cater was instrumental in arranging the purchase of the *Observer* by Atlantic Richfield.

unlike their British counterparts, American newspapers were – and remain – predominantly regional. For all the glory that deservedly accrued to it over Watergate, the *Washington Post* did not extend its influence – much less its circulation – in New York or Boston, Chicago or San Francisco, and did not presume to address political issues in those far-flung cities. If, as has been angrily alleged, the British possess 'local newspapers that are distributed nationally',[1] the Americans may be said to have a proportionately smaller number of local newspapers that are distributed locally.

'There is a good deal of over-simplification on the question of the extent to which popular newspapers do in fact influence the opinions of their readers,' Tom Driberg told the Royal Commissioners in 1948. He went on to suggest 'that people who deliberately buy the more 'serious', or ostensibly serious, newspapers ... are more likely to be influenced by editorial opinion than people who prefer lighter reading'. That, in time, stood revealed as yet another over-simplification. The number of 'serious' (or 'ostensibly serious') papers declined, and those that survived were increasingly erratic and sporadic in their attempts to exert influence. In evidence presented to the next Royal Commission in 1962 by 'certain members of the Young Fabian Group', it was postulated that 'the process of newspaper closures' would continue, but without any shrinkage of total consumption. It was seen as unlikely 'that the so-called "serious" newspapers will be able to cut any noticeable chunks' out of this market, however. Even in the cataclysmic event that 'the popular daily press [was] cut down to two papers', with 'the Sunday press not much bigger', the Young Fabians – lacking the optimism of their elders – did not believe 'that most people' would 'have the temperament to read newspapers like the *Observer*'. On that score, there was 'a good prima facie case for saying that it does not matter' which or how many newspapers continued to exist. The *News Chronicle* was to be mourned not for what it had been, latterly a product virtually indistinguishable from its competitors, but for 'what it might have become' if only 'the Newspaper business' were not merely 'a business'.[2]

That fraction of the public with the temperament to read papers like the *Observer* would also have had an exceptional degree of social and political awareness, hardly conducive to the unquestioning acceptance of journalistic pronouncements. The *Observer* itself quickly recognized this situation and was the first major newspaper to tailor its political comment accordingly. Less emphatically and perhaps less consciously, other newspapers followed suit. J. P. W. Mallalieu, 'a working journalist' and a Labour MP, had 'a habit of reading through all the principal papers in the morning' and would have been pleased 'to look through twice as many'. In his opinion, tendered to the first Royal Commission, only the *Daily Worker* practised political journalism on

---

[1] R. Boston, 'Growing Pains,' in Boston, ed., *The Press We Deserve* (London, 1970), p. 8.
[2] Evidence, Royal Commission on the Press, 1947-49, Cd. 7500, p. 5; Documentary Evidence, Royal Commission on the Press, 1961-62, Cd. 1812, V, 221-25.

the old model. 'I was very, very sad when the *Morning Post* went,' he testified. 'That paper had a Conservative slant that the *Daily Telegraph* never touches. I miss that, and the old *Daily Herald* too, which was a real Labour paper.' As early as the immediate post-war period, then, Mallalieu understood the change that many of his contemporaries mistook for an aberration. 'Except for the *Morning Post*, which had slavishly adhered to Victorian principles of political servitude, 'there has never been a Conservative paper', and the *Herald* was already a shadow of its former political self. Strictly according to nineteenth-century criteria, which most twentieth-century critics would have been loath to accept, the Conservatives were 'the Party which suffers most from lack of expression' in the press.[1]

Thereafter, at an accelerating pace, newspapers substituted what may be called political dispositions for what had been formal party allegiances. 'Although it is possible to identify the political complexion of the British press,' Stuart Hood wrote in 1972, 'there is today only one political newspaper – in the sense of a paper with party affiliations – at a national level', and that was the *Morning Star*, as the *Daily Worker* had been reincarnated in 1966. It, and it alone, was maintained 'to express the political line' of a particular party group, and it purveyed its orthodoxies to an estimated circulation of 65,000. Given that the Communist Party has not elected an MP since 1945, its fidelity to tradition has not been demonstrably rewarded.[2]

In other cases, political complexions were apt to flush and pale. 'Partisanship, of course, has not disappeared from the press,' remarked Jeremy Tunstall.[3] But that word, as he used it, was a far cry from its bygone definition. Over the decades, partisanship had come to mean something different to different people and even to the same people. To Beaverbrook, it meant something else in 1950–51 from what it had meant in the 1930s, let alone in Edwardian times, when he first accepted a silent interest in the *Daily Express*. To King, it meant something quite different in 1968 from what it had meant in 1945. To Dawson, its meaning in 1938 had changed from that in 1918. In Northcliffe's vocabulary, its usage in 1914 fundamentally contradicted its usage in 1895, when he was a Conservative candidate. Furthermore, as Tunstall has pointed out, partisanship became enmeshed with commercial considerations, making it difficult to tell which factor was the operative one. Voting preferences and newspaper choices were mutually correlated to social class, with the result that 'a big middle-class paper like the *Daily Telegraph*, for instance, may serve commercial as well as political aims by being itself Conservative'. Yet its Conservatism, like that of its middle-class readers, was more an outlook than a binding commitment, and technically undeserving of a capital 'C'.

Certainly, the practitioners of political journalism could no longer advance

---

[1] Evidence, Royal Commission on the Press, 1947-49, Cd. 7322, qq. 850-53.
[2] Hood, *The Mass Media*, p. 86; Butler and Stokes, *Political Change*, p. 229.
[3] Tunstall, *Westminster Lobby Correspondents*, p. 10.

the claims to public influence that John Thaddeus Delane had articulated privately and W. T. Stead publicly. 'The limitations of so-called power are painfully obvious to the publishers of all newspapers,' declared Cecil King in 1957, before they became still more 'painfully obvious' to him. Newspapers 'may speed up a movement of opinion of which they approve. They may slow down a movement of which they disapprove. What they cannot do, is to reverse public opinion.' That was not false modesty, never one of King's besetting sins. 'Every politician knows,' admitted Denis Healey, a Labour MP since 1952, 'and such studies as have been carried out confirm this, that . . . the extent to which people's effective opinions in the political sense, namely their voting habits, are determined by what they read is far less than most intellectuals believe.' Or, as one of those academic studies ascertained: 'A great deal of common information flows out to the mass of the British electorate through media which are heavily overlapping and which are describing political issues and events that they have seldom done anything to shape.'[1]

What about those intellectuals, particularly prominent on the Labour side, whom Healey ridiculed for their credulity? In the spring of 1961, John Freeman, the newly appointed editor of the *New Statesman*, braved sharp criticisms at Crossman's dinner-table. He replied, to his host's 'astonishment, . . . that 40 per cent of our readership are Tories and we can't disregard their views altogether' in the weekly contents. In view of this statistic, Freeman thought that the journal 'must show a certain detachment and balance'. Crossman was persuaded otherwise after hearing 'an amusing story' about 'a manufacturer in Leicester, a Tory, who has read the *Statesman* for years' not despite its socialist views, but because of them. 'What's wrong with it?' this gentleman had recently demanded of a friend. 'For three months now I've found nothing to be angry at and I only bought it to get angry.' To Crossman, that furnished 'a reminder that Tories may want some Socialist material in the paper', even if the pro-Labour management was reluctant to comply. Nine years later, when he finally had his own turn to edit the *New Statesman*, he aimed to restore it as 'a platform for constructive criticism' and proceeded to lose the circulation achieved by Freeman and already slipping during Paul Johnson's intervening editorship.[2]

For a brief moment in the mid-1960s, it appeared that the self-styled political weeklies, particularly the *New Statesman* and the *Spectator*, were the last bastions of party-oriented journalism. Their sales rose spectacularly, only to tumble at the close of the decade, when the vogue had passed and subscription rates began to spiral. From 1954, the *Spectator* had been owned by Ian Gilmour, who entered Parliament in 1962. Under Brian Inglis, his successor as

---

[1] King, *Future of the Press*, p. 89; Healey, BBC Third Programme, 25 May 1962, quoted in Windlesham, *Communication*, p. 25; Butler and Stokes, *Political Change*, p. 244.
[2] Entry of 17 May 1961, Crossman, *Backbench Diaries*, pp. 947-48; entry of 11 May 1970, Crossman, *Diaries*, III, 916.

editor, the paper achieved a weekly sale of 50,000. In 1963, Gilmour secured the editorial services of Iain Macleod, the Conservative MP for Enfield West and a fugitive from the 'magic circle' of Tory politics. Unlike Crossman, who came to his chair at the end of a ministerial career, Macleod was to return to the front bench. He resigned as editor in 1965 and, two years later, Gilmour disposed of the property. Thereafter, the *Spectator* became more and more politically self-effacing until 13 June 1981, when Alexander Chancellor, now editor, temporarily abolished the leading article that had been a standard feature since St Loe Strachey's time. 'For a start,' he explained, 'there is no such thing – in this paper at least – as a collective opinion; there is a variety of opinions of which the leading article has, in effect, been only one, dignified by anonymity and served up in larger type.' That was more or less what Rees-Mogg had said about *The Times* in his farewell message, three months earlier.[1]

Both the *New Statesman* and the *Spectator*, as well as the more prosperous *Economist*, with its increasingly mid-Atlantic character, henceforth delivered their political support conditionally, if at all. Within any single issue of either journal, regular columnists routinely contradict each other and outside contributors add to the diversity of perspective. Some of the most astringent criticism of successive Labour Party leaders has appeared in the *New Statesman*, where, most famously, Wilson was described on 26 May 1972 as 'The Lost Leader', whose 'very presence ... pollutes the atmosphere of politics'. The *Spectator* (9 March 1974) protested that it had been unfairly 'accused of a vindictive and personal dislike of Mr Heath', to whom it referred in the same breath as 'a squalid nuisance' who 'must now depart the Tory leadership as quickly as possible, and before he can do more damage'. Since 1979, the paper has not hesitated to feature attacks on Mrs Thatcher's policies, especially during the Falklands war. That manufacturer in Leicester, whose confusion was reported to Crossman, would not have known what to make of it at all.

Nor, for that matter, have most politicians known how to react. Being public persons with reputations first to be made and then to be defended, they remain naturally sensitive to what newspapers say about them. But force of circumstance has prevailed over force of habit, with the result that they no longer discriminate to any meaningful extent between the sources of censure or praise. In the nineteenth century, Gladstone could expect rough treatment from the Tory papers and could depend on the Liberal ones to counterbalance it; for Disraeli and Salisbury, the reverse held true. Later on, Asquith would have been perplexed and embarrassed by the embrace of the *Daily Mail*, just as Balfour was actually compromised by tender words from the *Daily News* and the *Westminster Gazette*. By the middle of the twentieth century, as the Suez crisis in 1956 showed most signally, editorial positions diverged from parlia-

---

[1] Nigel Fisher, *Iain Macleod* (London, 1973), ch. 14; Alan Watkins, *Brief Lives*, pp. 50-53; *also see* Philip Howard, 'How the politics of defeat has changed the tone of Britain's political weeklies,' *The Times*, 20 July 1976.

mentary party lines. Consequently, politicians have tended to collect whatever press support they can get and seldom to find it enough. On the understanding that quantity counts for more than quality, the political press is now considered to perform best when it performs chorally. To all intents and purposes, therefore, any persistent partisan preferences on the part of particular newspapers are irrelevant.

As a correspondent at the 1955 Conservative Party conference at Bournemouth, Crossman found it 'extraordinary how much room the *Mirror* takes up in the minds of politicians and how seriously it is regarded', to the point of its being the single paper to which R. A. Butler referred in a major speech. The time had come when the Tories were obliged to pay as much attention – if not more – to the *Mirror* as to the *Telegraph* or *The Times*. Conversely, Labour strategists could not afford to dismiss the *Telegraph*, the *Express*, or the *Financial Times*. For, in a general and cumulative way, newspapers affected the prevailing political climate. As Lord (formerly Sir Edward) Boyle recalled from his experience in the Macmillan and Douglas-Home administrations: 'The Cabinet increasingly, as the years go by, tends to be most concerned with the agenda that the press and media are setting out as the crucial issues before the nation at any one time.'[1]

In collaboration with other mass media with which its finances were often interlocked, the press achieved this quasi-meteorological power at the expense of other types of influence that it had once exerted more directly. The more successfully newspapers helped to shape or express a wider public consciousness, the more they were distracted from traditional political pursuits. Whether this shift of emphasis led to a diffusion of responsibilities or vice versa, the resultant differences were pronounced. A brief recapitulation may help to illustrate the contrast.

During previous generations, newspapers had functioned as important auxiliaries of parties or, alternatively, as the mouthpieces of personalities and factions within parties. Their preoccupations had mirrored and perhaps magnified affairs at Westminster. Leaving no doubt of their respective partisan attachments, which were underwritten and otherwise encouraged by party loyalists, newspapers had assisted – though perhaps less effectively than they convinced themselves they did – in the formulation of party doctrines. More manifestly, they had disseminated those doctrines. Year after year, they stirred the controversies that were the stuff of party politics. When elections approached, they rallied the faithful, appealed to the waverers, goaded the enemy, and, in short, raised the pitch of battle whenever there had existed a pitch to be raised.

Through the second half of the nineteenth century and well into the twentieth, newspapers had cooperated intimately and proudly with party

---

[1] Entry of 7 October 1955, Crossman, *Backbench Diaries*, p. 447; Boyle, quoted in Seymour-Ure, *Political Impact*, p. 36.

managers, who regarded their services as indispensable as much for reasons of prestige as for basic purposes of electioneering. For the sake of the cause, as they suitably defined it, they occasionally behaved underhandedly and thus abused the freedom they had won in the 1850s, when the repeal of the 'taxes on knowledge' had cleared the way for the rise of the modern political press. Yet newspapers perpetually gloried in that freedom, even when they subordinated it to party requirements. That, so to speak, was how they paid their way.

No less than the parliamentary figures whom they championed, the avowedly political journals of the past were frequently intoxicated by rhetoric, which was their stock in trade. They cannot, therefore, be trusted to appraise their own achievement which, however significant, was certainly more ephemeral and probably more peripheral than they cared to contemplate. Even in its heyday, the political press was vastly more important for what it reflected than for what it singlehandedly accomplished. How many votes it actually swayed either in parliamentary divisions or at the polls mattered less than how ardently it strove to sway them. The primary function of political journalism was to inspire confidence in a system of which it was, by design and consent, an integral part. Gradually, as that system lost confidence in itself and in the eyes of an expanding political community, the political press lost its bearings, its justification, and whatever efficacy it may have had.

At its worst, the political press had mischievously fanned passions and fed prejudices. At its best, it had focused ideas and inculcated democratic values. Together, the best and the worst conspired against it. By portraying their adversaries as contemptible and untrustworthy – as did *The Times* in 1886-87, the *Daily Mail* in 1915-16, or the *Daily Mirror* in 1951, to cite only three cases among many – newspapers brought their own political credentials into disrepute. More commendably, by inviting readers to exercise their judgment, they made their own tutelage expendable. Long before market surveys proved the point, people were reading newspapers for different reasons and coming away from them with antithetical conclusions. The 1st Baron (formerly Arthur) Ponsonby, a recruit from Liberalism to Labour, insisted to Collin Brooks that 'the influence of the press . . . works chiefly in reverse. I became a Socialist,' he revealed, 'not by reading the *Daily Herald* but by reading the *Morning Post*.'[1] By that criterion, the collapse of the *Morning Post* in 1937 was a greater blow to the Labour Party than the disappearance of the *Daily Herald* in 1964. Newspaper propaganda was always a double-edged weapon until those edges grew too blunt to cut either way.

* * *

---

[1] Brooks's diary, 15 July 1941. For a more sober account of Ponsonby's conversation, see Marvin Swartz, *The Union of Democratic Control in British Politics During the First World War* (Oxford, 1971).

On 25 August 1959, Hugh Cudlipp stopped to see Crossman 'on his way to lunch with Tony Crosland' and proclaimed himself 'available to steer the propaganda war' in the coming general election. Anthony Crosland, soon to re-enter Parliament as Labour MP for Grimsby, was already a distinguished party theoretician and might well have taught Cudlipp a thing or two. Three years later, in the wake of the second Royal Commission on the Press, Crosland wrote an article in *Encounter* on the ownership and conduct of the mass media.[1] He faulted the 'almost obsessive emotions both amongst apologists and critics', who were 'rigidly entrenched ... on both Right and Left' and who debated 'on the basis of breath-taking generalities for most of which no evidence of any kind exists'. Thereupon, Crosland presented his 'own position briefly and forthrightly' and, not least, with admirable cogency. 'Our aim should be the maximum degree of cultural pluralism and availability of different aesthetic goods,' he stated. In that regard, he found the situation in Britain 'extremely disquieting', for 'the range and variety of independent newspapers are below the requirements of a healthy democracy'.

Nevertheless, Crosland declined to 'share some popular views about the political power of the Press' and accepted that 'there is a limit to the number of national newspapers which any country can economically support'. Urging 'fresh legislation to enable the Government to examine and if necessary forbid any take-over, merger, or amalgamation which seriously restricts the degree of competition', he was prepared to 'go further, and give the Government power to unscramble *existing* concentrations' with the forlorn hope of saving the *Daily Herald* from the fatal clasp of the *Mirror* group. To protect the citizen – including royal personages? – against the intrusions of the 'more depraved and poisonous of the capitalist newspapers' (and from the 'often equally obnoxious' anti-capitalist ones), he proposed to strengthen the 'anaemic Press Council' by making it wholly 'independent of the industry', as the profession had long since become. The alleged 'influence of advertisers' caused him little worry: 'on major editorial policy, ... they could not care less' so long as 'the paper's circulation is satisfactory'.

Admittedly, the changes he broadly outlined would 'not provide an ideal solution. But there is no ideal solution to the problem of the media, for the sheer technical *scale* of operation limits the practical amount of diversity and competition'. Above all else, it was imperative to 'remember that the problem arises largely because of our poor educational provision. If we had more education, we should not only be more critical and "propaganda-safe" ..., but we should *insist* on higher standards.'

Here, Crosland was echoing Bright and Cobden, with their ennobling vision of a free press in an enlightened society. Yet, unlike them on the one

[1] Entry of 26 August 1959, Crossman, *Backbench Diaries*, p. 771; Crosland, 'The Mass Media,' *Encounter*, xix (November 1962), 3-14.

hand and more recent media moralists on the other, he was too realistic to demand perfection. 'The media have their dangers,' concluded Crosland,

> though they are far less sinister than most of the hypnotised critics think. But all too often we make them a scapegoat for deeper failings – for our national vices of philistinism and puritanism; for a deep-seated anti-Americanism; for our deplorable educational system; and, in the case of intellectuals, for personal failings of our own.

Two decades and countless crises later, his thoughtful arguments retain their validity. Precisely because they failed to stimulate official action, as he had hoped, they serve all the more pointedly as an epitaph.

MANUSCRIPT SOURCES

In addition to serial publications (usually identified in the text) and other published sources (cited in footnotes), this book rests on manuscript collections, as enumerated below. Only those collections are included from which direct quotations are made.

Christopher (1st Viscount) Addison Papers, Bodleian Library, Oxford.
Clifford Allen (Baron Allen of Hurtwood) Papers, The Library, University of South Carolina at Columbia.
Leo Amery Papers, courtesy of Mr Julian Amery, MP.
H. H. Asquith (1st Earl of Oxford and Asquith) Papers, Bodleian Library, Oxford.
Astor Papers, The University Library, Reading.
Stanley Baldwin (1st Earl Baldwin of Bewdley) Papers, Cambridge University Library.
A. J. Balfour (1st Earl of Balfour) Papers, British Library.
R. M. Barrington-Ward's diary, courtesy of Mr Mark Barrington-Ward.
Bathurst Papers, courtesy of the Earl Bathurst.
Bayford (Sir Robert Sanders, 1st Baron Bayford) Papers, Conservative Research Department.
Beaverbrook (Max Aitken, Baron Beaverbrook) Papers, House of Lords Record Office.
Arnold Bennett's journals, Berg Collection, New York Public Library.
E. C. Bentley's draft memoir, Bodleian Library, Oxford.
Robert Blatchford Papers, Central Library, Manchester.
R. D. Blumenfeld Papers, House of Lords Record Office.
Andrew Bonar Law Papers, House of Lords Record Office.
Collin Brooks's diary, courtesy of Miss Vivian Brooks.
Sir John Brunner Papers, Sydney Jones Library, University of Liverpool.
James (Viscount) Bryce Papers, Bodleian Library, Oxford.
John Burns Papers, British Library.
Cabinet Papers, Public Record Office.
George Cadbury Papers, The Library, University of Birmingham.
Sir Henry Campbell-Bannerman Papers, British Library.
Andrew Carnegie Papers, The Library of Congress, Washington, D.C.
Chamberlain Papers (Joseph, Austen, and Neville Chamberlain), The Library, University of Birmingham.
Chilston (Aretas Akers-Douglas, 1st Viscount Chilston) Papers, Kent Archives Office.
Conservative Party Archives, Conservative Research Department (since transferred to the Conservative Central Office, London, and the Bodleian Library, Oxford).
Sir Edward Cook Papers, courtesy of Mr Robin Duff and Professor J. E. Mennell.
Courtney (Leonard Courtney, Baron Courtney of Penwith) Papers, British Library of Political and Economic Science, London.
Cowdray (Sir Weetman Pearson and family) Papers, Science Museum Library, London.
W. M. Crook Papers, Bodleian Library, Oxford.
Curzon (1st Marquess Curzon) Papers, India Office Library.
Hugh (Baron) Dalton Papers, British Library of Political and Economic Science, London.
J.C.C. (1st Viscount) Davidson Papers, Bodleian Library, Oxford.
Geoffrey (Robinson) Dawson Papers, Bodleian Library, Oxford.

Derby (17th Earl of Derby) Papers, Liverpool Record Office.
Devonshire (8th Duke of Devonshire) Papers, Chatsworth.
Sir Charles Dilke Papers, British Library.
Sir Robert Donald Papers, House of Lords Record Office.
Tom Driberg (Baron Bradwell) Papers, Christ Church, Oxford.
W. M. Eager Papers, Reform Club, London.
Elibank (Alexander Murray, 1st Baron Murray of Elibank) Papers, National Library of Scotland, Edinburgh.
R. C. K. Ensor Papers, Corpus Christi College, Oxford.
T. H. S. Escott Papers, British Library.
Esher (Reginald Brett, 2nd Viscount Esher) Papers, Churchill College, Cambridge.
H. A. L. Fisher Papers, Bodleian Library, Oxford.
A. G. Gardiner Papers, British Library of Political and Economic Science, London.
J. L. Garvin Papers, University of Texas at Austin.
Viscount Gladstone (Herbert Gladstone) Papers, British Library.
Sir Edmund Gosse Papers, Brotherton Collection, The University Library, Leeds.
F. C. Gould, draft memoir, House of Lords Record Office.
Sir Edward Grigg (1st Baron Altrincham) Papers, courtesy of Mr John Grigg.
Guardian Archives, John Rylands University Library, Manchester.
H. A. Gwynne Papers, Bodleian Library, Oxford.
R. B. Haldane (Viscount Haldane of Cloan) Papers, National Library of Scotland, Edinburgh.
Sir Edward Hamilton's diary, British Library.
J. L. Hammond Papers, Bodleian Library, Oxford.
David Hannay Papers, University College, London.
Sir Patrick Hannon Papers, House of Lords Record Office.
Viscount Harcourt (L. V. Harcourt) Papers, Bodleian Library, Oxford.
Sir William Harcourt Papers, Bodleian Library, Oxford.
Frederic Harrison Papers, British Library of Political and Economic Science, London.
Oliver Harvey (1st Baron Harvey of Tasburgh) diary, British Library.
W. A. S. Hewins Papers, The University Library, Sheffield.
E. B. Iwan-Müller Papers, British Library.
Sir Richard Jebb Papers, Institute of Commonwealth Studies, University of London.
Thomas Jones Papers, copies courtesy of the Baroness White.
Earl Kitchener's correspondence with Lt-Col. R. J. Marker, British Library.
Earl Kitchener Papers, Public Record Office.
Labour Party Archives, Transport House, London.
George Lansbury Papers, British Library of Political and Economic Science, London.
Walter (1st Baron) Layton Papers, courtesy of the Hon Christopher Layton and Mr David Hubback.
R. C. Lehmann Papers, courtesy of Mr John Lehmann.
David Lloyd George (1st Earl Lloyd-George of Dwyfor) Papers, House of Lords Record Office.
Oliver Locker Lampson Papers, Norwich and Norfolk Record Office.
Marquess of Lothian (Philip Kerr) Papers, Scottish Record Office, Edinburgh.
J. Ramsay MacDonald Papers, Public Record Office.
Reginald McKenna Papers, Churchill College, Cambridge.
Sir Donald Maclean Papers, Bodleian Library, Oxford.
Arthur Mann Papers, courtesy of Mr E. Peter Wright.
Kingsley Martin Papers, The Library, University of Sussex.
Mass-Observation Archive, University of Sussex.
L. J. Maxse Papers, West Sussex Record Office.
Alfred (Viscount) Milner Papers, Bodleian Library, Oxford.
Minto (4th Earl of Minto) Papers, National Library of Scotland, Edinburgh.
C. E. Montague-Francis Dodd correspondence, British Library.
Gilbert Murray Papers, Bodleian Library, Oxford.
National Union of Conservative and Constitutional Associations, minutes and reports, Conservative Central Office.
H. W. Nevinson's diary, Bodleian Library, Oxford.

Sir William Robertson Nicoll Papers, courtesy of Mrs Mildred Kirkcaldy.
Sir Henry Norman Papers, courtesy of Lady Burke.
Northcliffe (Alfred Harmsworth, Viscount Northcliffe) Papers, British Library.
Oxford and Cambridge University Club, minutes, United Oxford and Cambridge University Club, London.
Passfield (Beatrice and Sidney Webb) Papers, British Library of Political and Economic Science, London.
S. Pearson & Son, Ltd. Papers, *see* Cowdray. (The papers of Sir C. Arthur Pearson, consulted by his biographer, were lost when his son emigrated to the United States.)
J. A. Pease (1st Baron Gainford) Papers, Nuffield College, Oxford.
Sir Robert Perks Papers, courtesy of Sir Malcolm Perks.
Rainbow Circle minute-books, courtesy of Mr Stephen Wilson.
S. K. Ratcliffe Papers, The Library, University of Wisconsin at Madison.
Reform Club, London, minutes.
Rosebery (5th Earl of Rosebery) Papers, National Library of Scotland, Edinburgh.
Rowntree Trust records, courtesy of Mr A. P. Duncum.
Walter Runciman (1st Viscount Runciman of Doxford) Papers, The University Library, Newcastle-upon-Tyne.
Salisbury (3rd Marquess of Salisbury) Papers, Hatfield House.
Herbert (Viscount) Samuel Papers, House of Lords Record Office.
J. S. Sandars Papers, Bodleian Library, Oxford.
D. H. and George Saunders Papers, Churchill College, Cambridge.
C. P. Scott Papers, British Library.
Selborne (2nd Earl of Selborne) Papers, Bodleian Library, Oxford.
Bernard Shaw Papers, British Library.
Sir John (1st Viscount) Simon Papers, Bodleian Library, Oxford.
Sir Archibald Sinclair (1st Viscount Thurso) Papers, Churchill College, Cambridge.
J. A. Spender Papers, British Library.
W. T. Stead Papers, courtesy of Professor Joseph O. Baylen.
Sir A. H. D. Steel-Maitland Papers, Scottish Record Office, Edinburgh.
J. St Loe Strachey Papers, House of Lords Record Office.
Frank Swinnerton Papers, University of Arkansas.
Times Archives, New Printing House Square, London.
TUC Archives, Congress House, London.
Wargrave (Sir Edward Goulding, 1st Baron Wargrave) Papers, House of Lords Record Office.
Frank Waters Papers, courtesy of Mrs Joan Woods (and since transferred to The Library, McMaster University, Hamilton, Ontario).
H. G. Wells Papers, The Library, University of Illinois at Champaign-Urbana.
Francis Williams (Baron Francis-Williams) Papers, Churchill College, Cambridge.
Oliver Woods Papers, courtesy of Mrs Joan Woods (and since transferred to The Library, McMaster University, Hamilton, Ontario).

INDEX

Abbey division, Westminster, by-election (1924), 435, 438
Abdication crisis, 562–67, 584, 590; *also see* Edward VIII
Aberconway, 1st Baron (Sir Charles McLaren), 193
Aberdeen Free Press, 211
Abyssinia crisis, 539, 540, 549, 550; *also see* Italy
Ackland, W. A., 125
Acland, Sir Richard, 637n.
Acland Hood, Sir A. F. (1st Baron St Audries), 70, 72, 116, 123, 124, 129, 162, 175
Action, 510, 511, 532, 572
Adams, John Coode, 168
Addison, Dr Christopher (1st Viscount), 292, 377
Addison, Paul, 430, 477
Advertisement duty, repealed (1853), 5
Advertising Service Guild, 631n.
Advertising World, 370
Aga Khan, 411, 649, 670
Agadir crisis, 210
Ainsworth, Harry, 407
Aitken, Sir Max (1st Baronet): *see* Beaverbrook, Baron
Aitken, Sir Max (2nd Baronet), 443, 673
Akerman, J. C., 513, 528, 530, 615
Alexandra, Queen, 76
All Souls College, Oxford, 202, 466
Allaun, Frank, 676
Allen, Clifford (Lord Allen of Hurtwood), 268, 409, 410
Allendale, 1st Viscount (W. C. B. Beaumont), 102, 191, 192, 193
Alliance magazine, 673n.
Allied Newspapers Ltd., 476
Allied Northern Newspapers Ltd., 476
Allighan, Garry, 625, 636, 637
'Alpha of the Plough', 293
Amalgamated Press Ltd., 98, 476, 559

Ambassadors Club, 488
Amery, Leo: as a Tariff Reformer, 21, 23, 25; nominated for *Observer*, 35; opposes Balfour, 49; as candidate, 107, 158, 160; relations with *Morning Post*, 108, 140; kept in check, 112; tries to entice Northcliffe, 120; promotes working-class Toryism, 128, 262; nominates Aitken, 161; relations with Bonar Law, 162–63, 414; backs Forward Movement, 183; as Halsbury Clubman, 185; laughs at Garvin, 218; wartime activities, 253, 310; defends press lords, 327; assists coalition, 339, 340–41; press relations, 451, 466, 499, 598; Beaverbrook confides in, 500; urges war cabinet, 587; quotes Cromwell, 599; mentioned, 28, 181, 199, 220, 322, 429, 454, 488, 588
Anderson, Sir John (1st Viscount Waverley), 624
Anderson, Robert O., 669, 670, 671
Andrews, W. L., 596
Angell, Sir Norman, 398, 410
Answers, 22, 97, 98
Anti-Waste League, 362, 377
Appeasement, 13, ch. xv *passim*
Apsley, Lord (Allen Algernon Bathurst), 382, 418, 435, 454, 561
Armistice, 348
Armstrong, G. G., 103, 104, 432, 459
Armstrong, Sir George, 25, 74–75, 169, 258
Army Act, amendment of, 230
Ascherson, Neal, 673
Ashley, Wilfrid (1st Baron Mount Temple), 122, 123
Asquith, Elizabeth (Princess Bibesco), 358
Asquith, H. H. (1st Earl of Oxford and Asquith): press relations, 10, 33, 47, 100, 107, 192, 233, 288, 300, 320, 366, 438, 601, 682; special relationship with *Westminster*, 79, 101–103, 174, 313; suffers press attacks, 138, 139, 271, 294, 300, 304, 338; derides

Index

Liberal press, 191; distributes press honours, 100, 103, 308; as Chancellor, 51, 82, 106; as pre-war premier, 99, 117, 128, 139, 140–41; serves tea to editors, 124; shouted down, 209; defends naval estimates, 212; willing to compromise, 226, 235; attends 'prayer-meeting', 241; appoints Kitchener, 254; upholds Liberal principles, 269–70; 'laziness & lack of ideas', 272; denies munitions shortage, 275; forms coalition, 277, 279–80, 281; relies on Kitchener, 284–86; 'a great man'? 287; weakened, 288–89, 291, 296; ends premiership, 297, 299, 301–302, 306; relations with Lloyd George, 292, 303–304, 305–306, 427, 448–49; as 'Wee Free' leader, 314, 317, 327–28, 331, 333; loses East Fife, 346–47, 348; immovable, 367, 370, 372–73; stands aside for Labour, 432, 495; in General Strike, 459; takes peerage and withdraws, 442, 466–67; mentioned, 5, 75, 166, 365, 447
Asquith, Margot (Countess of Oxford and Asquith), 99, 100, 279, 280, 284, 295, 305, 328, 373, 488, 525, 561–62
Asquith, Raymond, 75
Asquith family, 582
Asquith of Yarnbury, Baroness: *see* Bonham Carter, Lady Violet
Assheton, Ralph (1st Baron Clitheroe), 622
Associated Newspapers, 120, 515, 558, 568, 621, 653, 669, 673, 674
Astor, David, 609–10, 611, 612, 628, 635–36, 643–44, 668, 669, 670
Astor, Gavin (2nd Baron Astor of Hever), 636, 660, 661, 662
Astor, John Jacob (1st Baron Astor of Hever), 403, 408–9, 418, 431, 435, 450–1, 480, 589, 619, 622, 636, 660
Astor, Nancy (Viscountess Astor), 199, 232, 321, 363–64, 377, 403, 413, 441, 467, 480, 488, 584, 589, 612, 644n.
Astor, Waldorf (2nd Viscount): relations with Garvin, 175, 177, 182, 185, 202, 329, 333, 610–11; as Halsbury Clubman, 185; as party benefactor, 199–200; 'heartbroken', 232; almost loses *Observer*, 260–61; defines independence, 282–83, 385; relations with Carson, 285; sees Scott, 288; demands liquor controls, 320; inherits peerage, 363; in Plymouth politics, 377; offered share of *Spectator*, 406; evaluates Baldwin, 434; rumoured to be selling out, 491; wants to emulate *S. Times*, 560; commends Lloyd George, 600; selects new editor, 611–12; mentioned, 168, 190, 217, 226, 264, 279, 298, 301, 305, 321, 403, 467, 480, 487, 488, 589, 628, 644n.
Astor, William Waldorf (1st Viscount), 111, 168, 169, 171, 180, 199, 232, 259–61, 353, 403, 669
Astor family, 78, 258–61, 357, 476, 547, 583, 584, 589, 610, 661
Atlantic Richfield (Arco), 669–70, 678n.
Attlee, Clement (Earl Attlee), 540, 568, 580, 592, 595, 606, 623, 624, 632, 634, 638
Austin, Alfred, 18, 144
Austria, *Anschluss*, 527

Baird, John (1st Viscount Stonehaven), 281
Baistow, Tom, 651, 668
Baker, P. J. (Philip Noel-Baker), 250
Balcarres, Lord (27th Earl of Crawford), 175, 184
Baldwin, Oliver (2nd Earl Balfour of Bewdley), 438
Baldwin, Stanley (1st Earl Baldwin of Bewdley): feuds with press lords, 11, 223, 438, 439, 449–50, 468, 469, 477–78, 490, 498–504, 506–507, 536, 550; assists Bonar Law, 308; damns Lloyd George, 414; becomes Tory leader, 424–25; unites Liberals, 426–27; wages 1923 campaign, 428–30, 431, 434; 'keen' to save *Morning Post*, 436; forms second ministry, 442–43; achieves popularity, 451, 462, 549; fights General Strike, 452, 460, 461; Garvin dismisses, 467; press supports, 467, 480, 485; fails 'to save democracy', 487–88; pleases Berry brothers, 489; press relations, 496, 508; forced to accept Ramsay, 535–36; urged to accept Lloyd George, 536, 537; trades places with MacDonald, 539, 540, 548; in Abdication crisis, 563–67; leaves stage, 567, 568; mentioned, 3, 543, 675
Balfour, A. J. (1st Earl of Balfour): relations with newspapers, 7, 29–31, 73, 94, 97, 108, 124, 126, 130–31, 132, 143, 146–47, 150, 158–59, 177, 182–83, 187, 193, 219, 238, 306, 310, 392, 682; relies on journalists, 8, 30, 52–53, 110, 114–15, 142–43, 145n., 163, 164, 189; as Prime Minister, 18–19, 24; problems with Pearson, 28–29, 86, 88; kept abreast by Sandars, 80, 83n., 130, 161; balances factions, 32–33; loses seat, 34, 65, 67; disputes with Chamberlain, 48, 49, 50, 51, 70–72, 125; in 1910 campaigns, 136–37, 139–40, 141, 160; deserves 'another chance', 166; and Parliament Bill crisis, 182–83; decamps, 184; resigns leadership, 171, 184–86, 203; appoin-

ted to Admiralty, 277–78, 279; mentioned, 69, 95, 149, 214, 254, 288, 299, 316, 321, 358, 397, 459
'Balfour Must Go', 108, 179, 185
Ball, Sir Joseph, 551, 552, 554, 570–71
Balliol College, Oxford, 10, 202, 517
Banbury, 1st Baron (Sir Frederick Banbury), 436
Banker, The, 514
Baptist Times, 342, 538
Bareau, Paul, 519
Baring family, 89
Barnard Castle, by-election (1903), 43, 62
Barnes, George, 317
Barnes, Thomas, 202, 466, 643
Baron, Stanley, 546
Barran, Sir Rowland H., 103
Barrington-Ward, Adele, 590n.
Barrington-Ward, Robin: on *Observer*, 31n., 441; returns to *Times*, 467, 480; during General Strike, 457; guides *Times*, 488, 506, 508–9; reports two monkeys, 499; inspired by Neville, 503; in 1931 election, 511, 512; expects circulation gains, 512–13; keeps in 'touch with politics', 516–17; cites *Times*'s prestige, 550; relations with Churchill, 562, 616, 617–19, 628–29, 631; professional integrity, 533, 573, 574–75, 576; defends *Times*'s record, 585–86; fears Cabinet split, 589–90; scorns press honours, 597; protests against censorship, 604; named editor of *Times*, 608; sees post-war order, 622, 627–28, 632; resented by Tories, 634–35; dies, 643; mentioned, 435n., 563, 566, 580, 581, 601n., 609, 621, 636
Barry, Gerald, 524, 546–7, 600, 610, 626, 636
Bartholomew, H. H., 606, 625
Bartlett, Vernon, 466, 547, 582, 636
Bates, Sir Percy, 436, 453, 454, 460
Bathurst, Countess (Lilias Borthwick): inherits *Morning Post*, 18, 71, 108; pro-Chamberlain, 69, 70; relies on Ware, 114, 126, 140, 142, 144; hires Gwynne, 178–79; imposes restrictions, 180, 205–206; praises Garvin, 181; relies on Gwynne, 182–83, 186–87, 201, 218, 220, 225, 226, 244, 254–55, 264, 280, 285, 328, 332–33, 393–94, 418, 424, 431; reconciled to Bonar Law, 188; Northcliffe flatters, 209; criticizes paper, 234; refuses to take on *Globe*, 330; threatens to sell *Morning Post*, 262–63, 329, 430; becomes a fatalist, 435–36; sets record straight, 436–37; mentioned, 127, 321, 382
Bathurst, 7th Earl, 71, 179, 185, 186, 201, 264, 319

Bathurst, E. J., 165
Bathurst family, 159, 165, 290; *also see* Apsley, Lord
Baxter, Beverley, 464, 479, 480, 492, 499, 636
BBC, 390, 574, 593, 623, 638, 643; *also see* Radio and Television
Beaton, Neil S., 638
Beavan, John (Baron Ardwick), 655
Beaverbrook, Baron (Sir Max Aitken): buys into *Express*, 5, 123, 188, 223, 265–67, 308, 324; challenges Baldwin, 11, 438, 439, 498–504, 506–507, 536, 539; relations with Northcliffe, 161, 198, 349, 360, 363; plays go-between, 168, 298, 299, 301, 302; relations with Garvin, 176, 179–80, 190, 200, 220; discounts Smith, 184; as an MP, 193, 215; thwarts Locker Lampson, 194–98; influences Bonar Law, 187, 200–201, 204; relations with Rothermere, 224, 323, 362, 382–83, 396, 425–26, 469–70, 515, 533, 534; involved with *Globe*, 230, 233, 286; justifies secrecy, 237; entertains ambitions, 248; keeps 'look-out', 261; cooperates with Lloyd George, 293, 296–97, 306, 308–309, 328, 334–35, 341, 344, 345; has double identity, 298, 357; ennobled, 307–308; arouses resentment, 309, 318; takes office, 326–27, 340; plays at peacemaker, 345; asserts challenge, 355–56; regrets *S. Express*, 364–65; gives 'splendid support', 367; defends Canadian interests, 381; preaches independence, 386, 391–92, 394; gives the signal, 411–12; fights 1922 election, 417, 423; stays his hand, 424; acquires *Evening Standard*, 425; opposes 1923 election, 427–28, 428–30; celebrates 1924 as a bumper year, 433; welcomes Labour government, 434; sponsors Churchill, 435; shows moderation, 449–50; responds to General Strike, 452, 455, 457, 458, 460, 462; advises 'Bill' Berry, 474–75; opposes Tories, 479, 480; predicts 1929 result, 481, 487; as an 'untouchable', 488, 489; launches Empire Crusade, 490; tries by-election tactics, 502–503; courted by Neville, 504; leads the hobgoblins, 511, 513; relations with Cummings, 520, 531, 533–34, 538, 568; relations with Layton, 527, 648–49; as an isolationist, 538–39, 557–58, 571–72; scores Labour contradictions, 540; obeys 'inward monitor', 545; defends Hoare, 549; counts Dawson as leading pro-German, 550; hostility to government, 556, 557; invades Scotland, 558–59; as King's Man, 562, 564, 566; surveys press, 565; supports Neville, 567–68,

584; discounts threat of war, 590–91; on Halifax's claims, 600; recalls 'old days', 601; relations with Churchill, 571, 622, 623, 624, 627, 631; counsels moderation, 606, 618; shows latent radicalism, 608; suspected of wartime intrigue, 610, 611; notes decline of party allegiances, 613; preaches back to Bevan, 616–17; yearns for party warfare, 620; as virtual party manager, 622; tempts Percy Cudlipp, 633–34; employs 'contacts', 637; resents Royal Commission, 640; faces difficult choice, 646; offers terms to *News Chronicle*, 652, 653; commends Thomson, 660–61; dies, 673; mentioned 13, 121, 127, 257, 276, 277, 305, 329, 346, 358, 365, 402, 407, 443, 453, 454, 465, 508, 514, 519, 547, 553, 561, 595, 597n., 614, 618, 680
Beaverbrook Newspapers, 669, 673
Beckett, Sir Gervase, 3, 80, 387, 583
Beckett, John, 511
Beckett, Rupert, 387, 453, 454, 583–84
Begbie, Harold, 161
Belgium: neutrality of, 250; 'Hunnish' atrocities in, 257, 258, 275
Bell, Edward Price, 302
Bell, Stanley, 621
Bellenger, F. J., 636
Belloc, Hilaire, 77, 105, 171, 223, 293n.
Benn, Tony (Anthony Wedgwood Benn), 667, 675
Bennett, Arnold, 81, 102–3, 268, 276, 323–24, 340
Bentley, E. C., 55
Beresford, Lord Charles, 107, 126–27, 134
Berry brothers, 247, 335, 385, 421, 422, 425, 426, 445, 449, 453, 464, 470, 476–77, 484, 495, 553, 559, 584, 589, 635, 643, 677; *also see* Lords Buckland (H. Seymour Berry), Camrose (William Berry), *and* Kemsley (J. Gomer Berry)
Bevan, Aneurin, 604, 606, 608, 616–17, 636, 645, 646, 651n.
Bevin, Ernest, 369, 463, 482, 483, 497n., 509, 553, 556, 605, 606, 612, 615, 617, 627, 628
Biffen, John, 670, 671, 673
Binder, B. H., 527, 528, 529, 530, 531
Birk, Alma (Baroness Birk), 650n.
Birkenhead, 1st Earl of: *see* Smith, F. E.
Birmingham Daily Argus, 38
Birmingham Daily Gazette, 38–39, 175, 221
Birmingham Daily Post, 38, 66–67, 133, 153, 221n., 582
Birmingham Evening Dispatch, 39
Birmingham Sunday Mercury, 484

Birrell, Augustine, 56, 60, 61, 279
'Black Monday' (17 October 1960), 653–54
Blake, Robert, 220, 287, 413
Blatchford, Robert, 63, 134, 154, 252, 268, 343, 421, 434, 495, 496, 510
Blewett, Neal, 135–36, 141, 152
Blood, William F., 499n.
Blumenfeld, R. D.: evaluates 'mass thinking', 9; as a protectionist, 23, 225; position on the *Express*, 120, 121, 122, 123, 197, 204, 214, 221–22, 264–65, 267, 464; backslides, 153–54; funded by Aitken, 187–88, 194, 195–96, 223; asserts patriotism, 256–57; takes guidance, 302, 325; represents 'wool trade', 341–42; defends editorial independence, 356, 365, 392; blames Parliament, 518; joins January Club, 534; mentioned, 26, 60, 156, 159, 164–65, 179, 183, 236, 237, 253, 254, 255, 298, 357, 382, 412, 416, 431, 451, 467, 476, 507n.
Boer War, 6, 9, 15, 18, 19, 40, 47, 54, 55, 63, 99, 101, 210, 250; *also see* Transvaal
Bonar Law, Andrew: relations with Garvin, 31, 141, 176; relations with *Morning Post*, 108, 109, 158–59, 177, 205–206, 220; relies on Max, 123, 190, 204, 475, 571; disgruntled, 125–26; as Tariff Reformer, 134, 139–40; stands at Manchester, 146, 156–57, 160; emerges as leader, 187–89; relations with Northcliffe, 193, 216, 225, 283, 359; drawn into *Express* dealings, 194–95, 197–98, 266–67; weakens, 200–201; waxes extreme over Ireland, 201–202, 209, 214; bids farewell to Buckle, 203; meets Marlowe, 207; rescinds Referendum pledge, 214–15; suffers press criticism, 216–17, 229, 230, 318–19; advised about press, 222; willing to compromise, 226, 227; editorial contacts, 230, 232–33, 236, 237, 255, 256, 258; intervenes in press affairs, 259–61, 263–64, 298, 358; relations with Rothermere, 261, 362, 424, 469; agrees to coalition, 279, 281; loyalty to Asquith, 285, 290; challenged by Carson, 299; urges compromise, 303–304; stands by Lloyd George, 332, 341, 345, 379, 404; resigns from coalition, 381, 391; 'may revolt', 397; writes to *Times*, 411–12; lured from retirement, 413–17; falls ill and dies, 423–24; 'never got a chance', 567; mentioned, 80, 198, 219, 244, 282, 288, 291, 292, 296, 300, 308, 328, 329, 334, 355, 366, 392
Bonham Carter, Lady Violet (Baroness Asquith of Yarnbury), 100, 305, 564, 589, 590, 615n., 638, 640

Boot, Sir Jesse, 330, 331, 370n.
Boot, Lady, 331
Booth, F. Handel Booth, 293
Boothby, Robert (Baron Boothby), 550, 588
Boots, the Chemists, 513
Borden, Sir Robert, 450
Borthwick, Oliver, 21–22, 30, 188n.
Bottomley, Horatio, 148, 189, 248, 256–57, 268, 269, 275, 320, 321, 355, 392
Bowerman, C. W., 369
Boyle, Sir Edward (Baron Boyle of Handsworth), 683
Boynton, James, 127
Bracken, Brendan (1st Viscount), 455n, 492, 514–15, 516, 560, 593, 601, 610, 618, 622, 623, 624, 630–31, 635
Bradby, E. H., 57–58
Bradford Daily Telegraph, 353
Bradford Labour Echo, 64
Bradford Observer, 39, 44
Bradley, Jim, 654
Brailsford, H. N., 56, 58, 59, 105, 409–10, 411, 434, 444, 449, 463, 567
Brand, R. H. (1st Baron), 573
Bridgwater, by-election (1938), 581n., 582
Briggs, Asa, 390
Bright, John, 5, 16, 31, 101, 156, 642, 685
Brisbane, Arthur, 507
Bristol Times, 476
British Foreign and Colonial Corp., 477
British Gazette, 452, 454–56, 457, 458, 460–61, 592
British League for the Support of Ulster and the Union, 201
British Union of Fascists, 511, 533, 572–73
British Weekly, 101, 303, 373, 441, 538
British Worker, 452, 456
Brittain, Vera, 665
Broadcasting: *see* Radio and Television
Broadhurst, Henry, 56
Brooks, Collin, 3, 190, 439, 454n., 458, 465, 492, 515, 524, 534, 535, 536, 538, 545, 548, 549, 557, 558, 559, 561, 565–66, 568, 572, 574, 581, 594, 607n., 609, 611, 615, 621, 623, 684
Brown, Ivor, 611–12, 621, 622n., 643
Browne, George Ulick, 341–42
Brownlee, Leigh, 516
Broxbourne, Lord, 636
Bruce, Robert, 319, 416, 417
Brunner, Sir John (1st Baronet), 40, 41–42, 77, 85, 102, 193, 210, 211, 212–13, 229, 282, 373
Brunner, J. F. L. (2nd Baronet), 102, 229, 330, 373

Brunner, Roscoe, 85
Bryce, James (Viscount Bryce), 138, 275, 280, 314
Buccleuch, 7th Duke of, 436
Buchan, John (1st Baron Tweedsmuir), 41, 284, 313, 321, 324, 351, 406–407
Buchan, Norman, 665
Buchanan, Gray, 195
Buckland, 1st Baron (H. Seymour Berry), 471, 478, 489; *also see* Berry brothers
Buckle, G. E.: gives party service, 18, 37, 69, 70, 107, 112, 153, 181, 183–84, 185, 207; wobbles, 21, 115–16, 150; relations with Balfour, 29, 48, 94, 110, 124–25, 187, 189; disdains honours for journalists, 52–53; in transfer of *Times*, 85, 86–87, 88, 90, 93–94, 96–97, 119; celebrates 25th year as editor, 110; retires, 189, 202–203; Gwynne praises, 225; defines editorial responsibility, 231, 270; mentioned, 73, 132, 145, 157, 166, 198, 403
Buckmaster, Sir Stanley (1st Viscount), 240, 245, 276–77
Budget League, 123, 124, 138
Budget Protest League, 123
Bull, Sir William, 195, 499
Buller, H., 108
Bullock, Alan, 482
Bulmer-Thomas, Ivor, 586–87, 636
Bureau of Current Affairs, 639
Burgess, Guy, 665
Burnham, 1st Baron (Edward Levy Lawson), 1, 33, 52, 132, 149–50, 181, 209, 229
Burnham, 1st Viscount (Harry Lawson), 137, 144, 209, 241, 244, 255, 272, 301, 382, 393, 398, 422, 449, 453, 460
Burnham, 2nd Viscount, 464
Burns, John, 48, 51, 79–80, 100, 125n., 173, 205, 210, 280–81
Burton, Pomeroy, 120
Butes, Alfred, 87
Butler, David, 630, 664
Butler, Nicholas Murray, 564
Butler, R. A. (Baron Butler of Saffron Walden), 580, 584, 623–24, 683
Buxton, Noel (1st Baron Noel-Buxton), 502
Byers, Frank (Baron Byers), 633
Byles, W. P., 44

Cadbury, Edward, 340, 361, 494, 555
Cadbury, Egbert, 633, 649, 651, 652
Cadbury, George, 17, 42, 45, 56, 62, 77, 81, 227, 253, 311, 313, 331, 339, 361, 375, 486, 493, 494, 529

Index

Cadbury, Henry, 78, 81, 104, 148–49, 162n., 361, 365–66, 373, 385, 471, 472, 483, 486, 494, 522, 555, 578, 633, 646–47
Cadbury, Jocelyn, 621
Cadbury, Laurence, 385, 494, 522, 523, 524, 526–28, 530, 554–55, 582, 596, 597–98, 609, 614–15, 621, 631, 633, 636, 644, 647, 649, 651, 653–54
Cadbury, Paul, 582
Cadbury family, 43, 134, 147, 172, 365, 484, 490–94, 555, 573, 582, 615, 621, 647, 650, 654
Cadbury Trust, 484, 490, 493
Caird, Sir Andrew, 454, 461
Cambria Daily Leader, 488
Camden, Marquess of, 195
Campaign for Press Freedom, 675
Campbell, Alexander, 516
Campbell, J. R., 441
Campbell-Bannerman, Sir Henry, 15, 16, 39–40, 45, 47, 48, 50–51, 56, 71, 89, 90–91, 99, 141, 601
Camrose, 1st Viscount (William Berry), 247, 286n., 307, 364, 374, 426, 457, 474–75, 476, 478, 485, 489, 490, 501, 503, 514, 559, 560, 561, 567, 571, 583, 584, 587, 588, 589, 590, 595, 599, 607, 609, 614, 626, 627, 635, 640
Canivet, Mrs Mildred, 335, 336
Caretaker government, 623
Carlile, Sir Hildred, 195
Carlisle, Countess of, 60
Carlton Club, 3, 95, 186, 189, 413–14
Carnegie, Andrew, 40
Carr, E. H. 608, 616, 628
Carr, Henry, 584n.
Carson, Sir Edward, 84, 134, 187, 202, 226, 235–37, 255, 285, 290, 292, 298, 299, 304–306, 308, 325, 327, 332–33, 337, 366–67
Casey, William, 643
'Cassandra': see Connor, William
Cassel, Sir Ernest, 257
Castle, Barbara, 636, 666, 667
Castle, Ted (Baron), 667n.
Cater, Douglass, 678
Catlin, Sir George, 665
Catto, Sir Thomas (1st Baron Catto), 447, 471, 493, 528, 530
Cazalet, Victor, 442
Cecil, Lord Hugh, 7, 60, 90, 111, 127, 230, 283
Cecil, Lord Robert, 73, 111n., 126–27, 151, 240, 309, 310, 315, 325, 342–43, 360, 367, 372, 400
Cecil family, 48, 67, 90, 140
Central News Agency, 47
Chaco dispute, 550

Chamberlain, Sir Austen: becomes Chancellor, 24; relations with Garvin, 74, 167, 169, 181, 217; deals with *Morning Post*, 108, 127, 165–66, 329; breaks away, 159, 165, 185; bypassed for leadership, 184–88; relations with *Times* and Northcliffe, 216, 331, 338, 348, 391; downcast, 219, 269; shows 'splendid loyalty', 220; 'full of infamy', 327; supports coalition, 379, 399, 404–405, 413–14, 415, 416, 417, 419, 424; as Unionist leader, 393, 398; returns to fold, 439; mentioned, 7, 88, 144, 171, 254, 255–56, 364, 412, 429, 581
Chamberlain, Mrs Austen (Lady Chamberlain), 7, 581
Chamberlain, Joseph: cultivates press, 18, 19, 28, 29, 67–68, 149; espouses tariffs, 19–25, 31–32; uses Pearson, 37–38, 87, 88; tries to capture party, 47, 48, 49, 64–66, 68–71; suffers stroke, 72, 73, 82; retires, 127; militancy of his supporters, 94, 163–64; mentioned, 45, 137, 159, 160, 167, 184, 205, 210, 311, 557–58
Chamberlain, Neville: press relations, 3, 503, 546, 571, 582–84, 586, 587, 598–99, 601, 605, 610; organizes party, 488, 500–501, 502–504; resists Lloyd George, 537; hailed by Beaverbrook, 567–68, 584; goes to Munich, 577, 581; allegedly considers pre-war election, 581, 586–87, 591–92; wards off attacks, 588, 590; as wartime premier, 593, 595, 598–600; leaves office, 605–606; mentioned, 7, 310, 426, 428, 498, 543, 585, 611
Chamberlain, Mrs Neville, 581
Champion, H. H., 63
Chanak crisis, 411–12
Chancellor, Alexander, 682
Chancellor, Sir Christopher, 655
Channon, Sir Henry ('Chips'), 584, 585, 587, 588, 589, 598, 609
Chaplin, Henry (1st Viscount), 216
Chapman, Brian, 624
Chattaway, Edward, 497
Chelsea Pick and Shovel, 64
Chenery, Thomas, 202
Chesterton, Cecil, 171, 223
Chesterton, G. K., 15, 28, 57, 66n., 75, 105, 136
Chicago Daily News, 302
Chicago Tribune, 567
Chilcott, Sir W. S., 402
'Chinese Slavery', 54, 134, 486
Chiozza Money, L. G., 54
Chirol, Sir Valentine, 21, 30, 33, 48, 65–66, 82–83, 88–89, 90, 91, 92, 94, 112, 115, 124, 189, 351, 418

Chisholm, Hugh, 208, 282
Christiansen, Arthur, 457, 464–65, 517–18, 533, 545, 573, 603, 613, 617, 624, 631
Churchill, Clementine (Baroness Spencer-Churchill), 435, 536
Churchill, Randolph S., 462, 485, 535, 564–65, 588, 658
Churchill, Sir Winston S.: relations with the press, 12, 21–22, 27, 43, 46, 78–79, 100, 174, 230, 244, 259, 271, 294–95, 366, 450, 478, 479, 485, 501, 562, 581, 582–83, 587–88, 589–90, 591, 597, 602, 603–604, 605–607, 609, 611, 612, 613, 616, 617–18, 617–19; relations with Northcliffe, 34, 110, 114, 130, 166, 198–99, 269, 286, 398, 399; works with Lloyd George, 99, 106, 107, 140, 377, 406, 411; submits naval estimates, 210, 211–12, 213–14, 221, 230; speaks freely, 226; in 1915 Cabinet crisis, 273, 274, 276–77, 278, 279; in 1916 Cabinet crisis, 305, 306; Tories oppose, 319, 321, 348, 349; relations with Beaverbrook, 429, 435, 468, 557, 571; fights General Strike, 452–61; wages Indian mutiny, 503; denied office, 536, 539, 568; damages his credibility, 564, 565, 566; opposes appeasers, 574, 577; fears pre-war election, 591–92; becomes Prime Minister, 593, 600–601; mutterings against, 610; forms caretaker ministry, 622–23; campaigns in 1945, 623–24, 626–27, 629; skips leading articles, 631, 632; retains obsession with press, 634; endorses Royal Commission, 638; in 1950 election, 645–46; fingers the trigger, 647–48; mentioned, 209, 233, 272, 284, 319, 358, 415, 438, 443, 535, 548, 620, 621
Citrine, Sir Walter, 482, 509
Clarion, 63, 64, 154, 268, 343, 421
Clarke, Tom, 231, 245–46, 252, 254, 278, 288, 385, 395, 405, 491, 497, 517, 520, 521, 522, 524, 594, 673
Clement, William Innell, 40
Cliveden, 199, 466, 544, 546, 547, 589, 612
Clynes, J. R., 268, 364
Coalition Publicity Committee, 339
Cobden, Richard, 31, 101, 642, 685
Cockburn, Claud, 497, 580, 604, 612
Cole, G. D. H., 498, 518, 525, 526
Colman, J. J., 40
Colvin, Ian, 436, 546
Comic Cuts, 97
Coming Fashions, 407
Committee on Imperial Defence, 242
Committee on Privileges, 637
Commonweal, 63

Connaught, Duke of, 28
Connor, William ('Cassandra'), 605, 606
Conrad, Joseph, 57
Conservative Policy Secretariat, 426
Conservative Research Dept., 551, 553, 570, 575, 644–45
Contemporary Review, 47
Continental Daily Mail, 338, 346, 398, 405, 457, 484
Cook, Sir Edward, 9, 18, 22, 26, 27, 46, 55, 57, 91n., 176, 202, 231, 241, 244–45, 270, 272, 276–77, 308
Cooke, Sir C. Kinloch, 241n.
Cooper, Charles, 31, 32, 80
Cooper, Sir George, 195
Cooper, Sir Richard, 319
Cooper Brothers, 660
Coote, Sir Colin, 552, 553, 588
Council of Action, 537, 539, 540
Courtney of Penwith, 1st Baron (Leonard Courtney), 250
Cowdray, 1st Viscount (Sir Weetman Pearson), 43, 102, 191, 193, 312, 313, 315, 330, 334, 344, 371, 372, 374, 375, 385, 396, 445–46, 448–49, 471, 669, 673
Cowdray, 2nd Viscount (Harold Pearson), 331, 372n., 374, 423, 446, 448, 471, 472, 473–74, 483–84, 486, 490–91, 493, 497, 517, 520, 521, 522, 523
Cowdray, 3rd Viscount (W. J. C. Pearson), 522
Cowley, John, 149, 516, 598, 614
Cowling, Maurice, 369, 375–76
Cox, Harold, 159
Craig, Sir James (1st Viscount Craigavon), 436
Craik, Sir Henry, 491
Cranborne, Viscount (5th Marquess of Salisbury), 570
Cranfield, Arthur, 533, 636
Creed, Percy, 406
Crewe, 1st Marquess of, 284, 313
Crewe House, 593
Cripps, Sir Charles Alfred (1st Baron Parmoor), 111
Cripps, Sir Stafford, 612
Croal, J. P., 80, 290, 318–19, 416
Croft, Baron: *see* Page Croft, Sir Henry
Cromer, 1st Earl of, 89–90, 91, 92, 142, 159
Crook, W. M., 15
Crossfield, Bertram, 459n., 514, 647
Crosland, Anthony, 685–86
Crossley, Sir Saville (1st Baron Somerleyton), 229
Crossman, R. H. S., 11, 128n., 634, 636, 650n., 653, 657–58, 663, 664, 666, 667, 681, 682, 683

Crowther, Geoffrey, 611, 614, 643
Crozier, W. P., 362, 465–66, 547, 552, 570, 595, 613, 615, 616
Cruikshank, R. J., 497, 586, 603–604, 636, 649, 650
Crusader, 44
Cudlipp, Hugh (Baron), 465n., 598, 625, 633, 634, 651, 666, 685
Cudlipp, Percy, 545–46, 573, 597, 612–13, 633–34, 639, 649, 655
Cudlipp, Reginald, 598
Cummings, A. J., 388, 497, 498, 502, 511, 518n., 520, 521, 524, 527, 529, 531, 533–34, 538, 539, 546, 547–48, 552, 568, 571, 591, 596, 600, 603–604, 651n.
Curran, F. N., 123
Curran, James, 675
Cursley, Norman, 654n.
Curtis, Byron, 26, 27
Curtis, Lionel, 199
Curtis, Michael, 649, 651, 652, 670
Curzon, 1st Marquess, 130, 181, 182, 270, 284, 358, 406, 411, 414, 415, 424, 443
Cust, Henry, 30, 33, 199
Czechoslovakia: *see* Munich crisis

Daily Call, 264
Daily Chronicle: reconstructed under Donald, 9, 16, 26, 46–47; acquired by Lloyd George's syndicate, 5, 81, 313–14, 315, 334–37, 449; serves Liberals, 82, 106, 111, 135, 138, 144, 205, 319, 352, 353, 409, 472, 474; leaks Cabinet selections, 99–100; relations with Lloyd George, 213, 224, 285, 295, 311, 338, 373, 404, 426–27, 448, 467; wartime experience, 242, 246, 262, 284, 300, 302, 309, 323; hires Maurice, 333, 334, 335; reconstructed and merged, 361, 376, 379–80, 445, 446–47, 471–72, 484–85, 490, 492–93, 494–95, 519; mentioned, 1, 17, 39, 51, 55, 57, 61, 76, 78, 112, 161, 173, 185, 204, 211, 213, 227, 236, 251, 265, 271–72, 277, 289, 294, 328, 346, 383, 424, 432, 433, 441, 442, 459, 483, 484, 491, 513
Daily Citizen, 62, 65, 156, 190, 209, 234, 235, 245, 251–52, 267–68, 343
Daily Express: protectionism, 22, 23, 67; as Pearson's 'pet child', 27, 121; Blumenfeld's authority, 120; successive reconstructions, 120–23, 187–88, 190, 194–98, 221–23, 232, 258, 264–67, 308, 324–25, 430, 680; in party politics, 170, 179, 180, 183, 185, 224, 233, 278–79, 290, 300, 318, 367, 381–82, 431, 433, 435, 443, 468, 479, 480, 487, 550, 551, 564, 565, 566, 577, 598–99, 664; attacks Northcliffe, 218–19, 225; not contaminated by Germans, 257; demands compulsion, 275–76; decries Red peril, 325; unknown, 342; 'free and independent', 355–56, 358; during General Strike, 452, 455, 457, 458; improves quality and circulation, 467, 474, 484, 513, 517–18, 557, 560, 615–16, 644, 649; as Empire Crusader, 498–99; glorifies itself, 532–33, 534; commissions polls, 538–39, 645; says there will be 'no war', 545, 571–72, 591; editorial authority at, 464, 573, 617; snipes at MoI, 594; loses newsprint, 602; its vagaries, 616–17; fights 1945 election, 624, 625, 626, 627, 628, 630, 631n.; mentioned, 1, 3, 5, 9, 50, 76, 80, 135, 153, 156, 159, 165, 175, 231, 242, 253, 255, 309, 346, 396, 412, 416, 417, 451, 558, 613, 647, 677, 683
Daily Graphic, 1, 125, 135, 197, 222, 247, 364, 421, 431, 495, 635
Daily Herald, 5, 6, 62, 65, 190, 234–35, 245, 351–52, 354, 367, 368–69, 381, 389, 406, 408, 409, 420, 422, 427, 432–34, 437, 439–340, 443–44, 449, 452, 463, 481, 482–83, 487, 494, 496–97, 502, 509, 511, 517, 521, 524, 525, 530, 532, 536, 537, 540, 545–46, 547, 551, 552–53, 556, 559, 564–65, 569, 573, 578, 582–83, 591, 592, 594, 597–98, 599, 605, 607, 608, 610, 612–13, 615, 617, 624–25, 626, 627, 630, 631n., 633–34, 638, 644, 651, 652–54, 655–56, 658, 663, 680, 685; *also see Herald*
Daily Mail: in tariff conflict, 20, 22, 163–64, 165, 167–68, 219, 220; launches northern edition, 34, 68; prestige and influence, 35, 37, 52, 76, 117, 198; Northcliffe's favourite, 93, 94, 96, 276, 278, 302–303, 340, 395; relations with Garvin, 109, 134, 144, 150, 216; responds to People's Budget, 112, 113, 114, 115–16; in 1910 elections, 129–30, 133, 134, 135–36, 158, 159–60; structure of, 204, 206–207, 423, 464; flatters Lady Bathurst, 209; rides soft pedal, 223–24; attacks Kitchener, 243; circulates wartime rumours, 244, 256, 257; attacks Liberal ministers, 270, 271, 281, 293, 306, 349; circulation fluctuates, 283, 382, 467, 484, 513, 518, 525, 557, 558, 560, 615, 620–21, 649; relations with Lloyd George, 285, 309–10, 326, 345; relations with Labour, 343, 377, 420, 421, 432, 433, 434, 442; post-war partisanship, 405–406, 417, 428, 431, 438, 443, 451; in General Strike, 452, 454, 457–58; Beaverbrook vows to kill, 470; champions Hungary, 477; as Rothermere's sounding board, 516; cheers Black-

shirts, 533; celebrates Hitler, 547; lusts to arm, 549; opposes Baldwin, 551, 557, 563, 565; takes King's side, 564, 566; protests against wartime censorship, 595; commends Lloyd George, 600; grumbles, 605; not for sale, 615; in 1945 election, 625, 627, 630, 631n.; Attlee wonders about, 634; attacks Bevan, 645; absorbs *News Chronicle*, 647, 652–54; later partisanship, 664, 684; mentioned, 1, 3, 6, 8, 23, 27, 33, 59, 78–79, 80, 84–85, 87, 97, 121, 166, 179, 183, 245, 247, 252, 253, 254, 268, 269, 286, 287, 291, 316, 323, 332, 339, 351, 358, 366, 375, 389, 390, 397, 398, 445, 469, 491, 504, 517, 574, 595, 617, 676, 682
Daily Mail (and General) Trust, 470, 568
Daily Mirror, 1, 3, 11, 20–21, 33–34, 35, 84, 94, 97, 113, 135, 149, 222, 223, 231, 245, 246, 264, 346, 377, 382, 392, 408, 417, 423, 431, 467, 476, 515–16, 588, 592, 595, 598, 600, 601n., 605–607, 608, 624–30, 631n., 634, 636, 644, 646–52, 663, 664, 665, 666, 667, 683, 684
Daily News: revives under Cadbury management, 5, 16, 19, 26, 42, 44–46; intensifies partisanship, 47, 50, 51–52, 54–55, 66, 105, 161–62; structure and finances, 58, 78, 104, 119, 129, 134; offers platform to Labour, 62, 343, 344, 365–66, 368, 370, 432, 433, 448; attacks Northcliffe, 97, 112, 252–53, 279, 306, 325; opposes naval estimates, 119, 149, 213; relations with Lloyd George, 205, 243, 280, 285, 292–93, 294, 295, 299, 309, 312, 321, 322, 346, 404, 496; absorbs *Morning Leader*, 148, 172–73, 190; effects of wartime experience, 246, 250–51, 256, 284–85, 289, 290, 291, 303; identifies with McKenna and Runciman, 272–73, 317; deplores Beaverbrook's peerage, 308; editorial arrangements, 331, 361–62, 375; hires Maurice, 337, 412; post-war partisanship, 344, 352, 409, 420, 441–42, 472–74, 486; merges with other Liberal papers, 376, 396, 447, 459, 471–72, 483–85, 490, 492–93, 494–95, 519; proposal to revive its name, 650; mentioned, 1, 6, 22, 38, 39, 40, 56, 57, 61, 76, 79–80, 81, 116, 125n., 135, 136, 137, 138–39, 142, 169, 206–207, 210, 211, 227, 242, 323, 324, 373, 383, 385, 388, 502, 682
Daily News Ltd., 494
Daily News Trust, 493, 554–55, 647
Daily Paper, 2, 40–41
Daily Sketch, 222, 247, 421, 426, 431, 517, 584n., 598, 607, 609, 625–26, 627, 635, 652, 664

Daily Telegraph: and tariffs, 22, 25; belongs to 'Balfour clique', 30, 33, 49, 72, 255; evaluated, 52, 222; in 1906 campaign, 66, 67, 68; Garvin writes for, 120, 132, 144, 149–50, 168; in 1910 elections, 128, 135, 136–37, 138, 159; lacks partisan strength, 217, 218, 231; publishes Lansdowne letter, 243, 323; assists anti-Bolshevik campaign, 342–43; 'lumpy porridge', 351; coalitionism, 392–93, 419, 422; bets on Curzon, 424; backs Baldwin, 431; employs politicians, 451, 485, 562; in General Strike, 458; has 'faceless editors', 464; sold to Berrys, 470; shows impartiality, 501, 503; represents conservative values, 532; shows impartiality, 501, 503; represents conservative values, 532; 'almost negligible', 551; taken by Camrose, 559; absorbs *Morning Post*, 453, 561–62; in Abdication crisis, 564, 565, 567; partisanship in 1930s, 516, 569, 579, 583; editorial arrangements, 552, 573; supports Churchill, 587, 588, 590, 607, 609, 616; turns against Chamberlain, 598; wartime circulation, 603, 615, 616; later circulation, 625, 626, 627, 629, 645, 648, 652; like 'a neatly-rolled umbrella', 635; politics of its readers, 664; celebrates 125th birthday, 677; mentioned, 1, 80, 109, 162, 181, 209, 241, 247, 262, 301, 302, 318, 321, 324, 350, 382, 398, 412, 454, 474, 511, 512, 534, 572, 586, 599, 644, 647, 659, 661, 680, 683
Daily Worker, 532, 537, 563, 569, 572, 588, 604, 606, 607, 618, 667, 679; *also see Morning Star*.
Dalton, Hugh (Baron Dalton), 509, 585
Dalziel, Davison (1st Baron Dalziel of Wooler), 81, 120, 147, 177, 222, 263, 264, 282
Dalziel, Sir (James) Henry (1st Baron Dalziel of Kirkcaldy), 81, 112, 282, 290, 298, 303, 335, 336, 337, 340, 341, 344, 346, 361, 375, 380, 385, 449
Davidson, J. C. C. (1st Viscount Davidson), 180n., 308, 329, 345, 362, 387, 426, 442, 452–53, 454, 456, 460, 461, 468–69, 470, 476, 477, 478, 479, 485, 500–501, 566, 567
Davies, Clement, 552, 633
Davies, David (1st Baron Davies of Llandinam), 312, 313, 330, 338, 401
Davies, Haydn, 638
Dawson, Geoffrey (Geoffrey Robinson): defends his profession, 7; relations with Northcliffe, 96, 207, 209, 270, 271, 278, 316, 321, 331–32; takes over at *Times*, 202, 207, 219–20; defines editorial responsibilities, 223, 231, 255, 680; relations with Churchill,

221, 443, 457–58, 562; relations with Carson, 285, 298, 305–306; in 1916 crisis, 301, 304, 310; changes name, 317; refuses Lansdowne letter, 323; relations with Lloyd George, 325, 345; ends first editorship, 348–49, 350–51, 361, 400; returns to *Times*, 401, 403, 418, 422; relations with J. J. Astor, 450–51; sees Baldwin's strength, 451, 466, 504, 507–508, 517, 539; ridicules *Telegraph*, 512; anticipates Lloyd George, 536–37; reluctant to antagonize Germany, 544, 571, 579–80; takes a strong line, 550; crosses party lines, 552; in Abdication crisis, 563, 566–67; reflects and exerts influences, 548, 569–70, 573; shows snobbery, 574; welcomes new readers, 583; deplores 'silly talk', 585; awakened, 587; protests against censorship, 594; retires, 598; watches vote in Commons, 599; a conservative by nature, 608; an *Observer* tribune, 610; mentioned, 199, 235, 253, 269, 279, 318, 319, 380n., 387, 405, 467, 488, 499, 546, 561, 618, 657

Deedes, William, 677

Defence of the Realm Acts, 239–40, 245, 315, 604

Delane, J. T., 170, 202, 235, 270, 314, 466, 643, 681

Democrat, 406, 407, 420

Denman, Lady, 522, 523, 524, 528

Derby, 17th Earl of (Baron Stanley), 69, 94–95, 129, 146, 159, 215, 216, 218, 224, 262, 287–88, 290–91, 301, 307, 315, 316, 325, 378, 379, 397, 399, 412, 416, 417, 424, 451, 489

Derby Scheme, 287–88

Deutscher, Isaac, 628

Devonshire, 8th Duke of, 31, 32, 37, 48, 68

Devonshire, 9th Duke of, 403

Dibblee, G. B., 39, 78

Dicey, Edward, 2–3

Dinot, Frank, 209, 235, 252, 268

Disraeli, Benjamin (1st Earl of Beaconsfield), 5, 18, 21, 26, 202, 230, 412, 507, 677, 682

Dobson, Stanley, 637

Docker, Dudley, 195, 260, 269, 282, 286, 330, 365

Dodd, Francis, 133

Doidge, F. W., 487, 498

Donald, Sir Robert: early editorship at *Chronicle*, 10, 16, 55, 78, 204; relations with Northcliffe, 93, 209; relations with Lloyd George, 144, 205, 213, 214, 271–72, 295n., 296, 313–14, 319, 320, 333–37; relations with Bonar Law, 236, 298, 417; moves towards Asquith, 289, 296; calls for 'firmer methods', 300–301; banished, 335–36, 337, 361; buys provincial papers, 353, 371, 407; acquires *Globe*, 365, 385; foresees closures, 480; brings proposal to Cowdray, 483–84; works for MacDonald, 509–10; mentioned, 235, 247, 251, 302, 308n., 310, 311, 463

Donaldson, Frances, 567

Donner, Sir Patrick, 556

Douglas, James, 16, 319

Douglas-Home, Sir Alec (14th Earl of Home; Baron Home of the Hirsel), 672, 683

Douglas-Home, Charles, 672

Dove, John, 437

Downe, Dorothy, Viscountess, 572

Dreadnoughts, 105, 116–17

Driberg, Tom (Baron Bradwell), 613, 617, 631, 636, 640, 665

Drogheda, 11th Earl of, 662

Dublin Review, 108

du Cann, Edward, 670

Duff Cooper, Alfred (1st Viscount Norwich), 503, 504, 574, 581, 583, 593, 601, 603, 604

Dugdale, Sir Thomas (1st Baron Crathorne), 611

Dumphreys, John, 127

Dundee Advertiser, 211

Dunfermline Wroker, 64, 65

Dunn, J. Nicol, 30, 34, 69–70, 95, 157, 224

Dyer, General R. E. H., 378

Dyson, Will, 369–70

Eager, W. M., 459

East Fulham, survey of newspaper readership in, 630

East of England Newspaper Co. (Norwich), 36

Eastern Morning News, 211

Ecclestone, Jacob, 675

Echo, 1, 15, 16, 47–48, 56, 62, 121

Echo and Evening Chronicle, 246

Economist, The, 77, 111, 211, 282, 471, 498, 522, 611, 614, 615, 643, 666, 682

Edelman, Maurice, 625, 626, 634, 636, 646

Eden, Anthony (1st Earl of Avon), 387, 548, 570–71, 577, 578, 580, 582, 583, 587, 588, 589, 592, 596, 611, 617, 618n.

Edge, Sir William, 377

Edinburgh Evening News, 373, 446, 505–56

Edinburgh Review, 159

Edinger, George, 553

Education Act (1902), 19

Education Bill (1908), 108–109

Index

Edward VII, King, 1, 29n., 138, 141, 142, 143, 144, 154, 565
Edward VIII, King, 543, 562–67, 584, 590, 676
Edwards, Hamilton, 97, 98
Edwards, Ness, 658n.
Egremont, 1st Baron (John Wyndham), 662
Eighty Club, 370
Electra House, 593
Elias, J. S. (1st Viscount Southwood), 407, 454, 482, 483, 496, 525, 538, 545–66, 547, 564, 589, 610, 612
Elibank, Master of: *see* Murray, Alexander (Master of Elibank and 1st Baron Murray of Elibank)
Elizabeth, Queen (Queen Mother), 581
Elizabeth II, Queen, 676
Ellerman, Sir John, 166, 396, 401, 403, 514
Elliot, Arthur, 37
Elliott, Sydney, 625
Emergency Press (Glasgow), 458
Empire Crusade: *see* Empire Free Trade *and* United Empire Party
Empire Free Trade, 5, 451, 475, 490, 501, 502, 508, 532, 539, 557
Empire Review, 409
Encounter, 685
Encyclopaedia Britannica, 72
English Review, 636
English-Speaking Union, 363
Ensor, R. C. K., 48, 81, 172–73, 251, 337, 495, 519, 638
Esher, 2nd Viscount (Reginald Brett), 90, 93, 96, 145n., 149, 163, 164, 223, 270, 276, 330
European Economic Community, 669
Evans, Harold, 672, 673
Evans, Richardson, 27
Evans, Walter J., 206, 207
Evening News, 1, 12, 20, 24, 33, 35, 84, 94, 97, 150, 158, 166, 198, 223, 252, 253, 324, 325, 366, 377, 395, 398, 406, 417, 423, 429, 431, 501, 535, 588, 673
Evening Standard, 1, 27, 59, 67, 81, 120, 175, 177, 263, 276, 282, 302, 305, 315, 323, 325, 332, 363, 387, 394, 417, 425, 427, 430, 435, 437, 438, 452, 468, 470, 475, 487, 501, 502, 510, 517, 527, 558, 559, 562, 588, 598, 603, 608, 620, 637, 646, 673, 676
Evening Times, 148–49, 150
Everyman, 510
Everyman's Encyclopaedia, 633
Ewer, Norman, 444
Eyre and Spottiswoode, 455n., 514

Faber, 1st Baron (E. B. Faber), 229

Fabian Society, 8, 45, 55, 80, 247, 679
Fairbairn, A. D., 331
Falklands war, 682
Field, The, 353
Financial News, 465, 492, 513, 514, 515, 519, 615, 627, 635
Financial Times, 514, 515, 559, 598, 635, 662, 666, 668, 669, 683
Finer, S. E., 632, 678
First World War: effects on press, 4, 11, 16, 97, 157, 298, 383, 598, 630; British propaganda in, 592, 593; mentioned, 65, 214, 238, 249, 574
Fish, W. G., 358
Fisher, Baron (Admiral Sir John Fisher), 107, 134, 270, 273, 276, 277–78, 310, 319
Fisher, W. J., 39, 46
Fitzroy, Sir Almeric, 51
Fleet Holdings, 674
Fleming, Ian, 621n.
Flynn, E. F., 264
Foch, Marshal Ferdinand, 334
Foot, Sir Dingle, 628, 643–44
Foot, Michael, 598, 620, 627, 635n., 636, 638, 640, 644n., 646, 659–60
Foreign Office News Dept., 240
Foreign Policy Committee, 210
Foreign Policy Committee, 210
Forrest, William, 546–47, 553, 636n.
Forteviot, 1st Baron (Sir John Dewar), 330
Fortnightly Review, 30, 120, 431
Forward, 650n.
Forward movement, 183
Foster, Philip, 110
France: journalism in, 2, 66, 252; British relations with, 251, 253, 411, 478, 479, 547, 580
Franco, General Francisco, 591, 626
Frank, Sir Howard, 401
Fraser, Ivor, 453n.
Fraser, Sir J. Malcolm, 175, 205, 222, 232, 233, 258, 269, 393, 453n., 455, 460
Fraser, Lovat, 270, 271, 326
Fraser, Robert, 582–83
Freeman, G. S., 350
Freeman, John, 681
French, General Sir John (1st Earl of Ypres), 271, 277, 296
Furness, 1st Baron (Christopher Furness), 44, 101, 222
Future, The, 363
Fyfe, Hamilton: works for Northcliffe, 33–34, 208, 276, 343, 351; edits *Herald*, 408, 440, 449, 463; in General Strike, 452, 453, 455, 456, 459; mentioned, 113, 190, 410, 467

Index

Gaitskell, Dora (Baroness Gaitskell), 652
Gaitskell, Hugh, 649–50, 651, 652, 653, 655
Galloway, W. J., 34
Gallup Poll, 645, 646
Gardiner, A. G.: editorial authority, 10, 51–52, 78, 119, 173, 214, 298, 331, 464; early editorship, 16, 44–46, 54, 55, 62, 79, 99, 104–105; feuds with Northcliffe, 20, 97, 98, 209, 252–53, 294; assists Liberals, 106, 138–39, 161–62, 191; relations with Lloyd George, 205, 224, 292–93, 294, 299, 310–11, 319, 321, 340, 344–45; relations with Scott, 210, 212; scores commercialism, 247, 386; alleged to be pro-German, 249, 250; clings to Asquith, 272–73, 289–90, 303; has second thoughts about press freedom, 273; interprets 1915 crisis, 274, 280; advocates 'democratic' administration, 328; derides press lords, 308, 323, 618; removed from *Daily News*, 361, 375, 463; mentioned, 77, 107, 291, 317, 339, 344, 366, 408, 409, 480, 525, 611
Gardner Sinclair, William, 232–33, 258–61, 266
Garrick Club, 11
Garvin, Christina, 357
Garvin, J. L.: purveys gossip, 7, 145; as a political editor, 11, 13, 169–70, 204, 214, 235, 385; as a pluralist, 25, 30–31, 120, 133–34; appointed to *Observer*, 35, 74; leaves *Outlook*, 28, 77, 78, 96; relations with Balfour, 49, 50, 73, 128, 129, 132, 143, 146–47, 164, 179–80, 185–86; relations with Northcliffe, 73–74, 87–88, 93, 109, 113, 114–15, 116, 130, 131, 168–69, 216–17, 218, 219, 322; invests in the *World*, 98; as party strategist, 109, 111, 112, 124, 141, 144, 153, 154, 156, 159, 160, 167–68, 171; inspires *Telegraph*, 136, 149–50; as 'Master of Conservatism', 161, 162; takes over *Pall Mall*, 175–77, 190, 231–33; qualms about Beaverbrook, 179–80, 190, 357; welcomed to camp of reaction, 181, 182, 183; adheres to Austen, 187, 188; relations with Astors, 199, 259–60, 264, 282–83, 320, 329, 333, 491, 560, 573, 597, 610–11, 612; in leadership struggles, 200–201, 217, 219–20; in Irish affairs, 202, 209, 233–34; seeks inter-party accommodation, 226, 235–36; relations with Churchill, 230, 562, 589; enjoys wide contacts, 255, 298; relations with Lloyd George, 259, 285, 328, 404, 413, 537, 538, 600; nerves jangled, 266; in 1915 crisis, 274, 277–78, 280; preaches compulsion, 287, 288; rates morning papers, 351; fears telephone, 390–91; sees 'a miracle', 403; plays prophet, 420, 470–71, 507; relations with Baldwin, 428, 467, 487, 488, 539; sees Labour advance, 525; propounds 'golden rule', 545; urges rearmament, 548, 583; relations with Neville, 570, 590; Keynes quips about, 582; made a C.H., 597, 609; in 1945 election, 627; mentioned, 36, 90, 107, 120, 225, 237, 377, 386, 430, 457, 466–67, 471n., 547, 556, 571, 584
Garvin, Viola (J.L.'s daughter), 612
Garvin, Viola (J.L.'s second wife), 357
Geddes Report, 404
General Elections: (1906), 40, 46, 48, 53, 54, 56, 61, 64–65, 67, 68n., 119, 137, 486; (January 1910), 118, 126–27, 128–29, 132, 133, 135–38, 151, 152, 154, 161; (December 1910), 118, 142, 146, 151, 152, 153, 156, 157, 159, 160, 161; (1918) 338–39, 340, 343–44, 345–47, 348, 362; (1922), 390, 403, 404, 416–17, 419–20, 422; (1923), 390, 422, 427, 428–32; (1924), 422, 441–42; (1929), 469, 478–79, 480, 481, 482, 483, 485–88, 491, 495; (1931), 510, 511–12, 517; (1935), 530, 537, 539, 540, 549, 551; (1945), 13, 620, 623–32, 639, 644; (1950), 14, 644, 646–47; (1951), 14, 644, 647; (1955), 651; (1959), 654, 685; (1964), 634, 663, 664; (1966), 664–65; (1970), 668; (1974), 668; (1979), 668, 672; (1983), 674
General Strike, 353, 411, 452–62, 463, 467–68, 509, 604
Geneva, disarmament conference at, 522
Genoa Conference, 404, 405
George V, King, 163, 186, 201, 226, 228, 277, 283, 306, 307, 327, 341, 397, 405, 508, 535, 565
George VI, King, 567, 581, 600
George, William, 114
George Outram and Co., 558, 559
Germany: journalism in, 2, 4, 101; and British Liberal Press, 174, 249; pre-1914 policies, 134, 176, 203; settlement with, 346, 487, 547; arouses new fears, 536, 543, 544, 550, 555, 574, chapter xvi *passim*, 592, 604; *also see* First World War *and* Second World War
Gerothwohl, Professor M.A., 392
Gibbs, A. A., 459n.
Gibbs, Sir Philip, 56, 57, 60
Gilliat, George, 475
Gilmour, Ian, 681–82
Gladstone, Herbert (Viscount Gladstone), 39, 44, 45–46, 47, 52, 62, 90, 372n., 374

Gladstone, W. E., 9, 15, 16, 17, 19, 47, 211, 355, 601, 682
Glasgow Citizen, 558, 559, 603
Glasgow Daily Record, 158, 426
Glasgow Evening News, 558
Glasgow Evening Times, 558
Glasgow Forward, 406, 439
Glasgow Herald, 3, 67, 68, 125, 126, 133, 202, 219, 227, 319, 377, 416, 558, 575, 578, 597
Glasier, Bruce, 155
Glenconner, 1st Baron (Sir Edward Tennant), 166, 193
Glenesk, Lady, 71
Glenesk, Baron (Algernon Borthwick), 19n., 21, 52, 71, 73, 108, 188n., 436
Globe, 1, 21, 25, 49, 67, 70, 97, 75, 111, 121, 123, 144, 164, 168–69, 171, 181, 188, 195, 217, 224, 230, 233, 247, 255, 258, 260, 264, 276, 286, 305, 320–21, 322, 330, 332, 355, 365, 385
Goebbels, Joseph, 544, 575
Goldman, C. S., 28, 49, 73, 78, 168
Goldsmith, Sir James, 669, 670
Gollin, A. M., 163
Goodman, Baron (Arnold Goodman), 670
Göring, Hermann, 547
Gorst, Sir John, 230
Gosse, Sir Edmund, 296
Gould, F. Carruthers, 5
Goulding, Sir Edward (1st Baron Wargrave), 74, 126, 146, 147, 148, 159, 168, 183, 184, 187, 188, 233, 258, 307, 324, 330, 333, 362, 364, 365, 467, 468n., 470
Grant, John, 660
Greece, civil war in, 618
Greene, Sir Hugh, 670
Greenwood, Arthur, 362, 592, 595
Greenwood, Frederick, 28, 74
Greenwood, Sir Hamar (1st Viscount Greenwood), 330, 379n.
Gretton, John (1st Baron Gretton), 436, 443, 488–89
Grey, Sir Edward (Viscount Grey of Fallodon), 10, 50, 51, 76, 79, 82, 88, 89, 100, 107, 140, 173, 210, 212, 250, 251, 253, 279, 284, 286–87, 296, 302, 360, 367, 372, 374, 397, 400, 443, 459, 474, 486, 521, 581
Griffith-Boscawen, Sir Arthur, 381, 417
Grigg, Edward (1st Baron Altrincham), 73, 96, 99–100, 112, 199, 207, 380, 401, 405, 406, 413, 418, 420, 437–38, 536–37, 545, 548, 556, 610–11, 612
Grigor, Alexander, 229n.
Grimond, Jo, 654

Grotrian, Sir Herbert, 528, 529, 554
Guardian, The (Church weekly), 228
Guardian (successor to *Manchester Guardian*): see *Manchester Guardian*
Guest, F. E., 328, 329, 334–36, 339, 340–41, 345, 353, 361, 377, 379, 380, 548
Guinness, Walter (1st Baron Moyne), 73
Guinness family, 74n.
Gulland, John, 331, 344, 345
Gwynne, H. A.: edits *Standard*, 27, 29, 128; relations with Balfour, 49, 146, 184, 186–87; appointed to *Morning Post*, 78, 178–79; relations with Bonar Law, 156, 200, 220, 226; dislikes Northcliffe, 161, 218; relations with other journalists, 164, 177–78, 233–34, 265, 310, 392; editorial authority, 180, 205–206, 214, 225, 226, 332–33; in Unionist struggles, 182, 183, 185–86, 209–10, 217, 225; relations with Bathursts, 202, 329–30, 333, 393–94, 430; at outbreak of war, 244, 253, 254–55; collaborates with Asquithians, 256, 271, 328; refuses to be panicked, 262–63; disappointed by politicians, 266, 279–80, 281–82; campaigns for compulsion, 284, 285; relations with Lloyd George, 285, 392, 404, 426; pushes Carson, 290, 298; relations with Beaverbrook, 307, 332, 500, 503; duly modest, 415; professional views, 342, 386, 480–81; relations with Baldwin, 431, 435, 443, 485, 487–88; survives *Morning Post* reconstruction, 436–37, 454; in General Strike, 453, 455, 460–62; ends editorship, 560–62; mentioned, 258, 342, 357, 418, 422, 426, 466, 470, 501

Hadley, W. W., 595, 627
Haig, General Sir Douglas (1st Earl Haig), 296, 326, 334
Haldane, R. B. (Viscount Haldane of Cloan), 8, 51, 82, 123, 140, 173, 186, 212, 223–24, 233, 242, 245, 254, 256, 257, 267, 279, 280, 286, 302, 319, 320, 328, 332n., 657
Halévy, Élie, 238, 524
Haley, Sir William, 388, 466, 643, 659, 660, 662, 663, 672
Halifax, 1st Earl of (Edward Wood; 1st Baron Irwin), 468, 476, 548, 574, 579, 580, 587, 589, 593, 595, 600, 601, 605
Hall, Admiral Sir Reginald, 427, 460
Halsbury, 1st Earl of, 185, 186
Halsbury Club, 185–86
Hamilton, Sir Denis, 4, 662, 674, 675
Hamilton, Sir Edward, 19
Hammond, Barbara, 58

Index

Hammond, J. L., 56, 57–58, 77, 81, 250, 361–62, 495, 497, 513, 516, 599, 631
Hankey, Sir Maurice (1st Baron Hankey), 310, 592
Hannay, David, 28, 68, 72, 74
Hannon, Sir Patrick 557, 558n., 613
Harcourt, L. V. (1st Viscount Harcourt), 71, 140, 144, 178, 210, 279, 284, 321, 344, 374
Harcourt, Sir William, 71
Harcourt Kitchin, F., 201–202, 219, 227
Hardie, J. Keir, 62, 64, 79, 154, 155–56, 190, 409
Harmsworth, Alfred: *see* Northcliffe, Viscount
Harmsworth, Cecil (1st Baron Harmsworth), 21, 112–13, 297, 305, 329n., 345–46, 348
Harmsworth, Esmond (2nd Viscount Rothermere), 359, 416, 424, 461, 464, 478, 481, 502, 563, 565–66, 568, 594, 598, 605, 610, 611, 621, 653, 674
Harmsworth, Geraldine, 378, 396
Harmsworth, Harold: *see* Rothermere, 1st Viscount
Harmsworth, Sir Hildebrand, 21, 24, 75, 123
Harmsworth, Sir Leicester, 44, 377, 444–45, 484–85, 486, 490–91, 493, 494
Harmsworth, Vere (3rd Viscount Rothermere), 674
Harmsworth family, 11
Harris, Dr. F. Rutherfoord, 19
Harris, Wilson, 611, 636, 639
Harrison, Austin, 35
Harrison, Eric, 636
Harrison, William, 447, 471, 483, 484, 485, 490, 491, 492, 493, 495, 505, 513
Harvey, Oliver (1st Baron Harvey of Tasburgh), 593, 610
Hatry, Clarence, 365
Haworth, Sir Arthur, 192
Hazlitt, William, 570
Healey, Denis, 681
Hearst, William Randolph, 2, 246, 502, 507n., 605
Hearst syndicate, 459, 479
Heath, Edward, 664, 665, 670, 682
Heighway, Arthur, 637
Henderson, Sir Alexander (1st Baron Faringdon), 26, 83, 86, 122, 188, 195, 196, 197, 222, 223, 263–64, 265, 266, 267, 403
Henderson, Arthur, 43, 62, 233, 268, 317, 318, 319, 328, 343, 348, 364, 369, 370, 419–20, 440, 495, 509
Henderson, H. D., 376
Henry, Sir Charles, 101, 102, 191, 192, 193, 228–29, 312, 371

Herald (wartime weekly), 325, 343, 351; *also see Daily Herald*
Herbert, Sir Alan (A. P. Herbert), 636
Hereford Press and Printing Co., 370n.
Hetherington, Alastair, 659
Hewins, W. A. S., 21, 23, 38
Hichens, Lionel, 333
Hickman, Sir Alfred, 48
Hicks Beach, Sir Michael: *see* St Aldwyn, Earl
Higginbottom, F. J., 175–76, 179
Higham, Sir Charles, 339
Hill, James, 148, 353
Hill, William, 56
Hills, J. W., 108, 515
Hilton Young, Sir Edward (1st Baron Kennet), 514
Hirst, F. W., 77, 211, 212–13, 214, 282
History of The Times, The, 48, 252–53, 545, 569–70, 585n., 608, 657
Hitler, Adolf, 465, 522, 533, 543, 577, 582–83, 584n., 585, 587, 590, 592, 593, 600, 604; *also see* Second World War
Hoare, Geoffrey, 650, 651–52, 654
Hoare, Oliver, 324
Hoare, Sir Samuel (1st Viscount Templewood), 414, 415, 451, 468, 506n., 535, 549, 557, 585, 593, 595, 598
Hobhouse, Sir Charles, 47, 106, 283
Hobhouse, L. T., 55–56, 58–59, 61, 78, 119, 227, 229, 272, 288
Hobman, J. B., 375, 376
Hobson, J. A., 56, 59, 63, 352, 410
Hobson, Oscar, 513, 515, 519, 546, 549
Hodges, Frank, 369
Hodgson, Stuart, 362, 375, 376, 432, 459, 472, 497
Hogge, J. M., 317
Hohenlohe-Waldenburg, Princess Stefanie, 477
Holden, Anthony, 672
Hollis, Christopher, 636
Holmes, Sir Stanley (1st Baron Dovercourt), 445
Holt, R. W., 233
Home Rule: *see* Ireland
Honours for newspapermen, 33, 34, 52, 57, 100, 103, 202, 229n., 307–308, 341, 349, 384–85, 403, 414, 416, 425, 470, 471, 478, 482, 489, 510, 597, 608–609, 635, 669
Hood, Stuart, 680
Hooper, Stuart, 680
Hooper, Horace, 91
Hopkinson, Tom, 608

Hore-Belisha, Leslie (1st Baron Hore-Belisha), 479, 595
Horne, H. S., 484, 490
Horne, Sir Robert, 443
Horner, Arthur, 463
Horner, Lady (Frances Horner), 75
House, Col. Edward M., 291
House of Lords: as a Tory preserve, 75, 99, 107; precipitates constitutional crisis, 106, 112, 128, 133, 139, 140, 142, 201; as the 'real Newspaper Proprietors Association', 307
Houston, Lady, 535, 538, 560, 564, 572
Howard, Anthony, 671n.
Howard, Geoffrey, 300, 372
Howard de Walden, Lord, 122, 123, 195
Howarth, Mary, 33
Huddersfield Worker, 154
Hudson, Sir Robert, 148, 331, 353, 372, 396, 399, 419, 432, 448
Hudson and Stacey, 459n.
Hueffer, Ford Madox (Ford Madox Ford), 257
Hughes, J. Percival, 129, 157, 162, 175
Hulton, Sir Edward, 94–95, 125, 129, 321, 325, 341, 344, 355, 371, 385, 387, 394, 417, 421, 425, 426, 429, 553
Hulton family, 68, 247, 262, 264, 315, 476
Hurd, Anthony (Baron Hurd), 634, 636
Hungary, Rothermere's devotion to, 477–78, 506, 547
Hyndman, H. M., 63

Iliffe, Sir Edward (1st Baron Iliffe), 426, 476, 559
Illingworth, Percy, 123, 191, 193, 221
Illustrated Sunday Herald: see *Sunday Herald*
Imperial Fund, 262
Imperial Press Conference (1909), 238
Imperial Tobacco Co., 501
Independent Labour Party, 62, 63, 64, 80, 155, 409, 410, 525n.
Independent Television News, 582
India: reforms in, 82, 83, 109–10; disorders in, 378
Inglis, Brian, 681
Inman, P. A. (1st Baron Inman), 596
Institute of Journalists, 247, 475–76, 480, 496, 619
International Publishing Corp. (IPC), 655, 666, 667, 685
Inveresk Paper Co., 447, 490, 492, 525
Inverforth, 1st Baron: see Weir, Andrew
Ireland, 17–18, 37, 47, 49, 50, 89, 118, 139, 145, 146, 153, 160, 201, 203, 209–10, 214, 226, 233, 235–36, 244, 252, 360, 377–78, 401, 404, 418
Irwin, 3rd Viscount: see Halifax, 1st Earl of
Isaacs, Sir Rufus (1st Marquess of Reading), 85, 134, 175, 209, 224, 345, 379n., 447, 471–72
Islington Bulletin, 456
Islington Gazette, 370n.
Italy: journalism in, 506; sanctions against, 540, 549–50, 553; aggrieved, 547
Iveagh, 2nd Earl of (Rupert Guinness), 73, 74, 92, 195
Iwan-Müller, E. B., 8, 24, 30, 33, 49, 66–68, 69–70, 72, 137

Jackson, Frederick Huth, 125
Jackson, F. Stanley, 415, 425, 427, 436, 451, 460
Jackson, Holbrook, 81
Jacobson, Sydney (Baron Jacobson), 655
Jameson, Sir Leander Starr, 221
'Jane', 605
January Club, 534
Jarvis, Sir John, 514
Jebb, Richard, 108, 126, 178
Jeger, Baroness (Lena Jeger), 675
Jenkins, Hugh (Baron Jenkins of Putney), 665
Jenkins, Roy, 118, 666, 667
Jeune, Lady, 29
Johannesburg *Star*, 34, 207
John Bull, 148, 189, 256, 257, 268, 275, 279, 286, 338, 407, 408, 451
John Dicks Press Ltd., 174–55, 449
Johnson, Paul, 673, 681
Johnstone, Harcourt, 473, 520
Johnstone family, 25, 39
Joicey, James, 38
Jones, Harry, 300, 302, 336, 337
Jones, Kennedy, 60–61, 74, 92, 116, 124, 131, 144, 145n., 157, 158, 161, 164, 291–92, 309, 315, 385, 386
Jones, Sir Roderick, 586
Jones, Dr Thomas, 312–13, 321, 480, 502, 549, 563, 565, 609
Joseph Rowntree Social Service Trust, 42–43, 77, 227, 331, 372, 423; *also see* Rowntree, Joseph
Journal de Genève, 663
Jowitt, Sir William (1st Earl Jowitt), 482
Joynson Hicks, Sir William (1st Viscount Brentford), 458, 478, 479
Justice, 63

Index

Kahn, Otto, 196
Kaiser: *see* Wilhelm II, Kaiser
Kaufman, Gerald, 666
Kay, Ernest, 665
Kemsley, 1st Viscount (J. Gomer Berry), 364, 426, 457, 558, 559, 565, 571, 572, 573, 583, 584, 589, 590, 598, 607, 609, 611, 612, 634, 635, 639n., 646, 657
Kennedy, Joseph, 589, 590
Kennedy, Leo, 579
Kerr, Philip (11th Marquess of Lothian), 199, 321, 327, 363, 380, 385, 480, 521, 522-55, 584, 589, 612
Keynes, John Maynard, 376, 410, 514, 582
Keys, William, 674, 675
Kinealy, Alexander, 264
King, Cecil Harmsworth, 11, 467, 595, 605-607, 628, 634, 648, 649-51, 655, 666, 667, 674, 680, 681
Kinnear, Alfred, 47
Kipling, Rudyard, 57, 178, 179, 443, 504
Kitchener of Khartoum, 1st Earl, 243, 244, 254, 272, 275, 276, 278-79, 284-86, 287, 295, 315
Knollys, 1st Viscount, 163
Koch, Willy, 89, 91
Koestler, Arthur, 628

Labouchere, Henry, 28, 40, 46, 77, 609
Labour Elector, 63
Labour Leader, 62, 65, 154, 409; *also see New Leader*
Labour Press Agency, 235
Labour Press Co-operative Society, 665
Labour Representation Committee, 62, 64, 234
Lamb, Sir Larry, 672
Lancashire Daily Post, 227
Land and Water, 353
Lane-Fox, G. R. (1st Baron Bingley), 414, 454
Lang, Cosmo Gordon (Archbishop of Canterbury), 563, 564, 566
Lansbury, George, 6, 158, 190, 234, 235, 248, 325, 352, 354, 368, 369, 408, 411, 440, 443-44, 509
Lansbury's Labour Weekly, 411
Lansdowne, 5th Marquess of, 88, 115, 141, 163, 182, 183, 200, 216, 218, 219, 226, 229, 230, 323
Lansdowne letter, 243, 572
Lapworth, Charles, 234
Lascelles, Edward, 329
Laski, Harold, 591, 624
Law, Richard (1st Baron Coleraine), 628, 646
Law Times, 353
Lawrence, D.H., 257

Lawrence, Sir Joseph, 196, 197
Lawson, Fred (4th Baron Burnham), 589
Lawson, Harry: *see* Burnham, 1st Viscount
Lawson, Robertson, 221
Lawson Johnston, Sir George (1st Baron Luke), 195, 222, 223, 267, 308, 609
Layland-Barratt, Sir Francis, 193
Layton, Christopher, 673
Layton, Lady, 524
Layton, Michael (2nd Baron Layton), 647
Layton, Sir Walter (1st Baron Layton), 376, 471, 491, 493, 494, 520-21, 522, 523-27, 528, 529-30, 540, 547, 552, 554, 555, 556, 560, 564, 565, 575, 586, 589-90, 596, 600, 605, 609, 614, 615, 621, 626, 631, 644, 647, 648-50, 651, 652, 653
Leacock, Stephen, 391n.
League of Nations, 340, 538, 539, 543, 548, 549, 593
Leconfield, Baron, 195, 262, 436
Lederer, Lajos, 477, 515, 538n.
Lee, Alan J., 61
Lee of Fareham, 1st Viscount (Sir Arthur Lee), 363
Leeds Daily News, 44
Leeds Mercury, 44, 103, 388, 596
Lehmann, John, 506
Lehmann, R.C. 123
Leith of Fyvie, Lord, 319
Lenin, V.I., 408
Leopold, King of the Belgians, 135
LeSage, J.M., 128
Lethbridge, Sir Roper, 217-18
Lever, W.H. (1st Viscount Leverhulme), 84-85, 209, 334
Lever Brothers, 84-85, 87
Levin, Bernard, 675n.
Levy Lawson, Edward: *see* Burnham, 1st Viscount
Lewis, Henry, 145
L'Express, 669
Liberal Candidates' Association, 473
Liberal Central Association, 175, 447
Liberal Council, 473-74
Liberal League, 20, 90, 210
Liberal Unionist Council, 163
Liberal War Committee, 302
Lichnowsky, Prince Karl Max, 437
Litvinov, Maxim, 325
Liverpool Courier, 216, 290, 465
Liverpool Daily Post, 211, 212, 227, 229, 516
Liverpool, 2nd Earl of, 284
Lloyd, Edward, 40

Lloyd, Frank, 46, 78, 205, 265, 313, 334–37, 338, 375
Lloyd family, 495
Lloyd, George (1st Baron Lloyd), 253
Lloyd George, David (1st Earl Lloyd-George of Dwyfor): involvement with press transfers, 5, 45, 174–75, 335–37, 448; tangles with Northcliffe, 11, 110, 112–14, 224, 296–97, 305, 310, 316–17, 322, 338–40, 345–46, 351, 357–59, 399–400; Scott keeps his conscience, 42, 99, 141, 174, 366, 448, 495, 659; early relations with press, 46, 79, 80, 99–100, 101, 103; as Chancellor, 106–107, 109, 111, 114, 118, 119, 123, 131, 133, 141; mocks Garvin, 120, 133, 134, 181; assaults Lords, 140, 226–27; tells secrets, 144; launches Land Campaign, 204–205, 227; depends on Donald, 205, 214, 271–72, 510; opposes naval estimates, 210, 211–12, 213–14; survives Marconi scandal, 224, 331–32; courts press support, 227–28, 229, 236–37, 245, 248, 293, 298, 302–303, 309, 312–13, 314–15, 319–20, 325–27, 338, 344–45, 346, 353, 360–64, 370, 375, 379–80, 393–94, 446–47, 471, 476, 481, 520–21, 528–29, 548, 556, 596, 605; during First World War, 250–51, 272, 278, 279, 280, 284, 285, 286, 287, 290, 295, 299, 301; suffers press attacks, 243, 292–94, 322, 325, 329, 368, 403–404, 478, 485; as premier, 306, 307–308, 310–11, 317, 333, 341, 343, 348, 349, 367, 372, 378; grabs at *Westminster*, 373; works for fusion, 376–77; grows weaker, 384, 391, 392, 397–98, 405, 406; eyes *The Times*, 396, 401–402, 403, 662; falls from office, 411–15, 420, 601; left in isolation, 418–19, 423; re-emergence feared, 426, 442, 468–69, 472, 473, 533, 536, 537–38, 539–40, 600; relations with Baldwin, 427, 539; in 1923 election, 431–32; in General Strike, 458–59, 471n.; in 1929 election, 479, 480, 481, 486–88; deserted by Harrison, 491, 492; moves left, 495–96, 524–25; lectures Barrington-Ward, 552; admires Hitler, 557, advocates compromise peace, 606; mentioned, 48, 51, 173, 192, 429, 597
Lloyd George, Gwilym (1st Viscount Tenby), 446, 447
Lloyd George, Dame Margaret, 363, 375
Lloyd George family, 512, 540
Lloyd George Fund, 336, 432, 446–47, 483, 492, 496
Lloyd George, Lady Megan, 665
Lloyd George Liberal Magazine, 432
Lloyd's Bank, 471, 554

Lloyd's Weekly, 40, 334, 335; *also see Sunday News*
Locker Lampson, Oliver, 122, 194, 195–98, 258–59, 266, 354, 405
Lockhart, Bruce, 498
London Budget, 246
London County Council, elections in 1934, 525, 527
London Labour News, 651
London School of Economics, 59
Long, Walter (1st Viscount Long of Wraxall), 73, 123, 181, 184, 187, 188, 217, 255, 258, 310, 332, 334, 338, 364
Lonrho International 670, 673, 674, 676
Lonsdale, 5th Earl of, 122
Loreburn, 1st Earl of (Sir Robert Reid), 57, 71, 174, 210, 226, 280
Lothian, 11th Marquess of: *see* Kerr, Philip
Louis of Battenberg, Prince, 256
Low, David, 5, 475, 544, 587
Low, Sir Sidney, 26, 27, 178, 386
Lowther, Claude, 122, 195
Lucas, E.V., 74n
Lucas, Reginald, 18–19
Lucy, Sir Henry, 47, 297
Luke, Baron: *see* Lawson Johnston, Sir George
Lunn, Henry S., 15
Lupton, Arnold, 103
Lusitania, 184, 275
Lyman, R.W., 433n
Lynd, Robert, 464
Lyon, Laurance, 365
Lyttelton. Oliver (1st Viscount Chandos), 624

Mabane, William (1st Baron Mabane), 635
McCallum, R.B., 625, 646
MacCarthy, Desmond, 392
McCarthy, Ralph, 654n.
McCormick, Col. R.R., 567
McCurdy, C.A., 426, 446, 447, 467
MacDonald, J. Ramsay: cooperates with Liberals, 62, 173; develops Labour press, 268, 439–41, 449, 496–97, 509–10; as Labour leader, 235, 409, 483, 490, 506; accompanies Henderson, 317; nettled by press, 409, 410–11, 432–33, 444, 448, 451; inspires 'great expectations', 434; blamed for 'mess', 507; forms National Government, 508; calls 1931 election, 511; a liability, 535–36; makes way for Baldwin, 539, 548; mentioned, 190n., 381, 443, 597
McDonald, Iverach, 660
McDonnell, Sir Schomberg, 18
Mack Smith, Denis, 506

McKenna, Reginald, 100, 140, 149, 174, 212, 230, 244, 272–73, 276, 279, 284, 296, 327, 334, 344, 416, 425
McKibbin, Ross, 368, 444
McLachlan, Donald, 643, 652
Maclean, Sir Donald, 102, 193, 221, 330, 331, 336, 338, 353, 365–66, 370, 371, 372, 374, 423, 432, 445, 448, 472, 486, 490
Maclean, Stuart, 647
McLean, Iain, 581n.
Macleod, Iain, 682
Macmillan, Baron, 593, 594
Macmillan, Harold, 455, 488, 587, 591, 662, 683
Macmillan and Company, 455
McNeill, Ronald (1st Baron Cushendun), 25, 72, 209, 262, 282, 290, 418
McWhirter, W., 515
Madge, W.T., 74–75, 169, 233, 258, 264
Mail on Sunday, 676
Maisky, Ivan, 588
Majority, The, 65
Mallet, Bernard, 89
Mallalieu, J.P.W., 636, 679–80
Manchester City News, 28
Manchester Conservative and Unionist, 94
Manchester Courier, 30, 34–35, 69, 70, 94–95, 97, 132, 157, 160, 193, 210, 215, 219, 224, 245–46, 256, 261–62, 269
Manchester Daily Dispatch, 68, 94, 95, 126, 129, 143, 290, 513, 652
Manchester Evening Chronicle, 94, 95, 129, 262, 290
Manchester Evening Mail, 69, 246, 261, 262
Manchester Evening News, 423
Manchester Examiner, 262
Manchester Guardian (latterly, *The Guardian*): its reputation and appeal, 6, 39, 210, 211, 465, 517, 634, 652; financial and structural problems, 48–49, 56, 78, 81, 204, 324, 423, 560, 573, 615; favoured by Lloyd George, 42, 79, 141, 174, 224, 294–95, 309, 312, 346, 448, 537, 538; shows provincialism, 76, 388, 519, 554; considers move to London, 101, 228, 229, 445, 633, 648, 659, 668; preaches radicalism, 99, 100–101, 111, 119, 133, 135, 149, 165, 212, 213, 251; urges inter-party compromise, 226; wartime experience, 246, 256, 280, 288; sees humiliation of Asquith, 304; electioneers, 339, 417, 420, 422, 511; tries to conciliate Labour, 368, 433, 441, 497, 516, 626–27; in General Strike, 458; tempers partisanship, 424, 431, 473–74, 507, 570, 664; speaks out against appeasement, 571, 578, 582, 588, 598, 599; sales in Second World War, 602, 603; protests against censorship, 607; read by Churchill, 616; opposes Churchill, 618, 629; composition of its readership, 630; in recent elections, 645–46, 647, 641, 663; mentioned, 16, 26, 55, 104, 159, 172, 227, 277, 319, 323, 345, 352, 362, 377, 432, 495, 513, 532, 547, 579, 595, 613, 637n., 654, 661, 666, 677
Manchester Weekly Times, 262
Mann, Arthur, 3, 190, 315–16, 387–88, 393, 394, 414, 453, 508, 569, 575, 583–84, 592, 609, 610, 611, 621–22
Mansfield, John (3rd Baron Sandhurst), 57
Marconi, G., 390
Marconi scandal, 175, 204, 209, 223–24, 296
Margesson, David (1st Viscount Margesson), 535–36
Marks, H.H, 514
Marlborough, 9th Duke of, 142
Marlowe, Thomas, 78–79, 111n., 112, 138, 144, 166, 183, 204, 206–207, 253, 254, 255, 278, 298, 349, 358, 359, 360, 377, 405, 469, 503
Marshall, Archibald, 60
Martin Kinglsey, 497, 498, 499, 504, 514, 546, 634, 638, 639–40, 650n.
Mary, Queen, 572
Massey, Vincent, 565
Mass-Observation, 568, 630, 631n.
Massingham, H.W., 77, 78, 79, 106, 139, 140–41, 149, 205, 209, 210, 211, 212, 214, 224, 226, 228, 242, 249, 252, 272–73, 286, 289, 291, 343, 344, 375, 376, 400, 437, 463
Masterman, C.F.G., 46, 54, 79, 104, 106, 123, 140
Masterman, Lucy, 106
Matthews, Victor (Baron Matthews), 673, 674
Maude, F.W., 90
Maurice, Maj-Gen. Sir Frederick, 333, 334, 335, 337, 412
Maxse, Ivor, 70, 71, 80, 108, 179
Maxse, Leo, 18, 23, 49, 66, 70, 71, 72, 73, 79, 80, 91, 102, 108, 119, 128, 144, 146, 147, 154, 159, 170, 179, 180, 185, 186, 202, 214, 225, 227, 247, 255, 264, 267, 280, 285, 307, 320–21, 330, 365
Maxton, James, 525
Maxwell, Robert, 665n., 667, 677
Mellor, William, 444, 496
Merthyr Pioneer, 64
Meston, 1st Baron, 615n
Methodist Times, 538
Metternich, Count P., 33
Meynell, Francis, 369

Midland Bank, 425
Midland Daily Telegraph, 476
Midland Evening News, 48, 120
Midland Express Co., 39, 370n.
Midleton, 1st Earl of (St John Brodrick), 186
Military Service Bill (1916), 289, 292
Millwood, Philip, 444
Milner, 1st Viscount (Sir Alfred Milner), 8, 24, 27, 55, 72, 108, 128, 185, 199, 254, 255, 256, 270, 283–84, 296, 301, 305–56, 325, 326, 327, 332, 333, 346, 349, 418, 587
Miner, The, 62
Miners' Federation, 352, 463
Ministry of Information, 593–94, 595, 601, 603–604, 608, 630–31, 635
Minto, 4th Earl of, 110
Mirror group: *see* International Publishing Corp.
Mix, John, 195
Moberly Bell, C.F., 17, 21, 24, 31–32, 36–37, 48, 65, 85, 88, 91–93, 96–97, 107, 109, 115, 116, 119, 142, 152–53, 166, 189
Moberly Bell, Enid, 37, 91
Moberly Bell, Ethel, 351
Monckton, Sir Walter (1st Viscount Monckton), 604
Mond, Sir Alfred (1st Baron Melchett), 41, 102–103, 123, 191, 192, 228, 247, 312, 406, 427
Mond, Dr Ludwig, 102
Monopolies Commission, 662, 667, 670, 671
Montagu, Edwin, 305
Montague, C.E., 49, 133, 172
Montague, Fred (1st Baron Amwell), 456–57
Monypenny, W.F., 21, 28, 107, 202
Moore, Faith, 363n.
Moran, 1st Baron (Dr Charles Wilson), 623
Morgan, J.H., 46
Morden, Grant, 336, 407, 438–39
Morison, J.M.W., 215
Morison, Stanley, 574, 618n.
Morley, John (Viscount Morley of Blackburn), 17, 51, 82, 88, 93, 94, 100, 109–10, 119, 140, 210, 211, 212, 214, 230, 233, 291
Morley, Samuel, 40
Morning Advertiser, 1, 34, 222
Morning Herald, 121
Morning Leader, 1, 16, 41, 43, 55, 62, 76, 103, 106, 120, 135, 136, 141, 147–48, 172–73, 190, 495
'Morning News', 665
Morning Post: enjoys influence, 1, 76; goes 'Joeite', 18, 21–22, 49, 67, 69, 73, 94, 107–108, 109, 110; editorial arrangements, 27, 30, 34, 78, 119, 128, 178–79, 181, 205–206, 332–33; proprietorial adjustments, 71, 201, 363, 382, 396, 433, 435, 436–37; partisanship, 72, 107, 182, 185, 202, 222, 231, 233, 236, 237; as an organ of intransigence, 80, 111, 120, 126–27, 130, 132, 134, 135, 136, 142, 143–44, 146, 149, 153, 158–59, 160, 162, 165–66, 170; maintains traditions, 187, 208, 225, 328, 330, 532, 556; rivalry with *Times*, 198, 209, 218–19; wartime experience, 244, 253, 262–63, 270, 318, 325, 334; criticizes Liberal leaders, 271, 273, 275, 280, 204; asserts its independence, 281–82, 385, 409, 680; advocates compulsion, 283, 284; represents Carson, 290, 315; relations with Lloyd George, 295, 297, 299, 302, 309, 322, 404; mocks 'Lord Bunty', 307; defends right-wing movements, 319, 393, 466, 470, 474; breaks *Chronicle* story, 336, 337; fears red peril, 342, 343–44, 368, 547, 684; like 'cheap brandy', 351; discounts Carlton Club meeting, 414–15; in inter-war elections, 417–18, 485, 511; sides with Baldwin, 424, 430–31, 443; relations with Beaverbrook, 428, 500, 501; 'a coterie sheet', 429; fights General Strike, 453–55, 460–61; relations with Rothermere, 481, 485, 486, 501; 'not worth mentioning', 552; closes down, 560–62, 684; mentioned, 217, 321, 322, 323, 350, 357, 378, 398, 412, 451, 475, 503, 537, 565
Morning Star (1856–1869), 13
Morning Star (1966–   ), 681
Morrell, J.B., 43, 121, 370, 374, 484–85, 490, 494, 522, 526, 528, 554–55
Morris, Mowbray, 208
Morris, William, 63, 544–45
Morris, Sir William (1st Viscount Nuffield), 510
Morrison, Herbert (Baron Morrison of Lambeth), 497, 509, 540, 553, 599, 600, 604, 606, 607, 617, 624–25, 629, 637, 638, 645
Morrison, J.A., 149
Mosley, Sir Oswald, 506, 507, 510, 511, 519, 532–34, 548, 556–57, 564, 572-3, 575, 617
Muggeridge, Malcolm, 497
Muir, Ramsay, 376
Mullin, Chris, 676n.
Munich crisis, 545, 546–47, 553, 570, 575, 577, 583, 584, 592, 597, 618, 657
Murdoch, Sir Keith, 395
Murdoch, Rupert, 395, 655, 667, 669, 670, 671–72, 676
Murray, Alexander, Master of Elibank (1st

Baron Murray of Elibank), 75–76, 101–102, 145, 161–62, 174, 175, 191, 192–93, 236, 286, 297–98, 312, 373
Murray, Gilbert, 58, 250
Mussolini, Benito, 506, 533, 592

Nash, Vaughan, 57–58, 79, 139
Nathan, H.L. (1st Baron Nathan), 527, 530
Nathan, Lady, 527
Nation, 42, 62, 77, 78, 81, 97, 106, 111, 116, 139, 140–41, 200, 210, 211, 213, 243, 247, 251, 273, 284, 289, 295, 312, 322, 325, 343, 375, 376, 422, 495, 497, 514
National Administrative Council, Labour Party, 155, 156, 409, 411
National Co-operative Press, 449, 551
National Co-operative Society, 638
National Council of Evangelical Free Churches, 457, 538
National Council of Labour, 552
National Insurance, 173
National Labour Party, 510, 622
National Labour Press, Manchester, 155
National League of Airmen, 538
National Liberal Club, 55, 135, 211, 280–81, 295
National Liberal Federation, 109, 210, 211, 212–13, 521, 525
National News (*Sunday Illustrated*), 320
National Party, 318–19
National Press Agency, 43
National Publicity Bureau, 592–93
National Review, 18, 25, 30, 49, 66, 71, 72, 80, 102, 111, 120, 128, 154, 162, 181, 185, 186, 202, 223, 247, 255, 270, 320, 338, 392
National Service League, 283
National Unemployed Workers Movement, 532
National Union of Conservative and Constitutional Associations, 19, 40, 49, 72, 95, 163, 184, 186, 215, 439, 469
National Union of Journalists, 436, 513, 619, 620, 637, 638, 640n., 654
Nevinson, H.W., 17, 46, 59, 77–8, 104–105, 410, 463
New Age, 81, 154, 343
New Clarion, 497n.
New Democrat, 673n.
New Leader, 410–11, 433, 439, 440, 444, 449, 463; *also see Labour Leader*
New Liberal Review, 21
New Party, 507, 510, 519, 532
New Statesman, 247, 332n., 343, 362, 376, 409, 439, 441, 449, 458, 495, 497, 506, 514, 540, 550, 565, 573, 588, 590, 591, 636, 638, 650, 653–4, 666, 681, 682
New Writing, 506
New York Sun, 59
New York Times, 311, 397, 564
New York Tribune, 188n.
New York World, 507n.
Newcastle Daily Leader, 38
Newcastle Evening Leader, 25
Newcastle Evening Mail, 25
Newcastle Journal, 559
Newnes, Sir Frank, 8, 54, 81, 191, 192, 247
Newnes, Sir George, 8, 22, 40, 41–2, 50, 54, 81, 101, 191
Newport Industrial Council Central Strike Committee, 457
News Chronicle: founded, 447, 493–4; editorial arrangements, 466, 497, 521–2, 636, 649; takes Liberal side, 493, 494, 517, 519, 520–4, 525–31, 539–40, 551, 553, 556, 615; proprietorial adjustments, 494, 522–4, 530–1, 554–5, 573, 584, 609; responsive to Labour, 497, 525, 591, 608; circulation and finances, 513–4, 560, 615, 621, 630, 631, 644, 652; faces predicament, 520–1; follows Lloyd George, 536, 537, 538; covers foreign affairs, 546–7, 555–6; takes King's side, 564, 565; maps policy, 578, 586, 594, 600; backs Churchill, 582, 588; during Second World War, 603, 605, 607; run by 'geese', 616; in 1945 election, 626, 627, 631; needs 'a little punch', 633; commissions polls, 644–5; in 1950 election, 646–7; offered pact by Beaverbrook, 648–9; suffers an identity crisis, 650–51; shuts down, 653–4, 658; mourned, 679; mentioned, 385, 511, 532, 534, 547, 575, 583, 586, 597, 638, 664
News International, 674
News of the World, 103, 227, 246, 417, 471, 595, 598, 616, 664, 667
News-Letter, (National Labour Party), 510
Newspaper Press Directory, 494
Newspaper Press Fund, 676n.
Newspaper Proprietors Association, 307, 436, 453, 460–1
Newsprint Supply Company, 603
Newton, 2nd Baron, 182
Nicholas II, Tsar, 76
Nicholson, A.P., 113–14, 117, 131, 142, 157, 189, 198, 207, 230, 281, 289
Nicholson, Reginald, 142, 166
Nicolson, Sir Harold, 510, 511, 532, 563–64, 572, 577, 587, 599, 623n., 625
Nigeria Debate (8 November 1916), 299

1922 Club, 500, 608
1936 Club, 585
Nineteenth Century, 39
Norfolk, 15th duke of, 92
Norman, Sir Henry, 123-4, 129, 138, 227, 339
North-Devon Herald, 596
North-Devon Journal, 596
North Mail (Newcastle), 44, 559
North of England Newspaper Co., 42, 43, 370n.
Northcliffe, Lady, 150, 218, 321, 372
Northcliffe, Viscount (Alfred Harmsworth): stands for Parliament, 7-8, 34, 680; early partisanship, 18, 36; relations with Chamberlain, 20-1, 22, 23-34, 69, 219-20, 225; admires Balfour, 73, 151, 182, 255; outbid for *Standard*, 25, 26, 27; relations with Garvin, 30, 109, 131, 142-43, 150, 181; early properties, 33-5, 97, 121, 390; bids for *Times*, 34; owns *Observer*, 34, 35, 74, 147, 168-69; raised to peerage, 52; owns *Times*, 53, 60, 75, 83, 85-88, 92-93, 94, 95-7, 99, 119, 353; relations with editors, 78-9, 110-11, 183, 203, 270, 316, 323, 341, 348-51, 358, 391; ailments, 79, 84-5, 120, 129, 132-3, 150, 291, 359-60, 394, 398; retrenches, 97-8; travels, 116, 382, 397-8, 399; relations with Churchill, 110, 166, 198-9, 221; relations with Lloyd George, 110, 112-13, 114, 117, 296-7, 301-2, 306, 310, 332, 362, 339-40, 344, 345-6, 357, 359, 377, 399; gibes at 'wealthy people', 122; requires special handling, 130-2; evaluates rivals, 132, 145, 152, 153; relations with Bonar Law, 156-7, 187, 193, 230-1, 475; not his brothers' keeper, 158, 237, 397; faults Tories for neglect of press, 160-61; wields press power, 166-7, 168, 170, 189, 206-9; wearies, 183-4; relations with Beaverbrook, 190, 198, 308-9; Manchester operations, 193, 215, 216, 224; dislikes 'violent Ulster language', 202; shows gallantry, 209; 'a villain', 218-19; prophesies war, 223; unreliability, 223-24, 225, 232, 233, 248, 261, 264, 269, 283-4, 309-10, 313, 328, 331-32, 346; wartime activities, 244, 252-4, 257, 271, 276; attacks Kitchener, 278-9, 286, 295, 315; wins gratitude, 286-87; relations with Liberal editors, 289, 290, 294; kills 'Cock Robin', 11, 280-1, 297; as political powerhouse, 298; 'wants a smash', 305; deals with Americans, 311, 316-17; returns to England, 320-1; raised to a viscountcy, 322; a menace, 325; directs enemy propaganda, 326-7, 593; stipulates terms, 338-9,
341; gives Labour a 'fair show', 343, 344, 351, 368, 675; views solicited, 363, 366; prepared to back Grey, 372; invites flattery, 378; confident of *Times*, 382, 383; approaches the end, 384, 385, 395-6, 400, 401; dies, 402, 406; leaves will, 402-3; as 'Uncle Alfred', 467, 649, 650; remembered, 418, 469, 476, 485, 503, 560, 657; mentioned, 1, 12, 13, 40, 59, 102, 235, 247, 288, 306, 307, 337, 342, 405, 524, 553, 573, 621, 642, 673
Northcliffe Newspapers Ltd., 476
Northern Daily Mail, 44
Northern Echo (Darlington), 42, 43, 62, 103, 211, 372
Northern Liberal Federation, 525
Northumberland, 7th Duke of, 368, 382, 436, 453, 454, 470, 501
Norway, German invasion and occupation, 598, 599, 600, 602
Nottingham Daily Express Co., 370n.
Nottingham Evening News, 330
Nottingham Express, 212
Nottingham Journal, 330, 419
Nottingham Labour Echo, 64
Nottingham Strike Bulletin, 457
Now!, 669

O'Brien, Conor Cruise, 669, 670, 671n.
Observer, 2, 11, 31n., 34, 35, 47, 74, 86, 87, 91, 93, 94, 98, 109, 111, 112, 115, 120, 121, 128, 132, 133, 134, 138, 141, 145, 146, 147, 149, 150, 157, 159, 167-69, 175, 179, 180, 181, 182, 185, 188, 199, 201, 217, 219, 226, 232-33, 247, 259, 260-61, 264, 266, 271, 273, 277, 279, 287, 305, 320, 321, 329, 332, 353, 362, 364, 365, 379, 386, 392, 403, 404, 413, 428, 435n., 441, 457, 467, 470, 486, 487, 491, 525, 530, 537, 545, 554, 556, 560, 656, 570, 573, 583, 587, 597, 609-12, 616, 621-22, 627, 628, 629, 634, 643-44, 646, 653, 654n., 661, 663, 668-69, 670-71, 673, 676, 677, 679
O'Connor, T.P., 61, 213, 247, 311
O'Connor, Sir Terence, 488
Odhams Press, 320, 407, 454, 482, 483, 496, 652, 653, 655, 660
O'Donovan, Patrick, 677
Oliver, F.S., 144, 150, 154, 301, 333, 491
Olympia, BUF rally at (1934), 534
O'Neill, 3rd Baron, 621n.
O'Neill, Lady (Lady Rothermere; Mrs Ian Fleming), 621
Orage, A.R., 81, 343
Orwell, George, 607, 608, 628
Osborne Judgment, 151

Outlook, 28, 50, 73, 74, 77, 96, 168, 343n., 363
Owen, Frank, 598, 617
Oxford, by-election (1938), 581n.
Oxford and Asquith, Countess of: *see* Asquith, Margot
Oxford and Asquith, 1st Earl of: *see* Asquith, H.H.
Oxford and Cambridge Univerisity Club, 57, 517

'Pacificus': *see* Oliver, F.S.
Paderewski, Ignace, 83
Page, Walter H., 238, 287
Page Croft, Sir Henry (1st Baron Croft), 154, 225, 319, 436
Pall Mall Gazette, 1, 8, 22, 30, 33, 41, 46, 49, 58, 67, 76, 101, 121, 168, 169, 171, 175–86, 179, 181, 185, 190, 198, 199, 217, 218–19, 230, 231–33, 247, 259–61, 266, 273, 277, 279, 282, 337, 353, 355, 365, 425, 427
Palmer, Charles, 75, 230, 255, 286
Palmer, William ('Whiffley'), 496
Paper Duty, repealed (1861), 5
Parke, Ernest, 16, 103, 105, 119, 173, 210–11, 463, 494
Parker, Eric, 68, 72, 75
Parkinson, Hargreaves, 635
Parliament Act (1911), 154, 179, 182–83, 201
Partington, Sir Edward (1st Baron Doverdale), 192
Partington, Oswald (2nd Baron Doverdale), 101, 102, 191–92, 193, 283, 330, 334, 373, 419
Partisan Review, 607
Paul, Alexander, 22
Paul, Herbert, 16–17
Peace and Reconstruction movement: *see* Council of Action
Peace Ballot, 538
Peacock, E.R., 329
Pearson, Sir C. Arthur, 1, 21, 22–23, 25–29, 34, 36, 37–39, 40, 43, 59, 78, 83, 85–88, 89, 90, 91, 92, 93, 94, 109, 120–21, 132, 134, 147, 175, 177, 194, 196–97, 353
Pearson, Clive, 522, 523–24, 526, 527–28, 529, 530, 531, 554–55
Pearson, Harold: *see* Cowdray, 2nd Viscount
Pearson, Sir Weetman: *see* Cowdray, 1st Viscount
Pearson family, 662; *also see* Cowdray, 1st and 2nd Viscounts *and* Denman, Lady
Pearson's Weekly, 22, 23
Pease, J.A., 101–102, 103, 123, 144
Pease, W.E., 456
Pentland, 1st Baron, 140

People (later *Sunday People*), 25, 246, 258, 407–408, 438, 454, 482, 653, 663
Percy, Lord Eustace, 460
Perris, E.A., 335, 337, 376, 379, 432, 447, 492
Perry, Colin, 603
Perth, 16th Earl of (Sir Eric Drummond), 593, 594
Peters, Carl. 3–4
Pethick-Lawrence, F.W. (1st Baron Pethick-Lawrence), 16
Petter, Sir Ernest, 503
Phillips, G.A. 452, 458
Phillips, J.S.R., 80, 328
Phillipps, Vivian, 473–74
Picture Post, 608, 667n.
Pilling, John, 329
Pilot, 44
Pirrie, Viscount (W.J. Pirrie), 396
Plymouth Socialist, 64
Poland, British assurances to, 585, 592
Political and Economic Planning (PEP), 568–69
Pollock, Sir Frederick, 280
Ponsonby, 1st Baron (Arthur Ponsonby), 684
Pope, Wilson, 472, 497
'Popular Front', 578
Portal, 1st Viscount, 620–21
Portland, 6th Duke of, 195
Postgate, Raymond, 439
Praed, Herbert, 199–200
Pratt, J.W., 302
'Prerogative of the Harlot', 11, 504, 675
Press Association, 93, 350, 433, 584, 643
Press Bureau, 240, 241, 243–44, 245, 272, 311
Press Council, 640–41, 676, 685
Preston, Sir Walter, 435
Price, G. Ward: *see* Ward Price, G.
Priestley, J.B., 638, 639n.
Pringle, W.M.R., 317, 336–37
Printing House Square: *see Times, The*
Provincial Newspapers Ltd., 615
Prudential Assurance Co., 482
Pryor, S.J., 27, 59–60, 61, 129, 153
Public opinion polls, 644–45
Puck, 97
Pugh, Arthur, 482
Pulitzer, Joseph, 2, 507n.
Punch, 636

Radio and television, 12, 389–90, 631, 632, 658
Radio Times, 390
Rainbow Circle, 45, 62, 63, 352
Ramsden, John, 439
Ransome, Arthur, 497

Ratcliffe, S.K., 506–507
Rea, Walter (1st Baron Rea), 486
Reading, 1st Marquess of: *see* Isaacs, Sir Rufus
Reading Gazette, 559
'Red Crusader', 532
Red Magazine, 97
Redmond, John, 138, 140, 169
Reed International, 655, 666, 667, 674
Rees-Mogg, Sir William, 671, 672, 682
Referee, 407, 408
Reform Club, 63, 102, 231, 252, 445, 510, 529, 607n., 611
Reith, Sir John (1st Baron Reith), 593
Relugas Compact, 51
Repington, Col. Charles à Court, 82, 223, 276, 278, 326, 327–28, 334
Reuters, 27, 584, 589, 643
Reveille movement, 153–54, 155
Review of Reviews, 116, 120n.
Reynolds News (incorporating *Reynolds's Weekly Newspaper*, *Reynolds's Illustrated News*), 80–81, 135, 174–75, 246, 303, 314, 337, 449, 551, 567, 569, 578, 598, 638; *also see Sunday Citizen*
Rhodes, Cecil, 16, 94
Rhondda, Lady, 518, 596
Ribbentrop, Joachim von, 547n., 587
Riddell, Sir George (1st Baron Riddell), 103, 227, 246, 248n., 251, 272, 292, 298, 301, 310, 311, 335, 338–40, 342, 344, 346, 390, 394, 396, 417, 471
Ridley, 2nd Viscount (Matthew Ridley), 71, 262
Right of Reply, 676
Robbins, Baron (Lionel Robbins), 662
Roberts, Field-Marshal Earl, 168, 169, 179
Roberts, Sir James, 148
Robertson, E.J., 467–68, 479, 558–59, 640n., 644
Robertson, Field-Marshal Sir William, 295, 296, 320, 326, 334
Robertson Nicoll, Sir William, 101, 227, 303, 441
Robinson, Geoffrey: *see* Dawson, Geoffrey
Rolls-Royce Co., 161
Rosebery, 5th Earl of, 8–9, 15–16, 17–18, 19–20, 46, 47, 48, 50, 51, 59, 60, 90, 92, 94, 124, 149
Ross, Sir William David, 638
Rothermere, 1st Viscount (Harold Harmsworth): intervenes in politics, 127, 145; untamed by baronetcy, 158; takes over *Mirror*, 223; relations with Lloyd George, 224, 341, 344, 476, 537, 538; relations with Northcliffe, 158, 225, 237, 296, 395–6, 397; relations with Beaverbrook, 231, 325, 382–3, 425–6, 478, 475, 498, 500, 534; available for office, 279; promotes inter-party accord, 236, 237; covets *Observer*, 260–1, 264; admires Bottomley, 268–9; relations with Churchill, 306, 319, 435, 557, 562; squared, 320, 323–4, 326; expected to resign, 328; 'breast high' for an election, 338; 'a bounder', 340–1; disdains editors, 357, 464, 573–4; fears Bolshevism, 359, 396, 420; opposes 'Waste', 362, 392; expands his empire, 371, 403, 421, 423; administers pin-pricks, 373, 377; blows hot and cold, 393, 394; covets *Times*, 401–2; relations with Bonar Law, 413–14, 417, 423–24, 469; puts price on his support, 416, 424–5; competes with Berrys, 426, 484; prophesies doom, 428–30; opposes Baldwin, 431, 443, 462, 498–504, 549–50; Blatchford fires, 434; plays lion-tamer, 449–50; eyes *Morning Post*, 454, 501, 561; entertains Hungarian enthusiasms, 477–78; threatens to support Labour, 477, 481; thrives on controversy, 485–6, 487; blamed for defeat, 488, 489–90; eyes Harrison properties, 492; supports Mosley, 506, 532, 533, 534, 556–7, 572; falls into line, 511; economizes, 514, 515–16; as a 'monster', 518; hires Brooks, 534–5, 536; fears war, 545; confused, 547–8; disappointed by sales, 558; as a King's man, 564, 565–6; retires, 568, 572; pleads for election, 581; reassures Ribbentrop, 587; mentioned, 3, 11, 75, 149, 307, 321, 346, 348, 385, 386, 437, 444, 484, 560, 584, 598, 610
Rothermere, 2nd Viscount: *see* Harmsworth, Esmond
Rothermere, 3rd Viscount: *see* Harmsworth, Vere
Rothschild, 1st Baron, 92, 188
Rothschild family, 91
Rothwell, Alderman W.T., 97, 193, 224, 261–62
Round Table, The, 31, 437
Round Table Conference, 138, 144–45, 146
Round Table Group, 199
Rowland, Roland ('Tiny'), 670, 673
Rowntree, Arnold, 42, 43, 251
Rowntree, Joseph, 42–3, 147, 172, 292–3; *also see* Joseph Rowntree Social Service Trust
Rowntree family, 78, 147, 172
Royal Commissions on the Press: (1947–49) 14, 354, 383, 552, 555, 559, 575, 614, 615, 629, 632, 636, 637n., 638–9, 640–1, 643n., 644,

656, 679–80; (1961–62), 14, 641–2, 658, 679, 685; (1974–77), 14, 641, 642
Runciman, Walter (1st Baron Runciman), 330, 334, 353
Runciman, Walter (1st Viscount Runciman of Doxford), 100, 140, 171, 284, 317, 330, 353–4, 407, 528, 564
Russell, Bertrand 410, 628
Russell, Sir Edward, 229
Ryan, A.P., 574, 643, 665

St Aldwyn, 1st Earl (Sir Michael Hicks Beach), 24, 28–9, 181, 185
St Davids, 1st Viscount (J.W. Philips), 193, 371, 492
St George's, Westminster, by-election (1931), 503, 504
St James's Gazette, 1, 22, 25, 26, 27, 28, 68, 72, 120, 175, 208, 209
Salisbury, 3rd Marquess of, 15, 18, 24, 26, 682
Salt, Sir Titus, 148
Salvidge, Sir Archibald, 215, 417
Samuel, Sir Herbert (1st Viscount Samuel), 474, 512, 520, 521, 523, 539, 540, 568
Sandars, J.S., 28–9, 30, 31, 32, 33, 66, 70, 72, 80, 83n., 86, 90, 114, 115, 124–5, 127, 129–30, 131–2, 137, 141, 142–43, 145n, 149, 153, 158, 161, 163, 164, 165, 175, 180, 182, 184, 187, 310
Sanders, Sir Robert (1st Baron Bayford), 144, 160, 175, 187, 218, 219, 326–7, 339, 345, 348, 359, 366, 377, 381, 392, 393, 405, 416, 469n., 499–500
Sankey, 1st Viscount, 482
Saturday Review, 80, 314, 343n., 431, 535
Schmidt, Hermann, 221
Schofield, Guy, 637
Schuster, Ernest, 211
Scotsman, 3, 31, 32, 67, 80, 213, 226, 290, 319, 416, 428, 559, 597, 638, 660
Scott, C.P.: as an MP, 8; editorial authority, 10, 16, 39, 48–9, 56, 78, 81, 204, 214; keeps Lloyd George's conscience, 42, 99, 106, 141, 174, 205, 213–14, 227, 228, 294–5, 296, 303, 306, 318, 319, 322, 327, 333–4, 344, 366, 378, 432, 446, 448, 495, 659; in 1906 campaign, 55; antipathy to Asquith, 99, 272; relations with London Liberal papers, 104, 148, 173, 373, 376n., 422, 445–6; champions radicalism, 119, 139, 210; pursues inter-party accord, 235–6, 288; celebrates 70th birthday, 246; allegedly pro-German, 249–50; misjudges 1922 election, 418, 419; relations with Labour, 420, 433, 444, 463, 495; in General Strike, 458; relinquishes chair, 465: 'a feeble help', 497; dies, 513; mentioned 6, 57, 59, 101, 133, 172, 209, 298, 308, 313, 385, 466, 554, 597, 633
Scott, E.T. ('Ted'), 172, 458, 465, 495, 497, 511, 513, 516
Scott, John, 104, 228
Scott, Laurence (1877–1908)), 48–49, 81
Scott, Laurence (1909–   ) 648, 661
Scott family, 104, 554
Scott, Sir Samuel, 149
Scott-James, R.A., 2, 4, 10–11, 239
Scottish Daily Express, 558, 560, 597
Scottish Worker, 456
Second World War: impact on the press, 9, 11, 13, 389, 390, 598, 614–16; antecedents, 542, 574; declared, 592; censorship during, 593–4, 603–7; newsprint shortages, 602–3; effects on readership patterns, 630
Selborne, 2nd Earl of, 415
Select Committee on Education, Science and the Arts, 671
Sell's Directory, 68
Seymour-Ure, Colin, 387, 569, 664, 677–78
Shadwell, Arthur, 420
Shakespeare, Sir Geoffrey, 512
Sharp, Clifford, 332n., 362, 374, 514
Shaw, Bernard, 64, 77, 253, 343n., 410, 517, 561
Shaw, Tom, 369, 443
Shawcross, Baron (Sir Hartley Shawcross), 641, 646
Sheffield Daily Independent, 38, 43, 211, 370n., 372, 476
Sheffield Daily Telegraph, 427
Sheffield Mail, 476
'Shiver Sisters', 544, 587, 612
Shortt, Edward, 379n.
Sidebotham, Herbert, 49, 210
Silkin, John, 676n.
Simmons, J. Wagstaffe, 619
Simon, Sir John (1st Viscount Simon), 257, 279, 286n., 288, 364, 432, 441, 457, 459, 512, 521, 540, 582, 600, 601, 605, 606
Simon of Wythenshawe, 1st Baron (Sir Ernest Simon), 638
Simpson, Mrs Wallis (Duchess of Windsor), 562–67
Sinclair, Sir Archibald (1st Viscount Thurso), 568, 570, 588, 589, 591, 600, 613
Skidelsky, Robert, 509
Sloman, Anne, 664
Smalley, George, 188n.
Smith, A.C.H., 624, 651

Smith, F.E. (1st Earl of Birkenhead), 84, 98, 134, 143, 145n., 159, 161, 165, 181, 182, 183, 184, 185, 187, 213, 226, 243–44, 245, 284, 357, 360, 364, 366, 399, 402, 411, 417, 429, 443, 450, 451, 452, 475, 485, 488
Smith, Goldwin, 99
Smith, Sir Harold, 244
Smith, J. Parker, 31
Snowden, Philip (1st Viscount Snowden), 62, 343, 430, 509, 537, 548
Social Democratic Federation, 63, 64
Social Democratic Party, 672
Socialist League, 63
Socialist Review, 409, 411
SOGAT, 674
South African War: *see* Boer War
South Wales Daily News, 124, 211, 227, 379
South Wales Post, 488
Southern Daily Mail (Portsmouth), 34, 97
Southwood, 1st Viscount: *see* Elias, J.S.
Sowler family, 34
Spain, civil war in, 553, 555, 567
Speaker, 41, 42, 77, 81
S. Pearson and Son, Ltd., 522
Spectator, 21, 24, 27, 28, 36, 68, 71, 77, 88, 90, 108, 115, 126, 128, 133, 141, 154, 179, 216, 247, 291, 322, 328, 343n., 351, 378, 392, 406–407, 425, 428, 431, 467, 497, 585, 611, 636, 673, 681–82
Spen Valley, by-election (1919), 364, 365, 366
Spender, Harold, 17, 38–39, 124, 140, 173, 212, 241, 242–43, 247–48, 505
Spender, J.A., 9, 10, 16–17, 20, 27, 31, 41, 44, 47, 50, 51, 52n., 54–55, 76, 100–101, 102, 107, 119, 138–39, 149, 150–51, 171, 173, 174, 193, 204, 205, 209, 231, 238–39, 242, 243, 247–50, 253, 272, 276, 297, 298–99, 300, 308, 312–13, 330, 331, 336, 337, 338, 344, 373, 374–75, 386, 463, 466, 472, 491, 505, 517, 521, 525, 526, 528, 581–82, 584, 589, 601
Spender, Mary (Mrs J.A. Spender), 102, 374, 517
Spender, Sir Stephen, 505
Speyer, Sir Edgar, 91, 192, 257
Stalin, Joseph, 604
Stamfordham, 1st Baron, 412
Stamp Duty, repealed (1855), 5
Standard, 1, 6, 21, 23, 25–29, 37–38, 50, 57, 67, 70, 76, 78, 80, 85, 87, 94, 107, 110, 116, 120, 121, 125, 126, 127–28, 132, 134, 135, 146, 147, 156, 175, 177–78, 183, 185, 222, 263, 264, 276, 387
Stanley, Baron: *see* Derby, 17th Earl of
Stanley, Capt. Lord Edward, 316

Star, 1, 16, 41, 43, 55, 61, 76, 147–48, 172, 190, 227, 246, 252–53, 278, 284, 292, 293, 319, 324, 333, 344, 361, 370, 432, 459, 472, 480, 491, 493, 497, 530, 531, 538, 551, 555, 565, 605, 627, 630, 636, 638, 647, 648, 649, 653, 654
Starmer, Sir Charles, 42–43, 121, 370, 374, 375, 419, 445, 459, 490
Starmer-Morrell syndicate, 330–31, 355, 370–71; *also see*: Morrell, J.B.
Statist, The, 519
Staveley Hill, H.S., 120
Stead, W.T., 1, 8, 12, 40–41, 42, 79, 100, 107, 120n., 144, 176, 177, 199, 209, 235, 681
Steed, Wickham, 60, 83, 189, 253, 316–17, 320, 326, 349–51, 354, 357–58, 366, 377, 378, 391, 392, 395, 396, 397, 399, 400, 403, 405, 413, 415, 418, 574–76
Steel-Maitland, Sir Arthur, 122, 123, 153, 168, 175, 177, 184, 185, 186, 188, 193, 194, 196, 197, 200, 201, 207, 217, 221, 222, 223, 226–27, 232–33, 258, 259–51, 263, 264, 265, 266, 267, 269, 282, 291, 324
Steinkopff, Edward, 25
Stephenson, A.F., 69, 95, 215, 224, 246
Stevenson, Frances (Countess Lloyd-George), 284, 301, 359, 360, 536, 537
Stevenson, John, 532n.
Stevenson, W.H., 509
Stewart, Gershom, 215
Stewart, Margaret, 653–54
Stewart, William, 65
Stockman, H.R., 235
Stokes, Donald, 630
Stoppard, Tom, 14
Storey, Samuel, 40, 262, 371
Storr, Lancelot, 426
Strabolgi, 10th Baron (J.M. Kenworthy), 531
Strachey, John, 407, 628, 636, 646
Strachey, J. St Loe, 21, 23, 36, 51, 52, 59, 60, 71, 73, 88–90, 94, 98, 109, 128, 139, 141, 147–48, 150–51, 154, 179, 216, 291, 321, 322, 324, 328, 351, 368, 406–407, 418, 425, 434, 438, 682
Straight, Douglas, 49
Strathspey Herald, 379
Stuart, Sir Campbell, 349, 374, 378n., 395, 396, 398, 399, 403, 589, 593, 595
Stuart, James (1st Viscount Stuart of Findhorn), 622, 624
Stuart of Wortley, 1st Baron, 83
Suez crisis (1956), 668, 682–83
Sun (1893–1906), 1, 25, 74–75
Sun (1964–), 11, 655, 663, 664, 666–68, 672, 676

Sunday Citizen, 81, 267–68, 449, 663, 666
Sunday Companion, 97
Sunday Dispatch, 481, 534, 538, 549, 558, 574
Sunday Evening Telegram, 320
Sunday Express, 335, 364–65, 382, 386, 392, 434, 439, 452, 457, 479, 490, 553, 557, 558, 595, 634, 664
Sunday Graphic, 247, 447, 476, 587
Sunday Herald (formerly *Illustrated Sunday Herald*, later *Sunday Graphic*), 246–47
Sunday Mercury (Birmingham), 370
Sunday Mirror, 655
Sunday News (formerly *Lloyd's Weekly*), 446, 447, 476, 493, 495
Sunday People: see *People*
Sunday Pictorial, 149, 246, 268, 319–20, 323–24, 365, 382, 392, 423, 429–30, 468, 476, 515, 516, 588, 595, 598, 605, 606, 634, 655
Sunday Referee: see *Referee*
Sunday Telegraph, 664
Sunday Times, 221, 247, 335, 364, 365, 386, 392, 428, 457, 470, 501, 559, 560, 565, 583, 595, 607, 612, 616, 627, 635, 638, 659, 662, 666, 668, 671–72
Sunday Times Magazine, 667
Sutherland, 5th Duke of, 329
Sutherland, D.M., 282, 427
Sutherland, Sir William, 293, 295, 326, 329, 331, 332, 338, 362, 364, 365
Sutton, Sir George A., 87, 157, 558, 621
Swaffer, Hannen, 407, 464, 542n., 551, 553, 554, 627
Sydney *Evening News*, 395n.
Sykes, Sir Charles, 336
Szarvasy, F.A., 477, 478

Tablet, 636
Tactical Committee, Conservative Research Department, 644–45
Tariff Reform League, 20, 23 ff., 38, 67, 123, 197, 353
'Taxes on knowledge', 4, 5
Taylor, A.J.P., 121, 238, 248, 302, 346, 401, 465
Taylor, H.A., 389, 390, 447
Taylor, J.E., 16, 39, 56, 78, 101
Television: see Radio and Television
Tennant, Sir Edward: see Glenconner, 1st Baron
Thatcher, Denis, 677
Thatcher, Margaret, 672, 677, 682
Thomas, C.E., 606
Thomas, J.H., 268, 364, 443, 588
Thomasson, Franklin, 56, 57, 58–59, 60, 78

Thompson, A.M., 63, 268, 343
Thompson, E.R., 363, 475
Thompson, W.M., 80, 81
Thomson, Kenneth (2nd Baron Thomson of Fleet), 671, 672
Thomson, Roy (1st Baron Thomson of Fleet), 655, 660–61, 662–63, 668, 671
Thomson Organisation, 6, 671
Thursfield, James, 17, 36, 107
Tillett, Ben, 234, 482
Time and Tide, 497, 518, 591, 596, 665
Times, The: enjoys prestige, 1, 6, 67, 75, 76, 88, 117, 129, 312, 339, 474–75, 517, 531–32, 548–49, 550, 551, 580, 585, 659–60, 663; divided on tariffs, 21, 22, 37, 68–69, 165, 222–24; under Northcliffe, 35, 53, 69, 92–94, 95–96, 98, 102, 109, 119, 122, 132–33, 166, 208–209, 326, 327, 340, 353, 382, 383, 394–96, 399–400; professes independence, 36, 166–67, 331–32, 405, 569, 672–73, 682, 684; supports Unionists, 48, 49, 51–52, 53, 74, 80, 94; sees advent of Labour, 64, 65–66; letters to, 76, 181–82, 217, 226, 412, 471n., 572, 589–90, 659, 670, 672, 675n.; proprietary dissolved, 83; reacts to People's Budget, 107, 110, 112, 114–16, 124, 133; relations with Garvin, 109, 120; editorial arrangements, 110, 189, 202–203, 207, 348–51, 388, 418, 422, 464, 466, 467, 470, 552, 554, 569–70, 574, 643, 649, 672–73; relations with Churchill, 130, 230, 269–70, 366, 435, 562, 616, 618–19, 627–29, 631; relations with its rivals, 132, 134, 198, 218–19, 374, 435, 454, 499, 501, 561; in 1910 elections, 135, 138, 143, 144, 150, 152–53, 156, 157, 158, 159, 160, 162, 163; accepts Parliament Bill, 179, 181, 183; rejects physical force, 202; relations with Bonar Law, 216, 413; price and circulation, 225, 231, 283, 324, 382, 397, 398, 513, 517, 603; 644, 648, 660, 661; reports secrets, 236–37; wartime experience, 241, 242, 244, 245, 246, 251, 253, 257, 262; rejects Landsowne letter, 243, 323; argues for coalition, 270, 271, 273; publishes shells dispatch, 276–77; Margot threatens, 280; condemns weakness, 281, 286, 287, 301; 'runs the Cabinet', 288; assists rise of Lloyd George, 285, 302, 304, 309; attacks ministers, 309, 332, 346, 367, 377, 379, 391; as political guide, 315; scorns National Party, 319; accommodates Labour, 343; Esmond hopes to inherit, 359; gets a 'big flag', 360; commends Grey, 372,; Lloyd George covets, 404, 406; freed from a 'press gang', 408–409,;

eludes Rothermere, 423, 477n.; boosts Baldwin, 424–25, 427–28, 431, 450, 488, 508–509, 539; exhibits pro-Americanism, 451; in General Strike, 457–58; cites 'changed values', 462; revived Unionist label, 470–71; in 1929 election, 480; relations with Neville, 503, 589, 598–600; praises Mussolini, 506; gets facelift, 512; castigates Lloyd George, 536, 538; in Abyssinia crisis, 540–41, 549, 550; minds its own business, 544–45; appeases, 548, 553, 556, 573, 579–81, 584, 585–86; in Abdication crisis, 563–65, 566, 567; during Second World War, 602, 607, 608, 618, 622; in 1945 election, 627–28; relations with Labour government, 632, 634–35; acquired by Thomson, 662; vacates PHS, 668; sold to Murdoch, 671; mentioned, 6, 8, 17, 18, 28, 30, 31n., 59, 284, 291, 310, 321, 353, 378, 547, 637n., 645, 647, 652, 665, 683, 684

Times Book Club, 91
Times Newspapers Ltd., 662, 671–72, 676
Times Supplements, 672
Titanic, 173, 199
Tit-Bits, 22
'Top People', 659–60
Torch of Anarchy, 64
Tower, John, 579
T.P.'s Weekly, 247
Trades Disputes Acts (1927), 482
Trades Union Congress, 352, 369, 408, 452, 456–57, 463, 482, 509, 591, 615, 619, 644, 652, 653, 655, 674–75
Trades Unionist Tariff Reform Association, 128
Trafalgar House, 669, 673–74
Transport House, 645
Transvaal, 83, 221; *also see* Boer War
Trelford, Donald, 669–70, 671n.
Trevelyan, G.M., 250
Trevelyan, Sir George Otto, 314, 328
Tribune (daily, 1906–1908), 2, 48, 49, 55, 58–61, 67, 76, 80, 101, 119
Tribune (weekly, founded 1937), 497, 554n., 605, 609, 617, 646, 650, 666, 676n.
Truce of God, 143–44
Truth, 3, 28, 77, 169, 497, 609, 611
Tsar: *see* Nicholas II
Tunstall, Jeremy, 680
Turner, Ben, 369
Tweed, Col. Thomas, 459
Tyerman, Donald, 632, 643, 649, 674
Tyrrell, William (Baron Tyrrell), 89

Ulster: *see* Ireland
Union of Democratic Control, 251n.
Unionist Business Committee, 276
Unionist Democratic League, 127
Unionist News Bureau, 232, 258
United Empire Party, 499, 500; *also see* Empire Free Trade
United Newspapers Ltd., 5, 446, 492, 494, 527, 528, 554
United States of America: journalism in, 2, 79, 391, 563, 567, 618, 648, 678–79; investment capital from, 57–58, 59, 363; negotiates with Canada, 167, 178; sentiment against, 311, 316, 686; owed war debt, 423; *Times* espouses, 450–51
'Unspeakable Turk', 272, 412

Vallance, Aylmer, 522, 524, 526, 527, 528, 529, 530, 540, 639
Vansittart, Robert (list Baron Vansittart), 478, 579
Venizelos, E., 412
Versailles, Treaty of, 360, 361, 506, 548, 583, 587
Victoria, Queen, 143, 202, 394
Victoria House Printing Co., 408, 497n.
Voules, Horace, 77

Waddington, John, 195
Wadsworth, A.P., 355, 380, 615, 616, 626–27, 631, 632, 633, 643
Walkden, Evelyn, 637
Wallace, Edgar, 149, 495
Wallas, Graham, 55
Walter, Arthur, 52, 85, 86, 87, 88, 91, 92, 93
Walter, John, 166, 208, 219, 225, 270, 350, 378, 396, 400, 401, 402, 403, 418, 506, 549, 573, 580, 660
Walter family, 83, 86, 91, 400
Ward, Dudley, 211
Ward, W.P., 108
Ward Price, G., 501, 532, 547, 594
Wardell, Michael, 558n.
Ware, Fabian, 69, 71, 78, 108, 109, 111, 114, 119, 126, 127, 128, 132, 134, 140, 142, 143–44, 159, 178, 181, 189
Wargrave, 1st Baron: *see* Goulding, Edward
Warrington Guardian, 41–42
Warwick, Countess of, 154–55
Washington Post, 679
Watergate, 678
Waters, Frank, 558, 559, 580, 597, 602, 603, 608–609, 622, 632–33, 636, 640, 642–43, 644, 645, 647, 648–51, 652

Index

Waters, Sir George, 638
Waters, Joan (Mrs Frank Waters): *see* Woods, Joan
Watney, Charles T., 149
Watson, Angus, 538
Watson, Arthur, 464, 573
Webb, Beatrice, 8, 173, 332n., 369, 497, 602
Webb, Sir Henry, 192, 193, 330
Webb, Maurice, 636
Webb, Sidney (Baron Passfield), 8, 173, 332n., 369, 449n., 497, 602
Wedgwood Benn, Anthony (2nd Viscount Stansgate): *see* Benn, Tony
Week, The, 497, 580, 604
Weekly Dispatch, 209, 253, 309–10, 345, 365, 366, 395, 407, 423; *also see Sunday Dispatch*
Weeklies, 497–98, 681–82
Weir, Andrew (1st Baron Inverforth), 336, 361, 379, 396
Wells, H.G., 81, 394, 395, 410
Welsford, J.H., 143
Welsh Disestablishment, 153, 203, 210, 360
West of England Newspaper Co., 490
Western Daily Mercury, 211, 377
Western Evening Herald, 444
Western Mail, 471
Western Morning News, 377, 444
Westminster, 2nd Duke of, 123, 195, 262
Westminster Gazette: prestige, 1, 6, 9–10, 75–76, 79, 150–51, 266; proprietorship, 8, 41, 81, 101–103, 119, 121, 173, 190, 191–93, 194, 247, 308, 315, 330, 355, 371, 448–49; converts to morning publication, 10, 43, 338, 373, 374, 387; Liberal loyalty, 16, 38, 47, 48, 50, 54, 100, 105, 166, 280, 294, 300–301, 312, 344, 352, 365, 370, 381, 409, 419; shows tepidity, 111, 138–39, 171, 202, 211, 213, 226; experiences difficulties, 231, 243, 324, 444–45, 473; proposed merger with *Manchester Guardian*, 228; its 'letter-bag', 250; opposes Lloyd George, 309, 317, 367; escapes Lloyd George's clutches, 312–13, 320; responds to Lansdowne letter, 323; belittles Baldwin, 424; urges collaboration with Tories, 432; in General Strike, 459; absorbed by *Daily News*, 376, 471–72, 494; mentioned, 5, 31, 36, 56, 102, 109, 144, 153, 177, 673, 682
Westminster Press Ltd., 5, 43, 331, 372, 373, 374, 419, 444, 446, 448, 472, 483, 490, 494, 554, 582, 669
Wheler, Granville, 367
White, Arnold, 242, 255, 264
White, James, 336

Whitehall Securities, Ltd., 372, 423
Wigram, Col. Clive (1st Baron Wigram), 405
Wilhelm II, Kaiser, 252, 487
Wilkinson, Ellen, 525, 595
Wilkinson, Spenser, 108, 126, 143
William Jacks and Co., 195
Williams, Francis (Baron Francis-Williams), 426, 476, 496, 544–46, 552, 573, 597–98, 634, 639, 650n., 653, 678
Williams, Sir Herbert, 608
Williams, Marcia (Baroness Falkender), 666
Williams, Robert, 369, 444
Williams, Shirley, 157–58
Williams. W, Llewelyn, 289
Williamson, Sir Archibald (1st Baron Forres), 192, 379
Williamson, David, 54
Willis, Baron (Ted Willis), 665
Willis, Irene Cooper, 251n.
Willoughby de Broke, 19th Baron, 154
Wills brothers, 501
Wilson, F.W., 438, 439
Wilson, H.J., 42–43, 370n.
Wilson, H.W., 20, 22, 23, 112, 143, 145n., 150, 160, 163, 164, 204, 269, 358
Wilson, Sir Harold, 6, 11, 637n., 659, 662, 664, 665, 666, 667, 669, 682
Wilson, Sir Henry, 253, 301
Wilson, J.B., 23, 233n.
Wilson, P.W., 54, 79, 113
Wilson, Woodrow, 291, 311, 323, 361
Winn, Anthony, 581
Winterton, 6th Earl. 98, 143, 185, 585–86
Wintour, Charles, 676
Wit of Harold Wilson, The, 665
Withers, Hartley, 526
Wolfe, Humbert, 342
Woman Worker, 154
Wood, J.S., 197
Wood, Sir Kinglsey, 598, 605
Woodhouse. Percy, 290
Woods, Joan (Mrs Oliver Woods), 466, 609, 652
Woods, Maurice, 159n., 357
Woods, Oliver, 242–43, 357, 388, 466, 545, 612, 652, 659, 660, 663
Woodward, William 27, 177
Woolton, 1st Earl of, 598
Wootton, Barbara (Baroness Wootton of Abinger), 638
Worker, The, 234
Workers' Weekly (subsequently *Sunday Worker*, *Daily Worker*, and *Morning Star*), 440

Working-Men Candidates Funds, 127–28
World, 36, 97–98, 143, 190, 201
World's Press News, 637
Worthington-Evans, Sir Laming, 514
Wrench, Evelyn, 407

Yates, A., 6n.
Yates, Edmund, 98
Yorkshire Conservative Newspaper Co., 583, 584
Yorkshire Evening News, 123, 446
Yorkshire Observer, 148, 211, 353
Yorkshire Post 3, 66, 80, 116, 133, 212, 328, 350, 387–88, 393, 414, 415, 426, 427, 428, 430, 439, 453–54, 458, 465, 516, 572, 573, 575, 578–79, 583–84, 588, 592, 596, 597, 616, 668
Young, G.M., 638
Younger, Sir George (1st Viscount Younger of Leckie), 282, 324, 325–26, 353, 356, 357, 363, 365, 367, 379, 381, 414, 428
Yule, Sir David, 447

Zaharoff, Sir Basil, 221
Zec, Philip, 606, 625
Zinoviev, G., 442
Zinoviev letter, 442n.